World Directory of

ENVIRONMENTAL
RESEARCH CENTERS

Second Edition

World Directory of
ENVIRONMENTAL RESEARCH CENTERS

Second Edition

Sponsored by the
LAKE ERIE ENVIRONMENTAL
STUDIES (LEES) Program

Edited by William K. Wilson,
Morgan D. Dowd, Phyllis Sholtys

THE ORYX PRESS
Distributed by
R. R. BOWKER COMPANY
A Xerox Education Company
New York and London, 1974

Published by The Oryx Press
7632 East Edgemont Avenue, Scottsdale, Arizona 45251

Distributed by
R. R. Bowker Company, a Xerox Education Company
1180 Avenue of the Americas, New York, N. Y. 10036

Library of Congress Cataloging in Publication Data

Wilson, William K
  World directory of environmental research centers.

  First ed. published in 1970 under title: Directory
of organizations concerned with environmental research,
compiled by W. A. Mordy and P. A. Sholtys.
  "Sponsored by Lake Erie Environmental Studies (LEES)
Program"
  1. Environmental policy research — Directories.
I. Dowd, Morgan D., joint author. II. Sholtys,
Phyllis A., joint author. III. Title.
HC79.E5W54 1974   301.31'025   72-87536
ISBN 0-8352-0701-3

Contents

Foreword   ix

Preface   xi

BIOLOGY   1

General   1
    Educational Institute   1
    Field Station/Laboratory   10
    Foundation   12
    Government — Federal   12
    Government — State or Local   19
    Industrial/Commercial   20
    Professional Organizations   21
    Research Institute   22
    Unclassified   25

Biochemistry   26
    Educational Institute   26
    Field Station/Laboratory   26
    Government — Federal   26
    Government — State or Local   27
    Industrial/Commercial   27
    Professional Organizations   27
    Research Institute   27

Biophysics   27
    Educational Institute   27
    Field Station/Laboratory   27
    Government — State or Local   28
    Industrial/Commercial   28
    Research Institute   28

Ecology   28
    Educational Institute   28
    Field Station/Laboratory   33
    Foundation   34
    Government — Federal   38
    Government — State or Local   41
    Industrial/Commercial   46
    Professional Organizations   46
    Research Institute   50

CHEMISTRY   53

General   53
    Educational Institute   53
    Field Station/Laboratory   56
    Government — Federal   57
    Government — State or Local   57
    Industrial/Commercial   57
    Professional Organizations   57

    Research Institute   58
    Unclassified   58
Physical Chemistry   58
    Educational Institute   58
    Government — Federal   59
    Government — State or Local   59
    Research Institute   59

ENGINEERING   60

General   60
    Educational Institute   60
    Field Station/Laboratory   62
    Foundation   62
    Government — Federal   62
    Government — State or Local   65
    Industrial/Commercial   66
    Professional Organizations   68
    Research Institute   68

Agricultural Engineering   68
    Educational Institute   68
    Foundation   69
    Government — Federal   69
    Government — State or Local   71
    Industrial/Commercial   73
    Professional Organizations   73
    Research Institute   74

Chemical Engineering   75
    Educational Institute   75
    Field Station/Laboratory   75
    Government — Federal   75
    Government — State or Local   75
    Industrial/Commercial   75
    Research Institute   75

Pollution Abatement   76
    Educational Institute   76
    Field Station/Laboratory   78
    Foundation   78
    Government — Federal   78
    Government — State or Local   81
    Industrial/Commercial   94
    Professional Organizations   95
    Research Institute   96
    Unclassified   96

Water Resources   96
    Educational Institute   96
    Field Station/Laboratory   100
    Foundation   100

Government — Federal   100
Government — State or Local   105
Industrial/Commercial   110
Professional Organizations   110
Unclassified   111

GEOLOGY   112

General   112
Educational Institute   112
Field Station/Laboratory   114
Government — Federal   114
Government — State or Local   115
Industrial/Commercial   116
Professional Organizations   117
Research Institute   117

Geochemistry   117
Educational Institute   117
Government — Federal   117
Industrial/Commercial   118
Research Institute   118

Geophysics
Educational Institute   118
Foundation   118
Government — Federal   118
Industrial/Commercial   118
Research Institute   118
Unclassified   118

Paleontology   118
Educational Institute   118
Government — Federal   119
Research Institute   119

PHYSICS   120

General   120
Educational Institute   120
Field Station/Laboratory   121
Foundation   121
Government — Federal   121
Government — State or Local   122
Industrial/Commercial   122
Professional Organizations   122
Research Institute   123

SOCIAL SCIENCES/HUMANITIES   124

General   124
Educational Institute   124
Foundation   125
Government — Federal   125
Government — State or Local   125
Industrial/Commercial   125
Professional Organizations   125
Research Institute   126

Agriculture   126
Government — Federal   126

Community Development/Studies   126
Educational Institute   126
Foundation   126
Government — Federal   126
Government — State or Local   127
Industrial/Commercial   127
Professional Organizations   127
Research Institute   127

Education   127
Educational Institute   127
Foundation   128
Government — Federal   128
Government — State or Local   128
Industrial/Commercial   128
Professional Organizations   128
Research Institute   129
Unclassified   129

Employment/Unemployment   129
Government — Federal   129
Government — State or Local   129
Professional Organizations   129
Research Institute   129

Housing   129
Foundation   129
Government — Federal   129
Government — State or Local   129
Professional Organizations   129
Research Institute   130

Industrial Development   130
Educational Institute   130
Government — Federal   130
Government — State or Local   130
Industrial/Commercial   130
Professional Organizations   132

Juvenile Delinquency   132
Government — Federal   132
Government — State or Local   132
Research Institute   132

Labor Relations/Unions   132
Educational Institute   132
Government — Federal   132
Government — State or Local   132
Industrial/Commercial   133
Professional Organizations   133
Research Institute   133

Law/Legislation   133
Educational Institute   133
Foundation   133
Government — Federal   133

Government — State or Local   133
Professional Organizations   133
Research Institute   134

Mental Health   134
Educational Institute   134
Foundation   134
Government — Federal   134
Government — State or Local   134
Research Institute   134

Politics   134
Educational Institute   134
Government — Federal   135
Professional Organizations   135

Population Studies/Family Planning   135
Educational Institute   135
Foundation   135
Government — Federal   136
Government — State or Local   136
Professional Organizations   136
Research Institute   136

Psychology/Behavioral Science   136
Educational Institute   136
Foundation   137
Government — Federal   137
Professional Organizations   137
Research Institute   137

Recreation and Leisure   137
Educational Institute   137
Foundation   137
Government — Federal   137
Government — State or Local   138
Professional Organizations   138
Research Institute   138

Regional Planning   138
Educational Institute   138
Foundation   138
Government — State or Local   138

Professional Organizations   139
Research Institute   139

Rehabilitation   139
Foundation   139
Government — Federal   139
Government — State or Local   139
Research Institute   139

Transportation   139
Educational Institute   139
Government — Federal   139
Government — State or Local   139
Professional Organizations   139
Research Institute   139

Urban Problems   140
Educational Institute   140
Government — Federal   140
Research Institute   140

Welfare (Child, Public, Social)   140
Educational Institute   140
Government — Federal   140
Government — State or Local   140
Professional Organizations   141
Research Institute   141

INTERDISCIPLINARY   142

General   142
Educational Institute   142
Field Station/Laboratory   153
Foundation   154
Government — Federal   155
Government — State or Local   156
Industrial/Commercial   158
Professional Organizations   160
Research Institute   163
Unclassified   165

COUNTRY INDEX   171

Foreword

Since the late sixties, many countries have been attempting to resolve environmental problems not only by preventing pollution, but through research and educational programs, and by managing the environment. The State University of New York, College at Fredonia early recognized the need for free exchange of information between organizations interested in and doing research on the environment, and in 1967 President Oscar E. Lanford, with the approval of the State University of New York and the Board of Trustees of the State University of New York, began work on an environmental program which was to be known as Lake Erie Environmental Studies (LEES).

This second edition of the *World Directory of Environmental Research Centers* (the first edition was published in 1970 by the college itself, under a different title), is part of the LEES publication program; it represents what the authors believe to be the most comprehensive and accurate compilation of organizations in all countries doing research on the environment.

Uses for this Directory are many and varied; probably the most important, however, is to facilitate communications between individuals and organizations, so that those engaged in research projects will be able to share their results, thereby eliminating unnecessary duplication of effort. Second, this Directory provides an excellent management tool: in order to effectively manage any ecosystem, it is imperative that managers know what other individuals, groups, and learning institutions are doing in the areas of research, development, and management. This Directory will aid in the identification of vital research resources and in the pooling of these resources and ideas. The Directory also has many uses on the personal level. For example, it is a source of job opportunities for research personnel, and can be used by students interested in preparing for careers involving environmental problems.

It is the hope of the editors and of those working on the Lake Erie Environmental Studies program that this Directory will provide the kind of information needed to further the fields of environmental research, education, and management.

MORGAN D. DOWD, Dean
Graduate Studies and Research
State University of New York
College at Fredonia

Preface

Because of increasingly significant interest in environmental affairs, in pollution abatement, and in environmental management, the State University of New York, College at Fredonia decided to update and expand their directory of organizations engaged in environmental research, and to make it available to the general public through a commercial publisher. The first edition, published in 1970, listed only 1400 organizations located, for the most part, in the United States; the present edition includes over 4,800 research centers located throughout the world. A number of types of organizations are included in the Directory: educational institutions, field stations or laboratories, foundations, government organizations (federal, state, and local), industrial, commercial, or professional organizations, and research institutes.

The main section of the Directory is arranged by subject (Biology, Chemistry, Engineering, Geology, Physics, and Social Sciences), with subheadings listed under each of these major heads; organizations involved in multidisciplinary research are listed separately in the Interdisciplinary section.

Each entry in the main section includes the following information, if available: name and address of the research center; the name of its director; the size of the staff engaged in the research; the general environment being studied (oceanographic, terrestrial, limnologic, or atmospheric); and the specific interests being studied within those environments (prairie and temperate forests, polar, or tropical). The Country Index lists all research centers by country, or by state within the United States.

Although the editorial staff at the College at Fredonia has used its best efforts to include all active research centers engaged in work on the environment, no claim is made that the coverage is all-inclusive. The editors will be grateful for any comments or suggestions, whether favorable or critical, for use on future editions.

WILLIAM K. WILSON
Coordinator of Sponsored Research
State University of New York
College at Fredonia

Biology

GENERAL

Educational Institute

AGRICULTURAL MINISTRY, FAUNA DIVISION
FINCA LA HURORA,
GUATEMALA CITY, GUATEMALA
Director, Marvo Alberto Savedra Paz
General Environment: Oceanographic

AGRICULTURAL SCIENCES, GERMAN ACADEMY
MUGGELSEEDAMM 310
DDR 1162 BERLIN, WEST GERMANY
Director, Professor Diethelm Scheer
General Environment: Oceanographic

AGROMETEOROLOGY AND PLANT ECOLOGY
17-A LANE 31, YONG KANG STREET
TAIPEI, TAIWAN
Director, K T C Cheng

AIR ENVIRONMENT STUDY CENTER
328-B HAMMOND BUILDING
UNIVERSITY PARK, PA 16802
General Environment: Atmospheric

AQUATIC RESEARCH UNIT
INDIANA UNIVERSITY
BLOOMINGTON, IN 47401
Director, Dr Shelby D Gerking
General Environment: Oceanographic

ARCTIC BIOLOGY INSTITUTE
UNIVERSITY OF ALASKA
FAIRBANKS, ALASKA 85612
Director, Dr Lawrence Irving
Specific Interests: Polar (cold)

ARID LANDS PROGRAM, UNIVERSITY OF ARIZONA
TUCSON, AZ 85721
General Environment: Terrestrial
Specific Interests: Desert

BACTERIOLOGY DEPARTMENT
UNIVERSITY OF CALIFORNIA
DAVIS, CA 95616
Staff Size: 10 - 49

BAR-ILAN UNIVERSITY
RAMAT GAN, ISRAEL

BATH UNIVERSITY OF TECHNOLOGY
CLAVERTON DOWN
BATH, SOMERSET, ENGLAND
Director, Leonard Broadbent
Specific Interests: Prairie and Temperate Forest

BEHAVIORAL BIOLOGY DIVISION
JOHNS HOPKINS UNIVERSITY
BALTIMORE, MD 21201

BIOLOGICAL COLLEGE
HAKKAIDO UNIVERSITY
SAPPORO, JAPAN
Director, Dr Terugyoshi Kawamura
Specific Interests: Prairie and Temperate Forest

BIOLOGICAL FISHERIES DEPARTMENT, CATHOLIC UNIVERSITY OF VALPARAISO
AVENIDA BRAZIL 2950, CASILA
4059, VALPARAISO, CHILE
General Environment: Oceanographic

BIOLOGICAL FORSCHUNGSANSTALT
HIDDENSEE
KLOSTER AUF HIDDENSEE, EAST GERMANY
Director, Hans Schilimacher
Specific Interests: Prairie and Temperate Forest

BIOLOGICAL LABORATORY, UNIVERSITY OF CALIFORNIA
P O BOX 271
LA JOLLA, CA 92037
General Environment: Oceanographic

BIOLOGICAL RESEARCH BUREAU
RUTGERS UNIVERSITY
NEW BRUNSWICK, NJ 08903
Director, James Leathem

BIOLOGICAL SCIENCE SCHOOL
UNIVERSITY OF LAGOS
LAGOS (YABA), NIGERIA
Director, Professor Caleb J O Olaniyan
General Environment: Oceanographic

BIOLOGICAL SCIENCES CURRICULUM STUDY, UNIVERSITY OF COLORADO
POST OFFICE BOX 930
BOULDER, CO 80301
Staff Size: 10 - 49

BIOLOGICAL SCIENCES DEPARTMENT
DARTMOUTH COLLEGE
HANOVER, NH 03755

BIOLOGICAL SCIENCES DEPARTMENT, CALIFORNIA STATE COLLEGE
800 MONTE VISTA AVENUE
TURLOCK, CA 93726
Director, Steve J Grillos

BIOLOGICAL SCIENCES DIVISION
CORNELL UNIVERSITY
ITHACA, NY 14850
Director, Brooks Maylor

BIOLOGICAL STATION, USA
KOCHI UNIVERSITY
USA, JAPAN
Director, Dr Takeshi Yatsuka
General Environment: Oceanographic
Specific Interests: Prairie and Temperate Forest

BIOLOGICAL STATION, WALLA WALLA COLLEGE
RT 3 BOX 555 ROSARIO BEACH
ANACORTES, WA 98221
Director, Dr Harold G Coffin

BIOLOGICAL STRUCTURE DEPARTMENT, SCHOOL OF MEDICINE
UNIVERSITY OF WASHINGTON
SEATTLE, WA 98105
Director, R Blandau

BIOLOGICKY USTAV SAV
BRATISLAVA, KOLLAROVO
NAM 2, CZECHOSLOVAKIA
General Environment: Oceanographic
Staff Size: 10 - 49

BIOLOGY AND HEALTH SCIENCES
CALIFORNIA STATE COLLEGE AT HAWARD
HAWARD, CA 94542
Director, Harvey Scudder

BIOLOGY DEPARTMENT
UNIVERSITY OF YORK
YORK YO1500, ENGLAND
Director, Mark H Williamson
Staff Size: 10 - 49

BIOLOGY DEPARTMENT
BOSTON COLLEGE
CHESTNUT HILL, MA 02167
Specific Interests: Prairie and Temperate Forest

BIOLOGY DEPARTMENT
CALIFORNIA STATE POLYTECHNIC
   INSTITUTE
POMONA, CA 94366
Specific Interests: Prairie and Temperate
   Forest

BIOLOGY DEPARTMENT
UNIVERSITY OF SYDNEY
SYDNEY, VICTORIA, AUSTRALIA
Director, Dr Spencer Smith-White

BIOLOGY DEPARTMENT
AMERICAN UNIVERSITY OF BEIRUT
BEIRUT, LEBANON
General Environment: Oceanographic

BIOLOGY DEPARTMENT
CEDAR CREST COLLEGE
ALLENTOWN, PA 18104
Specific Interests: Prairie and Temperate
   Forest
Staff Size: 5 - 9

BIOLOGY DEPARTMENT
VICTORIA UNIVERSITY
VICTORIA, BRITISH COLUMBIA,
   CANADA
Director, G Fields
General Environment: Oceanographic

BIOLOGY DEPARTMENT
PRINCETON UNIVERSITY
PRINCETON, NJ 08540

BIOLOGY DEPARTMENT
MID-APPALACHIAN COLLEGE
   COUNCIL
KNOXVILLE, TN 37921
Specific Interests: Prairie and Temperate
   Forest

BIOLOGY DEPARTMENT
RICE UNIVERSITY
HOUSTON, TX 77001
Staff Size: 10 - 49

BIOLOGY DEPARTMENT
SAINT LOUIS UNIVERSITY
ST LOUIS, MO 63103

BIOLOGY DEPARTMENT
COLLEGE OF IDAHO
CALDWELL, ID 83605
Director, Lyle Stanford

BIOLOGY DEPARTMENT
DOMINICAN COLLEGE
RACINE, WI 53402
Specific Interests: Prairie and Temperate
   Forest
Staff Size: 1 - 4

BIOLOGY DEPARTMENT
NORTH TEXAS STATE UNIVERSITY
DENTON, TX 76203

BIOLOGY DEPARTMENT
CATHOLIC UNIVERSITY OF
   AMERICA
WASHINGTON, DC 20001

**BIOLOGY DEPARTMENT, PACE
   COLLEGE**
41 PARK ROW
NEW YORK, NY 10038
Director, Dolores Keller

**BIOLOGY DEPARTMENT,
   UNIVERSITY OF ALASKA**
POST OFFICE BOX 95175
COLLEGE, AK 99701
Head, Stephen Norrell

**BIOLOGY DEPARTMENT,
   UNIVERSITY OF HELSINKI**
UNIONINKATU 44
HELSINKI, FINLAND
Specific Interests: Prairie and Temperate
   Forest

**BIOLOGY DEPARTMENT,
   UNIVERSITY OF ROSTOCK**
DOBERANER STRASSE
ROSTOCK, EAST GERMANY
Director, Eike Libbert
Specific Interests: Prairie and Temperate
   Forest

BIOLOGY INSTITUTE
STR LATINA I
BUCHAREST, RUMANIA
Director, L Ludovic Rudescu
Specific Interests: Prairie and Temperate
   Forest

BIOLOGY INSTITUTE
TESLOVA 19
LJUBLJANA, YUGOSLAVIA
Director, Jovan Hadzi
Specific Interests: Prairie and Temperate
   Forest

**BIOLOGY INSTITUTE, TRAIAN
   SAVULESCU**
STR COGILNIC 35
BUCHAREST, RUMANIA
Director, I Theodor Busnita
Specific Interests: Prairie and Temperate
   Forest

BIOLOGY LABORATORY
HARVARD UNIVERSITY
CAMBRIDGE, MA 02138
Staff Size: 50 - 99

BOTANICAL INSTITUTION
UNIVERSITY OF LISBON
LISBON, PORTUGAL
Director, Flavio F P Resende

BOTANICAL SCIENCE INSTITUTE
UNIVERSITY OF MILAN, V GIUS
COLOMBO 60, MILAN, ITALY
Director, Sergio Tunzig

**BOTANY AND BOTANICAL
   GARDENS INSTITUTE**
TECHNOLOGY UNIVERSITY,
   MOMMSENSTRASSE
DRESDEN-A, EAST GERMANY
Director, Herbert Ulbricht
Specific Interests: Prairie and Temperate
   Forest

**BOTANY AND MICROBIOLOGY
   DEPARTMENT**
MONTANA STATE UNIVERSITY
BOZEMAN, MT 59715
Director, W Walter

**BOTANY AND PHYSIOLOGY
   INSTITUTE**
UNIVERSITY OF STOCKHOLM
STOCKHOLM, SWEDEN
Director, Torsten Hemberg
Specific Interests: Polar (cold)

**BOTANY AND PLANT PATHOLOGY
   DEPARTMENT**
COLORADO STATE UNIVERSITY
FORT COLLINS, CO 80521
General Environment: Terrestrial
Specific Interests: Prairie and Temperate
   Forest

BOTANY DEPARTMENT
HEBREW UNIVERSITY OF
   JERUSALEM
JERUSALEM, ISRAEL
Director, Dr I Friedman
General Environment: Oceanographic

BOTANY DEPARTMENT
PRIVATE BAG, RONDEBOSCH
CAPE TOWN, REP OF SOUTH
   AFRICA

**BOTANY DEPARTMENT,
   STANISLAUS STATE COLLEGE**
800 MONTE VISTA AVENUE
TURLOCK, CA 93940

**BOTANY DEPARTMENT,
   UNIVERSITY OF AUCKLAND**
POST OFFICE BOX 2175
AUCKLAND, NEW ZEALAND
Director, Professor V J Chapman
Specific Interests: Prairie and Temperate
   Forest
Staff Size: 10 - 49

**BOTANY INSTITUTION OF V L
   KOMAROV**
ULITSA POPOVA, 2
LENINGRAD, P-22, UNION OF
   SOVIET SOCIALIST REPUBLICS
Specific Interests: Polar (cold)

**BUENOS AIRES INSTITUTION OF
   TECHNOLOGY**
AVDA EDUARDO MADERO 351
BUENOS AIRES, ARGENTINA
General Environment: Oceanographic

CALIFORNIA INSTITUTE OF TECHNOLOGY
PASADENA, CA 91109
Director, Edward Lewis

CARLOS R DE ALBA P OCEAN
POST OFFICE BOX 453
ENSENADA, MEXICO
General Environment: Oceanographic
Staff Size: 10 - 49

CARTOGRAPHIC INSTITUTE
UNIVERSITY OF SANTO DOMINGO
SANTO DOMINGO, DOMINICAN REPUBLIC
General Environment: Oceanographic

CENTER BOTANICAL SOCIETY, INCORPORATED
NORTH CAROLINA STATE UNIVERSITY
RALEIGH, NC 27607
Director, L J Bradley
Staff Size: 50 - 99

CENTRAL INSTITUTION OF BIOLOGY, UNIVERSITY OF CONCEPCION
CASILLA 301
CONCEPCION, CHILE
Director, Dr H.l. Barrales

COMMUNITY UNIVERSITY OF PERU
HUACHO, PERU
General Environment: Oceanographic

CORAL REEF PROJECT
UNIVERSITY OF WEST INDIES
UWI KINGSTON, JAMAICA
Director, Dr T F Goreaw
General Environment: Oceanographic

EDUCATION ORTO BOTANICAL INSTITUTION, DELL UNIVERSITY PALERMO
V LINCOLN
PALERMO, ITALY
Director, Francesco Bruno

EGE UNIVERSITY
IZMIR, TURKEY
General Environment: Oceanographic

ENTOMOLOGY DEPARTMENT
SAN JOSE STATE COLLEGE
SAN JOSE, CA 95114
Professor, James Tilden

ENTOMOLOGY DIVISION, SCHOOL OF AGRICULTURE, UNIVERSITY OF ABERDEEN
ABERDEEN, ENGLAND
Director, George F Burnett
General Environment: Terrestrial
Specific Interests: Rural
Staff Size: 1 - 4

ENVIRONMENTAL AND BIOLOGICAL RESEARCH INSTITUTE
UTAH UNIVERSITY
SALT LAKE CITY, UT 84101
Director, Dr Don M Rees

ENVIRONMENTAL BIOLOGY
EASTERN NAZARENE COLLEGE
QUINCY, MA 02125
Specific Interests: Prairie and Temperate Forest

ENVIRONMENTAL BIOLOGY INSTITUTE
UNIVERSITY OF RHODE ISLAND
KINGSTON, RI 02836

ENVIRONMENTAL HEALTH CENTER
UNIVERSITY OF MISSOURI
COLUMBIA, MO 65201
Specific Interests: Prairie and Temperate Forest

ENVIRONMENTAL HEALTH DEPARTMENT, UNIVERSITY OF TEXAS
POST OFFICE BOX 20186
HOUSTON, TX 90007
Professor, Dr Leslie Chambers
General Environment: Oceanographic

ENVIRONMENTAL SCIENCES CENTER
SANTA ROSA JUNIOR COLLEGE
SANTA ROSA, CA 95402
Specific Interests: Prairie and Temperate Forest

ENVIRONMENTAL SCIENCES COLLEGE
UNIVERSITY OF WISCONSIN
GREEN BAY, WI 54301
Specific Interests: Prairie and Temperate Forest

ENVIRONMENTAL SCIENCES PROGRAM, DEPARTMENT OF MICROBIOLOGY
MCNEESE STATE UNIVERSITY
LAKE CHARLES, LA 70601
Chairman, Dr V Monsour
Staff Size: 5 - 9

ENVIRONMENTAL STRESS INSTITUTE
UNIVERSITY OF CALIFORNIA
SANTA BARBARA, CA 93106
Director, S Horvath
Staff Size: 50 - 99

ENVIRONMENTAL STUDIES
UNIVERSITY OF PORT ELIZABETH
PORT ELIZABETH, REPUBLIC OF SOUTH AFRICA
General Environment: Oceanographic

ENVIRONMENTAL STUDIES
UNIVERSITY COLLEGE
DURBAN, REPUBLIC OF SOUTH AFRICA
General Environment: Oceanographic

ENVIRONMENTAL STUDIES
HOLLINS COLLEGE
HOLLINS COLLEGE, VA 24020
Director, Dr Charles Morlang, Jr
Staff Size: 50 - 99

ENVIRONMENTAL STUDIES
UNIVERSITY OF TENNESSEE
KNOXVILLE, TN 37901

ENVIRONMENTAL STUDIES PROGRAM
BROWARD JUNIOR COLLEGE
FORT LAUDERDALE, FL 33334

ESTUARINE STUDIES CENTER
UNIVERSITY OF JACKSONVILLE
JACKSONVILLE, FL 32211
General Environment: Estuarine
Specific Interests: Prairie and Temperate Forest

EXPERIMENTAL RADIOLOGY, SCHOOL OF MEDICINE
UNIVERSITY OF ROCHESTER
ROCHESTER, NY 14600
Director, Louis Hempelmann

FISHERIES AND BIOLOGICAL UNITS
UNIVERSITY OF SINGAPORE
SINGAPORE
Director, Dr Tham Ah Kow
General Environment: Oceanographic
Specific Interests: Tropical (hot)

FISHERIES AND OCEANOGRAPHY, UNIVERSITY OF RIO GRANDE SUL
ENTREPOSTA DE PESCA
ESTADO RIO GRANDE SUL, BRAZIL
Director, Dr Boaventura Barcellos
General Environment: Oceanographic

FISHERIES CENTER, LABORATORY OF RADIATION BIOLOGY
UNIVERSITY OF WASHINGTON
SEATTLE, WA 98105
General Environment: Terrestrial

FISHERIES COLLEGE
UNIVERSITY OF PHILIPPINES
QUEZON CITY, PHILIPPINES
Director, Dean Nazario Pidlaon
Specific Interests: Prairie and Temperate Forest

FISHERIES COLLEGE
PENANG, MALAYSIA
General Environment: Oceanographic
Specific Interests: Tropical (hot)

**FISHERIES COLLEGE AT PUSAN,
PUSAN NATIONAL UNIVERSITY**
559 DAE YONG DONG
PUSAN, KOREA

Director, Chong Tae Yong
General Environment: Oceanographic
Specific Interests: Prairie and Temperate
Forest

**FISHERIES COLLEGE, KASETSART
UNIVERSITY**
BANGKHEN
BANGKOK, THAILAND

Director, Professor Chote Suvatti
General Environment: Oceanographic
Specific Interests: Tropical (hot)

FISHERIES DEPARTMENT
LYALLPUR AGRICULTURAL
UNIVERSITY
MYMENSINGH, PAKISTAN

Director, M Doha
General Environment: Oceanographic

**FISHERIES DEPARTMENT,
AGRICULTURE FACULTY**
HAKOZAKI-MACHI
FUKUOKA, JAPAN

General Environment: Oceanographic
Staff Size: 1 - 4

FISHERIES FACULTY
KINKI UNIVERSITY
FUSE, JAPAN

General Environment: Oceanographic
Specific Interests: Prairie and Temperate
Forest

FISHERIES FACULTY
HAKKAIDO UNIVERSITY
HAKODATE, JAPAN

Director, Dr Shinjro Kobayashi
General Environment: Oceanographic
Specific Interests: Prairie and Temperate
Forest

FISHERIES FACULTY
FISHERIES INSTITUTE
TOKYO, JAPAN

General Environment: Oceanographic
Specific Interests: Prairie and Temperate
Forest

FISHERIES INSTITUTE
MIYE PREFECTURAL UNIVERSITY
TSU MIYE, JAPAN

Director, Dr Sueo Shino
General Environment: Oceanographic
Specific Interests: Prairie and Temperate
Forest

FISHERIES INSTITUTE
NIHON UNIVERSITY
TOKYO, JAPAN

Director, Dr Nobuyuki Kawamoto
General Environment: Oceanographic
Specific Interests: Prairie and Temperate
Forest

FISHERIES INSTITUTE
KAGOSHIMA UNIVERSITY
KAGOSHIMA, JAPAN

Director, Dr Tada Takahashi
General Environment: Oceanographic
Specific Interests: Prairie and Temperate
Forest

FISHERIES INSTITUTE
OCHANOMIZU WOMEN'S
UNIVERSITY
TOKYO, JAPAN

General Environment: Oceanographic
Specific Interests: Prairie and Temperate
Forest

FISHERIES INSTITUTION
NAGASAKI UNIVERSITY
NAGASAKI, JAPAN

Director, Tetsuo Yamada
General Environment: Oceanographic
Specific Interests: Prairie and Temperate
Forest

FISHERIES RESEARCH CENTER
UNIVERSITY OF OKLAHOMA
NOBLE, OK 73068

Director, Dr Howard P Clemens
General Environment: Limnologic
Specific Interests: Desert

**FISHERIES RESOURCE INSTITUTE,
UNIVERSITY OF URUGUAY**
ALBERTO LASPLACES 1550
MONTEVIDEO, URUGUAY

Director, Dr Victor H Bertullo
General Environment: Oceanographic

FISHERIES STATION
TSUYAZAKI, FUKUOKA, JAPAN

Director, Dr Kiroshi Tsukahara
General Environment: Oceanographic
Specific Interests: Prairie and Temperate
Forest

**FISHERIES TECHNIQUES
DEPARTMENT**
UNIVERSITY OF SAO PAULO
SAO PAULO, BRAZIL

General Environment: Oceanographic

FISHERIES UNIVERSITY OF TOKYO
TOKYO, JAPAN

Director, Dr Michitaka Uda
General Environment: Oceanographic
Specific Interests: Prairie and Temperate
Forest

**FISHERY FACULTY, KAGOSHIMA
UNIVERSITY**
470 SHIMA, ARATA-CHO
KAGOSHIMA, JAPAN

Director, Dr K Konda
General Environment: Oceanographic

FOREST BOTANY INSTITUTE
BERTOLDSTRASSE 17
78 FREIBURG 1 BR, WEST GERMANY

Director, Hans Marquardt
General Environment: Terrestrial
Specific Interests: Prairie and Temperate
Forest
Staff Size: 5 - 9

**FOREST INSTITUTE FOR OCEAN
AND MOUNTAIN STUDY**
BOX 621 ROUTE 1
CARSON CITY, NV 89701

Director, Dr Richard Miller
General Environment: Oceanographic
Specific Interests: Mountainous

**FORESTRY INSTITUTION,
UNIVERSITY OF FREIBURG**
FREIBURG/BR
SONNHALDE 77, WEST GERMANY

Director, Karl Abetz
General Environment: Terrestrial
Specific Interests: Prairie and Temperate
Forest

**FRESHWATER BIOLOGICAL
LABORATORY, UNIVERSITY OF
COPENHAGEN**
51 HELSINGORSGADE DENMARK
3400
HILLEROD, DENMARK

Director, Professor E Nielsen
General Environment: Limnologic
Staff Size: 10 - 49

**FRESNO SCIENCE, DEPARTMENT
OF BIOLOGY**
SHAW AND CEDAR AVENUES
FRESNO, CA 93726

Director, Thomas Gunn

**GENERAL ANIMAL PHYSIOLOGY,
UNIVERSITY OF SOUTH PAULO**
CAIXA POSTA 11, 230 SOUTH P 9
SAO PAULO, BRAZIL

Director, Dr Paulo Sawaya

**GENETICS DEPARTMENT, NORTH
CAROLINA STATE UNIVERSITY**
POST OFFICE BOX 5356
RALEIGH, NC 27607

Specific Interests: Prairie and Temperate
Forest

**GENETICS DEPARTMENT, SCHOOL
OF MEDICINE**
UNIVERSITY OF WASHINGTON
SEATTLE, WA 98105

Director, S Gartler

GEOLOGY DEPARTMENT
UNIVERSITY OF EL SALVADOR
SAN SALVADOR, EL SALVADOR

Director, Dr Enrique Vinatea
General Environment: Oceanographic

**GEOLOGY INSTITUTE, INSTITUTE
OF APPLIED SCIENCE**
CIUDAD UNIVERSITARIA
MEXICO 20, DF, MEXICO

Director, Dr Guillermo P Salas
General Environment: Oceanographic
Staff Size: 50 - 99

HEALTH LAW CENTER
130 DESOTO STREET
PITTSBURGH, PA 15213

HUMAN PROTECTION CENTER
GREENSHORE COLLEGE
GREENSHORE, NC 27420

Specific Interests: Prairie and Temperate
  Forest

**HYDROBIOLOGICAL INSTITUTION,
  UNIVERSITY OF ISTANBUL**
BALTALIMANI
ISTANBUL, TURKEY

Director, Professor Muzaffer Demir
General Environment: Oceanographic

HYDROBIOLOGICAL LABORATORY
KANSAS STATE TEACHERS
  COLLEGE
PRATT, KS 67124

Director, Roy Schoonover
General Environment: Terrestrial

**HYDROBIOLOGICAL STATION AT
  OTSU**
OTSU, JAPAN

Director, Dr Syuiti Mori
General Environment: Limnologic
Staff Size: 5 - 9

**HYDROBIOLOGY AND
  FISCHEREIWISS INSTITUTE**
2 HAMBURG-ALTONA 1
OLBERSWEG 24, WEST GERMANY

Director, Professor Adolf Buckman
Specific Interests: Prairie and Temperate
  Forest

**HYDROBIOLOGY LABORATORY,
  INSTITUTE OF BIOLOGY**
CIUDAD UNIVERSITARIA
MEXICO 20, OF, MEXICO

Director, Dr Villalobos F Alejandro
General Environment: Oceanographic

HYDROLOGY INSTITUTE
UNIVERSITY OF TEHRAN
TEHRAN, IRAN

Director, Dr M Mozayeny
General Environment: Oceanographic

**INSTITUTION RUTLDE
  L'UNIVERSITY**
UNIVERSITY OF MONTPELLIER
MONTPELLIER, FRANCE

Director, Louis Emberger
Specific Interests: Prairie and Temperate
  Forest

**JORGE LADEO LOZANO,
  UNIVERSITY DE BOGOTA**
CALLE 23 NO 4-47
BOGOTA, COLOMBIA

Director, Luis Ortig Borda
General Environment: Oceanographic
Staff Size: 100 - 499

**LABORATORIES OF FRIDAY
  HARBOR**
UNIVERSITY OF WASHINGTON
FRIDAY HARBOR, WA 98250

General Environment: Oceanographic

**LIFE SCIENCES RESOURCES
  CENTER, KENT STATE
  UNIVERSITY**
AGASSIZ HOUSE
KENT, OH

Director, Dr Charles C Wilber

LIMNOLOGY DEPARTMENT
UNIVERSITY OF OSLO
OSLO, NORWAY

Director, Kaare Strom
General Environment: Limnologic
Specific Interests: Polar (cold)

**MARINE AND ATMOSPHERIC
  SCIENCE SCHOOL, UNIVERSITY
  OF MIAMI**
RICKENBACKER HIGHWAY
MIAMI, FL 33149

Dean, Dr F G Walton Smith
General Environment: Oceanographic
Staff Size: 100 - 499

**MARINE AND FOOD SCIENCES
  SCHOOL**
MONTEREY INSTITUTE OF
  TECHNOLOGY
GUAYMAS, SONORA, MEXICO

Dean, Dr Henry J Schafer
General Environment: Estuarine
Specific Interests: Tropical (hot)
Staff Size: 10 - 49

**MARINE BIOLOGICAL INSTITUTE
  OF OREGON**
UNIVERSITY OF OREGON
CHARLESTON, OR 97420

Director, Dr Peter W Frank
General Environment: Oceanographic

**MARINE BIOLOGICAL INSTITUTE
  OF SAO SEBASTIAO**
CAIXA POSTAL 11.230
SAO PAULO 9, BRAZIL

Director, Paulo Sawaya
General Environment: Oceanographic
Specific Interests: Tropical (hot)

**MARINE BIOLOGICAL
  LABORATORY**
SOUTHEAST ASIA TREATY
  ORGANIZATION
SHIRAHAMA, JAPAN

Director, Dr D Miyada
General Environment: Oceanographic
Specific Interests: Prairie and Temperate
  Forest

**MARINE BIOLOGICAL
  LABORATORY**
NIIGATA UNIVERSITY
SADO ISLAND, JAPAN

Director, Dr Keizo Aimi
General Environment: Oceanographic
Specific Interests: Prairie and Temperate
  Forest

**MARINE BIOLOGICAL
  LABORATORY AT WAGU**
OSAKA UNIVERSITY
WAGU, JAPAN

General Environment: Oceanographic
Specific Interests: Prairie and Temperate
  Forest

**MARINE BIOLOGICAL
  LABORATORY, UNIVERSITY OF
  COPENHAGEN**
GRONNEHAVE, HELSINGOR
COPENHAGEN, DENMARK

General Environment: Oceanographic
Specific Interests: Prairie and Temperate
  Forest

**MARINE BIOLOGICAL RESOURCES
  CENTER, UNIVERSITY OF
  BUENOS AIRES**
AVDA, ALBARELLOS Y
  CONSERVATION
BUENOS AIRES, ARGENTINA

Director, Dr Oscar Kuhnemann
General Environment: Oceanographic

**MARINE BIOLOGICAL SECTION,
  FACULTY OF SCIENCES**
UNIVERSITY COLUMBIA OF SIERRA
  LEONE
FREETOWN, SIERRA LEONE

General Environment: Oceanographic

MARINE BIOLOGICAL STATION
KUMATOTO UNIVERSITY
AITU, JAPAN

Director, Dr Makoto Yoshikura
General Environment: Oceanographic
Specific Interests: Prairie and Temperate
  Forest

MARINE BIOLOGICAL STATION
UNIVERSITY COLLEGE
KUNDUCHI, TANZANIA

General Environment: Oceanographic

MARINE BIOLOGICAL STATION
TOHOKU UNIVERSITY
ASAMUSHI, JAPAN

Director, Dr Etsuro Hirai
General Environment: Oceanographic
Specific Interests: Prairie and Temperate
  Forest

**MARINE BIOLOGICAL STATION AT
  OSHORO**
OSHORO, JAPAN

Director, Dr Shun Okada
General Environment: Oceanographic
Specific Interests: Prairie and Temperate
  Forest

MARINE BIOLOGICAL STATION AT SHIMODA
TOKYO UNIVERSITY OF EDUCATION
SHIMODA, JAPAN
Director, Dr Isokichi Harada
General Environment: Oceanographic
Specific Interests: Prairie and Temperate Forest

MARINE BIOLOGICAL STATION, HIROSHIMA UNIVERSITY
MUKAISHIMA, ONOMICHI P.O.
HIROSHIMA-KEN, JAPAN
Director, Professor Akihiko Inaba
General Environment: Oceanographic
Staff Size: 5 - 9

MARINE BIOLOGICAL STATION, TOMANO
OKAYAMA UNIVERSITY
TAMANO, JAPAN
Director, Dr Seiji Iwata
General Environment: Oceanographic
Specific Interests: Prairie and Temperate Forest

MARINE BIOLOGY
SAN JOSE STATE COLLEGE
SAN JOSE, CA 95114
Director, Professor Joseph Young
General Environment: Oceanographic

MARINE BIOLOGY DEPARTMENT
UNIVERSITY OF OSLO
OSLO, NORWAY
Director, Johan T Rudd
General Environment: Oceanographic
Specific Interests: Polar (cold)

MARINE BIOLOGY DEPARTMENT, DIVISION OF SCIENCE
UNIVERSITY OF LIBERIA
MONROVIA, LIBERIA
Directors, Dr P Gideon and Mrs Agnes C Dennis
General Environment: Oceanographic
Specific Interests: Tropical (hot)

MARINE BIOLOGY DEPARTMENT, UNIVERSITY OF KERALA
TRIVANDRUM 7
KERALA STATE, INDIA
General Environment: Oceanographic

MARINE BIOLOGY INSTITUTE
UNIVERSITY OF PUERTO RICO
MAYAGUEZ, PUERTO RICO
Director, Dr John E Randall
General Environment: Oceanographic

MARINE BIOLOGY INSTITUTE, INTER-UNIVERSITY
CASILLA DE CORREO 175
MAR DEL PLATO, ARGENTINA
Director, Dr Enrique E Boschi
General Environment: Oceanographic

MARINE BIOLOGY INSTITUTE, UNIVERSITY DE BORDEAUX
9 RUE PIERLOT, 33
BORDEAUX, FRANCE
Director, R Weill
General Environment: Oceanographic
Staff Size: 1 - 4

MARINE BIOLOGY STATION
SEOUL NATIONAL UNIVERSITY
SEOUL, KOREA
Director, Lee M Jai
General Environment: Oceanographic
Specific Interests: Prairie and Temperate Forest

MARINE BIOLOGY STATION, UNIVERSITY OF CHILE, NORTH ZONE
CASILLA 1240
ANTOFAGASTA, CHILE
General Environment: Oceanographic

MARINE BIOLOGY STATION, UNIVERSITY OF PHILIPPINES
PUERTO GALERA
ORIENTAL MINDORO, PHILIPPINES
General Environment: Oceanographic
Specific Interests: Prairie and Temperate Forest

MARINE BIOLOGY, NATIONAL TAIWAN UNIVERSITY
ROOSEVELT ROAD
TAIPEI, TAIWAN
Director, Professor Yun-Sheng Lian
General Environment: Oceanographic
Specific Interests: Tropical (hot)

MARINE FISHERIES DEPARTMENT, UNIVERSITY OF PHILIPPINES
BOSTON AND 23 STREET
PORT AREA, MANILA, PHILLIPPINES
Director, Dr Teodore G Megra
General Environment: Oceanographic
Specific Interests: Prairie and Temperate Forest

MARINE FISHERIES SCHOOLS
PENANG AND KUALA
TRENGGANU, MALAYSIA
Director, J L Carualho
General Environment: Oceanographic
Specific Interests: Tropical (hot)

MARINE GEOLOGICAL STATION
TOHOKU UNIVERSITY
SENDAI, JAPAN
Director, Dr Kiyoshi Asano
General Environment: Oceanographic
Specific Interests: Prairie and Temperate Forest

MARINE INSTITUTION
UNIVERSITY OF GEORGIA
SAPELO ISLAND, GA 31327
Director, Dr Vernon J Henry, Jr
General Environment: Oceanographic

MARINE LABORATORY, EAST PERCIVAL
UNIVERSITY OF CANTERBURY
KAIOURA, MARLBOROUGH, NEW ZEALAND
General Environment: Oceanographic
Specific Interests: Prairie and Temperate Forest
Staff Size: 1 - 4

MARINE LABORATORY, UNIVERSITY OF HAWAII
1801 UNIVERSITY AVENUE
HONOLULU 14, HI 96800
Director, Vernon E Brock
General Environment: Oceanographic

MARINE RESOURCES LABORATORY
UNIVERSITY OF CONNECTICUT
NOANK, CT 06340
Director, Dr John S Rankin Jr
General Environment: Oceanographic

MARINE RESOURCES, UNIVERSITY OF ALABAMA
P O BOX 188
DAUPHIN ISLAND, AL 36528
General Environment: Oceanographic

MARINE SCIENCE INSTITUTE
POST OFFICE BOX 809
MOREHEAD CITY, NC 28557
Director, Dr F Chestnut
General Environment: Oceanographic

MARINE SCIENCE INSTITUTE, UNIVERSITY OF KIEL
NIEMANNSWEG 11
23 KIEL, WEST GERMANY
Director, Professor Dr F Defant
General Environment: Oceanographic

MARINE SCIENCE SCHOOL, UNIVERSITY OF BAJA CALIFORNIA
CALLE PRIMERA 1838
ENSENADA, MEXICO
Subdirector, Ing Angel Garcia Gonzalez
General Environment: Oceanographic

MARINE SCIENCES CENTER
LEWES, DE 19958
General Environment: Oceanographic
Specific Interests: Prairie and Temperate Forest

MARINE SCIENCES CONSORTIUM OF PENNSYLVANIA
MILLERSVILLE, PA 17551
General Environment: Oceanographic
Specific Interests: Prairie and Temperate Forest

MARINE SCIENCES DEPARTMENT
CALIFORNIA STATE COLLEGE
LONG BEACH, CA 90801

Specific Interests: Prairie and Temperate
Forest

MARINE SCIENCES FACULTY
TOKAI UNIVERSITY
SHIMUZU, SHIZUOKA, JAPAN
Director, Dr Shoichiro Hayami
General Environment: Oceanographic
Specific Interests: Prairie and Temperate
Forest

**MARINE SCIENCES LABORATORY,
UNIVERSITY COLLEGE OF
NORTH WALES**
MENAI BRIDGE, WALES
Director, Dr D J Crisp, F R S
General Environment: Oceanographic

MARINE STATION
UNIVERSITY OF ALASKA
DOUGLAS, AK 99824
General Environment: Oceanographic
Specific Interests: Polar (cold)

**MARINE STATION AT
SHIRIGISHINAI**
SHIRIGISHINAI, JAPAN
General Environment: Oceanographic
Specific Interests: Prairie and Temperate
Forest

**MARINE STATION AT VICTORIA
UNIVERSITY**
ISLAND BAY
WELLINGTON, NEW ZEALAND
Director, Dr R E Pike
General Environment: Oceanographic
Specific Interests: Prairie and Temperate
Forest

**MAX-PLANCK INSTITUTION OF
BIOLOGY**
CORRENSSTRASSE 41
TUBINGEN, WEST GERMANY
Director, Georg Melchers
Specific Interests: Prairie and Temperate
Forest

**MEDICINE EPIDEMEOLOGY, LUNG
RESEARCH CENTER**
YALE UNIVERSITY
NEW HAVEN, CT 06510
Director, Professor Bouhuys
General Environment: Atmospheric
Staff Size: 10 - 49

**METEOROLOGY AND
OCEANOGRAPHY DEPARTMENT,
ANDHRA UNIVERSITY**
WALTAIR
ANDHRA PRADESH STATE, INDIA
General Environment: Oceanographic
Specific Interests: Tropical (hot)

**MICRO ENVIRONMENTAL
PHYSIOLOGY RESEARCH**
KEPPEL STATE, HYGIENE AND
TROPICAL MEDICINE
LONDON WCI, ENGLAND

Director, Joseph S Weiner
Specific Interests: Prairie and Temperate
Forest

**MICROBIOLOGICAL
SPECIFICATIONS COMMISSION
(INTERNATIONAL)**
4204 DRESDEN STREET
KENSINGTON, MD 20795
Director, Professor Glenn Slocum

MICROBIOLOGY DEPARTMENT
COLORADO STATE UNIVERSITY
FORT COLLINS, CO 80521

MICROBIOLOGY INSTITUTE
JAHNSTR 15
GREIFSWALD, EAST GERMANY
Director, Wilhem Schwartz
Specific Interests: Prairie and Temperate
Forest

**NATURAL RESOURCES POLICY
CENTER**
GEORGE WASHINGTON
UNIVERSITY
WASHINGTON, DC
Specific Interests: Prairie and Temperate
Forest

NATURAL RESOURCES SCHOOL
UNIVERSITY OF MICHIGAN
ANN ARBOR, MI 48101

NATURAL SCIENCES DEPARTMENT
CALIFORNIA STATE COLLEGE
BAKERSFIELD, CA 93306
Specific Interests: Prairie and Temperate
Forest

**NATURAL SCIENCES
DEPARTMENT, SONOMA STATE
COLLEGE**
1801 EAST COLATI AVENUE
ROHNERT PARK, CA 94928
Director, Clement E Falbo

**NUCLEAR MEDICINE DIVISION,
MEDICAL SCHOOL**
UNIVERSITY OF MIAMI
MIAMI, FL 33140
Staff Size: 50 - 99

**OBSTETRICS AND GYNECOLOGY
DEPARTMENT**
UNIVERSITY OF COLORADO
MEDICAL CENTER
DENVER, CO 80220
Director, D Hagerman

**OBSTETRICS AND GYNECOLOGY
DEPARTMENT, SCHOOL OF
MEDICINE**
VANDERBILT UNIVERSITY
NASHVILLE, TN 37203
Director, Marie Orgebin-Crist

**OBSTETRICS AND GYNECOLOGY
DEPARTMENT, SCHOOL OF
MEDICINE**
UNIVERSITY OF TEXAS
SAN ANTONIO, TX 78229
Director, J Seitchik

**OBSTETRICS AND GYNECOLOGY,
SCHOOL OF MEDICINE**
DUKE UNIVERSITY
DURHAM, NC 27706
Chairman, R Parker

**OBSTETRICS, GYNECOLOGY AND
ANATOMY DEPARTMENT**
UNIVERSITY OF KANSAS MEDICAL
CENTER
KANSAS CITY, KS 66103
Director, Gilbert Greenwald

**OCEANOGRAPHIC INSTITUTE AT
WOODS HOLE**
WOODS HOLE, MA 02543
Director, Dr Paul M Fye
General Environment: Oceanographic
Specific Interests: Prairie and Temperate
Forest

**OCEANOGRAPHIC INSTITUTE,
UNIVERSITY OF SAO PAULO**
CAIXA POSTA 9075, ALOMEDA
ED PRADO 698, SAO PAULO, BRAZIL
Director, Dr Martha Vannucci
General Environment: Oceanographic

OCEANOGRAPHIC LABORATORY
KERALA UNIVERSITY
ERNAKULAM, INDIA
Director, Dr C V Kurian
General Environment: Oceanographic
Specific Interests: Tropical (hot)

**OCEANOGRAPHIC RESEARCH
STATION**
TOKYO UNIVERSITY
TOKYO, JAPAN
Director, Yoshimitsu Ogura
General Environment: Oceanographic
Specific Interests: Prairie and Temperate
Forest

**OCEANOGRAPHY AND
BIOLOGICAL FISHERIES
DEPARTMENT**
UNIVERSITY OF SAO PAULO
SANTOS, BRAZIL
General Environment: Oceanographic

**OCEANOGRAPHY DEPARTMENT,
UNIVERSITY OF ALEXANDRIA**
MOHARREM BAY ALEXANDRIA
EL MISR, UNITED ARAB REPUBLIC
General Environment: Oceanographic

**OCEANOGRAPHY GROUP,
UNIVERSITY OF CALIFORNIA**
P O BOX 6207
SAN DIEGO, CA 92160

General Environment: Oceanographic
Staff Size: 10 - 49

**OCEANOGRAPHY GROUP,
ZOOLOGY DEPARTMENT**
KARACHI UNIVERSITY
KARACHI, PAKISTAN
Director, Dr S Mazhar-Ul Haq
General Environment: Oceanographic

OCEANOGRAPHY INSTITUTE
UNIVERSITY OF ALGIERS
ALGIERS, ALGERIA
Director, Dr F Bernard
General Environment: Oceanographic

**OCEANOGRAPHY INSTITUTE,
UNIVERSITY OF CAPETOWN**
RONDESBOSCH OF GOODHOPE
UNION, REPUBLIC OF SOUTH
AFRICA
Director, Dr J K Mallory
General Environment: Oceanographic

**OCEANOGRAPHY INSTITUTION,
UNIVERSITY OF THE SOUTH**
DARRAGUEIRA 216 BAHIA BLAN
BUENOS AIRES, ARGENTINA
Director, Dr Augusto Calmels
General Environment: Oceanographic

**OCEANOGRAPHY, ADVANCED
STUDY CENTER, ANNAMALAI
UNIVERSITY**
CHIDDAMBARAM
PORTO VOVO, SOUTH INDIA
Director, R V Seshaiya
General Environment: Oceanographic
Specific Interests: Tropical (hot)

**OCEANOGRAPHY, JOHNS HOPKINS
UNIVERSITY, CHESAPEAKE BAY
INSTITUTION**
CHARLES AND 34TH STREETS
BALTIMORE, MD 21218
General Environment: Estuarine

ORTHOPEDICS DIVISION
UNIVERSITY OF COLORADO
MEDICAL CENTER
DENVER, CO 80220
Department Head, Professor J Miles

**PACIFIC COOPERATIVE WATER
POLLUTION LABORATORY**
104 BIOLOGICAL SCIENCES
BUILDING, OREGON STATE
UNIVERSITY
CORVALLIS, OR 97331
Coordinator, Dr C Warren
General Environment: Limnologic
Staff Size: 10 - 49

PACIFIC MARINE STATION
UNIVERSITY OF THE PACIFIC
DILLON BEACH, CA 94929
Director, Dr Joel W Hedgpeth
General Environment: Oceanographic

**PATHOLOGY DEPARTMENT,
MOUNT SINAI SCHOOL OF
MEDICINE**
100TH AND FIFTH AVENUE
NEW YORK, NY 10029
Director, Hans Popper

PHYSIOLOGY DEPARTMENT
KINGSTON, JAMAICA
General Environment: Oceanographic

**PLANT ECOLOGY, VIETNAMESE
CONTRACT SCHOOL**
1135 BEACON AVENUE
PACIFIC GROVE, CA 93950
Director, Cao Thai Bao

PLANT PHYSIOLOGY DEPARTMENT
UNIVERSITY OF LAUSANNE
LAUSANNE, SWITZERLAND
Director, Paul-Emile Pilet
Specific Interests: Mountainous

**PLANT PHYSIOLOGY
DEPARTMENT, WARSAW
UNIVERSITY**
UL 3 MAJA5
WARSZAWA, POLAND
Specific Interests: Prairie and Temperate
Forest

PLANT PHYSIOLOGY INSTITUTE
UNIVERSITY OF LUND
LUND, SWEDEN
Director, Professor Hans Burstrom
Specific Interests: Polar (cold)

PLANT PHYSIOLOGY INSTITUTE
UNIVERSITY OF VIENNA
VIENNA, AUSTRIA
Director, Professor Karl Hofler
Specific Interests: Prairie and Temperate
Forest

PLANT SCIENCE DEPARTMENT
UTAH STATE UNIVERSITY
LOGAN, UT 84321
General Environment: Terrestrial
Specific Interests: Prairie and Temperate
Forest

**PUBLIC HEALTH LIBRARY
GRADUATE SCHOOL,
UNIVERSITY OF PITTSBURGH**
130 DESOTA STREET
PITTSBURGH, PA 15213

**PUBLIC HEALTH SCHOOL,
COLLEGE OF MEDICAL
SCIENCES**
UNIVERSITY OF MINNESOTA
MINNEAPOLIS, MN 55455
Director, Leonard Schuman

RESEARCH LABORATORY
CORNELL ORNAMENTALS
FARMINGDALE, NY 11735
General Environment: Limnologic

RESEARCH WATER BIOLOGY
GANNON COLLEGE
ERIE, PA 16501
Director, Autin O'Toole

RESOURCE LABORATORIES
KOMINATO FISHERIES
KOMINATO, JAPAN
Director, Dr Hiroshi Uno
General Environment: Oceanographic
Specific Interests: Prairie and Temperate
Forest

RIVER RESEARCH FOUNDATION
WINONA STATE COLLEGE
WINONA, MN 55987
Specific Interests: Prairie and Temperate
Forest

**SCIENCE AND TECHNOLOGY
FACULTY**
UNIVERSITY OF MADAGASCAR
TANANARIVE, MALAGASY
REPUBLIC
Director, Gerard Vassails
General Environment: Oceanographic

**SCIENCE AND TECHNOLOGY
RESEARCH COUNCIL OF TURKEY**
BAYINDER SOKAK 33,
VENISHEIR, ANKARA, TURKEY
General Environment: Oceanographic

**SCIENCE FACULTY,
CHULALONGKORN UNIVERSITY**
PATUMWAN
BANGKOK, THAILAND
Director, Professor Tab Nilandidhi
General Environment: Oceanographic
Specific Interests: Tropical (hot)

**SCIENCE INVESTIGATIONS
DEPARTMENT**
UNIVERSITY OF CHILE, NORTH
ZONE
ANTOFAGASTA, CHILE
General Environment: Oceanographic

**SCIENCES AND HUMANITIES
FACULTY**
CERRITO 73,
MONTEVIDEO, URUGUAY
General Environment: Oceanographic

**SCIENTIFIC STATION, BOWDOIN
COLLEGE**
KENT ISLAND
GRAND MANAN, CANADA
Director, Dr C E Huntington
General Environment: Oceanographic

**SCRIPPS INSTITUTE OF
OCEANOGRAPHY AT UNIVERSITY
OF CALIFORNIA**
8602 LA JOLLA DRIVE
LA JOLLA, CA 92037
Director, Dr Roger Revelle
General Environment: Oceanographic

SEA EXPERIMENT STATION
SCIENCES DEPARTMENT
AMAKUSA, JAPAN
General Environment: Oceanographic
Specific Interests: Prairie and Temperate
Forest

SEA INVERTEBRATE LABORATORY
BP 206 IFAN
DAKAR, SENEGAL
Director, R Roy
General Environment: Oceanographic

TECHNOLOGICAL UNIVERSITY OF ISTANBUL
MATERIALS RESEARCH UNITED
ISTANBUL, TURKEY
General Environment: Oceanographic

THE WEIZMANN INSTITUTE OF SCIENCE
POST OFFICE BOX 26
REHOVOTH, ISRAEL
Director, Professor Maschner
General Environment: Oceanographic

TROPICAL ZOOLOGY INSTITUTE
UNIVERSITY OF CENTRAL VENEZUELA
APARTADO SAB, VENEZUELA
Director, Dr Rafael Martinez
Specific Interests: Tropical (hot)

TRUJILLO NATIONAL UNIVERSITY
CASILLA POSTAL 315
TRUJILLO, PERU
Director, Felipe Ancieta Calderon
General Environment: Oceanographic
Staff Size: 10 - 49

UNIVERSITY OF BOMBAY
MAYO ROAD
FORT BOMBAY, INDIA
Director, Professor Rangnekar
General Environment: Oceanographic
Specific Interests: Tropical (hot)

UNIVERSITY OF TEHRAN
TEHRAN, IRAN
Director, Dr J S Saleh
General Environment: Oceanographic

UNIVERSITY OF WISCONSIN
BIOTRON, BIRGE HALL
MADISON, WI 53706
Director, Dr Harold Senn

URBAN ENVIRONMENT INSTITUTE
COLUMBIA UNIVERSITY
NEW YORK, NY 10023
Specific Interests: Urban

VETERINARY MEDICINE FACULTY
UNIVERSITY OF TEHRAN
TEHRAN, IRAN
Director, Dr Aziz Rafyi
General Environment: Oceanographic

VETERINARY PHYSIOLOGY AND PHARMACOLOGY DEPARTMENT
ROOM 205 UNIVERSITY OF MINNESOTA
ST PAUL, MN 55101
Director, P Hammond

WATER RESOURCES RESEARCH CENTER
1005 EAST 10TH STREET
BLOOMINGTON, IN 47401

WATER RESOURCES RESEARCH INSTITUTE, UNIVERSITY OF OREGON
114 COVELL HALL
CORVALLIS, OR 97331
General Environment: Oceanographic

WILDLIFE RESEARCH
BIOLOGICAL SCIENCES BUILDING, ROOM 214
TUCSON, AZ 85717

ZOOLOGIC ANSTALT BASEL
RHEINSPRUNG 9
BASEL, SWITZERLAND
Director, Adolf Portmann
Specific Interests: Mountainous

ZOOLOGIC INSTITUTION, JUSTUS LIEBIG UNIVERSITY
LUDWIGSTRASSE 23
GIESSEN, WEST GERMANY
Director, Wulf Emmo Ankel

ZOOLOGIC INVESTIGATION CENTER, UNIVERSITY OF CHILE
CASILLA 10135
SANTIAGO, CHILE
Director, Guillermo Mann

ZOOLOGICAL INSTITUTION, SOUTH UNIVERSITY OF CHILE
CASILLA 567
VALDIVIA, CHILE
Director, Dr Hugo Campos
Staff Size: 10 - 49

ZOOLOGICAL LABORATORY
UNIVERSITY OF PARIS
VILLEFRANCHE-SUR-MER, FRANCE
Director, Professor Bougis
General Environment: Oceanographic

ZOOLOGICAL RESOURCES LABORATORY
MADRAS UNIVERSITY
MADRAS, INDIA
Director, Dr G Krishnan
General Environment: Oceanographic
Specific Interests: Tropical (hot)

ZOOLOGY AND BIOLOGY, HISTORY OF SCIENCES, ADMINISTRATION
EVERGREEN STATE COLLEGE
OLYMPIA, WA 98501
Director, David Barry

ZOOLOGY AND HYDROBIOLOGY INSTITUTE
UNIVERSITY OF PERUGIA
PERUGIA, ITALY
Director, Giampaolo Moretti
General Environment: Limnologic

ZOOLOGY AND MARINE BIOLOGY DEPARTMENT, ANDHRA UNIVERSITY
WALTAIR
ANDHRA PRADESH STATE, INDIA
General Environment: Oceanographic
Specific Interests: Tropical (hot)

ZOOLOGY DEPARTMENT
UNIVERSITY COLLEGE
NAIROBI, KENYA

ZOOLOGY DEPARTMENT
UNIVERSITY OF NEW ENGLAND
ARMINDALE, NEW SOUTH WALES, AUSTRALIA
Director, Professor F O'farrell
General Environment: Terrestrial

ZOOLOGY DEPARTMENT
UNIVERSITY NEWCASTLE-UPON-TYNE
NEWCASTLE-UPON-TYNE,ENGLAND

ZOOLOGY DEPARTMENT
UNIVERSITY OF PADUA
PADUA, ITALY
General Environment: Oceanographic

ZOOLOGY DEPARTMENT
UNIVERSITY OF VIENNA
VIENNA, AUSTRIA
Director, Professor Wilhelm Kuhnelt
General Environment: Terrestrial
Staff Size: 5 - 9

ZOOLOGY DEPARTMENT, KINGSTON HARBOUR RESEARCH PROJECT
UNIVERSITY OF THE WEST INDIES
KINGSTON, JAMAICA
Director, Dr Barry Wade

ZOOLOGY DEPARTMENT, UNIVERSITY COLLEGE
POST OFFICE BOX 9184
DAR ES SALAAM, TANZANIA
Professor, I Griffiths
General Environment: Oceanographic

ZOOLOGY DEPARTMENT, UNIVERSITY OF CANTERBURY
PRIVATE BAG
CHRISTCHURCH, NEW ZEALAND
Director, Professor G Knox
Staff Size: 10 - 49

**ZOOLOGY DEPARTMENT,
    UNIVERSITY OF CEYLON**
THURSTAN ROAD
COLOMBO 2, CEYLON
Director, Hilary Crusz

ZOOLOGY INSTITUTE
61 DARMSTADT
BONN, WEST GERMANY
Director, Wolfgang Luther
Specific Interests: Prairie and Temperate
    Forest

**ZOOLOGY LABORATORY AND
    MUSEUM**
UNIVERSITY OF ATHENS
ATHENS, GREECE
Director, Dr Basil Kiortsis
General Environment: Oceanographic

**ZOOLOGY LABORATORY AND
    MUSEUM, UNIVERSITY OF
    ATHENS**
PANEPISTIMIOPOLIS (621)
ATHENS, GREECE
Director, Dr Basil Kiortsis
General Environment: Oceanographic
Staff Size: 5 - 9

**ZOOLOGY-ICHTHYOLOGY
    INSTITUTE**
USSR ACADEMY OF SCIENCES
LENINGRAD, UNION OF SOVIET
    SOCIALIST REPUBLICS
Director, Anatcli Ni Kolaevich
    Suetovidov
Specific Interests: Polar (cold)

Field Station/Laboratory

AL-GHARDAQA MARINE STATION
CAIRO, UNITED ARAB REPUBLIC
Director, Dr Abdel Rahman Al-Kholy
General Environment: Oceanographic

ANIMAL BEHAVIOR STATION
DUKE UNIVERSITY
DURHAM, NC 27706
Specific Interests: Prairie and Temperate
    Forest

**AQUATIC BIOLOGICAL
    LABORATORY**
OKLAHOMA STATE UNIVERSITY
STILLWATER, OK 74074
Director, Dr Troy C Doreis
General Environment: Limnologic

**BIOLOGICAL LABORATORY OF
    HONOLULU**
2570 DOLE STREET
HONOLULU, HI 96812
General Environment: Terrestrial

BIOLOGICAL STATION
PLACE LACAZE-DUTHIERS
ROSCOFF(FINISTERE), FRANCE
General Environment: Oceanographic

**BIRD PRESERVATION COUNCIL,
    UNITED STATES SECTION**
950 THIRD AVENUE
NEW YORK, NY 10022
Chairman, Roland C Clement
Staff Size: 50 - 99

CANANEIA MARINE STATION
UNIVERSITY OF SAO PAULO
CANANEIA, BRAZIL
General Environment: Oceanographic

CIVIC ENGINEERING LABORATORY
LISBON, PORTUGAL
General Environment: Oceanographic

COASTAL LABORATORY
NAOS ISLAND,
FOR AMADOR, PANAMA
General Environment: Oceanographic

CORK UNIVERSITY STATION
LOUGH INE SKIBBEREEN
COUNTY CORK, IRELAND
General Environment: Oceanographic

**DAGAT-DAGATAN SALT WATER
    FISHERIES EXPERIMENTAL
    STATION**
PHILLIPPINE FISHERIES
    COMMISSION, PO BOX 623
MANILA, PHILIPPINES
General Environment: Oceanographic

EAGLE LAKE FIELD STATION
CALIFORNIA STATE UNIVERSITY
CHICO, CA 95926
Director, Dr Robert I Ediger
Specific Interests: Mountainous
Staff Size: 1 - 4

**FATIO MARINE BIOLOGICAL
    LABORATORY, UNIVERSITY OF
    BOLOGNA**
VIALE ADRIATICO
PERSARO, ITALY
General Environment: Oceanographic

FISH HATCHERY STATION
LOURES RIVER, GREECE
General Environment: Oceanographic

**FISHERIES DEPARTMENT,
    TOHOKU UNIVERSITY**
KITA 6 BANCHO
SENDAI, JAPAN
General Environment: Oceanographic

**FISHERIES DIVISION,
    DEPARTMENT OF INDUSTRIES**
BEACH ROAD SEA POINT
CAPE TOWN, REPUBLIC OF SOUTH
    AFRICA
General Environment: Oceanographic

**FISHERIES EXPERIMENTATION
    STATION**
NO 16-2 KA, NANHANG DONG
PUSAN, SOUTH KOREA
General Environment: Oceanographic

FISHERIES HATCHERY STATION
EDESSA, GREECE
General Environment: Oceanographic

FISHERIES STATION
BENI SAF, ALGERIA
General Environment: Oceanographic
Staff Size: 5 - 9

**FISHERIES TECHNOLOGICAL
    LABORATORY**
KOZHIKODE 5
CALCUTTA, INDIA
Director, I George
General Environment: Oceanographic

FORESTRY PROJECT
HARVARD UNIVERSITY
PETERSHAM, MA 01366
Director, Dr M Zimmermann
Staff Size: 10 - 49

FRANZ T STONE LABORATORY
1735 NEIL AVENUE
COLUMBUS, OH 43210
General Environment: Limnologic

**FRESHWATER FISHERIES
    LABORATORY**
MAFF, 10 WHITEHALL PLACE
LONDON SW1, ENGLAND
Director, Richard Lloyd
General Environment: Limnologic
Specific Interests: Prairie and Temperate
    Forest

**HAKODATE MARINE
    OBSERVATORY**
180 AKAGAWA-DORI, KAMEDA
KAMEDA-GUN, HOKKAIDE, JAPAN
General Environment: Oceanographic

HYDROBIOLOGICAL LABORATORY
PIAZZA BORGHESE 91
ROME, ITALY
General Environment: Oceanographic

HYDROBIOLOGICAL STATION
THESSALONIKI, GREECE
General Environment: Oceanographic

HYDROBIOLOGICAL STATION
RHODES, GREECE
General Environment: Oceanographic

**HYDROBIOLOGY STATION OF
    GUARATUBA, ZOOLOGY
    DEPARTMENT**
UNIVERSITY OF PARANA
GUARATUBA, PARANA, BRAZIL
General Environment: Oceanographic

**HYDROBIOLOGY STATION,
LIMNOLOGY SOCIETY**
109 KANNONJI-MACHI
OTSU CITY, JAPAN
Director, Dr Masuzo Uello
General Environment: Limnologic
Specific Interests: Prairie and Temperate
Forest

**HYDROGEOLOGICAL PROBLEMS
LABORATORY**
ACADEMY OF SCIENCES
MOSCOW, UNION OF SOVIET
SOCIALIST REPUBLICS
Director, Dina R Gabe
Specific Interests: Polar (cold)

**JOAO M RATO MARINE
BIOLOGICAL STATION**
CP 1780
LOURENCO MARQUES,
MOZAMBIQUE
Director, Professor Dralberto X Dacunha
Marque
General Environment: Oceanographic

**KRISTINBERGS ZOOLOGICAL
STATION**
FISKBACKSKI, SWEDEN
General Environment: Oceanographic

LABORATORY ARAGO
BANYULS-SUR-MER, FRANCE
Director, Georges Petit
General Environment: Oceanographic
Specific Interests: Prairie and Temperate
Forest

**MARINE BIOLOGICAL
LABORATORY, FORT JOHNSON**
COLLEGE OF CHARLESTON, RT 1
CHARLESTON, SC 29401
Director, Dr Joseph R Merkel
General Environment: Oceanographic
Specific Interests: Prairie and Temperate
Forest

MARINE BIOLOGICAL STATION
SEA MUSEUM IFAN GOREE
BP 206, DAKAR, SENEGAL
General Environment: Oceanographic

**MARINE BIOLOGICAL STATION,
UNIVERSITY OF CHILE**
CASTILLA B-D
VINA DEL MAR, CHILE
Director, Parmenio Yanez Androde
General Environment: Oceanographic

**MARINE BIOLOGICAL STATION,
WEST HILL**
KOZHIKODE 5
CALCUTTA, INDIA
Director, I George
General Environment: Oceanographic

MARINE BIOLOGY LABORATORY
SAN SEBASTIAN, BRAZIL
General Environment: Oceanographic

MARINE FISHERIES LABORATORY
PORT-ETIENNE, MAURITANIA
General Environment: Oceanographic

**MARINE FISHERIES RESOURCES
LABORATORY ORGANIZATION
OF EAST AFRICA**
POST OFFICE BOX 668
ZANZIBAR
General Environment: Oceanographic

MARINE LABORATORY
MINAMUJAMATE-MACHI 5
NAGASAKI, JAPAN
General Environment: Oceanographic

MARINE LABORATORY
YEALM ROAD, NEWTON FERRERS
PLYMOUTH, DEVON, ENGLAND
Specific Interests: Prairie and Temperate
Forest

**MARINE LABORATORY,
CALIFORNIA INSTITUTE OF
TECHNOLOGY**
101 DAHLIA STREET
CORONA DEL MAR, CA 92625
Director, Dr Rl Sinsheimer
General Environment: Oceanographic
Staff Size: 10 - 49

MARINE SCIENCE INSTITUTE
UNIVERSITY OF CALIFORNIA
SANTA BARBARA, CA 93106
General Environment: Oceanographic

MARINE STATION
UNIVERSITY OF SAO PAULO
UBATUBA, BRAZIL
General Environment: Oceanographic

MARINE STATION
STANFORD UNIVERSITY
PACIFIC GROVE, CA 93950
Director, Dr John H Phillips
General Environment: Oceanographic
Specific Interests: Prairie and Temperate
Forest

**METEOROLOGICAL SERVICES
HEADQUARTERS**
35 BROWN ROAD
IKOYI, LAGOS, NIGERIA
Director, Caleb Igelege

MOTE MARINE LABORATORY
9501 BLIND PASS ROAD
SARASOTA, FL 33581
Director, Dr Eugene Clark
General Environment: Oceanographic
Specific Interests: Prairie and Temperate
Forest

**NAIKAI REGIONAL FISHERIES,
RESOURCES LABORATORY**
UJINA
HIROSHIMA, JAPAN
General Environment: Oceanographic

**OCEANOGRAPHIC LABORATORY,
SCOTLAND MARINE
BIOLOGICAL ASSOCIATION**
78 CRAIGHALL ROAD
EDINBURGH, SCOTLAND
General Environment: Oceanographic

**RAWSON ALGOLOGICAL
LABORATORY**
CHUBUT, ARGENTINA
General Environment: Oceanographic

RESEARCH STATION
POST OFFICE BOX 12
MALINDI, KENYA
Director, R Mendury
General Environment: Limnologic

RESEARCH STATION
POST OFFICE BOX 1146
MOMBASA, KENYA
General Environment: Limnologic

**SETO MARINE BIOLOGICAL
LABORATORY, KYOTO
UNIVERSITY**
SETO 3- CHOME SHIRAHAMA
WAKAYAMA PREFECTURE, JAPAN
General Environment: Oceanographic

**SOUTHWEST CENTER FOR
ADVANCED STUDIES**
POST OFFICE BOX 30365
DALLAS, TX 75230
Director, Claud Rupert

STATION MARINE DE BOU-ISMAIL
BOU-ISMAIL, ALGERIA
General Environment: Oceanographic
Staff Size: 5 - 9

**UNILEVER RESEARCH
LABORATORY**
COLWORTH HOUSE
SHARNBROOK, BEDFORD,
ENGLAND
Manager, Felix Franks
Specific Interests: Prairie and Temperate
Forest

VETERINARY LABORATORY
WEYBRIDGE
SURREY, ENGLAND
Specific Interests: Prairie and Temperate
Forest

ZOOLOGICAL STATION OF NAPLES
NAPLES, ITALY
General Environment: Oceanographic
Staff Size: 50 - 99

ZOOLOGICAL STATION OF VILLEFRANCHE
VILLEFRANCHE-SUR-MER H06, FRANCE
General Environment: Oceanographic
Staff Size: 10 - 49

Foundation

AMERICAN COMMISSION FOR INTERNATIONAL WILDLIFE
NEW YORK ZOOLOGICAL PARK
NEW YORK, NY 10060
Director, Richard Schaffer
General Environment: Terrestrial
Staff Size: 10 - 49

ATMOSPHERIC RESEARCH GENTER
POST OFFICE BOX 1470
BOULDER, CO 80302
Director, Dr John W Firor
General Environment: Atmospheric

BEAUDETTE FOUNDATION FOR BIOLOGICAL RESEARCH
P O BOX 229
MOSS LANDING, CA 95039
Staff Size: 10 - 49

INSTITUTION OCEANOGRAFICO DE UNIVERSITY DE SAO PAUL
AL EDUARDO PRADO 698
SAO PAULO, BRAZIL
General Environment: Oceanographic

LA SOCIETY FRANCO-JAPONAISE DES OCEAN
NICHIFUTSU-KAIKAN3 2-CHOME
KANDA, SURUGADAI, TOKYO, JAPAN
General Environment: Oceanographic
Specific Interests: Prairie and Temperate Forest

LIMNOLOGY DEPARTMENT
19TH STREET AND PARKWAY
PHILADELPHIA, PA 19100
General Environment: Estuarine

NATURAL HISTORY MUSEUM
SOSEAUA KISELEFF 1
BUCHAREST, RUMANIA
General Environment: Oceanographic
Specific Interests: Prairie and Temperate Forest

NIHON FISHERIES PROMOTION SOCIETY
15-CHOME TSUKIJI CHOU-KU
TOKYO, JAPAN
General Environment: Oceanographic
Specific Interests: Prairie and Temperate Forest

OCEANOGRAPHIC FOUNDATION
1 RICKENBACKER CAUSEWAY
VIRGINIA KEY, MIAMI, FL 33149
General Environment: Oceanographic

POLAR SECTION, NATURAL SCIENCES MUSEUM
UENO PARK
TAITO-KU, TOKYO, JAPAN
Director, Kiyoshie Sugie
Specific Interests: Prairie and Temperate Forest

RAPTOR RESEARCH FOUNDATION
UNIVERSITY OF SOUTH DAKOTA
VERMILLION, SD 57609
President, Byron E Harrell
Specific Interests: Prairie and Temperate Forest

Government — Federal

AGRICULTURE AND FISHERIE DEPARTMENT
BELIZE CITY, BRITISH HONDURAS
Director, C G Rosado

AGRICULTURE AND FISHERIES MINISTRY
ONE LOMBARD STREET
GEORGETOWN, GUYANA
Director, J C E Mccalmon
General Environment: Oceanographic

AGRICULTURE AND WATER MINISTRY
JIDDA, SAUDI ARABIA
General Environment: Oceanographic

AGRICULTURE, COMMERCE, AND INDUSTRY MINISTER
CALLE 39 Y AVENIDA, PO BOX 1631
PANAMA CITY, PANAMA
General Environment: Oceanographic

AMERICAN FISHERIES SOCIETY
1319 18TH STREET, NW, FOURTH FLOOR SUITE
WASHINGTON, DC 20036
General Environment: Estuarine

ANIMAL GENETICS DIVISION
POST OFFICE BOX 90
EPPING, NEW SOUTH WALES, AUSTRALIA
Specific Interests: Prairie and Temperate Forest

ANIMAL HEALTH DIVISION
PRIVATE BAG 1, POST OFFICE
PARKVILLE, VICTORIA, AUSTRALIA
Specific Interests: Prairie and Temperate Forest

ANIMAL HUSBANDRY DEPARTMENT
LOME, TOGO
Director, Salomon Amoussou

ANIMAL PHYSIOLOGY DIVISION
POST OFFICE BOX 239
BLACKTOWN, NEW SOUTH WALES, AUSTRALIA
Specific Interests: Prairie and Temperate Forest

ANTARCTIC INSTITUTE, NAVAL OPERATIONS COMMISSION
CERRITO 1248
BUENOS AIRES, ARGENTINA
Director, Rodolfo Panzarini
General Environment: Oceanographic
Specific Interests: Polar (cold)

ARMED FORCES RADIOBIOLOGY RESEARCH LIBRARY
BETHESDA, MD 20014
Specific Interests: Prairie and Temperate Forest

ATOMIC ENERGY COMMISSION
FISHERIES HARBOR, WEST WHARF
KARACHI, PAKISTAN
General Environment: Oceanographic

BIOLOGICAL AND MEDICAL SCIENCES DIVISION, NATIONAL SCIENCE FOUNDATION
1800 G STREET, NW
WASHINGTON, DC 20550

BIOLOGICAL CENTER, INDIAN OCEAN
ERNAKULAM, INDIA
Director, M Krishna Menon
General Environment: Oceanographic

BIOLOGICAL LABORATORY
BUREAU OF COMMISSION FISHERIES
OXFORD, MD 21654
Director, Arthur S Merrill
General Environment: Oceanographic
Staff Size: 10 - 49

BIOLOGICAL LABORATORY
2570 DOLE STREET, POST OFFICE BOX 3830
HONOLULU, HI 96812
Director, Dr Frank J Hester
Specific Interests: Tropical (hot)
Staff Size: 50 - 99

BIOLOGICAL LABORATORY
P O BOX 155
AUKE BAY, AK 99821
Director, William Smoker
Specific Interests: Prairie and Temperate Forest
Staff Size: 50 - 99

BIOLOGICAL LABORATORY
MILFORD, CT 06460
Director, Harry C Davis
Specific Interests: Prairie and Temperate
   Forest
Staff Size: 10 - 49

BIOLOGICAL LABORATORY
OXFORD, MD 21654
Director, Arthur S Merrill
General Environment: Oceanographic
Specific Interests: Prairie and Temperate
   Forest
Staff Size: 10 - 49

**BIOLOGICAL LABORATORY,
   BUREAU OF COMMISSION
   FISHERIES**
DEPARTMENT OF INTERIOR
MILFORD, CT 06460
Director, Harry C Davis
General Environment: Oceanographic
Staff Size: 10 - 49

**BIOLOGICAL LABORATORY,
   BUREAU OF COMMISSION
   FISHERIES**
75 33RD AVENUE
ST PETERSBURG BEACH, FL 33706
Director, James F Sykes
General Environment: Oceanographic
Staff Size: 10 - 49

**BIOLOGICAL SCIENCE, AMERICAN
   INSTITUTE**
3900 WISCONSIN AVENUE, NW
WASHINGTON, DC 20016
Director, John R Olive

BIOLOGY DEPARTMENT
AMERICAN UNIVERSITY OF BEIRUT
BEIRUT, LEBANON
Director, Dr Carl J George
General Environment: Oceanographic

BIOLOGY DEPARTMENT
CASILLA 5918
GUAYAQUIL, ECUADOR
Director, Dr Mario Cobo
General Environment: Oceanographic

**BIOLOGY SECTION, DEMOCRITUS
   NUCLEAR RESEARCH CENTER**
ATOMIC ENERGY COMMISSION
ATHENS, GREECE
Director, Panayiotis Demopoulos
General Environment: Geologic

**BIRD AND MAMMAL LABORATORY,
   NATIONAL MUSEUM**
10TH STREET AND CONSTITUTION
   AVENUE
WASHINGTON, DC 20560
Specific Interests: Prairie and Temperate
   Forest

**CENTRAL INLAND FISHERIES
   RESOURCES INSTITUTION**
BARRACKPORE
VIA CALCUTTA, INDIA
Director, Dr V G Jhingran
General Environment: Oceanographic
Specific Interests: Tropical (hot)

**CHARLES DARWIN RESOURCES
   STATION**
ISLA SANTA CRUZ
GALAPAGOS, GALAPAGOS ISLANDS
Director, Dr D W Snow

**COASTAL CONSERVATION
   COMMISSION**
CAIRO, UNITED ARAB REPUBLIC

**COUNCIL OF SCIENTIFIC AND
   INDUSTRIAL RESEARCH**
KARACHI, PAKISTAN
Director, Dr S Siddiqui
General Environment: Oceanographic

DE AGRICULTURE
DE RECURSOS MINISTRY
MANAGUA, NICARAGUA
Director, Ruben Camacho Saenz
General Environment: Limnologic
Staff Size: 50 - 99

DEFENSE MINISTRY
25 DEL MAYO 279
MONTEVIDEO, URUGUAY
General Environment: Oceanographic

**ECONOMICS AND NATIONAL
   RESOURCES MINISTRY**
MANAGUA, NICARAGUA
Director, Dr Sebastian Pavon Tapia 0902
General Environment: Oceanographic

ECONOMY AND MINING MINISTRY
BOITE POSTALE 548
LIBREVILLE, GABON
General Environment: Oceanographic

**ENTOMOLOGY RESOURCES
   DIVISION**
DEPARTMENT OF AGRICULTURE
BELTSVILLE, MD 20705
Staff Size: 500 - 999

**ENVIRONMENTAL AND
   SYSTEMATIC BIOLOGICAL
   SECTION**
1800 G STREET, NW
WASHINGTON, DC 20550
General Environment: Limnologic

**ENVIRONMENTAL RESEARCH
   NATIONAL COUNCIL**
HUNTINGDON, ENGLAND
Director, Monks Wood

**EXPLORATORY FISHING AND
   GEAR RESOURCES BASE**
STATE FISHERIES PIER
GLOUCESTER, MA 01930

Director, Keith Smith
General Environment: Oceanographic
Staff Size: 10 - 49

**EXPLORATORY FISHING AND
   GEAR RESOURCES BASE**
P O BOX 1668
JUNEAU, AK 99801
Director, Benjamin F Jones
General Environment: Oceanographic
Staff Size: 10 - 49

**EXPLORATORY FISHING AND
   GEAR RESOURCES BASE,
   BUREAU OF COMMISSION**
239 FREDERIC STREET, PO 1207
PASCAGULA, MS 39567
Director, Harvey R Bullis
General Environment: Oceanographic
Staff Size: 50 - 99

**EXPLORATORY FISHING AND
   GEAR RESOURCES BASE**
5 RESEARCH DRIVE
ANN ARBOR, MI 48103
Director, M R Greenwood
General Environment: Oceanographic
Staff Size: 10 - 49

**EXPLORATORY FISHING AND
   GEAR RESOURCES LABORATORY**
FEDERAL BUILDING-ROOM 308, PO
   280
BRUNSWICK, GA 31520
Director, Robert Cummins
General Environment: Oceanographic
Staff Size: 5 - 9

FEDERAL FISHERIES SERVICES
VICTORIA BH, PMB 12529
LAGOS, NIGERIA
Director, Donald R Niven
General Environment: Oceanographic
Staff Size: 10 - 49

FISHERIES
AVENUE CUAUHTEMOC 80
MEXICO 7 DF, MEXICO
Director, Echaniz R Jorge
General Environment: Oceanographic

**FISHERIES AND MARITIME ACT
   SECTION**
MINISTRY OF ECONOMY
SAN SALVADOR, EL SALVADOR

**FISHERIES AND OCEANOGRAPHY
   DIVISION**
CRONULLA, NEW SOUTH WALES,
   AUSTRALIA
Director, Dr G F Humphrey
General Environment: Oceanographic
Specific Interests: Tropical (hot)

**FISHERIES AND WILDLIFE
   DEPARTMENT**
MINISTRY OF AGRICULTURE
SAN JOSE, COSTA RICA
Director, Milton Lopez

**FISHERIES AND WILDLIFE
DEPARTMENT AGRICULTURE
MINISTRY**
SANTIAGO, CHILE
General Environment: Oceanographic

**FISHERIES AND WILDLIFE
SECTION**
DEPARTMENT OF FORESTS AND
NATURAL RESOURCES
BEIRUT, LEBANON
Director, Ismat B Boulos
General Environment: Geological

**FISHERIES AND WILDLIFE
SERVICE**
BUREAU COMMERICAL FISHERIES
WASHINGTON, DC 20240
General Environment: Oceanographic

**FISHERIES AND WILDLIFE
SERVICE**
18TH AND C STREETS, NW
WASHINGTON, DC 20240
Specific Interests: Prairie and Temperate
  Forest

FISHERIES BIOLOGICAL STATION
CASILLA 492 CORREO 2
SAN ANTONIO, CHILE
Director, Oscar Miranda Brandt
General Environment: Oceanographic

FISHERIES BUREAU
1688 CHUNGCHENG ROAD
TAIPEI, TAIWAN
Director, Kuo-Hsien Liu
General Environment: Oceanographic
Specific Interests: Tropical (hot)

**FISHERIES BUREAU,
AGRICULTURAL DEPARTMENT**
SUACCO, GBARNGA
CENTRAL PROVINCE, LIBERIA
Director, Peter Youn
General Environment: Oceanographic
Specific Interests: Tropical (hot)

**FISHERIES CENTER OF THE
SOUTHEAST**
75 VIRGINIA BEACH DRIVE
MIAMI, FL 33149
Director, Harvey R Bullis, Jr
General Environment: Oceanographic
Staff Size: 100 - 499

FISHERIES COMMISSION
INTRAMUROS
MANILA, PHILIPPINES
Director, Andres Manes
Specific Interests: Prairie and Temperate
  Forest

**FISHERIES COMMISSION BUREAU,
DEPARTMENT OF INTERIOR**
P O BOX 128
COLLEGE PK, MD 20740

Director, Roland Finch
General Environment: Oceanographic
Staff Size: 50 - 99

FISHERIES DEPARTMENT
KUALA LUMPUR, MALAYSIA
Director, Soong Min Kong
General Environment: Oceanographic
Specific Interests: Tropical (hot)

FISHERIES DEPARTMENT
GALLE FACE
COLOMBO, CEYLON
Director, L F Tissarerasinghe
General Environment: Oceanographic

FISHERIES DEPARTMENT
INDUSTRIAL MINISTRY
TRIPOLI, LIBYA
General Environment: Oceanographic

**FISHERIES DEPARTMENT,
AGRICULTURE AND NATURAL
RESOURCES MINISTRY**
NICOSIA, CYPRUS
Director, Andreas Dimitropoulos
General Environment: Oceanographic
Staff Size: 10 - 49

**FISHERIES DEPARTMENT,
FINANCE OFFICE**
TEHRAN, IRAN
General Environment: Oceanographic

**FISHERIES DEPARTMENT,
MINISTRY OF TOURISM AND
WILDLIFE**
POST OFFICE BOX 30027
NAIROBI, KENYA
General Environment: Limnologic

**FISHERIES DEVELOPMENT
INSTITUTION**
PERDO DE VALDIVA 2633
SANTIAGO, CHILE
Director, Antonio Bories
General Environment: Oceanographic

FISHERIES DIRECTORATE
RANGOON, BURMA
Director, Tiant Hlaing
General Environment: Oceanographic
Specific Interests: Tropical (hot)

FISHERIES DISEASE LABORATORY
SAND POINT NAVAL AIR STATION
SEATTLE, WA 98115
General Environment: Oceanographic

FISHERIES DIVISION
PRIMARY PRODUCTION
  DEPARTMENT
SINGAPORE
Director, Lim Ewe Hock
General Environment: Oceanographic
Specific Interests: Tropical (hot)

FISHERIES DIVISION
REDUIT, MAURITIUS

Director, E Cabon
General Environment: Oceanographic

FISHERIES DIVISION
ACCRA, GHANA
Director, Dr Zei
General Environment: Oceanographic

FISHERIES DIVISION
DEPARTMENT PRIMARY INDUSTRY
CANBERRA, AUSTRALIA
Assistant to the Secretary, C G Setter
General Environment: Oceanographic
Staff Size: 10 - 49

**FISHERIES DIVISION OF EAST
NIGERIA**
PMB 1027
ABA, NIGERIA
Director, S Savalingam
General Environment: Oceanographic

**FISHERIES DIVISION,
AGRICULTURE AND LANDS
MINISTRY**
FORESHORE RC
KINGSTON, JAMAICA
Director, a Kirton
General Environment: Oceanographic

**FISHERIES DIVISION,
AGRICULTURE AND NATURAL
RESOURCES MINISTRY**
KISSY DOCKYARD
FREETOWN, SIERRA LEONE
General Environment: Oceanographic
Staff Size: 5 - 9

**FISHERIES INSTITUTE OF
ECUADOR**
CASILLA 5991
GUAYAQUIL, ECUADOR
General Environment: Oceanographic

**FISHERIES INVESTIGATION
INSTITUTE**
HARINGKAPE 1, POST OFFICE BOX
68
IJMUIDEN, NETHERLANDS
General Environment: Oceanographic
Staff Size: 50 - 99

FISHERIES LABORATORY
REMEMBRANCE AVENUE
BURNHAM-ON-CROUCH, ESSEX,
  ENGLAND
Director, Peter C Wood
General Environment: Estuarine
Staff Size: 10 - 49

**FISHERIES NATIONAL
DIRECTORATE**
PHNOM-PENH, CAMBODIA
General Environment: Oceanographic
Specific Interests: Tropical (hot)

FISHERIES NATIONAL INSTITUTE
CASILLA 5918
GUAYAQUIL, ECUADOR

Director, Dr Luis Arriaga
General Environment: Oceanographic
Staff Size: 10 - 49

**FISHERIES NUTRITION
LABORATORY**
STAR ROUTE
COOK, WA 98615
General Environment: Oceanographic

**FISHERIES OCEAN CENTER,
BUREAU OF COMMISSION
FISHERIES**
8604 LA JOLLA SHORES DRIVE
LA JOLLA, CA 92037
Director, Alan R Longhurst
General Environment: Oceanographic
Staff Size: 50 - 99

FISHERIES OFFICE
AGRICULTURE MINISTRY
LATAKIA, SYRIA
General Environment: Oceanographic

FISHERIES OFFICE
MINISTRY OF AGRICULTURE
LATARIA, SYRIA

**FISHERIES PRODUCTS
DEPARTMENT**
CASILLA 5918
GUAYAQUIL, ECUADOR
Director, Errique Reyes
General Environment: Oceanographic

**FISHERIES RESEARCH AND
DEVELOPMENT AGENCY**
CHEJU REGIONAL BRANCH
CHEJU, KOREA
General Environment: Oceanographic
Specific Interests: Prairie and Temperate
Forest

**FISHERIES RESEARCH AND
DEVELOPMENT AGENCY**
16 2-KA NAM KANG DONE
PUSAN, KOREA
Director, Han Shin Wook
General Environment: Oceanographic
Specific Interests: Prairie and Temperate
Forest

**FISHERIES RESEARCH AND
DEVELOPMENT AGENCY**
SOUTH COAST REGION BRANCH
MOKPO, KOREA
General Environment: Oceanographic
Specific Interests: Prairie and Temperate
Forest

**FISHERIES RESEARCH AND
DEVELOPMENT AGENCY**
WEST COAST REGION BRANCH
KUNSAN, KOREA
General Environment: Oceanographic
Specific Interests: Prairie and Temperate
Forest

**FISHERIES RESEARCH AND
DEVELOPMENT AGENCY**
EAST COAST REGIONAL BRANCH
POHANG, KOREA
Director, Han Hak Soo
General Environment: Oceanographic
Specific Interests: Prairie and Temperate
Forest

FISHERIES RESEARCH INSTITUTE
125 HOU-I ROAD
KEELUNG, TAIWAN
Director, Dr Huo-Tu Heng
General Environment: Oceanographic
Specific Interests: Tropical (hot)

**FISHERIES RESEARCH
INSTITUTION**
GLUGOR
PENANG, MALAYSIA
Director, D Pathansali
General Environment: Oceanographic
Specific Interests: Tropical (hot)
Staff Size: 50 - 99

**FISHERIES RESEARCH
LABORATORY**
NIIGATA, JAPAN
Director, Dr Senji Tanida
General Environment: Oceanographic
Specific Interests: Prairie and Temperate
Forest

FISHERIES RESEARCH STATION
MINISTRY OF AGRICULTURE
SAMUT PRAKAN, THAILAND
Director, Dr Deb Menasveta
General Environment: Oceanographic
Specific Interests: Tropical (hot)

FISHERIES RESEARCH STATION
BOX 531, GALLE FACE
COLOMBO 3, CEYLON
Director, D T E Defonseca
General Environment: Oceanographic
Specific Interests: Tropical (hot)

**FISHERIES RESEARCH, FEDERAL
INSTITUTE**
PALMAILLE 9
HAMBURG-ALTONA, WEST
GERMANY
Director, Professor Ulrich Schmidt
General Environment: Oceanographic

**FISHERIES RESOURCE BOARD,
DEPARTMENT OF FISHERIES**
TUPPER BUILDING, CONFERENCE
HEIGHTS
OTTAWA, ONTARIO, CANADA
Director, Dr F R Hayes
General Environment: Oceanographic

**FISHERIES RESOURCE
DEPARTMENT**
BRASIL Y FLORENCIO SANCHEZ
BUENOS AIRES, ARGENTINA

Director, Dr Luis R Vazquez
General Environment: Oceanographic

**FISHERIES RESOURCE, MINISTRY
OF AGRICULTURAL AFFAIRS**
CALLE 51, LA PLATA
BUENOS ARIES, ARGENTINA
Director, Dr Paul Ringuelet
General Environment: Limnologic

FISHERIES SECTION
NATIONAL DEVELOPMENT
INSTITUTE
MANAGUA, NICARAGUA
General Environment: Oceanographic

**FISHERIES SERVICES,
AGRICULTURE MINISTRY**
BP 383,ONE RUE BEL-AIR
COTOMOV, DAHOMEY
General Environment: Oceanographic

FISHERIES STATION
BENI SAF, ALGERIA
General Environment: Oceanographic

**FISHERIES TECHNOLOGY
INSTITUTION**
12 DE OCTUBRE Y ACHA
MAR DEL PLATA, BUENOS AIRES,
ARGENTINA
General Environment: Oceanographic

FISHERY DEPARTMENT
24-89 AVENIDA BALBOA, PO BOX
3318
PANAMA CITY, PANAMA
Director, Dr Juan L De Obarrio
General Environment: Oceanographic

**FISHERY ECONOMICAL
DEPARTMENT**
CASILLA 5918
GUAYAQUIL, ECUADOR
Director, Ovidio Morla
General Environment: Oceanographic

**FISHERY PRODUCTS, ATLANTIC
TECHNOLOGY CENTER**
EMERSON AVENUE
GLOUCESTER, MA 01930
General Environment: Oceanographic
Staff Size: 10 - 49

FISHERY RESEARCH UNITED
BOX B62, COMMUNITY 2
TEMA, GHANA
Director, E Kwei
General Environment: Oceanographic

FISHERY SCIENCE
DEPARTMENT OF AGRICULTURE
PORT-AU-PRINCE, HAITI
Director, Emmanuel Garnier
General Environment: Oceanographic

FOREST, GAME, FISHERIES RESOURCES
EDIF BANCO, NAC DE FOMENTO
COMEYAGUELA, HONDURAS
Director, Aristides Diaz
General Environment: Oceanographic

FORESTS AND NATIONAL RESOURCES DEPARTMENT, AGRICULTURE MINISTRY
BEIRUT, LEBANON
General Environment: Oceanographic

FUNGICIDES AND GERMICIDES LABORATORY
UNITED STATES DEPARTMENT OF THE ARMY
NATICK, MA 01760
General Environment: Limnologic

GAME AND FISHERIES DEPARTMENT
POST OFFICE BOX 293
KHARTOUM, SUDAN
Director, Sayed Mirghani Mekki Medani
General Environment: Oceanographic

GEOLOGICAL SURVEY OF ISRAEL
30 MALKEY ISRAEL STREET
JERUSALEM, ISRAEL
General Environment: Oceanographic

GEOLOGY AND SUBSURFACE RESOURCES INSTITUTE
6 AMERIKIS STREET
ATHENS, GREECE
Director, Dr Kyriakos Zachos
General Environment: Oceanographic

GREAT LAKES FISHERY LABORATORY
1451 GREEN ROAD, P O BOX 640
ANN ARBOR, MI 48107
Director, G Y Harry
General Environment: Oceanographic
Staff Size: 50 - 99

GUAYMAS SUB-STATION
GUAYMAS
SONORA, MEXICO
Director, Rosales Fernando
General Environment: Oceanographic

HEALTH AND PHYSICS DIVISION
OAK RIDGE NATIONAL LABORATORY
OAK RIDGE, TN 37831
Director, Karl Morgan

HEALTH INSTITUTE
BETHESDA, MD 20014
Specific Interests: Prairie and Temperate Forest

HEALTH MINISTRY
DAVID HAMELECH STREET
JERUSALEM, ISRAEL

HIGH COUNCIL ON SCIENTIFIC RESEARCH
ALGIERS, ALGERIA
General Environment: Oceanographic

HOKKAIDO REGIONAL FISHERIES RESEARCH LABORATORY
YOICHI, JAPAN
Director, Dr Saburo Kawada
General Environment: Oceanographic
Specific Interests: Prairie and Temperate Forest

HUNTING AND FISHERIES OFFICE, AGRICULTURE MINISTRY
CARRERA 10 20-30, PISO 6
BOGOTA, COLOMBIA

HYDROBIOLOGY AND FISHERIES DIVISION, AGRICULTURE MINISTRY
BAGDAD, IRAQ
General Environment: Oceanographic

HYDROBIOLOGY LABORATORY, OSWALDO CRUZ INSTITUTE
CAIXA POSTA 926
RIO DE JANEIRO, BRAZIL
General Environment: Oceanographic

HYDROGRAPHIC DEPARTMENT, DOMINICAN NAVY
LA JEFATURA DE ESTADO MAYO
SANTO DOMINGO, DOMINICAN REPUBLIC
Director, Oscar Octavio Perer Mota
General Environment: Oceanographic

HYDROGRAPHIC SERVICE, ROYAL HELLENIC NAVY
MINISTRY OF NATIONAL DEFENSE
VOTANIKOS, ATHENS, GREECE
General Environment: Oceanographic

HYDROLOGY DEPARTMENT
ANKARA, TURKEY
General Environment: Oceanographic

HYDROLOGY-BIOLOGY INSTITUTE
KAYED BEY
ALEXANDRIA, UNITED ARAB REPUBLIC
General Environment: Oceanographic
Specific Interests: Tropical (hot)

INDUSTRIAL RESEARCH, OCEANOGRAPHIC INSTITUTION, DEPARTMENT OF SCIE
177 THORNDON QUAY
WELLINGTON, NEW ZEALAND
Director, James Brodie
General Environment: Oceanographic
Specific Interests: Prairie and Temperate Forest

INLAND FISHERIES DIRECTORATE
DJI. SALEMBA 17
DJAKARTA, INDONESIA

Director, Dr Amin Katamsi
General Environment: Terrestrial
Specific Interests: Tropical (hot)

INTER-BIOLOGICAL PROGRAM, UNITED STATES NATIONAL COMMISSION
2101 CONSTITUTION AVENUE, NW
WASHINGTON, DC 20418
General Environment: Oceanographic

ISLA MUJERES SUB-STATION
ISLA MUJERES
QUINTANA ROO, MEXICO
General Environment: Oceanographic

LABORATORY
POST OFFICE BOX 101, VICTORIA ROAD
ABERDEEN, SCOTLAND
General Environment: Oceanographic

LIGHTHOUSES AND HYDROLOGY
MEXICO 1, DF, MEXICO
General Environment: Oceanographic

LIVESTOCK AND AGRICULTURE MINISTRY
TORRES NORTE
CARACAS, VENEZUELA
General Environment: Oceanographic

MARINE BIOLOGICAL RESOURCES LABORATORY
FISHERIES HARBOR, WEST WHARF
KARACHI, PAKISTAN
General Environment: Oceanographic

MARINE BIOLOGICAL STATION
TAMPICO
TEMAULIPAS, MEXICO
General Environment: Oceanographic

MARINE BIOLOGICAL STATION AT CAMPECHE
CAMPECHE, MEXICO
Director, Fuentes C Dilio
General Environment: Oceanographic

MARINE BIOLOGICAL STATION AT ENSENDA
ENSENDA
BAJA CALIFORNIA, MEXICO
Director, Flores V Manuel
General Environment: Oceanographic

MARINE BIOLOGY AND FISHERIES MISSION
CP 1723
LOURENCO MARQUES, MOZAMBIQUE
General Environment: Oceanographic

MARINE CATCH OFFICE
BENGHAZI, LIBYA
General Environment: Oceanographic

MARINE DEPARTMENT
WORKS AND COMMUNICATION
MINISTRY
BATHURST, THE GAMBIA
General Environment: Oceanographic

**MARINE DEPARTMENT, FISHERIES
RESEARCH DIVISION**
327 WILLIS STREET
WELLINGTON, NEW ZEALAND
Director, G D Waugh
General Environment: Oceanographic
Specific Interests: Prairie and Temperate
Forest

**MARINE FISHERIES
DEVELOPMENT PROJECT**
CARRERA 10, !20-30 PISO 6
BOGOTA, COLOMBIA
General Environment: Oceanographic

MARINE FISHERIES OFFICE
KUCHING, MALAYSIA
General Environment: Oceanographic
Specific Interests: Tropical (hot)

**MARINE FISHERIES RESOURCE
CENTRAL INSTITUTE**
MANADAPAM CAMP P.O.
MADRAS STATE, INDIA
Director, S Jones
General Environment: Oceanographic
Specific Interests: Tropical (hot)

MARINE FISHERIES SERVICE
ROGERS AVENUE
MILFORD, CT 06460
Director, J T Graikowski
Specific Interests: Prairie and Temperate
Forest
Staff Size: 10 - 49

**MARINE FISHERIES SERVICE,
NORTHWEST FISHERIES CENTER**
2725 MONTLAKE BOULEVARD,
EAST
SEATTLE, WA 98112
Director, Gerald B Collins
General Environment: Estuarine
Staff Size: 100 - 499

**MARINE FISHERIES SYSTEMS
LABORATORY**
UNITED STATES NATIONAL
MUSEUM
WASHINGTON, DC 20560
Director, Daniel M Cohen
General Environment: Oceanographic
Staff Size: 5 - 9

**MARINE FISHERIES, SCIENCES
AND TECHNOLOGY INSTITUTE**
ALGIERS, ALGERIA
General Environment: Oceanographic

MARINE FISHING DEPARTMENT
EDIF BANCO, NAC FOMENTO
COMEYAGUELA, HONDURAS

Director, J E Mejia
General Environment: Oceanographic

MARINE LABORATORY
DEPARTMENT OF ZOOLOGY
PORT ROYAL, JAMAICA
Director, Dr J Goodbody
General Environment: Oceanographic

**MARINE LABORATORY,
DEPARTMENT OF AGRICULTURE
AND FISHERIES**
PO BOX 101
ABERDEEN AB9 8DB, SCOTLAND
Director, Mr B Parrish
General Environment: Oceanographic
Staff Size: 100 - 499

**MARINE LABORATORY, UNITED
STATES BUREAU OF SPORT
FISHERIES**
POST OFFICE BOX 98
TIBURON, CA 94920
General Environment: Oceanographic

MARINE MAMMAL DIVISION
NAVAL SUPPORT ACTIVITY, 192
SEATTLE, WA 98155
Director, Dr George Y Harry, Jr
General Environment: Oceanographic
Staff Size: 10 - 49

MARINE RESEARCH LABORATORY
WALVIS BAY
PRETORIA, REPUBLIC OF SOUTH
AFRICA
General Environment: Oceanographic

MARINE RESOURCES OFFICE
18TH & C STREETS, NW
WASHINGTON, DC 20240
General Environment: Oceanographic
Specific Interests: Prairie and Temperate
Forest

**MARINE SCIENCE NATIONAL
COMMITTEE**
BANGKOK, THAILAND
General Environment: Oceanographic
Specific Interests: Tropical (hot)

**MARINE SCIENCES AND
TECHNOLOGY NATIONAL
CENTER**
AODO 512 VERACRUZ
VERACRUZ, MEXICO
General Environment: Oceanographic

MARINE SECTION
PORT HARCOURT, NIGERIA
Director, E N C Eziuzo
General Environment: Oceanographic

MARITIME AUTHORITY
PORT-ETIENNE, MAURITANIA
General Environment: Oceanographic

MARITIME SERVICES
CP 262
LOURENCO MARQUES,
MOZAMBIQUE
General Environment: Oceanographic

**MAZATLAN MARINE BIOLOGICAL
STATION**
PALACIO FEDERAL
MAZATLAN, SINALOA, MEXICO
General Environment: Oceanographic

MEAT AND FISH DIRECTORATE
FISHERIES OFFICE
ANKARA, TURKEY
General Environment: Oceanographic

**MERCHANT MARINE AND SEA
FISHERIES DIRECTORATE**
NOVAKCHOTT, MAURITANIA
Director, Ali Kone
General Environment: Oceanographic

**MERCHANT MARINE, FEDERAL
SERVICE**
BP 416,
DOVALA, CAMEROON
Director, R Aubray
General Environment: Oceanographic

METEOROLOGICAL DEPARTMENT
FISHERIES HARBOR, WEST WHARF
KARACHI, PAKISTAN
General Environment: Oceanographic

**MIGRATORY BIRD CONSERVATION
COMMISSION**
DEPARTMENT OF THE INTERIOR
BUILDING
WASHINGTON, DC 20240

MINES AND HYDROLOGY OFFICE
EDIF BANCO, NAC DE FOMENTO
COMEYAGUELA, HONDURAS
General Environment: Oceanographic

MUSEUM OF SOUTH AFRICA
POST OFFICE BOX 61
CAPE TOWN, REPUBLIC OF SOUTH
AFRICA
Director, Dr T Barry
General Environment: Oceanographic

NACIONAL DE PESCA INSTITUTO
BIBLIOTECA
CHIAPAS 121, MEXICO CITY 7, DF,
MEXICO
Director, M E B Yolanda Mercader
General Environment: Oceanographic

**NAIKAI REGIONAL FISHERIES
RESEARCH LABORATORY**
HIROSHIMA, JAPAN
General Environment: Oceanographic
Specific Interests: Prairie and Temperate
Forest

NANKAI REGIONAL FISHERIES RESEARCH LABORATORY
KOCHI, JAPAN
General Environment: Oceanographic
Specific Interests: Prairie and Temperate Forest

NATIONAL OCEANIC AND ATMOSPHERIC ADMINISTRATION, COMMERCE DEPARTMENT
ROGERS AVENUE
MILFORD, CT 06460
General Environment: Oceanographic
Staff Size: 10 - 49

NATURAL HISTORY MUSEUM, MINISTRY OF CULTURE
BUENOS AIRES 652
MONTEVIDEO, URUGUAY
General Environment: Oceanographic

NATURAL RESOURCES MINISTRY
EDIFICIO BANCO, NAC FOMENT
COMEYAGUELA, HONDURAS
Director, Julio C Pineda
General Environment: Oceanographic

OCEAN RESEARCH LABORATORY, BUREAU OF COMMISSION FISHERIES
SOUTH ROTUNDA, STANFORD MUSEUM
STANFORD, CA 94305
Director, Oscar E Sette
General Environment: Oceanographic
Staff Size: 5 - 9

OCEAN RESEARCH OF CHINESE NATIONAL COMMISSION
NATIONAL TAIWAN UNIVERSITY-ROOSEVELT
TAIPEI, TAIWAN
Director, Dr Veichow C Juan
General Environment: Oceanographic
Specific Interests: Tropical (hot)

OCEANIC AND FISHERIES DIVISION
NATIONAL SCIENTIFIC AND TECHNOLOGICAL INSTITUTE
SALAMMBO, TUNISIA
Director, Mrs F Ktari
General Environment: Oceanographic

OCEANOGRAPHIC AND FISHERIES SERVICE
JULIO HERRERA Y OBES 1467
MONTEVIDEO, URUGUAY
General Environment: Oceanographic

OCEANOGRAPHIC DATA CENTER
M STREET AT 8TH STREET
WASHINGTON, DC 20390
General Environment: Oceanographic

OCEANOGRAPHIQUE INSTITUT
195 RUE SAINT-JACQUES
75 PARIS 5E, FRANCE
General Environment: Oceanographic

OCEANOGRAPHY AND EXPERIMENTAL FISHERIES DEPARTMENT
CASILLA 5918
GUAYAQUIL, ECUADOR
Director, Dr Jose Santoro
General Environment: Oceanographic

OCEANOGRAPHY AND FISHERIES BIOLOGICAL LABORATORY
CASILLA 183-V
VALPARAISO, CHILE
General Environment: Oceanographic

OCEANOGRAPHY AND FISHERIES INSTITUTE
CAIRO, UNITED ARAB REPUBLIC
Director, Professor H F Gohar
General Environment: Oceanographic

OCEANOGRAPHY AND FISHERIES RESEARCH INSTITUTE
16 POSSIDONOS AVENUE
OLD PHALERON, ATHENS, GREECE
General Environment: Oceanographic

OCEANOGRAPHY AND FISHING RESEARCH INSTITUTE
AGIOS KOSMAS-HELLINIKON
ATHENS, GREECE
General Environment: Oceanographic
Staff Size: 50 - 99

OCEANOGRAPHY AND LIMNOLOGY RESEARCH, NATIONAL COUNCIL RESEARCH
120 HA-AZMAUT ROAD
HAIFA, ISRAEL
Director, Commander Y Ben-Nun
General Environment: Oceanographic

OCEANOGRAPHY AND MARITIME FISHERIES DEPARTMENT
THIAROYE SURVEY MER, BP 2241
DAKAR, SENEGAL
Director, Magatte Lo
General Environment: Oceanographic
Staff Size: 10 - 49

OCEANOGRAPHY INSTITUTE OF SPAIN
MADRID, SPAIN
General Environment: Oceanographic

OCEANOGRAPHY INSTITUTE, ENVIRONMENTAL SCIENCES SERVICES ADMINISTRATION
GRAMAX BUILDING, 8060 13TH STREET
SILVER SPRING, MD 20910
General Environment: Estuarine

PACIFIC BIOLOGICAL STATION
POST OFFICE DRAWER 100
NANAIMO, CANADA
Staff Size: 100 - 499

PEARL AND FISHERY BOARD
MERCHANT STREET
RANGOON, BURMA
General Environment: Oceanographic
Specific Interests: Tropical (hot)

PEARL RESEARCH LABORATORY
AKO MIE, JAPAN
Director, Dr Shigeru Ota
General Environment: Oceanographic

PETROLEUM AND MINERAL RESOURCES MINISTRY
JIDDA, SAUDI ARABIA
General Environment: Oceanographic

PLANNING AND PROGRAMMING OFFICE
EDIF BANCO, NAC DE FOMENTO
COMEYAGUELA, HONDURAS
General Environment: Oceanographic

PUBLIC WORKS MINISTRY
KUWAIT
Director, Hassain Selim
General Environment: Oceanographic

RADIATION BIOLOGY LABORATORY
7901 KENTBURY DR
BETHESDA, MD 20014
Director, William H Klein

RADIOBIOLOGICAL LABORATORY, ARMED FORCES, DEPARTMENT OF DEFENSE
NATIONAL NAVAL MEDICAL CENTER
BETHESDA, MD 20014
Staff Size: 5 - 9

RADIOLOGICAL HEALTH BUREAU
12720 TWINBROOK PARKWAY
ROCKVILLE, MD 20852
Specific Interests: Prairie and Temperate Forest

RADIOLOGICAL PHYSICS DIVISION
9700 SOUTH CASS AVENUE
ARGONNE, IL 60439

RENEWABLE RESOURCES
MINISTRY OF AGRICULTURE
MANAGUA, NICARAGUA
Director, Ruben Camacho
General Environment: Oceanographic

SCIENCE AND TECHNOLOGY DEPARTMENT
JUAN LINDOLFO CUESTAS 1401
MONTEVIDEO, URUGUAY
Director, Dr Don Mario Siri
General Environment: Oceanographic

**SCIENCE RESOURCES, ALL-UNION
INSTITUTE OF OCEANOGRAPHY
MOSCOW, UNION OF SOVIET
SOCIALIST REPUBLICS**
Director, G K Tzhveskiy
General Environment: Oceanographic

**SCIENTIFIC AND TECHNICAL
RESOURCES**
31 BAYINDIRSOKAK
ANKARA, TURKEY
General Environment: Oceanographic

**SEA FISHERIES RESOURCES
STATION, DEPARTMENT OF
FISHERIES**
4 HABANKIN STREET
HAIFA, ISRAEL
Director, Dr O Oren
General Environment: Oceanographic

SEA INSTITUTE
LA PUNTA
CALLAO, PERU
General Environment: Oceanographic
Staff Size: 100 - 499

SEA RESEARCH INSTITUTE
BUITENHAVEN 27
DEN HELDER, NETHERLANDS
General Environment: Oceanographic

**SEIKAI REGIONAL FISHERIES
RESEARCH LABORATORY**
NAGASAKI, JAPAN
General Environment: Oceanographic
Specific Interests: Prairie and Temperate
Forest

**SMITHSONIAN TROPICAL
RESOURCES INSTITUTE**
POST OFFICE BOX 2072
BALBOA, CANAL ZONE
General Environment: Terrestrial
Specific Interests: Tropical (hot)
Staff Size: 100 - 499

**TECHNOLOGY INFORMATION
DEPARTMENT, BIOLOGICAL**
FORT DETRICK
FREDERICK, MD 21701
General Environment: Limnologic

**TECHNOLOGY LABORATORY,
BUREAU COMMISSION
FISHERIES**
239 FREDERIC STREET, PO 1207
PASCAGOULA, MS 39567
Director, Travis D Love
General Environment: Oceanographic
Staff Size: 5 - 9

**TECHNOLOGY LABORATORY,
BUREAU OF COMMERCIAL
FISHERIES**
622 MISSION STREET
KETCHIKAN, AK 99901

Director, Murray L Hayes
General Environment: Oceanographic
Specific Interests: Polar (cold)
Staff Size: 5 - 9

**TOHOKU REGIONAL FISHERIES
RESEARCH LABORATORY**
SHIOGAMA, JAPAN
Director, Dr Tokimi Tsusita
General Environment: Oceanographic
Specific Interests: Prairie and Temperate
Forest

**TOKAI REGIONAL FISHERIES
RESEARCH LABORATORY**
TOKYO, JAPAN
Director, Dr Taketatsu Hidaka
General Environment: Oceanographic
Specific Interests: Prairie and Temperate
Forest

**UNIVERSITY CORPORATION FOR
ATMOSPHERIC RESEARCH**
POST OFFICE BOX 1470
BOULDER, CO 80302
President, Dr Walter O Roberts
General Environment: Atmospheric
Staff Size: 100 - 499

WILDLIFE RESEARCH DIVISION
CANBERRA, AUSTRALIA
Specific Interests: Prairie and Temperate
Forest

**ZOOLOGICAL SURVEY
DEPARTMENT**
FISHERIES HARBOR, WEST WHARF
KARACHI, PAKISTAN

ZOOLOGICAL SURVEY OF INDIA
CALCUTTA, INDIA

**ZOOLOGY DEPARTMENT, NAVAL
RESOURCES INSTITUTE**
ILHA GOVENADOR, AVENUE
PRESIDENT,
RIO DE JANIERO, BRAZIL
General Environment: Oceanographic

Government — State or Local

**BIOLOGICAL EFFECTS
DEPARTMENT**
12720 TWINBROOK PARKWAY
ROCKVILLE, MD 20852
Secretary, Thomas Wagner

BOTANICAL GARDENS
KEW
RICHMOND, SURREY, ENGLAND
Director, J Heslop-Harrison

CONSERVATOIRE BOTANIQUE
192 RTE OF LAUSANNE
GENEVA, SWITZERLAND

Director, Dr J Miege
Staff Size: 50 - 99

**FISHERIES AND FAUNA
DEPARTMENT**
108 ADELAIDE TERRACE
PERTH, WEST AUSTRALIA,
AUSTRALIA
Director, J Fraser
Specific Interests: Tropical (hot)

**FISHERIES AND WILDLIFE
DEPARTMENT**
605 FLINDERS STREET
MELBOURNE, VICTORIA,
AUSTRALIA
Specific Interests: Tropical (hot)

FISHERIES COMMISSION
FRESHWATER LABORATORY
NARRANDERA, NEW SOUTH
WALES, AUSTRALIA
General Environment: Oceanographic
Specific Interests: Tropical (hot)

FISHERIES DEPARTMENT
KERALA, INDIA
Director, I George
General Environment: Oceanographic
Specific Interests: Tropical (hot)

FISHERIES DEPARTMENT
BOX 1191
ADELAIDE, SOUTH AUSTRALIA,
AUSTRALIA
Director, M Olsen
General Environment: Oceanographic
Staff Size: 5 - 9

FISHERIES DEPARTMENT
KONEDOBU
PAPUA, NEW GUINEA
General Environment: Oceanographic
Specific Interests: Tropical (hot)

FISHERIES DEPARTMENT
35-2 MOUNT ROAD
MADRAS 2, INDIA
General Environment: Oceanographic

FISHERIES SECTION
NORTHERN TERRITORY
ADMINISTRATION
DARWIN, NORTHERN
TERRITORIES, AUSTRALIA
Director, D Puffett
General Environment: Oceanographic
Specific Interests: Tropical (hot)

HARBORS DEPARTMENT
BOX 5094 G P O
BRISBANE, QUEENSLAND,
AUSTRALIA
Director, J Peel
General Environment: Oceanographic
Specific Interests: Tropical (hot)

**HEALTH, EDUCATION, AND
    WELFARE DEPARTMENT**
ALASKA OFFICE BUILDING
JUNEAU, AK 99801
General Environment: Marsh/Swamp
Specific Interests: Polar (cold)
Staff Size: 10 - 49

**MARINE BIOLOGICAL RESEARCH
    STATION**
RATNAGIRI
MAHARASHTRA STATE, INDIA
Director, Dr C V Kulkarni
General Environment: Oceanographic

MARINE BIOLOGICAL STATION
KANUDI TATANA ROAD
PORT MORESBY, NEW GUINEA
Director, W Charles
General Environment: Oceanographic
Specific Interests: Tropical (hot)

**RADIATION BIOLOGY DIVISION,
    DEPARTMENT OF RADIATION**
MEDICAL COLLEGE OF VIRGINIA
RICHMOND, VA 23219
Chairman, Stuart Lippincott

**STATE FISHERIES COORDINATOR-
    MISSION**
BOX 30 G P O
SYDNEY, NEW SOUTH WALES,
    AUSTRALIA
Director, Dr D D Francis
General Environment: Oceanographic
Specific Interests: Tropical (hot)

**TARAPOREVALA AQUARIUM AND
    MARINE BIOLOGY INSTITUTE**
NETAJI SUBHASH ROAD
BOMBAY, INDIA
Director, Dr C V Kulkarni
General Environment: Oceanographic

Industrial/Commercial

**ALIMENTOS INTERAMERICANOS,
    SOUTH AMERICA**
CORINTO, NICARAGUA
General Environment: Oceanographic

**ARABIAN AMERICAN OIL
    COMPANY**
JIDDA, SAUDI ARABIA
General Environment: Oceanographic

ARABIAN OIL COMPANY
POST OFFICE BOX 1641
KUWAIT
Director, Sinichi Satow
General Environment: Oceanographic

**BELCO PETROLEUM
    COORDINATOR**
411 TUCUA
LIMA, PERU
General Environment: Oceanographic

**BIOGEOLOGICAL SOCIETY
    NATIONAL SCIENCES MUSEUM**
UENO PARK
TAITO-KU, TOKYO, JAPAN
Director, Dr Yaichiro Okada
Specific Interests: Prairie and Temperate
    Forest

**BOOTH NICARAGUA, SOUTH
    AMERICA**
EL BLUFF, NICARAGUA
General Environment: Oceanographic

BUSH JOHNSONS LIMITED
WOODHAM MORTIMER HALL
MALDON, ESSEX, ENGLAND
Resources Director, Sydney Ellerton
General Environment: Terrestrial
Specific Interests: Prairie and Temperate
    Forest

CARIBBEAN PRODUCERS
GUANAJA, HONDURAS
General Environment: Oceanographic

CARLOS VERRANDO
JUNIV 358
LIMA, PERU
General Environment: Oceanographic

**COMPANIA INDUSTRIAL DE
    MARISCOS**
PUNTARENAS, COSTA RICA
Director, Rodrigo Calvo
General Environment: Oceanographic

**CYANAMID OF GREAT BRITAIN
    LIMITED**
154 FAREHAM ROAD
GOSPORT, HAMPSHIRE, ENGLAND
Manager, Ahmad Amara
Specific Interests: Prairie and Temperate
    Forest

**EUGENIO GARRON & SONS,
    LIMITED**
LIMON, COSTA RICA
Director, Francisco Garron
General Environment: Oceanographic

**FIGORIFICOS DE PUNTARENAS,
    SOUTH AMERICA**
PUNTARENAS, COSTA RICA
General Environment: Oceanographic

FISHERIES CORPORATION
GALLE FACE
COLOMBO 3, CEYLON
Director, D C L Amerasinghe
General Environment: Oceanographic

**FISHERIES DEPARTMENT AND
    ALLIED INDUSTRIAL
    BIOLOGICAL LABORATORY**
AQUILES, SERDAN 28 40 PISO
MEXICO 1 DF, MEXICO
General Environment: Oceanographic

**FISHERIES DEPARTMENT,
    MINISTRY OF AGRICULTURE**
PORT OF SPAIN, TRINIDAD
General Environment: Oceanographic

FISHERIES INDUSTRIES SOCIETY
BP 581
DOVALA, CAMEROON
General Environment: Oceanographic

FISHERMEN'S COOPERATIVE
SAN LORENZO, HONDURAS
General Environment: Oceanographic

**FUEL MINISTRY, ELECTRIC
    POWER AND INDUSTRIAL
    PROJECTS**
INDUSTRIAL PROJECTS
DAMASCUS, SYRIA
General Environment: Oceanographic

GETTY OIL COMPANY
JIDDA, SAUDI ARABIA
General Environment: Oceanographic

GULF FISHERIES BRANCH
POST OFFICE BOX 3389
KUWAIT
Director, Khalil Osman Mahmoud
General Environment: Oceanographic

HIELO Y FRIO, LIMITED
PUNTARENAS, COSTA RICA
General Environment: Oceanographic

HONDURAN FISHERIES INDUSTRY
GUANAJA, HONDURAS
General Environment: Oceanographic

**INTERNATIONAL FISHERIES
    CORPORATION**
POST OFFICE BOX 1262
KUWAIT
Director, Abdul Jaleel Behbehani
General Environment: Oceanographic

**KUWAIT NATIONAL FISHERIES
    COMPANY**
POST OFFICE BOX 3663
KUWAIT
Director, Hamid Al-Isa
General Environment: Oceanographic

**LANGOSTERA DE CARIBE,
    INCORPORATED**
CORN ISLAND, NICARAGUA
General Environment: Oceanographic

LIBERIA COLD STORES
MONROVIA, LIBERIA

General Environment: Oceanographic
Specific Interests: Tropical (hot)

MARGARITE MARINE BIOLOGICAL STATION
ESTADO NUEVA ESPARTA, VENEZUELA

MARISCOS DE GUATEMALA, SOUTH AMERICA
15 AVENUE 19-15, ZONE 13
GUATEMALA CITY, GUATEMALA
General Environment: Oceanographic

MARITIME FISHERIES SOCIETY
BP 84,MATADI,KONGO CENTRAL
KINSHASA, DEMOCRATIC REPUBLIC OF THE CONGO
Director, C Van Goethem
General Environment: Oceanographic

NATIONAL IRANIAN OIL COMPANY
TEHRAN, IRAN
General Environment: Oceanographic

NORTHERN FISHERMENS COOPERATIVE
NORTH FRONT STREET
BELIZE CITY, BRITISH HONDURAS
General Environment: Oceanographic

OCEANOGRAPHIC DEVELOPMENT CORPORATION
732 WILSON AVENUE, MEZZANINE
LIMA, PERU
General Environment: Oceanographic

PAKISTAN SHELL RAP
KARACHI, PAKISTAN
General Environment: Oceanographic

PESCANIA, SOUTH AMERICA
BLUEFIELDS, NICARAGUA
General Environment: Oceanographic

PETROLEOS MEXICANOS
JUAREZ 92,
MEXICO 1, DF, MEXICO
General Environment: Oceanographic

PRODUCTOS DE CARIBE, LIMITED
LIMON, COSTA RICA
Director, Stanley Lambert
General Environment: Oceanographic

PUERTO QUEQUEN HYDROBIOLOGY STATION
NECOCHEA
PUERTO QUEQUEN, ARGENTINA
Director, Enrique Balech
General Environment: Oceanographic

SHELL OIL COMPANY
KUWAIT
General Environment: Oceanographic

SIGNAL OIL AND GAS COMPANY
SAN LORENZO, HONDURAS
General Environment: Oceanographic

SIMON-HARTLEY LTP
STOKE-ON-TRENT, ST47B4, ENGLAND
Director, Dr J W Abson
Specific Interests: Urban
Staff Size: 100 - 499

TECHOQUIMICA
1152 COMINO A LA ATARJEA
LIMA, PERU
General Environment: Oceanographic

UNION OIL COMPANY
SAN LORENZO, HONDURAS
General Environment: Oceanographic

VEN DEVELOPMENT CORPORATION
EDIFICO N, CENTRO SI BOL
CARACUS, VENEZUELA

WILD FLOWER PRESERVATION SOCIETY
3740 OLIVER STREET, NW
WASHINGTON, DC 20015

WILLS BOWERS, INCORPORATED
CORN ISLAND, NICARAGUA
General Environment: Oceanographic

Professional Organizations

AMERICA LITTORAL SOCIETY
SANDY HOOK
HIGHLANDS, NJ 07732
President, John C Storr
Specific Interests: Prairie and Temperate Forest

AMERICAN FISHERIES SOCIETY
1404 NEW YORK AVENUE, NW
WASHINGTON, DC 20005
General Environment: Limnologic

BIOLOGICAL SCIENCES INSTITUTION
3900 WISCONSIN AVENUE, NW
WASHINGTON, DC 20016
Director, John R Olive
Specific Interests: Prairie and Temperate Forest
Staff Size: 1000 & Larger

BIOLOGISTS STATE ASSOCIATION
BOX 646
SANFORD, ME 04073

BIOLOGY TEACHERS NATIONAL ASSOCIATION
1420 N STREET, NW
WASHINGTON, DC 20005
President, Robert E Yager
Specific Interests: Prairie and Temperate Forest
Staff Size: 5000 - 9999

BIRD CLUBS FEDERATION OF NEW YORK STATE
STATE MUSEUM
ALBANY, NY 12224
President, Edgar M Reilly, Jr
Specific Interests: Prairie and Temperate Forest

BOTANICAL GARDENS, AMERICAN ASSOCIATION
UNIVERSITY OF WASHINGTON ARBORETUM
SEATTLE, WA 98105
President, Joseph Witt
Specific Interests: Prairie and Temperate Forest

CARTAGENA OFFICE, MAG AND SIVU VALL CORPORATION
CARRERA 14 25A-66 PISO 5
BOGOTA, COLOMBIA
General Environment: Oceanographic

CETACEAN SOCIETY OF AMERICA
4725 LINCOLN BOULEVARD
MARINA DEL REY, CA 90291
General Environment: Oceanographic

DESERT BIGHORN COUNCIL, DEPARTMENT OF BIOLOGICAL SCIENCES
UNIVERSITY OF NEVADA
LAS VEGAS, NV 89109
Chairman, William Graf
Specific Interests: Prairie and Temperate Forest

ENTOMOLOGICAL SOCIETY OF AMERICA
4603 CALVERT ROAD
COLLEGE PARK, MD 20740
Staff Size: 10 - 49

ENVIRONMENTAL RESEARCH COUNCIL
ALHAMBRA HOUSE, CHARING CROSS
LONDON, ENGLAND
Director, Gordon W Heath
General Environment: Terrestrial
Specific Interests: Prairie and Temperate Forest

GARDEN CLUBS NATIONAL COUNCIL
4401 MAGNOLIA AVENUE
ST LOUIS, MO 63110
President, Mrs William H Barton
General Environment: Terrestrial
Specific Interests: Prairie and Temperate Forest
Staff Size: 1000 & Larger

ICHTHYOLOGISTS SOCIETY OF AMERICA
NATIONAL MUSEUM OF NATURAL HISTORY
WASHINGTON, DC 20560

President, James Peters
Specific Interests: Prairie and Temperate
  Forest
Staff Size: 1000 - 4999

**INSTITUT POLYTECHNIQUE
  FEDERAL**
UNIVERSITS STRASSE 2
8006 ZURICH, SWITZERLAND

**INTERNATIONAL SHADE TREE
  CONFERENCE**
1827 NEIL AVENUE
COLUMBUS, OH 43210
General Environment: Terrestrial

**KATSURAHAMA MARINE SCIENCES
  MUSEUM**
778 URADO
KOCHI CITY, KOCHI, JAPAN
General Environment: Oceanographic
Specific Interests: Prairie and Temperate
  Forest

**MAMMALOGISTS SOCIETY OF
  AMERICA**
OKLAHOMA STATE UNIVERSITY
STILLWATER, OK 74074
Specific Interests: Prairie and Temperate
  Forest
Staff Size: 1000 - 4999

**NATURALISTS SOCIETY OF
  AMERICA**
WOOSTER COLLEGE
WOOSTER, OH 44691
Secretary, Professor Warren P Spencer
Specific Interests: Prairie and Temperate
  Forest
Staff Size: 500 - 999

**NATURALISTS SOCIETY, BIOLOGY
  DEPARTMENT**
SAN JOSE STATE COLLEGE
SAN JOSE, CA 95114
Director, James M Craig
Staff Size: 500 - 999

**ORNITHOLOGICAL SOCIETY OF
  ALABAMA**
POST OFFICE BOX 1448
BIRMINGHAM, AL 35201
President, Walter F Coxe
Specific Interests: Prairie and Temperate
  Forest
Staff Size: 100 - 499

**ORNITHOLOGICAL SOCIETY OF
  MARYLAND**
4915 GREENSPRING AVENUE
BALTIMORE, MD 21209
President, Dr Lawrence Zeleny
Specific Interests: Prairie and Temperate
  Forest
Staff Size: 1000 - 4999

**ORNITHOLOGISTS UNION OF
  AMERICA**
NATIONAL MUSEUM OF NATURAL
  HISTORY
WASHINGTON, DC 20560
Secretary, Richard C Banks

**RUFFED GROUSE SOCIETY OF
  AMERICA**
81 INDIAN SPRING LANE
ROCHESTER, NY 14618
President, George E Ford
Specific Interests: Prairie and Temperate
  Forest

**WHOOPING CRANE
  CONSERVATION ASSOCIATION**
216 WHITTON STREET
SIERRA VISTA, AZ 85635
Director, Jerome J Pratt
Staff Size: 100 - 499

**ZOOLOGICAL PARKS AND
  AQUARIUMS ASSOCIATION OF
  AMERICA**
OGLEBAY PARK
WHEELING, WV 26003
President, Gary K Clarke
Staff Size: 1 - 4

**ZOOLOGISTS SOCIETY OF
  AMERICA**
175 NATURAL RESOURCES
  BUILDING
URBANA, IL 61801
Secretary, Dr George Sprugel, Jr
Specific Interests: Prairie and Temperate
  Forest
Staff Size: 1000 - 4999

Research Institute

**ALGOLOGICAL RESEARCH
  INSTITUTE**
HOKKAIDO UNIVERSITY
MURORAN, 051, JAPAN
Director, Dr Yoshiteru Nakamura
General Environment: Oceanographic
Staff Size: 5 - 9

**ANTARCTIC INSTITUTION OF
  ARGENTINA**
CERITTO 1248
BUENOS AIRES, ARGENTINA
Director, Radm Rodolfo N Panzarina
General Environment: Oceanographic
Specific Interests: Polar (cold)

ARCTIC BIOLOGY INSTITUTE
UNIVERSITY OF ALASKA
FAIRBANKS, AK 99701
Director, Peter Morrison
Specific Interests: Polar (cold)
Staff Size: 100 - 499

BIOFYZIKALNI USTAV CSAV
BRNO 12
KRALOVOPOLSKA 135,
  CZECHOSLOVAKIA
Director, Ferdinand Hereik

BIOLOGIAI KUTATO
TIHANY, HUNGARY
Director, Dr Janos Salanki
General Environment: Limnologic

BIOLOGICAL INSTITUTE
DUBROVNIK, YUGOSLAVIA
Director, T Gamulin
General Environment: Oceanographic
Staff Size: 5 - 9

**BIOLOGICAL SCIENCES
  INTERNATIONAL UNION,
  BOTANISCH MUSEUM**
LANGE NIEUWSTRAAT 106
UTRECHT, NETHERLANDS

BIOLOGICKY USTAV SAV
BRATISLAVA, KOLLAROVO
NAM 2, CZECHOSLOVAKIA
Director, Dr Pavol Nemec

**BIOLOGY LABORATORY OF
  IMPERIAL HOUSEHOLD**
IMPERIAL PALACE
CHIYODA-KU, TOKYO, JAPAN
Specific Interests: Prairie and Temperate
  Forest
Staff Size: 1 - 4

**BIOMETEOROLOGY
  INTERNATIONAL SOCIETY**
HOFBROUCKERLAAN 54 OEGSTG
LEIDEN, NETHERLANDS
General Environment: Atmospheric

**BOTANICAL GARDENS
  (INTERNATIONAL CONGRESS),
  MUSEUM OF NATURAL HISTORY**
SMITHSONIAN INSTITUTE
WASHINGTON, DC 20025

**BOTANICAL SOCIETY, BOTANY
  DEPARTMENT, TOKYO
  UNIVERSITY**
1 MOTO-FUJI-CHO
BUNKYO-KU, TOKYO, JAPAN
Director, Tomoo Miwa
Specific Interests: Prairie and Temperate
  Forest

BOTANISCH STAATSSAMMIUNG
MENZINGER STRASSE 67
8000 MUNICH 19, WEST GERMANY
Specific Interests: Tropical (hot)

**BOTANY DEPARTMENT, SOCIETY
  OF PHYCOLOGY**
HOKKAIDO UNIVERSITY NISHI 5-
  CHOME
KITA 8-JO, SAPPORO CITY, JAPAN

Director, Dr Sachio Yamada
Specific Interests: Prairie and Temperate
Forest

BOYCE THOMPSON INSTITUTE
1086 NORTH BROADWAY
YONKERS, NY 10701
Plant Physiologist, Jay Jacobson
General Environment: Atmospheric
Staff Size: 1 - 4

**BROOKHAVEN NATIONAL
LABORATORY**
UPTON, NY 11973
Director, R Conard
General Environment: Atmospheric
Staff Size: 50 - 99

**CENTER SCIENCES STUDIES
RESOURCES BARRIETY**
B P 28 PLATEAU DE LATALAYE
BIARRITZ (B P), FRANCE
Director, L Barriety
General Environment: Oceanographic

CENTRAL MARINE FISHERIES
RAMANATHAPURAM DISTRICT
MADRAS STATE, INDIA
Director, S Jones
General Environment: Oceanographic

CLINICAL RESEARCH CENTER
NORTHWICK PARK
HARROW, MIDDLESEX, ENGLAND
Director, Robert G Milne
General Environment: Terrestrial
Specific Interests: Prairie and Temperate
Forest

**COMMONWEALTH INSTITUTE OF
BIOLOGICAL CONTROL**
C/O CAB, FARNHAM ROYAL
SLOUGH, BUCKINGHAMSHIRE,
ENGLAND
Director, Frederick J Simmonds
General Environment: Terrestrial
Specific Interests: Prairie and Temperate
Forest

DISEASES IN CENTRAL AFRICA
MEDECIN COLONEL LABUSQUIER
BP 4057, YAOUNPE, CAMEROON

**ECONOMIC RESOURCES
INSTITUTE**
UTAH STATE UNIVERSITY
LOGAN, UT 84321
General Environment: Limnologic

ELM RESEARCH INSTITUTE
60 WEST PROSPECT STREET
WALDWICK, NJ 07463
Executive Director, John P Hansel
General Environment: Terrestrial
Specific Interests: Prairie and Temperate
Forest
Staff Size: 100 - 499

ENTOMOLOGICKY USTAV CSAV
PRAHA 2-NOVE MESTO
VINICNA 7, CZECHOSLOVAKIA
Director, Dr Vladimir Landa
General Environment: Terrestrial

**EXPERIMENTAL
THALASSOGRAPHY, TRIESTE
INSTITUTE**
VIALE ROMOLO GESSI 2
TRIESTE, ITALY
Director, Dr Leopoldo Trotti
General Environment: Oceanographic

**FISH PROCESSING, INSTITUTE OF
SEA FISHERIES**
251 ROSTOCK-MARIENEHE
BERLIN, EAST GERMANY
Director, H Schneider
General Environment: Limnologic

**FISHERIES AND ANIMAL
HUSBANDRY FACULTY,
HIROSHIMA UNIVERSITY**
FUKAYASUCHO,
HIROSHIMA PREFECTURE, JAPAN
Director, Dr Yasuo Matsudaira
General Environment: Oceanographic

FISHERIES DEPARTMENT
NATIONAL POLYTECHNIC
INSTITUTE
QUITO, ECUADOR
Director, Dr Gustavo Villagmez
General Environment: Oceanographic

**FISHERIES FACULTY, PLANKTON
SOCIETY, HOKKAIDO
UNIVERSITY**
MINATO-MACHI
HAKODATE CITY, JAPAN
General Environment: Oceanographic
Specific Interests: Prairie and Temperate
Forest

FISHERIES RESEARCH INSTITUTE
CALTHROP ROAD
PENANG, MALAYSIA
Director, Soong Min Kong
General Environment: Oceanographic

**FISHERIES RESEARCH
LABORATORY MARINE
LABORATORY**
WELLINGTON, NEW ZEALAND
Director, G D Waugh
General Environment: Oceanographic

**FISHERIES RESOURCE CENTER,
BUENAVENTURA**
APARTADO AEREO 607
VALLE, COLOMBIA
General Environment: Oceanographic

FISHERIES SERVICES (OPEMA)
CONAKRY, GUINEA
Director, Dr Kekoura Sato
General Environment: Oceanographic

**FISHERIES-RESEARCH INSTITUTE
OF TAIWAN**
125 HOU-1 ROAD
KEELUNG, TAIWAN
Director, Hou-Tu Teng
General Environment: Oceanographic

**HYDROBIOLOGY INSTITUTE OF
ALEXANDRIA**
KAYED BAY ALEXANDRIA
EL MISR, UNITED ARAB REPUBLIC
General Environment: Oceanographic

**HYDROGRAPHIC OFFICE,
PORTUGUESE**
LISBON, PORTUGAL
Director, Dr Luciano Bastos
General Environment: Oceanographic

**LIMNOLOGY, MAX-PLANK-
INSTITUTION**
D-232 PLON (HOLSTEIN)
POSTFACH 165, WEST GERMANY
Professor, Harald Sioli
General Environment: Limnologic
Specific Interests: Tropical (hot)
Staff Size: 10 - 49

**MARINE BIOLOGICAL STATION AT
MISAKI**
MISAKI,KANAGAWA-KEN, JAPAN
Director, Professor Hideshi Kobayshi
General Environment: Oceanographic
Staff Size: 10 - 49

MARINE BIOLOGY INSTITUTE
ROVINJ, YUGOSLAVIA
Director, Dr N Allegretti
General Environment: Oceanographic

**MARINE BIOLOGY INSTITUTE,
CAUSILLA DECORR**
175-PLAYA GRANDE
MAR DEL PLATA, ARGENTINA
Director, Dr Erigue E Boschi
General Environment: Oceanographic

MARINE BIORESEARCH INSTITUTE
P O BOX 229
MOSS LANDING, CA 95039
Director, Dr J L Barnard
General Environment: Oceanographic

**MARINE FISHERIES INSTITUTION
OF MOROCCO**
RUE DE TIZNIT
CASABLANCA, MOROCCO
Director, Jean Collignon
General Environment: Oceanographic

**MARINE FISHERIES RESEARCH
ORGANIZATION OF EAST AFRICA**
POST OFFICE BOX 666
ZANZIBAR
Director, B E Bell
General Environment: Oceanographic

MARINE RESEARCH INSTITUTE
HANDELSHAFEN 12
BREMERHAVEN, WEST GERMANY
Director, H Gerlach
General Environment: Oceanographic

MARINE RESEARCH INSTITUTE
HELSINKI 4, FINLAND
Director, Dr Ilmo Hela
General Environment: Oceanographic
Specific Interests: Prairie and Temperate
Forest

MARINE RESEARCH INSTITUTE
POST OFFICE BOX 580 DAK
PASARIKAN
DJAKARTA KOTA, INDONESIA
Director, Gatot Raharoso Joenoes
General Environment: Oceanographic

**MARINE SCIENCES INSTITUTE OF
VIRGINIA**
WACHAPREAGUE, VA 23480
President, Jerome Williams
General Environment: Estuarine
Specific Interests: Prairie and Temperate
Forest
Staff Size: 100 - 499

MEDICAL DEPARTMENT
BROOKHAVEN NATIONAL
LABORATORY
UPTON, NY
Chairman, Victor Bond

**MEDICAL SCHOOL, UNIVERSITY
OF SOUTHERN CALIFORNIA**
2025 ZONAL AVENUE
LOS ANGELES, CA 90033
Professor, R P Sherman
General Environment: Atmospheric
Staff Size: 10 - 49

**MEDICAL SCHOOL, TULANE
UNIVERSITY**
1430 TULANE AVENUE
NEW ORLEANS, LA 70112
Head, Charles Dunlap

**METEOROLOGICAL AGENCY,
MARINE DIVISION**
OTEMACHI, CHIYODA-KU
TOKYO, JAPAN
Director, Dr K Wadachi
General Environment: Oceanographic

**MICROBIOLOGICAL SOCIETY,
DIVISION OF BIOSCIENCE**
NATIONAL RESEARCH COUNCIL
OTTAWA 2, ONTARIO, CANADA

**NATURAL RESOURCES
DEPARTMENT OF WEST
VIRGINIA**
1709 WASHINGTON STREET, EAST
CHARLESTON, WV 25311

**OCEANOGRAPHIC RESOURCES
INSTITUTION**
P O BOX 736, 2 WEST STREET
DURBAN, REPUBLIC OF SOUTH
AFRICA
Director, Dr E F Heydorn
General Environment: Oceanographic

OCEANOGRAPHIQUE CENTER
O R S T O M BP
4-NOUMEA, NEW CALEDONIA
Director, M Legand
General Environment: Oceanographic

OCEANOGRAPHIQUE INSTITUTE
JETEE NORD
ALGIERS, ALGERIA
Director, Professor Francis Bernard
General Environment: Oceanographic

**OCEANOGRAPHY AND FISHERIES
CENTER**
BP 1086 POINTE NOIRE
BRAZZAVILLE, DEMOCRATIC
REPUBLIC OF THE CONGO
General Environment: Oceanographic
Staff Size: 50 - 99

**OCEANOGRAPHY AND FISHERIES
INSTITUTE**
114 RT MARJONA
SPLIT, YUGOSLAVIA
Director, Miljenko Buljan
General Environment: Oceanographic

**OCEANOGRAPHY RED SEA
INSTITUTE**
AL-GHARDAQA
RED SEA, UNITED ARAB REPUBLIC
Director, Dr El Sayed M Hassan
General Environment: Oceanographic

**ORGANIZATION OF OVERSEAS
SCIENCE AND TECHNOLOGICAL
STATION**
TANANARIVE, MALAGASY
REPUBLIC
Director, Patrice Roederer
General Environment: Oceanographic

**OSTOM-MINISTRE DELA PRODUCE
ANIMALE BP**
18 ABIDJAN, IVORY COAST
Director, Dr G R Berrit

**PINEAPPLE RESEARCH
INSTITUTION OF HAWAII**
WAHIAWA
HONOLULU, HI 96786
Director, Dr D Williams
Staff Size: 10 - 49

**POTATOES AND BRASSICA
SECTION**
PLANT BREEDING INSTITUTE
TRUMPINGTON, CAMBRIDGE,
ENGLAND
General Environment: Terrestrial
Specific Interests: Prairie and Temperate
Forest

**RESEARCH CENTER AT
HUNTINGDON**
HUNTINGDON, NORTHAMPTON,
ENGLAND
Specific Interests: Prairie and Temperate
Forest
Staff Size: 500 - 999

**RESEARCH COUNCIL OF BRITISH
COLUMBIA**
UNIVERSITY OF BRITISH
COLUMBIA
VANCOUVER 8, BRITISH
COLUMBIA, CANADA
Director, Dr Paul C Trussell
General Environment: Oceanographic
Staff Size: 50 - 99

RESEARCH DEPARTMENT
BEMERODERSTRASSE 61
HANNOVER-KIRCHRONE, WEST
GERMANY

**RESEARCH LABORATORY,
HOKKAIDO**
HAMMANAKA, YOICHI
HOKKAIDO, JAPAN
Director, Dr Kohei Ogaki
General Environment: Oceanographic

RESEARCH LONG ASHTON
UNIVERSITY BRISTOL
BRISTOL, GLOUCESTER, ENGLAND
Director Plant Pathology Secretary, Dr R
Byrde
Specific Interests: Prairie and Temperate
Forest

**RESEARCH STATION AT EAST
MALLING**
EAST MALLING
KENT, ENGLAND
Director, Dr H C Pereira
General Environment: Terrestrial
Specific Interests: Rural
Staff Size: 100 - 499

**RESEARCH STATION OF BARRO
COLORADO**
GUTUN LAKE, PANAMA
General Environment: Oceanographic

SCIENCE ACADEMY OF AUSTRALIA
GORDON STREET
CANBERRA, AUSTRALIA
Director, Dr G F Humphrey
General Environment: Oceanographic
Specific Interests: Tropical (hot)

**SCIENCE ACADEMY OF
CALIFORNIA**
GOLDEN GATE PARK
SAN FRANCISCO, CA 94100
Director, Dr George E Lindsay
Staff Size: 100 - 499

SCIENCE AND FISHERIES SOCIETY, TOKYO UNIVERSITY OF FISHERIES
6-CHOME SHIBA KAIGAN-DORI
MINATO-KU, TOKYO, JAPAN
Director, Dr Morisaburo Tauchi
General Environment: Oceanographic
Specific Interests: Prairie and Temperate Forest

SCIENCE INSTITUTE, RABAT UNIVERSITY
AVENUE MOULAY CHERIF
RABAT, MOROCCO
Director, Mr Hajoub Msougar
General Environment: Oceanographic
Staff Size: 10 - 49

SCIENCE RESEARCH INSTITUTE
NEW MEXICO HIGHLANDS UNIVERSITY
LAS VEGAS, NM 87745
Professor of Biology, Stephen Norrel

SCIENTIFIC AND TECHNOLOGICAL INSTITUTE OF MARINE FISHERIES
59 AVENUE RAYMOND POINCARE
PARIS 16, FRANCE
Director, Jean Furnestin
General Environment: Oceanographic

SEA FISHERIES RESOURCES STATION
POST OFFICE BOX 699
HAIFA, ISRAEL
Director, O H Oren
General Environment: Oceanographic

SUISAN ZOSHOKU DANWAKAI FISHERIES-VETSCI
HIROSHIMA UNIVERSITY DAIMON-CHO
FUKUYAMA CITY, HIROSHIMA, JAPAN
Specific Interests: Prairie and Temperate Forest

THE MACAULAY INSTITUTE
CRAIGIEBUCKLER
ABERDEEN AB9 2QJ, SCOTLAND
General Environment: Terrestrial
Specific Interests: Prairie and Temperate Forest

TORRY RESEARCH STATION
ABERDEEN, SCOTLAND
Director, Robert M Love
General Environment: Oceanographic
Specific Interests: Polar (cold)
Staff Size: 100 - 499

VEGETABLE RESEARCH STATION, NATIONAL
WELLESBOURNE, WARWICK, ENGLAND
Director, Professor D W Wright
General Environment: Terrestrial

Specific Interests: Prairie and Temperate Forest
Staff Size: 50 - 99

WATER RESOURCES CENTER OF WASHINGTON
WASHINGTON STATE UNIVERSITY
PULLMAN, WA 99163

WEED RESEARCH ORGANIZATION
BEGBROKE HILL, YARNTON, OXFORD, OXSIPF, ENGLAND
Director, John D Fryer
General Environment: Terrestrial
Staff Size: 100 - 499

WHALE RESEARCH INSTITUTION
12-4 NISHIKAIGANDORI
TSUKISHIMAI CHOUKU, TOKYO, JAPAN
Director, Dr Hideo Omura
General Environment: Oceanographic
Specific Interests: Prairie and Temperate Forest

WILDERNESS RESEARCH CENTER, QUETICO-SUPERIOR
7335 CENTRAL AVENUE
ELY, MN 55731
Director, Clifford E Ahlgren
General Environment: Terrestrial
Specific Interests: Prairie and Temperate Forest
Staff Size: 1 - 4

WILDLIFE RESEARCH UNIT OF ALABAMA
AUBURN UNIVERSITY
AUBURN, AL 36830
Director, Maurice F Baker
General Environment: Terrestrial
Staff Size: 5 - 9

Unclassified

BIOLOGICAL STATION AT ALBERTA UNIVERSITY
TURNER VALLEY, ALBERTA, CANADA
Director, Dr D Boog
General Environment: Oceanographic

CENTRO INVESTIGACION BIOLOGIA MARIM
LIBERTAD 1235
BUENOS AIRES, ARGENTINA
Director, Dr Oscar Kiihnemann
General Environment: Oceanographic
Staff Size: 10 - 49

ENVIRONMENTAL AND HEALTH INSTITUTE
W5634 UNIVERSITY HOSPITAL
ANN ARBOR, MI 48100
Director, Dr Bertram Dinman

FISHERIES BUREAU, AGRICULTURE MINISTRY AT ARGENTINA
PASEO COLON 922
BUENOS AIRES, ARGENTINA
Director, Mr Juan Manuel Cordi
General Environment: Oceanographic

FISHERIES LABORATORY APPARTADO (NATIONAL)
ESTAGETA DE CALIDONIA
PANAMA CITY, PANAMA
Director, Dr Juan L De Obarrio
General Environment: Oceanographic

FISHERIES, TOKYO UNIVERSITY
5-7-4-CHOME KONAN
MINATOKU, TOKYO, JAPAN
President, Tomiyama Tetsuo
General Environment: Oceanographic

HYDROLOGY AND ENGINEERING INSTITUTE
POLISH ACADEMY OF SCIENCE
GDANSK, POLAND
Director, Dr S Huckl
General Environment: Estuarine

MARINE BIOLOGICAL RESOURCES LABORATORY
ISPAHANI BUILDING 183, MCLEOD ROAD
KARACHI, PAKISTAN
Director, Dr R Ranjha
General Environment: Oceanographic

MARINE BIOLOGY INSTITUTE
UNIVERSITY OF OSLO
OSLO, NORWAY

MARINE FISHERIES INSTITUTION
GDYNIA, POLAND
Director, Dr J Wolck
General Environment: Oceanographic

MARINE INSTITUTION
GDANSK, POLAND
Director, Dr R Zaorski
General Environment: Oceanographic

MARINE LABORATORY, DUKE UNIVERSITY
RIVERS ISLAND
BEAUFORT, NC 28516
Director, Dr Cazlyn G Bookhout
General Environment: Oceanographic

MARINE STUDIES
POLISH ACADEMY OF SCIENCE
SOPOT, POLAND
Director, Dr Stanislaw Szymborski
General Environment: Oceanographic

ORGANIC RESEARCH UNITED
MCMASTER UNIVERSITY
HAMILTON, ONTARIO, CANADA
Chairman, Dr Norman W Radforth
General Environment: Terrestrial

PERUVIAN SEA INSTITUTION ESQ GRAL VALLEY
GAMARRA CHUCUTIO
CALLAO, PERU
Director, Dr Alfredo V Freyre
General Environment: Oceanographic

TROPICAL AQUATIC BIOLOGICAL CENTER
LISBON, PORTUGAL
Director, Dr Pedro Guerreiro Da Franca
General Environment: Oceanographic
Specific Interests: Tropical (hot)

WATER RESOURCES OF THE NORWEGIAN INSTITUTE
OSLO, NORWAY
General Environment: Limnologic

ZOOLOGY DEPARTMENT, VICTORIA UNIVERSITY
POST OFFICE BOX 169
WELLINGTON, NEW ZEALAND
Professor, J T Salmon
Staff Size: 10 - 49

BIOCHEMISTRY

Educational Institute

AGRONOMY AND RANGE SCIENCE DEPARTMENT
UNIVERSITY OF CALIFORNIA
DAVIS, CA 95616
Professor, Frederick P Zcheile

BIOCHEMISTRY DEPARTMENT
STATE UNIVERSITY OF NEW JERSEY
NEW BRUNSWICK, NJ 08903
Director, Robert White-Stevens

BIOCHEMISTRY DEPARTMENT
OXFORD UNIVERSITY
OXFORD, ENGLAND

BIOCHEMISTRY DEPARTMENT
UNIVERSITY OF CALIFORNIA
RIVERSIDE, CA 92505
Professor, Franklin Turrell

BIOCHEMISTRY DEPARTMENT, AGRICULTURE AND LIFE SCIENCES COLLEGE
UNIVERSITY OF WISCONSIN
MADISON, WI 53706
Director, R Burris
General Environment: Limnologic
Staff Size: 1 - 4

BIOCHEMISTRY DEPARTMENT, OKLAHOMA CITY UNIVERSITY
2501 NORTH BLACKWELDER
OKLAHOMA CITY, OK 73106

Specific Interests: Prairie and Temperate Forest

BIOKEMIAI INTEZET MTA
KAROLINA UT 29
BUDAPEST XI, HUNGARY

CHEMISTRY DEPARTMENT
UNIVERSITY OF OREGON
EUGENE, OR 97403
Professor, V Boekelheide

CHIBA UNIVERSITY
CHIBA, JAPAN
Director, Dr Yasumi Ogura
Specific Interests: Prairie and Temperate Forest

GENETICS DEPARTMENT
STANFORD MEDICAL CENTER
STANFORD, CA 94305
Director, Henry Hulett

MARINE BIOLOGICAL LABORATORY
CITADEL HILL
PLYMOUTH, ENGLAND
Director, Leslie H N Cooper
General Environment: Oceanographic
Specific Interests: Prairie and Temperate Forests

MEDICAL COLLEGE
UNIVERSITY OF IOWA
IOWA CITY, IA 52240

MICROBIOLOGY INSTITUTE, RUTGERS UNIVERSITY
UNIVERSITY HEIGHTS CAMPUS
NEW BRUNSWICK, NJ 08901
General Environment: Terrestrial

NUTRITION DEPARTMENT, PUBLIC HEALTH SCHOOL
HARVARD UNIVERSITY
BOSTON, MA 02115
Professor, R Geyer
Staff Size: 10 - 49

PHARMACOLOGY DEPARTMENT
MICHIGAN STATE UNIVERSITY
EAST LANSING, MI 48823
Chairman, Theodore Brody

TECHNION
TECHNION CITY, HAIFA, ISRAEL
General Environment: Oceanographic

Field Station/Laboratory

ELECTRON MICROSCOPY AND EXPERIMENTATION LABORATORY
PRAHA 2-NOVE MESTO
ALBERTOV 4, CZECHOSLOVAKIA

LIMNI RESEARCH STATION
EUBOEA, GREECE
General Environment: Oceanographic

PLANT PATHOLOGY DEPARTMENT
WELSH PLANT BREEDING STATION
PLAS GOGERDDAU,
CARDIGANSHIRE, WALES
Director, Alec J H Carr
General Environment: Terrestrial
Specific Interests: Prairie and Temperate Forest

RADIATION, PHYSICAL AND CHEMICAL BIOLOGY INSTITUTE
UNITED SOVIET SOCIALISTS REPUBLIC ACADEMY OF SCIENCES
MOSCOW, UNION OF SOVIET SOCIALIST REPUBLICS
Director, Aleksandr Evseevich Braunshtein
Specific Interests: Polar (cold)

Government — Federal

ATOMIC ENERGY COMMISSION, DEMOCRITUS CENTER
BIOLOGY SECTION
ATHENS, GREECE
Director, Panaviotis Dempolous
General Environment: Oceanographic

ENVIRONMENTAL MUTAGEN INFORMATION CENTER, BIOLOGICAL DIVISION, OAK
POST OFFICE BOX Y
OAK RIDGE, TN 37830

FOOD PRESERVATION DIVISION
CAMDEN, AUSTRALIA
Specific Interests: Prairie and Temperate Forest

FOOD SCIENCE LABORATORY
2725 MONTLAKE BOULEVARD, EAST
SEATTLE, WA 98102
Director, Maurice E Stansby
Specific Interests: Prairie and Temperate Forest
Staff Size: 5 - 9

FOREST ENVIRONMENTAL RESEARCH DIVISION
14TH STREET AND INDEPENDENCE AVENUE
WASHINGTON, DC 20250
General Environment: Terrestrial
Specific Interests: Prairie and Temperate Forest

**FUNGICIDES AND GERMICIDES
LABORATORY**
NATICK LABORATORY
NATICK, MA 01760

Specific Interests: Prairie and Temperate
Forest

**HUMAN STUDIES BRANCH,
NATIONAL AERONAUTICS AND
SPACE ADMINISTRATION**
RESEARCH CENTER- M/S 239-17
MOFFETT FIELD, CA 94035

Director, John Greenleaf
Staff Size: 1 - 4

NATIONAL HEALTH LABORATORY
TOKYO, JAPAN

Director, Dr Nagamune Soda
Specific Interests: Prairie and Temperate
Forest

**NEUROCHEMISTRY LABORATORY,
NEUROLOGICAL DISEASES
INSTITUTE**
NATIONAL INSTITUTES OF
HEALTH- PUBLIC HEALTH
SERVICE
BETHESDA, MD 20014

Chief, Donald Tower
Staff Size: 10 - 49

RESEARCH GRANTS DIVISION
NATIONAL INSTITUTES OF HEALTH
BETHESDA, MD 20014

Staff Size: 100 - 499

**SCIENCE AND RESEARCH,
CHEMICAL AND
PHARMACEUTICAL INSTITUTE**
ZUBOVSKAYA ULITSA,7
MOSCOW, UNION OF SOVIET
SOCIALIST REPUBLICS

Staff Size: 10 - 49

TECHNOLOGICAL LABORATORY
239 FREDERIC STREET
PASCAGOULA, MS 39567

Director, Travis D Love
General Environment: Limnologic
Specific Interests: Prairie and Temperate
Forest
Staff Size: 5 - 9

Government — State or Local

**CALIFORNIA DEPARTMENT OF
PUBLIC HEALTH**
2151 BERKELEY WAY
BERKELEY, CA 94704

Director, Heriberto Thomas

Industrial/Commercial

**ABM INDUSTRIAL PRODUCTS
LIMITED**
POLEACRE LANE, WOODLEY
STOCKPORT, CHESHIRE, ENGLAND

Director, Eric Burbidge
Specific Interests: Prairie and Temperate
Forest

BIOCHEMISTRY DEPARTMENT
PFIZER LIMITED
SANDWICH, KENT, ENGLAND

Director, Walter D Butt
Specific Interests: Prairie and Temperate
Forest

**INDUSTRIAL HYGIENE SECTION,
STATE OF WASHINGTON**
DEPARTMENT OF LABOR AND
INDUSTRY
OLYMPIA, WA 98501

Chief, Lester Hansen

Professional Organizations

AYNSOME LABS, LIMITED
KENTSFORD ROAD
GRANGE-OVER-SANDS,
LANCASTERSHIRE, ENGLAND

Director, Alan H Ward
General Environment: Terrestrial
Specific Interests: Rural
Staff Size: 10 - 49

BIOLOGICAL CHEMISTS SOCIETY
9650 ROCKVILLE PIKE
BETHESDA, MD 20014

Executive Officer, R Harte
Specific Interests: Prairie and Temperate
Forest
Staff Size: 1000 - 4999

**OCEANOGRAPHIC SOCIETY,
HELLENIC**
ATHENS, GREECE

General Environment: Oceanographic
Staff Size: 1 - 4

Research Institute

**BIOCHEMISTRY DEPARTMENT,
BECKMAN INSTRUMENTS,
INCORPORATED**
2500 HARBOR BOULEVARD
FULLERTON, CA 92634

**BIOCHEMISTRY DEPARTMENT,
MACAULAY INSTITUTE FOR SOIL
RESEARCH**
ABERDEEN, SCOTLAND

General Environment: Terrestrial
Specific Interests: Prairie and Temperate
Forest

FOOD RESEARCH INSTITUTE
AGRICULTURAL RESEARCH
COUNCIL
NORWICH, ENGLAND

General Environment: Terrestrial
Specific Interests: Prairie and Temperate
Forest

**MARINE METEOROLOGY SOCIETY,
KOBE MARINE OBSERVATORY**
7 NAKA YA-MANOTE-DORI
IKUTA-KU, KOBE, HYOGO, JAPAN

Director, Saruto Narano
General Environment: Oceanographic
Specific Interests: Prairie and Temperate
Forest

MEDICAL RESEARCH INSTITUTE
751 SOUTH BASCOM AVENUE
SAN JOSE, CA 95128

Staff Size: 10 - 49

MORSKI INSTYTUT RYBACKI (MIR)
AL ZJEDNOCZENIA
GYDNIA, POLAND

General Environment: Limnologic
Staff Size: 5 - 9

**NATURAL ENVIRONMENT
RESEARCH COUNCIL**
UNIVERSITY OF ABERDEEN
TORRY, ABERDEEN, SCOTLAND

General Environment: Oceanographic
Specific Interests: Prairie and Temperate
Forest
Staff Size: 10 - 49

**SALT SCIENCES CENTRAL
RESEARCH INSTITUTION**
1390 2-CHOME TOYOMACHI
SHINAGAWA-KU, TOKYO, JAPAN

General Environment: Oceanographic
Specific Interests: Prairie and Temperate
Forest

BIOPHYSICS

Educational Institute

BIOPHYSICS DEPARTMENT
UNIVERSITY OF CHICAGO
CHICAGO, IL 60601

Field Station/Laboratory

**HYDROLOGY STATION OF
GUARATUBA, UNIVERSITY OF
PARANA**

CAIXA POSTAL 756
GUARATUBA, PARANA, BRAZIL
General Environment: Oceanographic

Government — State or Local

WATER QUALITY CONTROL
47 TRINITY AVENUE, SW
ATLANTA, GA 30334
General Environment: Oceanographic

Industrial/Commercial

BIOPHYSICS DIVISION, LITTON
SYSTEMS, INCORPORATED
3385 JUBILEE DRIVE
ENCINO, CA 91313
Director, Nichois Hazelwood

BIOPHYSICS DIVISION, MISSOURI
BOTANICAL GARDENS
2315 TOWER GROVE AVENUE
ST LOUIS, MO 63110
Director, David Gates

Research Institute

OCEANOGRAPHY AND MARINE
BIOLOGY INSTITUTE
POST OFFICE BOX 432
OYSTER BAY, NY 11711
General Environment: Oceanographic
Staff Size: 1 - 4

ECOLOGY

Educational Institute

AIR ENVIRONMENTAL STUDIES
CENTER
PENNSYLVANIA STATE UNIVERSITY
UNIVERSITY PARK, PA 16802

APPLIED BOTANY STATE
INSTITUTION, HAMBURG
UNIVERSITY
ERIKASTR 130
HAMBURG 20, WEST GERMANY
Director, Ulrich Ruge
Specific Interests: Prairie and Temperate
Forest

AQUACULTURE CENTER,
FISHERIES BUILDING
AUBURN UNIVERSITY
AUBURN, AL 36830
Director, Dr H S Swingle
General Environment: Limnologic
Staff Size: 10 - 49

AQUATIC ECOLOGY DEPARTMENT,
JOHN CARROLL UNIVERSITY
UNIVERSITY HEIGHTS
CLEVELAND, OH 44118
General Environment: Limnologic
Staff Size: 1 - 4

ATLANTIC SALMON EMERGENCY
COMMISSION
BOX 164
HANCOCK, NH 03449
Director, Richard Buck
Staff Size: 1 - 4

ATMOSPHERIC SCIENCES
RESEARCH CENTER
STATE UNIVERSITY OF NEW YORK
ALBANY, NY 12200
General Environment: Atmospheric

BIOLOGICAL AND
ENVIRONMENTAL SCIENCES
SCHOOL
UNIVERSITY OF ULSTER
COLERAINE, COUNTY
LONDONDERRY, NORTHERN
IRELAND
Specific Interests: Prairie and Temperate
Forest

BIOLOGICAL SCIENCES
DEPARTMENT
SAN JOSE STATE COLLEGE
SAN JOSE, CA 95114
Professor, James Heath

BIOLOGY DEPARTMENT
GEORGETOWN UNIVERSITY
WASHINGTON, DC 20007
Professor, Irving Gray

BIOLOGY DEPARTMENT, PAISLEY
COLLEGE OF TECHNOLOGY
HIGH STREET
PAISLEY, RENFREWSHIRE, PAI2BE,
SCOTLAND
Director, Dr John Smyth
General Environment: Limnologic

BIOLOGY DEPARTMENT, ROYAL
FREE HOSPITAL SCHOOL OF
MEDICINE
8 HUNTER STREET
LONDON WCI, ENGLAND
Director, Robert J Berry
Staff Size: 5 - 9

BIOLOGY DEPARTMENT, THE
GRAMMAR SCHOOL
CHELTENHAM, GLOUCESTER,
ENGLAND

Director, Donald P Bennett
Specific Interests: Prairie and Temperate
Forest

BIOLOGY DEPARTMENT,
UNIVERSITY OF EXETER
PRINCE OF WALES ROAD
EXETER, ENGLAND
Director, John Webster
Specific Interests: Prairie and Temperate
Forest

BOSTON ENVIRONMENT,
INCORPORATED
14 BEACON STREET
BOSTON, MA 02108
President, Charles M Ewing
Staff Size: 1 - 4

BOTANICAL GARDENS, OGROD
BOTANICZNY
UNIVERSITY OF WARSAW
AL UJAZDOWSKIE 4, WARSAW,
POLAND
Director, Luomila Karpowicz
Specific Interests: Prairie and Temperate
Forest

BOTANY DEPARTMENT
TEL AVIV UNIVERSITY
RAMAT AVIV, ISRAEL
Director, Dr J Lipkin
General Environment: Oceanographic

BOTANY DEPARTMENT
CONNECTICUT COLLEGE
NEW LONDON, CT 06320
Secretary, William Niering
Specific Interests: Prairie and Temperate
Forest
Staff Size: 1000 - 4999

BOTANY DEPARTMENT
AUCKLAND UNIVERSITY
AUCKLAND, NEW ZEALAND
Professor, Valentine J Chapman
Specific Interests: Prairie and Temperate
Forest

BOTANY SCHOOL
MAGDALENE COLLEGE
CAMBRIDGE, ENGLAND
Specific Interests: Prairie and Temperate
Forest

CONSERVATION AND
ENVIRONMENTAL SCIENCES
BUREAU
RUTGERS UNIVERSITY
NEW BRUNSWICK, NJ 08903
Chairman, Dr Billy Ray Wilson
Specific Interests: Prairie and Temperate
Forest

CONSERVE THE ENVIRONMENT,
STATEWIDE PROGRAM
BOX 757
CONCORD, NH 03301
Executive Director, Howard Dickinson
Staff Size: 1 - 4

CRISIS
SMITH HIGH SCHOOL
STORRS, CT 06268
Director, Marsha Smith

ECOLOGICAL RESEARCH CENTER
MERRY COLLEGE
DOBBS FERRY, NY 10522
Specific Interests: Prairie and Temperate
  Forest

ECOLOGICAL SOCIETY OF
  AMERICA, BOTANY
  DEPARTMENT
UNIVERSITY OF NORTH CAROLINA
CHAPEL HILL, NC 27514

ECOLOGICAL STUDIES INSTITUTE
UNIVERSITY OF NORTH DAKOTA
GRAND FORKS, ND 58201

ECOLOGY ACTION CLUB
78 AVENUE LOUIS PASTEUR
BOSTON, MA 02115
Director, Robert Akeson
Specific Interests: Urban
Staff Size: 10 - 49

ECOLOGY ACTION FOR RHODE
  ISLAND
286 THAYER STREET
PROVIDENCE, RI 02906
Staff Size: 5 - 9

ECOLOGY ACTION OF BOSTON
  UNIVERSITY
700 COMMONWEALTH AVENUE
BOSTON, MA 02215

ECOLOGY AND NATURAL
  RESOURCES INSTITUTE
UNIVERSITY OF GEORGIA
ATHENS, GA 30601

ECOLOGY CENTER
UTAH STATE UNIVERSITY
LOGAN, UT 84321

ECOLOGY CLUB, NATICK HIGH
  SCHOOL
MEGUNKO ROAD
NATICK, MA 01760
President, Michall Brown

ECOLOGY COALITION OF
  NORTHEASTERN UNIVERSITY
360 HUNTINGTON AVENUE
BOSTON, MA 02115

ECOLOGY DEPARTMENT
CHADRON STATE COLLEGE
CHADRON, NB 69337
Specific Interests: Prairie and Temperate
  Forest
Staff Size: 1 - 4

ECOLOGY INSTITUTE, POLISH
  ACADEMY OF SCIENCES
UL NOWY SWIAT 72
WARSZAWA, POLAND
Specific Interests: Prairie and Temperate
  Forest

ECOLOGY LABORATORY,
  ENVIRONMENT, POPULATION,
  AND ORGANIZED BIOLOGY
HALE SCIENCE BUILDING
BOULDER, CO 80304
General Environment: Terrestrial
Specific Interests: Mountainous

ECOLOGY-FRESH WATER,
  UNIVERSITY OF COPENHAGEN
HILLEROD
COPENHAGEN, DENMARK
Professor, Kaj Berg
General Environment: Limnologic
Specific Interests: Prairie and Temperate
  Forest

ECOLOGY, MARINE BIOLOGY
SAN JOSE STATE COLLEGE
SAN JOSE, CA 95114
Director, Estees Levine

ECONOMIC ACTION, CENTER FOR
  ENVIRONMENTAL STUDIES
WILLIAMSTOWN COLLEGE
WILLIAMSTOWN, MA 01267
Director, Bob Kaat

EFFLUENT SOCIETY
MEMORIAL UNION, UNIVERSITY
  OF MAINE
ORONO, ME 04473

ENVIRONMENT COMMISSION
275 EAST MAIN STREET
FRANKFORT, KY 40601

ENVIRONMENTAL ACTION, 207
  HAMPSHIRE HOUSE
UNIVERSITY OF MAINE
AMHERST, MA 01002

ENVIRONMENTAL AESTHETICS
SAN JOSE STATE COLLEGE
SAN JOSE, CA 95114
Director, Conrad Borovski

ENVIRONMENTAL CENTER OF
  THE LOWER HUDSON VALLEY
MERCY COLLEGE
DOBBS FERRY, NY 10522
Staff Size: 1 - 4

ENVIRONMENTAL CENTER
COLLEGE OF IDAHO
CALDWELL, ID 83605

ENVIRONMENTAL CONCERN
  GROUP, SEVERANCE HALL
WELLESLEY COLLEGE
WELLESLEY, MA 02181
Director, Flie Mccarthy

ENVIRONMENTAL EDUCATION
  ASSOCIATION OF SUSQUEHANNA
616 PHEASANT LANE
ENDWELL, NY 13760
Executive Director, Nancy Ayers
Staff Size: 1 - 4

ENVIRONMENTAL EDUCATION
  COMMITTEE
UNIVERSITY CENTER OF AVERY
  POINT
GROTON, CT 06340
Director, David Mckain

ENVIRONMENTAL EDUCATION,
  MADONNA COLLEGE
36600 SCHOOLCRAFT
LIVONIA, MI 48150
Director, Sr Dena M Barron

ENVIRONMENTAL GROUP OF
  HAWAII
POST OFFICE BOX 1618
HONOLULU, HI 96806
Specific Interests: Tropical (hot)

ENVIRONMENTAL HEALTH AND
  SAFETY
PUBLIC HEALTH SCHOOL,
  HARVARD UNIVERSITY
BOSTON, MA 02115

ENVIRONMENTAL HEALTH
  CENTER
WEST VIRGINIA UNIVERSITY
MORGANTOWN, WV 26505

ENVIRONMENTAL HEALTH
  DEPARTMENT, COLLEGE OF
  MEDICINE
UNIVERSITY OF CINCINNATI
CINCINNATI, OH 45219
Associate Professor, E Pfitzer
General Environment: Atmospheric

ENVIRONMENTAL HEALTH
  ENGINEERING PROGRAM
UNIVERSITY OF TEXAS
AUSTIN, TX 78701

ENVIRONMENTAL HEALTH
  INSTITUTE
UNIVERSITY OF CINCINNATI
CINCINNATI, OH 45221
Specific Interests: Prairie and Temperate
  Forest

ENVIRONMENTAL HEALTH
  INSTITUTE
PURDUE UNIVERSITY
LAFAYETTE, IN 47907
Specific Interests: Prairie and Temperate
  Forest
Staff Size: 100 - 499

ENVIRONMENTAL HEALTH PROGRAM
OREGON TECHNICAL INSTITUTE
KLAMUTH FALLS, OR 97601
Specific Interests: Prairie and Temperate Forest

ENVIRONMENTAL HEALTH SCIENCE CENTER
OREGON STATE UNIVERSITY
CORVALLIS, OR 97330

ENVIRONMENTAL HEALTH STUDIES INSTITUTE
UNIVERSITY OF NORTH CAROLINA
CHAPEL HILL, NC 27514

ENVIRONMENTAL INFORMATION COMMITTEE
POST OFFICE BOX 2281
GRAND RAPIDS, MI 49501
Director, Robert L Burnap

ENVIRONMENTAL INSTITUTE
MANKATO STATE COLLEGE
MANKATO, MN 56001
Director, Dr H Roger Smith
Staff Size: 10 - 49

ENVIRONMENTAL LAW SOCIETY
BOSTON UNIVERSITY
BOSTON, MA 02215

ENVIRONMENTAL LAW SOCIETY
HARVARD LAW SCHOOL
CAMBRIDGE, MA 02138

ENVIRONMENTAL LIVING, RACHAEL CARSON TRUST
8940 JONES MILL ROAD
WASHINGTON, DC 20015
Executive Director, S Briggs
Staff Size: 1 - 4

ENVIRONMENTAL MEDICINE INSTITUTE
NEW YORK UNIVERSITY MEDICAL CENTER
NEW YORK, NY 10016
Director, Norton Nelson

ENVIRONMENTAL PROGRAMS COMMISSION
UNIVERSITY OF VERMONT
BURLINGTON, VT 05401
Director, W Criukshank

ENVIRONMENTAL QUALITY COALITION
UNIVERSITY OF MASSACHUSETTS CAMPUS CENTER
AMHERST, MA 01002

ENVIRONMENTAL RESEARCH
COLORADO STATE UNIVERSITY
FORT COLLINS, CO 80521

Chairman, Dr Richard M Hansen
Specific Interests: Prairie and Temperate Forest

ENVIRONMENTAL RESEARCH CENTER
UNIVERSITY OF TULSA
TULSA, OK 74104
Specific Interests: Prairie and Temperate Forest

ENVIRONMENTAL SCIENCE CENTER
COLLEGE OF NEW ROCHELLE
NEW ROCHELLE, NY 10801
Director, Sr Estelle Ghidoni
Specific Interests: Prairie and Temperate Forest

ENVIRONMENTAL SCIENCE CENTER
MERCYHURST COLLEGE
ERIE, PA 16501

ENVIRONMENTAL SCIENCE CENTER
SANTA ROSA JUNIOR COLLEGE
SANTA ROSA, CA 95401

ENVIRONMENTAL SCIENCE CENTER
NORTH CAROLINA AGRICULTURE AND TECHNOLOGY STATE UNIVERSITY
GREENSBORO, NC 27401

ENVIRONMENTAL SCIENCE EDUCATION PROGRAM
NORTHEAST MISSOURI STATE
KIRKSVILLE, MO 63501

ENVIRONMENTAL SCIENCE PROGRAM
UNION COLLEGE AND UNIVERSITY
SCHENECTADY, NY 12301

ENVIRONMENTAL SCIENCE PROGRAM
WILKES COLLEGE
WILKES BARRE, PA 18701

ENVIRONMENTAL SCIENCE PROGRAM
WASHINGTON STATE UNIVERSITY
PULLMAN, WA 99163

ENVIRONMENTAL SCIENCES
BRANDEIS UNIVERSITY
WALTHAM, MA 02154
Specific Interests: Prairie and Temperate Forest

ENVIRONMENTAL SCIENCES AND ENGINEERING DEPARTMENT
UNIVERSITY OF NORTH CAROLINA
CHAPEL HILL, NC 27514
Professor, Stanley Eidenkope

ENVIRONMENTAL SCIENCES AND ENGINEERING PROGRAM
UNIVERSITY OF HOUSTON
HOUSTON, TX 77004
Specific Interests: Prairie and Temperate Forest

ENVIRONMENTAL SCIENCES CENTER
TULANE UNIVERSITY
NEW ORLEANS, LA 70101

ENVIRONMENTAL SCIENCES CENTER
UNIVERSITY OF CALGARY
CALGARY, ALBERTA, CANADA
Director, James B Cragg
Specific Interests: Prairie and Temperate Forest

ENVIRONMENTAL SCIENCES COLLEGE
UNIVERSITY OF WISCONSIN
GREEN BAY, WI 54301

ENVIRONMENTAL SCIENCES DEPARTMENT, CONSERVATION BUREAU
RUTGERS UNIVERSITY
NEW BRUNSWICK, NJ 08901

ENVIRONMENTAL SCIENCES EDUCATION PROGRAM
NORTHEAST MISSOURI STATE COLLEGE
KIRKSVILLE, MO 63501
Specific Interests: Prairie and Temperate Forest

ENVIRONMENTAL SCIENCES INSTITUTE
LOUISIANA STATE UNIVERSITY
BATON ROUGE, LA 70803
General Environment: Atmospheric
Staff Size: 1 - 4

ENVIRONMENTAL SCIENCES PROGRAM
MCNEESE STATE COLLEGE
LAKE CHARLES, LA 70601
Specific Interests: Prairie and Temperate Forest

ENVIRONMENTAL SCIENCES PROGRAM
UNION COLLEGE AND UNIVERSITY
SCHENECTADY, NY 12308
Specific Interests: Prairie and Temperate Forest

ENVIRONMENTAL STUDIES CENTER
ANTIOCH COLLEGE
YELLOW SPRINGS, OH 45387
Specific Interests: Prairie and Temperate Forest

ENVIRONMENTAL STUDIES GROUP
TEXAS CHRISTIAN UNIVERSITY
FORT WORTH, TX 76129
Director, Dr Leon W Newland
Specific Interests: Prairie and Temperate
 Forest

**ENVIRONMENTAL STUDIES
 GROUP, JOHNS HOPKINS
 UNIVERSITY**
615 NORTH WOLFE STREET
BALTIMORE, MD 21205
Professor, Anna Baetjer

**ENVIRONMENTAL STUDIES
 PROGRAM**
DRAKE UNIVERSITY
DES MOINES, IA 50301
General Environment: Limnologic

**ENVIRONMENTAL STUDIES
 PROGRAM**
TEXAS WOMANS UNIVERSITY
DENTON, TX 76204
Director, Dr Howard E Erdman

**ENVIRONMENTAL STUDIES
 PROGRAM**
MIDDLEBURY COLLEGE
MIDDLEBURY, VT 05753
Specific Interests: Prairie and Temperate
 Forest

**ENVIRONMENTAL STUDIES
 PROGRAM**
ALFRED UNIVERSITY
ALFRED, NY 14802
General Environment: Limnologic
Staff Size: 5 - 9

**ENVIRONMENTAL STUDIES
 PROGRAM**
STATE UNIVERSITY COLLEGE
BROCKPORT, NY 14420
Director, Dr Robert R Costa
General Environment: Limnologic
Staff Size: 5 - 9

**FELS RESEARCH INSTITUTE,
 SCHOOL OF MEDICINE**
TEMPLE UNIVERSITY
PHILADELPHIA, PA 19140
Director, Sidney Weinhouse

**FIELD STUDIES IN NATURAL
 HISTORY**
SAN JOSE STATE COLLEGE
SAN JOSE, CA 95114
Director, Thomas Harvey

FISHERIES FACULTY
HIROSHIMA UNIVERSITY
HIROSHIMA, JAPAN
Specific Interests: Prairie and Temperate
 Forest

FOREST METEOROLOGY
YALE UNIVERSITY
NEW HAVEN, CT 06520
Professor, William Reifsnyder
General Environment: Atmospheric
Specific Interests: Prairie and Temperate
 Forest
Staff Size: 10 - 49

FOREST RESEARCH FOUNDATION
LAVAL UNIVERSITY
QUEBEC, QUEBEC PROVINCE,
 CANADA
Director, Dr Andre Lafond
General Environment: Terrestrial
Specific Interests: Prairie and Temperate
 Forest

FORESTERS ASSOCIATION
STATE FOREST SERVICE,
 COLORADO STATE UNIVERSITY
FORT COLLINS, CO 80521
President, Thomas B Borden
General Environment: Terrestrial
Specific Interests: Prairie and Temperate
 Forest

FORESTRY DEPARTMENT
UNIVERSITY OF OXFORD
OXFORD, ENGLAND
General Environment: Terrestrial
Specific Interests: Prairie and Temperate
 Forest

FORESTRY GROUP
HARVARD UNIVERSITY
PETERSHAM, MA 01366
Director, Dr Hugh M Raud
General Environment: Terrestrial
Specific Interests: Prairie and Temperate
 Forest

FRIENDS OF AFRICA IN AMERICA
330 SOUTH BROADWAY
TARRYTOWN, NY 10591
President, Clement E Merowit
General Environment: Terrestrial
Staff Size: 1 - 4

GREAT LAKES STUDIES CENTER
UNIVERSITY OF WISCONSIN-
 MILWAUKEE
MILWAUKEE, WI 53201
Director, Clifford H Mortimer
General Environment: Limnologic
Specific Interests: Prairie and Temperate
 Forest
Staff Size: 10 - 49

HABITAT, INCORPORATED
BOX 136
BELMONT, MA 02178
President, D D Henry, Jr
Staff Size: 10 - 49

INSECT ECOLOGY
SAN JOSE STATE COLLEGE
SAN JOSE, CA 95114
Professor, William E Ferguson

**INSTITUTE ENVIRONMENTAL
 MEDICINE**
NEW YORK UNIVERSITY MEDICAL
 CENTER
NEW YORK, NY 10016
Director, Norton Nelson
Staff Size: 100 - 499

**INTERACT: COMMUNITY ACTION
 GROUP**
MASCONOMET REGIONAL H
 SOUTH
BOXFORD, MA 01921
President, Deborah Small

**LAKE ERIE ENVIRONMENTAL
 STUDIES**
STATE UNIVERSITY COLLEGE
FREDONIA, NY 14063
Director, Dr J Richard Mayer
General Environment: Limnologic
Staff Size: 10-49

LIMNOLOGIC INSTITUTE
UNIVERSITY OF UPPSALA
UPPSALA, SWEDEN
Director, Wilheim Rohde
General Environment: Limnologic
Specific Interests: Polar (cold)

**LIMNOLOGY FLUSSTATION,
 SCHLITZ**
STEINWEG 21, 6407 SCHLITZ
HESSEN, WEST GERMANY
Director, Karl Muller
General Environment: Limnologic
Specific Interests: Prairie and Temperate
 Forest

MAPLEVALE SCHOOL OF LIVING
CROSS CREEK, NEW BRUNSWICK,
 CANADA
Director, Judy Hinds
General Environment: Terrestrial
Specific Interests: Polar (cold)
Staff Size: 1 - 4

**MARINE BIOLOGY AND
 ECONOMICS DEPARTMENT**
TEL-AVIV UNIVERSITY
TEL-AVIV, ISRAEL
Professor, L Fishelson
General Environment: Oceanographic

**MARINE BIOLOGY DEPARTMENT,
 DIVISION OF SCIENCE**
UNIVERSITY OF LIBERIA
MONROVIA, LIBERIA
Director, Dr P W Gideon
General Environment: Estuarine

MARINE SCIENCES INSTITUTE
UNIVERSITY OF TEXAS
PORT ARANSAS, TX 78373
General Environment: Oceanographic
Staff Size: 10 - 49

MARINE SCIENCES INSTITUTE, UNIVERSITY OF MIAMI
RICKENBACKER CAUSEWAY
MIAMI, FL 33149

NATIONAL PARKS CONSERVATION ASSOCIATION
1701 18TH STREET, NW
WASHINGTON, DC 20009

NATURAL RESOURCE COUNCIL OF VERMONT
26 STATE STREET
MONTPELIER, VT 05602
Chairman, Mrs N C Garland
Staff Size: 5 - 9

NATURAL RESOURCES CENTER
UNIVERSITY OF MONTANA
MISSOULA, MT 59801

NATURAL RESOURCES RESEARCH INSTITUTION
PURDUE UNIVERSITY
LAFAYETTE, IN 47901

NATURAL RESOURCES SCHOOL
HUMBOLDT STATE COLLEGE
ARCATA, CA 95521
Dean, Richard Genelly

NATURAL RESOURCES SCHOOL
COLLEGE OF AGRICULTURE AND LIFE SCIENCES
MADISON, WI 53700
General Environment: Terrestrial

NATURE CONSERVANCY
UNIVERSITY OF NEW HAMPSHIRE
DURHAM, NH 03842

NATURE CONSERVATION, CONNECTICUT CHAPTER
151 BROOKDALE ROAD
STAMFORD, CT 06903
Chairman, Thomas Gaines

OCCUPATIONAL AND ENVIRONMENTAL HEALTH DEPARTMENT
WAYNE STATE UNIVERSITY, MEDICAL SCHOOL
DETROIT, MI 48207

OCEANOGRAPHY CENTER, ANNAMALAI UNIVERSITY
CHIDDAMBARAM
PORTO NOVO, SOUTH INDIA
Director, R V Seshaiya
General Environment: Oceanographic
Staff Size: 1 - 4

OCEANOGRAPHY DEPARTMENT
UNIVERSITY
SOUTHAMPTON 509, ENGLAND
Director, John E G Raymont
General Environment: Oceanographic
Staff Size: 10 - 49

ORNITHOLOGY LABORATORY
CORNELL UNIVERSITY
ITHACA, NY 14850
Director, O S Pettingill, Jr
Specific Interests: Prairie and Temperate Forest
Staff Size: 5 - 9

PLANT ECOLOGY
UNIVERSITY OF WARSAW
UJAZDOWSKIE 4, WARSAW, POLAND
Specific Interests: Prairie and Temperate Forest

POLLUTION RESEARCH CENTER
UTAH STATE UNIVERSITY
LOGAN, UT 84321
Specific Interests: Prairie and Temperate Forest

POPULATION BIOLOGY GROUP
PRINCETON UNIVERSITY, ENO HALL
PRINCETON, NJ 08540
Professor, Henry Horn
Staff Size: 5 - 9

PUBLIC HEALTH SCHOOL, HARVARD UNIVERSITY
665 HUNTINGTON AVENUE
BOSTON, MA 02115
Professor, Ross Mc Farland
Specific Interests: Urban

PUBLIC HEALTH SCHOOL, UNIVERSITY OF TEXAS
POST OFFICE BOX 20186
HOUSTON, TX 77025
Director, Arthur Atkisson
General Environment: Atmospheric
Specific Interests: Urban

RADIATION ECOLOGY LABORATORY, FISHERIES CENTER
UNIVERSITY OF WASHINGTON
SEATTLE, WA 98195
Staff Size: 10 - 49

RECYCLING REVOLUTION COOPERATIVE
14 PARK AVENUE
SOMERVILLE, MA 02144
Staff Size: 5 - 9

RESOURCE MANAGEMENT AND LAND PLANNING
SYRACUSE UNIVERSITY
SYRACUSE, NY 13210
Specific Interests: Prairie and Temperate Forest

RESOURCES DEVELOPMENT CENTER
UNIVERSITY OF NEW HAMPSHIRE
DURHAM, NH 03824

SCIENCES DIVISION, NORTHWEST MISSOURI STATE COLLEGE
KIRKSVILLE, MO 63501
Director, Dean Rosebery
Staff Size: 1 - 4

SCIENCES FACULTY
TOULOUSE, FRANCE
Director, Henri Gaussen
Specific Interests: Prairie and Temperate Forest

STUDENTS ACTUALLY CARE
FRAMINGHAM STATE COLLEGE
FRAMINGHAM, MA 01701
Director, Lenore Munro

STUDENTS CONCERNED FOR THE ENVIRONMENT
MIDDLEBURY UNION HIGH SCHOOL
MIDDLEBURY, VT 05753
Staff Size: 10 - 49

STUDENTS FOR ECOLOGY ACTION
SALEN ROAD, BEVERLY HIGH SCHOOL
BEVERLY, MA 01915

SYSTEMATIC GEOBOT INSTITUTION, GOTTINGEN UNIVERSITY
UNTERE KARSPULE 2
GOTTINGEN, WEST GERMANY
Director, Franz Firbas
Specific Interests: Prairie and Temperate Forest

TAXONOMIC BOTANY
UNIVERSITY OF LEIDEN
LEIDEN, NETHERLANDS
Director, J Van Steenis
Specific Interests: Prairie and Temperate Forest

TREE-RING RESOURCES LABORATORY
UNIVERSITY OF ARIZONA
TUCSON, AZ 85721
General Environment: Terrestrial
Staff Size: 10 - 49

WATER RESOURCE RESEARCH INSTITUTION, OREGON UNIVERSITY
114 COVELL HALL
CORVALLIS, OR 97331
General Environment: Oceanographic

WATER RESOURCES LABORATORY
UNIVERSITY OF LOUISVILLE
LOUISVILLE, KY 40208
Director, Dr Louis Krumholz
General Environment: Limnologic
Staff Size: 1 - 4

WATER RESOURCES RESEARCH CENTER
IOWA STATE UNIVERSITY
AMES, IA 50010
Specific Interests: Prairie and Temperate Forest

WATER RESOURCES RESEARCH CENTER
UNIVERSITY OF ARKANSAS
FAYETTEVILLE, AR 72701
General Environment: Oceanographic

WILDERNESS SOCIETY
729 15TH STREET, NW
WASHINGTON, DC 20005

ZOOLOGICAL RESEARCH LABORATORY
MADRAS UNIVERSITY
MADRAS, INDIA
Director, Dr G Krishnan
General Environment: Oceanographic
Staff Size: 5 - 9

ZOOLOGY DEPARTMENT
HEBREW UNIVERSITY OF JERUSALEM
JERUSALEM, ISRAEL
Director, H Steinitz
General Environment: Oceanographic

ZOOLOGY DEPARTMENT
UNIVERSITY OF ZURICH
ZURICH, SWITZERLAND
Professor, Hans Burla
Specific Interests: Mountainous

ZOOLOGY DEPARTMENT, UNIVERSITY OF GOTTINGEN
GOTTINGEN, WILHELMSPLATZL
BONN, WEST GERMANY
Professor, Peter Ax
General Environment: Oceanographic
Specific Interests: Prairie and Temperate Forest

ZOOLOGY INSTITUTE, UNIVERSITY OF ERLANGEN-NURNBERG
UNIVERSITATSSTRASSE 19
852 ERLANGEN, WEST GERMANY
Director, Hans-Jurgen Stammer
Specific Interests: Prairie and Temperate Forest

Field Station/Laboratory

AGRICULTURE, FISHERIES AND FOOD MINISTRY
FISHERIES LABORATORY, BURNHAM-ON-CROUH
ESSEX, ENGLAND
Director, Donald Hancock
Specific Interests: Prairie and Temperate Forest

BOTANICAL GARDENS
BROOKLYN,NY 10000
Director, Craig R Hibben
General Environment: Atmospheric

BOWDOINE SCIENCES STATION
KENT ISLAND, INGALLSHEAD
GRAND MANAN, NEW BRUNSWICK, CANADA
Director, Dr Charles Huntington
Staff Size: 1 - 4

ECOLOGY (GENERAL) LABORATORY
4 AVENUE DU PETIT CHATEAU
BRUNDY, FRANCE
Specific Interests: Prairie and Temperate Forest

ENTERIC REFERENCE LABORATORY, PUBLIC HEALTH LABORATORY SERVICE
COLINDALE AVENUE
LONDON NW9, ENGLAND
Director, Ephraim S Anderson
Specific Interests: Prairie and Temperate Forest

ENVIRONMENTAL LABORATORY OF LAKE ONTARIO
STATE UNIVERSITY OF NEW YORK AT OSWEGO
OSWEGO, NY 13126
Specific Interests: Prairie and Temperate Forest

ENVIRONMENTAL PROTECTION AGENCY LABORATORY
CHAMBLEE, GA 30005
Specific Interests: Prairie and Temperate Forest

ENVIRONMENTAL PROTECTION AGENCY LABORATORY
MONTGOMERY, AL 36101
Specific Interests: Prairie and Temperate Forest

ENVIRONMENTAL PROTECTION AGENCY LABORATORY
GROSS ILE
GROSSE ILE, MI 48138
Specific Interests: Prairie and Temperate Forest

ENVIRONMENTAL PROTECTION AGENCY LABORATORY
COLLEGE, AK 99701
Specific Interests: Prairie and Temperate Forest

ENVIRONMENTAL PROTECTION AGENCY LABORATORY
BEARS BLUFF, SC 29910
Specific Interests: Prairie and Temperate Forest

ENVIRONMENTAL PROTECTION AGENCY LABORATORY
DAUPHIN ISLAND, AL 36528
Specific Interests: Prairie and Temperate Forest

ENVIRONMENTAL PROTECTION AGENCY LABORATORY
GULF BREEZE, FL 32561
Specific Interests: Prairie and Temperate Forest

ENVIRONMENTAL PROTECTION AGENCY LABORATORY
NARRAGANSETT, RI 02882
Specific Interests: Prairie and Temperate Forest

ENVIRONMENTAL PROTECTION AGENCY LABORATORY
ROCKVILLE, MD 20801
Specific Interests: Prairie and Temperate Forest

ENVIRONMENTAL PROTECTION AGENCY LABORATORY
GIG HARBOR, WA 98335
Specific Interests: Urban

ENVIRONMENTAL PROTECTION AGENCY LABORATORY
PO BOX 190
PERRINE, FL 33157
Staff Size: 50 - 99

ENVIRONMENTAL PROTECTION AGENCY NATIONAL WATER QUALITY LABORATORY
DULUTH, MN 55804
Specific Interests: Prairie and Temperate Forest
Staff Size: 50 - 99

EXPERIMENTAL ECOLOGY
CARLSBERG LABORATORY
COPENHAGEN, DENMARK
Professor, Carsten Olsen
Specific Interests: Prairie and Temperate Forest

EXPERIMENTAL STATION OF MONKS WOOD
ABBOTS RIPTON
HUNTINGDON, ENGLAND
General Environment: Terrestrial
Specific Interests: Prairie and Temperate Forest

FISH BIOLOGY, MOSS LANDING LABORATORY
P O BOX 223
MOSS LANDING, CA 95039
Director, John Harville

FISHERIES EXPERIMENT STATION
CONWAY
CAERNS, ENGLAND

Director, Basil T Hepper
Specific Interests: Prairie and Temperate
Forest

FISHERIES LABORATORY
LOWESTOFT, ENGLAND

Director, David H Cushing
Specific Interests: Prairie and Temperate
Forest

FOREST INSTITUTE OF AMERICA
1619 MASSACHUSETTS AVENUE, NW
WASHINGTON, DC 20036

General Environment: Terrestrial

FORESTRY SCIENCES LABORATORY
MONTANA STATE UNIVERSITY
BOZEMAN, MT 59715

Director, Rulon Gardner
General Environment: Terrestrial
Specific Interests: Prairie and Temperate
Forest

LABORATORY
CITADEL HILL
PLYMOUTH, ENGLAND

Director, Alan J Southward
General Environment: Oceanographic
Specific Interests: Prairie and Temperate
Forest

LAND RESEARCH DIVISION
CANBERRA, AUSTRALIA

Director, Clive Hackett
General Environment: Terrestrial
Specific Interests: Prairie and Temperate
Forest

**MARINE BIOLOGICAL
LABORATORY AT AMAKUSA**
TOMIOKA, AMAKUSA
KUMAMOTO 863-25, JAPAN

Director, Dr Taiji Kikuchi
General Environment: Oceanographic
Staff Size: 1 - 4

MARINE LABORATORY
DUKE UNIVERSITY
RIVER'S ISLAND, BEAUFORT, NC
28516

Director, Dr Cazlyn G Bookhout
General Environment: Oceanographic
Specific Interests: Prairie and Temperate
Forest

**NATURE STUDY SOCIETY OF
AMERICA**
1144 EAST 3RD STREET
SALT LAKE CITY, UT 84101

**PESTICIDE INFESTATION
CONTROL LABORATORY**
MINISTRY OF AGRICULTURE,
TOLWORTH
SURREY, ENGLAND

Director, Ronald Davis
Specific Interests: Prairie and Temperate
Forest
Staff Size: 1 - 4

**PESTICIDE INFESTATION
LABORATORY**
LONDON ROAD
SLOUGH, BUCKINGHAMSHIRE,
ENGLAND

Director, Robert W Howe
Staff Size: 10 - 49

**PRESTON MONTFORD FIELD
CENTER**
SHREWSBURY, ENGLAND

Warden, Charles Sinker
General Environment: Terrestrial
Specific Interests: Prairie and Temperate
Forest

SAVE OUR SHORES
POST OFFICE BOX 103
NORTH QUINCY, MA 02171

Chairman, Mrs Saphin

SCIENTIFIC STATION AT BOWDOIN
BOWDOIN COLLEGE
BRUNSWICK, ME 04011

Director, Dr Charles Huntington
Staff Size: 1 - 4

WILLIAM F CLAPP LABORATORIES
WASHINGTON STREET
DUXBURY, MA 02332

Director, Dr Paul F Nace
General Environment: Oceanographic
Specific Interests: Prairie and Temperate
Forest

Foundation

**AMERICA'S FUTURE TREES
FOUNDATION**
1412 16TH STREET, NW
WASHINGTON, DC 20001

**AUDUBON COUNCIL OF
CONNECTICUT**
ORCHARD HILL ROAD
HARWINTON, CT 06790

President, E W Hutchinson

AUDUBON NATURALIST COUNCIL
BOX 509
BRUNSWICK, ME 04011

Executive Director, C M Packard

AUDUBON NATURALIST SOCIETY
8940 JONES MILL ROAD
WASHINGTON, DC 20015

Staff Size: 1000 - 4999

**AUDUBON NORTH CENTRAL
COUNCIL**
536 LAPLANT STREET
GREEN BAY, WI 54302

President, James Zimmerman
Specific Interests: Prairie and Temperate
Forest

AUDUBON SOCIETY (NATIONAL)
1130 FIFTH AVENUE
NEW YORK, NY 10028

Director, Carl W Buchheister
General Environment: Terrestrial
Staff Size: 1000 & Larger

**AUDUBON SOCIETY (NATIONAL),
INCORPORATED**
ORCHARD HILL ROAD
HARWINTON, CT 06790

**AUDUBON SOCIETY
INCORPORATED AT DARIEN**
POST OFFICE BOX 3313
DARIEN, CT 06820

President, H M Bubar

**AUDUBON SOCIETY
INCORPORATED AT HARTFORD**
POST OFFICE BOX 207
W HARTFORD, CT 06107

President, Allen C Morgan

**AUDUBON SOCIETY
INCORPORATED OF
LITCHFIELD HILLS**
BALDWIN HILL ROAD
LITCHFIELD, CT 06759

Vice President, Mrs John B Fahey

**AUDUBON SOCIETY
INCORPORATED, HOUSATONIC**
SHARON AUDUBON CENTER
SHARON, CT 06069

President, Dr M Oppenheimer

AUDUBON SOCIETY OF FLORIDA
POST OFFICE DRAWER 7
MAITLAND, FL 32701

Executive Director, Hal Scott
Specific Interests: Prairie and Temperate
Forest

**AUDUBON SOCIETY OF GREEN
MOUNTAIN**
POST OFFICE BOX 33
BURLINGTON, VT 05401

AUDUBON SOCIETY OF HAWAII
POST OFFICE BOX 5032
HONOLULU, HI 96814

President, Charles Kaigler
General Environment: Terrestrial
Specific Interests: Savanna and Rain
Forest
Staff Size: 5 - 9

AUDUBON SOCIETY OF MAINE
2203 BROADWAY
BANGOR, ME 04401

Director, Mrs Wayne Evans

AUDUBON SOCIETY OF MAINE
22 ELM STREET
PORTLAND, ME 04111

President, Helen C Frost

AUDUBON SOCIETY OF MASSACHUSETTS
SOUTH GREAT ROAD
LINCOLN, MA 01773
Staff Size: 100 - 499

AUDUBON SOCIETY OF MERRYMEETING
BOX 255
BRUNSWICK, ME 04011
President, H Tylen, Jr

AUDUBON SOCIETY OF MICHIGAN
7000 NORTH WESTNEDGE AVENUE
KALAMAZOO, MI 49007
President, Dr Harold Mahan
Specific Interests: Prairie and Temperate Forest

AUDUBON SOCIETY OF NEW HAMPSHIRE
NEW HAMPTON, NH 03256
President, Robert Smart

AUDUBON SOCIETY OF PROUTS NECK
11 BROWN STREET
CAMBRIDGE, MA 02138
Director, H W Pratt

AUDUBON SOCIETY OF SANTA CLARA VALLEY
945 MATADERO
PALO ALTO, CA 94306
Director, Howard Wolcott
General Environment: Terrestrial

AUDUBON SOCIETY OF SAUGATUCK VALLEY, INCORPORATED
BOX 684
WESTPORT, CT

AUDUBON SOCIETY OF YORK COUNTY
BRUEN PLACE
KENNEBUNK BEACH, ME 04045
President, Mrs Robert Ficker

BEAVER BROOK VALLEY PROJECT
DEPOT ROAD
BOXBOROUGH, MA 01719
Chairman, G C Krusen

CONSERVATION AND RESEARCH FOUNDATION,INCORPORATED
BOX 1445, CENTER COLLEGE
NEW LONDON, CT 06320
President, Richard H Goodwin

CONSERVATION COUNCIL OF INDIANA, INCORPORATED
6600 GUION ROAD
INDIANAPOLIS, IN 46268
President, William E Schmidt

CONSERVATION COUNCIL OF NEW YORK STATE
5 BROADWAY, ROOM 505
TROY, NY 12180
President, Martin Turner

CONSERVATION FEDERATION OF MINNESOTA
4313 SHADY OAK ROAD
HOPKINS, MN 55343
Executive Director, James T Shields

CONSERVATION FEDERATION OF MISSOURI
312 EAST CAPITOL AVENUE
JEFFERSON CITY, MO 65101
President, Dr C F Ljebbert
Staff Size: 1 - 4

CONSERVATION FOUNDATION
1717 MASSACHUSETTS AVENUE, NW
WASHINGTON, DC 20036

CONSERVATION LAW FOUNDATION
STATLER BUILDING, ROOM 506
BOSTON, MA 02116
Assistant Director, O Plimpton

CONSERVATION LEAGUE OF TENNESSEE
1507 COLLEGE HEIGHTS DRIVE
JOHNSON CITY, TN 37601
Secretary, John H Bailey

CONSERVATION TRUST OF MANCHESTER
85 BRIDGE STREET
MANCHESTER, MA 01944
Trustee, George G Loring

CONSERVATION UNITED OF MICHIGAN
BOX 2235
LANSING, MI 48911
Executive Director, Paul J Leach

ENVIRONMENTAL ACTION FOUNDATION, INCORPORATED
732 DUPONT CIRCLE BUILDING
WASHINGTON, DC 20036
Director, Mr Richard Dalsemer

ENVIRONMENTAL CONTROL NATIONAL FOUNDATION, INCORPORATED
151 TREMONT STREET
BOSTON, MA 02111
President, Chas Thibeau

ISAAC WALTON LEAGUE OF AMERICA
1800 NORTH KENT STREET, SUITE 806
ARLINGTON, VA 22209
Staff Size: 10 - 49

ISAAC WALTON LEAGUE OF AMERICA, MASSACHUSETTS CHAPTER
551 WATER STREET
ROCKLAND, MA 02370
President, Frank Bachoff

KESTREL TRUST FUND
650 EAST PLEASANT STREET
AMHERST, MA 01002
Director, Mrs Janet Dakin

LAND CONSERVATION TRUST OF DOVER
SPRINGDALE AVENUE
DOVER, MA 02030
Director, Ralph W Macallester
General Environment: Terrestrial
Specific Interests: Rural

LAND CONSERVATION TRUST OF LINCOLN
BOX 318
LINCOLN, MA 01773
Chairman, William M Preston
Specific Interests: Prairie and Temperate Forest

MARIA MOORS CABOT FOUNDATION
HARVARD UNIVERSITY
PETERSHAM, MA 01366
General Environment: Terrestrial
Specific Interests: Prairie and Temperate Forest

MARINA DIVISION
LA SALLE FOUNDATION
CARACAS, VENEZUELA
Director, Hermano Gines
General Environment: Oceanographic
Specific Interests: Tropical (hot)
Staff Size: 100 - 499

MAX MCGRAW WILDLIFE FOUNDATION
POST OFFICE BOX 194
DUNDEE, IL 60118
General Manager, George V Burger
Staff Size: 10 - 49

MOUNTAINEERS
719 DIKE STREET
SEATTLE, WA 98101
President, Max Hollenbeck
Specific Interests: Mountainous
Staff Size: 5000 - 9999

NATIONAL CAMPERS AND HIKERS ASSOCIATION
7172 TRANSIT ROAD
BUFFALO, NY 14221
National President, Jack L Skinner
Specific Interests: Prairie and Temperate Forest

NATIONAL WILDLIFE
REGION 1
BAR HARBOR, ME 04609
Director, Robert W Patterson

NATIONAL WILDLIFE
FEDERATION
REGION 11
JUNEAU, AK 99801
Director, Bud Boddy

NATIONAL WILDLIFE
FEDERATION
REGION 13
BOISE, ID 83701
Director, Ernest E Day

NATIONAL WILDLIFE
FEDERATION
REGION 12
RENO, NV 89501
Director, C Clifton Young

NATIONAL WILDLIFE
FEDERATION
REGION 4
TAVERNIER, FL 33070
Director, Herbert L Alley

NATIONAL WILDLIFE
FEDERATION
REGION 10
PHOENIX, AZ 85001
Director, N Bill Winter

NATIONAL WILDLIFE
FEDERATION
REGION 5
DRY RIDGE, KY 41035
Director, Frederick R Scroggin

NATIONAL WILDLIFE
FEDERATION
REGION 9
SIOUX FALLS, SD 57101
Director, Everett R Brue

NATIONAL WILDLIFE
FEDERATION
REGION 8
PORT ARTHUR, TX 77640
Director, Henry J Leblanc

NATIONAL WILDLIFE
FEDERATION
REGION 6
WOLCOTTVILLE, IN 46795
Director, Dwight Gallimore

NATURE CENTER AND MUSEUM
OF LITCHFIELD
WHITE MEMORIAL FOUNDATION
LITCHFIELD, CT 06759
Director, Gordon Loery

NATURE CONSERVANCY
BANCHORY
KINCARDINESHIRE, SCOTLAND

Director, Gordon R Miller
General Environment: Terrestrial
Specific Interests: Mountainous
Staff Size: 10 - 49

NATURE CONSERVANCY
FURZEBROOK RESOURCE STATION
WAREHAM, DORSET, ENGLAND
Director, Stephen P Chapman
General Environment: Terrestrial
Specific Interests: Prairie and Temperate
Forest

NATURE CONSERVANCY
12 HOPE TERRACE
EDINBURGH 9, SCOTLAND
Director, Peter S Maitland
General Environment: Limnologic
Specific Interests: Prairie and Temperate
Forest

NATURE CONSERVANCY
BOX 97
EAST BARRINGTON, NH 03825
Chairman, Albion R Hodgdon

NATURE CONSERVANCY
465 CONGRESS STREET
PORTLAND, ME 04111
Chairman, Edward T Richardson, Jr

NATURE CONSERVANCY
MANCHESTER, ME 04351
Director, Chas P Bradford

NATURE CONSERVANCY
21 SILVER BROOK ROAD
WESTPORT, CT 06880

NATURE CONSERVANCY
JERICHO, VT 05465
Chairman, Hubert Vogelman

NEPONSET VALLEY TRUST
20 CARPENTER ROAD
WALPOLE, MA 02081
Chairman, Lebaron R Briggs

OCEANOGRAPHY SECTION
NATIONAL SCIENCE FOUNDATION
WASHINGTON, DC 20550
General Environment: Oceanographic

OZARK SOCIETY, INCORPORATED
BOX 209
BENTONVILLE, AR 72712
President, Dr Neil Compton
Specific Interests: Mountainous
Staff Size: 500 - 999

PENNSYLVANIA FEDERATION OF
SPORTSMEN'S CLUBS
925 SOUTH JEFFERSON STREET
JEANNETTE, PA 15664
President, Joseph H Craig

PRESERVATION OF BIRDS
INTERNATIONAL COUNCIL,
BRITISH MUSEUM

CROMWELL ROAD
LONDON SW7, ENGLAND

PROTECT YOUR ENVIRONMENT
40 HIGHLAND AVENUE
ROWAYTON, CT 06853
Staff Size: 50 - 99

PROTECTION OF ANIMALS
NATIONAL SOCIETY
655 BOYLSTON STREET
BOSTON, MA 02166
General Environment: Terrestrial
Specific Interests: Prairie and Temperate
Forest
Staff Size: 10 - 49

PROTECTION OF NEW
HAMPSHIRES FORESTS SOCIETY
5 SOUTH STATE STREET
CONCORD, NH 03301
President, Lawrence W Rathburn
Specific Interests: Prairie and Temperate
Forest
Staff Size: 5 - 9

RURAL LAND FOUNDATION OF
LINCOLN
MACINTOSH LANE
LINCOLN, MA 01773
Director, Kenneth Bergen
General Environment: Terrestrial

SAVE NEW ENGLAND
50 WEST STREET
NORTHAMPTON, MA 01060
Executive Director, L Bogart

SAVE THE WETLANDS
COMMISSION, INCORPORATED
1087 BOSTON POST ROAD
MADISON, CT 06443
General Environment: Marsh/Swamp
Staff Size: 1 - 4

SCIENCE FOR YOUTH NATIONAL
FOUNDATION
145 EAST 52ND STREET
NEW YORK, NY 10022
Chairman of Building, Austin H
Maccormick
Specific Interests: Prairie and Temperate
Forest

SHELLFISH INSTITUTE OF NORTH
AMERICA
22 MAIN STREET
SAYVILLE, NY 11782
General Environment: Limnologic

SIERRA CLUB
STERLING ROAD
GREENWICH, CT 06830
Chairman, Emerson Stone

SIERRA CLUB
SEVEN TYLER LANE
RIVERSIDE, CT 06878
Vice Chairman, Wilbur Squire

SIERRA CLUB
1500 MILLS TOWER
SAN FRANCISCO, CA 94104
Executive Director, Michael Mccloskey
Staff Size: 50 - 99

SIERRA CLUB OF MAINE
POST OFFICE BOX 1324
BANGOR, ME 04401
Chairman, Stanley L Johnson

**SPORT FISHERY RESEARCH
    FOUNDATION**
SUITE 503, 719 13TH STREET NW
WASHINGTON, DC 20005
President, Cass S Hough
Specific Interests: Prairie and Temperate
    Forest

**SPORTSMENS CLUB OF NEW
    HAMPSHIRE**
123 SILVER LAKE ROAD
HOLLIS, NH 03049
Secretary, William Fitzgerald

**SPORTSMENS CLUB OF NEW
    HAMPSHIRE**
PUMPKIN HILL ROAD
WARNER, NH 03278
Director, John Hegerty

**SPORTSMENS COUNCIL OF
    WASHINGTON**
BOX 569
VANCOUVER, WA 98660
President, Norman Richardson

SPROTSMENS CLUBS OF TEXAS
311 VAUGHN BUILDING
AUSTIN, TX 78701
President, Henry J Leblanc, Sr

THOREAU FELLOWSHIP
POST OFFICE BOX 551
OLD TOWN, ME 04468
Secretary, Mrs Mary P Sherwood

**THORNE ECOLOGICAL
    FOUNDATION**
1229 UNIVERSITY BOULEVARD
BOULDER, CO 80302
President, Oakleigh Thorne
Specific Interests: Prairie and Temperate
    Forest

WELDER WILDLIFE FOUNDATION
BOX 1400
SINTON, TX 78387
Director, Clearance Cottam
General Environment: Marsh/Swamp
Specific Interests: Savanna and Rain
    Forest
Staff Size: 10 - 49

**WILDLIFE AND OUTDOOR
    RECREATION FEDERATION OF
    UTAH**

1102 WALKER BANK BUILDING
SALT LAKE CITY, UT 84111
President, F L Bud Sullivan

**WILDLIFE CONSERVATION OF
    NEW MEXICO**
BOX 1542
SANTA FE, NM 87501
President, Bobby Adee

WILDLIFE DEFENDERS
731 DUPONT CIRCLE BUILDING
WASHINGTON, DC 20036
Director, Mary Hatzell

**WILDLIFE FEDERATION OF
    ARIZONA**
POST OFFICE BOX 1769
PHOENIX, AZ 85001
Executive Director, Richard Small

**WILDLIFE FEDERATION OF
    ARKANSAS**
515 SOUTH MAIN STREET
STUTTGARD, AR 72106
President, Rex Hancock

**WILDLIFE FEDERATION OF
    ARKANSAS**
BOX 2277
LITTLE ROCK, AR 72201
Secretary, Bing Bennett

**WILDLIFE FEDERATION OF
    CALIFORNIA**
2644 JUDAH STREET
SAN FRANCISCO, CA 94112
President, V Schiavon

**WILDLIFE FEDERATION OF
    COLORADO**
BOX 1588
DENVER, CO 80201

**WILDLIFE FEDERATION OF
    COLORADO**
5123 JELLISON WAY
ARVADA, CO 80002
Secretary, Ronald M Stevens

**WILDLIFE FEDERATION OF
    CONNECTICUT**
82 SORRIES COURT
SOUTH MERIDEN, CT 06450
President, Walter Hylwa

**WILDLIFE FEDERATION OF
    DELAWARE**
1014 WASHINGTON STREET
WILMINGTON, DE 19801
President, James C Warren

**WILDLIFE FEDERATION OF
    FLORIDA**
5012 NE SECOND STREET
MIAMI, FL 33137
President, William F Theobald

**WILDLIFE FEDERATION OF
    HAWAII**
BOX 10113
HONOLULU, HI 96816
President, John Craft

**WILDLIFE FEDERATION OF
    IDAHO**
101 HORIZON DRIVE
BOISE, ID 83702
Secretary, W W Benson

**WILDLIFE FEDERATION OF
    IDAHO**
POST OFFICE BOX 849
COEUR D'ALENE, ID 83814
President, Robert G Thomas

**WILDLIFE FEDERATION OF
    ILLINOIS**
13005 SOUTH WESTERN AVENUE,
    BOX 116
BLUE ISLAND, IL 60406
President, John Worth
Staff Size: 1 - 4

WILDLIFE FEDERATION OF IOWA
601-1/2 NORTH MAIN STREET
BURLINGTON, IA 52601
Secretary, John C Welter

**WILDLIFE FEDERATION OF
    KANSAS**
RR 1
WAMEGO, KS 66547
President, Ted Cunningham

**WILDLIFE FEDERATION OF
    KANSAS**
1405 EISENHOWER DRIVE
JUNCTION CITY, KS 66441
Secretary, Clyde Obretch

**WILDLIFE FEDERATION OF
    LOUISIANA**
BOX 53112, ISTROUMA STATION
BATON ROUGE, LA 70805
Executive Director, Charles W Bosch

**WILDLIFE FEDERATION OF
    MARYLAND**
1002 WOODLAND WAY
HAGERSTOWN, MD 21740
President, Donald R Frush

**WILDLIFE FEDERATION OF
    MASSACHUSETTS**
BOX 343
NATICK, MA 01760
President, Chester S Spencer

**WILDLIFE FEDERATION OF
    MISSISSIPPI**
108 STATE STREET
BAY ST LOUIS, MS 39520
President, Clarence M Ladner

WILDLIFE FEDERATION OF MONTANA
410 WOODWORTH
MISSOULA, MT 59801
Executive Secretary, Don Aldrich

WILDLIFE FEDERATION OF NEVADA
POST OFFICE BOX 15205
LAS VEGAS, NV 89114
President, Philip T Gregory, Jr

WILDLIFE FEDERATION OF NORTH DAKOTA
POST OFFICE BOX 1694
BISMARCK, ND 58501

WILDLIFE FEDERATION OF OKLAHOMA
7404 NW 30TH STREET
BETHANY, OK 73008
President, Gene Dozier

WILDLIFE FEDERATION OF OREGON
811 SW 6TH AVENUE, ROOM 216
EXECUTIVE BUILDING
PORTLAND, OR 97204

WILDLIFE FEDERATION OF RHODE ISLAND
40 BOWEN STREET
PROVIDENCE, RI 02903
President, William H Lum

WILDLIFE FEDERATION OF SOUTH CAROLINA
LONE STAR ROAD
ELLORE, SC 29047
President, John E Bookhardt

WILDLIFE FEDERATION OF SOUTH DAKOTA
1217 SOUTH LAKE AVENUE
SIOUX FALLS, SD 57105
President, Raymond C Jacobson

WILDLIFE FEDERATION OF VIRGINIA
5608 WAYCROSS DRIVE
ALEXANDRIA, VA 22310
President, Carl Wiberg

WILDLIFE FEDERATION OF WEST VIRGINIA
BOX 38
DURBIN, WV 26264
President, David Brantner

WILDLIFE FEDERATION OF WISCONSIN
VISTA LANE
SUSSEX, W1, ENGLAND
President, James Wareing

WILDLIFE FEDERATION OF WYOMING
BOX 1406
CASPER, WY 82601
President, Guy H Williams

WILDLIFE MANAGEMENT INSTITUTE
200 AUDUBON LANE
FAIRFIELD, CT 06430
Field Conservation, Philip Barske
Staff Size: 5 - 9

WILDLIFE NATIONAL FEDERATION
1011 WASHINGTON STREET
WILMINGTON, DE 19801
Director, Edmund H Harvey

Government — Federal

AGRICULTURAL SCIENCE SERVICE, DEPARTMENT OF AGRICULTURE AND FISHER
EAST CRAIGS
EDINBURGH 12, SCOTLAND
Director, Dennis Graham
Specific Interests: Prairie and Temperate Forest
Staff Size: 10 - 49

AGRICULTURE COMMITTEE
HOUSE OFFICE BUILDING, SUITE 1301
WASHINGTON, DC 20515
Chairman, W R Poage

AIR POLLUTION CONTROL, NATIONAL CENTER
3RD AND C STREETS, SW
WASHINGTON, DC 20201
Specific Interests: Prairie and Temperate Forest

ATMOSPHERIC SCIENCES LIBRARY
ROOM 816, 8060 13TH STREET
SILVER SPRING, MD 20910

AUDUBON SOCIETY, NATIONAL
1130 5TH AVENUE
NEW YORK, NY 10028

BIOLOGICAL LABORATORY
75 33RD AVENUE
ST PETERSBURG, FL 33706
Acting Officer, J Kneeland Mcnulty
General Environment: Estuarine
Staff Size: 10 - 49

BIOLOGICAL LABORATORY
2725 MONTLAKE BOULEVARD, EAST
SEATTLE, WA 98102
Director, Gerald B Collins
General Environment: Oceanographic
Specific Interests: Prairie and Temperate Forest
Staff Size: 100 - 499

BIOLOGY LABORATORY, NATIONAL MARINE FISHERIES SERVICES
NATIONAL OCEANIC AND ATMOSPHERIC ADMINISTRATION
WEST BOOTHBAY HARBOR, ME 04575
Officer in Charge, George J Ridgway
General Environment: Oceanographic
Staff Size: 10 - 49

COMMERCE COMMITTEE
HOUSE OFFICE BUILDING, SUITE 5202
WASHINGTON, DC 20510
Chairman, Warren G Maguson

COMMERCIAL FISHERIES BUREAU
18TH AND C STREETS, NW
WASHINGTON, DC 20240
General Environment: Oceanographic

COMMUNITY ENVIRONMENTAL MANAGEMENT BUREAU
PARKLAWN BUILDING, ROOM 1587
ROCKVILLE, MD 20852
Specific Interests: Prairie and Temperate Forest

COMMUNITY ENVIRONMENTAL MANAGEMENT BUREAU
8717 POST OAK ROAD
POTOMAC, MD 20854

CONSERVATION AND RURAL DEVELOPMENT
1417 MONTAGUE DRIVE
VIENNA, VA 22180
Director, James D Keast
Specific Interests: Rural

CONSERVATION AND RURAL DEVELOPMENT
3833 ROBERTS LANE NORTH
ARLINGTON, VA 22207
Assistant Secretary, Thomas Cowden
Specific Interests: Rural

CROP ECOLOGY INSTITUTE
809 DALE DRIVE
SILVER SPRING, MD 20910

ECOLOGICAL SCIENCES INFORMATION CENTER, OAK RIDGE LABORATORY
BUILDING 3017
OAK RIDGE, TN 37830
Specific Interests: Prairie and Temperate Forest
Staff Size: 5 - 9

ECOLOGY AND ENVIRONMENTAL CONSERVATION OFFICE
6822 SORRELL DRIVE
MCLEAN, VA 22101
Director, William Aron

ECOLOGY OFFICE
SMITHSONIAN INSTITUTE
WASHINGTON, DC 20560

General Environment: Terrestrial
Staff Size: 10 - 49

ECOLOGY STUDIES PROGRAM
1616 HUNTER MILL ROAD
VIENNA, VA 22180

Director, Elwood Seaman

**ENERGY, NATURAL RESOURCES
AND ENVIRONMENT
SUBCOMMITTEE**
SENATE OFFICE BUILDING, SUITE
5202
WASHINGTON, DC 20510

Chairman, Philip Hart

**ENTOMOLOGY INFORMATION
SERVICE OF MILITARY**
FOREST GLEN SECTION
WASHINGTON, DC 20012

Staff Size: 10 - 49

ENVIRONMENT DEPARTMENT
PARLIAMENT BUILDING
OTTAWA, ONTARIO, CANADA

**ENVIRONMENTAL ACTION,
INCORPORATED**
1346 CONNECTICUT AVENUE, NW
WASHINGTON, DC 20036

**ENVIRONMENTAL CONTROL
ADMINISTRATION**
12720 TWINBROOK PARKWAY
ROCKVILLE, MD 20852

Specific Interests: Prairie and Temperate
Forest

**ENVIRONMENTAL EDUCATION,
NATIONAL PARK SERVICE**
UNITED STATES DEPARTMENT OF
INTERIOR
WASHINGTON, DC 20036

General Environment: Terrestrial

**ENVIRONMENTAL HEALTH
SECTION**
OFFICE OF SURGEON GENERAL
UNITED STATES AIR FORCE
WASHINGTON, DC 20333

Specific Interests: Prairie and Temperate
Forest

**ENVIRONMENTAL HYGIENE
AGENCY, UNITED STATES ARMY**
OFFICE OF SURGEON GENERAL
EDGEWOOD ARSENAL, MD 21010

Specific Interests: Prairie and Temperate
Forest

**ENVIRONMENTAL PROTECTION
AGENCY**
SOUTHEAST WATER LABORATORY
ATHENS, GA 30601

Staff Size: 100 - 499

**ENVIRONMENTAL PROTECTION
AGENCY**
3902 WATERSIDE MALL, ROOM 3105
WASHINGTON, DC 20460

**ENVIRONMENTAL QUALITY
CITIZENS ADVISORY
COMMISSION**
1700 PENNSYLVANIA AVENUE, NW
WASHINGTON, DC 20006

Specific Interests: Prairie and Temperate
Forest

**ENVIRONMENTAL QUALITY
COUNCIL**
6219 33RD STREET
WASHINGTON, DC 20015

Program Development Director, Alvin
Alm

**ENVIRONMENTAL RESEARCH
INSTITUTE**
WASHINGTON, DC 20234

**ENVIRONMENTAL RESEARCH
LABORATORY, WESTERN**
BOX 15027
LAS VEGAS, NV 89114

Staff Size: 100 - 499

**ENVIRONMENTAL RESEARCH
PROGRAM**
NEW YORK UNIVERSITY
NEW YORK, NY 10019

Specific Interests: Prairie and Temperate
Forest

**ENVIRONMENTAL SCIENCES
TRAINING COMMISSION**
DEPARTMENT OF MEDICINE AT
CORNELL
CORNELL, NY 10021

Chairman, L Hinkle
Staff Size: 1 - 4

**ENVIRONMENTAL SERVICES
COUNCIL**
560 NORTH STREET, SW
WASHINGTON, DC 20005

Director, James P Alexander

**FISHERIES LABORATORY OF
GREAT LAKES**
1451 GREEN ROAD
ANN ARBOR, MI 48107

Director, Howard D Tait
General Environment: Limnologic
Specific Interests: Prairie and Temperate
Forest
Staff Size: 50 - 99

**FISHERIES AND WILDLIFE
CONSERVATION
SUBCOMMITTEE**
HOUSE OFFICE BUILDING, SUITE
1334
WASHINGTON, DC 20515

Chairman, John D Dingell
General Environment: Oceanographic

**FISHERIES AND WILDLIFE
SERVICE**
BUREAU OF COMMERICAL
FISHERIES
WASHINGTON, DC 20240

**FISHERIES RESEARCH BOARD OF
CANADA**
BEDFORD INSTITUTION
OCEANOGRAPHY
DARTMOUTH, NOVA SCOTIA,
CANADA

Marine Ecologist, Dr L M Dickie
General Environment: Oceanographic
Specific Interests: Polar (cold)
Staff Size: 50 - 99

**FISHERY DIVISION, DEPARTMENT
OF AGRICULTURE**
POST OFFICE BOX 1232
ADDIS ABABA, ETHIOPIA

Director, Wolde Aregave Redda
General Environment: Oceanographic

**FISHERY RESEARCH DIVISION,
SPORT FISHERIES AND
WILDLIFE**
777 14TH STREET, NW
WASHINGTON, DC 20240

General Environment: Oceanographic

**FORESTRY AND SOIL
CONSERVATION DIVISION**
5708 18TH ROAD NORTH
ARLINGTON, VA 22205

**FORESTRY DEVELOPMENT
COMMISSION**
777 14TH STREET, NW
WASHINGTON, DC 20240

Specific Interests: Prairie and Temperate
Forest

**FORESTRY DEVELOPMENT
COMMISSION**
TENNESSEE VALLEY AUTHORITY
NORRIS, TN 37828

**FORESTRY DEVELOPMENT
COMMISSION**
UNITED STATES PUBLIC HEALTH
SERVICE
WASHINGTON, DC 20201

FORESTS SUBCOMMITTEE
HOUSE OFFICE BUILDING, SUITE
H218
WASHINGTON, DC 20515

Chairman, John L Mcmillan

FRIENDS OF THE EARTH
30 EAST 42ND STREET
NEW YORK, NY 10017

FUNGUS CULTURES, NATIONAL INDEX
NATICK LABS
NATICK, MA 01760

INDUSTRIAL HYGIENE ASSOCIATION
210 HADDON AVENUE
WESTMONT, NJ 08108
Staff Size: 5 - 9

INFORMATION PROCESSING OFFICE- UNITED STATES ARMY RESEARCH OFFICE
BOX CM, DUKE STATION
DURHAM, NC 27706
Specific Interests: Prairie and Temperate Forest

INTERNATIONAL ACTIVITIES OFFICE
SMITHSONIAN FOREIGN CURRENCY PROGRAM
WASHINGTON, DC 20560
Staff Size: 5 - 9

INTERNATIONAL JOINT COMMISSION, CANADIAN SECTION
ROOM 850, 151 SLATER STREET
OTTAWA, ONTARIO, CANADA

MARINE FISHERIES NATIONAL SERVICE
POST OFFICE BOX 6
WOODS HOLE, MA 02543
Director, R Edwards
General Environment: Oceanographic
Staff Size: 100 - 499

MARINE FISHERIES SERVICE, NATIONAL
2725 MONTLAKE BOULEVARD, EAST
SEATTLE, WA 98112
General Environment: Oceanographic
Staff Size: 100 - 499

MARINE MAMMAL DIVISION
NAVAL SUPPORT ACTIVITY 192
SEATTLE, WA 98115
Director, George Harry
General Environment: Oceanographic
Specific Interests: Prairie and Temperate Forest
Staff Size: 10 - 49

MARINE WATER QUALITY LABORATORY, NATIONAL
POST OFFICE BOX 277
WEST KINGSTON, RI 02892
General Environment: Estuarine
Staff Size: 50 - 99

MERCHANT MARINE AND FISHERIES COMMITTEE

HOUSE OFFICE BUILDING, SUITE 1334
WASHINGTON, DC 20515
Chairman, Edward Garmatz

MERCHANT MARINES AND FISHERIES, US HOUSE OF REPRESENTATIVES
ROOM 1334, LONGWORTH HOUSE BUILDING
WASHINGTON, DC 20515
General Environment: Limnologic

MIGRATORY BIRD CONSERVATION COMMISSION
DEPARTMENT OF INTERIOR BUILDING
WASHINGTON, DC 20240
Chairman, Rogers Morton

NATIONAL OCEANOGRAPHIC AND ATMOSPHERIC ADMINISTRATION
8060 13TH STREET
SILVER SPRING, MD 20910
General Environment: Atmospheric

NATURE CONSERVANCY
1522 K STREET, NW
WASHINGTON, DC 10036

NORTHERN PRAIRIE WILDLIFE RESEARCH CENTER
POST OFFICE BOX 1672
JAMESTOWN, ND 58401
General Environment: Marsh/Swamp
Specific Interests: Prairie and Temperate Forest
Staff Size: 50 - 99

OCEANOGRAPHY AND LIMNOLOGY OFFICE
10TH STREET AND CONSTITUTION AVENUE
WASHINGTON, DC 20560
General Environment: Oceanographic

OCEANOGRAPHY OFFICE
UNESCO
PARIS, FRANCE
Secretary, Sidney J Holt
General Environment: Oceanographic
Specific Interests: Prairie and Temperate Forest

ORGANIZATION OF AMERICAN STATES
PAN AMERICAN UNION
WASHINGTON, DC 20006

ORNITHOLOGISTS UNION OF NEBRASKA
UNIVERSITY OF NEBRASKA STATE MUSEUM
LINCOLN, NB 68508
President, C W Huntley

PAN-INDIAN OCEAN SCIENCE ASSOCIATION, BLOCK 95
PAKISTAN SECRETARIAT
KARACHI, PAKISTAN
General Environment: Oceanographic

PARKS AND RECREATION SUBCOMMITTEE
SENATE OFFICE BUILDING, SUITE 3106
WASHINGTON, DC 20510
Chairman, Alan Bible
General Environment: Terrestrial

PESTICIDE COMMISSION STUDIES DIVISION
ENVIRONMENTAL PROTECTION AGENCY
CHAMBLEE, GA 30341
Staff Size: 50 - 99

PLANT SCIENCE RESEARCH DIVISION
1714 EDGEWATER PARKWAY
SILVER SPRING, MD 20904
Director, H O Graumann

PLANT SCIENCES AND ENTOMOLOGY
3907 BEECHWOOD ROAD
HYATTSVILLE, MD 20782
Director, H R Thomas

RECLAMATION BUREAU
12821 HUNTSMAN WAY
POTOMAC, MD 20854
Commissioner, Ellis Armstrong

RESEARCH DEVELOPMENT DIVISION
UNITED STATES DEPARTMENT OF AGRICULTURE, SOIL CONSERVATION SERVICE
WASHINGTON, DC 20250
Director, Wallace Anderson
Staff Size: 10 - 49

RESEARCH MANAGEMENT
4633 DENPAT CENTER
ANNANDALE, VA 22003
Director, Eldon O Taylor

RESOURCES AND MANAGEMENT COMMISSION, NATIONAL ACADEMY OF SCIENCES
2101 CONSTITUTION AVENUE, NW
WASHINGTON, DC 20418

RIVERS AND HARBORS SUBCOMMITTEE
HOUSE OFFICE BUILDING, SUITE 2165
WASHINGTON, DC 20515
Chairman, John Blatnik
General Environment: Oceanographic

SIERRA CLUB
1050 MILLS TOWER
SAN FRANCISCO, CA 94104

SOIL CONSERVATION SERVICE
311 OLD FEDERAL BUILDING, 3RD
AND STATE STREETS
COLUMBUS, OH 43215
Staff Size: 100 - 499

SOIL CONSERVATION SERVICE
DEPARTMENT OF AGRICULTURE
WASHINGTON, DC 20250

SOIL CONSERVATION SERVICES
96 COLLEGE STREET
BURLINGTON, VT 05401
Staff Size: 50 - 99

SOIL CONSERVATION SERVICES
W 920 RIVERSIDE AVENUE
SPOKANE, WA 99201
State Conservationist, Mr Galen S Bridge
Staff Size: 100 - 499

SOIL CONSERVATION SERVICES
210 WALNUT STREET
DES MOINES, IA 50309
Staff Size: 100 - 499

SOLID WASTE MANAGEMENT
PROGRAMS
5016 BALTIC AVENUE
ROCKVILLE, MD 20853
Director, Hugh Connolly

SPORT FISHERIES AND WILDLIFE
BUREAU
18TH AND C STREETS
WASHINGTON, DC 20240
General Environment: Oceanographic

URBAN AND INDUSTRIAL HEALTH
NATIONAL CENTER
550 MAIN STREET
CINCINNATI, OH 45202
Specific Interests: Prairie and Temperate
Forest

WATER RESEARCH DIVISION,
GEOLOGICAL SURVEY
18TH AND F STREETS, NW
WASHINGTON, DC 20242
Specific Interests: Prairie and Temperate
Forest

WILDLIFE DIVISION, BUREAU OF
SPORT FISHERIES AND
WILDLIFE
DEPARTMENT OF THE INTERIOR
WASHINGTON, DC 20240

WILDLIFE RESEARCH CENTER,
PATUXENT
LAUREL, MD 20810
Staff Size: 100 - 499

Government — State or Local

ACTION CONSERVATION TRUST
42 TAYLOR ROAD
ACTON, MA 01720
President, James Donald

ACTION NOW CENTER,
INCORPORATED
152 TEMPLE STREET
NEW HAVEN, CT 06510
Chairman, Dan W Lufkin

AGRICULTURAL AND
CONSERVATION COMMISSION
DOVER-FOXCRAFT KIWANIS CLUB
DOVER-FOXCROFT, ME 04426
Chairman, G M Andrews

AIR AND WATER POLLUTION OF
MISSISSIPPI
POST OFFICE BOX 827
JACKSON, MS 39205

AIR POLLUTION REGIONAL
AUTHORITY OF PORTLAND
104 SW 5TH AVENUE
PORTLAND, OR 97204
General Environment: Atmospheric

APPALACHIAN MOUNTAIN CLUB
5 JOY STREET
BOSTON, MA 02108
President, John C Perry

APPALACHIAN MOUNTAIN CLUB
21 COLUMBIA AVENUE
BRUNSWICK, ME 04011
Director, Leroy D Cross

APPALACHIAN MOUNTAIN CLUB
55 MARVEL ROAD
NEW HAVEN, CT 06515
Chairman, Bente Morch

AREA DEVELOPMENT ECOLOGY-
ELECTRICITY
FALLS VILLAGE, CT 06031
President, James H Blodgett

ARROWSIC MARSHLANDS
ASSOCIATION
SPINNEY MILL ROAD
ARROWSIC, ME 04530
Secretary, Mrs George P Stafford

BERKSHIRE COUNTY LAND TRUST
100 WORTH STREET
PITTSFIELD, MA 01201

BIRD CLUB OF NEW HAVEN
26 MOWRY STREET
NEW HAVEN, CT 06518
President, G Denny Williams

BISCAY POND ASSOCIATION,
INCORPORATED
BRISTOL, ME 04539
President, W Benner

BOTANICAL INSTITUTE AND
GARDEN
UNIVERSITY OF PERUGIA
PERUGIA, ITALY
Director, Rodolfo E G Pichi-Sermolli
General Environment: Terrestrial
Specific Interests: Tropical (hot)
Staff Size: 10 - 49

CITIZENS FOR A CLEANER
ENVIRONMENT
814 ELM STREET
MANCHESTER, NH 03101
Director, Laurence Kelly

CITIZENS FOR A HEALTHY
ENVIRONMENT
36 PEMBERTON ROAD
COCHITUATE, MA 01778
Director, Lorraine Clough

CITIZENS FOR PARTICIPATION IN
ENVIRONMENTAL PROBLEMS
11 SOUTH STREET
BOSTON, MA 02111
Chairman, Mrs C Meyer

CITIZENS FOR PROPER
TRANSPORTATION PLANNING
14 BEACON STREET, ROOM 708
BOSTON, MA 02108
Coordinator Chairman, S P Crosby

COASTAL RESOURCES ACTION
COMMISSION
465 CONGRESS STREET, ROOM 507
PORTLAND, ME 04111
Director, H Hildreth, Jr

CONCERNED CITIZENS OF CAPE
ANN
ELM AVENUE, EASTERN POINT
GLOUCESTER, MA 01930
President, Mrs Katherine E Gross

CONCORD ENVIRONMENTAL
CORNER
129 MAIN STREET
CORNER, MA 01742
Director, Dan Monahan

CONSERVATION AND
DEVELOPMENT COMMISSION OF
SAN FRANCISCO BAY
30 VAN NESS AVENUE ROOM 2127
SAN FRANCISCO, CA 94102
Director, Joseph E Bodovitz
Staff Size: 10 - 49

CONSERVATION ASSOCIATION
CENTER
NORTHROP STREET
BRIDGEWATER, CT 06752
Executive Vice President, Robert F Kunz

CONSERVATION ASSOCIATION OF KENNEBEC VALLEY
POST OFFICE BOX 525
SKOWHEGAN, ME 04976
Secretary, J Leclair, Jr

CONSERVATION ASSOCIATION OF VERMONT
CHESTER DEPOT, VT 05144
President, Lloyd Jewett

CONSERVATION BILL OF RIGHTS COUNCIL OF MAINE
115-A STEVENS HALL, UNIVERSITY OF MAINE
ORONO, ME 04473
Director, Edward Schriver

CONSERVATION COMMISSION
TOWN HALL
BROOKLINE, MA 02146
Director, Mr Francis X Meaney

CONSERVATION COMMISSION CENTER, INCORPORATED
POST OFFICE BOX 177
W HARTFORD, CT 06107
President, Jack Gunther

CONSERVATION COMMISSION OF FAIRFIELD
739 OLD POST ROAD
FAIRFIELD, CT 06430
Director, Thomas J Steinke
Specific Interests: Urban
Staff Size: 1 - 4

CONSERVATION COMMISSION OF HOLLISTON
56 TEMI ROAD
HOLLISTON, MA 01746
Director, Brian Dextradeur
Staff Size: 10 - 49

CONSERVATION COMMISSIONS OF RHODE ISLAND
20 FIRGLADE AVENUE
EAST PROVIDENCE, RI 02915
Director, Edward J Doyle

CONSERVATION COMMITTEE OF ASHLAND
66 STROBUS LANE
ASHLAND, MA 01721
Director, John Schmidt

CONSERVATION COUNCIL OF BELMONT
BELMONT, MA 02178
Staff Size: 5 - 9

CONSERVATION COUNCIL OF FRAMINGHAM
94 PROSPECT STREET
FRAMINGHAM, MA 01701
President, Bert Rendell

CONSERVATION COUNCIL OF HANOVER
HANOVER, NH 03755
President, Robert Norman

CONSERVATION DEPARTMENT OF KANSAS
POST OFFICE BOX 600
SALINA, KS 67401

CONSERVATION FRIENDS
43 UNION STREET
MARSHFIELD, MA 02050
Director, Mrs Alan E Bates

CONSERVATION FRIENDS AT DENNIS
DENNIS, MA 02368
Director, Charles Vaughan

CONSERVATION FRIENDS OF DUXBURY
30 PINE HILL ROAD
DUXBURY, MA 02332
Director, Donald Connors

CONSERVATION GROUP, BEVERLY-GARDEN CITY
13 KING TERRACE
BEVERLY, MA 01915
Director, Mrs Philip C Parsons
General Environment: Nonspecific Not Available
General Environment: Nonspecific

CONSERVATION SERVICES, DEPARTMENT OF NATURAL RESOURCES
100 CAMBRIDGE
BOSTON, MA 02134

CONSERVATION SOCIETY OF PINE TREE
435 CONGRESS STREET
PORTLAND, ME 04111
Director, Vincent Mckusick

CONSERVATION SOCIETY OF SOUTHERN VERMONT
BOX 256
TOWNSHEND, VT 05353
Director, J W Stevens
Staff Size: 1 - 4

CULTURAL AND HISTORICAL SOCIETY OF LINCOLN COUNTY
BOX 61
WISCASSET, ME 04578
Director, Mrs John Raftin

DESIGN AND LANDMARKS, INCORPORATED
BUNGANUC ROAD
BRUNSWICK, ME 04011
Director, Brooks Stoddard

DEVELOPMENT ASSOCIATION OF CASCO BAY ISLAND
PEAKS ISLAND, ME 04108
Secretary, Mrs Winthrop K Deane

EARTH
60 BARKSDALE ROAD
W HARTFORD, CT 06107
Director, Laura De Costa
General Environment: Terrestrial

ECOLOGY ACTION
BOX ONE
WOODSTOCK, VT 05091

ECOLOGY ACTION FOR SOUTHERN RHODE ISLAND
PO BOX 9
KINGSTON, RI 02881

ECOLOGY ACTION LEAGUE OF HERMON
POST OFFICE BOX 922
MT HEROM, MA 01354

ECOLOGY ACTION NOTES
125 SILK STREET
BREWER, ME 04412
Director, Brian Damier

ECOLOGY ACTION OF BELMONT
80 MUNROE STREET
BELMONT, MA 02178
Publicity Director, Mrs Wolly Waugh

ECOLOGY ACTION OF BROCTON
116 DOVER STREET
BROCKTON, MA 02401
Secretary, Mrs Elizabeth Randall

ECOLOGY ACTION REACHING THROUGH HOUSEHOLDS
MAIN STREET
SPRINGFIELD, MA 01103

ECOLOGY ACTION, CENTER HUMAN SURVIVAL
52 MAIN STREET
WEST LEBANON, NH 03784

ECOLOGY CENTER OF NEW ENGLAND
891 MASSACHUSETTS AVENUE
CAMBRIDGE, MA 02139

ECOLOGY CENTER OF WASHINGTON
2000 AND STATE STREET, NW
SUITE 612
WASHINGTON, DC 20006

ECOLOGY CLUB OF DERBY
DERBY ACADEMY
HINGHAM, MA 02043
Director, Stephen Phillips

ECOLOGY DEPARTMENT
WASHINGTON STATE
OLYMPIA, WA 98504
Staff Size: 100 - 499

ECOLOGY LEAGUE
BOX 535
LAKEVILLE, CT 06039
President, Evon R Kochey

ECOLOGY LEAGUE
POST OFFICE BOX ONE
CORNWALL BRIDGE, CT 06754
President, Homer Page

ENVIRONMENT AND CONSUMER PROTECTION
PUBLIC HEALTH SERVICE
WASHINGTON, DC 20201
Chairman, Charles Johnson
Specific Interests: Urban

ENVIRONMENT TASK FORCE OF THE GOVERNMENT
ROOM 107, 100 CAMBRIDGE
BOSTON, MA 02202
Staff Size: 1 - 4

ENVIRONMENTAL ACTION COMMITTEE
BOX 99, BILLINGS CENTER
BURLINGTON, VT 05401
Director, Anne Ehrlich

ENVIRONMENTAL AWARENESS COMMITTEE
GREEN MOUNTAIN COLLEGE
POULTNEY, VT 05741
Director, Patricia G World

ENVIRONMENTAL CLUB
SOUTH BURLINGTON HIGH SCHOOL
SOUTH BURLINGTON, VT 05401

ENVIRONMENTAL CONSERVATION COUNCIL, BERKSHIRE-LITCHFIELD
POST OFFICE BOX 552
LAKEVILLE, CT 06039
President, Donald T Warner

ENVIRONMENTAL CONTROL ADMINISTRATION
12720 TWINBROOK PARKWAY
ROCKVILLE, MD 20852
Executive Secretary, Julius Sabo

ENVIRONMENTAL CONTROL ORGANIZATION OF STOUGHTON
60 HOLBROOK AVENUE
STOUGHTON, MN 02072
Director, Paul Mosier

ENVIRONMENTAL COUNCIL FAIRFIELD-LITCHFIELD
BETHEL, CT 06801
Chairman, Arthur Rickerby

ENVIRONMENTAL COUNCIL OF RHODE ISLAND
40 BOWEN STREET
PROVIDENCE, RI 02903
President, Al Harpell

ENVIRONMENTAL EDUCATION, NATIONAL PARK SERVICES SOUTHEAST OFFICE
POST OFFICE BOX 10008
RICHMOND, VA 23240
General Environment: Terrestrial

ENVIRONMENTAL EDUCATION, NATIONAL PARK SERVICES MIDWEST OFFICE
1709 JACKSON STREET
OMAHA, NB 68102
General Environment: Terrestrial

ENVIRONMENTAL EDUCATION, NATIONAL PARK SERVICES NORTHWEST OFFICE
4TH AND PIKE BUILDING
SEATTLE, WA 98101
General Environment: Terrestrial

ENVIRONMENTAL EDUCATION, NATIONAL PARK SERVICES
POST OFFICE BOX 728
SANTA FE, NM 87501
General Environment: Terrestrial

ENVIRONMENTAL EDUCATION, NATIONAL PARK SERVICES WESTERN OFFICE
450 GOLDEN GATE-BOX 36063
SAN FRANCISCO, CA 94102
General Environment: Terrestrial

ENVIRONMENTAL EPIDEMICS, DEPARTMENT OF PUBLIC HEALTH
2151 BERKELEY WAY
BERKELEY, CA 94704
Director, John Goldsmith

ENVIRONMENTAL GROUP OF HANOVER
CEDAR STREET
HANOVER, MA 02339
Director, Mrs Derek Jones

ENVIRONMENTAL HEALTH DIVISION, CITY HEALTH DEPARTMENT
6TH STREET, CITY HALL
LA CROSSE, WI 54601
Staff Size: 5 - 9

ENVIRONMENTAL HEALTH SCIENCES
NATIONAL INSTITUTES OF HEALTH
BETHESDA, MD 20014
Chairman, R Marston
Staff Size: 1 - 4

ENVIRONMENTAL LAW SOCIETY
41 TEMPLE STREET
BOSTON, MA 02114
Director, Thomas P Merlino

ENVIRONMENTAL PROTECTION DEPARTMENT
STATE OFFICE BUILDING
HARTFORD, CT 06115
General Environment: Terrestrial
Staff Size: 10 - 49

ENVIRONMENTAL QUALITY
15 GLIDDEN STREET
WATERVILLE, ME 04091
Chairman, Mrs Larry Seymour

ENVIRONMENTAL QUALITY
11 PIERSON DRIVE
SHELBURNE, VT 05482
Chairman, Mrs W White

ENVIRONMENTAL QUALITY
112 PINCKNEY STREET
BOSTON, MA 02114
Chairman, Mrs Ellen Robertson

ENVIRONMENTAL SERVICES DIVISION
HEALTH AND SOCIAL SERVICES DEPARTMENT
SANTA FE, NM 87501
Director, L Gordon

ENVIRONMENTAL STUDIES
11 ARCHER DR
NATICK, MA 01760
Director, Mrs G Forsythe

ENVIRONMENTAL STUDIES
143 SOUTH THIRD STREET
PHILADEPHIA, PA 19106
General Environment: Terrestrial

ENVIRONMENTAL TRUST OF MARYLAND
8 E MULBERRY STREET
BALTIMORE, MD 21202
Staff Size: 1 - 4

FOREST AND PARK ASSOCIATION CENTER
1010 MAIN STREET BOX 389
E HARTFORD, CT 06108
President, F M Callward

FOREST HISTORICAL SOCIETY
421 RIDGE ROAD
HAMDEN, CT 06517
President, Dr G Garratt

FRAMINGTON TOWN TRUST
4 WILLIAMS HEIGHTS
FRAMINGTON, MA 01701
Director, Dana Jost

**FRIENDS OF BROOKLINE
  CONSERVATION**
CRAFTS ROAD
BROOKLINE, MA 02167
President, Mrs C T Cohen

**GARDEN CLUB FEDERATION OF
  MAINE**
VILLA INTERLAKEN
FOREST BROOKTON, ME 04413
President, Mrs James L Pettit

**GRAFTON FOREST ASSOCIATION,
  INCORPORATED**
12 SOUTH STREET
GRAFTON, MA 01519
Director, Henry S Poler

HOSPITAL, DETROIT GENERAL
1326 ANTOINE STREET
DETROIT, MI 48226
Director, Donald Birmingham
Specific Interests: Urban

**IMPROVEMENT ASSOCIATION OF
  PEABODY**
18 TREMONT STREET
PEABODY, MA 01960
Director, Mrs Christine Roy

**IMPROVEMENT SOCIETY OF
  ANDOVER VILLAGE**
POST OFFICE BOX 90
ANDOVER, MA 01810
President, Robert L V French

LAKE ASSOCIATION OF CHINA
LAKEVIEW DRIVE
SOUTH CHINA, ME 04538
Director, Ben Dillenbeck

**LAKE ASSOCIATION OF
  DAMARISCOTTA**
ROAD ONE, BOX 126
NEWCASTLE, ME 04553
Secretary, Mrs Hazel M Tenny

**LAND CONSERVATION TRUST OF
  BEVERLY**
809 HALE STREET
BEVERLY FARMS, MA 01915
Director, James Polese

**LANDGUARD TRUST,
  INCORPORATED**
103 EXCHANGE STREET
PORTLAND, ME 04111
Executive Director, E T Richardson, Jr

**LOCAL INTERVENTION FOR
  ENVIRONMENT, INCORPORATED**
27 FAIR STREET
NEWBURYPORT, MA 01950
President, Mrs M R Eigerman

**MARINE SCIENCES INSTITUTE OF
  VIRGINIA**
SCHOOL OF MARINE SCIENCES,

WILLIAM AND MARY COLLEGE
GLOUCESTER POINT, VA 23062
General Environment: Estuarine
Staff Size: 100 - 499

MID-COAST AUDUBON
WALDOBORO, ME 04572
President, Milo Marsh

**MOUNTAIN DESERT ISLAND BIRD
  CLUB**
SALISBURY COVE, ME 04672
Director, Mrs Jere Jellison

NATCHAUG ORNITHOLOGICAL
RFD TWO, BOX 126
STORRS, CT 06268
Director, Leonard Seeber

NATURAL PRESERVES FORUM
5 SOUTH STATE STREET
CONCORD, NH 03301
Director, Leslie Clark

**NATURAL RESOURCE
  DEPARTMENT, STATE FORESTRY
  DEPARTMENT**
100 CAMBRIDGE
BOSTON, MA 02134

**NATURAL RESOURCES COUNCIL
  OF BERKSHIRE**
8 BANK BOW
PITTSFIELD, MA 01201
Executive Director, George S Wislocki
Staff Size: 1 - 4

**NATURAL RESOURCES
  DEPARTMENT**
270 WASHINGTON STREET, SW
ATLANTA, GA 30334

**NATURAL RESOURCES
  DEPARTMENT, PUBLIC ACCESS
  BOARD**
100 CAMBRIDGE
BOSTON, MA 02134

NATURAL SCIENCE CENTER
GREAT ESKER PARK
WEYMOUTH, MA 02188

**NATURALIST CLUB OF
  WATERBURY, INCORPORATED**
21 SUNRISE NOOK
WATERBURY, CT 06708

**NATURE CENTER OF LITCHFIELD,
  ECONOMIC-SIX**
LITCHFIELD NATURE CENTER
LITCHFIELD, CT 06759
Chairman, Gordon Loery

NATURE CLUB OF AUGUSTA
186 GREEN STREET
AUGUSTA, ME 04330
Director, Gwendolyn Stearns

**NATURE PROGRAMS FOR
  MCCLELLAN PARK CHILDREN**
MILLBRIDGE, ME 04658
Directors, Frank and Ada Graham

**NAUGATUCK PRIDE,
  INCORPORATED**
ORCHARD HILL ROAD
HARNINGTON, CT 06790
President, James Miller

**NEW ENVIRONMENTAL RESCUE
  ALLIANCE**
BOX 944
WEST CORNWALL, CT 06796
Chairman, Peter Mitchell

**OCCUPATIONAL HEALTH
  PROGRAM, ENVIRONMENTAL
  CONSERVATION
  ADMINISTRATION**
222 EAST CENTRAL PARKWAY
CINCINNATI, OH 45202
Secretary, Stanley Reno

**PRESERVATION OF CAPE COD
  ASSOCIATION**
BOX 325
EASTHAM, MA 02642
President, H E Whitlock

**PRESERVATION OF NEW
  HAMPSHIRES FORESTS SOCIETY**
5 SOUTH STATE STREET
CONCORD, NH 03301
Executive Director, Paul Bofinger

**PRESERVATION OF WILDLIFE
  AND NATURAL AREAS FUND**
ONE BOSTON PLACE
BOSTON, MA 02106
Director, Henry Lyman

**PROTECTIVE ASSOCIATION OF
  LAKE SUNAPEE**
BURPEE HILL ROAD
NEW LONDON, NH 03257

**PUBLIC AFFAIRS BUREAU,
  COMMITTEE TO KEEP
  MASSACHUSETTS BEAUTIFUL**
BOSTON COLLEGE
BOSTON, MA 02167
General Environment: Terrestrial

**RESEARCH COUNCIL OF NEW
  HAMPSHIRE, INCORPORATED**
5 SOUTH STATE STREET
CONCORD, NH 03301
Secretary, Leslie S Clark

**RESEARCH FOR CONSERVATION
  AND DEVELOPMENT OF NORTH
  COUNTRY**
POST OFFICE BOX 658
LITTLETON, NH 03561

RESOURCE DEVELOPMENT,
  DEPARTMENT OF NATURAL
  RESOURCES
STATE OFFICE BUILDING
MADISON, WI 53702

SLUM PREVENTION AND SMOKE
  ABATEMENT
1381 COOLIDGE HIGHWAY
RIVER ROUGE, MI 48218

SOIL AND WATER CONSERVATION
  ASSOCIATION
POST OFFICE BOX 128
PEORIA, AZ 85345
Director, Dr Charles E Huntington

SOIL AND WATER CONSERVATION
  ASSOCIATION OF RHODE ISLAND
TOURTELLOT HILL ROAD
CHEPACHET, RI 02814
Director, Domenic Marietti

SOIL CONSERVATION
POST OFFICE BOX 311
AUBURN, AL 36830

SOIL CONSERVATION
  ASSOCIATION OF NEW
  HAMPSHIRE
RFD TWO
EXETER, NH 03833
President, John W York

SOIL CONSERVATION SERVICE
5610 CRAWFORDSVILLE ROAD
INDIANAPOLIS, IN 46224

SOIL CONSERVATION SERVICE
1409 FORBES ROAD
LEXINGTON, KY 40505

SOIL CONSERVATION SERVICE
304 NORTH 8TH STREET, ROOM 345
BOISE, ID 83702

SOIL CONSERVATION SERVICE
UNITED STATES POST OFFICE
EAST GREENWICH, RI 02818

SOIL CONSERVATION SERVICE
FEDERAL BUILDING
DURHAM, NH 03824

SOIL CONSERVATION SERVICE
134 SOUTH 12TH STREET
LINCOLN, NB 68508

SOIL CONSERVATION SERVICE
FEDERAL BUILDING, POST OFFICE
  BOX 1458
BISMARK, ND 58501

SOIL CONSERVATION SERVICE
P O BOX 970
BOZEMAN, MT 59715

SOIL CONSERVATION SERVICE
1405 SOUTH HARRISON ROAD
EAST LANSING, MI 48823

SOIL CONSERVATION SERVICE
MANSFIELD PROFESSOR PARK, RT
  44A
STORRS, CT 06268

SOIL CONSERVATION SERVICE
27-29 COTTAGE STREET
AMHERST, MA 01002
Staff Size: 100 - 499

SOIL CONSERVATION SERVICE
PO BOX 2323, RM 5029, FEDERAL
  OFFICE BUILDING
LITTLE ROCK, AR

SOIL CONSERVATION SERVICE
2490 WEST 26TH AVENUE, ROOM
  313
DENVER, CO 80211

SOIL CONSERVATION SERVICES
FEDERAL BUILDING, 125 SOUTH
  STATE STREET, ROOM 4012
SALT LAKE CITY, UT 84111

SOIL CONSERVATION SERVICES
ROOM 522, HARTWICK BUILDING,
  4321 HARTWICK ROAD
COLLEGE PARK, MD 20740

SOIL CONSERVATION SERVICES
POST OFFICE BOX 678, 200 WEST
  CHURCH STREET
CHAMPAIGN, IL 61820

SOIL CONSERVATION SERVICES
FARM ROAD AND BRUMLEY
  STREET, AGRICULTURE
  BUILDING
STILLWATER, OK 74074

SOIL CONSERVATION SERVICES
FEDERAL BUILDING, 400 NORTH
  EIGHTH STREET, ROOM 7408
RICHMOND, VA 23240

SOIL CONSERVATION SERVICES
MIDTOWN PLAZA, ROOM 400, 700
  EAST WATER STREET
SYRACUSE, NY 13210

SOIL CONSERVATION SERVICES
ROOM 308, P O BUILDING, P O BOX
  4850
RENO, NV 89505

SOIL CONSERVATION SERVICES
TIOGA BUILDING, 2020 MILVIA
  STREET, ROOM 203
BERKELEY, CA 94704

SOIL CONSERVATION SERVICES
BOX 985, FEDERAL SQUARE
  STATION
HARRISBURG, PA 17108

SOIL CONSERVATION SERVICES
209 PRAIRIE AVENUE, PO BOX 865
MORGANTOWN, WV 26505

SOIL CONSERVATION SERVICES
1370 HAMILTON STREET, PO BOX
  219
SOMERSET, NJ 08873

SOIL CONSERVATION SERVICES
POST OFFICE BOX 1208
GAINESVILLE, FL 32601

SOIL CONSERVATION SERVICES
POST OFFICE BOX 610, MILNER
  BUILDING, ROOM 430
JACKSON, MS 39205

SOIL CONSERVATION SERVICES
4601 HAMMERSLEY ROAD, PO BOX
  4248
MADISON, WI 53711

SOIL CONSERVATION SERVICES
239 WISCONSIN AVENUE, SW, PO
  BOX 1357
HURON, SD 57350

SOIL CONSERVATION SERVICES
517 GOLD AVENUE, SW, PO BOX
  2007
ALBUQUERQUE, NM 87103

SOIL CONSERVATION SERVICES
316 NORTH ROBERT STREET, 200
  FEDERAL BUILDING
ST PAUL, MN 55101

SOIL CONSERVATION SERVICES
16-20 MAIN STREET, PO BOX 648
TEMPLE, TX 76501

SOIL CONSERVATION SERVICES
230 NORTH FIRST AVENUE, 6029
  FEDERAL BUILDING
PHOENIX, AZ 85025

SOIL CONSERVATION SERVICES
1218 SW WASHINGTON STREET
PORTLAND, OR 97205

SOIL CONSERVATION SERVICES,
  FEDERAL BUILDING
901 SUMTER STREET
COLUMBIA, SC 29201

SOIL CONSERVATION SERVICES,
  PARKADE PLAZA SHOPPING
  CENTER
TERRACE LEVEL-POST OFFICE
  BOX 459
COLUMBIA, MO 65201

**SOIL-WATER CONSERVATION, 204
SOILS BUILDING**
UNIVERSITY OF WISCONSIN
MADISON, WI 53706
Professor, Robert Muckenhirn
General Environment: Terrestrial
Specific Interests: Rural
Staff Size: 5 - 9

**TREFETHEN EVERGREEN
IMPROVEMENT ASSOCIATION**
BOARD OF GOVERNORS
PEAKS ISLAND, ME 04108

**VILLAGE IMPROVEMENT
ASSOCIATION**
MUNICIPAL BUILDING
BRUNSWICK, ME 04011
Chairman, Dana Little

**WHITE MOUNTAIN
ENVIRONMENTAL COMMITTEE**
5 SOUTH STATE STREET
CONCORD, NH 03301
Director, Paul Bofinger

**WILDFLOWER PRESERVATION
SOCIETY OF NEW ENGLAND**
HILLSBORO, NH 03244
Director, Annette Cottrell

**WILDFLOWER PRESERVATION
SOCIETY OF NEW ENGLAND**
6 PLEASANT STREET
CAMDEN, ME 04843

WILDLIFE FEDERATION CENTER
BOX 7
MIDDLETOWN, CT 06457
President, Walter Hylwa

**WILDLIFE FEDERATION OF
RHODE ISLAND**
40 BOWEN STREET
PROVIDENCE, RI 02903

**WILDLIFE RESEARCH CENTER OF
DENVER**
FEDERAL CENTER, BUILDING 16
DENVER, CO 80225

Industrial/Commercial

**AUDUBON SOCIETY OF SANTA
CLARA VALLEY**
945 MATADERO
PALO ALTO, CA 94306

CONSERVATION TRUST OF ESSEX
ESSEX, MA 01929
President, Peter Winslow

**ECOLOGY, AGROMETEOROLOGY,
DEPARTMENT OF TECHNOLOGY
OPERATIONS**
2500 HARBOR BOULEVARD
FULLERTON, CA 92634
Director, Paul Chase

**ENVIRONMENTAL SANITATION
AND HEALTH**
234 CHERRY STREET
SALINAS, CA 93901
Director, Walter Wong

**NATURAL SCIENCE MUSEUM OF
ARGENTINA**
ANGEL GALLARDO 470
BUENOS AIRES, ARGENTINA
Director, M Biraben
General Environment: Oceanographic

PLANT PROTECTION LIMITED
FERNHURST, HASLEMERE
SURREY, ENGLAND
Director, Dr Joseph Stubbs
General Environment: Terrestrial
Specific Interests: Urban
Staff Size: 1 - 4

PRIVATE RESEARCH
21-22 GREAT CASTLE STREET
LONDON W1, ENGLAND
Staff Size: 5 - 9

**RESEARCH DEPARTMENT, ICI
PLANT PROTECTION LIMITED**
YALDING
KENT, ENGLAND
Manager, Michael G Ashley
Specific Interests: Prairie and Temperate
Forest

**SCIENTIFIC RESOURCES
CORPORATION**
MONTGOMERYVILLE, PA 18936
Director, Charles Sackett

Professional Organizations

**AQUATIC INCORPORATED
CONSULTANTS**
1025 AIRPORT DRIVE
SOUTH BURLINGTON, VT 05401
President, George W Starbuck
Staff Size: 10 - 49

**BOTANICAL CLUB OF MICHIGAN,
INCORPORATED**
1800 DIXBORO ROAD
ANN ARBOR, MI 48105
President, Warren H Wagner, Jr
Specific Interests: Prairie and Temperate
Forest
Staff Size: 500 - 999

**CITIZENS COMMITTEE NATURAL
RESOURCE**
1346 CONNECTICUT AVENUE, NW
WASHINGTON, DC 20036

**CONSERVANCY OF GEORGIA,
INCORPORATED**
127 PEACHTREE STREET, NE
ATLANTA, GA 30303
President, Norman C Smith
Specific Interests: Prairie and Temperate
Forest
Staff Size: 1000 - 4999

**CONSERVANCY OF WESTERN
PENNSYLVANIA**
204 FIFTH AVENUE
PITTSBURGH, PA 15222
President, Joshua C Whetzel, Jr
Specific Interests: Prairie and Temperate
Forest
Staff Size: 10 - 49

**CONSERVATION COMMISSION OF
MASSACHUSETTS COUNCIL**
ROBIN FARM
BELCHERTOWN, MA 01007

**CONSERVATION COMMISSION OF
UPPER MISSISSIPPI RIVER**
322 FEDERAL BUILDING
DAVENPORT, IA 52801
Chairman, Jerry Kuehn
Specific Interests: Prairie and Temperate
Forest

**CONSERVATION COMMISSION,
INTERNATIONAL ASSOCIATION
FOR GAME**
1709 NEW YORK AVENUE, 3RD
FLOOR SUITE
WASHINGTON, DC 20006
Staff Size: 1 - 4

**CONSERVATION CONGRESS OF
OHIO**
6284 AUDREY, SW
CANTON, OH 44706
President, Cecil S Winters
Specific Interests: Prairie and Temperate
Forest
Staff Size: 1000 - 4999

**CONSERVATION COUNCIL FOR
HAWAII**
POST OFFICE BOX 2923
HONOLULU, HI 96802
President, Scott D Hamilton, Jr
Specific Interests: Prairie and Temperate
Forest

**CONSERVATION COUNCIL OF
ARIZONA**
POST OFFICE BOX 1771
SCOTTSDALE, AZ 85252

**CONSERVATION COUNCIL OF
MASSACHUSETTS**
1833 MASSACHUSETTS AVENUE
CAMBRIDGE, MA 02109

President, Roger Marshall
Specific Interests: Prairie and Temperate Forest

CONSERVATION COUNCIL OF MONTANA, INCORPORATED
BOX 175
MISSOULA, MT 59801
President, Don M Drummond
Specific Interests: Prairie and Temperate Forest

CONSERVATION COUNCIL OF NORTH CASCADES
POST OFFICE BOX 156, UNIVERSITY STATION
SEATTLE, WA 98501
President, Patrick D Goldsworthy
Specific Interests: Prairie and Temperate Forest
Staff Size: 1000 - 4999

CONSERVATION COUNCIL OF NORTHERN VIRGINIA
POST OFFICE BOX 304
ANNANDALE, VA 22003
President, W Woodworth
Specific Interests: Prairie and Temperate Forest
Staff Size: 100 - 499

CONSERVATION COUNCIL OF TEXAS
730 EAST FRIAR TUCK LANE
HOUSTON, TX 77024
Secretary, Mrs V Emmott
Specific Interests: Prairie and Temperate Forest

CONSERVATION OF NATURE AND NATURAL RESOURCES UNION
MORGES, SWITZERLAND
Staff Size: 10 - 49

CONSERVATION OF NATURE INTERNATIONAL UNION
1110 MORGES
BERN, SWITZERLAND
Secretary-General, E J H Berwick

CONSERVATION ROUNDUP OF FONTANA
FONTANA DAM, NC 28733
Executive Commission Chairman, Forrest V Durand 6180
Specific Interests: Prairie and Temperate Forest

CONSERVATION SOCIETY OF VIRGIN ISLANDS
BOX 750
ST THOMAS, VI 00801
President, Edward L Towle
Specific Interests: Tropical (hot)

DUCKS UNLIMITED
POST OFFICE BOX 66300
CHICAGO, IL 60666
Director, Dale E Whitesell
General Environment: Marsh/Swamp
Staff Size: 10 - 49

ECOLOGY ACTION
POST OFFICE BOX 9334
BERKELEY, CA 94709
President, Cliff Humphrey
Specific Interests: Prairie and Temperate Forest

ECOLOGY CENTER FOUNDATION
POST OFFICE BOX 1100
BERKELEY, CA 94701
Director, Mr Ray Balter

ECOS
POST OFFICE BOX 1055
CHAPEL HILL, NC 27514
Specific Interests: Prairie and Temperate Forest

ENCINO MEDICAL PLAZA
NORTHEAST
ALBUQUERQUE, NM 87106
Director, Robert Castillo
Specific Interests: Urban

ENVIRONMENT DEFENDERS OF FLORIDA, INCORPORATED
BOX 12063
GAINESVILLE, FL 32601

ENVIRONMENTAL ACTION
1346 CONNECTICUT AVENUE
WASHINGTON, DC 20036
Director, Dennis Hayes
Specific Interests: Prairie and Temperate Forest

ENVIRONMENTAL DEFENSE FUND, INCORPORATED
POST OFFICE BOX 740
STONY BROOK, NY 11790
Executive Director, Joseph D Hassett
Specific Interests: Prairie and Temperate Forest

ENVIRONMENTAL QUALITY
19 GYPSY TRAIL
WESTON, MA 02193
Chairman, Mrs Robert Haydock, Jr

ENVIRONMENTAL QUALITY, MASSACHUSETTS LEAGUE OF WOMEN VOTERS
120 BOYLSTON STREET
BOSTON, MA 02116
Chairman, Barbara Fegan

ENVIRONMENTAL SOUTH EAST COUNCIL, YUKON BRANCH
POST OFFICE BOX 31278
JACKSONVILLE, FL 32230
Director, Mrs Helen P Bird

FAMILY CAMPERS ASSOCIATION OF NORTH AMERICA
76 STATE STREET, BOX 308
NEWBURYPORT, MA 01950
Specific Interests: Prairie and Temperate Forest

FARMERS UNION (NATIONAL)
1575 SHERMAN STREET
DENVER, CO 80201
President, Tony T Dechant
Specific Interests: Prairie and Temperate Forest

FAUNA PRESERVATION SOCIETY
ZOOLOGICAL SOCIETY OF LONDON
REGENTS PARK, LONDON NW1, ENGLAND
President, the Marquis of Willingdon
Specific Interests: Prairie and Temperate Forest
Staff Size: 1000 - 4999

FISHERIES COUNCIL OF INDO-PACIFIC
FAO REGIONAL OFFICE, MALIWAN MANS, PHRA ATIT ROAD
BANGKOK 2, THAILAND
General Environment: Limnologic
Specific Interests: Tropical (hot)

FISHERIES INSTITUTE OF GULF AND CARIBBEAN
10 RICKENBACKER CAUSEWAY
MIAMI, FL 33149
General Environment: Oceanographic

FOREST AND PARK ASSOCIATION OF MASSACHUSETTS
1 COURT STREET
BOSTON, MA 02109
President, Herbert W Pratt
General Environment: Terrestrial
Specific Interests: Prairie and Temperate Forest

FOREST AND TRAINING ASSOCIATION OF WESTON
263 SOUTH AVENUE
WESTON, MA 02193
President, Hugo Uyterhoeven

FOREST HISTORY SOCIETY
BOX 1581
SANTA CRUZ, CA 95060
General Environment: Terrestrial
Specific Interests: Prairie and Temperate Forest
Staff Size: 500 - 999

FORESTERS SOCIETY, AMERICAN
1010 16TH STREET, NW
WASHINGTON, DC 20036
Director Professional Program, D R Theoe
General Environment: Terrestrial
Specific Interests: Prairie and Temperate Forest
Staff Size: 5 - 9

FORESTRY AND CONSERVATION ASSOCIATION
1326 AMERICAN BANK BUILDING
PORTLAND, OR 97205

President, Lee L White
General Environment: Terrestrial
Specific Interests: Prairie and Temperate
Forest

**FORESTRY ASSOCIATION OF
TENNESSEE**
SEWANEE, TN 37372

President, Charles E Cheston
Specific Interests: Prairie and Temperate
Forest

FORESTRY BUREAU
SOUTH PARKS ROAD
OXFORD, ENGLAND

Director, Christopher Swabey
General Environment: Terrestrial
Specific Interests: Prairie and Temperate
Forest

FRIENDS OF ANIMALS
256 GOODMAN HILL ROAD
SUDBURY, MA 01776

Director, Mrs Rex Trailer

**GARDEN CLUB FEDERATION OF
MASSACHUSETTS**
300 MASSACHUSETTS AVENUE
BOSTON, MA 02115

President, Miss Odoherty

GARDEN CLUB OF AMERICA
598 MADISON AVENUE
NEW YORK, NY 10022

President, Mrs Fredrick C Tanner
Specific Interests: Prairie and Temperate
Forest

GARDEN CLUB OF FRAMINGTON
25 LONGVIEW ROAD
FRAMINGTON, MA 01701

HARMONY
872 MASSACHUSSETTS AVENUE
CAMBRIDGE, MA 02139

**HORTICULTURAL SOCIETY OF
MASSACHUSETTS**
300 MASSACHUSETTS AVENUE
BOSTON, MA 02115

Executive Director, C B Lees
Staff Size: 10 - 49

**INTERCOLLEGIATE OUTING CLUB
ASSOCIATION**
310 NORTH 37TH STREET
PHILADELPHIA, PA 19104

Conservation Chairman, Cindy Barrett
Specific Interests: Prairie and Temperate
Forest

**JN DING DARLING FOUNDATION,
INCORPORATED**
C/O CENTRAL NATIONAL BANK
AND TRUST
DES MOINES, IA 50304

Chairman, Sherry R Fisher
Specific Interests: Prairie and Temperate
Forest

JONES RIVER VILLAGE CLUB
GROVE STREET
KINGSTON, MA 02364

Chairman, Samuel Babbitt
Staff Size: 10 - 49

**JUNIOR WOMENS CLUBS OF
HARWICK**
BOX 372
SOUTH HARWICK, MA 02661

President, Mrs R E Gomes

**KEEP AMERICA BEAUTIFUL,
INCORPORATED**
99 PARK AVENUE
NEW YORK, NY 10016

Executive Vice President, Roger W
Powers
Specific Interests: Prairie and Temperate
Forest
Staff Size: 10 - 49

KEEP OIL OUT
BOX 3721
PORTLAND, ME 04104

Director, Lee Eden

LAKE HIAWATHA ASSOCIATION
LAKE SHORE DRIVE
BELLINGHAM, MA 02019

President, Gerard Marcott

LEAGUE WOMEN VOTERS
73 BARBER ROAD
FRAMINGHAM, MA 01701

President, Marsha Rosenburg

LIFE SUPPORT GROUP
P O BOX 328
SUDBURY, MA 01776

**MARTHAS VINYARD CONCERNED
CITIZENS**
BOX 719
OAKS BLUFF, MA 02557

President, Tom Britt

**MERCK FOREST FOUNDATION,
INCORPORATED**
POST OFFICE BOX 485
MANCHESTER, VT 05254

Director, Hugh T Putnam, Jr
General Environment: Terrestrial
Specific Interests: Prairie and Temperate
Forest

**METROBOSTON CITIZENS
COALITION FOR CLEAN AIR**
131 CLARENDON STREET
BOSTON, MA 02116

Chairman, Paul Brountas
General Environment: Atmospheric
Specific Interests: Prairie and Temperate
Forest

MOUNTAINEERING LAND TRUST
19 CONGRESS STREET
BOSTON, MA 02109

Trustee, D Dawson
General Environment: Terrestrial
Specific Interests: Mountainous

**NATURAL AREAS COUNCIL OF
MICHIGAN**
1800 NORTH DIXBORO ROAD
ANN ARBOR, MI 48105

Specific Interests: Prairie and Temperate
Forest
Staff Size: 100 - 499

**NATURAL RESOURCE CENTER OF
NEW ENGLAND**
506 STATLER BUILDING
BOSTON, MA 02116

Director, Dr Charles H W Foster
Specific Interests: Prairie and Temperate
Forest

**NATURAL RESOURCE COUNCIL OF
MICHIGAN**
MASON BUILDING, DEPARTMENT
OF NATURAL RESOURCES
LANSING, MI 48926

Chairman, Norman F Billings
Specific Interests: Prairie and Temperate
Forest

**NATURAL RESOURCES
CONSERVATION ASSOCIATION
OF VERMONT**
CHESTER DEPOT, VT 05144

President, Lloyd Jewett
Specific Interests: Prairie and Temperate
Forest

**NATURAL RESOURCES COUNCIL
OF ILLINOIS**
ROUTE 2
JOLIET, IL 60431

Chairman, George H Woodruff
Specific Interests: Prairie and Temperate
Forest

**NATURAL RESOURCES COUNCIL
OF NEW HAMPSHIRE**
5 SOUTH STATE STREET
CONCORD, NH 03301

Chairman, Radcliff Pike
Specific Interests: Prairie and Temperate
Forest

**NATURE STUDY SOCIETY OF
AMERICA**
MILEWOOD ROAD
VERBANK, NY 12585

Secretary, Jane Geisler
Specific Interests: Prairie and Temperate
Forest
Staff Size: 500 - 999

**NORTHEASTERN FISHERIES
COMMISSION**
EAST BLOCK
LONDON, SW7, ENGLAND

General Environment: Oceanographic

OPERATION ROADBLOCK
HIGHLAND STREET
SOUTH EASTON, MA 02375
Chairman, Duncan Oliver

ORNITHOLOGICAL SOCIETY OF KANSAS
ST MARY OF PLAINS COLLEGE
DODGE CITY, KS 67801
Secretary, Mrs R Challans
Specific Interests: Prairie and Temperate Forest
Staff Size: 100 - 499

PLANNING AND CONSERVATION LEAGUE
909 12TH STREET
SACRAMENTO, CA 95814

PRESERVATION SOCIETY-BIRDS OF PREY
BOX 293
PACIFIC PALISADES, CA 90272
President, J Richard Hilton

PRESERVATION TRUST OF VAUGINS ISLAND
KENNEBUNK, ME 04046
President, Sterling Dow

PRESERVE BODEGA ASSOCIATION OF NORTHERN CALIFORNIA
HEAD AND HARBOR 341 MARKET STREET
SAN FRANCISCO, CA 94105
Secretary, David E Personnen
General Environment: Oceanographic
Specific Interests: Prairie and Temperate Forest

RANGE MANAGEMENT SOCIETY
2120 SOUTH BIRCH STREET
DENVER, CO 80222
General Environment: Terrestrial
Staff Size: 1 - 4

RESOURCES CONSERVATION COUNCIL OF WISCONSIN
BOX 707
MELLEN, WI 54546
President, Mrs G H Mccormick
Specific Interests: Prairie and Temperate Forest

ROADSIDE COUNCIL OF MASSACHUSETTS
66 NORTH STREET
LEXINGTON, MA 02173
Chairman, Mrs Ralph Davis
General Environment: Terrestrial
Specific Interests: Prairie and Temperate Forest

SAVE THE DUNES COUNCIL
1512 PARK DRIVE
MUNSTER, IN 46321

Executive Vice President, Sylvia Troy
Specific Interests: Prairie and Temperate Forest
Staff Size: 1000 - 4999

SAVE THE REDWOODS LEAGUE
114 SANSOME STREET, ROOM 605
SAN FRANCISCO, CA 94104
President, Newton B Drury
Specific Interests: Prairie and Temperate Forest

SCENIC RIVERS ASSOCIATION OF TENNESSEE
BOX 3104
NASHVILLE, TN 37219
President, Donald Bodley
General Environment: Limnologic
Specific Interests: Prairie and Temperate Forest
Staff Size: 100 - 499

SCIENTISTS INSTITUTION FOR PUBLIC INFORMATION
30 EAST 68TH STREET
NEW YORK, NY 10021
Specific Interests: Prairie and Temperate Forest

SHORTACRE
MAIN STREET
PETERSHAM, MA 01366

SIERRA CLUB, FRAMINGHAM-NATICK
27 WELLES STREET
FRAMINGHAM, MA 01701
President, Bill Grohs

SIERRA CLUB, LOMA PRIETA CHAPTER
P O BOX 143
MENLO PARK, CA 94025
Director, George Treichel

SOIL CONSERVATION SOCIETY OF AMERICA
7515 NORTH EAST ANKENY ROAD
ANKENY, IA 50021
President, Robert W Wikleberry
General Environment: Terrestrial
Specific Interests: Prairie and Temperate Forest
Staff Size: 1000 & Larger

SPORTSMEN LEAGUE OF KENTUCKY
610 HALBERT STREET
VANCEBURG, KY 41179
President, Reid Love
Specific Interests: Rural
Staff Size: 1 - 4

SPORTSMENS CLUB COUNCIL, INCORPORATED
19 GOULD AVENUE
MALDEN, MA 02148
Director, L Sullivan

SPORTSMENS CLUBS COUNCIL, INCORPORATED
220 NORTH MAIN STREET
ANDOVER, MA 01811
Director, Wilfred Svenson

STUDENT CONSERVATION ASSOCIATION
OLYMPIC VIEW DRIVE, ROUTE 1, BOX 573A
VASHON, WA 98070
Staff Size: 5 - 9

THEORETICAL AND APPLIED LIMNOLOGY ASSOCIATION (INTERNATIONAL)
KELLOGG BIOLOGICAL STATION, MICHIGAN STATE UNIVERSITY
HICKORY CORNERS, MI 49060
General Environment: Limnologic
Staff Size: 1000 - 4999

TRAILFINDERS, INCORPORATED
BOX 716
BANNING, CA 92220
President, Harry C James
Specific Interests: Prairie and Temperate Forest

TROUT UNLIMITED
5840 EAST JEWELL AVENUE
DENVER, CO 80222
President, Elliott Donnelley
General Environment: Limnologic
Specific Interests: Prairie and Temperate Forest

UNESCO
PLACE DE FONTENOY
75 PARIS, 7E, FRANCE

WILDERNESS PLANNING OF TENNESSEE CITIZENS
130 TABOR ROAD
OAK RIDGE, TN 37830
President, William L Russell
Specific Interests: Prairie and Temperate Forest

WILDLIFE FEDERATION NATIONAL ENDOWMENT
1412 16TH STREET, NW
WASHINGTON, DC 20036

WILDLIFE PROTECTION COUNCIL OF TEXAS
3132 LOVERS LANE
DALLAS, TX 75225
Secretary, Mrs Robert L Johnson
Specific Interests: Prairie and Temperate Forest
Staff Size: 100 - 499

WILDLIFE SOCIETY
SUITE S-176, 3900 WISCONSIN AVENUE
WASHINGTON, DC 20016

Specific Interests: Prairie and Temperate
Forest
Staff Size: 5000 - 9999

WOMEN VOTERS LEAGUE OF MASSACHUSETTS
120 BOYLSTON STREET
BOSTON, MA 02116
President, Mrs Norman Jacobsen

WOMENS CLUBS FEDERATION OF MASSACHUSETTS
115 NEWBURY STREET
BOSTON, MA 02116
President, M W Ross

YOUTH CONFERENCE ON NATURAL BEAUTY AND CONSERVATION, NATIONAL
C/O GIRL SCOUTS OF US, 830
THIRD AVENUE
NEW YORK, NY 10022
Specific Interests: Prairie and Temperate
Forest

Research Institute

BIOTOXICOLOGY INTERNATIONAL CENTER
WORLD LIFE RESEARCH
INSTITUTE
COLTON, CA 92324

BOTANY DEPARTMENT, INTERNATIONAL ASSOCIATION OF ECOLOGY
IMPERIAL COLLEGE
LONDON SW7, ENGLAND

CHESAPEAKE BAY INSTITUTION, JOHNS HOPKINS UNIVERSITY
CHARLES AND 34TH STREETS
BALTIMORE, MD 21218
Director, Dr Donald W Pritchard
General Environment: Oceanographic
Specific Interests: Prairie and Temperate
Forest

CHILDRENS HOSPITAL OF ST LOUIS
500 SOUTH KINGSHIGHWAY
ST LOUIS, MO 63110
Executive Director, B Perkins
Specific Interests: Urban

CLARKES FARMHOUSE
NORTHMOOR
OXON, ENGLAND
General Environment: Terrestrial
Specific Interests: Prairie and Temperate
Forest

COASTAL ECOLOGY RESEARCH STATION
NATURE CONSERVANCY, COLNEY
NORWICH, NORFOLK, ENGLAND

Director, Derek S Ranwell
Specific Interests: Prairie and Temperate
Forest
Staff Size: 10 - 49

COMMONWEALTH FORESTRY INSTITUTE
SOUTH PARKS ROAD
OXFORD, ENGLAND
General Environment: Terrestrial
Staff Size: 10 - 49

CONSERVATION COORDINATION COUNCIL OF NEW MEXICO
POST OFFICE BOX 142
ALBUQUERQUE, NM 87103
Specific Interests: Desert

DANUBE COMMISSION
BENCZUR UTCA 25
BUDAPEST VI, HUNGARY

EASTERN DECIDUOUS FOREST BIOME
OAK RIDGE NATIONAL
LABORATORY
OAK RIDGE, TN 37830
Director, Dr S I Averbach
General Environment: Terrestrial
Specific Interests: Prairie and Temperate
Forest
Staff Size: 100 - 499

ECOLOGY AND CONSERVATION
AUDUBON CANYON RANCH
STINSON BEACH, CA 94970
Director, Robert Reinhardt

ECOLOGY SOCIETY, BIOLOGY DEPARTMENT, TOHOKU UNIVERSITY
KATAHIRA-CHO
SENOAI CITY, MIYAGI, JAPAN
Director, Dr Denzaburo Miyaji
Specific Interests: Prairie and Temperate
Forest

ENVIRONMENTAL COUNCIL, NORTHERN
601 CHRISTIE BUILDING
DULUTH, MN 55802
Staff Size: 1 - 4

ENVIRONMENTAL HEALTH SCIENCES TRAINING COMMISSION
NATIONAL INSTITUTES OF HEALTH
BETHESDA, MD 20014
Executive Secretary, Bessey Otto

ENVIRONMENTAL PLANNING, RHM ASSOCIATES
POST OFFICE BOX 4116
CARMEL, CA 93921
Director, Ralph H Miner

ENVIRONMENTAL RESEARCH CENTER, NATIONAL
RESEARCH TRIANGLE PARK, NC
27709
Specific Interests: Prairie and Temperate
Forest

ENVIRONMENTAL RESEARCH CENTER, NATIONAL
CORVALLIS, OR 97330
Specific Interests: Prairie and Temperate
Forest

ENVIRONMENTAL RESEARCH INSTITUTE
CITADEL ROAD, PL1 3AX
PLYMOUTH, DEVON, ENGLAND
General Environment: Oceanographic
Specific Interests: Prairie and Temperate
Forest
Staff Size: 100 - 499

ENVIRONMENTAL RESEARCH INSTITUTE
BOX 156
MOOSE, WY 83012
Specific Interests: Prairie and Temperate
Forest

ENVIRONMENTAL RESEARCH INSTITUTION
YALE UNIVERSITY
NEW HAVEN, CT 06520
Specific Interests: Prairie and Temperate
Forest

ENVIRONMENTAL SCIENCES INSTITUTE
125 SOUTH 7TH STREET
SAN JOSE, CA 95114
Director, Jen-Yu Wang

ENVIRONMENTAL SCIENCES PROGRAM AT WILKES COLLEGE
ENVIRONMENTAL SCIENCES
RESEARCH INSTITUTION
WILKES BARRE, PA 18703
Specific Interests: Prairie and Temperate
Forest

FARMHOUSE
GREEN END, COMBERTON
CAMBRIDGE, ENGLAND
Director, Ronald K Murton
Specific Interests: Prairie and Temperate
Forest

FISHERIES COUNCIL OF THE MEDITERRANEAN
VIA DELLE TERME CARACALA
ROME, ITALY
General Environment: Oceanographic

FISHERIES OF NORTHWEST ATLANTIC, INTERNATIONAL COMMISSION

POST OFFICE BOX 638
DARTMOUTH, NOVA SCOTIA,
  CANADA
Staff Size: 5 - 9

FORESTRY RESEARCH INSTITUTE
KING'S BUILDINGS, MAYFIELD
  ROAD
EDINBURGH EH9 3JU, SCOTLAND
General Environment: Terrestrial
Specific Interests: Prairie and Temperate
  Forest

**FRESHWATER BIOLOGICAL
  ASSOCIATION**
RIVER LABORATORY, EAST STOKE
WAREHAM, PORSET, ENGLAND
General Environment: Limnologic
Specific Interests: Prairie and Temperate
  Forest
Staff Size: 10 - 49

**GEOLOGICAL SURVEY OF
  DENMARK**
PALAEOBOT DEPARTMENT
  THORAVEJ 3L
DK-2400 COPENHAGEN, DENMARK
State Geologist, Svend Anderson
Specific Interests: Prairie and Temperate
  Forest
Staff Size: 5 - 9

**INTERNATIONAL COUNCIL FOR
  THE EXPLORATION OF THE SEAS**
CHARLOTTENLUND SLOT
2920 CHARLOTTENLUND,
  DENMARK
General Environment: Oceanographic

**INTERNATIONAL OFFICE
  EPIZOOTICS**
12, RUE DE PRONY
PARIS 7, FRANCE

JOHN INNES INSTITUTE
COLNEY LANE
NORWICH, ENGLAND
Director, Norman Sunderland
General Environment: Terrestrial
Specific Interests: Prairie and Temperate
  Forest

LABORATORY AT PLYMOUTH
CITADEL HILL
PLYMOUTH, DEVON, ENGLAND
Director, James E Smith
General Environment: Oceanographic
Staff Size: 100 - 499

LIMNOLOGY INSTITUTE
UNIVERSITY OF LUND
S-220 03 LUND, SWEDEN
Professor, Sven Bjork
General Environment: Limnologic
Staff Size: 10 - 49

LITTORAL SOCIETY OF AMERICA
SANDY HOOK
HIGHLANDS, NJ 07732
General Environment: Estuarine

MARINE BIOLOGY STATION
UNIVERSITY OF BERGEN
N-5065 BLOMSTERDALEN, NORWAY
General Environment: Oceanographic
Specific Interests: Polar (cold)
Staff Size: 10 - 49

**MARINE ENVIRONMENTAL
  RESEARCH INSTITUTE**
CRAIGHALL ROAD
EDINBURGH EH6 4RQ, SCOTLAND
General Environment: Oceanographic
Specific Interests: Prairie and Temperate
  Forest
Staff Size: 100 - 499

MARINE FISHERIES SERVICE
WASHINGTON, DC 20240
General Environment: Oceanographic

**MARINE RESOURCES
  LABORATORY, DUNSTAFFNAGE**
POST OFFICE BOX 3
OBAN, ARGYLL, SCOTLAND
Director, Ronald I Currie
General Environment: Oceanographic
Staff Size: 50 - 99

MAURITIUS INSTITUTE
BP 54
PORT LOUIS, MAURITIUS
Director, C Michel
General Environment: Oceanographic
Staff Size: 1 - 4

NATURAL RESOURCE
COLORADO STATE UNIVERSITY
FORT COLLINS, CO 80521
Director, Dr George M Van Dyne
Specific Interests: Prairie and Temperate
  Forest
Staff Size: 50 - 99

**NATURAL RESOURCE COUNCIL OF
  MAINE**
20 WILLOW STREET
AUGUSTA, ME 04330
Executive Secretary, M F Burk
Staff Size: 1 - 4

NATURE CONSERVANCY
MERLEWOOD RESEARCH STATION
GRANGE-OVER-SANDS,
  LANCASTER, ENGLAND
Director, John N R Jeffers
General Environment: Terrestrial
Specific Interests: Prairie and Temperate
  Forest
Staff Size: 50 - 99

NATURE CONSERVANCY
19-20 BELGRAVE SQUARE
LONDON SW1, ENGLAND
Director, John F D Frazer
Specific Interests: Prairie and Temperate
  Forest

NATURE CONSERVANCY
PENRHOS ROAD
BANGOR, WALES
Director, Robert E Hughes
General Environment: Terrestrial
Specific Interests: Prairie and Temperate
  Forest

**NATURE PROTECTION RESEARCH
  CENTER**
KOPERNIKA 27
KRAKOW, POLAND
Director, Wladyslaw Szafer
Specific Interests: Prairie and Temperate
  Forest

**NATURE TRAINING SCHOOL,
  WORCESTER SCIENCE MUSEUM**
21 CEDAR STREET
WORCESTER, MA 01609
Director, R Stanhope

**NORMANDEAU ASSOCIATION,
  INCORPORATED**
686 MAST ROAD
MANCHESTER, NH 03102
Administration Assistant, John-Robert
  Curtin
General Environment: Oceanographic

**NUCLEAR SAFETY INFORMATION
  CENTER**
OAK RIDGE NATIONAL LIBRARY,
  POST OFFICE BOX Y
OAK RIDGE, TN 37830
Director, William B Cottrell
Staff Size: 50 - 99

OCEANOGRAPHY DEPARTMENT
FLORIDA STATE UNIVERSITY
TALLAHASSEE, FL 32306
General Environment: Oceanographic
Specific Interests: Prairie and Temperate
  Forest

**OVERSEAS PESTICIDE RESEARCH
  CENTER**
COLLEGE HOUSE, WRIGHTS LANE
LONDON W8, ENGLAND
Director, John Perfect
General Environment: Terrestrial
Specific Interests: Tropical (hot)
Staff Size: 5 - 9

**PHYSICAL PLANNING AND
  CONSTRUCTION RESOURCES,
  NATIONAL INSTITUTE**
ST MARTIN'S WATERLOO ROAD
DUBLIN 4, IRELAND
Specific Interests: Prairie and Temperate
  Forest

**PLANT GEOGRAPHY
  INTERNATIONAL SOCIETY**
3261 TODENMANN UBER RINTEN
BONN, WEST GERMANY

RESEARCH AGENCY
1416 NINTH STREET
SACRAMENTO, CA 95814

RESEARCH CENTER, TATE AND LYLE
KESTON
KENT, ENGLAND
Director, Brian Orchard
General Environment: Terrestrial
Specific Interests: Prairie and Temperate Forest

RESEARCH INSTITUTE
16 RUE DE BUFFON
PARIS, FRANCE
Professor, Andre Aubreville
General Environment: Terrestrial
Specific Interests: Tropical (hot)

RESEARCH INSTITUTE, ROWETT
BUCKSBURN
ABERDEEN, SCOTLAND
Director, Jean M Eadie
Specific Interests: Prairie and Temperate Forest

RESEARCH INSTITUTE, SRF
1500 CECIL COOK PLACE, PO BOX 580
GOLETA, CA 93017
President, Sidney R Frank

RESEARCH LABORATORY OF GULF COAST
POST OFFICE BOX AG
OCEAN SPRINGS, MS 39564
General Environment: Limnologic
Staff Size: 50 - 99

RESEARCH STATION AT LONG ASHTON
THE UNIVERSITY
BRISTOL, ENGLAND
Director, John P Hudson
General Environment: Terrestrial
Specific Interests: Rural
Staff Size: 50 - 99

RESEARCH STATION OF EAST MALLING
MAIDSTONE
KENT, ENGLAND
Director, Anne V Delap
General Environment: Terrestrial
Specific Interests: Prairie and Temperate Forest
Staff Size: 100 - 499

SCIENTIFIC EXPLORATION OF THE MEDITERRANEAN, INTERNATIONAL COMMISSION
16 BUILDING DE SUISSE
MONTE CARLO, MONACO
General Environment: Oceanographic

SOIL RESEARCH INSTITUTE, MACAULAY
CRAIGIEBUCKLER
ABERDEEN, SCOTLAND

Director, Sydney E Durno
General Environment: Terrestrial
Specific Interests: Prairie and Temperate Forest
Staff Size: 100 - 499

SOIL SCIENCE INTERNATIONAL SOCIETY, ROYAL TROPICAL INSTITUTE
63 MAURITSKADE
AMSTERDAM, NETHERLANDS
General Environment: Terrestrial

TRAINING AND RESEARCH INSTITUTE OF THE UNITED NATIONS
801 UNITED NATIONS PLAZA
NEW YORK, NY 10017

WILDLIFE RESEARCH COOPERATIVE OF COLORADO
COLORADO STATE UNIVERSITY, FORESTRY BUILDING
FORT COLLINS, CO 80521
Director, Dr Fred Glover
General Environment: Terrestrial
Specific Interests: Prairie and Temperate Forest

WORLD ECOLOGY INSTITUTE
P O BOX 4116
CARMEL, CA 93940
President, Ralph Miner

Chemistry

GENERAL

Educational Institute

**AGRONOMY INSTITUTE,
UNIVERSITY OF LOUVAIN**
72 AVENUE CARDINAL MERCIER
HEVERLE-LOUVAIN, BELGIUM
Professor, J J Fripiat
Specific Interests: Prairie and Temperate
Forest

**ANALYTICAL CHEMISTRY
LABORATORY**
NEIUWE ACHTERGRACHT 125
AMSTERDAM-C, NETHERLANDS
Specific Interests: Prairie and Temperate
Forest

CHEMICAL OCEANOGRAPHY
SAN JOSE STATE COLLEGE
SAN JOSE, CA 95114
Associate Professor, Arthur Stump
General Environment: Oceanographic

CHEMISTRY DEPARTMENT
UNIVERSITY OF ILLINOIS
CHICAGO, IL 60601

CHEMISTRY DEPARTMENT
RENSSELAER POLYTECHNIC
INSTITUTE
TROY, NY 12181
Professor, Herbert Clark

CHEMISTRY DEPARTMENT
MOSCOW UNIVERSITY
MOSCOW, UNION OF SOVIET
SOCIALIST REPUBLICS
Specific Interests: Polar (cold)

CHEMISTRY DEPARTMENT
OKLAHOMA CITY UNIVERSITY
OKLAHOMA CITY, OK 73106

CHEMISTRY DEPARTMENT
MASSACHUSETTS INSTITUTE OF
TECHNOLOGY
CAMBRIDGE, MA 02101

CHEMISTRY DEPARTMENT
WASHINGTON STATE UNIVERSITY
PULLMAN, WA 99163
Specific Interests: Prairie and Temperate
Forest

CHEMISTRY DEPARTMENT
UNIVERSITY OF CALIFORNIA
BERKELEY, CA 94701

CHEMISTRY DEPARTMENT
SAN JOSE STATE COLLEGE
SAN JOSE, CA 95114
Instructor of Chemistry, Sami Ibrahim

CHEMISTRY DEPARTMENT
UNIVERSITY OF CALIFORNIA
RIVERSIDE, CA 92502
Professor, James Pitts
General Environment: Atmospheric

CHEMISTRY DEPARTMENT
GLAMORGAN COLLEGE OF
TECHNOLOGY
TREFOREST, GLAMORGAN, WALES
Director, Leo H Thomas
Specific Interests: Prairie and Temperate
Forest

CHEMISTRY DEPARTMENT
KIEV UNIVERSITY
KIEV, UKRAINE, UNION OF SOVIET
SOCIALIST REPUBLICS
Specific Interests: Polar (cold)

CHEMISTRY DEPARTMENT
BROWN UNIVERSITY
PROVIDENCE, RI 02912
Professor, Harold R Ward
General Environment: Atmospheric
Specific Interests: Urban
Staff Size: 5 - 9

CHEMISTRY DEPARTMENT
UNIVERSITY OF CALIFORNIA
LA JOLLA, CA 92037

CHEMISTRY DEPARTMENT
UNIVERSITY COLLEGE OF WALES
ABERYSTWYTH, WALES
Specific Interests: Prairie and Temperate
Forest

**CHEMISTRY DEPARTMENT,
UNIVERSITY OF HARTFORD**
200 BLOOMFIELD AVENUE
WEST HARTFORD, CT 06107
Coordinator, T W Sharpless
Specific Interests: Urban
Staff Size: 5 - 9

**CHERKASSY PEDAGOGICAL
INSTITUTE**
ULITSA KARLA MARKSA 24
CHERKASSY, UNION OF SOVIET
SOCIALIST REPUBLICS
Director, T Tkanko
Staff Size: 5 - 9

**DYNAMIC AND MESO-
METEOROLOGY, DEPARTMENT
OF CHEMISTRY**
UNIVERSITY OF ARKANSAS
FAYETTEVILLE, AR 72701
Director, Tan Sun Chen

**ENVIRONMENTAL ADVISORY
PANEL AT COLGATE**
COLGATE UNIVERSITY
HAMILTON, NY 13346
Chairman, Dr Lawrence Przekop
Staff Size: 5 - 9

**ENVIRONMENTAL HEALTH
ENGINEERING**
CALIFORNIA INSTITUTE OF
TECHNOLOGY
PASADENA, CA 91109
Professor, James Morgan
General Environment: Limnologic
Staff Size: 5 - 9

**ENVIRONMENTAL SCIENCE
PROGRAM**
STATE UNIVERSITY COLLEGE
CORTLAND, NY 13045

**ENVIRONMENTAL SCIENCE
PROGRAM**
UNIVERSITY OF THE PACIFIC
STOCKTON, CA 95204
Academy Vice-President, Alistar Mccrone

**ENVIRONMENTAL SCIENCE
PROGRAM**
NEW MEXICO INSTITUTE OF
MINING AND TECHNOLOGY
SOCORRO, NM 87801

**ENVIRONMENTAL SCIENCE
PROGRAM**
CLARK UNIVERSITY
WORCESTER, MA 01610

**ENVIRONMENTAL SCIENCE
PROGRAM**
BRANDEIS UNIVERSTIY
WALTHAM, MA 02154

**ENVIRONMENTAL SCIENCE
PROGRAM**
LAWRENCE UNIVERSITY
APPLETON, WI 54911

**ENVIRONMENTAL SCIENCE
PROGRAM**
MURRAY STATE COLLEGE
MURRAY, KY 42071

ENVIRONMENTAL SCIENCE
PROGRAM
COLORADO COLLEGE
COLORADO SPRINGS, CO 80903

ENVIRONMENTAL SCIENCE
PROGRAM
WISCONSIN STATE UNIVERSITY -
STEVENS POINT
STEVENS POINT, WI 54481

ENVIRONMENTAL SCIENCE
PROGRAM
HAVERFORD COLLEGE
HAVERFORD, PA 19041

ENVIRONMENTAL SCIENCE
PROGRAM
BRYN MAWR COLLEGE
BRYN MAWR, PA 19010

ENVIRONMENTAL SCIENCE
PROGRAM
AMHERST COLLEGE
AMHERST, MA 01002

ENVIRONMENTAL SCIENCE
PROGRAM
INDIANA STATE UNIVERSITY
TERRE HAUTE, IN 47809

ENVIRONMENTAL SCIENCE
PROGRAM
UNIVERSITY OF CALIFORNIA
RIVERSIDE, CA 92502

ENVIRONMENTAL SCIENCE
PROGRAM
DEPAUW UNIVERSITY
GREENCASTLE, IN 46135

ENVIRONMENTAL SCIENCE
PROGRAM
UNIVERSITY OF EVANSVILLE
EVANSVILLE, IN 47704
Staff Size: 1 - 4

ENVIRONMENTAL SCIENCE
PROGRAM
KALAMAZOO COLLEGE
KALAMAZOO, MI 49001

ENVIRONMENTAL SCIENCE
PROGRAM
STATE UNIVERSITY OF NEW YORK
AT BINGHAMTON
BINGHAMTON, NY 13901

ENVIRONMENTAL SCIENCE
PROGRAM
RIDER COLLEGE
TRENTON, NJ 08602

ENVIRONMENTAL SCIENCE
PROGRAM
WELLS COLLEGE
AURORA, NY 13026

ENVIRONMENTAL SCIENCE
PROGRAM
STATE UNIVERSITY COLLEGE
OSWEGO, NY 13126

ENVIRONMENTAL SCIENCE
PROGRAM
MACALESTER COLLEGE
ST PAUL, MN 55101

ENVIRONMENTAL SCIENCE
PROGRAM
VASSAR COLLEGE
POUGHKEEPSIE, NY 12601

ENVIRONMENTAL SCIENCE
PROGRAM
LONG ISLAND UNIVERSITY
GREENVALE, NY 11548

ENVIRONMENTAL SCIENCE
PROGRAM
THIEL COLLEGE
GREENVILLE, PA 16125

ENVIRONMENTAL SCIENCE
PROGRAM
UNIVERSITY OF SCRANTON
SCRANTON, PA 18510

ENVIRONMENTAL SCIENCE
PROGRAM
PROVIDENCE COLLEGE
PROVIDENCE, RI 02918

ENVIRONMENTAL SCIENCE
PROGRAM
WESTMINSTER COLLEGE
NEW WILMINGTON, PA 16142

ENVIRONMENTAL SCIENCE
PROGRAM
WILLIAMS COLLEGE
WILLIAMSTOWN, MA 01267

ENVIRONMENTAL SCIENCE
PROGRAM
OHIO WESLEYAN UNIVERSITY
DELAWARE, OH 43015

ENVIRONMENTAL SCIENCE
PROGRAM
WELLESLEY COLLEGE
WELLESLEY, MA 02181

ENVIRONMENTAL SCIENCE
PROGRAM
WILLIAMETTE UNIVERSITY
SALEM, OR 97301

ENVIRONMENTAL SCIENCE
PROGRAM
COLLEGE OF THE HOLY CROSS
WORCESTER, MA 01610

ENVIRONMENTAL SCIENCE
PROGRAM
FISK UNIVERSITY
NASHVILLE, TN 37203

ENVIRONMENTAL SCIENCE
PROGRAM
BAYLOR UNIVERSITY
WACO, TX 76703

ENVIRONMENTAL SCIENCE
PROGRAM
TRINITY UNIVERSITY
SAN ANTONIO, TX 78212

ENVIRONMENTAL SCIENCE
PROGRAM
NORTH TEXAS STATE UNIVERSITY
DENTON, TX 76203

ENVIRONMENTAL SCIENCES
GROUP, ST JOSEPH'S COLLEGE
54TH AND CITY LINE AVENUE
PHILADELPHIA, PA 19131

ENVIRONMENTAL SCIENCES
GROUP, STATE UNIVERSITY
COLLEGE
1300 ELMWOOD AVENUE
BUFFALO, NY 14222

ENVIRONMENTAL SCIENCES
PROGRAM
TRINITY COLLEGE
HARTFORD, CT 06106

ENVIRONMENTAL SCIENCES
PROGRAM
AUGUSTANA COLLEGE
ROCK ISLAND, IL 61201

ENVIRONMENTAL SCIENCES
PROGRAM
2130 FULTON STREET
SAN FRANCISCO, CA 94117

ENVIRONMENTAL SCIENCES
PROGRAM, SAN FRANCISCO
STATE COLLEGE
1600 HOLLOWAY AVENUE
SAN FRANCISCO, CA 94132

ENVIRONMENTAL STUDIES
LOUISIANA STATE UNIVERSITY
BATON ROUGE, LA 70803
Professor of Chemistry, Philip West

ENVIRONMENTAL STUDIES
CENTER, QUEENS COLLEGE
65-30 KISSENA BOULEVARD
FLUSHING, NY 11367

ENVIRONMENTAL STUDIES
CENTER, XAVIER UNIVERSITY
DANA AVENUE AND VICTORIA
PARKWAY
CINCINNATI, OH 45207

ENVIRONMENTAL STUDIES
    GROUP, IMMACULATE HEART
    COLLEGE
2020 NORTH WESTERN AVENUE
LOS ANGELES, CA 90027

ENVIRONMENTAL STUDIES
    GROUP, ROCHESTER INSTITUTE
    OF TECHNOLOGY
1 LOMB DRIVE
ROCHESTER, NY 14623

ENVIRONMENTAL STUDIES
    PROGRAM
COLBY COLLEGE
WATERVILLE, ME 04901

ENVIRONMENTAL STUDIES
    PROGRAM
FURMAN UNIVERSITY
GREENVILLE, SC 29613

ENVIRONMENTAL STUDIES
    PROGRAM
MIDDLEBURY COLLEGE
MIDDLEBURY, VT 05753

ENVIRONMENTAL STUDIES
    PROGRAM
BOWDOIN COLLEGE
BRUNSWICK, ME 04011
President, Roger Howell, Jr

ENVIRONMENTAL STUDIES
    PROGRAM
BATES COLLEGE
LEWISTON, ME 04240

ENVIRONMENTAL STUDIES
    PROGRAM
OBERLIN COLLEGE
OBERLIN, OH 44074

ENVIRONMENTAL STUDIES
    PROGRAM
AUGUSTANA COLLEGE
SIOUX FALLS, SD 57102

ENVIRONMENTAL STUDIES
    PROGRAM
UNIVERSITY OF THE SOUTH
SEWANEE, TN 37375

ENVIRONMENTAL STUDIES
    PROGRAM
MEMPHIS STATE UNIVERSITY
MEMPHIS, TN 38111

ENVIRONMENTAL STUDIES
    PROGRAM
EAST TENNESSEE STATE
    UNIVERSITY
JOHNSON CITY, TN 37601

ENVIRONMENTAL STUDIES
    PROGRAM
NEW MEXICO HIGHLANDS
    UNIVERSITY
LAS VEGAS, NM 87701
President, Thomas C Donnelly

ENVIRONMENTAL STUDIES
    PROGRAM
WHEATON COLLEGE
NORTH, MA 02766
President, William C H Prentice

ENVIRONMENTAL STUDIES
    PROGRAM
ILLINOIS STATE UNIVERSITY
NORMAL, IL 61761
President, David Berlo

ENVIRONMENTAL STUDIES
    PROGRAM
MARSHALL UNIVERSITY
HUNTINGTON, WV 25701

ENVIRONMENTAL STUDIES
    PROGRAM
WILKES COLLEGE
WILKES-BARRE, PA 18703

ENVIRONMENTAL STUDIES
    PROGRAM
PACIFIC LUTHERAN UNIVERSITY
TACOMA, WA 98447

ENVIRONMENTAL STUDIES
    PROGRAM
MOUNT HOLYOKE COLLEGE
SOUTH HADLEY, MA 01075
President, David B Truman

ENVIRONMENTAL STUDIES
    PROGRAM
COLLEGE OF WILLIAM AND MARY
WILLIAMSBURG, VA 23185

ENVIRONMENTAL STUDIES
    PROGRAM
WISCONSIN STATE UNIVERSITY-
    EAU CLAIRE
EAU CLAIRE, WI 54701
Staff Size: 1 - 4

ENVIRONMENTAL STUDIES
    PROGRAM
BELOIT COLLEGE
BELOIT, WI 53511

ENVIRONMENTAL STUDIES
    PROGRAM
SMITH COLLEGE
NORTHAMPTON, MA 01060
President, Thomas C Mendenhall

ENVIRONMENTAL STUDIES
    PROGRAM
FAIRFIELD UNIVERSITY
FAIRFIELD, CT 06430

ENVIRONMENTAL STUDIES
    PROGRAM
UNIVERSITY OF REDLANDS
REDLANDS, CA 92373

ENVIRONMENTAL STUDIES
    PROGRAM
IDAHO STATE UNIVERSITY
POCATELLO, ID 83201

ENVIRONMENTAL STUDIES
    PROGRAM
WESLEYAN UNIVERSITY
MIDDLETOWN, CT 06457

ENVIRONMENTAL STUDIES
    PROGRAM
GOUCHER COLLEGE, TOWSON
BALTIMORE, MD 21204

ENVIRONMENTAL STUDIES
    PROGRAM
EARLHAM COLLEGE
RICHMOND, IN 47374

ENVIRONMENTAL STUDIES
    PROGRAM
UNIVERSITY OF CALIFORNIA, SAN
    DIEGO
LA JOLLA, CA 92037
Chancellor, William D Mcelroy

ENVIRONMENTAL STUDIES
    PROGRAM
WESTERN KENTUCKY UNIVERSITY
BOWLING GREEN, KY 42101

ENVIRONMENTAL STUDIES
    PROGRAM
WILLIAM SMITH COLLEGE
GENEVA, NY 14456

ENVIRONMENTAL STUDIES
    PROGRAM
LOWELL TECHNOLOGY INSTITUTE
LOWELL, MA 01854

ENVIRONMENTAL STUDIES
    PROGRAM
LOUISIANNA STATE UNIVERSITY IN
    NEW ORLEANS
NEW ORLEANS, LA 70122

ENVIRONMENTAL STUDIES
    PROGRAM
HOBART COLLEGE
GENEVA, NY 14456

ENVIRONMENTAL STUDIES
    PROGRAM, GEORGETOWN
    UNIVERSITY
37TH AND O STREETS, SW
WASHINGTON, DC 20007

ENVIRONMENTAL STUDIES
    PROGRAM, HERBERT H LEHMAN
    COLLEGE
BEDFORD PARK BOULEVARD WEST
NEW YORK, NY 10468

ENVIRONMENTAL STUDIES PROGRAM, LA SALLE COLLEGE
OLNEY AVENUE AT 20TH STREET
PHILADELPHIA, PA 19141

ENVIRONMENTAL STUDIES PROGRAM, MORGAN STATE COLLEGE
HILLEN STATE ROAD AND COLD SPRINGS LANE
BALTIMORE, MD 21212

ENVIRONMENTAL STUDIES PROGRAM, OCCIDENTAL COLLEGE
1600 CAMPUS ROAD
LOS ANGELES, CA 90041

ENVIRONMENTAL STUDIES PROGRAM, REED COLLEGE
3203 SOUTH EAST WOODSTOCK BOULEVARD
PORTLAND, OR 97202

ENVIRONMENTAL STUDIES PROGRAM, UNIVERSITY OF PORTLAND
5000 NORTH WILLIAMETTE BOULEVARD
PORTLAND, OR 97203

ENVIRONMENTAL STUDIES PROGRAM, VORONEZH STATE UNIVERSITY
PROSPEKT REVOLYUTSII,24
VORONEZH, UNION OF SOVIET SOCIALIST REPUBLICS
Director, Bi Mikhant-Yev
Staff Size: 10 - 49

ENVIRONMENTAL STUDIES PROGRAM, WAGNER COLLEGE
631 HOWARD AVENUE
STATEN ISLAND, NY 10301

ENVIRONMENTAL STUDIES, BUTLER UNIVERSITY
4600 SUNSET AVENUE
INDIANAPOLIS, IN 46208
President, Alexander E Jones

ENVIRONMENTAL STUDIES, CALIFORNIA POLYTECHNIC STATE UNIVERSITY
SAN LUIS OBISPO, CA 93401
Director, Robert E Kennedy

ENVIRONMENTAL STUDIES, CALIFORNIA STATE POLYTECHNIC COLLEGE
KELLOGG VOORHIS
POMONA, CA 91766

ENVIRONMENTAL STUDIES, CANADA COLLEGE
4200 FARM HILL BOULEVARD
REDWOOD CITY, CA 94061
Instructor of Chemistry, Ross Westover

ENVIRONMENTAL STUDIES, COLLEGE OF ST THOMAS
2115 SUMMIT AVENUE
ST PAUL, MN 55101

EPPLEY INSTITUTE FOR CANCER RESEARCH, UNIVERSITY OF NEBRASKA
42ND AND DEWEY AVENUE
OMAHA, NB 68105
Director, Phillippe Shubik

GEOCHEMICAL AND ANALYTICAL CHEMISTRY INSTITUTE
ACADEMY OF SCIENCES
MOSCOW, UNION OF SOVIET SOCIALIST REPUBLICS
Director, Aleksandr Pavlovich Vinograov
Specific Interests: Polar (cold)

GEOPHYSICS INSTITUTE
UNIVERSITY OF CALIFORNIA
LOS ANGELES, CA 90040

INSTITUTION OF BRENNSTOFFCHEM
RHEIN-WESTF TH AACHEN
BONN, WEST GERMANY
Specific Interests: Prairie and Temperate Forest

NUCLEAR SCIENCES AND ENGINEERING PROGRAM
UNIVERSITY OF CINCINNATI, 121 CHEMISTRY BUILDING
CINCINNATI, OH 45221

OCEANOGRAPHIC INSTITUTE
UNIVERSITY OF GOTEBORG
GOTEBORG, SWEDEN
General Environment: Oceanographic

OCEANOGRAPHY DEPARTMENT
UNIVERSITY OF LIVERPOOL
LIVERPOOL, ENGLAND
General Environment: Oceanographic
Staff Size: 10 - 49

ORGANIC CHEMISTRY INSTITUTE
UNIVERSITY OF NAPLES
NAPLES, ITALY

ORGANIC CHEMISTRY INSTITUTE, KAZAN BRANCH
ACADEMY OF SCIENCES
KAZAN, UNION OF SOVIET SOCIALIST REPUBLICS
Specific Interests: Polar (cold)

ORGANIC CHEMISTRY INSTITUTE, TECHNICAL UNIVERSITY
BERLIN, WEST GERMANY
Director, Ferdinand Bohlmann
Specific Interests: Prairie and Temperate Forest

ORGANIC CHEMISTRY INSTITUTE, UNIVERSITY OF GIESSEN
LUDUIGSTR 21
63 GIESSEN, WEST GERMANY
Director, Fritz Krohnke
Specific Interests: Prairie and Temperate Forest

PHARMACOLOGY DEPARTMENT, OAKDALE TOXICOLOGY CENTER
UNIVERSITY OF IOWA
OAKDALE, IA 52319
Professor, J Fouts

PHARMACOLOGY DEPARTMENT, SCHOOL OF MEDICINE
WASHINGTON UNIVERSITY
ST LOUIS, MO 63110
Associate Professor, R Burton

PHARMACY AND SCIENCE, PACIFIC COLLEGE
43RD AND KINGSESSING AVENUE
PHILADELPHIA, PA 19104

POLYMER SCIENCES SCHOOL
UNIVERSITY OF BRADFORD
BRADFORD, WEST RIDING, ENGLAND
Specific Interests: Prairie and Temperate Forest

PUBLIC HEALTH SCHOOL
UNIVERSITY OF MONTREAL, POST OFFICE BOX 6128
MONTREAL 101, PROVINCE OF QUEBEC, CANADA
General Environment: Atmospheric
Staff Size: 1 - 4

RESEARCH CENTER OF WESTERN NEW YORK
STATE UNIVERSITY OF NEW YORK
BUFFALO, NY 14210

WATER RESOURCES RESEARCH INSTITUTE, UNIVERSITY OF OREGON
114 COVELL HALL
CORVALLIS, OR 97331
General Environment: Oceanographic

Field Station/Laboratory

BIOREX LABORATORIES, RESEARCH DIVISION
198 CITY ROAD
LONDON, EC1, ENGLAND
Director, John C Turner
Specific Interests: Prairie and Temperate Forest

LABORATORIUM POLYMEROV SAV
BRATISLAVA-PATRONKA
DUBRAVSKA CESTA, CZECHOSLOVAKIA

ORGANIC CHEMISTRY LABORATORY
UNIVERSITY OF GHENT
GHENT, BELGIUM

Specific Interests: Prairie and Temperate Forest

Government — Federal

ATLANTIC OCEANOGRAPHIC LABORATORY
BEDFORD INSTITUTE
DARTMOUTH, NOVA SCOTIA, CANADA

Director, Dr Alan Walton
General Environment: Oceanographic
Staff Size: 10 - 49

CORROSION END ASSOCIATION (NATIONAL)
980 M & M BUILDING
HOUSTON, TEX 77002

General Environment: Limnologic

ENVIRONMENTAL CONSERVATION DIVISION, NORTHWEST FISHERIES CENTER
2725 MONTLAKE BOULEVARD EAST
SEATTLE, WA 98112

Director, M Stansby
General Environment: Oceanographic
Staff Size: 10 - 49

ENVIRONMENTAL PROTECTION AGENCY, REGION LABORATORY
15345 NE 36TH STREET
REDMOND, WA 98052

Staff Size: 10 - 49

OCCUPATIONAL SAFETY AND HEALTH DEPARTMENT
26 FEDERAL PLAZA
NEW YORK, NY 10007

General Environment: Atmospheric
Staff Size: 1 - 4

PACIFIC FISHERIES PRODUCTS TECHNOLOGY CENTER
2725 MONTLAKE BOULEVARD EAST
SEATTLE, WA 98112

Director, Maynard Steinberg
General Environment: Oceanographic
Staff Size: 10 - 49

TOXICOLOGY BRANCH
ARMED FORCES INSTITUTE OF PATHOLOGY
WASHINGTON, DC 20305

Assistant Chief, Abel Domingues

Government — State or Local

PESTICIDE CONTROL, UNIVERSITY OF ARIZONA EXPERIMENTAL STATION
POST OFFICE BOX 1130
MESA, AZ 85201

Director, Floyd Roberts

SCIENCE AND TECHNOLOGY MINISTRY
CHEMISTRY DEPARTMENT
SINGAPORE

Chief Chemist, Mr Chia Hong Hoe
General Environment: Estuarine
Specific Interests: Tropical (hot)
Staff Size: 50 - 99

STATE CHEMICAL LABORATORY
VERMILLON, SD 57069

State Chemist, D J Mitchell

THE NEW ALCHEMY INSTITUTION
BOX 432
WOODS HOLE, MA 02543

Director, John Todd

Industrial/Commercial

AMERICAN NUCLEONICS CORPORATION
1007 AIRWAY
GLENDALE, CA 91201

ASSOCIATED LEAD MANUFACTURERS, LIMITED
7 WADSWORTH ROAD
PERIVALE, GFD, MIDDLESEX, ENGLAND

Research Manager, Dr Edmund H Amstein
Specific Interests: Urban

CHEMISTRY DIVISION, AERE
HARWELL, BERKSHIRE, ENGLAND

Director, Colin B Amphlett
Specific Interests: Prairie and Temperate Forest

DETREX INDUSTRIAL CHEMISTRY, INCORPORATED
POST OFFICE BOX 501
DETROIT, MI 48232

Resources Manager, Charles Kircher
General Environment: Atmospheric

ENVIRONMENTAL HEALTH DEPARTMENT, HOOKER CHEMICAL COMPANY
277 PARK AVENUE
NEW YORK, NY 10017

HICKSON AND WELCH, LIMITED
CASTLEFORD, YORKSHIRE, ENGLAND

Chairman, Dennis W Adams
Specific Interests: Prairie and Temperate Forest

IMPERIAL CHEMICAL INDUSTRIES LIMITED
IMPERIAL CHEMISTRY HOUSE
MILLBANK, LONDON, ENGLAND

Chairman, E J Callard
Specific Interests: Prairie and Temperate Forest

MONSANTO CHEMICALS, LIMITED
10-18 VICTORIA STREET
LONDON, SW1, ENGLAND

Director, Cyril G Wickham
Specific Interests: Prairie and Temperate Forest

PARTICLE TECHNOLOGY INCORPORATED
734 NORTH PASTORIA AVENUE
SUNNYVALE, CA 94086

President, Mr Richard P Beck

RESEARCH AND DEVELOPMENT DEPARTMENT, BP CHEMICALS LIMITED
DEVONSHIRE HOUSE, MAYFAIR PLACE
PICCADILLY, LONDON, ENGLAND

Director, Godfrey P Armstrong
Specific Interests: Prairie and Temperate Forest

SCIENTIFIC SERVICES CENTER, CEGB
RATCLIFFE-ON-SOAR
NOTTINGHAM NG11 OEE, ENGLAND

Branch Head, Eric W F Gillham
General Environment: Terrestrial
Specific Interests: Rural
Staff Size: 100 - 499

SEAMAN NUCLEAR CORPORATION
3846 WEST WISCONSIN AVENUE
MILWAUKEE, WI 53208

Vice President, Mr J R Martin

SHELL RESEARCH, LIMITED
POST OFFICE BOX 1, THORNTON RESOURCES CENTER
CHESTER, CHESHIRE, ENGLAND

Director, Alun Thomas
Specific Interests: Prairie and Temperate Forest

Professional Organizations

ANALYTICAL CHEMISTS ASSOCIATION
BEN FRANKLIN STATION, 540
WASHINGTON, DC 20044

Research Institute

**AGRICULTURAL RESEARCH
CENTER, INCORPORATED**
1305 EAST MAIN STREET
LAKELAND, FL 33801
General Environment: Terrestrial
Specific Interests: Rural
Staff Size: 5 - 9

**ANALYTICAL CHEMISTRY
SOCIETY-GOVERNMENT
INDUSTRIAL CHEMISTRY RESEA**
1-1 MOTO-MACHI
SHIBUYA-KU, TOKYO, JAPAN
Specific Interests: Prairie and Temperate
Forest

**ATOMIC INDUSTRIAL FORUM,
TODEN BUILDING**
1-1 TAMURA-CHO SHIBA
MINATO-KU, TOKYO, JAPAN
Director, Keinosuke Suga
Specific Interests: Prairie and Temperate
Forest

BORAX RESEARCH CENTER
COX LANE
CHESSINGTON, SURREY, ENGLAND
Director, Raymond Thompson
Specific Interests: Prairie and Temperate
Forest

**CANCER RESEARCH AGENCY
INTERNATIONAL**
16 AVENUE MARECHAL FOCH
69 LYON, FRANCE

**CHEMISTRY AND METEOROLOGY
DIVISIONS**
433 VAN NESS
SANTA CRUZ, CA 95060
Director, Robert Kinzie

**CHEMISTRY RESEARCH AND
DEVELOPMENT**
GLAXO RESEARCH, LIMITED
GREENFORD, MIDDLESEX,
ENGLAND
Specific Interests: Prairie and Temperate
Forest

**COMMISSION FOR PROTECTION
OF POPULATION AGAINST
HAZARDS**
4 AVENUE DE L'OBSERVATOIRE
PARIS 6, FRANCE

**MARGARITA MARINE RESEARCH
STATION**
PUNTA DE PIEDRAS
ESTADO NUEYA ESPARTA,
VENEZUELA
General Environment: Oceanographic

MARINE SCIENCE INSTITUTE
UNIVERSITY OF ALASKA
COLLEGE, AK 99701
General Environment: Oceanographic
Specific Interests: Polar (cold)
Staff Size: 50 - 99

**NUCLEAR LABORATORY OF
ATMOSPHERIC SCIENCES**
POST OFFICE BOX 1470
BOULDER, CO 80302
Director, Dr William W Kellogg
General Environment: Atmospheric
Staff Size: 500 - 999

**OCEANOGRAPHY DIVISION,
SCRIPPS INSTITUTE**
LA JOLLA, CA 92037
General Environment: Atmospheric

PHYSICAL CHEMISTRY DIVISION
505 KING AVENUE, BATTELLE
MEMORIAL LIBRARY
COLUMBUS, OH 43201
Chief, Arthur Levy

**THEORETICAL CHEMISTRY, IBM
RESEARCH LABORATORY**
MONTEREY AND COTTLE ROADS
SAN JOSE, CA 95114
Chairman, Enrico Clementi

**THERMOCHEMISTRY AND
CHEMISTRY KINETICS
DEPARTMENT**
STANFORD RESEARCH INSTITUTE
MENLO PARK, CA 94025
Chairman, Sidney Benson

Unclassified

**ENVIRONMENTAL STUDIES
PROGRAM**
1104 7TH AVENUE SOUTH
MOORHEAD, MN 56560
President, Roland Dille
Staff Size: 1000 - 4999

PHYSICAL CHEMISTRY

Educational Institute

CHEMISTRY DEPARTMENT
ST AMBROSE COLLEGE
DAVENPORT, IA 52803
Chairman, James Resnick

**CHEMISTRY INSTITUTION
MARBURG**
L BAHNHOFSTRASSE 7
355 MARBURG, WEST GERMANY
Specific Interests: Prairie and Temperate
Forest

**MASSACHUSETTS GENERAL
HOSPITAL**
HARVARD MEDICAL SCHOOL
BOSTON, MA 02114
Professor, Edward Webster

OCEANOGRAPHY DEPARTMENT
PRIVATE BAG, RONDEBOSCH
CAPE TOWN, REPUBLIC OF SOUTH
AFRICA
General Environment: Oceanographic

**PHYSICAL CHEMISTRY
DEPARTMENT**
SAN JOSE STATE COLLEGE
SAN JOSE, CA 95114
Professor, Juana L Vivo Acrivos

PHYSICAL CHEMISTRY INSTITUTE
UKRAINIAN SOVIET SOCIALISTS
REPUBLIC ACADEMY OF
SCIENCES
KIEV, 28, UKRAINE, UNION OF
SOVIET SOCIALIST REPUBLICS
Specific Interests: Polar (cold)

**PHYSICS AND CHEMISTRY
RESEARCH INSTITUTE**
TOKYO, JAPAN
Specific Interests: Prairie and Temperate
Forest

**PHYSICS-CHEMISTRY INSTITUTE,
TECHNISCHE HOCHSCULE**
51 AACHEN, POSTFACH D TH
BONN, WEST GERMANY
Director, Ulrich F Franck
Specific Interests: Prairie and Temperate
Forest
Staff Size: 10 - 49

**RESEARCH AND GRADUATE
STUDIES**
UNIVERSITY OF KANSAS
LAWRENCE, KS 66044
Staff Size: 1000 - 4999

SCIENCES FACULTY
UNIVERSITY OF MADRID
MADRID 3, SPAIN
Specific Interests: Prairie and Temperate
Forest .

USTAV FYZIKY KOVOV SAV
BRATISLAVA UL FEBRUAROVEHO
VIT'AZSTVA 135, CZECHOSLOVAKIA

Government — Federal

INSTITUT KHIMICHESKOY FIZIKI
VOROB'YEVSKOYE SHOSSE, 2-A
MOSCOW, UNION OF SOVIET
SOCIALIST REPUBLICS
Staff Size: 10 - 49

**NUCLEAR EDUCATION AND
TRAINING DIVISION**
UNITED STATES ATOMIC ENERGY
COMMISSION
WASHINGTON, DC 20545
General Environment: Atmospheric

**OAK RIDGE ASSOCIATED
UNIVERSITIES**
POST OFFICE BOX 117
OAK RIDGE, TN 37830
General Environment: Atmospheric

OPERATIONAL SAFETY DIVISION
UNITED STATES ATOMIC ENERGY
COMMISSION
WASHINGTON, DC 20545
General Environment: Atmospheric

RADIOLOGICAL HEALTH BUREAU
5600 FISHERS LANE
ROCKVILLE, MD 20852
General Environment: Atmospheric

Government — State or Local

**ATOMIC ENERGY COMMISSION
CHICAGO OPERATIONS OFFICE**
9800 CASS AVENUE
ARGONNE, IL 60439
General Environment: Atmospheric

**ATOMIC ENERGY COMMISSION
GRAND JUNCTION OFFICE**
POST OFFICE BOX 2567
GRAND JUNCTION, CO 81501
General Environment: Atmospheric

**ATOMIC ENERGY COMMISSION
HEALTH AND SAFETY
LABORATORY**
376 HUDSON STREET
NEW YORK, NY 10014
General Environment: Atmospheric

**ATOMIC ENERGY COMMISSION
NEVADA OPERATIONS OFFICE**
POST OFFICE BOX 5400
ALBUQUERQUE, NM 87115
General Environment: Atmospheric

**ATOMIC ENERGY COMMISSION
OAK RIDGE OPERATIONS
OFFICE**
POST OFFICE BOX E
OAK RIDGE, TN 37830
General Environment: Atmospheric

**ATOMIC ENERGY COMMISSION
PITTSBURGH NAVAL REACTORS
OFFICE**
POST OFFICE BOX 109
WEST MIFFLIN, PA 15122
General Environment: Atmospheric

**ATOMIC ENERGY COMMISSION
RICHLAND OPERATIONS OFFICE**
POST OFFICE BOX 550
RICHLAND, WA 99352
General Environment: Atmospheric

**ATOMIC ENERGY COMMISSION
SAN FRANCISCO OPERATIONS**
2111 BANCROFT WAY
BERKELEY, CA 94704
General Environment: Atmospheric

**ATOMIC ENERGY COMMISSION
SAVANNAH RIVER OPERATIONS
OFFICE**
POST OFFICE BOX A
AIKEN, SC 29801
General Environment: Atmospheric

**ENVIRONMENTAL PROTECTION
AGENCY, REGION 5, LIBRARY**
1 NORTH WACKER DRIVE
CHICAGO, IL 60606

**RADIATION DIVISION,
ENVIRONMENTAL PROTECTION
AGENCY**
26 FEDERAL PLAZA, ROOM 847
NEW YORK, NY 10007

**RADIATION DIVISION,
ENVIRONMENTAL PROTECTION
AGENCY**
911 WALNUT STREET, ROOM 702
KANSAS CITY, MO 64106

**RADIATION DIVISION,
ENVIRONMENTAL PROTECTION
AGENCY**
1200 6TH AVENUE
SEATTLE, WA 98101

**RADIATION DIVISION,
ENVIRONMENTAL PROTECTION
AGENCY**
1114 COMMERCE STREET
DALLAS, TX 75202

**RADIATION DIVISION,
ENVIRONMENTAL PROTECTION
AGENCY**
1421 PEACHTREE STREET, NE
SUITE 300
ATLANTA, GA 30309

**RADIATION DIVISION,
ENVIRONMENTAL PROTECTION
AGENCY**
JOHN F KENNEDY FEDERAL
BUILDING, ROOM 2303
BOSTON, MA 02203

**RADIATION DIVISION,
ENVIRONMENTAL PROTECTION
AGENCY**
1860 LINCOLN STREET, ROOM 953,
LINCOLN TOWER BUILDING
DENVER, CO 80203

**RADIATION DIVISION,
ENVIRONMENTAL PROTECTION
AGENCY**
POST OFFICE BOX 12900
PHILADELPHIA, PA 19108

**RADIATION DIVISION,
ENVIRONMENTAL PROTECTION
AGENCY**
33 EAST CONGRESS PARKWAY
CHICAGO, IL 60605

Research Institute

**ICE AND SNOW STUDIES SOCIETY,
METEOROLOGY AGENCY**
7 1-CHOME OTE-MACHI
CHIYODA-KU, TOKYO, JAPAN
Director, Dr Hisano Hatareyama
Specific Interests: Prairie and Temperate
Forest

PHYSICAL CHEMISTRY INSTITUTE
SURFACE FORCES LABORATORY,
ACADEMY OF SCIENCES
MOSCOW, UNION OF SOVIET
SOCIALISTS REPUBLICS
Director, Boris Vladimirovich Deryagin

Engineering

GENERAL

Educational Institute

**AGRICULTURAL AND
ECONOMICAL LIBRARY,
GIANNINI FOUNDATION**
248 GIANNINI HALL, UNIVERSITY
OF CALIFORNIA
BERKELEY, CA 94720

**AGRICULTURAL, INDUSTRIAL,
MICROBIOLOGICAL INSTITUTE**
UNIVERSITY OF MASSACHUSETTS,
MARSHALL HALL
AMHERST, MA 01003

**ARCHITECTURAL ART AND
PLANNING COLLEGE**
CORNELL UNIVERSITY
ITHACA, NY 14850
Specific Interests: Urban

**ATMOSPHERIC PHYSICS
INSTITUTE, UNIVERSITY OF
ARIZONA**
TUCSON, AZ
General Environment: Atmospheric

**BALCONES RESEARCH CENTER,
UNIVERSITY OF TEXAS**
ROUTE 4 BOX 189
AUSTIN, TX 78700
Director, Professor J Neils Thompson

**CHEMICAL ENGINEERING
DEPARTMENT**
INSTITUTE OF TECHNOLOGY
MINNEAPOLIS, MN 55455

CHEMISTRY DEPARTMENT
UNIVERSITY OF CALIFORNIA
BERKELEY, CA 94720

**CHEMISTRY ENGINEERING AND
ENVIRONMENTAL HEALTH
ENGINEERING**
CIT
PASADENA, CA 91109
Professor, Sheldon Friedlander
General Environment: Atmospheric

CITY COLLEGE OF SAN FRANCISCO
50 PHELAN AVENUE
SAN FRANCISCO, CA 94112

CIVIL ENGINEERING
SAN JOSE STATE COLLEGE
SAN JOSE, CA 95114
Staff Size: 10 - 49

COOPER UNION
COOPER SQUARE
NEW YORK, NY 10003

**ELECTRICAL ENGINEERING
DEPARTMENT**
SAN JOSE STATE COLLEGE
SAN JOSE, CA 95114
Staff Size: 10 - 49

ENGINEERING COLLEGE
CLEMSON UNIVERSITY
CLEMSON, SC 29631
General Environment: Terrestrial
Staff Size: 10 - 49

ENGINEERING COLLEGE
UNIVERSITY OF IOWA
IOWA CITY, IA 52240

ENGINEERING COLLEGE
KANSAS STATE UNIVERSITY
MANHATTAN, KS 66502

ENGINEERING COLLEGE
UNIVERSITY OF TEXAS
AUSTIN, TX 78712

ENGINEERING DEPARTMENT
STATE UNIVERSITY OF NEW YORK
BUFFALO, NY 14210

**ENGINEERING DESIGN AND
ANALYSIS LABORATORY**
UNIVERSITY OF NEW HAMPSHIRE
DURHAM, NH 03824
General Environment: Oceanographic

ENGINEERING RESEARCH
UNIVERSITY OF COLORADO
CAMPUS
BOULDER, CO 80304

ENGINEERING RESEARCH CENTER
COLORADO STATE UNIVERSITY
FORT COLLINS, CO 80521

ENGINEERING SCHOOL
OREGON STATE UNIVERSITY
CORVALLIS, OR 97331

**ENVIRONMENTAL AND
RADIOLOGICAL SCIENCES**
BATTELLE NORTHWEST POST
OFFICE 999
RICHLAND, WA 99352
Manager, Richard Foster

**ENVIRONMENTAL AND WATER
RESEARCH, VANDERBILT
UNIVERSITY**

ENGINEERING DEPARTMENT
NASHVILLE, TN 37235
Director, Dr Barry Benedict
Staff Size: 10 - 49

**ENVIRONMENTAL ENGINEERING
AND SCIENCE, CIVIL
ENGINEERING DEPARTMENT**
MANHATTAN COLLEGE
BRONX, NY 10471
Director, Dr J Jeris
Specific Interests: Prairie and Temperate
Forest

**ENVIRONMENTAL ENGINEERING
DEPARTMENT**
ILLINOIS INSTITUTE OF
TECHNOLOGY
CHICAGO, IL 60601
Staff Size: 5 - 9

**ENVIRONMENTAL ENGINEERING
SCIENCE DEPARTMENT**
COLUMBIA-ENGINEERING,
UNIVERSITY OF FLORIDA
GAINESVILLE, FL 32601

**ENVIRONMENTAL MEDICINE
INSTITUTE**
NEW YORK UNIVERSITY MEDICAL
CENTER, LONG MEADOW
TUXEDO, NY 10987
Director, Merril Eisenbud

**ENVIRONMENTAL RESEARCH,
SCHOOL OF ENGINEERING AND
SCIENCES**
NEW YORK UNIVERSITY
NEW YORK, NY 10001

**ENVIRONMENTAL SCIENCE
ACTIVITIES**
UNIVERSITY OF FLORIDA
GAINESVILLE, FL 32601

**ENVIRONMENTAL SCIENCE AND
ENGINEERING**
COLUMBIA UNIVERSITY
NEW YORK, NY 10022

**ENVIRONMENTAL SCIENCE
PROGRAM**
UNIVERSITY OF HARTFORD
WEST HARTFORD, CT 06117

**ENVIRONMENTAL SCIENCE
PROGRAM**
WEBB INSTITUTE OF NAVAL
ARCHITECTURE
GLEN COVE, NY 11542

ENVIRONMENTAL SCIENCE
PROGRAM, ROOM 407
KIRKBRIDE HALL-WIDENER
COLUMBIA
CHESTER, PA 19013
Professor, J J Storlazzi

ENVIRONMENTAL SCIENCES AND
ENGINEERING PROGRAM
COLUMBIA UNIVERSITY
NEW YORK, NY 10023
Specific Interests: Prairie and Temperate
Forest

ENVIRONMENTAL STUDIES
UNIVERSITY OF STELLENBOSCH
STELLENBOSCH, REPUBLIC OF
SOUTH AFRICA
General Environment: Oceanographic

ENVIRONMENTAL STUDIES
PROGRAM
EMBRY RIDDLE AERONAUTICAL
DAYTONA BEACH, FL 32015
President, Jack R Hunt

ENVIRONMENTAL STUDIES
PROGRAM
GEORGE WASHINGTON
UNIVERSITY
WASHINGTON, DC 20006

ENVIRONMENTAL STUDIES
PROGRAM
TEXAS ARTS AND INDUSTRIES
UNIVERSITY
KINGSVILLE, TX 78363

ENVIRONMENTAL STUDIES
PROGRAM
MOUNTAIN COLLEGE OF
MINERAL SCIENCES
BUTTE, MT 59701

ENVIRONMENTAL STUDIES
PROGRAM
UNIVERSITY OF BRIDGEPORT
BRIDGEPORT, CT 06602

ENVIRONMENTAL STUDIES
PROGRAM
UNIVERSITY OF ALASKA
COLLEGE, AK 99701

ENVIRONMENTAL STUDIES
PROGRAM
STEVENS INSTITUTE OF
TECHNOLOGY
HOBOKEN, NJ 07030

ENVIRONMENTAL STUDIES
PROGRAM
OLD DOMINION UNIVERSITY
NORFOLK, VA 23508

ENVIRONMENTAL STUDIES
PROGRAM

NAVAL POSTGRADUATE SCHOOL
MONTEREY, CA 93940
Staff Size: 100 - 499

ENVIRONMENTAL STUDIES, ROSE
POLYTECHNICAL INSTITUTE
5500 WABASH AVENUE
TERRE HAUTE, IN 47803

EXPERIMENTAL PHYSICS
LABORATORY 11, TECHNOLOGY
UNIVERSITY OF ATHENS
POST OFFICE BOX 49
ATHENS, GREECE
Director, Paul E Santorini

FORSCHUNGSSTELLE
LIMNOLOGIE
ACADEMY OF SCIENCE
JENA-L, WEST GERMANY
General Environment: Limnologic
Specific Interests: Prairie and Temperate
Forest

GEOGRAPHY DEPARTMENT
UNIVERSITY OF LEEDS
LEEDS, WEST RIDING, ENGLAND
Director, J William Birch
General Environment: Terrestrial
Specific Interests: Prairie and Temperate
Forest

LINCOLN COLLEGE
CANTERBURY, NEW ZEALAND
General Environment: Terrestrial
Specific Interests: Tropical (hot)
Staff Size: 10 - 49

MANHATTAN COLLEGE
RIVERDALE
BRONX, NY 10471
General Environment: Estuarine
Staff Size: 5 - 9

MARINE STUDIES COLLEGE
UNIVERSITY OF DELAWARE
NEWARK, DE 19711

MECHANICAL ENGINEERING
OREGON STATE UNIVERSITY
CORVALLIS, OREGON 97331

MECHANICAL ENGINEERING
DEPARTMENT
WATERLOO UNIVERSITY
WATERLOO, ONTARIO, CANADA
Director, G T Csanady
Staff Size: 5 - 9

NUCLEAR ENGINEERING
DEPARTMENT, UNIVERSITY OF
WASHINGTON
303 BENSON HALL
SEATTLE, WA 98105

NUCLEAR ENGINEERING SCHOOL
GEORGIA INSTITUTE OF
TECHNOLOGY
ATLANTA, GA 30332
Director, Carlyle Roberts

PHYSICAL ENVIRONMENT UNIT,
UNIVERSITY OF ILLINOIS
208 MECHANICAL ENGINEERING
LABORATORY
URBANA, IL 61803
Director, Professor M K Fahnestock
General Environment: Terrestrial

POWER INSTITUTION, G M
KRZHIZHANOVSKII
LENINGSKII PROSPEKT, 19
MOSCOW, UNION OF SOVIET
SOCIALIST REPUBLICS
Specific Interests: Polar (cold)

PRATT INSTITUTE
215 RYERSON STREET
BROOKLYN, NY 11205

SANITARY ENGINEERING AND
WATER RESOURCES
DEPARTMENT
JOHNS HOPKINS UNIVERSITY, 513
AMES
BALTIMORE, MD 21218
Director, John Geyer
Specific Interests: Urban

SANITARY ENGINEERING
RESOURCES LABORATORY
UNIVERSITY OF CALIFORNIA
1301 SOUTH 46TH STREET
RICHMOND, CA 94800
Director, Professor P H Mcgauhey
General Environment: Atmospheric
Staff Size: 50 - 99

SCIENCE TECHNOLOGY
INSTITUTE, GREAT LAKES
DIVISION
NORTH UNIVERSITY BUILDING,
UNIVERSITY OF MICHIGAN
ANN ARBOR, MI 48104

SOIL MECHANICS AND
FOUNDATION
TECHNICAL UNIVERSITY
PRAGUE, CZECHOSLOVAKIA
Specific Interests: Prairie and Temperate
Forest

SURVEYING DEPARTMENT
PRIVATE BAG, RONDEBOSCH
CAPE TOWN, REPUBLIC OF SOUTH
AFRICA
General Environment: Oceanographic

WATER ENERGY INSTITUTE
ARMENIAN ACADEMY SCIENCES
MOSCOW, UNION OF SOVIET
SOCIALIST REPUBLICS
Director, Ivan Vasilevich Egiazarov
Specific Interests: Polar (cold)

WATER RESOURCE INSTITUTE
CHUNG-KU COLLEGE
TAEBU, KOREA
General Environment: Oceanographic
Specific Interests: Prairie and Temperate
Forest

WATER RESOURCES CENTER
UNIVERSITY OF DELAWARE
NEWARK, DE 19711

**WATER RESOURCES PROGRAM,
COLLEGE OF ENGINEERING**
UNIVERSITY OF MICHIGAN
ANN ARBOR, MI 48104
General Environment: Limnologic
Staff Size: 10 - 49

**WATER RESOURCES RESEARCH
INSTITUTE**
OKHOMA STATE UNIVERSITY
STILLWATER, OK 74074
General Environment: Limnologic

**WATER SCIENCES AND
ENGINEERING DEPARTMENT**
UNIVERSITY OF CALIFORNIA
DAVIS, CA 95616

Field Station/Laboratory

BELL TELEPHONE LABORATORIES
MURRAY HILL, NJ 07971
Director, G Wilkening

CINCINNATI GENERAL HOSPITAL
UNIVERSITY OF CINCINNATI
MEDICAL CENTER
CINCINNATI, OH 45229
Director, Leon Goldman

**ENVIRONMENTAL ENGINEERING
INTERSOCIETY BOARD**
P O BOX 9728
WASHINGTON, DC 20016
Director, Frank Butrico

**FOREST HYDROLOGY
LABORATORY**
ARIZONA STATE UNIVERSITY
TEMPE, AZ 85281
Director, Dr Hudson G Reynolds

**GEOTECHNICAL INSTITUTE OF
NORWAY**
OSLO, NORWAY
Director, Laurits Bjerrum
General Environment: Terrestrial
Staff Size: 50 - 99

**GREAT BARRIER REEF
COMMITTEE**
HERON ISLAND RESEARCH
STATION
GLADSTONE, QUEENSLAND,
AUSTRALIA
Director, Dr O Jones

**INDUSTRIAL MATERIALS
RESEARCH UNITED**

MILE END ROAD, QUEEN MARY
CORPORATION
LONDON E1 4NS, ENGLAND
Director, Derek Smith
Specific Interests: Prairie and Temperate
Forest

**INSTRUMENT SYSTEMATIC,
STANFORD RESOURCES
INSTITUTE**
124 LUNDY LANE
PALO ALTO, CA 94303

**NATURAL RESOURCE RESEARCH
INSTITUTE, COLLEGE OF
ENGINEERING, UNIVE**
BOX 3038, UNIVERSITY STATION
LARAMIE, WY 82070
Staff Size: 1 - 4

**NAUTICAL SOCIETY OF JAPAN,
TOKYO UNIVERSITY**
ETCHUJIMA-MACHI FUKAGAWA
KOTOKU, TOKYO, JAPAN
General Environment: Oceanographic
Specific Interests: Prairie and Temperate
Forest

Foundation

**BEACH AND SHORE
PRESERVATION OF AMERICA**
POST OFFICE BOX 1246
ROCKVILLE, MD 20850
Director, Richard Eaton
General Environment: Estuarine

ENGINEERING DIVISION
NATIONAL SCIENCE FOUNDATION
WASHINGTON, DC 20550

**FORESTRY FOUNDATION OF NEW
ENGLAND**
1 COURT STREET
BOSTON, MA 02108
President, Farnham W Smith
General Environment: Terrestrial
Specific Interests: Prairie and Temperate
Forest

**INSTITUTE DE STUDII CERCETARI
HIDROTEHNI**
BUCHARESTR
SPL INDEPENDENTEI 294,
BUCHARESTR, RUMANIA
Director, Ing Sorin Dumitresca
General Environment: Limnologic

**WATER RESOURCES
DEPARTMENT, RESOURCES
BUILDING**
1416 9TH STREET, POST OFFICE
BOX 388
SACRAMENTO, CA 95802

Government — Federal

**AGRICULTURE AND FISHERIES
(SABAH STATE MINISTRY OF)**
JESSELTON, MALAYSIA
Director, Chin Phui Kong
General Environment: Oceanographic
Specific Interests: Tropical (hot)

**AGRICULTURE AND FORESTRY
MINISTRY**
OFFICE OF FISHERIES
SEOUL, KOREA
Director, O J Keun
General Environment: Oceanographic
Specific Interests: Prairie and Temperate
Forest

**AGRICULTURE AND NATIONAL
RESOURCES DEPARTMENT**
MANILA, PHILIPPINES
Director, Fernando Lopez
Specific Interests: Prairie and Temperate
Forest

**AGRICULTURE DEPARTMENT,
CENTRAL PROJECT OFFICE**
14TH STREET AND
INDEPENDENCE AVENUE
WASHINGTON, DC 20250
General Environment: Limnologic

AGRICULTURE MINISTRY
DEPARTMENT OF FISHERIES
BANGKOK, THAILAND
Director, Nai Prida Karnasut
General Environment: Oceanographic
Specific Interests: Tropical (hot)

**APPLIED SCIENTIFIC RESEARCH
CORPORATION**
AGRICULTURAL RESEARCH
INSTITUTION
KHONKOEN, THAILAND
Director, Dr Frank C Nicholls
Specific Interests: Tropical (hot)

**ASTRONOMICAL OBSERVATORY AT
TASHKENT**
TASHKENT, UNION OF SOVIET
SOCIALIST REPUBLICS
Director, V P Sacheglov
Staff Size: 5 - 9

ATOMIC ENERGY BUREAU
TOKYO, JAPAN
Director, Hiroski Murata

**BHABHA ATOMIC RESEARCH
CENTER**
TROMBAY
BOMBAY, INDIA
Director, R Ramanna
Specific Interests: Tropical (hot)

COASTAL ENGINEERING RESOURCES CENTER
5201 LITTLE FALLS ROAD, NW
WASHINGTON, DC 20016
General Environment: Oceanographic
Staff Size: 100 - 499

COLD REGIONS RESEARCH ENGINEERING LABORATORY
POST OFFICE BOX 282
HANOVER, NH 03755
General Environment: Terrestrial
Specific Interests: Polar (cold)

ECONOMIC DEVELOPMENT BOARD
SINGAPORE
Director, Lim Hohup
Specific Interests: Tropical (hot)

ECONOMIC PLANNING AGENCY
WATER RESOURCES BRANCH
TOKYO, JAPAN
Director, Shigeru Matsumoto
Specific Interests: Prairie and Temperate Forest

ENGINEERING AND RESOURCES CENTER
DENVER FEDERAL CENTER, BUILDING 67
DENVER, CO 80225
Director, Bernard P Bellport

ENGINEERING, POST OFFICE DEPARTMENT
12TH AND PENNSYLVANIA AVENUES, NW
WASHINGTON, DC 20260
Director, Walter Rizzardi
Staff Size: 10 - 49

ENVIRONMENTAL CONTROL ADMINISTRATION
CONSUMER PROTECTION
ROCKVILLE, MD 20852
Director, Mr Julius J Sabo
Staff Size: 10 - 49

ENVIRONMENTAL RESOURCES DEVELOPMENT LABORATORY
UNITED STATES DEPARTMENT OF ARMY
FORT BELVOIR, VA 22060
General Environment: Limnologic

ENVIRONMENTAL SCIENCES SERVICES ADMINISTRATION
NATIONAL OCEANIC AND ATMOSPHERIC ADMINISTRATION
ROCKVILLE, MD 20852
General Environment: Oceanographic

EXTENSION SERVICE
DEPARTMENT OF AGRICULTURE
WASHINGTON, DC 20250

FEDERAL WORKING GROUP ON PESTICIDE MANAGEMENT
5600 FISHERS LANE, ROOM 17-92, PARKLAWN BUILDING
ROCKVILLE, MD 20852

FINANCE AND OIL MINISTRY
KUWAIT
Director, Mahmoud Adsani
General Environment: Terrestrial

FOOD AND DRUG ADMINISTRATION
200 C STREET, NW
WASHINGTON, DC 20204
Specific Interests: Prairie and Temperate Forest

FOREST PRESERVATION NATIONAL COMMISSION
3016 S BUILDING
WASHINGTON, DC 20250
General Environment: Terrestrial
Specific Interests: Prairie and Temperate Forest

FOREST PRODUCE INDUSTRIES OF AMERICA, INCORPORATED
1835 K STREET, NW
WASHINGTON, DC 20006
General Environment: Terrestrial

FORESTRY ASSOCIATION OF AMERICA
1319 18TH STREET, NW
WASHINGTON, DC 20036
General Environment: Terrestrial

GEODESY AND PHOTOGRAMMETRY, NATIONAL OCEANOGRAPHIC SURVEYS
NATIONAL OCEANIC AND ATMOSPHERIC ADMINISTRATION
ROCKVILLE, MD 20852
General Environment: Terrestrial

GEOGRAPHICAL SURVEY INSTITUTION
MINISTRY OF CONSTRUCTION
TOKYO, JAPAN
Director, Dr Motokiyo Aki

HYDROGRAPHIC DEPARTMENT
ROYAL THAI NAVY
BANGKOK, THAILAND
Director, Piti Tantivess
General Environment: Oceanographic
Specific Interests: Tropical (hot)
Staff Size: 100 - 499

HYDROGRAPHIC OFFICE, INDONESIAN NAVY
DJI. GUNUNG SAHARI I
DJAKARTA, INDONESIA
Director, Kolonel Pardjaman
General Environment: Oceanographic
Specific Interests: Tropical (hot)

HYDROGRAPHY AND NAVIGATION, MINISTRY OF NAVY
ILHA FISCAL
RIO DE JANEIRO, BRAZIL
Director, Ervesto De Mello Baptisa
General Environment: Oceanographic

INDUSTRIAL RESEARCH INSTITUTION
TOKYO, JAPAN
Specific Interests: Prairie and Temperate Forest

INDUSTRIAL SCIENCES AND TECHNOLOGY AGENCY
TOKYO, JAPAN
Director, Dr Akimasa Baba

INFORMATION DIVISION
UNITED STATES DEPARTMENT OF ARMY
WASHINGTON, DC 20315

INTERIOR COMMITTEE, INSULAR AFFAIRS, U S SENATE
ROOM 3106 NEW SENATE OFFICE BUILDING
WASHINGTON, DC 20510
General Environment: Limnologic

INTERNATIONAL BOUNDARIES AND WATER COMMISSION, US AND MEXICO
POST OFFICE BOX 1859
EL PASO, TX 79950
General Environment: Limnologic
Staff Size: 100 - 499

INTERNATIONAL JOINT COMMISSION, US AND CANADA
1711 NEW YORK AVENUE, NW
WASHINGTON, DC
General Environment: Limnologic

KAUNAS POLYTECHNICAL INSTITUTE
ULITSA DONELAYCHIO,35
KAUNAS, UNION OF SOVIET SOCIALIST REPUBLICS
Director, K M Barshaukas
Staff Size: 10 - 49

LAW AND NATIONAL DEVELOPMENT MINISTRY
PRIMARY PRODUCTION DEPARTMENT
SINGAPORE
Director, Cheng Tong Fatt
Specific Interests: Tropical (hot)

LENINGRAD HIGH ENGINEERING NAVAL ACADEMY, MAKARV
VASIL'YEVSKIY OSTROV,KL15A
LENINGRAD, UNION OF SOVIET SOCIALIST REPUBLICS
Staff Size: 10 - 49

LIMNOLOGICAL STATION
LOS BANOS
LAGUNA, PHILIPPINES

General Environment: Limnologic
Specific Interests: Prairie and Temperate
Forest

**MARINE OBSERVATORY OF
HAKODATE**
HAKODATE, JAPAN

Director, Mr Yoshiteru Ono
General Environment: Oceanographic
Specific Interests: Prairie and Temperate
Forest
Staff Size: 5 - 9

MARINE OBSERVATORY OF KOBE
KOBE, JAPAN

Director, Dr Yoshiyuki Fujii
General Environment: Oceanographic
Specific Interests: Prairie and Temperate
Forest

**MARINE RESOURCES INSTITUTE,
DEPARTMENT OF AGRICULTURE**
DJI SALEMBA 17
DJAKARTA, INDONESIA

Director, Hasanuddin Saanin
General Environment: Oceanographic
Specific Interests: Tropical (hot)

MARINE SAFETY ACADEMY
KURE, JAPAN

Director, Bungo Okumura
General Environment: Oceanographic
Specific Interests: Prairie and Temperate
Forest

MARINE SAFETY SCHOOL
MAIZURU, JAPAN

Director, Katoichi Watanabe
General Environment: Oceanographic
Specific Interests: Prairie and Temperate
Forest

**MEDICINE AND SURGERY
BUREAU, U S DEPARTMENT OF
NAVY**
CODE 7223
WASHINGTON, DC 20390

General Environment: Limnologic

**MINERAL RESOURCES
DEPARTMENT**
BANGKOK, THAILAND

Director, Nai Vija Sethaprts
Specific Interests: Tropical (hot)

MINES BUREAU
HERRAN STREET
MANILA, PHILIPPINES

Director, Fernando S Busuego Jr
Specific Interests: Prairie and Temperate
Forest

MINES BUREAU OF UNITED STATES
1600 EAST FIRST SOUTH STREET
SALT LAKE CITY, UT 84112

Staff Size: 100 - 499

**MISSISSIPPI RIVERS COMMISSION,
CORPORATION OF
ENGINEERING**
UNITED STATES ARMY, POST
OFFICE BOX 80
VICKSBURG, MS 39180

Specific Interests: Prairie and Temperate
Forest

**NUCLEAR SAFETY INFORMATION
CENTER**
PO BOX Y, OAK RIDGE NATIONAL
LABORATORY
OAK RIDGE, TN 37831

General Environment: Limnologic

**OCEANOGRAPHIC RESEARCH
NATIONAL COMMISSION**
DJAKARTA, INDONESIA

Director, Komodor Wardiman
General Environment: Oceanographic
Specific Interests: Tropical (hot)

**OCEANOGRAPHIC RESEARCH
UNITED**
YOUNGSFIELD
CAPE TOWN, REPUBLIC OF SOUTH
AFRICA

General Environment: Oceanographic

PEOPLE'S OIL INDUSTRY
604 MERCHANT STREET
RANGOON, BURMA

Specific Interests: Tropical (hot)

**PETROLEUM REFERENCE
ASSOCIATION**
1725 DE SALES STREET, NW
WASHINGTON, DC

General Environment: Terrestrial

PHILIPPINE NAVY
ROXAS BOULEVARD
MANILA, PHILIPPINES

Director, Commodore Pastor Viado
General Environment: Oceanographic
Specific Interests: Prairie and Temperate
Forest

**PORT AND HARBOR RESEARCH
INSTITUTE**
1-1 3-CHOME NAGASE
YOKOSUKA, JAPAN

Director, Dr Senri Tsuruta
General Environment: Oceanographic
Specific Interests: Prairie and Temperate
Forest

PORT OF SINGAPORE AUTHORITY
SINGAPORE

General Environment: Oceanographic
Specific Interests: Tropical (hot)

PREVENTIVE MEDICINE DIVISION
MAIN NAVY BUILDING
WASHINGTON, DC 20315

PUBLIC WORKS BUREAU
POST OFFICE BUILDING LAWTON
PLAZA
MANILA, PHILIPPINES

Director, Alejandro Delena
Specific Interests: Prairie and Temperate
Forest

PUBLIC WORKS MINISTRY
PHNOM-PENH, CAMBODIA

Specific Interests: Tropical (hot)

**RESEARCH AND ENGINEERING
BUREAU**
12TH AND PENNSYLVANIA
AVENUE, NW
WASHINGTON, DC 20260

Director, Mr Walter C Rizzardi

RESEARCH COUNCIL (NATIONAL)
BANGKOK, THAILAND

Director, General Netr Khemayodhin
Specific Interests: Tropical (hot)

RESOURCES RESEARCH INSTITUTE
KAWAGUCHI, JAPAN

Director, Dr Toshio Suzuki

**RIVERS AND HARBORS BOARD, US
DEPARTMENT OF ARMY**
2ND AND Q STREETS
WASHINGTON, DC 20024

General Environment: Limnologic

**RURAL DEVELOPMENT AND
CONSERVATION, DEPARTMENT
OF AGRICULTURE**
3833 ROBERTS LANE NORTH
ARLINGTON, VA 22207

Assistant Secretary, Thomas Cowden
Specific Interests: Rural

**SALT WATER FISHERIES
EXPERIMENTAL STATION**
DAGAT-DAGATAN, PHILIPPINES

Director, Dr Jose R Montilla
General Environment: Oceanographic
Specific Interests: Prairie and Temperate
Forest

**SCIENCE AND TECHNOLOGY
AGENCY**
TOKYO, JAPAN

Director, Keijiro Inoue

**SCIENCE AND TECHNOLOGY
INFORMATION DIVISION, NASA**
300 7TH STREET, NW
WASHINGTON, DC 20546

Specific Interests: Prairie and Temperate
Forest

**SCIENCE DEVELOPMENT BOARD
(NATIONAL)**
HERRAN STREET
MANILA, PHILIPPINES

Director, Dr Juan Salcedo, Jr
Specific Interests: Prairie and Temperate
Forest

SCIENCE-TECHNOLOGY
INFORMATION,
CLEARINGHOUSE
NATIONAL BUREAU OF
STANDARDS
SPRINGFIELD, VA 22151
General Environment: Limnologic

SCIENCES AND TECHNOLOGY
NATIONAL INSTITUTION
HERRAN STREET
MANILA, PHILIPPINES
Specific Interests: Prairie and Temperate
Forest

SEA FISHERIES RESEARCH
INSTITUTE
PASAR IKAN
DJAKARTA, INDONESIA
Director, Dr Singhi
General Environment: Oceanographic
Specific Interests: Tropical (hot)

SHIP TECHNICAL RESEARCH
INSTITUTION
TOKYO, JAPAN
Director, Dr Takuji Oe
General Environment: Oceanographic
Specific Interests: Prairie and Temperate
Forest

SHIPS DIVISION DEMARCATION
615 BOOTH STREET
OTTAWA, ONTARIO, CANADA
Director, D H Charles
General Environment: Oceanographic

SOIL CONSERVATION SERVICES,
ENGINEERING DIVISION
6312 24TH STREET, N
ARLINGTON, VA 22207
Director, John Phelan
Staff Size: 100 - 499

TECHNICAL LIBRARY DIVISION
UNITED STATES NAVY, CIVIL
ENGINEERING
PORT HUENEME, CA 93041
General Environment: Limnologic

TECHNOLOGICAL UTILIZATION
DIVISION, NASA
400 MARYLAND AVENUE, SW
WASHINGTON, DC 20546
General Environment: Atmospheric

UNITED STATES DEPARTMENT
INTERIOR
POST OFFICE DRAWER 1619
TULSA, OK 74101
Director, Administrator S W Power

WATER INDUSTRY AND
ENGINEERING SERVICES
DIVISION

UNITED STATES DEPARTMENT
COMMERCE
WASHINGTON, DC 20230
General Environment: Limnologic

WEATHER BUREAU
MANILA, PHILIPPINES
Director, Dr Roman Kintanar
General Environment: Atmospheric
Specific Interests: Prairie and Temperate
Forest

Government — State or Local

AIR POLLUTION AND
MECHANICAL EQUIPMENT
INSTITUTE
112 UNION STREET
PROVIDENCE, RI 02903
General Environment: Atmospheric

AIR POLLUTION TECHNOLOGY
ADVANCE BOARD
145 WEST BROAD STREET
SPARTANBURG, SC 29301
General Environment: Atmospheric

CONSERVATION INFORMATION,
AMERICAN ASSOCIATION
STATE CAPITOL BUILDING
LINCOLN, NB 68500
Director, Richard H Schaffer

COUNTY ENGINEERING
DEPARTMENT
COUNTY OF LOS ANGELES, 108
WEST 2ND STREET
LOS ANGELES, CA 90012
Engineer, Harvey T Brandt
Specific Interests: Urban
Staff Size: 1000 - 4999

ENVIRONMENTAL HEALTH
DIVISION, DUPAGE COUNTY
HEALTH DEPARTMENT
222 EAST WILLOW
WHEATON, IL 60187
Staff Size: 10 - 49

ENVIRONMENTAL HEALTH
SERVICES
3400 NORTH EASTERN AVENUE
OKLAHOMA CITY, OK 73105
General Environment: Limnologic

ENVIRONMENTAL QUALITY
DEPARTMENT
1234 SW MORRISON STREET
PORTLAND, OR 97205
General Environment: Limnologic

ENVIRONMENTAL SCIENCES
DIVISION

COGSWELL BUILDING
HELENA, MT 59601
Staff Size: 50 - 99

FIELD OPERATIONS DIVISION,
ENVIRONMENTAL PROTECTION
AGENCY
5600 FISHERS LANE
ROCKVILLE, MD 20852
Director, Mr Charles L Weaver

FISHERIES AND GAME
DEPARTMENT OF IDAHO
600 SOUTH WALNUT STREET
BOISE, ID 83707
President, Jack G Fisher
Specific Interests: Prairie and Temperate
Forest
Staff Size: 100 - 499

FOOD AND DRUG
ADMINISTRATION, BUREAU OF
SCIENCES
PUBLIC HEALTH SERVICE
WASHINGTON, DC 20204
Director, Drew Baker

HEALTH STATISTICS CENTER
3500 NORTH LOGAN STREET
LANSING, MI 48914
Director, Robert Lewis

INDUSTRIAL HYGIENE AND AIR
POLLUTION BUREAU
ROOM 406 CITY HALL
NEWARK, NJ 07102
General Environment: Atmospheric
Specific Interests: Urban

INTERIOR DEPARTMENT, PACIFIC
SOUTHWEST REGION
450 GOLDEN GATE AVENUE
SAN FRANCISCO, CA 94102
Specific Interests: Prairie and Temperate
Forest

NATURAL DISASTER DIVISION
17TH AND F STREETS, NW
WASHINGTON, DC 20504

NAVIGATION BUREAU
J FITCH PLAZA BOX 1889
TRENTON, NJ 08625
General Environment: Limnologic

OPERATING ENGINEERS
INTERNATIONAL UNION
WASHINGTON, DC 20036
Director, Alan Burch
Specific Interests: Urban

PUBLIC WORKS DEPARTMENT
1735 MAIN STREET
COLUMBIA, SC 29201
General Environment: Atmospheric

RADIATION PROTECTION
3 GATEWAY CENTER, BOX 2278
PITTSBURGH, PA 15230
Director, Edgar Barnes

SOIL CONSERVATION COMMISSION OF NORTH DAKOTA
CAPITOL BUILDING
BISMARK, ND 58501
General Environment: Limnologic

SOIL, WATER AND WEATHER DIVISION, WYOMING DEPARTMENT OF AGRICULTUR
313 CAPITOL BUILDING
CHEYENNE, WY 82001

TRAFFIC ENGINEERING
1785 LONG STREET
SAN JOSE, CA 95050
Project Engineer, Gene Mahoney

WATER DEPARTMENT OF PHILADELPHIA
1160 MUNICIPAL SERVICES BUILDING, JOHN KENNEDY AND 15TH STREETS
PHILADELPHIA, PA 19107
General Environment: Limnologic

WATER DIVISION, KENTUCKY DEPARTMENT OF NATURAL RESOURCES
CAPITOL ANNEX BUILDING
FRANKFORT, KY 40601
General Environment: Limnologic

WATER RESOURCES BOARD OF OKLAHOMA
2241 NW 40TH STREET
OKLAHOMA CITY, OK 73112
General Environment: Terrestrial
Staff Size: 10 - 49

Industrial/Commercial

AIR AND WATER CONTROL
INDUSTRIAL HARBOR WORKS
EAST CHICAGO, IN 46312
Director, John Brough

AIR PRODUCTS, LIMITED
KIRKHILL HOUSE, COLMONELL
AYRSHIRE, SCOTLAND
Director, William D Scott
General Environment: Atmospheric
Specific Interests: Prairie and Temperate Forest

APPLIED INSTRUMENT CORPORATION, ENGINEERING
1468 LUNING DRIVE
SAN JOSE, CA 95118
Director, Gerald W Albright

ARMCO ENVIRONMENTAL ENGINEERING
POST OFFICE BOX 1970
MIDDLETOWN, OH 45042
Director, J E Barker
General Environment: Atmospheric

ASAMERA OIL LIMITED
JAKARTA, INDONESIA
Specific Interests: Tropical (hot)

BPB INDUSTRIES, LIMITED RESEARCH DEVELOPMENT
EAST LEAKE
LOUGHBOROUGH, LEICESTERSHIRE, ENGLAND
Director, Dr John B Taylor
Staff Size: 100 - 499

BRITISH PETROLEUM COMPANY OF AUSTRALIA
1-29 ALBERT ROAD
MELBOURNE, VICTORIA, AUSTRALIA
Director, N R Seddon
General Environment: Terrestrial

BRITISH PETROLEUM COMPANY, LIMITED
BRITANNIC HOUSE, MOOR LANE
LONDON EC2, ENGLAND
Head, Patrick T W Akroyd
Specific Interests: Prairie and Temperate Forest

BRITISH PETROLEUM REFINERY OF SINGAPORE, LIMITED
SINGAPORE
Director, D B Robertson
Specific Interests: Tropical (hot)

CHINESE PETROLEUM CORPORATION
TAIPEI, TAIWAN
President, Mr Sin-Nan Hu,
Specific Interests: Tropical (hot)

COMMERCIAL FISHERMEN FEDERATION OF NEW ZEALAND
5857 P O BOX 597
CHRISTCHURCH, NEW ZEALAND
General Environment: Oceanographic
Specific Interests: Prairie and Temperate Forest

DELHI AUSTRALIAN PETROLEUM LIMITED
32 GRENFELL STREET
ADELAIDE, SOUTH AUSTRALIA, AUSTRALIA
Director, Charles T Easley
General Environment: Terrestrial
Specific Interests: Prairie and Temperate Forest

ENVIRONMENTAL CONTROL, FORD MOTOR COMPANY
THE AMERICA ROAD
DEARBORN, MI 48121
General Environment: Atmospheric

ESSO EXPLORATION INCORPORATED
SINGAPORE
Director, E C Salmon
Specific Interests: Tropical (hot)

FISHERIES AND INDUSTRIES COMPANY LIMITED OF SABAH
POST OFFICE BOX 591
SANDAKAN, SABAH, MALAYSIA
Director, C C Kanapi
General Environment: Oceanographic
Specific Interests: Tropical (hot)

FISHERIES AND MERCHANTS ASSOCIATION OF NEW ZEALAND
POST OFFICE BOX 857
WELLINGTON, NEW ZEALAND
General Environment: Oceanographic
Specific Interests: Prairie and Temperate Forest

FISHING COMPANY OF NORTH BORNEO
POST OFFICE BOX 591
SAN AAKAN, SABAH, MALAYSIA
Director, Kwan Yui Ming
General Environment: Oceanographic
Specific Interests: Tropical (hot)

GENERAL FOOD PROCESSING COMPANY, LIMITED
16 KOTA ROAD
TAIPING, PERAK, MALAYSIA
Director, Wee Tuck Lee
Specific Interests: Tropical (hot)

GLOBAL MARINE AUSTRALASIA PTY LIMITED
360 LONSDALE STREET
MELBOURNE, VICTORIA, AUSTRALIA
Director, James P Carroll
General Environment: Oceanographic
Specific Interests: Tropical (hot)

GRANITE CITY STEEL COMPANY
GRANITE CITY, IL 62040
Vice-President, D F Cairns
Staff Size: 5 - 9

INDUSTRIAL AND PUBLIC RELATIONS DEPARTMENT
BETHLEHEM STEEL CORPORATION
BETHLEHEM, PA 18016
Manager, D Brandt
General Environment: Atmospheric

INTERSTATE OIL LIMITED
95 COLLINS STREET
MELBOURNE, VICTORIA, AUSTRALIA

Director, Frank S Anderson
General Environment: Terrestrial

IRVING P KRICK INCORPORATED, OF TEXAS
611 SOUTH PALM CANYON DR
PALM SPRINGS, CA 92262
Director, Eddie F Choy
General Environment: Atmospheric
Staff Size: 10 - 49

JONES AND LAUGHLIN STEEL CORPORATION
3 GATEWAY CENTER
PITTSBURGH, PA 15230
Coordinator, Waino Jukkola
General Environment: Atmospheric

JURONG SHIPYARD
SINGAPORE
Specific Interests: Tropical (hot)

KAISER STEEL CORPORATION
PO BOX 217
FONTANA, CA 92335
Director, Jack Smith

KYUSHU OIL COMPANY
C/O PERMINA
DJAKARTA, INDONESIA
Specific Interests: Tropical (hot)

LOCKHEED MISSILE AND SPACE COMPANY
26565 ALTAMONT ROAD
LOS ALTOS HILLS, CA 94022
Director, Reynold W Cochran

MARINE INDUSTRIAL LIMITED OF MALAYSIA
RIVER ROAD
PENANG, MALAYSIA
Director, Chan Chi Lum
General Environment: Oceanographic
Specific Interests: Tropical (hot)

MOBIL EXPLORATION AUSTRALIA PTY LIMITED
31 QUEEN STREET
MELBOURNE, C1, VICTORIA, AUSTRALIA
Director, James H Macleod
General Environment: Terrestrial

MOBIL REFINING OF MALAYSIA, LIMITED
SINGAPORE
Directors, J R Kendall and H Lewis
Specific Interests: Tropical (hot)

NIPPON SUISAN KAISHA, LIMITED
NIPPON BUILDING, 2-6-2 OTEMACHI
CHIYODA-KU, TOKYO, JAPAN
President, Haruo Nakai
General Environment: Oceanographic
Specific Interests: Prairie and Temperate Forest
Staff Size: 1000 & Larger

OCEAN SCIENCE AND ENGINEERING COMPANY
DJAKARTA, INDONESIA
Specific Interests: Tropical (hot)

OIL DEVELOPMENT CORPORATION OF NORTH SUMATRA
C/O PERMINA
DJAKARTA, INDONESIA
Specific Interests: Tropical (hot)

OIL DRILLING AND EXPLORATION LIMITED
93 YORK STREET
SYDNEY, NEW SOUTH WALES, AUSTRALIA
Director, Douglas Davidson
General Environment: Terrestrial

PETROCARBON DEVELOPMENTS, LIMITED
SHARSTON ROAD, WYTHENSHAWE
MANCHESTER 22, ENGLAND
Director, Martin S W Ruhemann
Specific Interests: Prairie and Temperate Forest

PETROLEUM EXPLORATION COMPANY OF JAPAN
C/O PERMINA
DJAKARTA, INDONESIA
Specific Interests: Tropical (hot)

PETROLEUM PTY LIMITED OF WEST AUSTRALIA
167-187 KENT STREET
SYDNEY, NEW SOUTH WALES, AUSTRALIA
Director, G M Furnival
General Environment: Terrestrial
Specific Interests: Prairie and Temperate Forest

PHILIPS AUSTRALIAN OIL COMPANY
150 EDWARD STREET
BRISBANE, QUEENSLAND, AUSTRALIA
Director, J J Tanner
General Environment: Terrestrial

PLANNERS, ENGINEERS FOR LANDSCAPE ARCHITECTURE
1136 UNION HALL
HONOLULU, HI 96814

READING AND BATES PTY LIMITED
380 QUEENS STREET
BRISBANE, QUEENSLAND, AUSTRALIA
Director, Frank J Garnett

REPUBLIC STEEL CORPORATION
6801 BRECKSVILLE ROAD
INDEPENDENCE, OH 44131
Director, W E Sebesta

SANYO HYDROGRAPHIC COMPANY
23-7 5-CHOME SHINBASHI
MINATO-KU, TOKYO, JAPAN
Director, Kohei Ono
General Environment: Oceanographic
Specific Interests: Prairie and Temperate Forest

SHELL DEVELOPMENT PTY LIMITED
155 WILLIAM STREET
MELBOURNE, VICTORIA, AUSTRALIA
Director, Lewis Luxton Cbe
General Environment: Terrestrial

SHELL PETROLEUM COMPANY
C/O BRUNEI SHELL PETROLEUM
SERIA, BRUNEI, MALAYSIA
Specific Interests: Tropical (hot)

SHELL RESEARCH, LIMITED
SHELL CENTER
LONDON SEI, ENGLAND
Director, Charles N Thompson
Specific Interests: Prairie and Temperate Forest

SHIPBUILDING AND ENGINEERING OF WHYALLA
WHYALLA, SOUTH AUSTRALIA, AUSTRALIA
Director, B J Dalziell

SOUTHWESTERN DRILLING COMPANY
BRISBANE, QUEENSLAND, AUSTRALIA
Specific Interests: Prairie and Temperate Forest

ST LAWRENCE DEVELOPMENT COMPANY
SEAWAY CIRCLE
MASSENA, NY 13662

THAISARCO UNION CARBIDE EASTERN INCORPORATED
PHUKET, THAILAND
Specific Interests: Tropical (hot)

UNITED STATES STEEL CORPORATION
525 WILLIAM PENN PLACE
PITTSBURGH, PA 15230
Assistant, Herbert Dunsmore

WEATHER MODIFICATION, NATIONAL AND INTERNATIONAL
611 SOUTH PALM CANYON DR
PALM SPRINGS, CA 92262
Vice President, Newton Stone
General Environment: Atmospheric
Staff Size: 10 - 49

Professional Organizations

ACRES, INCORPORATED
1802 CHAPMAN ROAD
HUNTERTOWN, IN 46748
President, Robert Weber
General Environment: Terrestrial
Specific Interests: Prairie and Temperate
Forest

**ADIRONDACK MOUNTAIN CLUB,
INCORPORATED**
1113 CAMBRIDGE ROAD
TEANECK, NJ 07666
President, Frank J Oliver
General Environment: Terrestrial
Specific Interests: Mountainous
Staff Size: 1000 - 4999

**AMERICAN PETROLEUM
INSTITUTE**
1801 K STREET, NW
WASHINGTON, DC 20006

**CALIFORNIA ROADSIDE COUNCIL,
INCORPORATED**
2636 OCEAN AVENUE
SAN FRANCISCO, CA 94132
President, Mrs R Reynolds
Specific Interests: Prairie and Temperate
Forest

**CIVIL AND STRUCTURAL
ENGINEERING**
3104 MOUNTAIN CURVE AVENUE
ALTADENA, CA 91001
Director, Stanley Hart
General Environment: Terrestrial
Staff Size: 1 - 4

**CIVIL ENGINEER SOCIETY OF
AMERICA**
345 EAST 47TH STREET
NEW YORK, NY 10017
Executive Director, Dr Eugene Zwoyer
Staff Size: 50 - 99

**CONSERVANCY COUNCIL OF
MIDDLE TENNESSEE**
NASHVILLE CHILDRENS MUSEUM
NASHVILLE, TN 37210
President, Dennis Gibson
Specific Interests: Prairie and Temperate
Forest

**CONSERVATION INFORMATION
(AMERICAN ASSOCIATION)**
1416 9TH STREET
SACRAMENTO, CA 95814
Specific Interests: Prairie and Temperate
Forest

**FARM AND GARDEN ASSOCIATION
INCORPORATED OF NEW
ENGLAND**
45 NEWBURY STREET
BOSTON, MA 02116
President, Mrs M Clair

**INTERPROFESSIONAL
COMMISSION ON
ENVIRONMENTAL DESIGN**
1735 NEW YORK AVENUE, NW
WASHINGTON, DC 20006
Specific Interests: Prairie and Temperate
Forest

**LANDSCAPE ARCHITECTS
(AMERICAN SOCIETY)**
2013 E STREET, NW
WASHINGTON, DC 20006
Executive Director, Alfred B Lagasse
Specific Interests: Prairie and Temperate
Forest
Staff Size: 1000 - 4999

**MECHANICAL ENGINEERS
(AMERICAN SOCIETY)**
345 EAST 42ND STREET
NEW YORK, NY 10017
Specific Interests: Prairie and Temperate
Forest

**PETROLEUM GEOLOGISTS
(AMERICAN ASSOCIATION)**
BOX 979
TULSA, OK 74101
Specific Interests: Prairie and Temperate
Forest

**PUBLIC WORKS ASSOCIATION OF
AMERICA**
1313 EAST 60TH STREET
CHICAGO, IL 60637
Director, Robert D Bugher
Staff Size: 10 - 49

**RYCKMAN, EDGERLY, TOMLINSON
ASSOCIATION**
12161 LACKLAND ROAD
ST LOUIS, MO 63141
Senior Vice President, E Edgerley
Staff Size: 50 - 99

Research Institute

**CONSERVATION CORPORATION
OF THE CARRIBEAN**
APARTADO 896
SAN JOSE, COSTA RICA
Director, Guillermo Cruz

AGRICULTURAL
ENGINEERING

Educational Institute

**AGRICULTURAL AND
ENVIRONMENTAL SCIENCES
COLLEGE**

UNIVERSITY OF CALIFORNIA
DAVIS, CA 95616

**AGRICULTURAL AND NATURAL
RESOURCES COLLEGE**
MICHIGAN STATE UNIVERSITY
EAST LANSING, MI 48823

**AGRICULTURAL BOTANY
DEPARTMENT**
QUEEN'S UNIVERSITY
BT9/N BELFAST 6BB, NORTHERN
IRELAND
General Environment: Terrestrial
Specific Interests: Prairie and Temperate
Forest

**AGRICULTURAL CHEMISTRY AND
SOILS DEPARTMENT**
507 AGRICULTURAL SCIENCES
BUILDING
TUCSON, AZ 85721
Professor, Wallace Fuller

AGRICULTURAL DEPARTMENT
KYUSHU UNIVERSITY
FUKUOKA, JAPAN
Director, Dr Masuki Okamoto
Specific Interests: Prairie and Temperate
Forest

**AGRICULTURAL ENGINEERING
DEPARTMENT**
UNIVERSITY OF CALIFORNIA AT
DAVIS
DAVIS, CA 95616

**AGRICULTURAL ENGINEERING
DEPARTMENT**
IOWA STATE UNIVERSITY OF
SCIENCES
AMES, IA 50010

**AGRICULTURAL MEDICINE
INSTITUTE**
DEPARTMENT OF AGRICULTURE,
UNIVERSITY OF IOWA
OAKDALE, IA 52319
Specific Interests: Prairie and Temperate
Forest

**AGRICULTURAL MEDICINE
INSTITUTE**
ASR MEDICAL RESOURCES
FACILITY
OAKDALE, IA 52319
Associate Director, Clyde Berry

**AGRICULTURAL POLICY
INSTITUTE, NORTH CAROLINA
STATE UNIVERSITY**
P O BOX 5368
RALEIGH, NC 27607

AGRICULTURE COLLEGE
CORNELL UNIVERSITY
ITHACA, NY 14850

AGRICULTURE COLLEGE
UNIVERSITY OF CALIFORNIA
DAVIS, CA 95616
Specific Interests: Prairie and Temperate
Forest

AGRICULTURE COLLEGE
UNIVERSITY OF WISCONSIN
MADISON, WI 53706

AGRICULTURE COLLEGE
UNIVERSITY OF ILLINOIS
URBANA, IL 61801
Staff Size: 50 - 99

AGRICULTURE DEPARTMENT
UNIVERSITY OF CALIFORNIA
BERKELEY, CA 94720
Specific Interests: Prairie and Temperate
Forest

AGROMETEOROLGY
UNIVERSITY OF HAWAII
HONOLULU, HI 96822

**AIR POLLUTION DAMAGE TO
PLANTS IN COLORADO**
COLORADO STATE UNIVERSITY
FORT COLLINS, CO 80521
General Environment: Atmospheric

ARID LANDS PROGRAM
UNIVERSITY OF ARIZONA
TUCSON, AZ 85721
Director, W G Mcginnies
General Environment: Terrestrial
Specific Interests: Desert

**CONSERVATION EDUCATION
CENTER**
CLARION STATE COLLEGE
CLARION, PA 16214
Specific Interests: Prairie and Temperate
Forest

**ENVIRONMENTAL SCIENCE
PROGRAM**
OKLAHOMA STATE UNIVERSITY OF
AGRICULTURE
STILLWATER, OK 74074

ENVIRONMENTAL STUDIES
UNIVERSITY OF LIBYA
TRIPOLI, LIBYA
General Environment: Terrestrial

FACULTY OF AGRICULTURE
UNIVERSITY OF THE WEST INDIES
MONA, KINGSTON 7, JAMAICA
General Environment: Terrestrial
Specific Interests: Prairie and Temperate
Forest

**FISHERIES EXPERIMENTAL
STATION**
DEPARTMENT OF AGRICULTURE
TOKYO, JAPAN

Director, Yoshio Hiyama
General Environment: Oceanographic
Specific Interests: Prairie and Temperate
Forest

**FOOD PROTECTION AND
TOXICOLOGY**
UNIVERSITY OF CALIFORNIA
DAVIS, CA 95616

**LABORATORY FOR
AGRICULTURAL SENSING**
PURDUE UNIVERSITY
LAFAYETTE, IN 47901

**NUTRITION AND FOOD SCIENCES
DEPARTMENT**
MASSACHUSETTS INSTITUTE OF
TECHNOLOGY
CAMBRIDGE, MA 02139

**SANITARY SCIENCE, COLLEGE OF
AGRICULTURE**
UNIVERSITY OF MISSOURI
COLUMBIA, MO 65201
Staff Size: 1 - 4

**SOIL AND PLANT NUTRITION
DEPARTMENT**
UNIVERSITY OF CALIFORNIA
BERKELEY, CA 94720
General Environment: Terrestrial
Specific Interests: Prairie and Temperate
Forest

**SOILS DIVISION, AGRICULTURAL
INSTITUTION**
JOHNSTOWN CASTLE
WEXFORD, IRELAND
Director, Philip Moss
General Environment: Terrestrial
Specific Interests: Prairie and Temperate
Forest

Foundation

**AGRICULTURAL PRODUCERS,
INTERNATIONAL FEDERATION**
ROOM 401, BARR BUILDING, 910
17TH STREET, NW
WASHINGTON, DC 20006

AGRONOMY SOCIETY OF AMERICA
677 SOUTH SEGOE ROAD
MADISON, WI 43711
General Environment: Terrestrial

**DOCUMENTION AGRICOLE
SCIENT ET TECHNOLOGY**
6 BUILDING DRAGAN TZANCOV
SOFIA, BULGARIA
Director, Slavi Slavov
General Environment: Terrestrial

**FOOD AND AGRICULTURE
ORGANIZATION OF THE UNITED
NATIONS**
VIA DELLE TERME CARACALLA
ROME, ITALY

Government — Federal

**AGRICULTURAL ENGINEERING
RESOURCES DIVISION**
2819 DUVALL
BURONSVILLE, MD 20730
Director, W M Carleton
General Environment: Terrestrial

**AGRICULTURAL RESEARCH
SERVICE**
WASHINGTON,DC 20250
Specific Interests: Prairie and Temperate
Forest

AGRICULTURE
ROOM 1301, LONGWORTH HOUSE
WASHINGTON, DC 20515
Director, Representative William R
Poage
General Environment: Terrestrial

**AGRICULTURE AND FOREST
SENATE COMMITTEE**
245 SENATE OFFICE BUILDING
WASHINGTON, DC 20510
Director, Senator Allen J Ellender
General Environment: Terrestrial

AGRICULTURE DEPARTMENT
8822 FIRCREST PLACE
ALEXANDRIA, VA 22308
Under-Secretary, J Phil Campbell
General Environment: Terrestrial

AGRICULTURE DEPARTMENT
14TH STREET AND JEFFERSON
DRIVE, SW
WASHINGTON, DC 20250
Specific Interests: Prairie and Temperate
Forest

**AGRICULTURE LABORATORY,
NATIONAL**
U S DEPARTMENT OF
AGRICULTURE
BELTSVILLE, MD 20705
Specific Interests: Prairie and Temperate
Forest

AGRICULTURE MINISTRY
POST OFFICE BOX 630
ACCRA, GHANA
Director, J N N Adjetey

AGROMETEOROLOGY
B P 566 METEOROL NATIONALE
CONAKRY, GUINEA, WEST AFRICA
Director, Nouhou Tata Diallo

**AGRONOMY AND AGRICULTURAL
ECONOMICS, NATIONAL PLANT
AND FOOD INSTITUTE**
1700 K STREET, NW
WASHINGTON, DC 20006

**ANIMAL DISEASE AND PARASITE
RESEARCH DIVISION**
BELTSVILLE PARASITOLOGY
LABORATORY
BELTSVILLE, MD 20705
Specific Interests: Prairie and Temperate
Forest

**CONSUMER AND FOOD RESEARCH
DIVISION**
FEDERAL CENTER BUILDING
HYATTSVILLE, MD 20781
General Environment: Terrestrial
Specific Interests: Prairie and Temperate
Forest

**CONSUMER AND MARKETING
SERVICES**
14TH STREET AND
INDEPENDENCE AVENUE, SW
WASHINGTON, DC 20250
Specific Interests: Prairie and Temperate
Forest

**CURRENT RESEARCH
INFORMATION SYSTEM**
14TH STREET AND
INDEPENDENCE AVENUE, ROOM
6818
WASHINGTON, DC 20250
Specific Interests: Prairie and Temperate
Forest

FARMERS HOME ADMINISTRATION
14TH STREET AND
INDEPENDENCE AVENUE, SW
WASHINGTON, DC 20250
Specific Interests: Prairie and Temperate
Forest

**FOOD AND DRUG
ADMINISTRATION, DIVISION OF
COMMUNITY STUDIES**
4770 BUFORD HIGHWAY
CHAMBLEE, GA 30341
General Environment: Terrestrial

**FOREIGN AGRICULTURAL AND
SPECIAL PROGRAM DIVISION**
406 DEERFIELD AVENUE
SILVER SPRING, MD 20910
Director, Robert M Bor
General Environment: Terrestrial

**FOREST ENVIRONMENT
RESEARCH DIVISION**
14TH AND INDEPENDENCE
AVENUE, SW
WASHINGTON, DC 20250

Specific Interests: Prairie and Temperate
Forest

**FOREST SERVICE REGION 1
OFFICE**
FEDERAL BUILDING
MISSOULA, MT 59801
General Environment: Terrestrial
Specific Interests: Mountainous

**FOREST SERVICE REGION 10
OFFICE**
FEDERAL OFFICE BUILDING, BOX
1628
JUNEAU, AK 99801
General Environment: Terrestrial

**FOREST SERVICE REGION 2
OFFICE**
DENVER FEDERAL CENTER
BUILDING 85
DENVER, CO 80225
General Environment: Terrestrial
Specific Interests: Mountainous

**FOREST SERVICE REGION 3
OFFICE**
FEDERAL BUILDING, 517 GOLD
AVENUE, SW
ALBUQUERQUE, NM 87101
General Environment: Terrestrial
Specific Interests: Desert

**FOREST SERVICE REGION 5
OFFICE**
630 SANSOME STREET
SAN FRANCISCO, CA 94111
General Environment: Terrestrial
Specific Interests: Urban

**FOREST SERVICE REGION 6
OFFICE**
319 SW PINE STREET, BOX 3623
PORTLAND, OR 97208
General Environment: Terrestrial
Specific Interests: Prairie and Temperate
Forest

**FOREST SERVICE REGION 8
OFFICE**
1720 PEACHTREE, SUITE 800
ATLANTA, GA 30309
General Environment: Terrestrial

**FOREST SERVICE REGION 9
OFFICE**
633 WEST WISCONSIN AVENUE
MILWAUKE, WI 53203
General Environment: Terrestrial

**GRASSLAND HUSBANDRY,
AGRICULTURAL DEVELOPMENT
ADVANCE**
BLOCK C, GOVERNMENTAL
BUILDINGS
CAMBRIDGE, ENGLAND
Gwilym P Hughes
General Environment: Terrestrial
Specific Interests: Prairie and Temperate
Forest

**GULF COAST SHELLFISH
SANITATION RESEARCH CENTER**
POST OFFICE BOX 158
DAUPHIN ISLAND, AL 36528
General Environment: Oceanographic

**HUMAN NUTRITION RESEARCH
DIVISION**
AGRICULTURAL RESEARCH
CENTER
BELTSVILLE, MD 20705
General Environment: Terrestrial
Specific Interests: Prairie and Temperate
Forest

**HUMAN NUTRITION RESEARCH
DIVISION**
FEDERAL CENTER BUILDING
HYATTSVILLE, MD 20705
General Environment: Terrestrial
Specific Interests: Prairie and Temperate
Forest

**INFORMATION DIVISION,
FEDERAL CENTER BUILDING**
BELLCREST ROAD AND EAST-
WEST ROAD
HYATTSVILLE, MD 20781
Specific Interests: Prairie and Temperate
Forest

**INFORMATION OFFICE, U S
DEPARTMENT OF AGRICULTURE**
14TH STREET AND
INDEPENDENCE AVENUE
WASHINGTON, DC 20250
Specific Interests: Prairie and Temperate
Forest

**INSPECTION SERVICES OFFICE, U S
DEPARTMENT OF AGRICULTURE**
3202 DEVINE STREET, OFFICE H
COLUMBIA, SC 29205
Inspector, R Jones

LAND ECONOMY DEPARTMENT
SILVER STREET
CAMBRIDGE, ENGLAND
Director, Ford G Sturrock
General Environment: Terrestrial
Specific Interests: Prairie and Temperate
Forest

**MARKET QUALITY RESEARCH
DIVISION**
FEDERAL CENTER BUILDING
HYATTSVILLE, MD 20781
General Environment: Terrestrial
Specific Interests: Prairie and Temperate
Forest

**PESTICIDE BRANCH,
ENVIRONMENTAL PROTECTION
AGENCY**
1421 PEACHTREE, NE
ATLANTA, GA 30309
Section Head, T P Keller

PESTICIDE REGULATION DIVISION
POST OFFICE BOX 8348
RICHMOND, VA 23226

Inspector, H Howell

PESTICIDE REGULATION DIVISION
6400 FRANCE AVENUE, SOUTH
MINNEAPOLIS, MN 55435

Inspector, J Foley

**PESTICIDE REGULATION
DIVISION DEPARTMENT OF
AGRICULTURE**
SUITE 104, TILLMAN STREET
MEMPHIS, TN 38111

Inspection, N Stubbs

**PESTICIDE REGULATION
DIVISION, U S DEPARTMENT OF
AGRICULTURE**
226 WEST JACKSON BOULEVARD
CHICAGO, IL 60606

**PESTICIDE REGULATION
DIVISION, U S DEPARTMENT OF
AGRICULTURE**
511 NW BROADWAY
PORTLAND, OR 97207

Inspector, K Covert

**PESTICIDE REGULATION
DIVISION, U S DEPARTMENT OF
AGRICULTURE**
141 EAST TRINITY PLACE
DECATUR, GA 30030

**PESTICIDE REGULATION
DIVISION, U S DEPARTMENT OF
AGRICULTURE**
POST OFFICE BOX 6050
FORT WORTH, TX 76115

Inspector, W Pfister

**PESTICIDE REGULATION, US
DEPARTMENT OF AGRICULTURE**
1421 PEACHTREE, NE ROOM 200
ATLANTA, GA 30309

Secretary, Penny Gilmore

**ROCKY MOUNTAIN FOREST AND
RANGE EXPERIMENTAL STATION**
282 AGRICULTURE BUILDING
TEMPE, AZ 85281

Director, Dr Hudson G Renolds
General Environment: Terrestrial
Staff Size: 10 - 49

**SHELLFISH SANITATION
NORTHEAST RESEARCH CENTER**
NARRAGANSETT, RI 02882

General Environment: Oceanographic

**SHELLFISH SANITATION
NORTHWEST LABORATORY**
ROUTE 4, BOX 4519
GIG HARBOR, WA 98335

General Environment: Oceanographic

**SOIL AND WATER CONSERVATION
RESOURCES DIVISION**
POST OFFICE BOX 672
RIVERSIDE, CA 92502

Staff Size: 10 - 49

**SOIL AND WATER CONSERVATION
RESOURCES DIVISION**
AGRICULTURAL RESEARCH
SERVICE, U S DEPARTMENT OF
AGRICULTURE
BELTSVILLE,MD 20705

Director, R S Dyal
Staff Size: 100 - 499

**SOIL CLASS AND CORRELATION
DIVISION**
4613 BEECHWOOD ROAD
COLLEGE PARK, MD 20740

Director, Roy W Simonson
General Environment: Terrestrial

**SOIL CONSERVATION AND
FORESTRY SUBCOMMITTEE**
SENATE OFFICE BUILDING, SUITE
324
WASHINGTON, DC 20510

Chairman, James O Eastland
General Environment: Terrestrial

**SOIL CONSERVATION SERVICE,
SOIL SURVEY**
111 DEVERE DRIVE
SILVER SPRING, MD 20903

Deputy Administrator, William Johnson

**SOIL SURVEY INTERPRETATION
DIVISION**
915 NEWHALL STREET
SILVER SPRING, MD 20901

Director, Albert Klingebiel
General Environment: Terrestrial

**SOIL SURVEY INVESTIGATIONS
DIVISION**
64 40TH AVENUE
UNIVERSITY PARK, MD 20782

Director, Guy Smith
General Environment: Terrestrial

**SOIL SURVEY OPERATIONS
DIVISION**
1624 WOODMAN DRIVE
MCLEAN, VA 22101

Director, Dirk Van Der Voit
General Environment: Terrestrial

STATISTICAL REPORTING SERVICE
14TH STREET AND
INDEPENDENCE AVENUE, SW
WASHINGTON, DC 20250

Administrator, Harry C Trelogan
General Environment: Terrestrial

TROPICAL FORESTRY INSTITUTE
POST OFFICE BOX AQ
RIO PIEDRAS, PR 00923

Staff Size: 10 - 49

Government — State or Local

**AGRICULTURAL AND CHEMICAL
DEVELOPMENT OFFICE**
NATIONAL FERTILIZER
DEVELOPMENT CENTER
MUSCLE SHOALS, AL 35660

Specific Interests: Prairie and Temperate
Forest

**AGRICULTURAL CHEMISTRY
DIVISION**
BEARD BUILDING, BOX 3336
MONTGOMERY, AL 36109

Director, J Kirkpatrick
Staff Size: 10 - 49

**AGRICULTURAL EXPERIMENTAL
STATION OF CONNECTICUT**
POST OFFICE BOX 1106
NEW HAVEN, CT 06504

Director, J Hanna

**AGRICULTURAL LABORATORY
DEPARTMENT**
STATE HOUSE STATION, BOX 94693
LINCOLN, NB 68509

Director, G D Gilsdorf

AGRICULTURE DEPARTMENT
P O BOX 1209, 350 CAPITOL HILL
AVENUE
RENO, NV 89504

Chief Chemist, Harlan Specht

AGRICULTURE DEPARTMENT
ROOM 412, STATE CAPITOL
BUILDING
SALT LAKE CITY, UT 84114

State Chemist, H K Francis

AGRICULTURE DEPARTMENT
1525 SHERMAN STREET
DENVER, CO 80203

Director, Willard Snyder

AGRICULTURE DEPARTMENT
STATE OFFICE BUILDING
ST PAUL, MN 55101

Administrator, R Dennison
Staff Size: 100 - 499

AGRICULTURE DEPARTMENT
CAPITOL STATION
AUSTIN, TX 78710

Assistant Commissioner, Charlie
Chapman

AGRICULTURE DEPARTMENT
BOX 192B GPO
HOBART, TASMANIA

Director, R Mead
General Environment: Terrestrial
Specific Interests: Prairie and Temperate
Forest

**AGRICULTURE DEPARTMENT,
  STATE RECLAMATION BOARD**
100 CAMBRIDGE STREET
BOSTON, MA 02134

**AIR POLLUTION CONTROL,
  JOHNSON COUNTY HEALTH
  DEPARTMENT**
COURTHOUSE
OLATHE, KS 66061
General Environment: Atmospheric

**CHEMISTRY DIVISION,
  DEPARTMENT OF AGRICULTURE**
AGRICULTURAL BUILDING
RALEIGH, NC 27602
State Chemist, W Y Cobb

**CONSUMER PROTECTION,
  DEPARTMENT OF AGRICULTURE**
CAPITOL BUILDING, ROOM
  EAST-109
CHARLESTON, WV 25305
Director, C Amick

**CROP PESTICIDE STATE
  COMMISSION**
CLEMSON, SC 29631
Assistant State Entomologist, L H Senn

**ECONOMIC POISON SECTION,
  MARKETING CONSERVATION
  DIVISION**
POST OFFICE BOX 5425 PAWAA
  STATION
HONOLULU, HI 96814
Director, Stanley Tanaka

**ENTOMOLOGY DIVISION,
  DEPARTMENT OF AGRICULTURE**
122 STATE CAPITOL BUILDING
OKLAHOMA CITY, OK 73105
Director, Clyde Bower

**ENTOMOLOGY DIVISION,
  DEPARTMENT OF AGRICULTURE
  AND CONSERVATION**
83 PARK STREET
PROVIDENCE, RI 02903
Chief, Rudolf D'andrea

**ENTOMOLOGY DIVISION, STATE
  DEPARTMENT OF AGRICULTURE**
JEFFERSON BUILDING
JEFFERSON CITY, MO 65101
State Entomologist, Lester H Barrows

**ENVIRONMENTAL CONTROL,
  DEPARTMENT OF
  BIOCHEMISTRY**
PURDUE UNIVERSITY
LAFAYETTE, IN 47907

**FEED AND FERTILIZER CONTROL
  SERVICE**
COLLEGE STATION, TX 77843
Director, Reed Mcdonald

**FEEDS, FERTILIZER AND
  STABILIZATION STANDARDS
  DIVISION**
531 EAST SANGAMON STREET
SPRINGFIELD, IL 62706
Superintendent, John Staley

**FIELD CROPS AND
  AGRICULTURAL CHEMISTRY
  BUREAU**
1220 NORTH STREET
SACRAMENTO, CA 95814
Director, Van Entwistle

**FOOD AND DRUG DIVISION,
  DEPARTMENT OF AGRICULTURE**
BOX 9039, MELROSE STATION
NASHVILLE, TN 37204
Pesticide Chemist, J Jonakin

**GRAIN AND CHEMICAL DIVISION,
  U S DEPARTMENT OF
  AGRICULTURE**
BOX 128
OLYMPIA, WA 98501
Supervisor, Errett Deck, Jr

HEALTH DEPARTMENT
POST OFFICE BOX 9232
SAN JUAN, PR 00908
Specific Interests: Tropical (hot)

**INSPECTION DIVISION,
  DEPARTMENT OF AGRICULTURE**
POST OFFICE BOX 3150
LA CRUCES, NM 88001
Chief, Glen Horton

**LABORATORY SERVICES,
  DEPARTMENT OF AGRICULTURE**
635 CAPITOL NORTH EAST
SALEM, OR 97301
Chief Chemist, V Hiatt

**MARKETS AND STANDARDS
  DIVISION, DEPARTMENT OF
  AGRICULTURE**
STATE HOUSE ANNEX ROOM 106
CONCORD, NH 03301
Director, G Laramie

**MEAT AND POULTRY SURVEY,
  STATE DIVISION OF
  AGRICULTURE**
POST OFFICE BOX 490
JUNEAU, AK 99801
State Veterinarian, Dr F S Hosinger

**PESTICIDE COMPLIANCE,
  DEPARTMENT OF
  ENVIRONMENTAL PROTECTION**
STATE OFFICE BUILDING, ROOM
  G-3A
HARTFORD, CT 06115
Assistant Director, P J Wijga

**PESTICIDE CONSERVATION, STATE
  DIVISION OF AGRICULTURE**
BOX 800
PALMER, AK 99645
Director, Roland Snodgrass

**PESTICIDE CONTROL,
  DEPARTMENT OF AGRICULTURE**
POST OFFICE BOX 1888
TRENTON, NJ 08625
State Chemist, Delmar Myers

**PESTICIDE CONTROL,
  DEPARTMENT OF AGRICULTURE**
HILL FARM BUILDING, ROOM 202-B
MADISON, WI 53702
Director, H Halliday

**PESTICIDE CONTROL,
  LABORATORY DIVISION, STATE
  DEPARTMENT OF AGRICULTURE**
1615 SOUTH HARRISON ROAD
EAST LANSING, MI 48823
Director, C Carr
General Environment: Terrestrial

**PESTICIDE DIVISION, CHEMISTRY
  LABORATORY, AGRICULTURE
  DEPARTMENT**
EAST 7TH AND COURT STREETS
DES MOINES, IA 50319
Director, M Van Cleve
Specific Interests: Rural

**PESTICIDE DIVISION,
  DEPARTMENT OF AGRICULTURE**
CAPITOL SQUARE, SW
ATLANTA, GA 30334
Director, R Moncrieff

**PESTICIDE REGULATION,
  DEPARTMENT OF AGRICULTURE**
203 NORTH GOVERNOR STREET,
  ROOM 304
RICHMOND, VA 23219

**PESTICIDE SECTION, STATE
  DEPARTMENT OF AGRICULTURE**
MAYO BUILDING
TALLAHASSEE, FL 32304
Chief, E Winterle

**PLANT INDUSTRY BUREAU,
  DEPARTMENT OF AGRICULTURE**
POST OFFICE BOX 790
BOISE, ID 83701
Director, Wallace Fisher

**PLANT INDUSTRY DIVISION,
  DEPARTMENT OF AGRICULTURE**
REYNOLDSBURG, OH 43068
Chief, Harold Porter

**PLANT INDUSTRY DIVISION,
  DEPARTMENT OF AGRICULTURE
  AND MARKETS**

STATE CAMPUS BUILDING 8
ALBANY, NY 12226
Director, Henry Page

**PLANT INDUSTRY DIVISION,
DEPARTMENT OF AGRICULTURE**
PIERRE, SD 57501

**PLANT INDUSTRY DIVISION,
WYOMING DEPARTMENT OF
AGRICULTURE**
308 CAPITOL BUILDING
CHEYENNE, WY 82001
Director, Walter Patch

**PLANT PESTICIDE CONTROL
DIVISION**
DEPARTMENT OF AGRICULTURE
BOSTON, MA 02133
Specific Interests: Prairie and Temperate
  Forest
Staff Size: 50 - 99

**PLANT PESTICIDE CONTROL
DIVISION, DEPARTMENT OF
AGRICULTURE**
STATE OFFICE BUILDING, 116
  STREET
MONTPELIER, VT 05602
Director, J Scott
Staff Size: 10 - 49

SOIL CONSERVATION SERVICE
7504 VENICE COURT
FALLS CHURCH, VA 22043
Administrator, Kenneth E Grant

**STANDARDS AND INSPECTIONS
DIVISION**
DEPARTMENT OF AGRICULTURE
DOVER, DE 19901
Director, John Clough
Staff Size: 50 - 99

STATE BOARD OF AGRICULTURE
TOPEKA, KS 66612
Director, Robert H Guntert

**STATE LABORATORIES
DEPARTMENT**
BOX 937
BISMARCK, ND 58501
Food Commissioner, L Koehler

STATE PLANT BOARD
BOX 5207
STATE COLLEGE, MS 39762
Director, O Guice Jr

Industrial/Commercial

**AGRICULTURAL CHEMICALS,
NATIONAL ASSOCIATION**
1155-15TH STREET, NW
WASHINGTON, DC 20005

Science Coordinator, William Hollis

**CARIBENA PRODUCERS
COOPERATIVE**
SAN PEDRO SULA, AMBERGRIS
  CAYE
SAN PEDRO SULA, HONDURAS
General Environment: Terrestrial

COCONUT INDUSTRY BOARD
18 WATERLOO ROAD
KINGSTON 10, JAMAICA
Director, D H Romney
General Environment: Terrestrial
Specific Interests: Tropical (hot)

MILK MARKETING BOARD
THAMES DITTON, SURREY,
  ENGLAND
Director, Laurence K O'connor
Specific Interests: Prairie and Temperate
  Forest

NATIONAL CANNERS ASSOCIATION
1133 20TH STREET, NW
WASHINGTON, DC 20036
Specific Interests: Prairie and Temperate
  Forest
Staff Size: 500 - 999

PLANT PROTECTION LIMITED
FERNHURST
HASLEMERE, SURREY, ENGLAND
Management Director, William B Boon
General Environment: Terrestrial
Specific Interests: Prairie and Temperate
  Forest

**UKRAINIAN SCIENCES-RESOURCES
INSTITUTE KONSERVNOY**
ODESSA, UNION OF SOVIET
  SOCIALIST REPUBLICS
Director, Ye L Milnichenko
Staff Size: 5 - 9

Professional Organizations

**AGRICULTURAL DEVELOPMENT,
INTER AMERICAN COMMISSION**
1735 E STREET, NW, ROOM 1029
WASHINGTON, DC 20006

**AGRICULTURAL ENGINEERS
(AMERICAN SOCIETY OF)**
2950 NILES ROAD
ST JOSEPH, MI 49085
General Environment: Terrestrial
Staff Size: 10 - 49

AGRICULTURAL METEOROLOGY
METEOROLOGICAL OFFICE
POONA-5, INDIA
Director, Peruvemba Sreenivasan

**AGRICULTURAL RESEARCH
COUNCIL**
160 GREAT PORTLAND STREET
LONDON W1, ENGLAND
General Environment: Terrestrial
Specific Interests: Prairie and Temperate
  Forest

AGRONOMY SOCIETY OF AMERICA
677 SOUTH SEGOE ROAD
MADISON, WI 53711
Executive Secretary, Matthias Stelly
Specific Interests: Prairie and Temperate
  Forest
Staff Size: 5000 - 9999

**COMMISSION FOR NATIONAL
ARBOR DAY**
63 FITZRANDOLPH ROAD
WEST ORANGE, NJ 07052
National Executive Secretary, Harry J
  Banker
General Environment: Terrestrial
Specific Interests: Prairie and Temperate
  Forest

FARM BUREAU FEDERATION
BOX 238, NORTH MAIN STREET
CONCORD, NH 03301
Staff Size: 1 - 4

MASSACHUSETTS STATE GRANGE
757 WEST SAGAMORE STREET
E SANDWICH, MA 02537
Director, J Albert Torrey

NATIONAL GRANGE
1616 H STREET, NW
WASHINGTON, DC 20006
Master, John W Scott
General Environment: Terrestrial
Specific Interests: Prairie and Temperate
  Forest

NEW HAMPSHIRE STATE GRANGE
RFD ONE
SUNCOOK, NH 03275

POTATO MARKETING BOARD
50 HANS CRESCENT
LONDON SW1, ENGLAND
Director, Charles P Hampson
General Environment: Terrestrial
Specific Interests: Prairie and Temperate
  Forest

**SOIL CONSERVATION SOCIETY OF
AMERICA**
7515 NORTHEAST ANKENY ROAD
ANKENY, IA 50021
General Environment: Terrestrial
Specific Interests: Prairie and Temperate
  Forest

**WOMEN'S NATIONAL FARM AND
GARDEN ASSOCIATION**
BOX 204
VALENICIA, PA 10659

Chairman, Mrs Charles S Roberts
Specific Interests: Prairie and Temperate
Forest

Research Institute

**AGRICULTURAL AND CHEMURGIC
RESOURCES COUNCIL**
350 FIFTH AVENUE
NEW YORK, NY 10001
General Environment: Terrestrial
Specific Interests: Prairie and Temperate
Forest

**AGRICULTURAL ENGINEERING,
INTERNATIONAL COMMISSION**
19, AVENUE DU MAINE
PARIS 15, FRANCE
General Environment: Terrestrial

**AGRICULTURAL ENGINEERING,
NATIONAL INSTITUTE**
WREST PARK
SILSOE, BEDFORD, ENGLAND
Director, Gordon Shepperson
General Environment: Terrestrial
Specific Interests: Prairie and Temperate
Forest
Staff Size: 100 - 499

**AGRICULTURAL RESEARCH
COUNCIL, LETCOMBE
LABORATORY**
LETCOMBE REGIS
WANTAGE, BERKS, ENGLAND
Director, Robert S Russell
Specific Interests: Prairie and Temperate
Forest
Staff Size: 100 - 499

**AGRICULTURAL RESOURCE
INSTITUTE OF NORTHERN
IRELAND**
HILLSBOROUGH, COUNTY DOWN,
NORTHERN IRELAND
Director, John C Murdoch
General Environment: Terrestrial
Specific Interests: Prairie and Temperate
Forest

**AGRICULTURAL, ECONOMICAL,
RESOURCES COUNCIL**
212 POST OFFICE BUILDING
BERKELEY, CA 94701
General Environment: Terrestrial

**EUROPEAN AND MEDITERRANEAN
PLANT PROTECTION
ORGANIZATION**
1 RUE LA NOTRA
PARIS 16, FRANCE

**GLASSHOUSE CROPS RESEARCH
INSTITUTE**
WORTHING ROAD,
LITTLEHAMPTON, SUSSEX,
ENGLAND

Director, Peter B Flegg
General Environment: Terrestrial
Specific Interests: Prairie and Temperate
Forest

**GRASSLAND HUSBANDRY
DEPARTMENT**
WEST OF SCOTLAND
AGRICULTURAL COLLEGE
AUCHINCRUIVE, AYRSHIRE,
SCOTLAND
General Environment: Terrestrial
Specific Interests: Prairie and Temperate
Forest
Staff Size: 5 - 9

GRASSLAND RESEARCH INSTITUTE
MAIDENHEAD, BERKS, ENGLAND
Director, Albert J Heard
General Environment: Terrestrial
Specific Interests: Prairie and Temperate
Forest

HORTICULTURE DEPARTMENT
UNIVERSITY OF HAWAII
HONOLULU, HI 96822
General Environment: Terrestrial
Specific Interests: Tropical (hot)

L'VOV AGRICULTURAL INSTITUTE
PLOSHCHAD' BOG KAMEL'NIT, 1
L'VOV, UNION OF SOVIET
SOCIALIST REPUBLICS
Director, M T Gonchar
General Environment: Terrestrial
Specific Interests: Rural
Staff Size: 5 - 9

METEOROLOGY INSTITUTE
BUDAPEST
II KITAIBEL PAI U I, BUDAPEST,
HUNGARY
Director, Professor Frigyos Desi C S
General Environment: Atmospheric
Staff Size: 100 - 499

OFFICIAL SEED TESTING STATION
HUNTINGDON ROAD
CAMBRIDGE, ENGLAND
Chief Officer, David B Mackay
General Environment: Terrestrial
Specific Interests: Prairie and Temperate
Forest

**PLANT BREEDING STATION OF
SCOTLAND**
PENTLANDFIELD, ROSLIN
MIDLOTHIAN, SCOTLAND
General Environment: Terrestrial
Specific Interests: Prairie and Temperate
Forest

REGULATORY SERVICES DIVISION
KENTUCKY AGRICULTURAL
EXPERIMENT STATION
LEXINGTON, KY 40506
Director, H F Massey

**RESEARCH INSTITUTE FOR
CEREALS AND TECHNOLOGY
PLANTS**
STR POMPILIU ELIADE 4
BUCHAREST, RUMANIA
Director, E Nichifor Ceapolu
Specific Interests: Prairie and Temperate
Forest

RESEARCH STATION
ROTHWELL PLANT BREEDERS
CAISTOR, LANCASTER, ENGLAND
Director, Richard C F Macer
General Environment: Terrestrial
Specific Interests: Prairie and Temperate
Forest

**RESEARCH STATION AT
LEVINGTON**
LEVINGTON
IPSWICH, SUFFOLK, ENGLAND
Director, James G Hunter
General Environment: Terrestrial
Specific Interests: Rural
Staff Size: 100 - 499

**RESOURCES AND DEVELOPMENT,
GALLAHER LIMITED**
HENRY STREET
BELFAST BT 15 1JE, NORTHERN
IRELAND
Development Manager, Donald J
Mackenzie
General Environment: Terrestrial
Specific Interests: Prairie and Temperate
Forest

SHELL RESOURCES LIMITED
WOODSTOCK AGRICULTURAL
RESOURCES CENTER
SITTINGBOURNE, KENT, ENGLAND
Director, Trevor Chapman
General Environment: Terrestrial
Specific Interests: Prairie and Temperate
Forest

TROPICAL PRODUCTS INSTITUTE
56-62 GRAYS INN ROAD
LONDON WC1, ENGLAND
General Environment: Terrestrial
Specific Interests: Prairie and Temperate
Forest

**VEGETABLE RESEARCH NATIONAL
STATION**
WELLESBOURNE, WARWICK,
ENGLAND
Director, Professor D Wright
General Environment: Terrestrial
Staff Size: 100 - 499

VIESKH
MOSKVA-RYAZANSKOY Z DOROGI
STANTSIYA PLYUSHCHEVO, UNION
OF SOVIET SOCIALIST
REPUBLICS
General Environment: Terrestrial
Specific Interests: Rural

CHEMICAL ENGINEERING

Educational Institute

CHEMICAL ENGINEERING
SAN JOSE STATE COLLEGE
SAN JOSE, CA 95114
Associate Professor, David Mage

CHEMICAL ENGINEERING DEPARTMENT
GEORGIA INSTITUTE OF TECHNOLOGY, 225 NORTH AVENUE
ATLANTA, GA 30332
Professor, Clyde Orr, Jr
General Environment: Atmospheric

CHEMISTRY AND CHEMISTRY ENGINEERING DEPARTMENT
BATTELLE MEMORIAL INSTITUTION
COLUMBUS, OH 43201
Specific Interests: Prairie and Temperate Forest

CHEMISTRY ENGINEERING DEPARTMENT
UNIVERSITY OF TEXAS
AUSTIN, TX 78712
General Environment: Atmospheric
Staff Size: 1 - 4

TOXICITY LABORATORY, UNIVERSITY OF CHICAGO
930 EAST 58TH STREET
CHICAGO, IL 60637
Professor, Kenneth Du Bois

Field Station/Laboratory

SOIL SURVEY OF ENGLAND AND WALES
BOTHAMSTED EXPERIMENTAL STATION
HARPENDEN, HERTFORDSHIRE, ENGLAND
Director, Kenneth E Clare
General Environment: Terrestrial
Specific Interests: Prairie and Temperate Forest

Government — Federal

CHEMICAL ENGINEERING BRANCH, OFFICE OF MARINE SAFETY, US COAST GUARD
400 7TH STREET, SW
WASHINGTON, DC 20590
General Environment: Oceanographic
Staff Size: 10 - 49

EXTENSION SERVICE
DEPARTMENT OF AGRICULTURE
WASHINGTON, DC 20250
General Environment: Terrestrial

LARAMIE ENERGY RESEARCH
POST OFFICE BOX 3395 UNIVERSITY STATION
LARAMIE, WY 82070
General Environment: Terrestrial

MOTOR VEHICLE SAFETY PERFORMANCE SERVICE
6TH AND D STREETS, SW
WASHINGTON, DC 20591
General Environment: Atmospheric

NATURAL GAS BUREAU
441 G STREET, NW
WASHINGTON, DC 20426
General Environment: Limnologic
Staff Size: 100 - 499

PESTICIDE REGULATION DIVISION, DEPARTMENT OF AGRICULTURE
ROOM 208, NORWOOD POST OFFICE
NORWOOD, MA 02062
Inspector, S Colamaria

PESTICIDES PROGRAM
NATIONAL COMMUNICABLE DISEASE CENTER
ATLANTA, GA 30333
General Environment: Atmospheric

PESTICIDES PROGRAMS, TECHNICAL INFORMATION SERVICES, EPA
1626 K STREET, NW
WASHINGTON, DC 20460

PETROLEUM RESEARCH CENTER AT BARTLESVILLE
POST OFFICE BOX 1398
BARTLESVILLE, OK 74003
General Environment: Terrestrial

PLANT AND FOOD, NATIONAL INSTITUTE
1700 K STREET, NW
WASHINGTON, DC 20006
General Environment: Terrestrial

SALT AND MARINE CHEMISTRY RESOURCES CENTRAL INSTITUTE
BHAVNAGAR, INDIA
Director, Dr D S Datar

Government — State or Local

ENVIRONMENTAL HEALTH, STATE DEPARTMENT OF HEALTH AND MENTAL HYGIENE
610 NORTH HOWARD STREET
BALTIMORE, MD 21201
Director, Howard E Chaney
General Environment: Limnologic

PESTICIDE CONTROL, ENVIRONMENTAL SANITATION DIVISION
W F COGSWELL BUILDING
HELENA, MT 59601
Director, Claiborne Brinck

PESTICIDE CONTROL, FOOD AND DRUG DIVISION
ROOM 527, STATE HOUSE
BOSTON, MA 02133
Director, George Michael

PESTICIDE CONTROL, STATE INSPECTION SERVICE
UNIVERSITY OF MARYLAND
COLLEGE PARK, MD 20742
State Chemist, David Clarke
General Environment: Terrestrial

PESTICIDE REGULATION DIVISION, AGRICULTURE DEPARTMENT
BUILDING 402 AGRICULTURAL RESOURCES CENTER
BELTSVILLE, MD 20705
Inspector, F Hibbison

Industrial/Commercial

CHEMICAL ENGINEERING
2999 SAN YSIDRO
SANTA CLARA, CA 95051
Director, Michael Rothenberg

Research Institutes

NORTHWESTERN GAS BOARD
THOMAS STREET, STRETFORD
MANCHESTER, M32 ONJ, ENGLAND
Director, T Nicklin
General Environment: Terrestrial
Specific Interests: Prairie and Temperate Forest

POLLUTION ABATEMENT

Educational Institute

AGRICULTURAL TECHNOLOGY EXPERIMENTAL STATION
CORNELL UNIVERSITY
ITHACA, NY 14850
Director, Nyle Brady
General Environment: Atmospheric

AIR POLLUTION AND ALLERGIC DISEASES
UNIVERSITY OF MICHIGAN
MINNEAPOLIS, MN 55455
Environmental Research Director, Donald Cowan
General Environment: Atmospheric

AIR POLLUTION AND ENVIRONMENT CENTER, 226 ENGINEERING BUILDING
PENNSYLVANIA STATE UNIVERSITY
UNIVERSITY PARK, PA 16802
Director, William Moroz
General Environment: Atmospheric
Staff Size: 10 - 49

AIR POLLUTION EFFECTS ON TEXTILE FABRICS
UNIVERSITY CALIFORNIA
DAVIS, CA 95616
Researcher, Mary Morris
General Environment: Atmospheric

AIR POLLUTION RESEARCH UNIT, MRC
MEDICAL COLLEGE, ST BART'S
LONDON, ENGLAND
General Environment: Atmospheric
Specific Interests: Prairie and Temperate Forest

AIR POLLUTION RESOURCES
UNIVERSITY OF FLORIDA
GAINESVILLE, FL 30501
General Environment: Atmospheric

AIR POLLUTION RESOURCES CENTER
UNIVERSITY OF CALIFORNIA
RIVERSIDE, CA 92502
Director, Seymour Calvert
General Environment: Atmospheric

AIR RESOURCE PROGRAM
CIVIL ENGINEERING DEPARTMENT, 301 MORE HALL
SEATTLE, WA 98105
Professor, August Rossano
General Environment: Atmospheric

APPLIED SCIENCE DEPARTMENT
PO BOX 751, PORTLAND STATE UNIVERSITY
PORTLAND, OR 97207

Head, Dr Nan-Teh Hsu
General Environment: Atmospheric
Staff Size: 1 - 4

ATMOSPHERIC AND WATER POLLUTION, BIOLOGY DEPARTMENT
CARSON NEWMAN COLLEGE
JEFFERSON CITY, TN 37760
Director, Joseph Chapman

ATMOSPHERIC SCIENCES CENTER
UNIVERSITY OF ARKANSAS
FAYETTEVILLE, AR 72701
General Environment: Atmospheric

ATMOSPHERIC SCIENCES INSTITUTE
SOUTH DAKOTA SCHOOL OF MINES AND TECHNOLOGY
RAPID CITY, SD 57701
General Environment: Atmospheric

ATMOSPHERIC SCIENCES PROGRAM
UNIVERSITY OF FLORIDA
GAINESVILLE, FL 32601
Director, David T Williams
General Environment: Atmospheric

ATMOSPHERIC SCIENCES PROGRAM
COLORADO STATE UNIVERSITY
FORT COLLINS, CO 80521
General Environment: Atmospheric

ATMOSPHERIC SCIENCES PROGRAM
UNIVERSITY OF ARIZONA
TUCSON, AZ 85700
Director, Roy G Post
General Environment: Atmospheric

ATMOSPHERIC SCIENCES PROGRAM
LOYOLA UNIVERSITY
CHICAGO, IL 60600
General Environment: Atmospheric

ATMOSPHERIC SCIENCES PROGRAM
ST LOUIS UNIVERSITY
ST LOUIS, MO 63100
General Environment: Atmospheric

ATMOSPHERIC SCIENCES RESEARCH CENTER
STATE UNIVERSITY OF NEW YORK
ALBANY, NY 12224
General Environment: Atmospheric

ATMOSPHERIC STUDIES CENTER
UNIVERSITY OF CALIFORNIA
DAVIS, CA 95616
Director, K L Coulson
General Environment: Atmospheric

ATMOSPHERIC STUDIES CENTER
UNIVERSITY OF HOUSTON
HOUSTON, TX 77000

Director, William H Prengle, Jr
General Environment: Atmospheric

ATMOSPHERIC STUDIES PROGRAM
CLARKSON COLLEGE OF TECHNOLOGY
POTSDAM, NY 13676
Director, Milton Kerker
General Environment: Atmospheric

ATMOSPHERIC STUDIES PROGRAM
CASE WESTERN RESERVE UNIVERSITY
CLEVELAND, OH 44106
Associate Professor, Garnett Mcmillan
General Environment: Atmospheric

ATMOSPHERIC STUDIES PROGRAM
CALIFORNIA INSTITUTE OF TECHNOLOGY
PASADENA, CA 91100
Director, Sheldon K Friedlander
General Environment: Atmospheric

ATMOSPHERIC STUDIES PROGRAM, UNIVERSITY OF COLORADO
106 KETCHUM
BOULDER, CO 50304
Dean, Max Peters
General Environment: Atmospheric

AUTOMOTIVE ENGINEERING LABORATORY
UNIVERSITY OF MICHIGAN, NORTH CAMPUS
ANN ARBOR, MI 48104
Director, William Mirsky
General Environment: Atmospheric

BIO-ENVIRONMENTAL ENGINEERING DEPARTMENT
UNIVERSITY OF FLORIDA
GAINESVILLE, FL 32601
Professor, Roy Mccaldin
General Environment: Atmospheric

BIOLOGY DEPARTMENT
UNIVERSITY OF UTAH
SALT LAKE CITY, UT 84112
Professor, Clyde Hill
General Environment: Atmospheric

CELLULAR BIOLOGY INSTITUTE
UNIVERSITY OF NEBRASKA
LINCOLN, NB 68500

CHEMICAL ENGINEERING DEPARTMENT
UNIVERSITY OF TEXAS
AUSTIN, TX 78712
Professor, James Brock
General Environment: Atmospheric
Staff Size: 1 - 4

CHEMISTRY AND CHEMICAL ENGINEERING DEPARTMENT
UNIVERSITY OF ILLINOIS
URBANA, IL 61801

Professor, Richard Juvet
General Environment: Atmospheric

CHEMISTRY DEPARTMENT
OHIO STATE UNIVERSITY, 88 WEST
   18TH AVENUE
COLUMBUS, OH 43210
Chairman, Jack Calvert
General Environment: Atmospheric

CHEMISTRY DEPARTMENT
UNIVERSITY OF GEORGIA
ATHENS, GA 30601
General Environment: Atmospheric

**CHEMISTRY DEPARTMENT,
   PHARMACY COLLEGE**
UNIVERSITY OF ILLINOIS, PO BOX
   6998
CHICAGO, IL 60680
Director, Alfred Von Smolinski
General Environment: Atmospheric

**CIVIL ENGINEERING
   DEPARTMENT**
ENGINEERING COLLEGE,
   UNIVERSITY OF NOTRE DAME
NOTRE DAME, IN 46556
Staff Size: 10 - 49

**COASTAL ENGINEERING
   DEPARTMENT, BUILDING L**
UNIVERSITY OF FLORIDA
GAINESVILLE, FL 32601

**EARTH AND MINERAL SCIENCES
   COLLEGE**
PENNSYLVANIA STATE
   UNIVERSITY, 503 DEIKE
   BUILDING
UNIVERSITY PARK, PA 16802
Director, Hans Panofsky
General Environment: Atmospheric

ENGINEERING COLLEGE
WEST VIRGINIA UNIVERSITY
MORGANTOWN, WV 26506
Dean, Chester Arents
General Environment: Atmospheric

**ENVIRONMENTAL ENGINEERING
   PROGRAM, CIVIL ENGINEERING
   DEPARTMENT**
UNIVERSITY OF ILLINOIS
URBANA, IL 61801
Chairman, Richard Engelbrecht
Specific Interests: Urban
Staff Size: 5 - 9

**ENVIRONMENTAL HEALTH
   ADMINISTRATION, HEALTH AND
   MENTAL HYGIENE**
610 NORTH HOWARD STREET
BALTIMORE, MD 21201
Director, H Chaney
General Environment: Atmospheric

**ENVIRONMENTAL HEALTH
   INSTITUTE**
UNIVERSITY OF CINCINNATI
CINCINNATI, OH 45289

**ENVIRONMENTAL HEALTH
   PROGRAM**
OREGON TECHNOLOGY INSTITUTE
KLAMATH FALLS, OR 97601
General Environment: Limnologic

**ENVIRONMENTAL RESOURCES
   INSTITUTE**
KANSAS STATE UNIVERSITY
MANHATTAN, KS 66502
General Environment: Atmospheric

**ENVIRONMENTAL SCIENCE AND
   ENGINEERING PROGRAM**
RICE UNIVERSITY
HOUSTON, TX 77001
Director, Dr C H Ward
Staff Size: 10 - 49

**ENVIRONMENTAL SCIENCES
   COLLEGE**
UNIVERSITY OF WISCONSIN,
   GREEN BAY BX834
GREEN BAY, WI 54305
Dean, Frederick Sargent
General Environment: Atmospheric

**ENVIRONMENTAL SCIENCES
   INSTITUTE**
LOUISANA STATE UNIVERSITY
BATON ROUGE, LA 70801

**ENVIRONMENTAL SCIENCES,
   AGRICULTURAL COLLEGE**
RUTGERS STATE UNIVERSITY
NEW BRUNSWICK, NJ 08903
General Environment: Limnologic

GEOLOGIST GROUP
ILLINOIS STATE GEOLOGICAL
   SURVEY OF NATURAL
   RESOURCES
URBANA, IL 61801
Geologist, Jack Simon
General Environment: Atmospheric

**HYGIENE AND PUBLIC HEALTH
   SCHOOL**
615 NORTH WOLFE STREET,
   JOHN'S HOPKINS UNIVERSITY
BALTIMORE, MD 21205
Professor, Herbert Klarman
General Environment: Atmospheric

**INDUSTRIAL COOPERATION
   INSTITUTE, UNIVERSITY OF
   CALIFORNIA**
405 HILGARD AVENUE
LOS ANGELES, CA 90024
General Environment: Atmospheric

**INDUSTRIAL MEDICINE
   INSTITUTE, NEW YORK
   UNIVERSITY**

550 FIRST AVENUE
NEW YORK, NY 10016
General Environment: Atmospheric

INDUSTRIAL RESEARCH DIVISION
WASHINGTON STATE UNIVERSITY
PULLMAN, WA 94662
General Environment: Atmospheric
Staff Size: 10 - 49

**MECHANICAL ENGINEERING
   DEPARTMENT**
UNIVERSITY OF MICHIGAN,
   NORTH CAMPUS
ANN ARBOR, MI 48104
Professor, Jay Bolt
General Environment: Atmospheric

**MECHANICAL ENGINEERING
   DEPARTMENT**
TECHNOLOGY INSTITUTE,
   UNIVERSITY OF MINNESOTA
MINNEAPOLIS, MN 55455
Professor, Kenneth Whitby
General Environment: Atmospheric

MEDICAL SCHOOL
UNIVERSITY OF WASHINGTON
SEATTLE, WA 98105
Professor, James Mccarroll
General Environment: Atmospheric

**OCCUPATIONAL HEALTH
   DEPARTMENT**
GRADUATE SCHOOL OF PUBLIC
   HEALTH, UNIVERSITY OF
   PITTSBURGH
PITTSBURGH, PA 15213
Chairman, Morton Corn
General Environment: Atmospheric

PAPER CHEMISTRY INSTITUTE
1043 EAST SOUTH RIVER STREET
APPLETON, WI 54911
President, John G Strange
General Environment: Limnologic
Specific Interests: Prairie and Temperate
   Forest
Staff Size: 100 - 499

**PENOBSCOT RIVER OIL
   POLLUTION ABATEMENT
   COMMISSION**
101 BARROWS HALL, UNIVERSITY
   OF MAINE
ORONO, ME 04473

POLLUTION RESEARCH CENTER
UTAH STATE UNIVERSITY
LOGAN, UT 84321

**PREVENTIVE MEDICINE AND
   ENVIRONMENTAL DEPARTMENT**
MEDICAL INSTITUTE, UNIVERSITY
   OF IOWA
OAKDALE, IA 52319
General Environment: Atmospheric

PUBLIC ADMINISTRATION SCHOOL
UNIVERSITY OF SOUTH
CALIFORNIA, UNIVERSITY PARK
LOS ANGELES, CA 90007
Associate Director, William Leffland
General Environment: Atmospheric

PUBLIC HEALTH SCHOOL
UNIVERSITY OF MICHIGAN
ANN ARBOR, MI 48104
Professor, Ian Higgins
General Environment: Atmospheric

STUDENTS AGAINST POLLUTION
GRANITE STATE
LEOMINSTER, MA 01453

**TRACE LEVEL RESOURCES
INSTITUTE**
PURDUE UNIVERSITY
LAFAYETTE, IN 47907
Staff Size: 100 - 499

**URBAN AND ENVIRONMENTAL
STUDIES**
DREXEL UNIVERSITY
PHILADELPHIA, PA 19104
Director, P Walton Purdom
Specific Interests: Urban
Staff Size: 50 - 99

**WATER POLLUTION RESEARCH
ASSOCIATION**
MCLAUGHLIN HALL, UNIVERSITY
CALIFORNIA
BERKELEY, CA 94720
General Environment: Limnologic

**WATER POLLUTION, UNIVERSITY
OF CALIFORNIA**
104 WARREN HALL
BERKELEY, CA 94720
Professor, William Oswald
General Environment: Limnologic

WATER RESOURCES COMMISSION
PRINCETON UNIVERSITY
PRINCETON, NJ 08540
General Environment: Oceanographic

**WATER SUPPLY AND SEWAGE
PURIFICATION INSTITUTE**
PHYSIKSTRASSE 5
ZURICH 7, SWITZERLAND
Director, Otto Jaag
General Environment: Limnologic
Specific Interests: Mountainous

Field Station/Laboratory

AIR POLLUTION
1010 NORTHEAST COUCH STREET
PORTLAND, OR 97232
Director, Richard Hatchard
General Environment: Atmospheric

AQUATIC BIOLOGY LABORATORY
OKLAHOMA STATE UNIVERSITY
STILLWATER, OK 74074
Director, Dr Troy C Dorris
Specific Interests: Prairie and Temperate
Forest

**ATMOSPHERIC SCIENCES
RESEARCH CENTER
EXPERIMENTAL LABORATORY**
SCHENECTADY COUNTY AIRPORT
SCHENECTADY, NY 12329
General Environment: Atmospheric

FISHERIES LABORATORY
LOWESTOFT, SUFFOLK, ENGLAND
Director, Herbert Cole
Specific Interests: Prairie and Temperate
Forest

HYDRAULICS RESEARCH STATION
MINISTRY OF TECHNOLOGY
WALLINGFORD, BERKSHIRE,
ENGLAND
Executive Officer, John Grindley
General Environment: Estuarine
Specific Interests: Prairie and Temperate
Forest

PUBLIC HEALTH LABORATORIES
THRESH HOUSE, VERULAM
STREET, GRAYIS INN ROAD
LONDON, ENGLAND
Specific Interests: Prairie and Temperate
Forest

ROAD RESEARCH LABORATORY
CROWTHORNE, BERKSHIRE,
ENGLAND
Director, Philip T Sherwood
Specific Interests: Prairie and Temperate
Forest

WARREN SPRING LABORATORY
STEVENAGE, HERTFORDSHIRE,
ENGLAND
General Environment: Terrestrial
Specific Interests: Prairie and Temperate
Forest

**WATER POLLUTION AND
FISHERIES COOPERATIVE
RESEARCH LABORATORY**
315 EXTENSION HALL, OREGON
STATE UNIVERSITY
CORVALLIS, OR 97331
Director, Dr Charles Warren
Specific Interests: Prairie and Temperate
Forest

**WATER POLLUTION RESEARCH
LABORATORY**
STEVENAGE, HERTFORDSHIRE,
ENGLAND
Director, Morlais Owens
General Environment: Limnologic
Specific Interests: Prairie and Temperate
Forest

Foundation

**AEROSPACE AND SYSTEMS
DIVISION, SCIENCE CENTER**
NORTH AMERICAN ROCKWELL,
POST OFFICE BOX 1470
THOUSAND OAKS, CA 91360
General Environment: Atmospheric

BOTANICAL GARDENS
2135 TOWER GROVE AVENUE
ST LOUIS, MO 63110
Director, David Gates
General Environment: Atmospheric

MEDICAL STATISTICS SECTION
MAYO CLINIC AND MAYO
FOUNDATION
ROCHESTER, MN 55901
Professor, Leonard Kurland
General Environment: Atmospheric

USTAV FYZIKY ATMOSFERY CSAV
SPORTILOV, BOCNI II, NO 1401
PRAHA, CZECHOSLOVAKIA
General Environment: Atmospheric

**WATER POLLUTION CONTROL
FEDERATION**
3900 WISCONSIN AVENUE, NW
WASHINGTON, DC 20016
General Environment: Limnologic

ZAROMB RESEARCH FOUNDATION
PASSAIC, NJ 07055
Director, Solomon Zaromb
General Environment: Atmospheric

Government — Federal

**AIR AND WATER POLLUTION
SUBCOMMITTEE**
SENATE OFFICE BUILDING, SUITE
4204
WASHINGTON, DC 20510

**AIR POLLUTION CONTROL
BRANCH, ENVIRONMENTAL
PROTECTION AGENCY**
KENNEDY FEDERAL BUILDING,
GOVERNMENT CENTER, ROOM
2303
BOSTON, MA 02203
Specific Interests: Polar (cold)
Staff Size: 10 - 49

**AIR POLLUTION CONTROL
BRANCH, ENVIRONMENTAL
PROTECTION AGENCY**
1200 6TH AVENUE
SEATTLE, WA 98101
General Environment: Atmospheric
Staff Size: 10 - 49

AIR POLLUTION CONTROL BUREAU, ENVIRONMENTAL HEALTH CENTER
TUNNEY'S PASTURE
OTTAWA, ONTARIO, CANADA
General Environment: Atmospheric

AIR POLLUTION CONTROL OFFICE, RESEARCH GRANTS
POST OFFICE BOX 12055
RESEARCH TRIANGLE PARK, NC 27709
General Environment: Atmospheric

AIR POLLUTION CONTROL PROGRAM
1033 WADE AVENUE
RALEIGH, NC 27065
General Environment: Atmospheric

AIR PROGRAMS OFFICE, ENVIRONMENTAL PROTECTION AGENCY
AIR PROGRAMS LIBRARY
RESEARCH TRIANGLE PARK, NC 27711
Specific Interests: Polar (cold)
Staff Size: 100 - 499

AMERICAN WATERWAY OPERATIONS, INCORPORATED
1250 CONNECTICUT AVENUE, SUITE 502
WASHINGTON, DC 20036
General Environment: Limnologic

APPALACHIAN REGION-ANTHRACITE DEPOSITS, ENVIRONMENTAL AFFAIRS FIELD
19 NORTH MAIN STREET
WILKES-BARRE, PA 18701

ARMY CORPS OF ENGINEERS
DEPARTMENT OF THE ARMY
WASHINGTON, DC 20314

ATMOSPHERIC RESEARCH CENTER
BOULDER, CO 80302

ATOMIC ENERGY JOINT COMMITTEE
ROOM H-403, THE CAPITOL
WASHINGTON, DC 20500
General Environment: Atmospheric

BAY AREA AIR POLLUTION CONTROL DISTRICT
939 ELLIS STREET
SAN FRANCISCO, CA 94109
Director, D J Calcaghan
General Environment: Atmospheric
Staff Size: 50 - 99

BUILDINGS MANAGEMENT OFFICE
19TH AND F STREET, NW
WASHINGTON, DC 20405

CHEMISTRY AND PHYSICS DIVISION
NATIONAL AIR POLLUTION CONTROL, PUBLIC HEALTH SECTION
CINCINNATI, OH 45227
Director, Aubrey Altshuller
General Environment: Atmospheric

COAL DEPOSITS WESTERN, DENVER MINING RESEARCH CENTER
BUILDING 20, DENVER FEDERAL CENTER
DENVER, CO 80225

CRITERIA AND STANDARDS BUREAU
411 WEST CHAPEL HILL STREET
DURHAM, NC 27701
Specific Interests: Prairie and Temperate Forest

CRITERIA AND STANDARDS BUREAU
PUBLIC HEALTH SERVICE
DURHAM, NC 27701
Executive Secretary, Ernest Linde
General Environment: Atmospheric

ENGINEERING AND PHYSICAL SCIENCES BUREAU
1330 ST MARY'S STREET
RALEIGH, NC 27605
Specific Interests: Prairie and Temperate Forest

ENVIRONMENTAL CONSULTATION SERVICE, CAMBRIDGE RESEARCH LABORATORY
L.G. HANSCOM FIELD
BEDFORD, MA 01730

ENVIRONMENTAL PROTECTION AGENCY
401 M STREET, SW
WASHINGTON, DC 20460

ENVIRONMENTAL PROTECTION AGENCY
LABORATORY
ADA, OK 74820
Staff Size: 50 - 99

FISHERY PRODUCTS RESEARCH AND INSPECTION
NATIONAL MARINE FISHERIES SERVICES
WASHINGTON, DC 20235
Staff Specialist, David M Pressel
Staff Size: 1 - 4

GRANTS POLICY DIVISION, AIR POLLUTION OFFICE
1033 WADE AVENUE
RALEIGH, NC 27605
General Environment: Atmospheric

GRANTS PROGRAM OFFICE, OCCUPATIONAL SAFETY AND HEALTH
1014 BROADWAY
CINCINNATI, OH 45202

GULF COAST SHELLFISH SANITATION LABORATORY, PUBLIC HEALTH SERVICE
POST OFFICE BOX 158
DAUPHIN ISLAND, AL 36528
General Environment: Oceanographic
Specific Interests: Tropical (hot)

LIFE SUPPORT DIVISION
6570 AEROSPACE MEDICAL RESOURCE LABORATORY
WRIGHT-PATTERSON AF BASE, OH 45433
General Environment: Atmospheric

MARINE ENVIRONMENTAL PROTECTION DIVISION
11567 LINKS DRIVE
RESTON, VA 22070
Captain, Sidney Wallace
General Environment: Oceanographic
Staff Size: 1000 - 4999

MARITIME ADMINISTRATION, PUBLIC INFORMATION OFFICE
441 G STREET NW, ROOM 3037
WASHINGTON, DC 20235
General Environment: Oceanographic
Specific Interests: Prairie and Temperate Forest

MAYORS CONFERENCE OF THE UNITED STATES
1707 H STREET, NW ROOM 606
WASHINGTON, DC 20006
General Environment: Limnologic

METEOROLOGY CENTER
8060 13TH STREET, GRAMAX BUILDING
SILVER SPRING, MD 20910
General Environment: Atmospheric
Specific Interests: Prairie and Temperate Forest

MINES BUREAU, HEALTH AND SAFETY DIVISION
DEPARTMENT OF THE INTERIOR
WASHINGTON, DC 20240

MINING AND SAFETY RESEARCH CENTER, BUREAU OF MINES
4800 FORBES AVENUE
PITTSBURGH, PA 15213
Staff Size: 100 - 499

NATIONAL AEROMETRIC DATA BANK
ENVIRONMENTAL PROTECTION AGENCY
RESEARCH TRIANGLE PARK, NC 27711

General Environment: Atmospheric
Staff Size: 10 - 49

**NATIONAL AIR POLLUTION
    CONTROL**
801 NORTH RANDOLPH STREET
ARLINGTON, VA 22203
Director, Charles Walters
General Environment: Atmospheric

**NATIONAL AIR POLLUTION
    CONTROL ADMINISTRATION**
PUBLIC HEALTH SERVICE
ARLINGTON, VA 22203
Director, John Middleton
General Environment: Atmospheric

**NATIONAL AIR POLLUTION
    CONTROL ASSOCIATION**
9600 FISHERS LANE
ROCKVILLE, MD 20801
Director, Charles Kossack
General Environment: Atmospheric
Staff Size: 5 - 9

**NATIONAL INDUSTRIAL
    POLLUTION CONTROL COUNCIL**
5111 BATTERY LANE
BETHESDA, MD 20014
Director, Walter Hamilton

**NATIONAL SANITATION
    FOUNDATION, SCHOOL OF
    PUBLIC HEALTH**
MICHIGAN UNIVERSITY, P O BOX
    1468
ANN ARBOR, MI 48104
General Environment: Limnologic

**OCCUPATIONAL SAFETY AND
    HEALTH NATIONAL INSTITUTE**
50 FULTON STREET
SAN FRANCISCO, CA 94102
Program Director, Douglas L Johnson
Staff Size: 1 - 4

**POLLUTION CONTROL,
    DEPARTMENT OF JUSTICE**
500 23RD STREET
WASHINGTON, DC 20037
Director, Martin Green

**POLLUTION SURVEILLANCE
    DIVISION**
633 INDIANA AVENUE, NW
WASHINGTON, DC 20242
Specific Interests: Prairie and Temperate
    Forest

**PROGRAM SUPPORT BRANCH (AIR)
    ENVIRONMENTAL PROTECTION
    AGENCY**
1735 BALTIMORE, ROOM 265
KANSAS CITY, MO 64108
General Environment: Atmospheric
Staff Size: 10 - 49

**RADIATION OFFICE, RESEARCH
    AND TRAINING GRANTS BRANCH**
5600 FISHERS LANE, ROOM 18-67
ROCKVILLE, MD 20852
General Environment: Atmospheric

**RADIATION PROGRAM,
    ENVIRONMENTAL PROTECTION
    AGENCY, REGION 2**
100 CALIFORNIA STREET
SAN FRANCISCO, CA 94111
Staff Size: 1 - 4

**RADIATION SURVEILLANCE
    CENTER, RADIOLOGICAL
    HEALTH CENTER**
VAN NESS STREET AND
    CONSTITUTION
WASHINGTON, DC 20203
General Environment: Atmospheric

RADIOLOGICAL HEALTH BUREAU
12720 TWINBROOK PARKWAY
ROCKVILLE, MD 20852
General Environment: Atmospheric

RESEARCH AND TRAINING GRANTS
8120 WOODMONT AVENUE
BETHESDA, MD 20014
Specific Interests: Prairie and Temperate
    Forest

**SHELLFISH SANITATION
    LABORATORY (NORTHWEST),
    PUBLIC HEALTH SERVICE**
ROUTE 4, BOX 4519
GIG HARBOR, WA 98335

**SOLID WASTE MANAGEMENT
    BUREAU**
12720 TWINBROOK PARKWAY
ROCKVILLE, MD 20852
General Environment: Terrestrial

**SOLID WASTE RESEARCH
    DIVISIONAL**
NATIONAL ENVIRONMENTAL
    RESEARCH CENTER
CINCINNATI, OH 45268
Specialist for Technological Advances, C
    Clemons
General Environment: Terrestrial
Staff Size: 50 - 99

**SOUND SECTION, BUREAU OF
    STANDARDS**
METEOROLOGY DIVISION
WASHINGTON, DC 20234
General Environment: Atmospheric
Specific Interests: Urban

**STANDARDS AND COMPLIANCE
    OFFICE**
PUBLIC HEALTH SERVICE
ARLINGTON, VA 22203
Executive Secretary, Ebon Jones
General Environment: Atmospheric

TECHNICAL SERVICES DIVISION
633 INDIANA AVENUE, NW
WASHINGTON, DC 20242
Specific Interests: Prairie and Temperate
    Forest

**TECHNOLOGY CENTER,
    INFORMATION AND
    PUBLICATIONS OFFICE**
1330 ST MARY'S STREET
RALEIGH, NC 27605
Specific Interests: Prairie and Temperate
    Forest

**UNITED STATES COAST GUARD
    HEADQUARTERS**
400 7TH STREET, SW
WASHINGTON, DC 20590

**URBAN AND INDUSTRIAL HEALTH
    NATIONAL CENTER**
550 MAIN STREET
CINCINNATI, OH 45202
General Environment: Terrestrial

**WATER POLLUTION CONTROL
    ADMINISTRATION,
    DEPARTMENT OF THE INTERIOR**
633 INDIANA AVENUE, NW
WASHINGTON, DC 20242
General Environment: Limnologic

**WATER POLLUTION CONTROL
    ASSOCIATION, STATE AND
    INTERSTATE**
1100 HARRINGTON AVENUE
LITTLE ROCK, AR 72202
General Environment: Limnologic

**WATER POLLUTION RESEARCH
    ASSOCIATION INTERNATIONAL**
3900 WISCONSIN AVENUE, NW
WASHINGTON, DC 20016
Specific Interests: Prairie and Temperate
    Forest

**WATER POLLUTION RESEARCH
    LABORATORY**
ELDER WAY
STEVENAGE, HERTFORDSHIRE,
    ENGLAND
Director, L Downing
General Environment: Limnologic
Specific Interests: Urban
Staff Size: 100 - 499

**WATER RESOURCES AND
    ENGINEERING DIVISION**
14TH AND CONSTITUTION, NW
WASHINGTON, DC 20230
Specific Interests: Prairie and Temperate
    Forest

**WATER SUPPLY RESEARCH
    LABORATORY, ENVIRONMENTAL
    PROTECTION AGENCY**
SOUTH FERRY ROAD
NARRAGANSETT, RI 02882
General Environment: Oceanographic

Government — State or Local

AERONAUTICS COMMISSION
LOGAN AIRPORT
BOSTON, MA 02167
General Environment: Atmospheric

AGRICULTURE DEPARTMENT
BOX 16390 A
BATON ROUGE, LA 70803

AIR AND CLEAN WATER DIVISION
POST OFFICE BOX 1540
TRENTON, NJ 08608
Director, Richard Sullivan

**AIR AND OCCUPATIONAL
RADIATION HYGIENE, PUBLIC
HEALTH DEPARTMENT**
4210 EAST 11TH AVENUE
DENVER, CO 80220
General Environment: Atmospheric

**AIR AND WATER POLLUTION
CONTROL COMMISSION**
306 WEST JEFFERSON STREET
TALLAHASSEE, FL 32301
Director, Vincent Patton
General Environment: Limnologic

**AIR AND WATER POLLUTION
CONTROL DIVISION**
3600 W THIRD STREET
GARY, IN 46406
General Environment: Atmospheric

**AIR AND WATER PROGRAMS,
ENVIRONMENTAL PROTECTION
AGENCY, REGION 2**
26 FEDERAL PLAZA
NEW YORK, NY 10009
General Environment: Atmospheric

AIR CONSERVATION COMMISSION
BOX 1062
JEFFERSON CITY, MO 65101
General Environment: Atmospheric

AIR CONSERVATION COMMITTEE
60 COLLEGE STREET
NEW HAVEN, CT 06510
Director, Mrs R Samuel Howe
General Environment: Atmospheric

AIR CONSERVATION UNION
701 OCEAN STREET, ROOM 420
SANTA CRUZ, CA 95060
General Environment: Atmospheric
Staff Size: 5 - 9

AIR CONTROL BOARD
1100 WEST 49TH STREET
AUSTIN, TX 78756
General Environment: Atmospheric

AIR CONTROL COMMISSION
POST OFFICE BOX 60630
NEW ORLEANS, LA 70112
General Environment: Atmospheric

**AIR CONTROL SECTION, COUNTY
HEALTH DEPARTMENT**
300 SOUTH GEDDES STREET, BOX
1325
SYRACUSE, NY 13201
General Environment: Atmospheric

**AIR MANAGEMENT DIVISION,
ENVIRONMENTAL HEALTH
DEPARTMENT**
400 MARQUETTE, NW BOX 1293
ALBUQUERQUE, NM 87103
General Environment: Atmospheric
Staff Size: 10 - 49

**AIR MANAGEMENT SERVICES,
PHILADELPHIA DEPARTMENT
OF HEALTH**
1701 ARCH STREET, 6TH FLOOR
PHILADELPHIA, PA 19103
Assistant Health Commissioner, E Wilson
General Environment: Atmospheric
Specific Interests: Urban
Staff Size: 50 - 99

**AIR POLLUTION AND HEATING
INSPECTION DEPARTMENT**
CITY HALL
GREEN BAY, WI 54301
General Environment: Atmospheric

**AIR POLLUTION AND NOISE
ABATEMENT**
144 MERIDAN STREET
EAST BOSTON, MA 02128
General Environment: Atmospheric

AIR POLLUTION BOARD
CITY HALL, MICHIGAN AVENUE
LANSING, MI 48933
General Environment: Atmospheric

AIR POLLUTION BOARD
2211 SOUTH EIGHTH STREET
IRONTON, OH 45638
General Environment: Atmospheric

**AIR POLLUTION BUREAU, PUBLIC
SAFETY DEPARTMENT**
MUNICIPAL BUILDING
ERIE, PA 16501
General Environment: Atmospheric

**AIR POLLUTION CENTER,
PORTSMOUTH-IRONTON REGION**
CITY BUILDING, 740 SECOND
STREET
PORTSMOUTH, OH 45662
Director, James Weaver
General Environment: Atmospheric

AIR POLLUTION COMMISSION
49 MOUNT PLEASANT AVENUE
WEST ORANGE, NJ 07050
Director, Thomas Pluta
General Environment: Atmospheric
Staff Size: 5 - 9

AIR POLLUTION COMMITTEE
43 EAST STREET, CITY HALL
PITTSFIELD, MA 01210
General Environment: Atmospheric

AIR POLLUTION CONSORTIUM
31 WILDWOOD DRIVE
BEDFORD, MA 01730
Executive Director, Ted Rider
General Environment: Atmospheric

AIR POLLUTION CONTROL
5925 CALMUT AVENUE
HAMMOND, IN 46320
Chief, Ronald L Novak
General Environment: Atmospheric

AIR POLLUTION CONTROL
MUNICIPAL BUILDING, LIBERTY
AND HILLSIDE AVENUES
HILLSIDE, NJ 07205
General Environment: Atmospheric

AIR POLLUTION CONTROL
1601 EAST HAZELTON AVENUE
STOCKTON, CA 95201
General Environment: Atmospheric

AIR POLLUTION CONTROL
3575 11TH STREET
RIVERSIDE, CA 92501
Director, Galen R Kinley
General Environment: Atmospheric
Staff Size: 10 - 49

AIR POLLUTION CONTROL
MUNICIPAL BUILDING
MERIDIAN, MS 39301
General Environment: Atmospheric

AIR POLLUTION CONTROL
275 EAST MAIN STREET
FRANKFORT, KY 40601
General Environment: Atmospheric

AIR POLLUTION CONTROL
CITY HALL BUILDING
ASHEVILLE, NC 28807
General Environment: Atmospheric

AIR POLLUTION CONTROL
CITY HALL, 2935 MAYFIELD ROAD
CLEVELAND HEIGHTS, OH 44118
General Environment: Atmospheric

AIR POLLUTION CONTROL
CITY HALL, 1500 CHAPLINE STREET
WHEELING, WV 26003
General Environment: Atmospheric

AIR POLLUTION CONTROL
1216 W INNES
SALISBURY, NC 28144
General Environment: Atmospheric

AIR POLLUTION CONTROL
161 W ALAMEDA
TUCSON, AZ 85701
General Environment: Atmospheric

AIR POLLUTION CONTROL
200 EAST WASHINGTON STREET,
ROOM 1642
INDIANAPOLIS, IN 46204
General Environment: Atmospheric

AIR POLLUTION CONTROL
172 WEST 3RD STREET
SAN BERNARDINO, CA 92401
General Environment: Atmospheric

AIR POLLUTION CONTROL
BOX 6084, PRINCESS ANN STATION
VIRGINIA BEACH, VA 23450
General Environment: Atmospheric

AIR POLLUTION CONTROL
AUTHORITY
207 PIONEER BUILDING
MT VERNON, WA 98273
General Environment: Atmospheric
Staff Size: 5 - 9

AIR POLLUTION CONTROL
AUTHORITY
1200 FRANKLIN STREET
VANCOUVER, WA 98660
General Environment: Atmospheric

AIR POLLUTION CONTROL BOARD
601 W GERMANTOWN PIKE
PLYMOUTH MEETING, PA 19462
General Environment: Atmospheric

AIR POLLUTION CONTROL BOARD
9TH STREET, STATE OFFICE
BUILDING
RICHMOND, VA 23201
General Environment: Atmospheric
Staff Size: 50 - 99

AIR POLLUTION CONTROL BOARD
1330 W MICHIGAN STREET
INDIANAPOLIS, IN 46206
General Environment: Atmospheric

AIR POLLUTION CONTROL BOARD
MCCOOK, IL 60525
General Environment: Atmospheric

AIR POLLUTION CONTROL BOARD
OF GREATER YORK
32 WEST KING STREET
YORK, PA 17401
General Environment: Atmospheric

AIR POLLUTION CONTROL
BOARD, COOK COUNTY
309 CHICAGO CIVIC CENTER
CHICAGO, IL 60602
General Environment: Atmospheric

AIR POLLUTION CONTROL
BOARD, HEALTH DEPARTMENT
TOWN HALL
CHEEKTOWAGA, NY 14225
General Environment: Atmospheric

AIR POLLUTION CONTROL
BUREAU
CITY HALL, 11TH STREET
CHATTANOOGA, TN 37402
General Environment: Marsh/Swamp

AIR POLLUTION CONTROL
BUREAU
CITY HALL
HOPEWELL, VA 23860
General Environment: Atmospheric

AIR POLLUTION CONTROL
BUREAU
CITY HALL
ALPENA, MI 49707
General Environment: Atmospheric

AIR POLLUTION CONTROL
COMMISSION
4108 MACCORKLE AVENUE, SOUTH
EAST
CHARLESTON, WV 25304
General Environment: Atmospheric

AIR POLLUTION CONTROL
COMMISSION
61 SOUTH SPRING STREET
CONCORD, NH 03301
General Environment: Atmospheric
Staff Size: 10 - 49

AIR POLLUTION CONTROL
COMMISSION
6300 LINCOLN AVENUE
MORTON GROVE, IL 60053
General Environment: Atmospheric

AIR POLLUTION CONTROL
COMMITTEE
4937 WEST 25TH STREET
CICERO, IL 60650
General Environment: Atmospheric

AIR POLLUTION CONTROL
COMMITTEE
CITY HALL
BERWYN, IL 60402
General Environment: Atmospheric

AIR POLLUTION CONTROL
DEPARTMENT
320 NORTH CLARK STREET
CHICAGO, IL 60610
Director, William Stanley
General Environment: Atmospheric

AIR POLLUTION CONTROL
DEPARTMENT
CITY HALL
TEMPLE, TX 76501
General Environment: Atmospheric

AIR POLLUTION CONTROL
DEPARTMENT
CITY HALL
TORRINGTON, CT 06790
General Environment: Atmospheric
Staff Size: 50 - 99

AIR POLLUTION CONTROL
DEPARTMENT
209 CHURCH AVENUE, SW
ROANOKE, VA 24011
General Environment: Atmospheric

AIR POLLUTION CONTROL
DEPARTMENT
51 ASTOR PLACE
NEW YORK, NY 10003
General Environment: Atmospheric

AIR POLLUTION CONTROL
DEPARTMENT
9722 WEST WATERTOW PLANK
WAUWATOSA, WI 53226
General Environment: Atmospheric

AIR POLLUTION CONTROL
DEPARTMENT
POST OFFICE BOX 128
ARGO, IL 60501
General Environment: Atmospheric

AIR POLLUTION CONTROL
DISTRIBUTORS
1010 SOUTH HARBOR BOULEVARD
ANAHEIM, CA 92805
General Environment: Atmospheric

AIR POLLUTION CONTROL
DISTRICT
434 SOUTH SAN PEDRO STREET
LOS ANGELES, CA 90013
General Environment: Atmospheric
Staff Size: 100 - 499

AIR POLLUTION CONTROL
DISTRICT
2500 SOUTH THIRD STREET, 400
REYNOLDS BUILDING
LOUISVILLE, KY 40208
General Environment: Atmospheric

AIR POLLUTION CONTROL
DISTRICT
1516 MAIN STREET
NORTHAMPTON, PA 18067
General Environment: Atmospheric

AIR POLLUTION CONTROL
DISTRICT, LOWER PINE VALLEY
1414 STATE STREET
SPRINGFIELD, MA 01109
General Environment: Atmospheric

AIR POLLUTION CONTROL DISTRICT, SHASTA COUNTY HEALTH DEPARTMENT
2601 HOSPITAL LANE
REDDING, CA 96001
General Environment: Atmospheric
Specific Interests: Urban
Staff Size: 1 - 4

AIR POLLUTION CONTROL DIVISION
POST OFFICE BOX 9392
RALEIGH, NC 27603
General Environment: Atmospheric

AIR POLLUTION CONTROL DIVISION, CITY HEALTH DEPARTMENT
CITY HALL
CANTON, OH 44702
General Environment: Atmospheric

AIR POLLUTION CONTROL DIVISION, COUNTY HEALTH DEPARTMENT
826 EVERNIA STREET
WEST PALM BEACH, FL 33402
General Environment: Atmospheric

AIR POLLUTION CONTROL DIVISION, COUNTY HEALTH DEPARTMENT
10 KIRMAN AVENUE
RENO, NV 89502
General Environment: Atmospheric

AIR POLLUTION CONTROL DIVISION, COUNTY HEALTH DEPARTMENT
17 HARDING AVENUE
TERRE HAUTE, IN 47801
General Environment: Atmospheric

AIR POLLUTION CONTROL DIVISION, DEPARTMENT OF HEALTH
MUNICIPAL BUILDING
MIDDLETOWN, CT 06457
General Environment: Atmospheric

AIR POLLUTION CONTROL DIVISION, ENVIRONMENTAL HEALTH BUREAU
248 COX STREET
MOBILE, AL 36009
General Environment: Atmospheric

AIR POLLUTION CONTROL OFFICE
CITY HALL, 200 NIAGARA STREET
TONAWANDA, NY 14150
General Environment: Atmospheric

AIR POLLUTION CONTROL PROGRAM
403 GEORGE STREET
NEW BERN, NC 28560
General Environment: Atmospheric

AIR POLLUTION CONTROL PROGRAM, ENVIRONMENTAL HEALTH DIVISION
1936 AMELIA COURT
DALLAS, TX 75235
General Environment: Atmospheric

AIR POLLUTION CONTROL SECTION, COUNTY HEALTH DEPARTMENT
334 CALHOUN STREET
CHARLESTON, SC 29401
General Environment: Atmospheric
Staff Size: 5 - 9

AIR POLLUTION CONTROL SECTION, FIRE DEPARTMENT, CITY BUILDING
112 NORTH WASHINGTON STREET
KOKOMO, IN 46901
General Environment: Atmospheric

AIR POLLUTION CONTROL SECTION, FIRE HEADQUARTERS
LITTLE WASHINGTON STREET
POUGHKEEPSIE, NY 12601
General Environment: Atmospheric

AIR POLLUTION CONTROL SECTOR, PUBLIC HEALTH DEPARTMENT
455 MAIN STREET
WORCESTER, MA 01608
General Environment: Atmospheric

AIR POLLUTION CONTROL,
CITY HALL, 940 BOONVILLE STREET
SPRINGFIELD, MO 65802
General Environment: Atmospheric

AIR POLLUTION CONTROL, ALLEGHENY COUNTY HEALTH DEPARTMENT
301 39TH STREET
PITTSBURGH, PA 15201
General Environment: Atmospheric
Staff Size: 50 - 99

AIR POLLUTION CONTROL, BOARD OF HEALTH
5 BROAD STREET
SALEM, MA 01970
General Environment: Atmospheric

AIR POLLUTION CONTROL, BOARD OF HEALTH
916 GARDEN STREET
HOBOKEN, NJ 07030
General Environment: Atmospheric

AIR POLLUTION CONTROL, BOARD OF HEALTH
CITY HALL SQUARE
BROCKTON, MA 02401
General Environment: Atmospheric

AIR POLLUTION CONTROL, BOARD OF HEALTH
301 NORTH WOOD AVENUE, CITY HALL
LINDEN, NJ 07036
General Environment: Atmospheric

AIR POLLUTION CONTROL, BOARD OF HEALTH
CITY HALL
FITCHBURG, MA 01420
General Environment: Atmospheric
Staff Size: 5 - 9

AIR POLLUTION CONTROL, BOARD OF HEALTH, KIRBY HEALTH CENTER
71 NORTH FRANKLIN STREET
WILKES-BARRE, PA 18701
General Environment: Atmospheric

AIR POLLUTION CONTROL, BUILDING AND SAFETY DIVISION
4500 MAPLE AVENUE
DEARBORN, MI 48126
General Environment: Atmospheric

AIR POLLUTION CONTROL, BUILDING DEPARTMENT
1130 WASHINGTON AVENUE
MIAMI BEACH, FL 33139
General Environment: Atmospheric

AIR POLLUTION CONTROL, BUILDING DEPARTMENT
POST OFFICE BOX 708
MIAMI, FL 33133
General Environment: Atmospheric

AIR POLLUTION CONTROL, BUILDING INSPECTION DEPARTMENT
151 MARTIN STREET
BIRMINGHAM, MI 48012
General Environment: Atmospheric

AIR POLLUTION CONTROL, BUILDINGS AND SAFETY ENGINEERING DEPARTMENT
100 NORTH FIFTH STREET
ANN ARBOR, MI 48108
General Environment: Atmospheric

AIR POLLUTION CONTROL, BUILDINGS DEPARTMENT
241 WEST SOUTH STREET
KALAMAZOO, MI 49006
General Environment: Atmospheric

AIR POLLUTION CONTROL, BUREAU OF HEALTH AND SANITATION
1510 EAST PAPER MILL ROAD
PHILADELPHIA, PA 19118
General Environment: Atmospheric

**AIR POLLUTION CONTROL, CITY
    ENGINEERING OFFICE**
994 BIDDLE AVENUE
WYANDOTTE, MI 48192
General Environment: Atmospheric

**AIR POLLUTION CONTROL, CITY
    HEALTH DEPARTMENT**
513 KENTUCKY AVENUE
JOPLIN, MO 64801
General Environment: Atmospheric

**AIR POLLUTION CONTROL, CITY
    HEALTH DEPARTMENT**
CITY HALL
ST JOSEPH, MO 64501
General Environment: Atmospheric

**AIR POLLUTION CONTROL, CITY
    HEALTH DEPARTMENT**
817 NORTH JEFFERSON
SPOKANE, WA 99201
General Environment: Atmospheric

**AIR POLLUTION CONTROL, CITY
    HEALTH DEPARTMENT**
208 WEST SHAW
PASEDENA, TX 77502
General Environment: Atmospheric

**AIR POLLUTION CONTROL, CITY
    HEALTH DEPARTMENT**
210 SOUTH MAIN STREET
INDEPENDENCE, MO 64050
General Environment: Atmospheric

**AIR POLLUTION CONTROL, CITY
    HEALTH DEPARTMENT**
CITY HALL, 27 WEST MAIN STREET
NEW BRITAIN, CT 06051
General Environment: Atmospheric

**AIR POLLUTION CONTROL, CITY-
    COUNTY HEALTH UNIT**
1700 THIRD STREET
WITCHITA FALLS, TX 76301
General Environment: Atmospheric

**AIR POLLUTION CONTROL, CODE
    ENFORCEMENT AGENCY**
CITY HALL, 207 NORTH JAMES
    STREET
ROME, NY 13440
General Environment: Atmospheric

**AIR POLLUTION CONTROL,
    COUNTY BOARD OF HEALTH**
21 NORTH FOURTH STREET
WILMINGTON, NC 28401
General Environment: Atmospheric

**AIR POLLUTION CONTROL,
    COUNTY HEALTH DEPARTMENT**
COUNTY BUILDING, TERRACE
    STREET
MUSKEGON, MI 49440
General Environment: Atmospheric

**AIR POLLUTION CONTROL,
    COUNTY HEALTH DEPARTMENT**
712 SOUTH TEJON STREET
COLORADO SPRINGS, CO 80909
General Environment: Atmospheric

**AIR POLLUTION CONTROL,
    COUNTY HEALTH DEPARTMENT**
COUNTY OFFICE BUILDING
ROCKVILLE, MD 20850
General Environment: Atmospheric

**AIR POLLUTION CONTROL,
    COUNTY HEALTH DEPARTMENT**
625 SHADOW LANE
LAS VEGAS, NV 89106
General Environment: Atmospheric
Staff Size: 10 - 49

**AIR POLLUTION CONTROL,
    COUNTY HEALTH DEPARTMENT**
315 GROVER STREET
SHELBY, NC 28150
General Environment: Atmospheric

**AIR POLLUTION CONTROL,
    COUNTY HEALTH DEPARTMENT**
POST OFFICE BOX 2039
TYLER, TX 75701
General Environment: Atmospheric

**AIR POLLUTION CONTROL,
    COUNTY HEALTH DEPARTMENT**
515 PATTERSON AVENUE
GRAND JUNCTION, CO 81501
General Environment: Atmospheric

**AIR POLLUTION CONTROL,
    COUNTY HEALTH DEPARTMENT**
1200 BLYTHE BOULEVARD
CHARLOTTE, NC 28203
General Environment: Atmospheric

**AIR POLLUTION CONTROL,
    COUNTY HEALTH DEPARTMENT**
CITY BUILDING
SANDUSKY, OH 44870
General Environment: Atmospheric

**AIR POLLUTION CONTROL,
    COUNTY HEALTH DEPARTMENT**
445 FIRST STREET, SW
CEDAR RAPIDS, IA 52404
General Environment: Atmospheric
Staff Size: 5 - 9

**AIR POLLUTION CONTROL,
    COUNTY HEALTH DEPARTMENT**
520 SECOND AVENUE NORTH
ST PETERSBURG, FL 33731
General Environment: Atmospheric

**AIR POLLUTION CONTROL,
    COUNTY HEALTH DEPARTMENT**
1201 SOUTH 42ND STREET
OMAHA, NB 68105
General Environment: Atmospheric

**AIR POLLUTION CONTROL,
    COUNTY HEALTH DEPARTMENT**
260 SOUTH KIPLING STREET
LAKEWOOD, CO 80226
General Environment: Atmospheric

**AIR POLLUTION CONTROL,
    COUNTY HEALTH DEPARTMENT**
ROOM 301 COUNTY COURTHOUSE
MISSOULA, MT 59801
General Environment: Atmospheric

**AIR POLLUTION CONTROL,
    COUNTY HEALTH DEPARTMENT**
POST OFFICE BOX 1227
GREELEY, CO 80631
General Environment: Atmospheric

**AIR POLLUTION CONTROL,
    COUNTY HEALTH DEPARTMENT**
22 MARKET STREET
POUGHKEEPSIE, NY 12601
General Environment: Atmospheric

**AIR POLLUTION CONTROL,
    COUNTY HEALTH DEPARTMENT**
MERRIMAN ROAD
ELOISE, MI 48132
General Environment: Atmospheric
Specific Interests: Urban
Staff Size: 50 - 99

**AIR POLLUTION CONTROL,
    COUNTY HEALTH DEPARTMENT**
LIBERTY, MO 64068
General Environment: Atmospheric

**AIR POLLUTION CONTROL,
    COVINGTON-ALLEGHENY
    COUNTY**
COVINGTON, VA 24426
General Environment: Atmospheric

**AIR POLLUTION CONTROL,
    DEPARTMENT OF HEALTH**
CITY HALL
ELIZABETH, NJ 07201
General Environment: Atmospheric

**AIR POLLUTION CONTROL,
    ENGINEERING AND PUBLIC
    WORKS DEPARTMENT**
CITY-COUNTY MUNICIPAL
    BUILDING
AUGUSTA, GA 30902
General Environment: Atmospheric

**AIR POLLUTION CONTROL,
    ENVIRONMENTAL CONTROL
    DEPARTMENT**
1324 MOTOR PARKWAY
HAUPPAUGE, NY 11787
General Environment: Atmospheric
Staff Size: 10 - 49

AIR POLLUTION CONTROL,
ENVIRONMENTAL HEALTH
BUREAU
814 JEFFERSON AVENUE
MEMPHIS, TN 38105
General Environment: Atmospheric

AIR POLLUTION CONTROL,
ENVIRONMENTAL HEALTH
BUREAU
BALTIMORE COUNTY HEALTH
DEPARTMENT
TOWSON, MD 21204
General Environment: Atmospheric

AIR POLLUTION CONTROL,
ENVIRONMENTAL HEALTH
DIVISION
79 ELM STREET
HARTFORD, CT 06115
General Environment: Atmospheric

AIR POLLUTION CONTROL,
ENVIRONMENTAL HEALTH
SERVICES
3400 NORTH EASTERN BOULEVARD
OKLAHOMA CITY, OK 73105
General Environment: Atmospheric
Staff Size: 10 - 49

AIR POLLUTION CONTROL,
HAMTRACK FIRE DEPARTMENT
8523 JOSEPH CAMPAU AVENUE
HAMTRACK, MI 48212
General Environment: Atmospheric

AIR POLLUTION CONTROL,
HEALTH AND WELFARE
DEPARTMENT
CITY HALL, 30TH STREET AND
EAST AVENUE
BAYONNE, NJ 07002
General Environment: Atmospheric

AIR POLLUTION CONTROL,
HEALTH AND WELFARE
DEPARTMENT
61 SOUTH SPRING STREET
CONCORD, NH 03301
General Environment: Atmospheric
Staff Size: 10 - 49

AIR POLLUTION CONTROL,
HEALTH BUREAU
MUNICIPAL BUILDING
WASHINGTON, PA 15301
General Environment: Atmospheric

AIR POLLUTION CONTROL,
HEALTH DEPARTMENT
101 PASSAIC DRIVE
PASSAIC, NJ 07055
General Environment: Atmospheric

AIR POLLUTION CONTROL,
HEALTH DEPARTMENT

1938 LAUREL STREET POST OFFICE
2658
SARASOTA, FL 33579
General Environment: Atmospheric

AIR POLLUTION CONTROL,
HEALTH DEPARTMENT
CITY HALL, 105 JAY STREET
SCHENECTADY, NY 12305
General Environment: Atmospheric

AIR POLLUTION CONTROL,
HEALTH DEPARTMENT
204 HEALTH BUILDING
PROVIDENCE, RI 02908
General Environment: Atmospheric

AIR POLLUTION CONTROL,
HEALTH DEPARTMENT
151 CENTRAL MAIN
PUEBLO, CO 81003
General Environment: Atmospheric
Staff Size: 1 - 4

AIR POLLUTION CONTROL,
HEALTH DEPARTMENT
MAIN STREET
STRATFORD, CT 06497
General Environment: Atmospheric

AIR POLLUTION CONTROL,
HEALTH DEPARTMENT
2221 STOCKTON BOULEVARD
SACRAMENTO, CA 95817
General Environment: Atmospheric
Staff Size: 5 - 9

AIR POLLUTION CONTROL,
HEALTH DEPARTMENT
TOWN HALL, 739 OLD POST ROAD
FAIRFIELD, CT 06430
General Environment: Atmospheric

AIR POLLUTION CONTROL,
HEALTH DEPARTMENT
KENNEDY DRIVE
NOTLEY, NJ 07110
General Environment: Atmospheric
Staff Size: 10 - 49

AIR POLLUTION CONTROL,
HEALTH DEPARTMENT
229 NORTH STREET
STAMFORD, CT 06902
General Environment: Atmospheric

AIR POLLUTION CONTROL,
HEALTH DEPARTMENT
POST OFFICE BOX 90
HARRISBURG, PA 17120
General Environment: Atmospheric

AIR POLLUTION CONTROL,
HEALTH DEPARTMENT
33 WEST CENTRAL STREET
NATICK, MA 01760
General Environment: Atmospheric

AIR POLLUTION CONTROL,
HEALTH DEPARTMENT
1510 SMITH TOWER
SEATTLE, WA 98104
General Environment: Atmospheric

AIR POLLUTION CONTROL,
HEALTH DEPARTMENT
CITY HALL, 260 HIGH STREET
PERTH AMBOY, NJ 08861
General Environment: Atmospheric

AIR POLLUTION CONTROL,
HEALTH DEPARTMENT
BELVILLE, NJ 07109
General Environment: Atmospheric

AIR POLLUTION CONTROL,
HEALTH DEPARTMENT
CITY HALL
BEVERLY, MA 01915
General Environment: Atmospheric

AIR POLLUTION CONTROL,
HEALTH DEPARTMENT
TOWN HALL ANNEX, HAVEMEYER
PLACE
GREENWICH, CT 06830
General Environment: Atmospheric

AIR POLLUTION CONTROL,
HEALTH DEPARTMENT
414 CITY-COUNTY BUILDING
DETROIT, MI 48226
General Environment: Atmospheric

AIR POLLUTION CONTROL,
HEALTH DEPARTMENT
CITY HALL, ROOM 214
TRENTON, NJ 08608
General Environment: Atmospheric

AIR POLLUTION CONTROL,
HEALTH DEPARTMENT
1115 NORTH MACGREGOR STREET
HOUSTON, TX 77025
General Environment: Atmospheric

AIR POLLUTION CONTROL,
HEALTH DEPARTMENT
56 COVENTRY STREET
HARTFORD, CT 06112
General Environment: Atmospheric

AIR POLLUTION CONTROL,
HEALTH DEPARTMENT
65 CHESTNUT STREET
MONTCLAIR, NJ 07042
General Environment: Atmospheric

AIR POLLUTION CONTROL,
HEALTH DEPARTMENT
CITY HALL
OSKOSH, WI 54901
General Environment: Atmospheric

**AIR POLLUTION CONTROL,
HEALTH HOUSING AND
WELFARE DEPARTMENT**
CITY HALL
CAMDEN, NJ 08101
General Environment: Atmospheric

**AIR POLLUTION CONTROL,
INSPECTIONS DEPARTMENT**
CITY HALL, 305 M
MINNEAPOLIS, MN 55415
General Environment: Atmospheric

**AIR POLLUTION CONTROL,
MONTEREY COUNTY DISTRICT**
BOX 2137 1270 NATIVIDAD ROAD
SALINAS, CA 93901
General Environment: Atmospheric

**AIR POLLUTION CONTROL,
PUBLIC HEALTH AND WELFARE
DEPARTMENT**
2735 BROADWAY AVENUE
CLEVELAND, OH 44115
General Environment: Atmospheric

**AIR POLLUTION CONTROL,
PUBLIC HEALTH DEPARTMENT**
CITY HALL, 100 WEST MICHIGAN
BOULEVARD
MICHIGAN CITY, IN 46360
General Environment: Atmospheric
Staff Size: 1 - 4

**AIR POLLUTION CONTROL,
PUBLIC HEALTH DEPARTMENT**
727 CORDELL HULL BUILDING
NASHVILLE, TN 37219
General Environment: Atmospheric

**AIR POLLUTION CONTROL,
PUBLIC HEALTH DEPARTMENT**
1600 PACIFIC HIGHWAY
SAN DIEGO, CA 92101
General Environment: Atmospheric

**AIR POLLUTION CONTROL,
PUBLIC HEALTH DEPARTMENT**
30 CHURCH STREET
NEW ROCHELLE, NY 10805
General Environment: Atmospheric

**AIR POLLUTION CONTROL,
PUBLIC HEALTH DEPARTMENT**
3500 NORTH LOGAN STREET
LANSING, MI 48914
General Environment: Atmospheric

**AIR POLLUTION CONTROL,
PUBLIC SAFETY DEPARTMENT**
CITY HALL, BOX 7184
ASHEVILLE, NC 28807
General Environment: Atmospheric

**AIR POLLUTION CONTROL,
PUBLIC SAFETY DEPARTMENT**
1200 MARKET STREET
ST LOUIS, MO 63103

General Environment: Atmospheric
Staff Size: 10 - 49

**AIR POLLUTION CONTROL,
PUBLIC SAFETY DEPARTMENT**
181 SOUTH WASHINGTON
BOULEVARD
COLUMBUS, OH 43215
General Environment: Atmospheric

**AIR POLLUTION CONTROL,
PUBLIC SAFETY DEPARTMENT**
108 SOUTH 18TH STREET
OMAHA, NB 68102
General Environment: Atmospheric
Staff Size: 50 - 99

**AIR POLLUTION CONTROL,
PUBLIC SERVICE DEPARTMENT**
329 10TH STREET
LORAIN, OH 44052
General Environment: Atmospheric

**AIR POLLUTION CONTROL,
PUBLIC UTILITIES DEPARTMENT**
100 EAST 10TH STREET
ST PAUL, MN 55101
General Environment: Atmospheric
Staff Size: 10 - 49

**AIR POLLUTION CONTROL,
PUBLIC WORKS AND UTILITIES
DEPARTMENT**
1101 SOUTH SAGINAW, ROOM 210
FLINT, MI 48502
General Environment: Atmospheric

**AIR POLLUTION CONTROL,
PUBLIC WORKS DEPARTMENT**
SIXTH STREET AND BROADWAY
COLUMBIA, MO 65201
General Environment: Atmospheric

**AIR POLLUTION CONTROL,
SERVICES AND BUILDINGS
DEPARTMENT**
MUNICIPAL BUILDING, 101 WEST
THIRD STREET
DAYTON, OH 45402
General Environment: Atmospheric

**AIR POLLUTION CONTROL,
SEWERS DEPARTMENT**
2400 BEEKMAN STREET
CINCINNATI, OH 45214
General Environment: Atmospheric
Staff Size: 50 - 99

**AIR POLLUTION CONTROL,
VILLAGE OF HERKIMER**
120 GREEN STREET
HERKIMER, NY 13350
General Environment: Atmospheric

**AIR POLLUTION CONTROL,
WATER AND AIR RESOURCES**
POST OFFICE BOX 916
DOVER, DE 19901

AIR POLLUTION DEPARTMENT
MARKET STREET
STEUBENVILLE, OH 43952
General Environment: Atmospheric

**AIR POLLUTION DEPARTMENT,
COMMUNITY IMPROVEMENT
AND INSPECTION SERVICE**
509 WEALTHY STREET
GRAND RAPIDS, MI 49503
General Environment: Atmospheric

AIR POLLUTION DISTRICT
5630 SOUTH BROADWAY
EUREKA, CA 95501
General Environment: Atmospheric
Staff Size: 5 - 9

**AIR POLLUTION DIVISION, PUBLIC
HEALTH DEPARTMENT**
801 NORTH CAPITOL STREET, NE
WASHINGTON, DC 20002
General Environment: Atmospheric

AIR POLLUTION INSPECTION
MUNICIPAL BUILDING, MORGAN
STREET
ILION, NY 13357
General Environment: Atmospheric

**AIR POLLUTION PROGRAM,
ENVIRONMENTAL HEALTH
BUREAU**
1912 EIGHTH AVENUE SOUTH, BOX
2591
BIRMINGHAM, AL 35202
General Environment: Atmospheric
Staff Size: 10 - 49

**AIR POLLUTION REGULATION,
PUBLIC WORKS DEPARTMENT**
ROOM 109, CITY HALL
BATTLECREEK, MI 49014
General Environment: Atmospheric

**AIR POLLUTION SECTION,
ENVIRONMENTAL HEALTH
BUREAU**
1 STATE STREET
NEW HAVEN, CT 06511
General Environment: Atmospheric

**AIR POLLUTION SECTION,
HEALTH DEPARTMENT**
921 NE 23RD
OKLAHOMA CITY, OK 73105
Director, B Cranor
General Environment: Atmospheric
Staff Size: 10 - 49

**AIR POLLUTION,
ENVIRONMENTAL HEALTH,
COUNTY HEALTH DEPARTMENT**
240 OLD COUNTRY ROAD
MINEOLA, NY 11501
General Environment: Atmospheric

AIR POLLUTION, PUBLIC SAFETY DEPARTMENT
501 NORTH NINTH STREET
RICHMOND, VA 23219
General Environment: Atmospheric
Staff Size: 10 - 49

AIR QUALITY AND NOISE CONSERVATION, ENVIRONMENTAL RESOURCES
P O BOX 2351
HARRISBURG, PA 17105
General Environment: Atmospheric
Staff Size: 100 - 499

AIR QUALITY CONTROL BRANCH, PUBLIC WORKS DEPARTMENT
47 TRINITY AVENUE SW
ATLANTA, GA 30334
General Environment: Atmospheric

AIR QUALITY CONTROL BUREAU
610 NORTH HOWARD
BALTIMORE, MD 21201
General Environment: Atmospheric
Staff Size: 50 - 99

AIR QUALITY CONTROL DEPARTMENT
4525 INDIANAPOLIS BOULEVARD
EAST CHICAGO, IN 46312
General Environment: Atmospheric

AIR QUALITY CONTROL, BUILDING INSPECTION DEPARTMENT
CITY HALL, BOX 708
STATESVILLE, NC 28677
General Environment: Atmospheric

AIR QUALITY CONTROL, COUNTY HEALTH DEPARTMENT
101 SOUTH STREET
ANNAPOLIS, MD 21401
General Environment: Atmospheric

AIR RESOURCES BOARD
417 SOUTH HILL STREET
LOS ANGELES, CA 90013
General Environment: Atmospheric

AIR RESOURCES DIVISION, STATE HEALTH DEPARTMENT
84 HOLLAND AVENUE
ALBANY, NY 12208
General Environment: Atmospheric

AIR SANITATION BUREAU, STATE PUBLIC HEALTH DEPARTMENT
2151 BERKLEY WAY
BERKLEY, CA 94704
General Environment: Atmospheric

AIR SANITATION SECTION, HEALTH DEPARTMENT
P O BOX 3378
HONOLULU, HI 96801
General Environment: Atmospheric

AIR SANITATION, COUNTY HEALTH DEPARTMENT
POST OFFICE BOX 871
MARTINEZ, CA 94533
General Environment: Atmospheric

AIR USE MANAGEMENT, SANITARY ENGINEERING DIVISION
511 STATEHOUSE
BOSTON, MA 02133
General Environment: Atmospheric

ALASKA DEPARTMENT HEALTH & WELFARE
ALASKA OFFICE BUILDING
JUNEAU, AK 99801
Director, John S Mcdonald
General Environment: Atmospheric

ALEXANDRIA HEALTH DEPARTMENT
517 ST ASAPH STREET
ALEXANDRIA, VA 22314
General Environment: Atmospheric

ANTI-POLLUTION LEAGUE OF CONNECTICUT VALLEY
134 MAIN STREET
BRATTLEBORO, VT 05301

APPALACHIAN STUDIES AND DEVELOPMENT
295 COLISEUM
MORGANTOWN, WV 26506

ARKANSAS POLLUTION CONTROL COMMISSION
1100 HARRINGTON AVENUE
LITTLE ROCK, AR 72202
Director, S L Davies
General Environment: Limnologic

BAY AREA POLLUTION CONTROL DISTRICT
1418 MISSION STREET
SAN FRANCISCO, CA 94103
General Environment: Atmospheric

BIOLOGICAL-ENVIRONMENTAL SERVICES DIVISION
1602 BOULEVARD
JACKSONVILLE, FL 32202
General Environment: Atmospheric

BUILDING AND AIR POLLUTION CONTROL DEPARTMENT
CITY HALL, 225 WEST CENTER STREET
KINGSPORT, TN 37660
General Environment: Atmospheric

BUILDING DEPARTMENT
1501 OAK AVENUE
EVANSTON, IL 60204
General Environment: Atmospheric

BUILDING DEPARTMENT
EUCLID, OH 44123
General Environment: Atmospheric

BUILDING INSPECTION BUREAU
HAMPTON, VA 23369
General Environment: Atmospheric
Staff Size: 1 - 4

BUILDING INSPECTION DEPARTMENT, HEATING AND AIR POLLUTION
CITY HALL, WASHINGTON AVENUE
BAY CITY, MI 48706
General Environment: Atmospheric

CASPER-NATRONA COUNTY HEALTH DEPARTMENT
265 SOUTH WASHINGTON
CASPER, WY 82601
General Environment: Atmospheric

CITY MANAGER'S OFFICE
COURTHOUSE
CAPE GIRARDEAU, MO 63701
General Environment: Atmospheric

CITY MANAGER'S OFFICER
OLIVE AND EAST STREETS
BLOOMINGTON, IL 61701
General Environment: Atmospheric

CITY-COUNTY HEALTH DEPARTMENT
1202 JARVIS STREET, BOX 998
LUBBOCK, TX 79408
General Environment: Atmospheric

CLEAN AIR AND WATER DIVISION, HEALTH DEPARTMENT
POST OFFICE BOX 1540
TRENTON, NJ 08625

CLEAN AIR COMMISSION
14 ADAMS AVENUE
WALTHAM, MA 02154
President, Jack Koutoujian
General Environment: Atmospheric

CLEAN AIR POLLUTION
90 DOVER ROAD
WELLESLEY, MA 02181
General Environment: Atmospheric

CLEAN WATER COMMISSION
POST OFFICE BOX 154
JEFFERSON CITY, MO 65101
Executive Secretary, Jack K Smith
General Environment: Limnologic
Staff Size: 10 - 49

CLEANER AIR COALITION OF METROPOLITAN BOSTON
131 CLAREDON STREET
BOSTON, MA 02116
General Environment: Atmospheric

CLEAR AIR, CLEAN WATER, UNLIMITED
POST OFFICE BOX 311
ST PAUL, MN 55075

CODDO-SHREVEPORT HEALTH UNIT
1866 KINGS HIGHWAY
NEW ORLEANS, LA 71103
General Environment: Atmospheric

COOPERATIVE EXTENSION SERVICE
295 COLISEUM
MORGANTOWN, WV 26506

COUNTY HEALTH DEPARTMENT
2111 LAHOMA ROAD
ENID, OK 73701
General Environment: Atmospheric

DEVELOPMENT DEPARTMENT
65 SOUTH FRONT STREET
COLUMBUS, OH 43215

DEVELOPMENT OFFICE OF ALABAMA
MONTGOMERY, AL 36104

ENGINEERING AND SANITATION DIVISION, COUNTY HEALTH DEPARTMENT
POST OFFICE BOX 6148
SAVANNAH, GA 31405
General Environment: Atmospheric

ENGINEERING AND SANITATION DIVISION, HEALTH DEPARTMENT
STATEHOUSE
BOISE, ID 83701
General Environment: Atmospheric

ENGINEERING AND SANITATION DIVISION, STATE HEALTH DEPARTMENT
POST OFFICE BOX 640
BOISE, ID 83701
Director, Vaughn Anderson
General Environment: Limnologic

ENGINEERING AND SANITATION, PUBLIC HEALTH DEPARTMENT
4210 EAST 11TH AVENUE
DENVER, CO 80220

ENGINEERING DEPARTMENT, HEALTH DEPARTMENT
POST OFFICE BOX 118
COLUMBUS, OH 43216
General Environment: Atmospheric

ENGINEERING DIVISION, PUBLIC HEALTH DEPARTMENT
1800 UNIVERSITY DRIVE
FORT WORTH, TX 76107
General Environment: Atmospheric

ENGINEERING EXAMINERS AND BOILER INSPECTORS
2501 CITY HALL
BUFFALO, NY 14202
General Environment: Atmospheric

ENVIRONMENTAL HEALTH DEPARTMENT
3141 LOMA VISTA ROAD
VENTURA, CA 93001
General Environment: Atmospheric
Staff Size: 10 - 49

ENVIRONMENTAL CONTROL DEPARTMENT
320 NORTH CLARK STREET
CHICAGO, IL 60610
General Environment: Atmospheric

ENVIRONMENTAL ENGINEERING DIVISION, COUNTY HEALTH DEPARTMENT
202 SIXTH AVENUE EAST
BRADENTON, FL 33505
General Environment: Atmospheric

ENVIRONMENTAL ENGINEERING SERVICES, DEPARTMENT OF HEALTH
LUCAS STATE OFFICE BUILDING
DES MOINES, IA 50319
General Environment: Atmospheric
Staff Size: 50 - 99

ENVIRONMENTAL HEALTH AND AIR POLLUTION DIVISION, HEALTH DEPARTMENT
14 NORTH CENTRAL AVENUE
PHOENIX, AZ 85004
General Environment: Atmospheric

ENVIRONMENTAL HEALTH AND ENGINEERING, STATE DEPARTMENT OF HEALTH
STATE CAPITOL
BISMARCK, ND 58501
General Environment: Atmospheric

ENVIRONMENTAL HEALTH BUREAU
790 SUTRO STREET
RENO, NV 89502
General Environment: Atmospheric

ENVIRONMENTAL HEALTH BUREAU
401 COLLEY AVENUE
NORFOLK, VA 23507
Staff Size: 10 - 49

ENVIRONMENTAL HEALTH DIVISION, BERKLEY HEALTH DEPARTMENT
2121 MCKINLEY AVENUE
BERKLEY, CA 94703
General Environment: Atmospheric

ENVIRONMENTAL HEALTH DIVISION, CITY HEALTH DEPARTMENT
610 SOUTH SECOND STREET, EAST
SALT LAKE CITY, UT 84111
General Environment: Atmospheric

ENVIRONMENTAL HEALTH DIVISION, COUNTY HEALTH DEPARTMENT
300 EAST NORWOOD STREET
GREENSBORO, NC 27401
General Environment: Atmospheric

ENVIRONMENTAL HEALTH DIVISION, COUNTY HEALTH DEPARTMENT
4616 EAST 15TH STREET
TULSA, OK 74112
General Environment: Atmospheric

ENVIRONMENTAL HEALTH DIVISION, COUNTY HEALTH DEPARTMENT
4080 CHAIN BRIDGE ROAD
FAIRFAX, VA 22030
Specific Interests: Urban
Staff Size: 10 - 49

ENVIRONMENTAL HEALTH DIVISION, COUNTY HEALTH DEPARTMENT
615 NORTH HIGHLAND ROAD
GASTONIA, NC 28052
General Environment: Atmospheric

ENVIRONMENTAL HEALTH DIVISION, COUNTY HEALTH DEPARTMENT
1515 WASHINGTON STREET
WAUKEGAN, IL 60085
Staff Size: 10 - 49

ENVIRONMENTAL HEALTH DIVISION, COUNTY HEALTH DEPARTMENT
325 EAST CENTRAL PARKWAY
CINCINNATI, OH 45202
General Environment: Atmospheric

ENVIRONMENTAL HEALTH DIVISION, COUNTY HEALTH DEPARTMENT
2570 GRANT AVENUE
OGDEN, UT 84401
General Environment: Atmospheric

ENVIRONMENTAL HEALTH DIVISION, HEALTH DEPARTMENT
25 MILL STREET
PATERSON, NJ 07501
General Environment: Atmospheric

ENVIRONMENTAL HEALTH DIVISION, MILFORD HEALTH DEPARTMENT
EELS HILL ANNEX
MILFORD, CT 06460
General Environment: Atmospheric

ENVIRONMENTAL HEALTH DIVISION, PUBLIC HEALTH DEPARTMENT
P O BOX 3378
HONOLULU, HI 96801
Chief, Shinji Soneda
Staff Size: 10 - 49

ENVIRONMENTAL HEALTH DIVISION, STATE HEALTH DEPARTMENT
14 NORTH CENTRAL AVENUE
PHOENIX, AZ 85004
Director, Edmund Garthe
General Environment: Limnologic

ENVIRONMENTAL HEALTH SECTION, HEALTH DEPARTMENT
3450 BROADWAY, PO BOX 471
BOULDER, CO 80302
General Environment: Atmospheric

ENVIRONMENTAL HEALTH SECTION, STATE HEALTH DEPARTMENT
44 MEDICAL DRIVE
SALT LAKE CITY, UT 84113
General Environment: Atmospheric

ENVIRONMENTAL HEALTH SERVICE, COUNTY HEALTH DEPARTMENT
363 ALLEN STREET
HUDSON, NY 12534
General Environment: Atmospheric

ENVIRONMENTAL HEALTH SERVICES
TOPEKA, KS 66612
Director, J Lee Mayes
General Environment: Limnologic

ENVIRONMENTAL HEALTH SERVICES, BROOME COUNTY HEALTH DEPARTMENT
62068 WATER STREET
BINGHAMTON, NY 13901
General Environment: Atmospheric

ENVIRONMENTAL HEALTH SERVICES, COUNTY HEALTH DEPARTMENT
99 BUTLER STREET, SE
ATLANTA, GA 30303
General Environment: Atmospheric
Staff Size: 50 - 99

ENVIRONMENTAL HEALTH SERVICES, COUNTY HEALTH DEPARTMENT
311 BALDWIN STREET
ELMIRA, NY 14901
General Environment: Atmospheric

ENVIRONMENTAL HEALTH SERVICES, COUNTY HEALTH DEPARTMENT

COUNTY OFFICE BUILDING
LOCKPORT, NY 14094
General Environment: Atmospheric

ENVIRONMENTAL HEALTH SERVICES, COUNTY HEALTH DEPARTMENT
126 TRINITY PLACE WEST
DECATUR, GA 30030
General Environment: Atmospheric

ENVIRONMENTAL HEALTH SERVICES, HARTFORD HEALTH DEPARTMENT
28 SOUTH MAIN STREET
WEST HARTFORD, CT 06107
General Environment: Atmospheric

ENVIRONMENTAL HEALTH SERVICES, HEALTH DEPARTMENT
409 MADISON AVENUE
ALBANY, NY 12201
General Environment: Atmospheric

ENVIRONMENTAL HEALTH, COUNTY BOARD OF HEALTH
POST OFFICE BOX 2299
COLUMBUS, GA 31902
General Environment: Atmospheric

ENVIRONMENTAL HEALTH, METROPOLITAN HEALTH DEPARTMENT
131 WEST NUEVA STREET
SAN ANTONIO, TX 78285
General Environment: Atmospheric
Staff Size: 10 - 49

ENVIRONMENTAL HEALTH, WATER POLLUTION COMMISSION
44 MEDICAL DRIVE
SALT LAKE CITY, UT 84113
Director, L Thatcher
General Environment: Limnologic

ENVIRONMENTAL IMPROVEMENT COMMISSION
AUGUSTA, ME 04330
Staff Size: 50 - 99

ENVIRONMENTAL PROTECTION AGENCY REGION 3 OFFICE
POST OFFICE BOX 12900
PHILADEPHIA, PA 19108
General Environment: Atmospheric

ENVIRONMENTAL PROTECTION AGENCY REGION 4 OFFICE, SUITE 300
1421 PEACHTREE STREET, NE
ATLANTA, GA 30309
General Environment: Atmospheric

ENVIRONMENTAL PROTECTION AGENCY REGION 6 OFFICE
1114 COMMERCE STREET
DALLAS, TX 75202
General Environment: Atmospheric

ENVIRONMENTAL PROTECTION AGENCY REGION 8 OFFICE
1860 LINCOLN STREET, ROOM 953
DENVER, CO 80203
General Environment: Atmospheric

ENVIRONMENTAL QUALITY DEPARTMENT
1234 SOUTHWEST MORRISON STREET
PORTLAND, OR 97205
Staff Size: 100 - 499

ENVIRONMENTAL QUALITY DEPARTMENT
POST OFFICE BOX 1390
TRENTON, NJ 08625
General Environment: Atmospheric
Staff Size: 100 - 499

ENVIRONMENTAL SANITATION DIVISION
STATE OFFICE BUILDING
CHEYENNE, WY 82001
General Environment: Limnologic

ENVIRONMENTAL SANITATION DIVISION, COUNTY HEALTH DEPARTMENT
300 EAST MAIN STREET
DURHAM, NC 27701
General Environment: Atmospheric
Staff Size: 1 - 4

ENVIRONMENTAL SANITATION DIVISION, MONTANA BOARD OF HEALTH
STATE CAPITOL BUILDING
HELENA, MT 59601
General Environment: Limnologic

ENVIRONMENTAL SANITATION, HEALTH DEPARTMENT
406 ELIZABETH STREET
UTICA, NY 13501
General Environment: Atmospheric

ENVIRONMENTAL SANITATION, HEALTH DEPARTMENT
21ST FLOOR, CITY HALL
KANSAS CITY, MO 64106
General Environment: Atmospheric

ENVIRONMENTAL SANITATION, PUBLIC HEALTH DEPARTMENT
CITY HALL BUILDING
ROCKFORD, IL 61104
General Environment: Atmospheric

ENVIRONMENTAL SCIENCES AND ENGINEERING PROGRAM
UNIVERSITY OF HOUSTON-3801 CULLEN
HOUSTON, TX 77004
Director, Dr H Nugent Myrick
Staff Size: 10 - 49

**ENVIRONMENTAL SERVICES
DEPARTMENT**
104 SOUTH KENILWORTH STREET
ELMHURST, IL 60126
General Environment: Atmospheric

**ENVIRONMENTAL SERVICES,
HEALTH BUREAU**
CITY HALL
ALLENTOWN, PA 18101
General Environment: Atmospheric

**FIRE PREVENTION BUREAU, FIRE
DEPARTMENT**
470 EAST LINCOLN AVENUE
MT VERNON, NY 10550
General Environment: Atmospheric

**GAME AND FISHERIES
COMMISSION**
POST OFFICE BOX 451
JACKSON, MS 39205
General Environment: Limnologic

**GEOLOGICAL RESOURCES
DIVISION, NATURAL RESOURCES
DEPARTMENT**
1207 GRANDVIEW AVENUE
COLUMBUS, OH 43212
General Environment: Limnologic

GOVERNOR'S OFFICE
STATE OFFICE BUILDING
NASHVILLE, TN 37219

GOVERNOR'S OFFICE
STATE CAPITOL
RICHMOND, VA 23219

GOVERNOR'S OFFICE
STATE CAPITOL BUILDING
COLUMBIA, SC 29201

GOVERNOR'S OFFICE
116 WEST JONES STREET
RALEIGH, NC 27602

HARBOR POLLUTION COMMITTEE
MASSACHUSETTS PORT
   AUTHORITY, 470 ATLANTIC
   STREET
BOSTON, MA 02210

**HEALTH AND ENVIRONMENTAL
SANITATION, PUBLIC SAFETY
DEPARTMENT**
CITY HALL, 423 WALNUT STREET
HARRISBURG, PA 17101
General Environment: Atmospheric

**HEALTH AND WELFARE
DEPARTMENT**
CITY HALL, 280 GROVE STREET
JERSEY CITY, NJ 07302
General Environment: Atmospheric

**HEALTH AND WELFARE
DEPARTMENT**
709 SUTRO STREET
RENO, NV 89502
Director, Ernest Gregory
General Environment: Limnologic

HEALTH BUREAU
EIGHTH AND WASHINGTON
   STREETS
READING, PA 19601
General Environment: Atmospheric

HEALTH DEPARTMENT
770 HEMLOCK STREET
MACON, GA 31201
General Environment: Atmospheric

HEALTH DEPARTMENT
GRAND STREET
WATERBURY, CT 06702
General Environment: Atmospheric

HEALTH DEPARTMENT
504 EAST 2ND STREET
DULUTH, MN 55802
General Environment: Atmospheric
Staff Size: 1 - 4

HEALTH DEPARTMENT
STATE OFFICE BUILDING
DES MOINES, IA 50319
Commissioner, Dr Arthur Long
General Environment: Limnologic

HEALTH DEPARTMENT
18 NORTH JACKSON STREET
JANESVILLE, WI 53545
General Environment: Atmospheric

HEALTH DEPARTMENT
619 ANN AVENUE
KANSAS CITY, KS 66101
General Environment: Atmospheric

HEALTH DEPARTMENT
137 EAST AVENUE
NORWALK, CT 06851
General Environment: Atmospheric
Staff Size: 5 - 9

HEALTH DEPARTMENT
STATE HOUSE STATION
LINCOLN, NB 68509
Director, Dr Lynn Thompson
General Environment: Limnologic

HEALTH DEPARTMENT
801 SOUTH BRENTWOOD
   BOULEVARD
CLAYTON, MO 63105
Assistant Commander, Clifford Mitchell
General Environment: Atmospheric

HEALTH DEPARTMENT
COUNTY-CITY BUILDING
SOUTH BEND, IN 46601
General Environment: Atmospheric

HEALTH DEPARTMENT
1149 PEARL STREET, 601
   COURTHOUSE
BEAUMONT, TX 77701
General Environment: Atmospheric

HEALTH DEPARTMENT
148 MARITINE AVENUE
WHITE PLAINS, NY 10601
General Environment: Atmospheric

HEALTH DEPARTMENT
1085 SOUTH MAIN STREET
DECATUR, IL 62521
General Environment: Atmospheric
Staff Size: 5 - 9

HEALTH DEPARTMENT
311 23RD AVENUE NORTH
NASHVILLE, TN 37203
General Environment: Atmospheric

HEALTH DEPARTMENT
TOPEKA, KS 66612
Director, Dr Hugh E Dierker
General Environment: Limnologic

HEALTH DEPARTMENT
MUNICIPAL BUILDING, ROOM 353
HAMILTON, OH 45010
General Environment: Atmospheric

HEALTH DEPARTMENT
1207 OAK STREET
LA MARQUE, TX 77568
General Environment: Atmospheric
Specific Interests: Urban
Staff Size: 10 - 49

HEALTH DEPARTMENT
SAFETY BUILDING
EAU CLAIRE, WI 54701
General Environment: Atmospheric

HEALTH DEPARTMENT
CITY HALL, 225 NORTH ONEIDA
APPLETON, WI 54911
General Environment: Atmospheric

HEALTH DEPARTMENT
407 GRANT STREET
WAUSAU, WI 54401
General Environment: Atmospheric

HEALTH DEPARTMENT
1615 WEST EIGHTH STREET
TOPEKA, KS 66606
General Environment: Atmospheric

HEALTH DEPARTMENT
PIERRE, SD 57501
General Environment: Atmospheric

HEALTH DEPARTMENT
CITY HALL, 76 BAYARD AVENUE
NEW BRUNSWICK, NJ 08903
General Environment: Atmospheric

HEALTH DEPARTMENT
IRVING AND COLLEGE STREETS,
BOX 1751
SAN ANGELO, TX 76901
General Environment: Atmospheric

HEALTH DEPARTMENT
CITY OFFICE BUILDING
BELOIT, WI 53511
General Environment: Atmospheric

HEALTH DEPARTMENT LABORATORY
CITY HALL, 1323 BROADWAY
SUPERIOR, WI 54880
General Environment: Atmospheric

HEALTH DEPARTMENT OF COLORADO
4210 EAST 11TH AVENUE
DENVER, CO 80220
Director, Dr Cleere

HEALTH DEPARTMENT OF LINCOLN-LANCASTER COUNTY
2200 ST MARY'S AVENUE
LINCOLN, NB 68502
General Environment: Atmospheric
Staff Size: 5 - 9

HEALTH DEPARTMENT OF NUECES COUNTY
1811 NORTH SHORELINE DRIVE
CORPUS CHRISTI, TX 78403
General Environment: Atmospheric

HEALTH DISTRICT- LAKE COUNTY
121 LIBERTY STREET
PAINESVILLE, OH 44077
General Environment: Atmospheric

HEATING AND AIR POLLUTION DEPARTMENT
CITY HALL
WATERLOO, IA 50705
General Environment: Atmospheric

HIGHWAY DEPARTMENT BUILDING
HIGHWAY 45
TOPELO, MS 38801
Director of Appalachian Development
9340

HOUSING DIVISION, PLANNING AND DEVELOPMENT DEPARTMENT
655 LAKE STREET
OAK PARK, IL 60301
General Environment: Atmospheric

IN-STREAM POLLUTION CONTROL, BOARD OF HEALTH
1330 WEST MICHIGAN STREET
INDIANAPOLIS, IN 46206
General Environment: Limnologic

INDUSTRIAL HYGIENE BUREAU
BALTIMORE CITY HEALTH
DEPARTMENT
BALTIMORE, MD 21202
Director, Elkins Dahle, Jr
General Environment: Atmospheric
Staff Size: 10 - 49

INDUSTRIAL HYGIENE DIVISION, VERMONT HEALTH DEPARTMENT
32 SPAULDING BUILDING, BOX 607
BARRE, VT 05641
General Environment: Atmospheric
Staff Size: 10 - 49

INDUSTRIAL HYGIENE, PUBLIC HEALTH DEPARTMENT
STATE OFFICE BUILDING
CHEYENNE, WY 82001
General Environment: Atmospheric

INDUSTRIAL RADIATION AND AIR HYGIENE, ENVIRONMENTAL HEALTH SERVICE
10TH AND HARRISON STREETS
TOPEKA, KS 66612
General Environment: Atmospheric

INSPECTION AND SANITATION DIVISION
125 EAST AVENUE
HUTCHINSON, KS 67504
General Environment: Atmospheric

INSPECTION DEPARTMENT, AIR POLLUTION DEPARTMENT
419 FULTON STREET
PEORIA, IL 61602
General Environment: Atmospheric

INSPECTION DEPARTMENT, BUREAU OF PUBLIC WORKS
6801 DELMAR BOULEVARD
UNIVERSITY CITY, MO 63130
General Environment: Atmospheric

INSPECTION DIVISION, COUNTY HEALTH DEPARTMENT
EAST FIRST AND DES MOINES STREETS
DES MOINES, IA 50307
General Environment: Atmospheric

INSPECTION DIVISION, PUBLIC WORKS DEPARTMENT
427 PATTON STREET, BOX 1159
DANVILLE, VA 24541
General Environment: Atmospheric

INSPECTIONS DEPARTMENT
402 MUNICIPAL BUILDING
RALEIGH, NC 27602
General Environment: Atmospheric

INTERSTATE RELATIONS, GOVERNOR'S OFFICE
STATE CAPITOL
HARRISBURG, PA 17120

INTERSTATE SANITATION COMMISSION
10 COLUMBUS CIRCLE
NEW YORK, NY 10019
General Environment: Limnologic

KENTUCKY PROGRAM DEVELOPMENT
CAPITOL BUILDING, ROOM 157
FRANKFORT, KY 40601

LABORATORIES AND ENVIRONMENTAL HEALTH DIVISION, PUBLIC HEALTH
515 SOUTH CEDAR STREET
FRESNO, CA 93702
General Environment: Atmospheric

MORATORIUM ON POLLUTION
POST OFFICE BOX 143
PITTSFIELD, MA 01201
President, W I Hunter

OCCUPATIONAL HEALTH AND RADIATION CONTROL, ENVIRONMENTAL HEALTH
1100 WEST 49TH STREET
AUSTIN, TX 78756
General Environment: Atmospheric

OCCUPATIONAL HEALTH, AIR POLLUTION DIVISION, STATE HEALTH
408 GALISTEO STREET
SANTE FE, NM 87501
General Environment: Atmospheric
Staff Size: 10 - 49

OCCUPATIONAL SAFETY AND HEALTH DIVISION
300 SOUTH WACKER DRIVE, ROOM 2904
CHICAGO, IL 60606

OCCUPATIONAL SAFETY AND HEALTH DIVISION
50 7TH STREET, NE - ROOM 404
ATLANTA, GA 30323

OCCUPATIONAL SAFETY AND HEALTH INSTITUTE
601 EAST 12TH STREET
KANSAS CITY, MO 64106

OCCUPATIONAL SAFETY AND HEALTH, HEALTH, EDUCATION AND WELFARE
KENNEDY FEDERAL BUILDING, GOVERNMENT CENTER
BOSTON, MA 02203

OCCUPATIONAL SAFETY AND HEALTH, HEALTH, EDUCATION AND WELFARE
1114 COMMERCE STREET
DALLAS, TX 75202

OCCUPATIONAL SAFETY AND HEALTH, HEALTH, EDUCATION AND WELFARE
1321 SECOND AVENUE
SEATTLE, WA 98101

OCCUPATIONAL SAFETY AND HEALTH, HEALTH, EDUCATION AND WELFARE
POST OFFICE BOX 12900
PHILADELPHIA, PA 19108

ODESSA-ECTOR COUNTY HEALTH DEPARTMENT
200 WEST THIRD STREET
ODESSA, TX 79761
General Environment: Atmospheric

OIL AND GAS BOARD
BOX 1332
JACKSON, MS 39205
General Environment: Limnologic

PLANNING BUREAU
270 WASHINGTON STREET, ROOM 611
ATLANTA, GA 30334

POLLUTION ABATEMENT COMMISSION
COMMERCIAL STREET
PORTLAND, ME 04111
Chairman, Edward Langlois

POLLUTION CONTROL AGENCY
26 MAIN STREET
TOLEDO, OH 43605
Specific Interests: Urban
Staff Size: 10 - 49

POLLUTION CONTROL AUTHORITY
2600 BULL STREET, J MARION SIMS BUILDING
COLUMBIA, SC 29201
General Environment: Atmospheric

POLLUTION CONTROL COMMISSION
POST OFFICE BOX 281
WEST HARTFORD, CT 06107
Director, Anita Pericolosi

POLLUTION CONTROL DIVISION
7 COLLINSVILLE AVENUE
EAST ST LOUIS, IL 62201
Director, Joseph Iwasyzyn
General Environment: Atmospheric

POLLUTION CONTROL DIVISION, PUBLIC HEALTH DEPARTMENT
864 NORTHWEST 23RD STREET
MIAMI, FL 33127
Specific Interests: Urban
Staff Size: 50 - 99

POLLUTION CONTROL, BOARD OF HEALTH

UNIVERSITY CAMPUS
MINNEAPOLIS, MN 55440
General Environment: Atmospheric

POLLUTION UNLIMITED
872 BURT STREET
TAUNTON, MA 02780

PUBLIC HEALTH AND SAFETY BUREAU
400 SOUTH EIGHTH STREET
LEBANON, PA 17042
General Environment: Atmospheric

PUBLIC HEALTH CENTER
415 FOURTH STREETS, SE
ROCHESTER, MN 55901
General Environment: Atmospheric
Staff Size: 1 - 4

PUBLIC HEALTH DEPARTMENT
817 FRANKLIN STREET
MANITOWOC, WI 54220
General Environment: Atmospheric

PUBLIC HEALTH DEPARTMENT
CALIFORNIA STATE COLLEGE
BERKELEY, CA 94700
General Environment: Atmospheric

PUBLIC HEALTH DEPARTMENT
337 EAST WAYNE STREET
FORT WAYNE, IN 46802
General Environment: Atmospheric

PUBLIC HEALTH DEPARTMENT
425 WEST STATE STREET
ROCKFORD, IL 61101
General Environment: Atmospheric

PUBLIC HEALTH DEPARTMENT
CITY HALL, 1850 LEWIS AVENUE
NORTH CHICAGO, IL 60064
General Environment: Atmospheric

PUBLIC HEALTH DEPARTMENT OF COOK COUNTY
1425 SOUTH RACING AVENUE
CHICAGO, IL 60608
General Environment: Atmospheric

PUBLIC SAFETY DIVISION, HEALTH BUREAU
FIFTH AND WELSH STREETS
CHESTER, PA 19013
General Environment: Atmospheric

PUBLIC UTILITIES DEPARTMENT, TESTING LABORATORY
100 EAST 10TH STREET
ST PAUL, MN 55101
General Environment: Atmospheric

PUBLIC WORKS BOARD
LITTLE FALLS, NY 13365
Staff Size: 5 - 9

PUBLIC WORKS DEPARTMENT
226 WEST FOURTH STREET
DAVENPORT, IA 52801
General Environment: Atmospheric

PUBLIC WORKS DEPARTMENT
CITY HALL, 118 MAIN STREET
NEWPORT NEWS, VA 23601
General Environment: Atmospheric

PUBLIC WORKS DEPARTMENT
12TH AND OAK STREETS
KANSAS CITY, MO 64108
General Environment: Limnologic

PURE WATER DIVISION, STATE HEALTH DEPARTMENT
84 HOLLAND AVENUE
ALBANY, NY 12208
Assistant Commissioner, John Haberer
General Environment: Atmospheric

RADIOLOGICAL HEALTH DIVISION, ENVIRONMENTAL HEALTH DEPARTMENT
STATE OFFICE BUILDING
MONTGOMERY, AL 36104
General Environment: Atmospheric
Staff Size: 10 - 49

SAFETY AND PERMITS DEPARTMENT
CITY HALL, 1300 PERDIDO STREET
NEW ORLEANS, LA 70112
Director, E C Kurtz
General Environment: Atmospheric

SANITARY ENGINEERING AND ENVIRONMENTAL PROTECTION
DEPARTMENT OF HEALTH
PIERRE, SD 57501
General Environment: Limnologic
Staff Size: 5 - 9

SANITARY ENGINEERING DEPARTMENT
STATEHOUSE
AUGUSTA, ME 04330
General Environment: Atmospheric

SANITARY ENGINEERING, BOARD OF HEALTH
1217 PEARL STREET, BOX 210
JACKSONVILLE, FL 32201
General Environment: Atmospheric

SANITATION BUREAU, COUNTY HEALTH DEPARTMENT
1825 EAST ROOSEVELT DRIVE, BOX 2111
PHOENIX, AZ 85006
General Environment: Atmospheric

SANITATION ENGINEERING, STATE HEALTH DEPARTMENT
PIERRE, SD 57501
Director, Charles Carl
General Environment: Atmospheric

SEACOAST ANTIPOLLUTION LEAGUE
ROUTE 84
HAMPTON FALLS, NH 03844
President, Walter Tingle

SEWERAGE DIVISION, METROPOLITAN COMMISSION
20 SOMERSET
BOSTON, MA 02108

SMOKE ABATEMENT AND AIR POLLUTION CONTROL DEPARTMENT
724 O'CONNOR BUILDING, RIDGE ROAD
LACKAWANNA, NY 14218
General Environment: Atmospheric

SMOKE ABATEMENT AND BOILER INSPECTION DIVISION, INSPECTION SERVICE
711 NORTH 19TH STREET
BIRMINGHAM, AL 35203
General Environment: Atmospheric

SMOKE ABATEMENT COMMISSION
200 EAST THIRD STREET
JAMESTOWN, NY 14701
General Environment: Atmospheric

SMOKE AND AIR POLLUTION ADVISORY BOARD
2872 WEST JEFFERSON STREET
TRENTON, MI 48183
General Environment: Atmospheric

SMOKE AND AIR POLLUTION CONTROL BUREAU
217 ARSENAL STREET
WATERTOWN, NY 13601
General Environment: Atmospheric

SMOKE AND BOILER SECTION, LICENSES AND INSPECTIONS DEPARTMENT
DISTRICT BUILDING, 14TH AND E STREETS, NW
WASHINGTON, DC 20004
General Environment: Atmospheric

SMOKE CONTROL DIVISION, BUILDING DEPARTMENT
CITY HALL, 605 BANNOCK STREET
BOISE, ID 83702
General Environment: Atmospheric

SMOKE INSPECTION DEPARTMENT
CITY HALL
MONROE, MI 48161
General Environment: Atmospheric

SMOKE INSPECTION DIVISION, BUILDING INSPECTION DEPARTMENT
210 MONONA AVENUE
MADISON, WI 53709
General Environment: Atmospheric

SMOKE INSPECTIONS, PUBLIC HEALTH DEPARTMENT
41 WEST SECOND STREET
FOND DU LAC, WI 54935
General Environment: Atmospheric

STEAM CONTROL COMMISSION
POST OFFICE DRAWER FC, UNIVERSITY STATION
BATON ROUGE, LA 70803
General Environment: Limnologic

STEAM POLLUTION CONTROL DIVISION, PUBLIC HEALTH DEPARTMENT
620 CORDELL HULL BUILDING
NASHVILLE, TN 37219
General Environment: Limnologic

STREAM POLLUTION BOARD
1330 WEST MICHIGAN STREET
INDIANAPOLIS, IN 46207
General Environment: Estuarine

STREAM POLLUTION CONTROL, PUBLIC HEALTH DEPARTMENT
620 CORDELL HULL BUILDING
NASHVILLE, TN 37219
General Environment: Limnologic

URBAN HEALTH DEPARTMENT, COUNTY HEALTH CENTER
950 WEST MONROE STREET
JACKSON, MI 49202
General Environment: Atmospheric
Specific Interests: Desert

WATER AND AIR ENVIRONMENTAL IMPROVEMENT COMMISSION
STATE HOUSE
AUGUSTA, ME 04330
Chief Engineer, Raeburn W Macdonald
General Environment: Limnologic

WATER AND POLLUTION CONTROL ASSOCIATION
STATE BOARD OF HEALTH
COLUMBIA, SC 29201

WATER AND POLLUTION CONTROL ASSOCIATION
2746 LAURELWOOD ROAD
DORAVILLE, GA 30040
General Environment: Limnologic

WATER CONTROL BOARD
4010 WEST BROAD STREET
RICHMOND, VA 23230
General Environment: Limnologic

WATER DEPARTMENT
SIXTH AND TAYLOR STREETS
LYNCHBURG, VA 24501
General Environment: Atmospheric

WATER POLLUTION COMMISSION
FEDERAL AND WATER STREETS
DOVER, DE 19901
General Environment: Limnologic

WATER POLLUTION CONTROL AUTHORITY
J MARION SIMS BUILDING
COLUMBIA, SC 29201
Executive Director, W T Linton
General Environment: Limnologic

WATER POLLUTION CONTROL BOARD, HEALTH DEPARTMENT
POST OFFICE BOX 118
COLUMBUS, OH 43125
Chairman, Dr L Arnold
General Environment: Limnologic

WATER POLLUTION CONTROL COMMISSION
BOX 829
OLYMPIA, WA 98501
Director, Roy Harris
General Environment: Limnologic

WATER POLLUTION CONTROL COMMISSION
275 EAST MAIN STREET
FRANKFORT, KY 40601
General Environment: Limnologic

WATER POLLUTION CONTROL DIVISION, STATE HEALTH DEPARTMENT
335 STATE OFFICE BUILDING
PROVIDENCE, RI 02903
Chief, Carleton Maine
General Environment: Limnologic

WATER POLLUTION CONTROL, HEALTH DEPARTMENT
UNIVERSITY OF MINNESOTA CAMPUS
MINNEAPOLIS, MN 55440
General Environment: Limnologic

WATER POLLUTION COUNCIL
LABORATORY BUILDING
HELENA, MT 59601
General Environment: Atmospheric

WATER POLLUTION DIVISION, STATE HEALTH DEPARTMENT
STATE OFFICE BUILDING
DES MOINES, IA 50319
Director, R Schliekelman
General Environment: Limnologic

WATER QUALITY BOARD
311 WEST 11TH STREET
AUSTIN, TX 78701
Staff Size: 100 - 499

WATER QUALITY CONTROL BOARD
47 TRINITY AVENUE SW
ATLANTA, GA 30334
Director, R S Howard
General Environment: Limnologic

WATER QUALITY CONTROL DIVISION, HEALTH DEPARTMENT
300 INDIANA AVENUE, NW
WASHINGTON, DC 20001
Director, Arnold Speiser
General Environment: Limnologic

WATER RESOURCES COMMISSION
650 MAIN STREET
HARTFORD, CT 06115
Director, John Curry
General Environment: Limnologic

WATER RESOURCES COMMISSION
STEVENS T MASON BUILDING
LANSING, MI 48926
Executive Secretary, Ralph W Purdy
General Environment: Limnologic
Staff Size: 100 - 499

WATER RESOURCES COMMISSION
100 CAMBRIDGE AVENUE
BOSTON, MA 02202
Director, Thomas Mcmahon
General Environment: Limnologic

WATER RESOURCES CONTROL BUILDING
1416 NINTH STREET, 10TH FLOOR
SACRAMENTO, CA 95814
Chairman, W W Adams
General Environment: Limnologic

Industrial/Commercial

AIR POLLUTION DIVISION, MINE SAFETY APPLIANCE COMPANY
201 NORTH BRADDOCK AVENUE
PITTSBURGH, PA 15208
Sales Supervisor, William Dailey
General Environment: Atmospheric

AUTOMOTIVE EMISSIONS RESEARCH
MOBILE RESOURCES AND DEVELOPMENT CORPORATION
PAULSBORO, NJ 08066
Coordinator, Donald Osterhout
General Environment: Atmospheric

AUTOMOTIVE EMMISSIONS, FORD
WORLD HEADQUARTERS, AMERICAN ROAD
DEARBORN, MI 48121
Director, Donald Jensen
General Environment: Atmospheric

BITUMINOUS COAL RESOURCES, INCORPORATED
350 NORTH CLARKE STREET
MONROEVILLE, PA 15146

President, James Garvey
General Environment: Atmospheric

CIVIL ENGINEERING DEPARTMENT
EVANSDALE CAMPUS
MORGANTOWN, WV 26506
Professor, Benjamin Linsky
General Environment: Atmospheric

CONSOLIDATED EDISON CORPORATION OF NEW YORK, INCORPORATED
4 IRVING PLACE
NEW YORK, NY 10003
General Environment: Atmospheric

EMISSION CONTROL, GENERAL MOTORS
12 MILE AND MOUND ROADS
WARREN, MI 48090
Director, Frederick Bowditch
General Environment: Atmospheric

ENVIRONMENTAL ENGINEERING, ENGINEERING DEPARTMENT
E I DUPONT DE NEMOURS, AND COMPANY
WILMINGTON, DE 19898
Manager, James Parsons
General Environment: Atmospheric

ENVIRONMENTAL SERVICES, CROWN ZELLERBACH
904 NORTHWEST DRAKE STREET
CAMAS, WA 98607
Director, Herman Amberg
General Environment: Atmospheric
Staff Size: 10 - 49

EXXON RESEARCH AND ENGINEERING DEPARTMENT
POST OFFICE BOX 111
LINDEN, NJ 07036
President, Dr N V Hakala
General Environment: Atmospheric

HYDROLOGY AND METEOROLOGY INSTITUTE
2OU PODLES
WARSZAWA 32, PODLES, POLAND
General Environment: Oceanographic
Specific Interests: Polar (cold)

IMPERIAL CHEMISTRY INDUSTRY LIMITED, BRIXHAM RESOURCES
FRESHWATER QUARRY OVERGANG
BRIXHAM, SOUTH DEVON, ENGLAND
Sciences Administrator, Philip N J Chipperfield
Specific Interests: Prairie and Temperate Forest

INCINERATOR INSTITUTE OF AMERICA
ONE STONE PLACE
BRONXVILLE, NY 10708

Specific Interests: Prairie and Temperate Forest
Staff Size: 10 - 49

INDUSTRIAL GAS CLEANING DEPARTMENT
KOPPERS COMPANY, INCORPORATED
BALTIMORE, MD 21203
Manager, Earl Wilson
General Environment: Atmospheric

INDUSTRIAL GAS CLEANING INSTITUTE
1116 SUMMER STREET
STAMFORD, CT 06905
Specific Interests: Prairie and Temperate Forest
Staff Size: 10 - 49

IRON AND STEEL INSTITUTE
150 EAST 42D STREET
NEW YORK, NY 10017
General Environment: Limnologic

MANUFACTURING CHEMISTS ASSOCIATION
1825 CONNECTICUT AVENUE, NW
WASHINGTON, DC 20009
Staff Size: 50 - 99

NATIONAL AUTOMOTIVE MUFFLER ASSOCIATION
P O BOX 247
ALHAMBRA, CA 91802
Specific Interests: Prairie and Temperate Forest
Staff Size: 500 - 999

NATIONAL COAL POLICY CONFERENCE INCORPORATED
1000 16TH STREET, NW
WASHINGTON, DC 20036
Specific Interests: Prairie and Temperate Forest

NATIONAL COUNCIL FOR STREAM IMPROVEMENT
103 PARK AVENUE
NEW YORK, NY 10016
Specific Interests: Prairie and Temperate Forest
Staff Size: 100 - 499

NATIONAL PETROLEUM REFINERS ASSOCIATION
1725 DE SALES STREET, NW
WASHINGTON, DC 20036
Specific Interests: Prairie and Temperate Forest

NATIONAL WATER INSTITUTE
744 BROAD STREET, ROOM 3405
NEWARK, NJ 07102
Specific Interests: Prairie and Temperate Forest

**PAINT, VARNISH, AND LACQUER
(NATIONAL)**
1500 RHODE ISLAND AVENUE, NW
WASHINGTON, DC 20005
Technology Director, R Brown

**PERMUTIT COMPANY LIMITED,
PEMBERTON HOUSE**
LONDON ROAD
ISLEWORTH, MIDDLESEX,
ENGLAND
Technology Director, Thomas V Arden
Specific Interests: Prairie and Temperate
Forest

PULP AND PAPER ASSOCIATION
2633 EASTLAKE AVENUE EAST
SEATTLE, WA 98102
Staff Size: 1 - 4

**SEVERSKY ELECTRONATOM
CORPORATION**
30 ROCKEFELLER PLAZA
NEW YORK, NY 10020
President, James Fitzpatrick
General Environment: Atmospheric

SUN OIL COMPANY
POST OFFICE BOX 426
MARCUS HOOK, PA 19061
Resources Scientist, Paul Oberdorfer
General Environment: Atmospheric
Staff Size: 50 - 99

**TECHNOLOGY CENTER, PROCTOR
AND GAMBLE LIMITED**
GPO BOX FOREST HALL NO 2
NEWCASTLE-UPON-TYNE,
ENGLAND
Associate Manager, George K Ashforth
Specific Interests: Prairie and Temperate
Forest

**WATER AND CLEAN AIR
RESEARCH CENTER**
STRIP MILLS DIVISION OF BRITISH
STEEL
PORT TALBOT, GLAMORGANSHIRE,
WALES
Coordinator, Dr O'connor
Specific Interests: Urban

**WATER AND WASTEWATER
EQUIPMENT MANUFACTURING
ASSOCIATION**
744 BROAD STREET
NEWARK, NJ 07102
Specific Interests: Prairie and Temperate
Forest
Staff Size: 100 - 499

**WEATHER MEASURE
CORPORATION**
POST OFFICE BOX 41257
SACRAMENTO, CA 95841
President, Herbert S Dankman
General Environment: Atmospheric

Professional Organizations

**ACOUSTICAL SOCIETY OF
AMERICA**
335 EAST 45TH STREET
NEW YORK, NY 10017
Staff Size: 1000 - 4999

**AIR POLLUTION BUREAU, FIRE
DEPARTMENT**
274 MIDDLE STREET
BRIDGEPORT, CT 06603
General Environment: Atmospheric

**AIR POLLUTION CONTROL
ADMINISTRATION**
411 WEST CHAPEL HILL STREET
DURHAM, NC 27701
Director, Donald F Walters
General Environment: Atmospheric
Staff Size: 10 - 49

**AIR POLLUTION CONTROL
ASSOCIATION**
4400 FIFTH AVENUE
PITTSBURGH, PA 15213
General Environment: Atmospheric
Staff Size: 10 - 49

AIR POLLUTION CONTROL BOARD
POST OFFICE BOX 500
HUNTSVILLE, AL 35801
General Environment: Atmospheric

**AMERICAN SOCIETY OF SANITARY
ENGINEERING**
228 STANDARD BUILDING
CLEVELAND, OH 44113

**BEALL, GARNER AND GEARE,
INCORPORATED**
QUEEN CITY TRIANGLE
CUMBERLAND, MD 21502

**CITIZENS LEAGUE AGAINST SONIC
BOOM**
19 APPLE STREET
CAMBRIDGE, MA 02138
Director, William Shurcliffe
Specific Interests: Prairie and Temperate
Forest

**CLEAN AIR, CITIZEN'S
COMMITTEE**
598 MADISON AVENUE
NEW YORK, NY 10022
President, R Low
General Environment: Atmospheric
Specific Interests: Prairie and Temperate
Forest
Staff Size: 500 - 999

**ENVIRONMENTAL CONTROL
ASSOCIATION**
26 EAST EXCHANGE STREET
ST PAUL, MN 55101
President, Paul H Engstrom
Specific Interests: Prairie and Temperate
Forest
Staff Size: 1000 - 4999

**ENVIRONMENTAL ENGINEERING
INTERSOCIETY BOARD**
P O BOX 9728
WASHINGTON, DC 20016
Executive Secretary, Frank Butrico
Specific Interests: Prairie and Temperate
Forest
Staff Size: 1000 - 4999

**INSTRUMENT SOCIETY OF
AMERICA**
400 STANWIX STREET
PITTSBURGH, PA 15222
General Environment: Atmospheric
Specific Interests: Prairie and Temperate
Forest

LAKE CARRIERS ASSOCIATION
305 ROCKEFELLER BUILDING
CLEVELAND, OH 44121
General Environment: Limnologic
Specific Interests: Prairie and Temperate
Forest

**LAKE ERIE CLEANUP
COMMISSION, INCORPORATED**
3003 11TH STREET
MONROE, MI 48161
President, John Chascsa
General Environment: Limnologic
Specific Interests: Prairie and Temperate
Forest

**MARSHLANDS, TIDELANDS, AND
TIDEWATERS PRESERVATION
SOCIETY**
14 SHOREHAM STREET
QUINCY, MA 02171
President, J Slattery
General Environment: Marsh/Swamp

METEOROLOGICAL OFFICE
BRACKNELL, BERKSHIRE,
ENGLAND
Director, Patrick J Meade
General Environment: Atmospheric
Specific Interests: Prairie and Temperate
Forest

**SANITARY ENGINEERING
ASSOCIATION**
2A AVEIDA 0-61 ZONA 10
GUATEMALA CITY, GUATEMALA
Specific Interests: Tropical (hot)

**UNION OF CONCERNED
SCIENTISTS**
PO BOX 289, MASSACHUSETTS
INSTITUTE OF TECHNOLOGY
CAMBRIDGE, MA 02139
Specific Interests: Prairie and Temperate
Forest

**WATER POLLUTION CONTROL
ASSOCIATION**
607 BOYLSTON STREET
BOSTON, MA 02116
General Environment: Limnologic
Specific Interests: Prairie and Temperate
Forest

YACHT CLUB ASSOCIATION
18 MAVERICK STREET
MEDFORD, MA 02155
President, Harry Kane
General Environment: Oceanographic

Research Institute

AIR AND WATER POLLUTION DIVISION
3100 FLORA STREET
SAN LUIS OBISPO, CA 93401
Director, Chieko Mcinstry
General Environment: Atmospheric

AIR POLLUTION
P O BOX 2137
SALINAS, CA 93901
Director, Edward Munson
General Environment: Atmospheric

AIR POLLUTION
P O BOX 363
SAN JOSE, CA 95103
Director, Fay H Lew
General Environment: Atmospheric

AIR POLLUTION CONTROL
146 FERNBANK AVENUE
DELMER, NY 12054
Director, Benjamin Shen
General Environment: Atmospheric

ATMOSPHERIC RESEARCH GROUP
ALTADENA, CA 91001
General Environment: Atmospheric

ATMOSPHERIC SCIENCES RESEARCH CENTER
WHITEFACE MOUNTAIN FIELD STATION
WILMINGTON, NY 12997
General Environment: Atmospheric

BITUMINOUS COAL RESEARCH, INCORPORATED
350 HOCHBERG ROAD
MONROEVILLE, PA 15146
General Environment: Terrestrial

BRITISH COLUMBIA RESEARCH
3650 WESTBROOK CRESCENT
VANCOUVER 8, BRITISH COLUMBIA, CANADA
Director, Dr Paul C Trussell
Staff Size: 100 - 499

CENTRAL INLAND FISHERIES
POST OFFICE 24 PARGANAS
BARRACKPORE, WEST BENGAL, INDIA
Director, Dr U G Jhingran

COKE RESOURCES ASSOCIATION
CHESTERFIELD, DERBYSHIRE, ENGLAND

General Environment: Atmospheric
Specific Interests: Rural
Staff Size: 10 - 49

ENVIRONMENTAL POLLUTION
6104 NORTE 74 COLUMBIA SANCHEZ
MEXICO CITY, MEXICO
Director, Maria Lopez

ENVIRONMENTAL RESEARCH CENTER
CINCINNATI, OH 45201
Specific Interests: Prairie and Temperate Forest

FISHERIES RESEARCH, EXPERTS ON THE SCIENTIFIC ASPECTS OF MARINE POLLUTION
4160 MARINE DRIVE
WEST VANCOUVER, BRITISH COLUMBIA, CANADA
Director, Dr Waldichuck
General Environment: Oceanographic

MECHANICAL ENGINEERING DEPARTMENT, BATTELLE MEMORIAL LIBRARY
505 KING AVENUE
COLUMBUS, OH 43201
Consultant, William Reid
General Environment: Atmospheric

METEOROLOGY RESOURCES INCORPORATED
464 W WOODBURY ROAD
ALTADENA, CA 91001
President, Paul Maccready
General Environment: Atmospheric

NEW SCHOOL FOR SOCIAL RESEARCH
NEW YORK, NY 10001

POLLUTION CONTROL, LEATHER MANUFACTURING RESEARCH ASSOCIATION
MILTON PARK, EGHAM
SURREY, TW20 9UQ, ENGLAND
Director, Dr R L Sykes
Specific Interests: Prairie and Temperate Forest

POLLUTION RESEARCH UNIT, MATHEMATICS BUILDING
UNIVERSITY OF MANCHESTER
MANCHESTER M13 9PL, ENGLAND
Specific Interests: Prairie and Temperate Forest

SCIENCES RESEARCH INSTITUTE
PHILADELPHIA, PA 19100
General Environment: Terrestrial
Specific Interests: Urban

STANFORD RESEARCH INSTITUTION
333 RAVENSWOOD AVENUE
MENLO PARK, CA 94025
Staff Size: 1000 - 4999

SYSTEMS, SCIENCES AND SOFTWARE
P O BOX 1620
LA JOLLA, CA 92037
Director, Ralph Sklarew

WASTE WATER RENOVATION AND CONSERVATION PROJECT
PENNSYLVANIA STATE UNIVERSITY
UNIVERSITY PARK, PA 16802
Director, Dr Louis T Kardos
Specific Interests: Prairie and Temperate Forest

WATER CONDITIONING RESOURCES COUNCIL
325 WEST WESLEY STREET
WHEATON, IL 60187

WATER POLLUTION RESEARCH ASSOCIATION, HYDROBIOLOGIE INSTITUTE
PALMOILLE 55
2 HAMBURG-50, WEST GERMANY
General Environment: Limnologic

WORLD METEOROLOGICAL ORGANIZATION
41 AVENUE GIUSEPPE-MOTTA
GENEVA, SWITZERLAND
Secretary-General, Dr David Davies 8767
General Environment: Atmospheric

Unclassified

NORTHERN CALIFORNIA METPOL
11771 CARLISLE ROAD
SANTA ANA, CA 92705
Director, Leopold Cann
General Environment: Atmospheric

SOLID WASTE MANAGEMENT OFFICE, ENVIRONMENTAL PROTECTION AGENCY
P.O. BOX 597
CINCINNATI, OH 45201
General Environment: Atmospheric

WATER RESOURCES

Educational Institute

ARCTIC AND ALPINE RESOURCES INSTITUTE
HALE SCIENCE BUILDING, UNIVERSITY OF COLORADO
BOULDER, CO 80304
General Environment: Limnologic

ARID LANDS RESOURCES, UNIVERSITY OF ARIZONA
1242 EAST SPEEDWAY
TUCSON, AZ 85719
General Environment: Terrestrial
Specific Interests: Desert

BIOLOGICAL STATION, DEPARTMENT OF FISHERIES, DEFENSE RESOURCES
MISSISSIPPI RIVER AT 3RD
    AVENUE, SE
MINNEAPOLIS, MN 55414
Director, Dr J M Anderson
Staff Size: 10 - 49

CIVIL ENGINEERING DEPARTMENT
950 BEH, UNIVERSITY OF
    PITTSBURGH
PITTSBURGH, PA 15213
Staff Size: 5 - 9

COASTAL SEDIMENTATION UNIT
BEADON ROAD
TAUTON, SOMERSET, ENGLAND
Principal Science Officer, Alan Carr
General Environment: Oceanographic
Specific Interests: Prairie and Temperate
    Forest

CONSERVATION AND SURVEY DIVISION
UNIVERSITY OF NEBRASKA
LINCOLN, NB 68508
General Environment: Limnologic

DESERT RESEARCH INSTITUTE
UNIVERSITY OF NEVADA SYSTEM
RENO, NV 89507
Specific Interests: Desert
Staff Size: 10 - 49

EARTH SCIENCE DEPARTMENT
NORTHERN ILLINOIS UNIVERSITY
DE KALB, IL 60115
General Environment: Limnologic

ECOLOGY BUREAU AND GEOLOGY BUREAU
18TH AND RED RIVER STREET,
    BOX X UNIVERSITY STATION
AUSTIN, TX 78712
General Environment: Limnologic

ECOLOGY CENTER
P O BOX 1100
BERKELEY, CA 94701
Director, Raymond Bachelors
General Environment: Limnologic

ENGINEERING DEPARTMENT
UNIVERSITY OF CALIFORNIA
LOS ANGELES, CA 90024

ENGINEERING RESEARCH DIVISION, LA TECHNICAL UNIVERSITY
BOX 4875, TECHNOLOGY STATION
RUSTON, LA 71270
General Environment: Limnologic

ENGINEERING RESOURCES CENTER, COLLEGE OF ENGINEERING
UNIVERSITY OF COLORADO
BOULDER, CO 80304
General Environment: Limnologic

ENGINEERING SCHOOL
BOX 1826, STATION B, 24TH
    AVENUE, SOUTH
NASHVILLE, TN 37203

ENGINEERING-ECONOMIC PLANNING LIBRARY, STANFORD UNIVERSITY
ROOM 274 CIVIL ENGINEERING
    DEPARTMENT
STANFORD, CA 94305

ENVIRONMENTAL CONTROL ADMINISTRATION, BUREAU OF SOLID WASTE MANAGEMENT
5555 RIDGE AVENUE
CINCINNATI, OH 45213
General Environment: Terrestrial

ENVIRONMENTAL ENGINEERING AND SCIENCE GRADUATE PROGRAM
MANHATTAN COLLEGE
BRONX, NY 10711
Staff Size: 10 - 49

ENVIRONMENTAL HEALTH ENGINEERING LABORATORY
ENGINEERING LABORATORY
    BUILDING 305
AUSTIN, TX 78712
Director, Dr Ernest F Gloyna
General Environment: Oceanographic

ENVIRONMENTAL LABORATORY OF LAKE ONTARIO
STATE UNIVERSITY COLLEGE
OSWEGO, NY 13126
General Environment: Limnologic

ENVIRONMENTAL RESOURCES CENTER
GEORGIA INSTITUTE OF
    TECHNOLOGY
ATLANTA, GA 30332
General Environment: Oceanographic

ENVIRONMENTAL RESOURCES INSTITUTE
DEPARTMENT OF CHEMICAL
    ENGINEERING, UNIVERSITY OF
    SOUTH CAROLINA
COLUMBIA, SC 29208

ENVIRONMENTAL SCIENCE PROGRAM
WOODS HOLE OCEAN INSTITUTE
WOODS HOLE, MA 02543
General Environment: Oceanographic

ENVIRONMENTAL SCIENCES AND ENGINEERING LABORATORY
DEPARTMENT OF CHEMICAL
    ENGINEERING, RICE UNIVERSITY
HOUSTON, TX 77001

ENVIRONMENTAL STUDIES PROGRAM
ALPENA COMMUNITY COLLEGE
ALPENA, MI 49707
General Environment: Oceanographic

ENVIRONMENTAL STUDIES PROGRAM
CALIFORNIA STATE COLLEGE
LONG BEACH, CA 90835
General Environment: Oceanographic

ENVIRONMENTAL STUDIES PROGRAM
CALIFORNIA INSTITUTE OF
    TECHNOLOGY
PASADENA, CA 91148

ENVIRONMENTAL STUDIES, CHESAPEAKE BAY CENTER
ROUTE 4, BOX 622
EDGEWATER, MD 21037
General Environment: Oceanographic
Specific Interests: Prairie and Temperate
    Forest

ENVIRONMENTAL SYSTEMS ENGINEERING
CLEMSON UNIVERSITY
CLEMSON, SC 29631
Staff Size: 5 - 9

ESTUARINE STUDIES CENTER
UNIVERSITY OF JACKSON
JACKSONVILLE, FL 32201
General Environment: Estuarine

GEOLOGICAL SURVEY OF KENTUCKY, UNIVERSITY OF KENTUCKY
307 INDUSTRIES BUILDING
LEXINGTON, KY 40506
General Environment: Limnologic

GEOLOGY AND ENVIRONMENTAL ENGINEERING DEPARTMENT
THE JOHNS HOPKINS UNIVERSITY
BALTIMORE, MD 21201
Staff Size: 10 - 49

GEOLOGY DEPARTMENT
UNIVERSITY OF CHICAGO
CHICAGO, IL 60637
General Environment: Limnologic

HEALTH LAW CENTER
130 DE SOTO STREET
PITTSBURGH, PA 12513

HYDRAULIC LABORATORY OF ST ANTHONY FALLS, UNIVERSITY OF MINNESOTA
MISSISSIPPI RIVER AT 3RD AVENUE, SE
MINNEAPOLIS, MN 55414
General Environment: Limnologic

HYDRAULIC RESEARCH INSTITUTE
UNIVERSITY OF IOWA
IOWA CITY, IA 52240
General Environment: Limnologic

HYDROLOGY-SCIENCES INSTITUTE
64 GHADESSI STREET
TEHRAN, IRAN
Director, M Mgzaveny
General Environment: Limnologic

ICHTHYOLOGICAL LABORATORY AND MUSEUM
UNIVERSITY OF MIAMI
CORAL GABLES, FL 33146

INSTITUT ENERGETIKI I AVTOMATIKI
KISHINEV, UNION OF SOVIET SOCIALIST REPUBLICS

INTERNATIONAL COMMISSION ON LARGE DAMS
20 RUE DE L'ARCADE
PARIS 8, FRANCE
General Environment: Limnologic

IRRIGATION AND DRAINAGE COMMISSION
48 NYAYA MARG, CHANAKYAPURI
NEW DELHI 21, INDIA
General Environment: Limnologic

LAND AND WATER RESOURCES INSTITUTE, PENNSYLVANIA STATE UNIVERSITY
102 RESEARCH BUILDING 3
UNIVERSITY PARK, PA 16802
Director, Dr John C Frey

MARINE FISHERY RESOURCE RESEARCH CENTER OF JAPAN
MANDAI BUILDING KHOSIMACHI
TOKYO, JAPAN
Director, Takashi Hisamune
General Environment: Oceanographic
Staff Size: 10 - 49

MARINE LABORATORIES OF MOSS LANDING
FRESNO STATE COLLEGE
FRESNO, CA 93704
General Environment: Oceanographic

MARINE RESEARCH RESOURCES UNIT
GUILDHALL SQUARE
PORTSMOUTH, HANTS, ENGLAND
Director, Rowland L R Morgan
General Environment: Oceanographic
Specific Interests: Prairie and Temperate Forest

MARINE SCIENCES RESEARCH CENTER
STATE UNIVERSITY OF NEW YORK
STONY BROOK, NY 11790
General Environment: Oceanographic

MINES AND GEOLOGY BUREAU OF IDAHO
UNIVERSITY OF IDAHO
MOSCOW, ID 83843
General Environment: Terrestrial

MINES AND GEOLOGY BUREAU OF MONTANA
MAIN HALL, MONTANA COLLEGE, MINERAL SCIENCES DEPARTMENT
BUTTE, MT 59701
General Environment: Terrestrial

NATIONAL WATER RESOURCES ASSOCIATION
897 NATIONAL PRESS BUILDING
WASHINGTON, DC 20004

NATURAL RESOURCES INSTITUTION
124 W 17 AVENUE
COLUMBUS, OH 43210

OCEANOGRAPHY INSTITUTE
NATIONAL TAIWAN UNIVERSITY
TAIPEI, TAIWAN
Director, Tsu-You Chu
General Environment: Oceanographic

OCEANOGRAPHY, NATIONAL INSTITUTE
WORMLEY, GODALMING
SURREY, ENGLAND
Director, Professor H Charnock
General Environment: Oceanographic
Specific Interests: Prairie and Temperate Forest

PHYSICAL SCIENCES AND OCEANOGRAPHY, INTERNATIONAL ASSOCIATION
UNIVERSITY OF IOWA
IOWA CITY, IA 52240
Staff Size: 50 - 99

PULP MANUFACTURERS RESEARCH LEAGUE
P O BOX 436, 1043 EAST SOUTH RIVER STREET
APPLETON, WI 54911
General Environment: Limnologic

RECREATION AND WATERSHED RESOURCES DEPARTMENT
COLORADO STATE UNIVERSITY
FORT COLLINS, CO 80521

RESEARCH CENTER OF LAKE GEORGE
LAKE GEORGE, NY 12854
General Environment: Oceanographic

RESEARCH CENTER, COLLEGE OF ENGINEERING
UNIVERSITY OF COLORADO
BOULDER, CO 80302
Staff Size: 10 - 49

RESEARCH IN WATER CENTER, UNIVERSITY OF TEXAS AT AUSTIN
BALCONES RESEARCH CENTER-RT 4-189
AUSTIN, TX 78757
Director, Dr Earnest F Gloyna
General Environment: Limnologic
Staff Size: 10 - 49

RESEARCH INSTITUTE OF GREAT LAKES
1120 G DANIEL BALDWIN BUILDING
ERIE, PA 16501
Director, Fredrick D Buggie
General Environment: Limnologic

RESOURCES AND ECONOMIC DEVELOPMENT DEPARTMENT
UNIVERSITY NEW HAMPSHIRE
DURHAM, NH 03824
General Environment: Terrestrial

SANITARY ENGINEERING RESOURCE LABORATORY
UNIVERSITY OF CALIFORNIA
RICHMOND, CA 94801

SCIENCE AND HYDROLOGY, INTERNATIONAL ASSOCIATION
61 BRAEMSTAAT
GENTBRUGGE, BELGIUM
General Environment: Limnologic

SEA WATER CONVERSION LABORATORY
1301 SOUTH 46TH STREET
RICHMOND, CA 94804

SEA WATER TEST FACILITY
POST OFFICE BOX 109, UNIVERSITY OF CALIFORNIA
LA JOLLA, CA 92038

SOIL CONSERVATION COMMISSION OF MINNESOTA, MINNESOTA UNIVERSITY
201 SOIL SCIENCES BUILDING, ST PAUL, MN 55101
General Environment: Limnologic

SOIL CONSERVATION COMMISSION OF MISSISSIPPI
MISSISSIPPI STATE UNIVERSITY
STATE COLLEGE, MS 39762

General Environment: Limnologic

SOUTHERN RESEARCH INSTITUTE
2000 9TH AVENUE SOUTH
BIRMINGHAM, AL 35205

SOUTHWEST RESEARCH INSTITUTE
POST OFFICE BOX 2296
SAN ANTONIO, TX 78206

Specific Interests: Urban

STANFORD RESEARCH INSTITUTE
333 RAVENSWOOD AVENUE
MENLO PARK, CA 94025

General Environment: Estuarine
Specific Interests: Rural

USTAV HYDROLOGIE A HYDRAULIKY SAV
BRATISLAVA
TRNAVSKA 26, CZECHOSLOVAKIA

WASTE WATER RENOVATION AND CONSERVATION OF RESOURCES PROJECT
PACIFIC STATE UNIVERSITY
UNIVERSITY PARK, PA 16802

General Environment: Limnologic

WATER AND HYDRODYNAMICS LABORATORY
MASSACHUSETTS INSTITUTE OF TECHNOLOGY
CAMBRIDGE, MA 02139

Director, R Parsons
General Environment: Terrestrial
Staff Size: 50 - 99

WATER CONSERVATION FOR COLORADO WATERS
1525 SHERMAN STREET
DENVER, CO 80203

WATER INFORMATION CENTER, INCORPORATED
44 SIRTSINK DRIVE
PORT WASHINGTON, NY 11050

WATER POLLUTION ANALYSIS
MICHIGAN TECHNOLOGY UNIVERSITY
HOUGHTON, MI 49931

General Environment: Limnologic

WATER POLLUTION CONTROL ASSOCIATION OF ARKANSAS
COLLEGE OF ENGINEERING, UNIVERSITY OF ARKANSAS
FAYETTEVILLE, AR 72703

General Environment: Limnologic

WATER QUALITY SURVEY OF LORAINE COUNTY

147 DUMMOND ROAD
AVON LAKE, OH 44012

Director, Ef Noble
General Environment: Limnologic
Specific Interests: Urban
Staff Size: 5 - 9

WATER RESEARCH ASSOCIATION
MEDMENHAM
MARLOW, BUCKINGHAMSHIRE, ENGLAND

Director, R G Allen
General Environment: Limnologic
Staff Size: 100 - 499

WATER RESEARCH CENTER
CORNELL UNIVERSITY
ITHACA, NY 14850

General Environment: Limnologic

WATER RESOURCE RESEARCH CENTER
UNIVERSITY OF NEW HAMPSHIRE
DURHAM, NH 03824

General Environment: Limnologic

WATER RESOURCES
SAN JOSE STATE COLLEGE
SAN JOSE, CA 95114

WATER RESOURCES
2114 OLIVE AVENUE
FREMONT, CA 94538

Director, Carl Strandberg

WATER RESOURCES AND CONSERVATION DIVISION
107 WEST GAINES STREET
TALLAHASSEE, FL 32304

General Environment: Limnologic

WATER RESOURCES AND MARINE SCIENCES
CORNELL UNIVERSITY
ITHACA, NY 14850

General Environment: Oceanographic

WATER RESOURCES BUREAU
UNIVERSITY OF OKLAHOMA
NORMAN, OK 73069

General Environment: Limnologic

WATER RESOURCES CENTER
UNIVERSITY OF CALIFORNIA
LOS ANGELES, CA 90024

WATER RESOURCES CENTER
212-214 LORD HALL
ORONO, ME 04473

WATER RESOURCES CENTER
1000 WHITE AVENUE
KNOXVILLE, TN 37916

General Environment: Limnologic

WATER RESOURCES CENTER
UNIVERSITY OF CALIFORNIA
LOS ANGELES, CA 90024

WATER RESOURCES CENTER
UNIVERSITY OF MARYLAND, SHRIVER LABORATORY
COLLEGE PK, MD 20740

General Environment: Estuarine

WATER RESOURCES CENTER
GEORGIA INSTITUTION OF TECHNOLOGY
ATLANTA, GA 30332

General Environment: Limnologic

WATER RESOURCES CENTER
COLLEGE OF CIVIL ENGINEERING, TEXAS TECHNICAL COLLEGE
LUBBOCK, TX 79409

WATER RESOURCES CENTER HYDRAULICS-SANITATION LABORATORY
UNIVERSITY OF WISCONSIN
MADISON, WI 53706

General Environment: Limnologic

WATER RESOURCES CENTER OF RHODE ISLAND
UNIVERSITY OF RHODE ISLAND
KINGSTON, RI 02881

Director, Dr Ralph Thompson

WATER RESOURCES COMMISSION
PRINCETON UNIVERSITY
PRINCETON, NJ 08540

General Environment: Limnologic

WATER RESOURCES INSTITUTE
TEXAS A AND M UNIVERSITY
COLLEGE STATION, TX 77843

WATER RESOURCES INSTITUTE
UNIVERSITY OF CONNECTICUT
STORRS, CT 06268

Director, Dr William C Kennard

WATER RESOURCES INSTITUTE
WEST VIRGINIA UNIVERSITY
MORGANTOWN, WV 26505

General Environment: Limnologic

WATER RESOURCES INSTITUTE
MICHIGAN STATE UNIVERSITY
EAST LANSING, MI 48823

WATER RESOURCES INSTITUTE, INSTITUTE FOR NATURAL RESOURCES
UNIVERSITY OF GEORGIA
ATHENS, GA 30601

General Environment: Terrestrial
Staff Size: 5 - 9

WATER RESOURCES PROGRAM
PRINCETON UNIVERSITY, ENGINEERING QUAD
PRINCETON, NJ 08540

Staff Size: 5 - 9

WATER RESOURCES RESEARCH CENTER, UNIVERSITY OF MINNESOTA
2675 UNIVERSITY AVENUE, M 107, HUBBARD BUILDING
ST PAUL, MN 55114
General Environment: Limnologic

WATER RESOURCES RESEARCH INSTITUTE, NEW MEXICO STATE UNIVERSITY
POST OFFICE BOX 167
UNIVERSITY PARK, NM 88070
General Environment: Limnologic

WATER SCIENCES AND ENGINEERING DEPARTMENT
UNIVERSITY OF CALIFORNIA
DAVIS, CA 95616

WATER SUPPLY ASSOCIATION, INTERNATIONAL
34 PARK STREET
LONDON W1, ENGLAND
General Environment: Limnologic

WATER UTILIZATION INSTITUTE
UNIVERSITY OF ARIZONA
TUCSON, AZ 85721

WATERSHED COUNCIL FOR CENTER RIVER
125 COMBS ROAD
EASTHAMPTON, MA 01027
Executive Director, C Percy
Staff Size: 1 - 4

Field Station/Laboratory

DAVIDSON LABORATORY, STEVENS INSTITUTION TECHNOLOGY
CASTLE POINT STATION
IIOBOKEN, NJ 07030
General Environment: Limnologic

Foundation

BLACKSTONE RIVER WATERSHED ASSOCIATION
133 KENYON AVENUE
PAWTUCKET, RI 02801
Executive Director, David Rosser
Staff Size: 1 - 4

CHEMISTRY ABSTRACTS SERVICE, AMERICAN CHEMISTRY SOCIETY
OHIO STATE UNIVERSITY-OLENTANGY R ROAD
COLUMBUS, OH 43210
General Environment: Limnologic

FARM FOUNDATION
600 SOUTH MICHIGAN AVENUE
CHICAGO, IL 60605
General Environment: Estuarine

INTERGOVERNMENTAL SCIENCE PROGRAMS
NATIONAL SCIENCE FOUNDATION
WASHINGTON, DC 20550
General Environment: Oceanographic

JOINT REFERENCE LIBRARY, PUBLIC ADMINISTRATION SERVICE
1313 EAST 60TH STREET
CHICAGO, IL 60637
General Environment: Limnologic

SOIL AND WATER CONSERVATION FOUNDATION, DAVIS LIBRARY
P O BOX 776, 408 MAIN STREET
LEAGUE CITY, TX 77573

SOIL SCIENCES SOCIETY OF AMERICA
677 SOUTH SEGOE ROAD
MADISON, WI 53711
General Environment: Estuarine

WATER CONDITIONING FOUNDATIONS
POST OFFICE BOX 194
NORTHFIELD IL 60093
Executive Director, B Burnside

WATER DIVISION, DEPARTMENT OF NATURAL RESOURCES
100 NORTH SENATE AVENUE
INDIANAPOLIS, IN 46204

WATER POLLUTION CONTROL FEDERATION
3900 WISCONSIN AVENUE, NW
WASHINGTON, DC 20016
General Environment: Limnologic

WATER RESOURCES ASSOCIATION
21 SOUTH 12TH STREET
PHILADELPHIA, PA 19107
General Environment: Limnologic

Government — Federal

AGRICULTURAL RESOURCES INVENTORY ENGINEER, US ARMY MAP SERVICE
6500 BROOKS LANE NW
WASHINGTON, DC 20016
General Environment: Limnologic

AGRICULTURAL STABILIZATION AND CONSERVATION SERVICES
14TH STREET AND INDEPENDENCE AVENUE
WASHINGTON, DC 20250
General Environment: Limnologic

AGRICULTURE AND IRRIGATION MINISTRY
CAIRO, UNITED ARAB REPUBLIC

AGRICULTURE COMMITTEE, US HOUSE OF REPRESENTATIVES
ROOM 1301, LONGWORTH HOUSE OFFICE
WASHINGTON, DC 20515
General Environment: Limnologic

AIR POLLUTION CONTROL OFFICE
PARKLAWN BUILDING, 5600 FISHER LANE
ROCKVILLE, MD 20852
Specific Interests: Prairie and Temperate Forest

AMERICAN PETROLEUM INSTITUTE, TIME-LIFE BUILDING
1271 AVENUE OF THE AMERICAS
NEW YORK, NY 10020

APPROPRIATIONS COMMITTEE, US HOUSE OF REPRESENTATIVES
ROOM H-218, THE CAPITOL
WASHINGTON, DC 20515
General Environment: Oceanographic

AZERBAYDZAAN POLYTECHNICAL INSTITUTE
PROSPEKT NARIMANOVA,25
BAKU, UNION OF SOVIET SOCIALIST REPUBLICS
Staff Size: 5 - 9

BINGHAM OCEANOGRAPHIC LABORATORY, YALE UNIVERSITY
POST OFFICE BOX 2143
BILLINGS, MT 59103
General Environment: Terrestrial
Staff Size: 50 - 99

BIOLOGICAL LABORATORY
P O BOX 6
WOODS HOLE, MA 02543
Director, Herbert W Graham
Specific Interests: Prairie and Temperate Forest
Staff Size: 10 - 49

BONNEVILLE POWER ADMINISTRATION
P O BOX 3621
PORTLAND, OR 97208
General Environment: Limnologic

BUDGET BUREAU, EXECUTIVE OFFICE BUILDING
17TH AND PACIFIC AVENUE, NW
WASHINGTON, DC 20503

COASTAL AND GEODETIC SURVEY
UNITED STATES DEPARTMENT OF
  COMMERCE
WASHINGTON, DC 20230

General Environment: Oceanographic

COASTAL FISHERIES
CORPORATION (MIDDLE
ATLANTIC)
FISHERIES CENTER
HIGHLANDS, NJ 07732

Central Director, Carl Sinderman
General Environment: Oceanographic
Specific Interests: Prairie and Temperate
  Forest
Staff Size: 100 - 499

COMMERCIAL FISHERIES BUREAU
POST OFFICE BOX 3830
HONOLULU, HI 96812

General Environment: Atmospheric

COMMUNICABLE DISEASE CENTER
DEPARTMENT OF HEALTH,
  EDUCATION, AND WELFARE
ATLANTA, GA 30333

CRITERIA AND STANDARDS
BUREAU
411 W CHAPEL HILL STREET
DURHAM, NC 27701

Specific Interests: Prairie and Temperate
  Forest

ECONOMIC AND
TRANSPORTATION DIVISION
UNITED NATIONS PLAZA
NEW YORK, NY 10017

General Environment: Limnologic

ECONOMIC RESEARCH CENTER,
DEPARTMENT OF AGRICULTURE
500 12TH STREET, SW
WASHINGTON, DC 20250

General Environment: Limnologic

ENGINEERING AND PHYSICAL
SCIENCES BUREAU
1330 ST MARY'S STREET
RALEIGH, NC 27605

Specific Interests: Prairie and Temperate
  Forest

ENGINEERING DESIGN OFFICE,
TENNESSEE VALLEY AUTHORITY
607 UNION BUILDING
KNOXVILLE, TN 37902

General Environment: Limnologic

ENGINEERING OFFICE
UNITED STATES DEPARTMENT OF
  ARMY
WASHINGTON, DC 20315

ENVIRONMENTAL AFFAIRS
SECTION
1271 AVENUE OF AMERICAS
NEW YORK, NY 10020

Reference Librarian, Lois Schuermann
General Environment: Limnologic
Staff Size: 1 - 4

ENVIRONMENTAL CONTROL
ADMINISTRATION
12720 TWINBROOK PARKWAY
ROCKVILLE, MD 20852

Specific Interests: Prairie and Temperate
  Forest

ENVIRONMENTAL HYGIENE
AGENCY, OFFICE OF THE
SURGEON GENERAL
US DEPARTMENT OF THE ARMY
EDGEWOOD ARSENAL, MD 21010

General Environment: Limnologic

ENVIRONMENTAL QUALITY
COUNCIL
722 JACKSON PLACE, NW
WASHINGTON, DC 20006

Specific Interests: Prairie and Temperate
  Forest

EUTROPHICATION COMMISSION
SYMPOSIUM
2101 CONSTITUTION AVENUE, NW
WASHINGTON, DC 20418

General Environment: Limnologic

EXPERIMENTAL FISHING AND
GEAR RESOURCES FIELD
STATION
FEDERAL BUILDING, ROOM 308
BRUNSWICK, GA 31520

General Environment: Oceanographic
Specific Interests: Prairie and Temperate
  Forest
Staff Size: 5 - 9

EXPLORATORY FISHING AND
GEAR RESOURCES BASE
P O BOX 1668
JUNEAU, AK 99801

Director, Benjamine F Jones
Specific Interests: Prairie and Temperate
  Forest
Staff Size: 10 - 49

EXPLORATORY FISHING AND
GEAR RESOURCES BASE
5 RESEARCH DRIVE
ANN ARBOR, MI 48103

Director, M R Greenwood
Specific Interests: Prairie and Temperate
  Forest
Staff Size: 10 - 49

EXPLORATORY FISHING AND
GEAR RESOURCES BASE
2725 MONTLAKE BOULEVARD,
  EAST
SEATTLE, WA 98102

Director, Dayton L Anderson
Specific Interests: Prairie and Temperate
  Forest
Staff Size: 10 - 49

EXPLORATORY FISHING AND
GEAR RESOURCES BASE
239 FREDERIC STREET
PASCAGOULA, MS 39567

Director, Harvey R Bullis
Specific Interests: Prairie and Temperate
  Forest
Staff Size: 50 - 99

FARMERS HOME ADMINISTRATION
UNITED STATES DEPARTMENT OF
  AGRICULTURE
WASHINGTON, DC 20250

General Environment: Oceanographic

FEDERAL POWER COMMISSION
441 G STREET, NW
WASHINGTON, DC 20426

FISHERY OCEANOGRAPHIC
CENTER
8604 LA JOLLA SHORES DR
LA JOLLA, CA 92037

Director, Alan R Longhurst
General Environment: Oceanographic
Specific Interests: Prairie and Temperate
  Forest
Staff Size: 50 - 99

FLOOD CONTROL, RIVERS AND
HARBORS SUBCOMMITTEE
SENATE OFFICE BUILDING, SUITE
  3106
WASHINGTON, DC 20510

Chairman, Stephen M Young
General Environment: Oceanographic

FLORIDATION INFORMATION
SERVICE, DENTAL HEALTH
DIVISION, ROOM 508
DEPARTMENT OF HEALTH,
  EDUCATION, AND WELFARE
BETHESDA, MD 20014

FLUID MECHANICS LABORATORY,
NATIONAL BUREAU OF
STANDARDS
U S DEPARTMENT OF COMMERCE
WASHINGTON, DC 20234

FOREST SERVICE AND RESOURCE
BRANCH, DEPARTMENT OF
AGRICULTURE
14TH STREET AND
  INDEPENDENCE AVENUE
WASHINGTON, DC 20250

General Environment: Limnologic

FORESTRY DEVELOPMENT
DIVISION
TENNESSEE VALLEY AUTHORITY
NORRIS, TN 37828

FUNGICIDES AND GERMICIDES
LABORATORY
NATICK LABS
NATICK, MA 01760

GOVERNMENT OPERATIONS COMMITTEE
RAYBURN HOUSE OFFICE BUILDING
WASHINGTON, DC 20515

HEADQUARTERS, USAP (AFOCEKC)
WASHINGTON, DC 20330

HEALTH AND SAFETY DIVISION, TENNESSEE VALLEY AUTHORITY
715 EDNEY BUILDING, 11TH AND MARKET STREETS
CHATTANOOGA, TN 37401

HOME FEDERAL BUILDING
MARKET STREET
KNOXVILLE, TN 37902
General Environment: Oceanographic

HOUSING AND URBAN DEVELOPMENT DEPARTMENT
1626 K STREET, NW
WASHINGTON, DC 20410

HYDROLOGY OFFICE, NATIONAL WEATHER SERVICES, PACIFIC OFFICE
BOX 3650
HONOLULU, HI 96811
General Environment: Oceanographic

HYDROLOGY OFFICE, NATIONAL WEATHER SERVICES
8060 13TH STREET
SILVER SPRING, MD 20910
General Environment: Oceanographic

HYDROLOGY SERVICES OF CANADA
615 BOOTH STREET
OTTAWA, ONTARIO, CANADA
Director, G N Ewing
General Environment: Oceanographic
Staff Size: 100 - 499

INDIAN AFFAIRS BUREAU
ROOM 138, 1951 CONSTITUTION AVENUE
WASHINGTON, DC 20242

INDIAN HEALTH SERVICE OF OKLAHOMA CITY
388 OLD POST OFFICE AND COURTHOUSE BUILDING
OKLAHOMA CITY, OK 73102
Assistant Director, James Clark, Jr
General Environment: Terrestrial
Specific Interests: Rural
Staff Size: 100 - 499

INDIAN OCEAN PROGRAM, FISHERIES DEPARTMENT
VIA DELLE LERME DIVISION CARACALLA
ROME, ITALY
General Environment: Oceanographic

INDUSTRIAL HEALTH SERVICE
500 GOLD AVENUE, SW
ALBUQUERQUE, NM 87101
General Environment: Terrestrial
Staff Size: 50 - 99

INDUSTRY DIVISION, CENSUS BUREAU
UNITED STATES DEPARTMENT OF COMMERCE
WASHINGTON, DC 20233
Specific Interests: Urban

INSTITUT EKONOMIKI
ULITSA LENINA,15
KIEV, UNION OF SOVIET SOCIALIST REPUBLICS
General Environment: Limnologic

INSTITUT ENERGETIKI
ULITSA UYGURSKAYA
ALMA-ATA, UNION OF SOVIET SOCIALIST REPUBLICS
Staff Size: 1 - 4

INTERIOR AND INSULAR AFFAIRS COMMITTEE, US HOUSE OF REPRESENTATIVE
ROOM 1324, LONGWORTH HOUSE
WASHINGTON, DC 20515

LAND AND NATURAL RESOURCE DIVISION
CONSTITUTION AVENUE AND 10TH STREET
WASHINGTON, DC 20530

LAND MANAGEMENT
18TH AND E STREET
WASHINGTON, DC 20240

LARGE DAMS COMMISSION, ENGINEERS JOINT COUNCIL
345 EAST 47TH STREET
NEW YORK, NY 10017
General Environment: Limnologic

LAW ENFORCEMENT ADMINISTRATION
633 INDIANA AVENUE, NW
WASHINGTON, DC 20530
Specific Interests: Prairie and Temperate Forest

LIME ASSOCIATION (NATIONAL)
4000 BRANDYWINE STREET, NW
WASHINGTON, DC 20016

MARINE RESOURCES
5 MAYO AVENUE
ANNAPOLIS, MD 21403
Associate Administrator, David Wallace

MARINE SCIENCE DIVISION, 17TH COAST GUARD DISTRICT
BOX 3-5000, NEW FEDERAL BUILDING
JUNEAU, AK 99801

General Environment: Oceanographic
Specific Interests: Polar (cold)
Staff Size: 1 - 4

MARINE WATER QUALITY LABORATORY
P O BOX 277, LIBERTY LANE AND FAIRGROUNDS ROAD
WEST KINGSTON, RI 02892
General Environment: Oceanographic
Specific Interests: Prairie and Temperate Forest

MAYORS CONFERENCE
1707 H STREET, NW ROOM 606
WASHINGTON, DC 20006
General Environment: Limnologic

MISSISSIPPI VALLEY ASSOCIATION
225 SOUTH MERAMEE AVENUE
ST. LOUIS, MO 63105
General Environment: Limnologic

MISSOURI BASIN INTERAGENCY COMMISSION
P.O. BOX 103 DOWNTOWN STATION
OMAHA, NB 68101
Director, Colonel R. W. Love
General Environment: Limnologic

MUNICIPAL WASTE WATER PROGRAMS, WATER QUALITY OFFICE
ENVIRONMENTAL PROTECTION AGENCY
WASHINGTON, DC 20460
General Environment: Oceanographic

NATIONAL AGRICULTURAL LIBRARY
14TH STREET AND INDEPENDENCE AVENUE
WASHINGTON, DC 20250
General Environment: Limnologic

NATIONAL CENTER FOR SYSTEMATICS
10TH AND CONSTITUTION AVENUE, NW ROOM 57
WASHINGTON, DC 20242
Director, Daniel M Cohen
Specific Interests: Prairie and Temperate Forest
Staff Size: 5 - 9

NATIONAL LEAGUE OF CITIES
1612 K STREET, NW
WASHINGTON, DC 20006

NATIONAL MARINE FISHERIES SERVICE, HONOLULU LABORATORY
POST OFFICE BOX 3830
HONOLULU, HI 96812
General Environment: Oceanographic
Specific Interests: Tropical (hot)

NATIONAL PARKS ASSOCIATION
1300 NEW HAMPSHIRE AVENUE,
NW
WASHINGTON, DC 20036
General Environment: Terrestrial

**NATIONAL PETROLEUM REFINERS
ASSOCIATION**
1725 DE SALES STREET, NW
WASHINGTON, DC 20036

**NATIONAL RIVERS AND HARBORS
CONGRESS**
1028 CONNECTICUT AVENUE, NW
WASHINGTON, DC 20036
General Environment: Limnologic

NATIONAL WATER COMMISSION
800 NORTH QUINCY STREET
ARLINGTON, VA 22203
Director, Theodore M Schad
Staff Size: 5 - 9

**NATIONAL WEATHER SERVICE,
WESTERN REGION**
11188 FEDERAL BUILDING, 125
SOUTH STATE STREET
SALT LAKE CITY, UT 84111
General Environment: Atmospheric
Staff Size: 1 - 4

**NATIONAL WILDLIFE
FEDERATION**
1412 16TH STREET, NW
WASHINGTON, DC 20036
General Environment: Limnologic

**NATURAL RESOURCE ECONOMICS
DIVISIONAL**
14TH STREET AND
INDEPENDENCE AVENUE, SW
WASHINGTON, DC 20250
Specific Interests: Prairie and Temperate
Forest

NATURAL RESOURCES CENTER
702 19TH STREET, NW
WASHINGTON, DC 20006

**NAVAL FACILITIES ENGINEERING
COMMAND**
US DEPARTMENT OF NAVY, ROOM
2B27
WASHINGTON, DC 20390

**NAVAL HYDROLOGICAL SURVEY
OFFICE**
C/O MARITIME HEADQUARTERS,
YOUNGSFIELD
CAPE TOWN, REPUBLIC OF SOUTH
AFRICA
Director, Captain J C Walters

NAVAL OCEANOGRAPHIC OFFICE
US DEPARTMENT OF THE NAVY
WASHINGTON, DC 20390
General Environment: Oceanographic

OCEAN RESEARCH LABORATORY
SOUTH ROTUNDA, STANFORD
MUSEUM
STANFORD, CA 94305
Director, Oscar E Sette
General Environment: Oceanographic
Specific Interests: Prairie and Temperate
Forest
Staff Size: 5 - 9

OHIO BASIN REGIONAL LIBRARY
4676 COLUMBIA PARKWAY
CINCINNATI, OH 45226
Director, Robert Taft
Specific Interests: Prairie and Temperate
Forest

**OHIO VALLEY IMPROVEMENT
ASSOCIATION INCORPORATED**
4017 CAREW TOWER
CINCINNATI, OH 45202
General Environment: Limnologic

OUTDOOR RECREATION BUREAU
19TH AND C STREETS, NW
WASHINGTON, DC 20240
General Environment: Estuarine

**PACIFIC NORTHWEST WATER
LABORATORY**
PITTOCK BLOCK
PORTLAND, OR 97205
Specific Interests: Prairie and Temperate
Forest

PATENT OFFICE
14TH AND E STREETS, NW
WASHINGTON, DC 20231

**POLLUTION SURVEILLANCE
DIVISION**
633 INDIANA AVENUE, NW
WASHINGTON,DC 20242
Specific Interests: Prairie and Temperate
Forest

POWER BUREAU
441 G STREET, NW
WASHINGTON, DC 20426
General Environment: Estuarine

PROGRAM ENGINEERING SOCIETY
2029 K STREET, NW
WASHINGTON, DC 20006
General Environment: Limnologic

PUBLIC INFORMATION OFFICE
633 INDIANA AVENUE, NW
WASHINGTON,DC 20242
Specific Interests:Prairie and Temperate
Forest

PUBLIC WORKS COMMISSION
ROOM 4204, NEW SENATE
BUILDING
WASHINGTON, D C 20510
General Environment: Limnologic

**PUBLIC WORKS COMMITTEE, US
HOUSE OF REPRESENTATIVES**
ROOM 2165, RAYBURN HOUSE
OFFICE BUILDING
WASHINGTON, DC 20515

**REACTOR DEVELOPMENT AND
TECHNOLOGY DIVISION**
UNITED STATES ATOMIC ENERGY
COMMISSION
GERMANTOWN, MD 20545
General Environment: Limnologic

**RECLAMATION BUREAU,
DEPARTMENT OF THE INTERIOR**
BUILDING 67, DENVER FEDERAL
CENTER
DENVER, CO 80225
General Environment: Oceanographic

**RESEARCH AND DEVELOPMENT
OFFICE**
633 INDIANA AVENUE, NW
WASHINGTON,DC 20242
Specific Interests: Prairie and Temperate
Forest

**RESEARCH OFFICE, FEDERAL
HIGHWAYS ADMINISTRATION**
UNITED STATES DEPARTMENT OF
TRANSPORTATION
WASHINGTON, DC 20590
General Environment: Limnologic

**SALINE WATER OFFICE,
DEPARTMENT OF THE INTERIOR**
18TH AND C STREETS, NW
WASHINGTON, DC 20242
General Environment: Oceanographic

**SANITARY ENGINEERING
RESEARCH BRANCH**
UNITED STATES ARMY MEDICAL
RESEARCH DEVELOPMENT
COMMAND
WASHINGTON, DC 20314
General Environment: Limnologic

**SCIENCE AND TECHNOLOGY
COUNCIL**
EXECUTIVE OFFICE BUILDING
WASHINGTON, DC 20503

SEA GRANTS OFFICE
NATIONAL OCEANIC AND
ATMOSPHERIC ADMINISTRATION
ROCKVILLE, MD 20852
General Environment: Oceanographic
Staff Size: 10 - 49

**SMITHSONIAN INSTITUTION,
SCIENCES INFORMATION
EXCHANGE**
1730 M STREET, NW
WASHINGTON, DC 20036

SOIL AND WATER CONSERVATION AND RESOURCES DIVISION
PLANT INDUSTRY STATION, US DEPARTMENT OF AGRICULTURE
BELTSVILLE, MD 20705
General Environment: Limnologic

SOIL AND WATER CONSERVATION DISTRICTS ASSOCIATION
1025 VERMONT AVENUE, NW
WASHINGTON, DC 20005
General Environment: Limnologic

SOIL AND WATER CONSERVATION RESEARCH DIVISION
PLANT INDUSTRY STATION
BELTSVILLE, MD 20705
Specific Interests: Prairie and Temperate Forest
Staff Size: 500 - 999

SOIL CONSERVATION SERVICE
12TH STREET AND INDEPENDENCE AVENUE
WASHINGTON, DC 20250
General Environment: Limnologic

SOIL CONSERVATION SERVICES, RIVER BASIN DIVISION
5233 POMMEROY DRIVE
FAIRFAX, VA 22030
Director, Richard Kohnke

SOIL CONSERVATION SERVICES, WATERSHED PLANNING DIVISION
1318 JULIANA PLACE
ALEXANDRIA, VA 22304
Director, Joseph W Haas

SOLID WASTE MANAGEMENT BUREAU
12720 TWINBROOK PARKWAY
ROCKVILLE, MD 20852
Director, Richard D Vaughn
General Environment: Terrestrial

SOUTHEAST BASINS INTER-AGENCY COMMISSION
ROOM 402, NEW WALTON BUILDING
ATLANTA, GA 30303
Staff Size: 1 - 4

SOUTHEASTERN POWER ADMINISTRATION
DEPARTMENT OF THE INTERIOR
ELBERTON, GA 30635
General Environment: Oceanographic

TECHNICAL SERVICES DIVISION
633 INDIANA AVENUE, NW
WASHINGTON, DC 20242
Specific Interests: Prairie and Temperate Forest

TECHNOLOGICAL LABORATORY
622 MISSION STREET
KETCHIKAN, AK 99901
Director, Murray L Hayes
Specific Interests: Prairie and Temperate Forest
Staff Size: 5 - 9

TECHNOLOGICAL LABORATORY
2725 MONTLAKE BOULEVARD, EAST
SEATTLE, WA 98102
Director, Maynard Steinberg
Specific Interests: Prairie and Temperate Forest
Staff Size: 10 - 49

TENNESSEE-TOMBRIGBEE WATERWAY DEVELOPMENT AUTHORITY
POST OFFICE BOX 671
COLUMBUS, MS 39701
General Environment: Limnologic

TRAINING GRANTS BRANCH, MANPOWER TRAINING BRANCH
ENVIRONMENTAL PROTECTION AGENCY
WASHINGTON, DC 20460
General Environment: Oceanographic

UNITED STATES GEOLOGICAL SURVEY
DEPARTMENT OF THE INTERIOR
WASHINGTON, DC 20242

UPPER COLORADO RIVER COMMISSION
355 SOUTH FOURTH E STREET
SALT LAKE CITY, UT 84111
General Environment: Limnologic

UPPER MISSISSIPPI RIVER CONSERVATION CORPS
4TH AND PERRY STREET, 322 FEDERAL BUILDING
DAVENPORT, IA 52801
General Environment: Limnologic

US DEPARTMENT OF INTERIOR
18TH AND F STREETS, NW
WASHINGTON, DC 20006
General Environment: Oceanic

WATER COMMISSION, HYDROLOGICAL SERVICES
POST OFFICE BOX 6381
JERUSALEM, ISRAEL
Director, M Jacobs
General Environment: Terrestrial
Staff Size: 50 - 99

WATER CONTROL DIVISION, TENNESSEE VALLEY AUTHORITY
HOME FEDERAL BUILDING, MARKET STREET
KNOXVILLE, TN 37902

WATER HYGIENE
222 EAST CENTRAL PARKWAY
CINCINNATI, OH 45202

WATER QUALITY DATA STORAGE
POLLUTION SURVEILLANCE
WASHINGTON, DC 20242
Chief, Jesse L Lewis
General Environment: Limnologic
Staff Size: 10 - 49

WATER RESOURCES AND ENGINEERING SERVICES DIVISION
14TH STREET AND CONSTITUTION AVENUE
WASHINGTON, DC 20230
General Environment: Oceanographic

WATER RESOURCES AUTHORITY OF PUERTO RICO
POST OFFICE BOX 4267
SAN JUAN, PUERTO RICO 00905
General Environment: Limnologic

WATER RESOURCES COUNCIL
1025 VERMONT AVENUE, NW
WASHINGTON, DC 20005

WATER RESOURCES COUNCIL
10212 VALE ROAD
VIENNA, VA 22180
Director, W Don Maughan

WATER RESOURCES COUNCIL
2120 L STREET, NW
WASHINGTON, DC 20037

WATER RESOURCES COUNCIL, NATIONAL ACADEMY OF SCIENCES
2101 CONSTITUTION AVENUE, NW
WASHINGTON, DC 20418
General Environment: Limnologic

WATER RESOURCES DIVISION
NATIONAL PARK SERVICE
WASHINGTON, DC 20240
Staff Size: 10 - 49

WATER RESOURCES RESEARCH OFFICE
DEPARTMENT OF THE INTERIOR
WASHINGTON, DC 20240
General Environment: Oceanographic

WATER RESOURCES SCIENCES INFORMATION CENTER
DEPARTMENT OF INTERIOR
WASHINGTON, DC 20240
Manager, Ray Jenson
General Environment: Limnologic
Staff Size: 5 - 9

WATER SERVICE
MINISTRY OF PUBLIC WORKS
COTONOV, DAHOMEY

Director, Emile Paraiso
General Environment: Limnologic

WATER SUPPLY PROGRAM DIVISION
ENVIRONMENTAL PROTECTION AGENCY
WASHINGTON, DC 20201
Staff Size: 50 - 99

WATER SUPPLY RESEARCH LABORATORY
SOUTH FERRY ROAD
NARRAGANSETT, RI 02882
Staff Size: 10 - 49

WATERSHED ADMINISTRATION, SOIL CONSERVATION SERVICE
218 NORTH COLUMBUS STREET
ARLINGTON, VA 22203
Director, Hollis Williams

WATERSHED MANAGEMENT DIVISION, FOREST SERVICES
14TH STREET AND INDEPENDENCE AVENUE
WASHINGTON, DC 20250
General Environment: Limnologic

WATERSHED PLANNING, SOIL CONSERVATION SERVICES
9005 STRATFORD LANE
ALEXANDRIA, VA 22308
Assistant Deputy, Eugene Buie
Specific Interests: Rural
Staff Size: 10 - 49

WATERWAYS EXPERIMENT STATION
POST OFFICE BOX 631, HALLS FERRY ROAD
VICKSBURG, MS 39181
General Environment: Limnologic

Government — State or Local

AR-WHITE-RED BASINS COMMISSION, FEDERAL BUILDING
P O BOX 1467
MUSKOGEE, OK 74401
General Environment: Limnologic

BUSINESS ADMINISTRATION DEPARTMENT
POST OFFICE BOX 271, WATER RESOURCES BUILDING
JEFFERSON CITY, MO 65101
Staff Size: 5 - 9

CLEAN WATER INITIATIVE COMMISSION
7 BARROWS STREET
BRUNSWICK, ME 04011

Director, Edward Hanis
General Environment: Limnologic

COMPACT COMMISSION OF THE YELLOWSTONE RIVER
421 FEDERAL BUILDING
HELENA, MT 59601
General Environment: Limnologic

CONSERVATION COMMISSION OF MISSOURI
P.O. BOX 180
JEFFERSON CITY, MO 65101
General Environment: Limnologic

CONSTRUCTION DEPARTMENT
301 CITY HALL
ATLANTA, GA 30303
General Environment: Limnologic

COUNCIL OF STATE GOVERNMENTS
IRON WORKS PIKE
LEXINGTON, KY 40505
Executive Director, Brevard Crihfield

COUNCIL OF STATE GOVERNMENTS
1313 EAST 60TH STREET
CHICAGO, IL 60637

DELAWARE RIVER BASIN COMMISSION
25 SCOTCH ROAD
TRENTON, N J 08603

ECOLOGY ACTION CORPORATION OF THE CENTER RIVER
BOX 44
HADLEY, MA 01035
General Environment: Estuarine

ENGINEERING DEPARTMENT OF SEATTLE
910 MUNICIPAL BUILDING
SEATTLE, WA 98104

ENGINEERING DEPARTMENT OF WYOMING
STATE CAPITOL BUILDING
CHEYENNE, WY 82001
General Environment: Limnologic

ENGINEERING DIVISION OF STATE OF NEW MEXICO
STATE CAPITOL
SANTA FE, NM 87501
General Environment: Limnologic

ENGINEERING IN UTAH
442 CAPITOL BUILDING
SALT LAKE CITY, UT 84101
General Environment: Limnologic

ENVIRONMENTAL HEALTH AND

ENGINEERING SERVICES
STATE DEPARTMENT HEALTH
BISMARCK, ND 58501
Chief, W Van Heuvelen
General Environment: Limnologic

ENVIRONMENTAL HEALTH DIVISION
STATE DEPARTMENT HEALTH
MINNEAPOLIS, MN 55440
Director, Frederick Heisel
Staff Size: 50 - 99

ENVIRONMENTAL HEALTH DIVISION, KANSAS DEPARTMENT OF HEALTH
535 KANSAS AVENUE
TOPEKA, KS 66603
General Environment: Limnologic

ENVIRONMENTAL HEALTH DIVISION, KENTUCKY DEPARTMENT OF HEALTH
275 EAST MAIN STREET
FRANKFORT, KY 40601
General Environment: Limnologic

ENVIRONMENTAL HEALTH SERVICE, NEBRASKA DEPARTMENT OF HEALTH
POST OFFICE BOX 94757, STATE HOUSE STATION
LINCOLN, NB 68508
General Environment: Limnologic

ENVIRONMENTAL HEALTH SERVICES DIVISION
845 CENTRAL AVENUE
ALBANY, NY 12208
Assistant Commissioner, Meredith H Thompson
General Environment: Limnologic

ENVIRONMENTAL HEALTH, DEPARTMENT OF HEALTH
DAVIS STREET
PROVIDENCE, RI 02908

ENVIRONMENTAL MANPOWER OFFICE
50 WOLF ROAD
ALBANY, NY 12201
Director, Milton T Hill
Staff Size: 5 - 9

ENVIRONMENTAL QUALITY DEPARTMENT
1234 SW MORRISON STREET
PORTLAND, OR 97205
General Environment: Limnologic

ENVIRONMENTAL SANITATION BUREAU
CHARLOTTE AMALIE BOX 1442
ST THOMAS, VI 00801

FISHERIES AND GAME DIVISION, DEPARTMENT OF NATURAL RESOURCES
100 CAMBRIDGE
BOSTON, MA 02134

FISHERIES MANAGEMENT BUREAU, CONSERVATION AND ECONOMIC DEVELOPMENT
J FITCH PLAZA, PO BOX 1889
TRENTON, NJ 08625
General Environment: Limnologic

FLOOD CONSERVATION COMMISSION OF THE MERRIMACK RIVER VALLEY
4 PARK STREET
CONCORD, NH 03301
Executive Secretary, Miss Ruth E Matson
General Environment: Estuarine

FLOOD CONTROL COMMAND OF THE CENTER RIVER VALLEY
28 MECHANIC STREET
KEENE, NH 03431
Director, Nathan Tufts

FLOOD CONTROL DIVISION, DEPARTMENT OF ECOLOGY
335 GENERAL ADMINISTRATION BUILDING
OLYMPIA, WA 98501

GAME, FISHERIES AND PARKS DEPARTMENT OF SOUTH DAKOTA
PIERRE, SD 57501
General Environment: Limnologic

GEOLOGIC AND ECONOMIC SURVEY OF WEST VIRGINIA
WEST VIRGINIA UNIVERSITY
MORGANTOWN, WV 26505
General Environment: Oceanographic
Staff Size: 10 - 49

GEOLOGIC, TOPOGRAPHIC AND ECONOMIC SURVEY OF MISSISSIPPI
POST OFFICE BOX 4915, NORTH WEST STREET
JACKSON, MS 39216
General Environment: Limnologic

GEOLOGICAL AND MINERALOGICAL SERVICE OF UTAH
UNIVERSITY OF UTAH
SALT LAKE CITY, UT 84112
General Environment: Limnologic

GEOLOGICAL AND TOPOGRAPHY BUREAU
POST OFFICE BOX 1889, J FITCH PLAZA
TRENTON, NJ 08625
Staff Size: 10 - 49

GEOLOGICAL COMMISSION
STATE CAPITOL
LITTLE ROCK, AR 72201
General Environment: Limnologic

GEOLOGICAL SURVEY OF NORTH DAKOTA
UNIVERSITY STATION
GRAND FORKS, ND 58202
General Environment: Limnologic

GEOLOGY DIVISION, TENNESSEE DEPARTMENT OF CONSERVATION
G-5 STATE OFFICE BUILDING
NASHVILLE, TN 37219
General Environment: Limnologic

HEALTH DEPARTMENT OF WASHINGTON
PUBLIC HEALTH BUILDING
OLYMPIA, WA 98501

HEALTH DEPARTMENT, HAYDEN PLAZA WEST
4019 NORTH 33RD STREET
PHOENIX, AZ 85017

HEALTH DIVISION OF OREGON
1400 SW 5TH AVENUE, STATE OFFICE BUILDING
PORTLAND, OR 97201
General Environment: Limnologic
Staff Size: 100 - 499

HYDROLOGY OFFICE, NATIONAL WEATHER SERVICES, ALASKA OFFICE
632 SIXTH AVENUE
ANCHORAGE, AK 99501
General Environment: Oceanographic

HYDROLOGY OFFICE, NATIONAL WEATHER SERVICES, SOUTHERN OFFICE
ROOM 10E09, 819 TAYLOR STREET
FORT WORTH, TX 76102
General Environment: Oceanographic

HYDROLOGY OFFICE, NATIONAL WEATHER SERVICES, CENTRAL OFFICE
ROOM 1836, 601 EAST 12TH STREET
KANSAS CITY, MO 64104
General Environment: Oceanographic

HYDROLOGY RESEARCH AND DEVELOPMENT LABORATORY
NATIONAL WEATHER SERVICE
SILVER SPRING, MD 20910
General Environment: Terrestrial
Staff Size: 10 - 49

INDIAN HEALTH CENTER, ABERDEEN AREA
405 CITIZENS BUILDING
ABERDEEN, SD 57401
General Environment: Terrestrial

INDIAN HEALTH SERVICE, BILLINGS AREA
3 BILLINGS STREET WEST
BILLINGS, MT 59103
General Environment: Terrestrial

INDIAN HEALTH SERVICE, NAVAJO AREA
POST OFFICE BOX G
WINDOW ROCK, AZ 86515
General Environment: Terrestrial

INDIAN HEALTH SERVICE, OFFICE OF PROGRAM DEVELOPMENT
POST OFFICE BOX 11340
TUCSON, AZ 85706
General Environment: Terrestrial

INDIAN HEALTH SERVICE, PHOENIX AREA
801 EAST INDIAN SCHOOL ROAD
PHOENIX, AZ 85014
General Environment: Terrestrial

INDIAN HEALTH SERVICE, PORTLAND AREA
ROOM 200, 921 SW WASHINGTON STREET
PORTLAND, OR 97205
General Environment: Terrestrial

INFORMATION AND EDUCATION DIVISION, MAINE FOREST DEPARTMENT
STATE OFFICE BUILDING
AUGUSTA, ME 04330
General Environment: Limnologic

LABORATORIES DIVISION, UNIVERSITY OF WYOMING
P O BOX 3228, CHEMISTRY-ZOOLOGY BUILDING, ROOM 405
LARAMIE, WY 82071
General Environment: Limnologic

LAND AND NATURAL RESOURCES DEPARTMENT
465 SOUTH KING STREET, POST OFFICE BOX 373
HONOLULU, HI 96809
Manager, C Donald
Staff Size: 50 - 99

LAND TRUST OF THE NISSITISSIT RIVER, INCORPORATED
BOX 84
HOLLIS, NH 03049
General Environment: Estuarine

LEAGUE OF WOMEN VOTERS OF MASSACHUSETTS
120 BOYLSTON STREET
BOSTON, MA 02116

MARINE FISHERIES COMMISSION OF THE ATLANTIC STATES
100 CAMBRIDGE
BOSTON, MA 02134

MARINE SCIENCES DIVISION, 1ST COAST GUARD DISTRICT
KENNEDY BUILDING, GOVERNMENT CENTER
WASHINGTON, DC 02203
General Environment: Oceanographic

MARINE SCIENCES DIVISION, 13TH COAST GUARD DISTRICT
618 2ND AVENUE
SEATTLE, WA 98104
General Environment: Oceanographic

MARINE SCIENCES DIVISION, 14TH COAST GUARD DISTRICT
677 ALA MOANA
HONOLULU, HI 96813
General Environment: Oceanographic

MARINE SCIENCES DIVISION, 17TH COAST GUARD DISTRICT
709 WEST 9TH STREET
JUNEAU, AK 99801
General Environment: Oceanographic

MARINE SCIENCES DIVISION, 2ND COAST GUARD DISTRICT
1520 MARKET STREET, FEDERAL BUILDING
ST LOUIS, MO 63103
General Environment: Oceanographic

MARINE SCIENCES DIVISION, 8TH COAST GUARD DISTRICT
CUSTOM HOUSE
NEW ORLEANS, LA 70130
General Environment: Oceanographic

MARINE SCIENCES DIVISION, 9TH COAST GUARD DISTRICT
1240 EAST 9TH STREET
CLEVELAND, OH 44199
General Environment: Oceanographic

METROPOLITAN WATER DISTRICT OF SOUTH CAROLINA
1111 SUNSET BOULEVARD
LOS ANGELES, CA 90054
General Environment: Limnologic

NATIVE HEALTH SERVICE, ALASKA AREA
POST OFFICE BOX 7-741
ANCHORAGE, AK 99510
General Environment: Terrestrial

NATURAL RESOURCES DEPARTMENT OF WISCONSIN
POST OFFICE BOX 450
MADISON, WI 53701
General Environment: Limnologic
Staff Size: 1000 - 4999

NEW HAMPSHIRE COMMISSION FOR BETTER WATER
5 SOUTH STATE STREET
CONCORD, NH 03301

Director, John Dodge
General Environment: Limnologic

PARKS FOR RECREATION DIVISION, DEPARTMENT OF CONSERVATION
J FITCH PLAZA POST OFFICE BOX 1889
TRENTON, NJ 08625
General Environment: Limnologic

PHARMACOLOGY AND SCIENCE COLLEGE OF PHILADELPHIA
2301 NORTH CAMERON STREET
HARRISBURG, PA 17110
President, Arthur Osol
General Environment: Limnologic

PLANNING AND ZONING DEPARTMENT
701 NORTH 20 STREET
BIRMINGHAM, AL 35203

PLANNING OFFICE OF NEW MEXICO
SANTA FE, NM 87501
General Environment: Limnologic

POLLUTION CONTROL COMMISSION, NEW ENGLAND INTERSTATE WATER
ROOM 950, 73 TRENTON STREET
BOSTON, MA 02108
General Environment: Limnologic

PORT AUTHORITY OF MASSACHUSETTS
470 ATLANTIC AVENUE
BOSTON, MA 02167
General Environment: Oceanographic

PROTECTION OF THE LEE'S RIVER COMMISSION
22 LAWRENCE STREET
SWANSEA, MA 02777
Secretary, Mrs Janice Burrows
General Environment: Estuarine

PUBLIC WORKS DEPARTMENT OF DETROIT
528 CITY-COUNTY BUILDING
DETROIT, MI 48226

REGIONAL PLANNING COMMISSION OF SE WISCONSIN
916 NORTH EAST AVENUE
WAUKESHA, WI 53187
Specific Interests: Urban
Staff Size: 50 - 99

REPRESENTATIVE RIVER COMPACT ADMINISTRATION
1845 SHERMAN STREET, ROOM 101
DENVER, CO 80203
Staff Size: 100 - 499

RESOURCES BUREAU, WISCONSIN DEPARTMENT OF NATURAL RESOURCES
BOX 450
MADISON, WI 53701
General Environment: Limnologic

RESOURCES DEVELOPMENT DIVISION, DEPARTMENT OF NATURAL RESOURCES
1 WEST WILSON STREET
MADISON, WI 53702
Administrator, F Holman
General Environment: Limnologic

SANITARY ENGINEERING BUREAU
135 RIVERSIDE AVENUE
JACKSONVILLE, FL 32202

SANITARY ENGINEERING BUREAU, DEPARTMENT OF PUBLIC HEALTH
2151 BERKELEY WAY
BERKELEY, CA 94704
General Environment: Terrestrial
Staff Size: 50 - 99

SANITARY ENGINEERING BUREAU, DIVISION OF ENGINEERING
1314 EAST GRACE STREET
RICHMOND, VA 32319
Specific Interests: Rural

SANITARY ENGINEERING DIVISION, CONNECTICUT DEPARTMENT OF HEALTH
79 ELM STREET
HARTFORD, CT 06115

SANITARY ENGINEERING DIVISION, ILLINOIS DEPARTMENT PUBLIC HEALTH
STATE OFFICE BUILDING
SPRINGFIELD, IL 62700

SANITARY ENGINEERING DIVISION, WEST VIRGINIA HEALTH DEPARTMENT
1800 WASHINGTON STREET, EAST
CHARLESTON, WV 25311
General Environment: Limnologic

SANITARY ENGINEERING, MASSACHUSETTS DEPARTMENT OF PUBLIC HEALTH
511 STATE HOUSE
BOSTON, MASS 02133
General Environment: Limnologic

SCIENTIFIC RESEARCH IN SEWAGE AND SANITARY ENGINEERING
SOFIA, BUL P. NAPETOV 50
LA PAZ, BOLIVIA
Director, N Tchalukov
General Environment: Oceanographic

SOIL AND WATER CONSERVATION BUILDING
1014 FIRST NATIONAL BANK BUILDING
TEMPLE, TX 76501

SOIL AND WATER CONSERVATION COMMISSION OF NEBRASKA
POST OFFICE BOX 94725, STATE CAPITOL BUILDING
LINCOLN, NB 68509
General Environment: Limnologic

SOIL AND WATER CONSERVATION COMMISSION OF NEW MEXICO
ROOM 301, STATE CAPITOL
SANTA FE, NM 87501
General Environment: Limnologic

SOIL AND WATER CONSERVATION COMMISSION OF DELAWARE
P O BOX 567
GEORGETOWN, DE 19947

SOIL AND WATER CONSERVATION COMMISSION OF VIRGINIA
10 SOUTH 10TH STREET
RICHMOND, VA 23216

SOIL AND WATER CONSERVATION COMMISSION OF SOUTH DAKOTA
STATE CAPITOL
PIERRE, SD 57501

SOIL AND WATER CONSERVATION COMMISSION
2301 NORTH CAMERON STREET
HARRISBURG, PA 17120
Director, Walter Peechatka
General Environment: Terrestrial
Staff Size: 10 - 49

SOIL CONSERVATION COMMISSION OF KANSAS
ROOM 1252W STATE OFFICE BUILDING
TOPEKA, KS 66612
General Environment: Limnologic

SOIL CONSERVATION COMMITTEE
STATE OFFICE BUILDING
MONTGOMERY, AL 36104

STATE DEVELOPMENT BOARD OF SOUTH CAROLINA
WADE HAMPTON BOULEVARD, BOX 927
COLUMBIA, SC 29202

TEN MILE RIVER BASIN TASK FORCE
68 WINTHROP STREET
TAUNTON, MA 02780
Director, Tad Widby

UNITED SOUTH-EAST TRIBES PROGRAM
1970 MAIN STREET
SARASOTA, FL 33577
General Environment: Terrestrial

WATER ADMINISTRATION DEPARTMENT OF IDAHO
ROOM 107, STATEHOUSE
BOISE, ID 83701
General Environment: Limnologic
Staff Size: 50 - 99

WATER AMENDMENT BOARD
100 CAMBRIDGE STREET
BOSTON, MA 02167

WATER AND POWER DEPARTMENT OF LOS ANGELES
POST OFFICE BOX 111
LOS ANGELES, CA 90054
General Environment: Limnologic

WATER AND RELATED RESOURCES, DEPARTMENT OF ENVIRONMENTAL PROTECTION
STATE OFFICE BUILDING
HARTFORD, CT 06100

WATER COMMISSION OF NORTH DAKOTA
1301 STATE CAPITOL
BISMARK, ND 58501
General Environment: Limnologic

WATER COMMISSIONERS BOARD OF MISSISSIPPI
429 MISSISSIPPI STREET
JACKSON, MS 39201
General Environment: Limnologic

WATER CONSERVATION BOARD OF MONTANA
SAM W MITCHELL BUILDING
HELENA, MT 59601
General Environment: Limnologic

WATER CONSERVATION DISTRICT OF THE COLORADO RIVER
P O BOX 218
GLENWOOD SPRINGS, CO 81601
Secretary for Engineering, R C Fischer
General Environment: Limnologic

WATER CONTROL PLANNING DIVISION
HOME FEDERAL BUILDING, MARKET STREET
KNOXVILLE, TN 37902
Specific Interests: Prairie and Temperate Forest

WATER DEVELOPMENT BOARD OF TEXAS
POST OFFICE BOX 13087, CAPITAL STATION
AUSTIN, TX 78711
Staff Size: 100 - 499

WATER DIVISION, OHIO DEPARTMENT OF NATURAL RESOURCES
815 OHIO STATE OFFICE BUILDING
COLUMBUS, OH 43215
General Environment: Limnologic

WATER IMPROVEMENT COMMISSION
STATE OFFICE BUILDING
MONTGOMERY, AL 36104
Director, Arthur N Beck
General Environment: Limnologic

WATER POLICY AND SUPPLY DIVISION
JOHN FITCH PLAZA, P.O. BOX 1889
TRENTON, NJ 08625
General Environment: Limnologic

WATER POLLUTION CONTROL ASSOCIATION
POST OFFICE BOX 158
SCOTTSDALE, AZ 85252
General Environment: Limnologic

WATER POLLUTION CONTROL ASSOCIATION OF MONTANA
STATE CAPITOL BUILDING
HELENA, MT 59601
General Environment: Limnologic

WATER POLLUTION CONTROL OF NEW ENGLAND
511 STATE HOUSE
BOSTON, MA 02133
General Environment: Limnologic

WATER QUALITY BOARD OF TEXAS
1108 LAVACA STREET
AUSTIN, TX 78701
Executive Director, Hugh Yantis
General Environment: Limnologic

WATER QUALITY CONTROL DIVISION, DEPARTMENT OF PUBLIC HEALTH
300 INDIANA AVENUE, NW
WASHINGTON, DC 20001

WATER QUALITY CONTROL, NEW MEXICO ENVIRONMENTAL IMPROVEMENT AGENCY
POST OFFICE BOX 2348
SANTA FE, NM 87501
Director, John R Wright
General Environment: Limnologic

WATER QUALITY MANAGEMENT BUREAU
POST OFFICE BOX 2351, H AND W BUILDING
HARRISBURG, PA 17120
General Environment: Limnologic

WATER QUALITY SECTION, NMEIA
POST OFFICE BOX 2348
SANTA FE, NM 87501

Chief, John R Wright
General Environment: Limnologic
Staff Size: 10 - 49

WATER RESOURCES
20 LOCK STREET
NASHUA, NH 03060
Chairman, Mrs S. Taylor

WATER RESOURCES CENTER
COLLEGE OF FORESTRY
SYRACUSE, NY 13210
Director, Dr Robert Hennigan
General Environment: Limnologic

**WATER RESOURCES CENTER,
OHIO STATE UNIVERSITY**
1791 NEIL AVENUE
COLUMBUS, OH 43210
General Environment: Limnologic
Staff Size: 5 - 9

**WATER RESOURCES COMMISSION
OF NEW YORK STATE**
STATE OFFICE BUILDING
ALBANY, NY 12226
General Environment: Limnologic

**WATER RESOURCES COMMISSION
OF SOUTH DAKOTA**
STATE OFFICE BUILDING 1
PIERRE, SD 57501
Chief Engineer, J W Grimes
General Environment: Terrestrial
Staff Size: 10 - 49

WATER RESOURCES DEPARTMENT
STATE OFFICE BUILDING
ANNAPOLIS, MD 21401
Director, Paul Mckee
General Environment: Limnologic

WATER RESOURCES DEPARTMENT
STATE OFFICE BUILDING
MONTPELIER, VT 05602
Commissioner, Reinhold Thieme
General Environment: Limnologic

**WATER RESOURCES DEPARTMENT
OF NEBRASKA**
STATE CAPITOL
LINCOLN, NB 68509
General Environment: Limnologic

**WATER RESOURCES DEPARTMENT
OF NORTH CAROLINA**
P O BOX 9392
RALEIGH, NC 27603

**WATER RESOURCES DEPARTMENT
OF VERMONT**
STATE OFFICE BUILDING
MONTPELIER, VT 05602
Commissioner, Dr Martin Johnson
General Environment: Limnologic

**WATER RESOURCES DIVISION OF
COLORADO**

ROOM 101, 1845 SHERMAN STREET
DENVER, CO 80203
General Environment: Limnologic
Staff Size: 100 - 499

**WATER RESOURCES DIVISION,
DEPARTMENT NATURAL
RESOURCES**
201 SOUTH FALL STREET
CARSON CITY, NV 89701
General Environment: Limnologic

**WATER RESOURCES DIVISION,
DEPARTMENT OF NATURAL
RESOURCES**
1201 GREENBRIER STREET
CHARLESTON, WV 25311
General Environment: Limnologic

**WATER RESOURCES DIVISION,
DEPARTMENT OF
CONSERVATION**
2611 WEST END AVENUE
NASHVILLE, TN 37203
General Environment: Limnologic
Staff Size: 10 - 49

**WATER RESOURCES DIVISION,
MAINE PUBLIC UTILITIES
COMMISSION**
STATE HOUSE
AUGUSTA, ME 04330
General Environment: Limnologic

WATER RESOURCES DIVISION
100 CAMBRIDGE STREET
BOSTON, MA 02202
General Environment: Limnologic
Staff Size: 10 - 49

**WATER RESOURCES SECTION,
MOUNTAIN FISHERIES AND
GAME DEPARTMENT**
FISHERIES DEPARTMENT
HELENA, MT 59601
General Environment: Limnologic

**WATER SANITATION OF OHIO
RIVER VALLEY**
414 WALNUT STREET
CINCINNATI, OH 45202
General Environment: Estuarine

**WATER SUPPLY AND POLLUTION
CONTROL**
61 SOUTH SPRING STREET
CONCORD, NH 03301
Executive Director, William Healey
General Environment: Limnologic

**WATER SUPPLY AND POLLUTION
DIVISION, DEPARTMENT OF
HEALTH**
STATE CAPITOL BUILDING
BISMARCK, ND 58501
General Environment: Limnologic
Staff Size: 5 - 9

**WATER SUPPLY BUREAU,
DEPARTMENT**
3001 DRUID PARK DRIVE
BALTIMORE, MD 21215

**WATER SUPPLY, GAS AND
ELECTRICITY DEPARTMENT OF
NEW YORK CITY**
MUNICIPAL BUILDING
NEW YORK, NY 10007
General Environment: Limnologic

WATER SURVEY OF ILLINOIS
POST OFFICE BOX 232
URBANA, IL 61802
General Environment: Limnologic

**WATER WELL NATIONAL
ASSOCIATION**
1201 WAUKEGAN ROAD
GLENVIEW, ILL 60025
General Environment: Limnologic

**WATERSHED ASSOCIATION
COUNCIL OF THE MID-
ATLANTIC**
POST OFFICE BOX 171
PENNINGTON, NJ 08534
President, Mr Paul Felton
General Environment: Oceanographic
Specific Interests: Prairie and Temperate
   Forest

**WATERSHED ASSOCIATION OF
CHARLES RIVER**
2391 COMMONWEALTH AVENUE
AUBURNDALE, MA 02166
Executive Director, Kenneth H Wood

**WATERSHED ASSOCIATION OF
NASHUA RIVER, INCORPORATED**
GROTON, MA 01450
President, Mrs H F Stoddart

**WATERSHED ASSOCIATION OF
NEPONSET**
30 THOMPSON LANE
MILTON, MA 02187
Director, John Cronin

**WATERSHED ASSOCIATION OF
NORTH AND SOUTH RIVERS,
INCORPORATED**
POST OFFICE BOX 333
MARSHFIELD HILLS, MA 02051
President, Carl Smith
General Environment: Estuarine

**WATERSHED ASSOCIATION OF
THE HOUSATONIC RIVER**
11 HOUSATONIC STREET
LENOX, MA 01240

**WATERSHED ASSOCIATION,
INCORPORATED, OF THE
WESTFIELD RIVER**
POST OFFICE BOX 114
MIDDLEFIELD, MA 01243
President, W B Shepard, Jr

**WATERSHED ASSOCIATION,
INCORPORATED, OF THE
MERRIMACK RIVER**
105 EVERETT STREET
CONCORD, MA 01743

**WATERSHED COUNCIL OF
CENTER RIVER, INCORPORATED**
134 STEELE ROAD
W HARTFORD, CT 06119
President, E S Grant
General Environment: Limnologic

**WATERSHED COUNCIL OF THE
PARKER RIVER**
WASHINGTON STREET
W BOXFORD, MA 01885
President, Mrs R P Gowan

**WATERSHED PROTECTION
ASSOCIATION OF THE
SHAWSHEEN**
2 HADLEY ROAD
LEXINGTON, MA 02173
Director, Mrs Ann Briggs

**WATERWAYS DIVISION,
DEPARTMENT OF PUBLIC
WORKS**
1 CITY HALL SQUARE
BOSTON, MA 02129

**WATERWAYS DIVISION, PUBLIC
WORKS AND BUILDING
DEPARTMENT**
201 W MONROE STREET
SPRINGFIELD, IL 62706

WYOMING NATURAL
210 WEST 23RD STREET
CHEYENNE, WY 82001
General Environment: Limnologic

Industrial/Commercial

**AMERICAN TUNABOAT
ASSOCIATION**
ONE TUNA LANE
SAN DIEGO, CA 92101
Specific Interests: Prairie and Temperate
Forest
Staff Size: 100 - 499

**DESALINATION ENGINEERING
DEPARTMENT**
PO BOX 18041
TEL AVIV, ISRAEL
Director, Natan Berkman
General Environment: Oceanographic
Staff Size: 100 - 499

**MEKOROT WATER COMPANY,
LIMITED**
9 LINCOLN STREET
TEL AVIV, ISRAEL

Director, S Cantor
General Environment: Oceanographic

**NATIONAL WATERSHED
CONGRESS**
1025 VERMONT AVENUE, NW
WASHINGTON, DC 20005
Director, Gordon K Zimmerman
General Environment: Terrestrial
Specific Interests: Prairie and Temperate
Forest
Staff Size: 10 - 49

**TAHAL-WATER PLANNING FOR
ISRAEL, LIMITED**
54 IBN GVIROL STREET
TEL AVIV, ISRAEL
Director, Y Cahana
General Environment: Oceanographic

Professional Organizations

**AMERICAN BOTTLED WATER
ASSOCIATION**
1411 WEST OLYMPIC BOULEVARD
LOS ANGELES, CA 90015
Director, Fred H Jones
Staff Size: 1 - 4

**AMERICAN WATER RESOURCES
ASSOCIATION**
206 EAST UNIVERSITY AVENUE, BX
434
URBANA, IL 61801
Secretary, Dr J C Csallany
Staff Size: 5 - 9

**CIVIL ENGINEERS SOCIETY OF
BOSTON**
47 WINTER STREET
BOSTON, MA

**CONNECTICUT RIVER
WATERSHED COUNCIL,
INCORPORATED**
125 COMBS ROAD
EASTHAMPTON, MA 01027
Specific Interests: Prairie and Temperate
Forest

COOLING TOWER INSTITUTE
3003 YALE STREET
HOUSTON, TX 77018
Executive Secretary, Dorothy R Garrison
Specific Interests: Prairie and Temperate
Forest
Staff Size: 10 - 49

**DRAINAGE AND FLOOD CONTROL,
COMMITTEE ON IRRIGATION**
POST OFFICE BOX 15326
DENVER, CO 80215
General Environment: Limnologic

HYDRAULIC INSTITUTE
OSTER VOLDGAGE 10, DK-1350
COPENHAGEN K, DENMARK

Director, Torben Sorenson
General Environment: Oceanographic
Staff Size: 10 - 49

**INTERNATIONAL HYDROLOGY
DECADE COMMISSION**
2101 CONSTITUTION AVENUE, NW
WASHINGTON, DC 20418
General Environment: Terrestrial

**LAKE COCHITUATE WATERSHED
ASSOCIATION, INCORPORATED**
1143 WORCESTER STREET
NATICK, MA 01760
President, Paul Alphen
General Environment: Limnologic

LAKE HARRIS ASSOCIATION
9 SHORE DRIVE
BLACKSTONE, MA 01504
Director, Robert Heroux

**LEAGUE OF WOMEN VOTERS OF
UNITED STATES**
1730 M STREET, NW
WASHINGTON, DC 20036
President, Mrs Bruce B Benton
Specific Interests: Prairie and Temperate
Forest

POTOMAC BASIN CENTER
1250 CONNECTICUT AVENUE, NW
WASHINGTON, DC 20036
Executive Director, Robert T Dennis
Specific Interests: Prairie and Temperate
Forest

**WATER CONDITIONING
ASSOCIATION INTERNATIONAL**
325 WEST WESLEY STREET
WHEATON, IL 60188

WATER CONGRESS OF COLORADO
1200 LINCOLN STREET, SUITE 530
DENVER, CO 80203
Executive Director, Gordon H Scheer
Specific Interests: Prairie and Temperate
Forest

**WATER RESOURCES ASSOCIATION
OF DELAWARE RIVER BASIN**
21 SOUTH 12TH STREET
PHILADELPHIA, PA 19107
President, Robert H Young
Specific Interests: Prairie and Temperate
Forest

**WORKS CONFERENCE, NORTH
DAKOTA WATER AND
POLLUTION CONTROL**
STATION CAPITOL BUILDING
BISMARCK, ND 58501
General Environment: Limnologic
Staff Size: 5 - 9

Unclassified

**PLANNING AND INTERAGENCY
    PROGRAMS DIVISION**
WATER QUALITY OFFICE,
    ENVIRONMENTAL PROTECTION
    AGENCY
WASHINGTON, DC 20460
General Environment: Oceanographic

WATER RESOURCES INSTITUTE
SHAW UNIVERSITY, 124 RIDDICK
    BUILDING
RALEIGH, NC 27607
General Environment: Limnologic

**WATER RESOURCES RESEARCH
    INSTITUTE, UNIVERSITY OF
    WYOMING**
BOX 3038, UNIVERSITY STATION
LARAMIE, WY 82070
General Environment: Terrestrial
Staff Size: 10 - 49

Geology

GENERAL

Educational Institute

ARCTIC AND ALPINE RESEARCH INSTITUTE
HALE SCIENCES BLDG,
UNIVERSITY OF COLORADO
BOULDER, CO 80304
Director, Dr John W Marr
General Environment: Terrestrial
Specific Interests: Mountainous

ATMOSPHERIC SCIENCES DEPARTMENT
HEBREW UNIVERSITY OF JERUSALEM
JERUSALEM, ISRAEL
Director, Professor J Neumann
General Environment: Atmospheric

ATMOSPHERIC SCIENCES RESOURCES CENTER
STATE UNIVERSITY NEW YORK-ALBANY/SAROTOGA
SCOTIA, NY 12302
Director, Vincent Schaeffer
General Environment: Atmospheric

BERNARD PRICE INSTITUTE, WITWATERSRAND UNIVERSITY
TRANSVAAL
JOHANNESBURG, REPUBLIC OF SOUTH AFRICA
General Environment: Oceanographic

CONSERVATION AND NATURAL RESOURCES DIVISION
NORTHEASTERN UNIVERSITY, DEPARTMENT OF EARTH SCIENCES
BOSTON, MA 02115
Specific Interests: Prairie and Temperate Forest

ENVIRONMENTAL SCIENCE PROGRAM
COLLEGE OF WOOSTER
WOOSTER, OH 44691
General Environment: Terrestrial
Staff Size: 1 - 4

GEOCHEMICAL RESEARCH LABORATORY, HUNG ACADEMY OF SCIENCE
MUZEUM KORUT 4
BUDAPEST 8, HUNGARY
Director, Elemer Szadeczky-Kardoss
Specific Interests: Prairie and Temperate Forest

GEOCHRONOLOGY DEPARTMENT, EARTH SCIENCES SCHOOL
UNIVERSITY OF ARIZONA
TUCSON, AZ 85721
Specific Interests: Prairie and Temperate Forest

GEODESY AND GEOPHYSICS DEPARTMENT
MADINGLEY RISE
CAMBRIDGE, ENGLAND
Specific Interests: Prairie and Temperate Forest
Staff Size: 10 - 49

GEOGRAPHY DEPARTMENT, PURKYNE UNIVERSITY
BRNO 16
NAHORNT 14, CZECHOSLOVAKIA
Specific Interests: Prairie and Temperate Forest

GEOLOGICAL INSTITUTE
ACADEMY OF SCIENCES
MOSCOW, UNION OF SOVIET SOCIALIST REPUBLICS
Director, Aleksandr Leonidovich Yanshin
Specific Interests: Polar (cold)

GEOLOGICAL SURVEY OF SOUTH DAKOTA
SCIENCES CENTER, UNIVERSITY OF SOUTH DAKOTA
VERMILLION, SD 57069

GEOLOGICAL SURVEY OF VERMONT
UNIVERSITY OF VERMONT
BURLINGTON, VT 05401
General Environment: Terrestrial
Staff Size: 1 - 4

GEOLOGISCH-PALAONTOLOGISCHES INSTITUTION
DER TECHNOLOGY HOCHSCHULE DARMST
61 DARMSTADT, WEST GERMANY
Director, Gerhard Solle
Specific Interests: Prairie and Temperate Forest

GEOLOGY AND GEOGRAPHY DEPARTMENT, ACADEMY OF SCIENCES
LENIN PROSPEKT, 14
MOSCOW, UNION OF SOVIET SOCIALIST REPUBLICS
Specific Interests: Polar (cold)

GEOLOGY AND GEOPHYSICS INSTITUTE
SIBERIAN BRANCH, SCIENCE ACADEMY
MOSCOW, UNION OF SOVIET SOCIALIST REPUBLICS
Director, Andrei Alekseevich Trofimuk
Specific Interests: Polar (cold)

GEOLOGY AND PALEONTOLOGY INSTITUTE
TOHOKU UNIVERSITY
SENDAI, JAPAN
Director, Dr Kiyoshi Asano
Staff Size: 10 - 49

GEOLOGY DEPARTMENT
UNIVERSITY OF LEIDEN
LEIDEN, NETHERLANDS

GEOLOGY DEPARTMENT
CAIRO UNIVERSITY
CAIRO, UNITED ARAB REPUBLIC
Director, Dr Mohamed Taha El Ashry
General Environment: Oceanographic

GEOLOGY DEPARTMENT
UNIVERSITY OF STOCKHOLM
STOCKHOLM, SWEDEN
Director, Ivar Hessland
Specific Interests: Polar (cold)

GEOLOGY DEPARTMENT
UNIVERSITY OF PAVIA
ROME, ITALY
Director, Alfredo Boni
General Environment: Terrestrial
Specific Interests: Mountainous

GEOLOGY DEPARTMENT
UNIVERSITY OF MALAYA
KUALA LUMPUR, MALAYSIA
Specific Interests: Tropical (hot)

GEOLOGY DEPARTMENT
UNIVERSITY OF NEUCHATEL
BERN, SWITZERLAND
Director, Eugene Wegmann
Specific Interests: Mountainous

GEOLOGY DEPARTMENT
STATE JARACZA 3 M 4
KRAKOW, POLAND
Director, Andrzej Bolewski
Specific Interests: Prairie and Temperate Forest

GEOLOGY DEPARTMENT
SAN JOSE STATE COLLEGE
SAN JOSE, CA 95114

GEOLOGY DEPARTMENT
UNIVERSITY OF ROME
ROME, ITALY
Director, Bruno Accordi
General Environment: Terrestrial

GEOLOGY DEPARTMENT
UNIVERSITY OF CALIFORNIA
LOS ANGELES, CA 90001

GEOLOGY DEPARTMENT
UNIVERSITY OF WEST INDIES
KINGSTON, JAMAICA
Director, M E Robinson

GEOLOGY DEPARTMENT
UNIVERSITY OF FLORENCE
FLORENCE, ITALY
Director, Giovanni Merla

GEOLOGY DEPARTMENT
CARLI CAPLINA 31
BELGRADE, YUGOSLAVIA
Director, Kosta Petkovic
Specific Interests: Prairie and Temperate
Forest

GEOLOGY DEPARTMENT
HEBREW UNIVERSITY OF
JERUSALEM
JERUSALEM, ISRAEL
Director, Professor Y Ben-Tor
General Environment: Oceanographic

GEOLOGY DEPARTMENT,
UNIVERSITY GREIFSWALD
HAINSTRASSE 10
GREIFSWALD-ELDENA, EAST
GERMANY
Professor, Heinz Janert
General Environment: Terrestrial
Specific Interests: Prairie and Temperate
Forest

GEOLOGY DEPARTMENT,
UNIVERSITY OF DURHAM
SOUTH ROAD
DURHAM, ENGLAND
Director, George M Brown
Specific Interests: Prairie and Temperate
Forest

GEOLOGY INSTITUTE
UNIVERSITY OF PISA
VS MARIA 53, PISA, ITALY
Director, Livio Trevisan
General Environment: Terrestrial

GEOLOGY INSTITUTE
UNIVERSITY OF WURZBURG
WURZBURG, WEST GERMANY
Director, Georg W R Knetsch
Specific Interests: Prairie and Temperate
Forest

GEOLOGY INSTITUTE, ACADEMY
OF SCIENCE
PYZHEVSKII 7
MOSCOW, UNION OF SOVIET
SOCIALIST REPUBLICS
Specific Interests: Polar (cold)

GEOLOGY INSTITUTE, UNIVERSITY
OF BONN
NUSSALLEE 8
53 BONN, WEST GERMANY
Director, Roland Brinkman
Specific Interests: Prairie and Temperate
Forest

GEOLOGY INSTITUTE, UNIVERSITY
OF MILAN
PIAZZALE GORINI 15
MILAN, ITALY
Director, Ardito Desio

GEOLOGY INSTITUTION
UNIVERSITY OF BERGEN
BERGEN, NORWAY
Director, Niels-Henr Kolderup
Specific Interests: Polar (cold)

GEOLOGY-PALEONTOLOGY
INSTITUTE, UNIVERSITY MAINZ
MAINZ-GONSENHEIM
AN DER PRALL 1, WEST GERMANY
Director, Horst Falke
Specific Interests: Prairie and Temperate
Forest

GEOPHYSICAL COMMISSION,
ACADEMY OF SCIENCES
MOLODEZHNAYA, 3
MOSCOW, B-296, UNION OF SOVIET
SOCIALIST REPUBLICS
Director, Vladimir V Belousov
Specific Interests: Polar (cold)

GEOPHYSICAL INSTITUTE
UNIVERSITY OF ALASKA
COLLEGE, AK 72476
Specific Interests: Polar (cold)

GEOPHYSICAL INSTITUTE
UNIVERSITY OF TEHRAN
TEHRAN, IRAN
Director, Dr H Keshi-Afshar

GEOPHYSICAL SCIENCES
DEPARTMENT
5734 SOUTH ELLIS AVENUE
CHICAGO, IL 60637
Professor, David Atlas
General Environment: Atmospheric
Staff Size: 10 - 49

GEOPHYSICS INSTITUTE
GIVENBECKERS WEG 61
44 MUNSTER/WESTF, WEST
GERMANY
Specific Interests: Prairie and Temperate
Forest

GEOPHYSICS LABORATORY
UNIVERSITY OF TORONTO
TORONTO 5, ONTARIO, CANADA

HYDROLOGY DEPARTMENT,
KATEDRA HYDROMELIORACII,
STAVEBNAFAK
VYSOKA SKOLA TECHNICKA
BRATISLAVA, CZECHOSLOVAKIA
Specific Interests: Prairie and Temperate
Forest

LAMONT GEOLOGICAL
OBSERVATORY, COLUMBIA
UNIVERSITY
TORREY CLIFF
PALISADES, NY 10964
Director, Dr Maurice Ewing
General Environment: Oceanographic
Staff Size: 500 - 999

LOW TEMPERATURE SCIENCES
INSTITUTE
HOKKAIDO UNIVERSITY
SAPPORO, JAPAN
Director, Dr Jungo Yosida
Specific Interests: Prairie and Temperate
Forest

MARINE GEOLOGY
SAN JOSE STATE COLLEGE
SAN JOSE, CA 95114
General Environment: Oceanographic

MARINE SCIENCE DEPARTMENT
STATE UNIVERSITY OF NEW YORK
BINGHAMTON, NY 13904
General Environment: Terrestrial

MARINE SCIENCES INSTITUTE
UNIVERSITY OF ALASKA
COLLEGE, AK 72476
General Environment: Oceanographic
Specific Interests: Polar (cold)
Staff Size: 50 - 99

MECRESKUNDE INSTITUTE,
UNIVERSITY OF HAMBURG
HEIMHUDER STR 71
2 HAMBURG 13, WEST GERMANY
Director, Walter Hansen
General Environment: Oceanographic
Specific Interests: Prairie and Temperate
Forest

MECRESKUNDE, UNIVERSITY OF
KIEL
HOHENBERGSTR 2
KIEL, WEST GERMANY
Director, Gunter Dietrich
General Environment: Oceanographic
Specific Interests: Prairie and Temperate
Forest

METEOROLOGICAL OBSERVATION
AT BLUE HILLS
HARVARD UNIVERSITY
MILTON, MA 02186

Director, Dr Richard M Goody
General Environment: Terrestrial

METEOROLOGY
CALIFORNIA STATE UNIVERSITY,
   SAN JOSE
SAN JOSE, CA 95192
General Environment: Atmospheric
Specific Interests: Urban
Staff Size: 5 - 9

**MINERAL INSTITUTION,
   UNIVERSITY WURZBURG**
PLEICHERTORSTR 34
WURZBURG, WEST GERMANY
Director, Siegfried Matthes
Specific Interests: Prairie and Temperate
   Forest

MINERAL RESOURCES INSTITUTE
MICHIGAN TECHNICAL
   UNIVERSITY
HOUGHTON, MI 49931
General Environment: Terrestrial
Staff Size: 10 - 49

**MINES AND TECHNOLOGY
   SCHOOL OF SOUTH DAKOTA**
INSTITUTION OF ATMOSPHERIC
   SCIENCES
RAPID CITY, SD 57701
General Environment: Atmospheric
Specific Interests: Prairie and Temperate
   Forest

**MINES BUREAU OF ARIZONA,
   COLLEGE OF MINES**
UNIVERSITY OF ARIZONA
TUCSON, AZ 85721

NATURE CONSERVANCY
OAK COTTAGE, HYDE END LANE
BRIMPTON, NR READING,
   ENGLAND
Director, George P Black
Specific Interests: Prairie and Temperate
   Forest

OCEANOGRAPHIQUE INSTITUT
195, RUE ST-JACQUES
PARIS-5E, FRANCE
General Environment: Oceanographic
Specific Interests: Prairie and Temperate
   Forest

**OCEANOGRAPHY INSTITUTE,
   ACADEMY OF SCIENCES**
ULITSA BAKHRUSHINA, 8
MOSCOW, UNION OF SOVIET
   SOCIALIST REPUBLICS
Director, Vyeniamin Grigoryevich
   Bogorov
General Environment: Oceanographic
Specific Interests: Polar (cold)

**OCEANOGRAPHY INSTITUTE,
   MARINE EFFLUENTS UNIT**

PRIVATE BAG, RONDEBOSCH
CAPE TOWN, REPUBLIC OF SOUTH
   AFRICA
General Environment: Oceanographic

OIL INSTITUTE
ACADEMY OF SCIENCES
MOSCOW, UNION OF SOVIET
   SOCIALIST REPUBLICS
Specific Interests: Polar (cold)

**SCOTT POLAR RESEARCH
   INSTITUTION**
UNIVERSITY OF CAMBRIDGE
CAMBRIDGE, ENGLAND
Specific Interests: Polar (cold)

SEISMOLOGY INSTITUTE
NATIONAL OBSERVATORY OF
   ATHENS
ATHENS, GREECE
Director, George Galanpoulos

UNIVERSITY OF PRAGUE
VOLSINACH 38
PRAGUE, CZECHOSLOVAKIA
Professor, Frantisek Jermar

**WATER RESOURCES RESEARCH
   INSTITUTE, UNIVERSITY OF
   OREGON**
114 COVELL HALL
CORVALLIS, OR 97331
General Environment: Terrestrial

Field Station/Laboratory

**FOREST AND RANGE STATION,
   PACIFIC SOUTHWEST**
EXPERIMENTAL STATION
BERKELEY, CA 94703
General Environment: Terrestrial
Specific Interests: Prairie and Temperate
   Forest

**FOREST RESOURCES
   LABORATORY, SOUTHERN
   RESEARCH STATION**
MAPLE, ONTARIO, CANADA
General Environment: Terrestrial
Specific Interests: Prairie and Temperate
   Forest

**GEOLOGICAL AND MINERAL
   CONSERVATION MINISTRY**
BIRZHEVOI PROYEZD, 6
LENINGRAD, V-164, UNION OF
   SOVIET SOCIALIST REPUBLICS
Specific Interests: Polar (cold)

LIMNOLOGY LABORATORY
NABEREZHNAYA MAKAROVA 2
LENINGRAD, UNION OF SOVIET
   SOCIALIST REPUBLICS

Director, Stanislav Kalesnik
General Environment: Limnologic
Specific Interests: Polar (cold)

MT WASHINGTON OBSERVATORY
GORHAM, NH 03581
General Environment: Atmospheric

SUEZ BRANCH MARINE STATION
SUEZ, UNITED ARAB REPUBLIC
Director, Dr Mohammed Hassan
General Environment: Oceanographic
Staff Size: 1 - 4

Government — Federal

**ATOMIC ENERGY COMMISSION,
   ALBUQUERQUE OPERATIONS**
POST OFFICE BOX 5400
ALBUQUERQUE, NM 87115
General Environment: Atmospheric

**ATOMIC ENERGY COMMISSION,
   GRAND JUNCTION OFFICE**
POST OFFICE BOX 2567
GRAND JUNCTION, CO 81501
General Environment: Atmospheric

**ATOMIC ENERGY COMMISSION,
   IDAHO OPERATIONS OFFICE**
POST OFFICE BOX 2108
IDAHO FALLS, ID 83401
General Environment: Atmospheric

**ATOMIC ENERGY COMMISSION,
   NEW YORK OPERATIONS**
376 HUDSON STREET
NEW YORK, NY 10014
General Environment: Atmospheric

**ATOMIC ENERGY COMMISSION,
   OAK RIDGE OPERATIONS**
POST OFFICE BOX E
OAK RIDGE, TN 37830
General Environment: Atmospheric

**ATOMIC ENERGY COMMISSION,
   PITTSBURG NAVAL REACTORS
   OFFICE**
POST OFFICE BOX 109
WEST MIFFLIN, PA 15122
General Environment: Atmospheric

**ATOMIC ENERGY COMMISSION,
   RICHLAND OPERATIONS**
POST OFFICE BOX 550
RICHLAND, WA 99352
General Environment: Atmospheric

**ATOMIC ENERGY COMMISSION,
   SAN FRANCISCO OPERATIONS**
2111 BANCROFT WAY
BERKELEY, CA 94704
General Environment: Atmospheric

ATOMIC ENERGY COMMISSION, SAVANNAH RIVER OPERATIONS
POST OFFICE BOX A
AIKEN, SC 29801
General Environment: Atmospheric

ATOMIC ENERGY COMMISSION, SCHENECTADY NAVAL REACTORS OFFICE
POST OFFICE BOX 1069
SCHENECTADY, NY 12301
General Environment: Atmospheric

CHICAGO OPERATIONS OFFICE
9800 SOUTH CASS AVENUE
ARGONNE, IL 60439
General Environment: Atmospheric

COASTAL STUDIES DIVISION
MINISTRY OF TRANSPORTATION AND COMMUNICATION
ASHWOOD HARBOR, ISRAEL
Director, D Divon
General Environment: Oceanographic
Staff Size: 10 - 49

DEFENSE MINISTRY, INDUSTRIAL NAVY, NAVAL PHYSICS LABORATORY
NAVAL BASE
COCHIN, INDIA
Director, Dr D Srinivasa
General Environment: Oceanographic
Specific Interests: Tropical (hot)

DIVISION OF STATE AND LICENSEE RELATIONS
UNITED STATES ATOMIC ENERGY COMMISSION
WASHINGTON, DC 20545
General Environment: Atmospheric

ENERGY AND MINERAL RESOURCES MINISTRY
LAGOS, NIGERIA
Director, O Ukelonu

ENVIRONMENTAL STUDIES
468 HUNTER BUILDING, OCONNER STREET
OTTAWA, ONTARIO, CANADA
General Environment: Oceanographic

FINANCE AND OIL MINISTRY
DEPARTMENT OF OIL AFFAIRS
KUWAIT
Director, Mahmoud Adsani
General Environment: Oceanographic

GEOLOGICAL SURVEY
MINISTRY OF INTERNATIONAL TRADE AND INDUSTRY
TOKYO, JAPAN
Director, Dr Isamu Kobayashi
General Environment: Terrestrial
Staff Size: 100 - 499

GEOLOGICAL SURVEY OF UNITED STATES
MENLO PARK, CA 94025
Specific Interests: Prairie and Temperate Forest

GEOLOGICAL SURVEY OF UNITED STATES, DEPARTMENT OF INTERIOR
18TH AND F STREETS
WASHINGTON, DC 20006
General Environment: Terrestrial

GLACIOLOGY PANEL, NATIONAL ACADEMY OF SCIENCES
2101 CONSTITUTION AVENUE, NW
WASHINGTON, DC 20418
General Environment: Terrestrial

HYDROGRAPHIC SERVICE
MINISTRY OF DEFENSE, DEPARTMENT OF NAVY
KARACHI, PAKISTAN
General Environment: Oceanographic

HYDROGRAPHIC SERVICE, NAVAL OPERATIONS
MONTES DE OCA 2124
BUENOS AIRES, ARGENTINA
Director, E E Daviou
General Environment: Oceanographic

HYDROLOGY AND METEOROLOGY STATE INSTITUTE
UL, POPLESNAGI
WARSZAWA, POLAND
Director, Julian Lambor
General Environment: Atmospheric
Staff Size: 100 - 499

MARINE AND EARTH SCIENCES LIBRARY
NATIONAL OCEANIC AND ATMOSPHERIC ADMINISTRATION
ROCKVILLE, MD 20852
General Environment: Oceanographic

MARINE OBSERVATORY OF NAGASAKI
NAGASAKI, JAPAN
Director, Dr Kenkichi Fujita
Specific Interests: Prairie and Temperate Forest

METEOROLOGICAL OBSERVATION AGENCY
TOKYO, JAPAN
Director, Dr Yoshiji Shibata
General Environment: Atmospheric
Specific Interests: Prairie and Temperate Forest

METEOROLOGICAL RESEARCH INSTITUTE
TOKYO, JAPAN
Director, Dr Hidetoshi Arakawa
Specific Interests: Prairie and Temperate Forest

METEOROLOGICAL SERVICE (NATIONAL)
UNIVERSITY OF SANTO DOMINGO
SANTO DOMINGO, DOMINICAN REPUBLIC
General Environment: Atmospheric

METEOROLOGY WORLD DATA CENTER
NATIONAL WEATHER RECORDS CENTER
ASHVILLE, NC 28801
General Environment: Atmospheric

MINERAL INFORMATION OFFICE
18TH AND C STREETS, NW
WASHINGTON, DC 20240
Specific Interests: Prairie and Temperate Forest

MINES MINISTRY
POST OFFICE BOX 486
ADDIS ABABA, ETHIOPIA
Director, Assefa Lemma

OCEAN SURVEYS (NATIONAL)
NATIONAL OCEANIC AND ATMOSPHERIC ADMINISTRATION
ROCKVILLE, MD 20852
General Environment: Limnologic

OIL AND GAS OFFICE
18TH AND C STREETS, NW
WASHINGTON, DC 20240
Specific Interests: Prairie and Temperate Forest

PHYSICAL OCEANOGRAPHY DIVISION
ERNAKULAM, INDIA
Director, Dr V V R Varadachari
General Environment: Oceanographic

POLAR CONTROL SHELF PROJECT
880 WELLINGTON STREET
OTTAWA, ONTARIO, CANADA
General Environment: Oceanographic
Specific Interests: Polar (cold)

STATE HYDROLOGY WORKS
ANKARA, TURKEY
General Environment: Oceanographic

VNIGRI
DVORTSOVAYA NABEREZHNAYA 18
LENINGRAD, UNION OF SOVIET SOCIALIST REPUBLICS
Staff Size: 10 - 49

Government — State or Local

CONSERVATION DEPARTMENT, DIVISION OF GEOLOGY

G-5 STATE OFFICE BUILDING
NASHVILLE, TN 37219

**GEOLOGICAL SURVEY OF
    DELAWARE**
UNIVERSITY OF DELAWARE
NEWARK, DE 19711
Staff Size: 5 - 9

GEOLOGICAL SURVEY OF ILLINOIS
NATURAL RESOURCES BUILDING
URBANA, IL 61804
General Environment: Terrestrial
Staff Size: 100 - 499

GEOLOGICAL SURVEY OF KANSAS
KANSAS UNIVERSITY
LAWRENCE, KS 66044
General Environment: Terrestrial
Staff Size: 50 - 99

**GEOLOGICAL SURVEY OF
    MARYLAND, JOHNS HOPKINS
    UNIVERSITY**
214 LATROBE HALL
BALTIMORE, MD 21218
Staff Size: 10 - 49

**GEOLOGICAL SURVEY OF NORTH
    IRELAND**
20 COLLEGE GROUNDS
BELFAST BT9 6BS, IRELAND
Principal Geologist, Peter I Manning
General Environment: Terrestrial
Specific Interests: Prairie and Temperate
    Forest
Staff Size: 5 - 9

**GEOLOGICAL SURVEY OF
    OKLAHOMA**
830 VAN VLEET OVAL, ROOM 163
NORMAN, OK 73069
General Environment: Terrestrial
Staff Size: 10 - 49

**GEOLOGY BUREAU, DIVISION OF
    INTERIOR RESOURCES**
DEPARTMENT OF NATURAL
    RESOURCES
TALLAHASSE, FL 32302
Staff Size: 10 - 49

**METEOROLOGY DIVISION,
    NATIONAL AIR POLLUTION
    ADMINISTRATION**
PUBLIC HEALTH SERVICE
CINCINNATI, OH 45227
General Environment: Atmospheric

**MINERAL RESOURCES DIVISION,
    VIRGINIA DEPARTMENT OF
    CONSERVATION**
POST OFFICE BOX 3667
    UNIVERSITY STATION
CHARLOTTESVILLE, VA 22903
State Geologist, Dr James L Calver
General Environment: Terrestrial
Staff Size: 10 - 49

**SOIL CONSERVATION SOCIETY OF
    AMERICA**
STORRS, CT 06268
Secretary, E Offerman

**TOPOGRAPHY BUREAU,
    GEOLOGICAL SURVEY**
PENNSYLVANIA DEPARTMENT OF
    ENVIRONMENTAL RESOURCES
HARRISBURG, PA 17120
General Environment: Limnologic

Industrial/Commercial

**BRITISH PETROLEUM
    COORDINATOR LIMITED**
BRITANNIC HOUSE, MOOR LANE
LONDON EC2, ENGLAND
Manager, Percy E Kent
General Environment: Terrestrial
Specific Interests: Prairie and Temperate
    Forest
Staff Size: 100 - 499

**CEYLON MINERAL SANDS
    CORPORATION**
2211 THURSTAN ROAD
COLOMBO 7, CEYLON
Director, Sam S H Silvia

**CIVIL AND MARINE ENGINEERING
    CORPORATION, LIMITED**
65 HA-AZMAUT ROAD
HAIFA, ISRAEL
General Environment: Oceanographic

COPESA
GUAYAQUIL, ECUADOR
Director, Xavier Coronel
General Environment: Oceanographic

CORDINASA
GUAYAQUIL, ECUADOR
Director, Enrique Baquerizo
General Environment: Oceanographic

DEL MONTE DE ECUADOR
MANTA, ECUADOR
Director, Dr Juan Leirbonio
General Environment: Oceanographic

EMPACADORA NACIONAL (ENACA)
GUAYAQUIL, ECUADOR
Director, Harry Graham
General Environment: Oceanographic

**ENVIRONMENTAL SCIENCES
    GROUP, CLIMATE INSTRUCTION**
1240 BIRCHWOOD DRIVE
SUNNYVILLE, CA 94086
Manager, Mr Joseph Hicks
General Environment: Atmospheric

GEOMETRICS
914 INDUSTRIAL AVENUE
PALO ALTO, CA 94303
President, Sheldon Breiner
General Environment: Terrestrial
Staff Size: 50 - 99

INEPACA
MANTA, ECUADOR
Director, Augustin Gomez
General Environment: Oceanographic

IPESA
GUAYAQUIL, ECUADOR
Director, Manuel Sotero Da Silva
General Environment: Oceanographic

**IRAQ PETROLEUM CORPORATION,
    LIMITED**
33 CAVENDISH SQUARE
LONDON W1, ENGLAND
Manager, Harold V Dunnington
Specific Interests: Prairie and Temperate
    Forest

METEOROLOGY AND GEOLOGY
2751 SAN CARLOS LANE
COSTA MESA, CA 92626
Consultant, Donald Bradford

PAKISTAN SHELL RAP (FRENCH)
KARACHI, PAKISTAN
General Environment: Oceanographic

PAKISTAN SUN OIL CORPORATION
KARACHI, PAKISTAN
General Environment: Oceanographic

**PETROLEUM RESOURCES AND
    GEOPHYSICS INSTITUTE**
POST OFFICE BOX 120
AZOR, ISRAEL
General Environment: Oceanographic

PRODELMAR
MANTA, ECUADOR
Director, Enrique Baquerizo
General Environment: Oceanographic

SEISMOGRAPH SERVICES LIMITED
POST OFFICE BOX 607
ABA, NIGERIA
Director, M K Jenyon
General Environment: Oceanographic

SHELL OIL CORPORATION
POST OFFICE BOX 1641
KUWAIT
General Environment: Oceanographic

**STEETLEY ORGANIZATION
    RESOURCE DEPARTMENT**
CARLTON ROAD
WORKSOP, NOTTINGHAMSHIRE,
    ENGLAND

General Environment: Terrestrial
Specific Interests: Prairie and Temperate
 Forest

**UNITED GEOPHYSICS
 CORPORATION**
TINUBU SQUARE, POST OFFICE
 BOX 3545
LAGOS, NIGERIA
General Environment: Oceanographic

Professional Organizations

**GEODESY AND GEOPHYSICS
 SOCIETY OF ISRAEL**
54 IBN GVIROL STREET
TEL AVIV, ISRAEL
General Environment: Oceanographic

**UNDERSEA EXPLORATION
 SOCIETY, NATIONAL MARITIME
 MUSEUM**
198 ALENBY STREET
HAIFA, ISRAEL
Director, E Linder
General Environment: Oceanographic

Research Institute

**ASTRONOMICAL SOCIETY, TOKYO
 ASTRONOMICAL OBSERVATORY**
OSAWA
MITAKA CITY, TOKYO, JAPAN
Director, Dr Hideo Hirose
Specific Interests: Prairie and Temperate
 Forest

**BUREAU RECHERCHES
 GEOLOGICAL ET MINIERE**
RT11 UNIVERSITY. POST OFFICE
 BOX 268
NODAKAR-FANN, SENEGAL
General Environment: Terrestrial

ENDOUME MARINE STATION
RUE DE LA BATTERIE DES LIONS
MARSEILLES 7, FRANCE

**ENVIRONMENTAL RESOURCES
 COUNCIL (NATIONAL)**
27-33 CHARING CROSS
LONDON WC2, ENGLAND

**GEODETIC SOCIETY, MINISTRY OF
 CONSTRUCTION**
1900 7-CHOME KAMIMEGURO
MEGURO-KU, TOKYO, JAPAN
Director, Takahiro Hagiwara
Specific Interests: Prairie and Temperate
 Forest

**GEOLOGICAL SCIENCES
 INSTITUTE**
15-17 YOUNG STREET
LONDON W8, ENGLAND
General Environment: Terrestrial
Specific Interests: Prairie and Temperate
 Forest

GEOLOGICAL SCIENCES UNION
MELCHELSE STEENWEG 206
ANTWERP, BELGIUM

GRANT INSTITUTE OF GEOLOGY
WEST MAINS ROAD
EDINBURGH 9, SCOTLAND
General Environment: Terrestrial
Specific Interests: Prairie and Temperate
 Forest

**METEOROLOGY RESEARCH,
 INCORPORATED**
464 WOODBURY ROAD
ALTADENA, CA 91001
Vice President, J Robert Stinson
General Environment: Atmospheric

**MINERAL RESOURCES DIVISION,
 INSTITUTE OF GEOLOGICAL
 SCIENCES**
EXHIBITION ROAD
LONDON SW7, ENGLAND
Director, Arthur J G Notholt
General Environment: Terrestrial
Specific Interests: Prairie and Temperate
 Forest

MINERAL RESOURCES INSTITUTE
MICHIGAN TECHNOLOGY
 UNIVERSITY
HOUGHTON, MI 49931
General Environment: Terrestrial

**MINES, MINING AND GEOLOGY
 DEPARTMENT**
19 HUNTER STREET, SW
ATLANTA, GA 30303
General Environment: Oceanographic

NATURE CONSERVANCY
PENRHOS ROAD
BANGOR, CAERN, ENGLAND
Director, David F Ball
General Environment: Terrestrial
Specific Interests: Mountainous
Staff Size: 5 - 9

**OCEANOGRAPHIC INSTITUTE OF
 NEW ZEALAND**
D S I R BOX 8009
WELLINGTON, NEW ZEALAND
General Environment: Oceanographic
Staff Size: 10 - 49

**SEISMOLOGY AND EARTHQUAKE
 ENGINEERING INSTITUTE**
4-CHOME, HYAKUNIN-CHO
SHINJUKUKU, TOKYO, JAPAN
General Environment: Marsh/Swamp

**VOLCANO SOCIETY, EARTHQUAKE
 RESEARCH INSTITUTE**
TOKYO UNIVERSITY 1 MOTOFUJI-
 CHO
BUNKYO-KU, TOKYO, JAPAN
Director, Dr Hisashi Kuno
General Environment: Terrestrial
Specific Interests: Prairie and Temperate
 Forest

VOLTA BASIN RESEARCH PROJECT
LEGON, GHANA
General Environment: Oceanographic

GEOCHEMISTRY

Educational Institute

GEOCHEMISTRY DEPARTMENT
PRIVATE BAG, RONDEBOSCH
CAPE TOWN, REPUBLIC OF SOUTH
 AFRICA
Professor, L H Ahrens
General Environment: Oceanographic

**GEOLOGY AND MINERAL
 DEPARTMENT**
OXFORD UNIVERSITY, PARKS ROAD
OXFORD, ENGLAND
Director, Stephan Moorbath
General Environment: Terrestrial
Specific Interests: Prairie and Temperate
 Forest

**MINERAL INSTITUTION,
 UNIVERSITY OF SAARLANDES**
66 SAARBRUCKEN 15
BONN, WEST GERMANY
Director, F Rost
Specific Interests: Prairie and Temperate
 Forest

**MINERAL-PETROLEUM INSTITUTE,
 UNIVERSITY OF COLOGNE**
ZULPICHER STRASSE 47
COLOGNE, WEST GERMANY
Director, Karl Jasmund
Specific Interests: Prairie and Temperate
 Forest

**UNIVERSITY OF CALIFORNIA, SAN
 DIEGO**
LA JOLLA, CA 92037
Director, Dr Edward D Goldberg
General Environment: Oceanographic
Staff Size: 10 - 49

Government — Federal

FISHERIES SECTION
MINISTRY OF INDUSTRY AND

COMMERCE
MOGADISCIO, SOMALIA
General Environment: Oceanographic

Industrial/Commercial

NATIONAL PETROLEUM COUNCIL
BRASILIA, BRAZIL
General Environment: Oceanographic

Research Institute

**EARTH CHEMISTRY RESEARCH
ASSOCIATION, EARTH SCIENCE
DEPARTMENT**
NAGOYA UNIVERSITY FURO-CHO
CHIKUSA-KU, NAGOYA, AICHI,
JAPAN
General Environment: Terrestrial
Specific Interests: Prairie and Temperate
  Forest

GEOPHYSICS

Educational Institute

**FLUID DYNAMICS AND DIFFUSION
LABORATORY**
COLORADO STATE UNIVERSITY
FORT COLLINS, CO 80521
Director, Dr J E Cermak
General Environment: Atmospheric
Staff Size: 10 - 49

GEOLOGICAL INSTITUTE
BERGEN, NORWAY
Director, C L Godske
General Environment: Oceanographic

**GEOLOGY DEPARTMENT,
MASSACHUSETTS INSTITUTE OF
TECHNOLOGY**
77 MASSACHUSETTS AVENUE
CAMBRIDGE, MA 02139
General Environment: Oceanographic

GEOPHYSICAL INSTITUTE
UNIVERSITY OF ALASKA
COLLEGE, AK 99701
General Environment: Terrestrial

GEOPHYSICAL INSTITUTE
KYOTO UNIVERSITY
KYOTO, JAPAN
Director, Dr Shoitiro Hayami
Specific Interests: Prairie and Temperate
  Forest

**GEOPHYSICS AND PLANNING
PHYSICS INSTITUTE**
8602 LA JOLLA SHORES DRIVE
LA JOLLA, CA 92037
General Environment: Oceanographic
Staff Size: 10 - 49

GEOPHYSICS INSTITUTE
NATIONAL CENTRAL UNIVERSITY
MIAOLI, TAIWAN
General Environment: Terrestrial
Staff Size: 10 - 49

GEOPHYSICS INSTITUTE
UNIVERSITY OF HAWAII
HONOLULU, HI 96822

Foundation

GEOFYZIKALNI USTAV CSAV
SPORILOV, BOCNI II, NO 1401
PRAHA 4, CZECHOSLOVAKIA
General Environment: Terrestrial

ZAKLAND GEOFIZYKI
UL PASTEURA, WARSZAWA 22,
POLAND
General Environment: Terrestrial
Staff Size: 5 - 9

Government — Federal

**CAMBRIDGE RESOURCES
LABORATORY**
L.G. HANSCOM FIELD
BEDFORD, MA 01731

**GEOPHYSICS DIVISION, SCIENCE
AND INDUSTRIAL RESEARCH
DEPARTMENT**
156 THE TERRACE
WELLINGTON, NEW ZEALAND
Director, Dr T Hatherton
Specific Interests: Prairie and Temperate
  Forest

**GEOPHYSICS NATIONAL
INSTITUTE**
MADRID, SPAIN

Industrial/Commercial

**HUNTING GEOLOGY AND
GEOPHYSICS**
6 ELSTREE WAY
BOREHAM WOOD,
  HERTFORDSHIRE, ENGLAND

Manager, Derek B Morris
General Environment: Terrestrial
Specific Interests: Prairie and Temperate
  Forest

Research Institute

**SEISMOLOGICAL SOCIETY
GEOPHYSICS DEPARTMENT**
UNIVERSITY TOKYO 2-YAYOI-CHO
BUNKYO-KU, TOKYO, JAPAN
Director, Hitoshi Takeuchi
Specific Interests: Prairie and Temperate
  Forest

**SOUTHWEST CENTER FOR
ADVANCED STUDY**
BOX 8478
DALLAS, TX 75205
General Environment: Oceanographic
Staff Size: 100 - 499

**TERRESTRIAL ELECTRO-
MAGNETISM SOCIETY**
TOKYO UNIVERSITY 3 YAYOI-CHO
BUNKYO-KU, TOKYO, JAPAN
Director, Dr Yoshio Kato
General Environment: Terrestrial
Specific Interests: Prairie and Temperate
  Forest

Unclassified

GEOPHYSICS INSTITUTE
UNIVERSITY OF OSLO
OSLO, NORWAY
General Environment: Oceanographic

PALEONTOLOGY

Educational Institute

**GEOLOGICAL-PALEONTOLOGICAL
INSTITUTE AND MUSEUM**
UNIVERSITY HALLE/SAALE
HALLE, EAST GERMANY
Director, Horst W Matthes
Specific Interests: Prairie and Temperate
  Forest

**GEOLOGY DEPARTMENT,
PALEONTOLOGY INSTITUTE**
AM ST GEORGSFELD 43
GREIFSWALD, EAST GERMANY
Director, Hans Wehrli
Specific Interests: Prairie and Temperate
  Forest

GEOLOGY DEPARTMENT,
UNIVERSITY OF MUNICH
RICHARD WAGNER STRASSE 10-11
MUNICH 2, WEST GERMANY

Director, Richard Dehm
Specific Interests: Prairie and Temperate
Forest

MANCHESTER MUSEUM,
UNIVERSITY OF MANCHESTER
OXFORD ROAD
MANCHESTER, DORSET, ENGLAND

Director, David E Owen
General Environment: Limnologic
Specific Interests: Prairie and Temperate
Forest

PALEONTOLOGY DEPARTMENT,
UNIVERSITY OF BONN
NUSSALLEE 8
53 BONN, WEST GERMANY

Director, Heinrich Karl Erben
Specific Interests: Prairie and Temperate
Forest

PALEONTOLOGY INSTITUTE
ACADEMY OF SCIENCES
MOSCOW, UNION OF SOVIET
SOCIALIST REPUBLICS

Director, Aleksandr Grigorevich Vologdin
Specific Interests: Polar (cold)

PALEONTOLOGY INSTITUTION
UNIVERSITY OF VIENNA
VIENNA, AUSTRIA

Director, Othmar Kuehn
Specific Interests: Prairie and Temperate
Forest

Government — Federal

MINERAL INFORMATION OFFICE
18TH AND C STREETS, NW
WASHINGTON, DC 20240

General Environment: Terrestrial

MINERAL RESOURCE
DEVELOPMENT
18TH AND C STREETS, NW
WASHINGTON, DC 20240

General Environment: Terrestrial

Research Institute

PALEONTOLOGY DEPARTMENT,
BRITISH MUSEUM
CROMWELL ROAD
LONDON SW7, ENGLAND

Director, Kathlee I M Chesters
General Environment: Terrestrial
Specific Interests: Prairie and Temperate
Forest

Physics

GENERAL

Educational Institute

APPLIED GEOPHYSICS INSTITUTE
GLEBOVSKAYA ULITSA, 20-B
MOSCOW, UNION OF SOVIET
SOCIALIST REPUBLICS
Director, Yevgenii K Federov
Specific Interests: Polar (cold)

**APPLIED PHYSICS LABORATORY,
UNIVERSITY OF WASHINGTON**
1013 NE 40TH STREET
SEATTLE, WA 98105
General Environment: Oceanographic

ASTROPHYSICS LABORATORY
BOULDER, CO 80304
General Environment: Atmospheric

ATMOSPHERIC PHYSICS INSTITUTE
UNIVERSITY OF ARIZONA
TUCSON, AZ 85721
Director, Dr R Kassander
General Environment: Atmospheric
Specific Interests: Desert
Staff Size: 10 - 49

ATMOSPHERIC PHYSICS INSTITUTE
SASKATCHEWAN UNIVERSITY
SASKATOON, SASKATCHEWAN,
CANADA
Director, Dr B W Currie
General Environment: Atmospheric

**ATMOSPHERIC SCIENCE
DEPARTMENT**
STATE UNIVERSITY OF NEW YORK
ALBANY, NY 12224
General Environment: Atmospheric

**ENVIRONMENTAL RADIATION,
GRADUATE SCHOOL OF PUBLIC
HEALTH**
UNIVERSITY OF PITTSBURGH
PITTSBURGH, PA 15213

ENVIRONMENTAL STUDIES
UNIVERSITY OF CALIFORNIA
LOS ANGELES, CA 90024
General Environment: Atmospheric
Staff Size: 5 - 9

**ENVIRONMENTAL STUDIES,
UNIVERSITY OF SOUTH
CAROLINA**
1225 BELT LINE BOULEVARD
COLUMBIA, SC 29205

**EXPERIMENTAL PHYSICS
DEPARTMENT**
MOSCOW PHYSICO-TECHNOLOGY
INSTITUTION
MOSCOW, UNION OF SOVIET
SOCIALIST REPUBLICS
Director, Nikolai Eugenevich
Alekseevskii
Specific Interests: Polar (cold)

**GEOFIZICHESKI INSTUTUT PRI
BAN**
SOFIA
MOSKOUSKA 6, BULGARIA
Director, Professor Lyubomir Krustanov
General Environment: Atmospheric

**GEOPHYSICAL DEPARTMENT,
UNIVERSITY OF BUDAPEST**
L EOTVOS UNIVERSITY
BUDAPEST, HUNGARY
Director, L Egyed

GEOPHYSICAL INSTITUTE
UNIVERSITY OF CHICAGO
CHICAGO, IL 60600
General Environment: Atmospheric
Staff Size: 1 - 4

GEOPHYSICS DIVISION
KON NED MET INSTITUTION
DE BIUT, NETHERLANDS
Director, J Veldkamp
Specific Interests: Prairie and Temperate
Forest

**HIGH ALTITUDE OBSERVATORY
LIBRARY**
PO BOX 1558
BOULDER, CO 80301
General Environment: Atmospheric

**MECHANICS AND GEOPHYSICS,
DEPARTMENT OF ENGINEERING**
UNIVERSITY OF ICELAND
REYKJAVIK, ICELAND
Specific Interests: Polar (cold)

**METEOROLOGY AND
OCEANOGRAPHY DEPARTMENT,
FREE UNIVERSITY**
DE BOELELAAN
AMSTERDAM, NETHERLANDS
General Environment: Atmospheric
Staff Size: 1 - 4

METEOROLOGY DEPARTMENT
SAN JOSE STATE COLLEGE
SAN JOSE, CA 95114
General Environment: Atmospheric
Staff Size: 10 - 49

**PHYSICAL OCEANOGRAPHY AND
METEOROLOGY DEPARTMENT**
UNIVERSITY OF SAO PAULO
SAO PAULO, BRAZIL
General Environment: Oceanographic

**PHYSICAL SCIENCE SCHOOL,
UNIVERSITY OF ST ANDREWS**
NORTH HAUGH, ST ANDREWS
FIFE, KY16 955, SCOTLAND
Director, John F Allen
Specific Interests: Prairie and Temperate
Forest

PHYSICS DEPARTMENT
SAN JOSE STATE COLLEGE
SAN JOSE, CA 95114
Professor, Gareth Williams

PHYSICS DEPARTMENT
PRIVATE BAG, RONDEBOSCH
CAPE TOWN, REPUBLIC OF SOUTH
AFRICA
Director, Dr R D Cherry
Staff Size: 1 - 4

PHYSICS INSTITUTE
335 EAST 45TH STREET
NEW YORK, NY 10017
Secretary, Wallace Waterfall
Staff Size: 100 - 499

SOIL PHYSICS LABORATORY
DEPARTMENT OF CIVIL
ENGINEERING, CITY UNIVERSITY
LONDON EC1, ENGLAND
General Environment: Terrestrial
Specific Interests: Prairie and Temperate
Forest

**THERMOPHYSICAL PROPERTIES
RESEARCH CENTER, PURDUE
UNIVERSITY**
2595 YEAGER ROAD
WEST LAFAYETTE, IN 47906

**TIDAL INSTITUTE AND
OBSERVATORY, UNIVERSITY OF
LIVERPOOL**
BIDSTON
CHESHIRE, ENGLAND
Director, J R Rossiter
General Environment: Oceanographic

**UL'YANOV-LENIN STATE
UNIVERSITY**
ULITSA LENINA,18
KAZAN', UNION OF SOVIET
SOCIALIST REPUBLICS
Director, M T Nuzhin
Staff Size: 10 - 49

WATER RESOURCE RESEARCH
INSTITUTE, OREGON
UNIVERSITY
114 COVELL HALL
CORVALLIS, OR 97331
General Environment: Oceanographic

Field Station/Laboratory

APPLIED GEOPHYSICS INSTITUTE
THERESIEN STRASSE, UNIVERSITY
OF MUNICH
MUNICH 2, WEST GERMANY
Director, Gustav Agenheister
General Environment: Terrestrial

VOEKOV MAIN GEOPHYSICAL
OBSERVATION
MOSCOW, UNION OF SOVIET
SOCIALIST REPUBLICS
Director, Mikhael Ivanovich Bydiko
General Environment: Terrestrial
Specific Interests: Polar (cold)

Foundation

GEOPHYSICS RESEARCH BOARD,
NATIONAL ACADEMY OF
SCIENCE
2101 CONSTITUTION AVENUE, NW
WASHINGTON, DC 20418
Staff Size: 1 - 4

Government — Federal

AMES RESEARCH CENTER, NASA
MOFFETT FIELD, CA 94035
Director, Mr Clarence Sylvertson
General Environment: Atmospheric
Staff Size: 1000 - 4999

ATMOSPHERE ENVIRONMENT
SERVICE
4905 DUFFERIN STREET
DOWNSVILLE, ONTARIO, CANADA
Director, J R H Noble
General Environment: Atmospheric
Staff Size: 1000 - 4999

ATMOSPHERIC RESEARCH
CENTER HIGH ALTITUDE
OBSERVATORY LIBRARY
POST OFFICE BOX 1558
BOULDER, CO 80302
General Environment: Atmospheric

ENVIRONMENTAL CONSERVATION
SERVICE
CAMBRIDGE RESEARCH
LABORATORIES, L G HANSCOM
FIELD
BEDFORD, MA 01730
General Environment: Atmospheric
Staff Size: 1000 - 4999

ENVIRONMENTAL SATELLITE
CENTER
NATIONAL OCEANIC AND
ATMOSPHERIC
ADMINISTRATION, INTERIOR
DEPARTMENT
WASHINGTON, DC 20233
General Environment: Atmospheric

FAR-EASTERN STATE UNIVERSITY
PRIMORSKIY K, ULIT SVKHN,8
VLADIVOSTOK, UNION OF SOVIET
SOCIALIST REPUBLICS
Director, O N Andryushenko
Staff Size: 5 - 9

FIZIKI ATMOSFERY INSTITUTE
BOLISHAYA GRUZINSKAYA, V-10
MOSCOW, UNION OF SOVIET
SOCIALIST REPUBLICS
General Environment: Atmospheric
Staff Size: 10 - 49

FLUID MECHANICS BRANCH
UNITED STATES DEPARTMENT OF
COMMERCE
WASHINGTON, DC 20234
General Environment: Limnologic

FROZEN SEA RESEARCH GROUP,
ENVIRONMENTAL DEPARTMENT
825 DEVONSHIRE ROAD
VICTORIA, BRITISH COLUMBIA,
CANADA
General Environment: Oceanographic
Specific Interests: Polar (cold)
Staff Size: 10 - 49

GEOLOGY AND GEOPHYSICS
VIL'NYUS, UNION OF SOVIET
SOCIALIST REPUBLICS
General Environment: Atmospheric
Staff Size: 5 - 9

GEOPHYSICAL OBSERVATORY
LENINGRAD, UNION OF SOVIET
SOCIALIST REPUBLICS
Director, M I Budyko
General Environment: Atmospheric
Staff Size: 5 - 9

HYDROMETEOROLOGICAL
INSTITUTE
ULITSA CHKALOVA, 2-A
ODESSA, UNION OF SOVIET
SOCIALIST REPUBLICS
Staff Size: 5 - 9

HYDROMETEOROLOGICAL
INSTITUTION OF LENINGRAD
MALO-OKHTINSKIY PROSPEKT98
LENINGRAD, UNION OF SOVIET
SOCIALIST REPUBLICS
Director, P N Morozov
Staff Size: 5 - 9

HYDROMETEOROLOGICAL
RESEARCH CENTER
BOLSEHEVISTSKAYA STR 9-13
MOSCOW 123376, UNION OF
SOVIET SOCIALIST REPUBLICS
General Environment: Atmospheric
Staff Size: 500 - 999

JOINT METEOROLOGICAL
COMPUTER CENTER
MOSCOW, UNION OF SOVIET
SOCIALIST REPUBLICS
General Environment: Atmospheric

MARINE HYDROPHYSICS
INSTITUTE
SADOVAI ULITSA
LYUBLINO, MOSCOW, UNION OF
SOVIET SOCIALIST REPUBLICS
General Environment: Oceanographic

MARINE SCIENCE BRANCH, COAST
GUARD WESTERN AREA
630 SANSOME STREET
SAN FRANCISCO, CA 94126
General Environment: Oceanographic
Staff Size: 5 - 9

MATHEMATICS AND MECHANICAL
INSTITUTE
ASTRONOMICHESKIY TUPIK,11
TASHKENT, UNION OF SOVIET
SOCIALIST REPUBLICS
General Environment: Terrestrial
Staff Size: 10 - 49

METEOROLOGICAL DEPARTMENT
KARACHI, PAKISTAN
General Environment: Atmospheric

METEOROLOGICAL PHYSICS
DIVISION
MELBOURNE, VICTORIA,
AUSTRALIA
General Environment: Atmospheric
Specific Interests: Prairie and Temperate
Forest

METEOROLOGY DEPARTMENT
MINISTRY OF COMMUNICATIONS
SINGAPORE
Director, K Rajendram
General Environment: Atmospheric
Specific Interests: Tropical (hot)
Staff Size: 100 - 499

METEOROLOGY SERVICE
POST OFFICE BOX 25
BET DAGAN, ISRAEL

Director, Gideon Steinitz
General Environment: Atmospheric
Staff Size: 100 - 499

**NAVAL PHYSICAL LABORATORY,
MINISTRY OF DEFENSE**
NAVAL BASE
COCHIM, INDIA
Director, Dr D Scrinivasa
General Environment: Oceanographic

OCEANOGRAPHIC INSTITUTE
KROPOTKINSKIY PEREYOLOK
MOSCOW, DOM 6, UNION OF
    SOVIET SOCIALIST REPUBLICS
General Environment: Oceanographic

**PHYSICS AND APPLIED PHYSICS
DIVISION**
NATIONAL STANDARDS
    LABORATORY
SYDNEY, NEW SOUTH WALES,
    AUSTRALIA
Specific Interests: Prairie and Temperate
    Forest

POLAR GEOPHYSICS INSTITUTE
MURMANSK, UNION OF SOVIET
    SOCIALIST REPUBLICS
General Environment: Atmospheric
Specific Interests: Polar (cold)

**PRIKLADNOY GEOFIZIKI
INSTITUTE**
GLEBOVSKAYA ULITSA, 2-B
MOSCOW, UNION OF SOVIET
    SOCIALIST REPUBLICS
Staff Size: 10 - 49

RADIOLOGICAL HEALTH CENTER
VAN NESS STREET AND
    CONNECTICUT AVENUE, NW
WASHINGTON, DC 20203
Specific Interests: Prairie and Temperate
    Forest

**RESOURCE COUNCIL OF ALBERTA,
UNIVERSITY OF ALBERTA**
87TH AVENUE AND 114TH STREET
EDMONTON, ALBERTA, CANADA
General Environment: Atmospheric
Staff Size: 100 - 499

**TBILISI STATE UNIVERSITY IMENI
I V STALIN**
PROSPEKT CHAVCHAVADZE, 1
TBILISI, UNION OF SOVIET
    SOCIALIST REPUBLICS
General Environment: Atmospheric
Staff Size: 10 - 49

**TOMSK STATE UNIVERSITY IMENI
V V KUYBYSHEV**
PROSPEKT TIMIRYAZEVA,3
TOMSK, UNION OF SOVIET
    SOCIALIST REPUBLICS
Staff Size: 10 - 49

**VIL'NYUS UNIVERSITY IMENI V
KAPSUKAS**
ULITSA UNIVERSITETA,3
VIL'NYUS, UNION OF SOVIET
    SOCIALIST REPUBLICS
Director I P Kubilyus
Staff Size: 10 - 49

WEATHER BUREAU
8060 13TH STREET
SILVER SPRING, MD 20910
General Environment: Atmospheric
Staff Size: 5000 - 9999

Government — State or Local

**ATMOSPHERIC SCIENCES
RESOURCES CENTER**
STATE UNIVERSITY OF NEW YORK,
    1400 WASHINGTON AVENUE
ALBANY, NY 12203
General Environment: Atmospheric

**GEOLOGICAL AND NATURAL
HISTORY SURVEY**
SCIENCE HALL, UNIVERSITY OF
    WISCONSIN
MADISON, WI 53706
General Environment: Terrestrial

**GEOPHYSICAL FLUID DYNAMICS
LABORATORY**
PRINCETON UNIVERSITY,
    FORRESTAL
PRINCETON, NJ 08540
Director, Dr Joseph Smagorinsky
General Environment: Atmospheric
Staff Size: 10 - 49

HYDROGRAPHIC INSTITUTE
BERNIIARD NOCHT-STRASSE 78
HAMBURG 4, WEST GERMANY
President, Dr Hans Ulrich Roll
General Environment: Oceanographic
Staff Size: 500 - 999

METEOROLOGY
CALIFORNIA STATE UNIVERSITY,
    SAN JOSE
SAN JOSE, CA 95114
Professor, Jack Thompson
General Environment: Atmospheric
Staff Size: 10 - 49

NUCLEAR RESEARCH CENTER
STATE UNIVERSITY OF NEW YORK-
    BUFFALO, 3435 MAIN STREET
BUFFALO, NY 14214

WATER SURVEY
BOX 232
URBANA, IL 61801

Director, Dr William P Lowry
General Environment: Atmospheric
Staff Size: 1 - 4

Industrial/Commercial

**OSRODEK BADAWCZO-
ROZWOJOWY**
ELEKTRONIKI PROZNI OBREP
WARSAW, POLAND
Director, Professor Wieslaw Barwicz

**PHYSICS DEPARTMENT, PACKARD
BELL SASD**
649 LAWRENCE DRIVE
NEWBURY PARK, CA 91230
Director, Paul Metzger

RADIATION DETECTION COMPANY
385 LOGUE AVENUE
MOUNTAIN VIEW, CA 94042
President, Richard H Holden

**SYLVANIA ELECTRO-OPTICS
ORGANIZATION**
475 ELLIS STREET
MOUNTAIN VIEW, CA 94042
Manager, Burton Bernard

UKAEA, REACTOR GROUP
RISLEY, NR WARRINGTON
LANCASTERSHIRE, ENGLAND
Technology Manager, Ronald T Ackroyd
Specific Interests: Prairie and Temperate
    Forest

Professional Organizations

**ATMOSPHERIC ENVIRONMENT
SERVICE**
4905 DUFFER STREET
DOWNSVIEW, ONTARIO, CANADA
General Environment: Atmospheric

**ELECTROPLATERS SOCIETY OF
AMERICA**
443 BROAD STREET
NEWARK, NJ 07102
General Manager, Rodney Leeds
Specific Interests: Prairie and Temperate
    Forest
Staff Size: 5000 - 9999

NUCLEAR SOCIETY OF AMERICA
244 EAST OGDEN AVENUE
INSDALE, IL 60521
Executive Secretary, Octave J Dutemple
Staff Size: 10 - 49

Research Institute

**ANTARCTIC INSTITUTE OF
ARGENTINA**
CERITTO 1248
BUENOS AIRES, ARGENTINA

Director, Rear Admiral Rodolfo N
Panzarina
General Environment: Atmospheric
Specific Interests: Polar (cold)

**CHRISTIAN MICHELSENS
INSTITUTE**
NYGARDSGATEN 114
BERGEN, NORWAY

Director, Jan Andersen
General Environment: Oceanographic

CLOUD PHYSICS
464 W WOODBURY ROAD, POST
OFFICE 657
ALTADENA, CA 91001

**COASTAL OCEANOGRAPHY
INSTITUTE**
THE OBSERVATORY, BIDSTON,
CHESHIRE, ENGLAND

Director, John R Rossiter
General Environment: Oceanographic
Staff Size: 50 - 99

**FAR EAST SCIENCE RESEARCH
HYDROMETEOROLOGICAL
INSTITUTE**
VLADIVOSTOK, UNION OF SOVIET
SOCIALIST REPUBLICS

Director, P Uryvayev
General Environment: Atmospheric
Staff Size: 5 - 9

**GEOPHYSICAL INSTITUTE,
BULGARIAN ACADEMY OF
SCIENCE**
SOFIA
MOSKOVSKA 6, BULGARIA

Director, Professor Lyubomir Krustanov
General Environment: Atmospheric

**HYDROMETEOROLOGICAL
INSTITUTION, UKRAINIAN
SCIENCES-RESOURCES**
ULITSA TOLSTOGO,14
KIEV, UNION OF SOVIET
SOCIALIST REPUBLICS

Director, V Prevotko
General Environment: Atmospheric
Staff Size: 5 - 9

**HYDROMETEOROLOGY
INSTITUTION, KAZAH SCIENCES-
RESOURCES**
ALMA-ATA, UNION OF SOVIET
SOCIALIST REPUBLICS

General Environment: Atmospheric

INSTYTUT CHEMII FIZYCZNEJ PAN
UL KASPRZAKA 4452, WARSAW,
POLAND

Director, Dr Michal Smialowski

**METEOROLOGY AND
CLIMATOLOGY INSTITUTE,
SLOVAK ACADEMY**
BRATISLAVA
DUBRAVSKA CESTA,
CZECHOSLOVAKIA

Director, Dr Frantisek Smolen
General Environment: Atmospheric
Staff Size: 10 - 49

OCEANOGRAPHIC INSTITUTE
195 RUE SAINT JACQUES
PARIS 5, FRANCE

Director, Professor Andre Gougenheim
General Environment: Oceanographic

**OPERATIONS RESEARCH
ASSOCIATION, PHYSICS**
2370 CHARLESTON ROAD
MT VIEW, CA 94040

**RADIATION PROTECTION
(INTERNATIONAL)**
OAK RIDGE NATIONAL
LABORATORY
OAK RIDGE, TN 37830

General Environment: Atmospheric

**RADIATION RESEARCH SOCIETY
OF JAPAN**
250 KUROSUNA-MACHI
CHIABA CITY, CHIBA, JAPAN

Director, Dr Kemdo Tsukamoto
Specific Interests: Prairie and Temperate
Forest

**RADIOBIOLOGICAL PROTECTION
SERVICE**
CLIFTON AVENUE, BELMONT
SUTTON, SURREY CR4 4XY,
ENGLAND

Director, Michael J Butler
Specific Interests: Prairie and Temperate
Forest

SCIENCE AND SOFTWARE SYSTEMS
P O BOX 1620
LA JOLLA, CA 92037

Librarian, L S Lance

**SECTION OCEANOGRAPHIQUE
CENTER**
O R S T O M BP
4-NOUMEA, NEW CALEDONIA

Director, M Legand
General Environment: Oceanographic

**USTAV JADERNEHO VYZKUMU
CSAV (UJV)**
REZ-KLECANY, CZECHOSLOVAKIA

Director, Vladimir Svab

**VYZKUMNY USTAV
TELEKOMUNIKACI**
PRAHA 10-STRASNICE
TREBOHOSTICKA 987,
CZECHOSLOVAKIA

Director, Ing Bohumil Simek

**VYZKUMNY USTAV
VZDUCHOTECHNIKY**
PRAHA 10-MALESICE
POCERNICKA 96,
CZECHOSLOVAKIA

Director, Ing Miroslav Vaclavik

Social Sciences/Humanities

GENERAL

Educational Institute

ANTHROPOLOGY DEPARTMENT
UNIVERSITY OF TEXAS
AUSTIN, TX 78712
Associate Professor, F Johnston

APPLIED SOCIAL RESEARCH
605 WEST 115TH STREET-
COLUMBIA UNIVERSITY
NEW YORK, NY 10025
Director, Allen Barton
Staff Size: 50 - 99

**BUSINESS RESEARCH DIVISION,
SCHOOL OF COMMERCE, OHIO
STATE UNIVERS**
1775 SOUTH COLLEGE ROAD
COLUMBUS,OH 43210

**CONSERVATION SOCIETY OF
ALASKA**
BOX 80192
COLLEGE, AK 99701
Director, Ernst Mueller
Staff Size: 1 - 4

**ENVIRONMENTAL AND PUBLIC
HEALTH SCHOOL**
UNIVERSITY OF CALIFORNIA
IRVINE, CA 92664

**ENVIRONMENTAL STUDIES
CENTER**
ANTIOCH COLLEGE
YELLOW SPRINGS, OH 45387

**ENVIRONMENTAL STUDIES
PROGRAM**
UNIVERSITY OF WATERLOO
WATERLOO, ONTARIO, CANADA
Specific Interests: Prairie and Temperate
Forest

**ENVIRONMENTAL STUDIES
PROGRAM**
UNIVERSITY OF ROCHESTER
ROCHESTER, NY 14627
Specific Interests: Prairie and Temperate
Forest

**ENVIRONMENTAL STUDIES
PROGRAM**
ROCKLAND COUNTY CENTER
SUFFERN, NY 10901
Specific Interests: Urban

**ENVIRONMENTAL STUDIES
PROGRAM, UNIVERSITY OF
WISCONSIN**
3203 NORTH DOWNER AVENUE
MILWAUKEE, WI 53211

**FAMILY STUDY CENTER,
UNIVERSITY OF MINNESOTA**
1014 SOCIAL SCIENCES TOWER
MINNEAPOLIS MN 55455
Staff Size: 10 - 49

**GEOLOGY DEPARTMENT,
CALIFORNIA STATE UNIVERSITY**
18111 NORDHOFF
NORTHRIDGE, CA 91324
Director, John F Gaines
General Environment: Terrestrial
Specific Interests: Desert
Staff Size: 10 - 49

**GOVERNMENT RESEARCH
BUREAU, LYNDON B JOHNSON
SCHOOL OF PUBLIC AFFAIRS**
UNIVERSITY OF TEXAS
AUSTIN, TX 78712
Staff Size: 10 - 49

**GOVERNMENTAL STUDIES
INSTITUTE**
109 MOSES HALL, UNIVERSITY
CALIFORNIA
BERKELEY, CA 94720
Director, Dr Eugene C Lee
Staff Size: 10 - 49

HISTORICAL LIBRARY
BETHEL COLLEGE
NORTH NEWTON, KS 67117

**HOUSING AND ENVIRONMENTAL
STUDIES CENTER**
CORNELL UNIVERSITY
ITHACA, NY 14850

**HUMANITIES, ARTS, AND
POLITICAL SCIENCES SCHOOL**
SAN JOSE STATE COLLEGE
SAN JOSE, CA 95114

**HYGIENE AND PUBLIC HEALTH
SCHOOL, JOHN'S HOPKINS
UNIVERSITY**
615 NORTH WOLFE STREET
BALTIMORE, MD 21205
Associate Dean, Raymond Seltser

LIFE SCIENCES INSTITUTE
BROWN UNIVERSITY
PROVIDENCE, RI 02912
Director, Herman Chase

NEWBERRY LIBRARY
60 WEST WALTON STREET
CHICAGO,IL 60610

PUBLIC HEALTH DEPARTMENT
SIXTH AVENUE NORTH, CORDELL
HULL BUILDING
NASHVILLE, TN 37219
Director, Dr Eugene W Fowinkle

PUPLIC HEALTH INSTITUTE
UNIVERSITY OF TEHRAN
TEHRAN, IRAN

**SOCIAL ORGANIZATIONS
RESOURCES CENTER,
DEPARTMENT OF SOCIOLOGY**
UNIVERSITY OF MICHIGAN
ANN ARBOR, MI 48104

SOCIAL RESEARCH INSTITUTE
UNIVERSITY OF MICHIGAN
ANN ARBOR, MI 48104

**SOCIAL SCIENCE RESEARCH
CENTER**
UNIVERSITY OF PUERTO RICO
RIO PIEDRAS, PUERTO RICO 00931
Specific Interests: Tropical (hot)

**SOCIAL SCIENCES SECTION,
MOSCOW STATE UNIVERSITY**
MOKHOVAYA ULITSA
MOSCOW, UNION OF SOVIET
SOCIALIST REPUBLICS
Staff Size: 100 - 499

**SURVEY RESEARCH LABORATORY,
UNIVERSITY OF ILLINOIS**
437 DAVID KINLEY HALL
URBANA, IL 61801
Director, Robert Ferber
Staff Size: 50 - 99

URBAN ENVIRONMENTAL STUDIES
POLYTECHNICAL INSTITUTE OF
BROOKLYN
BROOKLYN, NY 11201
Specific Interests: Urban

URBAN ENVIRONMENTAL STUDIES
RENSSELAER POLYTECHNIC
INSTITUTE
TROY, NY 12181
Specific Interests: Urban

URBAN STUDIES INSTITUTE
SOUTHERN METHODIST
UNIVERSITY
DALLAS, TX 75222
Specific Interests: Urban

Foundation

ANTHROPOLOGY-SOCIOLOGY DIVISION
LA SALLE FOUNDATION
CARACAS, VENEZUELA
Director, Hermano Gines
Specific Interests: Tropical (hot)

ASTOR, LENOX AND TILDEN FOUNDATION, NEW YORK PUBLIC LIBRARY
FIFTH AND 42ND STREET
NEW YORK, NY 10018

FAMILY SERVICE ASSOCIATION OF AMERICA
44 EAST 23RD STREET
NEW YORK, NY 10010

PACIFIC SCIENTIFIC INFORMATION CENTER
1355 KALIHI STREET
HONOLULU, HI 96819

RESEARCH FOR THE FUTURE, INCORPORATED
1755 MASSACHUSETTS AVENUE, NW
WASHINGTON, DC 20036
Staff Size: 50 - 99

TWENTIETH CENTURY FUND
41 EAST 70TH STREET
NEW YORK, NY 10021

UNITED WAY OF AMERICA
801 NORTH FAIRFAX STREET
ALEXANDRIA, VA 22314

WORLD HEALTH ORGANIZATION
1211 GENEVA 27, SWITZERLAND

Government — Federal

CONSUMER PROTECTION AND ENVIRONMENTAL HEALTH SERVICES
PUBLIC AFFAIRS OFFICE
WASHINGTON, DC 20204

HEALTH ECONOMICS OFFICE
162 REGENT STREET
LONDON, WI, ENGLAND
Director, G T Smith
Specific Interests: Prairie and Temperate Forest

HEALTH MINISTRY
DAVID HAMELACH STREET
JERUSALEM, ISRAEL
Director, Dr R Gzebin
General Environment: Oceanographic

INTELLIGENCE AND RESOURCES BUREAU, EXTRAMURAL RESEARCH STAFF
2201 C STREET, NW
WASHINGTON, DC 20525

MEDICAL LIBRARY
8600 ROCKVILLE PIKE
BETHESDA, MD 20014
Director, Dr Martin M Cummings
Staff Size: 50 - 99

NATIONAL MUSEUM
HERRAN STREET
MANILA, PHILIPPINES
Specific Interests: Prairie and Temperate Forest

Government — State or Local

ECONOMIC AND SOCIAL ANALYSIS BUREAU, PUERTO RICO PLANNING
STOP 22
SANTURCE, PR 00909

EMPLOYERS MUTUAL OF WAUSAU
407 GRANT STREET
WAUSAU, WI 54402
Director, Betty Callow

HUMAN RESOURCES DEPARTMENT
25 K STREET, NE
WASHINGTON, DC 20009

MUSEUM OF THE STATE OF ARIZONA
UNIVERSITY OF ARIZONA
TUCSON, AZ 85721
Director, Dr Raymond H Thompson
Staff Size: 10 - 49

PLANNING SERVICES OFFICE
488 BROADWAY
ALBANY, NY 12207

Industrial/Commercial

CHESAPEAKE AND POTOMAC TELEPHONE
1710 H STREET, NW
WASHINGTON, DC 20006
Director, Lomas Wells

EXPLORATION INSTITUTE
2340 PRAIRIE AVENUE
EVANSTON, IL 60201

NATIONAL AFFAIRS BUREAU
1231 24TH STREET, NW
WASHINGTON, DC 20037
Specific Interests: Urban

Professional Organizations

AMERICAN ANTIQUARIAN SOCIETY
185 SALISBURY STREET
WORCESTER, MA 01609

AMERICAN GEOGRAPHICAL SOCIETY
BROADWAY AT 156TH STREET
NEW YORK,NY 10032

AMERICAN INSTITUTE FOR RESEARCH
410 AMBERSON AVENUE
PITTSBURGH,PA 15232

BOSTONIAN SOCIETY, OLD STATE HOUSE
206 WASHINGTON STREET
BOSTON,MA 02109

CONSERVATIONISTS COUNCIL
201 EAST 62ND STREET
NEW YORK, NY 10021
Director, Fred Smith
General Environment: Terrestrial
Specific Interests: Prairie and Temperate Forest

GEOPHYSICAL UNION
UNIVERSITY OF CHICAGO, 5828 UNIVERSITY DRIVE
CHICAGO, IL 60637

MEDICAL ACADEMY
2 EAST 103RD STREET
NEW YORK,NY 10029

OUTDOOR WRITERS ASSOCIATION OF AMERICA, INCORPORATED
4141 WEST BRADLEY ROAD
MILWAUKEE, WI 53209

SCENIC AND HISTORIC PRESERVATION SOCIETY
15 PINE STREET
NEW YORK,NY 10005

SOCIAL RESPONSES IN SCIENCES SOCIETY
37 HERMAN STREET
PHILADELPHIA,PA 19144

SOCIOLOGICAL ASSOCIATION OF AMERICA
1722 NORTH STREET, NW
WASHINGTON, DC 20036
Specific Interests: Urban

Research Institute

ARCTIC BIBLIOGRAPHIC PROJECT, ARCTIC INSTITUTE OF NORTH AMERICA
1619 NEW HAMPSHIRE AVENUE, NW
WASHINGTON, DC 20005
Specific Interests: Polar (cold)

FELS RESEARCH INSTITUTE
LIVERMORE STREET
YELLOW SPRINGS,OH 45387

MANKIND STUDY COUNCIL
POST OFFICE BOX 895
SANTA MONICA, CA 90406

POLITICAL SOCIAL SCIENCES ACADEMY
3937 CHESTNUT STREET
PHILADELPHIA, PA. 19104
Specific Interests: Urban

PUBLIC ADMINISTRATION INSTITUTE
55 WEST 44TH STREET
NEW YORK, NY 10036
Director, Mark W Cannon
Specific Interests: Urban

PUBLIC LIBRARY
325 SUPERIOR AVENUE
CLEVELAND, OH 44114

SOCIAL SCIENCE RESEARCH BUREAU, INCORPORATED
1200 17TH STREET
WASHINGTON, DC 20036
Staff Size: 50 - 99

AGRICULTURE

Government — Federal

AGRICULTURAL AND NATURAL RESOURCE MINISTRY
CAPE ST MARY VIA BATHURST
BATHURST, THE GAMBIA
Director, Stan G Trees

AGRICULTURAL AND NATURAL RESOURCE MINISTRY
DEPARTMENT OF FISHERIES
NICOSIA, CYPRUS
Director, Andreas Dimitropoulos
General Environment: Oceanographic

AGRICULTURAL AND NATURAL RESOURCE MINISTRY
LE REDUIT
PORT LOUIS, MAURITIUS
Director, M D Frenchmullen

AGRICULTURAL AND NATURAL RESOURCES MINISTRY
INDEPENDENCE BUILDING
LAGOS, NIGERIA
Director, George Ige

AGRICULTURAL STABILIZATION AND CONSERVATION SERVICES
DEPARTMENT OF AGRICULTURE
WASHINGTON, DC 20250

AGRICULTURE AND WATER MINISTRY
JIDDA, SAUDI ARABIA

COMMUNITY DEVELOPMENT/ STUDIES

Educational Institute

CITY PLANNING, LANDSCAPING, AND ARCHITECTURAL LIBRARY
203 MUMFORD HALL, UNIVERSITY OF ILLINOIS
URBANA, IL 61803

COMMUNITY DEVELOPMENT INSTITUTE
MICHIGAN STATE UNIVERSITY
EAST LANSING, MI 48823
Staff Size: 10 - 49

ECONOMICS DEPARTMENT
SAN JOSE STATE COLLEGE
SAN JOSE, CA 95114
Chairman, Norman Keiser

FOOD SCIENCES DEPARTMENT, UNIVERSITY OF WISCONSIN
BABCOCK HALL
MADISON, WI 53706
Staff Size: 10 - 49

FOREST SCIENCE DEPARTMENT
UNIVERSITY OF OXFORD, SOUTH PARK
OXFORD, ENGLAND
Director, Michael Gane
General Environment: Terrestrial
Specific Interests: Prairie and Temperate Forest

RESEARCH INSTITUTE OF STANFORD UNIVERSITY

333 RAVENSWOOD AVENUE
MENLO PARK, CA 94025
General Environment: Oceanographic

RESOURCES COUNCIL
UNIVERSITY OF BRITISH COLUMBIA
VANCOUVER 8, BRITISH COLUMBIA, CANADA

URBAN AMERICA
1717 MASSACHUSETTS AVENUE, NW
WASHINGTON, DC 20036
Specific Interests: Urban

URBAN RESOURCES BUREAU, PRINCETON UNIVERSITY
ARCHITECTURE BUILDING
PRINCETON, NJ 08540
Staff Size: 1 - 4

URBAN STUDIES CENTER
66 CHURCH STREET
CAMBRIDGE, MA 02139

Foundation

ALUMINUM CORPORATION OF AMERICA
1501 ALCOA BUILDING
PITTSBURGH, PA 15219
Vice President, Miles Colwell
Specific Interests: Urban

URBAN AMERICA, INCORPORATED.
15TH AND H STREETS, NW
WASHINGTON, DC 20005
Specific Interests: Urban

Government — Federal

AGRICULTURAL ECONOMICS
2440 VIRGINIA AVENUE
WASHINGTON, DC 20037
Director, Don Paarlberg

COMMUNITY ENVIRONMENT MANAGEMENT BUREAU
12720 TWINBROOK PARKWAY
ROCKVILLE, MD 20852
Director, Robert E Novick
General Environment: Terrestrial

COMMUNITY HEALTH SERVICES
3125 GARFIELD STREET
WASHINGTON, DC 20008
Director, Jordon J Popkin

COMMUNITY PLANNING AND MANAGEMENT

1855 UPSHUR STREET
WASHINGTON, DC 20011
Assistant Secretary, Samuel Jackson

ECONOMIC AFFAIRS MINISTRY
TAIPEI, TAIWAN
Specific Interests: Tropical (hot)

**HOUSING AND URBAN
   DEVELOPMENT**
451 7TH STREET, SW
WASHINGTON, DC 20410
Specific Interests: Urban

**PUBLIC WORKS OFFICE,
   ECONOMIC DEVELOPMENT
   ADMINISTRATION**
UNITED STATES DEPARTMENT OF
   COMMERCE
WASHINGTON, DC 20230
Specific Interests: Urban

**RURAL COMMUNITY
   DEVELOPMENT SERVICE**
INDEPENDENCE AVENUE
   BETWEEN 12TH AND 14TH
   STREETS
WASHINGTON, DC 20250
General Environment: Terrestrial

TRANSPORTATION MINISTRY
ECONOMIC PLANNING UNIT
KUALA LUMPUR, MALAYSIA
Specific Interests: Tropical (hot)

Government — State or Local

**CITY PLANNING COMMISSION,
   PHILADELPHIA**
JUNIPER AND FILBERT STREETS
PHILADELPHIA, PA 19107

FISHERIES BOARD
SOUTH BRISBANE, QUEENSLAND,
   AUSTRALIA

FISHERIES BOARD
TOWNSVILLE, QUEENSLAND,
   AUSTRALIA

**FISHERIES MARKETING
   AUTHORITY**
PYRMONT
SYDNEY, NEW SOUTH WALES,
   AUSTRALIA
Director, M Joseph

FISHERMAN'S COOPERATIVE
ADELAIDE, SOUTH AUSTRALIA,
   AUSTRALIA
Director, R M Fowler
General Environment: Oceanographic
Specific Interests: Tropical (hot)

**HARBORS AND LIGHTHOUSES
   DEPARTMENT**
ONE CLIFF STREET
FREEMANTLE, WESTERN
   AUSTRALIA, AUSTRALIA
General Environment: Oceanographic
Specific Interests: Tropical (hot)

HARBORS BOARD
VICTORIA SQUARE
ADELAIDE, SOUTH AUSTRALIA,
   AUSTRALIA
General Environment: Oceanographic
Specific Interests: Tropical (hot)

MARITIME SERVICES BOARD
CIRCULAR QUAY
SIDNEY, NEW SOUTH WALES,
   AUSTRALIA
General Environment: Oceanographic
Specific Interests: Tropical (hot)

**NAVIGATION AND SURVEY
   AUTHORITY**
GPO BOX 202B
HOBART, TASMANIA, AUSTRALIA
General Environment: Oceanographic
Specific Interests: Tropical (hot)

Industrial/Commercial

POLITICAL ECONOMY
1021 FOOTHILL STREET
SOUTH PASADENA, CA 91030
Director, Walter Wentz

Professional Organizations

**ARCHITECTS INSTITUTE OF
   AMERICA**
THE OCTAGON, 1735 NEW YORK
   AVENUE
WASHINGTON, DC 20006
Specific Interests: Urban

ECONOMIC ASSISTANCE COUNCIL
PETROVKA 14
MOSCOW K-31, UNION OF SOVIET
   SOCIALIST REPUBLICS

**PLANNERS INSTITUTE OF
   AMERICA**
917 15TH STREET, NW
WASHINGTON, DC 20005
Specific Interests: Urban

**PROTECTION OF NATIONAL AND
   HISTORICAL SITES AND
   MONUMENTS**
VIA MARSALA 8, 00185
ROME, ITALY

**RESEARCH FOUNDATION
   ASSOCIATION**
1001 CONNECTICUT AVENUE, NW
WASHINGTON, DC 20036

WORLD BANK
1818 H STREET, NW
WASHINGTON, DC 20433

Research Institute

**COMMUNITY SERVICE
   INCORPORATED**
114 EAST WHITEMAN STREET
YELLOW SPRINGS, OH 45387
Staff Size: 1 - 4

**DEVELOPMENT RESEARCH
   CENTER**
INDIANA UNIVERSITY
BLOOMINGTON, IN 47401
Director, William Siffin
Staff Size: 10 - 49

**WATER RESOURCES RESEARCH
   INSTITUTE, OREGON
   UNIVERSITY**
114 COVELL HALL
CORVALLIS, OR 97331
General Environment: Oceanographic

EDUCATION

Educational Institute

**ADULTS' LIBERAL EDUCATION
   STUDY CENTER**
BOSTON UNIVERSITY, 38
   MOUNTFORT STREET
BROOKLINE, MA 02146

**AGRICULTURAL SECONDARY
   SCHOOL**
SOUSSE, TUNISIA
General Environment: Oceanographic

ECOLOGY CENTER
2179 ALLSTON WAY
BERKELEY, CA 94704
Coordinator, Fred Budinger
Specific Interests: Prairie and Temperate
   Forest
Staff Size: 5 - 9

**EDUCATION AND CONSERVATION
   DEPARTMENT**
MONTCLAIR STATE COLLEGE
MONTCLAIR, NJ 07043
Specific Interests: Prairie and Temperate
   Forest

**EDUCATION MATERIALS
RESOURCES BUREAU**
COLLEGE OF EDUCATION,
LOUISIANA STATE UNIVERSITY
BATON ROUGE, LA 70803

**EDUCATION RESEARCH AND
SERVICES BUREAU**
CULLEN BOULEVARD, UNIVERSITY
OF HOUSTON
HOUSTON,TX 77002

**EDUCATION, PLANNING AND
DEVELOPMENT BUREAU**
UNIVERSITY OF MEXICO
ALBUQUERQUE, NM 87106
Director, Richard F Tonigan
Staff Size: 5 - 9

**EDUCATIONAL RESOURCES
BUREAU**
288 EDUCATION BUILDING,
UNIVERSITY OF ILLINOIS
URBANA, IL 61803

**ENVIRONMENTAL HEALTH
CENTER**
UNIVERSITY OF MISSOURI
COLUMBIA, MO 65201

**ENVIRONMENTAL SCIENCE
PROGRAM**
UNIVERSITY OF CONNECTICUT
STORRS, CT 06268

**ENVIRONMENTAL STUDIES
PROGRAM**
GALLAUDET COLLEGE, FLORIDA
AVENUE AND 7TH STREET, NE
WASHINGTON, DC 20002
Staff Size: 500 - 999

**HIGHER EDUCATION STUDY
CENTER**
UNIVERSITY OF MICHIGAN
ANN ARBOR, MI 48104

**INSTITUTIONAL RESOURCES
BUREAU**
330 BURTON HALL, MINNESOTA
UNIVERSITY
MINNEAPOLIS, MN 55455

MARINE ACADEMY
SOUSSE, TUNISIA
General Environment: Oceanographic

**NATURAL RESOURCES POLICY
CENTER**
GEORGE WASHINGTON
UNIVERSITY
WASHINGTON, DC 20001

**PROGRAMMED INSTRUCTION
CENTER**
TEACHERS COLLEGE, COLUMBIA
UNIVERSITY
NEW YORK, NY 10027

SOCIAL WORK SCHOOL
UNIVERSITY MICHIGAN
ANN ARBOR, MI 48104
Professor, H Wayne Vasey

Foundation

**CONSERVATION EDUCATION
ASSOCIATION**
BOX 450
MADISON, WI 53701
Staff Size: 500 - 999

Government — Federal

**ADULT EDUCATION PROGRAMS
DIVISION**
OFFICE OF EDUCATION
WASHINGTON, DC 20202

EDUCATION OFFICE
400 MARYLAND AVENUE
WASHINGTON, DC 20202

HEALTH AND WELFARE MINISTRY
TOKYO, JAPAN
Specific Interests: Prairie and Temperate
Forest

HIGHER EDUCATION MINISTRY
CAIRO, UNITED ARAB REPUBLIC
Director, Dr Ezzat Salama

NAUTICAL SCHOOL
ACCRA, GHANA
General Environment: Oceanographic

PEDAGOGICAL INSTITUTE
STALINIRI, UNION OF SOVIET
SOCIALIST REPUBLICS
Staff Size: 1 - 4

Government — State or Local

EDUCATION DEPARTMENT
HEROES MEMORIAL BUILDING
CARSON CITY,NV 89701

**EDUCATIONAL RESEARCH
DIVISION**
UNIVERSITY OF PUERTO RICO
RIO PIEDRAS, PR 00931

**ENVIRONMENTAL EDUCATION
OFFICE**
1114 COMMERCE STREET
DALLAS, TX 75202

**INDUSTRIAL RELATIONS AND
PUBLIC AFFAIRS OFFICE**
150 EAST 42ND STREET
NEW YORK, NY 10017
Vice President, Leo Teplow
Specific Interests: Urban

**RESOURCES EVALUATION
DIVISION**
110 LIVINGSTON STREET
BROOKLYN, NY 11201

SUPERIOR EDUCATION COUNCIL
UNIVERSITY OF PUERTO RICO
RIO PIEDRAS, PR 00931

Industrial/Commercial

ECONOMIC EDUCATION COUNCIL
2 WEST 46TH STREET
NEW YORK,NY 10036

**EDUCATIONAL FACILITIES
LABORATORIES, INCORPORATED**
477 MADISON AVENUE
NEW YORK, NY 10022

Professional Organizations

**AMERICAN ASSOCIATION OF
UNIVERSITY PROFESSORS**
1785 MASSACHUSETTS AVENUE, NW
WASHINGTON, DC 20036

**AMERICAN COUNCIL ON
EDUCATION**
ONE DUPONT CIRCLE
WASHINGTON, DC 20036
Specific Interests: Urban

**AMERICAN VOCATIONAL
ASSOCIATION INCORPORATED**
1510 H STREET, NW
WASHINGTON, DC 20005
Specific Interests: Urban

**CONSERVATION EDUCATION
ASSOCIATION**
GREEN HALL, UNIVERSITY OF
MINNESOTA
ST PAUL, MN 55101
President, Richard J Myshak
Specific Interests: Prairie and Temperate
Forest

EDUCATIONAL RECORDS BUREAU
21 AUDUBON AVENUE
NEW YORK,NY 10032

**GEOGRAPHIC EDUCATION
COUNCIL**

115 NORTH MARION STREET
OAK PARK, IL 60301
Staff Size: 1 - 4

**NATIONAL EDUCATION
ASSOCIATION**
1201 16TH STREET, NW
WASHINGTON, DC 20036

NATURE STUDY SOCIETY
1523 36TH STREET
OGDEN, UT 84403
President, Hal L Mickelson
Specific Interests: Prairie and Temperate
  Forest

SOCIAL STUDIES COUNCIL
1201 16TH STREET, NW
WASHINGTON,DC 20036

URBAN LAND INSTITUTE
ONE DU PONT CIRCLE, SUITE 500
WASHINGTON, DC 20036

Research Institute

**INTERNATIONAL EDUCATION
BUREAU**
809 UNITED NATIONS PLAZA
NEW YORK, NY 10017

**RESOURCES DIVISION, NATIONAL
EDUCATION ASSOCIATION**
1201 16TH STREET, NW
WASHINGTON, DC 20036

Unclassified

PRAIRIE PATHOLOGY
BX 1086/616 DELLES ROAD
WHEATON, IL 60187
President, William S Nemec
General Environment: Terrestrial
Specific Interests: Prairie and Temperate
  Forest
Staff Size: 1 - 4

EMPLOYMENT/
UNEMPLOYMENT

Government — Federal

DEFENSE AGENCY
JAPANESE MARITIME SELF
  DEFENSE
TOKYO, JAPAN

Director, Kaneshichi Masuda
General Environment: Oceanographic

**EMPLOYMENT SECURITY BUREAU,
LABOR DEPARTMENT**
14TH STREET AND CONSTITUTION
  AVENUE, NW
WASHINGTON, DC 20210

**FOREIGN SERVICE VOLUNTARY
AGENCY**
44 EAST 23RD STREET
NEW YORK,NY 10010

HYDROGRAPHIC DEPARTMENT
DEFENSE DEPARTMENT, NAVY
SYDNEY, NEW SOUTH WALES,
  AUSTRALIA
General Environment: Terrestrial
Specific Interests: Prairie and Temperate
  Forest

**POPULATION ASSOCIATION OF
AMERICA**
UNITED STATES PUBLIC HEALTH
  SERVICE
WASHINGTON, DC 20201
Specific Interests: Prairie and Temperate
  Forest
Staff Size: 1000 - 4999

**POPULATION RESEARCH
ADVISORY COMMISSION**
NATIONAL INSTITUTES OF HEALTH
BETHESDA, MD 20014
Executive Secretary, Ruth Crozier
Staff Size: 1 - 4

Government — State or Local

**EMPLOYMENT BUREAU,
DEPARTMENT OF LABOR**
165 NORTH CANAL STREET
CHICAGO, IL 60606

EMPLOYMENT DEPARTMENT
800 CAPITOL MALL
SACRAMENTO,CA 95814

**EMPLOYMENT SECURITY
DEPARTMENT**
P O BOX 2100
SALT LAKE CITY, UT 84110

Professional Organizations

**VOCATIONAL FOUNDATION
INCORPORATED**
353 PARK AVENUE SOUTH
NEW YORK, NY 10010

Research Institute

**HUMAN RESOURCES RESEARCH
ORGANIZATION**
300 NORTH WASHINGTON STREET
ALEXANDRIA, VA 22314

HOUSING

Foundation

**HOUSING AND PLANNING
FEDERATION**
43 WASSENAARSWEG,
THE HAGUE, THE NETHERLANDS

NEAR EAST FOUNDATION
54 EAST 64TH STREET
NEW YORK, NY 10021

**PLANNING AND HOUSING
ORGANIZATION**
4-A RING ROAD INDRAPRASTHA
NEW DELHI, INDIA

Government — Federal

**HOUSING AND URBAN
DEVELOPMENT DEPARTMENT**
451 7TH STREET, SW
WASHINGTON, DC 20410

Government — State or Local

**ENVIRONMENTAL PROTECTION
BUREAU, DEVELOPMENT
DEPARTMENT**
87 NEPPERHAN AVENUE
YONKERS, NY 10701
General Environment: Atmospheric

Professional Organizations

**HOUSING REDEVELOPMENT
OFFICE**
1413 K STREET, NW
WASHINGTON, DC 20005

Research Institute

RESEARCH BUREAU
294 WASHINGTON STREET
BOSTON, MA 02108
Specific Interests: Urban

INDUSTRIAL DEVELOPMENT

Educational Institute

BUSINESS RESEARCH BUREAU, BUSINESS ADMINISTRATION SCHOOL
UNIVERSITY OF MICHIGAN
ANN ARBOR, MI 48104

Government — Federal

AGRICULTURAL MINISTRY
TUNIS, TUNISIA
General Environment: Oceanographic

AQUATIC RESEARCH ORGANIZATION
CAIRO, UNITED ARAB REPUBLIC
General Environment: Oceanographic

DOMESTIC COMMERCE BUREAU
UNITED STATES DEPARTMENT OF COMMERCE
WASHINGTON, DC 20230

FISHERIES OFFICE
MAHDIA, TUNISIA
General Environment: Oceanographic

FISHERIES OFFICE
SFAX, TUNISIA
General Environment: Oceanographic

FISHERIES OFFICE
POST OFFICE BOX 73
MASSAWA, ETHIOPIA
Director, Osman Idris Aman
General Environment: Oceanographic

FISHERIES OFFICE
TUNIS, TUNISIA
General Environment: Oceanographic

FISHERIES OFFICE
GOULETTE, TUNISIA
General Environment: Oceanographic

FISHERIES SERVICE
LOME, TOGO
General Environment: Oceanographic

FISHERIES SERVICE
AGRICULTURAL MINISTRY
TANANARIVE, MALAGASY REPUBLIC
Director, Guy Nedelec
General Environment: Oceanographic

INDUSTRIAL OPERATIONS ADMINISTRATION
14TH AND CONSTITUTION AVENUE, NW
WASHINGTON, DC 20230
General Environment: Atmospheric

INDUSTRIAL PRODUCTION MINISTRY
BRAZZAVILLE, REPUBLIC OF THE CONGO
General Environment: Oceanographic

RURAL ECONOMY MINISTRY
BP 1095
LOME, TOGO
Director, Idrissou Abou Karim
General Environment: Oceanographic

SMALL BUSINESS ADMINISTRATION
811 VERMONT AVENUE, NW
WASHINGTON, DC 20416

Government — State or Local

COMMERCE DEPARTMENT
NEW CAPITOL ANNEX
FRANKFORT, KY 40601
Staff Size: 50 - 99

DEVELOPMENT OFFICE
STATE OFFICE BUILDING
HARTFORD, CT 06115
Specific Interests: Urban

INDUSTRIAL RELATIONS CENTER, BUSINESS ADMINISTRATION TOWER
UNIVERSITY OF MINNESOTA
MINNEAPOLIS, MN 55455

Industrial/Commercial

AFRICA-AZOTE
DAKAR, SENEGAL
Director, Mr Desire Pizano

AMERICAN FOREST PRODUCTS INDUSTRY INCORPORATED

1816 N STREET, NW
WASHINGTON, DC 20036
General Environment: Terrestrial
Specific Interests: Prairie and Temperate Forest

AMERICAN INTERNATIONAL OIL COMPANY
NOVAKCHOTT, MAURITANIA
General Environment: Oceanographic

AMERICAN OVERSEAS PETROLEUM LIMITED
8-10 BROAD STREET, PO BOX 1986
LAGOS, NIGERIA
Director, L D Pollard
General Environment: Oceanographic

AMOCO EGYPT OIL COMPANY
POST OFFICE BOX 2409
CAIRO, UNITED ARAB REPUBLIC
President, R W Craig

BAROID OF NIGERIA LIMITED
3 INDUSTRY ROAD, PO BOX 404
PORT HARCOURT, NIGERIA
General Environment: Oceanographic

BELL TELEPHONE COMPANY OF MICHIGAN
220 BAGLEY STREET, ROOM 850
DETROIT, MI 48226

BRITISH PETROLEUM, CONTINENTAL OIL CORPORATION
3-10 BROAD STREET, PO BOX 1253
LAGOS, NIGERIA
Director, D H Bingham, Jr
General Environment: Oceanographic

CANADALA, S P A
P O BOX 23
MOGADISCIO, SOMALIA
General Environment: Oceanographic

COMPANY FOR FROZEN FOODS OF SENEGAL
SOFRIGAL
DAKAR, SENEGAL
Director, Mr Alain Gras
General Environment: Oceanographic

COPETAD
IMMEUBLE BIAO, PLACE INDEPENDENCE, BP 2093
DAKAR, SENEGAL
Director, J M Ayme
General Environment: Oceanographic

CORE LABORATORIES,INCORPORATED
7 PORT HARCOURT/ABA ROAD
PMB 5148, PORT HARCOURT, NIGERIA
General Environment: Oceanographic

DIVCON INTERNATIONAL
FEDERAL PALACE HOTEL,
VICTORIA ISLE
POB 3720, LAGOS, NIGERIA
Director, Malcolm Williams
General Environment: Oceanographic

DOWELL SCHLUMBERGER
1300 FIRST CITY EAST BUILDING
HOUSTON, TX 77002
General Environment: Oceanographic

**EAST AFRICA OIL REFINERIES,
LIMITED**
MOMBASA, KENYA
General Environment: Oceanographic

**EASTMAN OIL WELL SURVEY
COMPANY**
SERVICES AND SUPPLY
CORPORATION WASHINGTON,
LIMITED
POB 387, PORT HARCOURT,
NIGERIA
Director, James Keene
General Environment: Oceanographic

**EGYPTIAN GENERAL PETROLEUM
CORPORATION**
CAIRO, UNITED ARAB REPUBLIC

EXXON
BUILDING MAGINOT, BP 1100
DAKAR, SENEGAL
Director, Max Aucel
General Environment: Oceanographic

EXXON EXPLORATION
22 RUE D'AZRO
RABAT, MOROCCO
General Environment: Oceanographic

**EXXON WEST AFRICA,
INCORPORATED**
8-10 BROAD STREET, PO BOX 176
LAGOS, NIGERIA
Director, James F Skane
General Environment: Oceanographic

**FISHERIES DEVELOPMENT
COMPANY**
ZANZIBAR
General Environment: Oceanographic

**FISHERIES DEVELOPMENT
CORPORATION**
POST OFFICE BOX 539
CAPE TOWN, REPUBLIC OF SOUTH
AFRICA
General Environment: Oceanographic

GHANA BOATYARD CORPORATION
TEMA, GHANA
General Environment: Oceanographic

GLOBAL MARINE EUROPA
127-129 BROAD STREET, PO BOX
3634

LAGOS, NIGERIA
General Environment: Oceanographic

**GREAT BASINS PETROLEUM
COMPANY LIMITED**
1-9 BERKLEY STREET, PO BOX 1236
LAGOS, NIGERIA
General Environment: Oceanographic

**GUIBERSON (DRESSER
INDUSTRIAL)**
POST OFFICE BOX 5123
PORT HARCOURT, NIGERIA
General Environment: Oceanographic

GULF OIL COMPANY
KINSHASA, REPUBLIC OF THE
CONGO
General Environment: Oceanographic

GULF OIL COMPANY OF ETHIOPIA
POST OFFICE BOX 2589
ADDIS ABABA, ETHIOPIA
Director, Assefa Yirdawo
General Environment: Oceanographic

GULF-GABON
LIBREVILLE, GABON
General Environment: Oceanographic

HABO S P A
P O BOX 23
MOGADISCIO, SOMALIA
General Environment: Oceanographic

HALLIBURTON LIMITED
TRANSPORATATION-AMADI
ESTATE, PO BOX 462
PORT HARCOURT, NIGERIA
General Environment: Oceanographic

INDUSTRIAL CONSTRUCTION SAIB
DAKAR, SENEGAL
Director, Mr Claude Shaeffer

**INTERNATIONAL DRILLING
COMPANY**
POST OFFICE BOX 538
PORT HARCOURT, NIGERIA
Director, William M Prindible
General Environment: Oceanographic

LANE WELLS DIVISION
PMB 5186
PORT HARCOURT, NIGERIA
Director, Harry Max
General Environment: Oceanographic

**MACOBAR DIVISION OF DRESSER
A G (ZUG)**
PMB 5123
PORT HARCOURT, NIGERIA
Director, James L Bryan
General Environment: Oceanographic

MARITIME FISHING COMPANY
LOME, TOGO

**MC DERMOTT OVERSEAS,
INCORPORATED**
1-9 BERKLEY STREET, PO BOX 2841
LAGOS, NIGERIA
General Environment: Oceanographic

**MILCHEM INTERNATIONAL
LIMITED**
4 AZIKIWE ROAD, PO BOX 669
PORT HARCOURT, NIGERIA
General Environment: Oceanographic

**MINED LAND CONSERVATION
CONFERENCE**
1130 17TH STREET, NW
WASHINGTON, DC 20036
Director, G Don Sullivan
General Environment: Terrestrial
Staff Size: 500 - 999

MOBIL OIL (EAST AFRICA) LIMITED
POST OFFICE BOX 1365
ADDIS ABABA, ETHOPIA
General Environment: Oceanographic

MOBIL OIL NIGERIA LIMITED
60 BROAD STREET, PMB 2054
LAGOS, NIGERIA
Director, Hugh M Keeley
General Environment: Oceanographic

NIGERIAN GULF OIL COMPANY
TINUBU SQUARE, PMB 2469
LAGOS, NIGERIA
General Environment: Oceanographic

**NIGERIAN PETROLEUM REFINING
CORPORATION, LIMITED**
PORT HARCOURT, NIGERIA
Director, J Bell
General Environment: Oceanographic

OTIS OF NIGERIA LIMITED
11 AZIKIWE ROAD, PO BOX 462
PORT HARCOURT, NIGERIA
Director, D J Allen
General Environment: Oceanographic

**PETROLEUM SOCIETY OF
EQUATORIAL AFRICA**
BOITE POSTALE 539
PORT GENTIL, GABON
General Environment: Oceanographic

**PHILIPS PETROLEUM
CORPORATION**
8-10 BROAD STREET, PMB 12612
LAGOS, NIGERIA
Director, J W Bruynzeel, Jr
General Environment: Oceanographic

PLANET OIL COMPANY
NOVAKCHOTT, MAURITANIA
General Environment: Oceanographic

SADAL TUNA FISHERIES CANNERY
DAKAR, SENEGAL
Director, Bernard Polo
General Environment: Oceanographic

SANTA FE DRILLING COMPANY
6 PORT HARCOURT/ABA ROAD
PMB 5019, PORT HARCOURT,
   NIGERIA
General Environment: Oceanographic

SCAF TUNA FISHERIES CANNERY
DAKAR, SENEGAL
Director, M Loiseau
General Environment: Oceanographic

SHELL-BRITISH PETROLEUM, SE
DRILL CORPORATION
POST OFFICE BOX 802
PORT HARCOURT, NIGERIA
Director, Elmer J Adkins
General Environment: Oceanographic

SOMALI AMERICAN FISHING
COMPANY
SOMALI CREDIT BANK
MOGADISCIO, SOMALIA
General Environment: Oceanographic

TENNECO OIL CORPORATION OF
NIGERIA
8-10 BROAD STREET, PO BOX 2119
LAGOS, NIGERIA
General Environment: Oceanographic

TEXACO AFRICA LIMITED
241 IGBOSERE ROAD, PO BOX 166
LAGOS, NIGERIA
Director, John O Sheldon
General Environment: Oceanographic

TIDELAND SIGNAL CORPORATION
SERVICES AND SUPPLY OF WEST
   AFRICA
POB 387, PORT HARCOURT,
   NIGERIA
Director, David Smith
General Environment: Oceanographic

TIDEX (NIGERIA) LIMITED
34 FRANCIS IHEKWOABA STREET
PMB 5187, PORT HARCOURT,
   NIGERIA
Director, Charles W Jones
General Environment: Oceanographic

TRANSWORLD DRILLING
CORPORATION LIMITED
21-25 BROAD STREET, P O BOX 3651
LAGOS, NIGERIA
General Environment: Oceanographic

WESTERN NIGERIA COOPERATIVE
FISHERIES ASSOCIATION

IJORA
LAGOS, NIGERIA
General Environment: Oceanographic

WILLIAMS BROTHERS COMPANY
MILE 101/2 ABA ROAD, PO BOX 649
PORT HARCOURT, NIGERIA
General Environment: Oceanographic

Professional Organizations

INDUSTRIAL HYGIENE
ASSOCIATION
14125 PREVOST
DETROIT, MI 48227
Specific Interests: Prairie and Temperate
   Forest

MANAGEMENT INSTITUTE
125 EAST 38TH STREET
NEW YORK, NY 10016
Specific Interests: Urban

JUVENILE DELINQUENCY

Government — Federal

JUVENILE DELINQUENCY, YOUTH
OFFICE
WELFAREE ADMINISTRATION,
DEPARTMENT OF HEALTH,
EDUCATION AND WELFARE
WASHINGTON, DC 20201

Government — State or Local

RESOURCES DIVISION,
CALIFORNIA YOUTH AUTHORITY
STATE OFFICE BUILDING NO. 1
SACRAMENTO, CA 95814

Research Institute

INFORMATION CENTER FOR
CRIME DELINQUENCY
NCCD CENTER
PARAMUS, NJ 07652

LABOR RELATIONS/ UNIONS

Educational Institute

INDUSTRIAL LABOR RELATIONS
LIBRARY
CORNELL UNIVERSITY
ITHACA, NY 14850

INDUSTRIAL RELATIONS BOARD,
WEST VIRGINIA UNIVERSITY
344 ARMSTRONG
MORGANTOWN, WV 26506
Staff Size: 5 - 9

INDUSTRIAL RELATIONS BUREAU,
BUSINESS ADMINISTRATION
SCHOOL
UNIVERSITY OF MICHIGAN
ANN ARBOR, MI 48104

INDUSTRIAL RELATIONS CENTER,
UNIVERSITY OF HAWAII
2500 CAMPUS ROAD
HONOLULU, HI 96822

INDUSTRIAL RELATIONS LIBRARY
INSTITUTE OF TECHNOLOGY
PASADENA, CA 91109

MANAGEMENT INSTITUTE, LABOR
RELATIONS DEPARTMENT
RYDER'S LANE, RUTGERS STATE
UNIVERSITY
NEW BRUNSWICK, NJ 08901

Government — Federal

LABOR, MANAGEMENT AND
WELFARE DEPARTMENT
8757 GEORGIA AVENUE
SILVER SPRING, MD 20910
Staff Size: 100 - 499

NATIONAL LABOR RELATIONS
BOARD
1717 PENNSYLVANIA AVENUE, NW
WASHINGTON, DC 20570

Government — State or Local

LABOR AND INDUSTRY
DEPARTMENT
GENERAL ADMINISTRATION
BUILDING
OLYMPIA, WA 98502

LABOR BUREAU OF IOWA
STATE HOUSE
DES MOINES, IA 50319

**LABOR STATISTICS OFFICE,
INDUSTRIAL RESEARCH
DEPARTMENT**
455 GOLDEN GATE AVENUE
SAN FRANCISCO, CA 94102
Staff Size: 10 - 49

**RESEARCH OFFICE, LABOR
DEPARTMENT**
1800 WASHINGTON STREET, EAST
CHARLESTON,WV 25305

Industrial/Commercial

**INDUSTRIAL RELATIONS COUNCIL
INFORMATION SERVICE**
1270 AVENUE OF THE AMERICAS
NEW YORK, NY 10020

Professional Organizations

AFL-CIO
AFL-CIO BUILDING, 815 16TH
STREET, NW
WASHINGTON, DC 20006
Specific Interests: Urban

**INTERNATIONAL LABOUR
ORGANIZATION**
GENEVA, SWITZERLAND

**WILLIAM GREEN HUMAN
RELATIONS LIBRARY**
25 EAST 78TH STREET
NEW YORK,NY 10021

Research Institute

**LABOR AND INDUSTRIES
DEPARTMENT**
STATE HOUSE, ROOM 473
BOSTON, MA 02133

**LABOR COLLEGE, DETROIT
PUBLIC LIBRARY**
5201 WOODWARD STREET
DETROIT, MI 48202

**RESEARCH DEPARTMENT,
INTERNATIONAL LADIES
GARMENT WORKERS UNION**
1710 BROADWAY
NEW YORK,NY 10019

LAW/LEGISLATION

Educational Institute

ENVIRONMENTAL LAW SOCIETY
HARVARD LAW SCHOOL
CAMBRIDGE, MA 02138

**FACULTY EXCHANGE, BUREAU OF
GOVERNMENT RESEARCH**
UNIVERSITY OF OKLAHOMA
NORMAN, OK 73069

**GOVERNMENT LIBRARY BUREAU,
UNIVERSITY OF MICHIGAN**
100-A RACKHAM BUILDING
ANN ARBOR, MI 48104

**HEALTH LAW CENTER,
UNIVERSITY OF PITTSBURGH**
130 DE SOTO STREET
PITTSBURGH,PA 15213

**MUNICIPAL GOVERNMENT
RESEARCH BUREAU**
HUBBARD HALL, BOWDOIN
COLLEGE
BRUNSWICK, ME 04011
Specific Interests: Urban

PUBLIC ADMINISTRATION BUREAU
LOUISIANA STATE UNIVERSITY
BATON ROUGE, LA 70803

Foundation

**CONSERVATION LAW
FOUNDATION OF NEW
ENGLAND, INCORPORATED**
95 NORTH MAIN STREET
CONCORD, NH 03301
President, Joan W Barto

RESPONSIVE LAW STUDY CENTER
POST OFFICE BOX 19367
WASHINGTON, DC 20036
Staff Size: 10 - 49

**SAVE AMERICA'S VITAL
ENVIRONMENT**
POST OFFICE BOX 52652
ATLANTA, GA 30305

Government — Federal

**AIR AND WATER DIVISION,
ENVIRONMENTAL PROTECTION
AGENCY**
WATERSIDE MALL, ROOM 3710
WASHINGTON, DC 20460

Director, D J Borchers
General Environment: Atmospheric
Staff Size: 100 - 499

**SOCIAL LEGISLATION
INFORMATION SERVICE
INSTITUTE**
1346 CONNECTICUT AVENUE, NW
WASHINGTON, DC 20036

Government — State or Local

**COUNCIL OF STATE
GOVERNMENTS**
IRON WORKS PIKE
LEXINGTON, KY 40505
Staff Size: 50 - 99

LEGISLATIVE COUNCIL SERVICES
201 STATE CAPITOL
SANTA FE, NM 87501

**LEGISLATIVE REFERENCE AND
RESEARCH DIVISION, STATE
LIBRARY**
109 STATE CAPITOL
OKLAHOMA CITY,OK 73105

**LEGISLATIVE REFERENCE
BUREAU**
STATE CAPITOL
MADISON,WI 53702

**LEGISLATIVE REFERENCE
LIBRARY**
EDUCATION BUILDING
ALBANY,NY 12224

**LEGISLATIVE RESOURCES
COMMISSION**
STATE CAPITOL BUILDING
FRANKFORT, KY 40601

**LEGISLATIVE RESOURCES
COUNCIL, SOUTH DAKOTA**
STATE CAPITOL
PIERRE, SD 57501

Professional Organizations

**CITIZENS COMMISSION FOR
NATURE CONSERVATION**
819 NORTH MAIN STREET
ROCKFORD, IL 61103
Specific Interests: Prairie and Temperate
Forest

**CONSERVATION LAW SOCIETY OF
AMERICA**
1500 MILLS TOWER, 220 BUSH
SAN FRANCISCO, CA 94104
Director, Robert W Jasperson
Staff Size: 1 - 4

**ENVIRONMENTAL DEFENSE FUND,
INCORPORATED**
162 OLD TOWN, EAST SETAUKET
NEW YORK, NY 11733

**GAME AND FRESH WATER
FISHERIES COMMISSION**
646 WEST TENNESEE STREET
TALLAHASSE, FL 32303
Director, D Aldrich
Staff Size: 10 - 49

**INTERNATIONAL COUNCIL FOR
ENVIRONMENTAL LAW**
GENEVA, SWITZERLAND

**INTERNATIONAL LAW
ASSOCIATION**
3 PAPER BUILDINGS, TEMPLE
SQUARE
LONDON, EC4, ENGLAND

LAW AND SOCIAL POLICY CENTER
1600 20TH STREET, NW
WASHINGTON, DC 20009
Staff Size: 5 - 9

POLITICAL SCIENCE ASSOCAITION
1726 MASSACHUSETTS AVENUE, NW
WASHINGTON, DC 20036
Specific Interests: Urban

Research Institute

CONSERVATION TRUSTEES
251 KEARNY STREET
SAN FRANCISCO, CA 94108
Director, William J Losh

ENVIRONMENTAL LAW INSTITUTE
1346 CONNECTICUT AVENUE
WASHINGTON, DC 20036
Staff Size: 10 - 49

**GOVERNMENTAL AFFAIRS
INSTITUTION**
1776 MASSACHUSETTS AVENUE, NW
WASHINGTON, DC 20036
Staff Size: 50 - 99

**POLLUTION RESEARCH
CONSORTUIM**
P O BOX 1248
ANN ARBOR, MI 48106

**PUBLIC POLICY RESEARCH
INSTITUTE**
1150 17TH STREET, NW
WASHINGTON, DC 20036
Specific Interests: Urban

MENTAL HEALTH

Educational Institute

**HOGG FOUNDATION FOR MENTAL
HEALTH**
UNIVERSITY OF TEXAS
AUSTIN, TX 78712

**MENTAL HEALTH RESEARCH
INSTITUTE, MICHIGAN
UNIVERSITY**
205 NORTH FOREST
ANN ARBOR, MI 48104

**MENTAL HEALTH RESOURCES
INSTITUTE**
UNIVERSITY OF MICHIGAN,
MEDICAL SCHOOL
ANN ARBOR, MI 48104

Foundation

**AMERICAN MENTAL HEALTH
FOUNDATION, INCORPORATED**
2 EAST 86TH STREET
NEW YORK, NY 10028
Specific Interests: Urban

Government — Federal

**HEALTH SERVICES AND MENTAL
HEALTH ADMINISTRATION**
14405 BARKWOOD DRIVE
ROCKVILLE, MD 20853
Administrator, Dr Vernon E Wilson

MENTAL HEALTH INSTITUTE
7817 GREENTWIG ROAD
BETHESDA, MD 20014
Director, Dr Bertram Brown

**MENTAL RETARDATION BRANCH,
CHILD HEALTH AND HUMAN
DEVELOPMENT**
NATIONAL INSTITUTE OF HEALTH,
PUBLIC HEALTH SERVICE
BETHESDA, MD 20014

**NATIONAL CLEARINGHOUSE FOR
MENTAL HEALTH**
NATIONAL INSTITUTION OF
MENTAL HEALTH
BETHESDA, MD 20014

Government — State or Local

**JUVENILE RESEARCH INSTITUTE,
DEPARTMENT OF MENTAL
HEALTH**
907 SOUTH WOLCOTT AVENUE
CHICAGO, IL 60612

**MENTAL HYGIENE DIVISION,
PUBLIC HEALTH DEPARTMENT**
STATE OFFICE BUILDING
MONTGOMERY, AL 36104

Research Institute

**INTRAMURAL RESEARCH,
NATIONAL INSTITUTE OF
MENTAL HEALTH**
HEALTH SERVICES AND MENTAL
HEALTH ADMINISTRATION
BETHESDA, MD 20014

**NATIONAL ASSOCIATION OF
RETARDED CHILDREN,
INCORPORATED**
420 LEXINGTON AVENUE
NEW YORK, NY 10017

POLITICS

Educational Institute

**B A ARNESON INSTITUTE OF
PRACTICAL POLLUTION**
OHIO WESLEYAN UNIVERSITY
DELEWARE, OH 43015

GOVERNMENT RESEARCH BUREAU
UNIVERSITY OF SOUTH DAKOTA
VERMILLION, SD 57069

**GOVERNMENTAL RESEARCH
BUREAU**
UNIVERSITY OF NEVADA
RENO, NV 89507

**GOVERNMENTAL RESOURCES
INSTITUTE**
124 DODD HALL, FLORIDA STATE
UNIVERSITY
TALLAHASSEE, FL. 32306

**INTERNATIONAL RELATIONS
COMMITTEE**
UNIVERSITY OF NOTRE DAME
NOTRE DAME, IN 46556

POLITICAL ECOLOGY
  DEPARTMENT
STATE UNIVERSITY OF NEW YORK
OLD WESTBURY, NY 11568
Specific Interests: Prairie and Temperate
  Forest

POLITICAL PSYCHOLOGY
  INSTITUTE, BROOKLYN
  COLLEGE
BEDFORD AVENUE AND AVENUE H
BROOKLYN, NY 11210
Specific Interests: Urban

POLITICAL SCIENCES
  LABORATORY
UNIVERSITY OF IOWA
IOWA CITY, IA 52240
Staff Size: 10 - 49

PUBLIC ADMINISTRATION
  INSTITUTE, INDIANA
  UNIVERSITY
BALLANTINE HALL 915
BLOOMINGTON, IN 47405

Government — Federal

ADVISORY COMMISSION ON
  INTERGOVERNMENTAL
  RELATIONS
726 JACKSON PLACE, NW
WASHINGTON, DC 20575
Staff Size: 10 - 49

Professional Organizations

ENVIRONMENTAL INFORMATION
  COMMISSION
438 NORTH SKINKER BOULEVARD
ST LOUIS, MO 63130
Director, Sheldon Novick
Specific Interests: Prairie and Temperate
  Forest

POPULATION
STUDIES/FAMILY
PLANNING

Educational Institute

BIOLOGICAL-MEDICAL DIVISION,
  POPULATION COUNCIL
ROCKEFELLER UNIVERSITY
NEW YORK, NY 10021
Director, S Segal

POPULATION AND FAMILY
  HEALTH DEPARTMENT
JOHNS HOPKINS UNIVERSITY
BALTIMORE, MD 21205
Director, J Rantner

POPULATION ASSOCIATION OF
  AMERICA
NATIONAL CENTER FOR HEALTH
  STATISTICS
WASHINGTON, DC 20201
Secretary, Anders S Lunde
Specific Interests: Prairie and Temperate
  Forest
Staff Size: 1000 - 4999

POPULATION COUNCIL
245 PARK AVENUE
NEW YORK, NY 10017
President, Bernard Berelson
Specific Interests: Prairie and Temperate
  Forest

POPULATION CRISIS COMMISSION
1730 K STREET, NW
WASHINGTON, DC 20006
National Chairman, James W
  Riddleberger

POPULATION DIVISION, PUBLIC
  HEALTH SCHOOL
UNIVERSITY OF PITTSBURGH
PITTSBURGH, PA 15213
Director, John Cutler
Staff Size: 10 - 49

POPULATION REFERENCE BUREAU
1755 MASSACHUSETTS AVENUE, NW
WASHINGTON, DC 20036
Director, William E Moran
Staff Size: 10 - 49

POPULATION RESEARCH AND
  CENSUS BUILDING
UNIVERSITY OF WASHINGTON
SEATTLE,WA 98105

POPULATION RESEARCH OFFICE
PRINCETON UNIVERSITY, 5 IVY
  LANE
PRINCETON, NJ 08540
Director, Ansley Coale
Staff Size: 10 - 49

POPULATION STUDIES CENTER
UNIVERSITY OF MICHIGAN
ANN ARBOR, MI 48104
Director, David Goldberg
Staff Size: 10 - 49

POPULATION STUDIES CENTER
UNIVERSITY OF PENNSYLVANIA,
  3718 LOCUST STREET
PHILADELPHIA, PA 19104
Director, Dr V Whitney
Staff Size: 10 - 49

Foundation

HUGH MOORE FUND
60 EAST 42ND STREET
NEW YORK, NY 10017

INTERNATIONAL PLANNED
  PARENTHOOD FEDERATION
18-20 LOWER REGENT STREET
LONDON, SW1, ENGLAND

OPTIMUM POPULATION,
  INCORPORATED
CHARLOTTE, VT 05445

PATHFINDER FUND
850 BOYLSTON STREET
CHESTNUT HILL, MA 02167

PLANNED PARENTHOOD LEAGUE
  OF MASSACHUSETTS
93 UNION STREET
NEWTON CENTRE, MA 02159

PLANNED PARENTHOOD, WORLD
  POPULATION DIVISION
810 7TH AVENUE
NEW YORK, NY 10019

POPULATION AND ENVIRONMENT
  COUNCIL
100 EAST OHIO STREET
CHICAGO, IL 60611
Director, Janet H Malone
Staff Size: 1 - 4

POPULATION STUDIES CENTER
HARVARD MEDICAL SCHOOL
BOSTON, MA 02115

RESOURCES STATION UNIT,
  EMPLOYMENT DEPARTMENT
P O BOX 602
CARSON CITY, NV 89701

SCRIPPS FOUNDATION FOR
  POPULATION RESEARCH
218 HARRISON HALL, MIAMI
  UNIVERSITY
OXFORD, OH 45056

ZERO POPULATION GROWTH
BOX 237
CONCORD, NH 03301

ZERO POPULATION GROWTH
210 ELM STREET
NORTHAMPTON, MA 01060

ZERO POPULATION GROWTH
14 BEACON STREET
BOSTON, MA

ZERO POPULATION GROWTH
POST OFFICE BOX 608
DURHAM, NH 03824

ZERO POPULATION GROWTH
29 ARCADIA STREET
LONGMEADOW, MA 01106

ZERO POPULATION GROWTH
BOX 422
HARTFORD, CT 06101
Staff Size: 1 - 4

ZERO POPULATION GROWTH
4080 FABIAN WAY
PALO ALTO, CA 94303
Staff Size: 10 - 49

ZERO POPULATION GROWTH
POST OFFICE BOX 47
FAIRFIELD, CT 06430
Staff Size: 1 - 4

ZERO POPULATION GROWTH
BOX 124
ORONO, ME 04473
Director, G Metz

ZERO POPULATION GROWTH
41 WASHINGTON STREET
NATICK, MA 01760
Director, Yale Hicks

ZERO POPULATION GROWTH
MOUNT HOLYOKE COLLEGE
SOUTH HADLEY, MA 01075

ZERO POPULATION GROWTH
BOX 2151, BRANDEIS UNIVERSITY
WALTHAM, MA 02154
Staff Size: 10 - 49

ZERO POPULATION GROWTH
BOX 0913
MIDDLEBURY, VT 05753

ZERO POPULATION GROWTH
36 CHURCH STREET
WESTBORO, MA 01581

ZERO POPULATION GROWTH
BOX 1947
NEW HAVEN, CT 06520

ZERO POPULATION GROWTH
PO BOX 81
STORRS, CT 06268

ZERO POPULATION GROWTH
THE HOTCHKISS SCHOOL
LAKEVILLE, CT 06036

ZERO POPULATION GROWTH
BOX 607
BRANFORD, CT 06405
Director, Mrs John Stannard

ZERO POPULATION GROWTH
BOX 599
HANOVER, NH 03755

ZERO POPULATION GROWTH
BOX 147
BRUNSWICK, ME 04011
Director, Lowell Finch

ZERO POPULATION GROWTH
367 STATE STREET
LOS ALTOS, CA 94022

ZERO POPULATION GROWTH
303 PEARL STREET
BURLINGTON, VT 05401
Director, Mrs Lynn Miller

ZERO POPULATION GROWTH
SHARON ROAD
PETERBOROUGH, NH 03458
Director, Dr William Preston

ZERO POPULATION GROWTH
POST OFFICE BOX 89
KINGSTON, RI 02881

**ZERO POPULATION GROWTH,
CONNECTICUT FEDERATION**
POST OFFICE BOX 422
HARTFORD, CT 06101
Staff Size: 1 - 4

Government — Federal

ECONOMIC RESEARCH SERVICE
14TH STREET AND
  INDEPENDENCE AVENUE
WASHINGTON, DC 20250

**FAMILY PLANNING SERVICE
  CENTER**
5600 FISHERS LANE
ROCKVILLE, MD 20852
Director, Dr Frank Beckles

Government — State or Local

**MOSKOVSKIY EKONOMIKO
  INSTITUT**
BOLSHOY STROCHENOVSKIY 18
MOSCOW, UNION OF SOVIET
  SOCIALIST REPUBLICS
Staff Size: 5 - 9

PUBLIC HEALTH DEPARTMENT
STATE OFFICE BUILDINGS
SPRINGFIELD,IL 62706

**RESEARCH OFFICE, HEALTH
  DEPARTMENT**
1250 PUNCHBOWL STREET, PO BOX
  3378
HONOLULU, HI 96801

**STATISTICAL RESEARCH AND
  RECORDS BUREAU, HEALTH
  DEPARTMENT**
301 PRESTON STREET
BALTIMORE,MD 21201

**VITAL STATISTICS DIVISION,
  HEALTH DEPARTMENT**
STATE OFFICE BUILDING
DES MOINES,IA 50319

Professional Organizations

**POPULATION STUDIES CENTER,
  INSTITUTION D'ETUDE
  DEMOGRAPHIQUES**
23 AVENUE FRANKLIN ROOSEVELT
PARIS 8, FRANCE

Research Institute

**MARGARET SANGER RESEARCH
  BUREAU, INCORPORATED**
17 WEST 16TH STREET
NEW YORK, NY 10011
Staff Size: 50 - 99

**PLANNED PARENTHOOD, WORLD
  POPULATION RESEARCH
  DEPARTMENT**
515 MADISON AVENUE
NEW YORK, NY 10022

**POPULATION AND ECONOMIC
  RESOURCES**
UNIVERSITY OF VIRGINIA
CHARLOTTESVILLE, VA 22903
Staff Size: 5 - 9

POPULATION RESEARCH CENTER
UNIVERSITY OF CHICAGO
CHICAGO, IL 60637
Director, Philip Hauser
Staff Size: 5 - 9

**WORLD NEIGHBORS,
  INCORPORATED**
5116 NORTH PORTLAND AVENUE
OKLAHOMA CITY, OK 73112

PSYCHOLOGY/ BEHAVIORAL SCIENCE

Educational Institute

**BEHAVIORAL RESEARCH
  INSTITUTE**

2426 LINDEN LANE
SILVER SPRING, MD 20910

BEHAVORIAL SCIENCE INSTITUTE
UNIVERSITY OF COLORADO
BOULDER, CO 80304

CLINIC COMPLEX
INDIANA UNIVERSITY
BLOOMINGTON, IN 47405

**EDUCATIONAL PSYCHOLOGY
LIBRARY, UNIVERSITY OF
CALIFORNIA**
405 HILGARD AVENUE
LOS ANGELES, CA 90024
Staff Size: 10 - 49

ETHNIC RESEARCH BUREAU
UNIVERSITY OF ARIZONA
TUCSON, AZ 85717
Director, Dr Thomas Weaver
Staff Size: 10 - 49

PSYCHOLOGY LIBRARY
GREEN HALL, PRINCETON
UNIVERSITY
PRINCETON, NJ 08540

**RESOURCES DIVISION, OHIO
STATE UNIVERSITY**
1775 SOUTH COLLEGE ROAD
COLUMBUS, OH 43210

**ROPER PUBLIC OPINION
RESEARCH CENTER**
WILLIAMS COLLEGE
WILLIAMSTOWN, MA 01267

SEXUAL RESEARCH INSTITUTE
INDIANA UNIVERSITY
BLOOMINGTON, IN 44058

**SOCIAL PSYCHOLOGY
DEPARTMENT, PUBLIC HEALTH
SCHOOL**
UNIVERSITY OF TEXAS
HOUSTON, TX 77025

**SOCIAL SCIENCES RESEARCH
CENTER, MISSISSIPPI STATE
UNIVERSITY**
P O BOX 238
STATE COLLEGE, MS 39762

Foundation

**HUMAN BEHAVIOR RESEARCH
FOUNDATION**
508 EAST WILLIAM STREET
ANN ARBOR, MI 48108

Government — Federal

**BEHAVIOR RESOURCES,
ANTHROPOMETRIC
LABORATORY**
ANTIOCH COLLEGE
YELLOW SPRINGS, OH 45387

**BEHAVIORAL SCIENCES DIVISION,
NATIONAL ACADEMY OF
SCIENCES**
2102 CONSTITUTION AVENUE, NW
WASHINGTON, DC 20418

**INTELLIGENCE AND RESEARCH
BUREAU**
2201 C STREET, NW
WASHINGTON, DC 20525

Professional Organizations

**AMERICAN PSYCHOLOGICAL
ASSOCIATION**
1200 17TH STREET, NW
WASHINGTON, DC 20036

Research Institute

**BIOSCIENCES INFORMATION
SERVICE**
2100 ARCH STREET
PHILADELPHIA, PA 19103

FELS RESEARCH INSTITUTE
LIVERMORE STREET
YELLOW SPRINGS, OH 45387
Staff Size: 50 - 99

**PSYCHOLOGICAL STUDIES
LABORATORY**
STEVENS INSTITUTE OF
TECHNOLOGY
HOBOKEN,NJ 07030

PSYCHOMETRIC SOCIETY
231 HILLCREST DR
CINCINNATI, OH 45215
Director, Dr W G Millenkopf

RECREATION AND LEISURE

Educational Institute

**GOOD OUTDOOR MANNERS
ASSOCIATION**

POST OFFICE BOX 7095
SEATTLE, WA 98133
President, June Mehrer
General Environment: Terrestrial
Staff Size: 10 - 49

**LAND MANAGEMENT
CURRICULUM**
UNIVERSITY OF WISCONSIN
RIVER FALLS, WI 54022
General Environment: Terrestrial
Specific Interests: Rural
Staff Size: 1 - 4

**RECREATION AND PARKS
ADMINISTRATION**
ARIZONA POLYTECHNICAL
COLLEGE
RUSSELLVILLE, AZ 72801
Staff Size: 1 - 4

Foundation

**FEDERATION OF WESTERN
OUTDOOR CLUBS**
3340 MAYFIELD AVENUE
SAN BERNARDINO, CA 92405
Director, Clark H Jones
General Environment: Terrestrial
Staff Size: 1000 & Larger

**FISHERIES AND GAME
COMMISSION**
EAST 4TH STREET AND COURT
AVENUE
DES MOINES, IA 50309
Staff Size: 10 - 49

Government — Federal

**JOB CORPS, MANPOWER
ADMINISTRATION**
1111 18TH STREET, NW
WASHINGTON, DC 20210

NATIONAL PARK SERVICE
C STREET, BETWEEN 18TH AND
19TH STREETS, NW
WASHINGTON, DC 20240

**NATIONAL PARK SERVICE,
INTERIOR DEPARTMENT**
18TH AND C STREETS
WASHINGTON, DC 20240

OUTDOOR RECREATION BUREAU
111 PRINCESS STREET
ALEXANDRIA, VA 22314
Director, G Douglas Hofe, Jr

RECREATION AND PARK ASSOCIATION
OGLEBAY PARK
WHEELING, WV 26003
General Environment: Limnologic

RECREATION DEPARTMENT
3005 10TH STREET, NE
WASHINGTON, DC 20018
Chairman, William Thomas

Government — State or Local

PARKS DIVISION, METRO DISTRICT COMMISSION
20 SOMERSET STREET
BOSTON, MA 02108

RECREATION SERVICE COMMISSION
BOX 856
CONCORD, NH 03301
Director, Richard Tapley

Professional Organizations

AMERICAN CAMPING ASSOCIATION
BRADFORD WOODS
MARTINSVILLE, IN 46151
Executive Director, Ernest F Schmidt
General Environment: Terrestrial
Staff Size: 10 - 49

APPALACHIAN MOUNTAIN CLUB
5 JOY STREET
BOSTON, MA 02108
President, Gardner W Moulton
Specific Interests: Prairie and Temperate Forest
Staff Size: 1000 & Larger

APPALACHIAN TRAIL CONFERENCE
1718 N STREET, NW
WASHINGTON, DC 20036
Chairman, Stanley Murray
Specific Interests: Prairie and Temperate Forest

FISHING AND GAME ADVISORY BOARD
SCHOOL STREET
MARLBOROUGH, NH 03455
Chairman, C W Richards
Specific Interests: Prairie and Temperate Forest

NATIONAL RIFLE ASSOCIATION
1600 RHODE ISLAND AVENUE, NW
WASHINGTON, DC 20036
Specific Interests: Prairie and Temperate Forest
Staff Size: 100 - 499

OUTBOARD BOATING CLUB OF AMERICA
333 NORTH MICHIGAN AVENUE
CHICAGO, IL 60601
Specific Interests: Prairie and Temperate Forest

PARKS AND RECREATION ASSOCIATION
60 EAST BROAD STREET
COLUMBUS, OH 43215
President, Dr Patricia Fehl
Staff Size: 1 - 4

PRAIRIE CLUB
28 EAST JACKSON AVENUE, ROOM 900
CHICAGO, IL 60604
President, Eugene Dissette
Specific Interests: Prairie and Temperate Forest

SAVE OUR SHORES
921 EAST SQUANTUM STREET
SQUANTUM, MA 02186
Chairman, Mrs Nelson Saphir
General Environment: Oceanographic
Specific Interests: Prairie and Temperate Forest

SPORT FISHING INSTITUTE
719 13TH STREET, NW SUITE 503
WASHINGTON, DC 20005
President, H G Shakespeare
Specific Interests: Prairie and Temperate Forest

SPORTSMENS CLUBS FEDERATION
RFO-WESTBORO
WESTBORO, VT 05494
President, Harry R Montague
Specific Interests: Prairie and Temperate Forest

SPORTSMENS CLUBS OF MASSACHUSETTS
290 NORTH STREET
FEEDING HILLS, MA 01030
Treasurer, Edmund J Gleason
Specific Interests: Prairie and Temperate Forest

TRAIL CONFERENCE
GPO BOX 2250
NEW YORK, NY 10001
President, George M Zoebelein
Specific Interests: Prairie and Temperate Forest
Staff Size: 1000 & Larger

Research Institute

NATIONAL RECREATION ASSOCIATION
8 WEST EIGHTH STREET
NEW YORK, NY 10011

REGIONAL PLANNING

Educational Institute

NEW YORK CITY AFFAIRS CENTER
NEW SCHOOL FOR SOCIAL RESEARCH
NEW YORK, NY 10001

UPHAM HALL
UNIVERSITY OF WISCONSIN, WHITEWATER
WHITEWATER, WI 53190
Staff Size: 10 - 49

URBAN RESEARCH BUREAU
PRINCETON UNIVERSITY
PRINCETON, NJ 08540
Specific Interests: Urban

Foundation

ROCKY MOUNTAIN CENTER ON ENVIRONMENTAL STUDIES
4260 EAST EVANS AVENUE
DENVER, CO 80222
Executive Director, Roger P Hansen
Specific Interests: Mountainous
Staff Size: 10 - 49

Government — State or Local

CITY AND REGIONAL PLANNERS SOCIETY
VAN DER LELYSTRAAT 18
DELFT, NETHERLANDS
General Environment: marsh/Swamp

ECONOMIC PLANNING AND DEVELOPMENT DEPARTMENT
210 W 23RD STREET
CHEYENNE, WY 82001

METROPOLITAN REGIONAL PLANNING COMMISSION
800 CADILLAC SQUARE BUILDING
DETROIT, MI 48226

Professional Organizations

CONSERVATION ASSOCIATES
MILLS TOWER, 220 BUSH STREET
SAN FRANCISCO, CA 94104
President, Dorothy Varian
Specific Interests: Prairie and Temperate
Forest

OPEN SPACE INSTITUTE
145 EAST 52ND STREET
NEW YORK, NY 10022
Specific Interests: Prairie and Temperate
Forest

**PLANNERS INSTITUTE OF
AMERICA**
917 FIFTEENTH STREET, NW
WASHINGTON, DC 20005
Specific Interests: Prairie and Temperate
Forest

**TRANSPORTATION ACADEMY OF
AMERICA**
2222 FULLER ROAD, ROOM 107-A
ANN ARBOR, MI 48105
Director, Herbert Norder
Specific Interests: Prairie and Temperate
Forest
Staff Size: 10 - 49

Research Institute

**CARIBBEAN CONSERVATION
ASSOCIATION**
COLLEGE OF THE VIRGIN ISLANDS
ST THOMAS, VI 00801
President, Edward L Towle
Specific Interests: Tropical (hot)
Staff Size: 1 - 4

PLANNING OFFICIALS SOCIETY
1313 EAST 60TH STREET
CHICAGO, IL 60637
Specific Interests: Urban
Staff Size: 10 - 49

**PLANNING SOCIETY, INTER-
AMERICA**
1505 PONCE DE LEON AVENIDA
SANTURCE, PR 00903

PRESERVATION ASSOCIATES
BOX 22
CORNISH FLAT, NH 03746
Director, Susan Van Rensselaer
General Environment: Terrestrial
Specific Interests: Rural

**REGIONAL PLANNING
ASSOCIATION, INCORPORATED**
235 EAST 45TH STREET
NEW YORK, NY 10017
President, John P Keith
Staff Size: 10 - 49

REHABILITATION

Foundation

**CRIPPLED CHILDREN AND
ADULTS NATIONAL SOCIETY**
2023 WEST OGDEN AVENUE
CHICAGO, IL 60612

FOREST PARK FOUNDATION
600 COMMERCIAL BANK BUILDING
PEORIA, IL 61602

Government — Federal

**REHABILITATION AND SOCIAL
SERVICE ADMINISTRATION**
330 14TH STREET, SW
WASHINGTON, DC 20201

Government — State or Local

**ALCOHOLIC REHABILITATION,
PUBLIC HEALTH DEPARTMENT**
2151 BERKELEY WAY
BERKELEY, CA 94704
Specific Interests: Urban

Research Institute

**CRIPPLED AND DISABLED
REHABILITATION INSTITUTE**
400 FIRST AVENUE
NEW YORK, NY 10010

TRANSPORTATION

Educational Institute

**ENGINEERING-TRANSPORTATION
LIBRARY**

UNIVERSITY OF MICHIGAN
ANN ARBOR, MI 48104

**TRANSPORTATION AND TRAFFIC
ENGINEERING INSTITUTE**
1301 SOUTH 46TH STREET
RICHMOND, CA 94804
Specific Interests: Urban
Staff Size: 10 - 49

**TRANSPORTATION CENTER
LIBRARY**
NORTHWESTERN UNIVERSITY
LIBRARY
EVANSTON, IL 60201

Government — Federal

**ENVIRONMENTAL AND URBAN
SYSTEMS, TRANSPORTATION
DEPARTMENT**
400 7TH STREET, SW
WASHINGTON, DC 20590
General Environment: Terrestrial
Staff Size: 10 - 49

**TRANSPORTATION, MINES, POST
AND TELEGRAPH MINISTRY**
BP 416
DOVALA, CAMEROON
General Environment: Oceanographic

Government — State or Local

HIGHWAY DEPARTMENT
DOVER, DE 19901

Professional Organizations

HIGHWAY RESOURCES BOARD
2101 CONSTITUTION AVENUE NE
WASHINGTON, DC 20418

**TRANSPORTATION CRISIS
COMMISSION**
56 BOYLSTON STREET
CAMBRIDGE, MA 02138
Specific Interests: Urban
Staff Size: 5 - 9

Research Institute

**HIGHWAY SAFETY RESEARCH
INSTITUTE, UNIVERSITY OF
MICHIGAN**

HURON PARKWAY AND BAXTER
  ROAD
ANN ARBOR, MI 48105
Director, Dr Robert Hess
General Environment: Terrestrial
Staff Size: 100 - 499

NATIONAL SAFETY COUNCIL
  RESEARCH DEPARTMENT
425 NORTH MICHIGAN AVENUE
CHICAGO, IL 60611

TRAFFIC AND TRANSPORTATION
  SOCIETY
22 WEST MADISON STREET, ROOM
  404
CHICAGO, IL 60602

URBAN INSTITUTE
2100 M STREET, NW
WASHINGTON, DC 20037
Specific Interests: Urban

URBAN PROBLEMS

Educational Institute

ENVIRONMENTAL SCIENCE
  PROGRAMS
UNIVERSITY OF NORTH CAROLINA
CHAPEL HILL, NC 27514

ENVIRONMENTAL STUDIES GROUP
UNIVERSITY OF SOUTHERN
  CALIFORNIA
LOS ANGELES, CA 90007

GOVERNMENT AFFAIRS
  INSTITUTE, UNIVERSITY OF
  WISCONSIN EXTENSION
610 LANGDON STREET
MADISON, WI 53706
Staff Size: 10 - 49

SUBURBAN AFFAIRS CENTER
ROCKLAND COMMUNITY COLLEGE
SUFFERN, NY 10901

URBAN AFFAIRS CENTER
UNIVERSITY OF SOUTHERN
  CALIFORNIA
LOS ANGELES, CA 90007
Director, J W Milliman
Specific Interests: Urban
Staff Size: 10-49

URBAN ENVIRONMENT INSTITUTE
COLUMBIA UNIVERSITY
NEW YORK, NY 10022
Specific Interests: Urban

URBAN ENVIRONMENTAL STUDIES
RENSSELAER POLYTECHNICAL
  INSTITUTE
TROY, NY 12100

URBAN ENVIRONMENTAL STUDIES
  CENTER
POLYTECHNICAL INSTITUTE OF
  BROOKLYN
BROOKLYN, NY 11201

URBAN STUDIES INSTITUTE
SOUTHERN METHODIST
  UNIVERSITY
DALLAS, TX 75201

Government — Federal

DRUG PROBLEM COMMISSION
NATIONAL BANK BUILDING, ROOM
  310
BETHESDA, MD 20014
Specific Interests: Urban

Research Institute

BROOKINGS INSTITUTION
1775 MASSACHUSETTS AVENUE, NW
WASHINGTON, DC 20036
Specific Interests: Urban

SOCIAL HEALTH ASSOCIATION
1790 BROADWAY
NEW YORK, NY 10024
Specific Interests: Urban

WELFARE (Child, Public, Social)

Educational Institute

CHILD STUDY INSTITUTE
UNIVERSITY OF MARYLAND
COLLEGE PARK, MD 20742

SOCIAL WELFARE CENTER
UNIVERSITY OF MINNESOTA
  LIBRARY
MINNEAPOLIS, MN 55455

SOCIAL WELFARE GRADUATE
  SCHOOL
BRANDEIS UNIVERSITY
WALTHAM, MA 02154

Government — Federal

CHILDREN'S BUREAU, WELFARE
  ADMINISTRATION
330 INDEPENDENCE AVENUE, SW
WASHINGTON, DC 20201

FAMILY SERVICE BUREAU,
  WELFARE ADMINISTRATION
330 INDEPENDENCE AVENUE, SW
WASHINGTON, DC 20201

HEALTH, EDUCATION, AND
  WELFARE DEPARTMENT, ROOM
  8A-24, BUILDING 31
9000 ROCKVILLE PIKE
BETHESDA, MD 20014

WELFARE ADMINISTRATION,
  RESEARCH DIVISION
US DEPARTMENT OF HEALTH,
  EDUCATION AND WELFARE
WASHINGTON, DC 20201

Government — State or Local

COMMON COUNCIL OF GREATER
  NEW YORK, INFORMATION
  BUREAU
225 PARK AVENUE SOUTH
NEW YORK, NY 10003
Specific Interests: Urban

HEALTH AND WELFARE
  DEPARTMENT
66 SOUTH STREET
CONCORD, NH 03301

PENSIONS AND SECURITY
  DEPARTMENT
STATE ADMINISTRATION
  BUILDING, 64 NORTH UNION
MONTGOMERY, AL 36104

PUBLIC WELFARE COMMISSION,
  OREGON
PUBLIC SERVICE BUILDING
SALEM, OR 97310

PUBLIC WELFARE DEPARTMENT
STATE OFFICE BUILDING
NASHVILLE, TN 37219

PUBLIC WELFARE DEPARTMENT
1632 WEST ADAMS STREET
PHOENIX, AZ 85007
Specific Interests: Urban

PUBLIC WELFARE DEPARTMENT,
  COLORADO
1600 SHERMAN STREET
DENVER, CO 80203

**PUBLIC WELFARE DEPARTMENT,
   FLORIDA**
POST OFFICE BOX 2050
JACKSONVILLE, FL 32203
Specific Interests: Urban

**PUBLIC WELFARE DEPARTMENT,
   MINNESOTA**
CENTENNIAL BUILDING
ST. PAUL, MN 55101

**RESEARCH DIVISION,
   DEPARTMENT OF SOCIAL
   WELFARE**
POST OFFICE BOX 8074
SACRAMENTO, CA 95818
Specific Interests: Urban

**SOCIAL WELFARE DEPARTMENT,
   RESEARCH DIVISION**
LEWIS CASE BUILDING
LANSING, MI 48913

Professional Organizations

**AMERICAN HOSPITAL
   ASSOCIATION**
840 NORTH LAKE SHORE DRIVE
CHICAGO, IL 60611
Specific Interests: Urban

Research Institute

**CHILD WELFARE LEAGUE OF
   AMERICA**
67 IRVING PLACE
NEW YORK, NY 10003

**CONSUMER'S RESEARCH,
   INCORPORATED**
WASHINGTON, NJ 07882

**CONSUMERS UNION OF THE
   UNITED STATES,INCORPORATED**
256 WASHINGTON STREET
MOUNT VERNON, NY 10553

Interdisciplinary

GENERAL

Educational Institute

AGRONOMY AND GEOSCIENCES DEPARTMENT
PURDUE UNIVERSITY
LAFAYETTE, IN 47907
Professor of Geosciences, James Newman

AIR ENVIRONMENT STUDY CENTER, PENNSYLVANIA STATE UNIVERSITY
226 CHEMICAL ENGINEERING II
UNIVERSITY PARK, PA 16802
General Environment: Atmospheric
Staff Size: 10 - 49

AIR POLLUTION DIVISION, COUNTY HEALTH DEPARTMENT
TEXAS TECHNOLOGY UNIVERSITY
LUBBOCK, TX 79409

ARCTIC AND ALPINE RESOURCE INSTITUTE
UNIVERSITY OF COLORADO
BOULDER, CO 80302
General Environment: Terrestrial
Specific Interests: Polar (cold)

AUDUBON SOCIETY INCORPORATED
SOUTH GREAT ROAD
LINCOLN, MA 01773
Staff Size: 100 - 499

AUDUBON SOCIETY OF CONNECTICUT
2325 BURR STREET
FAIRFIELD, CT 06430
Executive Director, Marshal T Case
Staff Size: 5 - 9

AUDUBON SOCIETY OF RHODE ISLAND
40 BOWEN STREET
PROVIDENCE, RI 02903
President, Richard M Field
Staff Size: 5 - 9

BELORUSSIAN INSTITUTE IMENI S M KIROV
ULITSA SVERDLOVA, 85
MINSK, UNION OF SOVIET SOCIALIST REPUBLICS

Director, I D Yurrevich
Specific Interests: Prairie and Temperate Forest

BIOLOGY DEPARTMENT
400 MIDDLEFORD ROAD
PALO ALTO, CA 94303
Instructor, Carol Sue Burger

BIOLOGY OF NATURAL SYSTEMS CENTER
WASHINGTON UNIVERSITY
ST LOUIS, MO 63130

BOSTON UNIVERSITY
625 HUNTINGTON AVENUE
BOSTON, MA 02115
President, John J O'neil

BROOKLYN COLLEGE
BEDFORD AVENUE AND AVENUE H
BROOKLYN, NY 11210
President, George Peck

BROWN UNIVERSITY
PROVIDENCE, RI 02912
Vice-President, Malcolm S Stevens

CALIFORNIA INSTITUTE OF TECHNOLOGY
1201 EAST BOULEVARD
PASADENA, CA 91109
President, Harold Brown

CHAUTAUQUA PROJECT
BOX 250
FREDONIA, NY 14063
Director, Richard Miga
Specific Interests: Prairie and Temperate Forest

CLIMATOLOGY AND METEOROLOGY DEPARTMENT
UNIVERSITY OF RIO DE JANEIRO
RIO DE JANEIRO, BRAZIL

CLIMATOLOGY, METEOROLOGY AND STATISTICS DEPARTMENT
CALIFORNIA STATE UNIVERSITY
NORTHRIDGE, CA 91324
General Environment: Atmospheric
Staff Size: 10 - 49

CONSERVATION AND ENVIRONMENTAL SCIENCES BUREAU AT RUTGERS
COLLEGE OF AGRICULTURAL AND ENVIRONMENTAL SCIENCES

NEW BRUNSWICK, NJ 08903
Chairman, Dr Robert White-Stevens

CONSERVATION ASSOCIATION INCORPORATED AT SHEEPSCOT VALLEY
POST OFFICE BOX 125
ALNA, ME 04535
Director, Nicholas Barth

CONSERVATION ASSOCIATION OF WHOOPING CRANE
RR1, BOX 323
KULA MAUI, HI 96790
Staff Size: 100 - 499

CONSERVATION DISTRICTS, NATIONAL ASSOCIATION
1025 VERMONT AVENUE, NW
WASHINGTON, DC 20005

CONSERVATION EDUCATION CENTER
CLARION STATE COLLEGE
CLARION, PA 16214

DEPARTMENT OF RADIOLOGY
UNIVERSITY OF WISCONSIN
MADISON, WI 53706

EAGLE LAKE FIELD STATION
CHICO STATE COLLEGE
CHICO, CA 95926

ECOLOGICAL STUDIES INSTITUTE
UNIVERSITY OF NORTH DAKOTA
GRAND FORKS, ND 58201
Director, Dr Paul B Kannowski
Specific Interests: Prairie and Temperate Forest
Staff Size: 10 - 49

ECOLOGY INSTITUTE
UNIVERSITY OF CALIFORNIA
DAVIS, CA 95616
Staff Size: 100 - 499

ENGINEERING SCOOL
TULANE UNIVERSITY
NEW ORLEANS, LA 70118
Director, Dr Frank W Macdonald

ENVIRONMENT AND RESOURCE ANALYSIS CENTER
UNIVERSITY OF MONTANA
MISSOULA, MT 59801
Specific Interests: Prairie and Temperate Forest

ENVIRONMENT AND RESOURCE
ANALYSIS CENTER
MISSOULA, MT 59801
Staff Size: 5 - 9

ENVIRONMENTAL AND WATER
RESOURCES ENGINEERING
DEPARTMENT
VANDERBILT UNIVERSITY
NASHVILLE, TN 37201

ENVIRONMENTAL CENTER OF
VERMONT
WOODSTOCK, VT 05091
Staff Size: 1 - 4

ENVIRONMENTAL CENTER, DUKE
UNIVERSITY
210 OLD CHEMISTRY BUILDING
DURHAM, NC 27706
Staff Size: 5 - 9

ENVIRONMENTAL DESIGN
SCHOOL
LOUISIANA STATE UNIVERSITY
BATON ROUGE, LA 70803
Director, Gerald J Mclindon
Specific Interests: Mountainous
Staff Size: 50 - 99

ENVIRONMENTAL DESIGN,
ANTHROPOLOGY
SAN JOSE STATE COLLEGE
SAN JOSE, CA 95114

ENVIRONMENTAL ENGINEERING
SCIENCE
CALIFORNIA INSTITUTE OF
TECHNOLOGY
PASADENA, CA 91109
Staff Size: 10 - 49

ENVIRONMENTAL HEALTH
SAN JOSE STATE COLLEGE
SAN JOSE, CA 95114

ENVIRONMENTAL HEALTH
DEPARTMENT, UNIVERSITY OF
WASHINGTON
F356 HEALTH SCIENCES
BUILDING, ROAD-94
SEATTLE, WA 98195
Specific Interests: Urban
Staff Size: 10 - 49

ENVIRONMENTAL INSTITUTE,
OKLAHOMA STATE UNIVERSITY
STILLWATER, OK 74074

ENVIRONMENTAL MEDICINE
INSTITUTE
NEW YORK UNIVERSITY MEDICAL
CENTER
NEW YORK, NY 10001

ENVIRONMENTAL MEDICINE,
SCHOOL OF HYGIENE AND
PUBLIC HEALTH

JOHNS HOPKINS UNIVERSITY
BALTIMORE, MD 21205
Director, E Radford

ENVIRONMENTAL PROGRAM
UNIVERSITY OF VERMONT
BURLINGTON, VT 05401

ENVIRONMENTAL QUALITY
GUIDENCE CENTER
UNIVERSITY OF MASSACHUSETTS
AMHERST, MA 01002
Staff Size: 1 - 4

ENVIRONMENTAL QUALITY
MANAGEMENT CENTER
CORNELL UNIVERSITY
ITHACA, NY 14850
Staff Size: 1 - 4

ENVIRONMENTAL QUALITY
PROGRAMS OFFICE
PENNSYLVANIA STATE UNIVERSITY
UNIVERSITY PARK, PA 16802

ENVIRONMENTAL RESEARCH AND
PLANNING CENTER
UNIVERSITY OF NEW MEXICO
ALBUQUERQUE, NM 87101

ENVIRONMENTAL RESEARCH
CENTER
WASHINGTON STATE UNIVERSITY
PULLMAN, WA 99163
Staff Size: 5 - 9

ENVIRONMENTAL SCIENCE
KOBE UNIVERSITY
KOBE, JAPAN
Specific Interests: Prairie and Temperate
Forest

ENVIRONMENTAL SCIENCE
CENTER
COLLEGE OF NEW ROCHELLE
NEW ROCHELLE, NY 10801

ENVIRONMENTAL SCIENCE
INSTITUTE
125 SOUTH SEVENTH STREET
SAN JOSE, CA 95114
Director, Dr J Y Wang
Staff Size: 100 - 499

ENVIRONMENTAL SCIENCE
PROGRAM
SEATTLE UNIVERSITY
SEATTLE, WA 98122

ENVIRONMENTAL SCIENCE
PROGRAM
UNIVERSITY OF VIRGINIA
CHARLOTTESVILLE, VA 22903

ENVIRONMENTAL SCIENCE
PROGRAM
UNIVERSITY OF WISCONSIN
MADISON, WI 53706

ENVIRONMENTAL SCIENCE
PROGRAM
UNION COLLEGE AND UNIVERSITY
SCHENECTADY, NY 12308

ENVIRONMENTAL SCIENCE
PROGRAM
ANTIOCH COLLEGE
YELLOW SPRINGS, OH 45387

ENVIRONMENTAL SCIENCE
PROGRAM
VALPARAISO UNIVERSITY
VALPARAISO, IN 46383

ENVIRONMENTAL SCIENCE
PROGRAM
YALE UNIVERSITY
NEW HAVEN, CT 06520

ENVIRONMENTAL SCIENCE
PROGRAM
UNIVERSITY OF ILLINOIS
URBANA, IL 61801
Director, J E Corbally

ENVIRONMENTAL SCIENCE
PROGRAM
UNIVERSITY OF COLORADO
BOULDER, CO 80302

ENVIRONMENTAL SCIENCE
PROGRAM
LOUISIANA STATE UNIVERSITY
BATON ROUGE, LA 70803

ENVIRONMENTAL SCIENCE
PROGRAM
COLORADO STATE UNIVERSITY
FORT COLLINS, CO 80521
Staff Size: 1000 - 4999

ENVIRONMENTAL SCIENCE
PROGRAM
UNIVERSITY OF IOWA
IOWA CITY, IA 52240

ENVIRONMENTAL SCIENCE
PROGRAM
LOUISIANA POLYTECHNICAL
INSTITUTE
RUSTON, LA 71270

ENVIRONMENTAL SCIENCE
PROGRAM
RENSSELAER POLYTECHNICAL
INSTITUTE
TROY, NY 12181

ENVIRONMENTAL SCIENCE
PROGRAM
UNIVERSITY OF KENTUCKY
LEXINGTON, KY 40506

ENVIRONMENTAL SCIENCE
PROGRAM
UNIVERSITY OF ARIZONA
TUCSON, AZ 85721

ENVIRONMENTAL SCIENCE PROGRAM
UNIVERSITY OF CALIFORNIA
SANTA BARBARA, CA 93106

ENVIRONMENTAL SCIENCE PROGRAM
UNIVERSITY OF NORTH CAROLINA
AT GREENSBORO
GREENSBORO, NC 27412
Director, James S Ferguson
Staff Size: 10 - 49

ENVIRONMENTAL SCIENCE PROGRAM
ARIZONA STATE UNIVERSITY
TEMPE, AZ 85281
Director, G H Durham

ENVIRONMENTAL SCIENCE PROGRAM
UNIVERSITY OF ALABAMA
UNIVERSITY, AL 35486

ENVIRONMENTAL SCIENCE PROGRAM
UNIVERSITY OF WASHINGTON
SEATTLE, WA 98105

ENVIRONMENTAL SCIENCE PROGRAM
UNIVERSITY OF RICHMOND
RICHMOND, VA 23173

ENVIRONMENTAL SCIENCE PROGRAM
WEST VIRGINIA UNIVERSITY
MORGANTOWN, WV 26506

ENVIRONMENTAL SCIENCE PROGRAM
DREW UNIVERSITY
MADISON, NJ 07940

ENVIRONMENTAL SCIENCE PROGRAM
UNIVERSITY OF NEW HAMPSHIRE
DURHAM, NH 03824

ENVIRONMENTAL SCIENCE PROGRAM
MONTANA STATE UNIVERSITY
BOZEMAN, MT 59715

ENVIRONMENTAL SCIENCE PROGRAM
FLORIDA STATE UNIVERSITY
TALLAHASSEE, FL 32306
Staff Size: 10 - 49

ENVIRONMENTAL SCIENCE PROGRAM
CALIFORNIA STATE UNIVERSITY,
NORTHRIDGE
NORTHRIDGE, CA 91324

ENVIRONMENTAL SCIENCE PROGRAM

TENNESSEE TECHNOLOGY UNIVERSITY
COOKEVILLE, TN 38501

ENVIRONMENTAL SCIENCE PROGRAM
ADAMS STATE COLLEGE
ALAMOSA, CO 81101
Director, Dr R C Peterson
Staff Size: 10 - 49

ENVIRONMENTAL SCIENCE PROGRAM
DARTMOUTH COLLEGE
HANOVER, NH 03755

ENVIRONMENTAL SCIENCE PROGRAM
SAM HOUSTON STATE COLLEGE
HUNTSVILLE, TX 77340
Specific Interests: Rural
Staff Size: 10 - 49

ENVIRONMENTAL SCIENCE PROGRAM
LEHIGH UNIVERSITY
BETHLEHEM, PA 18015

ENVIRONMENTAL SCIENCE PROGRAM
THE CITADEL
CHARLESTON, SC 29401

ENVIRONMENTAL SCIENCE PROGRAM
CLEMSON UNIVERSITY
CLEMSON, SC 29631

ENVIRONMENTAL SCIENCE PROGRAM
SOUTH DAKOTA SCHOOL OF
MINES & TECHNOLOGY
RAPID CITY, SD 57701

ENVIRONMENTAL SCIENCE PROGRAM
UNIVERSITY OF MARYLAND
COLLEGE PARK, MD 20742

ENVIRONMENTAL SCIENCE PROGRAM
HARVARD UNIVERSITY
CAMBRIDGE, MA 02138

ENVIRONMENTAL SCIENCE PROGRAM
AUBURN UNIVERSITY
AUBURN, AL 36830

ENVIRONMENTAL SCIENCE PROGRAM
UNIVERSITY OF ILLINOIS
URBANA, IL 61801

ENVIRONMENTAL SCIENCE PROGRAM
MASSACHUSETTS INSTITUTE OF
TECHNOLOGY
CAMBRIDGE, MA 02139

ENVIRONMENTAL SCIENCE PROGRAM
SIMMONS COLLEGE
BOSTON, MA 02115

ENVIRONMENTAL SCIENCE PROGRAM
UNIVERSITY OF MISSOURI AT
COLUMBIA
COLUMBIA, MO 65201

ENVIRONMENTAL SCIENCE PROGRAM
UNIVERSITY OF MISSISSIPPI
UNIVERSITY, MS 38677

ENVIRONMENTAL SCIENCE PROGRAM
TEXAS AGRICULTURAL AND
MECHANICAL UNIVERSITY
COLLEGE STATION, TX 77843

ENVIRONMENTAL SCIENCE PROGRAM
ALBION COLLEGE
ALBION, MI 49224

ENVIRONMENTAL SCIENCE PROGRAM
MICHIGAN TECHNOLOGICAL
UNIVERSITY
HOUGHTON, MI 49931

ENVIRONMENTAL SCIENCE PROGRAM
EASTERN MICHIGAN UNIVERSITY
YPSILANTI, MI 48197

ENVIRONMENTAL SCIENCE PROGRAM
WAYNE STATE UNIVERSITY
DETROIT, MI 48202

ENVIRONMENTAL SCIENCE PROGRAM
UNIVERSITY OF PENNSYLVANIA
PHILADELPHIA, PA 19104

ENVIRONMENTAL SCIENCE PROGRAM
TEXAS TECHNOLOGY COLLEGE
LUBBOCK, TX 79406

ENVIRONMENTAL SCIENCE PROGRAM
UNIVERSITY OF TEXAS AT
ARLINGTON
ARLINGTON, TX 76010

ENVIRONMENTAL SCIENCE PROGRAM
ADELPHI UNIVERSITY
GARDEN CITY, NY 11530

ENVIRONMENTAL SCIENCE PROGRAM
BRIGHAM YOUNG UNIVERSITY
PROVO, UT 84601

ENVIRONMENTAL SCIENCE
   PROGRAM
MIAMI UNIVERSITY
OXFORD, OH 45056

ENVIRONMENTAL SCIENCE
   PROGRAM
JOHNS HOPKINS UNIVESITY
BALTIMORE, MD 21218

ENVIRONMENTAL SCIENCE
   PROGRAM
ALLEGHENY COLLEGE
MEADVILLE, PA 16335
General Environment: Limnologic
Staff Size: 10 - 49

ENVIRONMENTAL SCIENCE
   PROGRAM
SETON HALL UNIVERSITY
SOUTH ORANGE, NJ 07079

ENVIRONMENTAL SCIENCE
   PROGRAM
UNIVERSITY OF UTAH
SALT LAKE CITY, UT 84112

ENVIRONMENTAL SCIENCE
   PROGRAM
UNIVERSITY OF TOLEDO
TOLEDO, OH 43606

ENVIRONMENTAL SCIENCE
   PROGRAM
OHIO STATE UNIVERSITY
COLUMBUS, OH 43210

ENVIRONMENTAL SCIENCE
   PROGRAM
WITTENBERG UNIVERSITY
SPRINGFIELD, OH 45501

ENVIRONMENTAL SCIENCE
   PROGRAM, AGRICULTURE AND
   SCIENCE DIVISION
NORTH DAKOTA UNIVERSITY
FARGO, ND 58102

ENVIRONMENTAL SCIENCE
   STUDIES
UNIVERSITY OF WESTERN
   AUSTRALIA
CANBERRA,AUSTRALIA

ENVIRONMENTAL SCIENCE
   TRAINING PROGRAM
UNIVERSITY OF CALIFORNIA
RIVERSIDE, CA 92575

ENVIRONMENTAL SCIENCE,
   DEPARTMENT OF SCIENCE
KANAZAWA UNIVERSITY
NOTO, JAPAN
Specific Interests: Prairie and Temperate
   Forest

ENVIRONMENTAL SCIENCES AND
   ENGINEERING DEPARTMENT

UNIVERSITY OF NORTH CAROLINA
CHAPEL HILL, NC 27514
Staff Size: 50 - 99

ENVIRONMENTAL SCIENCES AND
   ENGINEERING INSTITUTE
UNIVERSITY OF TORONTO
TORONTO 181, ONTARIO, CANADA
Staff Size: 10 - 49

ENVIRONMENTAL SCIENCES
   CENTER
UNIVERSITY OF MINNESOTA AT
   DULUTH
DULUTH, MN 55801
General Environment: Terrestrial

ENVIRONMENTAL SCIENCES
   GROUP, CALIFORNIA STATE
   COLLEGE
1000 EAST VICTORIA STREET
DOMINGUEZ HILLS, CA 90247
Dean, Robert Fischer

ENVIRONMENTAL SCIENCES
   GROUP, COLLEGE OF IDAHO
CALDWELL, ID 83605
Director, L M Stanford

ENVIRONMENTAL SCIENCES
   GROUP, DREXEL UNIVERSITY
32ND STREET AND CHESTNUT
   STREET
PHILADELPHIA, PA 19104
Director, William W Hagerty

ENVIRONMENTAL SCIENCES
   PROGRAM
UNIVERSITY OF FLORIDA
GAINESVILLE, FL 32601

ENVIRONMENTAL SCIENCES
   PROGRAM
SAN JOSE STATE COLLEGE
SAN JOSE, CA 95114

ENVIRONMENTAL SCIENCES
   PROGRAM
CALIFORNIA STATE UNIVERSITY,
   SAN DIEGO
SAN DIEGO, CA 92115
Director, Brage Golding

ENVIRONMENTAL SCIENCES
   PROGRAM, CASE WESTERN
   RESERVE UNIVERSITY
2040 ADELBERT ROAD
CLEVELAND, OH 44106

ENVIRONMENTAL SCIENCES
   PROJECT, DUQUESNE
   UNIVERSITY
600 FORBES AVENUE
PITTSBURGH, PA 15219

ENVIRONMENTAL STUDIES
UNIVERSITY OF QUEENSLAND
BRISBANE, QUEENSLAND,
   AUSTRALIA

ENVIRONMENTAL STUDIES
SOUTH DAKOTA STATE
   UNIVERSITY
BROOKINGS, SD 57006
Staff Size: 10 - 49

ENVIRONMENTAL STUDIES
UNIVERSITY OF NEBRASKA
LINCOLN, NB 68508
Director, Dr Howard W Ottoson

ENVIRONMENTAL STUDIES
UNIVERSITY OF CINCINNATI
CINCINNATI, OH 45221
Staff Size: 1000 & Larger

ENVIRONMENTAL STUDIES
SHIGA UNIVERSITY
OTSU, JAPAN
Director, Dr Kenji Miwa
Specific Interests: Prairie and Temperate
   Forest

ENVIRONMENTAL STUDIES
SCHOOL OF MEDICINE,
   UNIVERSITY OF MIAMI
MIAMI, FL 33152

ENVIRONMENTAL STUDIES
NORTH DAKOTA STATE HEALTH
   DEPARTMENT
BISMARK, ND 58501
Specific Interests: Urban

ENVIRONMENTAL STUDIES
SCHOOL OF PUBLIC HEALTH,
   UNIVERSITY OF CALIFORNIA AT
   BERKLELEY
BERKELEY, CA 94720
Staff Size: 10 - 49

ENVIRONMENTAL STUDIES
ROCKY MOUNTAIN BIOLOGICAL
   LABORATORY
CRESTED BUTTE, CO 81224
Staff Size: 100 - 499

ENVIRONMENTAL STUDIES
NATIONAL MERCHANT MARINE
   UNIVERSITY
TOKYO, JAPAN
General Environment: Oceanographic
Specific Interests: Prairie and Temperate
   Forest

ENVIRONMENTAL STUDIES
MIYAZAKI UNIVERSITY
MIYAZAKI, JAPAN
Specific Interests: Prairie and Temperate
   Forest

ENVIRONMENTAL STUDIES
NATIONAL MERCHANT MARINE
   UNIVERSITY
KOBE, JAPAN
General Environment: Oceanographic
Specific Interests: Prairie and Temperate
   Forest

ENVIRONMENTAL STUDIES
RUTGERS UNIVERSITY, STATE
  UNIVERSITY OF NEW JERSEY
NEW BRUNSWICK, NJ 08903

ENVIRONMENTAL STUDIES
POLYTECHNICAL INSTITUTE,
  CALIFORNIA STATE
POMONA, CA 91726

ENVIRONMENTAL STUDIES
OAKLAND UNIVERSITY
ROCHESTER, MI 48063
General Environment: Atmospheric

ENVIRONMENTAL STUDIES
  CENTER
PRINCETON UNIVERSITY,
  ENGINEERING QUAD
PRINCETON, NJ 08540
Director, Professor George T Reynolds
Staff Size: 10 - 49

ENVIRONMENTAL STUDIES
  CENTER
UNIVERSITY OF MAINE
ORONO, ME 04473

ENVIRONMENTAL STUDIES
  CENTER
WILLIAMS COLLEGE
WILLIAMSTOWN, MA 01267
Staff Size: 5 - 9

ENVIRONMENTAL STUDIES
  CENTER
VIRGINIA POLYTECHNICAL
  INSTITUTE AND UNIVERSITY
BLACKSBURG, VA 24061
Director, T Marshall Hahn, Jr

ENVIRONMENTAL STUDIES
  CENTER
UNIVERSITY OF OREGON
EUGENE, OR 97403
Director, Dr Stanton Cook

ENVIRONMENTAL STUDIES
  CENTER
WILLIAMS COLLEGE
WILLIAMSTOWN, MA 01267
Director, Thomas C Joaling
Staff Size: 5 - 9

ENVIRONMENTAL STUDIES
  CENTER OF BOWLING GREEN
BOWLING GREEN, OH 43402
Staff Size: 1 - 4

ENVIRONMENTAL STUDIES
  COLLEGE
HUXLEY COLLEGE
BELLINGHAM, WA 98225
Director, G E Miller
Staff Size: 10 - 49

ENVIRONMENTAL STUDIES
  DEPARTMENT
ADAMS STATE COLLEGE
ALAMOSA, CO 81101

Specific Interests: Mountainous
Staff Size: 5 - 9

ENVIRONMENTAL STUDIES
  FACULTY
4700 KEELE STREET, YORK
  UNIVERSITY
DOWNSVIEW, ONTARIO, CANADA
Director, Gerald Carrothers
Staff Size: 10 - 49

ENVIRONMENTAL STUDIES FOR
  NORTH ENGINEERING REGION
BECKET ACADEMY, BOX 21, RIVER
  ROAD
EAST HADDAM, CT 06423
Director, Sidney I Dupont
General Environment: Estuarine
Staff Size: 50 - 99

ENVIRONMENTAL STUDIES GROUP
TEXAS CHRISTIAN UNIVERSITY
FORT WORTH, TX 76101
General Environment: Limnologic
Staff Size: 10 - 49

ENVIRONMENTAL STUDIES GROUP
2500 CALIFORNIA STREET
OMAHA, NB 68131

ENVIRONMENTAL STUDIES
  GROUP, DRAKE UNIVERSITY
26TH STREET AND UNIVERSITY
  AVENUE
DES MOINES, IA 50311

ENVIRONMENTAL STUDIES
  INSTITUTE
BAYLOR UNIVERSITY
WACO, TX 76703
Director, Dr Owen T Lind
Staff Size: 10 - 49

ENVIRONMENTAL STUDIES
  INSTITUTE, CARNEGIE-MELLON
  UNIVERSITY
500 FORBES AVENUE
PITTSBURGH, PA 15213
Director, Dr William Grouse, Jr
Staff Size: 10 - 49

ENVIRONMENTAL STUDIES
  INSTITUTE, UNIVERSITY OF
  WISCONSIN
1225 W DAYTON STREET
MADISON, WI 53706
Director, Dr Reid Bryson
Staff Size: 100 - 499

ENVIRONMENTAL STUDIES
  PROGRAM
UNIVERSITY OF PUERTO RICO
RIO PIEDRAS, PR 00931

ENVIRONMENTAL STUDIES
  PROGRAM
VILLANOVA UNIVERSITY
VILLANOVA, PA 19085

ENVIRONMENTAL STUDIES
  PROGRAM
SWARTHMORE COLLEGE
SWARTHMORE, PA 19081

ENVIRONMENTAL STUDIES
  PROGRAM
BUCKNELL UNIVERSITY
LEWISBURG, PA 17837

ENVIRONMENTAL STUDIES
  PROGRAM
WASHINGTON STATE UNIVERSITY
PULLMAN, WA 99163

ENVIRONMENTAL STUDIES
  PROGRAM
UNIVERSITY OF PUGET SOUND
TACOMA, WA WAZ98416
Staff Size: 1 - 4

ENVIRONMENTAL STUDIES
  PROGRAM
UNIVERSITY OF WISCONSIN
SUPERIOR, WI 54880
Staff Size: 10 - 49

ENVIRONMENTAL STUDIES
  PROGRAM
UNIVERSITY OF SOUTH DAKOTA
VERMILLION, SD 57069
Staff Size: 100 - 499

ENVIRONMENTAL STUDIES
  PROGRAM
UNIVERSITY OF IDAHO
MOSCOW, ID 83843

ENVIRONMENTAL STUDIES
  PROGRAM
NORTHWESTERN UNIVERSITY
EVANSTON, IL 60201

ENVIRONMENTAL STUDIES
  PROGRAM
UNIVERSITY OF GEORGIA
ATHENS, GA 30601

ENVIRONMENTAL STUDIES
  PROGRAM
WHEATON COLLEGE
WHEATON, IL 60187
Staff Size: 1 - 4

ENVIRONMENTAL STUDIES
  PROGRAM
INDIANA UNIVERSITY
BLOOMINGTON, IN 47401

ENVIRONMENTAL STUDIES
  PROGRAM
UNIVERSITY OF SANTA CLARA
SANTA CLARA, CA 95053

ENVIRONMENTAL STUDIES
  PROGRAM
STATE UNIVERSITY COLLEGE
BUFFALO, NY 14201

ENVIRONMENTAL STUDIES
 PROGRAM
STATE UNIVERSITY COLLEGE
OSWEGO, NY 13126

ENVIRONMENTAL STUDIES
 PROGRAM
STATE UNIVERSITY COLLEGE
PLATTSBURGH, NY 12901
Staff Size: 5 - 9

ENVIRONMENTAL STUDIES
 PROGRAM
BOSTON COLLEGE
CHESTNUT HILL, MA 02109
General Environment: Terrestrial

ENVIRONMENTAL STUDIES
 PROGRAM
UNIVERSITY OF CALIFORNIA
SANTA CRUZ, CA 95060

ENVIRONMENTAL STUDIES
 PROGRAM
ALFRED UNIVERSITY
ALFRED, NY 14802
Staff Size: 1 - 4

ENVIRONMENTAL STUDIES
 PROGRAM
EASTERN NEW MEXICO
 UNIVERSITY
PORTALES, NM 88130
Director, P Buscemi
Specific Interests: Desert
Staff Size: 10 - 49

ENVIRONMENTAL STUDIES
 PROGRAM
UNIVERSITY OF NORTH
 COLORADO
GREELEY, CO 80631
Staff Size: 100 - 499

ENVIRONMENTAL STUDIES
 PROGRAM
UNIVERSITY OF MIAMI
CORAL GABLES, FL 30322

ENVIRONMENTAL STUDIES
 PROGRAM
COLORADO SCHOOL OF MINES
GOLDEN, CO 80401

ENVIRONMENTAL STUDIES
 PROGRAM
UNIVERSITY OF ALASKA
FAYETTEVILLE, AK 72701

ENVIRONMENTAL STUDIES
 PROGRAM
UNIVERSITY OF DELAWARE
NEWARK, DE 19711

ENVIRONMENTAL STUDIES
 PROGRAM
UNIVERSITY OF CONNECTICUT
STORRS, CT 06268

ENVIRONMENTAL STUDIES
 PROGRAM
NORTHERN ILLINOIS UNIVERSITY
DEKALB, IL 60115
Staff Size: 10 - 49

ENVIRONMENTAL STUDIES
 PROGRAM
KANSAS STATE COLLEGE
PITTSBURG, KS 66762
Staff Size: 10 - 49

ENVIRONMENTAL STUDIES
 PROGRAM
UNIVERSITY OF CALIFORNIA,
 BERKELEY
BERKELEY, CA 94720

ENVIRONMENTAL STUDIES
 PROGRAM
CALIFORNIA STATE UNIVERSITY,
 FRESNO
FRESNO, CA 93710
Director, Norman Baxter

ENVIRONMENTAL STUDIES
 PROGRAM
KANSAS STATE UNIVERSITY
MANHATTAN, KS 66502

ENVIRONMENTAL STUDIES
 PROGRAM
IOWA STATE UNIVERSITY
AMES, IA 50010

ENVIRONMENTAL STUDIES
 PROGRAM
DARTMOUTH COLLEGE
HANOVER, NH 03755
Director, Dr Gordon Macdonald
Staff Size: 10 - 49

ENVIRONMENTAL STUDIES
 PROGRAM
ALFRED UNIVERSITY
ALFRED, NY 14802
General Environment: Limnologic
Staff Size: 5 - 9

ENVIRONMENTAL STUDIES
 PROGRAM
BOWLING GREEN STATE
 UNIVERSITY
BOWLING GREEN, OH 43032
Staff Size: 1 - 4

ENVIRONMENTAL STUDIES
 PROGRAM
MIDDLEBURY COLLEGE
MIDDLEBURY, VT 05753
Staff Size: 5 - 9

ENVIRONMENTAL STUDIES
 PROGRAM
COLBY COLLEGE
WATERVILLE, ME 04901
Staff Size: 1 - 4

ENVIRONMENTAL STUDIES
 PROGRAM
UNIVERSITY OF NOTRE DAME
NOTRE DAME, IN 46556

ENVIRONMENTAL STUDIES
 PROGRAM
UNIVERSITY OF SOUTHWESTERN
 LA
LAFAYETTE, LA 70501

ENVIRONMENTAL STUDIES
 PROGRAM
EVERGREEN STATE COLLEGE
OLYMPIA, WA 98501

ENVIRONMENTAL STUDIES
 PROGRAM
5801 ELLIS AVENUE
CHICAGO, IL 62901

ENVIRONMENTAL STUDIES
 PROGRAM
BRADLEY UNIVERSITY
PEORIA, IL 61606

ENVIRONMENTAL STUDIES
 PROGRAM
PURDUE UNIVERSITY
WEST LAFAYETTE, IN 47907

ENVIRONMENTAL STUDIES
 PROGRAM
BROAD STREET AND
 MONTGOMERY AVENUE
PHILADELPHIA, PA 19122

ENVIRONMENTAL STUDIES
 PROGRAM
UNIVERSITY OF SOUTH CAROLINA
COLUMBIA, SC 29208

ENVIRONMENTAL STUDIES
 PROGRAM
LAMAR STATE COLLEGE OF
 TECHNOLOGY
BEAUMONT, TX 77704

ENVIRONMENTAL STUDIES
 PROGRAM
SOUTHERN METHODIST
 UNIVERSITY
DALLAS, TX 75222

ENVIRONMENTAL STUDIES
 PROGRAM
UNIVERSITY OF TEXAS AT AUSTIN
AUSTIN, TX 78712

ENVIRONMENTAL STUDIES
 PROGRAM
UNIVERSITY OF NORTH CAROLINA
 AT CHAPEL HILL
CHAPEL HILL, NC 27514

**ENVIRONMENTAL STUDIES
PROGRAM**
NORTH CAROLINA STATE
UNIVERSITY AT RALEIGH
RALEIGH, NC 27607

**ENVIRONMENTAL STUDIES
PROGRAM**
UTAH STATE UNIVERSITY
LOGAN, UT 84321

**ENVIRONMENTAL STUDIES
PROGRAM**
UNIVERSITY OF TEXAS AT EL PASO
EL PASO, TX 79999

**ENVIRONMENTAL STUDIES
PROGRAM**
UNIVERSITY OF UTAH GRADUATE
SCHOOL
SALT LAKE CITY, UT 84112

**ENVIRONMENTAL STUDIES
PROGRAM**
UNIVERSITY OF TEHRAN
TEHRAN, IRAN
Director, Dr J S Saleh

**ENVIRONMENTAL STUDIES
PROGRAM**
TUSKEGEE INSTITUTE
TUSKEGEE, AL 36088
President, Luther H Foster

**ENVIRONMENTAL STUDIES
PROGRAM**
RHODE ISLAND UNIVERSITY
KINGSTON, RI 02881
Director, Dr William Croasdale

**ENVIRONMENTAL STUDIES
PROGRAM**
WAKE FOREST UNIVERSITY
WINSTON-SALEM, NC 27106

**ENVIRONMENTAL STUDIES
PROGRAM**
UNIVERSITY OF NORTH DAKOTA
GRAND FORKS, ND 58201

**ENVIRONMENTAL STUDIES
PROGRAM**
UNIVERSITY OF ALASKA
COLLEGE, AK 99701
Director, Takeshi Ohtake
General Environment: Atmospheric
Specific Interests: Polar (cold)

**ENVIRONMENTAL STUDIES
PROGRAM**
BOWLING GREEN STATE
UNIVERSITY
BOWLING GREEN, OH 43402

**ENVIRONMENTAL STUDIES
PROGRAM**
4001 W MCNICHOLS ROAD
DETROIT, MI 48221

**ENVIRONMENTAL STUDIES
PROGRAM**
NEW MEXICO STATE UNIVERSITY
LAS CRUCES, NM 88001

**ENVIRONMENTAL STUDIES
PROGRAM**
STATE UNIVERSITY OF NEW YORK
AT STONY BROOK
STONY BROOK, NY 11790

**ENVIRONMENTAL STUDIES
PROGRAM**
ITHACA COLLEGE
ITHACA, NY 14850

**ENVIRONMENTAL STUDIES
PROGRAM**
CORNELL UNIVERSITY
ITHACA, NY 14850
Staff Size: 1000 - 4999

**ENVIRONMENTAL STUDIES
PROGRAM**
UNIVERSITY OF MONTANA
MISSOULA, MT 59801

**ENVIRONMENTAL STUDIES
PROGRAM**
UNIVERSITY OF NEW MEXICO
ALBUQUERQUE, NM 87106

**ENVIRONMENTAL STUDIES
PROGRAM**
FAIRLEIGH DICKINSON
UNIVERSITY
RUTHERFORD, NJ 07070

**ENVIRONMENTAL STUDIES
PROGRAM**
UNIVERSITY OF NEVADA, RENO
RENO, NV 89807

**ENVIRONMENTAL STUDIES
PROGRAM**
UNIVERSITY OF MICHIGAN
ANN ARBOR, MI 48104

**ENVIRONMENTAL STUDIES
PROGRAM**
SOUTHEAST MISSOURI STATE
COLLEGE
CAPE GIRARDEAU, MO 63701

**ENVIRONMENTAL STUDIES
PROGRAM**
UNIVERSITY OF SOUTHERN
MISSISSIPPI
HATTIESBURG, MS 39401

**ENVIRONMENTAL STUDIES
PROGRAM**
MISSISSIPPI STATE UNIVERSITY
STATE COLLEGE, MS 39762

**ENVIRONMENTAL STUDIES
PROGRAM**
PRINCETON UNIVERSITY
PRINCETON, NJ 08540

**ENVIRONMENTAL STUDIES
PROGRAM**
KENT STATE UNIVERSITY
KENT, OH 44240

**ENVIRONMENTAL STUDIES
PROGRAM**
CENTRAL MICHIGAN UNIVERSITY
MT PLEASANT, MI 48858

**ENVIRONMENTAL STUDIES
PROGRAM**
NORTHERN MICHIGAN
UNIVERSITY
MARQUETTER, MI 49855

**ENVIRONMENTAL STUDIES
PROGRAM**
MICHIGAN STATE UNIVERSITY
EAST LANSING, MI 48823

**ENVIRONMENTAL STUDIES
PROGRAM**
BOSTON COLLEGE
CHESTNUT HILL, MA 02167

**ENVIRONMENTAL STUDIES
PROGRAM**
UNIVERSITY OF MASSACHUSETTS
AMHERST, MA 01002

**ENVIRONMENTAL STUDIES
PROGRAM**
TUFTS UNIVERSITY
MEDFORD, MA 02155

**ENVIRONMENTAL STUDIES
PROGRAM**
NORTHWESTERN UNIVERSITY
BOSTON, MA 02115

**ENVIRONMENTAL STUDIES
PROGRAM**
OHIO UNIVERSITY
ATHENS, OH 45701

**ENVIRONMENTAL STUDIES
PROGRAM**
YOUNGSTOWN STATE UNIVERSITY
YOUNGSTOWN, OH 44503
Specific Interests: Urban
Staff Size: 100 - 499

**ENVIRONMENTAL STUDIES
PROGRAM**
OREGON STATE UNIVERSITY
CORVALLIS, OR 97331

**ENVIRONMENTAL STUDIES
PROGRAM**
UNIVERSITY OF OKLAHOMA
NORMAN, OK 73069

ENVIRONMENTAL STUDIES PROGRAM, CALIFORNIA STATE COLLEGE
6101 EAST 7TH STREET
LONG BEACH, CA 90801

ENVIRONMENTAL STUDIES PROGRAM, CANISIUS COLLEGE
2001 MAIN STREET
BUFFALO, NY 14208

ENVIRONMENTAL STUDIES PROGRAM, CITY COLLEGE
CONVENT AVENUE AT 138TH STREET
NEW YORK, NY 10031
Director, Joseph J Copeland

ENVIRONMENTAL STUDIES PROGRAM, CORNELL UNIVERSITY
SCHOOL OF AGRICULTURE
ITHACA, NY 14850

ENVIRONMENTAL STUDIES PROGRAM, HUNTER COLLEGE
695 PARK AVENUE
NEW YORK, NY 10021

ENVIRONMENTAL STUDIES PROGRAM, TEXAS CHRISTIAN UNIVERSITY
UNIVERSITY DRIVE
FORT WORTH, TX 76129

ENVIRONMENTAL STUDIES PROGRAM, UNIVERSITY OF AKRON
302 EAST BUCHTEL AVENUE
AKRON, OH 44304

ENVIRONMENTAL STUDIES PROGRAM, UNIVERSITY OF MISSOURI
5100 ROCKHILL ROAD
KANSAS CITY, MO 64110

ENVIRONMENTAL STUDIES PROGRAM, UNIVERSITY OF SOUTHERN CALIFORNIA
UNIVERSITY PARK
LOS ANGELES, CA 90007
Director, Norman H Topping

ENVIRONMENTAL STUDIES PROGRAM, UNIVERSITY OF TENNESSEE
CUMBERLAND AVENUE
KNOXVILLE, TN 37916

ENVIRONMENTAL STUDIES PROJECT, CATHOLIC UNIVERSITY OF AMERICA
4TH STREET AND MICHIGAN AVENUE, NE
WASHINGTON, DC 20017

ENVIRONMENTAL STUDIES PROJECT, CLEVELAND STATE UNIVERSITY
EUCLID AVENUE AT 24TH STREET
CLEVELAND, OH 44115

ENVIRONMENTAL STUDIES, HOWARD UNIVERSITY
2400 6TH STREET, NW
WASHINGTON, DC 20001

ENVIRONMENTAL STUDIES, HUXLEY COLLEGE
WESTERN WASHINGTON STATE COLLEGE
BELLINGTON, WA 98225
Director, Dean G Miller
Staff Size: 10 - 49

ENVIRONMENTAL STUDIES, ILLINOIS INSTITUTE OF TECHNOLOGY
3300 SOUTH FEDERAL STREET
CHICAGO, IL 60616

ENVIRONMENTAL STUDIES, LOYOLA UNIVERSITY OF LOS ANGELES
LOS ANGELES, CA 90045

ENVIRONMENTAL STUDIES, LOYOLA UNIVERSITY
6363 ST CHARLES AVENUE
NEW ORLEANS, LA 70118

ENVIRONMENTAL STUDIES, LOYOLA UNIVERSITY
820 NORTH MICHIGAN AVENUE
CHICAGO, IL 60611

ENVIRONMENTAL STUDIES, MARQUETTE UNIVERSITY
1131 WEST WISCONSIN AVENUE
MILWAUKEE, WI 53233

ENVIRONMENTAL STUDIES, MISSISSIPPI STATE UNIVERSITY
POST OFFICE DRAWER GH
STATE COLLEGE, MS 39762

ENVIRONMENTAL STUDIES, NEW YORK UNIVERSITY
WASHINGTON SQUARE
NEW YORK, NY 10003

ENVIRONMENTAL STUDIES, POLYTECHNICAL INSTITUTE OF BROOKLYN
333 JAY STREET
BROOKLYN, NY 11201

ENVIRONMENTAL STUDIES, RICE UNIVERSITY
POST OFFICE BOX 1982
HOUSTON, TX 77001
Staff Size: 500 - 999

ENVIRONMENTAL STUDIES, SAINT JOHN'S UNIVERSITY
GRAND CENTRAL AND UTOPIA PARKWAYS
JAMAICA, NY 11432

ENVIRONMENTAL STUDIES, SAINT LOUIS UNIVERSITY
221 NORTH GRAND BOULEVARD
ST LOUIS, MO 63103

ENVIRONMENTAL STUDIES, SAN JOSE STATE COLLEGE
300 ALPINE CREEK ROAD
LA HONDA, CA 94020

ENVIRONMENTAL STUDIES, UNIVERSITY OF CALIFORNIA AT LOS ANGELES
405 HILGARD AVENUE
LOS ANGELES, CA 90024
Director, Robert J Evel
Staff Size: 1000 - 4999

ENVIRONMENTAL STUDIES, UNIVERSITY OF CHICAGO
5801 ELLIS AVENUE
CHICAGO, IL 60637

ENVIRONMENTAL STUDIES, UNIVERSITY OF DAYTON
300 COLLEGE PARK AVENUE
DAYTON, OH 45409

ENVIRONMENTAL STUDIES, UNIVERSITY OF DENVER
2199 SOUTH UNIVERSITY BOULEVARD
DENVER, CO 80210

ENVIRONMENTAL STUDIES, UNIVERSITY OF HAWAII
2444 DOLE STREET
HONOLULU, HI 96822

ENVIRONMENTAL STUDIES, UNIVERSITY OF HOUSTON
3801 CULLEN ROAD
HOUSTON, TX 77004

ENVIRONMENTAL STUDIES, UNIVERSITY OF MINNESOTA, DELUTH
2400 OAKLAND AVENUE
DULUTH, MN 55812

ENVIRONMENTAL STUDIES, UNIVERSITY OF OTAGO
POST OFFICE BOX 56
DUNEDIN, NEW ZEALAND
Specific Interests: Prairie and Temperate Forest

ENVIRONMENTAL STUDIES, UNIVERSITY OF PITTSBURGH
5TH AND BIGELOW STREETS
PITTSBURGH, PA 15213

**ENVIRONMENTAL STUDIES,
UNIVERSITY OF ROCHESTER**
RIVER BOULEVARD
ROCHESTER, NY 14627

**ENVIRONMENTAL STUDIES,
UNIVERSITY OF TULSA**
600 SOUTH COLLEGE
TULSA, OH 74104

**ENVIRONMENTAL STUDIES,
VANDERBILT UNIVERSITY**
21ST AVENUE AND WEST END
NASHVILLE, TN 37203

**ENVIRONMENTAL STUDIES,
WICHITA STATE UNIVERSITY**
1845 FAIRMONT STREET
WICHITA, KS 67208

**ENVIRONMENTAL STUDY, STATE
UNIVERSITY OF NEW YORK AT
ALBANY**
1400 WASHINGTON AVENUE
ALBANY, NY 12222

**ENVIRONMENTAL SYSTEMS
MANAGEMENT**
AMERICAN UNIVERSITY
WASHINGTON, DC 20016
Specific Interests: Urban
Staff Size: 5 - 9

**ENVIRONMENTAL SYSTEMS
STUDIES PROGRAM**
WORCESTER POLYTECHNICAL
INSTITUTION
WORCESTER, MA 01609
Staff Size: 10 - 49

**EPIDEMICS AND PUBLIC HEALTH
DEPARTMENT, SCHOOL OF
MEDICINE**
YALE UNIVERSITY
NEW HAVEN, CT 06510

EPIDEMOIOLOGY DIVISION
UNIVERSITY OF MINNESOTA,
SCHOOL OF PUBLIC HEALTH
MINNEAPOLIS, MN 55455
Professor, Leonard Schuman
Specific Interests: Urban
Staff Size: 10 - 49

**ETHNIC RESEARCH BUREAU,
ANTHROPOLOGY DEPARTMENT**
UNIVERSITY OF ARIZONA
TUCSON, ARIZONA

**EXPERIMENTAL PATHOLOGY AND
TOXICOLOGY INSTITUTE**
ALBANY MEDICAL COLLEGE,
UNION
ALBANY, NY 12208
Director, L Golberg

FISHERIES COLLEGE
SHIMONOSEKI, JAPAN
Specific Interests: Prairie and Temperate
Forest

**FOOD AND NUTRITION
DEPARTMENT**
SCHOOL OF HOME ECONOMICS
TALLAHASSEE, FL 32306
Professor, Betty Watts

**FOOD SCIENCES AND HUMAN
NUTRITION DEPARTMENT**
MICHIGAN STATE UNIVERSITY
EAST LANSING, MI 48823
Chairman, G Leveille
Staff Size: 10 - 49

**FOOD TECHNOLOGY
DEPARTMENT, UNIVERSITY OF
CENTRAL VENEZUELA**
ORIENTE 10098
CARACAS, VENEZUELA
Staff Size: 10 - 49

FORDHAM UNIVERSITY
FORDHAM ROAD
BRONX, NY 10458

FOREST RESOURCES SCHOOL
UNIVERSITY OF GEORGIA
ATHENS, GA 30601
Staff Size: 10 - 49

FRESNO STATE COLLEGE
SHAW AND CEDAR AVENUE
FRESNO, CA 93726

GAKUGEI UNIVERSITY
OSAKA, JAPAN
Specific Interests: Prairie and Temperate
Forest

GEOGRAPHY DEPARTMENT
JOHN HOPKINS UNIVERSITY
BALTIMORE, MD 21218
Staff Size: 10 - 49

**GEOGRAPHY, CLIMATOLOGY
DEPARTMENT**
FRESNO STATE COLLEGE
FRESNO, CA 93726

**GEOLOGY AND HYDROGRAPHY
DEPARTMENT**
UNIVERSITY OF BERN
BERN, SWITZERLAND
Professor, Fritz Gygax
Specific Interests: Mountainous

GEOLOGY DEPARTMENT
FRESNO STATE COLLEGE
FRESNO, CA 93726
Director, R Montgomery
General Environment: Atmospheric
Staff Size: 10 - 49

GEOLOGY DEPARTMENT
UNIVERSITY OF CALIFORNIA
BERKELEY, CA 94720
Director, Mario Giovenetto

GEOLOGY DEPARTMENT
PRIVATE BAG, RONDEBOSCH
CAPE TOWN, REPUBLIC OF SOUTH
AFRICA
Professor, E S W Simpson
General Environment: Oceanographic

GEOLOGY DEPARTMENT
UNIVERSITY OF GUELPH
GUELPH, ONTARIO, CANADA
Director, Frederick Hung

**GEOLOGY DEPARTMENT, SAN
FERNANDO VALLEY COLLEGE**
ROOM 120, SIERRA HALL SOUTH
NORTHRIDGE, CA 91324
Director, J F Gaines
Staff Size: 10 - 49

**GEORGIA INSTITUTE OF
TECHNOLOGY**
225 NORTH AVENUE, NW
ATLANTA, GA 30332

GIMPO WOMEN'S COLLEGE
IGUCHI, HIROSHIMA, JAPAN
Specific Interests: Prairie and Temperate
Forest

GREAT LAKES INSTITUTE
UNIVERSITY OF TORONTO
TORONTO 5, ONTARIO, CANADA
Director, D Misner
General Environment: Limnologic
Staff Size: 10 - 49

**HEALTH LAW CENTER,
UNIVERSITY OF PITTSBURGH**
130 DE SOTO STREET
PITTSBURGH, PA 12513
General Environment: Limnologic

**HEBREW UNIVERSITY-HADASSAH
MEDICAL SCHOOL**
JERUSALEM, ISRAEL
Director, M Shilo

**HUMAN RESOURCES
CONSERVATION COMMITTEE**
COLUMBIA UNIVERSITY
NEW YORK, NY 10027
Director, Eli Ginzberg

**HYDRAULICS AND SANITATION
LABORATORY**
UNIVERSITY OF WISCONSIN
MADISON, WI 53706
General Environment: Limnologic

**ICHTHYOLOGICAL LABORATORY,
TUNGHAI UNIVERSITY**
TAICHUNG KANG ROAD
TAICHUNG, TAIWAN

Director, Dr Johnson Chen
Specific Interests: Tropical (hot)

**INLAND WATER RESOURCES
CENTER**
STATE UNIVERSITY OF NEW YORK
BUFFALO, NY 14214
Director, Dr Ralph Rumer
Staff Size: 10 - 49

**LAND AND WATER RESOURCE
INSTITUTE**
WATER RESOURCES CENTER
UNIVERSITY PARK, PA 16802
General Environment: Limnologic

**LAND LEAGUE OF
MASSACHUSETTS**
26 NELSON PLACE
WORCESTER, MA 01605
General Environment: Terrestrial
Specific Interests: Rural
Staff Size: 1 - 4

MAN IN HIS ENVIRONMENT
DOMINICAN COLLEGE
RACINE, WI 53401
Specific Interests: Urban

**MANAGEMENT AND HISTORY OF
ENVIRONMENT**
MINER INSTITUTE
CHAZY, NY 12921
Staff Size: 1 - 4

**MARINE BIOLOGICAL
OCEANOGRAPHIC INSTITUTE**
CAIXA POSTAL 1076
RECIFE PERNAMBUCO, BRAZIL
Director, Francois Ottman
General Environment: Oceanographic

**MARINE RESEARCH LABORATORY,
AUCKLAND UNIVERSITY**
LEIGH, AUCKLAND PROVINCE,
NEW ZEALAND
Director, Dr W M Ballantine
General Environment: Oceanographic
Staff Size: 5 - 9

MARINE SCIENCE CENTER
MCGILL UNIVERSITY
MONTREAL, PROVINCE OF
QUEBEC, CANADA
General Environment: Oceanographic

**MARINE SCIENCES AND MARITIME
RESOURCES, TEXAS A AND M
UNIVERSITY**
BUILDING 311 FT CROCKETT
GALVESTON, TX 77550
Director, Dr Sammy M Ray
General Environment: Oceanographic
Staff Size: 5 - 9

**MARINE SCIENCES FACULTY,
UNIVERSITY OF BOGOTA**
CALLE 23 / 4-43
BOGOTA, COLUMBIA

General Environment: Oceanographic
Staff Size: 5 - 9

**MARINE SCIENCES RESEARCH
CENTER**
STATE UNIVERSITY OF NEW YORK,
STONY BROOK
STONY BROOK, NY 11790
General Environment: Oceanographic
Staff Size: 50 - 99

**MEDICAL AND UNIVERSITY
RESEARCH DIVISION**
P O BOX 395
PRETORIA, REPUBLIC OF SOUTH
AFRICA
Director, J Zwamborn
General Environment: Oceanographic

MEDICAL DEPARTMENT
UNIVERSITY OF WASHINGTON
SEATTLE, WA 98105
Director, L Rowell

**METEOROLOGICAL SCIENCES
RESEARCH INSTITUTION**
OCEANOGRAPHIC LABORATORY
NAGASAKI, JAPAN
General Environment: Oceanographic
Specific Interests: Prairie and Temperate
Forest

METEOROLOGY DEPARTMENT
NAVAL POST-GRADUATE SCHOOL
MONTEREY, CA 93940
Director, George Haltiner

METEOROLOGY DEPARTMENT
UNIVERSITY OF RHODE ISLAND
KINGSTON, RI 02881

METEOROLOGY DEPARTMENT
SAN JOSE STATE COLLEGE
SAN JOSE, CA 95114
Professor of Meteorology, Robert Read

**METEOROLOGY INSTITUTE,
FEDERAL UNIVERSITY OF CEARA**
AVENIDA VISCONDE DE CAUIPE
FORTALEGA CEARA, BRAZIL
General Environment: Atmospheric
Staff Size: 500 - 999

METEOROLOGY PROGRAM
63 NORTH 5TH STREET
SAN JOSE, CA 95120

**MINERALOGY, INDUSTRIAL
HYGIENE**
MONTANA COLLEGE OF MINERAL
SCIENCE TECHNOLOGY
BUTTE, MT 59701

NATURAL FOODS ASSOCIATES
229 CONY STREET
AUGUSTA, ME 04330

NATURAL RESOURCE SCHOOL
CALIFORNIA STATE UNIVERSITY,
HUMBOLT
ARCATA, CA 95521

**NATURAL RESOURCES
DEPARTMENT**
ALPENA COMMUNITY COLLEGE
ALPENA, MI 49707
Specific Interests: Prairie and Temperate
Forest
Staff Size: 5 - 9

**NATURAL SCIENCES DIVISION,
CALIFORNIA STATE COLLEGE**
5500 STATE COLLEGE PARKWAY
SAN BERNARDINO, CA 92405
Chairman, Professor James Crum
Staff Size: 10 - 49

**NUCLEAR SCIENCES, ENRICO
FERMI INSTITUTE OF**
UNIVERSITY OF CHICAGO
CHICAGO, IL 60601
General Environment: Atmospheric
Specific Interests: Prairie and Temperate
Forest

**NUTRITION SCHOOL, SCHOOL OF
PUBLIC HEALTH**
HARVARD UNIVERSITY
BOSTON, MA 02115
Specific Interests: Prairie and Temperate
Forest

OCEAN RESOURCES PROGRAM
OREGON STATE UNIVERSITY
CORVALLIS, OR 97330
General Environment: Oceanographic
Staff Size: 100 - 499

OCEANOGRAPHIC INSTITUTE
PRIVATE BAG, RONDEBOSCH
CAPE TOWN, REPUBLIC OF SOUTH
AFRICA

OCEANOGRAPHIC INSTITUTE
UNIVERSITY OF BRITISH
COLUMBIA
VANCOUVER, BRITISH COLUMBIA,
CANADA
Director, Dr G L Pickard
General Environment: Oceanographic

OCEANOGRAPHIC INSTITUTE
UNIVERSITY OF ORIENTE, CUMANA
ESTADO SUCRE, VENEZUELA
Director, Jose Curra

**OCEANOGRAPHIC INSTITUTE AT
SCRIPPS**
UNIVERSITY OF CALIFORNIA AT
SAN DIEGO
LA JOLLA, CA 92037
Director, Dr William Nierenberg
General Environment: Oceanographic
Staff Size: 1000 - 4999

OCEANOGRAPHIC INSTITUTE, UNIVERSITY OF RECIFE
PRAIA DA PIEDADE
RECIFE, BRAZIL
General Environment: Oceanographic

OCEANOGRAPHIC RESEARCH UNITED
PRIVATE BAG, RONDEBOSCH
CAPE TOWN, REPUBLIC OF SOUTH AFRICA
General Environment: Oceanographic

OCEANOGRAPHY DEPARTMENT
UNITED STATES NAVAL POST GRADUATE SCHOOL
MONTEREY, CA 93940
General Environment: Oceanographic

OCEANOGRAPHY DEPARTMENT
UNIVERSITY OF WASHINGTON
SEATTLE, WA 98105
Professor, Richard Fleming
General Environment: Oceanographic

OCEANOGRAPHY DEPARTMENT
OREGON STATE UNIVERSITY
CORVALLIS, OR 97330
General Environment: Oceanographic
Staff Size: 100 - 499

OCEANOGRAPHY INSTITUTE
DALHOUSIE UNIVERSITY
HALIFAX, NOVA SCOTIA, CANADA
Director, Dr G Reiley
General Environment: Oceanographic

OCEANOGRAPHY INSTITUTE
UNIVERSITY OF BRITISH COLUMBIA
VANCOUVER 8, BRITISH COLUMBIA, CANADA
Director, G L Pickard
General Environment: Oceanographic

OCEANOGRAPHY INSTITUTE, UNIVERSITY ORIENTE
APARTADO 94 CUMANA
ESTADO SUCRE, VENEZUELA
Director, Luis E Herrera
General Environment: Oceanographic
Specific Interests: Tropical (hot)
Staff Size: 10 - 49

OCEANOGRAPHY RESEARCH PROGRAM, OREGON STATE UNIVERSITY
OCEANOGRAPHY BUILDING
CORVALLIS, OR 97331
General Environment: Oceanographic
Staff Size: 100 - 499

PATHOLOGY DEPARTMENT, UNIVERSITY OF MICHIGAN
1335 EAST CATHERINE STREET
ANN ARBOR, MI 48104
Director, S Hicks

PEDIATRICS DEPARTMENT, MEDICAL SCHOOL
UNIVERSITY OF IOWA
IOWA CITY, IA 52240
Associate Professor, Samuel Foman

PHYSICAL ENVIRONMENT STUDIES CENTER
UNIVERSITY OF MINNESOTA
MINNEAPOLIS, MN 55455

PHYSICAL ENVIRONMENT STUDIES CENTER, INSTITUTE OF TECHNOLOGY
UNIVERSITY OF MINNESOTA
MINNEAPOLIS, MN 55455
Specific Interests: Prairie and Temperate Forest

PHYSIOLOGY DEPARTMENT
INDIANA UNIVERSITY
BLOOMINGTON, IN 47401
Director, R Hullard

PREVENTIVE MEDICINE DEPARTMENT
WASHINGTON UNIVERSITY
ST LOUIS, MO 63110
Associate Professor, J Holloszy

PUBLIC HEALTH AND ADMINISTRATIVE MEDICINE SCHOOL
COLUMBIA UNIVERSITY
NEW YORK, NY 10027

RADIATION HEALTH, UNIVERSITY OF PITTSBURGH
508 SCAIFE HALL
PITTSBURGH, PA 15213

RESEARCH CENTER, GRADUATE
UNIVERSITY OF TEXAS
DALLAS, TX 75205

RESEARCH DEPARTMENT
CALIFORNIA STATE UNIVERSITY
LONG BEACH, CA 90840
Research Director, Dr Darwin L Mayfield
Staff Size: 1000 - 4999

RESEARCH DIVISION
CLARKSON COLLEGE OF TECHNOLOGY
POTSDAM, NY 13676
Associate Dean, Dr L Guy Donaruma

RESEARCH INSTITUTE OF DENVER
UNIVERSITY OF DENVER
DENVER, CO 80201
Staff Size: 100 - 499

RESOURCE CENTER OF VERMONT
UNIVERSITY OF VERMONT
BURLINGTON, VT 05410
General Environment: Limnologic

RESOURCE COUNCIL, UNIVERSITY OF ALBERTA
87TH AND 114TH STREET
EDMONTON, ALBERTA, CANADA

SCIENCE AND MATHEMATICS DIVISION
BEMIDJI STATE COLLEGE
BEMIDJI, MN 56601
Director, Dr Charles H Fuchsman
Specific Interests: Prairie and Temperate Forest
Staff Size: 10 - 49

SCIENCE DIVISION (NATIONAL), SONOMA STATE COLLEGE
1801 EAST COTATI AVENUE
ROHNERT PARK, CA 94928

SCIENCE FACULTY
ELIN SHAMS UNIVERSITY
CAIRO, UNITED ARAB REPUBLIC
Director, Dr Youssef Kotb

SCIENCE INSTITUTE, WEIZMANN
POST OFFICE BOX 26
REHOVOTH, ISRAEL
Director, Amos De Shalit
General Environment: Oceanographic

SCIENCE PROGRAM
UNIVERSITY OF MISSOURI AT ROLLA
ROLLA, MO 65401

SCIENCE SCHOOL, CALIFORNIA STATE POLYTECHNICAL UNIVERSITY
3801 WEST TEMPLE AVENUE
POMONA, CA 91768
Director, Vincent Parker
Staff Size: 50 - 99

SCIENTIFIC LAND MANAGEMENT CURRICULUM
WISCONSIN STATE UNIVERSITY
RIVER FALLS, WI 54022
Director, Dr J Beaver
General Environment: Terrestrial

SEA DISASTER RESEARCH FACILITY
APPLIED DYNAMICS RESEARCH INSTITUTE
TSUYAZARI, FURUORO, JAPAN
Director, Dr Furuzo Taboko
General Environment: Oceanographic
Specific Interests: Prairie and Temperate Forest

SEX-RACE EQUALITY, AFFIRMATIVE ACTION
1902 PALO ALTO WAY
MENLO PARK, CA 94025

SOIL CONSERVATION COUNCIL OF VERMONT

UNIVERSITY OF VERMONT
BURLINGTON, VT 05401

SPACE SCIENCES LABORATORY
UNIVERSITY OF CALIFORNIA
BERKELEY, CA 94720

General Environment: Atmospheric
Staff Size: 100 - 499

STATE UNIVERSITY OF NEW YORK
OFFICES, SUITE 500
1730 RHODE ISLAND AVENUE, NW
WASHINGTON, DC 20036

Director, Charles Cohen

SYNOPTIC METEOROLOGY,
OPERATIONAL FORECA
SAN JOSE STATE COLLEGE
SAN JOSE, CA 95114

Director, Harold Bulk

SYSTEMATIC RESEARCH
INSTITUTE
8049 PROSPECT WAY
LA MESA, CA 92041

Director, M Anderson

TECHNICIAN TRAINING PROGRAM
BROOME TECHNICAL COLLEGE
BINGHAMTON, NY 13904

TECHNICIAN TRAINING PROGRAM
MORRISVILLE AGRICULTURAL-
TECHNOLOGY
MORRISVILLE, NY 13408

TECHNICIAN TRAINING PROGRAM
HUDSON VALLEY COMMISSION
COLLEGE
TROY, NY 12151

Staff Size: 100 - 499

TECHNICIAN TRAINING PROGRAM
SULLIVAN COUNTY COMMUNITY
COLLEGE
SOUTH FALLSBURG, NY 12779

TREE-RING RESEARCH
LABORATORY
UNIVERSITY OF ARIZONA
TUCSON, AZ 85717

General Environment: Atmospheric
Staff Size: 10 - 49

TROPICAL METEOROLOGY
INSTITUTE
UNIVERSITY OF PUERTO RICO
RIO PIEDRAS, PR 00931

Director, D Clay Mcdowell
General Environment: Atmospheric
Specific Interests: Tropical (hot)
Staff Size: 1 - 4

UNESCO
PLACE DE FONTENOV
PARIS (7E), FRANCE

Director, Luis Capurro
General Environment: Oceanographic
Staff Size: 1000 - 4999

UNIVERSITY DIGEST SERVICES
POST OFFICE BOX 343
TROY, MI 48084

WATER CHEMISTRY PROGRAM
UNIVERSITY OF WISCONSIN
MADISON, WI 53706

WATER RESOURCES CENTER
PURDUE UNIVERSITY LIFE
SCIENCES BUILDING
LAFAYETTE, IN 47907

Staff Size: 50 - 99

WATER RESOURCES INSTITUTION
MARY MARTIN HALL, AUBURN
UNIVERSITY
AUBURN, AL 36830

WATER RESOURCES INSTITUTION,
OREGON UNIVERSITY
114 COVELL HALL
CORVALLIS, OR 97331

General Environment: Limnologic

WATER RESOURCES LIBRARY
UNIVERSITY OF LOUISVILLE
LOUISVILLE, KY 40208

Staff Size: 5 - 9

WATERSHED ASSOCIATION OF
LAKE COCHITUATE
61 LAKE SHORE ROAD
NATICK, MA 01760

General Environment: Limnologic
Specific Interests: Urban
Staff Size: 1 - 4

ZOOLOGY DEPARTMENT
UNIVERSITY OF WISCONSIN
MADISON, WI 53706

Professor, Roland Meyer

ZOOLOGY DEPARTMENT
UNIVERSITY OF TEXAS
AUSTIN, TX 78712

Professor, H Sutton

Field Station/Laboratory

AMERICAN COUNCIL OF
INDEPENDENT LABS,
INCORPORATED
1026 17TH STREET, NW
WASHINGTON, DC 20036

ATMOSPHERIC SCIENCES
RESEARCH CENTER
LABORATORY
100 FULLER ROAD
ALBANY, NY 12224

BIOLOGICAL STATION
UNIVERSITY OF MONTANA
MISSOULA, MT 59801

General Environment: Limnologic
Specific Interests: Mountainous
Staff Size: 10 - 49

LABORATORY AT FRIDAY HARBOR
WASHINGTON UNIVERSITY
FRIDAY HARBOR, WA 98250

Director, Robert L Fernald
General Environment: Oceanographic

LIMNOLOGY LABORATORY
UNIVERSITY OF WISCONSIN
MADISON, WI 53706

General Environment: Limnologic

MARINE BIOLOGICAL STATION
(SOUTHERN)
USHUAIA
TIERRA DEL FUEGO, ARGENTINA

General Environment: Oceanographic

MARINE LABS AT MOSS LANDING
CALIFORNIA STATE UNIVERSITY,
FRESNO
FRESNO, CA 93710

Marine Science Coordinator
General Environment: Oceanographic
Staff Size: 10 - 49

MARINE SCIENCE LABS, NERC
UNITED
MENAI BRIDGE
ANGLESEY, WALES

James Nott
Specific Interests: Prairie and Temperate
Forest

MARINE STATION, UNIVERSITY OF
OTAGO
PORTOBELLO
DUNEDIN, NEW ZEALAND

Director, Dr E J Batham
General Environment: Oceanographic
Staff Size: 1 - 4

PACIFIC NORTHWEST
LABORATORY
P O BOX 999
RICHLAND, WA 99352

WEATHER MEASURE NORTHWEST
P O BOX 1776
EUGENE, OR 97401

Director, Donna Mcdonough

WETLANDS INSTITUTE OF SOUTH
JERSEY
LEHIGH UNIVERSITY (CMES)
STONE HARBOR, NJ 08247

Director, Dr Sidney S Herman
General Environment: Estuarine
Staff Size: 10 - 49

Foundation

**ADIRONDACK MOUNTAINS
PROTECTION ASSOCIATION**
POST OFFICE BOX 951
SCHENECTADY, NY 12301
Director, Richard H Pough
Staff Size: 100 - 499

ANTARCTIC PROGRAMS OFFICE
NATIONAL SCIENCE FOUNDATION
WASHINGTON, DC 20550
Specific Interests: Polar (cold)

**ARCHITECTURAL AND
ENVIRONMENTAL ARTS
PROGRAMS**
NATIONAL ENDOWMENT FOR
ARTS
WASHINGTON, DC 20506

AUCKLAND MUSEUM
NEWMARKET
AUCKLAND, NEW ZEALAND
Specific Interests: Prairie and Temperate
Forest

**AUDUBON SOCIETY OF
GREENWICH, INCORPORATED**
109 GREENWICH AVENUE
GREENWICH, CT 06830
President, Paul Vanderstricht
Staff Size: 5 - 9

BEAVER BROOK ASSOCIATION
BROWN LANE
HOLLIS, NH 03049
Director, Kurt Olson
Specific Interests: Rural
Staff Size: 1 - 4

**BOTANICAL CLUB OF NEW
ENGLAND**
22 DIVINITY STREET
CAMBRIDGE, MA 02138

BOY SCOUTS OF AMERICA
NORTH BRUNSWICK, NJ 08902
Executive Director, Alden Barber
Specific Interests: Prairie and Temperate
Forest
Staff Size: 1000 - 4999

BOYS CLUBS OF AMERICA
771 FIRST AVENUE
NEW YORK, NY 10017
National Director, John M Gleason
Specific Interests: Prairie and Temperate
Forest

CAMP FIRE GIRLS
1740 BROADWAY
NEW YORK, NY 10019
National Director, Hester Turner
Specific Interests: Prairie and Temperate
Forest
Staff Size: 500 - 999

**CENTRO NATION DE
INFORMACION Y
DOCUMENTACION**
AGUSTINAS 853, OFFICINA 547
SANTIAGO, CHILE

COHASSET CONSERVATION TRUST
31 NICHOLS ROAD
COHASSET, MA 02025
Director, Edward B Long

COMITE D'ETAT DES EAUX
BOUL GRAL MAGHARU 6-8
BUCURESTI 22, RUMANIA
Director, Al Nissim

CONSERVATION (YARMOUTH)
351 NORTH DENNIS ROAD
YARMOUTH PORT, MA 02675
Director, Theodore Frothingham

**CONSERVATION AND RESEARCH
FOUNDATION**
CONNECTICUT COLLEGE
NEW LONDON, CT 06320

CONSERVATION CITIZENS
3535 MOORES RIVER DRIVE
LANSING, MI 48910
Director, Clarence Case

**CONSERVATION DISTRICTS
FOUNDATION**
1025 VERMONT AVENUE, NW
WASHINGTON, DC 20005

**CONSERVATION DISTRICTS
FOUNDATIONS, DAVIS
CONSERVATION LIBRARY**
PO BOX 776, 408 MAIN STREET
LEAGUE CITY, TX 77573

CONSERVATION FOUNDATION
1250 CONNECTICUT AVENUE, NW
WASHINGTON, DC 20036
Director, Russell E Train
Staff Size: 10 - 49

**CONSERVATION FOUNDATION OF
CATHAM, INCORPORATED**
QUEEN ANNE ROAD
CATHAM, MA 02633
President, Edward Jacob

**CONSERVATION FOUNDATION OF
NANTUCKET, INCORPORATED**
POST OFFICE BOX 31
NANTUCKET, MA 02554
Secretary, R F Mooney

**CONSERVATION FOUNDATION-
PUBLIC AFFAIRS**
1717 MASSACHUSETTS AVENUE, NW
WASHINGTON, DC 20036
Director, T J Adams
Staff Size: 10 - 49

**CONSERVATION TRUST OF
LITTLETON**
WILDERNESS ROAD
LITTLETON, MA 01460
President, Dr H S Harvey
Specific Interests: Rural

**CONSERVATORY FOUNDATION OF
WEST NEWBURY**
102 MAIN STREET
WEST NEWBURY, MA 01985

CYCLICAL STUDIES FOUNDATION
124 SOUTH HIGHLAND AVENUE
PITTSBURGH, PA 15206
Staff Size: 10 - 49

DESERT PROTECTIVE COUNCIL
POST OFFICE BOX 33
BANNING, CA 92220
Director, Robert G Bear
General Environment: Terrestrial
Specific Interests: Desert
Staff Size: 500 - 999

EXTENSION SERVICES, 4-H CLUBS
DEPARTMENT OF AGRICULTURE
WASHINGTON, DC 20250
National Director, Mylo S Downey
Specific Interests: Prairie and Temperate
Forest
Staff Size: 100 - 499

**FOOD COOPERATIVE OF WEST
SOMERVILLE**
14 PARK AVENUE
WEST SOMERVILLE, MA 02144

GEOPHYSICAL UNION OF AMERICA
2100 PENNSYLVANIA AVENUE, NW,
SUITE 435
WASHINGTON, DC 20037

GIRL SCOUTS OF USA
830 THIRD AVENUE
NEW YORK, NY 10022
National Executive Director, Louise
Wood
Specific Interests: Prairie and Temperate
Forest
Staff Size: 1000 - 4999

**HEALTH PLANNING COUNCIL
INCORPORATED**
WILMINGTON, DE 19810
Executive Director, C Foster
Staff Size: 5 - 9

**HISTORIC PRESERVATION TRUST,
NATIONAL**
748 JACKSON PLACE, NW
WASHINGTON, DC 20006
Specific Interests: Prairie and Temperate
Forest
Staff Size: 100 - 499

**INTERPRETIVE NATURE
    ASSOCIATION**
5956 NORTH HAGADORN ROAD
EAST LANSING, MI 48823
Director, H B Guillaume
Staff Size: 100 - 499

**ISLAND RESOURCES
    FOUNDATION, INCORPORATED**
POST OFFICE BOX 4187
ST THOMAS, VI 00801
President, Edward L Towle
Specific Interests: Tropical (hot)
Staff Size: 10 - 49

**IZAAK WALTON LEAGUE OF
    AMERICA**
1326 WAUKEGAN ROAD
GLENVILLE, IL 60025
General Environment: Terrestrial
Staff Size: 1000 & Larger

**LAND CONSERVATION TRUST OF
    SCITUATE**
50 COLE PARKWAY
SCITUATE, MA 02066
Chairman, E P Ryan
General Environment: Marsh/Swamp

**LAND USE FOUNDATION OF NEW
    HAMPSHIRE**
SEVEN SOUTH STATE STREET
CONCORD, NH 03301
President, R J Hill
General Environment: Terrestrial
Staff Size: 1 - 4

MARINE ECOLOGICAL INSTITUTE
811 HARBOR BOULEVARD
REDWOOD CITY, CA 94063
President, Robert Rutherford
General Environment: Estuarine
Specific Interests: Urban
Staff Size: 10 - 49

NATIONAL GEOGRAPHIC SOCIETY
1146 SIXTEENTH STREET
WASHINGTON, DC 20036

NATIONAL SCIENCE FOUNDATION
1800 G STREET, NW
WASHINGTON, DC 20550

**NATURAL RESOURCES
    DEPARTMENT OF WEST
    VIRGINIA**
1709 WASHINGTON STREET EAST
CHARLESTON, WV 25311
General Environment: Limnologic

**NATURAL RESOURCES, CITIZENS
    COMMISSION**
712 DUPONT CIRCLE BUILDING
WASHINGTON, DC 20006
Director, Spenser M Smith

**NEWTON CONSERVATORS,
    INCORPORATED**
319 AUBURN STREET
AUBURNDALE, MA 02166
Director, Mrs Arno H Heyn
Specific Interests: Urban

**NORTH JERSEY CONSERVATION
    FOUNDATION**
300 MENDHAM ROAD
MORRISTOWN, NJ 07960
President, Dr David Reisner
Staff Size: 5 - 9

OCEANOGRAPHIC DATA CENTER
2ND AND M STREETS, SE
WASHINGTON, DC 20390
General Environment: Oceanographic

**OCEANOGRAPHY MUSEUM OF
    MONACO**
MONTE CARLO, MONACO
Director, Jacques Y Cousteau
General Environment: Oceanographic
Staff Size: 50 - 99

**PETROLEUM INDUSTRY
    RESOURCES FOUNDATION**
60 EAST 42ND STREET
NEW YORK, NY 10017
Specific Interests: Prairie and Temperate
    Forest
Staff Size: 1 - 4

POLAR PROGRAM OFFICE
NATIONAL SCIENCE FOUNDATION
WASHINGTON, DC 20550
Specific Interests: Polar (cold)
Staff Size: 10 - 49

**PRE-COLLEGE SCIENCE
    EDUCATION DIVISION**
NATIONAL SCIENCE FOUNDATION
WASHINGTON, DC 20550
Staff Size: 1 - 4

RESERVATIONS
244 ADAMS STREET
MILTON, MA 02186
Director, G Abbott, Jr
Staff Size: 10 - 49

S R F RESEARCH INSTITUTE
SANTA BARBARA MUNICIPAL
    AIRPORT
GOLETA, CA 93017
General Environment: Atmospheric

**SCIENCE INFORMATION SERVICE
    OFFICE**
NATIONAL SCIENCE FOUNDATION
WASHINGTON, DC 20550

**SHERBORN FOREST AND TRAIL
    ASSOCIATION**

28 MILL STATE
SHERBORN, MA 01770
President, Harold Sossen
General Environment: Terrestrial
Staff Size: 100 - 499

SIERRA CLUB FOUNDATION
220 BUSH STREET
SAN FRANCISCO, CA 94101
Staff Size: 10 - 49

**UNDERGRADUATE EDUCATION IN
    SCIENCE DIVISION**
NATIONAL SCIENCE FOUNDATION
WASHINGTON, DC 20550

**WATERSHED ASSOCIATION,OF
    UPPER RARITAW**
POST OFFICE BOX 44
FARNILLS, NJ 07931
Executive Director, P W Larson
Specific Interests: Urban
Staff Size: 1 - 4

Government — Federal

**HEALTH, EDUCATION AND
    WELFARE REGION 1 OFFICE**
FEDERAL BUILDING,
    GOVERNMENT CENTER
BOSTON, MA 02203

**HEALTH, EDUCATION AND
    WELFARE REGION 10 OFFICE**
1321 SECOND AVENUE
SEATTLE, WA 98101

**HEALTH, EDUCATION AND
    WELFARE REGION 2 OFFICE**
26 FEDERAL PLAZA
NEW YORK, NY 10007

**HEALTH, EDUCATION AND
    WELFARE REGION 4 OFFICE**
50 7TH STREET NE -ROOM 404
ATLANTA, GA 30323

**HEALTH, EDUCATION AND
    WELFARE REGION 5 OFFICE,
    P.O. BUILDING**
433 WEST VAN BUREN STREET
CHICAGO, IL 60607

**HEALTH, EDUCATION AND
    WELFARE REGION 6 OFFICE**
1114 COMMERCE STREET
DALLAS, TX 75202

**HEALTH, EDUCATION AND
    WELFARE REGION 8 OFFICE**
19TH & STOUT STREETS
DENVER, CO 80202

RESEARCH OFFICE UNITED STATES ARMY
BOX CM, DUKE STATION
DURHAM, NC 27706

Government — State or Local

ADMINISTRATION BUILDING AT SANTA CLARA COUNTY
70 WEST HEDDING STREET
SAN JOSE, CA 95110
Planning Director, Mr Roy Cameron

AGRICULTURE AND RESOURCE MINISTRY OF WESTERN NIGERIA
IBADAN, NIGERIA
Director, T S B Arisisala

AGRICULTURE DEPARTMENT
14TH STREET AND
    INDEPENDENCE AVENUE, SW
WASHINGTON,DC 20250
General Environment: Terrestrial
Specific Interests: Prairie and Temperate
    Forest

AIR AND WATER POLLUTION CONTROL, HARRIS COUNTY HEALTH DEPARTMENT
BOX 6031
PASADENA, TX 77502
Staff Size: 10 - 49

AIR AND WATER RESOURCES OFFICE
POST OFFICE BOX 27687
RALEIGH, NC 27611
Assistant Director, Earle Hubbard
Staff Size: 100 - 499

ATOMIC ENERGY COMMISSION, IDAHO OPERATIONS OFFICE
POST OFFICE BOX 2108
IDAHO FALLS, ID 83401

ATOMIC ENERGY COMMISSION, NEVADA OPERATIONS
POST OFFICE BOX 14100
LAS VEGAS, NV 89114
Staff Size: 10 - 49

BELKNAP COMMITTEE ON BEAUTIFICATION
LACONIA, NH 03246
Secretary, Marjorie Powell

BOSTON PUBLIC LIBRARY
COPLEY SQUARE
BOSTON, MA 02117
Staff Size: 500 - 999

COMMUNITY ENVIRONMENTAL MANAGEMENT BUREAU
5555 RIDGE AVENUE
CINCINNATI, OH 45213
Director, Joseph Schock
Staff Size: 10 - 49

CONSERVATION (WEYMOUTH)
TOWN HALL
WEYMOUTH, MA 02188

CONSERVATION ASSOCIATION OF MASSACHUSETTS
147 BEECHWOOD ROAD
WESTWOOD, MA 02090
Director, Thomas R Darcy

CONSERVATION ASSOCIATION OF NEPONSET, INCORPORATED
76 WINTER STREET
NORWOOD, MA 02062
Secretary, Mrs Stanley Cottrell

CONSERVATION ASSOCIATION OF SMITHS FERRY
RESERVATION ROAD
HOLYOKE, MA 01040
Director, Dr Robert Moriarty

CONSERVATION COMMISSION
HOLDERNESS, NH 03245
Director, Malcolm Taylor
Staff Size: 5 - 9

CONSERVATION COMMISSION OF BOSTON
BOSTON CITY HALL, ROOM 913
BOSTON, MA 02201
Director, Mr Bonoff
Specific Interests: Urban
Staff Size: 1 - 4

CONSERVATION COMMISSION OF NATICK
139 NORTH MAIN STREET
NATICK, MA 01760
Director, G H Wallace

CONSERVATION COMMISSION OF SHERBORN
FARM ROAD
SHERBORN, MA 01770
Director, H King

CONSERVATION COMMISSION OF SUDBURY
NINE BENT BROOK ROAD
SUDBURY, MA 01776
Vice-Chairman, Margaret Langmuire

CONSERVATION COMMITTEE OF NEEDHAM
45 FAIRFIELD STREET
NEEDHAM, MA 02192

CONSERVATION COMMITTEES ASSOCIATION OF MASSACHUSETTS

84 STATE STREET
BOSTON, MA 02109
Executive Director, Stuart Debard

CONSERVATION COUNCIL OF FRAMINGHAM
POST OFFICE BOX 2407
FRAMINGHAM, MA 01701
President, Bertram Rendell

CONSERVATION COUNCIL OF MASSACHUSETTS, INCORPORATED
POST OFFICE BOX 315
LINCOLN CENTER, MA 01773
President, Roger Marshall

CONSERVATION COUNCIL OF SOUTH MIDDLESEX
66 STROBUS LANE
ASHLAND, MA 01721
Director, J Schmidt

CONSERVATION FOUNDATION AT CARLISLE
57 WOODLAND ROAD
CARLISLE, MA 01741
Trustee, R Mcwalter

CONSERVATION GROUP OF REVERE
77 LIBERTY AVENUE
REVERE, MA 02151
President, C Castinetti

CONSERVATION OF WELLESLEY
32 SKYLINE DRIVE
WELLESLEY, MA 02181
President, Franklin Sanders

CONSERVATION SOCIETY OF SOUTH HADLEY
THREE WOODBRIDGE STREET
SOUTH HADLEY, MA 01075
President, Richard L Johnson

CONSERVATION SOCIETY, INCORPORATED
VINEYARD HAVEN, MA 02568
Director, R Woodruff

CONSERVATION TRUST OF WEST NEWBURY
102 MAIN STREET
WEST NEWBURY, MA 01985
Director, Peter Haack

CONSERVATION TRUST OF WESTWOOD
521 HARTFORD STREET
WESTWOOD, MA 02090
Chairman, Mr C K Mullin

ENVIRONMENT
ONE W ELM STREET
GREENWICH, CT 06830

**ENVIRONMENTAL ACTION OF
    COHASSET**
POST OFFICE BOX 31
COHASSET, MA 02025
President, Eric Gjesteby

**ENVIRONMENTAL ASSOCIATION
    OF SCITUATE**
245 FIRST PARISH ROAD
SCITUATE, MA 02066
President, Carl Smith

**ENVIRONMENTAL CONCERNS
    COMMISSION OF AMHERST**
19 APPLEWOOD LANE
AMHERST, MA 01002
Chairman, James F Walker
Specific Interests: Rural
Staff Size: 100 - 499

**ENVIRONMENTAL CONSERVATION
    ASSOCIATION OF PEMBROKE**
132 HIGH STREET
PEMBROOKE, MA 02359
President, William H Christmann

**ENVIRONMENTAL CONSERVATION
    DEPARTMENT**
POUCH O
JUNEAU, AK 99801
Director, James Anderegg
Staff Size: 10 - 49

**ENVIRONMENTAL CONSERVATION
    ORGANIZATION**
POST OFFICE BOX 121
GROVELAND, MA 01330
President, John Osborne

**ENVIRONMENTAL HEALTH
    ASSOCIATION, NATIONAL**
NORTH MAIN STREET
BREWER, ME 04412
President, Charles W Heddering

**ENVIRONMENTAL INFORMATION
    COMMITTEE OF MICHIGAN**
P O BOX 2281
GRAND RAPIDS, MI 49501
Director, Robert Burnap

**ENVIRONMENTAL PROTECTION
    AGENCY OF ILLINOIS**
2200 CHURCHILL ROAD
SPRINGFIELD, IL 67206
Director, William Blaser
Staff Size: 500 - 999

**ENVIRONMENTAL PROTECTION
    COMMISSION OF
    HILLSBOROUGH COUNTY**
906 JACKSON STREET
TAMPA, FL 33602
Director, Roger Stewart
Staff Size: 10 - 49

**ENVIRONMENTAL QUALITY
    DEPARTMENT, GREATER
    ANCHORAGE AREA BOROUGH**

3500 TUDOR ROAD
ANCHORAGE, AK 99507
Staff Size: 50 - 99

**ENVIRONMENTAL RESCUE
    ALLIANCE**
BOX 944
WEST CORNWALL, CT 06796
Chairman, Peter Mitchell

**ENVIRONMENTAL SCIENCE AND
    FORESTRY COLLEGE**
STATE UNIVERSITY OF NEW YORK
    AT SYRACUSE
SYRACUSE, NY 13210
Director, Dr Richard E Pentony
Staff Size: 100 - 499

**GEOLOGICAL SURVEY OF
    ALABAMA**
P O DRAWER O, UNIVERSITY OF
    ALABAMA
TUSCALOOSA, AL 35486
Staff Size: 50 - 99

**GULF COAST RESEARCH
    LABORATORY**
OCEAN SPRINGS, MS 39564
Director, Harold D Howse
General Environment: Oceanographic
Staff Size: 50 - 99

**HEALTH DEPARTMENT OF KERN
    COUNTY**
POST OFFICE BOX 997
BAKERSFIELD, CA 93302
Staff Size: 10 - 49

**HEALTH, FOOD, AND DRUGS
    DEPARTMENT**
1624 WEST ADAMS STREET
PHOENIX, AZ 85007
Director, Dr George Spendlove

**HINGHAM FRIENDS OF
    CONSERVATION**
25 ROCKWOOD ROAD
HINGHAM, MA 02043
President, Charles Malme

**HOPKINTON CONSERVATION
    COMMISSION**
20 MAYHEW STREET
HOPKINTON, MA 01748
Director, Nelson Mcintire

**IMPROVEMENT ASSOCIATION OF
    FRAMINGHAM**
6 VERNON STREET
FRAMINGHAM, MA 01701
Director, J Maddocks

**IMPROVEMENT SOCIETY OF
    NORTH ANDOVER**
JOHNSON STREET
NORTH ANDOVER, MA 01845
Director, Mr William Enright

**LAND CONSERVATION TRUST OF
    CONCORD**
81 ESTABROOK ROAD
CONCORD, MA 01742
Director, David Emerson

**LAND CONSERVATION TRUST OF
    SEEKONK**
JACOBS STREET
SEEKONK, MA 02771
President, Mrs C Wilson

**LEAGUE OF WOMEN VOTERS OF
    CONNECTICUT**
60 CONNOLLY PARKWAY
HAMDEN, CT 06514
President, Mrs James Welch

**LEXINGTON CITIZENS FOR
    CONSERVATION**
21 LONGFELLOW ROAD
LEXINGTON, MA 02173
Director, Mrs John Ross

**MASSACHUSETTS SOCIETY FOR
    THE PREVENTION OF CRUELTY
    TO ANIMALS**
180 LONGWOOD AVENUE
BOSTON, MA 02115

**METALLURGY RESEARCH CENTER,
    BUREAU OF MINES**
COLLEGE PARK METALLURGY
    RESEARCH CENTER
COLLEGE PARK, MD 20740
General Environment: Terrestrial
Staff Size: 100 - 499

MUSEUM OF SCIENCE
SCIENCE PARK
BOSTON, MA 02114
Director, Bradford Washburn

**NASHOBA CONSERVATION TRUST,
    INCORPORATED**
WHEELER STREET
PEPPERELL, MA 01463
Director, Bruce Wetherbee

**NATURAL HISTORY CLUB OF
    TERRYVILLE**
102 GREYSTONE AVENUE
BRISTOL, CT 06010
President, Alphonse Marcotte

**NATURAL RESOURCE
    DEPARTMENT**
100 CAMBRIDGE STREET
BOSTON, MA MAIZ02134

**NATURAL RESOURCES COUNCIL
    OF CONNECTICUT**
POST OFFICE BOX 352
WEST HAVEN, CT 06516
Secretary, Charles Barr

NATURAL RESOURCES TRUST OF EASTON
BOX 187
SOUTH EASTON, MA 02375
President, Mrs Donald C Reusch

NATURAL RESOURCES TRUST OF MANSFIELD
255 FRUIT STREET
MANSFIELD, MA 02048
President, Mrs Doris Webb

NATURE CENTER, SOUTH SHORE
MAPLE STREET
NORWELL, MA 02061

NAVAL POST-GRADUATE SCHOOL
MONTEREY, CA 93940
Director, Admiral R W Mcnitt

NISSITISSIT RIVER LAND TRUST
LAWRENCE STREET
PEPPERELL, MA 01463
Vice-President, Trescott T Abele

OCCUPATIONAL HEALTH PROGRAM
NEW JERSEY DEPARTMENT OF HEALTH
TRENTON, NJ 08625
Chief, Lynn Schall

OCCUPATIONAL SAFETY AND HEALTH BUREAU
12720 TWINBROOK PARKWAY
ROCKVILLE, MD 20852
Chairman, Marcus Key

OCCUPATIONAL SAFETY AND HEALTH DIVISION
STATE HEALTH OFFICE
PIERRE, SD 57501
Staff Size: 1 - 4

PROTECT YOUR ENVIRONMENT OF STRATFORD, INCORPORATED
66 JEFFERSON STREET
STRATFORD, CT 06497
President, Py Epler, Jr

PROTECTION OF THE ENVIRONMENT OF PROVINCETOWN
GENERAL DELIVERY
PROVINCETOWN, MA 02657

PROTECTIVE ASSOCIATION OF MT GREYLOCK
LANESBORO, MA 01237
President, Mr William Tague

PUBLIC HEALTH DIVISION, DEPARTMENT OF HEALTH AND WELFARE
POUCH H
JUNEAU, AK 98801

PUBLIC HEALTH SERVICE
222 EAST CENTRAL PARKWAY
CINCINNATI, OH 45202
Executive Secretary, Alan Stevens

RADIOLOGICAL HEALTH DIVISION, STATE HEALTH OFFICE
STATE DEPARTMENT OF HEALTH
PIERRE, SD 57501
Staff Size: 1 - 4

RESERVATIONS, TRUSTEES OF
244 ADAMS STREET
MILTON, MA 02186
Director, G Abbot Jr

RESOURCE CONSERVATION DIVISION
1416 9TH STREET, ROOM 1354
SACRAMENTO, CA 95814
General Environment: Terrestrial
Staff Size: 10 - 49

SALT POND AREAS BIRD SANCTUARIES
231 MAIN STREET
FALMOUTH, MA 02540
President, Ermine Lovell

SAVE SCENIC MONTEREY
BOX 125
MONTEREY, MA 01245
President, T F Gillis

SCIENCE CENTER OF SQUAM LAKE
US ROUTE THREE, BOX 146
HOLDERNESS, NH 03245
Director, Gilbert Merrill

SCIENCE INVESTIGATIONS INSTITUTE OF VENEZUELA
APARTADO 1827
CARACAS, VENEZUELA
Director, Dr Marcel Roche

SOIL AND WATER CONSERVATION ASSOCIATION OF MAINE
R F D
EAST CORNINTH, ME 04427
Director, John Fogler

SOIL AND WATER CONSERVATION COMMISSION OF ARKANSAS
STATE CAPITOL
LITTLE ROCK, AR 72201
General Environment: Terrestrial

SOIL CONSERVATION AND MANAGEMENT DIVISION
400 STATE OFFICE BUILDING
PHOENIX, AZ 85007
Director, Wayne Kessler

SOIL CONSERVATION SERVICE
204 EAST 5TH-ROOM 217
ANCHORAGE, AK 99645
Staff Size: 10 - 49

STOP UNNECESSARY ROAD BUILDING
OAK STREET
NORTON, MA 02766
Director, Helen Landis

TUBERCULOSIS AND HEALTH ASSOCIATION OF MAINE
20 WILLOW STREET
AUGUSTA, ME 04330

UNITED STATES NAVY
3406 FIDDLERS GREEN
FALLS CHURCH, VA 22044
Vice Admiral, William Behrens, Jr
General Environment: Oceanographic

WEATHER MODIFICATION PROGRAM, NATIONAL SCIENCE FOUNDATION
WASHINGTON, DC 20550
General Environment: Atmospheric
Staff Size: 1 - 4

WILDFLOWER PRESERVATION SOCIETY OF NEW ENGLAND
300 MASSACHUSETTS AVENUE
BOSTON, MA 02115
Executive Director, Mrs B Green

WILDLIFE FEDERATION OF MASSACHUSETTS, INCORPORATED
BOX 343
NATICK, MA 01760
President, Charles Strumski

WOMEN'S CLUBS, MAINE FEDERATION
37 MCLAUGHLIN STREET
BANGOR, ME 04401
President, Mrs Arthur Rogers

WOODROW WILSON INTERNATIONAL CENTER FOR SCHOLARS
SMITHSONIAN INSTITUTION BUILDING
WASHINGTON, DC 20560

ZOOLOGICAL SOCIETY OF MASSACHUSETTS
1904 CANTON AVENUE
MILTON, MA 02186

Industrial/Commercial

ADVANCED TECHNOLOGY OPERATIONS, BECKMAN INSTITUTE
2500 HARBOR BOULEVARD
FULLERTON, CA 92634
Director, Dr Robert Gafford

ARABIAN AMERICAN OIL
JIDDA, SAUDI ARABIA
General Environment: Oceanographic

ARTKAM CORPORATION (OMEGA)
858 SAN ANTONIO ROAD
PALO ALTO, CA 94303
President, Arthur W Strametz

**CAMARA PUNTARENENSE DE
  PESCADORES**
PUNTARENAS, COSTA RICA
Director, Jose Moreno Arellano
General Environment: Oceanographic

**CARTWRIGHT AERIAL SURVEYS,
  INCORPORATED**
MUNICIPAL AIRPORT
SACRAMENTO, CA 95834
President, Vern W Cartwright

COMMUNICATIONS, CYBERNETICS
674 HAMILTON LANE
SANTA CLARA, CA 95051
Director, Charles Aldrich
Staff Size: 1 - 4

**COMPANIA ENLATADORA
  NACIONAL**
PUNTARENAS, COSTA RICA
Director, Fernando Palau Curco
General Environment: Oceanographic

COMSIS CORPORATION
3448 DE LA CRUZ BOULEVARD
SANTA CLARA, CA 95050
Director, Paul Whiting Jr
General Environment: Atmospheric

**CONSERVATION
  COMMUNICATIONS
  ASSOCIATION**
POST OFFICE BOX 310
LUFKIN, TX 75901
Director, George R Chase
General Environment: Terrestrial
Staff Size: 100 - 499

**CONSULTANTS COMPUTATION
  BUREAU**
594 HOWARD STREET
SAN FRANISCO, CA 94105
President, Zulfikar O Cumali

**DATA AND PLANNING DIVISION,
  NIO**
KRISHI BHAVAN
NEW DELHI, INDIA
Director, R Jayaraman

**ENVIRONMENTAL SCIENCES
  LABORATORY, GENERAL
  ELECTRIC COMPANY**
POST OFFICE BOX 8555
PHILADELPHIA, PA 19101
Manager, Dr Sinclaire M Scala
Staff Size: 100 - 499

**EUGENIO GARRON AND SONS,
  LIMITED**
LIMON, COSTA RICA
Director, Francisco Garron
General Environment: Oceanographic

**FISHERIES CORPORATION AT
  CEYLON**
GALLE FACE
COLOMBO 3, CEYLON
Director, D C L Amerasinghe
General Environment: Oceanographic

**FISHERMAN'S PRODUCE
  CORPORATION (NATIONAL)**
ANGEL LANE
BELIZE CITY, HONDURAS
General Environment: Oceanographic

**FOREST PRODUCTS ASSOCIATION
  (NATIONAL)**
1619 MASSACHUSETTS AVENUE, NW
WASHINGTON, DC 20036
General Environment: Terrestrial
Specific Interests: Prairie and Temperate
  Forest
Staff Size: 50 - 99

GETTY OIL COMPANY
JIDDA, SAUDI ARABIA
General Environment: Oceanographic

HANES CORPORATION
WINSTON SALEM, NC 27100
Chairman, Gordon Hanes

**HYDROLOGY PRODUCTION,
  DIVISION OF DILLINGHAM
  CORPORATION**
POST OFFICE BOX 2528
SAN DIEGO, CA 92112
Sales Manager, C L Strickland

IAAPCO/SINCLAIR
DENVER CLUB BUILDING
DENVER, CO 80202

IBM RESEARCH LABORATORY
MONTEREY AND COTTLE ROADS
SAN JOSE, CA 95114
Director, H Eschenfelder

**IMPERIAL CHEMICAL INDUSTRIES
  LIMITED**
JEALOTTS HILL RESOURCES
  STATION
BRACKNELL, BERKSHIRE,
  ENGLAND
Manager, Alan Calderbank
Staff Size: 50 - 99

**IRVING P KRICK ASSOCIATES,
  INCORPORATED**
611 SOUTH PALM CANYON DR
PALM SPRINGS, CA 92262
President, Irving P Krick
General Environment: Atmospheric
Staff Size: 10 - 49

**ISHIKAWAJIMA HARIMA
  DOCKYARD**
YOKOHAMA, JAPAN
General Environment: Oceanographic
Specific Interests: Prairie and Temperate
  Forest

**KAHL SCIENTIFIC INSTRUMENT
  CORPORATION**
P O BOX 1166
EL CAJON, CA 92022
President, Joseph Kahl
General Environment: Oceanographic
Staff Size: 10 - 49

**LABOR AND HEALTH INSTITUTE
  AT SAINT LOUIS**
1641 SOUTH KINGSHIGHWAY
  BOULE
ST LOUIS, NC 27100
Director, Edward Berger

**LOBSTERMEN'S ASSOCIATION OF
  MAINE**
427 MAIN STREET
ROCKLAND, MA 04841
President, Leslie Dyer
Specific Interests: Prairie and Temperate
  Forest
Staff Size: 1000 - 4999

**MELLONICS ENVIRONMENTAL
  SCIENCES**
654 SUNSET DRIVE
PACIFIC GROVE, CA 93950
Manager, William Woodworth

METEOROLOGY
785 WEST END AVENUE, APT 6-C
NEW YORK, NY 10025
Director, Adolfo Eduardo Baca

METEOROLOGY, OCEANOGRAPHY
1570 WAKEFIELD TERRACE
LOS ALTOS, CA 94022
Director, Leighton Koehler
General Environment: Oceanographic

**METEOROLOGY, VANCE
  ASSOCIATES**
P O BOX 682
CORONA DEL MAR, CA 92625
Senior Consultant, Willison Vance

**NATURAL RESOURCES COUNCIL
  OF AMERICA**
719 13TH STREET, NW, ROOM 509
WASHINGTON, DC
Director, Carl W Buchheister
General Environment: Terrestrial
Staff Size: 10 - 49

**NATURE AND NATURAL
  RESOURCES INTERNATIONAL
  UNION FOR CONSERVATION**
200 P STREET, NW
WASHINGTON, DC 20001

Director, Harold J Coolidge
General Environment: Oceanographic
Staff Size: 100 - 499

**OCEANOGRAPHIC
INSTRUMENTATION**
11803 SORRENTO VALLEY ROAD
SAN DIEGO, CA 92112
Director, C L Strickland
General Environment: Oceanographic

**OYSTER INSTITUTE OF NORTH
AMERICA**
22 MAIN STREET
SAYVILLE, NY 11782
Specific Interests: Prairie and Temperate
Forest
Staff Size: 100 - 499

PAGE INCORPORATED
CEBU, PHILIPPINES
Director, Mrs Emmanuel Page
Specific Interests: Prairie and Temperate
Forest

PAPER CHEMISTRY INSTITUTE
POST OFFICE BOX 1048
APPLETON, WI 54911
Chief, Mr Averill J Wiley
General Environment: Terrestrial
Specific Interests: Prairie and Temperate
Forest
Staff Size: 10 - 49

**PESTICIDE CONTROL
ASSOCIATION (NATIONAL)**
250 WEST JERSEY STREET
ELIZABETH, NJ 07202
Specific Interests: Prairie and Temperate
Forest
Staff Size: 1000 - 4999

**PLACENCIA PRODUCERS
COMPANY-OPERATIONS**
TEGUCIGALPA, HONDURAS

PRODUCTOS ALTAMAR LIMITED,
PUNTARENAS, COSTA RICA
Director, Gerald Lippman

**RESEARCH AND DEVELOPMENT
MANAGEMENT, ICI LIMITED**
MONO DIVISION, POST OFFICE
BOX 8
THE HEATH, RUNCORD,
CHESHIRE, ENGLAND
Director, E C Allberry
Specific Interests: Prairie and Temperate
Forest

**ROYCO INSTRUMENTS,
INCORPORATED**
141 JEFFERSON DRIVE
MENLO PARK, CA 94025
Research Director, Mr Alvin Lieberman

**SAINT HUBERT SOCIETY OF
AMERICA**
STUDIO 1, 5 TUDOR CITY PLACE
NEW YORK, NY 10017

Director, John J Poister
Staff Size: 100 - 499

**SCIENCE AND INDUSTRIAL
RESOURCE INSTITUTE AT
CEYLON**
BAUDDHALOKA MAWATHA
COLOMBO 7, CEYLON
Director, Dr George Ponnamperuma

SCIENTIFIC ADMINISTRATION
1041 DESCO AVENUE
CAMARILLO, CA 93010
Director, Roy Nelson

SOUTHERN FISHERIES COMPANY
TEHRAN, IRAN
Director, Rear Admiral Asghar Zadeh

STANDARD OIL COMPANY
910 SOUTH MICHIGAN AVENUE
CHICAGO, IL 60605
Director, Dr Peter Wolkonsky
Staff Size: 10 - 49

THE ARROW COMPANY
3385 SOUTH BANNOCK STREET
ENGLEWOOD, CO 80110
Staff Size: 1 - 4

VARIAN ASSOCIATES
611 HANSEN WAY
PALO ALTO, CA 94303

**WATER FOWL ADVISORY
COMMITTEE**
UNITED STATES DEPARTMENT OF
INTERIOR
WASHINGTON, DC 20240

**WEATHER MEASURE
CORPORATION**
P O BOX 41257
SACRAMENTO, CA 95841
President, Herbert Dankman

WILDERNESS SOCIETY
729 5TH STREET, NW
WASHINGTON, DC 20005
Director, Stewart M Brandborg
Staff Size: 1000 & Larger

**WILDLIFE FEDERATION
(NATIONAL)**
1412 16TH STREET, NW
WASHINGTON, DC 20036
General Environment: Terrestrial
Staff Size: 1000 & Larger

**WILDLIFE FOUNDATION OF
NORTH AMERICA**
709 WIRE BUILDING
WASHINGTON, DC 20005
Director, C R Gutemuth
Staff Size: 100 - 499

ZAPATE-ODE
CANBERRA, AUSTRALIA

Professional Organizations

A.K.F.A.
BOX 171
FALLS VILLAGE, CT 06031
Director, David Dewolfe
Staff Size: 1 - 4

**AMERICAN ASSOCIATION OF
UNIVERSITY WOMEN**
2401 VIRGINIA AVENUE
WASHINGTON, DC 20037
Staff Size: 1 - 4

AMERICAN CHEMISTRY SOCIETY
1155 SIXTEENTH STREET, NW
WASHINGTON, DC 20036
Executive Secretary, B R Stonerson
Specific Interests: Prairie and Temperate
Forest
Staff Size: 1000 & Larger

**AMERICAN FORESTRY
ASSOCIATION**
919-17TH STREET, NW
WASHINGTON, DC 20006
Director, Fred E Hornaday
General Environment: Terrestrial
Specific Interests: Prairie and Temperate
Forest
Staff Size: 1000 and Larger

**ASSOCIATION EXECUTIVES
SOCIETY**
2000 K STREET, NW
WASHINGTON, DC 20006
Executive Vice President, Norman E Bess
Specific Interests: Prairie and Temperate
Forest
Staff Size: 1000 - 4999

**AUDUBON COUNCIL OF
CONNECTICUT**
ORCHARD HILL ROAD
HARWINTON, CT 06790
President, Stanley Barnes
Specific Interests: Prairie and Temperate
Forest
Staff Size: 5000 - 9999

**AUDUBON SOCIETY OF ARKANSAS,
INCORPORATED**
180 NORTH BROADWAY
EL DORADO, AR 71730
President, H H Shugart
Specific Interests: Prairie and Temperate
Forest
Staff Size: 500 - 999

**AUDUBON SOCIETY OF
CONNECTICUT**
2325 BURR STREET
FAIRCHILD, CT 06430

President, Paul Mooney
Specific Interests: Prairie and Temperate
  Forest
Staff Size: 1000 - 4999

AUDUBON SOCIETY OF ILLINOIS
ROOSEVELT AND LAKE SHORE
  DRIVES
CHICAGO, IL 60605
President, Raymond Mostek
Specific Interests: Prairie and Temperate
  Forest

AUDUBON SOCIETY OF INDIANA
MARY GRAY BIRD SANCTUARY, RR 6
CONNERSVILLE, IN 47331
President, Charles D Wise
Specific Interests: Prairie and Temperate
  Forest

AUDUBON SOCIETY OF MISSOURI
403 SOUTH FREDERICK
MARYVILLE, MO 64466
President, David Casterra
Specific Interests: Prairie and Temperate
  Forest

**AUDUBON SOCIETY OF NEW
  HAMPSHIRE**
63 NORTH MAIN STREET
CONCORD, NH 03301
Director, Tudor Richards
Specific Interests: Prairie and Temperate
  Forest

**AUDUBON SOCIETY OF NEW
  JERSEY**
790 EWING AVENUE
FRANKLIN LAKES, NJ 07417
President, Burton Dezendorf
Specific Interests: Prairie and Temperate
  Forest

AUDUBON SOCIETY OF OHIO
3530 EPWORTH AVENUE
CINCINNATI, OH 45211
President, Irene M Lammers
Specific Interests: Prairie and Temperate
  Forest

BERNICE P BISHOP MUSEUM
1355 KALIHI STREET
HONOLULU, HI 96819
Specific Interests: Tropical (hot)

**BIRD BANDING ASSOCIATION
  (INLAND)**
BOX 152
BAILEYS HARBOR, WI 54202
President, Roy Lukes
Specific Interests: Prairie and Temperate
  Forest

**BIRD BANDING ASSOCIATION
  (NORTHEAST)**
MASSACHUSETTS AUDUBON
  SOCIETY
LINCOLN, MA 01773

President, James Baird
Specific Interests: Prairie and Temperate
  Forest

**BIRD BANDING ASSOCIATION
  (WESTERN)**
3041 ELDRIDGE
BELLINGHAM, WA 98225
President, Terence R Wahl
Specific Interests: Prairie and Temperate
  Forest
Staff Size: 100 - 499

**BOONE AND CROCKETT CLUB,
  CARNEGIE MELLON UNIVERSITY**
4400 FORBES AVENUE
PITTSBURG, PA 15213
President, F C Pullman
Specific Interests: Prairie and Temperate
  Forest

**BOSTON ENVIRONMENT
  INCORPORATED**
14 BEACON STREET, ROOM 710
BOSTON, MA 02108
Director, John W Putnam
Specific Interests: Prairie and Temperate
  Forest

BROADMOAR SANCTUARY
SOUTH STREET
SOUTH NATICK, MA 01760
Staff Size: 1 - 4

**BROOKS BIRD CLUB,
  INCORPORATED**
707 WARWOOD AVENUE
WHEELING, WV 26003
President, George Koch
Specific Interests: Prairie and Temperate
  Forest

**BROTHERHOOD OF THE JUNGLE
  COCK, INCORPORATED**
10 EAST FAYETTE STREET
BALTIMORE, MD 21202
President, John Hunter, Jr
Specific Interests: Prairie and Temperate
  Forest

CALIFORNIA TOMORROW
681 MARKET STREET
SAN FRANCISCO, CA 94105
President, Alfred Heller

CAMPFIRE CLUB OF AMERICA
19 RECTOR STREET
NEW YORK, NY 10006
Specific Interests: Prairie and Temperate
  Forest

CONCERNED SCIENTISTS UNION
PO BOX 289
CAMBRIDGE, MA 02139
Director, J J Mackenzie

CONSERVATION FORUM
101 ENGLEWOOD AVENUE
BUFFALO, NY 14214

President, Charles I Joudry
Specific Interests: Prairie and Temperate
  Forest

**CONSERVATION LAW
  FOUNDATION, INCORPORATED**
506 STATLER OFFICE BUILDING
BOSTON, MA 02116
President, Arnold W Hunnewell, Jr
Specific Interests: Prairie and Temperate
  Forest

**COOPER ORNITHOLOGICAL
  SOCIETY**
CALIFORNIA ACADEMY OF
  SCIENCES, GOLDEN GATE PARK
SAN FRANCISCO, CA 94118
President, William H Behle

ECOLOGY ACTION, BOSTON AREA
925 MASSACHUSETTS AVENUE
CAMBRIDGE, MA 02139
Specific Interests: Prairie and Temperate
  Forest

ENVIRONMENTAL POLICY CENTER
28 PEABODY TERRACE
CAMBRIDGE, MA 02138
Director, Barbara M Heller

**ENVIRONMENTAL SCIENCES
  INSTITUTE**
940 EAST NORTHWEST HIGHWAY
MT PROSPECT, IL 60056
Director, B L Peterson
General Environment: Terrestrial
Staff Size: 50 - 99

**ENVIRONMENTAL, PUBLIC AND
  OCCUPATIONAL HEALTH
  DEPARTMENT**
535 NORTH DEARBORN STREET
CHICAGO, IL 60610
Staff Size: 10 - 49

**FOREST AND PARK ASSOCIATION
  OF CONNECTICUT**
1010 MAIN STREET, P O BOX 389
EAST HARTFORD, CT 06108
President, Floyd M Callward
Specific Interests: Prairie and Temperate
  Forest

**FORESTRY AND CONSERVATION
  ASSOCIATION (WESTERN)**
1326 AMERICAN BANK BUILDING
PORTLAND, OR 97205
Director, H R Glascock
General Environment: Terrestrial
Specific Interests: Prairie and Temperate
  Forest
Staff Size: 500 - 999

**FORESTRY ASSOCIATION
  EXECUTIVES NATIONAL
  COUNCIL**
1040 MAIN STREET
EAST HARTFORD, CT 06108

General Environment: Terrestrial
Specific Interests: Prairie and Temperate
Forest

FORESTRY ASSOCIATION EXECUTIVES NATIONAL COUNCIL
301 EAST FRANKLIN STREET
RICHMOND, VA 23219
Director, William E Cooper
General Environment: Terrestrial
Specific Interests: Prairie and Temperate
Forest
Staff Size: 10 - 49

FRIENDS OF THE WILDERNESS
3515 EAST FOURTH STREET
DULUTH, MN 55804
President, Ernest C Oberholtzer
Specific Interests: Prairie and Temperate
Forest

GAME AND FISHERIES COMMISSION, NORTH EAST ASSOCIATION
NORTH STREET
DOVER, DE 19901
Chairman, Norman G Wilder
Specific Interests: Prairie and Temperate
Forest

GAME BREEDERS OF NORTH AMERICA, SHOOTING PREVENTION ASSOCIATION
EAST MOUNTAIN ROAD, ROAD 2
HEGINS, PA 18947
Specific Interests: Prairie and Temperate
Forest

GAME CONSERVATION SOCIETY
BOX 54
ARMONK, NY 10504
President, Otto Oustechy
Specific Interests: Prairie and Temperate
Forest

GAME FISHERIES COMMISSIONERS WESTERN ASSOCIATION
BOX 25
BOISE, ID 83707
Secretary, Robert L Salter
Staff Size: 5 - 9

GAME FISHERIES COMMISSIONERS WESTERN ASSOCIATION
PARLIAMENT BUILDINGS
VICTORIA, BRITISH COLUMBIA, CANADA
Specific Interests: Prairie and Temperate
Forest

INDUSTRIAL MISSION OF BOSTON
56 BOYLSTON STREET
CAMBRIDGE, MA 02138
Director, Scott Paradise
Specific Interests: Prairie and Temperate
Forest

INTERPRETIVE NATURALISTS ASSOCIATION
1251 EAST BROAD STREET
COLUMBUS, OH 43205
Specific Interests: Prairie and Temperate
Forest
Staff Size: 500 - 999

KANNONZAKI FISHERY MUSEUM
KAMOI-MINAMINON
YOKOSUKA CITY, KANAGAWA, JAPAN
General Environment: Oceanographic
Specific Interests: Prairie and Temperate
Forest

LIMNOLOGY AND OCEANOGRAPHY SOCIETY OF AMERICA
UNIVERSITY OF MICHIGAN
ANN ARBOR, MI 48104
Director, Dr George Saunders
General Environment: Oceanographic
Staff Size: 1 - 4

MARINE TECHNOLOGY SOCIETY
1730 M STREET, NW
WASHINGTON, DC 20036
Director, Dr Robert W Niblock
General Environment: Oceanographic
Staff Size: 5 - 9

NATIONAL EDUCATION ASSOCIATION
1201 16TH STREET, NW
WASHINGTON, DC 20036
Specific Interests: Prairie and Temperate
Forest

NATIONAL OCEANOGRAPHIC ASSOCIATION
1900 L STREET, NW
WASHINGTON, DC 20036
Director, Carlton B Hamm
General Environment: Oceanographic

NATURAL HISTORY MUSEUM OF AMERICA
CENTRAL PARK WEST AT 79TH STREET
NEW YORK, NY 10024
Staff Size: 500 - 999

NATURAL HISTORY MUSEUM OF CHICAGO
ROOSEVELT ROAD AND LAKE SHORE
CHICAGO,IL 60605

NATURAL RESOURCES ASSOCIATION OF WISCONSIN
RT 1, BOX 390
STEVENS POINT, WI 54481
President, F Baumgartner
Specific Interests: Prairie and Temperate
Forest

NATURAL RESOURCES CENTER OF NEW ENGLAND
506 STATLER BUILDING
BOSTON, MA 02116
Director, Dr Perry R Hagenstein
Specific Interests: Prairie and Temperate
Forest
Staff Size: 1 - 4

NATURE AND NATURAL RESOURCES CONSERVATION UNION
110 MORGES
BERN, SWITZERLAND

NATURE STUDY SOCIETY OF AMERICA
1501 GRANADA BOULEVARD
ANN ARBOR, MI 48103
Specific Interests: Prairie and Temperate
Forest
Staff Size: 500 - 999

NUCLEAR ENERGY COMMISSION (INTERNATIONAL/AMERICAN)
PAN AMERICAN UNION
WASHINGTON, DC 20006

OCEANOGRAPHIC FOUNDATION, INTERNATIONAL
ONE RICKENBACKER CAUSEWAY
VIRGINIA KEY, MIAMI, FL 33149
Director, F G W Smith
General Environment: Oceanographic
Staff Size: 1000 & Larger

ORNITHOLOGICAL SOCIETY OF WISCONSIN
288 EAST SOMO AVENUE
TOMAHAWK, WI 54487
President, Donald J Hendrick
Specific Interests: Prairie and Temperate
Forest

ORNITHOLOGY SOCIETY OF VIRGINIA
6207 NEWMAN ROAD
FAIRFAX, VA 22030
President, J W Eike
Specific Interests: Prairie and Temperate
Forest

OUTDOOR CIRCLE
200 NORTH VINEYARD BOULEVARD
HONOLULU, HI 96817
Specific Interests: Prairie and Temperate
Forest

OUTDOOR WRITER'S ASSOCIATION
244 RICHMOND DR
WARWICK, RI 02888
President, John S Carroll
Specific Interests: Prairie and Temperate
Forest

PRAIRIE GROUSE TECHNOLOGY COUNCIL
P O BOX 567- WILDLIFE RESEARCH CENTER
FORT COLLINS, CO 80521

Chairman, Donald M Hoffman
General Environment: Terrestrial
Specific Interests: Prairie and Temperate
Forest
Staff Size: 100 - 499

RESOURCES FOR THE FUTURE
1755 MASSACHUSETTS AVENUE, NW
WASHINGTON, DC 20036

Secretary, John E Herbert
Staff Size: 10 - 49

SCIENCES ACADEMY OF CALIFORNIA
GOLDEN GATE PARK
SAN FRANCISCO, CA 94118

Director, Dr George E Linsay
Staff Size: 100 - 499

SCIENTIFIC ADVANCEMENT ASSOCIATION
1515 MASSACHUSETTS AVENUE, NW
WASHINGTON, DC 20005

Executive Officer, Dael Wolfle
Specific Interests: Prairie and Temperate
Forest
Staff Size: 1000 and Larger

SIERRA CLUB, LOMA PRIETA CHAPTER
POST OFFICE BOX 143
MENLO PARK, CA 94025

Director, George Treichel
General Environment: Terrestrial

STATE FORESTERS NATIONAL ASSOCIATION
2705 SPURGIN ROAD
MISSOULA, MT 59801

Director, G C Moon
General Environment: Terrestrial
Specific Interests: Prairie and Temperate
Forest
Staff Size: 10 - 49

TYMPANUCHUS CUPIDO PINNATUS SOCIETY
611 EAST WISCONSIN AVENUE, P O
BOX 1156
MILWAUKEE, WI 53201

President, Willis G Sullivan
Specific Interests: Prairie and Temperate
Forest
Staff Size: 1000 - 4999

UENO ZOO AQUARIUM
UENO PARK
TAITO-KU, TOKYO, JAPAN

Specific Interests: Prairie and Temperate
Forest

WATERFOWL COUNCIL, IDAHO FISHERIES AND GAME DEPARTMENT
P O BOX 25
BOISE, ID 83707

Director, John R Woodworth
Specific Interests: Prairie and Temperate
Forest

WATERSHED ASSOCIATION OF FARMINGTON RIVER
MURRAY HILL, NJ 07971

President, Hiram P Maxim

WATERSHEDS (STONYBROOK-MILLSTONE)
POST OFFICE BOX 171
PENNINSTON, NJ 08534

Executive Director, Ian R Walter
Specific Interests: Urban
Staff Size: 1 - 4

WILD ANIMAL PROPAGATION TRUST
OGLEBAY PARK
WHEELING, WV 26003

President, Don G Davis

WILDLIFE MANAGEMENT INSTITUTE
709 WIRE BUILDING
WASHINGTON, DC 20005

Director, Daniel Poole

WILDLIFE RESTORATION FOUNDATION
17 WEST 60TH STREET
NEW YORK, NY 10023

Director, Amos L Horst
General Environment: Terrestrial
Specific Interests: Prairie and Temperate
Forest
Staff Size: 1000 - 4999

WILSON ORNITHOLOGICAL SOCIETY
8728 OXWELL LANE
LAUREL, MD 20810

Secretary, Jeff Swinebroad
Specific Interests: Prairie and Temperate
Forest

WORLD MEDICAL ASSOCIATION
10 COLUMBUS CIRCLE
NEW YORK, NY 10019

WORLD WILDLIFE FUND
1816 JEFFERSON PLACE, NW
WASHINGTON, DC 20036

Director, Lloyd W Smith

ZOOLOGICAL SOCIETY OF NEW YORK
THE ZOOLOGICAL PARK
BRONX, NY 10460

Chairman of Building, Fairfield Osborn
Specific Interests: Prairie and Temperate
Forest

Research Institute

AIR AND SPACECRAFT REMOTE SENSING

AMES RESEARCH CENTER
MOFFETT FIELD, CA 94035

Director, John Arvesen

AIR POLLUTION RESEARCH CENTER
UNIVERSITY OF CALIFORNIA
RIVERSIDE, CA 92502

Director, James N Pitts
General Environment: Atmospheric
Specific Interests: Urban
Staff Size: 50 - 99

ANTARCTIC BRITISH SURVEY
30 GILLINGHAM STREET
LONDON, SW1, ENGLAND

Director, Sir Vivian Fuchs
Specific Interests: Polar (cold)
Staff Size: 100 - 499

APPLIED RESEARCH ENVIRONMENTAL SCIENCE, NATURE CONSERVATION
POST OFFICE BOX P
ST MICHAELS, MD 21663

Director, Dr Edgar Garbisch
General Environment: Estuarine
Staff Size: 5 - 9

ARCTIC INSTITUTE OF NORTH AMERICA
3458 REDPATH DRIVE
MONTREAL, QUEBEC, CANADA

Specific Interests: Polar (cold)

ATOMIC FORUM, EUROPEAN
26 RUE DE CLICHY
PARIS 9, FRANCE

CHARLES DARWIN FOUNDATION, GALAPAGOS ISLE
1 RUE DUCALE
BRUSSELS 1, BELGIUM

Specific Interests: Tropical (hot)

CONSERVATION ENGINEERING ASSOCIATION
EAST 7TH AND COURT AVENUE
DES MOINES, IA 50309

Director, D M Hill
General Environment: Estuarine

DESERT RESEARCH INSTITUTE
RENO, NV 89507

Staff Size: 100 - 499

ENVIRONMENTAL AND PUBLIC HEALTH COUNCIL
535 NORTH DEARBORN STREET
CHICAGO, IL 60610

Executive Secretary, Frank Barton
Staff Size: 10 - 49

ENVIRONMENTAL HEALTH
369 EAST REED STREET
SAN JOSE, CA 95112

Director, Theresa Gautefald

ENVIRONMENTAL MEDICINE
55 GOLDEN OAK DRIVE
PORTOLA VALLEY, CA 94025
Director, John Billingham

**ENVIRONMENTAL QUALITY
LABORATORY**
CALIFORNIA INSTITUTION OF
TECHNOLOGY
PASADENA, CA 91109
Staff Size: 10 - 49

**ENVIRONMENTAL SCIENCES
OFFICE**
SMITHSONIAN INSTITUTION
WASHINGTON, DC 20560
Director, William L Eilers

**ENVIRONMENTAL SCIENCES
SERVICES ADMINISTRATION**
BOULDER, CO 80302
Specific Interests: Prairie and Temperate
Forest

**ENVIRONMENTAL STUDIES
CENTER**
VIRGINIA POLYTECHNIC
INSTITUTE/STATE UNIVERSITY
BLACKSBURG, VA 24061
Director, Dr John Cairns Jr
Staff Size: 50 - 99

**ENVIRONMENTAL STUDIES,
BATTELLE MEMORIAL
INSTITUTE**
505 KING AVENUE
COLUMBUS, OHIO
President, S L Fawcett
Staff Size: 5000 - 9999

**ENVIRONMENTAL STUDIES, JOHN
MUIR INSTITUTE**
1098 MILLS TOWER
SAN FRANCISCO, CA 94104
President, Max K Linn
Staff Size: 5 - 9

**EUROPEAN ATOMIC ENERGY
SOCIETY**
VIA BELISARIO 15
ROME, ITALY

FOREST INSTITUTE OF THE SOUTH
SUITE 280, 1 CORPORATION
SQUARE, NE
ATLANTA, GA 30329
General Environment: Terrestrial
Specific Interests: Prairie and Temperate
Forest

**FUND INSTITUTE OF BLACK
AFRICA**
C/O UNIVERSITY OF DAKAR
DAKAR, SENEGAL
Director, Vincent Monteill

**GENETICS DEPARTMENT, AMES
RESOURCES CENTER, NASA**
MOFFETT FIELD, CA 94035
Director, Ellen Weaver

**GEOGRAPHY DEPARTMENT,
ASSOCIATION QUARTERNARY
RESEARCH**
TOKYO UNIVERSITY I MISSOURI-
TOFUJI-CYO
BUNKYO-KU, TOKYO, JAPAN
Director, Professor Soki Yamamoto
Specific Interests: Prairie and Temperate
Forest

GEOLOGICAL SOCIETY OF TOKYO
12 NIBAN-CHO, CHIYODA-KU
TOKYO, JAPAN
Director, Moritatsu Hosokawa
Specific Interests: Prairie and Temperate
Forest

**GEOLOGICAL SOCIETY, GEOLOGY
DEPARTMENT**
TOKYO UNIVERSITY 1 MISSOURI-
TOFUJI-CHO
BUNKYO-KU, TOKYO, JAPAN
Director, Dr Takeo Wantanabe
Specific Interests: Prairie and Temperate
Forest

**GEOLOGY AND GEOPHYSICS
DEPARTMENT AT M I T**
77 MASSACHUSETTS AVENUE
CAMBRIDGE, MA 02139

**GREAT LAKES RESEARCH
INSTITUTE**
1120 G DANIEL BALDWIN
BUILDING
ERIE, PA 16501
President, Frederick D Buggie
General Environment: Limnologic

HOLLY SOCIETY OF AMERICA
407 FOUNTAIN GREEN ROAD
BEL AIR, MD 21014
Secretary Treasurer, B C Green Jr
General Environment: Terrestrial
Specific Interests: Prairie and Temperate
Forest
Staff Size: 1000 - 4999

HYDROBIOLOGICAL INSTITUTE
ATHENS, GREECE
Director, J Xanthakidis
General Environment: Oceanographic

**INDUSTRIAL HEALTH
FOUNDATION**
5231 CENTER AVENUE
PITTSBURGH, PA 15232
Specific Interests: Prairie and Temperate
Forest

**INSTITUTE DE CERCETARI
PROIETARI PISCOLE**

BUILDING ANA JPATESCU
BUCURESTI, 46, RUMANIA
Director, Ing Gheorghe Mirica

**INSTYTUT GOSPODARKI WODNEJ
(IGW)**
WARSZAWA 10, POLAND
Director, Dr Kazimierz Matul

**INTERNATIONAL COUNCIL OF
SCIENTIFIC UNIONS**
VIA CORNELIO CELSO 7
00161 ROME, ITALY

**MAIMONIDES HOSPITAL OF
BROOKLYN**
4802 TENTH AVENUE
BROOKLYN, NY 11219
Director, David Grob

**MARINE AND ENVIRONMENTAL
STUDIES CENTER**
LEHIGH UNIVERSITY
BETHLEHEM, PA 18015
Staff Size: 10 - 49

MARINE REARCH INSTITUTE
5000 BERGEN, NORWAY
Director, Gunnar Saetersdal
General Environment: Oceanographic
Staff Size: 100 - 499

MARINE RESEARCH INSTITUTE
SKULAGOTA 4
REYKJAVIK, ICELAND
Director, Jon Jonsson
General Environment: Oceanographic

**MEDICAL RESEARCH
DEPARTMENT**
SAINT LUKES HOSPITAL
CLEVELAND, OH 44104
Head, George Wright

**MEDICINE FOLLOW-UP AGENCY,
SCIENCE ACADEMY RESEARCH
CENTER**
2101 CONSTITUTION AVENUE, NW
WASHINGTON, DC 20418
Director, B Gilbert

METEOROLOGIYA PRI BAN
SOPHIA, LENIN 154, BULGARIA
Director, I Marinov
General Environment: Atmospheric

**METEOROLOGY RESOURCES
INCORPORATED**
464 W WOODBURY ROAD
ALTADENA, CA 91001
Vice President, Robert Stinson

**NATURAL RESOURCES COUNCIL
OF MAINE**
20 WILLOW STREET
AUGUSTA, ME 04330
Staff Size: 5 - 9

OCEANIC INSTITUTE
MAKAPUU POINT
WAIMANALO OAHU, HI 96795
General Environment: Oceanographic
Specific Interests: Tropical (hot)
Staff Size: 10 - 49

OCEANOGRAPHIC INSTITUTE OF
   WOODS HOLE
OFFICE OF ENVIRONMENTAL
   QUALITY
WOODS HOLE, MA 02543
Associate Director, Bostwick H Ketchum
General Environment: Oceanographic
Staff Size: 500 - 999

OCEANOGRAPHY, SCRIPPS
   INSTITUTE
UNIVERSITY OF CALIFORNIA
SAN DIEGO, CA 92172
Staff Size: 1000 - 4999

ORSZAGOS METEOROLOGIAI
   INTEZET
KITAIBEL PAL U I
BUDAPEST, HUNGARY
Director, Frigyos Desi

POLAR RESEARCH, SCOTT
   INSTITUTE
LENSFIELD ROAD
CAMBRIDGE, ENGLAND
Director, Brian Roberts
Specific Interests: Polar (cold)

POLLUTION ABSTRACTS
POST OFFICE BOX 2369
LA JOLLA, CA 92037
Staff Size: 10 - 49

PUBLIC AFFAIRS INSTITUTE
WESTERN MICHIGAN UNIVERSITY
KALAMAZOO, MI 49001
Director, Dr Robert Kaufman
General Environment: Terrestrial
Specific Interests: Urban
Staff Size: 100 - 499

PUBLIC LIBRARY AT CLEVELAND
325 SUPERIOR AVENUE
CLEVELAND, OH 44101

RESEARCH GRANTS DIVISION
NATIONAL INSTITUTES OF HEALTH
BETHESDA, MD 20014
Director, John Dalton

RESEARCH INSTITUTE FOR
   ADVANCE STUDY
1450 SOUTH ROLLING ROAD
BALTIMORE, MD 21227
Staff Size: 100 - 499

RESEARCH INSTITUTE OF
   STANFORD UNIVERSITY
333 RAVENSWOOD DR
MENLO PARK, CA 94025

RESEARCH LABORATORY
BENJAMIN FRANKLIN PARKWAY
PHILADELPHIA, PA 19103
Staff Size: 100 - 499

RUA DR SATTAMINI
   AGROMETEOROLOGY
91-APT 105 TIJUCA
RIO DE JANEIRO, BRAZIL
Director, Marlene Pinto

SCIENCE AND TECHNOLOGY
   INSTITUTE OF KOREA
9-CHONG-RO 2-KA CHONGRO-KU
POBOX 38,KWANG-KWANMOON,
   KOREA
Director, Dr Choi Hyung
Specific Interests: Prairie and Temperate
   Forest

SCIENCE INFORMATION
   EXCHANGE
1730 M STREET, NW
WASHINGTON, DC 20036

SCIENCES AND TECHNOLOGY
   RESEARCH COUNCIL OF TURKEY
31 BAYINDIRSOKAK
ANKARA, TURKEY
Director, Professor Mustafa Uluoz

SCIENTIFIC INSTITUTE OF LEBU
APARTADO 123
LEBU, CHILE
Director, Dr Alberto Zapata Barra

SMITHSONIAN INSTITUTION,
   CENTER FOR SHORT-LIVED
   PHENOMENA
60 GARDEN STREET
CAMBRIDGE, MA 02138
Staff Size: 5 - 9

SOUTH WESTERN RESEARCH
   INSTITUTE
LIBRARY 8500 CULEBRA, P O
   DRAWER 28510
SAN ANTONIO, TX 78284
Staff Size: 1000 - 4999

SPACE RESEARCH COMMITTEE
55 BUILDING MALESHERBES
PARIS 8, FRANCE
General Environment: Atmospheric

SYSTEMATIC RESEARCH
   INSTITUTE
8049 PROSPECT WAY
LA MESA, CA 92041
Director, M Anderson

SYSTEMS ANALYSIS DIVISION,
   STANFORD RESEARCH
   INSTITUTE
333 RAVENSWOOD AVENUE
MENLO PARK, CA 94025
Operations Analyst, Richard C Sandys

WATER RESOURCES CENTER
10 WEST 35TH STREET
CHICAGO, IL 60616
General Environment: Limnologic
Staff Size: 1000 - 4999

WILDLIFE REHABILITATION
   CENTER
GROVE STREET
UPTON, MA 01568
President, P B Stanton
Staff Size: 1 - 4

WINZEN RESEARCH
   INCORPORATED
8401 LYNDALE AVENUE
MINNEAPOLIS, MN 55420
General Environment: Atmospheric

ZAKLAD GEOFIZYKI
UL PASTEURA 3 .
WARSZAWA 22, POLAND
Director, Professor Stephan Manczarski

Unclassified

ACADEMIA SINICA
SECTION 2, 128 YENCHIU ROAD
NANKANG, TAIWAN
Director, Dr Shih-Chieh Wang
Specific Interests: Tropical (hot)

ADMINISTRATION INSTITUTE
CASILLA 5918
GUAYAQUIL, ECUADOR
Director, Rene Calle

AIR POLLUTION TECHNOLOGY
   INFORMATION CENTER
RESEARCH TRIANGLE PARK, NJ
   27709
Director, Peter Halpin
General Environment: Atmospheric
Staff Size: 10 - 49

ALLIED HEALTH MANPOWER,
   HEALTH MANPOWER
   EDUCATION BUREAU
NATIONAL INSTITUTES OF HEALTH
BETHESDA, MD 20014
Director, T Hatch

ANIMAL PARASITOLOGY
   INSTITUTE
NATIONAL AGRICULTURAL
   RESEARCH CENTER
BELTSVILLE, MD 20705
General Environment: Terrestrial
Specific Interests: Rural
Staff Size: 100 - 499

ANTARCTIC PROGRAMS OFFICE,
   DIVISION OF ENVIRONMENTAL
   SCIENCES

1800 G STREET, NW
WASHINGTON, DC 20550
Specific Interests: Polar (cold)

**APPALACHIAN REGIONAL
  COMMISSION**
1666 CONNECTICUT AVENUE, NW
WASHINGTON, DC 20235
Staff Size: 10 - 49

APPLIED RESEARCH INSTITUTE
KANBE
RANGOON, BURMA
Director, Dr F Ba Hli
Specific Interests: Tropical (hot)

**ARMY ENVIRONMENTAL HYGIENE
  AGENCY**
OFFICE OF SURGEON GENERAL
EDGEWOOD ARSENAL, MD 21010

**ATLANTIC OCEANOGRAPHY
  LABORATORY, BEDFORD
  INSTITUTION**
POST OFFICE BOX 1006
DARTMOUTH, NOVA SCOTIA,
  CANADA
Director, Dr William Ford
General Environment: Oceanographic
Staff Size: 500 - 999

**BIOGEOCHEMISTRY-ECOLOGY
  INFORMATION CENTER, OAK
  RIDGE NATIONAL LAB**
BUILDING 2001, X-10
OAK RIDGE, TN 37830

BUREAU OF CUSTOMS
PORT AREA
MANILA, PHILIPPINES
Director, Juan Ponce Enrile
Specific Interests: Prairie and Temperate
  Forest

BUREAU OF LAND MANAGEMENT
18TH AND C STREETS, NW
WASHINGTON, DC 20240
Staff Size: 1000 - 4999

**CENTRAL SALT AND MARINE
  CHEMISTRY RESEARCH**
SCIENTIFIC AND INDUSTRIAL
  RESEARCH COUNCIL
HAVNAGAR, INDIA
Director, Dr D S Datar

**CIVIL AEROMEDICAL INSTITUTE,
  FEDERAL AVIATION
  ADMINISTRATION**
POST OFFICE BOX 25082
OKLAHOMA CITY, OK 73125
Chief, P Iampietro
Staff Size: 10 - 49

**CLEARING HOUSE FOR FEDERAL
  SCIENCES-TECHNOLOGY
  INFORMATION**
5285 PORT ROYAL ROAD
SPRINGFIELD, VA 22151

Specific Interests: Prairie and Temperate
  Forest

COAST AND GEODETIC SURVEY
WASHINGTON SCIENCES CENTER,
  BUILDING 1
ROCKVILLE, MD 20852

COAST GUARD EASTERN AREA
GOVERNORS ISLAND
NEW YORK, NY 10004
General Environment: Oceanographic
Specific Interests: Polar (cold)
Staff Size: 5 - 9

**COASTAL ENGINEERING
  RESEARCH CENTER**
5201 LITTLE FALLS ROAD, NW
WASHINGTON, DC 20016

**COLD REGIONS BIBLIOGRAPHY
  PROJECT**
SCIENCES AND TECHNOLOGY
  DIVISION, LIBRARY OF
  CONGRESS
WASHINGTON, DC 20540
Head, Dr Geza T Thurony
Specific Interests: Polar (cold)
Staff Size: 5 - 9

**COMMERCE AND INDUSTRY
  DEPARTMENT**
DIVISION OF SEA FISHERIES
CAPE TOWN, REPUBLIC OF SOUTH
  AFRICA
Director, C G Duplessis

**COMMONWEALTH SCIENTIFIC
  AND RESEARCH ORGANIZATION**
MELBOURNE, NEW SOUTH WALES,
  AUSTRALIA

CONSERVATION VOTERS LEAGUE
324 C STREET, SW
WASHINGTON, DC 20003
Staff Size: 1 - 4

**CONSUMER PROTECTION AND
  ENVIRONMENTAL HEALTH
  SERVICES**
FEDERAL BUILDING 8, 200 C
  STREET, SW
WASHINGTON, DC 20204
Specific Interests: Prairie and Temperate
  Forest

**COOPERATIVE STATE RESEARCH
  SERVICE**
14TH STREET AND
  INDEPENDENCE AVENUE, SW
WASHINGTON, DC 20250
Staff Size: 50 - 99

DATA AND PLANNING DIVISION
KRISHI BHAVAN
NEW DELHI, INDIA
Director, R Jayaraman
General Environment: Oceanographic

DEFENSE DEPARTMENT
6304 STONEHAM LANE
MCLEAN, VA 22101

**DEFENSE DEPARTMENT,
  CANADIAN AIR FORCE**
125 ELGIN STREET
OTTAWA, ONTARIO, CANADA
Director, Dr R J Uffen
General Environment: Oceanographic

**DEFENSE DOCUMENTATION
  CENTER, DEFENSE SUPPLY
  AGENCY**
DEPARTMENT DEFENSE,
  CAMERON STATION
ALEXANDRIA, VA 22314
Staff Size: 100 - 499

**DEFENSE MINISTRY (NATIONAL),
  ROYAL RESEARCH**
VOTANIKOS
ATHENS, GREECE
Director, Captain Hercules Kolokythas

**DEFENSE MINISTRY,
  DEPARTMENT OF
  HYDROGRAPHY AND
  NAVIGATION**
CUBUKLU
ISTANBUL, TURKEY
Director, Captain Nedret Berkay
General Environment: Oceanographic

**EARTH SCIENCES BRANCH,
  DIVISION OF BIOLOGICAL AND
  MEDICAL SCIENCES**
ATOMIC ENERGY COMMISSION
WASHINGTON, DC 20545
Chief, Dr Rudolf J Engelmann
Staff Size: 10 - 49

ECUADOREAN NAVY
CASILLA
GUAYAQUIL, ECUADOR

EDUCATION DEPARTMENT
ARROCEROS
MANILA, PHILIPPINES
Director, Dr Carlos P Romulo, Minister
Specific Interests: Prairie and Temperate
  Forest

EDUCATION MINISTRY
SINGAPORE
Specific Interests: Tropical (hot)

EDUCATION MINISTRY
TOKYO, JAPAN
Director, Toshihiro Kennoki

EDUCATION MINISTRY
TAIWAN, CHINA
Specific Interests: Tropical (hot)

**EDUCATION MINISTRY, APPLIED
  RESEARCH INSTITUTE**
PORTO NOVO, DAHOMEY

**ENGINEERING AGENCY FOR
RESOURCES INVENTION**
6500 BROOKS LANE
WASHINGTON, DC 20315

**ENVIRONMENTAL AFFAIRS
OFFICE, GENERAL SERVICES
ADMINISTRATION**
18TH AND F STREETS, NW
WASHINGTON, DC 20405
Staff Size: 1 - 4

**ENVIRONMENTAL CONTROL
ADMINISTRATION**
12720 TWINBROOK PARKWAY
ROCKVILLE, MD 20852

**ENVIRONMENTAL CONTROL
ADMINISTRATION**
222 EAST CENTRAL PARKWAY
CINCINNATI, OH 45202

ENVIRONMENTAL DATA SERVICE
9403 CALDRAN DRIVE
CLINTON, MD 20735
Director, Thomas Austin

**ENVIRONMENTAL MONITORING
AND PREDICTING SECTION**
6815 BUTTERMERE LANE
BETHESDA, MD 20034
Associate Administrator, Richard
Hallgren

**ENVIRONMENTAL PROTECTION
AGENCY REGION 10**
1200 SIXTH AVENUE
SEATTLE, WA 98101
Staff Size: 100 - 499

**ENVIRONMENTAL PROTECTION
AGENCY, REGION 9**
100 CALIFORNIA STREET
SAN FRANCISCO, CA 94111

**ENVIRONMENTAL PROTECTION
AGENCY, REGION 2**
26 FEDERAL PLAZA
NEW YORK, NY 10007
Staff Size: 100 - 499

**ENVIRONMENTAL RESEARCH
INSTITUTE**
30TH STREET AND ARAPAHOE
AVENUE
BOULDER, CO 80302

**ENVIRONMENTAL RESOURCES
LABORATORY**
4927 IDYLWILD TRAIL
BOULDER, CO 80302
Director, Wilmont Hess

**ENVIRONMENTAL SCIENCE
DIVISION, NATIONAL SCIENCE
FOUNDATION**
1800 G STREET, NW
WASHINGTON, DC 20550

**ENVIRONMENTAL SCIENCES
INFORMATION CENTER**
NATIONAL OCEANIC AND
ATMOSPHERIC ADMINISTRATION
ROCKVILLE, MD 20852
Staff Size: 50 - 99

**ENVIRONMENTAL SCIENCES
SERVICES ADMINISTRATION**
1666 CONNECTICUT AVENUE, NW
WASHINGTON, DC 20230
General Environment: Atmospheric

**ENVIRONMENTAL STUDIES
DIVISION**
NATIONAL SCIENCE FOUNDATION
WASHINGTON, DC 20550
Staff Size: 10 - 49

**ENVIRONMENTAL STUDIES
PROGRAM**
SAINT LAWRENCE UNIVERSITY
CANTON, NY 13617
President, Frank P Piskor
General Environment: Terrestrial
Staff Size: 5 - 9

**ENVIRONMENTAL STUDIES
PROGRAM**
228 MARK HALL, UNIVERSITY OF
CALIFORNIA
DAVIS, CA 95616
Dean, F Mccalla
Staff Size: 10 - 49

EXTERNAL AFFAIRS DEPARTMENT
OTTAWA, ONTARIO, CANADA
Director, Paul Martin
General Environment: Oceanographic

FEDERAL EXTENSION SERVICE
14TH STREET AND
INDEPENDENCE AVENUE
WASHINGTON, DC 20250
Staff Size: 100 - 499

FEDERAL POWER COMMISSION
441 G STREET, NW
WASHINGTON, DC 20426

FEDERAL RADIATION COUNCIL
17TH STREET AND PACIFIC
AVENUE, NW
WASHINGTON,DC 20503
Specific Interests: Prairie and Temperate
Forest

**FEDERAL WATER POLLUTION
CONTROL ADMINISTRATION**
1921 JEFFERSON DAVIS HIGHWAY
ARLINGTON, VA 22212
Director, David D Dominick

FINANCE MINISTRY
DEPARTMENT OF FISHERIES
TEHRAN, IRAN
General Environment: Oceanographic

**FISHERIES AND HYDROBIOLOGY
DEPARTMENT**
MINISTRY OF AGRICULTURE
BAGHDAD, IRAQ
Director, Dr Mahmoud Ibrahim Alhamid
General Environment: Oceanographic

**FISHERIES INVESTIGATION
CENTER**
CUMANA
ESTADO SUCRE, VENEZUELA
General Environment: Oceanographic

**FOOD PROTECTION COMMISSION,
BIOLOGY AND AGRICULTURE
DIVISION**
2101 CONSTITUTION AVENUE, NW
WASHINGTON, DC 20418

**FOREST RESERVATION
COMMISSION, (NATIONAL)**
DEPARTMENT OF AGRICULTURE,
SOUTH BUILDING
WASHINGTON, DC 20240
President, Robert F Froehlke

FORESTRY COMMISSION
25 SAVILE ROW
LONDON WIX2AY, ENGLAND
Public Officer, Herbert L Edlin
General Environment: Terrestrial
Specific Interests: Prairie and Temperate
Forest

FORESTRY DEPARTMENT
LOME, TOGO
General Environment: Terrestrial

**FROZEN SEA RESEARCH GROUP
FOR DEMARCATION**
825 DEVONSHIRE ROAD
ESQUIMALT, BRITISH COLUMBIA,
CANADA
General Environment: Oceanographic
Specific Interests: Polar (cold)

**FUEL, ELECTRIC POWER AND
INDUSTRIAL PROGRAMS
MINISTRY**
GENERAL PETROLEUM
ESTABLISHMENT
DAMASCUS, SYRIA
Director, Ishan Sarkis
General Environment: Oceanographic

**GULF COAST WATER SUPPLY
RESEARCH LABORATORY**
POST OFFICE BOX 158
DAUPHIN ISLAND, AL 36528
Director, R J Hammerstrom
Specific Interests: Prairie and Temperate
Forest

**HEALTH SERVICES AND MENTAL
HEALTH ADMINISTRATION**
5600 FISHERS LANE, ROOM 1587
ROCKVILLE, MD 20852
Staff Size: 50 - 99

**HEALTH, EDUCATION, AND
WELFARE DEPARTMENT**
1100 CREST LANE
MCLEAN, VA 22010

**HEALTH, EDUCATION, AND
WELFARE REGION 3**
POST OFFICE BOX 12900
PHILADELPHIA, PA 19108
Staff Size: 1 - 4

**HEALTH, EDUCATION, AND
WELFARE REGION 7**
601 EAST 12TH STREET
KANSAS CITY, MO 64106
Staff Size: 1 - 4

**HYDROGRAPHIC DEPARTMENT,
TURKISH NAVY**
CUBUKULU, ISTANBUL, TURKEY
Director, Captain H Akoglu
General Environment: Oceanographic

**INDIAN NATIONAL COMMANDER
ON OCEAN RESEARCH**
RAFI MARG
NEW DELHI, INDIA
Director, Dr D N Wadia
General Environment: Oceanographic
Staff Size: 100 - 499

**INDUSTRY AND MINING HIGH
COMMISSION**
NOVAKCHOTT, MAURITANIA
Director, Dr Fall Papa Daouda

INTERIOR AND INSULAR AFFAIRS
ROOM 3106, SENATE OFFICE
BUILDING
WASHINGTON, DC 20510
Director, Senator Henry M Jackson

INTERIOR AND INSULAR AFFAIRS
ROOM 1324, LONGWORTH HOUSE
WASHINGTON, DC 20515
Director, Representative Wayne N
Aspinall

INTERIOR DEPARTMENT
1951 CONSTITUTION AVENUE, NW
WASHINGTON, DC 20240

**INTERNATIONAL SCIENTIFIC AND
TECHNOLOGIC AFFAIRS
DIVISION**
2201 C STREET, NW
WASHINGTON, DC 20525
Staff Size: 10 - 49

**JOINT COMMITTEE ON ATOMIC
ENERGY**
CAPITOL BUILDING, ROOM H-403
WASHINGTON, DC 20510
Director, Edward Bauser
Staff Size: 10 - 49

LAND AND MINE MINISTRY
KUALA LUMPUR, MALAYSIA

Director, Mahayuddin Bin Haji Moho
Zain
General Environment: Terrestrial
Specific Interests: Tropical (hot)

**LAND AND NATURAL RESOURCES
DIVISION, DEPARTMENT OF
JUSTICE**
700 NEW HAMPSHIRE AVENUE
WASHINGTON, DC 20037

**LENINGRAD ORDER LENIN STATE
UNIVERSITY, LGV**
UNIVERSITY NABEREZHNAYA,7/9
LENINGRAD, UNION OF SOVIET
SOCIALIST REPUBLICS
Director, D Aleksandrov
Staff Size: 100 - 499

MARINE FISHERIES DEPARTMENT
FISHERIES HARBOR, WEST WHARF
KARACHI, PAKISTAN
General Environment: Oceanographic

MARINELAND
RFD 1, BOX 122
ST AUGUSTINE, FL 32084
General Manager, B C Townsend, Jr
General Environment: Oceanographic
Specific Interests: Prairie and Temperate
Forest

**MARINELAND OF PACIFIC
RESEARCH LABORATORY**
PALOS VERDES DRIVE SOUTH
PALOS VERDES ESTATES, CA 90274
Curator, John H Prescott
General Environment: Oceanographic
Specific Interests: Prairie and Temperate
Forest

MARITIME SAFETY AGENCY
TOKYO, JAPAN
Director, Dr Mitsuo Sato
Specific Interests: Prairie and Temperate
Forest

**MEAT AND FISHERIES
DIRECTORATE**
FISHERIES OFFICE
ANKARA, TURKEY
General Environment: Oceanographic

**METEOROLOGICAL INSTITUTE,
(INTERNATIONAL)**
STOCKHOLM, SWEDEN
Director, Bert Bolin
General Environment: Atmospheric

MINISTRY OF AGRICULTURE
DEPARTMENT OF FORESTS AND
NATURAL RESOURCES
BEIRUT, LEBANON

**MOBILE SOURCE POLLUTION
CONTROL PROGRAM**
2565 PLYMOUTH ROAD
ANN ARBOR, MI 48105
General Environment: Atmospheric
Staff Size: 100 - 499

NATIONAL ACADEMY OF SCIENCES
2101 CONSTITUTION AVENUE, NW
WASHINGTON, DC 20418
Staff Size: 500 - 999

**NATIONAL CLEAN-UP, PAINT-UP,
FIX-UP BUREAU**
1500 RHODE ISLAND AVENUE, NW
WASHINGTON, DC 20005
Director, R H Hackendahl
Specific Interests: Prairie and Temperate
Forest

NATIONAL DEFENSE MINISTRY
TAIPEI, TAIWAN
Specific Interests: Tropical (hot)

**NATIONAL ENVIRONMENTAL
RESEARCH CENTER**
OFFICE OF PUBLIC AFFAIRS
CINCINNATI, OH 45268
Director, Gilbert M Gigliotti

**NATIONAL INSTITUTE OF
ENVIRONMENTAL HEALTH
SCIENCES**
POST OFFICE BOX 12233
RESEARCH TRIANGLE PARK, NC
27709
General Environment: Terrestrial

**NATIONAL OCEANIC AND
ATMOSPHERIC
ADMINISTRATION**
DEPARTMENT OF COMMERCE,
ENVIRONMENTAL RESEARCH
LABORATORY
BOULDER, CO 80302
Director, Dr W Hess
Staff Size: 1000 - 4999

**NATIONAL OCEANIC AND
ATMOSPHERIC
ADMINISTRATION**
8306 MELODY CENTER
BETHESDA, MD 20034
Administrator, Robert M White

**NATIONAL OCEANIC AND
ATMOSPHERIC
ADMINISTRATION**
DEPARTMENT OF COMMERCE
ROCKVILLE, MD 20910
Staff Size: 1000 & Larger

NATIONAL REFERRAL CENTER
LIBRARY OF CONGRESS
WASHINGTON, DC 20540
Staff Size: 10 - 49

NATIONAL RESOURCES COUNCIL
OXFORD STREET
HALIFAX, NOVA SCOTIA, CANADA
Director, Dr C Neish
Staff Size: 50 - 99

NATIONAL WATER COMMISSION
800 NORTH QUINCY STREET
ARLINGTON, VA 22203
Staff Size: 10 - 49

**NATURAL HISTORY CENTRAL
    LIBRARY**
10TH STREET & CONSTITUTION
    AVENUE
WASHINGTON, DC 20560

**NATURAL RESOURCE AND TRADE
    MINISTRY**
BELIZE CITY, HONDURAS

**NATURAL RESOURCE ECONOMICS
    DIVISION**
14TH STREET AND
    INDEPENDENCE AVENUE
WASHINGTON, DC 20250
Specific Interests: Prairie and Temperate
    Forest

**NOISE ABATEMENT, FEDERAL
    AVIATION ADMINISTRATION
    REGIONAL OFFICE**
632 SIXTH AVENUE
ANCHORAGE, AK 99501
Director, Lyle K Brown

NORSE POLAR INSTITUTT
OSLO, NORWAY
Director, Tore Gjelsvik
Specific Interests: Polar (cold)

**NORTH-WEST WATER SUPPLY
    RESEARCH LABORATORY**
6702 TYEE DRIVE
GIG HARBOR, WA 98335
General Environment: Limnologic
Specific Interests: Prairie and Temperate
    Forest
Staff Size: 10 - 49

**NORWEGIAN DEFENSE
    RESOURCES ESTABLISHMENT**
BOX 115
3191 HORTEN, NORWAY
General Environment: Oceanographic

**OCEANOGRAPHIC DATA CENTER
    FOR DEMARCATION OF CANADA**
185 SOMERSET STREET WEST
OTTAWA, CANADA
Director, C D Sauer
General Environment: Oceanographic

OCEANOGRAPHIC INSTITUTE
LUZHNIKOVSKAYA ULITSA 8
MOSCOW, UNION OF SOVIET
    SOCIALIST REPUBLICS
General Environment: Oceanographic

**OCEANOGRAPHIC INSTITUTE OF
    HYDROLOGY AND
    METEOROLOGY**
CDYNIA, POLAND

**OCEANOGRAPHIC INSTITUTE,
    (NATIONAL)**
WORMLEY, ENGLAND
General Environment: Oceanographic

**OCEANOGRAPHIC RESEARCH,
    NATIONAL COMMISSION**
ISLAMABAD, PAKISTAN
General Environment: Oceanographic

**OCEANOGRAPHIC STUDIES OF
    ARGENTINA**
BUENOS AIRES, ARGENTINA
General Environment: Oceanographic

OCEANOGRAPHY BRANCH
615 BOOTH STREET
OTTAWA, ONTARIO, CANADA
Director, Dr N J Campbell
General Environment: Oceanographic
Staff Size: 50 - 99

**OCEANOGRAPHY COMMISSION OF
    CANADA**
REGIONAL WORK GROUP
OTTAWA, ONTARIO, CANADA
General Environment: Oceanographic

**OCEANOGRAPHY DEPARTMENT,
    ARCTIC AND ANTARCTIC
    RESEARCH INSTITUTE**
FONTANKA 34
LENINGRAD, UNION OF SOVIET
    SOCIALIST REPUBLICS
Director, V Frolov
General Environment: Oceanographic
Specific Interests: Polar (cold)

**OCEANOGRAPHY DIVISION,
    NATIONAL PHYSICAL
    RESOURCES LABORATORY**
KING GEORGE V AVENUE
DURBAN, REPUBLIC OF SOUTH
    AFRICA
Director, F P Anderson
General Environment: Oceanographic
Staff Size: 10 - 49

**OCEANOGRAPHY INSTITUTE,
    (NATIONAL)**
ERNAKULAM, INDIA
Director, Dr N K Panikkar
General Environment: Oceanographic

OFFICE OF BASIC MATERIALS
14TH STREET AND CONSTITUTION
    AVENUE, NW
WASHINGTON, DC 20230
Director, James M Owens

PANAMA CANAL COMPANY
BOX M
BALBOA HEIGHTS, CANAL ZONE
General Environment: Limnologic
Specific Interests: Tropical (hot)
Staff Size: 10 - 49

**PESTICIDE INFESTATION
    CONTROL LABORATORY**
LONDON ROAD
SLOUGH, BUCKINGHAMSHIRE,
    ENGLAND
Head of Chemistry Department, William
    B Burns
Staff Size: 100 - 499

**PESTICIDES COMMUNITY STUDIES
    DIVISION**
ENVIRONMENTAL PROTECTION
    AGENCY
CHAMBLEE, GA 30341
General Environment: limnologic

**PESTICIDES REGULATION
    DIVISION**
14TH STREET AND
    INDEPENDENCE AVENUE
WASHINGTON, DC 20250
Staff Size: 100 - 499

**PETROLEUM AND MINERAL
    RESOURCES MINISTRY**
JIDDA, SAUDI ARABIA

**PHILIPPINE ATOMIC ENERGY
    COMMISSION**
727 HERRAN STREET
MANILA, PHILIPPINES
Commissioner, Dr Librado D Ibe
Specific Interests: Tropical (hot)
Staff Size: 5 - 9

PLANNING ORGANIZATION
TEHRAN, IRAN
Director, Dr Rassekh
General Environment: Oceanographic

PLANT INDUSTRY STATION
SOIL AND WATER CONSERVATION
    RESOURCES
BELTSVILLE, MD 20705
Specific Interests: Rural
Staff Size: 500 - 999

POPULATION RESEARCH CENTER
NATIONAL INSTITUTES OF HEALTH
BETHESDA, MD 20014
Director, Dr B S Liljeroot
Staff Size: 10 - 49

**PORT AND NAVIGATION
    ORGANIZATION**
MINISTRY OF ROADS
TEHRAN, IRAN
Director, Admiral Sheyrant

PUBLIC INFORMATION OFFICE
WASHINGTON SCIENCES CENTER,
    BUILDING 5
ROCKVILLE, MD 20852
Specific Interests: Prairie and Temperate
    Forest

RADIATION PROGRAMS
ROOM 18-67 5600 FISHERS LANE,
    PARKLAWN BUILDING
ROCKVILLE, MD 20852
Staff Size: 100 - 499

**RADIATION PROGRAMS OFFICE,
    ENVIRONMENTAL PROTECTION
    AGENCY**
5600 FISHERS LANE, ROOM 18B46
ROCKVILLE, MD 20852
Staff Size: 10 - 49

RADIOLOGICAL HEALTH BUREAU
12720 TWINBROOK PARKWAY
ROCKVILLE, MD 20852
Specific Interests: Prairie and Temperate Forest

RESEARCH OFFICE AND UNIVERSITY RELATIONS (TA/RUR)
BUREAU OF TECHNOLOGY, ASSISTANCE AID
WASHINGTON, DC 20523
Staff Size: 10 - 49

RESEARCH SUPPORT BRANCH
NATIONAL INSTITUTES OF HEALTH
BETHESDA, MD 20014

RESOURCE CENTER FOR DISASTER PREVENTION, (NATIONAL)
15-1, GINZA 6-CHOME
CHUO-KU, TOKYO 104, JAPAN
Director, Masami Sugawara
Specific Interests: Prairie and Temperate Forest

RURAL ECONOMY AND HANDICRAFT MINISTRY
CONAKRY, GUINEA
Director, Fodeba Keita

SCIENCE AND TECHNOLOGY DIVISION, LIBRARY OF CONGRESS
10 FIRST STREET, SE
WASHINGTON, DC 20540
Chief, Marvin Mcfarland
Staff Size: 50 - 99

SCIENCE AND TECHNOLOGY MINISTRY
SEOUL, KOREA
Director, Kim Kee Hyong
Specific Interests: Prairie and Temperate Forest

SCIENCE AND TECHNOLOGY NATIONAL REFERRAL CENTER
1ST STREET & INDEPENDENCE AVENUE
WASHINGTON, DC 20540

SCIENCE AND TECHNOLOGY RESOURCE COUNCIL, (NATIONAL)
RIVADAVIA 1917
BUENOS AIRES, ARGENTINA
Director, Luis Capurro
General Environment: Oceanographic

SCIENCE INFORMATION EXCHANGE
1730 M STREET, NW
WASHINGTON, DC 20036

SCIENCE RESEARCH COUNCIL
STATE HOUSE, HIGH HOLBORN
LONDON, WC1, ENGLAND

SCIENCES RESEARCH INSTITUTE
CP 1780
LOURENCO MARQUES, MOZAMBIQUE
Director, Professor Alberto X Dacunha Marques

SCIENCES-TECHNOLOGY-GOVERNMENT PROGRAM
AMERICAN UNIVERSITY
WASHINGTON, DC 20216
Specific Interests: Prairie and Temperate Forest

SCIENTIFIC AND INDUSTRIAL RESEARCH COUNCIL
DURBAN, REPUBLIC OF SOUTH AFRICA
Director, T F W Harri
General Environment: Oceanographic

SCIENTIFIC AND INDUSTRIAL RESEARCH COUNCIL
KARACHI, PAKISTAN
Director, Dr S Siddiqui

SCIENTIFIC RESEARCH SUPREME COUNCIL
CAIRO, UNITED ARAB REPUBLIC
Director, Professor Ahmed Riad Turky

SHORT-LIVED PHENOMENA CENTER
60 GARDEN STREET
CAMBRIDGE, MA 02138

SMITHSONIAN INSTITUTION
1000 JEFFERSON DRIVE, SW
WASHINGTON, DC 20560
Director, H Dillon Ripley

SOIL AND WATER CONSERVATION RESOURCES DIVISION
8601 LAVERNE DRIVE
HYATTSVILLE, MD 20783
Director, J Van Schilfgaarde

SOIL CONSERVATION SERVICE
FEDERAL OFFICE BUILDING, POST OFFICE BOX 2440
CASPER, WY 82601
Staff Size: 100 - 499

SOIL CONSERVATION SERVICE
468 NORTH MILLEGE AVENUE, PO BOX 832
ATHENS, GA 30601
Staff Size: 100 - 499

SOIL CONSERVATION SERVICE
561 UNITED STATES COURT HOUSE
NASHVILLE, TN 37203

SOIL CONSERVATION SERVICE
DEPARTMENT OF AGRICULTURE BUILDING, UNIVERSITY OF MAINE
ORONO, ME 04473

State Conservationist, Donald Dinsmore
General Environment: Terrestrial
Staff Size: 50 - 99

SOIL CONSERVATION SERVICES
FEDERAL OFFICE BUILDING, POST OFFICE BOX 27307
RALEIGH, NC 27611
Staff Size: 1 - 4

SOIL CONSERVATION SERVICES, CARIBBEAN AREA
GPO BOX 4868
SAN JUAN, PR 00936
General Environment: Terrestrial
Specific Interests: Tropical (hot)
Staff Size: 50 - 99

SOIL, WATER AND ENGINEERING
8303 CURRY PLACE
ADELPHI, MD 20783
Deputy Administrator, W Cooper

SOUTHWEST AFRICAN ADMINISTRATION
PRETORIA, REPUBLIC OF SOUTH AFRICA

SPORT FISHERIES AND WILDLIFE BUREAU
8207 DUSINANE CENTER
MCLEAN, VA 22101
Director, Spencer Smith

STATENS NATURVARDSVERK
FACK
S-171 20 SOLNA 1, SWEDEN
Forskning Sekretariatet, L Hannerz 1006

STATIONARY SOURCE ENFORCEMENT DIVISION
ENVIRONMENTAL PROTECTION AGENCY
ROCKVILLE, MD 20852
Director, William Megonnell
General Environment: Atmospheric
Staff Size: 100 - 499

WAR MINISTRY, IMPERIAL IRANIAN NAVY
TEHRAN, IRAN
Director of Administration, Farajollah Rasai
General Environment: Oceanographic

WATER RESOURCE INSTITUTE, (NATIONAL)
KING GEORGE V AVENUE
DURBAN, REPUBLIC OF SOUTH AFRICA
Director, W D Oliff
General Environment: Oceanographic

WILDLIFE FEDERATION (NATIONAL)
1412 16TH STREET, SW
WASHINGTON, DC 20036

COUNTRY INDEX

ALGERIA

FISHERIES STATION
BENI SAF, ALGERIA
See Biology: General; Field Station/Laboratory

HIGH COUNCIL ON SCIENTIFIC RESEARCH
ALGIERS, ALGERIA
See Biology: General; Government-Federal

MARINE FISHERIES, SCIENCES AND TECHNOLOGY INSTITUTE
ALGIERS, ALGERIA
See Biology: General; Government-Federal

OCEANOGRAPHIQUE INSTITUTE
JETEE NORD
ALGIERS, ALGERIA
See Biology: General; Research Institute

OCEANOGRAPHY INSTITUTE
UNIVERSITY OF ALGIERS
ALGIERS, ALGERIA
See Biology: General; Educational Institute

STATION MARINE DE BOU-ISMAIL
BOU-ISMAIL, ALGERIA
See Biology: General; Field Station/Laboratory

ARGENTINA

ANTARCTIC INSTITUTE OF ARGENTINA
CERITTO 1248
BUENOS AIRES, ARGENTINA
See Physics: General; Research Institute

BUENOS AIRES INSTITUTION OF TECHNOLOGY
AVDA EDUARDO MADERO 351
BUENOS AIRES, ARGENTINA
See Biology: General; Educational Institute

CENTRO INVESTIGACION BIOLOGIA MARIM
LIBERTAD 1235
BUENOS AIRES, ARGENTINA
See Biology: General; Unclassified

FISHERIES BUREAU, AGRICULTURE MINISTRY AT ARGENTINA
PASEO COLON 922
BUENOS AIRES, ARGENTINA
See Biology: General; Unclassified

FISHERIES RESOURCE DEPARTMENT
BRASIL Y FLORENCIO SANCHEZ
BUENOS AIRES, ARGENTINA
See Biology: General; Government-Federal

FISHERIES RESOURCE, MINISTRY OF AGRICULTURAL AFFAIRS
CALLE 51, LA PLATA
BUENOS AIRES, ARGENTINA
See Biology: General; Government-Federal

FISHERIES TECHNOLOGY INSTITUTION
12 DE OCTUBRE Y ACHA
MAR DEL PLATA, BUENOS AIRES, ARGENTINA
See Biology: General; Government-Federal

HYDROGRAPHIC SERVICE, NAVAL OPERATIONS
MONTES DE OCA 2124
BUENOS AIRES, ARGENTINA
See Geology: General; Government-Federal

MARINE BIOLOGICAL RESOURCES CENTER, UNIVERSITY OF BUENOS AIRES
AVDA, ALBARELLOS Y CONSERVATION
BUENOS AIRES, ARGENTINA
See Biology: General; Educational Institute

MARINE BIOLOGICAL STATION (SOUTHERN)
USHUAIA
TIERRA DEL FUEGO, ARGENTINA
See Interdisciplinary: General; Field Station/Laboratory

MARINE BIOLOGY INSTITUTE, INTER-UNIVERSITY
CASILLA DE CORREO 175
MAR DEL PLATO, ARGENTINA
See Biology: General; Educational Institute

NATURAL SCIENCE MUSEUM OF ARGENTINA
ANGEL GALLARDO 470
BUENOS AIRES, ARGENTINA
See Biology: Ecology; Industrial/Commercial

OCEANOGRAPHIC STUDIES OF ARGENTINA
BUENOS AIRES, ARGENTINA
See Interdisciplinary: General; Unclassified

OCEANOGRAPHY INSTITUTION, UNIVERSITY OF THE SOUTH
DARRAGUEIRA 216 BAHIA BLAN
BUENOS AIRES, ARGENTINA
See Biology: General; Educational Institute

PUERTO QUEQUEN HYDROBIOLOGY STATION
NECOCHEA
PUERTO QUEQUEN, ARGENTINA
See Biology: General; Industrial/Commercial

RAWSON ALGOLOGICAL LABORATORY
CHUBUT, ARGENTINA
See Biology: General; Field Station/Laboratory

SCIENCE AND TECHNOLOGY RESOURCE COUNCIL, (NATIONAL)
RIVADAVIA 1917
BUENOS AIRES, ARGENTINA
See Interdisciplinary: General; Unclassified

AUSTRALIA

ANIMAL GENETICS DIVISION
POST OFFICE BOX 90
EPPING, NEW SOUTH WALES, AUSTRALIA
See Biology: General; Government-Federal

ANIMAL HEALTH DIVISION
PRIVATE BAG 1, POST OFFICE
PARKVILLE, VICTORIA, AUSTRALIA
See Biology: General; Government-Federal

ANIMAL PHYSIOLOGY DIVISION
POST OFFICE BOX 239
BLACKTOWN, NEW SOUTH WALES, AUSTRALIA
See Biology: General; Government-Federal

BIOLOGY DEPARTMENT
UNIVERSITY OF SYDNEY
SYDNEY, VICTORIA, AUSTRALIA
See Biology: General; Educational Institute

BRITISH PETROLEUM COMPANY OF AUSTRALIA
1-29 ALBERT ROAD
MELBOURNE, VICTORIA, AUSTRALIA
See Engineering: General; Industrial/Commercial

COMMONWEALTH SCIENTIFIC AND RESEARCH ORGANIZATION
MELBOURNE, NEW SOUTH WALES, AUSTRALIA
See Interdisciplinary: General; Unclassified

**DELHI AUSTRALIAN PETROLEUM
    LIMITED**
32 GRENFELL STREET
ADELAIDE, SOUTH AUSTRALIA,
AUSTRALIA
See Engineering: General; Industrial/
Commercial

**ENVIRONMENTAL SCIENCE
    STUDIES**
UNIVERSITY OF WESTERN
    AUSTRALIA
CANBERRA, AUSTRALIA
See Interdisciplinary: General; Educa-
tional Institute

ENVIRONMENTAL STUDIES
UNIVERSITY OF QUEENSLAND
BRISBANE, QUEENSLAND,
AUSTRALIA
See Interdisciplinary: General; Educa-
tional Institute

**FISHERIES AND FAUNA
    DEPARTMENT**
108 ADELAIDE TERRACE
PERTH, WEST AUSTRALIA,
AUSTRALIA
See Biology: General; Government-State
or Local

**FISHERIES AND OCEANOGRAPHY
    DIVISION**
CRONULLA, NEW SOUTH WALES,
AUSTRALIA
See Biology: General; Government-Fed-
eral

**FISHERIES AND WILDLIFE
    DEPARTMENT**
605 FLINDERS STREET
MELBOURNE, VICTORIA,
AUSTRALIA
See Biology: General; Government-State
or Local

FISHERIES BOARD
SOUTH BRISBANE, QUEENSLAND,
AUSTRALIA
See Social Sciences/Humanities: Commu-
nity Development/Studies; Govern-
ment-State or Local

FISHERIES BOARD
TOWNSVILLE, QUEENSLAND,
AUSTRALIA
See Social Sciences/Humanities: Commu-
nity Development/Studies; Govern-
ment-State or Local

FISHERIES COMMISSION
FRESHWATER LABORATORY
NARRANDERA, NEW SOUTH
WALES, AUSTRALIA
See Biology: General; Government-State
or Local

FISHERIES DEPARTMENT
BOX 1191
ADELAIDE, SOUTH AUSTRALIA,

AUSTRALIA
See Biology: General; Government-State
or Local

FISHERIES DIVISION
DEPARTMENT PRIMARY INDUSTRY
CANBERRA, AUSTRALIA
See Biology: General; Government-Fed-
eral

**FISHERIES MARKETING
    AUTHORITY**
PYRMONT
SYDNEY, NEW SOUTH WALES,
AUSTRALIA
See Social Sciences/Humanities: Commu-
nity Development/Studies; Govern-
ment-State or Local

FISHERIES SECTION
NORTHERN TERRITORY
    ADMINISTRATION
DARWIN, NORTHERN
TERRITORIES, AUSTRALIA
See Biology: General; Government-State
or Local

FISHERMAN'S COOPERATIVE
ADELAIDE, SOUTH AUSTRALIA,
AUSTRALIA
See Social Sciences/Humanities: Commu-
nity Development/Studies; Govern-
ment-State or Local

FOOD PRESERVATION DIVISION
CAMDEN, AUSTRALIA
See Biology: Biochemistry; Government-
Federal

**GLOBAL MARINE AUSTRALASIA
    PTY LIMITED**
360 LONSDALE STREET
MELBOURNE, VICTORIA,
AUSTRALIA
See Engineering: General; Industrial/
Commercial

**GREAT BARRIER REEF
    COMMITTEE**
HERON ISLAND RESEARCH
    STATION
GLADSTONE, QUEENSLAND,
AUSTRALIA
See Engineering: General; Field Station/
Laboratory

**HARBORS AND LIGHTHOUSES
    DEPARTMENT**
ONE CLIFF STREET
FREEMANTLE, WESTERN
AUSTRALIA, AUSTRALIA
See Social Sciences/Humanities: Commu-
nity Development/Studies; Govern-
ment-State or Local

HARBORS BOARD
VICTORIA SQUARE
ADELAIDE, SOUTH AUSTRALIA,
AUSTRALIA
See Social Sciences/Humanities: Commu-
nity Development/Studies; Govern-
ment-State or Local

HARBORS DEPARTMENT
BOX 5094 G P O
BRISBANE, QUEENSLAND,
AUSTRALIA
See Biology: General; Government-State
or Local

HYDROGRAPHIC DEPARTMENT
DEFENSE DEPARTMENT, NAVY
SYDNEY, NEW SOUTH WALES,
AUSTRALIA
See Social Sciences/Humanities: Employ-
ment/Unemployment;   Government-
Federal

INTERSTATE OIL LIMITED
95 COLLINS STREET
MELBOURNE, VICTORIA,
AUSTRALIA
See Engineering: General; Industrial/
Commercial

LAND RESEARCH DIVISION
CANBERRA, AUSTRALIA
See Biology: Ecology; Field Station/Lab-
oratory

MARITIME SERVICES BOARD
CIRCULAR QUAY
SIDNEY, NEW SOUTH WALES,
AUSTRALIA
See Social Sciences/Humanities: Commu-
nity Development/Studies; Govern-
ment-State or Local

**METEOROLOGICAL PHYSICS
    DIVISION**
MELBOURNE, VICTORIA,
AUSTRALIA
See Physics: General; Government-Feder-
al

**MOBIL EXPLORATION AUSTRALIA
    PTY LIMITED**
31 QUEEN STREET
MELBOURNE, C1, VICTORIA,
AUSTRALIA
See Engineering: General; Industrial/
Commercial

**NAVIGATION AND SURVEY
    AUTHORITY**
GPO BOX 202B
HOBART, TASMANIA, AUSTRALIA
See Social Sciences/Humanities: Commu-
nity Development/Studies; Govern-
ment-State or Local

**OIL DRILLING AND EXPLORATION
    LIMITED**
93 YORK STREET
SYDNEY, NEW SOUTH WALES,
AUSTRALIA
See Engineering: General; Industrial/
Commercial

**PETROLEUM PTY LIMITED OF
    WEST AUSTRALIA**
167-187 KENT STREET
SYDNEY, NEW SOUTH WALES,

AUSTRALIA
See Engineering: General; Industrial/Commercial

PHILIPS AUSTRALIAN OIL COMPANY
150 EDWARD STREET
BRISBANE, QUEENSLAND, AUSTRALIA
See Engineering: General; Industrial/Commercial

PHYSICS AND APPLIED PHYSICS DIVISION
NATIONAL STANDARDS LABORATORY
SYDNEY, NEW SOUTH WALES, AUSTRALIA
See Physics: General; Government-Federal

READING AND BATES PTY LIMITED
380 QUEENS STREET
BRISBANE, QUEENSLAND, AUSTRALIA
See Engineering: General; Industrial/Commercial

SCIENCE ACADEMY OF AUSTRALIA
GORDON STREET
CANBERRA, AUSTRALIA
See Biology: General; Research Institute

SHELL DEVELOPMENT PTY LIMITED
155 WILLIAM STREET
MELBOURNE, VICTORIA, AUSTRALIA
See Engineering: General; Industrial/Commercial

SHIPBUILDING AND ENGINEERING OF WHYALLA
WHYALLA, SOUTH AUSTRALIA, AUSTRALIA
See Engineering: General; Industrial/Commercial

SOUTHWESTERN DRILLING COMPANY
BRISBANE, QUEENSLAND, AUSTRALIA
See Engineering: General; Industrial/Commercial

STATE FISHERIES COORDINATOR-MISSION
BOX 30 G P O
SYDNEY, NEW SOUTH WALES, AUSTRALIA
See Biology: General; Government-State or Local

WILDLIFE RESEARCH DIVISION
CANBERRA, AUSTRALIA
See Biology: General; Government-Federal

ZAPATE-ODE
CANBERRA, AUSTRALIA
See Interdisciplinary: General; Industrial/Commercial

ZOOLOGY DEPARTMENT
UNIVERSITY OF NEW ENGLAND
ARMINDALE, NEW SOUTH WALES, AUSTRALIA
See Biology: General; Educational Institute

AUSTRIA

PALEONTOLOGY INSTITUTION
UNIVERSITY OF VIENNA
VIENNA, AUSTRIA
See Geology: Paleontology; Educational Institute

PLANT PHYSIOLOGY INSTITUTE
UNIVERSITY OF VIENNA
VIENNA, AUSTRIA
See Biology: General; Educational Institute

ZOOLOGY DEPARTMENT
UNIVERSITY OF VIENNA
VIENNA, AUSTRIA
See Biology: General; Educational Institute

BELGIUM

AGRONOMY INSTITUTE, UNIVERSITY OF LOUVAIN
72 AVENUE CARDINAL MERCIER
HEVERLE-LOUVAIN, BELGIUM
See Chemistry: General; Educational Institute

CHARLES DARWIN FOUNDATION, GALAPAGOS ISLE
1 RUE DUCALE
BRUSSELS 1, BELGIUM
See Interdisciplinary: General; Research Institute

GEOLOGICAL SCIENCES UNION
MELCHELSE STEENWEG 206
ANTWERP, BELGIUM
See Geology: General; Research Institute

ORGANIC CHEMISTRY LABORATORY
UNIVERSITY OF GHENT
GHENT, BELGIUM
See Chemistry: General; Field Station/Laboratory

SCIENCE AND HYDROLOGY, INTERNATIONAL ASSOCIATION
61 BRAEMSTAAT
GENTBRUGGE, BELGIUM
See Engineering: Water Resources; Educational Institute

BOLIVIA

SCIENTIFIC RESEARCH IN SEWAGE AND SANITARY ENGINEERING
SOFIA, BUL P. NAPETOV 50
LA PAZ, BOLIVIA
See Engineering: Water Resources; Government-State or Local

BRAZIL

CANANEIA MARINE STATION
UNIVERSITY OF SAO PAULO
CANANEIA, BRAZIL
See Biology: General; Field Station/Laboratory

CLIMATOLOGY AND METEOROLOGY DEPARTMENT
UNIVERSITY OF RIO DE JANEIRO
RIO DE JANEIRO, BRAZIL
See Interdisciplinary: General; Educational Institute

FISHERIES AND OCEANOGRAPHY, UNIVERSITY OF RIO GRANDE SUL
ENTREPOSTA DE PESCA
ESTADO RIO GRANDE SUL, BRAZIL
See Biology: General; Educational Institute

FISHERIES TECHNIQUES DEPARTMENT
UNIVERSITY OF SAO PAULO
SAO PAULO, BRAZIL
See Biology: General; Educational Institute

GENERAL ANIMAL PHISIOLOGY, UNIVERSITY OF SOUTH PAULO
CAIXA POSTA 11, 230 SOUTH P 9
SAO PAULO, BRAZIL
See Biology: General; Educational Institute

HYDROBIOLOGY LABORATORY, OSWALDO CRUZ INSTITUTE
CAIXA POSTA 926
RIO DE JANEIRO, BRAZIL
See Biology: General; Government-Federal

HYDROBIOLOGY STATION OF GUARATUBA, ZOOLOGY DEPARTMENT
UNIVERSITY OF PARANA
GUARATUBA, PARANA, BRAZIL
See Biology: General; Field Station/Laboratory

HYDROGRAPHY AND NAVIGATION, MINISTRY OF NAVY

ILHA FISCAL
RIO DE JANEIRO, BRAZIL
See Engineering: General; Government-
Federal

**HYDROLOGY STATION OF
    GUARATUBA, UNIVERSITY OF
    PARANA**
CAIXA POSTAL 756
GUARATUBA, PARANA, BRAZIL
See Biology: Biophysics; Field Station/
Laboratory

**INSTITUTION OCEANOGRAFICO
    DE UNIVERSITY DE SAO PAUL**
AL EDUARDO PRADO 698
SAO PAULO, BRAZIL
See Biology: General; Foundation

**MARINE BIOLOGICAL INSTITUTE
    OF SAO SEBASTIAO**
CAIXA POSTAL 11.230
SAO PAULO 9, BRAZIL
See Biology: General; Educational Insti-
tute

**MARINE BIOLOGICAL
    OCEANOGRAPHIC INSTITUTE**
CAIXA POSTAL 1076
RECIFE PERNAMBUCO, BRAZIL
See Interdisciplinary: General; Educa-
tional Institute

MARINE BIOLOGY LABORATORY
SAN SEBASTIAN, BRAZIL
See Biology: General; Field Station/Lab-
oratory

MARINE STATION
UNIVERSITY OF SAO PAULO
UBATUBA, BRAZIL
See Biology: General; Field Station/Lab-
oratory

**METEOROLOGY INSTITUTE,
    FEDERAL UNIVERSITY OF CEARA**
AVENIDA VISCONDE DE CAUIPE
FORTALEGA CEARA, BRAZIL
See Interdisciplinary: General; Educa-
tional Institute

NATIONAL PETROLEUM COUNCIL
BRASILIA, BRAZIL
See Geology: Geochemistry; Industrial/
Commercial

**OCEANOGRAPHIC INSTITUTE,
    UNIVERSITY OF RECIFE**
PRAIA DA PIEDADE
RECIFE, BRAZIL
See Interdisciplinary: General; Educa-
tional Institute

**OCEANOGRAPHIC INSTITUTE,
    UNIVERSITY OF SAO PAULO**
CAIXA POSTA 9075, ALOMEDA
ED PRADO 698, SAO PAULO, BRAZIL
See Biology: General; Educational Insti-
tute

**OCEANOGRAPHY AND
    BIOLOGICAL FISHERIES
    DEPARTMENT**
UNIVERSITY OF SAO PAULO
SANTOS, BRAZIL
See Biology: General; Educational Insti-
tute

**PHYSICAL OCEANOGRAPHY AND
    METEOROLOGY DEPARTMENT**
UNIVERSITY OF SAO PAULO
SAO PAULO, BRAZIL
See Physics: General; Educational Insti-
tute

**RUA DR SATTAMINI
    AGROMETEOROLOGY**
91-APT 105 TIJUCA
RIO DE JANEIRO, BRAZIL
See Interdisciplinary: General; Research
Institute

**ZOOLOGY DEPARTMENT, NAVAL
    RESOURCES INSTITUTE**
ILHA GOVENADOR, AVENUE
    PRESIDENT,
RIO DE JANIERO, BRAZIL
See Biology: General; Government-Fed-
eral

BRITISH HONDURAS

**AGRICULTURE AND FISHERIES
    DEPARTMENT**
BELIZE CITY, BRITISH HONDURAS
See Biology: General; Government-Fed-
eral

**NORTHERN FISHERMEN'S
    COOPERATIVE**
NORTH FRONT STREET
BELIZE CITY, BRITISH HONDURAS
See Biology: General; Industrial/Com-
mercial

BULGARIA

**DOCUMENTION AGRICOLE
    SCIENT ET TECHNOLOGY**
6 BUILDING DRAGAN TZANCOV
SOFIA, BULGARIA
See Engineering: Agricultural Engineering; Foundation

**GEOPHYSICAL INSTITUTE,
    BULGARIAN ACADEMY OF
    SCIENCE**
SOFIA
MOSKOVSKA 6, BULGARIA
See Physics: General; Research Institute

METEOROLOGIYA PRI BAN
SOFIA, LENIN 154, BULGARIA
See Interdisciplinary: General; Research
Institute

BURMA

APPLIED RESEARCH INSTITUTE
KANBE
RANGOON, BURMA
See Interdisciplinary: General; Unclassi-
fied

FISHERIES DIRECTORATE
RANGOON, BURMA
See Biology: General; Government-Fed-
eral

PEARL AND FISHERY BOARD
MERCHANT STREET
RANGOON, BURMA
See Biology: General; Government-Fed-
eral

PEOPLE'S OIL INDUSTRY
604 MERCHANT STREET
RANGOON, BURMA
See Engineering: General; Government-
Federal

CAMBODIA

**FISHERIES NATIONAL
    DIRECTORATE**
PHNOM-PENH, CAMBODIA
See Biology: General; Government-Fed-
cral

PUBLIC WORKS MINISTRY
PHNOM-PENH, CAMBODIA
See Engineering: General; Government-
Federal

CAMEROON

DISEASES IN CENTRAL AFRICA
MEDECIN COLONEL LABUSQUIER
BP 4057, YAOUNPE, CAMEROON
See Biology: General; Research Institute

FISHERIES INDUSTRIES SOCIETY
BP 581
DOVALA, CAMEROON
See Biology: General; Industrial/Com-
mercial

**MERCHANT MARINE, FEDERAL
SERVICE**
BP 416,
DOVALA, CAMEROON
See Biology: General; Government-Federal

**TRANSPORTATION, MINES, POST
AND TELEGRAPH MINISTRY**
BP 416
DOVALA, CAMEROON
See Social Sciences/Humanities: Transportation; Government-Federal

CANADA

**AIR POLLUTION CONTROL
BUREAU, ENVIRONMENTAL
HEALTH CENTER**
TUNNEY'S PASTURE
OTTAWA, ONTARIO, CANADA
See Engineering: Pollution Abatement;
Government-Federal

**ARCTIC INSTITUTE OF NORTH
AMERICA**
3458 REDPATH DRIVE
MONTREAL, QUEBEC, CANADA
See Interdisciplinary: General; Research
Institute

**ATLANTIC OCEANOGRAPHIC
LABORATORY**
BEDFORD INSTITUTE
DARTMOUTH, NOVA SCOTIA,
CANADA
See Chemistry: General; Government-Federal

**ATMOSPHERIC ENVIRONMENT
SERVICE**
4905 DUFFER STREET
DOWNSVIEW, ONTARIO, CANADA
See Physics: General; Professional Organizations

ATMOSPHERIC PHYSICS INSTITUTE
SASKATCHEWAN UNIVERSITY
SASKATOON, SASKATCHEWAN,
CANADA
See Physics: General; Educational Institute

**BIOLOGICAL STATION AT
ALBERTA UNIVERSITY**
TURNER VALLEY, ALBERTA,
CANADA
See Biology: General; Unclassified

BIOLOGY DEPARTMENT
VICTORIA UNIVERSITY
VICTORIA, BRITISH COLUMBIA,
CANADA
See Biology: General; Educational Institute

BOWDOINE SCIENCES STATION
KENT ISLAND, INGALLSHEAD
GRAND MANAN, NEW BRUNSWICK,
CANADA
See Biology: Ecology; Field Station/Laboratory

BRITISH COLUMBIA RESEARCH
3650 WESTBROOK CRESCENT
VANCOUVER 8, BRITISH
COLUMBIA, CANADA
See Engineering: Pollution Abatement;
Research Institute

**DEFENSE DEPARTMENT,
CANADIAN AIR FORCE**
125 ELGIN STREET
OTTAWA, ONTARIO, CANADA
See Interdisciplinary: General; Unclassified

ENVIRONMENT DEPARTMENT
PARLIAMENT BUILDING
OTTAWA, ONTARIO, CANADA
See Biology: Ecology; Government-Federal

**ENVIRONMENTAL SCIENCES AND
ENGINEERING INSTITUTE**
UNIVERSITY OF TORONTO
TORONTO 181, ONTARIO, CANADA
See Interdisciplinary: General; Educational Institute

**ENVIRONMENTAL SCIENCES
CENTER**
UNIVERSITY OF CALGARY
CALGARY, ALBERTA, CANADA
See Biology: Ecology; Educational Institute

ENVIRONMENTAL STUDIES
468 HUNTER BUILDING, OCONNER
STREET
OTTAWA, ONTARIO, CANADA
See Geology: General; Government-Federal

**ENVIRONMENTAL STUDIES
FACULTY**
4700 KEELE STREET, YORK
UNIVERSITY
DOWNSVIEW, ONTARIO, CANADA
See Interdisciplinary: General; Educational Institute

**ENVIRONMENTAL STUDIES
PROGRAM**
UNIVERSITY OF WATERLOO
WATERLOO, ONTARIO, CANADA
See Social Sciences/Humanities: General;
Educational Institute

EXTERNAL AFFAIRS DEPARTMENT
OTTAWA, ONTARIO, CANADA
See Interdisciplinary: General; Unclassified

**FISHERIES OF NORTHWEST
ATLANTIC, INTERNATIONAL
COMMISSION**

POST OFFICE BOX 638
DARTMOUTH, NOVA SCOTIA,
CANADA
See Biology: Ecology; Research Institute

**FISHERIES RESEARCH BOARD OF
CANADA**
BEDFORD INSTITUTION
OCEANOGRAPHY
DARTMOUTH, NOVA SCOTIA,
CANADA
See Biology: Ecology; Government-Federal

FISHERIES RESEARCH
4160 MARINE DRIVE
WEST VANCOUVER, BRITISH
COLUMBIA, CANADA
See Engineering: Pollution Abatement;
Research Institute

**FISHERIES RESOURCE BOARD,
DEPARTMENT OF FISHERIES**
TUPPER BUILDING, CONFERENCE
HEIGHTS
OTTAWA, ONTARIO, CANADA
See Biology: General; Government-Federal

FOREST RESEARCH FOUNDATION
LAVAL UNIVERSITY
QUEBEC, QUEBEC PROVINCE,
CANADA
See Biology: Ecology; Educational Institute

**FOREST RESOURCES
LABORATORY, SOUTHERN
RESEARCH STATION**
MAPLE, ONTARIO, CANADA
See Geology: General; Field Station/Laboratory

**FROZEN SEA RESEARCH GROUP,
ENVIRONMENTAL DEPARTMENT**
825 DEVONSHIRE ROAD
VICTORIA, BRITISH COLUMBIA,
CANADA
See Physics: General; Government-Federal

**GAME FISHERIES COMMISSIONERS
WESTERN ASSOCIATION**
PARLIAMENT BUILDINGS
VICTORIA, BRITISH COLUMBIA,
CANADA
See Interdisciplinary: General; Professional Organizations

GEOLOGY DEPARTMENT
UNIVERSITY OF GUELPH
GUELPH, ONTARIO, CANADA
See Interdisciplinary: General; Educational Institute

GEOPHYSICS LABORATORY
UNIVERSITY OF TORONTO
TORONTO 5, ONTARIO, CANADA
See Geology: General; Educational Institute

GREAT LAKES INSTITUTE
UNIVERSITY OF TORONTO
TORONTO 5, ONTARIO, CANADA
See Interdisciplinary: General; Educational Institute

HYDROLOGY SERVICES OF CANADA
615 BOOTH STREET
OTTAWA, ONTARIO, CANADA
See Engineering: Water Resources; Government-Federal

INTERNATIONAL JOINT COMMISSION, CANADIAN SECTION
ROOM 850, 151 SLATER STREET
OTTAWA, ONTARIO, CANADA
See Biology: Ecology; Government-Federal

MAPLEVALE SCHOOL OF LIVING
CROSS CREEK, NEW BRUNSWICK, CANADA
See Biology: Ecology; Educational Institute

MARINE SCIENCE CENTER
MCGILL UNIVERSITY
MONTREAL, PROVINCE OF QUEBEC, CANADA
See Interdisciplinary: General; Educational Institute

MECHANICAL ENGINEERING DEPARTMENT
WATERLOO UNIVERSITY
WATERLOO, ONTARIO, CANADA
See Engineering: General; Educational Institute

MICROBIOLOGICAL SOCIETY, DIVISION OF BIOSCIENCE
NATIONAL RESEARCH COUNCIL
OTTAWA 2, ONTARIO, CANADA
See Biology: General; Research Institute

NATIONAL RESOURCES COUNCIL
OXFORD STREET
HALIFAX, NOVA SCOTIA, CANADA
See Interdisciplinary: General; Unclassified

OCEANOGRAPHIC DATA CENTER FOR DEMARCATION OF CANADA
185 SOMERSET STREET WEST
OTTAWA, CANADA
See Interdisciplinary: General; Unclassified

OCEANOGRAPHIC INSTITUTE
UNIVERSITY OF BRITISH COLUMBIA
VANCOUVER, BRITISH COLUMBIA, CANADA
See Interdisciplinary: General; Educational Institute

OCEANOGRAPHY BRANCH
615 BOOTH STREET
OTTAWA, ONTARIO, CANADA
See Interdisciplinary: General; Unclassified

OCEANOGRAPHY COMMISSION OF CANADA
REGIONAL WORK GROUP
OTTAWA, ONTARIO, CANADA
See Interdisciplinary: General; Unclassified

OCEANOGRAPHY INSTITUTE
DALHOUSIE UNIVERSITY
HALIFAX, NOVA SCOTIA, CANADA
See Interdisciplinary: General; Educational Institute

ORGANIC RESEARCH UNITED
MCMASTER UNIVERSITY
HAMILTON, ONTARIO, CANADA
See Biology: General; Unclassified

PACIFIC BIOLOGICAL STATION
POST OFFICE DRAWER 100
NANAIMO, CANADA
See Biology: General; Government-Federal

POLAR CONTROL SHELF PROJECT
880 WELLINGTON STREET
OTTAWA, ONTARIO, CANADA
See Geology: General; Government-Federal

PUBLIC HEALTH SCHOOL
UNIVERSITY OF MONTREAL, POST OFFICE BOX 6128
MONTREAL 101, PROVINCE OF QUEBEC, CANADA
See Chemistry: General; Educational Institute

RESEARCH COUNCIL OF BRITISH COLUMBIA
UNIVERSITY OF BRITISH COLUMBIA
VANCOUVER 8, BRITISH COLUMBIA, CANADA
See Biology: General; Research Institute

RESOURCE COUNCIL, UNIVERSITY OF ALBERTA
87TH AND 114TH STREET
EDMONTON, ALBERTA, CANADA
See Interdisciplinary: General; Educational Institute

RESOURCES COUNCIL
UNIVERSITY OF BRITISH COLUMBIA
VANCOUVER 8, BRITISH COLUMBIA, CANADA
See Social Sciences/Humanities: Community Development/Studies; Educational Institute

SHIPS DIVISION DEMARCATION
615 BOOTH STREET
OTTAWA, ONTARIO, CANADA
See Engineering: General; Government-Federal

CANAL ZONE

PANAMA CANAL COMPANY
BOX M
BALBOA HEIGHTS, CANAL ZONE
See Interdisciplinary: General; Unclassified

SMITHSONIAN TROPICAL RESOURCES INSTITUTE
P.O. BOX 2072
BALBOA, CANAL ZONE
See Biology: General; Government-Federal

CEYLON

CEYLON MINERAL SANDS CORPORATION
2211 THURSTAN ROAD
COLOMBO 7, CEYLON
See Geology: General; Industrial/Commercial

FISHERIES CORPORATION AT CEYLON
GALLE FACE
COLOMBO 3, CEYLON
See Interdisciplinary: General; Industrial/Commercial

SCIENCE AND INDUSTRIAL RESOURCE INSTITUTE AT CEYLON
BAUDDHALOKA MAWATHA
COLOMBO 7, CEYLON
See Interdisciplinary: General; Industrial/Commercial

ZOOLOGY DEPARTMENT, UNIVERSITY OF CEYLON
THURSTAN ROAD
COLOMBO 2, CEYLON
See Biology: General; Educational Institute

CHILE

BIOLOGICAL FISHERIES DEPARTMENT, CATHOLIC UNIVERSITY OF VALPARAISO
AVENIDA BRAZIL 2950, CASILA 4059, VALPARAISO, CHILE
See Biology: General; Educational Institute

CENTRAL INSTITUTION OF BIOLOGY, UNIVERSITY OF CONCEPCION

CASILLA 301
CONCEPCION, CHILE
See Biology: General; Educational Institute

**CENTRO NATION DE
INFORMACION Y
DOCUMENTACION**
AGUSTINAS 853, OFFICINA 547
SANTIAGO, CHILE
See Interdisciplinary: General; Foundation

**FISHERIES AND WILDLIFE
DEPARTMENT, AGRICULTURE
MINISTRY**
SANTIAGO, CHILE
See Biology: General; Government-Federal

FISHERIES BIOLOGICAL STATION
CASILLA 492 CORREO 2
SAN ANTONIO, CHILE
See Biology: General; Government-Federal

**FISHERIES DEVELOPMENT
INSTITUTION**
PERDO DE VALDIVA 2633
SANTIAGO, CHILE
See Biology: General; Government-Federal

**MARINE BIOLOGICAL STATION,
UNIVERSITY OF CHILE**
CASTILLA B-D
VINA DEL MAR, CHILE
See Biology: General; Field Station/Laboratory

**MARINE BIOLOGY STATION,
UNIVERSITY OF CHILE, NORTH
ZONE**
CASILLA 1240
ANTOFAGASTA, CHILE
See Biology: General; Educational Institute

**OCEANOGRAPHY AND FISHERIES
BIOLOGICAL LABORATORY**
CASILLA 183-V
VALPARAISO, CHILE
See Biology: General; Government-Federal

**SCIENCE INVESTIGATIONS
DEPARTMENT**
UNIVERSITY OF CHILE, NORTH
ZONE
ANTOFAGASTA, CHILE
See Biology: General; Educational Institute

SCIENTIFIC INSTITUTE OF LEBU
APARTADO 123
LEBU, CHILE
See Interdisciplinary: General; Research Institute

**ZOOLOGIC INVESTIGATION
CENTER, UNIVERSITY OF CHILE**
CASILLA 10135
SANTIAGO, CHILE
See Biology: General; Educational Institute

**ZOOLOGICAL INSTITUTION,
SOUTH UNIVERSITY OF CHILE**
CASILLA 567
VALDIVIA, CHILE
See Biology: General; Educational Institute

COLOMBIA

**FISHERIES RESOURCE CENTER,
BUENAVENTURA**
APARTADO AEREO 607
VALLE, COLOMBIA
See Biology: General; Research Institute

**HUNTING AND FISHERIES OFFICE,
AGRICULTURE MINISTRY**
CARRERA 10 20-30, PISO 6
BOGOTA, COLOMBIA
See Biology: General; Government-Federal

**JORGE LADEO LOZANO,
UNIVERSITY DE BOGOTA**
CALLE 23 NO 4-47
BOGOTA, COLOMBIA
See Biology: General; Educational Institute

**MARINE FISHERIES
DEVELOPMENT PROJECT**
CARRERA 10, !20-30 PISO 6
BOGOTA, COLOMBIA
See Biology: General; Government-Federal

**CARTAGENA OFFICE, MAG AND
SIVU VALL CORPORATION**
CARRERA 14 25A-66 PISO 5
BOGOTA, COLOMBIA
See Biology: General; Professional Organizations

**MARINE SCIENCES FACULTY,
UNIVERSITY OF BOGOTA**
CALLE 23 / 4-43
BOGOTA, COLOMBIA
See Interdisciplinary: General; Educational Institute

COSTA RICA

**CAMARA PUNTARENENSE DE
PESCADORES**
PUNTARENAS, COSTA RICA
See Interdisciplinary: General; Industrial/Commercial

**COMPANIA ENLATADORA
NACIONAL**
PUNTARENAS, COSTA RICA
See Interdisciplinary: General; Industrial/Commercial

**COMPANIA INDUSTRIAL DE
MARISCOS**
PUNTARENAS, COSTA RICA
See Biology: General; Industrial/Commercial

**CONSERVATION CORPORATION
OF THE CARRIBEAN**
APARTADO 896
SAN JOSE, COSTA RICA
See Engineering: General; Research Institute

**EUGENIO GARRON & SONS,
LIMITED**
LIMON, COSTA RICA
See Biology: General; Industrial/Commercial

**FIGORIFICOS DE PUNTARENAS,
SOUTH AMERICA**
PUNTARENAS, COSTA RICA
See Biology: General; Industrial/Commercial

**FISHERIES AND WILDLIFE
DEPARTMENT**
MINISTRY OF AGRICULTURE
SAN JOSE, COSTA RICA
See Biology: General; Government-Federal

HIELO Y FRIO, LIMITED
PUNTARENAS, COSTA RICA
See Biology: General; Industrial/Commercial

PRODUCTOS ALTAMAR LIMITED,
PUNTARENAS, COSTA RICA
See Interdisciplinary: General; Industrial/Commercial

PRODUCTOS DE CARIBE, LIMITED
LIMON, COSTA RICA
See Biology: General; Industrial/Commercial

CYPRUS

**FISHERIES DEPARTMENT,
AGRICULTURE AND NATURAL
RESOURCES MINISTRY**
NICOSIA, CYPRUS
See Biology: General; Government-Federal

CZECHOSLOVAKIA

BIOFYZIKALNI USTAV CSAV
BRNO 12
KRALOVOPOLSKA 135,
CZECHOSLOVAKIA
See Biology: General; Research Institute

BIOLOGICKY USTAV SAV
BRATISLAVA, KOLLAROVO
NAM 2, CZECHOSLOVAKIA
See Biology: General; Research Institute

**ELECTRON MICROSCOPY AND
    EXPERIMENTATION
    LABORATORY**
PRAHA 2-NOVE MESTO
ALBERTOV 4, CZECHOSLOVAKIA
See Biology: Biochemistry; Field Station/
Laboratory

ENTOMOLOGICKY USTAV CSAV
PRAHA 2-NOVE MESTO
VINICNA 7, CZECHOSLOVAKIA
See Biology: General; Research Institute

GEOFYZIKALNI USTAV CSAV
SPORILOV, BOCNI II, NO 1401
PRAHA 4, CZECHOSLOVAKIA
See Geology: Geophysics; Foundation

**GEOGRAPHY DEPARTMENT,
    PURKYNE UNIVERSITY**
BRNO 16
NAHORNT 14, CZECHOSLOVAKIA
See Geology: General; Educational Institute

**HYDROLOGY DEPARTMENT,
    KATEDRA HYDROMELIORACII,
    STAVEBNAFAK**
VYSOKA SKOLA TECHNICKA
BRATISLAVA, CZECHOSLOVAKIA
See Geology: General; Educational Institute

LABORATORIUM POLYMEROV SAV
BRATISLAVA-PATRONKA
DUBRAVSKA CESTA,
CZECHOSLOVAKIA
See Chemistry: General; Field Station/
Laboratory

**METEOROLOGY AND
    CLIMATOLOGY INSTITUTE,
    SLOVAK ACADEMY**
BRATISLAVA
DUBRAVSKA CESTA,
CZECHOSLOVAKIA
See Physics: General; Research Institute

**SOIL MECHANICS AND
    FOUNDATION**
TECHNICAL UNIVERSITY
PRAGUE, CZECHOSLOVAKIA
See Engineering: General; Educational
Institute

UNIVERSITY OF PRAGUE
VOLSINACH 38
PRAGUE, CZECHOSLOVAKIA
See Geology: General; Educational Institute

USTAV FYZIKY ATMOSFERY CSAV
SPORTILOV, BOCNI II, NO 1401
PRAHA, CZECHOSLOVAKIA
See Engineering: Pollution Abatement;
Foundation

USTAV FYZIKY KOVOV SAV
BRATISLAVA UL FEBRUAROVEHO
VIT'AZSTVA 135, CZECHOSLOVAKIA
See Chemistry: Physical Chemistry; Educational Institute

**USTAV HYDROLOGIE A
    HYDRAULIKY SAV**
BRATISLAVA
TRNAVSKA 26, CZECHOSLOVAKIA
See Engineering: Water Resources; Educational Institute

**USTAV JADERNEHO VYZKUMU
    CSAV (UJV)**
REZ-KLECANY, CZECHOSLOVAKIA
See Physics: General; Research Institute

**VYZKUMNY USTAV
    TELEKOMUNIKACI**
PRAHA 10-STRASNICE
TREBOHOSTICKA 987,
CZECHOSLOVAKIA
See Physics: General; Research Institute

**VYZKUMNY USTAV
    VZDUCHOTECHNIKY**
PRAHA 10-MALESICE
POCERNICKA 96,
CZECHOSLOVAKIA
See Physics: General; Research Institute

DAHOMEY

**EDUCATION MINISTRY, APPLIED
    RESEARCH INSTITUTE**
PORTO NOVO, DAHOMEY
See Interdisciplinary: General; Unclassified

**FISHERIES SERVICES,
    AGRICULTURE MINISTRY**
BP 383,ONE RUE BEL-AIR
COTONOU, DAHOMEY
See Biology: General; Government-Federal

WATER SERVICE
MINISTRY OF PUBLIC WORKS
COTONOU, DAHOMEY
See Engineering: Water Resources; Government-Federal

DEMOCRATIC REPUBLIC OF THE CONGO

MARITIME FISHERIES SOCIETY
BP 84,MATADI,KONGO CENTRAL
KINSHASA, DEMOCRATIC
REPUBLIC OF THE CONGO
See Biology: General; Industrial/Commercial

**OCEANOGRAPHY AND FISHERIES
    CENTER**
BP 1086 POINTE NOIRE
BRAZZAVILLE,, DEMOCRATIC
REPUBLIC OF THE CONGO
See Biology: General; Research Institute

DENMARK

**ECOLOGY-FRESH WATER,
    UNIVERSITY OF COPENHAGEN**
HILLEROD
COPENHAGEN, DENMARK
See Biology: Ecology; Educational Institute

EXPERIMENTAL ECOLOGY
CARLSBERG LABORATORY
COPENHAGEN, DENMARK
See Biology: Ecology; Field Station/Laboratory

**FRESHWATER BIOLOGICAL
    LABORATORY, UNIVERSITY OF
    COPENHAGEN**
51 HELSINGORSGADE DENMARK
3400
HILLEROD, DENMARK
See Biology: General; Educational Institute

**GEOLOGICAL SURVEY OF
    DENMARK**
PALAEOBOT DEPARTMENT
THORAVEJ 3L
DK-2400 COPENHAGEN, DENMARK
See Biology: Ecology; Research Institute

HYDRAULIC INSTITUTE
OSTER VOLDGAGE 10, DK-1350
COPENHAGEN K, DENMARK
See Engineering: Water Resources; Professional Organizations

**INTERNATIONAL COUNCIL FOR
    THE EXPLORATION OF THE SEAS**
CHARLOTTENLUND SLOT
2920 CHARLOTTENLUND,
DENMARK
See Biology: Ecology; Research Institute

MARINE BIOLOGICAL
    LABORATORY, UNIVERSITY OF
    COPENHAGEN
GRONNEHAVE, HELSINGOR
COPENHAGEN, DENMARK
See Biology: General; Educational Institute

DOMINICAN REPUBLIC

CARTOGRAPHIC INSTITUTE
UNIVERSITY OF SANTO DOMINGO
SANTO DOMINGO, DOMINICAN
REPUBLIC
See Biology: General; Educational Institute

HYDROGRAPHIC DEPARTMENT,
    DOMINICAN NAVY
LA JEFATURA DE ESTADO MAYO
SANTO DOMINGO, DOMINICAN
REPUBLIC
See Biology: General; Government-Federal

METEOROLOGICAL SERVICE
    (NATIONAL)
UNIVERSITY OF SANTO DOMINGO
SANTO DOMINGO, DOMICAN
REPUBLIC
See Geology: General; Government-Federal

EAST GERMANY

BIOLOGICAL
    FORSCHUNGSANSTALT
HIDDENSEE
KLOSTER AUF HIDDENSEE, EAST
GERMANY
See Biology: General; Educational Institute

BIOLOGY DEPARTMENT,
    UNIVERSITY OF ROSTOCK
DOBERANER STRASSE
ROSTOCK, EAST GERMANY
See Biology: General; Educational Institute

BOTANY AND BOTANICAL
    GARDENS INSTITUTE
TECHNOLOGY UNIVERSITY,
    MOMMSENSTRASSE
DRESDEN-A, EAST GERMANY
See Biology: General; Educational Institute

FISH PROCESSING, INSTITUTE OF
    SEA FISHERIES
251 ROSTOCK-MARIENEHE
BERLIN, EAST GERMANY
See Biology: General; Research Institute

GEOLOGICAL-PALEONTOLOGICAL
    INSTITUTE AND MUSEUM
UNIVERSITY HALLE/SAALE
HALLE, EAST GERMANY
See Geology: Paleontology; Educational Institute

GEOLOGY DEPARTMENT,
    PALEONTOLOGY INSTITUTE
AM ST GEORGSFELD 43
GREIFSWALD, EAST GERMANY
See Geology: Paleontology; Educational Institute

GEOLOGY DEPARTMENT,
    UNIVERSITY GREIFSWALD
HAINSTRASSE 10
GREIFSWALD-ELDENA, EAST
GERMANY
See Geology: General; Educational Institute

MICROBIOLOGY INSTITUTE
JAHNSTR 15
GREIFSWALD, EAST GERMANY
See Biology: General; Educational Institute

ECUADOR

ADMINISTRATION INSTITUTE
CASILLA 5918
GUAYAQUIL, ECUADOR
See Interdisciplinary: General; Unclassified

BIOLOGY DEPARTMENT
CASILLA 5918
GUAYAQUIL, ECUADOR
See Biology: General; Government-Federal

DEL MONTE DE ECUADOR
MANTA, ECUADOR
See Geology: General; Industrial/Commercial

ECUADOREAN NAVY
CASILLA
GUAYAQUIL, ECUADOR
See Interdisciplinary: General; Unclassified

EMPACADORA NACIONAL (ENACA)
GUAYAQUIL, ECUADOR
See Geology: General; Industrial/Commercial

FISHERIES DEPARTMENT
NATIONAL POLYTECHNIC
    INSTITUTE
QUITO, ECUADOR
See Biology: General; Research Institute

FISHERIES INSTITUTE OF
    ECUADOR
CASILLA 5991
GUAYAQUIL, ECUADOR
See Biology: General; Government-Federal

FISHERIES NATIONAL INSTITUTE
CASILLA 5918
GUAYAQUIL, ECUADOR
See Biology: General; Government-Federal

INEPACA
MANTA, ECUADOR
See Geology: General; Industrial/Commercial

PRODELMAR
MANTA, ECUADOR
See Geology: General; Industrial/Commercial

EL SALVADOR

FISHERIES AND MARITIME ACT
    SECTION
MINISTRY OF ECONOMY
SAN SALVADOR, EL SALVADOR
See Biology: General; Government-Federal

GEOLOGY DEPARTMENT
UNIVERSITY OF EL SALVADOR
SAN SALVADOR, EL SALVADOR
See Biology: General; Educational Institute

ENGLAND

ABM INDUSTRIAL PRODUCTS
    LIMITED
POLEACRE LANE, WOODLEY
STOCKPORT, CHESHIRE, ENGLAND
See Biology: Biochemistry; Industrial/Commercial

AGRICULTURAL ENGINEERING,
    NATIONAL INSTITUTE
WREST PARK
SILSOE, BEDFORD, ENGLAND
See Engineering: Agricultural Engineering; Research Institute

AGRICULTURAL RESEARCH COUNCIL
160 GREAT PORTLAND STREET
LONDON W1, ENGLAND
See Engineering: Agricultural Engineering; Professional Organizations

AGRICULTURAL RESEARCH COUNCIL, LETCOMBE LABORATORY
LETCOMBE REGIS, WANTAGE
WANTAGE, BERKS, ENGLAND
See Engineering: Agricultural Engineering; Research Institute

AGRICULTURE, FISHERIES AND FOOD MINISTRY
FISHERIES LABORATORY,
BURNHAM-ON-CROUH
ESSEX, ENGLAND
See Biology: Ecology; Field Station/Laboratory

AIR POLLUTION RESEARCH UNIT, MRC
MEDICAL COLLEGE, ST BART'S
LONDON, ENGLAND
See Engineering: Pollution Abatement; Educational Institute

ANTARCTIC BRITISH SURVEY
30 GILLINGHAM STREET
LONDON, SW1, ENGLAND
See Interdisciplinary: General; Research Institute

ASSOCIATED LEAD MANUFACTURERS, LIMITED
7 WADSWORTH ROAD
PERIVALE, GFD, MIDDLESEX,
ENGLAND
See Chemistry: General; Industrial/Commercial

AYNSOME LABS, LIMITED
KENTSFORD ROAD
GRANGE-OVER-SANDS,
LANCASTERSHIRE, ENGLAND
See Biology: Biochemistry; Professional Organizations

BATH UNIVERSITY OF TECHNOLOGY
CLAVERTON DOWN
BATH, SOMERSET, ENGLAND
See Biology: General; Educational Institute

BIOCHEMISTRY DEPARTMENT
OXFORD UNIVERSITY
OXFORD, ENGLAND
See Biology: Biochemistry; Educational Institute

BIOCHEMISTRY DEPARTMENT
PFIZER LIMITED
SANDWICH, KENT, ENGLAND
See Biology: Biochemistry; Industrial/Commercial

BIOLOGY DEPARTMENT
UNIVERSITY OF YORK
YORK YO1500, ENGLAND
See Biology: General; Educational Institute

BIOLOGY DEPARTMENT, ROYAL FREE HOSPITAL SCHOOL OF MEDICINE
8 HUNTER STREET
LONDON WCI, ENGLAND
See Biology: Ecology; Educational Institute

BIOLOGY DEPARTMENT, THE GRAMMAR SCHOOL
CHELTENHAM, GLOUCESTER,
ENGLAND
See Biology: Ecology; Educational Institute

BIOLOGY DEPARTMENT, UNIVERSITY OF EXETER
PRINCE OF WALES ROAD
EXETER, ENGLAND
See Biology: Ecology; Educational Institute

BIOREX LABORATORIES, RESEARCH DIVISION
198 CITY ROAD
LONDON, EC1, ENGLAND
See Chemistry: General; Field Station/Laboratory

BORAX RESEARCH CENTER
COX LANE
CHESSINGTON, SURREY, ENGLAND
See Chemistry: General; Research Institute

BOTANICAL GARDENS
KEW
RICHMOND, SURREY, ENGLAND
See Biology: General; Government-State or Local

BOTANY DEPARTMENT, INTERNATIONAL ASSOCIATION OF ECOLOGY
IMPERIAL COLLEGE
LONDON SW7, ENGLAND
See Biology: Ecology; Research Institute

BOTANY SCHOOL
MAGDALENE COLLEGE
CAMBRIDGE, ENGLAND
See Biology: Ecology; Educational Institute

BPB INDUSTRIES, LIMITED RESEARCH DEVELOPMENT
EAST LEAKE
LOUGHBOROUGH,
LEICESTERSHIRE, ENGLAND
See Engineering: General; Industrial/Commercial

BRITISH PETROLEUM COMPANY, LIMITED
BRITANNIC HOUSE, MOOR LANE
LONDON EC2, ENGLAND
See Engineering: General; Industrial/Commercial

BUSH JOHNSONS LIMITED
WOODHAM MORTIMER HALL
MALDON, ESSEX, ENGLAND
See Biology: General; Industrial/Commercial

CHEMISTRY DIVISION, AERE
HARWELL, BERKSHIRE, ENGLAND
See Chemistry: General; Industrial/Commercial

CHEMISTRY RESEARCH AND DEVELOPMENT
GLAXO RESEARCH, LIMITED
GREENFORD, MIDDLESEX,
ENGLAND
See Chemistry: General; Research Institute

CLARKES FARMHOUSE
NORTHMOOR
OXON, ENGLAND
See Biology: Ecology; Research Institute

CLINICAL RESEARCH CENTER
NORTHWICK PARK
HARROW, MIDDLESEX, ENGLAND
See Biology: General; Research Institute

COASTAL ECOLOGY RESEARCH STATION
NATURE CONSERVANCY, COLNEY
NORWICH, NORFOLK, ENGLAND
See Biology: Ecology; Research Institute

COASTAL OCEANOGRAPHY INSTITUTE
THE OBSERVATORY, BIDSTON,
CHESHIRE, ENGLAND
See Physics: General; Research Institute

COASTAL SEDIMENTATION UNIT
BEADON ROAD
TAUTON, SOMERSET, ENGLAND
See Engineering: Water Resources; Educational Institute

COKE RESOURCES ASSOCIATION
CHESTERFIELD, DERBYSHIRE,
ENGLAND
See Engineering: Pollution Abatement; Research Institute

COMMONWEALTH FORESTRY INSTITUTE
SOUTH PARKS ROAD
OXFORD, ENGLAND
See Biology: Ecology; Research Institute

COMMONWEALTH INSTITUTE OF BIOLOGICAL CONTROL
C/O CAB, FARNHAM ROYAL
SLOUGH, BUCKINGHAMSHIRE,
ENGLAND
See Biology: General; Research Institute

CYANAMID OF GREAT BRITAIN LIMITED
154 FAREHAM ROAD
GOSPORT, HAMPSHIRE, ENGLAND
See Biology: General; Industrial/Commercial

**ENTERIC REFERENCE
   LABORATORY, PUBLIC HEALTH
   LABORATORY SERVICE**
COLINDALE AVENUE
LONDON NW9, ENGLAND
See Biology: Ecology; Field Station/Lab-
   oratory

**ENVIRONMENTAL RESEARCH
   COUNCIL**
ALHAMBRA HOUSE, CHARING
   CROSS
LONDON, ENGLAND
See Biology: General; Professional Organ-
   izations

**ENVIRONMENTAL RESEARCH
   INSTITUTE**
CITADEL ROAD, PL1 3AX
PLYMOUTH, DEVON, ENGLAND
See Biology: Ecology; Research Institute

**ENVIRONMENTAL RESEARCH
   NATIONAL COUNCIL**
HUNTINGDON, ENGLAND
See Biology: General; Government-Fed-
   eral

**ENVIRONMENTAL RESOURCES
   COUNCIL (NATIONAL)**
27-33 CHARING CROSS
LONDON WC2, ENGLAND
See Geology: General; Research Institute

**EXPERIMENTAL STATION OF
   MONKS WOOD**
ABBOTS RIPTON
HUNTINGDON, ENGLAND
See Biology: Ecology; Field Station/Lab-
   oratory

FARMHOUSE
GREEN END, COMBERTON
CAMBRIDGE, ENGLAND
See Biology: Ecology; Research Institute

FAUNA PRESERVATION SOCIETY
ZOOLOGICAL SOCIETY OF
   LONDON
REGENTS PARK, LONDON NW1,
   ENGLAND
See Biology: Ecology; Professional
   Organizations

FISHERIES EXPERIMENT STATION
CONWAY
CAERNS, ENGLAND
See Biology: Ecology; Field Station/
   Laboratory

FISHERIES LABORATORY
LOWESTOFT, SUFFOLK, ENGLAND
See Engineering: Pollution Abatement;
   Field Station/Laboratory

FISHERIES LABORATORY
REMEMBRANCE AVENUE
BURNHAM-ON-CROUCH, ESSEX,
   ENGLAND
See Biology: General; Government-Fed-
   eral

FOOD RESEARCH INSTITUTE
AGRICULTURAL RESEARCH
   COUNCIL

NORWICH, ENGLAND
See Biology: Biochemistry; Research Institute

FOREST SCIENCE DEPARTMENT
UNIVERSITY OF OXFORD, SOUTH
   PARK
OXFORD, ENGLAND
See Social Sciences/Humanities: Commu-
   nity Development/Studies; Education-
   al Institute

FORESTRY BUREAU
SOUTH PARKS ROAD
OXFORD, ENGLAND
See Biology: Ecology; Professional Organ-
   izations

FORESTRY COMMISSION
25 SAVILE ROW
LONDON WIX2AY, ENGLAND
See Interdisciplinary: General; Unclassified

**FRESHWATER BIOLOGICAL
   ASSOCIATION**
RIVER LABORATORY, EAST STOKE
WAREHAM, DORSET, ENGLAND
See Biology: Ecology; Research Institute

**FRESHWATER FISHERIES
   LABORATORY**
MAFF, 10 WHITEHALL PLACE
LONDON SW1, ENGLAND
See Biology: General; Field Station/Lab-
   oratory

**GEODESY AND GEOPHYSICS
   DEPARTMENT**
MADINGLEY RISE
CAMBRIDGE, ENGLAND
See Geology: General; Educational Insti-
   tute

GEOGRAPHY DEPARTMENT
UNIVERSITY OF LEEDS
LEEDS, WEST RIDING, ENGLAND
See Engineering: General; Educational
   Institute

**GEOLOGICAL SCIENCES
   INSTITUTE**
15-17 YOUNG STREET
LONDON W8, ENGLAND
See Geology: General; Research Institute

**GEOLOGY AND MINERAL
   DEPARTMENT**
OXFORD UNIVERSITY, PARKS ROAD
OXFORD, ENGLAND
See Geology: Geochemistry; Educational
   Institute

**GEOLOGY DEPARTMENT,
   UNIVERSITY OF DURHAM**
SOUTH ROAD
DURHAM, ENGLAND
See Geology: General; Educational Insti-
   tute

**GLASSHOUSE CROPS RESEARCH
   INSTITUTE**
WORTHING ROAD,

LITTLEHAMPTON, SUSSEX,
   ENGLAND
See Engineering: Agricultural Engineer-
   ing; Research Institute

**GRASSLAND HUSBANDRY,
   AGRICULTURAL DEVELOPMENT
   ADVANCE**
BLOCK C, GOVERNMENTAL
   BUILDINGS
CAMBRIDGE, ENGLAND
See Engineering: Agricultural Engineer-
   ing; Government-Federal

GRASSLAND RESEARCH INSTITUTE
HURLEY, MAIDENHEAD
MAIDENHEAD, BERKS, ENGLAND
See Engineering: Agricultural Engineer-
   ing; Research Institute

HEALTH ECONOMICS OFFICE
162 REGENT STREET
LONDON, WI, ENGLAND
See Social Sciences/Humanities: General;
   Government-Federal

HICKSON AND WELCH, LIMITED
CASTLEFORD, YORKSHIRE,
   ENGLAND
See Chemistry: General; Industrial/Com-
   mercial

**HUNTING GEOLOGY AND
   GEOPHYSICS**
6 ELSTREE WAY
BOREHAM WOOD,
   HERTFORDSHIRE, ENGLAND
See Geology: Geophysics; Industrial/
   Commercial

HYDRAULICS RESEARCH STATION
MINISTRY OF TECHNOLOGY
WALLINGFORD, BERKSHIRE,
   ENGLAND
See Engineering: Pollution Abatement;
   Field Station/Laboratory

**IMPERIAL CHEMICAL INDUSTRIES
   LIMITED**
IMPERIAL CHEMISTRY HOUSE
MILLBANK, LONDON, ENGLAND
See Chemistry: General; Industrial/
   Commercial

**IMPERIAL CHEMICAL INDUSTRIES
   LIMITED**
JEALOTTS HILL RESOURCES
   STATION
BRACKNELL, BERKSHIRE,
   ENGLAND
See Interdisciplinary: General;
   Industrial/Commercial

**IMPERIAL CHEMISTRY INDUSTRY
   LIMITED, BRIXHAM RESOURCES**
FRESHWATER QUARRY OVERGANG
BRIXHAM, SOUTH DEVON,
   ENGLAND
See Engineering: Pollution Abatement;
   Industrial/Commercial

**INDUSTRIAL MATERIALS
   RESEARCH UNITED**
MILE END ROAD, QUEEN MARY
   CORPORATION

LONDON E1 4NS, ENGLAND
See Engineering: General; Field Station/
Laboratory

**INTERNATIONAL LAW
ASSOCIATION**
3 PAPER BUILDINGS, TEMPLE
SQUARE
LONDON, EC4, ENGLAND
See Social Sciences/Humanities: Law/
Legislation; Professional Organizations

**INTERNATIONAL PLANNED
PARENTHOOD FEDERATION**
18-20 LOWER REGENT STREET
LONDON, SW1, ENGLAND
See Social Sciences/Humanities: Population Studies/Family Planning; Foundation

**IRAQ PETROLEUM CORPORATION,
LIMITED**
33 CAVENDISH SQUARE
LONDON W1, ENGLAND
See Geology: General; Industrial/Com-
mercial

JOHN INNES INSTITUTE
COLNEY LANE
NORWICH, ENGLAND
See Biology: Ecology; Research Institute

LABORATORY
CITADEL HILL
PLYMOUTH, ENGLAND
See Biology: Ecology; Field Station/Lab-
oratory

LAND ECONOMY DEPARTMENT
SILVER STREET
CAMBRIDGE, ENGLAND
See Engineering: Agricultural Engineer-
ing; Government-Federal

**MANCHESTER MUSEUM,
UNIVERSITY OF MANCHESTER**
OXFORD ROAD
MANCHESTER, DORSET, ENGLAND
See Geology: Paleontology; Educational
Institute

MARINE LABORATORY
YEALM ROAD, NEWTON FERRERS
PLYMOUTH, DEVON, ENGLAND
See Biology: General; Field Station/Lab-
oratory

**MARINE RESEARCH RESOURCES
UNIT**
GUILDHALL SQUARE
PORTSMOUTH, HANTS, ENGLAND
See Engineering: Water Resources; Edu-
cational Institute

METEOROLOGICAL OFFICE
BRACKNELL, BERKSHIRE,
ENGLAND
See Engineering: Pollution Abatement;
Professional Organizations

**MICRO ENVIRONMENTAL
PHYSIOLOGY RESEARCH**
KEPPEL STATE, HYGIENE AND
TROPICAL MEDICINE

LONDON WCI, ENGLAND
See Biology: General; Educational Institute

MILK MARKETING BOARD
THAMES DITTON, SURREY,
ENGLAND
See Engineering: Agricultural Engineer-
ing; Industrial/Commercial

**MINERAL RESOURCES DIVISION,
INSTITUTE OF GEOLOGICAL
SCIENCES**
EXHIBITION ROAD
LONDON SW7, ENGLAND
See Geology: General; Research Institute

MONSANTO CHEMICALS, LIMITED
10-18 VICTORIA STREET
LONDON, SW1, ENGLAND
See Chemistry: General; Industrial/Com-
mercial

NATURE CONSERVANCY
FURZEBROOK RESOURCE STATION
WAREHAM, DORSET, ENGLAND
See Biology: Ecology; Foundation

NATURE CONSERVANCY
MERLEWOOD RESEARCH STATION
GRANGE-OVER-SANDS,
LANCASTER, ENGLAND
See Biology: Ecology; Research Institute

NATURE CONSERVANCY
OAK COTTAGE, HYDE END LANE
BRIMPTON, NR READING,
ENGLAND
See Geology: General; Educational Insti-
tute

NATURE CONSERVANCY
PENRHOS ROAD
BANGOR, CAERN, ENGLAND
See Geology: General; Research Institute

NATURE CONSERVANCY
19-20 BELGRAVE SQUARE
LONDON SW1, ENGLAND
See Biology: Ecology; Research Institute

**NORTHEASTERN FISHERIES
COMMISSION**
EAST BLOCK
LONDON, SW7, ENGLAND
See Biology: Ecology; Professional Organ-
izations

NORTHWESTERN GAS BOARD
THOMAS STREET, STRETFORD
MANCHESTER, M32 ONJ, ENGLAND
See Engineering: Chemical Engineering;
Research Institute

OCEANOGRAPHY DEPARTMENT
UNIVERSITY
SOUTHAMPTON 509, ENGLAND
See Biology: Ecology; Educational Insti-
tute

OCEANOGRAPHY DEPARTMENT
UNIVERSITY OF LIVERPOOL
LIVERPOOL, ENGLAND
See Chemistry: General; Educational In-
stitute

**OCEANOGRAPHY, NATIONAL
INSTITUTE**
WORMLEY, GODALMING
SURREY, ENGLAND
See Engineering: Water Resources; Edu-
cational Institute

OFFICIAL SEED TESTING STATION
HUNTINGDON ROAD
CAMBRIDGE, ENGLAND
See Engineering: Agricultural Engineer-
ing; Research Institute

**OVERSEAS PESTICIDE RESEARCH
CENTER**
COLLEGE HOUSE, WRIGHTS LANE
LONDON W8, ENGLAND
See Biology: Ecology; Research Institute

**PALEONTOLOGY DEPARTMENT,
BRITISH MUSEUM**
CROMWELL ROAD
LONDON SW7, ENGLAND
See Geology: Paleontology; Research In-
stitute

**PERMUTIT COMPANY LIMITED,
PEMBERTON HOUSE**
LONDON ROAD
ISLEWORTH, MIDDLESEX,
ENGLAND
See Engineering: Pollution Abatement;
Industrial/Commercial

**PESTICIDE INFESTATION
CONTROL LABORATORY**
LONDON ROAD
SLOUGH, BUCKINGHAMSHIRE,
ENGLAND
See Interdisciplinary: General; Unclassi-
fied

**PESTICIDE INFESTATION
CONTROL LABORATORY**
MINISTRY OF AGRICULTURE,
TOLWORTH
SURREY, ENGLAND
See Biology: Ecology; Field Station/Lab-
oratory

**PETROCARBON DEVELOPMENTS,
LIMITED**
SHARSTON ROAD, WYTHENSHAWE
MANCHESTER 22, ENGLAND
See Engineering: General; Industrial/
Commercial

PLANT PROTECTION LIMITED
FERNHURST
HASLEMERE, SURREY, ENGLAND
See Engineering: Agricultural Engineer-
ing; Industrial/Commercial

**POLAR RESEARCH, SCOTT
INSTITUTE**
LENSFIELD ROAD
CAMBRIDGE, ENGLAND
See Interdisciplinary: General; Research
Institute

**POLLUTION CONTROL, LEATHER
MANUFACTURING RESEARCH
ASSOCIATION**
MILTON PARK, EGHAM

SURREY, TW20 9UQ, ENGLAND
See Engineering: Pollution Abatement;
Research Institute

**POLLUTION RESEARCH UNIT,
MATHEMATICS BUILDING**
UNIVERSITY OF MANCHESTER
MANCHESTER M13 9PL, ENGLAND
See Engineering: Pollution Abatement;
Research Institute

POLYMER SCIENCES SCHOOL
UNIVERSITY OF BRADFORD
BRADFORD, WEST RIDING,
ENGLAND
See Chemistry: General; Educational In-
stitute

POTATO MARKETING BOARD
50 HANS CRESCENT
LONDON SW1, ENGLAND
See Engineering: Agricultural Engineering; Professional Organizations

**POTATOES AND BRASSICA
SECTION**
PLANT BREEDING INSTITUTE
TRUMPINGTON, CAMBRIDGE,
ENGLAND
See Biology: General; Research Institute

**PRESERVATION OF BIRDS
INTERNATIONAL COUNCIL,
BRITISH MUSEUM**
CROMWELL ROAD
LONDON SW7, ENGLAND
See Biology: Ecology; Foundation

**PRESTON MONTFORD FIELD
CENTER**
SHREWSBURY, ENGLAND
See Biology: Ecology; Field Station/Lab-
oratory

PRIVATE RESEARCH
21-22 GREAT CASTLE STREET
LONDON W1, ENGLAND
See Biology: Ecology; Industrial/Com-
mercial

PUBLIC HEALTH LABORATORIES
THRESH HOUSE, VERULAM
STREET, GRAYIS INN ROAD
LONDON, ENGLAND
See Engineering: Pollution Abatement;
Field Station/Laboratory

**RADIOBIOLOGICAL PROTECTION
SERVICE**
CLIFTON AVENUE, BELMONT
SUTTON, SURREY CR4 4XY,
ENGLAND
See Physics: General; Research Institute

**RESEARCH AND DEVELOPMENT
DEPARTMENT, BP CHEMICALS
LIMITED**
DEVONSHIRE HOUSE, MAYFAIR
PLACE
PICCADILLY, LONDON, ENGLAND
See Chemistry: General; Industrial/Com-
mercial

**RESEARCH AND DEVELOPMENT
MANAGEMENT, ICI LIMITED**
MONO DIVISION, POST OFFICE
BOX 8
THE HEATH, RUNCORD,
CHESHIRE, ENGLAND
See Interdisciplinary: General; Industrial/
Commercial

**RESEARCH CENTER AT
HUNTINGDON**
HUNTINGDON, NORTHAMPTON,
ENGLAND
See Biology: General; Research Institute

**RESEARCH CENTER, TATE AND
LYLE**
KESTON
KENT, ENGLAND
See Biology: Ecology; Research Institute

**RESEARCH DEPARTMENT, ICI
PLANT PROTECTION LIMITED**
YALDING
KENT, ENGLAND
See Biology: Ecology; Industrial/Com-
mercial

RESEARCH LONG ASHTON
UNIVERSITY OF BRISTOL
BRISTOL, GLOUCESTER, ENGLAND
See Biology: General; Research Institute

RESEARCH STATION
ROTHWELL PLANT BREEDERS
CAISTOR, LANCASTER, ENGLAND
See Engineering: Agricultural Engineer-
ing; Research Institute

**RESEARCH STATION AT EAST
MALLING**
EAST MALLING
KENT, ENGLAND
See Biology: General; Research Institute

**RESEARCH STATION AT
LEVINGTON**
LEVINGTON
IPSWICH, SUFFOLK, ENGLAND
See Engineering: Agricultural Engineer-
ing; Research Institute

**RESEARCH STATION AT LONG
ASHTON**
THE UNIVERSITY
BRISTOL, ENGLAND
See Biology: Ecology; Research Institute

**RESEARCH STATION OF EAST
MALLING**
MAIDSTONE
KENT, ENGLAND
See Biology: Ecology; Research Institute

ROAD RESEARCH LABORATORY
CROWTHORNE, BERKSHIRE,
ENGLAND
See Engineering: Pollution Abatement;
Field Station/Laboratory

SCIENCE RESEARCH COUNCIL
STATE HOUSE, HIGH HOLBORN
LONDON, WC1, ENGLAND
See Interdisciplinary: General; Unclassi-
fied

**SCIENTIFIC SERVICES CENTER,
CEGB**
RATCLIFFE-ON-SOAR
NOTTINGHAM NG11 OEE,
ENGLAND
See Chemistry: General; Industrial/Com-
mercial

**SCOTT POLAR RESEARCH
INSTITUTION**
UNIVERSITY OF CAMBRIDGE
CAMBRIDGE, ENGLAND
See Geology: General; Educational Insti-
tute

SHELL RESEARCH, LIMITED
POST OFFICE BOX 1, THORNTON
RESOURCES CENTER
CHESTER, CHESHIRE, ENGLAND
See Chemistry: General; Industrial/Com-
mercial

SHELL RESEARCH, LIMITED
SHELL CENTER
LONDON SEI, ENGLAND
See Engineering: General; Industrial/
Commercial

SHELL RESOURCES LIMITED
WOODSTOCK AGRICULTURAL
RESOURCES CENTER
SITTINGBOURNE, KENT, ENGLAND
See Engineering: Agricultural Engineer-
ing; Research Institute

SIMON-HARTLEY LTP
STOKE-ON-TRENT, ST47B4,
ENGLAND
See Biology: General; Industrial/Com-
mercial

SOIL PHYSICS LABORATORY
DEPARTMENT OF CIVIL
ENGINEERING, CITY UNIVERSITY
LONDON EC1, ENGLAND
See Physics: General; Educational Insti-
tute

**SOIL SURVEY OF ENGLAND AND
WALES**
BOTHAMSTED EXPERIMENTAL.
STATION
HARPENDEN, HERTFORDSHIRE,
ENGLAND
See Engineering: Chemical Engineering;
Field Station/Laboratory

**STEETLEY ORGANIZATION
RESOURCE DEPARTMENT**
CARLTON ROAD
WORKSOP, NOTTINGHAMSHIRE,
ENGLAND
See Geology: General; Industrial/Com-
mercial

**TECHNOLOGY CENTER, PROCTOR
AND GAMBLE LIMITED**
GPO BOX FOREST HALL NO 2
NEWCASTLE-UPON-TYNE,
ENGLAND
See Engineering: Pollution Abatement;
Industrial/Commercial

TIDAL INSTITUTE AND OBSERVATORY, UNIVERSITY OF LIVERPOOL
BIDSTON
CHESHIRE, ENGLAND
See Physics: General; Educational Institute

TROPICAL PRODUCTS INSTITUTE
56-62 GRAYS INN ROAD
LONDON WC1, ENGLAND
See Engineering: Agricultural Engineering; Research Institute

UKAEA, REACTOR GROUP
RISLEY, NR WARRINGTON
LANCASTERSHIRE, ENGLAND
See Physics: General; Industrial/Commercial

UNILEVER RESEARCH LABORATORY
COLWORTH HOUSE
SHARNBROOK, BEDFORD,
ENGLAND
See Biology: General; Field Station/Laboratory

VEGETABLE RESEARCH NATIONAL STATION
WELLESBOURNE, WARWICK,
ENGLAND
See Engineering: Agricultural Engineering; Research Institute

VETERINARY LABORATORY
WEYBRIDGE
SURREY, ENGLAND
See Biology: General; Field Station/Laboratory

WARREN SPRING LABORATORY
STEVENAGE, HERTFORDSHIRE,
ENGLAND
See Engineering: Pollution Abatement; Field Station/Laboratory

WATER POLLUTION RESEARCH LABORATORY
ELDER WAY
STEVENAGE, HERTFORDSHIRE,
ENGLAND
See Engineering: Pollution Abatement; Government-Federal

WATER RESEARCH ASSOCIATION
MEDMENHAM
MARLOW, BUCKINGHAMSHIRE,
ENGLAND
See Engineering: Water Resources; Educational Institute

WATER SUPPLY ASSOCIATION, INTERNATIONAL
34 PARK STREET
LONDON W1, ENGLAND
See Engineering: Water Resources; Educational Institute

WEED RESEARCH ORGANIZATION
BEGBROKE HILL, YARNTON,
OXFORD, OXSIPF, ENGLAND
See Biology: General; Research Institute

WILDLIFE FEDERATION OF WISCONSIN
VISTA LANE
SUSSEX, W1, ENGLAND
See Biology: Ecology; Foundation

ZOOLOGY DEPARTMENT
UNIVERSITY NEWCASTLE-UPON-TYNE
NEWCASTLE-UPON-TYNE,ENGLAND
See Biology: General; Educational Institute

ETHIOPIA

FISHERIES OFFICE
POST OFFICE BOX 73
MASSAWA, ETHIOPIA
See Social Sciences/Humanities: Industrial Development; Government-Federal

FISHERY DIVISION, DEPARTMENT OF AGRICULTURE
POST OFFICE BOX 1232
ADDIS ABABA, ETHIOPIA
See Biology: Ecology; Government-Federal

GULF OIL COMPANY OF ETHIOPIA
POST OFFICE BOX 2589
ADDIS ABABA ETHIOPIA
See Social Sciences/Humanities: Industrial Development; Industrial/Commercial

MINES MINISTRY
POST OFFICE BOX 486
ADDIS ABABA, ETHIOPIA
See Geology: General; Government-Federal

MOBIL OIL (EAST AFRICA)LIMITED
POST OFFICE BOX 1365
ADDIS ABABA ETHIOPIA
See Social Sciences/Humanities: Industrial Development; Industrial/Commercial

FINLAND

BIOLOGY DEPARTMENT, UNIVERSITY OF HELSINKI
UNIONINKATU 44
HELSINKI, FINLAND
See Biology: General; Educational Institute

MARINE RESEARCH INSTITUTE
HELSINKI 4, FINLAND
See Biology: General; Research Institute

FRANCE

AGRICULTURAL ENGINEERING, INTERNATIONAL COMMISSION
19, AVENUE DU MAINE
PARIS 15, FRANCE
See Engineering: Agricultural Engineering; Research Institute

ATOMIC FORUM, EUROPEAN
26 RUE DE CLICHY
PARIS 9, FRANCE
See Interdisciplinary: General; Research Institute

BIOLOGICAL STATION
PLACE LACAZE-DUTHIERS
ROSCOFF(FINISTERE), FRANCE
See Biology: General; Field Station/Laboratory

CANCER RESEARCH AGENCY INTERNATIONAL
16 AVENUE MARECHAL FOCH
69 LYON, FRANCE
See Chemistry: General; Research Institute

CENTER SCIENCES STUDIES RESOURCES BARRIETY
B P 28 PLATEAU DE LATALAYE
BIARRITZ (B P), FRANCE
See Biology: General; Research Institute

COMMISSION FOR PROTECTION OF POPULATION AGAINST HAZARDS
4 AVENUE DE L'OBSERVATOIRE
PARIS 6, FRANCE
See Chemistry: General; Research Institute

ECOLOGY (GENERAL) LABORATORY
4 AVENUE DU PETIT CHATEAU
BRUNDY, FRANCE
See Biology: Ecology; Field Station/Laboratory

ENDOUME MARINE STATION
RUE DE LA BATTERIE DES LIONS
MARSEILLES 7, FRANCE
See Geology: General; Research Institute

EUROPEAN AND MEDITERRANEAN PLANT PROTECTION ORGANIZATION
1 RUE LA NOTRA
PARIS 16, FRANCE
See Engineering: Agricultural Engineering; Research Institute

INSTITUTION RUTLDE L'UNIVERSITY
UNIVERSITY OF MONTPELLIER
MONTPELLIER, FRANCE
See Biology: General; Educational Institute

INTERNATIONAL COMMISSION ON LARGE DAMS
20 RUE DE L'ARCADE

PARIS 8, FRANCE
See Engineering: Water Resources; Educational Institute

**INTERNATIONAL OFFICE
EPIZOOTICS**
12, RUE DE PRONY
PARIS 7, FRANCE
See Biology: Ecology; Research Institute

LABORATORY ARAGO
BANYULS-SUR-MER, FRANCE
See Biology: General; Field Station/Laboratory

**MARINE BIOLOGY INSTITUTE,
UNIVERSITY DE BORDEAUX**
9 RUE PIERLOT, 33
BORDEAUX, FRANCE
See Biology: General; Educational Institute

OCEANOGRAPHIC INSTITUTE
195 RUE SAINT JACQUES
PARIS 5, FRANCE
See Physics: General; Research Institute

**POPULATION STUDIES CENTER,
INSTITUTION D'ETUDE
DEMOGRAPHIQUES**
23 AVENUE FRANKLIN ROOSEVELT
PARIS 8, FRANCE
See Social Sciences/Humanities: Population Studies/Family Planning; Professional Organizations

RESEARCH INSTITUTE
16 RUE DE BUFFON
PARIS, FRANCE
See Biology: Ecology; Research Institute

SCIENCES FACULTY
TOULOUSE, FRANCE
See Biology: Ecology; Educational Institute

**SCIENTIFIC AND
TECHNOLOGICAL INSTITUTE OF
MARINE FISHERIES**
59 AVENUE RAYMOND POINCARE
PARIS 16, FRANCE
See Biology: General; Research Institute

SPACE RESEARCH COMMITTEE
55 BUILDING MALESHERBES
PARIS 8, FRANCE
See Interdisciplinary: General; Research Institute

UNESCO
PLACE DE FONTENOY
75 PARIS, 7E, FRANCE
See Biology: Ecology; Professional Organizations

ZOOLOGICAL LABORATORY
UNIVERSITY OF PARIS
VILLEFRANCHE-SUR-MER, FRANCE
See Biology: General; Educational Institute

GABON

ECONOMY AND MINING MINISTRY
BOITE POSTALE 548
LIBREVILLE, GABON
See Biology: General; Government-Federal

GULF-GABON
LIBREVILLE, GABON
See Social Sciences/Humanities: Industrial Development; Industrial/Commercial

**PETROLEUM SOCIETY OF
EQUATORIAL AFRICA**
BOITE POSTALE 539
PORT GENTIL, GABON
See Social Sciences/Humanities: Industrial Development; Industrial/Commercial

GALAPAGOS ISLANDS

**CHARLES DARWIN RESOURCES
STATION**
ISLA SANTA CRUZ
GALAPAGOS, GALAPAGOS ISLANDS
See Biology: General; Government-Federal

GAMBIA

**AGRICULTURAL AND NATURAL
RESOURCE MINISTRY**
CAPE ST MARY VIA BATHURST
BATHURST, THE GAMBIA
See Social Sciences/Humanities: Agriculture; Government-Federal

MARINE DEPARTMENT
WORKS AND COMMUNICATION
MINISTRY
BATHURST, THE GAMBIA
See Biology: General; Government-Federal

GHANA

AGRICULTURE MINISTRY
POST OFFICE BOX 630
ACCRA, GHANA
See Engineering: Agricultural Engineering; Government-Federal

FISHERIES DIVISION
ACCRA, GHANA

See Biology: General; Government-Federal

FISHERY RESEARCH UNITED
BOX B62, COMMUNITY 2
TEMA, GHANA
See Biology: General; Government-Federal

GHANA BOATYARD CORPORATION
TEMA, GHANA
See Social Sciences/Humanities: Industrial Development; Industrial/Commercial

NAUTICAL SCHOOL
ACCRA, GHANA
See Social Sciences/Humanities: Education; Government-Federal

VOLTA BASIN RESEARCH PROJECT
LEGON, GHANA
See Geology: General; Research Institute

GREECE

**BIOLOGY SECTION, DEMOCRITUS
NUCLEAR RESEARCH CENTER**
ATOMIC ENERGY COMMISSION
ATHENS, GREECE
See Biology: General; Government-Federal

**DEFENSE MINISTRY (NATIONAL),
ROYAL RESEARCH**
VOTANIKOS
ATHENS, GREECE
See Interdisciplinary: General; Unclassified

**EXPERIMENTAL PHYSICS
LABORATORY 11, TECHNOLOGY
UNIVERSITY**
POST OFFICE BOX 49
ATHENS, GREECE
See Engineering: General; Educational Institute

FISH HATCHERY STATION
LOURES RIVER, GREECE
See Biology: General; Field Station/Laboratory

FISHERIES HATCHERY STATION
EDESSA, GREECE
See Biology: General; Field Station/Laboratory

**GEOLOGY AND SUBSURFACE
RESOURCES INSTITUTE**
6 AMERIKIS STREET
ATHENS, GREECE
See Biology: General; Government-Federal

HYDROBIOLOGICAL INSTITUTE
ATHENS, GREECE
See Interdisciplinary: General; Research Institute

HYDROBIOLOGICAL STATION
RHODES, GREECE
See Biology: General; Field Station/Laboratory

HYDROBIOLOGICAL STATION
THESSALONIKI, GREECE
See Biology: General; Field Station/Laboratory

HYDROGRAPHIC SERVICE, ROYAL HELLENIC NAVY
MINISTRY OF NATIONAL DEFENSE
VOTANIKOS, ATHENS, GREECE
See Biology: General; Government-Federal

LIMNI RESEARCH STATION
EUBOEA, GREECE
See Biology: Biochemistry; Field Station/Laboratory

OCEANOGRAPHIC SOCIETY, HELLENIC
ATHENS, GREECE
See Biology: Biochemistry; Professional Organizations

OCEANOGRAPHY AND FISHING RESEARCH INSTITUTE
AGIOS KOSMAS-HELLINIKON
ATHENS, GREECE
See Biology: General; Government-Federal

SEISMOLOGY INSTITUTE
NATIONAL OBSERVATORY OF ATHENS
ATHENS, GREECE
See Geology: General; Educational Institute

ZOOLOGY LABORATORY AND MUSEUM
UNIVERSITY OF ATHENS
ATHENS, GREECE
See Biology: General; Educational Institute

GUATEMALA

AGRICULTURAL MINISTRY, FAUNA DIVISION
FINCA LA HURORA,
GUATEMALA CITY, GUATEMALA
See Biology: General; Educational Institute

MARISCOS DE GUATEMALA, SOUTH AMERICA
15 AVENUE 19-15, ZONE 13
GUATEMALA CITY, GUATEMALA
See Biology: General; Industrial/Commercial

SANITARY ENGINEERING ASSOCIATION
2A AVEIDA 0-61 ZONA 10
GUATEMALA CITY, GUATEMALA
See Engineering: Pollution Abatement; Professional Organizations

GUINEA

FISHERIES SERVICES (OPEMA)
CONAKRY, GUINEA
See Biology: General; Research Institute

RURAL ECONOMY AND HANDICRAFT MINISTRY
CONAKRY, GUINEA
See Interdisciplinary: General; Unclassified

GUYANA

AGRICULTURE AND FISHERIES MINISTRY
ONE LOMBARD STREET
GEORGETOWN, GUYANA
See Biology: General; Government-Federal

HAITI

FISHERY SCIENCE
DEPARTMENT OF AGRICULTURE
PORT-AU-PRINCE, HAITI
See Biology: General; Government-Federal

HONDURAS

CARIBBEAN PRODUCERS
GUANAJA, HONDURAS
See Biology: General; Industrial/Commercial

CARIBENA PRODUCERS COOPERATIVE
SAN PEDRO SULA, HONDURAS
See Engineering: Agricultural Engineering; Industrial/Commercial

FISHERMAN'S PRODUCE CORPORATION (NATIONAL)
ANGEL LANE
BELIZE CITY, HONDURAS
See Interdisciplinary: General; Industrial/Commercial

FISHERMEN'S COOPERATIVE
SAN LORENZO, HONDURAS
See Biology: General; Industrial/Commercial

FOREST, GAME, FISHERIES RESOURCES
EDIF BANCO, NAC DE FOMENTO
COMEYAGUELA, HONDURAS
See Biology: General; Government-Federal

HONDURAN FISHERIES INDUSTRY
GUANAJA, HONDURAS
See Biology: General; Industrial/Commercial

MARINE FISHING DEPARTMENT
EDIF BANCO, NAC DE FOMENTO
COMEYAGUELA, HONDURAS
See Biology: General; Government-Federal

MINES AND HYDROLOGY OFFICE
EDIF BANCO, NAC DE FOMENTO
COMEYAGUELA, HONDURAS
See Biology: General; Government-Federal

NATURAL RESOURCE AND TRADE MINISTRY
BELIZE CITY, HONDURAS
See Interdisciplinary: General; Unclassified

NATURAL RESOURCES MINISTRY
EDIF BANCO, NAC DE FOMENT
COMEYAGUELA, HONDURAS
See Biology: General; Government-Federal

PLACENCIA PRODUCERS COMPANY-OPERATIONS
TEGUCIGALPA, HONDURAS
See Interdisciplinary: General; Industrial/Commercial

PLANNING AND PROGRAMMING OFFICE
EDIF BANCO, NAC DE FOMENTO
COMEYAGUELA, HONDURAS
See Biology: General; Government-Federal

SIGNAL OIL AND GAS COMPANY
SAN LORENZO, HONDURAS
See Biology: General; Industrial/Commercial

UNION OIL COMPANY
SAN LORENZO, HONDURAS
See Biology: General; Industrial/Commercial

HUNGARY

BIOKEMIAI INTEZET MTA
KAROLINA UT 29
BUDAPEST XI, HUNGARY
See Biology: Biochemistry; Educational Institute

BIOLOGIAI KUTATO
TIHANY, HUNGARY
See Biology: General; Research Institute

DANUBE COMMISSION
BENCZUR UTCA 25
BUDAPEST VI, HUNGARY
See Biology: Ecology; Research Institute

**GEOCHEMICAL RESEARCH
LABORATORY, HUNG ACADEMY
OF SCIENCE**
MUZEUM KORUT 4
BUDAPEST 8, HUNGARY
See Geology: General; Educational Institute

**GEOPHYSICAL DEPARTMENT,
UNIVERSITY OF BUDAPEST**
L EOTVOS UNIVERSITY
BUDAPEST, HUNGARY
See Physics: General; Educational Institute

**ORSZAGOS METEOROLOGIAI
INTEZET**
KITAIBEL PAL U I
BUDAPEST, HUNGARY
See Interdisciplinary: General; Research Institute

ICELAND

MARINE RESEARCH INSTITUTE
SKULAGOTA 4
REYKJAVIK, ICELAND
See Interdisciplinary: General; Research Institute

**MECHANICS AND GEOPHYSICS,
DEPARTMENT OF ENGINEERING**
UNIVERSITY OF ICELAND
REYKJAVIK, ICELAND
See Physics: General; Educational Institute

INDIA

AGRICULTURAL METEOROLOGY
METEOROLOGICAL OFFICE
POONA-5, INDIA
See Engineering: Agricultural Engineering; Professional Organizations

**BHABHA ATOMIC RESEARCH
CENTER**
TROMBAY
BOMBAY, INDIA
See Engineering: General; Government-Federal

**BIOLOGICAL CENTER, INDIAN
OCEAN**
ERNAKULAM, INDIA
See Biology: General; Government-Federal

CENTRAL INLAND FISHERIES
POST OFFICE 24 PARGANAS
BARRACKPORE, WEST BENGAL, INDIA
See Engineering: Pollution Abatement; Research Institute

**CENTRAL INLAND FISHERIES
RESOURCES INSTITUTION**
BARRACKPORE
VIA CALCUTTA, INDIA
See Biology: General; Government-Federal

CENTRAL MARINE FISHERIES
RAMANATHAPURAM DISTRICT
MADRAS STATE, INDIA
See Biology: General; Research Institute

**CENTRAL SALT AND MARINE
CHEMISTRY RESEARCH**
SCIENTIFIC AND INDUSTRIAL
RESEARCH COUNCIL
HAVNAGAR, INDIA
See Interdisciplinary: General; Unclassified

**DATA AND PLANNING DIVISION,
NIO**
KRISHI BHAVAN
NEW DELHI, INDIA
See Interdisciplinary: General; Industrial/Commercial

**DEFENSE MINISTRY, INDUSTRIAL
NAVY, NAVAL PHYSICS
LABORATORY**
NAVAL BASE
COCHIN, INDIA
See Geology: General; Government-Federal

FISHERIES DEPARTMENT
KERALA, INDIA
See Biology: General; Government-State or Local

FISHERIES DEPARTMENT
35-2 MOUNT ROAD
MADRAS 2, INDIA
See Biology: General; Government-State or Local

**FISHERIES TECHNOLOGICAL
LABORATORY**
KOZHIKODE 5
CALCUTTA, INDIA
See Biology: General; Field Station/Laboratory

**INDIAN NATIONAL COMMANDER
ON OCEAN RESEARCH**
RAFI MARG
NEW DELHI, INDIA
See Interdisciplinary: General; Unclassified

**IRRIGATION AND DRAINAGE
COMMISSION**
48 NYAYA MARG, CHANAKYAPURI
NEW DELHI 21, INDIA
See Engineering: Water Resources; Educational Institute

**MARINE BIOLOGICAL RESEARCH
STATION**
RATNAGIRI
MAHARASHTRA STATE, INDIA
See Biology: General; Government-State or Local

**MARINE BIOLOGICAL STATION,
WEST HILL**
KOZHIKODE 5
CALCUTTA, INDIA
See Biology: General; Field Station/Laboratory

**MARINE BIOLOGY DEPARTMENT,
UNIVERSITY OF KERALA**
TRIVANDRUM 7
KERALA STATE, INDIA
See Biology: General; Educational Institute

**MARINE FISHERIES RESOURCE
CENTRAL INSTITUTE**
MANADAPAM CAMP P.O.
MADRAS STATE, INDIA
See Biology: General; Government-Federal

**METEOROLOGY AND
OCEANOGRAPHY DEPARTMENT,
ANDHRA UNIVERSITY**
WALTAIR
ANDHRA PRADESH STATE, INDIA
See Biology: General; Educational Institute

**NAVAL PHYSICAL LABORATORY,
MINISTRY OF DEFENSE**
NAVAL BASE
COCHIN, INDIA
See Physics: General; Government-Federal

OCEANOGRAPHIC LABORATORY
KERALA UNIVERSITY
ERNAKULAM, INDIA
See Biology: General; Educational Institute

**PHYSICAL OCEANOGRAPHY
DIVISION**
ERNAKULAM, INDIA
See Geology: General; Government-Federal

**PLANNING AND HOUSING
ORGANIZATION**
4-A RING ROAD INDRAPRASTHA
NEW DELHI, INDIA
See Social Sciences/Humanities: Housing; Foundation

**SALT AND MARINE CHEMISTRY
RESOURCES CENTRAL
INSTITUTE**
BHAVNAGAR, INDIA
See Engineering: Chemical Engineering;
Government-Federal

**TARAPOREVALA AQUARIUM AND
MARINE BIOLOGY INSTITUTE**
NETAJI SUBHASH ROAD
BOMBAY, INDIA
See Biology: General; Government-State
or Local

UNIVERSITY OF BOMBAY
MAYO ROAD
FORT BOMBAY, INDIA
See Biology: General; Educational Institute

**ZOOLOGICAL RESEARCH
LABORATORY**
MADRAS UNIVERSITY
MADRAS, INDIA
See Biology: Ecology; Educational Institute

ZOOLOGICAL SURVEY OF INDIA
CALCUTTA, INDIA
See Biology: General; Government-Federal

**ZOOLOGY AND MARINE BIOLOGY
DEPARTMENT, ANDHRA
UNIVERSITY**
WALTAIR
ANDHRA PRADESH STATE, INDIA
See Biology: General; Educational Institute

INDONESIA

ASAMERA OIL LIMITED
JAKARTA, INDONESIA
See Engineering: General; Industrial/
Commercial

**HYDROGRAPHIC OFFICE,
INDONESIAN NAVY**
DJI. GUNUNG SAHARI I
DJAKARTA, INDONESIA
See Engineering: General; Government-
Federal

INLAND FISHERIES DIRECTORATE
DJI. SALEMBA 17
DJAKARTA, INDONESIA
See Biology: General; Government-Federal

KYUSHU OIL COMPANY
C/O PERMINA
DJAKARTA, INDONESIA
See Engineering: General; Industrial/
Commercial

MARINE RESEARCH INSTITUTE
POST OFFICE BOX 580 DAK
PASARIKAN
DJAKARTA KOTA, INDONESIA
See Biology: General; Research Institute

**MARINE RESOURCES INSTITUTE,
DEPARTMENT OF AGRICULTURE**
DJI SALEMBA 17
DJAKARTA, INDONESIA
See Engineering: General; Government-
Federal

**OCEAN SCIENCE AND
ENGINEERING COMPANY**
DJAKARTA, INDONESIA
See Engineering: General; Industrial/
Commercial

**OCEANOGRAPHIC RESEARCH
NATIONAL COMMISSION**
DJAKARTA, INDONESIA
See Engineering: General; Government-
Federal

**OIL DEVELOPMENT
CORPORATION OF NORTH
SUMATRA**
C/O PERMINA
DJAKARTA, INDONESIA
See Engineering: General; Industrial/
Commercial

**PETROLEUM EXPLORATION
COMPANY OF JAPAN**
C/O PERMINA
DJAKARTA, INDONESIA
See Engineering: General; Industrial/
Commercial

**SEA FISHERIES RESEARCH
INSTITUTE**
PASAR IKAN
DJAKARTA, INDONESIA
See Engineering: General; Government-
Federal

IRAN

**ENVIRONMENTAL STUDIES
PROGRAM**
UNIVERSITY OF TEHRAN
TEHRAN, IRAN
See Interdisciplinary: General; Educational Institute

FINANCE MINISTRY
DEPARTMENT OF FISHERIES
TEHRAN, IRAN
See Interdisciplinary: General; Unclassified

**FISHERIES DEPARTMENT,
FINANCE OFFICE**
TEHRAN, IRAN
See Biology: General; Government-Federal

GEOPHYSICAL INSTITUTE
UNIVERSITY OF TEHRAN
TEHRAN, IRAN
See Geology: General; Educational Institute

HYDROLOGY INSTITUTE
UNIVERSITY OF TEHRAN
TEHRAN, IRAN
See Biology: General; Educational Institute

NATIONAL IRANIAN OIL COMPANY
TEHRAN, IRAN
See Biology: General; Industrial/Commercial

**PORT AND NAVIGATION
ORGANIZATION**
MINISTRY OF ROADS
TEHRAN, IRAN
See Interdisciplinary: General; Unclassified

PUPLIC HEALTH INSTITUTE
UNIVERSITY OF TEHRAN
TEHRAN, IRAN
See Social Sciences/Humanities: General;
Educational Institute

SOUTHERN FISHERIES COMPANY
TEHRAN, IRAN
See Interdisciplinary: General; Industrial/
Commercial

VETERINARY MEDICINE FACULTY
UNIVERSITY OF TEHRAN
TEHRAN, IRAN
See Biology: General; Educational Institute

**WAR MINISTRY, IMPERIAL
IRANIAN NAVY**
TEHRAN, IRAN
See Interdisciplinary: General; Unclassified

IRAQ

**FISHERIES AND HYDROBIOLOGY
DEPARTMENT**
MINISTRY OF AGRICULTURE
BAGHDAD, IRAQ
See Interdisciplinary: General; Unclassified

IRELAND

CORK UNIVERSITY STATION
LOUGH INE SKIBBEREEN
COUNTY CORK, IRELAND

ITALY 191

See Biology: General; Field Station/Laboratory

GEOLOGICAL SURVEY OF NORTH IRELAND
20 COLLEGE GROUNDS
BELFAST BT9 6BS, IRELAND
See Geology: General; Government-State or Local

PHYSICAL PLANNING AND CONSTRUCTION RESOURCES, NATIONAL INSTITUTE
ST MARTIN'S WATERLOO ROAD
DUBLIN 4, IRELAND
See Biology: Ecology; Research Institute

SOILS DIVISION, AGRICULTURAL INSTITUTION
JOHNSTOWN CASTLE
WEXFORD, IRELAND
See Engineering: Agricultural Engineering; Educational Institute

ISRAEL

ATMOSPHERIC SCIENCES DEPARTMENT
HEBREW UNIVERSITY OF JERUSALEM
JERUSALEM, ISRAEL
See Geology: General; Educational Institute

BAR-ILAN UNIVERSITY
RAMAT GAN, ISRAEL
See Biology: General; Educational Institute

BOTANY DEPARTMENT
HEBREW UNIVERSITY OF JERUSALEM
JERUSALEM, ISRAEL
See Biology: General; Educational Institute

BOTANY DEPARTMENT
TEL AVIV UNIVERSITY
RAMAT AVIV, ISRAEL
See Biology: Ecology; Educational Institute

CIVIL AND MARINE ENGINEERING CORPORATION, LIMITED
65 HA-AZMAUT ROAD
HAIFA, ISRAEL
See Geology: General; Industrial/Commercial

COASTAL STUDIES DIVISION
MINISTRY OF TRANSPORTATION AND COMMUNICATION
ASHWOOD HARBOR, ISRAEL
See Geology: General; Government-Federal

DESALINATION ENGINEERING DEPARTMENT
PO BOX 18041
TEL AVIV, ISRAEL
See Engineering: Water Resources; Industrial/Commercial

GEODESY AND GEOPHYSICS SOCIETY OF ISRAEL
54 IBN GVIROL STREET
TEL AVIV, ISRAEL
See Geology: General; Professional Organizations

GEOLOGICAL SURVEY OF ISRAEL
30 MALKEY ISRAEL STREET
JERUSALEM, ISRAEL
See Biology: General; Government-Federal

GEOLOGY DEPARTMENT
HEBREW UNIVERSITY OF JERUSALEM
JERUSALEM, ISRAEL
See Geology: General; Educational Institute

HEALTH MINISTRY
DAVID HAMELACH STREET
JERUSALEM, ISRAEL
See Social Sciences/Humanities: General; Government-Federal

HEBREW UNIVERSITY-HADASSAH MEDICAL SCHOOL
JERUSALEM, ISRAEL
See Interdisciplinary: General; Educational Institute

MARINE BIOLOGY AND ECONOMICS DEPARTMENT
TEL-AVIV UNIVERSITY
TEL-AVIV, ISRAEL
See Biology: Ecology; Educational Institute

MEKOROT WATER COMPANY, LIMITED
9 LINCOLN STREET
TEL AVIV,ISRAEL
See Engineering: Water Resources; Industrial/Commercial

METEOROLOGY SERVICE
POST OFFICE BOX 25
BET DAGAN, ISRAEL
See Physics: General; Government-Federal

OCEANOGRAPHY AND LIMNOLOGY RESEARCH, NATIONAL COUNCIL RESEARCH
120 HA-AZMAUT ROAD
HAIFA, ISRAEL
See Biology: General; Government-Federal

PETROLEUM RESOURCES AND GEOPHYSICS INSTITUTE
POST OFFICE BOX 120
AZOR, ISRAEL
See Geology: General; Industrial/Commercial

SEA FISHERIES RESOURCES STATION
POST OFFICE BOX 699
HAIFA, ISRAEL
See Biology: General; Research Institute

TAHAL-WATER PLANNING FOR ISRAEL, LIMITED
54 IBN GVIROL STREET
TEL AVIV, ISRAEL
See Engineering: Water Resources; Industrial/Commercial

TECHNION
TECHNION CITY, HAIFA, ISRAEL
See Biology: Biochemistry; Educational Institute

THE WEIZMANN INSTITUTE OF SCIENCE
POST OFFICE BOX 26
REHOVOTH, ISRAEL
See Biology: General; Educational Institute

UNDERSEA EXPLORATION SOCIETY, NATIONAL MARITIME MUSEUM
198 ALENBY STREET
HAIFA, ISRAEL
See Geology: General; Professional Organizations

WATER COMMISSION, HYDROLOGICAL SERVICES
POST OFFICE BOX 6381
JERUSALEM, ISRAEL
See Engineering: Water Resources; Government-Federal

ZOOLOGY DEPARTMENT
HEBREW UNIVERSITY OF JERUSALEM
JERUSALEM, ISRAEL
See Biology: Ecology; Educational Institute

ISTANBUL

HYDROBIOLOGICAL INSTITUTION
ISTANBUL UNIVERSITY
BALTA LIMANI, ISTANBUL
See Biology: General; Educational Institute

ITALY

BOTANICAL INSTITUTE AND GARDEN
UNIVERSITY OF PERUGIA
PERUGIA, ITALY

See Biology: Ecology; Government-State
or Local

BOTANICAL SCIENCE INSTITUTE
UNIVERSITY OF MILAN, V GIUS
COLOMBO 60, MILAN, ITALY
See Biology: General; Educational Institute

**EDUCATION ORTO BOTANICAL
INSTITUTION, DELL UNIVERSITY
PALERMO**
V LINCOLN
PALERMO, ITALY
See Biology: General; Educational Institute

**EUROPEAN ATOMIC ENERGY
SOCIETY**
VIA BELISARIO 15
ROME, ITALY
See Interdisciplinary: General; Research
Institute

**EXPERIMENTAL
THALASSOGRAPHY, TRIESTE
INSTITUTE**
VIALE ROMOLO GESSI 2
TRIESTE, ITALY
See Biology: General; Research Institute

**FATIO MARINE BIOLOGICAL
LABORATORY, UNIVERSITY OF
BOLOGNA**
VIALE ADRIATICO
PERSARO, ITALY
See Biology: General; Field Station/Laboratory

**FISHERIES COUNCIL OF THE
MEDITERRANEAN**
VIA DELLE TERME CARACALA
ROME, ITALY
See Biology: Ecology; Research Institute

**FOOD AND AGRICULTURE
ORGANIZATION OF THE UNITED
NATIONS**
VIA DELLE TERME CARACALLA
ROME, ITALY
See Engineering: Agricultural Engineering; Foundation

GEOLOGY DEPARTMENT
UNIVERSITY OF FLORENCE
FLORENCE, ITALY
See Geology: General; Educational Institute

GEOLOGY DEPARTMENT
UNIVERSITY OF PAVIA
ROME, ITALY
See Geology: General; Educational Institute

GEOLOGY DEPARTMENT
UNIVERSITY OF ROME
ROME, ITALY
See Geology: General; Educational Institute

GEOLOGY INSTITUTE
UNIVERSITY OF PISA
VS MARIA 53, PISA, ITALY
See Geology: General; Educational Institute

**GEOLOGY INSTITUTE, UNIVERSITY
OF MILAN**
PIAZZALE GORINI 15
MILAN, ITALY
See Geology: General; Educational Institute

HYDROBIOLOGICAL LABORATORY
PIAZZA BORGHESE 91
ROME, ITALY
See Biology: General; Field Station/Laboratory

**INDIAN OCEAN PROGRAM,
FISHERIES DEPARTMENT**
VIA DELLE LERME DIVISION
CARACALLA
ROME, ITALY
See Engineering: Water Resources; Government-Federal

**INTERNATIONAL COUNCIL OF
SCIENTIFIC UNIONS**
VIA CORNELIO CELSO 7
00161 ROME, ITALY
See Interdisciplinary: General; Research
Institute

ORGANIC CHEMISTRY INSTITUTE
UNIVERSITY OF NAPLES
NAPLES, ITALY
See Chemistry: General; Educational Institute

**PROTECTION OF NATIONAL AND
HISTORICAL SITES AND
MONUMENTS**
VIA MARSALA 8, 00185
ROME, ITALY
See Social Sciences/Humanities: Community Development/Studies; Professional Organizations

ZOOLOGICAL STATION OF NAPLES
NAPLES, ITALY
See Biology: General; Field Station/Laboratory

**ZOOLOGY AND HYDROBIOLOGY
INSTITUTE**
UNIVERSITY OF PERUGIA
PERUGIA, ITALY
See Biology: General; Educational Institute

ZOOLOGY DEPARTMENT
UNIVERSITY OF PADUA
PADUA, ITALY
See Biology: General; Educational Institute

IVORY COAST

**OSTOM-MINISTRE DELA PRODUCE
ANIMALE BP**
18 ABIDJAN, IVORY COAST
See Biology: General; Research Institute

JAMAICA

COCONUT INDUSTRY BOARD
18 WATERLOO ROAD
KINGSTON 10, JAMAICA
See Engineering: Agricultural Engineering; Industrial/Commercial

CORAL REEF PROJECT
UNIVERSITY OF WEST INDIES
UWI KINGSTON, JAMAICA
See Biology: General; Educational Institute

FACULTY OF AGRICULTURE
UNIVERSITY OF THE WEST INDIES
MONA, KINGSTON 7, JAMAICA
See Engineering: Agricultural Engineering; Educational Institute

**FISHERIES DIVISION,
AGRICULTURE AND LANDS
MINISTRY**
FORESHORE RC
KINGSTON, JAMAICA
See Biology: General; Government-Federal

GEOLOGY DEPARTMENT
UNIVERSITY OF WEST INDIES
KINGSTON,JAMAICA
See Geology: General; Educational Institute

MARINE LABORATORY
DEPARTMENT OF ZOOLOGY
PORT ROYAL, JAMAICA
See Biology: General; Government-Federal

PHYSIOLOGY DEPARTMENT
KINGSTON, JAMAICA
See Biology: General; Educational Institute

**ZOOLOGY DEPARTMENT,
KINGSTON HARBOUR RESEARCH
PROJECT**
UNIVERSITY OF THE WEST INDIES
KINGSTON, JAMAICA
See Biology: General; Educational Institute

JAPAN

AGRICULTURAL DEPARTMENT
KYUSHU UNIVERSITY
FUKUOKA, JAPAN
See Engineering: Agricultural Engineering; Educational Institute

**ALGOLOGICAL RESEARCH
INSTITUTE**
HOKKAIDO UNIVERSITY
MURORAN, 051, JAPAN
See Biology: General; Research Institute

ANALYTICAL CHEMISTRY SOCIETY
1-1 MOTO-MACHI
SHIBUYA-KU, TOKYO, JAPAN
See Chemistry: General; Research Institute

**ASTRONOMICAL SOCIETY, TOKYO
ASTRONOMICAL OBSERVATORY**
OSAWA
MITAKA CITY, TOKYO, JAPAN
See Geology: General; Research Institute

ATOMIC ENERGY BUREAU
TOKYO, JAPAN
See Engineering: General; Government-Federal

**ATOMIC INDUSTRIAL FORUM,
TODEN BUILDING**
1-1 TAMURA-CHO SHIBA
MINATO-KU, TOKYO, JAPAN
See Chemistry: General; Research Institute

**BIOGEOLOGICAL SOCIETY
NATIONAL SCIENCES MUSEUM**
UENO PARK
TAITO-KU, TOKYO, JAPAN
See Biology: General; Industrial/Commercial

BIOLOGICAL COLLEGE
HAKKAIDO UNIVERSITY
SAPPORO, JAPAN
See Biology: General; Educational Institute

BIOLOGICAL STATION, USA
KOCHI UNIVERSITY
USA, JAPAN
See Biology: General; Educational Institute

**BIOLOGY LABORATORY OF
IMPERIAL HOUSEHOLD**
IMPERIAL PALACE
CHIYODA-KU, TOKYO, JAPAN
See Biology: General; Research Institute

**BOTANICAL SOCIETY, BOTANY
DEPARTMENT, TOKYO
UNIVERSITY**
1 MOTO-FUJI-CHO
BUNKYO-KU, TOKYO, JAPAN
See Biology: General; Research Institute

**BOTANY DEPARTMENT, SOCIETY
OF PHYCOLOGY**
HOKKAIDO UNIVERSITY NISHI 5-
CHOME
KITA 8-JO, SAPPORO CITY, JAPAN
See Biology: General; Research Institute

CHIBA UNIVERSITY
CHIBA, JAPAN
See Biology: Biochemistry; Educational Institute

DEFENSE AGENCY
JAPANESE MARITIME SELF
DEFENSE
TOKYO, JAPAN
See Social Sciences/Humanities: Employment/Unemployment; Government-Federal

**EARTH CHEMISTRY RESEARCH
ASSOCIATION, EARTH SCIENCE
DEPARTMENT**
NAGOYA UNIVERSITY FURO-CHO
CHIKUSA-KU, NAGOYA, AICHI,
JAPAN
See Geology: Geochemistry; Research Institute

**ECOLOGY SOCIETY, BIOLOGY
DEPARTMENT, TOHOKU
UNIVERSITY**
KATAHIRA-CHO
SENOAI CITY, MIYAGI, JAPAN
See Biology: Ecology; Research Institute

ECONOMIC PLANNING AGENCY
WATER RESOURCES BRANCH
TOKYO, JAPAN
See Engineering: General; Government-Federal

EDUCATION MINISTRY
TOKYO, JAPAN
See Interdisciplinary: General; Unclassified

ENVIRONMENTAL SCIENCE
KOBE UNIVERSITY
KOBE, JAPAN
See Interdisciplinary: General; Educational Institute

**ENVIRONMENTAL SCIENCE,
DEPARTMENT OF SCIENCE**
KANAZAWA UNIVERSITY
NOTO, JAPAN
See Interdisciplinary: General; Educational Institute

ENVIRONMENTAL STUDIES
MIYAZAKI UNIVERSITY
MIYAZAKI, JAPAN
See Interdisciplinary: General; Educational Institute

ENVIRONMENTAL STUDIES
NATIONAL MERCHANT MARINE
UNIVERSITY
KOBE, JAPAN

See Interdisciplinary: General; Educational Institute

ENVIRONMENTAL STUDIES
NATIONAL MERCHANT MARINE
UNIVERSITY
TOKYO, JAPAN
See Interdisciplinary: General; Educational Institute

ENVIRONMENTAL STUDIES
SHIGA UNIVERSITY
OTSU, JAPAN
See Interdisciplinary: General; Educational Institute

**FISHERIES AND ANIMAL
HUSBANDRY FACULTY,
HIROSHIMA UNIVERSITY**
FUKAYASUCHO,
HIROSHIMA PREFECTURE, JAPAN
See Biology: General; Research Institute

FISHERIES COLLEGE
SHIMONOSEKI, JAPAN
See Interdisciplinary: General; Educational Institute

**FISHERIES DEPARTMENT,
AGRICULTURE FACULTY**
HAKOZAKI-MACHI
FUKUOKA, JAPAN
See Biology: General; Educational Institute

**FISHERIES DEPARTMENT,
TOHOKU UNIVERSITY**
KITA 6 BANCHO
SENDAI, JAPAN
See Biology: General; Field Station/Laboratory

**FISHERIES EXPERIMENTAL
STATION**
DEPARTMENT OF AGRICULTURE
TOKYO, JAPAN
See Engineering: Agricultural Engineering; Educational Institute

FISHERIES FACULTY
FISHERIES INSTITUTE
TOKYO, JAPAN
See Biology: General; Educational Institute

FISHERIES FACULTY
KINKI UNIVERSITY
FUSE, JAPAN
See Biology: General; Educational Institute

**FISHERIES FACULTY, PLANKTON
SOCIETY, HOKKAIDO
UNIVERSITY**
MINATO-MACHI
HAKODATE CITY, JAPAN
See Biology: General; Research Institute

FISHERIES INSTITUTE
KAGOSHIMA UNIVERSITY

KAGOSHIMA, JAPAN
See Biology: General; Educational Institute

FISHERIES INSTITUTE
MIYE PREFECTURAL UNIVERSITY
TSU MIYE, JAPAN
See Biology: General; Educational Institute

FISHERIES INSTITUTE
NIHON UNIVERSITY
TOKYO, JAPAN
See Biology: General; Educational Institute

FISHERIES INSTITUTE
OCHANOMIZU WOMEN'S
UNIVERSITY
TOKYO, JAPAN
See Biology: General; Educational Institute

FISHERIES INSTITUTION
NAGASAKI UNIVERSITY
NAGASAKI, JAPAN
See Biology: General; Educational Institute

**FISHERIES RESEARCH
LABORATORY**
NIIGATA, JAPAN
See Biology: General; Government-Federal

FISHERIES STATION
TSUYAZAKI, FUKUOKA, JAPAN
See Biology: General; Educational Institute

FISHERIES, TOKYO UNIVERSITY
5-7-4-CHOME KONAN
MINATOKU, TOKYO, JAPAN
See Biology: General; Unclassified

**FISHERY FACULTY, KAGOSHIMA
UNIVERSITY**
470 SHIMA, ARATA-CHO
KAGOSHIMA, JAPAN
See Biology: General; Educational Institute

GAKUGEI UNIVERSITY
OSAKA, JAPAN
See Interdisciplinary: General; Educational Institute

**GEODETIC SOCIETY, MINISTRY OF
CONSTRUCTION**
1900 7-CHOME KAMIMEGURO
MEGURO-KU, TOKYO, JAPAN
See Geology: General; Research Institute

**GEOGRAPHICAL SURVEY
INSTITUTION**
MINISTRY OF CONSTRUCTION
TOKYO, JAPAN
See Engineering: General; Government-Federal

**GEOGRAPHY DEPARTMENT,
ASSOCIATION QUARTERNARY
RESEARCH**
TOKYO UNIVERSITY I MISSOURI-
TOFUJI-CYO
BUNKYO-KU, TOKYO, JAPAN
See Interdisciplinary: General; Research Institute

GEOLOGICAL SOCIETY OF TOKYO
12 NIBAN-CHO, CHIYODA-KU
TOKYO, JAPAN
See Interdisciplinary: General; Research Institute

**GEOLOGICAL SOCIETY, GEOLOGY
DEPARTMENT**
TOKYO UNIVERSITY 1 MISSOURI-
TOFUJI-CHO
BUNKYO-KU, TOKYO, JAPAN
See Interdisciplinary: General; Research Institute

GEOLOGICAL SURVEY
MINISTRY OF INTERNATIONAL
TRADE AND INDUSTRY
TOKYO, JAPAN
See Geology: General; Government-Federal

**GEOLOGY AND PALEONTOLOGY
INSTITUTE**
TOHOKU UNIVERSITY
SENDAI, JAPAN
See Geology: General; Educational Institute

GEOPHYSICAL INSTITUTE
KYOTO UNIVERSITY
KYOTO, JAPAN
See Geology: Geophysics; Educational Institute

GIMPO WOMEN'S COLLEGE
IGUCHI, HIROSHIMA, JAPAN
See Interdisciplinary: General; Educational Institute

**HAKODATE MARINE
OBSERVATORY**
180 AKAGAWA-DORI, KAMEDA
KAMEDA-GUN, HOKKAIDO, JAPAN
See Biology: General; Field Station/Laboratory

HEALTH AND WELFARE MINISTRY
TOKYO, JAPAN
See Social Sciences/Humanities: Education; Government-Federal

**HOKKAIDO REGIONAL FISHERIES
RESEARCH LABORATORY**
YOICHI, JAPAN
See Biology: General; Government-Federal

**HYDROBIOLOGICAL STATION AT
OTSU**
OTSU, JAPAN
See Biology: General; Educational Institute

**HYDROBIOLOGY STATION,
LIMNOLOGY SOCIETY**
109 KANNONJI-MACHI
OTSU CITY, JAPAN
See Biology: General; Field Station/Laboratory

**ICE AND SNOW STUDIES SOCIETY,
METEOROLOGY AGENCY**
7 1-CHOME OTE-MACHI
CHIYODA-KU, TOKYO, JAPAN
See Chemistry: Physical Chemistry; Research Institute

**INDUSTRIAL RESEARCH
INSTITUTION**
TOKYO, JAPAN
See Engineering: General; Government-Federal

**INDUSTRIAL SCIENCES AND
TECHNOLOGY AGENCY**
TOKYO, JAPAN
See Engineering: General; Government-Federal

**ISHIKAWAJIMA HARIMA
DOCKYARD**
YOKOHAMA, JAPAN
See Interdisciplinary: General; Industrial/Commercial

KANNONZAKI FISHERY MUSEUM
KAMOI-MINAMINON
YOKOSUKA CITY, KANAGAWA,
JAPAN
See Interdisciplinary: General; Professional Organizations

**KATSURAHAMA MARINE SCIENCES
MUSEUM**
778 URADO
KOCHI CITY, KOCHI, JAPAN
See Biology: General; Professional Organizations

**LA SOCIETY FRANCO-JAPONAISE
DES OCEAN**
NICHIFUTSU-KAIKAN3 2-CHOME
KANDA, SURUGADAI, TOKYO,
JAPAN
See Biology: General; Foundation

**LOW TEMPERATURE SCIENCES
INSTITUTE**
HOKKAIDO UNIVERSITY
SAPPORO, JAPAN
See Geology: General; Educational Institute

**MARINE BIOLOGICAL
LABORATORY**
NIIGATA UNIVERSITY
SADO ISLAND, JAPAN
See Biology: General; Educational Institute

**MARINE BIOLOGICAL
LABORATORY**
SOUTHEAST ASIA TREATY
ORGANIZATION

SHIRAHAMA, JAPAN
See Biology: General; Educational Institute

**MARINE BIOLOGICAL
LABORATORY AT AMAKUSA**
TOMIOKA, AMAKUSA
KUMAMOTO 863-25, JAPAN
See Biology: Ecology; Field Station/Laboratory

**MARINE BIOLOGICAL
LABORATORY AT WAGU**
OSAKA UNIVERSITY
WAGU, JAPAN
See Biology: General; Educational Institute

MARINE BIOLOGICAL STATION
KUMAMOTO UNIVERSITY
AITU, JAPAN
See Biology: General; Educational Institute

MARINE BIOLOGICAL STATION
TOHOKU UNIVERSITY
ASAMUSHI, JAPAN
See Biology: General; Educational Institute

**MARINE BIOLOGICAL STATION AT
MISAKI**
MISAKI,KANAGAWA-KEN, JAPAN
See Biology: General; Research Institute

**MARINE BIOLOGICAL STATION AT
OSHORO**
OSHORO, JAPAN
See Biology: General; Educational Institute

**MARINE BIOLOGICAL STATION AT
SHIMODA**
TOKYO UNIVERSITY OF
EDUCATION
SHIMODA, JAPAN
See Biology: General; Educational Institute

**MARINE BIOLOGICAL STATION,
HIROSHIMA UNIVERSITY**
MUKAISHIMA, ONOMICHI P.O.
HIROSHIMA-KEN, JAPAN
See Biology: General; Educational Institute

**MARINE BIOLOGICAL STATION,
TOMANO**
OKAYAMA UNIVERSITY
TAMANO, JAPAN
See Biology: General; Educational Institute

**MARINE FISHERY RESOURCE
RESEARCH CENTER OF JAPAN**
MANDAI BUILDING KHOSIMACHI
TOKYO, JAPAN
See Engineering: Water Resources; Educational Institute

MARINE GEOLOGICAL STATION
TOHOKU UNIVERSITY
SENDAI, JAPAN
See Biology: General; Educational Institute

MARINE LABORATORY
MINAMUJAMATE-MACHI 5
NAGASAKI, JAPAN
See Biology: General; Field Station/Laboratory

**MARINE METEOROLOGY SOCIETY,
KOBE MARINE OBSERVATORY**
7 NAKA YA-MANOTE-DORI
IKUTA-KU, KOBE, HYOGO, JAPAN
See Biology: Biochemistry; Research Institute

**MARINE OBSERVATORY OF
HAKODATE**
HAKODATE, JAPAN
See Engineering: General; Government-Federal

MARINE OBSERVATORY OF KOBE
KOBE, JAPAN
See Engineering: General; Government-Federal

**MARINE OBSERVATORY OF
NAGASAKI**
NAGASAKI, JAPAN
See Geology: General; Government-Federal

MARINE SAFETY ACADEMY
KURE, JAPAN
See Engineering: General; Government-Federal

MARINE SAFETY SCHOOL
MAIZURU, JAPAN
See Engineering: General; Government-Federal

MARINE SCIENCES FACULTY
TOKAI UNIVERSITY
SHIMUZU, SHIZUOKA, JAPAN
See Biology: General; Educational Institute

**MARINE STATION AT
SHIRIGISHINAI**
SHIRIGISHINAI, JAPAN
See Biology: General; Educational Institute

MARITIME SAFETY AGENCY
TOKYO, JAPAN
See Interdisciplinary: General; Unclassified

**METEOROLOGICAL AGENCY,
MARINE DIVISION**
OTEMACHI, CHIYODA-KU
TOKYO, JAPAN
See Biology: General; Research Institute

**METEOROLOGICAL OBSERVATION
AGENCY**
TOKYO, JAPAN
See Geology: General; Government-Federal

**METEOROLOGICAL RESEARCH
INSTITUTE**
TOKYO, JAPAN
See Geology: General; Government-Federal

**METEOROLOGICAL SCIENCES
RESEARCH INSTITUTION**
OCEANOGRAPHIC LABORATORY
NAGASAKI, JAPAN
See Interdisciplinary: General; Educational Institute

**NAIKAI REGIONAL FISHERIES,
RESOURCES LABORATORY**
UJINA
HIROSHIMA, JAPAN
See Biology: General; Field Station/Laboratory

NATIONAL HEALTH LABORATORY
TOKYO, JAPAN
See Biology: Biochemistry; Government-Federal

**NAUTICAL SOCIETY OF JAPAN,
TOKYO UNIVERSITY**
ETCHUJIMA-MACHI FUKAGAWA
KOTOKU, TOKYO, JAPAN
See Engineering: General; Field Station/Laboratory

**NIHON FISHERIES PROMOTION
SOCIETY**
15-CHOME TSUKIJI CHOU-KU
TOKYO, JAPAN
See Biology: General; Foundation

NIPPON SUISAN KAISHA, LIMITED
NIPPON BUILDING, 2-6-2
OTEMACHI
CHIYODA-KU, TOKYO, JAPAN
See Engineering: General; Industrial/Commercial

**OCEANOGRAPHIC RESEARCH
STATION**
TOKYO UNIVERSITY
TOKYO, JAPAN
See Biology: General; Educational Institute

PEARL RESEARCH LABORATORY
AKO MIE, JAPAN
See Biology: General; Government-Federal

**PHYSICS AND CHEMISTRY
RESEARCH INSTITUTE**
TOKYO, JAPAN
See Chemistry: Physical Chemistry; Educational Institute

POLAR SECTION, NATURAL SCIENCES MUSEUM
UENO PARK
TAITO-KU, TOKYO, JAPAN
See Biology: General; Foundation

PORT AND HARBOR RESEARCH INSTITUTE
1-1 3-CHOME NAGASE
YOKOSUKA, JAPAN
See Engineering: General; Government-Federal

RADIATION RESEARCH SOCIETY OF JAPAN
250 KUROSUNA-MACHI
CHIABA CITY, CHIBA, JAPAN
See Physics: General; Research Institute

RESEARCH LABORATORY, HOKKAIDO
HAMMANAKA, YOICHI
HOKKAIDO, JAPAN
See Biology: General; Research Institute

RESOURCE CENTER FOR DISASTER PREVENTION, (NATIONAL)
15-1, GINZA 6-CHOME
CHUO-KU, TOKYO 104, JAPAN
See Interdisciplinary: General; Unclassified

RESOURCE LABORATORIES
KOMINATO FISHERIES
KOMINATO, JAPAN
See Biology: General; Educational Institute

RESOURCES RESEARCH INSTITUTE
KAWAGUCHI, JAPAN
See Engineering: General; Government-Federal

SALT SCIENCES CENTRAL RESEARCH INSTITUTION
1390 2-CHOME TOYOMACHI
SHINAGAWA-KU, TOKYO, JAPAN
See Biology: Biochemistry; Research Institute

SANYO HYDROGRAPHIC COMPANY
23-7 5-CHOME SHINBASHI
MINATO-KU, TOKYO, JAPAN
See Engineering: General; Industrial/Commercial

SCIENCE AND FISHERIES SOCIETY, TOKYO UNIVERSITY OF FISHERIES
6-CHOME SHIBA KAIGAN-DORI
MINATO-KU, TOKYO, JAPAN
See Biology: General; Research Institute

SCIENCE AND TECHNOLOGY AGENCY
TOKYO, JAPAN
See Engineering: General; Government-Federal

SEA DISASTER RESEARCH FACILITY
APPLIED DYNAMICS RESEARCH INSTITUTE
TSUYAZARI, FURUORO, JAPAN
See Interdisciplinary: General; Educational Institute

SEA EXPERIMENT STATION
SCIENCES DEPARTMENT
AMAKUSA, JAPAN
See Biology: General; Educational Institute

SEIKAI REGIONAL FISHERIES RESEARCH LABORATORY
NAGASAKI, JAPAN
See Biology: General; Government-Federal

SEISMOLOGICAL SOCIETY GEOPHYSICS DEPARTMENT
UNIVERSITY TOKYO 2-YAYOI-CHO
BUNKYO-KU, TOKYO, JAPAN
See Geology: Geophysics; Research Institute

SEISMOLOGY AND EARTHQUAKE ENGINEERING INSTITUTE
4-CHOME, HYAKUNIN-CHO
SHINJUKUKU, TOKYO, JAPAN
See Geology: General; Research Institute

SETO MARINE BIOLOGICAL LABORATORY, KYOTO UNIVERSITY
SETO 3- CHOME SHIRAHAMA
WAKAYAMA PREFECTURE, JAPAN
See Biology: General; Field Station/Laboratory

SHIP TECHNICAL RESEARCH INSTITUTION
TOKYO, JAPAN
See Engineering: General; Government-Federal

SUISAN ZOSHOKU DANWAKAI FISHERIES-VETSCI
HIROSHIMA UNIVERSITY DAIMON-CHO
FUKUYAMA CITY, HIROSHIMA, JAPAN
See Biology: General; Research Institute

TERRESTRIAL ELECTRO-MAGNETISM SOCIETY
TOKYO UNIVERSITY 3 YAYOI-CHO
BUNKYO-KU, TOKYO, JAPAN
See Geology: Geophysics; Research Institute

TOHOKU REGIONAL FISHERIES RESEARCH LABORATORY
SHIOGAMA, JAPAN
See Biology: General; Government-Federal

TOKAI REGIONAL FISHERIES RESEARCH LABORATORY
TOKYO, JAPAN

See Biology: General; Government-Federal

UENO ZOO AQUARIUM
UENO PARK
TAITO-KU, TOKYO, JAPAN
See Interdisciplinary: General; Professional Organizations

VOLCANO SOCIETY, EARTHQUAKE RESEARCH INSTITUTE
TOKYO UNIVERSITY 1 MOTOFUJI-CHO
BUNKYO-KU, TOKYO, JAPAN
See Geology: General; Research Institute

WHALE RESEARCH INSTITUTION
12-4 NISHIKAIGANDORI
TSUKISHIMAI CHOUKU, TOKYO, JAPAN
See Biology: General; Research Institute

KENYA

EAST AFRICA OIL REFINERIES, LIMITED
MOMBASA, KENYA
See Social Sciences/Humanities: Industrial Development; Industrial/Commercial

FISHERIES DEPARTMENT, MINISTRY OF TOURISM AND WILDLIFE
POST OFFICE BOX 30027
NAIROBI, KENYA
See Biology: General; Government-Federal

RESEARCH STATION
POST OFFICE BOX 1146
MOMBASA, KENYA
See Biology: General; Field Station/Laboratory

RESEARCH STATION
POST OFFICE BOX 12
MALINDI, KENYA
See Biology: General; Field Station/Laboratory

ZOOLOGY DEPARTMENT
UNIVERSITY COLLEGE
NAIROBI, KENYA
See Biology: General; Educational Institute

KOREA

AGRICULTURE AND FORESTRY MINISTRY
OFFICE OF FISHERIES

SEOUL, KOREA
See Engineering: General; Government-Federal

FISHERIES COLLEGE AT PUSAN, PUSAN NATIONAL UNIVERSITY
559 DAE YONG DONG
PUSAN, KOREA
See Biology: General; Educational Institute

FISHERIES RESEARCH AND DEVELOPMENT AGENCY
CHEJU REGIONAL BRANCH
CHEJU, KOREA
See Biology: General; Government-Federal

FISHERIES RESEARCH AND DEVELOPMENT AGENCY
EAST COAST REGIONAL BRANCH
POHANG, KOREA
See Biology: General; Government-Federal

FISHERIES RESEARCH AND DEVELOPMENT AGENCY
SOUTH COAST REGION BRANCH
MOKPO, KOREA
See Biology: General; Government-Federal

FISHERIES RESEARCH AND DEVELOPMENT AGENCY
WEST COAST REGION BRANCH
KUNSAN, KOREA
See Biology: General; Government-Federal

FISHERIES RESEARCH AND DEVELOPMENT AGENCY
16 2-KA NAM KANG DONE
PUSAN, KOREA
See Biology: General; Government-Federal

MARINE BIOLOGY STATION
SEOUL NATIONAL UNIVERSITY
SEOUL, KOREA
See Biology: General; Educational Institute

SCIENCE AND TECHNOLOGY INSTITUTE OF KOREA
9-CHONG-RO 2-KA CHONGRO-KU
POBOX 38,KWANG-KWANMOON, KOREA
See Interdisciplinary: General; Research Institute

SCIENCE AND TECHNOLOGY MINISTRY
SEOUL, KOREA
See Interdisciplinary: General; Unclassified

WATER RESOURCE INSTITUTE
CHUNG-KU COLLEGE
TAEBU, KOREA
See Engineering: General; Educational Institute

KUWAIT

ARABIAN OIL COMPANY
POST OFFICE BOX 1641
KUWAIT
See Biology: General; Industrial/Commercial

FINANCE AND OIL MINISTRY
KUWAIT
See Engineering: General; Government-Federal

GULF FISHERIES BRANCH
POST OFFICE BOX 3389
KUWAIT
See Biology: General; Industrial/Commercial

INTERNATIONAL FISHERIES CORPORATION
POST OFFICE BOX 1262
KUWAIT
See Biology: General; Industrial/Commercial

KUWAIT NATIONAL FISHERIES COMPANY
POST OFFICE BOX 3663
KUWAIT
See Biology: General; Industrial/Commercial

PUBLIC WORKS MINISTRY
KUWAIT
See Biology: General; Government-Federal

SHELL OIL CORPORATION
POST OFFICE BOX 1641
KUWAIT
See Geology: General; Industrial/Commercial

LEBANON

BIOLOGY DEPARTMENT
AMERICAN UNIVERSITY OF BEIRUT
BEIRUT, LEBANON
See Biology: General; Government-Federal

FISHERIES AND WILDLIFE SECTION
DEPARTMENT OF FORESTS AND NATURAL RESOURCES
BEIRUT, LEBANON
See Biology: General; Government-Federal

FORESTS AND NATIONAL RESOURCES DEPARTMENT, AGRICULTURE MINISTRY

BEIRUT, LEBANON
See Biology: General; Government-Federal

LIBERIA

FISHERIES BUREAU, AGRICULTURAL DEPARTMENT
SUACCO, GBARNGA
CENTRAL PROVINCE, LIBERIA
See Biology: General; Government-Federal

LIBERIA COLD STORES
MONROVIA, LIBERIA
See Biology: General; Industrial/Commercial

MARINE BIOLOGY DEPARTMENT, DIVISION OF SCIENCE
UNIVERSITY OF LIBERIA
MONROVIA, LIBERIA
See Biology: General; Educational Institute

LIBYA

ENVIRONMENTAL STUDIES
UNIVERSITY OF LIBYA
TRIPOLI, LIBYA
See Engineering: Agricultural Engineering; Educational Institute

FISHERIES DEPARTMENT
INDUSTRIAL MINISTRY
TRIPOLI, LIBYA
See Biology: General; Government-Federal

MARINE CATCH OFFICE
BENGHAZI, LIBYA
See Biology: General; Government-Federal

MALAGASY REPUBLIC

FISHERIES SERVICE
AGRICULTURAL MINISTRY
TANANARIVE, MALAGASY REPUBLIC
See Social Sciences/Humanities: Industrial Development; Government-Federal

ORGANIZATION OF OVERSEAS
   SCIENCE AND TECHNOLOGICAL
   STATION
TANANARIVE, MALAGASY
REPUBLIC
See Biology: General; Research Institute

SCIENCE AND TECHNOLOGY
   FACULTY
UNIVERSITY OF MADAGASCAR
TANANARIVE, MALAGASY
REPUBLIC
See Biology: General; Educational Insti-
   tute

MALAYSIA

AGRICULTURE AND FISHERIES
   (SABAH STATE MINISTRY OF)
JESSELTON, MALAYSIA
See Engineering: General; Government-
   Federal

FISHERIES AND INDUSTRIES
   COMPANY LIMITED OF SABAH
POST OFFICE BOX 591
SANDAKAN, SABAH, MALAYSIA
See Engineering: General; Industrial/
   Commercial

FISHERIES COLLEGE
PENANG, MALAYSIA
See Biology: General; Educational Insti-
   tute

FISHERIES DEPARTMENT
KUALA LUMPUR, MALAYSIA
See Biology: General; Government-Fed-
   eral

FISHERIES RESEARCH INSTITUTE
CALTHROP ROAD
PENANG, MALAYSIA
See Biology: General; Research Institute

FISHERIES RESEARCH
   INSTITUTION
GLUGOR
PENANG, MALAYSIA
See Biology: General; Government-Fed-
   eral

FISHING COMPANY OF NORTH
   BORNEO
POST OFFICE BOX 591
SAN AAKAN, SABAH, MALAYSIA
See Engineering: General; Industrial/
   Commercial

GENERAL FOOD PROCESSING
   COMPANY, LIMITED
16 KOTA ROAD
TAIPING, PERAK, MALAYSIA
See Engineering: General; Industrial/
   Commercial

GEOLOGY DEPARTMENT
UNIVERSITY OF MALAYA
KUALA LUMPUR, MALAYSIA
See Geology: General; Educational Insti-
   tute

LAND AND MINE MINISTRY
KUALA LUMPUR, MALAYSIA
See Interdisciplinary: General; Unclassi-
   fied

MARINE FISHERIES OFFICE
KUCHING, MALAYSIA
See Biology: General; Government-Fed-
   eral

MARINE FISHERIES SCHOOLS
PENANG AND KUALA
TRENGGANU, MALAYSIA
See Biology: General; Educational Insti-
   tute

MARINE INDUSTRIAL LIMITED OF
   MALAYSIA
RIVER ROAD
PENANG, MALAYSIA
See Engineering: General; Industrial/
   Commercial

SHELL PETROLEUM COMPANY
C/O BRUNEI SHELL PETROLEUM
SERIA, BRUNEI, MALAYSIA
See Engineering: General; Industrial/
   Commercial

TRANSPORTATION MINISTRY
ECONOMIC PLANNING UNIT
KUALA LUMPUR, MALAYSIA
See Social Sciences/Humanities: Commu-
   nity Development/Studies; Govern-
   ment-Federal

MAURITANIA

AMERICAN INTERNATIONAL OIL
   COMPANY
NOVAKCHOTT, MAURITANIA
See Social Sciences/Humanities: Indus-
   trial Development; Industrial/Com-
   mercial

INDUSTRY AND MINING HIGH
   COMMISSION
NOVAKCHOTT, MAURITANIA
See Interdisciplinary: General; Unclassi-
   fied

MARINE FISHERIES LABORATORY
PORT-ETIENNE, MAURITANIA
See Biology: General; Field Station/Lab-
   oratory

MARITIME AUTHORITY
PORT-ETIENNE, MAURITANIA
See Biology: General; Government-Fed-
   eral

MERCHANT MARINE AND SEA
   FISHERIES DIRECTORATE
NOVAKCHOTT, MAURITANIA
See Biology: General; Government-Fed-
   eral

PLANET OIL COMPANY
NOVAKCHOTT, MAURITANIA
See Social Sciences/Humanities: Industrial Development; Industrial/Com-
   mercial

MAURITIUS

AGRICULTURAL AND NATURAL
   RESOURCE MINISTRY
LE REDUIT
PORT LOUIS, MAURITIUS
See Social Sciences/Humanities: Agricul-
   ture; Government-Federal

FISHERIES DIVISION
REDUIT
REDUIT, MAURITIUS
See Biology: General; Government-Fed-
   eral

MAURITIUS INSTITUTE
BP 54
PORT LOUIS, MAURITIUS
See Biology: Ecology; Research Institute

MEXICO

CARLOS R DE ALBA P OCEAN
POST OFFICE BOX 453
ENSENADA, MEXICO
See Biology: General; Educational Insti-
   tute

ENVIRONMENTAL POLLUTION
6104 NORTE 74 COLUMBIA
   SANCHEZ
MEXICO CITY, MEXICO
See Engineering: Pollution Abatement;
   Research Institute

FISHERIES
AVENUE CUAUHTEMOC 80
MEXICO 7 DF, MEXICO
See Biology: General; Government-Fed-
   eral

FISHERIES DEPARTMENT AND
   ALLIED INDUSTRIAL
   BIOLOGICAL LABORATORY
AQUILES, SERDAN 28 40 PISO
MEXICO 1 DF, MEXICO
See Biology: General; Industrial/Com-
   mercial

GEOLOGY INSTITUTE, INSTITUTE OF APPLIED SCIENCE
CIUDAD UNIVERSITARIA
MEXICO 20, DF, MEXICO
See Biology: General; Educational Institute

GUAYMAS SUB-STATION
SONORA, MEXICO
See Biology: General; Government-Federal

HYDROBIOLOGY LABORATORY, INSTITUTE OF BIOLOGY
CIUDAD UNIVERSITARIA
MEXICO 20, OF, MEXICO
See Biology: General; Educational Institute

ISLA MUJERES SUB-STATION
QUINTANA ROO, MEXICO
See Biology: General; Government-Federal

LIGHTHOUSES AND HYDROLOGY
MEXICO 1, DF, MEXICO
See Biology: General; Government-Federal

MARINE AND FOOD SCIENCES SCHOOL
MONTEREY INSTITUTE OF TECHNOLOGY
GUAYMAS, SONORA, MEXICO
See Biology: General; Educational Institute

MARINE BIOLOGICAL STATION
TAMPICO
TEMAULIPAS, MEXICO
See Biology: General; Government-Federal

MARINE BIOLOGICAL STATION AT CAMPECHE
CAMPECHE, MEXICO
See Biology: General; Government-Federal

MARINE SCIENCE SCHOOL, UNIVERSITY OF BAJA CALIFORNIA
CALLE PRIMERA 1838
ENSENADA, MEXICO
See Biology: General; Educational Institute

MARINE SCIENCES AND TECHNOLOGY NATIONAL CENTER
AODO 512 VERACRUZ
VERACRUZ, MEXICO
See Biology: General; Government-Federal

MAZATLAN MARINE BIOLOGICAL STATION
PALACIO FEDERAL
MAZATLAN, SINALOA, MEXICO
See Biology: General; Government-Federal

NACIONAL DE PESCA INSTITUTO
BIBLIOTECA
CHIAPAS 121, MEXICO CITY 7, DF, MEXICO
See Biology: General; Government-Federal

PETROLEOS MEXICANOS
JUAREZ 92,
MEXICO 1, DF, MEXICO
See Biology: General; Industrial/Commercial

MONACO

OCEANOGRAPHY MUSEUM OF MONACO
MONTE CARLO, MONACO
See Interdisciplinary: General; Foundation

SCIENTIFIC EXPLORATION OF THE MEDITERRANEAN, INTERNATIONAL COMMISSION
16 BUILDING DE SUISSE
MONTE CARLO, MONACO
See Biology: Ecology; Research Institute

MOROCCO

EXXON EXPLORATION
22 RUE D'AZRO
RABAT, MOROCCO
See Social Sciences/Humanities: Industrial Development; Industrial/Commercial

MARINE FISHERIES INSTITUTION OF MOROCCO
RUE DE TIZNIT
CASABLANCA, MOROCCO
See Biology: General; Research Institute

SCIENCE INSTITUTE, RABAT UNIVERSITY
AVENUE MOULAY CHERIF
RABAT, MOROCCO
See Biology: General; Research Institute

MOZAMBIQUE

MARINE BIOLOGY AND FISHERIES MISSION
CP 1723

LOURENCO MARQUES, MOZAMBIQUE
See Biology: General; Government-Federal

MARITIME SERVICES
CP 262
LOURENCO MARQUES, MOZAMBIQUE
See Biology: General; Government-Federal

SCIENCES RESEARCH INSTITUTE
CP 1780
LOURENCO MARQUES, MOZAMBIQUE
See Interdisciplinary: General; Unclassified

NETHERLANDS

ANALYTICAL CHEMISTRY LABORATORY
NEIUWE ACHTERGRACHT 125
AMSTERDAM-C, NETHERLANDS
See Chemistry: General; Educational Institute

BIOLOGICAL SCIENCES INTERNATIONAL UNION, BOTANISCH MUSEUM
LANGE NIEUWSTRAAT 106
UTRECHT, NETHERLANDS
See Biology: General; Research Institute

BIOMETEOROLOGY INTERNATIONAL SOCIETY
HOFBROUCKERLAAN 54 OEGSTG
LEIDEN, NETHERLANDS
See Biology: General; Research Institute

CITY AND REGIONAL PLANNERS SOCIETY
VAN DER LELYSTRAAT 18
DELFT, NETHERLANDS
See Social Sciences/Humanities: Regional Planning; Government-State or Local

FISHERIES INVESTIGATION INSTITUTE
HARINGKAPE 1, POST OFFICE BOX 68
IJMUIDEN, NETHERLANDS
See Biology: General; Government-Federal

GEOLOGY DEPARTMENT
UNIVERSITY OF LEIDEN
LEIDEN, NETHERLANDS
See Geology: General; Educational Institute

GEOPHYSICS DIVISION
KON NED MET INSTITUTION

DE BIUT, NETHERLANDS
See Physics: General; Educational Institute

HOUSING AND PLANNING FEDERATION
43 WASSENAARSWEG,
THE HAGUE, NETHERLANDS
See Social Sciences/Humanities: Housing; Foundation

METEOROLOGY AND OCEANOGRAPHY DEPARTMENT, FREE UNIVERSITY
DE BOELELAAN
AMSTERDAM, NETHERLANDS
See Physics: General; Educational Institute

SEA RESEARCH INSTITUTE
BUITENHAVEN 27
DEN HELDER, NETHERLANDS
See Biology: General; Government-Federal

SOIL SCIENCE INTERNATIONAL SOCIETY, ROYAL TROPICAL INSTITUTE
63 MAURITSKADE
AMSTERDAM, NETHERLANDS
See Biology: Ecology; Research Institute

TAXONOMIC BOTANY
UNIVERSITY OF LEIDEN
LEIDEN, NETHERLANDS
See Biology: Ecology; Educational Institute

NEW CALEDONIA

OCEANOGRAPHIQUE CENTER
O R S T O M BP
4-NOUMEA, NEW CALEDONIA
See Biology: General; Research Institute

NEW GUINEA

FISHERIES DEPARTMENT
KONEDOBU
PAPUA, NEW GUINEA
See Biology: General; Government-State or Local

MARINE BIOLOGICAL STATION
KANUDI TATANA ROAD
PORT MORESBY, NEW GUINEA
See Biology: General; Government-State or Local

NEW ZEALAND

AUCKLAND MUSEUM
NEWMARKET
AUCKLAND, NEW ZEALAND
See Interdisciplinary: General; Foundation

BOTANY DEPARTMENT
AUCKLAND UNIVERSITY
AUCKLAND, NEW ZEALAND
See Biology: Ecology; Educational Institute

COMMERCIAL FISHERMEN FEDERATION OF NEW ZEALAND
5857 P O BOX 597
CHRISTCHURCH, NEW ZEALAND
See Engineering: General; Industrial/Commercial

ENVIRONMENTAL STUDIES, UNIVERSITY OF OTAGO
POST OFFICE BOX 56
DUNEDIN, NEW ZEALAND
See Interdisciplinary: General; Educational Institute

FISHERIES AND MERCHANTS ASSOCIATION OF NEW ZEALAND
POST OFFICE BOX 857
WELLINGTON, NEW ZEALAND
See Engineering: General; Industrial/Commercial

FISHERIES RESEARCH LABORATORY MARINE LABORATORY
WELLINGTON, NEW ZEALAND
See Biology: General; Research Institute

GEOPHYSICS DIVISION, SCIENCE AND INDUSTRIAL RESEARCH DEPARTMENT
156 THE TERRACE
WELLINGTON, NEW ZEALAND
See Geology: Geophysics; Government-Federal

INDUSTRIAL RESEARCH, OCEANOGRAPHIC INSTITUTION
177 THORNDON QUAY
WELLINGTON, NEW ZEALAND
See Biology: General; Government-Federal

LINCOLN COLLEGE
CANTERBURY, NEW ZEALAND
See Engineering: General; Educational Institute

MARINE DEPARTMENT, FISHERIES RESEARCH DIVISION
327 WILLIS STREET
WELLINGTON, NEW ZEALAND
See Biology: General; Government-Federal

MARINE LABORATORY, EAST PERCIVAL
UNIVERSITY OF CANTERBURY
KAIOURA, MARLBOROUGH, NEW ZEALAND
See Biology: General; Educational Institute

MARINE RESEARCH LABORATORY, AUCKLAND UNIVERSITY
LEIGH, AUCKLAND PROVINCE, NEW ZEALAND
See Interdisciplinary: General; Educational Institute

MARINE STATION AT VICTORIA UNIVERSITY
ISLAND BAY
WELLINGTON, NEW ZEALAND
See Biology: General; Educational Institute

MARINE STATION, UNIVERSITY OF OTAGO
PORTOBELLO
DUNEDIN, NEW ZEALAND
See Interdisciplinary: General; Field Station/Laboratory

OCEANOGRAPHIC INSTITUTE OF NEW ZEALAND
D S I R BOX 8009
WELLINGTON, NEW ZEALAND
See Geology: General; Research Institute

ZOOLOGY DEPARTMENT, UNIVERSITY OF CANTERBURY
PRIVATE BAG
CHRISTCHURCH, NEW ZEALAND
See Biology: General; Educational Institute

ZOOLOGY DEPARTMENT, VICTORIA UNIVERSITY
POST OFFICE BOX 169
WELLINGTON, NEW ZEALAND
See Biology: General; Unclassified

NICARAGUA

ALIMENTOS INTERAMERICANOS, SOUTH AMERICA
CORINTO, NICARAGUA
See Biology: General; Industrial/Commercial

BOOTH NICARAGUA, SOUTH AMERICA
EL BLUFF, NICARAGUA
See Biology: General; Industrial/Commercial

ECONOMICS AND NATIONAL RESOURCES MINISTRY
MANAGUA, NICARAGUA

See Biology: General; Government-Federal

FISHERIES SECTION
NATIONAL DEVELOPMENT
INSTITUTE
MANAGUA, NICARAGUA
See Biology: General; Government-Federal

LANGOSTERA DE CARIBE, INCORPORATED
CORN ISLAND, NICARAGUA
See Biology: General; Industrial/Commercial

PESCANIA, SOUTH AMERICA
BLUEFIELDS, NICARAGUA
See Biology: General; Industrial/Commercial

RENEWABLE RESOURCES
MINISTRY OF AGRICULTURE
MANAGUA, NICARAGUA
See Biology: General; Government-Federal

WILLS BOWERS, INCORPORATED
CORN ISLAND, NICARAGUA
See Biology: General; Industrial/Commercial

NIGERIA

AGRICULTURAL AND NATURAL RESOURCES MINISTRY
INDEPENDENCE BUILDING
LAGOS, NIGERIA
See Social Sciences/Humanities: Agriculture; Government-Federal

AGRICULTURE AND RESOURCE MINISTRY OF WESTERN NIGERIA
IBADAN, NIGERIA
See Interdisciplinary: General; Government-State or Local

AMERICAN OVERSEAS PETROLEUM LIMITED
8-10 BROAD STREET, PO BOX 1986
LAGOS, NIGERIA
See Social Sciences/Humanities: Industrial Development; Industrial/Commercial

BAROID OF NIGERIA LIMITED
3 INDUSTRY ROAD, PO BOX 404
PORT HARCOURT, NIGERIA
See Social Sciences/Humanities: Industrial Development; Industrial/Commercial

BIOLOGICAL SCIENCE SCHOOL
UNIVERSITY OF LAGOS
LAGOS (YABA), NIGERIA

See Biology: General; Educational Institute

BRITISH PETROLEUM, CONTINENTAL OIL CORPORATION
3-10 BROAD STREET, PO BOX 1253
LAGOS, NIGERIA
See Social Sciences/Humanities: Industrial Development; Industrial/Commercial

CORE LABORATORIES,INCORPORATED
7 PORT HARCOURT/ABA ROAD
PMB 5148, PORT HARCOURT, NIGERIA
See Social Sciences/Humanities: Industrial Development; Industrial/Commercial

DIVCON INTERNATIONAL
FEDERAL PALACE HOTEL, VICTORIA ISLE
POB 3720, LAGOS, NIGERIA
See Social Sciences/Humanities: Industrial Development; Industrial/Commercial

EASTMAN OIL WELL SURVEY COMPANY
SERVICES AND SUPPLY
CORPORATION WASHINGTON, LIMITED
POB 387, PORT HARCOURT, NIGERIA
See Social Sciences/Humanities: Industrial Development; Industrial/Commercial

ENERGY AND MINERAL RESOURCES MINISTRY
LAGOS, NIGERIA
See Geology: General; Government-Federal

EXXON WEST AFRICA, INCORPORATED
8-10 BROAD STREET, PO BOX 176
LAGOS, NIGERIA
See Social Sciences/Humanities: Industrial Development; Industrial/Commercial

FEDERAL FISHERIES SERVICES
VICTORIA BH, PMB 12529
LAGOS, NIGERIA
See Biology: General; Government-Federal

FISHERIES DIVISION OF EAST NIGERIA
PMB 1027
ABA, NIGERIA
See Biology: General; Government-Federal

GLOBAL MARINE EUROPA
127-129 BROAD STREET, PO BOX 3634

LAGOS, NIGERIA
See Social Sciences/Humanities: Industrial Development; Industrial/Commercial

GREAT BASINS PETROLEUM COMPANY LIMITED
1-9 BERKLEY STREET, PO BOX 1236
LAGOS, NIGERIA
See Social Sciences/Humanities: Industrial Development; Industrial/Commercial

GUIBERSON (DRESSER INDUSTRIAL)
POST OFFICE BOX 5123
PORT HARCOURT, NIGERIA
See Social Sciences/Humanities: Industrial Development; Industrial/Commercial

HALLIBURTON LIMITED
TRANSPORATATION-AMADI
ESTATE, PO BOX 462
PORT HARCOURT, NIGERIA
See Social Sciences/Humanities: Industrial Development; Industrial/Commercial

INTERNATIONAL DRILLING COMPANY
POST OFFICE BOX 538
PORT HARCOURT, NIGERIA
See Social Sciences/Humanities: Industrial Development; Industrial/Commercial

LANE WELLS DIVISION
PMB 5186
PORT HARCOURT, NIGERIA
See Social Sciences/Humanities: Industrial Development; Industrial/Commercial

MACOBAR DIVISION OF DRESSER A G (ZUG)
PMB 5123
PORT HARCOURT, NIGERIA
See Social Sciences/Humanities: Industrial Development; Industrial/Commercial

MARINE SECTION
PORT HARCOURT, NIGERIA
See Biology: General; Government-Federal

MC DERMOTT OVERSEAS, INCORPORATED
1-9 BERKLEY STREET, PO BOX 2841
LAGOS, NIGERIA
See Social Sciences/Humanities: Industrial Development; Industrial/Commercial

METEOROLOGICAL SERVICES HEADQUARTERS
35 BROWN ROAD
IKOYI, LAGOS, NIGERIA
See Biology: General; Field Station/Laboratory

**MILCHEM INTERNATIONAL
LIMITED**
4 AZIKIWE ROAD, PO BOX 669
PORT HARCOURT, NIGERIA
See Social Sciences/Humanities: Industrial Development; Industrial/Commercial

MOBIL OIL NIGERIA LIMITED
60 BROAD STREET, PMB 2054
LAGOS, NIGERIA
See Social Sciences/Humanities: Industrial Development; Industrial/Commercial

NIGERIAN GULF OIL COMPANY
TINUBU SQUARE,PMB 2469
LAGOS, NIGERIA
See Social Sciences/Humanities: Industrial Development; Industrial/Commercial

**NIGERIAN PETROLEUM REFINING
CORPORATION, LIMITED**
PORT HARCOURT, NIGERIA
See Social Sciences/Humanities: Industrial Development; Industrial/Commercial

OTIS OF NIGERIA LIMITED
11 AZiKIWE ROAD, PO BOX 462
PORT HARCOURT, NIGERIA
See Social Sciences/Humanities: Industrial Development; Industrial/Commercial

**PHILIPS PETROLEUM
CORPORATION**
8-10 BROAD STREET, PMB 12612
LAGOS, NIGERIA
See Social Sciences/Humanities: Industrial Development; Industrial/Commercial

SANTA FE DRILLING COMPANY
6 PORT HARCOURT/ABA ROAD
PMB 5019, PORT HARCOURT,
NIGERIA
See Social Sciences/Humanities: Industrial Development; Industrial/Commercial

SEISMOGRAPH SERVICES LIMITED
POST OFFICE BOX 607
ABA, NIGERIA
See Geology: General; Industrial/Commercial

**SHELL-BRITISH PETROLEUM, SE
DRILL CORPORATION**
POST OFFICE BOX 802
PORT HARCOURT, NIGERIA
See Social Sciences/Humanities: Industrial Development; Industrial/Commercial

**TENNECO OIL CORPORATION OF
NIGERIA**
8-10 BROAD STREET, PO BOX 2119
LAGOS, NIGERIA

See Social Sciences/Humanities: Industrial Development; Industrial/Commercial

TEXACO AFRICA LIMITED
241 IGBOSERE ROAD, PO BOX 166
LAGOS, NIGERIA
See Social Sciences/Humanities: Industrial Development; Industrial/Commercial

TIDELAND SIGNAL CORPORATION
SERVICES AND SUPPLY OF WEST
 AFRICA
POB 387, PORT HARCOURT,
NIGERIA
See Social Sciences/Humanities: Industrial Development; Industrial/Commercial

TIDEX (NIGERIA) LIMITED
34 FRANCIS IHEKWOABA STREET
PMB 5187, PORT HARCOURT,
NIGERIA
See Social Sciences/Humanities: Industrial Development; Industrial/Commercial

**TRANSWORLD DRILLING
CORPORATION LIMITED**
21-25 BROAD STREET, P O BOX 3651
LAGOS, NIGERIA
See Social Sciences/Humanities: Industrial Development; Industrial/Commercial

**UNITED GEOPHYSICS
CORPORATION**
TINUBU SQUARE, POST OFFICE
 BOX 3545
LAGOS, NIGERIA
See Geology: General; Industrial/Commercial

**WESTERN NIGERIA COOPERATIVE
FISHERIES ASSOCIATION**
IJORA
LAGOS, NIGERIA
See Social Sciences/Humanities: Industrial Development; Industrial/Commercial

WILLIAMS BROTHERS COMPANY
MILE 101/2 ABA ROAD, PO BOX 649
PORT HARCOURT, NIGERIA
See Social Sciences/Humanities: Industrial Development; Industrial/Commercial

NORTHERN IRELAND

**AGRICULTURAL BOTANY
 DEPARTMENT**
QUEEN'S UNIVERSITY
BT9/N BELFAST 6BB, NORTHERN
IRELAND

See Engineering: Agricultural Engineering; Educational Institute

**AGRICULTURAL RESOURCE
INSTITUTE OF NORTHERN
IRELAND**
HILLSBOROUGH, COUNTY DOWN,
NORTHERN IRELAND
See Engineering: Agricultural Engineering; Research Institute

**BIOLOGICAL AND
ENVIRONMENTAL SCIENCES
SCHOOL**
UNIVERSITY OF ULSTER
COLERAINE, COUNTY
LONDONDERRY, NORTHERN
IRELAND
See Biology: Ecology; Educational Institute

**RESOURCES AND DEVELOPMENT,
GALLAHER LIMITED**
HENRY STREET
BELFAST BT 15 1JE, NORTHERN
IRELAND
See Engineering: Agricultural Engineering; Research Institute

NORWAY

**CHRISTIAN MICHELSENS
INSTITUTE**
NYGARDSGATEN 114
BERGEN, NORWAY
See Physics: General; Research Institute

GEOLOGY INSTITUTION
UNIVERSITY OF BERGEN
BERGEN, NORWAY
See Geology: General; Educational Institute

GEOPHYSICS INSTITUTE
UNIVERSITY OF OSLO
OSLO, NORWAY
See Geology: Geophysics; Unclassified

**GEOTECHNICAL INSTITUTE OF
NORWAY**
OSLO, NORWAY
See Engineering: General; Field Station/
Laboratory

LIMNOLOGY DEPARTMENT
UNIVERSITY OF OSLO
OSLO, NORWAY
See Biology: General; Educational Institute

MARINE BIOLOGY DEPARTMENT
UNIVERSITY OF OSLO
OSLO, NORWAY
See Biology: General; Educational Institute

MARINE BIOLOGY STATION
UNIVERSITY OF BERGEN
N-5065 BLOMSTERDALEN, NORWAY
See Biology: Ecology; Research Institute

MARINE RESEARCH INSTITUTE
5000 BERGEN, NORWAY
See Interdisciplinary: General; Research
Institute

NORSE POLAR INSTITUTT
OSLO, NORWAY
See Interdisciplinary: General; Unclassified

**NORWEGIAN DEFENSE
RESOURCES ESTABLISHMENT**
BOX 115
3191 HORTEN, NORWAY
See Interdisciplinary: General; Unclassified

**WATER RESOURCES OF THE
NORWEGIAN INSTITUTE**
OSLO, NORWAY
See Biology: General; Unclassified

PAKISTAN

ATOMIC ENERGY COMMISSION
FISHERIES HARBOR, WEST WHARF
KARACHI, PAKISTAN
See Biology: General; Government-Federal

**COUNCIL OF SCIENTIFIC AND
INDUSTRIAL RESEARCH**
KARACHI, PAKISTAN
See Biology: General; Government-Federal

FISHERIES DEPARTMENT
LYALLPUR AGRICULTURAL
UNIVERSITY
MYMENSINGH, PAKISTAN
See Biology: General; Educational Institute

HYDROGRAPHIC SERVICE
MINISTRY OF DEFENSE,
DEPARTMENT OF NAVY
KARACHI, PAKISTAN
See Geology: General; Government-Federal

**MARINE BIOLOGICAL RESOURCES
LABORATORY**
FISHERIES HARBOR, WEST WHARF
KARACHI, PAKISTAN
See Biology: General; Government-Federal

**MARINE BIOLOGICAL RESOURCES
LABORATORY**
ISPAHANI BUILDING 183, MCLEOD
ROAD

KARACHI, PAKISTAN
See Biology: General; Unclassified

MARINE FISHERIES DEPARTMENT
FISHERIES HARBOR, WEST WHARF
KARACHI, PAKISTAN
See Interdisciplinary: General; Unclassified

METEOROLOGICAL DEPARTMENT
FISHERIES HARBOR, WEST WHARF
KARACHI, PAKISTAN
See Biology: General; Government-Federal

**OCEANOGRAPHIC RESEARCH,
NATIONAL COMMISSION**
ISLAMABAD, PAKISTAN
See Interdisciplinary: General; Unclassified

**OCEANOGRAPHY GROUP,
ZOOLOGY DEPARTMENT**
KARACHI UNIVERSITY
KARACHI, PAKISTAN
See Biology: General; Educational Institute

PAKISTAN SHELL RAP
KARACHI, PAKISTAN
See Biology: General; Industrial/Commercial

PAKISTAN SUN OIL CORPORATION
KARACHI, PAKISTAN
See Geology: General; Industrial/Commercial

**PAN-INDIAN OCEAN SCIENCE
ASSOCIATION, BLOCK 95**
PAKISTAN SECRETARIAT
KARACHI, PAKISTAN
See Biology: Ecology; Government-Federal

**SCIENTIFIC AND INDUSTRIAL
RESEARCH COUNCIL**
KARACHI, PAKISTAN
See Interdisciplinary: General; Unclassified

**ZOOLOGICAL SURVEY
DEPARTMENT**
FISHERIES HARBOR, WEST WHARF
KARACHI, PAKISTAN
See Biology: General; Government-Federal

PANAMA

**AGRICULTURE, COMMERCE, AND
INDUSTRY MINISTER**
CALLE 39 Y AVENIDA, PO BOX 1631
PANAMA CITY, PANAMA
See Biology: General; Government-Federal

COASTAL LABORATORY
NAOS ISLAND,
FOR AMADOR, PANAMA
See Biology: General; Field Station/Laboratory

**FISHERIES LABORATORY
APPARTADO (NATIONAL)**
ESTAGETA DE CALIDONIA
PANAMA CITY, PANAMA
See Biology: General; Unclassified

FISHERY DEPARTMENT
24-89 AVENIDA BALBOA, PO BOX
3318
PANAMA CITY, PANAMA
See Biology: General; Government-Federal

**RESEARCH STATION OF BARRO
COLORADO**
GUTUN LAKE, PANAMA
See Biology: General; Research Institute

PERU

**BELCO PETROLEUM
COORDINATOR**
411 TUCUA
LIMA, PERU
See Biology: General; Industrial/Commercial

CARLOS VERRANDO
JUNIV 358
LIMA, PERU
See Biology: General; Industrial/Commercial

COMMUNITY UNIVERSITY OF PERU
HUACHO, PERU
See Biology: General; Educational Institute

**OCEANOGRAPHIC DEVELOPMENT
CORPORATION**
732 WILSON AVENUE, MEZZANINE
LIMA, PERU
See Biology: General; Industrial/Commercial

**PERUVIAN SEA INSTITUTION ESQ
GRAL VALLEY**
GAMARRA CHUCUTIO
CALLAO, PERU
See Biology: General; Unclassified

TECHOQUIMICA
1152 COMINO A LA ATARJEA
LIMA, PERU
See Biology: General; Industrial/Commercial

TRUJILLO NATIONAL UNIVERSITY
CASILLA POSTAL 315
TRUJILLO, PERU
See Biology: General; Educational Institute

PHILIPPINES

AGRICULTURE AND NATIONAL RESOURCES DEPARTMENT
MANILA, PHILIPPINES
See Engineering: General; Government-Federal

BUREAU OF CUSTOMS
PORT AREA
MANILA, PHILIPPINES
See Interdisciplinary: General; Unclassified

DAGAT-DAGATAN SALT WATER FISHERIES EXPERIMENTAL STATION
PHILLIPPINE FISHERIES COMMISSION, PO BOX 623
MANILA, PHILIPPINES
See Biology: General; Field Station/Laboratory

EDUCATION DEPARTMENT
ARROCEROS
MANILA, PHILIPPINES
See Interdisciplinary: General; Unclassified

FISHERIES COLLEGE
UNIVERSITY OF PHILIPPINES
QUEZON CITY, PHILIPPINES
See Biology: General; Educational Institute

FISHERIES COMMISSION
INTRAMUROS
MANILA, PHILIPPINES
See Biology: General; Government-Federal

LIMNOLOGICAL STATION
LOS BANOS
LAGUNA, PHILIPPINES
See Engineering: General; Government-Federal

MARINE BIOLOGY STATION, UNIVERSITY OF PHILIPPINES
PUERTO GALERA
ORIENTAL MINDORO, PHILIPPINES
See Biology: General; Educational Institute

MARINE FISHERIES DEPARTMENT, UNIVERSITY OF PHILIPPINES
BOSTON AND 23 STREET
PORT AREA, MANILA, PHILLIPPINES

See Biology: General; Educational Institute

MINES BUREAU
HERRAN STREET
MANILA, PHILIPPINES
See Engineering: General; Government-Federal

NATIONAL MUSEUM
HERRAN STREET
MANILA, PHILIPPINES
See Social Sciences/Humanities: General; Government-Federal

PAGE INCORPORATED
CEBU, PHILIPPINES
See Interdisciplinary: General; Industrial/Commercial

PHILIPPINE ATOMIC ENERGY COMMISSION
727 HERRAN STREET
MANILA, PHILIPPINES
See Interdisciplinary: General; Unclassified

PHILIPPINE NAVY
ROXAS BOULEVARD
MANILA, PHILIPPINES
See Engineering: General; Government-Federal

PUBLIC WORKS BUREAU
POST OFFICE BUILDING LAWTON PLAZA
MANILA, PHILIPPINES
See Engineering: General; Government-Federal

SALT WATER FISHERIES EXPERIMENTAL STATION
DAGAT-DAGATAN, PHILIPPINES
See Engineering: General; Government-Federal

SCIENCE DEVELOPMENT BOARD (NATIONAL)
HERRAN STREET
MANILA, PHILIPPINES
See Engineering: General; Government-Federal

WEATHER BUREAU
MANILA, PHILIPPINES
See Engineering: General; Government-Federal

POLAND

BOTANICAL GARDENS, OGROD BOTANICZNY
UNIVERSITY OF WARSAW
AL UJAZDOWSKIE 4, WARSAW, POLAND
See Biology: Ecology; Educational Institute

ECOLOGY INSTITUTE, POLISH ACADEMY OF SCIENCES
UL NOWY SWIAT 72
WARSZAWA, POLAND
See Biology: Ecology; Educational Institute

GEOLOGY DEPARTMENT
STATE JARACZA 3 M 4
KRAKOW, POLAND
See Geology: General; Educational Institute

HYDROLOGY AND ENGINEERING INSTITUTE
POLISH ACADEMY OF SCIENCE
GDANSK, POLAND
See Biology: General; Unclassified

HYDROLOGY AND METEOROLOGY INSTITUTE
2OU PODLES
WARSZAWA 32, PODLES, POLAND
See Engineering: Pollution Abatement; Industrial/Commercial

HYDROLOGY AND METEOROLOGY STATE INSTITUTE
UL, POPLESNAGI
WARSZAWA, POLAND
See Geology: General; Government-Federal

INSTYTUT CHEMII FIZYCZNEJ PAN
UL KASPRZAKA 4452, WARSAW, POLAND
See Physics: General; Research Institute

INSTYTUT GOSPODARKI WODNEJ (IGW)
WARSZAWA 10, POLAND
See Interdisciplinary: General; Research Institute

MARINE FISHERIES INSTITUTION
GDYNIA, POLAND
See Biology: General; Unclassified

MARINE INSTITUTION
GDANSK, POLAND
See Biology: General; Unclassified

MARINE STUDIES
POLISH ACADEMY OF SCIENCE
SOPOT, POLAND
See Biology: General; Unclassified

MORSKI INSTYTUT RYBACKI (MIR)
AL ZJEDNOCZENIA
GDYNIA POLAND
See Biology: Biochemistry; Research Institute

NATURE PROTECTION RESEARCH CENTER
KOPERNIKA 27
KRAKOW, POLAND
See Biology: Ecology; Research Institute

OCEANOGRAPHIC INSTITUTE OF HYDROLOGY AND METEOROLOGY
GDYNIA POLAND
See Interdisciplinary: General; Unclassified

OSRODEK BADAWCZO-ROZWOJOWY
ELEKTRONIKI PROZNI OBREP
WARSAW, POLAND
See Physics: General; Industrial/Commercial

PLANT ECOLOGY
UNIVERSITY OF WARSAW
UJAZDOWSKIE 4, WARSAW, POLAND
See Biology: Ecology; Educational Institute

PLANT PHYSIOLOGY DEPARTMENT, WARSAW UNIVERSITY
UL 3 MAJA5
WARSZAWA, POLAND
See Biology: General; Educational Institute

ZAKLAD GEOFIZYKI
UL PASTEURA 3
WARSZAWA 22, POLAND
See Interdisciplinary: General; Research Institute

ZAKLAND GEOFIZYKI
UL PASTEURA, WARSZAWA 22, POLAND
See Geology: Geophysics; Foundation

PORTUGAL

BOTANICAL INSTITUTION
UNIVERSITY OF LISBON
LISBON, PORTUGAL
See Biology: General; Educational Institute

CIVIC ENGINEERING LABORATORY
LISBON, PORTUGAL
See Biology: General; Field Station/Laboratory

HYDROGRAPHIC OFFICE, PORTUGUESE
LISBON, PORTUGAL
See Biology: General; Research Institute

TROPICAL AQUATIC BIOLOGICAL CENTER
LISBON, PORTUGAL
See Biology: General; Unclassified

REPUBLIC OF SOUTH AFRICA

BERNARD PRICE INSTITUTE, WITWATERSRAND UNIVERSITY
TRANSVAAL
JOHANNESBURG, REPUBLIC OF SOUTH AFRICA
See Geology: General; Educational Institute

BOTANY DEPARTMENT
PRIVATE BAG, RONDEBOSCH
CAPE TOWN, REPUBLIC OF SOUTH AFRICA
See Biology: General; Educational Institute

COMMERCE AND INDUSTRY DEPARTMENT
DIVISION OF SEA FISHERIES
CAPE TOWN, REPUBLIC OF SOUTH AFRICA
See Interdisciplinary: General; Unclassified

ENVIRONMENTAL STUDIES
UNIVERSITY COLLEGE
DURBAN, REPUBLIC OF SOUTH AFRICA
See Biology: General; Educational Institute

ENVIRONMENTAL STUDIES
UNIVERSITY OF PORT ELIZABETH
PORT ELIZABETH, REPUBLIC OF SOUTH AFRICA
See Biology: General; Educational Institute

ENVIRONMENTAL STUDIES
UNIVERSITY OF STELLENBOSCH
STELLENBOSCH, REPUBLIC OF SOUTH AFRICA
See Engineering: General; Educational Institute

FISHERIES DEVELOPMENT CORPORATION
POST OFFICE BOX 539
CAPE TOWN, REPUBLIC OF SOUTH AFRICA
See Social Sciences/Humanities: Industrial Development; Industrial/Commercial

FISHERIES DIVISION, DEPARTMENT OF INDUSTRIES
BEACH ROAD SEA POINT
CAPE TOWN, REPUBLIC OF SOUTH AFRICA
See Biology: General; Field Station/Laboratory

GEOCHEMISTRY DEPARTMENT
PRIVATE BAG, RONDEBOSCH
CAPE TOWN, REPUBLIC OF SOUTH AFRICA

See Geology: Geochemistry; Educational Institute

GEOLOGY DEPARTMENT
PRIVATE BAG, RONDEBOSCH
CAPE TOWN, REPUBLIC OF SOUTH AFRICA
See Interdisciplinary: General; Educational Institute

MARINE RESEARCH LABORATORY
WALVIS BAY
PRETORIA, REPUBLIC OF SOUTH AFRICA
See Biology: General; Government-Federal

MEDICAL AND UNIVERSITY RESEARCH DIVISION
P O BOX 395
PRETORIA, REPUBLIC OF SOUTH AFRICA
See Interdisciplinary: General; Educational Institute

MUSEUM OF SOUTH AFRICA
POST OFFICE BOX 61
CAPE TOWN, REPUBLIC OF SOUTH AFRICA
See Biology: General; Government-Federal

NAVAL HYDROLOGICAL SURVEY OFFICE
C/O MARITIME HEADQUARTERS, YOUNGSFIELD
CAPE TOWN, REPUBLIC OF SOUTH AFRICA
See Engineering: Water Resources; Government-Federal

OCEANOGRAPHIC INSTITUTE
PRIVATE BAG, RONDEBOSCH
CAPE TOWN, REPUBLIC OF SOUTH AFRICA
See Interdisciplinary: General; Educational Institute

OCEANOGRAPHIC RESEARCH UNITED
YOUNGSFIELD
CAPE TOWN, REPUBLIC OF SOUTH AFRICA
See Engineering: General; Government-Federal

OCEANOGRAPHIC RESOURCES INSTITUTION
P O BOX 736, 2 WEST STREET
DURBAN, REPUBLIC OF SOUTH AFRICA
See Biology: General; Research Institute

OCEANOGRAPHY DEPARTMENT
PRIVATE BAG, RONDEBOSCH
CAPE TOWN, REPUBLIC OF SOUTH AFRICA
See Chemistry: Physical Chemistry; Educational Institute

OCEANOGRAPHY DIVISION, NATIONAL PHYSICAL RESOURCES LABORATORY
KING GEORGE V AVENUE
DURBAN, REPUBLIC OF SOUTH AFRICA
See Interdisciplinary: General; Unclassified

OCEANOGRAPHY INSTITUTE, MARINE EFFLUENTS UNIT
PRIVATE BAG, RONDEBOSCH
CAPE TOWN, REPUBLIC OF SOUTH AFRICA
See Geology: General; Educational Institute

OCEANOGRAPHY INSTITUTE, UNIVERSITY OF CAPETOWN
RONDESBOSCH OF GOODHOPE UNION, REPUBLIC OF SOUTH AFRICA
See Biology: General; Educational Institute

PHYSICS DEPARTMENT
PRIVATE BAG, RONDEBOSCH
CAPE TOWN, REPUBLIC OF SOUTH AFRICA
See Physics: General; Educational Institute

SCIENTIFIC AND INDUSTRIAL RESEARCH COUNCIL
DURBAN, REPUBLIC OF SOUTH AFRICA
See Interdisciplinary: General; Unclassified

SOUTHWEST AFRICAN ADMINISTRATION
PRETORIA, REPUBLIC OF SOUTH AFRICA
See Interdisciplinary: General; Unclassified

SURVEYING DEPARTMENT
PRIVATE BAG, RONDEBOSCII
CAPE TOWN, REPUBLIC OF SOUTH AFRICA
See Engineering: General; Educational Institute

WATER RESOURCE INSTITUTE, (NATIONAL)
KING GEORGE V AVENUE
DURBAN, REPUBLIC OF SOUTH AFRICA
See Interdisciplinary: General; Unclassified

RUMANIA

BIOLOGY INSTITUTE
STR LATINA I
BUCHAREST, RUMANIA
See Biology: General; Educational Institute

BIOLOGY INSTITUTE, TRAIAN SAVULESCU
STR COGILNIC 35
BUCHAREST, RUMANIA
See Biology: General; Educational Institute

COMITE D'ETAT DES EAUX
BOUL GRAL MAGHARU 6-8
BUCURESTI 22, RUMANIA
See Interdisciplinary: General; Foundation

INSTITUTE DE CERCETARI PROIETARI PISCOLE
BUILDING ANA JPATESCU
BUCURESTI, 46, RUMANIA
See Interdisciplinary: General; Research Institute

INSTITUTE DE STUDII CERCETARI HIDROTEHNI
SPL INDEPENDENTEI 294,
BUCHAREST, RUMANIA
See Engineering: General; Foundation

NATURAL HISTORY MUSEUM
SOSEAUA KISELEFF 1
BUCHAREST, RUMANIA
See Biology: General; Foundation

RESEARCH INSTITUTE FOR CEREALS AND TECHNOLOGY PLANTS
STR POMPILIU ELIADE 4
BUCHAREST, RUMANIA
See Engineering: Agricultural Engineering; Research Institute

SAUDI ARABIA

AGRICULTURE AND WATER MINISTRY
JIDDA, SAUDI ARABIA
See Biology: General; Government-Federal

ARABIAN OIL COMPANY
JIDDA, SAUDI ARABIA
See Biology: General; Industrial/Commercial

GETTY OIL COMPANY
JIDDA, SAUDI ARABIA
See Biology: General; Industrial/Commercial

PETROLEUM AND MINERAL RESOURCES MINISTRY
JIDDA, SAUDI ARABIA
See Biology: General; Government-Federal

SCOTLAND

AGRICULTURAL SCIENCE SERVICE, DEPARTMENT OF AGRICULTURE
EAST CRAIGS
EDINBURGH 12, SCOTLAND
See Biology: Ecology; Government-Federal

AIR PRODUCTS, LIMITED
KIRKHILL HOUSE, COLMONELL
AYRSHIRE, SCOTLAND
See Engineering: General; Industrial/Commercial

BIOCHEMISTRY DEPARTMENT, MACAULAY INSTITUTE FOR SOIL RESEARCH
ABERDEEN, SCOTLAND
See Biology: Biochemistry; Research Institute

BIOLOGY DEPARTMENT, PAISLEY COLLEGE OF TECHNOLOGY
HIGH STREET
PAISLEY, RENFREWSHIRE, PAI2BE, SCOTLAND
See Biology: Ecology; Educational Institute

FORESTRY RESEARCH INSTITUTE
KING'S BUILDINGS, MAYFIELD ROAD
EDINBURGH EH9 3JU, SCOTLAND
See Biology: Ecology; Research Institute

GRANT INSTITUTE OF GEOLOGY
WEST MAINS ROAD
EDINBURGH 9, SCOTLAND
See Geology: General; Research Institute

GRASSLAND HUSBANDRY DEPARTMENT
WEST OF SCOTLAND AGRICULTURAL COLLEGE
AUCHINCRUIVE, AYRSHIRE, SCOTLAND
See Engineering: Agricultural Engineering; Research Institute

MARINE ENVIRONMENTAL RESEARCH INSTITUTE
CRAIGHALL ROAD
EDINBURGH EH6 4RQ, SCOTLAND
See Biology: Ecology; Research Institute

MARINE LABORATORY, DEPARTMENT OF AGRICULTURE AND FISHERIES
PO BOX 101
ABERDEEN AB9 8DB, SCOTLAND
See Biology: General; Government-Federal

MARINE RESOURCES LABORATORY, DUNSTAFFNAGE
POST OFFICE BOX 3

OBAN, ARGYLL, SCOTLAND
See Biology: Ecology; Research Institute

**NATURAL ENVIRONMENT
RESEARCH COUNCIL**
UNIVERSITY OF ABERDEEN
TORRY, ABERDEEN, SCOTLAND
See Biology: Biochemistry; Research Institute

NATURE CONSERVANCY
BANCHORY
KINCARDINESHIRE, SCOTLAND
See Biology: Ecology; Foundation

NATURE CONSERVANCY
12 HOPE TERRACE
EDINBURGH 9, SCOTLAND
See Biology: Ecology; Foundation

**OCEANOGRAPHIC LABORATORY,
SCOTLAND MARINE
BIOLOGICAL ASSOCIATION**
78 CRAIGHALL ROAD
EDINBURGH, SCOTLAND
See Biology: General; Field Station/Laboratory

**PHYSICAL SCIENCE SCHOOL,
UNIVERSITY OF ST ANDREWS**
NORTH HAUGH, ST ANDREWS
FIFE, KY16 955, SCOTLAND
See Physics: General; Educational Institute

**PLANT BREEDING STATION OF
SCOTLAND**
PENTLANDFIELD, ROSLIN
MIDLOTHIAN, SCOTLAND
See Engineering: Agricultural Engineering; Research Institute

RESEARCH INSTITUTE, ROWETT
BUCKSBURN
ABERDEEN, SCOTLAND
See Biology: Ecology; Research Institute

THE MACAULAY INSTITUTE
CRAIGIEBUCKLER
ABERDEEN AB9 2QJ, SCOTLAND
See Biology: General; Research Institute

TORRY RESEARCH STATION
ABERDEEN, SCOTLAND
See Biology: General; Research Institute

SENEGAL

AFRICA-AZOTE
DAKAR, SENEGAL
See Social Sciences/Humanities: Industrial Development; Industrial/Commercial

**BUREAU RECHERCHES
GEOLOGICAL ET MINIERE**
RT11 UNIVERSITY. POST OFFICE
BOX 268
NODAKAR-FANN, SENEGAL
See Geology: General; Research Institute

**COMPANY FOR FROZEN FOODS OF
SENEGAL**
SOFRIGAL
DAKAR, SENEGAL
See Social Sciences/Humanities: Industrial Development; Industrial/Commercial

COPETAD
IMMEUBLE BIAO, PLACE
INDEPENDENCE, BP 2093
DAKAR, SENEGAL
See Social Sciences/Humanities: Industrial Development; Industrial/Commercial

EXXON
BUILDING MAGINOT, BP 1100
DAKAR, SENEGAL
See Social Sciences/Humanities: Industrial Development; Industrial/Commercial

**FUND INSTITUTE OF BLACK
AFRICA**
C/O UNIVERSITY OF DAKAR
DAKAR, SENEGAL
See Interdisciplinary: General; Research Institute

INDUSTRIAL CONSTRUCTION SAIB
DAKAR, SENEGAL
See Social Sciences/Humanities: Industrial Development; Industrial/Commercial

MARINE BIOLOGICAL STATION
SEA MUSEUM IFAN GOREE
BP 206, DAKAR, SENEGAL
See Biology: General; Field Station/Laboratory

**OCEANOGRAPHY AND MARITIME
FISHERIES DEPARTMENT**
THIAROYE SURVEY MER, BP 2241
DAKAR, SENEGAL
See Biology: General; Government-Federal

SADAL TUNA FISHERIES CANNERY
DAKAR, SENEGAL
See Social Sciences/Humanities: Industrial Development; Industrial/Commercial

SCAF TUNA FISHERIES CANNERY
DAKAR, SENEGAL
See Social Sciences/Humanities: Industrial Development; Industrial/Commercial

SEA INVERTEBRATE LABORATORY
BP 206 IFAN

DAKAR, SENEGAL
See Biology: General; Educational Institute

SIERRA LEONE

**FISHERIES DIVISION,
AGRICULTURE AND NATURAL
RESOURCES MINISTRY**
KISSY DOCKYARD
FREETOWN, SIERRA LEONE
See Biology: General; Government-Federal

**MARINE BIOLOGICAL SECTION,
FACULTY OF SCIENCES**
UNIVERSITY COLUMBIA OF SIERRA
LEONE
FREETOWN, SIERRA LEONE
See Biology: General; Educational Institute

SINGAPORE

**BRITISH PETROLEUM REFINERY
OF SINGAPORE, LIMITED**
SINGAPORE
See Engineering: General; Industrial/Commercial

**ECONOMIC DEVELOPMENT
BOARD**
SINGAPORE
See Engineering: General; Government-Federal

EDUCATION MINISTRY
SINGAPORE
See Interdisciplinary: General; Unclassified

**ESSO EXPLORATION
INCORPORATED**
SINGAPORE
See Engineering: General; Industrial/Commercial

**FISHERIES AND BIOLOGICAL
UNITS**
UNIVERSITY OF SINGAPORE
SINGAPORE
See Biology: General; Educational Institute

FISHERIES DIVISION
PRIMARY PRODUCTION
DEPARTMENT
SINGAPORE
See Biology: General; Government-Federal

JURONG SHIPYARD
SINGAPORE
See Engineering: General; Industrial/
Commercial

**LAW AND NATIONAL
    DEVELOPMENT MINISTRY**
PRIMARY PRODUCTION
    DEPARTMENT
SINGAPORE
See Engineering: General; Government-
Federal

METEOROLOGY DEPARTMENT
MINISTRY OF COMMUNICATIONS
SINGAPORE
See Physics: General; Government-Feder-
al

**MOBIL REFINING OF MALAYSIA,
    LIMITED**
SINGAPORE
See Engineering: General; Industrial/
Commercial

PORT OF SINGAPORE AUTHORITY
SINGAPORE
See Engineering: General; Government-
Federal

**SCIENCE AND TECHNOLOGY
    MINISTRY**
CHEMISTRY DEPARTMENT
SINGAPORE
See Chemistry: General; Government-
State or Local

SOMALIA

CANADALA, S P A
P O BOX 23
MOGADISCIO, SOMALIA
See Social Sciences/Humanities: Indus-
trial Development; Industrial/Com-
mercial

FISHERIES SECTION
MINISTRY OF INDUSTRY AND
    COMMERCE
MOGADISCIO, SOMALIA
See Geology: Geochemistry; Govern-
ment-Federal

HABO S P A
P O BOX 23
MOGADISCIO, SOMALIA
See Social Sciences/Humanities: Indus-
trial Development; Industrial/Com-
mercial

**SOMALI AMERICAN FISHING
    COMPANY**
SOMALI CREDIT BANK
MOGADISCIO, SOMALIA

See Social Sciences/Humanities: Industrial Development; Industrial/Com-
mercial

SOUTH INDIA

**OCEANOGRAPHY CENTER,
    ANNAMALAI UNIVERSITY**
CHIDDAMBARAM
PORTO NOVO, SOUTH INDIA
See Biology: Ecology; Educational Insti-
tute

SPAIN

**GEOPHYSICS NATIONAL
    INSTITUTE**
MADRID, SPAIN
See Geology: Geophysics; Government-
Federal

**OCEANOGRAPHY INSTITUTE OF
    SPAIN**
MADRID, SPAIN
See Biology: General; Government-Fed-
eral

SCIENCES FACULTY
UNIVERSITY OF MADRID
MADRID 3, SPAIN
See Chemistry: Physical Chemistry; Edu-
cational Institute

SUDAN

**GAME AND FISHERIES
    DEPARTMENT**
POST OFFICE BOX 293
KHARTOUM, SUDAN
See Biology: General; Government-Fed-
eral

SWEDEN

**BOTANY AND PHYSIOLOGY
    INSTITUTE**
UNIVERSITY OF STOCKHOLM
STOCKHOLM, SWEDEN
See Biology: General; Educational Insti-
tute

GEOLOGY DEPARTMENT
UNIVERSITY OF STOCKHOLM
STOCKHOLM, SWEDEN
See Geology: General; Educational Insti-
tute

**KRISTINBERGS ZOOLOGICAL
    STATION**
FISKBACKSKI, SWEDEN
See Biology: General; Field Station/Lab-
oratory

LIMNOLOGIC INSTITUTE
UNIVERSITY OF UPPSALA
UPPSALA, SWEDEN
See Biology: Ecology; Educational Insti-
tute

LIMNOLOGY INSTITUTE
UNIVERSITY OF LUND
S-220 03 LUND, SWEDEN
See Biology: Ecology; Research Institute

**METEOROLOGICAL INSTITUTE,
    (INTERNATIONAL)**
STOCKHOLM, SWEDEN
See Interdisciplinary: General; Unclassi-
fied

OCEANOGRAPHIC INSTITUTE
UNIVERSITY OF GOTEBORG
GOTEBORG, SWEDEN
See Chemistry: General; Educational In-
stitute

PLANT PHYSIOLOGY INSTITUTE
UNIVERSITY OF LUND
LUND, SWEDEN
See Biology: General; Educational Insti-
tute

STATENS NATURVARDSVERK
FACK
S-171 20 SOLNA 1, SWEDEN
See Interdisciplinary: General; Unclassi-
fied

SWITZERLAND

**CONSERVATION OF NATURE
    INTERNATIONAL UNION**
1110 MORGES
BERN, SWITZERLAND
See Biology: Ecology; Professional Organizations

CONSERVATOIRE BOTANIQUE
192 RTE OF LAUSANNE
GENEVA, SWITZERLAND
See Biology: General; Government-State
or Local

**GEOLOGY AND HYDROGRAPHY
    DEPARTMENT**
UNIVERSITY OF BERN
BERN, SWITZERLAND

See Interdisciplinary: General; Educational Institute

GEOLOGY DEPARTMENT
UNIVERSITY OF NEUCHATEL
BERN, SWITZERLAND
See Geology: General; Educational Institute

INSTITUT POLYTECHNIQUE FEDERAL
UNIVERSITS STRASSE 2
8006 ZURICH, SWITZERLAND
See Biology: General; Professional Organizations

INTERNATIONAL COUNCIL FOR ENVIRONMENTAL LAW
GENEVA, SWITZERLAND
See Social Sciences/Humanities: Law/Legislation; Professional Organizations

INTERNATIONAL LABOUR ORGANIZATION
GENEVA, SWITZERLAND
See Social Sciences/Humanities: Labor/Relations/Unions; Professional Organizations

NATURE AND NATURAL RESOURCES CONSERVATION UNION
110 MORGES
BERN, SWITZERLAND
See Interdisciplinary: General; Professional Organizations

PLANT PHYSIOLOGY DEPARTMENT
UNIVERSITY OF LAUSANNE
LAUSANNE, SWITZERLAND
See Biology: General; Educational Institute

WATER SUPPLY AND SEWAGE PURIFICATION INSTITUTE
PHYSIKSTRASSE 5
ZURICH 7, SWITZERLAND
See Engineering: Pollution Abatement; Educational Institute

WORLD HEALTH ORGANIZATION
1211 GENEVA 27, SWITZERLAND
See Social Sciences/Humanities: General; Foundation

WORLD METEOROLOGICAL ORGANIZATION
41 AVENUE GIUSEPPE-MOTTA
GENEVA, SWITZERLAND
See Engineering: Pollution Abatement; Research Institute

ZOOLOGIC ANSTALT BASEL
RHEINSPRUNG 9
BASEL, SWITZERLAND
See Biology: General; Educational Institute

ZOOLOGY DEPARTMENT
UNIVERSITY OF ZURICH
ZURICH, SWITZERLAND
See Biology: Ecology; Educational Institute

SYRIA

FISHERIES OFFICE
AGRICULTURE MINISTRY
LATAKIA, SYRIA
See Biology: General; Government-Federal

FUEL MINISTRY, ELECTRIC POWER AND INDUSTRIAL PROJECTS
INDUSTRIAL PROJECTS
DAMASCUS, SYRIA
See Biology: General; Industrial/Commercial

TAIWAN

ACADEMIA SINICA
SECTION 2, 128 YENCHIU ROAD
NANKANG, TAIWAN
See Interdisciplinary: General; Unclassified

AGROMETEOROLOGY AND PLANT ECOLOGY
17-A LANE 31, YONG KANG STREET
TAIPEI, TAIWAN
See Biology: General; Educational Institute

CHINESE PETROLEUM CORPORATION
TAIPEI, TAIWAN
See Engineering: General; Industrial/Commercial

ECONOMIC AFFAIRS MINISTRY
TAIPEI, TAIWAN
See Social Sciences/Humanities: Community Development/Studies; Government-Federal

EDUCATION MINISTRY
TAIWAN, CHINA
See Interdisciplinary: General; Unclassified

FISHERIES BUREAU
1688 CHUNGCHENG ROAD
TAIPEI, TAIWAN
See Biology: General; Government-Federal

FISHERIES RESEARCH INSTITUTE
125 HOU-I ROAD
KEELUNG, TAIWAN
See Biology: General; Government-Federal

GEOPHYSICS INSTITUTE
NATIONAL CENTRAL UNIVERSITY
MIAOLI, TAIWAN

See Geology: Geophysics; Educational Institute

ICHTHYOLOGICAL LABORATORY, TUNGHAI UNIVERSITY
TAICHUNG KANG ROAD
TAICHUNG, TAIWAN
See Interdisciplinary: General; Educational Institute

MARINE BIOLOGY, NATIONAL TAIWAN UNIVERSITY
ROOSEVELT ROAD
TAIPEI, TAIWAN 107
See Biology: General; Educational Institute

NATIONAL DEFENSE MINISTRY
TAIPEI, TAIWAN
See Interdisciplinary: General; Unclassified

OCEAN RESEARCH OF CHINESE NATIONAL COMMISSION
NATIONAL TAIWAN UNIVERSITY-ROOSEVELT
TAIPEI, TAIWAN
See Biology: General; Government-Federal

OCEANOGRAPHY INSTITUTE
NATIONAL TAIWAN UNIVERSITY
TAIPEI, TAIWAN
See Engineering: Water Resources; Educational Institute

TANZANIA

ZOOLOGY DEPARTMENT, UNIVERSITY COLLEGE
POST OFFICE BOX 9184
DAR ES SALAAM, TANZANIA
See Biology: General; Educational Institute

THAILAND

AGRICULTURE MINISTRY
DEPARTMENT OF FISHERIES
BANGKOK, THAILAND
See Engineering: General; Government-Federal

APPLIED SCIENTIFIC RESEARCH CORPORATION
AGRICULTURAL RESEARCH INSTITUTION
KHONKOEN, THAILAND
See Engineering: General; Government-Federal

**FISHERIES COLLEGE, KASETSART
UNIVERSITY**
BANGKHEN
BANGKOK, THAILAND
See Biology: General; Educational Institute

**FISHERIES COUNCIL OF INDO-
PACIFIC**
FAO REGIONAL OFFICE, MALIWAN
MANS, PHRA ATIT ROAD
BANGKOK 2, THAILAND
See Biology: Ecology; Professional Organizations

FISHERIES RESEARCH STATION
MINISTRY OF AGRICULTURE
SAMUT PRAKAN, THAILAND
See Biology: General; Government-Federal

HYDROGRAPHIC DEPARTMENT
ROYAL THAI NAVY
BANGKOK, THAILAND
See Engineering: General; Government-Federal

**MARINE SCIENCE NATIONAL
COMMITTEE**
BANGKOK, THAILAND
See Biology: General; Government-Federal

**MINERAL RESOURCES
DEPARTMENT**
BANGKOK, THAILAND
See Engineering: General; Government-Federal

RESEARCH COUNCIL (NATIONAL)
BANGKOK, THAILAND
See Engineering: General; Government-Federal

**SCIENCE FACULTY,
CHULALONGKORN UNIVERSITY**
PATUMWAN
BANGKOK, THAILAND
See Biology: General; Educational Institute

**THAISARCO UNION CARBIDE
EASTERN INCORPORATED**
PHUKET, THAILAND
See Engineering: General; Industrial/Commercial

TOGO

**ANIMAL HUSBANDRY
DEPARTMENT**
LOME, TOGO
See Biology: General; Government-Federal

FISHERIES SERVICE
LOME, TOGO
See Social Sciences/Humanities: Industrial Development; Government-Federal

FORESTRY DEPARTMENT
LOME, TOGO
See Interdisciplinary: General; Unclassified

MARITIME FISHING COMPANY
LOME, TOGO
See Social Sciences/Humanities: Industrial Development; Industrial/Commercial

RURAL ECONOMY MINISTRY
BP 1095
LOME, TOGO
See Social Sciences/Humanities: Industrial Development; Government-Federal

TRINIDAD

**FISHERIES DEPARTMENT,
MINISTRY OF AGRICULTURE**
PORT OF SPAIN, TRINIDAD
See Biology: General; Industrial/Commercial

TUNISIA

AGRICULTURAL MINISTRY
TUNIS, TUNISIA
See Social Sciences/Humanities: Industrial Development; Government-Federal

**AGRICULTURAL SECONDARY
SCHOOL**
SOUSSE, TUNISIA
See Social Sciences/Humanities: Education; Educational Institute

FISHERIES OFFICE
GOULETTE, TUNISIA
See Social Sciences/Humanities: Industrial Development; Government-Federal

FISHERIES OFFICE
MAHDIA, TUNISIA
See Social Sciences/Humanities: Industrial Development; Government-Federal

FISHERIES OFFICE
SFAX, TUNISIA
See Social Sciences/Humanities: Industrial Development; Government-Federal

FISHERIES OFFICE
TUNIS, TUNISIA
See Social Sciences/Humanities: Industrial Development; Government-Federal

MARINE ACADEMY
SOUSSE, TUNISIA
See Social Sciences/Humanities: Education; Educational Institute

**OCEANIC AND FISHERIES
DIVISION**
NATIONAL SCIENTIFIC AND
TECHNOLOGICAL INSTITUTE
SALAMMBO, TUNISIA
See Biology: General; Government-Federal

TURKEY

**DEFENSE MINISTRY,
DEPARTMENT OF
HYDROGRAPHY AND
NAVIGATION**
CUBUKLU
ISTANBUL, TURKEY
See Interdisciplinary: General; Unclassified

EGE UNIVERSITY
IZMIR, TURKEY
See Biology: General; Educational Institute

**HYDROBIOLOGICAL INSTITUTION,
UNIVERSITY OF ISTANBUL**
BALTALIMANI
ISTANBUL, TURKEY
See Biology: General; Educational Institute

**HYDROGRAPHIC DEPARTMENT,
TURKISH NAVY**
CUBUKULU, ISTANBUL, TURKEY
See Interdisciplinary: General; Unclassified

HYDROLOGY DEPARTMENT
ANKARA, TURKEY
See Biology: General; Government-Federal

**MEAT AND FISHERIES
DIRECTORATE**
FISHERIES OFFICE
ANKARA, TURKEY
See Interdisciplinary: General; Unclassified

**SCIENCE AND TECHNOLOGY
  RESEARCH COUNCIL OF TURKEY**
BAYINDER SOKAK 33,
VENISHEIR, ANKARA, TURKEY
See Biology: General; Educational Institute

STATE HYDROLOGY WORKS
ANKARA, TURKEY
See Geology: General; Government-Federal

**TECHNOLOGICAL UNIVERSITY OF
  ISTANBUL**
MATERIALS RESEARCH UNITED
ISTANBUL, TURKEY
See Biology: General; Educational Institute

UNION OF SOVIET SOCIALIST REPUBLICS

APPLIED GEOPHYSICS INSTITUTE
GLEBOVSKAYA ULITSA, 20-B
MOSCOW, UNION OF SOVIET
SOCIALIST REPUBLICS
See Physics: General; Educational Institute

**ASTRONOMICAL OBSERVATORY AT
  TASHKENT**
TASHKENT, UNION OF SOVIET
SOCIALIST REPUBLICS
See Engineering: General; Government-Federal

**AZERBAYDZAAN POLYTECHNICAL
  INSTITUTE**
PROSPEKT NARIMANOVA,25
BAKU, UNION OF SOVIET
SOCIALIST REPUBLICS
See Engineering: Water Resources; Government-Federal

**BELORUSSIAN INSTITUTE IMENI S
  M KIROV**
ULITSA SVERDLOVA, 85
MINSK, UNION OF SOVIET
SOCIALIST REPUBLICS
See Interdisciplinary: General; Educational Institute

**BOTANY INSTITUTION OF V L
  KOMAROV**
ULITSA POPOVA, 2
LENINGRAD, P-22, UNION OF
SOVIET SOCIALIST REPUBLICS
See Biology: General; Educational Institute

CHEMISTRY DEPARTMENT
KIEV UNIVERSITY
KIEV, UKRAINE, UNION OF SOVIET
SOCIALIST REPUBLICS
See Chemistry: General; Educational Institute

CHEMISTRY DEPARTMENT
MOSCOW UNIVERSITY
MOSCOW, UNION OF SOVIET
SOCIALIST REPUBLICS
See Chemistry: General; Educational Institute

**CHERKASSY PEDAGOGICAL
  INSTITUTE**
ULITSA KARLA MARKSA 24
CHERKASSY, UNION OF SOVIET
SOCIALIST REPUBLICS
See Chemistry: General; Educational Institute

ECONOMIC ASSISTANCE COUNCIL
PETROVKA 14
MOSCOW K-31, UNION OF SOVIET
SOCIALIST REPUBLICS
See Social Sciences/Humanities: Community Development/Studies; Professional Organizations

**ENVIRONMENTAL STUDIES
  PROGRAM, VORONEZH STATE
  UNIVERSITY**
PROSPEKT REVOLYUTSII,24
VORONEZH, UNION OF SOVIET
SOCIALIST REPUBLICS
See Chemistry: General; Educational Institute

**EXPERIMENTAL PHYSICS
  DEPARTMENT**
MOSCOW PHYSICO-TECHNOLOGY
INSTITUTION
MOSCOW, UNION OF SOVIET
SOCIALIST REPUBLICS
See Physics: General; Educational Institute

**FAR EAST SCIENCE RESEARCH
  HYDROMETEOROLOGICAL
  INSTITUTE**
VLADIVOSTOK, UNION OF SOVIET
SOCIALIST REPUBLICS
See Physics: General; Research Institute

FAR-EASTERN STATE UNIVERSITY
PRIMORSKIY K, ULIT SVKHN,8
VLADIVOSTOK, UNION OF SOVIET
SOCIALIST REPUBLICS
See Physics: General; Government-Federal

FIZIKI ATMOSFERY INSTITUTE
BOLISHAYA GRUZINSKAYA, V-10
MOSCOW, UNION OF SOVIET
SOCIALIST REPUBLICS
See Physics: General; Government-Federal

**GEOCHEMICAL AND ANALYTICAL
  CHEMISTRY INSTITUTE**
ACADEMY OF SCIENCES
MOSCOW, UNION OF SOVIET
SOCIALIST REPUBLICS
See Chemistry: General; Educational Institute

**GEOLOGICAL AND MINERAL
  CONSERVATION MINISTRY**
BIRZHEVOI PROYEZD, 6
LENINGRAD, V-164, UNION OF
SOVIET SOCIALIST REPUBLICS
See Geology: General; Field Station/Laboratory

GEOLOGICAL INSTITUTE
ACADEMY OF SCIENCES
MOSCOW, UNION OF SOVIET
SOCIALIST REPUBLICS
See Geology: General; Educational Institute

**GEOLOGY AND GEOGRAPHY
  DEPARTMENT, ACADEMY OF
  SCIENCES**
LENIN PROSPEKT, 14
MOSCOW, UNION OF SOVIET
SOCIALIST REPUBLICS
See Geology: General; Educational Institute

GEOLOGY AND GEOPHYSICS
VIL'NYUS, UNION OF SOVIET
SOCIALIST REPUBLICS
See Physics: General; Government-Federal

**GEOLOGY AND GEOPHYSICS
  INSTITUTE**
SIBERIAN BRANCH, SCIENCE
ACADEMY
MOSCOW, UNION OF SOVIET
SOCIALIST REPUBLICS
See Geology: General; Educational Institute

**GEOLOGY INSTITUTE, ACADEMY
  OF SCIENCE**
PYZHEVSKII 7
MOSCOW, UNION OF SOVIET
SOCIALIST REPUBLICS
See Geology: General; Educational Institute

**GEOPHYSICAL COMMISSION,
  ACADEMY OF SCIENCES**
MOLODEZHNAYA, 3
MOSCOW, B-296, UNION OF SOVIET
SOCIALIST REPUBLICS
See Geology: General; Educational Institute

GEOPHYSICAL OBSERVATORY
LENINGRAD, UNION OF SOVIET
SOCIALIST REPUBLICS
See Physics: General; Government-Federal

**HYDROGEOLOGICAL PROBLEMS
  LABORATORY**
ACADEMY OF SCIENCES
MOSCOW, UNION OF SOVIET
SOCIALIST REPUBLICS
See Biology: General; Field Station/Laboratory

HYDROMETEOROLOGICAL INSTITUTE
ULITSA CHKALOVA, 2-A
ODESSA, UNION OF SOVIET
SOCIALIST REPUBLICS
See Physics: General; Government-Federal

HYDROMETEOROLOGICAL INSTITUTION OF LENINGRAD
MALO-OKHTINSKIY PROSPEKT98
LENINGRAD, UNION OF SOVIET
SOCIALIST REPUBLICS
See Physics: General; Government-Federal

HYDROMETEOROLOGICAL INSTITUTION, UKRAINIAN SCIENCES-RESOURCES
ULITSA TOLSTOGO,14
KIEV UNION OF SOVIET SOCIALIST
REPUBLICS
See Physics: General; Research Institute

HYDROMETEOROLOGICAL RESEARCH CENTER
BOLSEHEVISTSKAYA STR 9-13
MOSCOW 123376, UNION OF
SOVIET SOCIALIST REPUBLIC
See Physics: General; Government-Federal

HYDROMETEOROLOGY INSTITUTION, KAZAH SCIENCES-RESOURCES
ALMA-ATA, UNION OF SOVIET
SOCIALIST REPUBLICS
See Physics: General; Research Institute

INSTITUT EKONOMIKI
ULITSA LENINA,15
KIEV, UNION OF SOVIET
SOCIALIST REPUBLICS
See Engineering: Water Resources; Government-Federal

INSTITUT ENERGETIKI
ULITSA UYGURSKAYA
ALMA-ATA, UNION OF SOVIET
SOCIALIST REPUBLICS
See Engineering: Water Resources; Government-Federal

INSTITUT ENERGETIKI I AVTOMATIKI
KISHINEV, UNION OF SOVIET
SOCIALIST REPUBLICS
See Engineering: Water Resources; Educational Institute

INSTITUT KHIMICHESKOY FIZIKI
VOROB'YEVSKOYE SHOSSE, 2-A
MOSCOW, UNION OF SOVIET
SOCIALIST REPUBLICS
See Chemistry: Physical Chemistry; Government-Federal

JOINT METEOROLOGICAL COMPUTER CENTER
MOSCOW, UNION OF SOVIET
SOCIALIST REPUBLICS

See Physics: General; Government-Federal

KAUNAS POLYTECHNICAL INSTITUTE
ULITSA DONELAYCHIO,35
KAUNAS, UNION OF SOVIET
SOCIALIST REPUBLICS
See Engineering: General; Government-Federal

L'VOV AGRICULTURAL INSTITUTE
PLOSHCHAD' BOG KAMEL'NIT, 1
L'VOV, UNION OF SOVIET
SOCIALIST REPUBLICS
See Engineering: Agricultural Engineering; Research Institute

LENINGRAD HIGH ENGINEERING NAVAL ACADEMY, MAKARV
VASIL'YEVSKIY OSTROV,KL15A
LENINGRAD, UNION OF SOVIET
SOCIALIST REPUBLICS
See Engineering: General; Government-Federal

LENINGRAD ORDER LENIN STATE UNIVERSITY, LGV
UNIVERSITY NABEREZHNAYA,7/9
LENINGRAD, UNION OF SOVIET
SOCIALIST REPUBLICS
See Interdisciplinary: General; Unclassified

LIMNOLOGY LABORATORY
NABEREZHNAYA MAKAROVA 2
LENINGRAD, UNION OF SOVIET
SOCIALIST REPUBLICS
See Geology: General; Field Station/Laboratory

MARINE HYDROPHYSICS INSTITUTE
SADOVAI ULITSA
LYUBLINO, MOSCOW, UNION OF
SOVIET SOCIALIST REPUBLICS
See Physics: General; Government-Federal

MATHEMATICS AND MECHANICAL INSTITUTE
ASTRONOMICHESKIY TUPIK,11
TASHKENT, UNION OF SOVIET
SOCIALIST REPUBLICS
See Physics: General; Government-Federal

MOSKOVSKIY EKONOMIKO INSTITUT
BOLSHOY STROCHENOVSKIY 18
MOSCOW, UNION OF SOVIET
SOCIALIST REPUBLICS
See Social Sciences/Humanities: Population Studies/Family Planning; Government-State or Local

OCEANOGRAPHIC INSTITUTE
KROPOTKINSKIY PEREYOLOK
MOSCOW, DOM 6, UNION OF
SOVIET SOCIALIST REPUBLIC
See Physics: General; Government-Federal

OCEANOGRAPHY DEPARTMENT, ARCTIC AND ANTARCTIC RESEARCH INSTITUTE
FONTANKA 34
LENINGRAD, UNION OF SOVIET
SOCIALIST REPUBLICS
See Interdisciplinary: General; Unclassified

OCEANOGRAPHY INSTITUTE, ACADEMY OF SCIENCES
ULITSA BAKHRUSHINA, 8
MOSCOW, UNION OF SOVIET
SOCIALIST REPUBLICS
See Geology: General; Educational Institute

OIL INSTITUTE
ACADEMY OF SCIENCES
MOSCOW, UNION OF SOVIET
SOCIALIST REPUBLICS
See Geology: General; Educational Institute

ORGANIC CHEMISTRY INSTITUTE, KAZAN BRANCH
ACADEMY OF SCIENCES
KAZAN, UNION OF SOVIET
SOCIALIST REPUBLICS
See Chemistry: General; Educational Institute

PALEONTOLOGY INSTITUTE
ACADEMY OF SCIENCES
MOSCOW, UNION OF SOVIET
SOCIALIST REPUBLICS
See Geology: Paleontology; Educational Institute

PEDAGOGICAL INSTITUTE
STALINIRI, UNION OF SOVIET
SOCIALIST REPUBLICS
See Social Sciences/Humanities: Education; Government-Federal

PHYSICAL CHEMISTRY INSTITUTE
SURFACE FORCES LABORATORY,
ACADEMY OF SCIENCES
MOSCOW, UNION OF SOVIET
SOCIALISTS REPUBLICS
See Chemistry: Physical Chemistry; Research Institute

PHYSICAL CHEMISTRY INSTITUTE
UKRAINIAN SOVIET SOCIALISTS
REPUBLIC ACADEMY OF
SCIENCES
KIEV, 28, UKRAINE, UNION OF
SOVIET SOCIALIST REPUBLICS
See Chemistry: Physical Chemistry; Educational Institute

POLAR GEOPHYSICS INSTITUTE
MURMANSK, UNION OF SOVIET
SOCIALIST REPUBLICS
See Physics: General; Government-Federal

POWER INSTITUTION, G M KRZHIZHANOVSKII
LENINGSKII PROSPEKT, 19

MOSCOW, UNION OF SOVIET
SOCIALIST REPUBLICS
See Engineering: General; Educational
Institute

**PRIKLADNOY GEOFIZIKI
INSTITUTE**
GLEBOVSKAYA ULITSA, 2-B
MOSCOW, UNION OF SOVIET
SOCIALIST REPUBLICS
See Physics: General; Government-Federal

**RADIATION, PHYSICAL AND
CHEMICAL BIOLOGY INSTITUTE**
MOSCOW, UNION OF SOVIET
SOCIALIST REPUBLICS
See Biology: Biochemistry; Field Station/
Laboratory

**SCIENCE AND RESEARCH,
CHEMICAL AND
PHARMACEUTICAL INSTITUTE**
ZUBOVSKAYA ULITSA,7
MOSCOW, UNION OF SOVIET
SOCIALIST REPUBLICS
See Biology: Biochemistry; Government-
Federal

SCIENCE RESOURCES, ALL-UNION
INSTITUTE OF OCEANOGRAPHY
MOSCOW, UNION OF SOVIET
SOCIALIST REPUBLICS
See Biology: General; Government-Federal

**SOCIAL SCIENCES SECTION,
MOSCOW STATE UNIVERSITY**
MOKHOVAYA ULITSA
MOSCOW, UNION OF SOVIET
SOCIALIST REPUBLICS
See Social Sciences/Humanities: General;
Educational Institute

**TBILISI STATE UNIVERSITY IMENI
I V STALIN**
PROSPEKT CHAVCHAVADZE, 1
TBILISI, UNION OF SOVIET
SOCIALIST REPUBLICS
See Physics: General; Government-Federal

**TOMSK STATE UNIVERSITY IMENI
V V KUYBYSHEV**
PROSPEKT TIMIRYAZEVA,3
TOMSK, UNION OF SOVIET
SOCIALIST REPUBLICS
See Physics: General; Government-Federal

**UKRAINIAN SCIENCES-RESOURCES
INSTITUTE KONSERVNOY**
ODESSA, UNION OF SOVIET
SOCIALIST REPUBLICS
See Engineering: Agricultural Engineering; Industrial/Commercial

**UL'YANOV-LENIN STATE
UNIVERSITY**
ULITSA LENINA,18

KAZAN', UNION OF SOVIET
SOCIALIST REPUBLICS
See Physics: General; Educational Institute

VIESKH
MOSKVA-RYAZANSKOY Z DOROGI
STANTSIYA PLYUSHCHEVO, UNION
OF SOVIET SOCIALIST REPUBLICS
See Engineering: Agricultural Engineering; Research Institute

**VIL'NYUS UNIVERSITY IMENI V
KAPSUKAS**
ULITSA UNIVERSITETA,3
VIL'NYUS, UNION OF SOVIET
SOCIALIST REPUBLICS
See Physics: General; Government-Federal

VNIGRI
DVORTSOVAYA NABEREZHNAYA 18
LENINGRAD, UNION OF SOVIET
SOCIALIST REPUBLICS
See Geology: General; Government-Federal

**VOEKOV MAIN GEOPHYSICAL
OBSERVATION**
MOSCOW, UNION OF SOVIET
SOCIALIST REPUBLICS
See Physics: General; Field Station/Laboratory

WATER ENERGY INSTITUTE
ARMENIAN ACADEMY SCIENCES
MOSCOW, UNION OF SOVIET
SOCIALIST REPUBLICS
See Engineering: General; Educational
Institute

**ZOOLOGY-ICHTHYOLOGY
INSTITUTE**
USSR ACADEMY OF SCIENCES
LENINGRAD, UNION OF SOVIET
SOCIALIST REPUBLICS
See Biology: General; Educational Institute

UNITED ARAB
REPUBLIC

**AGRICULTURE AND IRRIGATION
MINISTRY**
CAIRO, UNITED ARAB REPUBLIC
See Engineering: Water Resources; Government-Federal

AL-GHARDAQA MARINE STATION
CAIRO, UNITED ARAB REPUBLIC
See Biology: General; Field Station/Laboratory

AMOCO EGYPT OIL COMPANY
POST OFFICE BOX 2409
CAIRO, UNITED ARAB REPUBLIC
See Social Sciences/Humanities: Industrial Development; Industrial/Commercial

**AQUATIC RESEARCH
ORGANIZATION**
CAIRO, UNITED ARAB REPUBLIC
See Social Sciences/Humanities: Industrial Development; Government-Federal

**COASTAL CONSERVATION
COMMISSION**
CAIRO, UNITED ARAB REPUBLIC
See Biology: General; Government-Federal

**EGYPTIAN GENERAL PETROLEUM
CORPORATION**
CAIRO, UNITED ARAB REPUBLIC
See Social Sciences/Humanities: Industrial Development; Industrial/Commercial

HIGHER EDUCATION MINISTRY
CAIRO, UNITED ARAB REPUBLIC
See Social Sciences/Humanities: Education; Government-Federal

**HYDROBIOLOGY INSTITUTE OF
ALEXANDRIA**
KAYED BAY ALEXANDRIA
EL MISR, UNITED ARAB REPUBLIC
See Biology: General; Research Institute

**OCEANOGRAPHY AND FISHERIES
INSTITUTE**
CAIRO, UNITED ARAB REPUBLIC
See Biology: General; Government-Federal

**OCEANOGRAPHY DEPARTMENT,
UNIVERSITY OF ALEXANDRIA**
MOHARREM BAY ALEXANDRIA
EL MISR, UNITED ARAB REPUBLIC
See Biology: General; Educational Institute

**OCEANOGRAPHY RED SEA
INSTITUTE**
AL-GHARDAQA
RED SEA, UNITED ARAB REPUBLIC
See Biology: General; Research Institute

SCIENCE FACULTY
ELIN SHAMS UNIVERSITY
CAIRO, UNITED ARAB REPUBLIC
See Interdisciplinary: General; Educational Institute

**SCIENTIFIC RESEARCH SUPREME
COUNCIL**
CAIRO, UNITED ARAB REPUBLIC
See Interdisciplinary: General; Unclassified

SUEZ BRANCH MARINE STATION
SUEZ, UNITED ARAB REPUBLIC
See Geology: General; Field Station/Laboratory

UNITED STATES

Alaska

ALASKA DEPARTMENT HEALTH & WELFARE
ALASKA OFFICE BUILDING
JUNEAU, AK 99801
See Engineering: Pollution Abatement; Government-State or Local

ARCTIC BIOLOGY INSTITUTE
UNIVERSITY OF ALASKA
FAIRBANKS, AK 99701
See Biology: General; Research Institute

BIOLOGICAL LABORATORY
P O BOX 155
AUKE BAY, AK 99821
See Biology: General; Government-Federal

BIOLOGY DEPARTMENT, UNIVERSITY OF ALASKA
POST OFFICE BOX 95175
COLLEGE, AK 99701
See Biology: General; Educational Institute

ENVIRONMENTAL CONSERVATION DEPARTMENT
POUCH O
JUNEAU, AK 99801
See Interdisciplinary: General; Government-State or Local

ENVIRONMENTAL PROTECTION AGENCY LABORATORY
COLLEGE, AK 99701
See Biology: Ecology; Field Station/Laboratory

ENVIRONMENTAL QUALITY DEPARTMENT, GREATER ANCHORAGE AREA BOROUGH
3500 TUDOR ROAD
ANCHORAGE, AK 99507
See Interdisciplinary: General; Government-State or Local

ENVIRONMENTAL STUDIES PROGRAM
UNIVERSITY OF ALASKA
COLLEGE, AK 99701
See Interdisciplinary: General; Educational Institute

EXPLORATORY FISHING AND GEAR RESOURCES BASE
P O BOX 1668
JUNEAU, AK 99801
See Biology: General; Government-Federal

FOREST SERVICE REGION 10 OFFICE
FEDERAL OFFICE BUILDING, BOX 1628
JUNEAU, AK 99801
See Engineering: Agricultural Engineering; Government-Federal

GEOPHYSICAL INSTITUTE
UNIVERSITY OF ALASKA
COLLEGE, AK 72476
See Geology: General; Educational Institute

HEALTH, EDUCATION, AND WELFARE DEPARTMENT
ALASKA OFFICE BUILDING
JUNEAU, AK 99801
See Biology: General; Government-State or Local

HYDROLOGY OFFICE, NATIONAL WEATHER SERVICES, ALASKA OFFICE
632 SIXTH AVENUE
ANCHORAGE, AK 99501
See Engineering: Water Resources; Government-State or Local

MARINE SCIENCE DIVISION, 17TH COAST GUARD DISTRICT
BOX 3-5000, NEW FEDERAL BUILDING
JUNEAU, AK 99801
See Engineering: Water Resources; Government-Federal

MARINE SCIENCE INSTITUTE
UNIVERSITY OF ALASKA
COLLEGE, AK 99701
See Chemistry: General; Research Institute

MARINE STATION
UNIVERSITY OF ALASKA
DOUGLAS, AK 99824
See Biology: General; Educational Institute

MEAT AND POULTRY SURVEY, STATE DIVISION OF AGRICULTURE
POST OFFICE BOX 490
JUNEAU, AK 99801
See Engineering: Agricultural Engineering; Government-State or Local

NATIONAL WILDLIFE FEDERATION
REGION 11
JUNEAU, AK 99801
See Biology: Ecology; Foundation

NATIVE HEALTH SERVICE, ALASKA AREA
POST OFFICE BOX 7-741
ANCHORAGE, AK 99510
See Engineering: Water Resources; Government-State or Local

NOISE ABATEMENT, FEDERAL AVIATION ADMINISTRATION REGIONAL OFFICE
632 SIXTH AVENUE
ANCHORAGE, AK 99501
See Interdisciplinary: General; Unclassified

PESTICIDE CONSERVATION, STATE DIVISION OF AGRICULTURE
BOX 800
PALMER, AK 99645
See Engineering: Agricultural Engineering; Government-State or Local

SOIL CONSERVATION SERVICE
204 EAST 5TH-ROOM 217
ANCHORAGE, AK 99645
See Interdisciplinary: General; Government-State or Local

TECHNOLOGY LABORATORY, BUREAU OF COMMERCIAL FISHERIES
622 MISSION STREET
KETCHIKAN, AK 99901
See Biology: General; Government-Federal

Alabama

AGRICULTURAL AND CHEMICAL DEVELOPMENT OFFICE
NATIONAL FERTILIZER DEVELOPMENT CENTER
MUSCLE SHOALS, AL 35660
See Engineering: Agricultural Engineering; Government-State or Local

AGRICULTURAL CHEMISTRY DIVISION
BEARD BUILDING, BOX 3336
MONTGOMERY, AL 36109
See Engineering: Agricultural Engineering; Government-State or Local

AIR POLLUTION CONTROL BOARD
POST OFFICE BOX 500
HUNTSVILLE, AL 35801
See Engineering: Pollution Abatement; Professional Organizations

AIR POLLUTION CONTROL DIVISION, ENVIRONMENTAL HEALTH BUREAU
248 COX STREET
MOBILE, AL 36009
See Engineering: Pollution Abatement; Government-State or Local

AIR POLLUTION PROGRAM, ENVIRONMENTAL HEALTH BUREAU
1912 EIGHTH AVENUE SOUTH, BOX 2591
BIRMINGHAM, AL 35202
See Engineering: Pollution Abatement; Government-State or Local

AQUACULTURE CENTER, FISHERIES BUILDING
AUBURN UNIVERSITY
AUBURN, AL 36830
See Biology: Ecology; Educational Institute

DEVELOPMENT OFFICE OF ALABAMA
MONTGOMERY, AL 36104
See Engineering: Pollution Abatement; Government-State or Local

ENVIRONMENTAL PROTECTION AGENCY LABORATORY
DAUPHIN ISLAND, AL 36528
See Biology: Ecology; Field Station/Laboratory

ENVIRONMENTAL PROTECTION AGENCY LABORATORY
MONTGOMERY, AL 36101
See Biology: Ecology; Field Station/Laboratory

ENVIRONMENTAL SCIENCE PROGRAM
AUBURN UNIVERSITY
AUBURN, AL 36830
See Interdisciplinary: General; Educational Institute

ENVIRONMENTAL SCIENCE PROGRAM
UNIVERSITY OF ALABAMA
UNIVERSITY, AL 35486
See Interdisciplinary: General; Educational Institute

ENVIRONMENTAL STUDIES PROGRAM
TUSKEGEE INSTITUTE
TUSKEGEE, AL 36088
See Interdisciplinary: General; Educational Institute

GEOLOGICAL SURVEY OF ALABAMA
P O DRAWER O, UNIVERSITY OF ALABAMA
TUSCALOOSA, AL 35486
See Interdisciplinary: General; Government-State or Local

GULF COAST SHELLFISH SANITATION RESEARCH CENTER
POST OFFICE BOX 158
DAUPHIN ISLAND, AL 36528
See Engineering: Agricultural Engineering; Government-Federal

GULF COAST WATER SUPPLY RESEARCH LABORATORY
POST OFFICE BOX 158
DAUPHIN ISLAND, AL 36528
See Interdisciplinary: General; Unclassified

MARINE RESOURCES, UNIVERSITY OF ALABAMA
P O BOX 188

DAUPHIN ISLAND, AL 36528
See Biology: General; Educational Institute

MENTAL HYGIENE DIVISION, PUBLIC HEALTH DEPARTMENT
STATE OFFICE BUILDING
MONTGOMERY, AL 36104
See Social Sciences/Humanities: Mental Health; Government-State or Local

ORNITHOLOGICAL SOCIETY OF ALABAMA
POST OFFICE BOX 1448
BIRMINGHAM, AL 35201
See Biology: General; Professional Organizations

PENSIONS AND SECURITY DEPARTMENT
STATE ADMINISTRATION BUILDING, 64 NORTH UNION
MONTGOMERY, AL 36104
See Social Sciences/Humanities: Welfare(Child Public Social); Government-State or Local

PLANNING AND ZONING DEPARTMENT
701 NORTH 20 STREET
BIRMINGHAM, AL 35203
See Engineering: Water Resources; Government-State or Local

RADIOLOGICAL HEALTH DIVISION, ENVIRONMENTAL HEALTH DEPARTMENT
STATE OFFICE BUILDING
MONTGOMERY, AL 36104
See Engineering: Pollution Abatement; Government-State or Local

SMOKE ABATEMENT AND BOILER INSPECTION DIVISION, INSPECTION SERVICE
711 NORTH 19TH STREET
BIRMINGHAM, AL 35203
See Engineering: Pollution Abatement; Government-State or Local

SOIL CONSERVATION
POST OFFICE BOX 311
AUBURN, AL 36830
See Biology: Ecology; Government-State or Local

SOIL CONSERVATION COMMITTEE
STATE OFFICE BUILDING
MONTGOMERY, AL 36104
See Engineering: Water Resources; Government-State or Local

SOUTHERN RESEARCH INSTITUTE
2000 9TH AVENUE SOUTH
BIRMINGHAM, AL 35205
See Engineering: Water Resources; Educational Institute

WATER IMPROVEMENT COMMISSION
STATE OFFICE BUILDING

MONTGOMERY, AL 36104
See Engineering: Water Resources; Government-State or Local

WATER RESOURCES INSTITUTION
MARY MARTIN HALL, AUBURN UNIVERSITY
AUBURN, AL 36830
See Interdisciplinary: General; Educational Institute

WILDLIFE RESEARCH UNIT OF ALABAMA
AUBURN UNIVERSITY
AUBURN, AL 36830
See Biology: General; Research Institute

Arkansas

ARKANSAS POLLUTION CONTROL COMMISSION
1100 HARRINGTON AVENUE
LITTLE ROCK, AR 72202
See Engineering: Pollution Abatement; Government-State or Local

ATMOSPHERIC SCIENCES CENTER
UNIVERSITY OF ARKANSAS
FAYETTEVILLE, AR 72701
See Engineering: Pollution Abatement; Educational Institute

AUDUBON SOCIETY OF ARKANSAS, INCORPORATED
180 NORTH BROADWAY
EL DORADO, AR 71730
See Interdisciplinary: General; Professional Organizations

DYNAMIC AND MESO-METEOROLOGY, DEPARTMENT OF CHEMISTRY
UNIVERSITY OF ARKANSAS
FAYETTEVILLE, AR 72701
See Chemistry: General; Educational Institute

GEOLOGICAL COMMISSION
STATE CAPITOL
LITTLE ROCK, AR 72201
See Engineering: Water Resources; Government-State or Local

OZARK SOCIETY, INCORPORATED
BOX 209
BENTONVILLE, AR 72712
See Biology: Ecology; Foundation

SOIL AND WATER CONSERVATION COMMISSION OF ARKANSAS
STATE CAPITOL
LITTLE ROCK, AR 72201
See Interdisciplinary: General; Government-State or Local

**WATER POLLUTION CONTROL
ASSOCIATION OF ARKANSAS**
COLLEGE OF ENGINEERING,
UNIVERSITY OF ARKANSAS
FAYETTEVILLE, AR 72703
See Engineering: Water Resources; Educational Institute

**WATER POLLUTION CONTROL
ASSOCIATION, STATE AND
INTERSTATE**
1100 HARRINGTON AVENUE
LITTLE ROCK, AR 72202
See Engineering: Pollution Abatement;
Government-Federal

**WATER RESOURCES RESEARCH
CENTER**
UNIVERSITY OF ARKANSAS
FAYETTEVILLE, AR 72701
See Biology: Ecology; Educational Institute

**WILDLIFE FEDERATION OF
ARKANSAS**
BOX 2277
LITTLE ROCK, AR 72201
See Biology: Ecology; Foundation

**WILDLIFE FEDERATION OF
ARKANSAS**
515 SOUTH MAIN STREET
STUTTGARD, AR 72106
See Biology: Ecology; Foundation

Arizona

**AGRICULTURAL CHEMISTRY AND
SOILS DEPARTMENT**
507 AGRICULTURAL SCIENCES
BUILDING
TUCSON, AZ 85721
See Engineering: Agricultural Engineering; Educational Institute

AIR POLLUTION CONTROL
161 W ALAMEDA
TUCSON, AZ 85701
See Engineering: Pollution Abatement;
Government-State or Local

ARID LANDS PROGRAM
UNIVERSITY OF ARIZONA
TUCSON, AZ 85721
See Engineering: Agricultural Engineering; Educational Institute

ATMOSPHERIC PHYSICS INSTITUTE
UNIVERSITY OF ARIZONA
TUCSON, AZ 85721
See Physics: General; Educational Institute

**CONSERVATION COUNCIL OF
ARIZONA**
POST OFFICE BOX 1771
SCOTTSDALE, AZ 85252

See Biology: Ecology; Professional Organizations

**ENVIRONMENTAL HEALTH
DIVISION, STATE HEALTH
DEPARTMENT**
14 NORTH CENTRAL AVENUE
PHOENIX, AZ 85004
See Engineering: Pollution Abatement;
Government-State or Local

**ENVIRONMENTAL SCIENCE
PROGRAM**
ARIZONA STATE UNIVERSITY
TEMPE, AZ 85281
See Interdisciplinary: General; Educational Institute

**ENVIRONMENTAL SCIENCE
PROGRAM**
UNIVERSITY OF ARIZONA
TUCSON, AZ 85721
See Interdisciplinary: General; Educational Institute

**ETHNIC RESEARCH BUREAU,
ANTHROPOLOGY DEPARTMENT**
UNIVERSITY OF ARIZONA
TUCSON, ARIZONA
See Interdisciplinary: General; Educational Institute

**FOREST HYDROLOGY
LABORATORY**
ARIZONA STATE UNIVERSITY
TEMPE, AZ 85281
See Engineering: General; Field Station/
Laboratory

**GEOCHRONOLOGY DEPARTMENT,
EARTH SCIENCES SCHOOL**
UNIVERSITY OF ARIZONA
TUCSON, AZ 85721
See Geology: General; Educational Institute

**HEALTH DEPARTMENT, HAYDEN
PLAZA WEST**
4019 NORTH 33RD STREET
PHOENIX, AZ 85017
See Engineering: Water Resources; Government-State or Local

**HEALTH, FOOD, AND DRUGS
DEPARTMENT**
1624 WEST ADAMS STREET
PHOENIX, AZ 85007
See Interdisciplinary: General; Government-State or Local

**INDIAN HEALTH SERVICE,
NAVAJO AREA**
POST OFFICE BOX G
WINDOW ROCK, AZ 86515
See Engineering: Water Resources; Government-State or Local

**INDIAN HEALTH SERVICE, OFFICE
OF PROGRAM DEVELOPMENT**
POST OFFICE BOX 11340
TUCSON, AZ 85706

See Engineering: Water Resources; Government-State or Local

**INDIAN HEALTH SERVICE,
PHOENIX AREA**
801 EAST INDIAN SCHOOL ROAD
PHOENIX, AZ 85014
See Engineering: Water Resources; Government-State or Local

**MINES BUREAU OF ARIZONA,
COLLEGE OF MINES**
UNIVERSITY OF ARIZONA
TUCSON, AZ 85721
See Geology: General; Educational Institute

**MUSEUM OF THE STATE OF
ARIZONA**
UNIVERSITY OF ARIZONA
TUCSON, AZ 85721
See Social Sciences/Humanities: General;
Government-State or Local

**NATIONAL WILDLIFE
FEDERATION**
REGION 10
PHOENIX, AZ 85001
See Biology: Ecology; Foundation

**PESTICIDE CONTROL, UNIVERSITY
OF ARIZONA EXPERIMENTAL
STATION**
POST OFFICE BOX 1130
MESA, AZ 85201
See Chemistry: General; Government-
State or Local

PUBLIC WELFARE DEPARTMENT
1632 WEST ADAMS STREET
PHOENIX, AZ 85007
See Social Sciences/Humanities:
Welfare(Child Public Social);
Government-State or Local

**RECREATION AND PARKS
ADMINISTRATION**
ARIZONA POLYTECHNICAL
COLLEGE
RUSSELLVILLE, AZ 72801
See Social Sciences/Humanities:
Recreation and Leisure; Educational
Institute

**ROCKY MOUNTAIN FOREST AND
RANGE EXPERIMENTAL STATION**
282 AGRICULTURE BUILDING
TEMPE, AZ 85281
See Engineering: Agricultural Engineering; Government-Federal

**SANITATION BUREAU, COUNTY
HEALTH DEPARTMENT**
1825 EAST ROOSEVELT DRIVE, BOX
2111
PHOENIX, AZ 85006
See Engineering: Pollution Abatement;
Government-State or Local

**SOIL AND WATER CONSERVATION
ASSOCIATION**
POST OFFICE BOX 128

PEORIA, AZ 85345
See Biology: Ecology; Government-State or Local

SOIL CONSERVATION AND MANAGEMENT DIVISION
400 STATE OFFICE BUILDING
PHOENIX, AZ 85007
See Interdisciplinary: General; Government-State or Local

SOIL CONSERVATION SERVICES
230 NORTH FIRST AVENUE, 6029 FEDERAL BUILDING
PHOENIX, AZ 85025
See Biology: Ecology; Government-State or Local

TREE-RING RESEARCH LABORATORY
UNIVERSITY OF ARIZONA
TUCSON, AZ 85717
See Interdisciplinary: General; Educational Institute

WATER POLLUTION CONTROL ASSOCIATION
POST OFFICE BOX 158
SCOTTSDALE, AZ 85252
See Engineering: Water Resources; Government-State or Local

WATER UTILIZATION INSTITUTE
UNIVERSITY OF ARIZONA
TUCSON, AZ 85721
See Engineering: Water Resources; Educational Institute

WHOOPING CRANE CONSERVATION ASSOCIATION
216 WHITTON STREET
SIERRA VISTA, AZ 85635
See Biology: General; Professional Organizations

WILDLIFE FEDERATION OF ARIZONA
POST OFFICE BOX 1769
PHOENIX, AZ 85001
See Biology: Ecology; Foundation

WILDLIFE RESEARCH
BIOLOGICAL SCIENCES BUILDING, ROOM 214
TUCSON, AZ 85717
See Biology: General; Educational Institute

California

ADMINISTRATION BUILDING AT SANTA CLARA COUNTY
70 WEST HEDDING STREET
SAN JOSE, CA 95110
See Interdisciplinary: General; Government-State or Local

ADVANCED TECHNOLOGY OPERATIONS, BECKMAN INSTITUTE
2500 HARBOR BOULEVARD
FULLERTON, CA 92634
See Interdisciplinary: General; Industrial/Commercial

AEROSPACE AND SYSTEMS DIVISION, SCIENCE CENTER
NORTH AMERICAN ROCKWELL, POST OFFICE BOX 1470
THOUSAND OAKS, CA 91360
See Engineering: Pollution Abatement; Foundation

AGRICULTURAL AND ECONOMICAL LIBRARY, GIANNINI FOUNDATION
248 GIANNINI HALL, UNIVERSITY OF CALIFORNIA
BERKELEY, CA 94720
See Engineering: General; Educational Institute

AGRICULTURAL AND ENVIRONMENTAL SCIENCES COLLEGE
UNIVERSITY OF CALIFORNIA
DAVIS, CA 95616
See Engineering: Agricultural Engineering; Educational Institute

AGRICULTURAL, ECONOMICAL, RESOURCES COUNCIL
212 POST OFFICE BUILDING
BERKELEY, CA 94701
See Engineering: Agricultural Engineering; Research Institute

AGRICULTURE COLLEGE
UNIVERSITY OF CALIFORNIA
DAVIS, CA 95616
See Engineering: Agricultural Engineering; Educational Institute

AGRICULTURE DEPARTMENT
UNIVERSITY OF CALIFORNIA
BERKELEY, CA 94720
See Engineering: Agricultural Engineering; Educational Institute

AGRONOMY AND RANGE SCIENCE DEPARTMENT
UNIVERSITY OF CALIFORNIA
DAVIS, CA 95616
See Biology: Biochemistry; Educational Institute

AIR AND SPACECRAFT REMOTE SENSING
AMES RESEARCH CENTER
MOFFETT FIELD, CA 94035
See Interdisciplinary: General; Research Institute

AIR AND WATER POLLUTION DIVISION
3100 FLORA STREET
SAN LUIS OBISPO, CA 93401
See Engineering: Pollution Abatement; Research Institute

AIR CONSERVATION UNION
701 OCEAN STREET, ROOM 420
SANTA CRUZ, CA 95060
See Engineering: Pollution Abatement; Government-State or Local

AIR POLLUTION
P O BOX 363
SAN JOSE, CA 95103
See Engineering: Pollution Abatement; Research Institute

AIR POLLUTION CONTROL
1601 EAST HAZELTON AVENUE
STOCKTON, CA 95201
See Engineering: Pollution Abatement; Government-State or Local

AIR POLLUTION CONTROL
172 WEST 3RD STREET
SAN BERNARDINO, CA 92401
See Engineering: Pollution Abatement; Government-State or Local

AIR POLLUTION CONTROL
3575 11TH STREET
RIVERSIDE, CA 92501
See Engineering: Pollution Abatement; Government-State or Local

AIR POLLUTION CONTROL DISTRIBUTORS
1010 SOUTH HARBOR BOULEVARD
ANAHEIM, CA 92805
See Engineering: Pollution Abatement; Government-State or Local

AIR POLLUTION CONTROL DISTRICT
434 SOUTH SAN PEDRO STREET
LOS ANGELES, CA 90013
See Engineering: Pollution Abatement; Government-State or Local

AIR POLLUTION CONTROL DISTRICT, SHASTA COUNTY HEALTH DEPARTMENT
2601 HOSPITAL LANE
REDDING, CA 96001
See Engineering: Pollution Abatement; Government-State or Local

AIR POLLUTION CONTROL, HEALTH DEPARTMENT
2221 STOCKTON BOULEVARD
SACRAMENTO, CA 95817
See Engineering: Pollution Abatement; Government-State or Local

AIR POLLUTION CONTROL, MONTEREY COUNTY DISTRICT
BOX 2137 1270 NATIVIDAD ROAD
SALINAS, CA 93901
See Engineering: Pollution Abatement; Government-State or Local

AIR POLLUTION CONTROL, PUBLIC HEALTH DEPARTMENT
1600 PACIFIC HIGHWAY
SAN DIEGO, CA 92101

See Engineering: Pollution Abatement; Government-State or Local

AIR POLLUTION DISTRICT
5630 SOUTH BROADWAY
EUREKA, CA 95501
See Engineering: Pollution Abatement; Government-State or Local

AIR POLLUTION EFFECTS ON TEXTILE FABRICS
UNIVERSITY OF CALIFORNIA
DAVIS, CA 95616
See Engineering: Pollution Abatement; Educational Institute

AIR POLLUTION RESOURCES CENTER
UNIVERSITY OF CALIFORNIA
RIVERSIDE, CA 92507
See Engineering: Pollution Abatement; Educational Institute

AIR RESOURCES BOARD
417 SOUTH HILL STREET
LOS ANGELES, CA 90013
See Engineering: Pollution Abatement; Government-State or Local

AIR SANITATION BUREAU, STATE PUBLIC HEALTH DEPARTMENT
2151 BERKELEY WAY
BERKELEY, CA 94704
See Engineering: Pollution Abatement; Government-State or Local

AIR SANITATION, COUNTY HEALTH DEPARTMENT
POST OFFICE BOX 871
MARTINEZ, CA 94533
See Engineering: Pollution Abatement; Government-State or Local

ALCOHOLIC REHABILITATION, PUBLIC HEALTH DEPARTMENT
2151 BERKELEY WAY
BERKELEY, CA 94704
See Social Sciences/Humanities: Rehabilitation; Government-State or Local

AMERICAN BOTTLED WATER ASSOCIATION
1411 WEST OLYMPIC BOULEVARD
LOS ANGELES, CA 90015
See Engineering: Water Resources; Professional Organizations

AMERICAN NUCLEONICS CORPORATION
1007 AIRWAY
GLENDALE, CA 91201
See Chemistry: General; Industrial/Commercial

AMERICAN TUNABOAT ASSOCIATION
ONE TUNA LANE
SAN DIEGO, CA 92101
See Engineering: Water Resources; Industrial/Commercial

AMES RESEARCH CENTER, NASA
MOFFETT FIELD, CA 94035
See Physics: General; Government-Federal

APPLIED INSTRUMENT CORPORATION, ENGINEERING
1468 LUNING DRIVE
SAN JOSE, CA 95118
See Engineering: General; Industrial/Commercial

ARTKAM CORPORATION (OMEGA)
858 SAN ANTONIO ROAD
PALO ALTO, CA 94303
See Interdisciplinary: General; Industrial/Commercial

ATMOSPHERIC RESEARCH GROUP
ALTADENA, CA 91001
See Engineering: Pollution Abatement; Research Institute

ATMOSPHERIC STUDIES CENTER
UNIVERSITY OF CALIFORNIA
DAVIS, CA 95616
See Engineering: Pollution Abatement; Educational Institute

ATMOSPHERIC STUDIES PROGRAM
CALIFORNIA INSTITUTE OF TECHNOLOGY
PASADENA, CA 91100
See Engineering: Pollution Abatement; Educational Institute

ATOMIC ENERGY COMMISSION SAN FRANCISCO OPERATIONS
2111 BANCROFT WAY
BERKELEY, CA 94704
See Chemistry: Physical Chemistry; Government-State or Local

AUDUBON SOCIETY OF SANTA CLARA VALLEY
945 MATADERO
PALO ALTO, CA 94306
See Biology: Ecology; Industrial/Commercial

BACTERIOLOGY DEPARTMENT
UNIVERSITY OF CALIFORNIA
DAVIS, CA 95616
See Biology: General; Educational Institute

BAY AREA AIR POLLUTION CONTROL DISTRICT
939 ELLIS STREET
SAN FRANCISCO, CA 94109
See Engineering: Pollution Abatement; Government-Federal

BAY AREA POLLUTION CONTROL DISTRICT
1418 MISSION STREET
SAN FRANCISCO, CA 94103
See Engineering: Pollution Abatement; Government-State or Local

BEAUDETTE FOUNDATION FOR BIOLOGICAL RESEARCH
P O BOX 229
MOSS LANDING, CA 95039
See Biology: General; Foundation

BIOCHEMISTRY DEPARTMENT
UNIVERSITY OF CALIFORNIA
RIVERSIDE, CA 92505
See Biology: Biochemistry; Educational Institute

BIOCHEMISTRY DEPARTMENT, BECKMAN INSTRUMENTS, INCORPORATED
2500 HARBOR BOULEVARD
FULLERTON, CA 92634
See Biology: Biochemistry; Research Institute

BIOLOGICAL LABORATORY, UNIVERSITY OF CALIFORNIA
P O BOX 271
LA JOLLA, CA 92037
See Biology: General; Educational Institute

BIOLOGICAL SCIENCES DEPARTMENT
SAN JOSE STATE COLLEGE
SAN JOSE, CA 95114
See Biology: Ecology; Educational Institute

BIOLOGICAL SCIENCES DEPARTMENT, CALIFORNIA STATE COLLEGE
800 MONTE VISTA AVENUE
TURLOCK, CA 93726
See Biology: General; Educational Institute

BIOLOGY AND ECOLOGY DEPARTMENT
SAN JOSE STATE COLLEGE
SAN JOSE, CA 95114
See Biology: Ecology; Educational Institute

BIOLOGY AND HEALTH SCIENCES
CALIFORNIA STATE COLLEGE AT HAWARD
HAWARD, CA 94542
See Biology: General; Educational Institute

BIOLOGY DEPARTMENT
CALIFORNIA STATE POLYTECHNIC INSTITUTE
POMONA, CA 94366
See Biology: General; Educational Institute

BIOLOGY DEPARTMENT
400 MIDDLEFORD ROAD
PALO ALTO, CA 94303
See Interdisciplinary: General; Educational Institute

BIOPHYSICS DIVISION, LITTON SYSTEMS, INCORPORATED
3385 JUBILEE DRIVE
ENCINO, CA 91313
See Biology: Biophysics; Industrial/Commercial

BIOTOXICOLOGY INTERNATIONAL CENTER
WORLD LIFE RESEARCH INSTITUTE
COLTON, CA 92324
See Biology: Ecology; Research Institute

BOTANY DEPARTMENT, STANISLAUS STATE COLLEGE
800 MONTE VISTA AVENUE
TURLOCK, CA 93940
See Biology: General; Educational Institute

CALIFORNIA DEPARTMENT OF PUBLIC HEALTH
2151 BERKELEY WAY
BERKELEY, CA 94704
See Biology: Biochemistry; Government-State or Local

CALIFORNIA INSTITUTE OF TECHNOLOGY
1201 EAST BOULEVARD
PASADENA, CA 91109
See Interdisciplinary: General; Educational Institute

CALIFORNIA ROADSIDE COUNCIL, INCORPORATED
2636 OCEAN AVENUE
SAN FRANCISCO, CA 94132
See Engineering: General; Professional Organizations

CALIFORNIA TOMORROW
681 MARKET STREET
SAN FRANCISCO, CA 94105
See Interdisciplinary: General; Professional Organizations

CARTWRIGHT AERIAL SURVEYS, INCORPORATED
MUNICIPAL AIRPORT
SACRAMENTO, CA 95834
See Interdisciplinary: General; Industrial/Commercial

CETACEAN SOCIETY OF AMERICA
4725 LINCOLN BOULEVARD
MARINA DEL REY, CA 90291
See Biology: General; Professional Organizations

CHEMICAL ENGINEERING
SAN JOSE STATE COLLEGE
SAN JOSE, CA 95114
See Engineering: Chemical Engineering; Educational Institute

CHEMICAL ENGINEERING
2999 SAN YSIDRO
SANTA CLARA, CA 95051
See Engineering: Chemical Engineering; Industrial/Commercial

CHEMICAL OCEANOGRAPHY
SAN JOSE STATE COLLEGE
SAN JOSE, CA 95114
See Chemistry: General; Educational Institute

CHEMISTRY AND METEOROLOGY DIVISIONS
433 VAN NESS
SANTA CRUZ, CA 95060
See Chemistry: General; Research Institute

CHEMISTRY DEPARTMENT
UNIVERSITY OF CALIFORNIA
BERKELEY, CA 94720
See Engineering: General; Educational Institute

CHEMISTRY DEPARTMENT
UNIVERSITY OF CALIFORNIA
LA JOLLA, CA 92037
See Chemistry: General; Educational Institute

CHEMISTRY DEPARTMENT
UNIVERSITY OF CALIFORNIA, RIVERSIDE
RIVERSIDE, CA 92502
See Chemistry: General; Educational Institute

CHEMISTRY ENGINEERING AND ENVIRONMENTAL HEALTH ENGINEERING
CIT
PASADENA, CA 91109
See Engineering: General; Educational Institute

CITY COLLEGE OF SAN FRANCISCO
50 PHELAN AVENUE
SAN FRANCISCO, CA 94112
See Engineering: General; Educational Institute

CIVIL AND STRUCTURAL ENGINEERING
3104 MOUNTAIN CURVE AVENUE
ALTADENA, CA 91001
See Engineering: General; Professional Organizations

CIVIL ENGINEERING
SAN JOSE STATE COLLEGE
SAN JOSE, CA 95114
See Engineering: General; Educational Institute

CLIMATOLOGY, METEOROLOGY AND STATISTICS DEPARTMENT
CALIFORNIA STATE UNIVERSITY
NORTHRIDGE, CA 91324
See Interdisciplinary: General; Educational Institute

CLOUD PHYSICS
464 W WOODBURY ROAD, POST OFFICE 657
ALTADENA, CA 91001
See Physics: General; Research Institute

COMMUNICATIONS, CYBERNETICS
674 HAMILTON LANE
SANTA CLARA, CA 95051
See Interdisciplinary: General; Industrial/Commercial

COMSIS CORPORATION
3448 DE LA CRUZ BOULEVARD
SANTA CLARA, CA 95050
See Interdisciplinary: General; Industrial/Commercial

CONSERVATION AND DEVELOPMENT COMMISSION OF SAN FRANCISCO BAY
30 VAN NESS AVENUE ROOM 2127
SAN FRANCISCO, CA 94102
See Biology: Ecology; Government-State or Local

CONSERVATION ASSOCIATES
MILLS TOWER, 220 BUSH STREET
SAN FRANCISCO, CA 94104
See Social Sciences/Humanities: Regional Planning; Professional Organizations

CONSERVATION INFORMATION (AMERICAN ASSOCIATION)
1416 9TH STREET
SACRAMENTO, CA 95814
See Engineering: General; Professional Organizations

CONSERVATION LAW SOCIETY OF AMERICA
1500 MILLS TOWER, 220 BUSH
SAN FRANCISCO, CA 94104
See Social Sciences/Humanities: Law/Legislation; Professional Organizations

CONSERVATION TRUSTEES
251 KEARNY STREET
SAN FRANCISCO, CA 94108
See Social Sciences/Humanities: Law/Legislation; Research Institute

CONSULTANTS COMPUTATION BUREAU
594 HOWARD STREET
SAN FRANISCO, CA 94105
See Interdisciplinary: General; Industrial/Commercial

COOPER ORNITHOLOGICAL SOCIETY
CALIFORNIA ACADEMY OF SCIENCES, GOLDEN GATE PARK
SAN FRANCISCO, CA 94118
See Interdisciplinary: General; Professional Organizations

COUNTY ENGINEERING DEPARTMENT
COUNTY OF LOS ANGELES, 108 WEST 2ND STREET
LOS ANGELES, CA 90012
See Engineering: General; Government-State or Local

DESERT PROTECTIVE COUNCIL
POST OFFICE BOX 33
BANNING, CA 92220
See Interdisciplinary: General; Foundation

EAGLE LAKE FIELD STATION
CHICO STATE COLLEGE
CHICO, CA 95926
See Interdisciplinary: General; Educational Institute

ECOLOGY ACTION
POST OFFICE BOX 9334
BERKELEY, CA 94709
See Biology: Ecology; Professional Organizations

ECOLOGY AND CONSERVATION
AUDUBON CANYON RANCH
STINSON BEACH, CA 94970
See Biology: Ecology; Research Institute

ECOLOGY CENTER
P O BOX 1100
BERKELEY, CA 94701
See Engineering: Water Resources; Educational Institute

ECOLOGY INSTITUTE
UNIVERSITY OF CALIFORNIA
DAVIS, CA 95616
See Interdisciplinary: General; Educational Institute

ECOLOGY, AGROMETEOROLOGY, DEPARTMENT OF TECHNOLOGY OPERATIONS
2500 HARBOR BOULEVARD
FULLERTON, CA 92634
See Biology: Ecology; Industrial/Commercial

ECOLOGY, MARINE BIOLOGY
SAN JOSE STATE COLLEGE
SAN JOSE, CA 95114
See Biology: Ecology; Educational Institute

ECONOMICS DEPARTMENT
SAN JOSE STATE COLLEGE
SAN JOSE, CA 95114
See Social Sciences/Humanities: Community Development/Studies; Educational Institute

EDUCATIONAL PSYCHOLOGY LIBRARY, UNIVERSITY OF CALIFORNIA
405 HILGARD AVENUE
LOS ANGELES, CA 90024
See Social Sciences/Humanities: Psychology/Behavioral Science; Educational Institute

ELECTRICAL ENGINEERING DEPARTMENT
SAN JOSE STATE COLLEGE
SAN JOSE, CA 95114
See Engineering: General; Educational Institute

EMPLOYMENT DEPARTMENT
800 CAPITOL MALL
SACRAMENTO,CA 95814
See Social Sciences/Humanities: Employment/Unemployment; Government-State or Local

ENGINEERING DEPARTMENT
UNIVERSITY OF CALIFORNIA
LOS ANGELES, CA 90024
See Engineering: Water Resources; Educational Institute

ENGINEERING-ECONOMIC PLANNING LIBRARY, STANFORD UNIVERSITY
ROOM 274 CIVIL ENGINEERING DEPARTMENT
STANFORD, CA 94305
See Engineering: Water Resources; Educational Institute

ENTOMOLOGY DEPARTMENT
SAN JOSE STATE COLLEGE
SAN JOSE, CA 95114
See Biology: General; Educational Institute

ENVIROMENTAL HEALTH DEPARTMENT
3141 LOMA VISTA ROAD
VENTURA, CA 93001
See Engineering: Pollution Abatement; Government-State or Local

ENVIRONMENTAL AESTHETICS
SAN JOSE STATE COLLEGE
SAN JOSE, CA 95114
See Biology: Ecology; Educational Institute

ENVIRONMENTAL AND PUBLIC HEALTH SCHOOL
UNIVERSITY OF CALIFORNIA
IRVINE, CA 92664
See Social Sciences/Humanities: General; Educational Institute

ENVIRONMENTAL DESIGN, ANTHROPOLOGY
SAN JOSE STATE COLLEGE
SAN JOSE, CA 95114
See Interdisciplinary: General; Educational Institute

ENVIRONMENTAL EDUCATION, NATIONAL PARK SERVICES WESTERN OFFICE
450 GOLDEN GATE-BOX 36063
SAN FRANCISCO, CA 94102
See Biology: Ecology; Government-State or Local

ENVIRONMENTAL ENGINEERING SCIENCE
CALIFORNIA INSTITUTE OF TECHNOLOGY
PASADENA, CA 91109
See Interdisciplinary: General; Educational Institute

ENVIRONMENTAL EPIDEMICS, DEPARTMENT OF PUBLIC HEALTH
2151 BERKELEY WAY
BERKELEY, CA 94704
See Biology: Ecology; Government-State or Local

ENVIRONMENTAL HEALTH
SAN JOSE STATE COLLEGE
SAN JOSE, CA 95114
See Interdisciplinary: General; Educational Institute

ENVIRONMENTAL HEALTH
369 EAST REED STREET
SAN JOSE, CA 95112
See Interdisciplinary: General; Research Institute

ENVIRONMENTAL HEALTH ENGINEERING
CALIFORNIA INSTITUTE OF TECHNOLOGY
PASADENA, CA 91109
See Chemistry: General; Educational Institute

ENVIRONMENTAL INFORMATION CENTER
CALIFORNIA STATE UNIVERSITY-SAN JOSE
SAN JOSE, CA 95114
See Biology: Ecology; Educational Institute

ENVIRONMENTAL MEDICINE
55 GOLDEN OAK DRIVE
PORTOLA VALLEY, CA 94025
See Interdisciplinary: General; Research Institute

ENVIRONMENTAL PLANNING, RHM ASSOCIATES
POST OFFICE BOX 4116
CARMEL, CA 93921
See Biology: Ecology; Research Institute

ENVIRONMENTAL PROTECTION AGENCY, REGION 9
100 CALIFORNIA STREET
SAN FRANCISCO, CA 94111
See Interdisciplinary: General; Unclassified

ENVIRONMENTAL QUALITY LABORATORY
CALIFORNIA INSTITUTION OF TECHNOLOGY
PASADENA, CA 91109
See Interdisciplinary: General; Research Institute

ENVIRONMENTAL SANITATION AND HEALTH
234 CHERRY STREET
SALINAS, CA 93901
See Biology: Ecology; Industrial/Commercial

ENVIRONMENTAL SCIENCE
CENTER
SANTA ROSA JUNIOR COLLEGE
SANTA ROSA, CA 95401
See Biology: Ecology; Educational Institute

ENVIRONMENTAL SCIENCE
INSTITUTE
125 SOUTH SEVENTH STREET
SAN JOSE, CA 95114
See Interdisciplinary: General; Educational Institute

ENVIRONMENTAL SCIENCE
PROGRAM
CALIFORNIA STATE UNIVERSITY,
NORTHRIDGE
NORTHRIDGE, CA 91324
See Interdisciplinary: General; Educational Institute

ENVIRONMENTAL SCIENCE
PROGRAM
UNIVERSITY OF CALIFORNIA
SANTA BARBARA, CA 93106
See Interdisciplinary: General; Educational Institute

ENVIRONMENTAL SCIENCE
PROGRAM
UNIVERSITY OF CALIFORNIA,
RIVERSIDE
RIVERSIDE, CA 92502
See Chemistry: General; Educational Institute

ENVIRONMENTAL SCIENCE
PROGRAM
UNIVERSITY OF THE PACIFIC
STOCKTON, CA 95204
See Chemistry: General; Educational Institute

ENVIRONMENTAL SCIENCES
CENTER
SANTA ROSA JUNIOR COLLEGE
SANTA ROSA, CA 95402
See Biology: General; Educational Institute

ENVIRONMENTAL SCIENCES
GROUP, CALIFORNIA STATE
COLLEGE
1000 EAST VICTORIA STREET
DOMINGUEZ HILLS, CA 90247
See Interdisciplinary: General; Educational Institute

ENVIRONMENTAL SCIENCES
GROUP, CLIMATE INSTRUCTION
1240 BIRCHWOOD DRIVE
SUNNYVILLE, CA 94086
See Geology: General; Industrial/Commercial

ENVIRONMENTAL SCIENCES
INSTITUTE
125 SOUTH 7TH STREET
SAN JOSE, CA 95114
See Biology: Ecology; Research Institute

ENVIRONMENTAL SCIENCES
PROGRAM
CALIFORNIA STATE UNIVERSITY,
SAN DIEGO
SAN DIEGO, CA 92115
See Interdisciplinary: General; Educational Institute

ENVIRONMENTAL SCIENCES
PROGRAM
SAN JOSE STATE COLLEGE
SAN JOSE, CA 95114
See Interdisciplinary: General; Educational Institute

ENVIRONMENTAL SCIENCES
PROGRAM
2130 FULTON STREET
SAN FRANCISCO, CA 94117
See Chemistry: General; Educational Institute

ENVIRONMENTAL SCIENCES
PROGRAM, SAN FRANCISCO
STATE COLLEGE
1600 HOLLOWAY AVENUE
SAN FRANCISCO, CA 94132
See Chemistry: General; Educational Institute

ENVIRONMENTAL STRESS
INSTITUTE
UNIVERSITY OF CALIFORNIA
SANTA BARBARA, CA 93106
See Biology: General; Educational Institute

ENVIRONMENTAL STUDIES
POLYTECHNICAL INSTITUTE,
CALIFORNIA STATE
POMONA, CA 91726
See Interdisciplinary: General; Educational Institute

ENVIRONMENTAL STUDIES
SCHOOL OF PUBLIC HEALTH,
UNIVERSITY OF CALIFORNIA AT
BERKLELEY
BERKELEY, CA 94720
See Interdisciplinary: General; Educational Institute

ENVIRONMENTAL STUDIES
UNIVERSITY OF CALIFORNIA
LOS ANGELES, CA 90024
See Physics: General; Educational Institute

ENVIRONMENTAL STUDIES GROUP
UNIVERSITY OF SOUTHERN
CALIFORNIA
LOS ANGELES, CA 90007
See Social Sciences/Humanities: Urban Problems; Educational Institute

ENVIRONMENTAL STUDIES
GROUP, IMMACULATE HEART
COLLEGE
2020 NORTH WESTERN AVENUE
LOS ANGELES, CA 90027

See Chemistry: General; Educational Institute

ENVIRONMENTAL STUDIES
PROGRAM
CALIFORNIA INSTITUTE OF
TECHNOLOGY
PASADENA, CA 91148
See Engineering: Water Resources; Educational Institute

ENVIRONMENTAL STUDIES
PROGRAM
CALIFORNIA STATE COLLEGE
LONG BEACH, CA 90835
See Engineering: Water Resources; Educational Institute

ENVIRONMENTAL STUDIES
PROGRAM
CALIFORNIA STATE UNIVERSITY,
FRESNO
FRESNO, CA 93710
See Interdisciplinary: General; Educational Institute

ENVIRONMENTAL STUDIES
PROGRAM
NAVAL POSTGRADUATE SCHOOL
MONTEREY, CA 93940
See Engineering: General; Educational Institute

ENVIRONMENTAL STUDIES
PROGRAM
UNIVERSITY OF CALIFORNIA
SANTA CRUZ, CA 95060
See Interdisciplinary: General; Educational Institute

ENVIRONMENTAL STUDIES
PROGRAM
UNIVERSITY OF CALIFORNIA,
BERKELEY
BERKELEY, CA 94720
See Interdisciplinary: General; Educational Institute

ENVIRONMENTAL STUDIES
PROGRAM
UNIVERSITY OF CALIFORNIA, SAN
DIEGO
LA JOLLA, CA 92037
See Chemistry: General; Educational Institute

ENVIRONMENTAL STUDIES
PROGRAM
UNIVERSITY OF REDLANDS
REDLANDS, CA 92373
See Chemistry: General; Educational Institute

ENVIRONMENTAL STUDIES
PROGRAM
UNIVERSITY OF SANTA CLARA
SANTA CLARA, CA 95053
See Interdisciplinary: General; Educational Institute

**ENVIRONMENTAL STUDIES
PROGRAM**
228 MARK HALL, UNIVERSITY OF
CALIFORNIA
DAVIS, CA 95616
See Interdisciplinary: General; Unclassi-
fied

**ENVIRONMENTAL STUDIES
PROGRAM, CALIFORNIA STATE
COLLEGE**
6101 EAST 7TH STREET
LONG BEACH, CA 90801
See Interdisciplinary: General; Educa-
tional Institute

**ENVIRONMENTAL STUDIES
PROGRAM, OCCIDENTAL
COLLEGE**
1600 CAMPUS ROAD
LOS ANGELES, CA 90041
See Chemistry: General; Educational In-
stitute

**ENVIRONMENTAL STUDIES
PROGRAM, UNIVERSITY OF
SOUTHERN CALIFORNIA**
UNIVERSITY PARK
LOS ANGELES, CA 90007
See Interdisciplinary: General; Educa-
tional Institute

**ENVIRONMENTAL STUDIES,
CALIFORNIA POLYTECHNIC
STATE UNIVERSITY**
SAN LUIS OBISPO, CA 93401
See Chemistry: General; Educational In-
stitute

**ENVIRONMENTAL STUDIES,
CALIFORNIA STATE
POLYTECHNIC COLLEGE**
KELLOGG VOORHIS
POMONA, CA 91766
See Chemistry: General; Educational In-
stitute

**ENVIRONMENTAL STUDIES,
CANADA COLLEGE**
4200 FARM HILL BOULEVARD
REDWOOD CITY, CA 94061
See Chemistry: General; Educational In-
stitute

**ENVIRONMENTAL STUDIES, JOHN
MUIR INSTITUTE**
1098 MILLS TOWER
SAN FRANCISCO, CA 94104
See Interdisciplinary: General; Research
Institute

**ENVIRONMENTAL STUDIES,
LOYOLA UNIVERSITY OF LOS
ANGELES**
LOS ANGELES, CA 90045
See Interdisciplinary: General; Educa-
tional Institute

**ENVIRONMENTAL STUDIES, SAN
JOSE STATE COLLEGE**
300 ALPINE CREEK ROAD

LA HONDA, CA 94020
See Interdisciplinary: General; Educational Institute

**ENVIRONMENTAL STUDIES,
UNIVERSITY OF CALIFORNIA AT
LOS ANGELES**
405 HILGARD AVENUE
LOS ANGELES, CA 90024
See Interdisciplinary: General; Educa-
tional Institute

**FEDERATION OF WESTERN
OUTDOOR CLUBS**
3340 MAYFIELD AVENUE
SAN BERNARDINO, CA 92405
See Social Sciences/Humanities: Recrea-
tion and Leisure; Foundation

**FIELD CROPS AND
AGRICULTURAL CHEMISTRY
BUREAU**
1220 NORTH STREET
SACRAMENTO, CA 95814
See Engineering: Agricultural Engineer-
ing; Government-State or Local

**FIELD STUDIES IN NATURAL
HISTORY**
SAN JOSE STATE COLLEGE
SAN JOSE, CA 95114
See Biology: Ecology; Educational Insti-
tute

**FISH BIOLOGY, MOSS LANDING
LABORATORY**
P O BOX 223
MOSS LANDING, CA 95039
See Biology: Ecology; Field Station/Lab-
oratory

**FISHERIES OCEAN CENTER,
BUREAU OF COMMISSION
FISHERIES**
8604 LA JOLLA SHORES DRIVE
LA JOLLA, CA 92037
See Biology: General; Government-Fed-
eral

**FISHERY OCEANOGRAPHIC
CENTER**
8604 LA JOLLA SHORES DR
LA JOLLA, CA 92037
See Engineering: Water Resources; Gov-
ernment-Federal

**FOOD PROTECTION AND
TOXICOLOGY**
UNIVERSITY OF CALIFORNIA
DAVIS, CA 95616
See Engineering: Agricultural Engineer-
ing; Educational Institute

**FOREST AND RANGE STATION,
PACIFIC SOUTHWEST**
EXPERIMENTAL STATION
BERKELEY, CA 94703
See Geology: General; Field Station/Lab-
oratory

FOREST HISTORY SOCIETY
BOX 1581
SANTA CRUZ, CA 95060
See Biology: Ecology; Professional Organ-
izations

**FOREST SERVICE REGION 5
OFFICE**
630 SANSOME STREET
SAN FRANCISCO, CA 94111
See Engineering: Agricultural Engineer-
ing; Government-Federal

**FRESNO SCIENCE, DEPARTMENT
OF BIOLOGY**
SHAW AND CEDAR AVENUES
FRESNO, CA 93726
See Biology: General; Educational Insti-
tute

FRESNO STATE COLLEGE
SHAW AND CEDAR AVENUE
FRESNO, CA 93726
See Interdisciplinary: General; Educa-
tional Institute

GENETICS DEPARTMENT
STANFORD MEDICAL CENTER
STANFORD, CA 94305
See Biology: Biochemistry; Educational
Institute

**GENETICS DEPARTMENT, AMES
RESOURCES CENTER, NASA**
MOFFETT FIELD, CA 94035
See Interdisciplinary: General; Research
Institute

**GEOGRAPHY, CLIMATOLOGY
DEPARTMENT**
FRESNO STATE COLLEGE
FRESNO, CA 93726
See Interdisciplinary: General; Educa-
tional Institute

**GEOLOGICAL SURVEY OF UNITED
STATES**
MENLO PARK, CA 94025
See Geology: General; Government-Fed-
eral

GEOLOGY DEPARTMENT
FRESNO STATE COLLEGE
FRESNO, CA 93726
See Interdisciplinary: General; Educa-
tional Institute

GEOLOGY DEPARTMENT
SAN JOSE STATE COLLEGE
SAN JOSE, CA 95114
See Geology: General; Educational Insti-
tute

GEOLOGY DEPARTMENT
UNIVERSITY OF CALIFORNIA
BERKELEY, CA 94720
See Interdisciplinary: General; Educa-
tional Institute

GEOLOGY DEPARTMENT
UNIVERSITY OF CALIFORNIA
LOS ANGELES, CA 90001
See Geology: General; Educational Institute

**GEOLOGY DEPARTMENT,
CALIFORNIA STATE UNIVERSITY**
18111 NORDHOFF
NORTHRIDGE, CA 91324
See Social Sciences/Humanities: General;
Educational Institute

**GEOLOGY DEPARTMENT, SAN
FERNANDO VALLEY COLLEGE**
ROOM 120, SIERRA HALL SOUTH
NORTHRIDGE, CA 91324
See Interdisciplinary: General; Educational Institute

GEOMETRICS
914 INDUSTRIAL AVENUE
PALO ALTO, CA 94303
See Geology: General; Industrial/Commercial

**GEOPHYSICS AND PLANNING
PHYSICS INSTITUTE**
8602 LA JOLLA SHORES DRIVE
LA JOLLA, CA 92037
See Geology: Geophysics; Educational Institute

GEOPHYSICS INSTITUTE
UNIVERSITY OF CALIFORNIA
LOS ANGELES, CA 90040
See Chemistry: General; Educational Institute

**GOVERNMENTAL STUDIES
INSTITUTE**
109 MOSES HALL, UNIVERSITY OF
CALIFORNIA
BERKELEY, CA 94720
See Social Sciences/Humanities: General;
Educational Institute

**HEALTH DEPARTMENT OF KERN
COUNTY**
POST OFFICE BOX 997
BAKERSFIELD, CA 93302
See Interdisciplinary: General; Government-State or Local

**HUMAN STUDIES BRANCH,
NATIONAL AERONAUTICS AND
SPACE ADMINISTRATION**
RESEARCH CENTER- M/S 239-17
MOFFETT FIELD, CA 94035
See Biology: Biochemistry; Government-Federal

**HUMANITIES, ARTS, AND
POLITICAL SCIENCES SCHOOL**
SAN JOSE STATE COLLEGE
SAN JOSE, CA 95114
See Social Sciences/Humanities: General;
Educational Institute

**HYDROLOGY PRODUCTION,
DIVISION OF DILLINGHAM
CORPORATION**
POST OFFICE BOX 2528
SAN DIEGO, CA 92112
See Interdisciplinary: General; Industrial/Commercial

IBM RESEARCH LABORATORY
MONTEREY AND COTTLE ROADS
SAN JOSE, CA 95114
See Interdisciplinary: General; Industrial/Commercial

**INDUSTRIAL COOPERATION
INSTITUTE, UNIVERSITY OF
CALIFORNIA**
405 HILGARD AVENUE
LOS ANGELES, CA 90024
See Engineering: Pollution Abatement;
Educational Institute

INDUSTRIAL RELATIONS LIBRARY
INSTITUTE OF TECHNOLOGY
PASADENA, CA 91109
See Social Sciences/Humanities: Labor/
Relations/Unions; Educational Institute

INSECT ECOLOGY
SAN JOSE STATE COLLEGE
SAN JOSE, CA 95114
See Biology: Ecology; Educational Institute

**INSTRUMENT SYSTEMATIC,
STANFORD RESOURCES
INSTITUTE**
124 LUNDY LANE
PALO ALTO, CA 94303
See Engineering: General; Field Station/
Laboratory

**INTERIOR DEPARTMENT, PACIFIC
SOUTHWEST REGION**
450 GOLDEN GATE AVENUE
SAN FRANCISCO, CA 94102
See Engineering: General; Government-State or Local

**IRVING P KRICK ASSOCIATES,
INCORPORATED**
611 SOUTH PALM CANYON DR
PALM SPRINGS, CA 92262
See Interdisciplinary: General; Industrial/
Commercial

**KAHL SCIENTIFIC INSTRUMENT
CORPORATION**
P O BOX 1166
EL CAJON, CA 92022
See Interdisciplinary: General; Industrial/
Commercial

KAISER STEEL CORPORATION
PO BOX 217
FONTANA, CA 92335
See Engineering: General; Industrial/
Commercial

**LABOR STATISTICS OFFICE,
INDUSTRIAL RESEARCH
DEPARTMENT**
455 GOLDEN GATE AVENUE
SAN FRANCISCO, CA 94102
See Social Sciences/Humanities: Labor/
Relations/Unions; Government-State
or Local

**LABORATORIES AND
ENVIRONMENTAL HEALTH
DIVISION**
515 SOUTH CEDAR STREET
FRESNO, CA 93702
See Engineering: Pollution Abatement;
Government-State or Local

**LOCKHEED MISSILE AND SPACE
COMPANY**
26565 ALTAMONT ROAD
LOS ALTOS HILLS, CA 94022
See Engineering: General; Industrial/
Commercial

MANKIND STUDY COUNCIL
POST OFFICE BOX 895
SANTA MONICA, CA 90406
See Social Sciences/Humanities: General;
Research Institute

MARINE BIOLOGY
SAN JOSE STATE COLLEGE
SAN JOSE, CA 95114
See Biology: General; Educational Institute

MARINE BIORESEARCH INSTITUTE
P O BOX 229
MOSS LANDING, CA 95039
See Biology: General; Research Institute

MARINE ECOLOGICAL INSTITUTE
811 HARBOR BOULEVARD
REDWOOD CITY, CA 94063
See Interdisciplinary: General; Foundation

MARINE GEOLOGY
SAN JOSE STATE COLLEGE
SAN JOSE, CA 95114
See Geology: General; Educational Institute

**MARINE LABORATORIES OF MOSS
LANDING**
FRESNO STATE COLLEGE
FRESNO, CA 93704
See Engineering: Water Resources; Educational Institute

**MARINE LABORATORY,
CALIFORNIA INSTITUTE OF
TECHNOLOGY**
101 DAHLIA STREET
CORONA DEL MAR, CA 92625
See Biology: General; Field Station/Laboratory

**MARINE LABORATORY, UNITED
STATES BUREAU OF SPORT
FISHERIES**

POST OFFICE BOX 98
TIBURON, CA 94920
See Biology: General; Government-Federal

MARINE LABS AT MOSS LANDING
CALIFORNIA STATE UNIVERSITY,
FRESNO
FRESNO, CA 93710
See Interdisciplinary: General; Field Station/Laboratory

**MARINE SCIENCE BRANCH, COAST
GUARD WESTERN AREA**
630 SANSOME STREET
SAN FRANCISCO, CA 94126
See Physics: General; Government-Federal

MARINE SCIENCE INSTITUTE
UNIVERSITY OF CALIFORNIA
SANTA BARBARA, CA 93106
See Biology: General; Field Station/Laboratory

MARINE SCIENCES DEPARTMENT
CALIFORNIA STATE COLLEGE
LONG BEACH, CA 90801
See Biology: General; Educational Institute

MARINE STATION
STANFORD UNIVERSITY
PACIFIC GROVE, CA 93950
See Biology: General; Field Station/Laboratory

**MARINELAND OF PACIFIC
RESEARCH LABORATORY**
PALOS VERDES DRIVE SOUTH
PALOS VERDES ESTATES, CA 90274
See Interdisciplinary: General; Unclassified

MEDICAL RESEARCH INSTITUTE
751 SOUTH BASCOM AVENUE
SAN JOSE, CA 95128
See Biology: Biochemistry; Research Institute

**MEDICAL SCHOOL, UNIVERSITY
OF SOUTHERN CALIFORNIA**
2025 ZONAL AVENUE
LOS ANGELES, CA 90033
See Biology: General; Research Institute

**MELLONICS ENVIRONMENTAL
SCIENCES**
654 SUNSET DRIVE
PACIFIC GROVE, CA 93950
See Interdisciplinary: General; Industrial/Commercial

METEOROLOGY AND GEOLOGY
2751 SAN CARLOS LANE
COSTA MESA, CA 92626
See Geology: General; Industrial/Commercial

METEOROLOGY DEPARTMENT
NAVAL POST-GRADUATE SCHOOL
MONTEREY, CA 93940
See Interdisciplinary: General; Educational Institute

METEOROLOGY DEPARTMENT
SAN JOSE STATE COLLEGE
SAN JOSE, CA 95114
See Interdisciplinary: General; Educational Institute

METEOROLOGY PROGRAM
63 NORTH 5TH STREET
SAN JOSE, CA 95120
See Interdisciplinary: General; Educational Institute

**METEOROLOGY RESOURCES
INCORPORATED**
464 W WOODBURY ROAD
ALTADENA, CA 91001
See Interdisciplinary: General; Research Institute

METEOROLOGY, OCEANOGRAPHY
1570 WAKEFIELD TERRACE
LOS ALTOS, CA 94022
See Interdisciplinary: General; Industrial/Commercial

**METEOROLOGY, VANCE
ASSOCIATES**
P O BOX 682
CORONA DEL MAR, CA 92625
See Interdisciplinary: General; Industrial/Commercial

**METEOROLOGY RESEARCH,
INCORPORATED**
464 WOODBURY ROAD
ALTADENA, CA 91001
See Geology: General; Research Institute

METROPOLITAN WATER DISTRICT
LOS ANGELES, CA 90054
See Engineering: Water Resources; Government-State or Local

**NATIONAL AUTOMOTIVE
MUFFLER ASSOCIATION**
P O BOX 247
ALHAMBRA, CA 91802
See Engineering: Pollution Abatement; Industrial/Commercial

NATURAL RESOURCES SCHOOL
HUMBOLDT STATE COLLEGE
ARCATA, CA 95521
See Biology: Ecology; Educational Institute

NATURAL SCIENCES DEPARTMENT
CALIFORNIA STATE COLLEGE
BAKERSFIELD, CA 93306
See Biology: General; Educational Institute

**NATURAL SCIENCES
DEPARTMENT, SONOMA STATE
COLLEGE**
1801 EAST COLATI AVENUE
ROHNERT PARK, CA 94928
See Biology: General; Educational Institute

**NATURAL SCIENCES DIVISION,
CALIFORNIA STATE COLLEGE**
5500 STATE COLLEGE PARKWAY
SAN BERNARDINO, CA 92405
See Interdisciplinary: General; Educational Institute

**NATURALISTS SOCIETY, BIOLOGY
DEPARTMENT**
SAN JOSE STATE COLLEGE
SAN JOSE, CA 95114
See Biology: General; Professional Organizations

NAVAL POST-GRADUATE SCHOOL
MONTEREY, CA 93940
See Interdisciplinary: General; Government-State or Local

NORTHERN CALIFORNIA METPOL
11771 CARLISLE ROAD
SANTA ANA, CA 92705
See Engineering: Pollution Abatement; Unclassified

**OCCUPATIONAL SAFETY AND
HEALTH NATIONAL INSTITUTE**
50 FULTON STREET
SAN FRANCISCO, CA 94102
See Engineering: Pollution Abatement; Government-Federal

OCEAN RESEARCH LABORATORY
SOUTH ROTUNDA, STANFORD
MUSEUM
STANFORD, CA 94305
See Engineering: Water Resources; Government-Federal

**OCEAN RESEARCH LABORATORY,
BUREAU OF COMMISSION
FISHERIES**
SOUTH ROTUNDA, STANFORD
MUSEUM
STANFORD, CA 94305
See Biology: General; Government-Federal

**OCEANOGRAPHIC INSTITUTE AT
SCRIPPS**
UNIVERSITY OF CALIFORNIA AT
SAN DIEGO
LA JOLLA, CA 92037
See Interdisciplinary: General; Educational Institute

**OCEANOGRAPHIC
INSTRUMENTATION**
11803 SORRENTO VALLEY ROAD
SAN DIEGO, CA 92112
See Interdisciplinary: General; Industrial/Commercial

OCEANOGRAPHY DEPARTMENT
UNITED STATES NAVAL POST
  GRADUATE SCHOOL
MONTEREY, CA 93940
See Interdisciplinary: General; Educational Institute

**OCEANOGRAPHY GROUP,
  UNIVERSITY OF CALIFORNIA**
P O BOX 6207
SAN DIEGO, CA 92160
See Biology: General; Educational Institute

**OPERATIONS RESEARCH
  ASSOCIATION, PHYSICS**
2370 CHARLESTON ROAD
MT VIEW, CA 94040
See Physics: General; Research Institute

PACIFIC MARINE STATION
UNIVERSITY OF THE PACIFIC
DILLON BEACH, CA 94929
See Biology: General; Educational Institute

**PARTICLE TECHNOLOGY
  INCORPORATED**
734 NORTH PASTORIA AVENUE
SUNNYVALE, CA 94086
See Chemistry: General; Industrial/Commercial

**PHYSICAL CHEMISTRY
  DEPARTMENT**
SAN JOSE STATE COLLEGE
SAN JOSE, CA 95114
See Chemistry: Physical Chemistry; Educational Institute

PHYSICS DEPARTMENT
SAN JOSE STATE COLLEGE
SAN JOSE, CA 95114
See Physics: General; Educational Institute

**PHYSICS DEPARTMENT, PACKARD
  BELL SASD**
649 LAWRENCE DRIVE
NEWBURY PARK, CA 91230
See Physics: General; Industrial/Commercial

**PLANNING AND CONSERVATION
  LEAGUE**
909 12TH STREET
SACRAMENTO, CA 95814
See Biology: Ecology; Professional Organizations

**PLANT ECOLOGY, VIETNAMESE
  CONTRACT SCHOOL**
1135 BEACON AVENUE
PACIFIC GROVE, CA 93950
See Biology: General; Educational Institute

POLITICAL ECONOMY
1021 FOOTHILL STREET
SOUTH PASADENA, CA 91030

See Social Sciences/Humanities: Community Development/Studies; Industrial/Commercial

POLLUTION ABSTRACTS
POST OFFICE BOX 2369
LA JOLLA, CA 92037
See Interdisciplinary: General; Research Institute

**PRESERVATION SOCIETY-BIRDS OF
  PREY**
BOX293
PACIFIC PALISADES, CA 90272
See Biology: Ecology; Professional Organizations

**PRESERVE BODEGA ASSOCIATION
  OF NORTHERN CALIFORNIA**
HEAD AND HARBOR 341 MARKET
  STREET
SAN FRANCISCO, CA 94105
See Biology: Ecology; Professional Organizations

PUBLIC ADMINISTRATION SCHOOL
UNIVERSITY OF SOUTH
  CALIFORNIA, UNIVERSITY PARK
LOS ANGELES, CA 90007
See Engineering: Pollution Abatement; Educational Institute

PUBLIC HEALTH DEPARTMENT
CALIFORNIA STATE COLLEGE
BERKELEY, CA 94700
See Engineering: Pollution Abatement; Government-State or Local

RADIATION DETECTION COMPANY
385 LOGUE AVENUE
MOUNTAIN VIEW, CA 94042
See Physics: General; Industrial/Commercial

**RADIATION PROGRAM,
  ENVIRONMENTAL PROTECTION
  AGENCY, REGION 2**
100 CALIFORNIA STREET
SAN FRANCISCO, CA 94111
See Engineering: Pollution Abatement; Government-Federal

RESEARCH AGENCY
1416 NINTH STREET
SACRAMENTO, CA 95814
See Biology: Ecology; Research Institute

RESEARCH DEPARTMENT
CALIFORNIA STATE UNIVERSITY
LONG BEACH, CA 90840
See Interdisciplinary: General; Educational Institute

**RESEARCH DIVISION,
  DEPARTMENT OF SOCIAL
  WELFARE**
POST OFFICE BOX 8074
SACRAMENTO, CA 95818

See Social Sciences/Humanities: Welfare(child Public Social); Government-State or Local

**RESEARCH INSTITUTE OF
  STANFORD UNIVERSITY**
333 RAVENSWOOD AVENUE
MENLO PARK, CA 94025
See Social Sciences/Humanities: Community Development/Studies; Educational Institute

RESEARCH INSTITUTE, SRF
1500 CECIL COOK PLACE, PO BOX
  580
GOLETA, CA 93017
See Biology: Ecology; Research Institute

**RESOURCE CONSERVATION
  DIVISION**
1416 9TH STREET, ROOM 1354
SACRAMENTO, CA 95814
See Interdisciplinary: General; Government-State or Local

**RESOURCES DIVISION,
  CALIFORNIA YOUTH AUTHORITY**
STATE OFFICE BUILDING NO. 1
SACRAMENTO, CA 95814
See Social Sciences/Humanities: Juvenile Delinquency; Government-State or Local

**ROYCO INSTRUMENTS,
  INCORPORATED**
141 JEFFERSON DRIVE
MENLO PARK, CA 94025
See Interdisciplinary: General; Industrial/Commercial

S R F RESEARCH INSTITUTE
SANTA BARBARA MUNICIPAL
  AIRPORT
GOLETA, CA 93017
See Interdisciplinary: General; Foundation

**SANITARY ENGINEERING BUREAU,
  DEPARTMENT OF PUBLIC
  HEALTH**
2151 BERKELEY WAY
BERKELEY, CA 94704
See Engineering: Water Resources; Government-State or Local

**SANITARY ENGINEERING
  RESOURCES LABORATORY
  UNIVERSITY OF CALIFORNIA**
1301 SOUTH 46TH STREET
RICHMOND, CA 94800
See Engineering: General; Educational Institute

SAVE THE REDWOODS LEAGUE
114 SANSOME STREET, ROOM 605
SAN FRANCISCO, CA 94104
See Biology: Ecology; Professional Organizations

**SCIENCE ACADEMY OF
  CALIFORNIA**
GOLDEN GATE PARK

SAN FRANCISCO, CA 94100
See Biology: General; Research Institute

SCIENCE AND SOFTWARE SYSTEMS
P O BOX 1620
LA JOLLA, CA 92037
See Physics: General; Research Institute

SCIENCE DIVISION (NATIONAL), SONOMA STATE COLLEGE
1801 EAST COTATI AVENUE
ROHNERT PARK, CA 94928
See Interdisciplinary: General; Educational Institute

SCIENCE SCHOOL, CALIFORNIA STATE POLYTECHNICAL UNIVERSITY
3801 WEST TEMPLE AVENUE
POMONA, CA 91768
See Interdisciplinary: General; Educational Institute

SCIENCES ACADEMY OF CALIFORNIA
GOLDEN GATE PARK
SAN FRANCISCO, CA 94118
See Interdisciplinary: General; Professional Organizations

SCIENTIFIC ADMINISTRATION
1041 DESCO AVENUE
CAMARILLO, CA 93010
See Interdisciplinary: General; Industrial/Commercial

SCRIPPS INSTITUTE OF OCEANOGRAPHY AT UNIVERSITY OF CALIFORNIA
8602 LA JOLLA DRIVE
LA JOLLA, CA 92037
See Biology: General; Educational Institute

SEA WATER CONVERSION LABORATORY
1301 SOUTH 46TH STREET
RICHMOND, CA 94804
See Engineering: Water Resources; Educational Institute

SEA WATER TEST FACILITY
POST OFFICE BOX 109, UNIVERSITY OF CALIFORNIA
LA JOLLA, CA 92038
See Engineering: Water Resources; Educational Institute

SEX-RACE EQUALITY, AFFIRMATIVE ACTION
1902 PALO ALTO WAY
MENLO PARK, CA 94025
See Interdisciplinary: General; Educational Institute

SIERRA CLUB FOUNDATION
220 BUSH STREET
SAN FRANCISCO, CA 94101
See Interdisciplinary: General; Foundation

SIERRA CLUB, LOMA PRIETA CHAPTER
P O BOX 143
MENLO PARK, CA 94025
See Biology: Ecology; Professional Organizations

SOIL AND PLANT NUTRITION DEPARTMENT
UNIVERSITY OF CALIFORNIA
BERKELEY, CA 94720
See Engineering: Agricultural Engineering; Educational Institute

SOIL AND WATER CONSERVATION RESOURCES DIVISION
POST OFFICE BOX 672
RIVERSIDE, CA 92502
See Engineering: Agricultural Engineering; Government-Federal

SOIL CONSERVATION SERVICES
TIOGA BUILDING, 2020 MILVIA STREET, ROOM 203
BERKELEY, CA 94704
See Biology: Ecology; Government-State or Local

SPACE SCIENCES LABORATORY
UNIVERSITY OF CALIFORNIA
BERKELEY, CA 94720
See Interdisciplinary: General; Educational Institute

STANFORD RESEARCH INSTITUTE
333 RAVENSWOOD AVENUE
MENLO PARK, CA 94025
See Engineering: Water Resources; Educational Institute

SYLVANIA ELECTRO-OPTICS ORGANIZATION
475 ELLIS STREET
MOUNTAIN VIEW, CA 94042
See Physics: General; Industrial/Commercial

SYNOPTIC METEOROLOGY
SAN JOSE STATE COLLEGE
SAN JOSE, CA 95114
See Interdisciplinary: General; Educational Institute

SYSTEMATIC RESEARCH INSTITUTE
8049 PROSPECT WAY
LA MESA, CA 92041
See Interdisciplinary: General; Educational Institute

SYSTEMS, SCIENCES AND SOFTWARE
P O BOX 1620
LA JOLLA, CA 92037
See Engineering: Pollution Abatement; Research Institute

TECHNICAL LIBRARY DIVISION
UNITED STATES NAVY, CIVIL ENGINEERING

PORT HUENEME, CA 93041
See Engineering: General; Government-Federal

THEORETICAL CHEMISTRY, IBM RESEARCH LABORATORY
MONTEREY AND COTTLE ROADS
SAN JOSE, CA 95114
See Chemistry: General; Research Institute

THERMOCHEMISTRY AND CHEMISTRY KINETICS DEPARTMENT
STANFORD RESEARCH INSTITUTE
MENLO PARK, CA 94025
See Chemistry: General; Research Institute

TRAFFIC ENGINEERING
1785 LONG STREET
SAN JOSE, CA 95050
See Engineering: General; Government-State or Local

TRAILFINDERS, INCORPORATED
BOX 716
BANNING, CA 92220
See Biology: Ecology; Professional Organizations

TRANSPORTATION AND TRAFFIC ENGINEERING INSTITUTE
1301 SOUTH 46TH STREET
RICHMOND, CA 94804
See Social Sciences/Humanities: Transportation; Educational Institute

URBAN AFFAIRS CENTER
UNIVERSITY OF SOUTHERN CALIFORNIA
LOS ANGELES, CA 90007
See Social Sciences/Humanities: Urban Problems; Educational Institute

VARIAN ASSOCIATES
611 HANSEN WAY
PALO ALTO, CA 94303
See Interdisciplinary: General; Industrial/Commercial

WATER AND POWER DEPARTMENT OF LOS ANGELES
POST OFFICE BOX 111
LOS ANGELES, CA 90054
See Engineering: Water Resources; Government-State or Local

WATER POLLUTION, UNIVERSITY OF CALIFORNIA
104 WARREN HALL
BERKELEY, CA 94720
See Engineering: Pollution Abatement; Educational Institute

WATER RESOURCES
SAN JOSE STATE COLLEGE
SAN JOSE, CA 95114
See Engineering: Water Resources; Educational Institute

WATER RESOURCES
2114 OLIVE AVENUE
FREMONT, CA 94538
See Engineering: Water Resources; Educational Institute

WATER RESOURCES CENTER
UNIVERSITY OF CALIFORNIA
LOS ANGELES, CA 90024
See Engineering: Water Resources; Educational Institute

WATER RESOURCES CONTROL BUILDING
1416 NINTH STREET, 10TH FLOOR
SACRAMENTO, CA 95814
See Engineering: Pollution Abatement; Government-State or Local

WATER RESOURCES DEPARTMENT, RESOURCES BUILDING
1416 9TH STREET, POST OFFICE BOX 388
SACRAMENTO, CA 95802
See Engineering: General; Foundation

WATER SCIENCES AND ENGINEERING DEPARTMENT
UNIVERSITY OF CALIFORNIA
DAVIS, CA 95616
See Engineering: General; Educational Institute

WEATHER MEASURE CORPORATION
POST OFFICE BOX 41257
SACRAMENTO, CA 95841
See Engineering: Pollution Abatement; Industrial/Commercial

WEATHER MODIFICATION, NATIONAL AND INTERNATIONAL
611 SOUTH PALM CANYON DR
PALM SPRINGS, CA 92262
See Engineering: General; Industrial/Commercial

WILDLIFE FEDERATION OF CALIFORNIA
2644 JUDAH STREET
SAN FRANCISCO, CA 94112
See Biology: Ecology; Foundation

WORLD ECOLOGY INSTITUTE
P O BOX 4116
CARMEL, CA 93940
See Biology: Ecology; Research Institute

ZERO POPULATION GROWTH
367 STATE STREET
LOS ALTOS, CA 94022
See Social Sciences/Humanities: Population Studies/Family Planning; Foundation

ZERO POPULATION GROWTH
4080 FABIAN WAY
PALO ALTO, CA 94303

See Social Sciences/Humanities: Population Studies/Family Planning; Foundation

Colorado

AGRICULTURE DEPARTMENT
1525 SHERMAN STREET
DENVER, CO 80203
See Engineering: Agricultural Engineering; Government-State or Local

AIR AND OCCUPATIONAL RADIATION HYGIENE, PUBLIC HEALTH DEPARTMENT
4210 EAST 11TH AVENUE
DENVER, CO 80220
See Engineering: Pollution Abatement; Government-State or Local

AIR POLLUTION CONTROL, COUNTY HEALTH DEPARTMENT
POST OFFICE BOX 1227
GREELEY, CO 80631
See Engineering: Pollution Abatement; Government-State or Local

AIR POLLUTION CONTROL, COUNTY HEALTH DEPARTMENT
260 SOUTH KIPLING STREET
LAKEWOOD, CO 80226
See Engineering: Pollution Abatement; Government-State or Local

AIR POLLUTION CONTROL, COUNTY HEALTH DEPARTMENT
515 PATTERSON AVENUE
GRAND JUNCTION, CO 81501
See Engineering: Pollution Abatement; Government-State or Local

AIR POLLUTION CONTROL, COUNTY HEALTH DEPARTMENT
712 SOUTH TEJON STREET
COLORADO SPRINGS, CO 80909
See Engineering: Pollution Abatement; Government-State or Local

AIR POLLUTION CONTROL, HEALTH DEPARTMENT
151 CENTRAL MAIN
PUEBLO, CO 81003
See Engineering: Pollution Abatement; Government-State or Local

AIR POLLUTION DAMAGE TO PLANTS IN COLORADO
COLORADO STATE UNIVERSITY
FORT COLLINS, CO 80521
See Engineering: Agricultural Engineering; Educational Institute

ARCTIC AND ALPINE RESEARCH INSTITUTE
HALE SCIENCES BLDG,
UNIVERSITY OF COLORADO
BOULDER, CO 80304
See Geology: General; Educational Institute

ASTROPHYSICS LABORATORY
BOULDER, CO 80304
See Physics: General; Educational Institute

ATMOSPHERIC RESEARCH CENTER
POST OFFICE BOX 1470
BOULDER, CO 80302
See Biology: General; Foundation

ATMOSPHERIC RESEARCH CENTER HIGH ALTITUDE OBSERVATORY LIBRARY
POST OFFICE BOX 1558
BOULDER, CO 80302
See Physics: General; Government-Federal

ATMOSPHERIC SCIENCES PROGRAM
COLORADO STATE UNIVERSITY
FORT COLLINS, CO 80521
See Engineering: Pollution Abatement; Educational Institute

ATMOSPHERIC STUDIES PROGRAM, UNIVERSITY OF COLORADO
106 KETCHUM
BOULDER, CO 50304
See Engineering: Pollution Abatement; Educational Institute

ATOMIC ENERGY COMMISSION GRAND JUNCTION OFFICE
POST OFFICE BOX 2567
GRAND JUNCTION, CO 81501
See Chemistry: Physical Chemistry; Government-State or Local

BEHAVORIAL SCIENCE INSTITUTE
UNIVERSITY OF COLORADO
BOULDER, CO 80304
See Social Sciences/Humanities: Psychology/Behavioral Science; Educational Institute

BIOLOGICAL SCIENCES CURRICULUM STUDY, UNIVERSITY OF COLORADO
POST OFFICE BOX 930
BOULDER, CO 80301
See Biology: General; Educational Institute

BOTANY AND PLANT PATHOLOGY DEPARTMENT
COLORADO STATE UNIVERSITY
FORT COLLINS, CO 80521
See Biology: General; Educational Institute

COAL DEPOSITS WESTERN, DENVER MINING RESEARCH CENTER
BUILDING 20, DENVER FEDERAL CENTER
DENVER, CO 80225

See Engineering: Pollution Abatement;
Government-Federal

**DRAINAGE AND FLOOD CONTROL,
COMMITTEE ON IRRIGATION**
POST OFFICE BOX 15326
DENVER, CO 80215
See Engineering: Water Resources; Professional Organizations

**ECOLOGY LABORATORY,
ENVIRONMENT, POPULATION,
AND ORGANIZED BIOLOGY**
HALE SCIENCE BUILDING
BOULDER, CO 80304
See Biology: Ecology; Educational Institute

**ENGINEERING AND RESOURCES
CENTER**
DENVER FEDERAL CENTER,
BUILDING 67
DENVER, CO 80225
See Engineering: General; Government-Federal

**ENGINEERING AND SANITATION,
PUBLIC HEALTH DEPARTMENT**
4210 EAST 11TH AVENUE
DENVER, CO 80220
See Engineering: Pollution Abatement;
Government-State or Local

ENGINEERING RESEARCH CENTER
COLORADO STATE UNIVERSITY
FORT COLLINS, CO 80521
See Engineering: General; Educational
Institute

**ENGINEERING RESOURCES
CENTER, COLLEGE OF
ENGINEERING**
UNIVERSITY OF COLORADO
BOULDER, CO 80304
See Engineering: Water Resources; Educational Institute

**ENVIRONMENTAL HEALTH
SECTION, HEALTH
DEPARTMENT**
3450 BROADWAY, PO BOX 471
BOULDER, CO 80302
See Engineering: Pollution Abatement;
Government-State or Local

**ENVIRONMENTAL PROTECTION
AGENCY REGION 8 OFFICE**
1860 LINCOLN STREET, ROOM 953
DENVER, CO 80203
See Engineering: Pollution Abatement;
Government-State or Local

ENVIRONMENTAL RESEARCH
COLORADO STATE UNIVERSITY
FORT COLLINS, CO 80521
See Biology: Ecology; Educational Institute

**ENVIRONMENTAL RESEARCH
INSTITUTE**
30TH STREET AND ARAPAHOE
AVENUE

BOULDER, CO 80302
See Interdisciplinary: General; Unclassified

**ENVIRONMENTAL RESOURCES
LABORATORY**
4927 IDYLWILD TRAIL
BOULDER, CO 80302
See Interdisciplinary: General; Unclassified

**ENVIRONMENTAL SCIENCE
PROGRAM**
ADAMS STATE COLLEGE
ALAMOSA, CO 81101
See Interdisciplinary: General; Educational Institute

**ENVIRONMENTAL SCIENCE
PROGRAM**
COLORADO COLLEGE
COLORADO SPRINGS, CO 80903
See Chemistry: General; Educational Institute

**ENVIRONMENTAL SCIENCE
PROGRAM**
COLORADO STATE UNIVERSITY
FORT COLLINS, CO 80521
See Interdisciplinary: General; Educational Institute

**ENVIRONMENTAL SCIENCE
PROGRAM**
UNIVERSITY OF COLORADO
BOULDER, CO 80302
See Interdisciplinary: General; Educational Institute

**ENVIRONMENTAL SCIENCES
SERVICES ADMINISTRATION**
BOULDER, CO 80302
See Interdisciplinary: General; Research Institute

ENVIRONMENTAL STUDIES
ROCKY MOUNTAIN BIOLOGICAL
LABORATORY
CRESTED BUTTE, CO 81224
See Interdisciplinary: General; Educational Institute

**ENVIRONMENTAL STUDIES
PROGRAM**
COLORADO SCHOOL OF MINES
GOLDEN, CO 80401
See Interdisciplinary: General; Educational Institute

**ENVIRONMENTAL STUDIES
PROGRAM**
UNIVERSITY OF NORTH
COLORADO
GREELEY, CO 80631
See Interdisciplinary: General; Educational Institute

**ENVIRONMENTAL STUDIES,
UNIVERSITY OF DENVER**
2199 SOUTH UNIVERSITY
BOULEVARD
DENVER, CO 80210
See Interdisciplinary: General; Educational Institute

FARMERS UNION (NATIONAL)
1575 SHERMAN STREET
DENVER, CO 80201
See Biology: Ecology; Professional Organizations

**FLUID DYNAMICS AND DIFFUSION
LABORATORY**
COLORADO STATE UNIVERSITY
FORT COLLINS, CO 80521
See Geology: Geophysics; Educational Institute

FOREST SERVICE REGION 2
DENVER FEDERAL CENTER
BUILDING 85
DENVER, CO 80225
See Engineering: Agricultural Engineering; Government-Federal

FORESTERS ASSOCIATION
STATE FOREST SERVICE,
COLORADO STATE UNIVERSITY
FORT COLLINS, CO 80521
See Biology: Ecology; Educational Institute

**HEALTH DEPARTMENT OF
COLORADO**
4210 EAST 11TH AVENUE
DENVER, CO 80220
See Engineering: Pollution Abatement;
Government-State or Local

**HEALTH, EDUCATION AND
WELFARE REGION 8 OFFICE**
19TH & STOUT STREETS
DENVER, CO 80202
See Interdisciplinary: General; Government-Federal

**HIGH ALTITUDE OBSERVATORY
LIBRARY**
PO BOX 1558
BOULDER, CO 80301
See Physics: General; Educational Institute

IAAPCO/SINCLAIR
DENVER CLUB BUILDING
DENVER, CO 80202
See Interdisciplinary: General; Industrial/
Commercial

MICROBIOLOGY DEPARTMENT
COLORADO STATE UNIVERSITY
FORT COLLINS, CO 80521
See Biology: General; Educational Institute

**NATIONAL OCEANIC AND
ATMOSPHERIC
ADMINISTRATION**

DEPARTMENT OF COMMERCE,
ENVIRONMENTAL RESEARCH
LABORATORY
BOULDER, CO 80302
See Interdisciplinary: General; Unclassified

NUCLEAR LABORATORY OF
ATMOSPHERIC SCIENCES
POST OFFICE BOX 1470
BOULDER, CO 80302
See Chemistry: General; Research Institute

OBSTETRICS AND GYNECOLOGY
DEPARTMENT
UNIVERSITY OF COLORADO
MEDICAL CENTER
DENVER, CO 80220
See Biology: General; Educational Institute

PRAIRIE GROUSE TECHNOLOGY
COUNCIL
P O BOX 567- WILDLIFE RESEARCH
CENTER
FORT COLLINS, CO 80521
See Interdisciplinary: General; Professional Organizations

PUBLIC WELFARE DEPARTMENT,
COLORADO
1600 SHERMAN STREET
DENVER, CO 80203
See Social Sciences/Humanities:
Welfare(Child Public Social);
Government-State or Local

RADIATION DIVISION,
ENVIRONMENTAL PROTECTION
AGENCY
1860 LINCOLN STREET, ROOM 953,
LINCOLN TOWER BUILDING
DENVER, CO 80203
See Chemistry: Physical Chemistry; Government-State or Local

RANGE MANAGEMENT SOCIETY
2120 SOUTH BIRCH STREET
DENVER, CO 80222
See Biology: Ecology; Professional Organizations

RECLAMATION BUREAU,
DEPARTMENT OF THE INTERIOR
BUILDING 67, DENVER FEDERAL
CENTER
DENVER, CO 80225
See Engineering: Water Resources; Government-Federal

RECREATION AND WATERSHED
RESOURCES DEPARTMENT
COLORADO STATE UNIVERSITY
FORT COLLINS, CO 80521
See Engineering: Water Resources; Educational Institute

REPRESENTATIVE RIVER
COMPACT ADMINISTRATION
1845 SHERMAN STREET, ROOM 101
DENVER, CO 80203
See Engineering: Water Resources; Government-State or Local

RESEARCH CENTER, COLLEGE OF
ENGINEERING
UNIVERSITY OF COLORADO
BOULDER, CO 80302
See Engineering: Water Resources; Educational Institute

RESEARCH INSTITUTE OF DENVER
UNIVERSITY OF DENVER
DENVER, CO 80201
See Interdisciplinary: General; Educational Institute

ROCKY MOUNTAIN CENTER ON
ENVIRONMENTAL STUDIES
4260 EAST EVANS AVENUE
DENVER, CO 80222
See Social Sciences/Humanities: Regional Planning; Foundation

SOIL CONSERVATION SERVICE
2490 WEST 26TH AVENUE, ROOM
313
DENVER, CO 80211
See Biology: Ecology; Government-State or Local

THE ARROW COMPANY
3385 SOUTH BANNOCK STREET
ENGLEWOOD, CO 80110
See Interdisciplinary: General; Industrial/Commercial

THORNE ECOLOGICAL
FOUNDATION
1229 UNIVERSITY BOULEVARD
BOULDER, CO 80302
See Biology: Ecology; Foundation

TROUT UNLIMITED
5840 EAST JEWELL AVENUE
DENVER, CO 80222
See Biology: Ecology; Professional Organizations

UNIVERSITY CORPORATION FOR
ATMOSPHERIC RESEARCH
POST OFFICE BOX 1470
BOULDER, CO 80302
See Biology: General; Government-Federal

WATER CONGRESS OF COLORADO
1200 LINCOLN STREET, SUITE 530
DENVER, CO 80203
See Engineering: Water Resources; Professional Organizations

WATER CONSERVATION DISTRICT
OF THE COLORADO RIVER
P O BOX 218
GLENWOOD SPRINGS, CO 81601
See Engineering: Water Resources; Government-State or Local

WATER CONSERVATION FOR
COLORADO WATERS
1525 SHERMAN STREET
DENVER, CO 80203
See Engineering: Water Resources; Educational Institute

WATER RESOURCES DIVISION OF
COLORADO
ROOM 101, 1845 SHERMAN STREET
DENVER, CO 80203
See Engineering: Water Resources; Government-State or Local

WILDLIFE FEDERATION OF
COLORADO
BOX 1588
DENVER, CO 80201
See Biology: Ecology; Foundation

WILDLIFE FEDERATION OF
COLORADO
5123 JELLISON WAY
ARVADA, CO 80002
See Biology: Ecology; Foundation

WILDLIFE RESEARCH CENTER OF
DENVER
FEDERAL CENTER, BUILDING 16
DENVER, CO 80225
See Biology: Ecology; Government-State or Local

WILDLIFE RESEARCH
COOPERATIVE OF COLORADO
COLORADO STATE UNIVERSITY,
FORESTRY BUILDING
FORT COLLINS, CO 80521
See Biology: Ecology; Research Institute

Connecticut

A.K.F.A.
BOX 171
FALLS VILLAGE, CT 06031
See Interdisciplinary: General; Professional Organizations

ACTION NOW CENTER,
INCORPORATED
152 TEMPLE STREET
NEW HAVEN, CT 06510
See Biology: Ecology; Government-State or Local

AGRICULTURAL EXPERIMENTAL
STATION OF CONNECTICUT
POST OFFICE BOX 1106
NEW HAVEN, CT 06504
See Engineering: Agricultural Engineering; Government-State or Local

AIR CONSERVATION COMMITTEE
60 COLLEGE STREET
NEW HAVEN, CT 06510
See Engineering: Pollution Abatement;
Government-State or Local

AIR POLLUTION BUREAU, FIRE DEPARTMENT
274 MIDDLE STREET
BRIDGEPORT, CT 06603
See Engineering: Pollution Abatement;
Professional Organizations

AIR POLLUTION CONTROL DEPARTMENT
CITY HALL
TORRINGTON, CT 06790
See Engineering: Pollution Abatement;
Government-State or Local

AIR POLLUTION CONTROL DIVISION, DEPARTMENT OF HEALTH
MUNICIPAL BUILDING
MIDDLETOWN, CT 06457
See Engineering: Pollution Abatement;
Government-State or Local

AIR POLLUTION CONTROL, CITY HEALTH DEPARTMENT
CITY HALL, 27 WEST MAIN STREET
NEW BRITAIN, CT 06051
See Engineering: Pollution Abatement;
Government-State or Local

AIR POLLUTION CONTROL, HEALTH DEPARTMENT
MAIN STREET
STRATFORD, CT 06497
See Engineering: Pollution Abatement;
Government-State or Local

AIR POLLUTION CONTROL, HEALTH DEPARTMENT
TOWN HALL ANNEX, HAVEMEYER PLACE
GREENWICH, CT 06830
See Engineering: Pollution Abatement;
Government-State or Local

AIR POLLUTION CONTROL, HEALTH DEPARTMENT
TOWN HALL, 739 OLD POST ROAD
FAIRFIELD, CT 06430
See Engineering: Pollution Abatement;
Government-State or Local

AIR POLLUTION CONTROL, HEALTH DEPARTMENT
229 NORTH STREET
STAMFORD, CT 06902
See Engineering: Pollution Abatement;
Government-State or Local

AIR POLLUTION CONTROL, HEALTH DEPARTMENT
56 COVENTRY STREET
HARTFORD, CT 06112
See Engineering: Pollution Abatement;
Government-State or Local

AIR POLLUTION SECTION, ENVIRONMENTAL HEALTH BUREAU
1 STATE STREET
NEW HAVEN, CT 06511

See Engineering: Pollution Abatement;
Government-State or Local

APPALACHIAN MOUNTAIN CLUB
55 MARVEL ROAD
NEW HAVEN, CT 06515
See Biology: Ecology; Government-State
or Local

AREA DEVELOPMENT ECOLOGY-ELECTRICITY
FALLS VILLAGE, CT 06031
See Biology: Ecology; Government-State
or Local

AUDUBON COUNCIL OF CONNECTICUT
ORCHARD HILL ROAD
HARWINTON, CT 06790
See Biology: Ecology; Foundation

AUDUBON SOCIETY INCORPORATED AT DARIEN
POST OFFICE BOX 3313
DARIEN, CT 06820
See Biology: Ecology; Foundation

AUDUBON SOCIETY INCORPORATED AT HARTFORD
POST OFFICE BOX 207
W HARTFORD, CT 06107
See Biology: Ecology; Foundation

AUDUBON SOCIETY INCORPORATED OF LITCHFIELD HILLS
BALDWIN HILL ROAD
LITCHFIELD, CT 06759
See Biology: Ecology; Foundation

AUDUBON SOCIETY INCORPORATED, HOUSATONIC
SHARON AUDUBON CENTER
SHARON, CT 06069
See Biology: Ecology; Foundation

AUDUBON SOCIETY OF CONNECTICUT
2325 BURR STREET
FAIRFIELD, CT 06430
See Interdisciplinary: General; Educational Institute

AUDUBON SOCIETY OF GREENWICH, INCORPORATED
109 GREENWICH AVENUE
GREENWICH, CT 06830
See Interdisciplinary: General; Foundation

AUDUBON SOCIETY OF SAUGATUCK VALLEY, INCORPORATED
BOX 684
WESTPORT, CT
See Biology: Ecology; Foundation

BIOLOGICAL LABORATORY, BUREAU OF COMMISSION FISHERIES

DEPARTMENT OF INTERIOR
MILFORD, CT 06460
See Biology: General; Government-Federal

BIRD CLUB OF NEW HAVEN
26 MOWRY STREET
NEW HAVEN, CT 06518
See Biology: Ecology; Government-State
or Local

BOTANY DEPARTMENT
CONNECTICUT COLLEGE
NEW LONDON, CT 06320
See Biology: Ecology; Educational Institute

CHEMISTRY DEPARTMENT, UNIVERSITY OF HARTFORD
200 BLOOMFIELD AVENUE
WEST HARTFORD, CT 06107
See Chemistry: General; Educational Institute

CONSERVATION AND RESEARCH FOUNDATION
CONNECTICUT COLLEGE
NEW LONDON, CT 06320
See Interdisciplinary: General; Foundation

CONSERVATION ASSOCIATION CENTER
NORTHROP STREET
BRIDGEWATER, CT 06752
See Biology: Ecology; Government-State
or Local

CONSERVATION COMMISSION CENTER, INCORPORATED
POST OFFICE BOX 177
WEST HARTFORD, CT 06107
See Biology: Ecology; Government-State
or Local

CONSERVATION COMMISSION OF FAIRFIELD
739 OLD POST ROAD
FAIRFIELD, CT 06430
See Biology: Ecology; Government-State
or Local

CRISIS
SMITH HIGH SCHOOL
STORRS, CT 06268
See Biology: Ecology; Educational Institute

DEVELOPMENT OFFICE
STATE OFFICE BUILDING
HARTFORD, CT 06115
See Social Sciences/Humanities: Industrial Development; Government-State
or Local

EARTH
60 BARKSDALE ROAD
WEST HARTFORD, CT 06107
See Biology: Ecology; Government-State
or Local

ECOLOGY LEAGUE
BOX 535
LAKEVILLE, CT 06039
See Biology: Ecology; Government-State
or Local

ECOLOGY LEAGUE
POST OFFICE BOX ONE
CORNWALL BRIDGE, CT 06754
See Biology: Ecology; Government-State
or Local

ENVIRONMENT
ONE W ELM STREET
GREENWICH, CT 06830
See Interdisciplinary: General; Govern-
ment-State or Local

**ENVIRONMENTAL CONSERVATION
COUNCIL, BERKSHIRE-
LITCHFIELD**
POST OFFICE BOX 552
LAKEVILLE, CT 06039
See Biology: Ecology; Government-State
or Local

ENVIRONMENTAL COUNCIL
FAIRFIELD-LITCHFIELD
BETHEL, CT 06801
See Biology: Ecology; Government-State
or Local

**ENVIRONMENTAL EDUCATION
COMMITTEE**
UNIVERSITY CENTER OF AVERY
POINT
GROTON, CT 06340
See Biology: Ecology; Educational Insti-
tute

**ENVIRONMENTAL HEALTH
DIVISION, MILFORD HEALTH
DEPARTMENT**
EELS HILL ANNEX
MILFORD, CT 06460
See Engineering: Pollution Abatement;
Government-State or Local

**ENVIRONMENTAL HEALTH
SERVICES, HARTFORD HEALTH
DEPARTMENT**
28 SOUTH MAIN STREET
WEST HARTFORD, CT 06107
See Engineering: Pollution Abatement;
Government-State or Local

**ENVIRONMENTAL PROTECTION
DEPARTMENT**
STATE OFFICE BUILDING
HARTFORD, CT 06115
See Biology: Ecology; Government-State
or Local

**ENVIRONMENTAL RESCUE
ALLIANCE**
BOX 944
WEST CORNWALL, CT 06796
See Interdisciplinary: General; Govern-
ment-State or Local

**ENVIRONMENTAL RESEARCH
INSTITUTION**
YALE UNIVERSITY
NEW HAVEN, CT 06520
See Biology: Ecology; Research Institute

**ENVIRONMENTAL SCIENCE
PROGRAM**
UNIVERSITY OF CONNECTICUT
STORRS, CT 06268
See Social Sciences/Humanities: Educa-
tion; Educational Institute

**ENVIRONMENTAL SCIENCE
PROGRAM**
UNIVERSITY OF HARTFORD
WEST HARTFORD, CT 06117
See Engineering: General; Educational
Institute

**ENVIRONMENTAL SCIENCE
PROGRAM**
YALE UNIVERSITY
NEW HAVEN, CT 06520
See Interdisciplinary: General; Educa-
tional Institute

**ENVIRONMENTAL SCIENCES
PROGRAM**
TRINITY COLLEGE
HARTFORD, CT 06106
See Chemistry: General; Educational In-
stitute

**ENVIRONMENTAL STUDIES FOR
NORTH ENGINEERING REGION**
BECKET ACADEMY, BOX 21, RIVER
ROAD
EAST HADDAM, CT 06423
See Interdisciplinary: General; Educa-
tional Institute

**ENVIRONMENTAL STUDIES
PROGRAM**
FAIRFIELD UNIVERSITY
FAIRFIELD, CT 06430
See Chemistry: General; Educational In-
stitute

**ENVIRONMENTAL STUDIES
PROGRAM**
UNIVERSITY OF BRIDGEPORT
BRIDGEPORT, CT 06602
See Engineering: General; Educational
Institute

**ENVIRONMENTAL STUDIES
PROGRAM**
UNIVERSITY OF CONNECTICUT
STORRS, CT 06268
See Interdisciplinary: General; Educa-
tional Institute

**ENVIRONMENTAL STUDIES
PROGRAM**
WESLEYAN UNIVERSITY
MIDDLETOWN, CT 06457
See Chemistry: General; Educational In-
stitute

**EPIDEMICS AND PUBLIC HEALTH
DEPARTMENT, SCHOOL OF
MEDICINE**
YALE UNIVERSITY
NEW HAVEN, CT 06510
See Interdisciplinary: General; Educa-
tional Institute

**FOREST AND PARK ASSOCIATION
OF CONNECTICUT**
1010 MAIN STREET, P O BOX 389
EAST HARTFORD, CT 06108
See Interdisciplinary: General; Profession-
al Organizations

FOREST HISTORICAL SOCIETY
421 RIDGE ROAD
HAMDEN, CT 06517
See Biology: Ecology; Government-State
or Local

FOREST METEOROLOGY
YALE UNIVERSITY
NEW HAVEN, CT 06520
See Biology: Ecology; Educational Insti-
tute

**FORESTRY ASSOCIATION
EXECUTIVES NATIONAL
COUNCIL**
1040 MAIN STREET
EAST HARTFORD, CT 06108
See Interdisciplinary: General; Profession-
al Organizations

HEALTH DEPARTMENT
GRAND STREET
WATERBURY, CT 06702
See Engineering: Pollution Abatement;
Government-State or Local

HEALTH DEPARTMENT
137 EAST AVENUE
NORWALK, CT 06851
See Engineering: Pollution Abatement;
Government-State or Local

**INDUSTRIAL GAS CLEANING
INSTITUTE**
1116 SUMMER STREET
STAMFORD, CT 06905
See Engineering: Pollution Abatement;
Industrial/Commercial

**LEAGUE OF WOMEN VOTERS OF
CONNECTICUT**
60 CONNOLLY PARKWAY
HAMDEN, CT 06514
See Interdisciplinary: General; Govern-
ment-State or Local

MARINE FISHERIES SERVICE
ROGERS AVENUE
MILFORD, CT 06460
See Biology: General; Government-Fed-
eral

MARINE RESOURCES LABORATORY
UNIVERSITY OF CONNECTICUT
NOANK, CT 06340

See Biology: General; Educational Institute

MEDICINE EPIDEMEOLOGY LUNG RESEARCH CENTER
YALE UNIVERSITY
NEW HAVEN, CT 06510
See Biology: General; Educational Institute

NATCHAUG ORNITHOLOGICAL
RFD TWO, BOX 126
STORRS, CT 06268
See Biology: Ecology; Government-State or Local

NATIONAL OCEANIC AND ATMOSPHERIC ADMINISTRATION
ROGERS AVENUE
MILFORD, CT 06460
See Biology: General; Government-Federal

NATURAL HISTORY CLUB OF TERRYVILLE
102 GREYSTONE AVENUE
BRISTOL, CT 06010
See Interdisciplinary: General; Government-State or Local

NATURAL RESOURCES COUNCIL OF CONNECTICUT
POST OFFICE BOX 352
WEST HAVEN, CT 06516
See Interdisciplinary: General; Government-State or Local

NATURALIST CLUB OF WATERBURY, INCORPORATED
21 SUNRISE NOOK
WATERBURY, CT 06708
See Biology: Ecology; Government-State or Local

NATURE CENTER AND MUSEUM OF LITCHFIELD
WHITE MEMORIAL FOUNDATION
LITCHFIELD, CT 06759
See Biology: Ecology; Foundation

NATURE CONSERVANCY
21 SILVER BROOK ROAD
WESTPORT, CT 06880
See Biology: Ecology; Foundation

NATURE CONSERVATION, CONNECTICUT CHAPTER
151 BROOKDALE ROAD
STAMFORD, CT 06903
See Biology: Ecology; Educational Institute

NAUGATUCK PRIDE, INCORPORATED
ORCHARD HILL ROAD
HARNINGTON, CT 06790
See Biology: Ecology; Government-State or Local

NEW ENVIRONMENTAL RESCUE ALLIANCE
BOX 944
WEST CORNWALL, CT 06796
See Biology: Ecology; Government-State or Local

PESTICIDE COMPLIANCE, DEPARTMENT OF ENVIRONMENTAL PROTECTION
STATE OFFICE BUILDING, ROOM G-3A
HARTFORD, CT 06115
See Engineering: Agricultural Engineering; Government-State or Local

POLLUTION CONTROL COMMISSION
POST OFFICE BOX 281
WEST HARTFORD, CT 06107
See Engineering: Pollution Abatement; Government-State or Local

PROTECT YOUR ENVIRONMENT
40 HIGHLAND AVENUE
ROWAYTON, CT 06853
See Biology: Ecology; Foundation

PROTECT YOUR ENVIRONMENT OF STRATFORD, INCORPORATED
66 JEFFERSON STREET
STRATFORD, CT 06497
See Interdisciplinary: General; Government-State or Local

SANITARY ENGINEERING DIVISION, CONNECTICUT DEPARTMENT OF HEALTH
79 ELM STREET
HARTFORD, CT 06115
See Engineering: Water Resources; Government-State or Local

SAVE THE WETLANDS COMMISSION, INCORPORATED
1087 BOSTON POST ROAD
MADISON, CT 06443
See Biology: Ecology; Foundation

SIERRA CLUB
SEVEN TYLER LANE
RIVERSIDE, CT 06878
See Biology: Ecology; Foundation

SIERRA CLUB
STERLING ROAD
GREENWICH, CT 06830
See Biology: Ecology; Foundation

SOIL CONSERVATION SOCIETY OF AMERICA
STORRS, CT 06268
See Geology: General; Government-State or Local

WATER AND RELATED RESOURCES
STATE OFFICE BUILDING
HARTFORD, CT 06100
See Engineering: Water Resources; Government-State or Local

WATER RESOURCES COMMISSION
650 MAIN STREET
HARTFORD, CT 06115
See Engineering: Pollution Abatement; Government-State or Local

WATER RESOURCES INSTITUTE
UNIVERSITY OF CONNECTICUT
STORRS, CT 06268
See Engineering: Water Resources; Educational Institute

WATERSHED COUNCIL OF CENTER RIVER, INCORPORATED
134 STEELE ROAD
W HARTFORD, CT 06119
See Engineering: Water Resources; Government-State or Local

WILDLIFE FEDERATION CENTER
BOX 7
MIDDLETOWN, CT 06457
See Biology: Ecology; Government-State or Local

WILDLIFE FEDERATION OF CONNECTICUT
82 SORRIES COURT
SOUTH MERIDEN, CT 06450
See Biology: Ecology; Foundation

WILDLIFE MANAGEMENT INSTITUTE
200 AUDUBON LANE
FAIRFIELD, CT 06430
See Biology: Ecology; Foundation

ZERO POPULATION GROWTH
BOX 1947
NEW HAVEN, CT 06520
See Social Sciences/Humanities: Population Studies/Family Planning; Foundation

ZERO POPULATION GROWTH
BOX 422
HARTFORD, CT 06101
See Social Sciences/Humanities: Population Studies/Family Planning; Foundation

ZERO POPULATION GROWTH
BOX 607
BRANFORD, CT 06405
See Social Sciences/Humanities: Population Studies/Family Planning; Foundation

ZERO POPULATION GROWTH
PO BOX 81
STORRS, CT 06268
See Social Sciences/Humanities: Population Studies/Family Planning; Foundation

ZERO POPULATION GROWTH
POST OFFICE BOX 47
FAIRFIELD, CT 06430

See Social Sciences/Humanities: Population Studies/Family Planning; Foundation

ZERO POPULATION GROWTH
THE HOTCHKISS SCHOOL
LAKEVILLE, CT 06036
See Social Sciences/Humanities: Population Studies/Family Planning; Foundation

ZERO POPULATION GROWTH, CONNECTICUT FEDERATION
POST OFFICE BOX 422
HARTFORD, CT 06101
See Social Sciences/Humanities: Population Studies/Family Planning; Foundation

District of Columbia

ADULT EDUCATION PROGRAMS DIVISION
OFFICE OF EDUCATION
WASHINGTON, DC 20202
See Social Sciences/Humanities: Education; Government-Federal

ADVISORY COMMISSION ON INTERGOVERNMENTAL RELATIONS
726 JACKSON PLACE, NW
WASHINGTON, DC 20575
See Social Sciences/Humanities: Politics; Government-Federal

AFL-CIO
AFL-CIO BUILDING, 815 16TH STREET, NW
WASHINGTON, DC 20006
See Social Sciences/Humanities: Labor/Relations/Unions; Professional Organizations

AGRICULTURAL CHEMICALS, NATIONAL ASSOCIATION
1155-15TH STREET, NW
WASHINGTON, DC 20005
See Engineering: Agricultural Engineering; Industrial/Commercial

AGRICULTURAL DEVELOPMENT, INTER AMERICAN COMMISSION
1735 E STREET, NW, ROOM 1029
WASHINGTON, DC 20006
See Engineering: Agricultural Engineering; Professional Organizations

AGRICULTURAL ECONOMICS
2440 VIRGINIA AVENUE
WASHINGTON, DC 20037
See Social Sciences/Humanities: Community Development/Studies; Government-Federal

AGRICULTURAL PRODUCERS, INTERNATIONAL FEDERATION
ROOM 401, BARR BUILDING, 910 17TH STREET, NW

WASHINGTON, DC 20006
See Engineering: Agricultural Engineering; Foundation

AGRICULTURAL RESEARCH SERVICE
WASHINGTON, DC 20250
See Engineering: Agricultural Engineering; Government-Federal

AGRICULTURAL RESOURCES INVENTORY ENGINEER, US ARMY MAP SERVICE
6500 BROOKS LANE NW
WASHINGTON, DC 20016
See Engineering: Water Resources; Government-Federal

AGRICULTURAL STABILIZATION AND CONSERVATION SERVICES
14TH STREET AND INDEPENDENCE AVENUE
WASHINGTON, DC 20250
See Engineering: Water Resources; Government-Federal

AGRICULTURE
ROOM 1301, LONGWORTH HOUSE
WASHINGTON, DC 20515
See Engineering: Agricultural Engineering; Government-Federal

AGRICULTURE AND FORESTRY COMMITTEE
SENATE OFFICE BUILDING, SUITE 324
WASHINGTON, DC 20510
See Engineering: Agricultural Engineering; Government-Federal

AGRICULTURE COMMITTEE, US HOUSE OF REPRESENTATIVES
ROOM 1301, LONGWORTH HOUSE OFFICE
WASHINGTON, DC 20515
See Engineering: Water Resources; Government-Federal

AGRICULTURE DEPARTMENT
14TH STREET AND INDEPENDENCE AVENUE, SW
WASHINGTON, DC 20250
See Interdisciplinary: General; Government-State or Local

AGRONOMY AND AGRICULTURAL ECONOMICS
1700 K STREET, NW
WASHINGTON, DC 20006
See Engineering: Agricultural Engineering; Government-Federal

AIR AND WATER DIVISION, ENVIRONMENTAL PROTECTION AGENCY
WATERSIDE MALL, ROOM 3710
WASHINGTON, DC 20460
See Social Sciences/Humanities: Law/Legislation; Government-Federal

AIR AND WATER POLLUTION SUBCOMMITTEE
SENATE OFFICE BUILDING, SUITE 4204
WASHINGTON, DC 20510
See Engineering: Pollution Abatement; Government-Federal

AIR POLLUTION CONTROL, NATIONAL CENTER
3RD AND C STREETS, SW
WASHINGTON, DC 20201
See Biology: Ecology; Government-Federal

AIR POLLUTION DIVISION, PUBLIC HEALTH DEPARTMENT
801 NORTH CAPITOL STREET, NE
WASHINGTON, DC 20002
See Engineering: Pollution Abatement; Government-State or Local

AMERICA'S FUTURE TREES FOUNDATION
1412 16TH STREET, NW
WASHINGTON, DC 20001
See Biology: Ecology; Foundation

AMERICAN ASSOCIATION OF UNIVERSITY PROFESSORS
1785 MASSACHUSETTS AVENUE, NW
WASHINGTON, DC 20036
See Social Sciences/Humanities: Education; Professional Organizations

AMERICAN ASSOCIATION OF UNIVERSITY WOMEN
2401 VIRGINIA AVENUE
WASHINGTON, DC 20037
See Interdisciplinary: General; Professional Organizations

AMERICAN CHEMISTRY SOCIETY
1155 SIXTEENTH STREET, NW
WASHINGTON, DC 20036
See Interdisciplinary: General; Professional Organizations

AMERICAN COUNCIL OF INDEPENDENT LABS, INCORPORATED
1026 17TH STREET, NW
WASHINGTON, DC 20036
See Interdisciplinary: General; Field Station/Laboratory

AMERICAN COUNCIL ON EDUCATION
ONE DUPONT CIRCLE
WASHINGTON, DC 20036
See Social Sciences/Humanities: Education; Professional Organizations

AMERICAN FISHERIES SOCIETY
1319 18TH STREET, NW, FOURTH FLOOR SUITE
WASHINGTON, DC 20036
See Biology: General; Government-Federal

AMERICAN FOREST PRODUCTS INDUSTRY INCORPORATED
1816 N STREET, NW
WASHINGTON,DC 20036
See Social Sciences/Humanities: Industrial Development; Industrial/Commercial

AMERICAN FORESTRY ASSOCIATION
919-17TH STREET, NW
WASHINGTON, DC 20006
See Interdisciplinary: General; Professional Organizations

AMERICAN PETROLEUM INSTITUTE
1801 K STREET, NW
WASHINGTON, DC 20006
See Engineering: General; Professional Organizations

AMERICAN PSYCHOLOGICAL ASSOCIATION
1200 17TH STREET, NW
WASHINGTON, DC 20036
See Social Sciences/Humanities: Psychology/Behavioral Science; Professional Organizations

AMERICAN VOCATIONAL ASSOCIATION INCORPORATED
1510 H STREET, NW
WASHINGTON, DC 20005
See Social Sciences/Humanities: Education; Professional Organizations

AMERICAN WATERWAY OPERATIONS, INCORPORATED
1250 CONNECTICUT AVENUE, SUITE 502
WASHINGTON, DC 20036
See Engineering: Pollution Abatement; Government-Federal

ANALYTICAL CHEMISTS ASSOCIATION
BEN FRANKLIN STATION, 540
WASHINGTON, DC 20044
See Chemistry: General; Professional Organizations

ANTARCTIC PROGRAMS OFFICE, DIVISION OF ENVIRONMENTAL SCIENCES
1800 G STREET, NW
WASHINGTON, DC 20550
See Interdisciplinary: General; Unclassified

APPALACHIAN REGIONAL COMMISSION
1666 CONNECTICUT AVENUE, NW
WASHINGTON, DC 20235
See Interdisciplinary: General; Unclassified

APPALACHIAN TRAIL CONFERENCE
1718 N STREET, NW

WASHINGTON, DC 20036
See Social Sciences/Humanities: Recreation and Leisure; Professional Organizations

APPROPRIATIONS COMMITTEE, U S SENATE
ROOM 1235 NEW SENATE OFFICE BUILDING
WASHINGTON, DC 20510
See Engineering: General; Government-Federal

APPROPRIATIONS COMMITTEE, US HOUSE OF REPRESENTATIVES
ROOM H-218, THE CAPITOL
WASHINGTON, DC 20515
See Engineering: Water Resources; Government-Federal

ARCHITECTS INSTITUTE OF AMERICA
THE OCTAGON, 1735 NEW YORK AVENUE
WASHINGTON, DC 20006
See Social Sciences/Humanities: Community Development/Studies; Professional Organizations

ARCHITECTURAL AND ENVIRONMENTAL ARTS PROGRAMS
NATIONAL ENDOWMENT FOR ARTS
WASHINGTON, DC 20506
See Interdisciplinary: General; Foundation

ARCTIC BIBLIOGRAPHIC PROJECT, ARCTIC INSTITUTE OF NORTH AMERICA
1619 NEW HAMPSHIRE AVENUE, NW
WASHINGTON, DC 20005
See Social Sciences/Humanities: General; Research Institute

ARMY CORPS OF ENGINEERS
DEPARTMENT OF THE ARMY
WASHINGTON, DC 20314
See Engineering: Pollution Abatement; Government-Federal

ASSOCIATION EXECUTIVES SOCIETY
2000 K STREET, NW
WASHINGTON, DC 20006
See Interdisciplinary: General; Professional Organizations

ATOMIC ENERGY JOINT COMMITTEE
ROOM H-403, THE CAPITOL
WASHINGTON, DC 20500
See Engineering: Pollution Abatement; Government-Federal

AUDUBON NATURALIST SOCIETY
8940 JONES MILL ROAD
WASHINGTON, DC 20015
See Biology: Ecology; Foundation

BEHAVIORAL SCIENCES DIVISION, NATIONAL ACADEMY OF SCIENCES
2102 CONSTITUTION AVENUE, NW
WASHINGTON, DC 20418
See Social Sciences/Humanities: Psychology/Behavioral Science; Government-Federal

BIOLOGICAL AND MEDICAL SCIENCES DIVISION, NATIONAL SCIENCE FOUNDATION
1800 G STREET, NW
WASHINGTON, DC 20550
See Biology: General; Government-Federal

BIOLOGICAL SCIENCES INSTITUTION
3900 WISCONSIN AVENUE, NW
WASHINGTON, DC 20016
See Biology: General; Professional Organizations

BIOLOGY DEPARTMENT
CATHOLIC UNIVERSITY OF AMERICA
WASHINGTON, DC 20001
See Biology: General; Educational Institute

BIOLOGY DEPARTMENT
GEORGETOWN UNIVERSITY
WASHINGTON, DC 20007
See Biology: Ecology; Educational Institute

BIOLOGY TEACHERS NATIONAL ASSOCIATION
1420 N STREET, NW
WASHINGTON, DC 20005
See Biology: General; Professional Organizations

BIRD AND MAMMAL LABORATORY, NATIONAL MUSEUM
10TH STREET AND CONSTITUTION AVENUE
WASHINGTON, DC 20560
See Biology: General; Government-Federal

BOTANICAL GARDENS (INTERNATIONAL CONGRESS), MUSEUM OF NATURAL HISTORY
SMITHSONIAN INSTITUTE
WASHINGTON, DC 20025
See Biology: General; Research Institute

BROOKINGS INSTITUTION
1775 MASSACHUSETTS AVENUE, NW
WASHINGTON, DC 20036
See Social Sciences/Humanities: Urban Problems; Research Institute

BUDGET BUREAU, EXECUTIVE OFFICE BUILDING
17TH AND PACIFIC AVENUE, NW
WASHINGTON, DC 20503

See Engineering: Water Resources; Government-Federal

BUILDINGS MANAGEMENT OFFICE
19TH AND F STREET, NW
WASHINGTON, DC 20405
See Engineering: Pollution Abatement; Government-Federal

BUREAU OF LAND MANAGEMENT
18TH AND C STREETS, NW
WASHINGTON, DC 20240
See Interdisciplinary: General; Unclassified

CHEMICAL ENGINEERING BRANCH, OFFICE OF MARINE SAFETY, US COAST GUARD
400 7TH STREET, SW
WASHINGTON, DC 20590
See Engineering: Chemical Engineering; Government-Federal

CHESAPEAKE AND POTOMAC TELEPHONE
1710 H STREET, NW
WASHINGTON, DC 20006
See Social Sciences/Humanities: General; Industrial/Commercial

CHILDREN'S BUREAU, WELFARE ADMINISTRATION
330 INDEPENDENCE AVENUE, SW
WASHINGTON, DC 20201
See Social Sciences/Humanities: Welfare(Child Public Social); Government-Federal

CITIZENS COMMITTEE NATURAL RESOURCE
1346 CONNECTICUT AVENUE, NW
WASHINGTON, DC 20036
See Biology: Ecology; Professional Organizations

COASTAL AND GEODETIC SURVEY
UNITED STATES DEPARTMENT OF COMMERCE
WASHINGTON, DC 20230
See Engineering: Water Resources; Government-Federal

COASTAL ENGINEERING RESOURCES CENTER
5201 LITTLE FALLS ROAD, NW
WASHINGTON, DC 20016
See Engineering: General; Government-Federal

COLD REGIONS BIBLIOGRAPHY PROJECT
SCIENCES AND TECHNOLOGY DIVISION, LIBRARY OF CONGRESS
WASHINGTON, DC 20540
See Interdisciplinary: General; Unclassified

COMMERCE COMMITTEE
HOUSE OFFICE BUILDING, SUITE 5202
WASHINGTON, DC 20510

See Biology: Ecology; Government-Federal

COMMERCE COMMITTEE, U S SENATE
ROOM 5202 NEW SENATE OFFICE BUILDING
WASHINGTON, DC 20510
See Engineering: General; Government-Federal

COMMERCIAL FISHERIES BUREAU
18TH AND C STREETS, NW
WASHINGTON, DC 20240
See Biology: Ecology; Government-Federal

COMMUNITY HEALTH SERVICES
3125 GARFIELD STREET
WASHINGTON, DC 20008
See Social Sciences/Humanities: Community Development/Studies; Government-Federal

COMMUNITY PLANNING AND MANAGEMENT
1855 UPSHUR STREET
WASHINGTON, DC 20011
See Social Sciences/Humanities: Community Development/Studies; Government-Federal

CONSERVATION COMMISSION, INTERNATIONAL ASSOCIATION FOR GAME
1709 NEW YORK AVENUE, 3RD FLOOR SUITE
WASHINGTON, DC 20006
See Biology: Ecology; Professional Organizations

CONSERVATION DISTRICTS FOUNDATION
1025 VERMONT AVENUE, NW
WASHINGTON, DC 20005
See Interdisciplinary: General; Foundation

CONSERVATION FOUNDATION
1717 MASSACHUSETTS AVENUE, NW
WASHINGTON, DC 20036
See Biology: Ecology; Foundation

CONSERVATION VOTERS LEAGUE
324 C STREET, SW
WASHINGTON, DC 20003
See Interdisciplinary: General; Unclassified

CONSUMER AND MARKETING SERVICES
14TH STREET AND INDEPENDENCE AVENUE, SW
WASHINGTON, DC 20250
See Engineering: Agricultural Engineering; Government-Federal

CONSUMER PROTECTION AND ENVIRONMENTAL HEALTH SERVICES

FEDERAL BUILDING 8, 200 C STREET, SW
WASHINGTON, DC 20204
See Interdisciplinary: General; Unclassified

COOPERATIVE STATE RESEARCH SERVICE
14TH STREET AND INDEPENDENCE AVENUE, SW
WASHINGTON, DC 20250
See Interdisciplinary: General; Unclassified

CURRENT RESEARCH INFORMATION SYSTEM
14TH STREET AND INDEPENDENCE AVENUE, ROOM 6818
WASHINGTON, DC 20250
See Engineering: Agricultural Engineering; Government-Federal

DIVISION OF STATE AND LICENSEE RELATIONS
UNITED STATES ATOMIC ENERGY COMMISSN
WASHINGTON, DC 20545
See Geology: General; Government-Federal

DOCUMENTS SUPERINTENDENT
GOVERNMENT PRINTING OFFICE
WASHINGTON, DC 20402
See Engineering: Water Resources; Government-Federal

DOMESTIC COMMERCE BUREAU
UNITED STATES DEPARTMENT OF COMMERCE
WASHINGTON, DC 20230
See Social Sciences/Humanities: Industrial Development; Government-Federal

EARTH SCIENCES BRANCH, DIVISION OF BIOLOGICAL AND MEDICAL SCIENCES
ATOMIC ENERGY COMMISSION
WASHINGTON, DC 20545
See Interdisciplinary: General; Unclassified

ECOLOGY CENTER OF WASHINGTON
2000 AND STATE STREET, NW SUITE 612
WASHINGTON, DC 20006
See Biology: Ecology; Government-State or Local

ECOLOGY OFFICE
SMITHSONIAN INSTITUTE
WASHINGTON, DC 20560
See Biology: Ecology; Government-Federal

ECONOMIC RESEARCH CENTER, DEPARTMENT OF AGRICULTURE
500 12TH STREET, SW

WASHINGTON, DC 20250
See Engineering: Water Resources; Government-Federal

ECONOMIC RESEARCH SERVICE
14TH STREET AND
INDEPENDENCE AVENUE
WASHINGTON, DC 20250
See Social Sciences/Humanities: Population Studies/Family Planning; Government-Federal

EDUCATION OFFICE
400 MARYLAND AVENUE
WASHINGTON, DC 20202
See Social Sciences/Humanities: Education; Government-Federal

EMPLOYMENT SECURITY BUREAU, LABOR DEPARTMENT
14TH STREET AND CONSTITUTION
AVENUE, NW
WASHINGTON, DC 20210
See Social Sciences/Humanities: Employment/Unemployment; Government-Federal

ENERGY, NATURAL RESOURCES AND ENVIRONMENT SUBCOMMITTEE
SENATE OFFICE BUILDING, SUITE 5202
WASHINGTON, DC 20510
See Biology: Ecology; Government-Federal

ENGINEERING AGENCY FOR RESOURCES INVENTION
6500 BROOKS LANE
WASHINGTON, DC 20315
See Interdisciplinary: General; Unclassified

ENGINEERING DIVISION
NATIONAL SCIENCE FOUNDATION
WASHINGTON, DC 20550
See Engineering: General; Foundation

ENGINEERING OFFICE
UNITED STATES DEPARTMENT OF ARMY
WASHINGTON, DC 20315
See Engineering: Water Resources; Government-Federal

ENGINEERING, POST OFFICE DEPARTMENT
12TH AND PENNSYLVANIA
AVENUES, NW
WASHINGTON, DC 20260
See Engineering: General; Government-Federal

ENTOMOLOGY INFORMATION SERVICE OF MILITARY
FOREST GLEN SECTION
WASHINGTON, DC 20012
See Biology: Ecology; Government-Federal

ENVIRONMENT AND CONSUMER PROTECTION
PUBLIC HEALTH SERVICE
WASHINGTON, DC 20201
See Biology: Ecology; Government-State or Local

ENVIRONMENTAL ACTION FOUNDATION, INCORPORATED
732 DUPONT CIRCLE BUILDING
WASHINGTON, DC 20036
See Biology: Ecology; Foundation

ENVIRONMENTAL ACTION, INCORPORATED
1346 CONNECTICUT AVENUE, NW
WASHINGTON, DC 20036
See Biology: Ecology; Government-Federal

ENVIRONMENTAL AFFAIRS OFFICE, GENERAL SERVICES ADMINISTRATION
18TH AND F STREETS, NW
WASHINGTON, DC 20405
See Interdisciplinary: General; Unclassified

ENVIRONMENTAL AND SYSTEMATIC BIOLOGICAL SECTION
1800 G STREET, NW
WASHINGTON, DC 20550
See Biology: General; Government-Federal

ENVIRONMENTAL AND URBAN SYSTEMS, TRANSPORTATION DEPARTMENT
400 7TH STREET, SW
WASHINGTON, DC 20590
See Social Sciences/Humanities: Transportation; Government-Federal

ENVIRONMENTAL EDUCATION, NATIONAL PARK SERVICE
UNITED STATES DEPARTMENT OF INTERIOR
WASHINGTON, DC 20036
See Biology: Ecology; Government-Federal

ENVIRONMENTAL ENGINEERING INTERSOCIETY BOARD
P O BOX 9728
WASHINGTON, DC 20016
See Engineering: General; Field Station/Laboratory

ENVIRONMENTAL HEALTH SECTION
OFFICE OF SURGEON GENERAL
UNITED STATES AIR FORCE
WASHINGTON, DC 20333
See Biology: Ecology; Government-Federal

ENVIRONMENTAL LAW INSTITUTE
1346 CONNECTICUT AVENUE
WASHINGTON, DC 20036

See Social Sciences/Humanities: Law/Legislation; Research Institute

ENVIRONMENTAL LIVING, RACHAEL CARSON TRUST
8940 JONES MILL ROAD
WASHINGTON, DC 20015
See Biology: Ecology; Educational Institute

ENVIRONMENTAL PROTECTION AGENCY
3902 WATERSIDE MALL, ROOM 3105
WASHINGTON, DC 20460
See Biology: Ecology; Government-Federal

ENVIRONMENTAL PROTECTION AGENCY
401 M STREET, SW
WASHINGTON, DC 20460
See Engineering: Pollution Abatement; Government-Federal

ENVIRONMENTAL QUALITY CITIZENS ADVISORY COMMISSION
1700 PENNSYLVANIA AVENUE, NW
WASHINGTON, DC 20006
See Biology: Ecology; Government-Federal

ENVIRONMENTAL QUALITY COUNCIL
6219 33RD STREET
WASHINGTON, DC 20015
See Biology: Ecology; Government-Federal

ENVIRONMENTAL QUALITY COUNCIL
722 JACKSON PLACE, NW
WASHINGTON, DC 20006
See Engineering: Water Resources; Government-Federal

ENVIRONMENTAL RESEARCH INSTITUTE
WASHINGTON, DC 20234
See Biology: Ecology; Government-Federal

ENVIRONMENTAL SATELLITE CENTER
NATIONAL OCEANIC AND ATMOSPHERIC ADMINISTRATION, INTERIOR DEPARTMENT
WASHINGTON, DC 20233
See Physics: General; Government-Federal

ENVIRONMENTAL SCIENCE DIVISION, NATIONAL SCIENCE FOUNDATION
1800 G STREET, NW
WASHINGTON, DC 20550
See Interdisciplinary: General; Unclassified

ENVIRONMENTAL SCIENCES OFFICE
SMITHSONIAN INSTITUTION
WASHINGTON, DC 20560
See Interdisciplinary: General; Research Institute

ENVIRONMENTAL SCIENCES SERVICES ADMINISTRATION
1666 CONNECTICUT AVENUE, NW
WASHINGTON, DC 20230
See Interdisciplinary: General; Unclassified

ENVIRONMENTAL SERVICES COUNCIL
560 NORTH STREET, SW
WASHINGTON, DC 20005
See Biology: Ecology; Government-Federal

ENVIRONMENTAL STUDIES DIVISION
NATIONAL SCIENCE FOUNDATION
WASHINGTON, DC 20550
See Interdisciplinary: General; Unclassified

ENVIRONMENTAL STUDIES PROGRAM
GALLAUDET COLLEGE, FLORIDA AVENUE AND 7TH STREET, NE
WASHINGTON, DC 20002
See Social Sciences/Humanities: Education; Educational Institute

ENVIRONMENTAL STUDIES PROGRAM
GEORGE WASHINGTON UNIVERSITY
WASHINGTON, DC 20006
See Engineering: General; Educational Institute

ENVIRONMENTAL STUDIES PROGRAM, GEORGETOWN UNIVERSITY
37TH AND O STREETS, SW
WASHINGTON, DC 20007
See Chemistry: General; Educational Institute

ENVIRONMENTAL STUDIES PROJECT, CATHOLIC UNIVERSITY OF AMERICA
4TH STREET AND MICHIGAN AVENUE, NE
WASHINGTON, DC 20017
See Interdisciplinary: General; Educational Institute

ENVIRONMENTAL STUDIES, HOWARD UNIVERSITY
2400 6TH STREET, NW
WASHINGTON, DC 20001
See Interdisciplinary: General; Educational Institute

ENVIRONMENTAL SYSTEMS MANAGEMENT
AMERICAN UNIVERSITY
WASHINGTON, DC 20016

See Interdisciplinary: General; Educational Institute

EUTROPHICATION COMMISSION SYMPOSIUM
2101 CONSTITUTION AVENUE, NW
WASHINGTON, DC 20418
See Engineering: Water Resources; Government-Federal

EXTENSION SERVICES, 4-H CLUBS
DEPARTMENT OF AGRICULTURE
WASHINGTON, DC 20250
See Interdisciplinary: General; Foundation

FAMILY SERVICE BUREAU, WELFARE ADMINISTRATION
330 INDEPENDENCE AVENUE, SW
WASHINGTON, DC 20201
See Social Sciences/Humanities: Welfare(Child Public Social); Government-Federal

FARMERS HOME ADMINISTRATION
14TH STREET AND INDEPENDENCE AVENUE, SW
WASHINGTON, DC 20250
See Engineering: Agricultural Engineering; Government-Federal

FEDERAL POWER COMMISSION
441 G STREET, NW
WASHINGTON, DC 20426
See Engineering: Water Resources; Government-Federal

FEDERAL RADIATION COUNCIL
17TH STREET AND PACIFIC AVENUE, NW
WASHINGTON,DC 20503
See Interdisciplinary: General; Unclassified

FISHERIES AND WILDLIFE CONSERVATION SUBCOMMITTEE
HOUSE OFFICE BUILDING, SUITE 1334
WASHINGTON, DC 20515
See Biology: Ecology; Government-Federal

FISHERIES AND WILDLIFE SERVICE
18TH AND C STREETS, NW
WASHINGTON, DC 20240
See Biology: General; Government-Federal

FISHERY PRODUCTS RESEARCH AND INSPECTION
NATIONAL MARINE FISHERIES SERVICES
WASHINGTON, DC 20235
See Engineering: Pollution Abatement; Government-Federal

FISHERY RESEARCH DIVISION, SPORT FISHERIES AND WILDLIFE

777 14TH STREET, NW
WASHINGTON, DC 20240
See Biology: Ecology; Government-Federal

FLOOD CONTROL, RIVERS AND HARBORS SUBCOMMITTEE
SENATE OFFICE BUILDING, SUITE 3106
WASHINGTON, DC 20510
See Engineering: Water Resources; Government-Federal

FLUID MECHANICS LABORATORY, NATIONAL BUREAU OF STANDARDS
U S DEPARTMENT OF COMMERCE
WASHINGTON, DC 20234
See Engineering: Water Resources; Government-Federal

FOOD AND DRUG ADMINISTRATION
200 C STREET, NW
WASHINGTON, DC 20204
See Engineering: General; Government-Federal

FOOD PROTECTION COMMISSION, BIOLOGY AND AGRICULTURE DIVISION
2101 CONSTITUTION AVENUE, NW
WASHINGTON, DC 20418
See Interdisciplinary: General; Unclassified

FOREST ENVIRONMENT RESEARCH DIVISION
14TH AND INDEPENDENCE AVENUE, SW
WASHINGTON, DC 20250
See Engineering: Agricultural Engineering; Government-Federal

FOREST INSTITUTE OF AMERICA
1619 MASSACHUSETTS AVENUE, NW
WASHINGTON, DC 20036
See Biology: Ecology; Field Station/Laboratory

FOREST PRESERVATION NATIONAL COMMISSION
3016 S BUILDING
WASHINGTON, DC 20250
See Engineering: General; Government-Federal

FOREST PRODUCE INDUSTRIES OF AMERICA, INCORPORATED
1835 K STREET, NW
WASHINGTON, DC 20006
See Engineering: General; Government-Federal

FOREST PRODUCTS ASSOCIATION (NATIONAL)
1619 MASSACHUSETTS AVENUE, NW
WASHINGTON, DC 20036
See Interdisciplinary: General; Industrial/Commercial

FOREST RESERVATION COMMISSION, (NATIONAL)
DEPARTMENT OF AGRICULTURE, SOUTH BUILDING
WASHINGTON, DC 20240
See Interdisciplinary: General; Unclassified

FOREST SERVICE AND RESOURCE BRANCH, DEPARTMENT OF AGRICULTURE
14TH STREET AND INDEPENDENCE AVENUE
WASHINGTON, DC 20250
See Engineering: Water Resources; Government-Federal

FORESTERS SOCIETY, AMERICAN
1010 16TH STREET, NW
WASHINGTON, DC 20036
See Biology: Ecology; Professional Organizations

FORESTRY ASSOCIATION OF AMERICA
1319 18TH STREET, NW
WASHINGTON, DC 20036
See Engineering: General; Government-Federal

FORESTRY DEVELOPMENT COMMISSION
777 14TH STREET, NW
WASHINGTON, DC 20240
See Biology: Ecology; Government-Federal

FORESTS SUBCOMMITTEE
HOUSE OFFICE BUILDING, SUITE H218
WASHINGTON, DC 20515
See Biology: Ecology; Government-Federal

GEOLOGICAL SURVEY OF UNITED STATES, DEPARTMENT OF INTERIOR
18TH AND F STREETS
WASHINGTON, DC 20006
See Geology: General; Government-Federal

GEOPHYSICAL UNION OF AMERICA
2100 PENNSYLVANIA AVENUE, NW, SUITE 435
WASHINGTON, DC 20037
See Interdisciplinary: General; Foundation

GEOPHYSICS RESEARCH BOARD, NATIONAL ACADEMY OF SCIENCE
2101 CONSTITUTION AVENUE, NW
WASHINGTON, DC 20418
See Physics: General; Foundation

GLACIOLOGY PANEL, NATIONAL ACADEMY OF SCIENCES

2101 CONSTITUTION AVENUE, NW
WASHINGTON, DC 20418
See Geology: General; Government-Federal

GOVERNMENT OPERATIONS COMMITTEE
RAYBURN HOUSE OFFICE BUILDING
WASHINGTON, DC 20515
See Engineering: Water Resources; Government-Federal

GOVERNMENTAL AFFAIRS INSTITUTION
1776 MASSACHUSETTS AVENUE, NW
WASHINGTON, DC 20036
See Social Sciences/Humanities: Law/Legislation; Research Institute

HIGHWAY RESOURCES BOARD
2101 CONSTITUTION AVENUE NE
WASHINGTON, DC 20418
See Social Sciences/Humanities: Transportation; Professional Organizations

HISTORIC PRESERVATION TRUST, NATIONAL
748 JACKSON PLACE, NW
WASHINGTON, DC 20006
See Interdisciplinary: General; Foundation

HOUSING AND URBAN DEVELOPMENT
451 7TH STREET, SW
WASHINGTON, DC 20410
See Social Sciences/Humanities: Community Development/Studies; Government-Federal

HOUSING REDEVELOPMENT OFFICE
1413 K STREET, NW
WASHINGTON, DC 20005
See Social Sciences/Humanities: Housing; Professional Organizations

HUMAN RESOURCES DEPARTMENT
25 K STREET, NE
WASHINGTON, DC 20009
See Social Sciences/Humanities: General; Government-State or Local

ICHTHYOLOGISTS SOCIETY OF AMERICA
NATIONAL MUSEUM OF NATURAL HISTORY
WASHINGTON, DC 20560
See Biology: General; Professional Organizations

INDIAN AFFAIRS BUREAU
ROOM 138, 1951 CONSTITUTION AVENUE
WASHINGTON, DC 20242
See Engineering: Water Resources; Government-Federal

INDUSTRIAL OPERATIONS ADMINISTRATION
14TH AND CONSTITUTION AVENUE, NW
WASHINGTON, DC 20230
See Social Sciences/Humanities: Industrial Development; Government-Federal

INDUSTRY DIVISION, CENSUS BUREAU
UNITED STATES DEPARTMENT OF COMMERCE
WASHINGTON, DC 20233
See Engineering: Water Resources; Government-Federal

INFORMATION DIVISION
UNITED STATES DEPARTMENT OF ARMY
WASHINGTON, DC 20315
See Engineering: General; Government-Federal

INFORMATION OFFICE, U S DEPARTMENT OF AGRICULTURE
14TH STREET AND INDEPENDENCE AVENUE
WASHINGTON, DC 20250
See Engineering: Agricultural Engineering; Government-Federal

INTELLIGENCE AND RESOURCES BUREAU, EXTRAMURAL RESEARCH STAFF
2201 C STREET, NW
WASHINGTON, DC 20525
See Social Sciences/Humanities: General; Government-Federal

INTER-BIOLOGICAL PROGRAM, UNITED STATES NATIONAL COMMISSION
2101 CONSTITUTION AVENUE, NW
WASHINGTON, DC 20418
See Biology: General; Government-Federal

INTERGOVERNMENTAL SCIENCE PROGRAMS
NATIONAL SCIENCE FOUNDATION
WASHINGTON, DC 20550
See Engineering: Water Resources; Foundation

INTERIOR AND INSULAR AFFAIRS
ROOM 1324, LONGWORTH HOUSE
WASHINGTON, DC 20515
See Interdisciplinary: General; Unclassified

INTERIOR AND INSULAR AFFAIRS
ROOM 3106, SENATE OFFICE BUILDING
WASHINGTON, DC 20510
See Interdisciplinary: General; Unclassified

INTERIOR DEPARTMENT
1951 CONSTITUTION AVENUE, NW
WASHINGTON, DC 20240
See Interdisciplinary: General; Unclassified

INTERNATIONAL ACTIVITIES OFFICE
SMITHSONIAN FOREIGN CURRENCY PROGRAM
WASHINGTON, DC 20560
See Biology: Ecology; Government-Federal

INTERNATIONAL HYDROLOGY DECADE COMMISSION
2101 CONSTITUTION AVENUE, NW
WASHINGTON, DC 20418
See Engineering: Water Resources; Professional Organizations

INTERNATIONAL JOINT COMMISSION, US AND CANADA
1711 NEW YORK AVENUE, NW
WASHINGTON, DC
See Engineering: General; Government-Federal

INTERNATIONAL SCIENTIFIC AND TECHNOLOGIC AFFAIRS DIVISION
2201 C STREET, NW
WASHINGTON, DC 20525
See Interdisciplinary: General; Unclassified

INTERPROFESSIONAL COMMISSION ON ENVIRONMENTAL DESIGN
1735 NEW YORK AVENUE, NW
WASHINGTON, DC 20006
See Engineering: General; Professional Organizations

JOB CORPS, MANPOWER ADMINISTRATION
1111 18TH STREET, NW
WASHINGTON, DC 20210
See Social Sciences/Humanities: Recreation and Leisure; Government-Federal

JOINT COMMITTEE ON ATOMIC ENERGY
CAPITOL BUILDING, ROOM H-403
WASHINGTON, DC 20510
See Interdisciplinary: General; Unclassified

JUVENILE DELINQUENCY, YOUTH OFFICE
WELFARE ADMINISTRATION, DEPARTMENT OF HEALTH, EDUCATION AND WELFAR
WASHINGTON, DC 20201
See Social Sciences/Humanities: Juvenile Delinquency; Government-Federal

LAND AND NATURAL RESOURCE DIVISION
CONSTITUTION AVENUE AND 10TH STREET
WASHINGTON, DC 20530
See Engineering: Water Resources; Government-Federal

LAND MANAGEMENT
18TH AND E STREET
WASHINGTON, DC 20240
See Engineering: Water Resources; Government-Federal

LANDSCAPE ARCHITECTS (AMERICAN SOCIETY)
2013 E STREET, NW
WASHINGTON, DC 20006
See Engineering: General; Professional Organizations

LAW AND SOCIAL POLICY CENTER
1600 20TH STREET, NW
WASHINGTON, DC 20009
See Social Sciences/Humanities: Law/Legislation; Professional Organizations

LAW ENFORCEMENT ADMINISTRATION
633 INDIANA AVENUE, NW
WASHINGTON, DC 20530
See Engineering: Water Resources; Government-Federal

LEAGUE OF WOMEN VOTERS OF UNITED STATES
1730 M STREET, NW
WASHINGTON, DC 20036
See Engineering: Water Resources; Professional Organizations

LIME ASSOCIATION (NATIONAL)
4000 BRANDYWINE STREET, NW
WASHINGTON, DC 20016
See Engineering: Water Resources; Government-Federal

MANUFACTURING CHEMISTS ASSOCIATION
1825 CONNECTICUT AVENUE, NW
WASHINGTON, DC 20009
See Engineering: Pollution Abatement; Industrial/Commercial

MARINE FISHERIES SERVICE
WASHINGTON, DC 20240
See Biology: Ecology; Research Institute

MARINE FISHERIES SYSTEMS LABORATORY
UNITED STATES NATIONAL MUSEUM
WASHINGTON, DC 20560
See Biology: General; Government-Federal

MARINE RESOURCES OFFICE
18TH & C STREETS, NW
WASHINGTON, DC 20240
See Biology: General; Government-Federal

MARINE SCIENCES DIVISION, 1ST COAST GUARD DISTRICT
KENNEDY BUILDING, GOVERNMENT CENTER
WASHINGTON, DC 02203
See Engineering: Water Resources; Government-State or Local

MARINE TECHNOLOGY SOCIETY
1730 M STREET, NW
WASHINGTON, DC 20036
See Interdisciplinary: General; Professional Organizations

MARITIME ADMINISTRATION, PUBLIC INFORMATION OFFICE
441 G STREET NW, ROOM 3037
WASHINGTON, DC 20235
See Engineering: Pollution Abatement; Government-Federal

MAYORS CONFERENCE OF THE UNITED STATES
1707 H STREET, NW ROOM 606
WASHINGTON, DC 20006
See Engineering: Pollution Abatement; Government-Federal

MEDICINE AND SURGERY BUREAU, U S DEPARTMENT OF NAVY
CODE 7223
WASHINGTON, DC 20390
See Engineering: General; Government-Federal

MEDICINE FOLLOW-UP AGENCY, SCIENCE ACADEMY RESEARCH CENTER
2101 CONSTITUTION AVENUE, NW
WASHINGTON, DC 20418
See Interdisciplinary: General; Research Institute

MERCHANT MARINES AND FISHERIES, US HOUSE OF REPRESENTATIVES
ROOM 1334, LONGWORTH HOUSE BUILDING
WASHINGTON, DC 20515
See Biology: Ecology; Government-Federal

MIGRATORY BIRD CONSERVATION COMMISSION
DEPARTMENT OF INTERIOR BUILDING
WASHINGTON, DC 20240
See Biology: Ecology; Government-Federal

MINED LAND CONSERVATION CONFERENCE
1130 17TH STREET, NW
WASHINGTON, DC 20036
See Social Sciences/Humanities: Industrial Development; Industrial/Commercial

MINERAL INFORMATION OFFICE
18TH AND C STREETS, NW
WASHINGTON, DC 20240
See Geology: General; Government-Federal

**MINERAL RESOURCE
DEVELOPMENT**
18TH AND C STREETS, NW
WASHINGTON, DC 20240
See Geology: Paleontology; Government-Federal

MINES BUREAU
UNITED STATES DEPARTMENT OF
THE INTERIOR
WASHINGTON, DC 20240
See Engineering: Pollution Abatement;
Government-Federal

**MOTOR VEHICLE SAFETY
PERFORMANCE SERVICE**
6TH AND D STREETS, SW
WASHINGTON, DC 20591
See Engineering: Chemical Engineering;
Government-Federal

**MUNICIPAL WASTE WATER
PROGRAMS, WATER QUALITY
OFFICE**
ENVIRONMENTAL PROTECTION
AGENCY
WASHINGTON, DC 20460
See Engineering: Water Resources; Government-Federal

NATIONAL ACADEMY OF SCIENCES
2101 CONSTITUTION AVENUE, NW
WASHINGTON, DC 20418
See Interdisciplinary: General; Unclassified

NATIONAL AFFAIRS BUREAU
1231 24TH STREET, NW
WASHINGTON, DC 20037
See Social Sciences/Humanities: General;
Industrial/Commercial

**NATIONAL AGRICULTURAL
LIBRARY**
14TH STREET AND
INDEPENDENCE AVENUE
WASHINGTON, DC 20250
See Engineering: Water Resources; Government-Federal

NATIONAL CANNERS ASSOCIATION
1133 20TH STREET, NW
WASHINGTON, DC 20036
See Engineering: Agricultural Engineering; Industrial/Commercial

**NATIONAL CENTER FOR
SYSTEMATICS**
10TH AND CONSTITUTION
AVENUE, NW ROOM 57
WASHINGTON, DC 20242
See Engineering: Water Resources; Government-Federal

**NATIONAL CLEAN-UP, PAINT-UP,
FIX-UP BUREAU**
1500 RHODE ISLAND AVENUE, NW
WASHINGTON, DC 20005
See Interdisciplinary: General; Unclassified

**NATIONAL COAL POLICY
CONFERENCE INCORPORATED**
1000 16TH STREET, NW
WASHINGTON, DC 20036
See Engineering: Pollution Abatement;
Industrial/Commercial

**NATIONAL EDUCATION
ASSOCIATION**
1201 16TH STREET, NW
WASHINGTON, DC 20036
See Interdisciplinary: General; Professional Organizations

NATIONAL GEOGRAPHIC SOCIETY
1146 SIXTEENTH STREET
WASHINGTON, DC 20036
See Interdisciplinary: General; Foundation

NATIONAL GRANGE
1616 H STREET, NW
WASHINGTON, DC 20006
See Engineering: Agricultural Engineering; Professional Organizations

**NATIONAL LABOR RELATIONS
BOARD**
1717 PENNSYLVANIA AVENUE, NW
WASHINGTON, DC 20570
See Social Sciences/Humanities: Labor/
Relations/Unions; Government-Federal

NATIONAL LEAGUE OF CITIES
1612 K STREET, NW
WASHINGTON, DC 20006
See Engineering: Water Resources; Government-Federal

**NATIONAL OCEANOGRAPHIC
ASSOCIATION**
1900 L STREET, NW
WASHINGTON, DC 20036
See Interdisciplinary: General; Professional Organizations

**NATIONAL PARK SERVICE,
INTERIOR DEPARTMENT**
18TH AND C STREETS
WASHINGTON, DC 20240
See Social Sciences/Humanities: Recreation and Leisure; Government-Federal

NATIONAL PARKS ASSOCIATION
1300 NEW HAMPSHIRE AVENUE,
NW
WASHINGTON, DC 20036
See Engineering: Water Resources; Government-Federal

**NATIONAL PARKS CONSERVATION
ASSOCIATION**
1701 18TH STREET, NW

WASHINGTON, DC 20009
See Biology: Ecology; Educational Institute

**NATIONAL PETROLEUM REFINERS
ASSOCIATION**
1725 DE SALES STREET, NW
WASHINGTON, DC 20036
See Engineering: Pollution Abatement;
Industrial/Commercial

NATIONAL REFERRAL CENTER
LIBRARY OF CONGRESS
WASHINGTON, DC 20540
See Interdisciplinary: General; Unclassified

NATIONAL RIFLE ASSOCIATION
1600 RHODE ISLAND AVENUE, NW
WASHINGTON, DC 20036
See Social Sciences/Humanities: Recreation and Leisure; Professional Organizations

**NATIONAL RIVERS AND HARBORS
CONGRESS**
1028 CONNECTICUT AVENUE, NW
WASHINGTON, DC 20036
See Engineering: Water Resources; Government-Federal

NATIONAL SCIENCE FOUNDATION
1800 G STREET, NW
WASHINGTON, DC 20550
See Interdisciplinary: General; Foundation

**NATIONAL WATER RESOURCES
ASSOCIATION**
897 NATIONAL PRESS BUILDING
WASHINGTON, DC 20004
See Engineering: Water Resources; Educational Institute

**NATIONAL WATERSHED
CONGRESS**
1025 VERMONT AVENUE, NW
WASHINGTON, DC 20005
See Engineering: Water Resources; Industrial/Commercial

**NATIONAL WILDLIFE
FEDERATION**
1412 16TH STREET, NW
WASHINGTON, DC 20036
See Engineering: Water Resources; Government-Federal

NATURAL DISASTER DIVISION
17TH AND F STREETS, NW
WASHINGTON, DC 20504
See Engineering: General; Government-State or Local

NATURAL GAS BUREAU
441 G STREET, NW
WASHINGTON, DC 20426
See Engineering: Chemical Engineering;
Government-Federal

**NATURAL HISTORY CENTRAL
  LIBRARY**
10TH STREET & CONSTITUTION
  AVENUE
WASHINGTON, DC 20560
See Interdisciplinary: General; Unclassified

**NATURAL RESOURCE ECONOMICS
  DIVISIONAL**
14TH STREET AND
  INDEPENDENCE AVENUE, SW
WASHINGTON, DC 20250
See Engineering: Water Resources; Government-Federal

NATURAL RESOURCES CENTER
702 19TH STREET, NW
WASHINGTON, DC 20006
See Engineering: Water Resources; Government-Federal

**NATURAL RESOURCES COUNCIL
  OF AMERICA**
719 13TH STREET, NW, ROOM 509
WASHINGTON, DC
See Interdisciplinary: General; Industrial/
Commercial

**NATURAL RESOURCES POLICY
  CENTER**
GEORGE WASHINGTON
  UNIVERSITY
WASHINGTON, DC 20001
See Social Sciences/Humanities: Education; Educational Institute

**NATURAL RESOURCES, CITIZENS
  COMMISSION**
712 DUPONT CIRCLE BUILDING
WASHINGTON, DC 20006
See Interdisciplinary: General; Foundation

**NATURE AND NATURAL
  RESOURCES INTERNATIONAL
  UNION FOR CONSERVATION**
200 P STREET, NW
WASHINGTON, DC 20001
See Interdisciplinary: General; Industrial/
Commercial

NATURE CONSERVANCY
1522 K STREET, NW
WASHINGTON, DC 10036
See Biology: Ecology; Government-Federal

**NAVAL FACILITIES ENGINEERING
  COMMAND**
US DEPARTMENT OF NAVY, ROOM
  2B27
WASHINGTON, DC 20390
See Engineering: Water Resources; Government-Federal

NAVAL OCEANOGRAPHIC OFFICE
US DEPARTMENT OF THE NAVY
WASHINGTON, DC 20390

See Engineering: Water Resources; Government-Federal

**NUCLEAR EDUCATION AND
  TRAINING DIVISION**
UNITED STATES ATOMIC ENERGY
  COMMISSION
WASHINGTON, DC 20545
See Chemistry: Physical Chemistry; Government-Federal

**NUCLEAR ENERGY COMMISSION
  (INTERNATIONAL/AMERICAN), O
  A S**
PAN AMERICAN UNION
WASHINGTON, DC 20006
See Interdisciplinary: General; Professional Organizations

OCEANOGRAPHIC DATA CENTER
M STREET AT 8TH STREET
WASHINGTON, DC 20390
See Biology: General; Government-Federal

**OCEANOGRAPHY AND
  LIMNOLOGY OFFICE**
10TH STREET AND CONSTITUTION
  AVENUE
WASHINGTON, DC 20560
See Biology: Ecology; Government-Federal

OCEANOGRAPHY SECTION
NATIONAL SCIENCE FOUNDATION
WASHINGTON, DC 20550
See Biology: Ecology; Foundation

OFFICE OF BASIC MATERIALS
14TH STREET AND CONSTITUTION
  AVENUE, NW
WASHINGTON, DC 20230
See Interdisciplinary: General; Unclassified

OIL AND GAS OFFICE
18TH AND C STREETS, NW
WASHINGTON, DC 20240
See Geology: General; Government-Federal

**OPERATING ENGINEERS
  INTERNATIONAL UNION**
WASHINGTON, DC 20036
See Engineering: General; Government-State or Local

OPERATIONAL SAFETY DIVISION
UNITED STATES ATOMIC ENERGY
  COMMISSION
WASHINGTON, DC 20545
See Chemistry: Physical Chemistry; Government-Federal

**ORGANIZATION OF AMERICAN
  STATES**
PAN AMERICAN UNION
WASHINGTON, DC 20006
See Biology: Ecology; Government-Federal

**ORNITHOLOGISTS UNION OF
  AMERICA**
NATIONAL MUSEUM OF NATURAL
  HISTORY
WASHINGTON, DC 20560
See Biology: General; Professional Organizations

OUTDOOR RECREATION BUREAU
19TH AND C STREETS, NW
WASHINGTON, DC 20240
See Engineering: Water Resources; Government-Federal

**PAINT, VARNISH, AND LACQUER
  (NATIONAL)**
1500 RHODE ISLAND AVENUE, NW
WASHINGTON, DC 20005
See Engineering: Pollution Abatement;
Industrial/Commercial

**PARKS AND RECREATION
  SUBCOMMITTEE**
SENATE OFFICE BUILDING, SUITE
  3106
WASHINGTON, DC 20510
See Biology: Ecology; Government-Federal

PATENT OFFICE
14TH AND E STREETS, NW
WASHINGTON, DC 20231
See Engineering: Water Resources; Government-Federal

**PESTICIDES PROGRAMS,
  TECHNICAL INFORMATION
  SERVICES, EPA**
1626 K STREET, NW
WASHINGTON, DC 20460
See Engineering: Chemical Engineering;
Government-Federal

**PESTICIDES REGULATION
  DIVISION**
14TH STREET AND
  INDEPENDENCE AVENUE
WASHINGTON, DC 20250
See Interdisciplinary: General; Unclassified

**PETROLEUM REFERENCE
  ASSOCIATION**
1725 DE SALES STREET, NW
WASHINGTON, DC
See Engineering: General; Government-Federal

**PLANNERS INSTITUTE OF
  AMERICA**
917 15TH STREET, NW
WASHINGTON, DC 20005
See Social Sciences/Humanities: Community Development/Studies; Professional Organizations

**PLANNING AND INTERAGENCY
  PROGRAMS DIVISION**
WATER QUALITY OFFICE,

ENVIRONMENTAL PROTECTION
AGENCY
WASHINGTON, DC 20460
See Engineering: Water Resources; Un-
classified

PLANT AND FOOD, NATIONAL
INSTITUTE
1700 K STREET, NW
WASHINGTON, DC 20006
See Engineering: Chemical Engineering;
Government-Federal

POLAR PROGRAM OFFICE
NATIONAL SCIENCE FOUNDATION
WASHINGTON, DC 20550
See Interdisciplinary: General; Founda-
tion

POLITICAL SCIENCE ASSOCIATION
1726 MASSACHUSETTS AVENUE, NW
WASHINGTON, DC 20036
See Social Sciences/Humanities: Law/
Legislation; Professional Organizations

POLLUTION CONTROL,
DEPARTMENT OF JUSTICE
500 23RD STREET
WASHINGTON, DC 20037
See Engineering: Pollution Abatement;
Government-Federal

POLLUTION SURVEILLANCE
DIVISION
633 INDIANA AVENUE, NW
WASHINGTON, DC 20242
See Engineering: Pollution Abatement;
Government-Federal

POPULATION ASSOCIATION OF
AMERICA
NATIONAL CENTER FOR HEALTH
STATISTICS
WASHINGTON, DC 20201
See Social Sciences/Humanities: Popula-
tion Studies/Family Planning; Educa-
tional Institute

POPULATION CRISIS COMMISSION
1730 K STREET, NW
WASHINGTON, DC 20006
See Social Sciences/Humanities: Population Studies/Family Planning; Educational Institute

POPULATION REFERENCE BUREAU
1755 MASSACHUSETTS AVENUE, NW
WASHINGTON, DC 20036
See Social Sciences/Humanities: Population Studies/Family Planning; Educational Institute

POTOMAC BASIN CENTER
1250 CONNECTICUT AVENUE, NW
WASHINGTON, DC 20036
See Engineering: Water Resources; Professional Organizations

POWER BUREAU
441 G STREET, NW
WASHINGTON, DC 20426
See Engineering: Water Resources; Government-Federal

PRE-COLLEGE SCIENCE
EDUCATION DIVISION
NATIONAL SCIENCE FOUNDATION
WASHINGTON, DC 20550
See Interdisciplinary: General; Founda-
tion

PREVENTIVE MEDICINE DIVISION
MAIN NAVY BUILDING
WASHINGTON, DC 20315
See Engineering: General; Government-
Federal

PROGRAM ENGINEERING SOCIETY
2029 K STREET, NW
WASHINGTON, DC 20006
See Engineering: Water Resources; Government-Federal

PUBLIC INFORMATION OFFICE
633 INDIANA AVENUE, NW
WASHINGTON,DC 20242
See Engineering: Water Resources; Government-Federal

PUBLIC POLICY RESEARCH
INSTITUTE
1150 17TH STREET, NW
WASHINGTON, DC 20036
See Social Sciences/Humanities: Law/
Legislation; Research Institute

PUBLIC WORKS COMMISSION
ROOM 4204, NEW SENATE
BUILDING
WASHINGTON, D C 20510
See Engineering: Water Resources; Gov-
ernment-Federal

PUBLIC WORKS COMMITTEE, US
HOUSE OF REPRESENTATIVES
ROOM 2165, RAYBURN HOUSE
OFFICE BUILDING
WASHINGTON, DC 20515
See Engineering: Water Resources; Gov-
ernment-Federal

PUBLIC WORKS OFFICE,
ECONOMIC DEVELOPMENT
ADMINISTRATION
UNITED STATES DEPARTMENT OF
COMMERCE
WASHINGTON, DC 20230
See Social Sciences/Humanities: Commu-
nity Development/Studies; Govern-
ment-Federal

RADIOLOGICAL HEALTH CENTER
VAN NESS STREET AND
CONNECTICUT AVENUE, NW
WASHINGTON, DC 20203
See Physics: General; Government-Feder-
al

RECREATION DEPARTMENT
3005 10TH STREET, NE
WASHINGTON, DC 20018
See Social Sciences/Humanities: Recreation and Leisure; Government-Federal

REHABILITATION AND SOCIAL
SERVICE ADMINISTRATION
330 14TH STREET, SW
WASHINGTON, DC 20201
See Social Sciences/Humanities: Rehabil-
itation; Government-Federal

RESEARCH AND DEVELOPMENT
OFFICE
633 INDIANA AVENUE, NW
WASHINGTON,DC 20242
See Engineering: Water Resources; Gov-
ernment-Federal

RESEARCH AND ENGINEERING
BUREAU
12TH AND PENNSYLVANIA
AVENUE, NW
WASHINGTON, DC 20260
See Engineering: General; Government-
Federal

RESEARCH DEVELOPMENT
DIVISION
UNITED STATES DEPARTMENT OF
AGRICULTURE, SOIL
CONSERVATION SERVICE
WASHINGTON, DC 20250
See Biology: Ecology; Government-Fed-
eral

RESEARCH FOR THE FUTURE,
INCORPORATED
1755 MASSACHUSETTS AVENUE, NW
WASHINGTON, DC 20036
See Social Sciences/Humanities: General;
Foundation

RESEARCH FOUNDATION
ASSOCIATION
1001 CONNECTICUT AVENUE, NW
WASHINGTON, DC 20036
See Social Sciences/Humanities: Community Development/Studies; Professional Organizations

RESEARCH OFFICE AND
UNIVERSITY RELATIONS (TA/
RUR)
BUREAU OF TECHNOLOGY,
ASSISTANCE AID
WASHINGTON, DC 20523
See Interdisciplinary: General; Unclassi-
fied

RESEARCH OFFICE, FEDERAL
HIGHWAYS ADMINISTRATION
UNITED STATES DEPARTMENT OF
TRANSPORTATION
WASHINGTON, DC 20590
See Engineering: Water Resources; Gov-
ernment-Federal

RESOURCES AND MANAGEMENT
COMMISSION, NATIONAL
ACADEMY OF SCIENCES
2101 CONSTITUTION AVENUE, NW
WASHINGTON, DC 20418
See Biology: Ecology; Government-Fed-
eral

RESOURCES DIVISION, NATIONAL EDUCATION ASSOCIATION
1201 16TH STREET, NW
WASHINGTON, DC 20036
See Social Sciences/Humanities: Education; Research Institute

RESOURCES FOR THE FUTURE
1755 MASSACHUSETTS AVENUE, NW
WASHINGTON, DC 20036
See Interdisciplinary: General; Professional Organizations

RESPONSIVE LAW STUDY CENTER
POST OFFICE BOX 19367
WASHINGTON, DC 20036
See Social Sciences/Humanities: Law/Legislation; Foundation

RIVERS AND HARBORS BOARD, US DEPARTMENT OF ARMY
2ND AND Q STREETS
WASHINGTON, DC 20024
See Engineering: General; Government-Federal

RIVERS AND HARBORS SUBCOMMITTEE
HOUSE OFFICE BUILDING, SUITE 2165
WASHINGTON, DC 20515
See Biology: Ecology; Government-Federal

RURAL COMMUNITY DEVELOPMENT SERVICE
INDEPENDENCE AVENUE BETWEEN 12TH AND 14TH STREETS
WASHINGTON, DC 20250
See Social Sciences/Humanities: Community Development/Studies; Government-Federal

SALINE WATER OFFICE, DEPARTMENT OF THE INTERIOR
18TH AND C STREETS, NW
WASHINGTON, DC 20242
See Engineering: Water Resources; Government-Federal

SANITARY ENGINEERING RESEARCH BRANCH
UNITED STATES ARMY MEDICAL RESEARCH DEVELOPMENT COMMAND
WASHINGTON, DC 20314
See Engineering: Water Resources; Government-Federal

SCIENCE AND TECHNOLOGY COUNCIL
EXECUTIVE OFFICE BUILDING
WASHINGTON, DC 20503
See Engineering: Water Resources; Government-Federal

SCIENCE AND TECHNOLOGY DIVISION, LIBRARY OF CONGRESS

10 FIRST STREET, SE
WASHINGTON, DC 20540
See Interdisciplinary: General; Unclassified

SCIENCE AND TECHNOLOGY INFORMATION DIVISION, NASA
300 7TH STREET, NW
WASHINGTON, DC 20546
See Engineering: General; Government-Federal

SCIENCE AND TECHNOLOGY NATIONAL REFERRAL CENTER
1ST STREET & INDEPENDENCE AVENUE
WASHINGTON, DC 20540
See Interdisciplinary: General; Unclassified

SCIENCE INFORMATION EXCHANGE
1730 M STREET, NW
WASHINGTON, DC 20036
See Interdisciplinary: General; Unclassified

SCIENCE INFORMATION SERVICE OFFICE
NATIONAL SCIENCE FOUNDATION
WASHINGTON, DC 20550
See Interdisciplinary: General; Foundation

SCIENCES-TECHNOLOGY-GOVERNMENT PROGRAM
AMERICAN UNIVERSITY
WASHINGTON, DC 20216
See Interdisciplinary: General; Unclassified

SCIENTIFIC ADVANCEMENT ASSOCIATION
1515 MASSACHUSETTS AVENUE, NW
WASHINGTON, DC 20005
See Interdisciplinary: General; Professional Organizations

SMALL BUSINESS ADMINISTRATION
811 VERMONT AVENUE, NW
WASHINGTON, DC 20416
See Social Sciences/Humanities: Industrial Development; Government-Federal

SMITHSONIAN INSTITUTION
1000 JEFFERSON DRIVE, SW
WASHINGTON, DC 20560
See Interdisciplinary: General; Unclassified

SMITHSONIAN INSTITUTION, SCIENCES INFORMATION EXCHANGE
1730 M STREET, NW
WASHINGTON, DC 20036
See Engineering: Water Resources; Government-Federal

SMOKE AND BOILER SECTION, LICENSES AND INSPECTIONS DEPARTMENT
DISTRICT BUILDING, 14TH AND E STREETS, NW
WASHINGTON, DC 20004
See Engineering: Pollution Abatement; Government-State or Local

SOCIAL LEGISLATION INFORMATION SERVICE INSTITUTE
1346 CONNECTICUT AVENUE, NW
WASHINGTON, DC 20036
See Social Sciences/Humanities: Law/Legislation; Government-Federal

SOCIAL SCIENCE RESEARCH BUREAU, INCORPORATED
1200 17TH STREET
WASHINGTON, DC 20036
See Social Sciences/Humanities: General; Research Institute

SOCIAL STUDIES COUNCIL
1201 16TH STREET, NW
WASHINGTON,DC 20036
See Social Sciences/Humanities: Education; Professional Organizations

SOCIOLOGICAL ASSOCIATION OF AMERICA
1722 NORTH STREET, NW
WASHINGTON, DC 20036
See Social Sciences/Humanities: General; Professional Organizations

SOIL AND WATER CONSERVATION DISTRICTS ASSOCIATION
1025 VERMONT AVENUE, NW
WASHINGTON, DC 20005
See Engineering: Water Resources; Government-Federal

SOIL CONSERVATION AND FORESTRY SUBCOMMITTEE
SENATE OFFICE BUILDING, SUITE 324
WASHINGTON, DC 20510
See Engineering: Agricultural Engineering; Government-Federal

SOIL CONSERVATION SERVICE
DEPARTMENT OF AGRICULTURE
WASHINGTON, DC 20250
See Biology: Ecology; Government-Federal

SOUND SECTION, BUREAU OF STANDARDS
METEOROLOGY DIVISION
WASHINGTON, DC 20234
See Engineering: Pollution Abatement; Government-Federal

SPORT FISHERIES AND WILDLIFE BUREAU
18TH AND C STREETS
WASHINGTON, DC 20240
See Biology: Ecology; Government-Federal

**SPORT FISHERY RESEARCH
  FOUNDATION**
SUITE 503, 719 13TH STREET NW
WASHINGTON, DC 20005
See Biology: Ecology; Foundation

SPORT FISHING INSTITUTE
719 13TH STREET, NW SUITE 503
WASHINGTON, DC 20005
See Social Sciences/Humanities: Recreation and Leisure; Professional Organizations

**STATE UNIVERSITY OF NEW YORK
  OFFICES, SUITE 500**
1730 RHODE ISLAND AVENUE, NW
WASHINGTON, DC 20036
See Interdisciplinary: General; Educational Institute

STATISTICAL REPORTING SERVICE
14TH STREET AND
  INDEPENDENCE AVENUE, SW
WASHINGTON, DC 20250
See Engineering: Agricultural Engineering; Government-Federal

TECHNICAL SERVICES DIVISION
633 INDIANA AVENUE, NW
WASHINGTON, DC 20242
See Engineering: Water Resources; Government-Federal

**TECHNOLOGICAL UTILIZATION
  DIVISION, NASA**
400 MARYLAND AVENUE, SW
WASHINGTON, DC 20546
See Engineering: General; Government-Federal

TOXICOLOGY BRANCH
ARMED FORCES INSTITUTE OF
  PATHOLOGY
WASHINGTON, DC 20305
See Chemistry: General; Government-Federal

**TRAINING GRANTS BRANCH,
  MANPOWER TRAINING BRANCH**
ENVIRONMENTAL PROTECTION
  AGENCY
WASHINGTON, DC 20460
See Engineering: Water Resources; Government-Federal

**UNDERGRADUATE EDUCATION IN
  SCIENCE DIVISION**
NATIONAL SCIENCE FOUNDATION
WASHINGTON, DC 20550
See Interdisciplinary: General; Foundation

**UNITED STATES COAST GUARD
  HEADQUARTERS**
400 7TH STREET, SW
WASHINGTON, DC 20590
See Engineering: Pollution Abatement; Government-Federal

**UNITED STATES GEOLOGICAL
  SURVEY**
DEPARTMENT OF THE INTERIOR
WASHINGTON, DC 20242
See Engineering: Water Resources; Government-Federal

URBAN AMERICA
1717 MASSACHUSETTS AVENUE, NW
WASHINGTON, DC 20036
See Social Sciences/Humanities: Community Development/Studies; Educational Institute

URBAN AMERICA, INCORPORATED.
15TH AND H STREETS, NW
WASHINGTON, DC 20005
See Social Sciences/Humanities: Community Development/Studies; Foundation

URBAN INSTITUTE
2100 M STREET, NW
WASHINGTON, DC 20037
See Social Sciences/Humanities: Transportation; Research Institute

URBAN LAND INSTITUTE
ONE DU PONT CIRCLE, SUITE 500
WASHINGTON, DC 20036
See Social Sciences/Humanities: Education; Professional Organizations

US DEPARTMENT OF INTERIOR
18TH AND F STREETS, NW
WASHINGTON, DC 20006
See Engineering: Water Resources; Government-Federal

**WATER FOWL ADVISORY
  COMMITTEE**
UNITED STATES DEPARTMENT OF
  INTERIOR
WASHINGTON, DC 20240
See Interdisciplinary: General; Industrial/Commercial

**WATER INDUSTRY AND
  ENGINEERING SERVICES
  DIVISION**
UNITED STATES DEPARTMENT
  COMMERCE
WASHINGTON, DC 20230
See Engineering: General; Government-Federal

**WATER POLLUTION CONTROL
  ADMINISTRATION**
DEPARTMENT OF THE INTERIOR
WASHINGTON, DC 20242
See Engineering: Pollution Abatement; Government-Federal

**WATER POLLUTION CONTROL
  FEDERATION**
3900 WISCONSIN AVENUE, NW
WASHINGTON, DC 20016
See Engineering: Pollution Abatement; Foundation

**WATER POLLUTION RESEARCH
  ASSOCIATION INTERNATIONAL**
3900 WISCONSIN AVENUE, NW
WASHINGTON, DC 20016
See Engineering: Pollution Abatement; Government-Federal

**WATER QUALITY
  ADMINISTRATION**
DEPARTMENT OF THE INTERIOR
WASHINGTON, DC 20242
See Engineering: Pollution Abatement; Government-Federal

**WATER QUALITY CONTROL
  DIVISION, DEPARTMENT OF
  PUBLIC HEALTH**
300 INDIANA AVENUE, NW
WASHINGTON, DC 20001
See Engineering: Water Resources; Government-State or Local

WATER QUALITY DATA STORAGE
POLLUTION SURVEILLANCE
WASHINGTON, DC 20242
See Engineering: Water Resources; Government-Federal

**WATER RESEARCH DIVISION,
  GEOLOGICAL SURVEY**
18TH AND F STREETS, NW
WASHINGTON, DC 20242
See Biology: Ecology; Government-Federal

**WATER RESOURCES AND
  ENGINEERING DIVISION**
14TH AND CONSTITUTION, NW
WASHINGTON, DC 20230
See Engineering: Pollution Abatement; Government-Federal

**WATER RESOURCES AND
  ENGINEERING SERVICES
  DIVISION**
14TH STREET AND CONSTITUTION
  AVENUE
WASHINGTON, DC 20230
See Engineering: Water Resources; Government-Federal

WATER RESOURCES COUNCIL
1025 VERMONT AVENUE, NW
WASHINGTON, DC 20005
See Engineering: Water Resources; Government-Federal

WATER RESOURCES COUNCIL
2120 L STREET, NW
WASHINGTON, DC 20037
See Engineering: Water Resources; Government-Federal

**WATER RESOURCES COUNCIL,
  NATIONAL ACADEMY OF
  SCIENCES**
2101 CONSTITUTION AVENUE, NW
WASHINGTON, DC 20418
See Engineering: Water Resources; Government-Federal

WATER RESOURCES DIVISION
NATIONAL PARK SERVICE
WASHINGTON, DC 20240
See Engineering: Water Resources; Government-Federal

WATER RESOURCES RESEARCH OFFICE
DEPARTMENT OF THE INTERIOR
WASHINGTON, DC 20240
See Engineering: Water Resources; Government-Federal

WATER RESOURCES SCIENCES INFORMATION CENTER
DEPARTMENT OF INTERIOR
WASHINGTON, DC 20240
See Engineering: Water Resources; Government-Federal

WATER SUPPLY PROGRAM DIVISION
ENVIRONMENTAL PROTECTION AGENCY
WASHINGTON, DC 20201
See Engineering: Water Resources; Government-Federal

WATERSHED MANAGEMENT DIVISION, FOREST SERVICES
14TH STREET AND INDEPENDENCE AVENUE
WASHINGTON, DC 20250
See Engineering: Water Resources; Government-Federal

WEATHER MODIFICATION PROGRAM, NATIONAL SCIENCE FOUNDATION
WASHINGTON, DC 20550
See Interdisciplinary: General; Government-State or Local

WELFARE ADMINISTRATION, RESEARCH DIVISION
US DEPARTMENT OF HEALTH, EDUCATION AND WELFARE
WASHINGTON, DC 20201
See Social Sciences/Humanities: Welfare(Child Public Social); Government-Federal

WILD FLOWER PRESERVATION SOCIETY
3740 OLIVER STREET, NW
WASHINGTON, DC 20015
See Biology: General; Industrial/Commercial

WILDERNESS SOCIETY
729 15TH STREET, NW
WASHINGTON, DC 20005
See Biology: Ecology; Educational Institute

WILDLIFE DEFENDERS
731 DUPONT CIRCLE BUILDING
WASHINGTON, DC 20036
See Biology: Ecology; Foundation

WILDLIFE DIVISION, BUREAU OF SPORT FISHERIES AND WILDLIFE
DEPARTMENT OF THE INTERIOR
WASHINGTON, DC 20240
See Biology: Ecology; Government-Federal

WILDLIFE FEDERATION NATIONAL ENDOWMENT
1412 16TH STREET, NW
WASHINGTON, DC 20036
See Biology: Ecology; Professional Organizations

WILDLIFE FOUNDATION OF NORTH AMERICA
709 WIRE BUILDING
WASHINGTON, DC 20005
See Interdisciplinary: General; Industrial/Commercial

WILDLIFE MANAGEMENT INSTITUTE
709 WIRE BUILDING
WASHINGTON, DC 20005
See Interdisciplinary: General; Professional Organizations

WILDLIFE SOCIETY
SUITE S-176, 3900 WISCONSIN AVENUE
WASHINGTON, DC 20016
See Biology: Ecology; Professional Organizations

WOODROW WILSON INTERNATIONAL CENTER FOR SCHOLARS
SMITHSONIAN INSTITUTION BUILDING
WASHINGTON, DC 20560
See Interdisciplinary: General; Government-State or Local

WORLD BANK
1818 H STREET, NW
WASHINGTON, DC 20433
See Social Sciences/Humanities: Community Development/Studies; Professional Organizations

WORLD WILDLIFE FUND
1816 JEFFERSON PLACE, NW
WASHINGTON, DC 20036
See Interdisciplinary: General; Professional Organizations

Delaware

AIR POLLUTION CONTROL, WATER AND AIR RESOURCES
POST OFFICE BOX 916
DOVER, DE 19901
See Engineering: Pollution Abatement; Government-State or Local

ENVIRONMENTAL ENGINEERING, ENGINEERING DEPARTMENT
E I DUPONT DE NEMOURS, AND COMPANY
WILMINGTON, DE 19898
See Engineering: Pollution Abatement; Industrial/Commercial

ENVIRONMENTAL STUDIES PROGRAM
UNIVERSITY OF DELAWARE
NEWARK, DE 19711
See Interdisciplinary: General; Educational Institute

GAME AND FISHERIES COMMISSION, NORTH EAST ASSOCIATION
NORTH STREET
DOVER, DE 19901
See Interdisciplinary: General; Professional Organizations

GEOLOGICAL SURVEY OF DELAWARE
UNIVERSITY OF DELAWARE
NEWARK, DE 19711
See Geology: General; Government-State or Local

HEALTH PLANNING COUNCIL INCORPORATED
WILMINGTON, DE 19810
See Interdisciplinary: General; Foundation

HIGHWAY DEPARTMENT
DOVER, DE 19901
See Social Sciences/Humanities: Transportation; Government-State or Local

MARINE SCIENCES CENTER
LEWES, DE 19958
See Biology: General; Educational Institute

MARINE STUDIES COLLEGE
UNIVERSITY OF DELAWARE
NEWARK, DE 19711
See Engineering: General; Educational Institute

SOIL AND WATER CONSERVATION COMMISSION OF DELAWARE
P O BOX 567
GEORGETOWN, DE 19947
See Engineering: Water Resources; Government-State or Local

STANDARDS AND INSPECTIONS DIVISION
DEPARTMENT OF AGRICULTURE
DOVER, DE 19901
See Engineering: Agricultural Engineering; Government-State or Local

WATER POLLUTION COMMISSION
FEDERAL AND WATER STREETS
DOVER, DE 19901
See Engineering: Pollution Abatement; Government-State or Local

WATER RESOURCES CENTER
UNIVERSITY OF DELAWARE
NEWARK, DE 19711
See Engineering: General; Educational Institute

**WILDLIFE FEDERATION OF
DELAWARE**
1014 WASHINGTON STREET
WILMINGTON, DE 19801
See Biology: Ecology; Foundation

**WILDLIFE NATIONAL
FEDERATION**
1011 WASHINGTON STREET
WILMINGTON, DE 19801
See Biology: Ecology; Foundation

Florida

**AGRICULTURAL RESEARCH
CENTER, INCORPORATED**
1305 EAST MAIN STREET
LAKELAND, FL 33801
See Chemistry: General; Research Institute

**AIR AND WATER POLLUTION
CONTROL COMMISSION**
306 WEST JEFFERSON STREET
TALLAHASSEE, FL 32301
See Engineering: Pollution Abatement;
Government-State or Local

**AIR POLLUTION CONTROL
DIVISION, COUNTY HEALTH
DEPARTMENT**
826 EVERNIA STREET
WEST PALM BEACH, FL 33402
See Engineering: Pollution Abatement;
Government-State or Local

**AIR POLLUTION CONTROL,
BUILDING DEPARTMENT**
POST OFFICE BOX 708
MIAMI, FL 33133
See Engineering: Pollution Abatement;
Government-State or Local

**AIR POLLUTION CONTROL,
BUILDING DEPARTMENT**
1130 WASHINGTON AVENUE
MIAMI BEACH, FL 33139
See Engineering: Pollution Abatement;
Government-State or Local

**AIR POLLUTION CONTROL,
COUNTY HEALTH DEPARTMENT**
520 SECOND AVENUE NORTH
ST PETERSBURG, FL 33731
See Engineering: Pollution Abatement;
Government-State or Local

**AIR POLLUTION CONTROL,
HEALTH DEPARTMENT**
1938 LAUREL STREET POST OFFICE
2658
SARASOTA, FL 33579
See Engineering: Pollution Abatement;
Government-State or Local

AIR POLLUTION RESOURCES
UNIVERSITY OF FLORIDA
GAINESVILLE, FL 30501

See Engineering: Pollution Abatement;
Educational Institute

**ATMOSPHERIC SCIENCES
PROGRAM**
UNIVERSITY OF FLORIDA
GAINESVILLE, FL 32601
See Engineering: Pollution Abatement;
Educational Institute

AUDUBON SOCIETY OF FLORIDA
POST OFFICE DRAWER 7
MAITLAND, FL 32701
See Biology: Ecology; Foundation

**BIO-ENVIRONMENTAL
ENGINEERING DEPARTMENT**
UNIVERSITY OF FLORIDA
GAINESVILLE, FL 32601
See Engineering: Pollution Abatement;
Educational Institute

**BIOLOGICAL LABORATORY,
BUREAU OF COMMISSION
FISHERIES**
75 33RD AVENUE
ST PETERSBURG BEACH, FL 33706
See Biology: General; Government-Federal

**BIOLOGICAL-ENVIRONMENTAL
SERVICES DIVISION**
1602 BOULEVARD
JACKSONVILLE, FL 32202
See Engineering: Pollution Abatement;
Government-State or Local

**COASTAL ENGINEERING
DEPARTMENT, BUILDING L**
UNIVERSITY OF FLORIDA
GAINESVILLE, FL 32601
See Engineering: Pollution Abatement;
Educational Institute

**ENVIRONMENT DEFENDERS OF
FLORIDA, INCORPORATED**
BOX 12063
GAINESVILLE, FL 32601
See Biology: Ecology; Professional Organizations

**ENVIRONMENTAL ENGINEERING
DIVISION, COUNTY HEALTH
DEPARTMENT**
202 SIXTH AVENUE EAST
BRADENTON, FL 33505
See Engineering: Pollution Abatement;
Government-State or Local

**ENVIRONMENTAL PROTECTION
AGENCY LABORATORY**
GULF BREEZE, FL 32561
See Biology: Ecology; Field Station/Laboratory

**ENVIRONMENTAL PROTECTION
AGENCY LABORATORY**
PO BOX 190
PERRINE, FL 33157

See Biology: Ecology; Field Station/Laboratory

**ENVIRONMENTAL PROTECTION
COMMISSION OF
HILLSBOROUGH COUNTY**
906 JACKSON STREET
TAMPA, FL 33602
See Interdisciplinary: General; Government-State or Local

**ENVIRONMENTAL SCIENCE
ACTIVITIES**
UNIVERSITY OF FLORIDA
GAINESVILLE, FL 32601
See Engineering: General; Educational
Institute

**ENVIRONMENTAL SCIENCE
PROGRAM**
FLORIDA STATE UNIVERSITY
TALLAHASSEE, FL 32306
See Interdisciplinary: General; Educational Institute

**ENVIRONMENTAL SOUTH EAST
COUNCIL, YUKON BRANCH**
POST OFFICE BOX 31278
JACKSONVILLE, FL 32230
See Biology: Ecology; Professional Organizations

ENVIRONMENTAL STUDIES
SCHOOL OF MEDICINE,
UNIVERSITY OF MIAMI
MIAMI, FL 33152
See Interdisciplinary: General; Educational Institute

**ENVIRONMENTAL STUDIES
PROGRAM**
BROWARD JUNIOR COLLEGE
FORT LAUDERDALE, FL 33334
See Biology: General; Educational Institute

**ENVIRONMENTAL STUDIES
PROGRAM**
EMBRY RIDDLE AERONAUTICAL
DAYTONA BEACH, FL 32015
See Engineering: General; Educational
Institute

**ENVIRONMENTAL STUDIES
PROGRAM**
UNIVERSITY OF MIAMI
CORAL GABLES, FL 30322
See Interdisciplinary: General; Educational Institute

ESTAURINE STUDIES CENTER
UNIVERSITY OF JACKSON
JACKSONVILLE, FL 32201
See Engineering: Water Resources; Educational Institute

**FISHERIES CENTER OF THE
SOUTHEAST**
75 VIRGINIA BEACH DRIVE
MIAMI, FL 33149
See Biology: General; Government-Federal

**FISHERIES INSTITUTE OF GULF
AND CARIBBEAN**
10 RICKENBACKER CAUSEWAY
MIAMI, FL 33149
See Biology: Ecology; Professional Organizations

**FOOD AND NUTRITION
DEPARTMENT**
SCHOOL OF HOME ECONOMICS
TALLAHASSEE, FL 32306
See Interdisciplinary: General; Educational Institute

**GAME AND FRESH WATER
FISHERIES COMMISSION**
646 WEST TENNESEE STREET
TALLAHASSE, FL 32303
See Social Sciences/Humanities: Law/Legislation; Professional Organizations

**GEOLOGY BUREAU, DIVISION OF
INTERIOR RESOURCES**
DEPARTMENT OF NATURAL
RESOURCES
TALLAHASSE, FL 32302
See Geology: General; Government-State or Local

**ICHTHYOLOGICAL LABORATORY
AND MUSEUM**
UNIVERSITY OF MIAMI
CORAL GABLES, FL 33146
See Engineering: Water Resources; Educational Institute

**MARINE AND ATMOSPHERIC
SCIENCE SCHOOL, UNIVERSITY
OF MIAMI**
RICKENBACKER HIGHWAY
MIAMI, FL 33149
See Biology: General; Educational Institute

MARINELAND
RFD 1, BOX 122
ST AUGUSTINE, FL 32084
See Interdisciplinary: General; Unclassified

MOTE MARINE LABORATORY
9501 BLIND PASS ROAD
SARASOTA, FL 33581
See Biology: General; Field Station/Laboratory

**NATIONAL WILDLIFE
FEDERATION**
REGION 4
TAVERNIER, FL 33070
See Biology: Ecology; Foundation

**NUCLEAR MEDICINE DIVISION,
MEDICAL SCHOOL**
UNIVERSITY OF MIAMI
MIAMI, FL 33140

See Biology: General; Educational Institute

**OCEANOGRAPHIC FOUNDATION,
INTERNATIONAL**
ONE RICKENBACKER CAUSEWAY
VIRGINIA KEY, MIAMI, FL 33149
See Interdisciplinary: General; Professional Organizations

OCEANOGRAPHY DEPARTMENT
FLORIDA STATE UNIVERSITY
TALLAHASSEE, FL 32306
See Biology: Ecology; Research Institute

**PESTICIDE SECTION, STATE
DEPARTMENT OF AGRICULTURE**
MAYO BUILDING
TALLAHASSEE, FL 32304
See Engineering: Agricultural Engineering; Government-State or Local

**POLLUTION CONTROL DIVISION,
PUBLIC HEALTH DEPARTMENT**
864 NORTHWEST 23RD STREET
MIAMI, FL 33127
See Engineering: Pollution Abatement; Government-State or Local

**PUBLIC WELFARE DEPARTMENT,
FLORIDA**
POST OFFICE BOX 2050
JACKSONVILLE, FL 32203
See Social Sciences/Humanities: Welfare(Child Public Social); Government-State or Local

**SANITARY ENGINEERING, BOARD
OF HEALTH**
1217 PEARL STREET, BOX 210
JACKSONVILLE, FL 32201
See Engineering: Pollution Abatement; Government-State or Local

SOIL CONSERVATION SERVICES
POST OFFICE BOX 1208
GAINESVILLE, FL 32601
See Biology: Ecology; Government-State or Local

**UNITED SOUTH-EAST TRIBES
PROGRAM**
1970 MAIN STREET
SARASOTA, FL 33577
See Engineering: Water Resources; Government-State or Local

**WATER RESOURCES AND
CONSERVATION DIVISION**
107 WEST GAINES STREET
TALLAHASSEE, FL 32304
See Engineering: Water Resources; Educational Institute

**WILDLIFE FEDERATION OF
FLORIDA**
5012 NE SECOND STREET
MIAMI, FL 33137
See Biology: Ecology; Foundation

Georgia

**AIR POLLUTION CONTROL,
ENGINEERING AND PUBLIC
WORKS DEPARTMENT**
CITY-COUNTY MUNICIPAL
BUILDING
AUGUSTA, GA 30902
See Engineering: Pollution Abatement; Government-State or Local

**AIR QUALITY CONTROL BRANCH,
PUBLIC WORKS DEPARTMENT**
47 TRINITY AVENUE SW
ATLANTA, GA 30334
See Engineering: Pollution Abatement; Government-State or Local

**CHEMICAL ENGINEERING
DEPARTMENT**
GEORGIA INSTITUTE OF
TECHNOLOGY, 225 NORTH
AVENUE
ATLANTA, GA 30332
See Engineering: Chemical Engineering; Educational Institute

CHEMISTRY DEPARTMENT
UNIVERSITY OF GEORGIA
ATHENS, GA 30601
See Engineering: Pollution Abatement; Educational Institute

COMMUNICABLE DISEASE CENTER
DEPARTMENT OF HEALTH,
EDUCATION, AND WELFARE
ATLANTA, GA 30333
See Engineering: Water Resources; Government-Federal

**CONSERVANCY OF GEORGIA,
INCORPORATED**
127 PEACHTREE STREET, NE
ATLANTA, GA 30303
See Biology: Ecology; Professional Organizations

CONSTRUCTION DEPARTMENT
301 CITY HALL
ATLANTA, GA 30303
See Engineering: Water Resources; Government-State or Local

**ECOLOGY AND NATURAL
RESOURCES INSTITUTE**
UNIVERSITY OF GEORGIA
ATHENS, GA 30601
See Biology: Ecology; Educational Institute

ECOLOGY INSTITUTE
UNIVERSITY OF GEORGIA
ATHENS, GA 30601
See Biology: Ecology; Educational Institute

**ENGINEERING AND SANITATION
DIVISION, COUNTY HEALTH
DEPARTMENT**

POST OFFICE BOX 6148
SAVANNAH, GA 31405
See Engineering: Pollution Abatement;
Government-State or Local

**ENVIRONMENTAL HEALTH
SERVICES, COUNTY HEALTH
DEPARTMENT**
126 TRINITY PLACE WEST
DECATUR, GA 30030
See Engineering: Pollution Abatement;
Government-State or Local

**ENVIRONMENTAL HEALTH
SERVICES, COUNTY HEALTH
DEPARTMENT**
99 BUTLER STREET, SE
ATLANTA, GA 30303
See Engineering: Pollution Abatement;
Government-State or Local

**ENVIRONMENTAL HEALTH,
COUNTY BOARD OF HEALTH**
POST OFFICE BOX 2299
COLUMBUS, GA 31902
See Engineering: Pollution Abatement;
Government-State or Local

**ENVIRONMENTAL PROTECTION
AGENCY**
SOUTHEAST WATER LABORATORY
ATHENS, GA 30601
See Biology: Ecology; Government-Federal

**ENVIRONMENTAL PROTECTION
AGENCY LABORATORY**
CHAMBLEE, GA 30005
See Biology: Ecology; Field Station/Laboratory

**ENVIRONMENTAL PROTECTION
AGENCY REGION 4 OFFICE,
SUITE 300**
1421 PEACHTREE STREET, NE
ATLANTA, GA 30309
See Engineering: Pollution Abatement;
Government-State or Local

**ENVIRONMENTAL RESOURCES
CENTER**
GEORGIA INSTITUTE OF
TECHNOLOGY
ATLANTA, GA 30332
See Engineering: Water Resources; Educational Institute

**ENVIRONMENTAL STUDIES
PROGRAM**
UNIVERSITY OF GEORGIA
ATHENS, GA 30601
See Interdisciplinary: General; Educational Institute

**EXPERIMENTAL FISHING AND
GEAR RESOURCES FIELD
STATION**
FEDERAL BUILDING, ROOM 308
BRUNSWICK, GA 31520
See Engineering: Water Resources; Government-Federal

**FOOD AND DRUG
ADMINISTRATION, DIVISION OF
COMMUNITY STUDIES**
4770 BUFORD HIGHWAY
CHAMBLEE, GA 30341
See Engineering: Agricultural Engineering; Government-Federal

FOREST INSTITUTE OF THE SOUTH
SUITE 280, 1 CORPORATION
SQUARE, NE
ATLANTA, GA 30329
See Interdisciplinary: General; Research
Institute

FOREST RESOURCES SCHOOL
UNIVERSITY OF GEORGIA
ATHENS, GA 30601
See Interdisciplinary: General; Educational Institute

**FOREST SERVICE REGION 8
OFFICE**
1720 PEACHTREE, SUITE 800
ATLANTA, GA 30309
See Engineering: Agricultural Engineering; Government-Federal

**GEORGIA INSTITUTE OF
TECHNOLOGY**
225 NORTH AVENUE, NW
ATLANTA, GA 30332
See Interdisciplinary: General; Educational Institute

HEALTH DEPARTMENT
770 HEMLOCK STREET
MACON, GA 31201
See Engineering: Pollution Abatement;
Government-State or Local

**HEALTH, EDUCATION AND
WELFARE REGION 4 OFFICE**
50 7TH STREET NE -ROOM 404
ATLANTA, GA 30323
See Interdisciplinary: General; Government-Federal

MARINE INSTITUTION
UNIVERSITY OF GEORGIA
SAPELO ISLAND, GA 31327
See Biology: General; Educational Institute

**MINES, MINING AND GEOLOGY
DEPARTMENT**
19 HUNTER STREET, SW
ATLANTA, GA 30303
See Geology: General; Research Institute

**NATURAL RESOURCES
DEPARTMENT**
270 WASHINGTON STREET, SW
ATLANTA, GA 30334
See Biology: Ecology; Government-State
or Local

NUCLEAR ENGINEERING SCHOOL
GEORGIA INSTITUTE OF
TECHNOLOGY

ATLANTA, GA 30332
See Engineering: General; Educational
Institute

**OCCUPATIONAL SAFETY AND
HEALTH DIVISION**
50 7TH STREET, NE - ROOM 404
ATLANTA, GA 30323
See Engineering: Pollution Abatement;
Government-State or Local

**PESTICIDE BRANCH,
ENVIRONMENTAL PROTECTION
AGENCY**
1421 PEACHTREE, NE
ATLANTA, GA 30309
See Engineering: Agricultural Engineering; Government-Federal

**PESTICIDE COMMISSION STUDIES
DIVISION**
ENVIRONMENTAL PROTECTION
AGENCY
CHAMBLEE, GA 30341
See Biology: Ecology; Government-Federal

**PESTICIDE DIVISION,
DEPARTMENT OF AGRICULTURE**
CAPITOL SQUARE, SW
ATLANTA, GA 30334
See Engineering: Agricultural Engineering; Government-State or Local

**PESTICIDE REGULATION
DIVISION, U S DEPARTMENT OF
AGRICULTURE**
141 EAST TRINITY PLACE
DECATUR, GA 30030
See Engineering: Agricultural Engineering; Government-Federal

**PESTICIDE REGULATION, US
DEPARTMENT OF AGRICULTURE**
1421 PEACHTREE, NE ROOM 200
ATLANTA, GA 30309
See Engineering: Agricultural Engineering; Government-Federal

**PESTICIDES COMMUNITY STUDIES
DIVISION**
ENVIRONMENTAL PROTECTION
AGENCY
CHAMBLEE, GA 30341
See Interdisciplinary: General; Unclassified

PESTICIDES PROGRAM
NATIONAL COMMUNICABLE
DISEASE CENTER
ATLANTA, GA 30333
See Engineering: Chemical Engineering;
Government-Federal

PLANNING BUREAU
270 WASHINGTON STREET, ROOM
611
ATLANTA, GA 30334

See Engineering: Pollution Abatement;
Government-State or Local

**RADIATION DIVISION,
ENVIRONMENTAL PROTECTION
AGENCY**
1421 PEACHTREE STREET, NE
SUITE 300
ATLANTA, GA 30309
See Chemistry: Physical Chemistry; Government-State or Local

**SAVE AMERICA'S VITAL
ENVIRONMENT**
POST OFFICE BOX 52652
ATLANTA, GA 30305
See Social Sciences/Humanities: Law/
Legislation; Foundation

SOIL CONSERVATION SERVICE
468 NORTH MILLEGE AVENUE, PO
BOX 832
ATHENS, GA 30601
See Interdisciplinary: General; Unclassified

**SOUTHEAST BASINS INTER-
AGENCY COMMISSION**
ROOM 402, NEW WALTON
BUILDING
ATLANTA, GA 30303
See Engineering: Water Resources; Government-Federal

**SOUTHEASTERN POWER
ADMINISTRATION**
DEPARTMENT OF THE INTERIOR
ELBERTON, GA 30635
See Engineering: Water Resources; Government-Federal

**WATER AND POLLUTION
CONTROL ASSOCIATION**
2746 LAURELWOOD ROAD
DORAVILLE, GA 30040
See Engineering: Pollution Abatement;
Government-State or Local

WATER QUALITY CONTROL BOARD
47 TRINITY AVENUE SW
ATLANTA, GA 30334
See Engineering: Pollution Abatement;
Government-State or Local

WATER RESOURCES CENTER
GEORGIA INSTITUTION OF
TECHNOLOGY
ATLANTA, GA 30332
See Engineering: Water Resources; Educational Institute

**WATER RESOURCES INSTITUTE,
INSTITUTE FOR NATURAL
RESOURCES**
UNIVERSITY OF GEORGIA
ATHENS, GA 30601
See Engineering: Water Resources; Educational Institute

Hawaii

AGROMETEOROLGY
UNIVERSITY OF HAWAII
HONOLULU, HI 96822
See Engineering: Agricultural Engineering; Educational Institute

**AIR SANITATION SECTION,
HEALTH DEPARTMENT**
P O BOX 3378
HONOLULU, HI 96801
See Engineering: Pollution Abatement;
Government-State or Local

AUDUBON SOCIETY OF HAWAII
POST OFFICE BOX 5032
HONOLULU, HI 96814
See Biology: Ecology; Foundation

BERNICE P BISHOP MUSEUM
1355 KALIHI STREET
HONOLULU, HI 96819
See Interdisciplinary: General; Professional Organizations

BIOLOGICAL LABORATORY
2570 DOLE STREET, POST OFFICE
BOX 3830
HONOLULU, HI 96812
See Biology: General; Government-Federal

**BIOLOGICAL LABORATORY OF
HONOLULU**
2570 DOLE STREET
HONOLULU, HI 96812
See Biology: General; Field Station/Laboratory

COMMERCIAL FISHERIES BUREAU
POST OFFICE BOX 3830
HONOLULU, HI 96812
See Engineering: Water Resources; Government-Federal

**CONSERVATION ASSOCIATION OF
WHOOPING CRANE**
RR1, BOX 323
KULA MAUI, HI 96790
See Interdisciplinary: General; Educational Institute

**CONSERVATION COUNCIL FOR
HAWAII**
POST OFFICE BOX 2923
HONOLULU, HI 96802
See Biology: Ecology; Professional Organizations

**ECONOMIC POISON SECTION,
MARKETING CONSERVATION
DIVISION**
POST OFFICE BOX 5425 PAWAA
STATION
HONOLULU, HI 96814
See Engineering: Agricultural Engineering; Government-State or Local

**ENVIRONMENTAL GROUP OF
HAWAII**
POST OFFICE BOX 1618
HONOLULU, HI 96806
See Biology: Ecology; Educational Institute

**ENVIRONMENTAL HEALTH
DIVISION, PUBLIC HEALTH
DEPARTMENT**
P O BOX 3378
HONOLULU, HI 96801
See Engineering: Pollution Abatement;
Government-State or Local

**ENVIRONMENTAL STUDIES,
UNIVERSITY OF HAWAII**
2444 DOLE STREET
HONOLULU, HI 96822
See Interdisciplinary: General; Educational Institute

GEOPHYSICS INSTITUTE
UNIVERSITY OF HAWAII
HONOLULU, HI 96822
See Geology: Geophysics; Educational Institute

HORTICULTURE DEPARTMENT
UNIVERSITY OF HAWAII
HONOLULU, HI 96822
See Engineering: Agricultural Engineering; Research Institute

**HYDROLOGY OFFICE, NATIONAL
WEATHER SERVICES, PACIFIC
OFFICE**
BOX 3650
HONOLULU, HI 96811
See Engineering: Water Resources; Government-Federal

**INDUSTRIAL RELATIONS CENTER,
UNIVERSITY OF HAWAII**
2500 CAMPUS ROAD
HONOLULU, HI 96822
See Social Sciences/Humanities: Labor/
Relations/Unions; Educational Institute

**LAND AND NATURAL RESOURCES
DEPARTMENT**
465 SOUTH KING STREET, POST
OFFICE BOX 373
HONOLULU, HI 96809
See Engineering: Water Resources; Government-State or Local

**MARINE LABORATORY,
UNIVERSITY OF HAWAII**
1801 UNIVERSITY AVENUE
HONOLULU 14, HI 96800
See Biology: General; Educational Institute

**MARINE SCIENCES DIVISION, 14TH
COAST GUARD DISTRICT**
677 ALA MOANA
HONOLULU, HI 96813

See Engineering: Water Resources; Government-State or Local

NATIONAL MARINE FISHERIES SERVICE, HONOLULU LABORATORY
POST OFFICE BOX 3830
HONOLULU, HI 96812
See Engineering: Water Resources; Government-Federal

OCEANIC INSTITUTE
MAKAPUU POINT
WAIMANALO OAHU, HI 96795
See Interdisciplinary: General; Research Institute

OUTDOOR CIRCLE
200 NORTH VINEYARD BOULEVARD
HONOLULU, HI 96817
See Interdisciplinary: General; Professional Organizations

PACIFIC SCIENTIFIC INFORMATION CENTER
1355 KALIHI STREET
HONOLULU, HI 96819
See Social Sciences/Humanities: General; Foundation

PINEAPPLE RESEARCH INSTITUTION OF HAWAII
WAHIAWA
HONOLULU, HI 96786
See Biology: General; Research Institute

PLANNERS, ENGINEERS FOR LANDSCAPE ARCHITECTURE
1136 UNION HALL
HONOLULU, HI 96814
See Engineering: General; Industrial/Commercial

RESEARCH OFFICE, HEALTH DEPARTMENT
1250 PUNCHBOWL STREET, PO BOX 3378
HONOLULU, HI 96801
See Social Sciences/Humanities: Population Studies/Family Planning; Government-State or Local

WILDLIFE FEDERATION OF HAWAII
BOX 10113
HONOLULU, HI 96816
See Biology: Ecology; Foundation

Iowa

AGRICULTURAL ENGINEERING DEPARTMENT
IOWA STATE UNIVERSITY OF SCIENCES
AMES, IA 50010
See Engineering: Agricultural Engineering; Educational Institute

AGRICULTURAL MEDICINE INSTITUTE
DEPARTMENT OF AGRICULTURE, UNIVERSITY OF IOWA
OAKDALE, IA 52319
See Engineering: Agricultural Engineering; Educational Institute

AIR POLLUTION CONTROL, COUNTY HEALTH DEPARTMENT
445 FIRST STREET, SW
CEDAR RAPIDS, IA 52404
See Engineering: Pollution Abatement; Government-State or Local

CHEMISTRY DEPARTMENT
ST AMBROSE COLLEGE
DAVENPORT, IA 52803
See Chemistry: Physical Chemistry; Educational Institute

CONSERVATION COMMISSION OF UPPER MISSISSIPPI RIVER
322 FEDERAL BUILDING
DAVENPORT, IA 52801
See Biology: Ecology; Professional Organizations

CONSERVATION ENGINEERING ASSOCIATION
EAST 7TH AND COURT AVENUE
DES MOINES, IA 50309
See Interdisciplinary: General; Research Institute

ENGINEERING COLLEGE
UNIVERSITY IOWA
IOWA CITY, IA 52240
See Engineering: General; Educational Institute

ENVIRONMENTAL ENGINEERING SERVICES, DEPARTMENT OF HEALTH
LUCAS STATE OFFICE BUILDING
DES MOINES, IA 50319
See Engineering: Pollution Abatement; Government-State or Local

ENVIRONMENTAL SCIENCE PROGRAM
UNIVERSITY OF IOWA
IOWA CITY, IA 52240
See Interdisciplinary: General; Educational Institute

ENVIRONMENTAL STUDIES GROUP, DRAKE UNIVERSITY
26TH STREET AND UNIVERSITY AVENUE
DES MOINES, IA 50311
See Interdisciplinary: General; Educational Institute

ENVIRONMENTAL STUDIES PROGRAM
IOWA STATE UNIVERSITY
AMES, IA 50010
See Interdisciplinary: General; Educational Institute

FISHERIES AND GAME COMMISSION
EAST 4TH STREET AND COURT AVENUE
DES MOINES, IA 50309
See Social Sciences/Humanities: Recreation and Leisure; Foundation

HEALTH DEPARTMENT
STATE OFFICE BUILDING
DES MOINES, IA 50319
See Engineering: Pollution Abatement; Government-State or Local

HEATING AND AIR POLLUTION DEPARTMENT
CITY HALL
WATERLOO, IA 50705
See Engineering: Pollution Abatement; Government-State or Local

HYDRAULIC RESEARCH INSTITUTE
UNIVERSITY OF IOWA
IOWA CITY, IA 52240
See Engineering: Water Resources; Educational Institute

INSPECTION DIVISION, COUNTY HEALTH DEPARTMENT
EAST FIRST AND DES MOINES STREETS
DES MOINES, IA 50307
See Engineering: Pollution Abatement; Government-State or Local

JN DING DARLING FOUNDATION, INCORPORATED
C/O CENTRAL NATIONAL BANK AND TRUST
DES MOINES, IA 50304
See Biology: Ecology; Professional Organizations

LABOR BUREAU OF IOWA
STATE HOUSE
DES MOINES, IA 50319
See Social Sciences/Humanities: Labor/Relations/Unions; Government-State or Local

MEDICAL COLLEGE
UNIVERSITY OF IOWA
IOWA CITY, IA 52240
See Biology: Biochemistry; Educational Institute

PEDIATRICS DEPARTMENT, MEDICAL SCHOOL
UNIVERSITY OF IOWA
IOWA CITY, IA 52240
See Interdisciplinary: General; Educational Institute

PESTICIDE DIVISION, CHEMISTRY LABORATORY, AGRICULTURE DEPARTMENT
EAST 7TH AND COURT STREETS
DES MOINES, IA 50319
See Engineering: Agricultural Engineering; Government-State or Local

**PHARMACOLOGY DEPARTMENT,
OAKDALE TOXICOLOGY CENTER**
UNIVERSITY OF IOWA
OAKDALE, IA 52319
See Chemistry: General; Educational Institute

**PHYSICAL SCIENCES AND
OCEANOGRAPHY,
INTERNATIONAL ASSOCIATION**
UNIVERSITY OF IOWA
IOWA CITY, IA 52240
See Engineering: Water Resources; Educational Institute

**POLITICAL SCIENCES
LABORATORY**
UNIVERSITY OF IOWA
IOWA CITY, IA 52240
See Social Sciences/Humanities: Politics; Educational Institute

**PREVENTIVE MEDICINE AND
ENVIRONMENTAL DEPARTMENT**
MEDICAL INSTITUTE, UNIVERSITY
OF IOWA
OAKDALE, IA 52319
See Engineering: Pollution Abatement; Educational Institute

PUBLIC WORKS DEPARTMENT
226 WEST FOURTH STREET
DAVENPORT, IA 52801
See Engineering: Pollution Abatement; Government-State or Local

SOIL CONSERVATION SERVICES
210 WALNUT STREET
DES MOINES, IA 50309
See Biology: Ecology; Government-Federal

**SOIL CONSERVATION SOCIETY OF
AMERICA**
7515 NORTHEAST ANKENY ROAD
ANKENY, IA 50021
See Engineering: Agricultural Engineering; Professional Organizations

**UPPER MISSISSIPPI RIVER
CONSERVATION CORPS**
4TH AND PERRY STREET, 322
FEDERAL BUILDING
DAVENPORT, IA 52801
See Engineering: Water Resources; Government-Federal

**VITAL STATISTICS DIVISION,
HEALTH DEPARTMENT**
STATE OFFICE BUILDING
DES MOINES,IA 50319
See Social Sciences/Humanities: Population Studies/Family Planning; Government-State or Local

**WATER POLLUTION DIVISION,
STATE HEALTH DEPARTMENT**
STATE OFFICE BUILDING
DES MOINES, IA 50319
See Engineering: Pollution Abatement; Government-State or Local

**WATER RESOURCES RESEARCH
CENTER**
IOWA STATE UNIVERSITY
AMES, IA 50010
See Biology: Ecology; Educational Institute

WILDLIFE FEDERATION OF IOWA
601-1/2 NORTH MAIN STREET
BURLINGTON, IA 52601
See Biology: Ecology; Foundation

Idaho

**ATOMIC ENERGY COMMISSION,
IDAHO OPERATIONS OFFICE**
POST OFFICE BOX 2108
IDAHO FALLS, ID 83401
See Geology: General; Government-Federal

BIOLOGY DEPARTMENT
COLLEGE OF IDAHO
CALDWELL, ID 83605
See Biology: General; Educational Institute

**ENGINEERING AND SANITATION
DIVISION, STATE HEALTH
DEPARTMENT**
POST OFFICE BOX 640
BOISE, ID 83701
See Engineering: Pollution Abatement; Government-State or Local

**ENVIRONMENTAL CENTER,
REGIONAL**
COLLEGE OF IDAHO
CALDWELL, ID 83605
See Biology: Ecology; Educational Institute

**ENVIRONMENTAL SCIENCES
GROUP, COLLEGE OF IDAHO**
CALDWELL, ID 83605
See Interdisciplinary: General; Educational Institute

**ENVIRONMENTAL STUDIES
PROGRAM**
IDAHO STATE UNIVERSITY
POCATELLO, ID 83201
See Chemistry: General; Educational Institute

**ENVIRONMENTAL STUDIES
PROGRAM**
UNIVERSITY OF IDAHO
MOSCOW, ID 83843
See Interdisciplinary: General; Educational Institute

**FISHERIES AND GAME
DEPARTMENT OF IDAHO**
600 SOUTH WALNUT STREET
BOISE, ID 83707
See Engineering: General; Government-State or Local

**GAME FISHERIES COMMISSIONERS
WESTERN ASSOCIATION**
BOX 25
BOISE, ID 83707
See Interdisciplinary: General; Professional Organizations

**MINES AND GEOLOGY BUREAU OF
IDAHO**
UNIVERSITY OF IDAHO
MOSCOW, ID 83843
See Engineering: Water Resources; Educational Institute

**NATIONAL WILDLIFE
FEDERATION**
REGION 13
BOISE, ID 83701
See Biology: Ecology; Foundation

**PLANT INDUSTRY BUREAU,
DEPARTMENT OF AGRICULTURE**
POST OFFICE BOX 790
BOISE, ID 83701
See Engineering: Agricultural Engineering; Government-State or Local

**SMOKE CONTROL DIVISION,
BUILDING DEPARTMENT**
CITY HALL, 605 BANNOCK STREET
BOISE, ID 83702
See Engineering: Pollution Abatement; Government-State or Local

SOIL CONSERVATION SERVICE
304 NORTH 8TH STREET, ROOM 345
BOISE, ID 83702
See Biology: Ecology; Government-State or Local

**WATER ADMINISTRATION
DEPARTMENT OF IDAHO**
ROOM 107, STATEHOUSE
BOISE, ID 83701
See Engineering: Water Resources; Government-State or Local

**WATERFOWL COUNCIL, IDAHO
FISHERIES AND GAME
DEPARTMENT**
P O BOX 25
BOISE, ID 83707
See Interdisciplinary: General; Professional Organizations

**WILDLIFE FEDERATION OF
IDAHO**
POST OFFICE BOX 849
COEUR D'ALENE, ID 83814
See Biology: Ecology; Foundation

**WILDLIFE FEDERATION OF
IDAHO**
101 HORIZON DRIVE
BOISE, ID 83702
See Biology: Ecology; Foundation

Illinois

AGRICULTURE COLLEGE
UNIVERSITY OF ILLINOIS
URBANA, IL 61801
See Engineering: Agricultural Engineering; Educational Institute

AIR POLLUTION CONTROL BOARD
MCCOOK, IL 60525
See Engineering: Pollution Abatement; Government-State or Local

AIR POLLUTION CONTROL BOARD, COOK COUNTY
309 CHICAGO CIVIC CENTER
CHICAGO, IL 60602
See Engineering: Pollution Abatement; Government-State or Local

AIR POLLUTION CONTROL COMMISSION
6300 LINCOLN AVENUE
MORTON GROVE, IL 60053
See Engineering: Pollution Abatement; Government-State or Local

AIR POLLUTION CONTROL COMMITTEE
CITY HALL
BERWYN, IL 60402
See Engineering: Pollution Abatement; Government-State or Local

AIR POLLUTION CONTROL COMMITTEE
4937 WEST 25TH STREET
CICERO, IL 60650
See Engineering: Pollution Abatement; Government-State or Local

AIR POLLUTION CONTROL DEPARTMENT
POST OFFICE BOX 128
ARGO, IL 60501
See Engineering: Pollution Abatement; Government-State or Local

AIR POLLUTION CONTROL DEPARTMENT
320 NORTH CLARK STREET
CHICAGO, IL 60610
See Engineering: Pollution Abatement; Government-State or Local

AMERICAN HOSPITAL ASSOCIATION
840 NORTH LAKE SHORE DRIVE
CHICAGO, IL 60611
See Social Sciences/Humanities: Welfare(Child Public Social); Professional Organizations

AMERICAN WATER RESOURCES ASSOCIATION
206 EAST UNIVERSITY AVENUE, BX 434
URBANA, IL 61801
See Engineering: Water Resources; Professional Organizations

ATMOSPHERIC SCIENCES PROGRAM
LOYOLA UNIVERSITY
CHICAGO, IL 60600
See Engineering: Pollution Abatement; Educational Institute

ATOMIC ENERGY COMMISSION CHICAGO OPERATIONS OFFICE
9800 CASS AVENUE
ARGONNE, IL 60439
See Chemistry: Physical Chemistry; Government-State or Local

AUDUBON SOCIETY OF ILLINOIS
ROOSEVELT AND LAKE SHORE DRIVES
CHICAGO, IL 60605
See Interdisciplinary: General; Professional Organizations

BIOPHYSICS DEPARTMENT
UNIVERSITY OF CHICAGO
CHICAGO, IL 60601
See Biology: Biophysics; Educational Institute

BUILDING DEPARTMENT
1501 OAK AVENUE
EVANSTON, IL 60204
See Engineering: Pollution Abatement; Government-State or Local

CHEMISTRY AND CHEMICAL ENGINEERING DEPARTMENT
UNIVERSITY OF ILLINOIS
URBANA, IL 61801
See Engineering: Pollution Abatement; Educational Institute

CHEMISTRY DEPARTMENT, PHARMACY COLLEGE
UNIVERSITY OF ILLINOIS, PO BOX 6998
CHICAGO, IL 60680
See Engineering: Pollution Abatement; Educational Institute

CITIZENS COMMISSION FOR NATURE CONSERVATION
819 NORTH MAIN STREET
ROCKFORD, IL 61103
See Social Sciences/Humanities: Law/Legislation; Professional Organizations

CITY MANAGER'S OFFICER
OLIVE AND EAST STREETS
BLOOMINGTON, IL 61701
See Engineering: Pollution Abatement; Government-State or Local

CITY PLANNING, LANDSCAPING, AND ARCHITECTURAL LIBRARY
203 MUMFORD HALL, UNIVERSITY OF ILLINOIS
URBANA, IL 61803
See Social Sciences/Humanities: Community Development/Studies; Educational Institute

COUNCIL OF STATE GOVERNMENTS
1313 EAST 60TH STREET
CHICAGO, IL 60637
See Engineering: Water Resources; Government-State or Local

CRIPPLED CHILDREN AND ADULTS NATIONAL SOCIETY
2023 WEST OGDEN AVENUE
CHICAGO, IL 60612
See Social Sciences/Humanities: Rehabilitation; Foundation

DUCKS UNLIMITED
POST OFFICE BOX 66300
CHICAGO, IL 60666
See Biology: Ecology; Professional Organizations

EARTH SCIENCE DEPARTMENT
NORTHERN ILLINOIS UNIVERSITY
DE KALB, IL 60115
See Engineering: Water Resources; Educational Institute

EDUCATIONAL RESOURCES BUREAU
288 EDUCATION BUILDING, UNIVERSITY OF ILLINOIS
URBANA, IL 61803
See Social Sciences/Humanities: Education; Educational Institute

EMPLOYMENT BUREAU, DEPARTMENT OF LABOR
165 NORTH CANAL STREET
CHICAGO, IL 60606
See Social Sciences/Humanities: Employment/Unemployment; Government-State or Local

ENVIRONMENTAL AND PUBLIC HEALTH COUNCIL
535 NORTH DEARBORN STREET
CHICAGO, IL 60610
See Interdisciplinary: General; Research Institute

ENVIRONMENTAL CONTROL DEPARTMENT
320 NORTH CLARK STREET
CHICAGO, IL 60610
See Engineering: Pollution Abatement; Government-State or Local

ENVIRONMENTAL ENGINEERING DEPARTMENT
ILLINOIS INSTITUTE OF TECHNOLOGY
CHICAGO, IL 60601
See Engineering: General; Educational Institute

ENVIRONMENTAL ENGINEERING PROGRAM, CIVIL ENGINEERING DEPARTMENT
UNIVERSITY OF ILLINOIS
URBANA, IL 61801

See Engineering: Pollution Abatement;
Educational Institute

**ENVIRONMENTAL HEALTH
DIVISION, COUNTY HEALTH
DEPARTMENT**
1515 WASHINGTON STREET
WAUKEGAN, IL 60085
See Engineering: Pollution Abatement;
Government-State or Local

**ENVIRONMENTAL HEALTH
DIVISION, DUPAGE COUNTY
HEALTH DEPARTMENT**
222 EAST WILLOW
WHEATON, IL 60187
See Engineering: General; Government-
State or Local

**ENVIRONMENTAL PROTECTION
AGENCY OF ILLINOIS**
2200 CHURCHILL ROAD
SPRINGFIELD, IL 67206
See Interdisciplinary: General; Govern-
ment-State or Local

**ENVIRONMENTAL PROTECTION
AGENCY, REGION 5, LIBRARY**
1 NORTH WACKER DRIVE
CHICAGO, IL 60606
See Chemistry: Physical Chemistry; Gov-
ernment-State or Local

**ENVIRONMENTAL SANITATION,
PUBLIC HEALTH DEPARTMENT**
CITY HALL BUILDING
ROCKFORD, IL 61104
See Engineering: Pollution Abatement;
Government-State or Local

**ENVIRONMENTAL SCIENCE
PROGRAM**
UNIVERSITY OF ILLINOIS
URBANA, IL 61801
See Interdisciplinary: General; Educa-
tional Institute

**ENVIRONMENTAL SCIENCES
INSTITUTE**
940 EAST NORTHWEST HIGHWAY
MT PROSPECT, IL 60056
See Interdisciplinary: General; Profession-
al Organizations

**ENVIRONMENTAL SCIENCES
PROGRAM**
AUGUSTANA COLLEGE
ROCK ISLAND, IL 61201
See Chemistry: General; Educational In-
stitute

**ENVIRONMENTAL SERVICES
DEPARTMENT**
104 SOUTH KENILWORTH STREET
ELMHURST, IL 60126
See Engineering: Pollution Abatement;
Government-State or Local

**ENVIRONMENTAL STUDIES
PROGRAM**
BRADLEY UNIVERSITY
PEORIA, IL 61606
See Interdisciplinary: General; Educa-
tional Institute

**ENVIRONMENTAL STUDIES
PROGRAM**
ILLINOIS STATE UNIVERSITY
NORMAL, IL 61761
See Chemistry: General; Educational In-
stitute

**ENVIRONMENTAL STUDIES
PROGRAM**
NORTHERN ILLINOIS UNIVERSITY
DEKALB, IL 60115
See Interdisciplinary: General; Educa-
tional Institute

**ENVIRONMENTAL STUDIES
PROGRAM**
NORTHWESTERN UNIVERSITY
EVANSTON, IL 60201
See Interdisciplinary: General; Educa-
tional Institute

**ENVIRONMENTAL STUDIES
PROGRAM**
WHEATON COLLEGE
WHEATON, IL 60187
See Interdisciplinary: General; Educa-
tional Institute

**ENVIRONMENTAL STUDIES,
ILLINOIS INSTITUTE OF
TECHNOLOGY**
3300 SOUTH FEDERAL STREET
CHICAGO, IL 60616
See Interdisciplinary: General; Educa-
tional Institute

**ENVIRONMENTAL STUDIES,
LOYOLA UNIVERSITY**
820 NORTH MICHIGAN AVENUE
CHICAGO, IL 60611
See Interdisciplinary: General; Educa-
tional Institute

**ENVIRONMENTAL STUDIES,
UNIVERSITY OF CHICAGO**
5801 ELLIS AVENUE
CHICAGO, IL 60637
See Interdisciplinary: General; Educa-
tional Institute

**ENVIRONMENTAL, PUBLIC AND
OCCUPATIONAL HEALTH
DEPARTMENT**
535 NORTH DEARBORN STREET
CHICAGO, IL 60610
See Interdisciplinary: General; Profession-
al Organizations

EXPLORATION INSTITUTE
2340 PRAIRIE AVENUE
EVANSTON, IL 60201
See Social Sciences/Humanities: General;
Industrial/Commercial

FARM FOUNDATION
600 SOUTH MICHIGAN AVENUE
CHICAGO, IL 60605
See Engineering: Water Resources; Foundation

**FEEDS, FERTILIZER AND
STABILIZATION STANDARDS
DIVISION**
531 EAST SANGAMON STREET
SPRINGFIELD, IL 62706
See Engineering: Agricultural Engineer-
ing; Government-State or Local

FOREST PARK FOUNDATION
600 COMMERCIAL BANK BUILDING
PEORIA, IL 61602
See Social Sciences/Humanities: Rehabilitation; Foundation

**GEOGRAPHIC EDUCATION
COUNCIL**
115 NORTH MARION STREET
OAK PARK, IL 60301
See Social Sciences/Humanities: Educa-
tion; Professional Organizations

GEOLOGICAL SURVEY OF ILLINOIS
NATURAL RESOURCES BUILDING
URBANA, IL 61804
See Geology: General; Government-State
or Local

GEOLOGIST GROUP
ILLINOIS STATE GEOLOGICAL
SURVEY OF NATURAL
RESOURCES
URBANA, IL 61801
See Engineering: Pollution Abatement;
Educational Institute

GEOLOGY DEPARTMENT
UNIVERSITY OF CHICAGO
CHICAGO, IL 60637
See Engineering: Water Resources; Edu-
cational Institute

GEOPHYSICAL INSTITUTE
UNIVERSITY OF CHICAGO
CHICAGO, IL 60600
See Physics: General; Educational Insti-
tute

**GEOPHYSICAL SCIENCES
DEPARTMENT**
5734 SOUTH ELLIS AVENUE
CHICAGO, IL 60637
See Geology: General; Educational Insti-
tute

GEOPHYSICAL UNION
UNIVERSITY OF CHICAGO, 5828
UNIVERSITY DRIVE
CHICAGO, IL 60637
See Social Sciences/Humanities: General;
Professional Organizations

GRANITE CITY STEEL COMPANY
GRANITE CITY, IL 62040
See Engineering: General; Industrial/
Commercial

HEALTH DEPARTMENT
1085 SOUTH MAIN STREET
DECATUR, IL 62521
See Engineering: Pollution Abatement;
Government-State or Local

**HEALTH, EDUCATION AND
WELFARE REGION 5 OFFICE,
P.O. BUILDING**
433 WEST VAN BUREN STREET
CHICAGO, IL 60607
See Interdisciplinary: General; Government-Federal

**HOUSING DIVISION, PLANNING
AND DEVELOPMENT
DEPARTMENT**
655 LAKE STREET
OAK PARK, IL 60301
See Engineering: Pollution Abatement;
Government-State or Local

**INSPECTION DEPARTMENT, AIR
POLLUTION DEPARTMENT**
419 FULTON STREET
PEORIA, IL 61602
See Engineering: Pollution Abatement;
Government-State or Local

**IZAAK WALTON LEAGUE OF
AMERICA**
1326 WAUKEGAN ROAD
GLENVILLE, IL 60025
See Interdisciplinary: General; Foundation

**JOINT REFERENCE LIBRARY,
PUBLIC ADMINISTRATION
SERVICE**
1313 EAST 60TH STREET
CHICAGO, IL 60637
See Engineering: Water Resources; Foundation

**JUVENILE RESEARCH INSTITUTE,
DEPARTMENT OF MENTAL
HEALTH**
907 SOUTII WOLCOTT AVENUE
CHICAGO, IL 60612
See Social Sciences/Humanities: Mental
Health; Government-State or Local

**MAX MCGRAW WILDLIFE
FOUNDATION**
POST OFFICE BOX 194
DUNDEE, IL 60118
See Biology: Ecology; Foundation

**NATIONAL SAFETY COUNCIL
RESEARCH DEPARTMENT**
425 NORTH MICHIGAN AVENUE
CHICAGO, IL 60611
See Social Sciences/Humanities: Transportation; Research Institute

**NATURAL HISTORY MUSEUM OF
CHICAGO**
ROOSEVELT ROAD AND LAKE
SHORE
CHICAGO,IL 60605

See Interdisciplinary: General; Professional Organizations

**NATURAL RESOURCES COUNCIL
OF ILLINOIS**
ROUTE 2
JOLIET, IL 60431
See Biology: Ecology; Professional Organizations

NEWBERRY LIBRARY
60 WEST WALTON STREET
CHICAGO,IL 60610
See Social Sciences/Humanities: General;
Educational Institute

**NUCLEAR SCIENCES, ENRICO
FERMI INSTITUTE OF**
UNIVERSITY OF CHICAGO
CHICAGO, IL 60601
See Interdisciplinary: General; Educational Institute

NUCLEAR SOCIETY OF AMERICA
244 EAST OGDEN AVENUE
INSDALE, IL 60521
See Physics: General; Professional Organizations

**OCCUPATIONAL SAFETY AND
HEALTH DIVISION**
300 SOUTH WACKER DRIVE, ROOM
2904
CHICAGO, IL 60606
See Engineering: Pollution Abatement;
Government-State or Local

**OUTBOARD BOATING CLUB OF
AMERICA**
333 NORTH MICHIGAN AVENUE
CHICAGO, IL 60601
See Social Sciences/Humanities: Recreation and Leisure; Professional Organizations

**PESTICIDE REGULATION
DIVISION, U S DEPARTMENT OF
AGRICULTURE**
226 WEST JACKSON BOULEVARD
CHICAGO, IL 60606
See Engineering: Agricultural Engineering; Government-Federal

**PHYSICAL ENVIRONMENT UNIT,
UNIVERSITY OF ILLINOIS**
208 MECHANICAL ENGINEERING
LABORATORY
URBANA, IL 61803
See Engineering: General; Educational
Institute

PLANNING OFFICIALS SOCIETY
1313 EAST 60TH STREET
CHICAGO, IL 60637
See Social Sciences/Humanities: Regional
Planning; Research Institute

POLLUTION CONTROL DIVISION
7 COLLINSVILLE AVENUE
EAST ST LOUIS, IL 62201
See Engineering: Pollution Abatement;
Government-State or Local

**POPULATION AND ENVIRONMENT
COUNCIL**
100 EAST OHIO STREET
CHICAGO, IL 60611
See Social Sciences/Humanities: Population Studies/Family Planning; Foundation

POPULATION RESEARCH CENTER
UNIVERSITY OF CHICAGO
CHICAGO, IL 60637
See Social Sciences/Humanities: Population Studies/Family Planning; Research Institute

PRAIRIE CLUB
28 EAST JACKSON AVENUE, ROOM
900
CHICAGO, IL 60604
See Social Sciences/Humanities: Recreation and Leisure; Professional Organizations

PRAIRIE PATHOLOGY
BX 1086/616 DELLES ROAD
WHEATON, IL 60187
See Social Sciences/Humanities: Education; Unclassified

PUBLIC HEALTH DEPARTMENT
CITY HALL, 1850 LEWIS AVENUE
NORTH CHICAGO, IL 60064
See Engineering: Pollution Abatement;
Government-State or Local

PUBLIC HEALTH DEPARTMENT
STATE OFFICE BUILDINGS
SPRINGFIELD,IL 62706
See Social Sciences/Humanities: Population Studies/Family Planning; Government-State or Local

PUBLIC HEALTH DEPARTMENT
425 WEST STATE STREET
ROCKFORD, IL 61101
See Engineering: Pollution Abatement;
Government-State or Local

**PUBLIC HEALTH DEPARTMENT OF
COOK COUNTY**
1425 SOUTH RACING AVENUE
CHICAGO, IL 60608
See Engineering: Pollution Abatement;
Government-State or Local

**PUBLIC WORKS ASSOCIATION OF
AMERICA**
1313 EAST 60TH STREET
CHICAGO, IL 60637
See Engineering: General; Professional
Organizations

**RADIATION DIVISION,
ENVIRONMENTAL PROTECTION
AGENCY**
33 EAST CONGRESS PARKWAY
CHICAGO, IL 60605
See Chemistry: Physical Chemistry; Government-State or Local

RADIOLOGICAL PHYSICS DIVISION
9700 SOUTH CASS AVENUE
ARGONNE, IL 60439
See Biology: General; Government-Federal

**SANITARY ENGINEERING
DIVISION, ILLINOIS
DEPARTMENT PUBLIC HEALTH**
STATE OFFICE BUILDING
SPRINGFIELD, IL 62700
See Engineering: Water Resources; Government-State or Local

SOIL CONSERVATION SERVICES
POST OFFICE BOX 678, 200 WEST
CHURCH STREET
CHAMPAIGN, IL 61820
See Biology: Ecology; Government-State or Local

STANDARD OIL COMPANY
910 SOUTH MICHIGAN AVENUE
CHICAGO, IL 60605
See Interdisciplinary: General; Industrial/Commercial

**SURVEY RESEARCH LABORATORY,
UNIVERSITY OF ILLINOIS**
437 DAVID KINLEY HALL
URBANA, IL 61801
See Social Sciences/Humanities: General;
Educational Institute

**TOXICITY LABORATORY,
UNIVERSITY OF CHICAGO**
930 EAST 58TH STREET
CHICAGO, IL 60637
See Engineering: Chemical Engineering;
Educational Institute

**TRAFFIC AND TRANSPORTATION
SOCIETY**
22 WEST MADISON STREET, ROOM
404
CHICAGO, IL 60602
See Social Sciences/Humanities: Transportation; Research Institute

**TRANSPORTATION CENTER
LIBRARY**
NORTHWESTERN UNIVERSITY
LIBRARY
EVANSTON, IL 60201
See Social Sciences/Humanities: Transportation; Educational Institute

**WATER CONDITIONING
FOUNDATIONS**
POST OFFICE BOX 194
NORTHFIELD IL 60093
See Engineering: Water Resources; Foundation

WATER RESOURCES CENTER
10 WEST 35TH STREET
CHICAGO, IL 60616
See Interdisciplinary: General; Research
Institute

WATER SURVEY
BOX 232
URBANA, IL 61801
See Physics: General; Government-State
or Local

**WATER WELL NATIONAL
ASSOCIATION**
1201 WAUKEGAN ROAD
GLENVIEW, ILL 60025
See Engineering: Water Resources; Government-State or Local

**WATERWAYS DIVISION, PUBLIC
WORKS AND BUILDING
DEPARTMENT**
201 W MONROE STREET
SPRINGFIELD, IL 62706
See Engineering: Water Resources; Government-State or Local

**WILDLIFE FEDERATION OF
ILLINOIS**
13005 SOUTH WESTERN AVENUE,
BOX 116
BLUE ISLAND, IL 60406
See Biology: Ecology; Foundation

**ZOOLOGISTS SOCIETY OF
AMERICA**
175 NATURAL RESOURCES
BUILDING
URBANA, IL 61801
See Biology: General; Professional Organizations

Indiana

ACRES, INCORPORATED
1802 CHAPMAN ROAD
HUNTERTOWN, IN 46748
See Engineering: General; Professional
Organizations

**AGRONOMY AND GEOSCIENCES
DEPARTMENT**
PURDUE UNIVERSITY
LAFAYETTE, IN 47907
See Interdisciplinary: General; Educational Institute

AIR AND WATER CONTROL
INDUSTRIAL HARBOR WORKS
EAST CHICAGO, IN 46312
See Engineering: General; Industrial/Commercial

**AIR AND WATER POLLUTION
CONTROL DIVISION**
3600 W THIRD STREET
GARY, IN 46406
See Engineering: Pollution Abatement;
Government-State or Local

AIR POLLUTION CONTROL
200 EAST WASHINGTON STREET,
ROOM 1642
INDIANAPOLIS, IN 46204
See Engineering: Pollution Abatement;
Government-State or Local

AIR POLLUTION CONTROL
5925 CALMUT AVENUE
HAMMOND, IN 46320
See Engineering: Pollution Abatement;
Government-State or Local

AIR POLLUTION CONTROL BOARD
1330 W MICHIGAN STREET
INDIANAPOLIS, IN 46206
See Engineering: Pollution Abatement;
Government-State or Local

**AIR POLLUTION CONTROL
DIVISION, COUNTY HEALTH
DEPARTMENT**
17 HARDING AVENUE
TERRE HAUTE, IN 47801
See Engineering: Pollution Abatement;
Government-State or Local

**AIR POLLUTION CONTROL
SECTION, FIRE DEPARTMENT,
CITY BUILDING**
112 NORTH WASHINGTON STREET
KOKOMO, IN 46901
See Engineering: Pollution Abatement;
Government-State or Local

**AIR POLLUTION CONTROL,
PUBLIC HEALTH DEPARTMENT**
CITY HALL, 100 WEST MICHIGAN
BOULEVARD
MICHIGAN CITY, IN 46360
See Engineering: Pollution Abatement;
Government-State or Local

**AIR QUALITY CONTROL
DEPARTMENT**
4525 INDIANAPOLIS BOULEVARD
EAST CHICAGO, IN 46312
See Engineering: Pollution Abatement;
Government-State or Local

**AMERICAN CAMPING
ASSOCIATION**
BRADFORD WOODS
MARTINSVILLE, IN 46151
See Social Sciences/Humanities: Recreation and Leisure; Professional Organizations

AQUATIC RESEARCH UNIT
INDIANA UNIVERSITY
BLOOMINGTON, IN 47401
See Biology: General; Educational Institute

AUDUBON SOCIETY OF INDIANA
MARY GRAY BIRD SANCTUARY, RR 6
CONNERSVILLE, IN 47331
See Interdisciplinary: General; Professional Organizations

**CIVIL ENGINEERING
DEPARTMENT**
ENGINEERING COLLEGE,
UNIVERSITY OF NOTRE DAME
NOTRE DAME, IN 46556
See Engineering: Pollution Abatement;
Educational Institute

CLINIC COMPLEX
INDIANA UNIVERSITY
BLOOMINGTON, IN 47405
See Social Sciences/Humanities: Psychology/Behavioral Science; Educational Institute

CONSERVATION COUNCIL OF INDIANA, INCORPORATED
6600 GUION ROAD
INDIANAPOLIS, IN 46268
See Biology: Ecology; Foundation

DEVELOPMENT RESEARCH CENTER
INDIANA UNIVERSITY
BLOOMINGTON, IN 47401
See Social Sciences/Humanities: Community Development/Studies; Research Institute

ENVIRONMENTAL CONTROL, DEPARTMENT OF BIOCHEMISTRY
PURDUE UNIVERSITY
LAFAYETTE, IN 47907
See Engineering: Agricultural Engineering; Government-State or Local

ENVIRONMENTAL HEALTH INSTITUTE
PURDUE UNIVERSITY
LAFAYETTE, IN 47901
See Biology: Ecology; Educational Institute

ENVIRONMENTAL SCIENCE PROGRAM
DEPAUW UNIVERSITY
GREENCASTLE, IN 46135
See Chemistry: General; Educational Institute

ENVIRONMENTAL SCIENCE PROGRAM
INDIANA STATE UNIVERSITY
TERRE HAUTE, IN 47809
See Chemistry: General; Educational Institute

ENVIRONMENTAL SCIENCE PROGRAM
UNIVERSITY OF EVANSVILLE
EVANSVILLE, IN 47704
See Chemistry: General; Educational Institute

ENVIRONMENTAL SCIENCE PROGRAM
VALPARAISO UNIVERSITY
VALPARAISO, IN 46383
See Interdisciplinary: General; Educational Institute

ENVIRONMENTAL STUDIES PROGRAM
EARLHAM COLLEGE
RICHMOND, IN 47374
See Chemistry: General; Educational Institute

ENVIRONMENTAL STUDIES PROGRAM
INDIANA UNIVERSITY
BLOOMINGTON, IN 47401
See Interdisciplinary: General; Educational Institute

ENVIRONMENTAL STUDIES PROGRAM
PURDUE UNIVERSITY
WEST LAFAYETTE, IN 47907
See Interdisciplinary: General; Educational Institute

ENVIRONMENTAL STUDIES PROGRAM
UNIVERSITY OF NOTRE DAME
NOTRE DAME, IN 46556
See Interdisciplinary: General; Educational Institute

ENVIRONMENTAL STUDIES, BUTLER UNIVERSITY
4600 SUNSET AVENUE
INDIANAPOLIS, IN 46208
See Chemistry: General; Educational Institute

ENVIRONMENTAL STUDIES, ROSE POLYTECHNICAL INSTITUTE
5500 WABASH AVENUE
TERRE HAUTE, IN 47803
See Engineering: General; Educational Institute

HEALTH DEPARTMENT
COUNTY-CITY BUILDING
SOUTH BEND, IN 46601
See Engineering: Pollution Abatement; Government-State or Local

IN-STREAM POLLUTION CONTROL, BOARD OF HEALTH
1330 WEST MICHIGAN STREET
INDIANAPOLIS, IN 46206
See Engineering: Pollution Abatement; Government-State or Local

INTERNATIONAL RELATIONS COMMITTEE
UNIVERSITY OF NOTRE DAME
NOTRE DAME, IN 46556
See Social Sciences/Humanities: Politics; Educational Institute

LABORATORY FOR AGRICULTURAL SENSING
PURDUE UNIVERSITY
LAFAYETTE, IN 47901
See Engineering: Agricultural Engineering; Educational Institute

NATIONAL WILDLIFE FEDERATION
REGION 6
WOLCOTTVILLE, IN 46795
See Biology: Ecology; Foundation

NATURAL RESOURCES RESEARCH INSTITUTION
PURDUE UNIVERSITY
LAFAYETTE, IN 47901
See Biology: Ecology; Educational Institute

PHYSIOLOGY DEPARTMENT
INDIANA UNIVERSITY
BLOOMINGTON, IN 47401
See Interdisciplinary: General; Educational Institute

PUBLIC ADMINISTRATION INSTITUTE, INDIANA UNIVERSITY
BALLANTINE HALL 915
BLOOMINGTON, IN 47405
See Social Sciences/Humanities: Politics; Educational Institute

PUBLIC HEALTH DEPARTMENT
337 EAST WAYNE STREET
FORT WAYNE, IN 46802
See Engineering: Pollution Abatement; Government-State or Local

SAVE THE DUNES COUNCIL
1512 PARK DRIVE
MUNSTER, IN 46321
See Biology: Ecology; Professional Organizations

SEXUAL RESEARCH INSTITUTE
INDIANA UNIVERSITY
BLOOMINGTON, IN 44058
See Social Sciences/Humanities: Psychology/Behavioral Science; Educational Institute

SOIL CONSERVATION SERVICE
5610 CRAWFORDSVILLE ROAD
INDIANAPOLIS, IN 46224
See Biology: Ecology; Government-State or Local

STREAM POLLUTION BOARD
1330 WEST MICHIGAN STREET
INDIANAPOLIS, IN 46207
See Engineering: Pollution Abatement; Government-State or Local

THERMOPHYSICAL PROPERTIES RESEARCH CENTER, PURDUE UNIVERSITY
2595 YEAGER ROAD
WEST LAFAYETTE, IN 47906
See Physics: General; Educational Institute

TRACE LEVEL RESOURCES INSTITUTE
PURDUE UNIVERSITY
LAFAYETTE, IN 47907
See Engineering: Pollution Abatement; Educational Institute

WATER DIVISION, DEPARTMENT OF NATURAL RESOURCES
100 NORTH SENATE AVENUE
INDIANAPOLIS, IN 46204
See Engineering: Water Resources; Foundation

WATER RESOURCES CENTER
PURDUE UNIVERSITY LIFE
SCIENCES BUILDING
LAFAYETTE, IN 47907
See Interdisciplinary: General; Educational Institute

**WATER RESOURCES RESEARCH
CENTER**
1005 EAST 10TH STREET
BLOOMINGTON, IN 47401
See Biology: General; Educational Institute

Kansas

**AIR POLLUTION CONTROL,
JOHNSON COUNTY HEALTH
DEPARTMENT**
COURTHOUSE
OLATHE, KS 66061
See Engineering: Agricultural Engineering; Government-State or Local

**CONSERVATION DEPARTMENT OF
KANSAS**
POST OFFICE BOX 600
SALINA, KS 67401
See Biology: Ecology; Government-State or Local

ENGINEERING COLLEGE
KANSAS STATE UNIVERSITY
MANHATTAN, KS 66502
See Engineering: General; Educational Institute

**ENVIRONMENTAL HEALTH
DIVISION, KANSAS DEPARTMENT
OF HEALTH**
535 KANSAS AVENUE
TOPEKA, KS 66603
See Engineering: Water Resources; Government-State or Local

**ENVIRONMENTAL HEALTH
SERVICES**
TOPEKA, KS 66612
See Engineering: Pollution Abatement; Government-State or Local

**ENVIRONMENTAL RESOURCES
INSTITUTE**
KANSAS STATE UNIVERSITY
MANHATTAN, KS 66502
See Engineering: Pollution Abatement; Educational Institute

**ENVIRONMENTAL STUDIES
PROGRAM**
KANSAS STATE COLLEGE
PITTSBURG, KS 66762
See Interdisciplinary: General; Educational Institute

**ENVIRONMENTAL STUDIES
PROGRAM**
KANSAS STATE UNIVERSITY

MANHATTAN, KS 66502
See Interdisciplinary: General; Educational Institute

**ENVIRONMENTAL STUDIES,
WICHITA STATE UNIVERSITY**
1845 FAIRMONT STREET
WICHITA, KS 67208
See Interdisciplinary: General; Educational Institute

GEOLOGICAL SURVEY OF KANSAS
KANSAS UNIVERSITY
LAWRENCE, KS 66044
See Geology: General; Government-State or Local

HEALTH DEPARTMENT
1615 WEST EIGHTH STREET
TOPEKA, KS 66606
See Engineering: Pollution Abatement; Government-State or Local

HEALTH DEPARTMENT
619 ANN AVENUE
KANSAS CITY, KS 66101
See Engineering: Pollution Abatement; Government-State or Local

HISTORICAL LIBRARY
BETHEL COLLEGE
NORTH NEWTON, KS 67117
See Social Sciences/Humanities: General; Educational Institute

HYDROBIOLOGICAL LABORATORY
KANSAS STATE TEACHERS
COLLEGE
PRATT, KS 67124
See Biology: General; Educational Institute

**INDUSTRIAL RADIATION AND AIR
HYGIENE, ENVIRONMENTAL
HEALTH SERVICE**
10TH AND HARRISON STREETS
TOPEKA, KS 66612
See Engineering: Pollution Abatement; Government-State or Local

**INSPECTION AND SANITATION
DIVISION**
125 EAST AVENUE
HUTCHINSON, KS 67504
See Engineering: Pollution Abatement; Government-State or Local

**OBSTETRICS, GYNECOLOGY AND
ANATOMY DEPARTMENT**
UNIVERSITY OF KANSAS MEDICAL
CENTER
KANSAS CITY, KS 66103
See Biology: General; Educational Institute

**ORNITHOLOGICAL SOCIETY OF
KANSAS**
ST MARY OF PLAINS COLLEGE
DODGE CITY, KS 67801

See Biology: Ecology; Professional Organizations

**RESEARCH AND GRADUATE
STUDIES**
UNIVERSITY OF KANSAS
LAWRENCE, KS 66044
See Chemistry: Physical Chemistry; Educational Institute

**SOIL CONSERVATION
COMMISSION OF KANSAS**
ROOM 1252W STATE OFFICE
BUILDING
TOPEKA, KS 66612
See Engineering: Water Resources; Government-State or Local

STATE BOARD OF AGRICULTURE
TOPEKA, KS 66612
See Engineering: Agricultural Engineering; Government-State or Local

**WILDLIFE FEDERATION OF
KANSAS**
1405 EISENHOWER DRIVE
JUNCTION CITY, KS 66441
See Biology: Ecology; Foundation

Kentucky

AIR POLLUTION CONTROL
275 EAST MAIN STREET
FRANKFORT, KY 40601
See Engineering: Pollution Abatement; Government-State or Local

**AIR POLLUTION CONTROL
DISTRICT**
2500 SOUTH THIRD STREET, 400
REYNOLDS BUILDING
LOUISVILLE, KY 40208
See Engineering: Pollution Abatement; Government-State or Local

COMMERCE DEPARTMENT
NEW CAPITOL ANNEX
FRANKFORT, KY 40601
See Social Sciences/Humanities: Industrial Development; Government-State or Local

**COUNCIL OF STATE
GOVERNMENTS**
IRON WORKS PIKE
LEXINGTON, KY 40505
See Social Sciences/Humanities: Law/Legislation; Government-State or Local

ENVIRONMENT COMMISSION
275 EAST MAIN STREET
FRANKFORT, KY 40601
See Biology: Ecology; Educational Institute

**ENVIRONMENTAL HEALTH
DIVISION, KENTUCKY
DEPARTMENT OF HEALTH**

275 EAST MAIN STREET
FRANKFORT, KY 40601
See Engineering: Water Resources; Government-State or Local

**ENVIRONMENTAL SCIENCE
PROGRAM**
MURRAY STATE COLLEGE
MURRAY, KY 42071
See Chemistry: General; Educational Institute

**ENVIRONMENTAL SCIENCE
PROGRAM**
UNIVERSITY OF KENTUCKY
LEXINGTON, KY 40506
See Interdisciplinary: General; Educational Institute

**ENVIRONMENTAL STUDIES
PROGRAM**
WESTERN KENTUCKY UNIVERSITY
BOWLING GREEN, KY 42101
See Chemistry: General; Educational Institute

**GEOLOGICAL SURVEY OF
KENTUCKY, UNIVERSITY OF
KENTUCKY**
307 INDUSTRIES BUILDING
LEXINGTON, KY 40506
See Engineering: Water Resources; Educational Institute

**KENTUCKY PROGRAM
DEVELOPMENT**
CAPITOL BUILDING, ROOM 157
FRANKFORT, KY 40601
See Engineering: Pollution Abatement; Government-State or Local

**LEGISLATIVE RESOURCES
COMMISSION**
STATE CAPITOL BUILDING
FRANKFORT, KY 40601
See Social Sciences/Humanities: Law/Legislation; Government-State or Local

**NATIONAL WILDLIFE
FEDERATION**
REGION 5
DRY RIDGE, KY 41035
See Biology: Ecology; Foundation

REGULATORY SERVICES DIVISION
KENTUCKY AGRICULTURAL
EXPERIMENT STATION
LEXINGTON, KY 40506
See Engineering: Agricultural Engineering; Research Institute

SOIL CONSERVATION SERVICE
1409 FORBES ROAD
LEXINGTON, KY 40505
See Biology: Ecology; Government-State or Local

**SPORTSMEN LEAGUE OF
KENTUCKY**
610 HALBERT STREET

VANCEBURG, KY 41179
See Biology: Ecology; Professional Organizations

**WATER DIVISION, KENTUCKY
DEPARTMENT OF NATURAL
RESOURCES**
CAPITOL ANNEX BUILDING
FRANKFORT, KY 40601
See Engineering: General; Government-State or Local

**WATER POLLUTION CONTROL
COMMISSION**
275 EAST MAIN STREET
FRANKFORT, KY 40601
See Engineering: Pollution Abatement; Government-State or Local

WATER RESOURCES LABORATORY
UNIVERSITY OF LOUISVILLE
LOUISVILLE, KY 40208
See Biology: Ecology; Educational Institute

Louisiana

AGRICULTURE DEPARTMENT
BOX 16390 A
BATON ROUGE, LA 70803
See Engineering: Pollution Abatement; Government-State or Local

AIR CONTROL COMMISSION
POST OFFICE BOX 60630
NEW ORLEANS, LA 70112
See Engineering: Pollution Abatement; Government-State or Local

**CODDO-SHREVEPORT HEALTH
UNIT**
1866 KINGS HIGHWAY
NEW ORLEANS, LA 71103
See Engineering: Pollution Abatement; Government-State or Local

**EDUCATION MATERIALS
RESOURCES BUREAU**
COLLEGE OF EDUCATION,
LOUISIANA STATE UNIVERSITY
BATON ROUGE, LA 70803
See Social Sciences/Humanities: Education; Educational Institute

**ENGINEERING RESEARCH
DIVISION, LA TECHNICAL
UNIVERSITY**
BOX 4875, TECHNOLOGY STATION
RUSTON, LA 71270
See Engineering: Water Resources; Educational Institute

ENGINEERING SCOOL
TULANE UNIVERSITY
NEW ORLEANS, LA 70118
See Interdisciplinary: General; Educational Institute

ENVIRONMENTAL DESIGN

SCHOOL
LOUISIANA STATE UNIVERSITY
BATON ROUGE, LA 70803
See Interdisciplinary: General; Educational Institute

**ENVIRONMENTAL SCIENCE
PROGRAM**
LOUISIANA POLYTECHNICAL
INSTITUTE
RUSTON, LA 71270
See Interdisciplinary: General; Educational Institute

**ENVIRONMENTAL SCIENCE
PROGRAM**
LOUISIANA STATE UNIVERSITY
BATON ROUGE, LA 70803
See Interdisciplinary: General; Educational Institute

**ENVIRONMENTAL SCIENCES
CENTER**
TULANE UNIVERSITY
NEW ORLEANS, LA 70101
See Biology: Ecology; Educational Institute

**ENVIRONMENTAL SCIENCES
PROGRAM**
MCNEESE STATE COLLEGE
LAKE CHARLES, LA 70601
See Biology: Ecology; Educational Institute

**ENVIRONMENTAL STUDIES
PROGRAM**
LOUISIANA STATE UNIVERSITY IN
NEW ORLEANS
NEW ORLEANS, LA 70122
See Chemistry: General; Educational Institute

**ENVIRONMENTAL STUDIES
PROGRAM**
UNIVERSITY OF SOUTHWESTERN
LA
LAFAYETTE, LA 70501
See Interdisciplinary: General; Educational Institute

**ENVIRONMENTAL STUDIES,
LOYOLA UNIVERSITY**
6363 ST CHARLES AVENUE
NEW ORLEANS, LA 70118
See Interdisciplinary: General; Educational Institute

**MARINE SCIENCES DIVISION, 8TH
COAST GUARD DISTRICT**
CUSTOM HOUSE
NEW ORLEANS, LA 70130
See Engineering: Water Resources; Government-State or Local

**MEDICAL SCHOOL, TULANE
UNIVERSITY**
1430 TULANE AVENUE
NEW ORLEANS, LA 70112
See Biology: General; Research Institute

PUBLIC ADMINISTRATION BUREAU
LOUISIANA STATE UNIVERSITY
BATON ROUGE, LA 70803
See Social Sciences/Humanities: Law/
Legislation; Educational Institute

**SAFETY AND PERMITS
DEPARTMENT**
CITY HALL, 1300 PERDIDO STREET
NEW ORLEANS, LA 70112
See Engineering: Pollution Abatement;
Government-State or Local

STEAM CONTROL COMMISSION
POST OFFICE DRAWER FC,
UNIVERSITY STATION
BATON ROUGE, LA 70803
See Engineering: Pollution Abatement;
Government-State or Local

**WILDLIFE FEDERATION OF
LOUISIANA**
BOX 53112, ISTROUMA STATION
BATON ROUGE, LA 70805
See Biology: Ecology; Foundation

Massachusetts

ACTION CONSERVATION TRUST
42 TAYLOR ROAD
ACTON, MA 01720
See Biology: Ecology; Government-State
or Local

**ADULTS' LIBERAL EDUCATION
STUDY CENTER**
BOSTON UNIVERSITY, 38
MOUNTFORT STREET
BROOKLINE, MA 02146
See Social Sciences/Humanities: Educa-
tion; Educational Institute

AERONAUTICS COMMISSION
LOGAN'AIRPORT
BOSTON, MA 02167
See Engineering: Pollution Abatement;
Government-State or Local

**AGRICULTURAL, INDUSTRIAL,
MICROBIOLOGICAL INSTITUTE**
UNIVERSITY OF MASSACHUSETTS,
MARSHALL HALL
AMHERST, MA 01003
See Engineering: General; Educational
Institute

**AGRICULTURE DEPARTMENT,
STATE RECLAMATION BOARD**
100 CAMBRIDGE STREET
BOSTON, MA 02134
See Engineering: Agricultural Engineer-
ing; Government-State or Local

**AIR POLLUTION AND NOISE
ABATEMENT**
144 MERIDAN STREET
EAST BOSTON, MA 02128
See Engineering: Pollution Abatement;
Government-State or Local

AIR POLLUTION COMMITTEE
43 EAST STREET, CITY HALL
PITTSFIELD, MA 01210
See Engineering: Pollution Abatement;
Government-State or Local

AIR POLLUTION CONSORTIUM
31 WILDWOOD DRIVE
BEDFORD, MA 01730
See Engineering: Pollution Abatement;
Government-State or Local

**AIR POLLUTION CONTROL
BRANCH, ENVIRONMENTAL
PROTECTION AGENCY**
KENNEDY FEDERAL BUILDING,
GOVERNMENT CENTER, ROOM
2303
BOSTON, MA 02203
See Engineering: Pollution Abatement;
Government-Federal

**AIR POLLUTION CONTROL
DISTRICT, LOWER PINE VALLEY**
1414 STATE STREET
SPRINGFIELD, MA 01109
See Engineering: Pollution Abatement;
Government-State or Local

**AIR POLLUTION CONTROL
SECTOR, PUBLIC HEALTH
DEPARTMENT**
455 MAIN STREET
WORCESTER, MA 01608
See Engineering: Pollution Abatement;
Government-State or Local

**AIR POLLUTION CONTROL,
BOARD OF HEALTH**
CITY HALL
FITCHBURG, MA 01420
See Engineering: Pollution Abatement;
Government-State or Local

**AIR POLLUTION CONTROL,
BOARD OF HEALTH**
CITY HALL SQUARE
BROCKTON, MA 02401
See Engineering: Pollution Abatement;
Government-State or Local

**AIR POLLUTION CONTROL,
BOARD OF HEALTH**
5 BROAD STREET
SALEM, MA 01970
See Engineering: Pollution Abatement;
Government-State or Local

**AIR POLLUTION CONTROL,
HEALTH DEPARTMENT**
CITY HALL
BEVERLY, MA 01915
See Engineering: Pollution Abatement;
Government-State or Local

**AIR POLLUTION CONTROL,
HEALTH DEPARTMENT**
33 WEST CENTRAL STREET
NATICK, MA 01760
See Engineering: Pollution Abatement;
Government-State or Local

**AIR USE MANAGEMENT, SANITARY
ENGINEERING DIVISION**
511 STATEHOUSE
BOSTON, MA 02133
See Engineering: Pollution Abatement;
Government-State or Local

AMERICAN ANTIQUARIAN SOCIETY
185 SALISBURY STREET
WORCESTER, MA 01609
See Social Sciences/Humanities: General;
Professional Organizations

APPALACHIAN MOUNTAIN CLUB
5 JOY STREET
BOSTON, MA 02108
See Biology: Ecology; Government-State
or Local

**AUDUBON SOCIETY OF
MASSACHUSETTS**
SOUTH GREAT ROAD
LINCOLN, MA 01773
See Biology: Ecology; Foundation

**AUDUBON SOCIETY OF PROUTS
NECK**
11 BROWN STREET
CAMBRIDGE, MA 02138
See Biology: Ecology; Foundation

BEAVER BROOK VALLEY PROJECT
DEPOT ROAD
BOXBOROUGH, MA 01719
See Biology: Ecology; Foundation

BERKSHIRE COUNTY LAND TRUST
100 WORTH STREET
PITTSFIELD, MA 01201
See Biology: Ecology; Government-State
or Local

BIOLOGICAL LABORATORY
P O BOX 6
WOODS HOLE, MA 02543
See Engineering: Water Resources; Gov-
ernment-Federal

BIOLOGY DEPARTMENT
BOSTON COLLEGE
CHESTNUT HILL, MA 02167
See Biology: General; Educational Insti-
tute

BIOLOGY LABORATORY
HARVARD UNIVERSITY
CAMBRIDGE, MA 02138
See Biology: General; Educational Insti-
tute

**BIRD BANDING ASSOCIATION
(NORTHEAST)**
MASSACHUSETTS AUDUBON
SOCIETY
LINCOLN, MA 01773
See Interdisciplinary: General; Profession-
al Organizations

BOSTON ENVIRONMENT, INCORPORATED
14 BEACON STREET
BOSTON, MA 02108
See Biology: Ecology; Educational Institute

BOSTON PUBLIC LIBRARY
COPLEY SQUARE
BOSTON, MA 02117
See Interdisciplinary: General; Government-State or Local

BOSTON UNIVERSITY
625 HUNTINGTON AVENUE
BOSTON, MA 02115
See Interdisciplinary: General; Educational Institute

BOSTONIAN SOCIETY, OLD STATE HOUSE
206 WASHINGTON STREET
BOSTON,MA 02109
See Social Sciences/Humanities: General; Professional Organizations

BOTANICAL CLUB OF NEW ENGLAND
22 DIVINITY STREET
CAMBRIDGE, MA 02138
See Interdisciplinary: General; Foundation

BROADMOAR SANCTUARY
SOUTH STREET
SOUTH NATICK, MA 01760
See Interdisciplinary: General; Professional Organizations

CAMBRIDGE RESOURCES LABORATORY
L.G. HANSCOM FIELD
BEDFORD, MA 01731
See Geology: Geophysics; Government-Federal

CHEMISTRY DEPARTMENT
MASSACHUSETTS INSTITUTE OF TECHNOLOGY
CAMBRIDGE, MA 02101
See Chemistry: General; Educational Institute

CITIZENS FOR A HEALTHY ENVIRONMENT
36 PEMBERTON ROAD
COCHITUATE, MA 01778
See Biology: Ecology; Government-State or Local

CITIZENS FOR PARTICIPATION IN ENVIRONMENTAL PROBLEMS
11 SOUTH STREET
BOSTON, MA 02111
See Biology: Ecology; Government-State or Local

CITIZENS FOR PROPER TRANSPORTATION PLANNING
14 BEACON STREET, ROOM 708
BOSTON, MA 02108

See Biology: Ecology; Government-State or Local

CITIZENS LEAGUE AGAINST SONIC BOOM
19 APPLE STREET
CAMBRIDGE, MA 02138
See Engineering: Pollution Abatement; Professional Organizations

CIVIL ENGINEERS SOCIETY OF BOSTON
47 WINTER STREET
BOSTON, MA
See Engineering: Water Resources; Professional Organizations

CLEAN AIR COMMISSION
14 ADAMS AVENUE
WALTHAM, MA 02154
See Engineering: Pollution Abatement; Government-State or Local

CLEAN AIR POLLUTION
90 DOVER ROAD
WELLESLEY, MA 02181
See Engineering: Pollution Abatement; Government-State or Local

CLEANER AIR COALITION OF METROPOLITAN BOSTON
131 CLAREDON STREET
BOSTON, MA 02116
See Engineering: Pollution Abatement; Government-State or Local

COHASSET CONSERVATION TRUST
31 NICHOLS ROAD
COHASSET, MA 02025
See Interdisciplinary: General; Foundation

CONCERNED CITIZENS OF CAPE ANN
ELM AVENUE, EASTERN POINT
GLOUCESTER, MA 01930
See Biology: Ecology; Government-State or Local

CONCERNED SCIENTISTS UNION
PO BOX 289
CAMBRIDGE, MA 02139
See Interdisciplinary: General; Professional Organizations

CONCORD ENVIRONMENTAL CORNER
129 MAIN STREET
CORNER, MA 01742
See Biology: Ecology; Government-State or Local

CONNECTICUT RIVER WATERSHED COUNCIL, INCORPORATED
125 COMBS ROAD
EASTHAMPTON, MA 01027
See Engineering: Water Resources; Professional Organizations

CONSERVATION (WEYMOUTH)
TOWN HALL
WEYMOUTH, MA 02188
See Interdisciplinary: General; Government-State or Local

CONSERVATION (YARMOUTH)
351 NORTH DENNIS ROAD
YARMOUTH PORT, MA 02675
See Interdisciplinary: General; Foundation

CONSERVATION AND NATURAL RESOURCES DIVISION
NORTHEASTERN UNIVERSITY, DEPARTMENT OF EARTH SCIENCES
BOSTON, MA 02115
See Geology: General; Educational Institute

CONSERVATION ASSOCIATION OF MASSACHUSETTS
147 BEECHWOOD ROAD
WESTWOOD, MA 02090
See Interdisciplinary: General; Government-State or Local

CONSERVATION ASSOCIATION OF NEPONSET, INCORPORATED
76 WINTER STREET
NORWOOD, MA 02062
See Interdisciplinary: General; Government-State or Local

CONSERVATION ASSOCIATION OF SMITHS FERRY
RESERVATION ROAD
HOLYOKE, MA 01040
See Interdisciplinary: General; Government-State or Local

CONSERVATION COMMISSION
TOWN HALL
BROOKLINE, MA 02146
See Biology: Ecology; Government-State or Local

CONSERVATION COMMISSION OF BOSTON
BOSTON CITY HALL, ROOM 913
BOSTON, MA 02201
See Interdisciplinary: General; Government-State or Local

CONSERVATION COMMISSION OF FRAMINGHAM
14 CRESTWOOD DRIVE
FRAMINGHAM, MA 01701
See Biology: Ecology; Government-State or Local

CONSERVATION COMMISSION OF HOLLISTON
56 TEMI ROAD
HOLLISTON, MA 01746
See Biology: Ecology; Government-State or Local

CONSERVATION COMMISSION OF MASSACHUSETTS COUNCIL
ROBIN FARM
BELCHERTOWN, MA 01007
See Biology: Ecology; Professional Organizations

CONSERVATION COMMISSION OF NATICK
139 NORTH MAIN STREET
NATICK, MA 01760
See Interdisciplinary: General; Government-State or Local

CONSERVATION COMMISSION OF SHERBORN
FARM ROAD
SHERBORN, MA 01770
See Interdisciplinary: General; Government-State or Local

CONSERVATION COMMISSION OF SUDBURY
NINE BENT BROOK ROAD
SUDBURY, MA 01776
See Interdisciplinary: General; Government-State or Local

CONSERVATION COMMITTEE OF ASHLAND
66 STROBUS LANE
ASHLAND, MA 01721
See Biology: Ecology; Government-State or Local

CONSERVATION COMMITTEE OF NEEDHAM
45 FAIRFIELD STREET
NEEDHAM, MA 02192
See Interdisciplinary: General; Government-State or Local

CONSERVATION COMMITTEES ASSOCIATION OF MASSACHUSETTS
84 STATE STREET
BOSTON, MA 02109
See Interdisciplinary: General; Government-State or Local

CONSERVATION COUNCIL OF BELMONT
BELMONT, MA 02178
See Biology: Ecology; Government-State or Local

CONSERVATION COUNCIL OF FRAMINGHAM
94 PROSPECT STREET
FRAMINGHAM, MA 01701
See Biology: Ecology; Government-State or Local

CONSERVATION COUNCIL OF MASSACHUSETTS
1833 MASSACHUSETTS AVENUE
CAMBRIDGE, MA 02109
See Biology: Ecology; Professional Organizations

CONSERVATION COUNCIL OF MASSACHUSETTS, INCORPORATED
POST OFFICE BOX 315
LINCOLN CENTER, MA 01773
See Interdisciplinary: General; Government-State or Local

CONSERVATION COUNCIL OF SOUTH MIDDLESEX
66 STROBUS LANE
ASHLAND, MA 01721
See Interdisciplinary: General; Government-State or Local

CONSERVATION FOUNDATION AT CARLISLE
57 WOODLAND ROAD
CARLISLE, MA 01741
See Interdisciplinary: General; Government-State or Local

CONSERVATION FOUNDATION OF CATHAM, INCORPORATED
QUEEN ANNE ROAD
CATHAM, MA 02633
See Interdisciplinary: General; Foundation

CONSERVATION FOUNDATION OF NANTUCKET, INCORPORATED
POST OFFICE BOX 31
NANTUCKET, MA 02554
See Interdisciplinary: General; Foundation

CONSERVATION FRIENDS
43 UNION STREET
MARSHFIELD, MA 02050
See Biology: Ecology; Government-State or Local

CONSERVATION FRIENDS AT DENNIS
DENNIS, MA 02368
See Biology: Ecology; Government-State or Local

CONSERVATION FRIENDS OF DUXBURY
30 PINE HILL ROAD
DUXBURY, MA 02332
See Biology: Ecology; Government-State or Local

CONSERVATION GROUP OF REVERE
77 LIBERTY AVENUE
REVERE, MA 02151
See Interdisciplinary: General; Government-State or Local

CONSERVATION GROUP, BEVERLY-GARDEN CITY
13 KING TERRACE
BEVERLY, MA 01915
See Biology: Ecology; Government-State or Local

CONSERVATION LAW FOUNDATION, INCORPORATED
506 STATLER OFFICE BUILDING
BOSTON, MA 02116
See Interdisciplinary: General; Professional Organizations

CONSERVATION OF SOIL AND WATER, STATE COMMITTEE
100 CAMBRIDGE
BOSTON, MA 02134
See Biology: Ecology; Government-State or Local

CONSERVATION OF WELLESLEY
32 SKYLINE DRIVE
WELLESLEY, MA 02181
See Interdisciplinary: General; Government-State or Local

CONSERVATION SERVICES, DEPARTMENT OF NATURAL RESOURCES
100 CAMBRIDGE
BOSTON, MA 02134
See Biology: Ecology; Government-State or Local

CONSERVATION SOCIETY OF SOUTH HADLEY
THREE WOODBRIDGE STREET
SOUTH HADLEY, MA 01075
See Interdisciplinary: General; Government-State or Local

CONSERVATION SOCIETY, INCORPORATED
VINEYARD HAVEN, MA 02568
See Interdisciplinary: General; Government-State or Local

CONSERVATION TRUST OF ESSEX
ESSEX, MA 01929
See Biology: Ecology; Industrial/Commercial

CONSERVATION TRUST OF LITTLETON
WILDERNESS ROAD
LITTLETON, MA 01460
See Interdisciplinary: General; Foundation

CONSERVATION TRUST OF MANCHESTER
85 BRIDGE STREET
MANCHESTER, MA 01944
See Biology: Ecology; Foundation

CONSERVATION TRUST OF WEST NEWBURY
102 MAIN STREET
WEST NEWBURY, MA 01985
See Interdisciplinary: General; Government-State or Local

CONSERVATION TRUST OF WESTWOOD
521 HARTFORD STREET
WESTWOOD, MA 02090

See Interdisciplinary: General; Government-State or Local

CONSERVATORY FOUNDATION OF WEST NEWBURY
102 MAIN STREET
WEST NEWBURY, MA 01985
See Interdisciplinary: General; Foundation

ECOLOGY ACTION CLUB
78 AVENUE LOUIS PASTEUR
BOSTON, MA 02115
See Biology: Ecology; Educational Institute

ECOLOGY ACTION CORPORATION OF THE CENTER RIVER
BOX 44
HADLEY, MA 01035
See Engineering: Water Resources; Government-State or Local

ECOLOGY ACTION LEAGUE OF HERMON
POST OFFICE BOX 922
MT HEROM, MA 01354
See Biology: Ecology; Government-State or Local

ECOLOGY ACTION OF BELMONT
80 MUNROE STREET
BELMONT, MA 02178
See Biology: Ecology; Government-State or Local

ECOLOGY ACTION OF BOSTON UNIVERSITY
700 COMMONWEALTH AVENUE
BOSTON, MA 02215
See Biology: Ecology; Educational Institute

ECOLOGY ACTION OF BROCTON
116 DOVER STREET
BROCKTON, MA 02401
See Biology: Ecology; Government-State or Local

ECOLOGY ACTION REACHING THROUGH HOUSEHOLDS
MAIN STREET
SPRINGFIELD, MA 01103
See Biology: Ecology; Government-State or Local

ECOLOGY ACTION, BOSTON AREA
925 MASSACHUSETTS AVENUE
CAMBRIDGE, MA 02139
See Interdisciplinary: General; Professional Organizations

ECOLOGY CENTER OF NEW ENGLAND
891 MASSACHUSETTS AVENUE
CAMBRIDGE, MA 02139
See Biology: Ecology; Government-State or Local

ECOLOGY CLUB OF DERBY
DERBY ACADEMY
HINGHAM, MA 02043
See Biology: Ecology; Government-State or Local

ECOLOGY CLUB, NATICK HIGH SCHOOL
MEGUNKO ROAD
NATICK, MA 01760
See Biology: Ecology; Educational Institute

ECOLOGY COALITION OF NORTHEASTERN UNIVERSITY
360 HUNTINGTON AVENUE
BOSTON, MA 02115
See Biology: Ecology; Educational Institute

ECONOMIC ACTION, CENTER FOR ENVIRONMENTAL STUDIES
WILLIAMSTOWN COLLEGE
WILLIAMSTOWN, MA 01267
See Biology: Ecology; Educational Institute

ENVIRONMENT TASK FORCE OF THE GOVERNMENT
ROOM 107, 100 CAMBRIDGE
BOSTON, MA 02202
See Biology: Ecology; Government-State or Local

ENVIRONMENTAL ACTION OF COHASSET
POST OFFICE BOX 31
COHASSET, MA 02025
See Interdisciplinary: General; Government-State or Local

ENVIRONMENTAL ACTION, 207 HAMPSHIRE HOUSE
UNIVERSITY OF MAINE
AMHERST, MA 01002
See Biology: Ecology; Educational Institute

ENVIRONMENTAL ASSOCIATION OF SCITUATE
245 FIRST PARISH ROAD
SCITUATE, MA 02066
See Interdisciplinary: General; Government-State or Local

ENVIRONMENTAL BIOLOGY
EASTERN NAZARENE COLLEGE
QUINCY, MA 02125
See Biology: General; Educational Institute

ENVIRONMENTAL CONCERN GROUP, SEVERANCE HALL
WELLESLEY COLLEGE
WELLESLEY, MA 02181
See Biology: Ecology; Educational Institute

ENVIRONMENTAL CONCERNS COMMISSION OF AMHERST
19 APPLEWOOD LANE

AMHERST, MA 01002
See Interdisciplinary: General; Government-State or Local

ENVIRONMENTAL CONSERVATION ASSOCIATION OF PEMBROKE
132 HIGH STREET
PEMBROOKE, MA 02359
See Interdisciplinary: General; Government-State or Local

ENVIRONMENTAL CONSERVATION ORGANIZATION
POST OFFICE BOX 121
GROVELAND, MA 01330
See Interdisciplinary: General; Government-State or Local

ENVIRONMENTAL CONSULTATION SERVICE, CAMBRIDGE RESEARCH LABORATORY
L.G. HANSCOM FIELD
BEDFORD, MA 01730
See Engineering: Pollution Abatement; Government-Federal

ENVIRONMENTAL CONTROL NATIONAL FOUNDATION, INCORPORATED
151 TREMONT STREET
BOSTON, MA 02111
See Biology: Ecology; Foundation

ENVIRONMENTAL GROUP OF HANOVER
CEDAR STREET
HANOVER, MA 02339
See Biology: Ecology; Government-State or Local

ENVIRONMENTAL HEALTH AND SAFETY
PUBLIC HEALTH SCHOOL, HARVARD UNIVERSITY
BOSTON, MA 02115
See Biology: Ecology; Educational Institute

ENVIRONMENTAL LAW SOCIETY
BOSTON UNIVERSITY
BOSTON, MA 02215
See Biology: Ecology; Educational Institute

ENVIRONMENTAL LAW SOCIETY
HARVARD LAW SCHOOL
CAMBRIDGE, MA 02138
See Biology: Ecology; Educational Institute

ENVIRONMENTAL LAW SOCIETY
41 TEMPLE STREET
BOSTON, MA 02114
See Biology: Ecology; Government-State or Local

ENVIRONMENTAL POLICY CENTER
28 PEABODY TERRACE
CAMBRIDGE, MA 02138
See Interdisciplinary: General; Professional Organizations

ENVIRONMENTAL QUALITY
112 PINCKNEY STREET
BOSTON, MA 02114
See Biology: Ecology; Government-State
or Local

ENVIRONMENTAL QUALITY
19 GYPSY TRAIL
WESTON, MA 02193
See Biology: Ecology; Professional Organizations

**ENVIRONMENTAL QUALITY
COALITION**
UNIVERSITY OF MASSACHUSETTS
CAMPUS CENTER
AMHERST, MA 01002
See Biology: Ecology; Educational Institute

**ENVIRONMENTAL QUALITY,
MASSACHUSETTS LEAGUE OF
WOMEN VOTERS**
120 BOYLSTON STREET
BOSTON, MA 02116
See Biology: Ecology; Professional Organizations

**ENVIRONMENTAL SCIENCE
PROGRAM**
AMHERST COLLEGE
AMHERST, MA 01002
See Chemistry: General; Educational Institute

**ENVIRONMENTAL SCIENCE
PROGRAM**
BRANDEIS UNIVERSTIY
WALTHAM, MA 02154
See Chemistry: General; Educational Institute

**ENVIRONMENTAL SCIENCE
PROGRAM**
CLARK UNIVERSITY
WORCESTER, MA 01610
See Chemistry: General; Educational Institute

**ENVIRONMENTAL SCIENCE
PROGRAM**
COLLEGE OF THE HOLY CROSS
WORCESTER, MA 01610
See Chemistry: General; Educational Institute

**ENVIRONMENTAL SCIENCE
PROGRAM**
HARVARD UNIVERSITY
CAMBRIDGE, MA 02138
See Interdisciplinary: General; Educational Institute

**ENVIRONMENTAL SCIENCE
PROGRAM**
MASSACHUSETTS INSTITUTION OF
TECHNOLOGY
CAMBRIDGE, MA 02139
See Interdisciplinary: General; Educational Institute

**ENVIRONMENTAL SCIENCE
PROGRAM**
SIMMONS COLLEGE
BOSTON, MA 02115
See Interdisciplinary: General; Educational Institute

**ENVIRONMENTAL SCIENCE
PROGRAM**
WELLESLEY COLLEGE
WELLESLEY, MA 02181
See Chemistry: General; Educational Institute

**ENVIRONMENTAL SCIENCE
PROGRAM**
WILLIAMS COLLEGE
WILLIAMSTOWN, MA 01267
See Chemistry: General; Educational Institute

**ENVIRONMENTAL SCIENCE
PROGRAM**
WOODS HOLE OCEAN INSTITUTE
WOODS HOLE, MA 02543
See Engineering: Water Resources; Educational Institute

ENVIRONMENTAL SCIENCES
BRANDEIS UNIVERSITY
WALTHAM, MA 02154
See Biology: Ecology; Educational Institute

ENVIRONMENTAL STUDIES
11 ARCHER DR
NATICK, MA 01760
See Biology: Ecology; Government-State
or Local

**ENVIRONMENTAL STUDIES
PROGRAM**
BOSTON COLLEGE
CHESTNUT HILL, MA 02109
See Interdisciplinary: General; Educational Institute

**ENVIRONMENTAL STUDIES
PROGRAM**
LOWELL TECHNOLOGY INSTITUTE
LOWELL, MA 01854
See Chemistry: General; Educational Institute

**ENVIRONMENTAL STUDIES
PROGRAM**
MOUNT HOLYOKE COLLEGE
SOUTH HADLEY, MA 01075
See Chemistry: General; Educational Institute

**ENVIRONMENTAL STUDIES
PROGRAM**
NORTHWESTERN UNIVERSITY
BOSTON, MA 02115
See Interdisciplinary: General; Educational Institute

**ENVIRONMENTAL STUDIES
PROGRAM**
SMITH COLLEGE
NORTHAMPTON, MA 01060
See Chemistry: General; Educational Institute

**ENVIRONMENTAL STUDIES
PROGRAM**
TUFTS UNIVERSITY
MEDFORD, MA 02155
See Interdisciplinary: General; Educational Institute

**ENVIRONMENTAL STUDIES
PROGRAM**
UNIVERSITY OF MASSACHUSETTS
AMHERST, MA 01002
See Interdisciplinary: General; Educational Institute

**ENVIRONMENTAL STUDIES
PROGRAM**
WHEATON COLLEGE
NORTH, MA 02766
See Chemistry: General; Educational Institute

**ENVIRONMENTAL SYSTEMS
STUDIES PROGRAM**
WORCESTER POLYTECHNICAL
INSTITUTION
WORCESTER, MA 01609
See Interdisciplinary: General; Educational Institute

**EXPLORATORY FISHING AND
GEAR RESOURCES BASE**
STATE FISHERIES PIER
GLOUCESTER, MA 01930
See Biology: General; Government-Federal

**FAMILY CAMPERS ASSOCIATION
OF NORTH AMERICA**
76 STATE STREET, BOX 308
NEWBURYPORT, MA 01950
See Biology: Ecology; Professional Organizations

**FARM AND GARDEN ASSOCIATION
INCORPORATED OF NEW
ENGLAND**
45 NEWBURY STREET
BOSTON, MA 02116
See Engineering: General; Professional Organizations

**FISHERIES AND GAME DIVISION,
DEPARTMENT OF NATURAL
RESOURCES**
100 CAMBRIDGE
BOSTON, MA 02134
See Engineering: Water Resources; Government-State or Local

**FISHERY PRODUCTS, ATLANTIC
TECHNOLOGY CENTER**
EMERSON AVENUE
GLOUCESTER, MA 01930
See Biology: General; Government-Federal

FOOD COOPERATIVE OF WEST SOMERVILLE
14 PARK AVENUE
WEST SOMERVILLE, MA 02144
See Interdisciplinary: General; Foundation

FOREST AND PARK ASSOCIATION OF MASSACHUSETTS
1 COURT STREET
BOSTON, MA 02109
See Biology: Ecology; Professional Organizations

FOREST AND TRAINING ASSOCIATION OF WESTON
263 SOUTH AVENUE
WESTON, MA 02193
See Biology: Ecology; Professional Organizations

FORESTRY FOUNDATION OF NEW ENGLAND
1 COURT STREET
BOSTON, MA 02108
See Engineering: General; Foundation

FORESTRY GROUP
HARVARD UNIVERSITY
PETERSHAM, MA 01366
See Biology: Ecology; Educational Institute

FRAMINGTON TOWN TRUST
4 WILLIAMS HEIGHTS
FRAMINGTON, MA 01701
See Biology: Ecology; Government-State or Local

FRIENDS OF ANIMALS
256 GOODMAN HILL ROAD
SUDBURY, MA 01776
See Biology: Ecology; Professional Organizations

FRIENDS OF BROOKLINE CONSERVATION
CRAFTS ROAD
BROOKLINE, MA 02167
See Biology: Ecology; Government-State or Local

FUNGICIDES AND GERMICIDES LABORATORY
NATICK LABORATORY
NATICK, MA 01760
See Biology: Biochemistry; Government-Federal

FUNGICIDES AND GERMICIDES LABORATORY
UNITED STATES DEPARTMENT OF THE ARMY
NATICK, MA 01760
See Biology: General; Government-Federal

FUNGUS CULTURES, NATIONAL INDEX
NATICK LABS
NATICK, MA 01760
See Biology: Ecology; Government-Federal

GARDEN CLUB FEDERATION OF MASSACHUSETTS
300 MASSACHUSETTS AVENUE
BOSTON, MA 02115
See Biology: Ecology; Professional Organizations

GARDEN CLUB OF FRAMINGTON
25 LONGVIEW ROAD
FRAMINGTON, MA 01701
See Biology: Ecology; Professional Organizations

GEOLOGY AND GEOPHYSICS DEPARTMENT AT M I T
77 MASSACHUSETTS AVENUE
CAMBRIDGE, MA 02139
See Interdisciplinary: General; Research Institute

GRAFTON FOREST ASSOCIATION, INCORPORATED
12 SOUTH STREET
GRAFTON, MA 01519
See Biology: Ecology; Government-State or Local

HABITAT, INCORPORATED
BOX 136
BELMONT, MA 02178
See Biology: Ecology; Educational Institute

HARBOR POLLUTION COMMITTEE
MASSACHUSETTS PORT AUTHORITY, 470 ATLANTIC STREET
BOSTON, MA 02210
See Engineering: Pollution Abatement; Government-State or Local

HARMONY
872 MASSACHUSSETTS AVENUE
CAMBRIDGE, MA 02139
See Biology: Ecology; Professional Organizations

HEALTH, EDUCATION AND WELFARE REGION 1 OFFICE
FEDERAL BUILDING, GOVERNMENT CENTER
BOSTON, MA 02203
See Interdisciplinary: General; Government-Federal

HINGHAM FRIENDS OF CONSERVATION
25 ROCKWOOD ROAD
HINGHAM, MA 02043
See Interdisciplinary: General; Government-State or Local

HOPKINTON CONSERVATION COMMISSION
20 MAYHEW STREET
HOPKINTON, MA 01748
See Interdisciplinary: General; Government-State or Local

HORTICULTURAL SOCIETY OF MASSACHUSETTS
300 MASSACHUSETTS AVENUE
BOSTON, MA 02115
See Biology: Ecology; Professional Organizations

IMPROVEMENT ASSOCIATION OF FRAMINGHAM
6 VERNON STREET
FRAMINGHAM, MA 01701
See Interdisciplinary: General; Government-State or Local

IMPROVEMENT ASSOCIATION OF PEABODY
18 TREMONT STREET
PEABODY, MA 01960
See Biology: Ecology; Government-State or Local

IMPROVEMENT SOCIETY OF ANDOVER VILLAGE
POST OFFICE BOX 90
ANDOVER, MA 01810
See Biology: Ecology; Government-State or Local

IMPROVEMENT SOCIETY OF NORTH ANDOVER
JOHNSON STREET
NORTH ANDOVER, MA 01845
See Interdisciplinary: General; Government-State or Local

INDUSTRIAL MISSION OF BOSTON
56 BOYLSTON STREET
CAMBRIDGE, MA 02138
See Interdisciplinary: General; Professional Organizations

INTERACT: COMMUNITY ACTION GROUP
MASCONOMET REGIONAL H SOUTH
BOXFORD, MA 01921
See Biology: Ecology; Educational Institute

ISAAC WALTON LEAGUE OF AMERICA
MASSACHUSETTS STATE DIVISION, BOX 47
LUDLOW, MA 01046
See Biology: Ecology; Foundation

ISAAC WALTON LEAGUE OF AMERICA, MASSACHUSETTS CHAPTER
551 WATER STREET
ROCKLAND, MA 02370
See Biology: Ecology; Foundation

JONES RIVER VILLAGE CLUB
GROVE STREET
KINGSTON, MA 02364
See Biology: Ecology; Professional Organizations

JUNIOR WOMENS CLUBS OF HARWICK
BOX 372
SOUTH HARWICK, MA 02661
See Biology: Ecology; Professional Organizations

KESTREL TRUST FUND
650 EAST PLEASANT STREET
AMHERST, MA 01002
See Biology: Ecology; Foundation

LABOR AND INDUSTRIES DEPARTMENT
STATE HOUSE, ROOM 473
BOSTON, MA 02133
See Social Sciences/Humanities: Labor/Relations/Unions; Research Institute

LAKE COCHITUATE WATERSHED ASSOCIATION, INCORPORATED
1143 WORCESTER STREET
NATICK, MA 01760
See Engineering: Water Resources; Professional Organizations

LAKE HARRIS ASSOCIATION
9 SHORE DRIVE
BLACKSTONE, MA 01504
See Engineering: Water Resources; Professional Organizations

LAKE HIAWATHA ASSOCIATION
LAKE SHORE DRIVE
BELLINGHAM, MA 02019
See Biology: Ecology; Professional Organizations

LAND CONSERVATION TRUST OF BEVERLY
809 HALE STREET
BEVERLY FARMS, MA 01915
See Biology: Ecology; Government-State or Local

LAND CONSERVATION TRUST OF CONCORD
81 ESTABROOK ROAD
CONCORD, MA 01742
See Interdisciplinary: General; Government-State or Local

LAND CONSERVATION TRUST OF DOVER
SPRINGDALE AVENUE
DOVER, MA 02030
See Biology: Ecology; Foundation

LAND CONSERVATION TRUST OF LINCOLN
BOX 318
LINCOLN, MA 01773
See Biology: Ecology; Foundation

LAND CONSERVATION TRUST OF SCITUATE
50 COLE PARKWAY
SCITUATE, MA 02066
See Interdisciplinary: General; Foundation

LAND CONSERVATION TRUST OF SEEKONK
JACOBS STREET
SEEKONK, MA 02771
See Interdisciplinary: General; Government-State or Local

LAND LEAGUE OF MASSACHUSETTS
26 NELSON PLACE
WORCESTER, MA 01605
See Interdisciplinary: General; Educational Institute

LEAGUE OF WOMEN VOTERS OF MASSACHUSETTS
120 BOYLSTON STREET
BOSTON, MA 02116
See Engineering: Water Resources; Government-State or Local

LEAGUE OF WOMEN VOTERS
73 BARBER ROAD
FRAMINGHAM, MA 01701
See Biology: Ecology; Professional Organizations

LEXINGTON CITIZENS FOR CONSERVATION
21 LONGFELLOW ROAD
LEXINGTON, MA 02173
See Interdisciplinary: General; Government-State or Local

LIFE SUPPORT GROUP
P O BOX 328
SUDBURY, MA 01776
See Biology: Ecology; Professional Organizations

LOBSTERMEN'S ASSOCIATION OF MAINE
427 MAIN STREET
ROCKLAND, MA 04841
See Interdisciplinary: General; Industrial/Commercial

LOCAL INTERVENTION FOR ENVIRONMENT, INCORPORATED
27 FAIR STREET
NEWBURYPORT, MA 01950
See Biology: Ecology; Government-State or Local

MARIA MOORS CABOT FOUNDATION
HARVARD UNIVERSITY
PETERSHAM, MA 01366
See Biology: Ecology; Foundation

MARINE FISHERIES ADVISORY COMMISSION, DIVISION OF NATURAL RESOURCE
100 CAMBRIDGE STREET
BOSTON, MA 02134
See Engineering: Water Resources; Government-State or Local

MARINE FISHERIES NATIONAL SERVICE
POST OFFICE BOX 6
WOODS HOLE, MA 02543
See Biology: Ecology; Government-Federal

MARSHLANDS, TIDELANDS, AND TIDEWATERS PRESERVATION SOCIETY
14 SHOREHAM STREET
QUINCY, MA 02171
See Engineering: Pollution Abatement; Professional Organizations

MARTHAS VINYARD CONCERNED CITIZENS
BOX 719
OAKS BLUFF, MA 02557
See Biology: Ecology; Professional Organizations

MASSACHUSETTS GENERAL HOSPITAL
HARVARD MEDICAL SCHOOL
BOSTON, MA 02114
See Chemistry: Physical Chemistry; Educational Institute

MASSACHUSETTS SOCIETY FOR THE PREVENTION OF CRUELTY TO ANIMALS
180 LONGWOOD AVENUE
BOSTON, MA 02115
See Interdisciplinary: General; Government-State or Local

MASSACHUSETTS STATE GRANGE
757 WEST SAGAMORE STREET
E SANDWICH, MA 02537
See Engineering: Agricultural Engineering; Professional Organizations

METEOROLOGICAL OBSERVATION AT BLUE HILLS
HARVARD UNIVERSITY
MILTON, MA 02186
See Geology: General; Educational Institute

METROBOSTON CITIZENS COALITION FOR CLEAN AIR
131 CLARENDON STREET
BOSTON, MA 02116
See Biology: Ecology; Professional Organizations

MORATORIUM ON POLLUTION
POST OFFICE BOX 143
PITTSFIELD, MA 01201
See Engineering: Pollution Abatement; Government-State or Local

MOUNTAINEERING LAND TRUST
19 CONGRESS STREET
BOSTON, MA 02109
See Biology: Ecology; Professional Organizations

MUSEUM OF SCIENCE
SCIENCE PARK
BOSTON, MA 02114
See Interdisciplinary: General; Government-State or Local

NASHOBA CONSERVATION TRUST, INCORPORATED
WHEELER STREET
PEPPERELL, MA 01463
See Interdisciplinary: General; Government-State or Local

NATURAL RESOURCE DEPARTMENT, STATE FORESTRY DEPARTMENT
100 CAMBRIDGE
BOSTON, MA 02134
See Biology: Ecology; Government-State or Local

NATURAL RESOURCES CENTER OF NEW ENGLAND
506 STATLER BUILDING
BOSTON, MA 02116
See Interdisciplinary: General; Professional Organizations

NATURAL RESOURCES COUNCIL OF BERKSHIRE
8 BANK BOW
PITTSFIELD, MA 01201
See Biology: Ecology; Government-State or Local

NATURAL RESOURCES TRUST OF EASTON
BOX 187
SOUTH EASTON, MA 02375
See Interdisciplinary: General; Government-State or Local

NATURAL RESOURCES TRUST OF MANSFIELD
255 FRUIT STREET
MANSFIELD, MA 02048
See Interdisciplinary: General; Government-State or Local

NATURAL SCIENCE CENTER
GREAT ESKER PARK
WEYMOUTH, MA 02188
See Biology: Ecology; Government-State or Local

NATURE CENTER, SOUTH SHORE
MAPLE STREET
NORWELL, MA 02061
See Interdisciplinary: General; Government-State or Local

NATURE TRAINING SCHOOL, WORCESTER SCIENCE MUSEUM
21 CEDAR STREET
WORCESTER, MA 01609
See Biology: Ecology; Research Institute

NEPONSET VALLEY TRUST
20 CARPENTER ROAD
WALPOLE, MA 02081
See Biology: Ecology; Foundation

NEWTON CONSERVATORS, INCORPORATED
319 AUBURN STREET
AUBURNDALE, MA 02166
See Interdisciplinary: General; Foundation

NISSITISSIT RIVER LAND TRUST
LAWRENCE STREET
PEPPERELL, MA 01463
See Interdisciplinary: General; Government-State or Local

NUTRITION AND FOOD SCIENCES DEPARTMENT
MASSACHUSETTS INSTITUTE OF TECHNOLOGY
CAMBRIDGE, MA 02139
See Engineering: Agricultural Engineering; Educational Institute

NUTRITION DEPARTMENT, PUBLIC HEALTH SCHOOL
HARVARD UNIVERSITY
BOSTON, MA 02115
See Biology: Biochemistry; Educational Institute

OCCUPATIONAL SAFETY AND HEALTH, HEALTH, EDUCATION AND WELFARE
KENNEDY FEDERAL BUILDING, GOVERNMENT CENTER
BOSTON, MA 02203
See Engineering: Pollution Abatement; Government-State or Local

OCEANOGRAPHIC INSTITUTE OF WOODS HOLE
OFFICE OF ENVIRONMENTAL QUALITY
WOODS HOLE, MA 02543
See Interdisciplinary: General; Research Institute

OPERATION ROADBLOCK
HIGHLAND STREET
SOUTH EASTON, MA 02375
See Biology: Ecology; Professional Organizations

PARKS DIVISION, METRO DISTRICT COMMISSION
20 SOMERSET STREET
BOSTON, MA 02108
See Social Sciences/Humanities: Recreation and Leisure; Government-State or Local

PATHFINDER FUND
850 BOYLSTON STREET
CHESTNUT HILL, MA 02167
See Social Sciences/Humanities: Population Studies/Family Planning; Foundation

PESTICIDE CONTROL, FOOD AND DRUG DIVISION
ROOM 527, STATE HOUSE
BOSTON, MA 02133
See Engineering: Chemical Engineering; Government-State or Local

PESTICIDE REGULATION DIVISION, DEPARTMENT OF AGRICULTURE
ROOM 208, NORWOOD POST OFFICE
NORWOOD, MA 02062
See Engineering: Chemical Engineering; Government-Federal

PLANNED PARENTHOOD LEAGUE OF MASSACHUSETTS
93 UNION STREET
NEWTON CENTRE, MA 02159
See Social Sciences/Humanities: Population Studies/Family Planning; Foundation

PLANT PESTICIDE CONTROL DIVISION
DEPARTMENT OF AGRICULTURE
BOSTON, MA 02133
See Engineering: Agricultural Engineering; Government-State or Local

POLLUTION CONTROL COMMISSION, NEW ENGLAND INTERSTATE WATER
ROOM 950, 73 TRENTON STREET
BOSTON, MA 02108
See Engineering: Water Resources; Government-State or Local

POLLUTION UNLIMITED
872 BURT STREET
TAUNTON, MA 02780
See Engineering: Pollution Abatement; Government-State or Local

POPULATION STUDIES CENTER
HARVARD MEDICAL SCHOOL
BOSTON, MA 02115
See Social Sciences/Humanities: Population Studies/Family Planning; Foundation

PORT AUTHORITY OF MASSACHUSETTS
470 ATLANTIC AVENUE
BOSTON, MA 02167
See Engineering: Water Resources; Government-State or Local

PRESERVATION OF CAPE COD ASSOCIATION
BOX 325
EASTHAM, MA 02642
See Biology: Ecology; Government-State or Local

PRESERVATION OF WILDLIFE AND NATURAL AREAS FUND
ONE BOSTON PLACE
BOSTON, MA 02106
See Biology: Ecology; Government-State or Local

**PROTECTION OF ANIMALS
NATIONAL SOCIETY**
655 BOYLSTON STREET
BOSTON, MA 02166
See Biology: Ecology; Foundation

**PROTECTION OF THE
ENVIRONMENT OF
PROVINCETOWN**
GENERAL DELIVERY
PROVINCETOWN, MA 02657
See Interdisciplinary: General; Government-State or Local

**PROTECTION OF THE LEE'S RIVER
COMMISSION**
22 LAWRENCE STREET
SWANSEA, MA 02777
See Engineering: Water Resources; Government-State or Local

**PROTECTIVE ASSOCIATION OF MT
GREYLOCK**
LANESBORO, MA 01237
See Interdisciplinary: General; Government-State or Local

**PUBLIC AFFAIRS BUREAU,
COMMITTEE TO KEEP
MASSACHUSETTS BEAUTIFUL**
BOSTON COLLEGE
BOSTON, MA 02167
See Biology: Ecology; Government-State or Local

**PUBLIC HEALTH SCHOOL,
HARVARD UNIVERSITY**
665 HUNTINGTON AVENUE
BOSTON, MA 02115
See Biology: Ecology; Educational Institute

**RADIATION DIVISION,
ENVIRONMENTAL PROTECTION
AGENCY**
JOHN F KENNEDY FEDERAL
BUILDING, ROOM 2303
BOSTON, MA 02203
See Chemistry: Physical Chemistry; Government-State or Local

**RECYCLING REVOLUTION
COOPERATIVE**
14 PARK AVENUE
SOMERVILLE, MA 02144
See Biology: Ecology; Educational Institute

RESEARCH BUREAU
294 WASHINGTON STREET
BOSTON, MA 02108
See Social Sciences/Humanities:
Housing; Research Institute

RESERVATIONS, TRUSTEES OF
244 ADAMS STREET
MILTON, MA 02186
See Interdisciplinary: General; Government-State or Local

**ROADSIDE COUNCIL OF
MASSACHUSETTS**
66 NORTH STREET
LEXINGTON, MA 02173
See Biology: Ecology; Professional Organizations

**ROPER PUBLIC OPINION
RESEARCH CENTER**
WILLIAMS COLLEGE
WILLIAMSTOWN, MA 01267
See Social Sciences/Humanities: Psychology/Behavioral Science; Educational Institute

**RURAL LAND FOUNDATION OF
LINCOLN**
MACINTOSH LANE
LINCOLN, MA 01773
See Biology: Ecology; Foundation

**SALT POND AREAS BIRD
SANCTUARIES**
231 MAIN STREET
FALMOUTH, MA 02540
See Interdisciplinary: General; Government-State or Local

**SANITARY ENGINEERING,
MASSACHUSETTS DEPARTMENT
OF PUBLIC HEALTH**
511 STATE HOUSE
BOSTON, MASS 02133
See Engineering: Water Resources; Government-State or Local

SAVE NEW ENGLAND
50 WEST STREET
NORTHAMPTON, MA 01060
See Biology: Ecology; Foundation

SAVE OUR SHORES
921 EAST SQUANTUM STREET
SQUANTUM, MA 02186
See Social Sciences/Humanities: Recreation and Leisure; Professional Organizations

SAVE SCENIC MONTEREY
BOX 125
MONTEREY, MA 01245
See Interdisciplinary: General; Government-State or Local

**SEWERAGE DIVISION,
METROPOLITAN COMMISSION**
20 SOMERSET
BOSTON, MA 02108
See Engineering: Pollution Abatement; Government-State or Local

**SHERBORN FOREST AND TRAIL
ASSOCIATION**
28 MILL STATE
SHERBORN, MA 01770
See Interdisciplinary: General; Foundation

SHORTACRE
MAIN STREET

PETERSHAM, MA 01366
See Biology: Ecology; Professional Organizations

**SIERRA CLUB, FRAMINGHAM-
NATICK**
27 WELLES STREET
FRAMINGHAM, MA 01701
See Biology: Ecology; Professional Organizations

**SMITHSONIAN INSTITUTION,
CENTER FOR SHORT-LIVED
PHENOMENA**
60 GARDEN STREET
CAMBRIDGE, MA 02138
See Interdisciplinary: General; Research Institute

**SOCIAL WELFARE GRADUATE
SCHOOL**
BRANDEIS UNIVERSITY
WALTHAM, MA 02154
See Social Sciences/Humanities:
Welfare(Child Public Social);
Educational Institute

SOIL CONSERVATION SERVICE
27-29 COTTAGE STREET
AMHERST, MA 01002
See Biology: Ecology; Government-State or Local

**SPORTSMENS CLUB COUNCIL,
INCORPORATED**
19 GOULD AVENUE
MALDEN, MA 02148
See Biology: Ecology; Professional Organizations

**SPORTSMENS CLUBS COUNCIL,
INCORPORATED**
220 NORTH MAIN STREET
ANDOVER, MA 01811
See Biology: Ecology; Professional Organizations

**SPORTSMENS CLUBS OF
MASSACHUSETTS**
290 NORTH STREET
FEEDING HILLS, MA 01030
See Social Sciences/Humanities: Recreation and Leisure; Professional Organizations

**STOP UNNECESSARY ROAD
BUILDING**
OAK STREET
NORTON, MA 02766
See Interdisciplinary: General; Government-State or Local

STUDENTS ACTUALLY CARE
FRAMINGHAM STATE COLLEGE
FRAMINGHAM, MA 01701
See Biology: Ecology; Educational Institute

STUDENTS AGAINST POLLUTION
GRANITE STATE
LEOMINSTER, MA 01453

See Engineering: Pollution Abatement; Educational Institute

STUDENTS FOR ECOLOGY ACTION
SALEN ROAD, BEVERLY HIGH
SCHOOL
BEVERLY, MA 01915
See Biology: Ecology; Educational Institute

TEN MILE RIVER BASIN TASK FORCE
68 WINTHROP STREET
TAUNTON, MA 02780
See Engineering: Water Resources; Government-State or Local

THE NEW ALCHEMY INSTITUTION
BOX 432
WOODS HOLE, MA 02543
See Chemistry: General; Government-State or Local

TRANSPORTATION CRISIS COMMISSION
56 BOYLSTON STREET
CAMBRIDGE, MA 02138
See Social Sciences/Humanities: Transportation; Professional Organizations

UNION OF CONCERNED SCIENTISTS
PO BOX 289, MASSACHUSETTS
INSTITUTE OF TECHNOLOGY
CAMBRIDGE, MA 02139
See Engineering: Pollution Abatement; Professional Organizations

URBAN STUDIES CENTER
66 CHURCH STREET
CAMBRIDGE, MA 02139
See Social Sciences/Humanities: Community Development/Studies; Educational Institute

WATER AMENDMENT BOARD
100 CAMBRIDGE STREET
BOSTON, MA 02167
See Engineering: Water Resources; Government-State or Local

WATER AND HYDRODYNAMICS LABORATORY
MASSACHUSETTS INSTITUTION OF
TECHNOLOGY
CAMBRIDGE, MA 02139
See Engineering: Water Resources; Educational Institute

WATER POLLUTION CONTROL ASSOCIATION
607 BOYLSTON STREET
BOSTON, MA 02116
See Engineering: Pollution Abatement; Professional Organizations

WATER POLLUTION CONTROL OF NEW ENGLAND
511 STATE HOUSE
BOSTON, MA 02133

See Engineering: Water Resources; Government-State or Local

WATER RESOURCES COMMISSION
100 CAMBRIDGE AVENUE
BOSTON, MA 02202
See Engineering: Pollution Abatement; Government-State or Local

WATERSHED ASSOCIATION OF CHARLES RIVER
2391 COMMONWEALTH AVENUE
AUBURNDALE, MA 02166
See Engineering: Water Resources; Government-State or Local

WATERSHED ASSOCIATION OF LAKE COCHITUATE
61 LAKE SHORE ROAD
NATICK, MA 01760
See Interdisciplinary: General; Educational Institute

WATERSHED ASSOCIATION OF NASHUA RIVER, INCORPORATED
GROTON, MA 01450
See Engineering: Water Resources; Government-State or Local

WATERSHED ASSOCIATION OF NEPONSET
30 THOMPSON LANE
MILTON, MA 02187
See Engineering: Water Resources; Government-State or Local

WATERSHED ASSOCIATION OF NORTH AND SOUTH RIVERS, INCORPORATED
POST OFFICE BOX 333
MARSHFIELD HILLS, MA 02051
See Engineering: Water Resources; Government-State or Local

WATERSHED ASSOCIATION OF THE HOUSATONIC RIVER
11 HOUSATONIC STREET
LENOX, MA 01240
See Engineering: Water Resources; Government-State or Local

WATERSHED ASSOCIATION, INCORPORATED, OF THE WESTFIELD RIVER
POST OFFICE BOX 114
MIDDLEFIELD, MA 01243
See Engineering: Water Resources; Government-State or Local

WATERSHED ASSOCIATION, INCORPORATED, OF THE MERRIMACK RIVER
105 EVERETT STREET
CONCORD, MA 01743
See Engineering: Water Resources; Government-State or Local

WATERSHED COUNCIL FOR CENTER RIVER
125 COMBS ROAD
EASTHAMPTON, MA 01027
See Engineering: Water Resources; Educational Institute

WATERSHED COUNCIL OF THE PARKER RIVER
WASHINGTON STREET
W BOXFORD, MA 01885
See Engineering: Water Resources; Government-State or Local

WATERSHED PROTECTION ASSOCIATION OF THE SHAWSHEEN
2 HADLEY ROAD
LEXINGTON, MA 02173
See Engineering: Water Resources; Government-State or Local

WATERWAYS DIVISION, DEPARTMENT OF PUBLIC WORKS
1 CITY HALL SQUARE
BOSTON, MA 02129
See Engineering: Water Resources; Government-State or Local

WILDFLOWER PRESERVATION SOCIETY OF NEW ENGLAND
300 MASSACHUSETTS AVENUE
BOSTON, MA 02115
See Interdisciplinary: General; Government-State or Local

WILDLIFE FEDERATION OF MASSACHUSETTS
BOX 343
NATICK, MA 01760
See Biology: Ecology; Foundation

WILDLIFE REHABILITATION CENTER
GROVE STREET
UPTON, MA 01568
See Interdisciplinary: General; Research Institute

WILLIAM F CLAPP LABORATORIES
WASHINGTON STREET
DUXBURY, MA 02332
See Biology: Ecology; Field Station/Laboratory

WOMEN VOTERS LEAGUE OF MASSACHUSETTS
120 BOYLSTON STREET
BOSTON, MA 02116
See Biology: Ecology; Professional Organizations

WOMENS CLUBS FEDERATION OF MASSACHUSETTS
115 NEWBURY STREET
BOSTON, MA 02116
See Biology: Ecology; Professional Organizations

YACHT CLUB ASSOCIATION
18 MAVERICK STREET
MEDFORD, MA 02155
See Engineering: Pollution Abatement;
Professional Organizations

ZERO POPULATION GROWTH
BOX 2151, BRANDEIS UNIVERSITY
WALTHAM, MA 02154
See Social Sciences/Humanities: Population Studies/Family Planning; Foundation

ZERO POPULATION GROWTH
MOUNT HOLYOKE COLLEGE
SOUTH HADLEY, MA 01075
See Social Sciences/Humanities: Population Studies/Family Planning; Foundation

ZERO POPULATION GROWTH
14 BEACON STREET
BOSTON, MA
See Social Sciences/Humanities: Population Studies/Family Planning; Foundation

ZERO POPULATION GROWTH
210 ELM STREET
NORTHAMPTON, MA 01060
See Social Sciences/Humanities: Population Studies/Family Planning; Foundation

ZERO POPULATION GROWTH
29 ARCADIA STREET
LONGMEADOW, MA 01106
See Social Sciences/Humanities: Population Studies/Family Planning; Foundation

ZERO POPULATION GROWTH
36 CHURCH STREET
WESTBORO, MA 01581
See Social Sciences/Humanities: Population Studies/Family Planning; Foundation

ZERO POPULATION GROWTH
41 WASHINGTON STREET
NATICK, MA 01760
See Social Sciences/Humanities: Population Studies/Family Planning; Foundation

**ZOOLOGICAL SOCIETY OF
  MASSACHUSETTS**
1904 CANTON AVENUE
MILTON, MA 02186
See Interdisciplinary: General; Government-State or Local

Maryland

**AGRICULTURAL ENGINEERING
  RESOURCES DIVISION**
2819 DUVALL
BURONSVILLE, MD 20730

See Engineering: Agricultural Engineering; Government-Federal

**AGRICULTURE LABORATORY,
  NATIONAL**
U S DEPARTMENT OF
  AGRICULTURE
BELTSVILLE, MD 20705
See Engineering: Agricultural Engineering; Government-Federal

AIR POLLUTION CONTROL OFFICE
PARKLAWN BUILDING, 5600
  FISHER LANE
ROCKVILLE, MD 20852
See Engineering: Water Resources; Government-Federal

**AIR POLLUTION CONTROL,
  COUNTY HEALTH DEPARTMENT**
COUNTY OFFICE BUILDING
ROCKVILLE, MD 20850
See Engineering: Pollution Abatement;
Government-State or Local

**AIR POLLUTION CONTROL,
  ENVIRONMENTAL HEALTH
  BUREAU**
BALTIMORE COUNTY HEALTH
  DEPARTMENT
TOWSON, MD 21204
See Engineering: Pollution Abatement;
Government-State or Local

AIR QUALITY CONTROL BUREAU
610 NORTH HOWARD
BALTIMORE, MD 21201
See Engineering: Pollution Abatement;
Government-State or Local

**AIR QUALITY CONTROL, COUNTY
  HEALTH DEPARTMENT**
101 SOUTH STREET
ANNAPOLIS, MD 21401
See Engineering: Pollution Abatement;
Government-State or Local

**ALLIED HEALTH MANPOWER,
  HEALTH MANPOWER
  EDUCATION BUREAU**
NATIONAL INSTITUTES OF HEALTH
BETHESDA, MD 20014
See Interdisciplinary: General; Unclassified

**ANIMAL DISEASE AND PARASITE
  RESEARCH DIVISION**
BELTSVILLE PARASITOLOGY
  LABORATORY
BELTSVILLE, MD 20705
See Engineering: Agricultural Engineering; Government-Federal

**APPLIED RESEARCH
  ENVIRONMENTAL SCIENCE,
  NATURE CONSERVATION**
POST OFFICE BOX P
ST MICHAELS, MD 21663

See Interdisciplinary: General; Research
Institute

**ARMED FORCES RADIOBIOLOGY
  RESEARCH LIBRARY**
BETHESDA, MD 20014
See Biology: General; Government-Federal

**ARMY ENVIRONMENTAL HYGIENE
  AGENCY**
OFFICE OF SURGEON GENERAL
EDGEWOOD ARSENAL, MD 21010
See Interdisciplinary: General; Unclassified

ATMOSPHERIC SCIENCES LIBRARY
ROOM 816, 8060 13TH STREET
SILVER SPRING, MD 20910
See Biology: Ecology; Government-Federal

**BEACH AND SHORE
  PRESERVATION OF AMERICA**
POST OFFICE BOX 1246
ROCKVILLE, MD 20850
See Engineering: General; Foundation

**BEALL, GARNER AND GEARE,
  INCORPORATED**
QUEEN CITY TRIANGLE
CUMBERLAND, MD 21502
See Engineering: Pollution Abatement;
Professional Organizations

BEHAVIORAL BIOLOGY DIVISION
JOHNS HOPKINS UNIVERSITY
BALTIMORE, MD 21201
See Biology: General; Educational Institute

**BEHAVIORAL RESEARCH
  INSTITUTE**
2426 LINDEN LANE
SILVER SPRING, MD 20910
See Social Sciences/Humanities: Psychology/Behavioral Science; Educational
Institute

BIOLOGICAL CHEMISTS SOCIETY
9650 ROCKVILLE PIKE
BETHESDA, MD 20014
See Biology: Biochemistry; Professional
Organizations

**BIOLOGICAL EFFECTS
  DEPARTMENT**
12720 TWINBROOK PARKWAY
ROCKVILLE, MD 20852
See Biology: General; Government-State
or Local

BIOLOGICAL LABORATORY
BUREAU OF COMMISSION
  FISHERIES
OXFORD, MD 21654
See Biology: General; Government-Federal

**BROTHERHOOD OF THE JUNGLE
  COCK, INCORPORATED**
10 EAST FAYETTE STREET

BALTIMORE, MD 21202
See Interdisciplinary: General; Professional Organizations

CHESAPEAKE BAY INSTITUTION, JOHNS HOPKINS UNIVERSITY
CHARLES AND 34TH STREETS
BALTIMORE, MD 21218
See Biology: Ecology; Research Institute

CHILD STUDY INSTITUTE
UNIVERSITY OF MARYLAND
COLLEGE PARK, MD 20742
See Social Sciences/Humanities: Welfare(Child Public Social); Educational Institute

COAST AND GEODETIC SURVEY
WASHINGTON SCIENCES CENTER, BUILDING 1
ROCKVILLE, MD 20852
See Interdisciplinary: General; Unclassified

COMMUNITY ENVIRONMENT MANAGEMENT BUREAU
12720 TWINBROOK PARKWAY
ROCKVILLE, MD 20852
See Social Sciences/Humanities: Community Development/Studies; Government-Federal

COMMUNITY ENVIRONMENTAL MANAGEMENT BUREAU
8717 POST OAK ROAD
POTOMAC, MD 20854
See Biology: Ecology; Government-Federal

CONSUMER AND FOOD RESEARCH DIVISION
FEDERAL CENTER BUILDING
HYATTSVILLE, MD 20781
See Engineering: Agricultural Engineering; Government-Federal

CROP ECOLOGY INSTITUTE
809 DALE DRIVE
SILVER SPRING, MD 20910
See Biology: Ecology; Government-Federal

DRUG PROBLEM COMMISSION
NATIONAL BANK BUILDING, ROOM 310
BETHESDA, MD 20014
See Social Sciences/Humanities: Urban Problems; Government-Federal

ENTOMOLOGICAL SOCIETY OF AMERICA
4603 CALVERT ROAD
COLLEGE PARK, MD 20740
See Biology: General; Professional Organizations

ENTOMOLOGY RESOURCES DIVISION
DEPARTMENT OF AGRICULTURE
BELTSVILLE, MD 20705

See Biology: General; Government-Federal

ENVIRONMENTAL CONTROL ADMINISTRATION
12720 TWINBROOK PARKWAY
ROCKVILLE, MD 20852
See Biology: Ecology; Government-Federal

ENVIRONMENTAL CONTROL ADMINISTRATION
5600 FISHERS LANE
ROCKVILLE, MD 20852
See Biology: Ecology; Government-Federal

ENVIRONMENTAL DATA SERVICE
9403 CALDRAN DRIVE
CLINTON, MD 20735
See Interdisciplinary: General; Unclassified

ENVIRONMENTAL HEALTH ADMINISTRATION, HEALTH AND MENTAL HYGIENE
610 NORTH HOWARD STREET
BALTIMORE, MD 21201
See Engineering: Pollution Abatement; Educational Institute

ENVIRONMENTAL HEALTH SCIENCES TRAINING COMMISSION
NATIONAL INSTITUTES OF HEALTH
BETHESDA, MD 20014
See Biology: Ecology; Research Institute

ENVIRONMENTAL HYGIENE AGENCY, OFFICE OF THE SURGEON GENERAL
US DEPARTMENT OF THE ARMY
EDGEWOOD ARSENAL, MD 21010
See Engineering: Water Resources; Government-Federal

ENVIRONMENTAL MEDICINE, SCHOOL OF HYGIENE AND PUBLIC HEALTH
JOHNS HOPKINS UNIVERSITY
BALTIMORE, MD 21205
See Interdisciplinary: General; Educational Institute

ENVIRONMENTAL MONITORING AND PREDICTING SECTION
6815 BUTTERMERE LANE
BETHESDA, MD 20034
See Interdisciplinary: General; Unclassified

ENVIRONMENTAL PROTECTION AGENCY LABORATORY
ROCKVILLE, MD 20801
See Biology: Ecology; Field Station/Laboratory

ENVIRONMENTAL SCIENCE PROGRAM
JOHNS HOPKINS UNIVESITY

BALTIMORE, MD 21218
See Interdisciplinary: General; Educational Institute

ENVIRONMENTAL SCIENCE PROGRAM
UNIVERSITY OF MARYLAND
COLLEGE PARK, MD 20742
See Interdisciplinary: General; Educational Institute

ENVIRONMENTAL SCIENCES SERVICES ADMINISTRATION
NATIONAL OCEANIC AND ATMOSPHERIC ADMINISTRATION
ROCKVILLE, MD 20852
See Engineering: General; Government-Federal

ENVIRONMENTAL STUDIES GROUP, JOHNS HOPKINS UNIVERSITY
615 NORTH WOLFE STREET
BALTIMORE, MD 21205
See Biology: Ecology; Educational Institute

ENVIRONMENTAL STUDIES PROGRAM
GOUCHER COLLEGE, TOWSON
BALTIMORE, MD 21204
See Chemistry: General; Educational Institute

ENVIRONMENTAL STUDIES PROGRAM, MORGAN STATE COLLEGE
HILLEN STATE ROAD AND COLD SPRINGS LANE
BALTIMORE, MD 21212
See Chemistry: General; Educational Institute

ENVIRONMENTAL STUDIES, CHESAPEAKE BAY CENTER
ROUTE 4, BOX 622
EDGEWATER, MD 21037
See Engineering: Water Resources; Educational Institute

ENVIRONMENTAL TRUST OF MARYLAND
8 E MULBERRY STREET
BALTIMORE, MD 21202
See Biology: Ecology; Government-State or Local

FAMILY PLANNING SERVICE CENTER
5600 FISHERS LANE
ROCKVILLE, MD 20852
See Social Sciences/Humanities: Population Studies/Family Planning; Government-Federal

FEDERAL WORKING GROUP ON PESTICIDE MANAGEMENT
5600 FISHERS LANE, ROOM 17-92, PARKLAWN BUILDING
ROCKVILLE, MD 20852
See Engineering: General; Government-Federal

ᅟ

ᅟ

UNITED STATES   271

FIELD OPERATIONS DIVISION, ENVIRONMENTAL PROTECTION AGENCY
5600 FISHERS LANE
ROCKVILLE, MD 20852
See Engineering: General; Government-State or Local

FISHERIES COMMISSION BUREAU, DEPARTMENT OF INTERIOR
P O BOX 128
COLLEGE PK, MD 20740
See Biology: General; Government-Federal

FLORIDATION INFORMATION SERVICE, DENTAL HEALTH DIVISION, ROOM 508
DEPARTMENT OF HEALTH, EDUCATION, AND WELFARE
BETHESDA, MD 20014
See Engineering: Water Resources; Government-Federal

FOREIGN AGRICULTURAL AND SPECIAL PROGRAM DIVISION
406 DEERFIELD AVENUE
SILVER SPRING, MD 20910
See Engineering: Agricultural Engineering; Government-Federal

GEODESY AND PHOTOGRAMMETRY, NATIONAL OCEANOGRAPHIC SURVEYS
NATIONAL OCEANIC AND ATMOSPHERIC ADMINISTRATION
ROCKVILLE, MD 20852
See Engineering: General; Government-Federal

GEOLOGICAL SURVEY OF MARYLAND, JOHNS HOPKINS UNIVERSITY
214 LATROBE HALL
BALTIMORE, MD 21218
See Geology: General; Government-State or Local

GEOLOGY AND ENVIRONMENTAL ENGINEERING DEPARTMENT
THE JOHNS HOPKINS UNIVERSITY
BALTIMORE, MD 21201
See Engineering: Water Resources; Educational Institute

HEALTH INSTITUTE
BETHESDA, MD 20014
See Biology: General; Government-Federal

HEALTH SERVICES AND MENTAL HEALTH ADMINISTRATION
14405 BARKWOOD DRIVE
ROCKVILLE, MD 20853
See Social Sciences/Humanities: Mental Health; Government-Federal

HEALTH SERVICES AND MENTAL HEALTH ADMINISTRATION
5600 FISHERS LANE, ROOM 1587
ROCKVILLE, MD 20852
See Interdisciplinary: General; Unclassified

HEALTH, EDUCATION, AND WELFARE DEPARTMENT, ROOM 8A-24, BUILDING 31
9000 ROCKVILLE PIKE
BETHESDA, MD 20014
See Social Sciences/Humanities: Welfare(Child Public Social); Government-Federal

HOLLY SOCIETY OF AMERICA
407 FOUNTAIN GREEN ROAD
BEL AIR, MD 21014
See Interdisciplinary: General; Research Institute

HUMAN NUTRITION RESEARCH DIVISION
AGRICULTURAL RESEARCH CENTER
BELTSVILLE, MD 20705
See Engineering: Agricultural Engineering; Government-Federal

HUMAN NUTRITION RESEARCH DIVISION
FEDERAL CENTER BUILDING
HYATTSVILLE, MD 20705
See Engineering: Agricultural Engineering; Government-Federal

HYDROLOGY OFFICE, NATIONAL WEATHER SERVICES
8060 13TH STREET
SILVER SPRING, MD 20910
See Engineering: Water Resources; Government-Federal

HYDROLOGY RESEARCH AND DEVELOPMENT LABORATORY
NATIONAL WEATHER SERVICE
SILVER SPRING, MD 20910
See Engineering: Water Resources; Government-State or Local

HYGIENE AND PUBLIC HEALTH SCHOOL, JOHNS HOPKINS UNIVERSITY
615 NORTH WOLFE STREET
BALTIMORE, MD 21205
See Social Sciences/Humanities: General; Educational Institute

INDUSTRIAL GAS CLEANING DEPARTMENT
KOPPERS COMPANY, INCORPORATED
BALTIMORE, MD 21203
See Engineering: Pollution Abatement; Industrial/Commercial

INDUSTRIAL HYGIENE BUREAU
BALTIMORE CITY HEALTH DEPARTMENT
BALTIMORE, MD 21202
See Engineering: Pollution Abatement; Government-State or Local

INFORMATION DIVISION, FEDERAL CENTER BUILDING

BELLCREST ROAD AND EAST-WEST ROAD
HYATTSVILLE, MD 20781
See Engineering: Agricultural Engineering; Government-Federal

INTRAMURAL RESEARCH, NATIONAL INSTITUTE OF MENTAL HEALTH
HEALTH SERVICES AND MENTAL HEALTH ADMINISTRATION
BETHESDA, MD 20014
See Social Sciences/Humanities: Mental Health; Research Institute

LABOR, MANAGEMENT AND WELFARE DEPARTMENT
8757 GEORGIA AVENUE
SILVER SPRING, MD 20910
See Social Sciences/Humanities: Labor/Relations/Unions; Government-Federal

MARINE AND EARTH SCIENCES LIBRARY
NATIONAL OCEANIC AND ATMOSPHERIC ADMINISTRATION
ROCKVILLE, MD 20852
See Geology: General; Government-Federal

MARINE RESOURCES
5 MAYO AVENUE
ANNAPOLIS, MD 21403
See Engineering: Water Resources; Government-Federal

MARKET QUALITY RESEARCH DIVISION
FEDERAL CENTER BUILDING
HYATTSVILLE, MD 20781
See Engineering: Agricultural Engineering; Government-Federal

MEDICAL LIBRARY
8600 ROCKVILLE PIKE
BETHESDA, MD 20014
See Social Sciences/Humanities: General; Government-Federal

MENTAL HEALTH INSTITUTE
7817 GREENTWIG ROAD
BETHESDA, MD 20014
See Social Sciences/Humanities: Mental Health; Government-Federal

MENTAL RETARDATION BRANCH, CHILD HEALTH AND HUMAN DEVELOPMENT
NATIONAL INSTITUTE OF HEALTH, PUBLIC HEALTH SERVICE
BETHESDA, MD 20014
See Social Sciences/Humanities: Mental Health; Government-Federal

METALLURGY RESEARCH CENTER, BUREAU OF MINES
COLLEGE PARK METALLURGY RESEARCH CENTER
COLLEGE PARK, MD 20740
See Interdisciplinary: General; Government-State or Local

METEOROLOGY CENTER
8060 13TH STREET, GRAMAX
BUILDING
SILVER SPRING, MD 20910
See Engineering: Pollution Abatement;
Government-Federal

**MICROBIOLOGICAL
SPECIFICATIONS COMMISSION
(INTERNATIONAL)**
4204 DRESDEN STREET
KENSINGTON, MD 20795
See Biology: General; Educational Institute

**NATIONAL AIR POLLUTION
CONTROL ASSOCIATION**
9600 FISHERS LANE
ROCKVILLE, MD 20801
See Engineering: Pollution Abatement;
Government-Federal

**NATIONAL CLEARINGHOUSE FOR
MENTAL HEALTH**
NATIONAL INSTITUTION OF
MENTAL HEALTH
BETHESDA, MD 20014
See Social Sciences/Humanities: Mental
Health; Government-Federal

**NATIONAL INDUSTRIAL
POLLUTION CONTROL COUNCIL**
5111 BATTERY LANE
BETHESDA, MD 20014
See Engineering: Pollution Abatement;
Government-Federal

**NATIONAL OCEANIC AND
ATMOSPHERIC
ADMINISTRATION**
DEPARTMENT OF COMMERCE
ROCKVILLE, MD 20910
See Interdisciplinary: General; Unclassified

**NATIONAL OCEANIC AND
ATMOSPHERIC
ADMINISTRATION**
8306 MELODY CENTER
BETHESDA, MD 20034
See Interdisciplinary: General; Unclassified

**NATIONAL OCEANOGRAPHIC AND
ATMOSPHERIC
ADMINISTRATION**
8060 13TH STREET
SILVER SPRING, MD 20910
See Biology: Ecology; Government-Federal

**NEUROCHEMISTRY LABORATORY,
NEUROLOGICAL DISEASES
INSTITUTE**
NATIONAL INSTITUTES OF
HEALTH- PUBLIC HEALTH
SERVICE
BETHESDA, MD 20014
See Biology: Biochemistry; Government-Federal

**OCCUPATIONAL SAFETY AND
HEALTH BUREAU**
12720 TWINBROOK PARKWAY
ROCKVILLE, MD 20852
See Interdisciplinary: General; Government-State or Local

OCEAN SURVEYS (NATIONAL)
NATIONAL OCEANIC AND
ATMOSPHERIC ADMINISTRATION
ROCKVILLE, MD 20852
See Geology: General; Government-Federal

**OCEANOGRAPHY INSTITUTE,
ENVIRONMENTAL SCIENCES
SERVICES ADMINISTRA**
GRAMAX BUILDING, 8060 13TH
STREET
SILVER SPRING, MD 20910
See Biology: General; Government-Federal

**OCEANOGRAPHY, JOHNS HOPKINS
UNIVERSITY, CHESAPEAKE BAY
INSTITUTION**
CHARLES AND 34TH STREETS
BALTIMORE, MD 21218
See Biology: General; Educational Institute

**ORNITHOLOGICAL SOCIETY OF
MARYLAND**
4915 GREENSPRING AVENUE
BALTIMORE, MD 21209
See Biology: General; Professional Organizations

**PESTICIDE CONTROL, STATE
INSPECTION SERVICE**
UNIVERSITY OF MARYLAND
COLLEGE PARK, MD 20742
See Engineering: Chemical Engineering;
Government-State or Local

**PESTICIDE REGULATION
DIVISION, AGRICULTURE
DEPARTMENT**
BUILDING 402 AGRICULTURAL
RESOURCES CENTER
BELTSVILLE, MD 20705
See Engineering: Chemical Engineering;
Government-State or Local

PLANT INDUSTRY STATION
SOIL AND WATER CONSERVATION
RESOURCES
BELTSVILLE, MD 20705
See Interdisciplinary: General; Unclassified

**PLANT SCIENCE RESEARCH
DIVISION**
1714 EDGEWATER PARKWAY
SILVER SPRING, MD 20904
See Biology: Ecology; Government-Federal

**PLANT SCIENCES AND
ENTOMOLOGY**
3907 BEECHWOOD ROAD

HYATTSVILLE, MD 20782
See Biology: Ecology; Government-Federal

**POPULATION AND FAMILY
HEALTH DEPARTMENT**
JOHNS HOPKINS UNIVERSITY
BALTIMORE, MD 21205
See Social Sciences/Humanities: Population Studies/Family Planning; Educational Institute

POPULATION RESEARCH CENTER
NATIONAL INSTITUTES OF HEALTH
BETHESDA, MD 20014
See Interdisciplinary: General; Unclassified

PUBLIC INFORMATION OFFICE
WASHINGTON SCIENCES CENTER,
BUILDING 5
ROCKVILLE, MD 20852
See Interdisciplinary: General; Unclassified

**RADIATION BIOLOGY
LABORATORY**
7901 KENTBURY DR
BETHESDA, MD 20014
See Biology: General; Government-Federal

**RADIATION PROGRAMS OFFICE,
ENVIRONMENTAL PROTECTION
AGENCY**
5600 FISHERS LANE, ROOM 18B46
ROCKVILLE, MD 20852
See Interdisciplinary: General; Unclassified

**RADIOBIOLOGICAL LABORATORY,
ARMED FORCES, DEPARTMENT
OF DEFENSE**
NATIONAL NAVAL MEDICAL
CENTER
BETHESDA, MD 20014
See Biology: General; Government-Federal

RADIOLOGICAL HEALTH BUREAU
12720 TWINBROOK PARKWAY
ROCKVILLE, MD 20852
See Biology: General; Government-Federal

**REACTOR DEVELOPMENT AND
TECHNOLOGY DIVISION**
UNITED STATES ATOMIC ENERGY
COMMISSION
GERMANTOWN, MD 20545
See Engineering: Water Resources; Government-Federal

RECLAMATION BUREAU
12821 HUNTSMAN WAY
POTOMAC, MD 20854
See Biology: Ecology; Government-Federal

RESEARCH AND TRAINING GRANTS
8120 WOODMONT AVENUE
BETHESDA, MD 20014
See Engineering: Pollution Abatement;
Government-Federal

RESEARCH GRANTS DIVISION
NATIONAL INSTITUTES OF HEALTH
BETHESDA, MD 20014
See Interdisciplinary: General; Research
Institute

**RESEARCH INSTITUTE FOR
ADVANCE STUDY**
1450 SOUTH ROLLING ROAD
BALTIMORE, MD 21227
See Interdisciplinary: General; Research
Institute

RESEARCH SUPPORT BRANCH
NATIONAL INSTITUTES OF HEALTH
BETHESDA, MD 20014
See Interdisciplinary: General; Unclassi-
fied

**SANITARY ENGINEERING AND
WATER RESOURCES
DEPARTMENT**
JOHNS HOPKINS UNIVERSITY, 513
AMES
BALTIMORE, MD 21218
See Engineering: General; Educational
Institute

SEA GRANTS OFFICE
NATIONAL OCEANIC AND
ATMOSPHERIC ADMINISTRATION
ROCKVILLE, MD 20852
See Engineering: Water Resources; Gov-
ernment-Federal

**SOIL AND WATER CONSERVATION
AND RESOURCES DIVISION**
PLANT INDUSTRY STATION, US
DEPARTMENT OF AGRICULTURE
BELTSVILLE, MD 20705
See Engineering: Water Resources; Gov-
ernment-Federal

**SOIL AND WATER CONSERVATION
RESOURCES DIVISION**
8601 LAVERNE DRIVE
HYATTSVILLE, MD 20783
See Interdisciplinary: General; Unclassi-
fied

**SOIL CLASS AND CORRELATION
DIVISION**
4613 BEECHWOOD ROAD
COLLEGE PARK, MD 20740
See Engineering: Agricultural Engineer-
ing; Government-Federal

**SOIL CONSERVATION SERVICE,
SOIL SURVEY**
111 DEVERE DRIVE
SILVER SPRING, MD 20903
See Engineering: Agricultural Engineer-
ing; Government-Federal

SOIL CONSERVATION SERVICES
ROOM 522, HARTWICK BUILDING,
4321 HARTWICK ROAD
COLLEGE PARK, MD 20740
See Biology: Ecology; Government-State
or Local

**SOIL SURVEY INTERPRETATION
DIVISION**
915 NEWHALL STREET
SILVER SPRING, MD 20901
See Engineering: Agricultural Engineer-
ing; Government-Federal

**SOIL SURVEY INVESTIGATIONS
DIVISION**
64 40TH AVENUE
UNIVERSITY PARK, MD 20782
See Engineering: Agricultural Engineer-
ing; Government-Federal

SOIL, WATER AND ENGINEERING
8303 CURRY PLACE
ADELPHI, MD 20783
See Interdisciplinary: General; Unclassified

**SOLID WASTE MANAGEMENT
BUREAU**
12720 TWINBROOK PARKWAY
ROCKVILLE, MD 20852
See Engineering: Water Resources; Gov-
ernment-Federal

**SOLID WASTE MANAGEMENT
PROGRAMS**
5016 BALTIC AVENUE
ROCKVILLE, MD 20853
See Biology: Ecology; Government-Fed-
eral

**STATIONARY SOURCE
ENFORCEMENT DIVISION**
ENVIRONMENTAL PROTECTION
AGENCY
ROCKVILLE, MD 20852
See Interdisciplinary: General; Unclassi-
fied

**STATISTICAL RESEARCH AND
RECORDS BUREAU, HEALTH
DEPARTMENT**
301 PRESTON STREET
BALTIMORE,MD 21201
See Social Sciences/Humanities: Popula-
tion Studies/Family Planning; Govern-
ment-State or Local

**TECHNOLOGY INFORMATION
DEPARTMENT, BIOLOGICAL, US
DEPARTMENT OF THE ARMY**
FORT DETRICK
FREDERICK, MD 21701
See Biology: General; Government-Fed-
eral

WATER RESOURCES CENTER
UNIVERSITY OF MARYLAND,
SHRIVER LABORATORY
COLLEGE PK, MD 20740
See Engineering: Water Resources; Edu-
cational Institute

WATER RESOURCES DEPARTMENT
STATE OFFICE BUILDING
ANNAPOLIS, MD 21401
See Engineering: Water Resources; Gov-
ernment-State or Local

**WATER SUPPLY BUREAU,
DEPARTMENT**
3001 DRUID PARK DRIVE
BALTIMORE, MD 21215
See Engineering: Water Resources; Gov-
ernment-State or Local

WEATHER BUREAU
8060 13TH STREET
SILVER SPRING, MD 20910
See Physics: General; Government-Federal

**WILDLIFE FEDERATION OF
MARYLAND**
1002 WOODLAND WAY
HAGERSTOWN, MD 21740
See Biology: Ecology; Foundation

**WILDLIFE RESEARCH CENTER,
PATUXENT**
LAUREL, MD 20810
See Biology: Ecology; Government-Fed-
eral

**WILSON ORNITHOLOGICAL
SOCIETY**
8728 OXWELL LANE
LAUREL, MD 20810
See Interdisciplinary: General; Profession-
al Organizations

Maine

**AGRICULTURAL AND
CONSERVATION COMMISSION**
DOVER-FOXCRAFT KIWANIS CLUB
DOVER-FOXCROFT, ME 04426
See Biology: Ecology; Government-State
or Local

APPALACHIAN MOUNTAIN CLUB
21 COLUMBIA AVENUE
BRUNSWICK, ME 04011
See Biology: Ecology; Government-State
or Local

**ARROWSIC MARSHLANDS
ASSOCIATION**
SPINNEY MILL ROAD
ARROWSIC, ME 04530
See Biology: Ecology; Government-State
or Local

AUDUBON NATURALIST COUNCIL
BOX 509
BRUNSWICK, ME 04011
See Biology: Ecology; Foundation

AUDUBON SOCIETY OF MAINE
22 ELM STREET
PORTLAND, ME 04111
See Biology: Ecology; Foundation

AUDUBON SOCIETY OF MAINE
2203 BROADWAY
BANGOR, ME 04401
See Biology: Ecology; Foundation

AUDUBON SOCIETY OF MAINE
57 BAXTER BOULEVARD
PORTLAND, ME 04101
See Biology: Ecology; Foundation

**AUDUBON SOCIETY OF
  MERRYMEETING**
BOX 255
BRUNSWICK, ME 04011
See Biology: Ecology; Foundation

**AUDUBON SOCIETY OF YORK
  COUNTY**
BRUEN PLACE
KENNEBUNK BEACH, ME 04045
See Biology: Ecology; Foundation

BIOLOGISTS STATE ASSOCIATION
BOX 646
SANFORD, ME 04073
See Biology: General; Professional Organizations

**BIOLOGY LABORATORY,
  NATIONAL MARINE FISHERIES
  SERVICES**
NATIONAL OCEANIC AND
ATMOSPHERIC ADMINISTRATION
WEST BOOTHBAY HARBOR, ME
04575
See Biology: Ecology; Government-Federal

**BISCAY POND ASSOCIATION,
  INCORPORATED**
BRISTOL, ME 04539
See Biology: Ecology; Government-State
or Local

**CLEAN WATER INITIATIVE
  COMMISSION**
7 BARROWS STREET
BRUNSWICK, ME 04011
See Engineering: Water Resources; Government-State or Local

**COASTAL RESOURCES ACTION
  COMMISSION**
465 CONGRESS STREET, ROOM 507
PORTLAND, ME 04111
See Biology: Ecology; Government-State
or Local

**CONSERVATION ASSOCIATION
  INCORPORATED AT SHEEPSCOT
  VALLEY**
POST OFFICE BOX 125
ALNA, ME 04535
See Interdisciplinary: General; Educational Institute

**CONSERVATION ASSOCIATION OF
  KENNEBEC VALLEY**
POST OFFICE BOX 525

SKOWHEGAN, ME 04976
See Biology: Ecology; Government-State
or Local

**CONSERVATION BILL OF RIGHTS
  COUNCIL OF MAINE**
115-A STEVENS HALL, UNIVERSITY
OF MAINE
ORONO, ME 04473
See Biology: Ecology; Government-State
or Local

**CONSERVATION SOCIETY OF PINE
  TREE**
435 CONGRESS STREET
PORTLAND, ME 04111
See Biology: Ecology; Government-State
or Local

**CULTURAL AND HISTORICAL
  SOCIETY OF LINCOLN COUNTY**
BOX 61
WISCASSET, ME 04578
See Biology: Ecology; Government-State
or Local

**DESIGN AND LANDMARKS,
  INCORPORATED**
BUNGANUC ROAD
BRUNSWICK, ME 04011
See Biology: Ecology; Government-State
or Local

**DEVELOPMENT ASSOCIATION OF
  CASCO BAY ISLAND**
PEAKS ISLAND, ME 04108
See Biology: Ecology; Government-State
or Local

ECOLOGY ACTION NOTES
125 SILK STREET
BREWER, ME 04412
See Biology: Ecology; Government-State
or Local

EFFLUENT SOCIETY
MEMORIAL UNION, UNIVERSITY
OF MAINE
ORONO, ME 04473
See Biology: Ecology; Educational Institute

**ENVIRONMENTAL HEALTH
  ASSOCIATION, NATIONAL**
NORTH MAIN STREET
BREWER, ME 04412
See Interdisciplinary: General; Government-State or Local

**ENVIRONMENTAL IMPROVEMENT
  COMMISSION**
AUGUSTA, ME 04330
See Engineering: Pollution Abatement;
Government-State or Local

ENVIRONMENTAL QUALITY
15 GLIDDEN STREET
WATERVILLE, ME 04091
See Biology: Ecology; Government-State
or Local

**ENVIRONMENTAL STUDIES
  CENTER**
UNIVERSITY OF MAINE
ORONO, ME 04473
See Interdisciplinary: General; Educational Institute

**ENVIRONMENTAL STUDIES
  PROGRAM**
BATES COLLEGE
LEWISTON, ME 04240
See Chemistry: General; Educational Institute

**ENVIRONMENTAL STUDIES
  PROGRAM**
BOWDOIN COLLEGE
BRUNSWICK, ME 04011
See Chemistry: General; Educational Institute

**ENVIRONMENTAL STUDIES
  PROGRAM**
COLBY COLLEGE
WATERVILLE, ME 04901
See Chemistry: General; Educational Institute

**GARDEN CLUB FEDERATION OF
  MAINE**
VILLA INTERLAKEN
FOREST BROOKTON, ME 04413
See Biology: Ecology; Government-State
or Local

**INFORMATION AND EDUCATION
  DIVISION, MAINE FOREST
  DEPARTMENT**
STATE OFFICE BUILDING
AUGUSTA, ME 04330
See Engineering: Water Resources; Government-State or Local

KEEP OIL OUT
BOX 3721
PORTLAND, ME 04104
See Biology: Ecology; Professional Organizations

LAKE ASSOCIATION OF CHINA
LAKEVIEW DRIVE
SOUTH CHINA, ME 04538
See Biology: Ecology; Government-State
or Local

**LAKE ASSOCIATION OF
  DAMARISCOTTA**
ROAD ONE, BOX 126
NEWCASTLE, ME 04553
See Biology: Ecology; Government-State
or Local

**LANDGUARD TRUST,
  INCORPORATED**
103 EXCHANGE STREET
PORTLAND, ME 04111
See Biology: Ecology; Government-State
or Local

MID-COAST AUDUBON
WALDOBORO, ME 04572
See Biology: Ecology; Government-State or Local

MOUNTAIN DESERT ISLAND BIRD CLUB
SALISBURY COVE, ME 04672
See Biology: Ecology; Government-State or Local

MUNICIPAL GOVERNMENT RESEARCH BUREAU
HUBBARD HALL, BOWDOIN COLLEGE
BRUNSWICK, ME 04011
See Social Sciences/Humanities: Law/Legislation; Educational Institute

NATIONAL WILDLIFE
REGION 1
BAR HARBOR, ME 04609
See Biology: Ecology; Foundation

NATURAL FOODS ASSOCIATES
229 CONY STREET
AUGUSTA, ME 04330
See Interdisciplinary: General; Educational Institute

NATURAL RESOURCES COUNCIL OF MAINE
20 WILLOW STREET
AUGUSTA, ME 04330
See Interdisciplinary: General; Research Institute

NATURE CLUB OF AUGUSTA
186 GREEN STREET
AUGUSTA, ME 04330
See Biology: Ecology; Government-State or Local

NATURE CONSERVANCY
MANCHESTER, ME 04351
See Biology: Ecology; Foundation

NATURE CONSERVANCY
465 CONGRESS STREET
PORTLAND, ME 04111
See Biology: Ecology; Foundation

NATURE PROGRAMS FOR MCCLELLAN PARK CHILDREN
MILLBRIDGE, ME 04658
See Biology: Ecology; Government-State or Local

PENOBSCOT RIVER OIL POLLUTION ABATEMENT COMMISSION
101 BARROWS HALL, UNIVERSITY OF MAINE
ORONO, ME 04473
See Engineering: Pollution Abatement; Educational Institute

POLLUTION ABATEMENT COMMISSION
COMMERCIAL STREET

PORTLAND, ME 04111
See Engineering: Pollution Abatement; Government-State or Local

PRESERVATION TRUST OF VAUGINS ISLAND
KENNEBUNK, ME 04046
See Biology: Ecology; Professional Organizations

SANITARY ENGINEERING DEPARTMENT
STATEHOUSE
AUGUSTA, ME 04330
See Engineering: Pollution Abatement; Government-State or Local

SCIENTIFIC STATION AT BOWDOIN
BOWDOIN COLLEGE
BRUNSWICK, ME 04011
See Biology: Ecology; Field Station/Laboratory

SIERRA CLUB OF MAINE
POST OFFICE BOX 1324
BANGOR, ME 04401
See Biology: Ecology; Foundation

SOIL AND WATER CONSERVATION ASSOCIATION OF MAINE
R F D
EAST CORNINTH, ME 04427
See Interdisciplinary: General; Government-State or Local

SOIL CONSERVATION SERVICE
DEPARTMENT OF AGRICULTURE BUILDING, UNIVERSITY OF MAINE
ORONO, ME 04473
See Interdisciplinary: General; Unclassified

THOREAU FELLOWSHIP
POST OFFICE BOX 551
OLD TOWN, ME 04468
See Biology: Ecology; Foundation

TREFETHEN EVERGREEN IMPROVEMENT ASSOCIATION
BOARD OF GOVERNORS
PEAKS ISLAND, ME 04108
See Biology: Ecology; Government-State or Local

TUBERCULOSIS AND HEALTH ASSOCIATION OF MAINE
20 WILLOW STREET
AUGUSTA, ME 04330
See Interdisciplinary: General; Government-State or Local

VILLAGE IMPROVEMENT ASSOCIATION
MUNICIPAL BUILDING
BRUNSWICK, ME 04011
See Biology: Ecology; Government-State or Local

WATER AND AIR ENVIRONMENTAL IMPROVEMENT COMMISSION
STATE HOUSE
AUGUSTA, ME 04330
See Engineering: Pollution Abatement; Government-State or Local

WATER RESOURCES CENTER
212-214 LORD HALL
ORONO, ME 04473
See Engineering: Water Resources; Educational Institute

WATER RESOURCES DIVISION, MAINE PUBLIC UTILITIES COMMISSION
STATE HOUSE
AUGUSTA, ME 04330
See Engineering: Water Resources; Government-State or Local

WILDFLOWER PRESERVATION SOCIETY OF NEW ENGLAND
6 PLEASANT STREET
CAMDEN, ME 04843
See Biology: Ecology; Government-State or Local

WOMEN'S CLUBS, MAINE FEDERATION
37 MCLAUGHLIN STREET
BANGOR, ME 04401
See Interdisciplinary: General; Government-State or Local

ZERO POPULATION GROWTH
BOX 124
ORONO, ME 04473
See Social Sciences/Humanities: Population Studies/Family Planning; Foundation

ZERO POPULATION GROWTH
BOX 147
BRUNSWICK, ME 04011
See Social Sciences/Humanities: Population Studies/Family Planning; Foundation

Michigan

AGRICULTURAL AND NATURAL RESOURCES COLLEGE
MICHIGAN STATE UNIVERSITY
EAST LANSING, MI 48823
See Engineering: Agricultural Engineering; Educational Institute

AGRICULTURAL ENGINEERS (AMERICAN SOCIETY OF)
2950 NILES ROAD
ST JOSEPH, MI 49085
See Engineering: Agricultural Engineering; Professional Organizations

AIR POLLUTION BOARD
CITY HALL, MICHIGAN AVENUE
LANSING, MI 48933
See Engineering: Pollution Abatement;
Government-State or Local

**AIR POLLUTION CONTROL
BUREAU**
CITY HALL
ALPENA, MI 49707
See Engineering: Pollution Abatement;
Government-State or Local

**AIR POLLUTION CONTROL,
BUILDING AND SAFETY
DIVISION**
4500 MAPLE AVENUE
DEARBORN, MI 48126
See Engineering: Pollution Abatement;
Government-State or Local

**AIR POLLUTION CONTROL,
BUILDING INSPECTION
DEPARTMENT**
151 MARTIN STREET
BIRMINGHAM, MI 48012
See Engineering: Pollution Abatement;
Government-State or Local

**AIR POLLUTION CONTROL,
BUILDINGS AND SAFETY
ENGINEERING DEPARTMENT**
100 NORTH FIFTH STREET
ANN ARBOR, MI 48108
See Engineering: Pollution Abatement;
Government-State or Local

**AIR POLLUTION CONTROL,
BUILDINGS DEPARTMENT**
241 WEST SOUTH STREET
KALAMAZOO, MI 49006
See Engineering: Pollution Abatement;
Government-State or Local

**AIR POLLUTION CONTROL, CITY
ENGINEERING OFFICE**
994 BIDDLE AVENUE
WYANDOTTE, MI 48192
See Engineering: Pollution Abatement;
Government-State or Local

**AIR POLLUTION CONTROL,
COUNTY HEALTH DEPARTMENT**
COUNTY BUILDING, TERRACE
STREET
MUSKEGON, MI 49440
See Engineering: Pollution Abatement;
Government-State or Local

**AIR POLLUTION CONTROL,
COUNTY HEALTH DEPARTMENT**
MERRIMAN ROAD
ELOISE, MI 48132
See Engineering: Pollution Abatement;
Government-State or Local

**AIR POLLUTION CONTROL,
HAMTRACK FIRE DEPARTMENT**
8523 JOSEPH CAMPAU AVENUE
HAMTRACK, MI 48212
See Engineering: Pollution Abatement;
Government-State or Local

**AIR POLLUTION CONTROL,
HEALTH DEPARTMENT**
414 CITY-COUNTY BUILDING
DETROIT, MI 48226
See Engineering: Pollution Abatement;
Government-State or Local

**AIR POLLUTION CONTROL,
PUBLIC HEALTH DEPARTMENT**
3500 NORTH LOGAN STREET
LANSING, MI 48914
See Engineering: Pollution Abatement;
Government-State or Local

**AIR POLLUTION CONTROL,
PUBLIC WORKS AND UTILITIES
DEPARTMENT**
1101 SOUTH SAGINAW, ROOM 210
FLINT, MI 48502
See Engineering: Pollution Abatement;
Government-State or Local

**AIR POLLUTION DEPARTMENT,
COMMUNITY IMPROVEMENT
AND INSPECTION SERVICE**
509 WEALTHY STREET
GRAND RAPIDS, MI 49503
See Engineering: Pollution Abatement;
Government-State or Local

**AIR POLLUTION REGULATION,
PUBLIC WORKS DEPARTMENT**
ROOM 109, CITY HALL
BATTLECREEK, MI 49014
See Engineering: Pollution Abatement;
Government-State or Local

AUDUBON SOCIETY OF MICHIGAN
7000 NORTH WESTNEDGE AVENUE
KALAMAZOO, MI 49007
See Biology: Ecology; Foundation

AUTOMOTIVE EMMISSIONS, FORD
WORLD HEADQUARTERS,
AMERICAN ROAD
DEARBORN, MI 48121
See Engineering: Pollution Abatement;
Industrial/Commercial

**AUTOMOTIVE ENGINEERING
LABORATORY**
UNIVERSITY OF MICHIGAN,
NORTH CAMPUS
ANN ARBOR, MI 48104
See Engineering: Pollution Abatement;
Educational Institute

**BELL TELEPHONE COMPANY OF
MICHIGAN**
220 BAGLEY STREET, ROOM 850
DETROIT, MI 48226
See Social Sciences/Humanities: Industrial Development; Industrial/Com-
mercial

**BOTANICAL CLUB OF MICHIGAN,
INCORPORATED**
1800 DIXBORO ROAD
ANN ARBOR, MI 48105
See Biology: Ecology; Professional Organ-
izations

**BUILDING INSPECTION
DEPARTMENT, HEATING AND
AIR POLLUTION DEPARTMENT**
CITY HALL, WASHINGTON AVENUE
BAY CITY, MI 48706
See Engineering: Pollution Abatement;
Government-State or Local

**BUSINESS RESEARCH BUREAU,
BUSINESS ADMINISTRATION
SCHOOL**
UNIVERSITY OF MICHIGAN
ANN ARBOR, MI 48104
See Social Sciences/Humanities: Indus-
trial Development; Educational Insti-
tute

**COMMUNITY DEVELOPMENT
INSTITUTE**
MICHIGAN STATE UNIVERSITY
EAST LANSING, MI 48823
See Social Sciences/Humanities: Commu-
nity Development/Studies; Education-
al Institute

CONSERVATION CITIZENS
3535 MOORES RIVER DRIVE
LANSING, MI 48910
See Interdisciplinary: General; Foundation

**CONSERVATION UNITED OF
MICHIGAN**
BOX 2235
LANSING, MI 48911
See Biology: Ecology; Foundation

**DETREX INDUSTRIAL CHEMISTRY,
INCORPORATED**
POST OFFICE BOX 501
DETROIT, MI 48232
See Chemistry: General; Industrial/Com-
mercial

**EMISSION CONTROL, GENERAL
MOTORS**
12 MILE AND MOUND ROADS
WARREN, MI 48090
See Engineering: Pollution Abatement;
Industrial/Commercial

**ENGINEERING-TRANSPORTATION
LIBRARY**
UNIVERSITY OF MICHIGAN
ANN ARBOR,MI 48104
See Social Sciences/Humanities: Trans-
portation; Educational Institute

**ENVIRONMENTAL AND HEALTH
INSTITUTE**
W5634 UNIVERSITY HOSPITAL
ANN ARBOR, MI 48100
See Biology: General; Unclassified

**ENVIRONMENTAL CONTROL,
FORD MOTOR COMPANY**
THE AMERICA ROAD
DEARBORN, MI 48121
See Engineering: General; Industrial/
Commercial

ENVIRONMENTAL EDUCATION, MADONNA COLLEGE
36600 SCHOOLCRAFT
LIVONIA, MI 48150
See Biology: Ecology; Educational Institute

ENVIRONMENTAL INFORMATION COMMITTEE OF MICHIGAN
P O BOX 2281
GRAND RAPIDS, MI 49501
See Interdisciplinary: General; Government-State or Local

ENVIRONMENTAL PROTECTION AGENCY LABORATORY
GROSSE ILE, MI 48138
See Biology: Ecology; Field Station/Laboratory

ENVIRONMENTAL SCIENCE PROGRAM
ALBION COLLEGE
ALBION, MI 49224
See Interdisciplinary: General; Educational Institute

ENVIRONMENTAL SCIENCE PROGRAM
EASTERN MICHIGAN UNIVERSITY
YPSILANTI, MI 48197
See Interdisciplinary: General; Educational Institute

ENVIRONMENTAL SCIENCE PROGRAM
KALAMAZOO COLLEGE
KALAMAZOO, MI 49001
See Chemistry: General; Educational Institute

ENVIRONMENTAL SCIENCE PROGRAM
MICHIGAN TECHNOLOGICAL UNIVERSITY
HOUGHTON, MI 49931
See Interdisciplinary: General; Educational Institute

ENVIRONMENTAL SCIENCE PROGRAM
WAYNE STATE UNIVERSITY
DETROIT, MI 48202
See Interdisciplinary: General; Educational Institute

ENVIRONMENTAL STUDIES
OAKLAND UNIVERSITY
ROCHESTER, MI 48063
See Interdisciplinary: General; Educational Institute

ENVIRONMENTAL STUDIES PROGRAM
ALPENA COMMUNITY COLLEGE
ALPENA, MI 49707
See Engineering: Water Resources; Educational Institute

ENVIRONMENTAL STUDIES PROGRAM
CENTRAL MICHIGAN UNIVERSITY
MT PLEASANT, MI 48858
See Interdisciplinary: General; Educational Institute

ENVIRONMENTAL STUDIES PROGRAM
MICHIGAN STATE UNIVERSITY
EAST LANSING, MI 48823
See Interdisciplinary: General; Educational Institute

ENVIRONMENTAL STUDIES PROGRAM
NORTHERN MICHIGAN UNIVERSITY
MARQUETTER, MI 49855
See Interdisciplinary: General; Educational Institute

ENVIRONMENTAL STUDIES PROGRAM
UNIVERSITY OF MICHIGAN
ANN ARBOR, MI 48104
See Interdisciplinary: General; Educational Institute

ENVIRONMENTAL STUDIES PROGRAM
4001 W MCNICHOLS ROAD
DETROIT, MI 48221
See Interdisciplinary: General; Educational Institute

EXPLORATORY FISHING AND GEAR RESOURCES BASE
5 RESEARCH DRIVE
ANN ARBOR, MI 48103
See Engineering: Water Resources; Government-Federal

FOOD SCIENCES AND HUMAN NUTRITION DEPARTMENT
MICHIGAN STATE UNIVERSITY
EAST LANSING, MI 48823
See Interdisciplinary: General; Educational Institute

GOVERNMENT LIBRARY BUREAU, UNIVERSITY OF MICHIGAN
100-A RACKHAM BUILDING
ANN ARBOR, MI 48104
See Social Sciences/Humanities: Law/Legislation; Educational Institute

GREAT LAKES FISHERY LABORATORY
1451 GREEN ROAD, P O BOX 640
ANN ARBOR, MI 48107
See Biology: General; Government-Federal

HEALTH STATISTICS CENTER
3500 NORTH LOGAN STREET
LANSING, MI 48914
See Engineering: General; Government-State or Local

HIGHER EDUCATION STUDY CENTER
UNIVERSITY OF MICHIGAN
ANN ARBOR, MI 48104
See Social Sciences/Humanities: Education; Educational Institute

HIGHWAY SAFETY RESEARCH INSTITUTE, UNIVERSITY OF MICHIGAN
HURON PARKWAY AND BAXTER ROAD
ANN ARBOR, MI 48105
See Social Sciences/Humanities: Transportation; Research Institute

HOSPITAL, DETROIT GENERAL
1326 ANTOINE STREET
DETROIT, MI 48226
See Biology: Ecology; Government-State or Local

HUMAN BEHAVIOR RESEARCH FOUNDATION
508 EAST WILLIAM STREET
ANN ARBOR, MI 48108
See Social Sciences/Humanities: Psychology/Behavioral Science; Foundation

INDUSTRIAL HYGIENE ASSOCIATION
14125 PREVOST
DETROIT, MI 48227
See Social Sciences/Humanities: Industrial Development; Professional Organizations

INDUSTRIAL RELATIONS BUREAU, BUSINESS ADMINISTRATION SCHOOL
UNIVERSITY OF MICHIGAN
ANN ARBOR, MI 48104
See Social Sciences/Humanities: Labor/Relations/Unions; Educational Institute

INTERPRETIVE NATURE ASSOCIATION
5956 NORTH HAGADORN ROAD
EAST LANSING, MI 48823
See Interdisciplinary: General; Foundation

LABOR COLLEGE, DETROIT PUBLIC LIBRARY
5201 WOODWARD STREET
DETROIT, MI 48202
See Social Sciences/Humanities: Labor/Relations/Unions; Research Institute

LAKE ERIE CLEANUP COMMISSION, INCORPORATED
3003 11TH STREET
MONROE, MI 48161
See Engineering: Pollution Abatement; Professional Organizations

LIMNOLOGY AND OCEANOGRAPHY SOCIETY OF AMERICA
UNIVERSITY OF MICHIGAN

ANN ARBOR, MI 48104
See Interdisciplinary: General; Professional Organizations

MECHANICAL ENGINEERING DEPARTMENT
UNIVERSITY OF MICHIGAN, NORTH CAMPUS
ANN ARBOR, MI 48104
See Engineering: Pollution Abatement; Educational Institute

MENTAL HEALTH RESEARCH INSTITUTE, MICHIGAN UNIVERSITY
205 NORTH FOREST
ANN ARBOR, MI 48104
See Social Sciences/Humanities: Mental Health; Educational Institute

MENTAL HEALTH RESOURCES INSTITUTE
UNIVERSITY OF MICHIGAN, MEDICAL SCHOOL
ANN ARBOR, MI 48104
See Social Sciences/Humanities: Mental Health; Educational Institute

METROPOLITAN REGIONAL PLANNING COMMISSION
800 CADILLAC SQUARE BUILDING
DETROIT, MI 48226
See Social Sciences/Humanities: Regional Planning; Government-State or Local

MINERAL RESOURCES INSTITUTE
MICHIGAN TECHNOLOGY UNIVERSITY
HOUGHTON, MI 49931
See Geology: General; Research Institute

MOBILE SOURCE POLLUTION CONTROL PROGRAM
2565 PLYMOUTH ROAD
ANN ARBOR, MI 48105
See Interdisciplinary: General; Unclassified

NATIONAL SANITATION FOUNDATION, SCHOOL OF PUBLIC HEALTH
MICHIGAN UNIVERSITY, P O BOX 1468
ANN ARBOR, MI 48104
See Engineering: Pollution Abatement; Government-Federal

NATURAL AREAS COUNCIL OF MICHIGAN
1800 NORTH DIXBORO ROAD
ANN ARBOR, MI 48105
See Biology: Ecology; Professional Organizations

NATURAL RESOURCE COUNCIL OF MICHIGAN
MASON BUILDING, DEPARTMENT OF NATURAL RESOURCES
LANSING, MI 48926
See Biology: Ecology; Professional Organizations

NATURAL RESOURCES DEPARTMENT
ALPENA COMMUNITY COLLEGE
ALPENA, MI 49707
See Interdisciplinary: General; Educational Institute

NATURAL RESOURCES SCHOOL
UNIVERSITY OF MICHIGAN
ANN ARBOR, MI 48101
See Biology: General; Educational Institute

NATURE STUDY SOCIETY OF AMERICA
1501 GRANADA BOULEVARD
ANN ARBOR, MI 48103
See Interdisciplinary: General; Professional Organizations

OCCUPATIONAL AND ENVIRONMENTAL HEALTH DEPARTMENT
WAYNE STATE UNIVERSITY, MEDICAL SCHOOL
DETROIT, MI 48207
See Biology: Ecology; Educational Institute

PATHOLOGY DEPARTMENT, UNIVERSITY OF MICHIGAN
1335 EAST CATHERINE STREET
ANN ARBOR, MI 48104
See Interdisciplinary: General; Educational Institute

PESTICIDE CONTROL, LABORATORY DIVISION, STATE DEPARTMENT OF AGRICULTURE
1615 SOUTH HARRISON ROAD
EAST LANSING, MI 48823
See Engineering: Agricultural Engineering; Government-State or Local

PHARMACOLOGY DEPARTMENT
MICHIGAN STATE UNIVERSITY
EAST LANSING, MI 48823
See Biology: Biochemistry; Educational Institute

POLLUTION RESEARCH CONSORTIUM
P O BOX 1248
ANN ARBOR, MI 48106
See Social Sciences/Humanities: Law/Legislation; Research Institute

POPULATION STUDIES CENTER
UNIVERSITY OF MICHIGAN
ANN ARBOR, MI 48104
See Social Sciences/Humanities: Population Studies/Family Planning; Educational Institute

PUBLIC AFFAIRS INSTITUTE
WESTERN MICHIGAN UNIVERSITY
KALAMAZOO, MI 49001
See Interdisciplinary: General; Research Institute

PUBLIC HEALTH SCHOOL
UNIVERSITY OF MICHIGAN
ANN ARBOR, MI 48104
See Engineering: Pollution Abatement; Educational Institute

PUBLIC WORKS DEPARTMENT OF DETROIT
528 CITY-COUNTY BUILDING
DETROIT, MI 48226
See Engineering: Water Resources; Government-State or Local

SCIENCE TECHNOLOGY INSTITUTE, GREAT LAKES DIVISION
NORTH UNIVERSITY BUILDING, UNIVERSITY MICHIGAN
ANN ARBOR, MI 48104
See Engineering: General; Educational Institute

SLUM PREVENTION AND SMOKE ABATEMENT
1381 COOLIDGE HIGHWAY
RIVER ROUGE, MI 48218
See Biology: Ecology; Government-State or Local

SMOKE AND AIR POLLUTION ADVISORY BOARD
2872 WEST JEFFERSON STREET
TRENTON, MI 48183
See Engineering: Pollution Abatement; Government-State or Local

SMOKE INSPECTION DEPARTMENT
CITY HALL
MONROE, MI 48161
See Engineering: Pollution Abatement; Government-State or Local

SOCIAL ORGANIZATIONS RESOURCES CENTER, DEPARTMENT OF SOCIOLOGY
UNIVERSITY OF MICHIGAN
ANN ARBOR, MI 48104
See Social Sciences/Humanities: General; Educational Institute

SOCIAL RESEARCH INSTITUTE
UNIVERSITY OF MICHIGAN
ANN ARBOR, MI 48104
See Social Sciences/Humanities: General; Educational Institute

SOCIAL WELFARE DEPARTMENT, RESEARCH DIVISION
LEWIS CASE BUILDING
LANSING, MI 48913
See Social Sciences/Humanities: Welfare(Child Public Social); Government-State or Local

SOCIAL WORK SCHOOL
UNIVERSITY MICHIGAN
ANN ARBOR, MI 48104
See Social Sciences/Humanities: Education; Educational Institute

SOIL CONSERVATION SERVICE
1405 SOUTH HARRISON ROAD
EAST LANSING, MI 48823
See Biology: Ecology; Government-State
or Local

**THEORETICAL AND APPLIED
LIMNOLOGY ASSOCIATION
(INTERNATIONAL)**
KELLOGG BIOLOGICAL STATION,
MICHIGAN STATE UNIVERSITY
HICKORY CORNERS, MI 49060
See Biology: Ecology; Professional Organizations

**TRANSPORTATION ACADEMY OF
AMERICA**
2222 FULLER ROAD, ROOM 107-A
ANN ARBOR, MI 48105
See Social Sciences/Humanities: Regional
Planning; Professional Organizations

UNIVERSITY DIGEST SERVICES
POST OFFICE BOX 343
TROY, MI 48084
See Interdisciplinary: General; Educational Institute

**URBAN HEALTH DEPARTMENT,
COUNTY HEALTH CENTER**
950 WEST MONROE STREET
JACKSON, MI 49202
See Engineering: Pollution Abatement;
Government-State or Local

WATER POLLUTION ANALYSIS
MICHIGAN TECHNOLOGY
UNIVERSITY
HOUGHTON, MI 49931
See Engineering: Water Resources; Educational Institute

WATER RESOURCES COMMISSION
STEVENS T MASON BUILDING
LANSING, MI 48926
See Engineering: Pollution Abatement;
Government-State or Local

WATER RESOURCES INSTITUTE
MICHIGAN STATE UNIVERSITY
EAST LANSING, MI 48823
See Engineering: Water Resources; Educational Institute

**WATER RESOURCES PROGRAM,
COLLEGE OF ENGINEERING**
UNIVERSITY OF MICHIGAN
ANN ARBOR, MI 48104
See Engineering: General; Educational
Institute

Minnesota

AGRICULTURE DEPARTMENT
STATE OFFICE BUILDING
ST PAUL, MN 55101
See Engineering: Agricultural Engineering; Government-State or Local

**AIR POLLUTION AND ALLERGIC
DISEASES**
UNIVERSITY OF MICHIGAN
MINNEAPOLIS, MN 55455
See Engineering: Pollution Abatement;
Educational Institute

**AIR POLLUTION CONTROL,
INSPECTIONS DEPARTMENT**
CITY HALL, 305 M
MINNEAPOLIS, MN 55415
See Engineering: Pollution Abatement;
Government-State or Local

**AIR POLLUTION CONTROL,
PUBLIC UTILITIES DEPARTMENT**
100 EAST 10TH STREET
ST PAUL, MN 55101
See Engineering: Pollution Abatement;
Government-State or Local

**BIOLOGICAL STATION,
DEPARTMENT OF FISHERIES,
DEFENSE RESOURCES BOARD**
MISSISSIPPI RIVER AT 3RD
AVENUE, SE
MINNEAPOLIS, MN 55414
See Engineering: Water Resources; Educational Institute

**CHEMICAL ENGINEERING
DEPARTMENT**
INSTITUTE OF TECHNOLOGY
MINNEAPOLIS, MN 55455
See Engineering: General; Educational
Institute

**CLEAR AIR, CLEAN WATER,
UNLIMITED**
POST OFFICE BOX 311
ST PAUL, MN 55075
See Engineering: Pollution Abatement;
Government-State or Local

**CONSERVATION EDUCATION
ASSOCIATION**
GREEN HALL, UNIVERSITY OF
MINNESOTA
ST PAUL, MN 55101
See Social Sciences/Humanities: Education; Professional Organizations

**CONSERVATION FEDERATION OF
MINNESOTA**
4313 SHADY OAK ROAD
HOPKINS, MN 55343
See Biology: Ecology; Foundation

**ENVIRONMENTAL CONTROL
ASSOCIATION**
26 EAST EXCHANGE STREET
ST PAUL, MN 55101
See Engineering: Pollution Abatement;
Professional Organizations

**ENVIRONMENTAL CONTROL
ORGANIZATION OF STOUGHTON**
60 HOLBROOK AVENUE
STOUGHTON, MN 02072
See Biology: Ecology; Government-State
or Local

**ENVIRONMENTAL COUNCIL,
NORTHERN**
601 CHRISTIE BUILDING
DULUTH, MN 55802
See Biology: Ecology; Research Institute

**ENVIRONMENTAL HEALTH
DIVISION**
STATE DEPARTMENT HEALTH
MINNEAPOLIS, MN 55440
See Engineering: Water Resources; Government-State or Local

ENVIRONMENTAL INSTITUTE
MANKATO STATE COLLEGE
MANKATO, MN 56001
See Biology: Ecology; Educational Institute

**ENVIRONMENTAL PROTECTION
AGENCY NATIONAL WATER
QUALITY LABORATORY**
DULUTH, MN 55804
See Biology: Ecology; Field Station/Laboratory

**ENVIRONMENTAL SCIENCE
PROGRAM**
MACALESTER COLLEGE
ST PAUL, MN 55101
See Chemistry: General; Educational Institute

**ENVIRONMENTAL SCIENCES
CENTER**
UNIVERSITY OF MINNESOTA AT
DULUTH
DULUTH, MN 55801
See Interdisciplinary: General; Educational Institute

**ENVIRONMENTAL STUDIES
PROGRAM**
1104 7TH AVENUE SOUTH
MOORHEAD, MN 56560
See Chemistry: General; Unclassified

**ENVIRONMENTAL STUDIES,
COLLEGE OF ST THOMAS**
2115 SUMMIT AVENUE
ST PAUL, MN 55101
See Chemistry: General; Educational Institute

EPIDEMEOLOGY DIVISION
UNIVERSITY OF MINNESOTA,
SCHOOL OF PUBLIC HEALTH
MINNEAPOLIS, MN 55455
See Interdisciplinary: General; Educational Institute

**FAMILY STUDY CENTER,
UNIVERSITY OF MINNESOTA**
1014 SOCIAL SCIENCES TOWER
MINNEAPOLIS MN 55455
See Social Sciences/Humanities: General;
Educational Institute

FRIENDS OF THE WILDERNESS
3515 EAST FOURTH STREET
DULUTH, MN 55804

See Interdisciplinary: General; Professional Organizations

HEALTH DEPARTMENT
504 EAST 2ND STREET
DULUTH, MN 55802
See Engineering: Pollution Abatement; Government-State or Local

HYDRAULIC LABORATORY OF ST ANTHONY FALLS, UNIVERSITY OF MINNESOTA
MISSISSIPPI RIVER AT 3RD AVENUE, SE
MINNEAPOLIS, MN 55414
See Engineering: Water Resources; Educational Institute

INDUSTRIAL RELATIONS CENTER, BUSINESS ADMINISTRATION TOWER
UNIVERSITY OF MINNESOTA
MINNEAPOLIS, MN 55455
See Social Sciences/Humanities: Industrial Development; Government-State or Local

INSTITUTIONAL RESOURCES BUREAU
330 BURTON HALL, MINNESOTA UNIVERSITY
MINNEAPOLIS, MN 55455
See Social Sciences/Humanities: Education; Educational Institute

MECHANICAL ENGINEERING DEPARTMENT
TECHNOLOGY INSTITUTE, UNIVERSITY OF MINNESOTA
MINNEAPOLIS, MN 55455
See Engineering: Pollution Abatement; Educational Institute

MEDICAL STATISTICS SECTION
MAYO CLINIC AND MAYO FOUNDATION
ROCHESTER, MN 55901
See Engineering: Pollution Abatement; Foundation

PESTICIDE REGULATION DIVISION
6400 FRANCE AVENUE, SOUTH
MINNEAPOLIS, MN 55435
See Engineering: Agricultural Engineering; Government-Federal

PHYSICAL ENVIRONMENT STUDIES CENTER, INSTITUTE OF TECHNOLOGY
UNIVERSITY OF MINNESOTA
MINNEAPOLIS, MN 55455
See Interdisciplinary: General; Educational Institute

POLLUTION CONTROL, BOARD OF HEALTH
UNIVERSITY CAMPUS
MINNEAPOLIS, MN 55440
See Engineering: Pollution Abatement; Government-State or Local

PUBLIC HEALTH CENTER
415 FOURTH STREETS, SE
ROCHESTER, MN 55901
See Engineering: Pollution Abatement; Government-State or Local

PUBLIC HEALTH SCHOOL, COLLEGE OF MEDICAL SCIENCES
UNIVERSITY OF MINNESOTA
MINNEAPOLIS, MN 55455
See Biology: General; Educational Institute

PUBLIC UTILITIES DEPARTMENT, TESTING LABORATORY
100 EAST 10TH STREET
ST PAUL, MN 55101
See Engineering: Pollution Abatement; Government-State or Local

PUBLIC WELFARE DEPARTMENT, MINNESOTA
CENTENNIAL BUILDING
ST. PAUL, MN 55101
See Social Sciences/Humanities: Welfare(Child Public Social); Government-State or Local

RIVER RESEARCH FOUNDATION
WINONA STATE COLLEGE
WINONA, MN 55987
See Biology: General; Educational Institute

SCIENCE AND MATHEMATICS DIVISION
BEMIDJI STATE COLLEGE
BEMIDJI, MN 56601
See Interdisciplinary: General; Educational Institute

SOCIAL WELFARE CENTER
UNIVERSITY OF MINNESOTA LIBRARY
MINNEAPOLIS, MN 55455
See Social Sciences/Humanities: Welfare(Child Public Social); Educational Institute

SOIL CONSERVATION COMMISSION OF MINNESOTA, MINNESOTA UNIVERSITY
201 SOIL SCIENCES BUILDING, ST PAUL, MN 55101
See Engineering: Water Resources; Educational Institute

VETERINARY PHYSIOLOGY AND PHARMACOLOGY DEPARTMENT
ROOM 205 TEH, UNIVERSITY OF MINNESOTA
ST PAUL, MN 55101
See Biology: General; Educational Institute

WATER POLLUTION CONTROL, HEALTH DEPARTMENT
UNIVERSITY OF MINNESOTA CAMPUS
MINNEAPOLIS, MN 55440

See Engineering: Pollution Abatement; Government-State or Local

WATER RESOURCES RESEARCH CENTER, UNIVERSITY OF MINNESOTA
2675 UNIVERSITY AVENUE, M 107, HUBBARD BUILDING
ST PAUL, MN 55114
See Engineering: Water Resources; Educational Institute

WILDERNESS RESEARCH CENTER, QUETICO-SUPERIOR
7335 CENTRAL AVENUE
ELY, MN 55731
See Biology: General; Research Institute

WINZEN RESEARCH INCORPORATED
8401 LYNDALE AVENUE
MINNEAPOLIS, MN 55420
See Interdisciplinary: General; Research Institute

Missouri

AIR CONSERVATION COMMISSION
BOX 1062
JEFFERSON CITY, MO 65101
See Engineering: Pollution Abatement; Government-State or Local

AIR POLLUTION CONTROL,
CITY HALL, 940 BOONVILLE STREET
SPRINGFIELD, MO 65802
See Engineering: Pollution Abatement; Government-State or Local

AIR POLLUTION CONTROL, CITY HEALTH DEPARTMENT
CITY HALL
ST JOSEPH, MO 64501
See Engineering: Pollution Abatement; Government-State or Local

AIR POLLUTION CONTROL, CITY HEALTH DEPARTMENT
210 SOUTH MAIN STREET
INDEPENDENCE, MO 64050
See Engineering: Pollution Abatement; Government-State or Local

AIR POLLUTION CONTROL, CITY HEALTH DEPARTMENT
513 KENTUCKY AVENUE
JOPLIN, MO 64801
See Engineering: Pollution Abatement; Government-State or Local

AIR POLLUTION CONTROL, COUNTY HEALTH DEPARTMENT
LIBERTY, MO 64068
See Engineering: Pollution Abatement; Government-State or Local

**AIR POLLUTION CONTROL,
PUBLIC SAFETY DEPARTMENT**
1200 MARKET STREET
ST LOUIS, MO 63103
See Engineering: Pollution Abatement;
Government-State or Local

**AIR POLLUTION CONTROL,
PUBLIC WORKS DEPARTMENT**
SIXTH STREET AND BROADWAY
COLUMBIA, MO 65201
See Engineering: Pollution Abatement;
Government-State or Local

**ATMOSPHERIC SCIENCES
PROGRAM**
ST LOUIS UNIVERSITY
ST LOUIS, MO 63100
See Engineering: Pollution Abatement;
Educational Institute

AUDUBON SOCIETY OF MISSOURI
403 SOUTH FREDERICK
MARYVILLE, MO 64466
See Interdisciplinary: General; Professional Organizations

BIOLOGY DEPARTMENT
SAINT LOUIS UNIVERSITY
ST LOUIS, MO 63103
See Biology: General; Educational Insti-
tute

**BIOLOGY OF NATURAL SYSTEMS
CENTER**
WASHINGTON UNIVERSITY
ST LOUIS, MO 63130
See Interdisciplinary: General; Educa-
tional Institute

BOTANICAL GARDENS
2135 TOWER GROVE AVENUE
ST LOUIS, MO 63110
See Engineering: Pollution Abatement;
Foundation

**BUSINESS ADMINISTRATION
DEPARTMENT**
POST OFFICE BOX 271, WATER
RESOURCES BUILDING
JEFFERSON CITY, MO 65101
See Engineering: Water Resources; Gov-
ernment-State or Local

**CHILDRENS HOSPITAL OF ST
LOUIS**
500 SOUTH KINGSHIGHWAY
ST LOUIS, MO 63110
See Biology: Ecology; Research Institute

CITY MANAGER'S OFFICE
COURTHOUSE
CAPE GIRARDEAU, MO 63701
See Engineering: Pollution Abatement;
Government-State or Local

CLEAN WATER COMMISSION
POST OFFICE BOX 154
JEFFERSON CITY, MO 65101
See Engineering: Pollution Abatement;
Government-State or Local

**CONSERVATION COMMISSION OF
MISSOURI**
P.O. BOX 180
JEFFERSON CITY, MO 65101
See Engineering: Water Resources; Gov-
ernment-State or Local

**CONSERVATION FEDERATION OF
MISSOURI**
312 EAST CAPITOL AVENUE
JEFFERSON CITY, MO 65101
See Biology: Ecology; Foundation

**ENTOMOLOGY DIVISION, STATE
DEPARTMENT OF AGRICULTURE**
JEFFERSON BUILDING
JEFFERSON CITY, MO 65101
See Engineering: Agricultural Engineer-
ing; Government-State or Local

**ENVIRONMENTAL HEALTH
CENTER**
UNIVERSITY OF MISSOURI
COLUMBIA, MO 65201
See Biology: General; Educational Insti-
tute

**ENVIRONMENTAL INFORMATION
COMMISSION**
438 NORTH SKINKER BOULEVARD
ST LOUIS, MO 63130
See Social Sciences/Humanities: Politics;
Professional Organizations

**ENVIRONMENTAL SANITATION,
HEALTH DEPARTMENT**
21ST FLOOR, CITY HALL
KANSAS CITY, MO 64106
See Engineering: Pollution Abatement;
Government-State or Local

**ENVIRONMENTAL SCIENCE
EDUCATION PROGRAM**
NORTHEAST MISSOURI STATE
KIRKSVILLE, MO 63501
See Biology: Ecology; Educational Insti-
tute

**ENVIRONMENTAL SCIENCE
PROGRAM**
UNIVERSITY OF MISSOURI AT
COLUMBIA
COLUMBIA, MO 65201
See Interdisciplinary: General; Educa-
tional Institute

**ENVIRONMENTAL SCIENCES
EDUCATION PROGRAM**
NORTHEAST MISSOURI STATE
COLLEGE
KIRKSVILLE, MO 63501
See Biology: Ecology; Educational Insti-
tute

**ENVIRONMENTAL STUDIES
PROGRAM**
SOUTHEAST MISSOURI STATE
COLLEGE
CAPE GIRARDEAU, MO 63701
See Interdisciplinary: General; Educa-
tional Institute

**ENVIRONMENTAL STUDIES
PROGRAM, UNIVERSITY OF
MISSOURI**
5100 ROCKHILL ROAD
KANSAS CITY, MO 64110
See Interdisciplinary: General; Educa-
tional Institute

**ENVIRONMENTAL STUDIES, SAINT
LOUIS UNIVERSITY**
221 NORTH GRAND BOULEVARD
ST LOUIS, MO 63103
See Interdisciplinary: General; Educa-
tional Institute

**GARDEN CLUBS NATIONAL
COUNCIL**
4401 MAGNOLIA AVENUE
ST LOUIS, MO 63110
See Biology: General; Professional Organ-
izations

HEALTH DEPARTMENT
801 SOUTH BRENTWOOD
BOULEVARD
CLAYTON, MO 63105
See Engineering: Pollution Abatement;
Government-State or Local

**HEALTH, EDUCATION, AND
WELFARE REGION 7**
601 EAST 12TH STREET
KANSAS CITY, MO 64106
See Interdisciplinary: General; Unclassi-
fied

**HYDROLOGY OFFICE, NATIONAL
WEATHER SERVICES, CENTRAL
OFFICE**
ROOM 1836, 601 EAST 12TH STREET
KANSAS CITY, MO 64104
See Engineering: Water Resources; Gov-
ernment-State or Local

**INSPECTION DEPARTMENT,
BUREAU OF PUBLIC WORKS**
6801 DELMAR BOULEVARD
UNIVERSITY CITY, MO 63130
See Engineering: Pollution Abatement;
Government-State or Local

**MARINE SCIENCES DIVISION, 2ND
COAST GUARD DISTRICT**
1520 MARKET STREET, FEDERAL
BUILDING
ST LOUIS, MO 63103
See Engineering: Water Resources; Gov-
ernment-State or Local

MISSISSIPPI VALLEY ASSOCIATION
225 SOUTH MERAMEE AVENUE
ST. LOUIS, MO 63105
See Engineering: Water Resources; Government-Federal

**OCCUPATIONAL SAFETY AND
HEALTH INSTITUTE**
601 EAST 12TH STREET
KANSAS CITY, MO 64106
See Engineering: Pollution Abatement;
Government-State or Local

PHARMACOLOGY DEPARTMENT, SCHOOL OF MEDICINE
WASHINGTON UNIVERSITY
ST LOUIS, MO 63110
See Chemistry: General; Educational Institute

PREVENTIVE MEDICINE DEPARTMENT
WASHINGTON UNIVERSITY
ST LOUIS, MO 63110
See Interdisciplinary: General; Educational Institute

PROGRAM SUPPORT BRANCH (AIR) ENVIRONMENTAL PROTECTION AGENCY
1735 BALTIMORE, ROOM 265
KANSAS CITY, MO 64108
See Engineering: Pollution Abatement; Government-Federal

PUBLIC WORKS DEPARTMENT
12TH AND OAK STREETS
KANSAS CITY, MO 64108
See Engineering: Pollution Abatement; Government-State or Local

RADIATION DIVISION, ENVIRONMENTAL PROTECTION AGENCY
911 WALNUT STREET, ROOM 702
KANSAS CITY, MO 64106
See Chemistry: Physical Chemistry; Government-State or Local

RYCKMAN, EDGERLY, TOMLINSON ASSOCIATION
12161 LACKLAND ROAD
ST LOUIS, MO 63141
See Engineering: General; Professional Organizations

SANITARY SCIENCE, COLLEGE OF AGRICULTURE
UNIVERSITY OF MISSOURI
COLUMBIA, MO 65201
See Engineering: Agricultural Engineering; Educational Institute

SCIENCE PROGRAM
UNIVERSITY OF MISSOURI AT ROLLA
ROLLA, MO 65401
See Interdisciplinary: General; Educational Institute

SCIENCES DIVISION, NORTHWEST MISSOURI STATE COLLEGE
KIRKSVILLE, MO 63501
See Biology: Ecology; Educational Institute

SOIL CONSERVATION SERVICES, PARKADE PLAZA SHOPPING CENTER
TERRACE LEVEL-POST OFFICE BOX 459
COLUMBIA, MO 65201
See Biology: Ecology; Government-State or Local

Mississippi

AIR AND WATER POLLUTION OF MISSISSIPPI
POST OFFICE BOX 827
JACKSON, MS 39205
See Biology: Ecology; Government-State or Local

AIR POLLUTION CONTROL
MUNICIPAL BUILDING
MERIDIAN, MS 39301
See Engineering: Pollution Abatement; Government-State or Local

ENVIRONMENTAL SCIENCE PROGRAM
UNIVERSITY OF MISSISSIPPI
UNIVERSITY, MS 38677
See Interdisciplinary: General; Educational Institute

ENVIRONMENTAL STUDIES PROGRAM
MISSISSIPPI STATE UNIVERSITY
STATE COLLEGE, MS 39762
See Interdisciplinary: General; Educational Institute

ENVIRONMENTAL STUDIES PROGRAM
UNIVERSITY OF SOUTHERN MISSISSIPPI
HATTIESBURG, MS 39401
See Interdisciplinary: General; Educational Institute

ENVIRONMENTAL STUDIES, MISSISSIPPI STATE UNIVERSITY
POST OFFICE DRAWER GH
STATE COLLEGE, MS 39762
See Interdisciplinary: General; Educational Institute

EXPLORATORY FISHING AND GEAR RESOURCES BASE
239 FREDERIC STREET
PASCAGOULA, MS 39567
See Engineering: Water Resources; Government-Federal

GAME AND FISHERIES COMMISSION
POST OFFICE BOX 451
JACKSON, MS 39205
See Engineering: Pollution Abatement; Government-State or Local

GEOLOGIC, TOPOGRAPHIC AND ECONOMIC SURVEY OF MISSISSIPPI
POST OFFICE BOX 4915, NORTH WEST STREET
JACKSON, MS 39216
See Engineering: Water Resources; Government-State or Local

GULF COAST RESEARCH LABORATORY
OCEAN SPRINGS, MS 39564
See Interdisciplinary: General; Government-State or Local

HIGHWAY DEPARTMENT BUILDING
HIGHWAY 45
TOPELO, MS 38801
See Engineering: Pollution Abatement; Government-State or Local

MISSISSIPPI RIVERS COMMISSION, CORPORATION OF ENGINEERING
UNITED STATES ARMY, POST OFFICE BOX 80
VICKSBURG, MS 39180
See Engineering: General; Government-Federal

OIL AND GAS BOARD
BOX 1332
JACKSON, MS 39205
See Engineering: Pollution Abatement; Government-State or Local

RESEARCH LABORATORY OF GULF COAST
POST OFFICE BOX AG
OCEAN SPRINGS, MS 39564
See Biology: Ecology; Research Institute

SOCIAL SCIENCES RESEARCH CENTER, MISSISSIPPI STATE UNIVERSITY
P O BOX 238
STATE COLLEGE, MS 39762
See Social Sciences/Humanities: Psychology/Behavioral Science; Educational Institute

SOIL CONSERVATION COMMISSION OF MISSISSIPPI
MISSISSIPPI STATE UNIVERSITY
STATE COLLEGE, MS 39762
See Engineering: Water Resources; Educational Institute

SOIL CONSERVATION SERVICES
POST OFFICE BOX 610, MILNER BUILDING, ROOM 430
JACKSON, MS 39205
See Biology: Ecology; Government-State or Local

STATE PLANT BOARD
BOX 5207
STATE COLLEGE, MS 39762
See Engineering: Agricultural Engineering; Government-State or Local

TECHNOLOGY LABORATORY, BUREAU COMMISSION FISHERIES, DEPARTMENT OF
239 FREDERIC STREET, PO 1207
PASCAGOULA, MS 39567
See Biology: General; Government-Federal

TENNESSEE-TOMBRIGBEE WATERWAY DEVELOPMENT AUTHORITY
POST OFFICE BOX 671
COLUMBUS, MS 39701
See Engineering: Water Resources; Government-Federal

WATER COMMISSIONERS BOARD OF MISSISSIPPI
429 MISSISSIPPI STREET
JACKSON, MS 39201
See Engineering: Water Resources; Government-State or Local

WATERWAYS EXPERIMENT STATION
POST OFFICE BOX 631, HALLS FERRY ROAD
VICKSBURG, MS 39181
See Engineering: Water Resources; Government-Federal

WILDLIFE FEDERATION OF MISSISSIPPI
108 STATE STREET
BAY ST LOUIS, MS 39520
See Biology: Ecology; Foundation

Montana

AIR POLLUTION CONTROL, COUNTY HEALTH DEPARTMENT
ROOM 301 COUNTY COURTHOUSE
MISSOULA, MT 59801
See Engineering: Pollution Abatement; Government-State or Local

BINGHAM OCEANOGRAPHIC LABORATORY, YALE UNIVERSITY
POST OFFICE BOX 2143
BILLINGS, MT 59103
See Engineering: Water Resources; Government-Federal

BIOLOGICAL STATION
UNIVERSITY OF MONTANA
MISSOULA, MT 59801
See Interdisciplinary: General; Field Station/Laboratory

BOTANY AND MICROBIOLOGY DEPARTMENT
MONTANA STATE UNIVERSITY
BOZEMAN, MT 59715
See Biology: General; Educational Institute

COMPACT COMMISSION OF THE YELLOWSTONE RIVER
421 FEDERAL BUILDING

HELENA, MT 59601
See Engineering: Water Resources; Government-State or Local

CONSERVATION COUNCIL OF MONTANA, INCORPORATED
BOX 175
MISSOULA, MT 59801
See Biology: Ecology; Professional Organizations

ENVIRONMENT AND RESOURCE ANALYSIS CENTER
UNIVERSITY OF MONTANA
MISSOULA, MT 59801
See Interdisciplinary: General; Educational Institute

ENVIRONMENTAL SANITATION DIVISION, MONTANA BOARD OF HEALTH
STATE CAPITOL BUILDING
HELENA, MT 59601
See Engineering: Pollution Abatement; Government-State or Local

ENVIRONMENTAL SCIENCE PROGRAM
MONTANA STATE UNIVERSITY
BOZEMAN, MT 59715
See Interdisciplinary: General; Educational Institute

ENVIRONMENTAL SCIENCES DIVISION
COGSWELL BUILDING
HELENA, MT 59601
See Engineering: General; Government-State or Local

ENVIRONMENTAL STUDIES PROGRAM
MOUNTAIN COLLEGE OF MINERAL SCIENCES
BUTTE, MT 59701
See Engineering: General; Educational Institute

ENVIRONMENTAL STUDIES PROGRAM
UNIVERSITY OF MONTANA
MISSOULA, MT 59801
See Interdisciplinary: General; Educational Institute

FOREST SERVICE REGION 1 OFFICE
FEDERAL BUILDING
MISSOULA, MT 59801
See Engineering: Agricultural Engineering; Government-Federal

FORESTRY SCIENCES LABORATORY
MONTANA STATE UNIVERSITY
BOZEMAN, MT 59715
See Biology: Ecology; Field Station/Laboratory

INDIAN HEALTH SERVICE, BILLINGS AREA
3 BILLINGS STREET WEST
BILLINGS, MT 59103
See Engineering: Water Resources; Government-State or Local

MINERALOGY, INDUSTRIAL HYGIENE
MONTANA COLLEGE OF MINERAL SCIENCE TECHNOLOGY
BUTTE, MT 59701
See Interdisciplinary: General; Educational Institute

MINES AND GEOLOGY BUREAU OF MONTANA
MAIN HALL, MONTANA COLLEGE, MINERAL SCIENCES DEPARTMENT
BUTTE, MT 59701
See Engineering: Water Resources; Educational Institute

NATURAL RESOURCES CENTER
UNIVERSITY OF MONTANA
MISSOULA, MT 59801
See Biology: Ecology; Educational Institute

PESTICIDE CONTROL, ENVIRONMENTAL SANITATION DIVISION
W F COGSWELL BUILDING
HELENA, MT 59601
See Engineering: Chemical Engineering; Government-State or Local

SOIL CONSERVATION SERVICE
P O BOX 970
BOZEMAN, MT 59715
See Biology: Ecology; Government-State or Local

STATE FORESTERS NATIONAL ASSOCIATION
2705 SPURGIN ROAD
MISSOULA, MT 59801
See Interdisciplinary: General; Professional Organizations

WATER CONSERVATION BOARD OF MONTANA
SAM W MITCHELL BUILDING
HELENA, MT 59601
See Engineering: Water Resources; Government-State or Local

WATER POLLUTION CONTROL ASSOCIATION OF MONTANA
STATE CAPITOL BUILDING
HELENA, MT 59601
See Engineering: Water Resources; Government-State or Local

WATER POLLUTION COUNCIL
LABORATORY BUILDING
HELENA, MT 59601
See Engineering: Pollution Abatement; Government-State or Local

**WATER RESOURCES SECTION,
MOUNTAIN FISHERIES AND
GAME DEPARTMENT**
FISHERIES DEPARTMENT
HELENA, MT 59601
See Engineering: Water Resources; Government-State or Local

**WILDLIFE FEDERATION OF
MONTANA**
410 WOODWORTH
MISSOULA, MT 59801
See Biology: Ecology; Foundation

Nebraska

**AGRICULTURAL LABORATORY
DEPARTMENT**
STATE HOUSE STATION, BOX 94693
LINCOLN, NB 68509
See Engineering: Agricultural Engineering; Government-State or Local

**AIR POLLUTION CONTROL,
COUNTY HEALTH DEPARTMENT**
1201 SOUTH 42ND STREET
OMAHA, NB 68105
See Engineering: Pollution Abatement;
Government-State or Local

**AIR POLLUTION CONTROL,
PUBLIC SAFETY DEPARTMENT**
108 SOUTH 18TH STREET
OMAHA, NB 68102
See Engineering: Pollution Abatement;
Government-State or Local

CELLULAR BIOLOGY INSTITUTE
UNIVERSITY OF NEBRASKA
LINCOLN, NB 68500
See Engineering: Pollution Abatement;
Educational Institute

**CONSERVATION AND SURVEY
DIVISION**
UNIVERSITY OF NEBRASKA
LINCOLN, NB 68508
See Engineering: Water Resources; Educational Institute

**CONSERVATION INFORMATION,
AMERICAN ASSOCIATION**
STATE CAPITOL BUILDING
LINCOLN, NB 68500
See Engineering: General; Government-State or Local

ECOLOGY DEPARTMENT
CHADRON STATE COLLEGE
CHADRON, NB 69337
See Biology: Ecology; Educational Institute

**ENVIRONMENTAL EDUCATION,
NATIONAL PARK SERVICES
MIDWEST OFFICER**
1709 JACKSON STREET
OMAHA, NB 68102

See Biology: Ecology; Government-State
or Local

**ENVIRONMENTAL HEALTH
SERVICE, NEBRASKA
DEPARTMENT OF HEALTH**
POST OFFICE BOX 94757, STATE
HOUSE STATION
LINCOLN, NB 68508
See Engineering: Water Resources; Government-State or Local

ENVIRONMENTAL STUDIES
UNIVERSITY OF NEBRASKA
LINCOLN, NB 68508
See Interdisciplinary: General; Educational Institute

ENVIRONMENTAL STUDIES GROUP
2500 CALIFORNIA STREET
OMAHA, NB 68131
See Interdisciplinary: General; Educational Institute

**EPPLEY INSTITUTE FOR CANCER
RESEARCH, UNIVERSITY OF
NEBRASKA**
42ND AND DEWEY AVENUE
OMAHA, NB 68105
See Chemistry: General; Educational Institute

HEALTH DEPARTMENT
STATE HOUSE STATION
LINCOLN, NB 68509
See Engineering: Pollution Abatement;
Government-State or Local

**HEALTH DEPARTMENT OF
LINCOLN-LANCASTER COUNTY**
2200 ST MARY'S AVENUE
LINCOLN, NB 68502
See Engineering: Pollution Abatement;
Government-State or Local

**MISSOURI BASIN INTERAGENCY
COMMISSION**
P.O. BOX 103 DOWNTOWN STATION
OMAHA, NB 68101
See Engineering: Water Resources; Government-Federal

**ORNITHOLOGISTS UNION OF
NEBRASKA**
UNIVERSITY OF NEBRASKA STATE
MUSEUM
LINCOLN, NB 68508
See Biology: Ecology; Government-Federal

**SOIL AND WATER CONSERVATION
COMMISSION OF NEBRASKA**
POST OFFICE BOX 94725, STATE
CAPITOL BUILDING
LINCOLN, NB 68509
See Engineering: Water Resources; Government-State or Local

SOIL CONSERVATION SERVICE
134 SOUTH 12TH STREET
LINCOLN, NB 68508
See Biology: Ecology; Government-State
or Local

**WATER RESOURCES DEPARTMENT
OF NEBRASKA**
STATE CAPITOL
LINCOLN, NB 68509
See Engineering: Water Resources; Government-State or Local

North Carolina

**AGRICULTURAL POLICY
INSTITUTE, NORTH CAROLINA
STATE UNIVERSITY**
P O BOX 5368
RALEIGH, NC 27607
See Engineering: Agricultural Engineering; Educational Institute

**AIR AND WATER RESOURCES
OFFICE**
POST OFFICE BOX 27687
RALEIGH, NC 27611
See Interdisciplinary: General; Government-State or Local

AIR POLLUTION CONTROL
CITY HALL BUILDING
ASHEVILLE, NC 28807
See Engineering: Pollution Abatement;
Government-State or Local

AIR POLLUTION CONTROL
1216 W INNES
SALISBURY, NC 28144
See Engineering: Pollution Abatement;
Government-State or Local

**AIR POLLUTION CONTROL
ADMINISTRATION**
411 WEST CHAPEL HILL STREET
DURHAM, NC 27701
See Engineering: Pollution Abatement;
Professional Organizations

**AIR POLLUTION CONTROL
DIVISION**
POST OFFICE BOX 9392
RALEIGH, NC 27603
See Engineering: Pollution Abatement;
Government-State or Local

**AIR POLLUTION CONTROL
OFFICE, RESEARCH GRANTS
OFFICE**
POST OFFICE BOX 12055
RESEARCH TRIANGLE PARK, NC
27709
See Engineering: Pollution Abatement;
Government-Federal

**AIR POLLUTION CONTROL
PROGRAM**
1033 WADE AVENUE
RALEIGH, NC 27065
See Engineering: Pollution Abatement;
Government-Federal

**AIR POLLUTION CONTROL
  PROGRAM**
403 GEORGE STREET
NEW BERN, NC 28560
See Engineering: Pollution Abatement;
  Government-State or Local

**AIR POLLUTION CONTROL,
  COUNTY BOARD OF HEALTH**
21 NORTH FOURTH STREET
WILMINGTON, NC 28401
See Engineering: Pollution Abatement;
  Government-State or Local

**AIR POLLUTION CONTROL,
  COUNTY HEALTH DEPARTMENT**
1200 BLYTHE BOULEVARD
CHARLOTTE, NC 28203
See Engineering: Pollution Abatement;
  Government-State or Local

**AIR POLLUTION CONTROL,
  COUNTY HEALTH DEPARTMENT**
315 GROVER STREET
SHELBY, NC 28150
See Engineering: Pollution Abatement;
  Government-State or Local

**AIR POLLUTION CONTROL,
  PUBLIC SAFETY DEPARTMENT**
CITY HALL, BOX 7184
ASHEVILLE, NC 28807
See Engineering: Pollution Abatement;
  Government-State or Local

**AIR POLLUTION TRAINING
  INSTITUTE, MANPOWER
  DEVELOPMENT STAFF**
ENVIRONMENTAL PROTECTION
  AGENCY
RESEARCH TRIANGLE PARK, NC
27711
See Engineering: Pollution Abatement;
  Government-Federal

**AIR PROGRAMS OFFICE,
  ENVIRONMENTAL PROTECTION
  AGENCY**
AIR PROGRAMS LIBRARY
RESEARCH TRIANGLE PARK, NC
27711
See Engineering: Pollution Abatement;
  Government-Federal

**AIR QUALITY CONTROL,
  BUILDING INSPECTION
  DEPARTMENT**
CITY HALL, BOX 708
STATESVILLE, NC 28677
See Engineering: Pollution Abatement;
  Government-State or Local

ANIMAL BEHAVIOR STATION
DUKE UNIVERSITY
DURHAM, NC 27706
See Biology: General; Field Station/Lab-
  oratory

**CENTER BOTANICAL SOCIETY,
  INCORPORATED**
NORTH CAROLINA STATE
  UNIVERSITY

RALEIGH, NC 27607
See Biology: General; Educational Institute

**CHEMISTRY DIVISION,
  DEPARTMENT OF AGRICULTURE**
AGRICULTURAL BUILDING
RALEIGH, NC 27602
See Engineering: Agricultural Engineer-
  ing; Government-State or Local

**CONSERVATION ROUNDUP OF
  FONTANA**
FONTANA DAM, NC 28733
See Biology: Ecology; Professional Organ-
  izations

**CRITERIA AND STANDARDS
  BUREAU**
411 W CHAPEL HILL STREET
DURHAM, NC 27701
See Engineering: Water Resources; Gov-
  ernment-Federal

**ECOLOGICAL SOCIETY OF
  AMERICA, BOTANY
  DEPARTMENT**
UNIVERSITY OF NORTH CAROLINA
CHAPEL HILL, NC 27514
See Biology: Ecology; Educational Insti-
  tute

ECOS
POST OFFICE BOX 1055
CHAPEL HILL, NC 27514
See Biology: Ecology; Professional Organ-
  izations

**ENGINEERING AND PHYSICAL
  SCIENCES BUREAU**
1330 ST MARY'S STREET
RALEIGH, NC 27605
See Engineering: Water Resources; Gov-
  ernment-Federal

**ENVIRONMENTAL CENTER, DUKE
  UNIVERSITY**
210 OLD CHEMISTRY BUILDING
DURHAM, NC 27706
See Interdisciplinary: General; Educa-
  tional Institute

**ENVIRONMENTAL HEALTH
  DIVISION, COUNTY HEALTH
  DEPARTMENT**
300 EAST NORWOOD STREET
GREENSBORO, NC 27401
See Engineering: Pollution Abatement;
  Government-State or Local

**ENVIRONMENTAL HEALTH
  DIVISION, COUNTY HEALTH
  DEPARTMENT**
615 NORTH HIGHLAND ROAD
GASTONIA, NC 28052
See Engineering: Pollution Abatement;
  Government-State or Local

**ENVIRONMENTAL HEALTH
  STUDIES INSTITUTE**
UNIVERSITY OF NORTH CAROLINA

CHAPEL HILL, NC 27514
See Biology: Ecology; Educational Institute

**ENVIRONMENTAL RESEARCH
  CENTER, NATIONAL**
RESEARCH TRIANGLE PARK, NC
27709
See Biology: Ecology; Research Institute

**ENVIRONMENTAL SANITATION
  DIVISION, COUNTY HEALTH
  DEPARTMENT**
300 EAST MAIN STREET
DURHAM, NC 27701
See Engineering: Pollution Abatement;
  Government-State or Local

**ENVIRONMENTAL SCIENCE
  CENTER**
NORTH CAROLINA AGRICULTURE
  AND TECHNOLOGY STATE
  UNIVERSITY
GREENSBORO, NC 27401
See Biology: Ecology; Educational Insti-
  tute

**ENVIRONMENTAL SCIENCE
  PROGRAM**
UNIVERSITY OF NORTH CAROLINA
  AT GREENSBORO
GREENSBORO, NC 27412
See Interdisciplinary: General; Educa-
  tional Institute

**ENVIRONMENTAL SCIENCES AND
  ENGINEERING DEPARTMENT**
UNIVERSITY OF NORTH CAROLINA
CHAPEL HILL, NC 27514
See Interdisciplinary: General; Educa-
  tional Institute

**ENVIRONMENTAL STUDIES
  PROGRAM**
NORTH CAROLINA STATE
  UNIVERSITY AT RALEIGH
RALEIGH, NC 27607
See Interdisciplinary: General; Educa-
  tional Institute

**ENVIRONMENTAL STUDIES
  PROGRAM**
UNIVERSITY OF NORTH CAROLINA
  AT CHAPEL HILL
CHAPEL HILL, NC 27514
See Interdisciplinary: General; Educa-
  tional Institute

**ENVIRONMENTAL STUDIES
  PROGRAM**
WAKE FOREST UNIVERSITY
WINSTON-SALEM, NC 27106
See Interdisciplinary: General; Educa-
  tional Institute

**GENETICS DEPARTMENT, NORTH
  CAROLINA STATE UNIVERSITY**
POST OFFICE BOX 5356
RALEIGH, NC 27607
See Biology: General; Educational Insti-
  tute

GRANTS POLICY DIVISION, AIR POLLUTION OFFICE
1033 WADE AVENUE
RALEIGH, NC 27605
See Engineering: Pollution Abatement; Government-Federal

HANES CORPORATION
WINSTON SALEM, NC 27100
See Interdisciplinary: General; Industrial/Commercial

HUMAN PROTECTION CENTER
GREENSHORE COLLEGE
GREENSHORE, NC 27420
See Biology: General; Educational Institute

INFORMATION PROCESSING OFFICE- UNITED STATES ARMY RESEARCH OFFICE
BOX CM, DUKE STATION
DURHAM, NC 27706
See Biology: Ecology; Government-Federal

INSPECTIONS DEPARTMENT
402 MUNICIPAL BUILDING
RALEIGH, NC 27602
See Engineering: Pollution Abatement; Government-State or Local

LABOR AND HEALTH INSTITUTE AT SAINT LOUIS
1641 SOUTH KINGSHIGHWAY BOULE
ST LOUIS, NC 27100
See Interdisciplinary: General; Industrial/Commercial

MARINE LABORATORY
DUKE UNIVERSITY
RIVER'S ISLAND, BEAUFORT, NC 28516
See Biology: Ecology; Field Station/Laboratory

MARINE SCIENCE INSTITUTE
POST OFFICE BOX 809
MOREHEAD CITY, NC 28557
See Biology: General; Educational Institute

METEOROLOGY WORLD DATA CENTER
NATIONAL WEATHER RECORDS CENTER
ASHVILLE, NC 28801
See Geology: General; Government-Federal

NATIONAL AEROMETRIC DATA BANK
ENVIRONMENTAL PROTECTION AGENCY
RESEARCH TRIANGLE PARK, NC 27711
See Engineering: Pollution Abatement; Government-Federal

NATIONAL INSTITUTE OF ENVIRONMENTAL HEALTH SCIENCES
POST OFFICE BOX 12233
RESEARCH TRIANGLE PARK, NC 27709
See Interdisciplinary: General; Unclassified

OBSTETRICS AND GYNECOLOGY, SCHOOL OF MEDICINE
DUKE UNIVERSITY
DURHAM, NC 27706
See Biology: General; Educational Institute

RESEARCH OFFICE UNITED STATES ARMY
BOX CM, DUKE STATION
DURHAM, NC 27706
See Interdisciplinary: General; Government-Federal

SOIL CONSERVATION SERVICES
FEDERAL OFFICE BUILDING, POST OFFICE BOX 27307
RALEIGH, NC 27611
See Interdisciplinary: General; Unclassified

TECHNOLOGY CENTER, INFORMATION AND PUBLICATIONS OFFICE
1330 ST MARY'S STREET
RALEIGH, NC 27605
See Engineering: Pollution Abatement; Government-Federal

WATER RESOURCES DEPARTMENT OF NORTH CAROLINA
P O BOX 9392
RALEIGH, NC 27603
See Engineering: Water Resources; Government-State or Local

WATER RESOURCES INSTITUTE
SHAW UNIVERSITY, 124 RIDDICK BUILDING
RALEIGH, NC 27607
See Engineering: Water Resources; Unclassified

North Dakota

ECOLOGICAL STUDIES INSTITUTE
UNIVERSITY OF NORTH DAKOTA
GRAND FORKS, ND 58201
See Biology: Ecology; Educational Institute

ENVIRONMENTAL HEALTH AND ENGINEERING, STATE DEPARTMENT OF HEALTH
STATE CAPITOL
BISMARCK, ND 58501
See Engineering: Pollution Abatement; Government-State or Local

ENVIRONMENTAL SCIENCE PROGRAM, AGRICULTURE AND SCIENCE DIVISION
NORTH DAKOTA UNIVERSITY
FARGO, ND 58102
See Interdisciplinary: General; Educational Institute

ENVIRONMENTAL STUDIES PROGRAM
UNIVERSITY OF NORTH DAKOTA
GRAND FORKS, ND 58201
See Interdisciplinary: General; Educational Institute

GEOLOGICAL SURVEY OF NORTH DAKOTA
UNIVERSITY STATION
GRAND FORKS, ND 58202
See Engineering: Water Resources; Government-State or Local

NORTHERN PRAIRIE WILDLIFE RESEARCH CENTER
POST OFFICE BOX 1672
JAMESTOWN, ND 58401
See Biology: Ecology; Government-Federal

SOIL CONSERVATION SERVICE
FEDERAL BUILDING, POST OFFICE BOX 1458
BISMARCK, ND 58501
See Biology: Ecology; Government-State or Local

STATE LABORATORIES DEPARTMENT
BOX 937
BISMARCK, ND 58501
See Engineering: Agricultural Engineering; Government-State or Local

WATER SUPPLY AND POLLUTION DIVISION, DEPARTMENT OF HEALTH
STATE CAPITOL BUILDING
BISMARCK, ND 58501
See Engineering: Water Resources; Government-State or Local

WILDLIFE FEDERATION OF NORTH DAKOTA
POST OFFICE BOX 1694
BISMARCK, ND 58501
See Biology: Ecology; Foundation

WORKS CONFERENCE, NORTH DAKOTA WATER AND POLLUTION CONTROL
STATION CAPITOL BUILDING
BISMARCK, ND 58501
See Engineering: Water Resources; Professional Organizations

New Hampshire

AIR POLLUTION CONTROL, HEALTH AND WELFARE DEPARTMENT

61 SOUTH SPRING STREET
CONCORD, NH 03301
See Engineering: Pollution Abatement;
Government-State or Local

**ATLANTIC SALMON EMERGENCY
COMMISSION**
BOX 164
HANCOCK, NH 03449
See Biology: Ecology; Educational Institute

**AUDUBON SOCIETY OF NEW
HAMPSHIRE**
NEW HAMPTON, NH 03256
See Biology: Ecology; Foundation

**AUDUBON SOCIETY OF NEW
HAMPSHIRE**
63 NORTH MAIN STREET
CONCORD, NH 03301
See Interdisciplinary: General; Professional Organizations

BEAVER BROOK ASSOCIATION
BROWN LANE
HOLLIS, NH 03049
See Interdisciplinary: General; Foundation

**BELKNAP COMMITTEE ON
BEAUTIFICATION**
LACONIA, NH 03246
See Interdisciplinary: General; Government-State or Local

**BIOLOGICAL SCIENCES
DEPARTMENT**
DARTMOUTH COLLEGE
HANOVER, NH 03755
See Biology: General; Educational Institute

**CITIZENS FOR A CLEANER
ENVIRONMENT**
814 ELM STREET
MANCHESTER, NH 03101
See Biology: Ecology; Government-State or Local

**COLD REGIONS RESEARCH
ENGINEERING LABORATORY**
POST OFFICE BOX 282
HANOVER, NH 03755
See Engineering: General; Government-Federal

CONSERVATION COMMISSION
HOLDERNESS, NH 03245
See Interdisciplinary: General; Government-State or Local

**CONSERVATION COUNCIL OF
HANOVER**
HANOVER, NH 03755
See Biology: Ecology; Government-State or Local

**CONSERVATION LAW
FOUNDATION OF NEW
ENGLAND, INCORPORATED**
95 NORTH MAIN STREET

CONCORD, NH 03301
See Social Sciences/Humanities: Law/
Legislation; Foundation

**CONSERVE THE ENVIRONMENT,
STATEWIDE PROGRAM**
BOX 757
CONCORD, NH 03301
See Biology: Ecology; Educational Institute

**ECOLOGY ACTION, CENTER
HUMAN SURVIVAL**
52 MAIN STREET
WEST LEBANON, NH 03784
See Biology: Ecology; Government-State or Local

**ENGINEERING DESIGN AND
ANALYSIS LABORATORY**
UNIVERSITY OF NEW HAMPSHIRE
DURHAM, NH 03824
See Engineering: General; Educational Institute

**ENVIRONMENTAL SCIENCE
PROGRAM**
UNIVERSITY OF NEW HAMPSHIRE
DURHAM, NH 03824
See Interdisciplinary: General; Educational Institute

**ENVIRONMENTAL STUDIES
PROGRAM**
DARTMOUTH COLLEGE
HANOVER, NH 03755
See Interdisciplinary: General; Educational Institute

FARM BUREAU FEDERATION
BOX 238, NORTH MAIN STREET
CONCORD, NH 03301
See Engineering: Agricultural Engineering; Professional Organizations

**FISHING AND GAME ADVISORY
BOARD**
SCHOOL STREET
MARLBOROUGH, NH 03455
See Social Sciences/Humanities: Recreation and Leisure; Professional Organizations

**FLOOD CONSERVATION
COMMISSION OF THE
MERRIMACK RIVER VALLEY**
4 PARK STREET
CONCORD, NH 03301
See Engineering: Water Resources; Government-State or Local

**FLOOD CONTROL COMMAND OF
THE CENTER RIVER VALLEY**
28 MECHANIC STREET
KEENE, NH 03431
See Engineering: Water Resources; Government-State or Local

**HEALTH AND WELFARE
DEPARTMENT**
66 SOUTH STREET
CONCORD, NH 03301

See Social Sciences/Humanities:
Welfare(Child Public Social);
Government-State or Local

**LAND TRUST OF THE NISSITISSIT
RIVER, INCORPORATED**
BOX 84
HOLLIS, NH 03049
See Engineering: Water Resources; Government-State or Local

**LAND USE FOUNDATION OF NEW
HAMPSHIRE**
SEVEN SOUTH STATE STREET
CONCORD, NH 03301
See Interdisciplinary: General; Foundation

**MARKETS AND STANDARDS
DIVISION, DEPARTMENT OF
AGRICULTURE**
STATE HOUSE ANNEX ROOM 106
CONCORD, NH 03301
See Engineering: Agricultural Engineering; Government-State or Local

MT WASHINGTON OBSERVATORY
GORHAM, NH 03581
See Geology: General; Field Station/Laboratory

NATURAL PRESERVES FORUM
5 SOUTH STATE STREET
CONCORD, NH 03301
See Biology: Ecology; Government-State or Local

**NATURAL RESOURCES COUNCIL
OF NEW HAMPSHIRE**
5 SOUTH STATE STREET
CONCORD, NH 03301
See Biology: Ecology; Professional Organizations

NATURE CONSERVANCY
BOX 97
EAST BARRINGTON, NH 03825
See Biology: Ecology; Foundation

NATURE CONSERVANCY
UNIVERSITY OF NEW HAMPSHIRE
DURHAM, NH 03842
See Biology: Ecology; Educational Institute

**NEW HAMPSHIRE COMMISSION
FOR BETTER WATER**
5 SOUTH STATE STREET
CONCORD, NH 03301
See Engineering: Water Resources; Government-State or Local

NEW HAMPSHIRE STATE GRANGE
RFD NO ONE
SUNCOOK, NH 03275
See Engineering: Agricultural Engineering; Professional Organizations

**NORMANDEAU ASSOCIATION,
INCORPORATED**
686 MAST ROAD
MANCHESTER, NH 03102
See Biology: Ecology; Research Institute

PRESERVATION ASSOCIATES
BOX 22
CORNISH FLAT, NH 03746
See Social Sciences/Humanities: Regional
Planning; Research Institute

**PROTECTION OF NEW
HAMPSHIRES FORESTS SOCIETY**
5 SOUTH STATE STREET
CONCORD, NH 03301
See Biology: Ecology; Foundation

**PROTECTIVE ASSOCIATION OF
LAKE SUNAPEE**
BURPEE HILL ROAD
NEW LONDON, NH 03257
See Biology: Ecology; Government-State
or Local

**RECREATION SERVICE
COMMISSION**
BOX 856
CONCORD, NH 03301
See Social Sciences/Humanities: Recrea-
tion and Leisure; Government-State or
Local

**RESEARCH COUNCIL OF NEW
HAMPSHIRE, INCORPORATED**
5 SOUTH STATE STREET
CONCORD, NH 03301
See Biology: Ecology; Government-State
or Local

**RESEARCH FOR CONSERVATION
AND DEVELOPMENT OF NORTH
COUNTRY**
POST OFFICE BOX 658
LITTLETON, NH 03561
See Biology: Ecology; Government-State
or Local

**RESOURCES AND ECONOMIC
DEVELOPMENT DEPARTMENT**
UNIVERSITY NEW HAMPSHIRE
DURHAM, NH 03824
See Engineering: Water Resources; Edu-
cational Institute

**RESOURCES DEVELOPMENT
CENTER**
UNIVERSITY OF NEW HAMPSHIRE
DURHAM, NH 03824
See Biology: Ecology; Educational Insti-
tute

SCIENCE CENTER OF SQUAW LAKE
US ROUTE THREE, BOX 146
HOLDERNESS, NH 03245
See Interdisciplinary: General; Govern-
ment-State or Local

**SEACOAST ANTIPOLLUTION
LEAGUE**
ROUTE 84
HAMPTON FALLS, NH 03844
See Engineering: Pollution Abatement;
Government-State or Local

**SOIL CONSERVATION
ASSOCIATION OF NEW
HAMPSHIRE**
RFD TWO
EXETER, NH 03833
See Biology: Ecology; Government-State
or Local

SOIL CONSERVATION SERVICE
FEDERAL BUILDING
DURHAM, NH 03824
See Biology: Ecology; Government-State
or Local

**SPORTSMENS CLUB OF NEW
HAMPSHIRE**
PUMPKIN HILL ROAD
WARNER, NH 03278
See Biology: Ecology; Foundation

**SPORTSMENS CLUB OF NEW
HAMPSHIRE**
123 SILVER LAKE ROAD
HOLLIS, NH 03049
See Biology: Ecology; Foundation

**WATER RESOURCE RESEARCH
CENTER**
UNIVERSITY OF NEW HAMPSHIRE
DURHAM, NH 03824
See Engineering: Water Resources; Edu-
cational Institute

WATER RESOURCES
20 LOCK STREET
NASHUA, NH 03060
See Engineering: Water Resources; Government-State or Local

**WATER SUPPLY AND POLLUTION
CONTROL**
61 SOUTH SPRING STREET
CONCORD, NH 03301
See Engineering: Water Resources; Gov-
ernment-State or Local

**WHITE MOUNTAIN
ENVIRONMENTAL COMMITTEE**
5 SOUTH STATE STREET
CONCORD, NH 03301
See Biology: Ecology; Government-State
or Local

**WILDFLOWER PRESERVATION
SOCIETY OF NEW ENGLAND**
HILLSBORO, NH 03244
See Biology: Ecology; Government-State
or Local

ZERO POPULATION GROWTH
BOX 237
CONCORD, NH 03301
See Social Sciences/Humanities: Popula-
tion Studies/Family Planning; Founda-
tion

ZERO POPULATION GROWTH
BOX 599
HANOVER, NH 03755
See Social Sciences/Humanities: Popula-
tion Studies/Family Planning; Founda-
tion

ZERO POPULATION GROWTH
POST OFFICE BOX 608
DURHAM, NH 03824
See Social Sciences/Humanities: Popula-
tion Studies/Family Planning; Founda-
tion

ZERO POPULATION GROWTH
SHARON ROAD
PETERBOROUGH, NH 03458
See Social Sciences/Humanities: Popula-
tion Studies/Family Planning; Founda-
tion

New Jersey

**ADIRONDACK MOUNTAIN CLUB,
INCORPORATED**
1113 CAMBRIDGE ROAD
TEANECK, NJ 07666
See Engineering: General; Professional
Organizations

AIR AND CLEAN WATER DIVISION
POST OFFICE BOX 1540
TRENTON, NJ 08608
See Engineering: Pollution Abatement;
Government-State or Local

AIR POLLUTION COMMISSION
49 MOUNTAIN PLEASANT AVENUE
WEST ORANGE, NJ 07050
See Engineering: Pollution Abatement;
Government-State or Local

AIR POLLUTION CONTROL
MUNICIPAL BUILDING, LIBERTY
AND HILLSIDE AVENUES
HILLSIDE, NJ 07205
See Engineering: Pollution Abatement;
Government-State or Local

**AIR POLLUTION CONTROL,
BOARD OF HEALTH**
301 NORTH WOOD AVENUE, CITY
HALL
LINDEN, NJ 07036
See Engineering: Pollution Abatement;
Government-State or Local

**AIR POLLUTION CONTROL,
BOARD OF HEALTH**
916 GARDEN STREET
HOBOKEN, NJ 07030
See Engineering: Pollution Abatement;
Government-State or Local

**AIR POLLUTION CONTROL,
DEPARTMENT OF HEALTH**
CITY HALL

ELIZABETH, NJ 07201
See Engineering: Pollution Abatement;
Government-State or Local

**AIR POLLUTION CONTROL,
HEALTH AND WELFARE
DEPARTMENT**
CITY HALL, 30TH STREET AND
EAST AVENUE
BAYONNE, NJ 07002
See Engineering: Pollution Abatement;
Government-State or Local

**AIR POLLUTION CONTROL,
HEALTH DEPARTMENT**
BELVILLE, NJ 07109
See Engineering: Pollution Abatement;
Government-State or Local

**AIR POLLUTION CONTROL,
HEALTH DEPARTMENT**
CITY HALL, ROOM 214
TRENTON, NJ 08608
See Engineering: Pollution Abatement;
Government-State or Local

**AIR POLLUTION CONTROL,
HEALTH DEPARTMENT**
CITY HALL, 260 HIGH STREET
PERTH AMBOY, NJ 08861
See Engineering: Pollution Abatement;
Government-State or Local

**AIR POLLUTION CONTROL,
HEALTH DEPARTMENT**
KENNEDY DRIVE
NUTLEY, NJ 07110
See Engineering: Pollution Abatement;
Government-State or Local

**AIR POLLUTION CONTROL,
HEALTH DEPARTMENT**
101 PASSAIC DRIVE
PASSAIC, NJ 07055
See Engineering: Pollution Abatement;
Government-State or Local

**AIR POLLUTION CONTROL,
HEALTH DEPARTMENT**
65 CHESTNUT STREET
MONTCLAIR, NJ 07042
See Engineering: Pollution Abatement;
Government-State or Local

**AIR POLLUTION CONTROL,
HEALTH HOUSING AND
WELFARE DEPARTMENT**
CITY HALL
CAMDEN, NJ 08101
See Engineering: Pollution Abatement;
Government-State or Local

AMERICA LITTORAL SOCIETY
SANDY HOOK
HIGHLANDS, NJ 07732
See Biology: General; Professional Organizations

**AUDUBON SOCIETY OF NEW
JERSEY**
790 EWING AVENUE
FRANKLIN LAKES, NJ 07417

See Interdisciplinary: General; Professional Organizations

**AUTOMOTIVE EMISSIONS
RESEARCH**
MOBILE RESOURCES AND
DEVELOPMENT CORPORATION
PAULSBORO, NJ 08066
See Engineering: Pollution Abatement;
Industrial/Commercial

BELL TELEPHONE LABORATORIES
MURRAY HILL, NJ 07971
See Engineering: General; Field Station/
Laboratory

BIOCHEMISTRY DEPARTMENT
STATE UNIVERSITY OF NEW JERSEY
NEW BRUNSWICK, NJ 08903
See Biology: Biochemistry; Educational
Institute

BIOLOGICAL RESEARCH BUREAU
RUTGERS UNIVERSITY
NEW BRUNSWICK, NJ 08903
See Biology: General; Educational Institute

BIOLOGY DEPARTMENT
PRINCETON UNIVERSITY
PRINCETON, NJ 08540
See Biology: General; Educational Institute

BOY SCOUTS OF AMERICA
NORTH BRUNSWICK, NJ 08902
See Interdisciplinary: General; Foundation

**CLEAN AIR AND WATER DIVISION,
HEALTH DEPARTMENT**
POST OFFICE BOX 1540
TRENTON, NJ 08625
See Engineering: Pollution Abatement;
Government-State or Local

**COASTAL FISHERIES
CORPORATION (MIDDLE
ATLANTIC)**
FISHERIES CENTER
HIGHLANDS, NJ 07732
See Engineering: Water Resources; Government-Federal

**COMMISSION FOR NATIONAL
ARBOR DAY**
63 FITZRANDOLPH ROAD
WEST ORANGE, NJ 07052
See Engineering: Agricultural Engineering; Professional Organizations

**CONSERVATION AND
ENVIRONMENTAL SCIENCES
BUREAU**
RUTGERS UNIVERSITY
NEW BRUNSWICK, NJ 08903
See Biology: Ecology; Educational Institute

**CONSUMER'S RESEARCH,
INCORPORATED**
WASHINGTON, NJ 07882
See Social Sciences/Humanities:
Welfare(Child Public Social); Research
Institute

**DAVIDSON LABORATORY, STEVENS
INSTITUTE OF TECHNOLOGY**
CASTLE POINT STATION
HOBOKEN, NJ 07030
See Engineering: Water Resources; Field
Station/Laboratory

**DELAWARE RIVER BASIN
COMMISSION**
25 SCOTCH ROAD
TRENTON, N J 08603
See Engineering: Water Resources; Government-State or Local

**EDUCATION AND CONSERVATION
DEPARTMENT**
MONTCLAIR STATE COLLEGE
MONTCLAIR, NJ 07043
See Social Sciences/Humanities: Education; Educational Institute

**ELECTROPLATERS SOCIETY OF
AMERICA**
443 BROAD STREET
NEWARK, NJ 07102
See Physics: General; Professional Organizations

ELM RESEARCH INSTITUTE
60 WEST PROSPECT STREET
WALDWICK, NJ 07463
See Biology: General; Research Institute

**ENVIRONMENTAL HEALTH
DIVISION, HEALTH
DEPARTMENT**
25 MILL STREET
PATERSON, NJ 07501
See Engineering: Pollution Abatement;
Government-State or Local

**ENVIRONMENTAL QUALITY
DEPARTMENT**
POST OFFICE BOX 1390
TRENTON, NJ 08625
See Engineering: Pollution Abatement;
Government-State or Local

**ENVIRONMENTAL SCIENCE
PROGRAM**
DREW UNIVERSITY
MADISON, NJ 07940
See Interdisciplinary: General; Educational Institute

**ENVIRONMENTAL SCIENCE
PROGRAM**
RIDER COLLEGE
TRENTON, NJ 08602
See Chemistry: General; Educational Institute

ENVIRONMENTAL SCIENCE PROGRAM
SETON HALL UNIVERSITY
SOUTH ORANGE, NJ 07079
See Interdisciplinary: General; Educational Institute

ENVIRONMENTAL SCIENCES, AGRICULTURAL COLLEGE
RUTGERS STATE UNIVERSITY
NEW BRUNSWICK, NJ 08903
See Engineering: Pollution Abatement; Educational Institute

ENVIRONMENTAL STUDIES CENTER
PRINCETON UNIVERSITY, ENGINEERING QUAD
PRINCETON, NJ 08540
See Interdisciplinary: General; Educational Institute

ENVIRONMENTAL STUDIES PROGRAM
FAIRLEIGH DICKINSON UNIVERSITY
RUTHERFORD, NJ 07070
See Interdisciplinary: General; Educational Institute

ENVIRONMENTAL STUDIES PROGRAM
PRINCETON UNIVERSITY
PRINCETON, NJ 08540
See Interdisciplinary: General; Educational Institute

ENVIRONMENTAL STUDIES PROGRAM
STEVENS INSTITUTE OF TECHNOLOGY
HOBOKEN, NJ 07030
See Engineering: General; Educational Institute

EXXON RESEARCH AND ENGINEERING DEPARTMENT
POST OFFICE BOX 111
LINDEN, NJ 07036
See Engineering: Pollution Abatement; Industrial/Commercial

FISHERIES MANAGEMENT BUREAU, CONSERVATION AND ECONOMIC DEVELOPMENT
J FITCH PLAZA, PO BOX 1889
TRENTON, NJ 08625
See Engineering: Water Resources; Government-State or Local

GEOLOGICAL AND TOPOGRAPHY BUREAU
POST OFFICE BOX 1889, J FITCH PLAZA
TRENTON, NJ 08625
See Engineering: Water Resources; Government-State or Local

GEOPHYSICAL FLUID DYNAMICS LABORATORY
PRINCETON UNIVERSITY, FORRESTAL
PRINCETON, NJ 08540
See Physics: General; Government-State or Local

HEALTH AND WELFARE DEPARTMENT
CITY HALL, 280 GROVE STREET
JERSEY CITY, NJ 07302
See Engineering: Pollution Abatement; Government-State or Local

HEALTH DEPARTMENT
CITY HALL, 76 BAYARD AVENUE
NEW BRUNSWICK, NJ 08903
See Engineering: Pollution Abatement; Government-State or Local

INDUSTRIAL HYGIENE AND AIR POLLUTION BUREAU
ROOM 406 CITY HALL
NEWARK, NJ 07102
See Engineering: General; Government-State or Local

INDUSTRIAL HYGIENE ASSOCIATION
210 HADDON AVENUE
WESTMONT, NJ 08108
See Biology: Ecology; Government-Federal

INFORMATION CENTER FOR CRIME DELINQUENCY
NCCD CENTER
PARAMUS, NJ 07652
See Social Sciences/Humanities: Juvenile Delinquency; Research Institute

LITTORAL SOCIETY OF AMERICA
SANDY HOOK
HIGHLANDS, NJ 07732
See Biology: Ecology; Research Institute

MANAGEMENT INSTITUTE, LABOR RELATIONS DEPARTMENT
RYDER'S LANE, RUTGERS STATE UNIVERSITY
NEW BRUNSWICK, NJ 08901
See Social Sciences/Humanities: Labor/Relations/Unions; Educational Institute

MICROBIOLOGY INSTITUTE, RUTGERS UNIVERSITY
UNIVERSITY HEIGHTS CAMPUS
NEW BRUNSWICK, NJ 08901
See Biology: Biochemistry; Educational Institute

NATIONAL WATER INSTITUTE
744 BROAD STREET, ROOM 3405
NEWARK, NJ 07102
See Engineering: Pollution Abatement; Industrial/Commercial

NAVIGATION BUREAU
J FITCH PLAZA BOX 1889
TRENTON, NJ 08625
See Engineering: General; Government-State or Local

NORTH JERSEY CONSERVATION FOUNDATION
300 MENDHAM ROAD
MORRISTOWN, NJ 07960
See Interdisciplinary: General; Foundation

OCCUPATIONAL HEALTH PROGRAM
NEW JERSEY DEPARTMENT OF HEALTH
TRENTON, NJ 08625
See Interdisciplinary: General; Government-State or Local

PARKS FOR RECREATION DIVISION, DEPARTMENT OF CONSERVATION
J FITCH PLAZA POST OFFICE BOX 1889
TRENTON, NJ 08625
See Engineering: Water Resources; Government-State or Local

PESTICIDE CONTROL ASSOCIATION (NATIONAL)
250 WEST JERSEY STREET
ELIZABETH, NJ 07202
See Interdisciplinary: General; Industrial/Commercial

PESTICIDE CONTROL, DEPARTMENT OF AGRICULTURE
POST OFFICE BOX 1888
TRENTON, NJ 08625
See Engineering: Agricultural Engineering; Government-State or Local

POPULATION BIOLOGY GROUP
PRINCETON UNIVERSITY, ENO HALL
PRINCETON, NJ 08540
See Biology: Ecology; Educational Institute

POPULATION RESEARCH LIBRARY
PRINCETON UNIVERSITY
PRINCETON, NJ 08540
See Social Sciences/Humanities: Population Studies/Family Planning; Educational Institute

PSYCHOLOGICAL STUDIES LABORATORY
STEVENS INSTITUTE OF TECHNOLOGY
HOBOKEN, NJ 07030
See Social Sciences/Humanities: Psychology/Behavioral Science; Research Institute

PSYCHOLOGY LIBRARY
GREEN HALL, PRINCETON UNIVERSITY
PRINCETON, NJ 08540

See Social Sciences/Humanities: Psychology/Behavioral Science; Educational Institute

SOIL CONSERVATION SERVICES
1370 HAMILTON STREET, PO BOX 219
SOMERSET, NJ 08873
See Biology: Ecology; Government-State or Local

URBAN RESOURCES BUREAU, PRINCETON UNIVERSITY
ARCHITECTURE BUILDING
PRINCETON, NJ 08540
See Social Sciences/Humanities: Community Development/Studies; Educational Institute

WATER AND WASTEWATER EQUIPMENT MANUFACTURING ASSOCIATION
744 BROAD STREET
NEWARK, NJ 07102
See Engineering: Pollution Abatement; Industrial/Commercial

WATER RESOURCES COMMISSION
PRINCETON UNIVERSITY
PRINCETON, NJ 08540
See Engineering: Water Resources; Educational Institute

WATERSHED ASSOCIATION COUNCIL OF THE MID-ATLANTIC
POST OFFICE BOX 171
PENNINGTON, NJ 08534
See Engineering: Water Resources; Government-State or Local

WATERSHED ASSOCIATION OF FARMINGTON RIVER
MURRAY HILL, NJ 07971
See Interdisciplinary: General; Professional Organizations

WATERSHED ASSOCIATION OF UPPER RARITAN
POST OFFICE BOX 44
FARNILLS, NJ 07931
See Interdisciplinary: General; Foundation

WATERSHEDS (STONYBROOK-MILLSTONE)
POST OFFICE BOX 171
PENNINSTON, NJ 08534
See Interdisciplinary: General; Professional Organizations

WETLANDS INSTITUTE OF SOUTH JERSEY
LEHIGH UNIVERSITY (CMES)
STONE HARBOR, NJ 08247
See Interdisciplinary: General; Field Station/Laboratory

ZAROMB RESEARCH FOUNDATION
PASSAIC, NJ 07055
See Engineering: Pollution Abatement; Foundation

New Mexico

AIR MANAGEMENT DIVISION, ENVIRONMENTAL HEALTH DEPARTMENT
400 MARQUETTE, NW BOX 1293
ALBUQUERQUE, NM 87103
See Engineering: Pollution Abatement; Government-State or Local

ATOMIC ENERGY COMMISSION, ALBUQUERQUE OPERATIONS
POST OFFICE BOX 5400
ALBUQUERQUE, NM 87115
See Geology: General; Government-Federal

CONSERVATION COORDINATION COUNCIL OF NEW MEXICO
POST OFFICE BOX 142
ALBUQUERQUE, NM 87103
See Biology: Ecology; Research Institute

EDUCATION, PLANNING AND DEVELOPMENT BUREAU
UNIVERSITY OF MEXICO
ALBUQUERQUE, NM 87106
See Social Sciences/Humanities: Education; Educational Institute

ENCINO MEDICAL PLAZA
NORTHEAST
ALBUQUERQUE, NM 87106
See Biology: Ecology; Professional Organizations

ENGINEERING DIVISION OF STATE OF NEW MEXICO
STATE CAPITOL
SANTA FE, NM 87501
See Engineering: Water Resources; Government-State or Local

ENVIRONMENTAL EDUCATION, NATIONAL PARK SERVICES
POST OFFICE BOX 728
SANTA FE, NM 87501
See Biology: Ecology; Government-State or Local

ENVIRONMENTAL RESEARCH AND PLANNING CENTER
UNIVERSITY OF NEW MEXICO
ALBUQUERQUE, NM 87101
See Interdisciplinary: General; Educational Institute

ENVIRONMENTAL SCIENCE PROGRAM
NEW MEXICO INSTITUTE OF MINING AND TECHNOLOGY
SOCORRO, NM 87801
See Chemistry: General; Educational Institute

ENVIRONMENTAL SERVICES DIVISION
HEALTH AND SOCIAL SERVICES DEPARTMENT
SANTA FE, NM 87501
See Biology: Ecology; Government-State or Local

ENVIRONMENTAL STUDIES PROGRAM
EASTERN NEW MEXICO UNIVERSITY
PORTALES, NM 88130
See Interdisciplinary: General; Educational Institute

ENVIRONMENTAL STUDIES PROGRAM
NEW MEXICO HIGHLANDS UNIVERSITY
LAS VEGAS, NM 87701
See Chemistry: General; Educational Institute

ENVIRONMENTAL STUDIES PROGRAM
NEW MEXICO STATE UNIVERSITY
LAS CRUCES, NM 88001
See Interdisciplinary: General; Educational Institute

ENVIRONMENTAL STUDIES PROGRAM
UNIVERSITY OF NEW MEXICO
ALBUQUERQUE, NM 87106
See Interdisciplinary: General; Educational Institute

FOREST SERVICE REGION 3 OFFICE
FEDERAL BUILDING, 517 GOLD AVENUE, SW
ALBUQUERQUE, NM 87101
See Engineering: Agricultural Engineering; Government-Federal

INDUSTRIAL HEALTH SERVICE
500 GOLD AVENUE, SW
ALBUQUERQUE, NM 87101
See Engineering: Water Resources; Government-Federal

INSPECTION DIVISION, DEPARTMENT OF AGRICULTURE
POST OFFICE BOX 3150
LA CRUCES, NM 88001
See Engineering: Agricultural Engineering; Government-State or Local

LEGISLATIVE COUNCIL SERVICES
201 STATE CAPITOL
SANTA FE, NM 87501
See Social Sciences/Humanities: Law/Legislation; Government-State or Local

OCCUPATIONAL HEALTH, AIR POLLUTION DIVISION, STATE HEALTH DEPARTMENT
408 GALISTEO STREET
SANTE FE, NM 87501
See Engineering: Pollution Abatement; Government-State or Local

**PLANNING OFFICE OF NEW
MEXICO**
SANTA FE, NM 87501
See Engineering: Water Resources; Gov-
ernment-State or Local

SCIENCE RESEARCH INSTITUTE
NEW MEXICO HIGHLANDS
UNIVERSITY
LAS VEGAS, NM 87745
See Biology: General; Research Institute

**SOIL AND WATER CONSERVATION
COMMISSION OF NEW MEXICO**
ROOM 301, STATE CAPITOL
SANTA FE, NM 87501
See Engineering: Water Resources; Gov-
ernment-State or Local

SOIL CONSERVATION SERVICES
517 GOLD AVENUE, SW PO BOX 2007
ALBUQUERQUE, NM 87103
See Biology: Ecology; Government-State
or Local

**WATER QUALITY CONTROL, NEW
MEXICO ENVIRONMENTAL
IMPROVEMENT AGENCY**
POST OFFICE BOX 2348
SANTA FE, NM 87501
See Engineering: Water Resources; Gov-
ernment-State or Local

**WATER RESOURCES RESEARCH
INSTITUTE, NEW MEXICO STATE
UNIVERSITY**
POST OFFICE BOX 167
UNIVERSITY PARK, NM 88070
See Engineering: Water Resources; Edu-
cational Institute

**WILDLIFE CONSERVATION OF
NEW MEXICO**
BOX 1542
SANTA FE, NM 87501
See Biology: Ecology; Foundation

Nevada

AGRICULTURE DEPARTMENT
P O BOX 1209, 350 CAPITOL HILL
AVENUE
RENO, NV 89504
See Engineering: Agricultural Engineer-
ing; Government-State or Local

**AIR POLLUTION CONTROL
DIVISION, COUNTY HEALTH
DEPARTMENT**
10 KIRMAN AVENUE
RENO, NV 89502
See Engineering: Pollution Abatement;
Government-State or Local

**AIR POLLUTION CONTROL,
COUNTY HEALTH DEPARTMENT**
625 SHADOW LANE

LAS VEGAS, NV 89106
See Engineering: Pollution Abatement;
Government-State or Local

**ATOMIC ENERGY COMMISSION,
NEVADA OPERATIONS**
POST OFFICE BOX 14100
LAS VEGAS, NV 89114
See Interdisciplinary: General; Govern-
ment-State or Local

**DESERT BIGHORN COUNCIL,
DEPARTMENT OF BIOLOGICAL
SCIENCES**
UNIVERSITY OF NEVADA
LAS VEGAS, NV 89109
See Biology: General; Professional Organ-
izations

DESERT RESEARCH INSTITUTE
UNIVERSITY OF NEVADA SYSTEM
RENO, NV 89507
See Engineering: Water Resources; Edu-
cational Institute

EDUCATION DEPARTMENT
HEROES MEMORIAL BUILDING
CARSON CITY,NV 89701
See Social Sciences/Humanities: Educa-
tion; Government-State or Local

**ENVIRONMENTAL HEALTH
BUREAU**
790 SUTRO STREET
RENO, NV 89502
See Engineering: Pollution Abatement;
Government-State or Local

**ENVIRONMENTAL RESEARCH
LABORATORY, WESTERN**
BOX 15027
LAS VEGAS, NV 89114
See Biology: Ecology; Government-Fed-
eral

**ENVIRONMENTAL STUDIES
PROGRAM**
UNIVERSITY OF NEVADA, RENO
RENO, NV 89807
See Interdisciplinary: General; Educa-
tional Institute

**FOREST INSTITUTE FOR OCEAN
AND MOUNTAIN STUDY**
BOX 621 ROUTE 1
CARSON CITY, NV 89701
See Biology: General; Educational Insti-
tute

**GOVERNMENTAL RESEARCH
BUREAU**
UNIVERSITY OF NEVADA
RENO, NV 89507
See Social Sciences/Humanities: Politics;
Educational Institute

**HEALTH AND WELFARE
DEPARTMENT**
709 SUTRO STREET
RENO, NV 89502

See Engineering: Pollution Abatement;
Government-State or Local

**NATIONAL WILDLIFE
FEDERATION**
REGION 12
RENO, NV 89501
See Biology: Ecology; Foundation

**RESOURCES STATION UNIT,
EMPLOYMENT DEPARTMENT**
P O BOX 602
CARSON CITY, NV 89701
See Social Sciences/Humanities: Popula-
tion Studies/Family Planning; Founda-
tion

SOIL CONSERVATION SERVICES
ROOM 308, P O BUILDING, P O BOX
4850
RENO, NV 89505
See Biology: Ecology; Government-State
or Local

**WATER RESOURCES DIVISION,
DEPARTMENT NATURAL
RESOURCES AND
CONSERVATION**
201 SOUTH FALL STREET
CARSON CITY, NV 89701
See Engineering: Water Resources; Gov-
ernment-State or Local

**WILDLIFE FEDERATION OF
NEVADA**
POST OFFICE BOX 15205
LAS VEGAS, NV 89114
See Biology: Ecology; Foundation

New York

**ACOUSTICAL SOCIETY OF
AMERICA**
335 EAST 45TH STREET
NEW YORK, NY 10017
See Engineering: Pollution Abatement;
Professional Organizations

**ADIRONDACK MOUNTAINS
PROTECTION ASSOCIATION**
POST OFFICE BOX 951
SCHENECTADY, NY 12301
See Interdisciplinary: General; Founda-
tion

**AGRICULTURAL AND CHEMURGIC
RESOURCES COUNCIL**
350 FIFTH AVENUE
NEW YORK, NY 10001
See Engineering: Agricultural Engineer-
ing; Research Institute

**AGRICULTURAL TECHNOLOGY
EXPERIMENTAL STATION**
CORNELL UNIVERSITY
ITHACA, NY 14850
See Engineering: Pollution Abatement;
Educational Institute

AIR AND WATER PROGRAMS, ENVIRONMENTAL PROTECTION AGENCY, REGION 2
26 FEDERAL PLAZA
NEW YORK, NY 10009
See Engineering: Pollution Abatement; Government-State or Local

AIR CONTROL SECTION, COUNTY HEALTH DEPARTMENT
300 SOUTH GEDDES STREET, BOX 1325
SYRACUSE, NY 13201
See Engineering: Pollution Abatement; Government-State or Local

AIR POLLUTION CONTROL
146 FERNBANK AVENUE
DELMER, NY 12054
See Engineering: Pollution Abatement; Research Institute

AIR POLLUTION CONTROL BOARD, HEALTH DEPARTMENT
TOWN HALL
CHEEKTOWAGA, NY 14225
See Engineering: Pollution Abatement; Government-State or Local

AIR POLLUTION CONTROL DEPARTMENT
51 ASTOR PLACE
NEW YORK, NY 10003
See Engineering: Pollution Abatement; Government-State or Local

AIR POLLUTION CONTROL OFFICE
CITY HALL, 200 NIAGARA STREET
TONAWANDA, NY 14150
See Engineering: Pollution Abatement; Government-State or Local

AIR POLLUTION CONTROL SECTION, FIRE HEADQUARTERS
LITTLE WASHINGTON STREET
POUGHKEEPSIE, NY 12601
See Engineering: Pollution Abatement; Government-State or Local

AIR POLLUTION CONTROL, CODE ENFORCEMENT AGENCY
CITY HALL, 207 NORTH JAMES STREET
ROME, NY 13440
See Engineering: Pollution Abatement; Government-State or Local

AIR POLLUTION CONTROL, COUNTY HEALTH DEPARTMENT
22 MARKET STREET
POUGHKEEPSIE, NY 12601
See Engineering: Pollution Abatement; Government-State or Local

AIR POLLUTION CONTROL, ENVIRONMENTAL CONTROL DEPARTMENT
1324 MOTOR PARKWAY
HAUPPAUGE, NY 11787
See Engineering: Pollution Abatement; Government-State or Local

AIR POLLUTION CONTROL, HEALTH DEPARTMENT
CITY HALL, 105 JAY STREET
SCHENECTADY, NY 12305
See Engineering: Pollution Abatement; Government-State or Local

AIR POLLUTION CONTROL, PUBLIC HEALTH DEPARTMENT
30 CHURCH STREET
NEW ROCHELLE, NY 10805
See Engineering: Pollution Abatement; Government-State or Local

AIR POLLUTION CONTROL, VILLAGE OF HERKIMER
120 GREEN STREET
HERKIMER, NY 13350
See Engineering: Pollution Abatement; Government-State or Local

AIR POLLUTION INSPECTION
MUNICIPAL BUILDING, MORGAN STREET
ILION, NY 13357
See Engineering: Pollution Abatement; Government-State or Local

AIR POLLUTION, ENVIRONMENTAL HEALTH, COUNTY HEALTH DEPARTMENT
240 OLD COUNTRY ROAD
MINEOLA, NY 11501
See Engineering: Pollution Abatement; Government-State or Local

AIR RESOURCES DIVISION, STATE HEALTH DEPARTMENT
84 HOLLAND AVENUE
ALBANY, NY 12208
See Engineering: Pollution Abatement; Government-State or Local

AMERICAN COMMISSION FOR INTERNATIONAL WILDLIFE
NEW YORK ZOOLOGICAL PARK
NEW YORK, NY 10060
See Biology: General; Foundation

AMERICAN GEOGRAPHICAL SOCIETY
BROADWAY AT 156TH STREET
NEW YORK,NY 10032
See Social Sciences/Humanities: General; Professional Organizations

AMERICAN MENTAL HEALTH FOUNDATION, INCORPORATED
2 EAST 86TH STREET
NEW YORK, NY 10028
See Social Sciences/Humanities: Mental Health; Foundation

AMERICAN PETROLEUM INSTITUTE, TIME-LIFE BUILDING
1271 AVENUE OF THE AMERICAS
NEW YORK, NY 10020
See Engineering: Water Resources; Government-Federal

APPLIED SOCIAL RESEARCH
605 WEST 115TH STREET-COLUMBIA UNIVERSITY
NEW YORK, NY 10025
See Social Sciences/Humanities: General; Educational Institute

ARCHITECTURAL ART AND PLANNING COLLEGE
CORNELL UNIVERSITY
ITHACA, NY 14850
See Engineering: General; Educational Institute

ASTOR, LENOX AND TILDEN FOUNDATION, NEW YORK PUBLIC LIBRARY
FIFTH AND 42ND STREET
NEW YORK, NY 10018
See Social Sciences/Humanities: General; Foundation

ATMOSPHERIC SCIENCES RESEARCH CENTER
STATE UNIVERSITY OF NEW YORK
ALBANY, NY 12224
See Engineering: Pollution Abatement; Educational Institute

ATMOSPHERIC SCIENCES RESEARCH CENTER
WHITEFACE MOUNTAIN FIELD STATION
WILMINGTON, NY 12997
See Engineering: Pollution Abatement; Research Institute

ATMOSPHERIC SCIENCES RESEARCH CENTER EXPERIMENTAL LABORATORY
SCHENECTADY COUNTY AIRPORT
SCHENECTADY, NY 12329
See Engineering: Pollution Abatement; Field Station/Laboratory

ATMOSPHERIC SCIENCES RESEARCH CENTER LABORATORY
100 FULLER ROAD
ALBANY, NY 12224
See Interdisciplinary: General; Field Station/Laboratory

ATMOSPHERIC SCIENCES RESEARCH CENTER
STATE UNIVERSITY NEW YORK-ALBANY/SAROTOGA
SCOTIA, NY 12302
See Geology: General; Educational Institute

ATMOSPHERIC STUDIES PROGRAM
CLARKSON COLLEGE OF TECHNOLOGY
POTSDAM, NY 13676
See Engineering: Pollution Abatement; Educational Institute

ATOMIC ENERGY COMMISSION HEALTH AND SAFETY LABORATORY
376 HUDSON STREET
NEW YORK, NY 10014
See Chemistry: Physical Chemistry; Government-State or Local

ATOMIC ENERGY COMMISSION, SCHENECTADY NAVAL REACTORS OFFICE
POST OFFICE BOX 1069
SCHENECTADY, NY 12301
See Geology: General; Government-Federal

AUDUBON SOCIETY (NATIONAL)
1130 FIFTH AVENUE
NEW YORK, NY 10028
See Biology: Ecology; Foundation

BIOLOGICAL SCIENCES DIVISION
CORNELL UNIVERSITY
ITHACA, NY 14850
See Biology: General; Educational Institute

BIOLOGICAL-MEDICAL DIVISION, POPULATION COUNCIL
ROCKEFELLER UNIVERSITY
NEW YORK, NY 10021
See Social Sciences/Humanities: Population Studies/Family Planning; Educational Institute

BIOLOGY DEPARTMENT, PACE COLLEGE
41 PARK ROW
NEW YORK, NY 10038
See Biology: General; Educational Institute

BIRD CLUBS FEDERATION OF NEW YORK STATE
STATE MUSEUM
ALBANY, NY 12224
See Biology: General; Professional Organizations

BIRD PRESERVATION COUNCIL, UNITED STATES SECTION
950 THIRD AVENUE
NEW YORK, NY 10022
See Biology: General; Field Station/Laboratory

BOTANICAL GARDENS
BROOKLYN
BROOKLYN, NY 10000
See Biology: Ecology; Field Station/Laboratory

BOYCE THOMPSON INSTITUTE
1086 NORTH BROADWAY
YONKERS, NY 10701
See Biology: General; Research Institute

BOYS CLUBS OF AMERICA
771 FIRST AVENUE
NEW YORK, NY 10017
See Interdisciplinary: General; Foundation

BROOKHAVEN NATIONAL LABORATORY
UPTON, NY 11973
See Biology: General; Research Institute

BROOKLYN COLLEGE
BEDFORD AVENUE AND AVENUE H
BROOKLYN, NY 11210
See Interdisciplinary: General; Educational Institute

CAMP FIRE GIRLS
1740 BROADWAY
NEW YORK, NY 10019
See Interdisciplinary: General; Foundation

CAMPFIRE CLUB OF AMERICA
19 RECTOR STREET
NEW YORK, NY 10006
See Interdisciplinary: General; Professional Organizations

CHAUTAUQUA PROJECT
BOX 250
FREDONIA, NY 14063
See Interdisciplinary: General; Educational Institute

CHEMISTRY DEPARTMENT
RENSSELAER POLYTECHNIC INSTITUTE
TROY, NY 12181
See Chemistry: General; Educational Institute

CHILD WELFARE LEAGUE OF AMERICA
67 IRVING PLACE
NEW YORK, NY 10003
See Social Sciences/Humanities: Welfare(Child Public Social); Research Institute

CIVIL ENGINEER SOCIETY OF AMERICA
345 EAST 47TH STREET
NEW YORK, NY 10017
See Engineering: General; Professional Organizations

CLEAN AIR, CITIZEN'S COMMITTEE
598 MADISON AVENUE
NEW YORK, NY 10022
See Engineering: Pollution Abatement; Professional Organizations

COAST GUARD EASTERN AREA
GOVERNORS ISLAND
NEW YORK, NY 10004
See Interdisciplinary: General; Unclassified

COMMON COUNCIL OF GREATER NEW YORK, INFORMATION BUREAU
225 PARK AVENUE SOUTH
NEW YORK, NY 10003
See Social Sciences/Humanities: Welfare(Child Public Social); Government-State or Local

CONSERVATION COUNCIL OF NEW YORK STATE
5 BROADWAY, ROOM 505
TROY, NY 12180
See Biology: Ecology; Foundation

CONSERVATION FORUM
101 ENGLEWOOD AVENUE
BUFFALO, NY 14214
See Interdisciplinary: General; Professional Organizations

CONSERVATIONISTS COUNCIL
201 EAST 62ND STREET
NEW YORK, NY 10021
See Social Sciences/Humanities: General; Professional Organizations

CONSOLIDATED EDISON CORPORATION OF NEW YORK, INCORPORATED
4 IRVING PLACE
NEW YORK, NY 10003
See Engineering: Pollution Abatement; Industrial/Commercial

CONSUMERS UNION OF THE UNITED STATES, INCORPORATED
256 WASHINGTON STREET
MOUNT VERNON, NY 10553
See Social Sciences/Humanities: Welfare(Child Public Social); Research Institute

COOPER UNION
COOPER SQUARE
NEW YORK, NY 10003
See Engineering: General; Educational Institute

CRIPPLED AND DISABLED REHABILITATION INSTITUTE
400 FIRST AVENUE
NEW YORK, NY 10010
See Social Sciences/Humanities: Rehabilitation; Research Institute

ECOLOGICAL RESEARCH CENTER
MERRY COLLEGE
DOBBS FERRY, NY 10522
See Biology: Ecology; Educational Institute

ECONOMIC AND TRANSPORTATION DIVISION
UNITED NATIONS PLAZA
NEW YORK, NY 10017
See Engineering: Water Resources; Government-Federal

ECONOMIC EDUCATION COUNCIL
2 WEST 46TH STREET
NEW YORK,NY 10036
See Social Sciences/Humanities: Education; Industrial/Commercial

EDUCATIONAL FACILITIES
LABORATORIES, INCORPORATED
477 MADISON AVENUE
NEW YORK, NY 10022
See Social Sciences/Humanities: Education; Industrial/Commercial

EDUCATIONAL RECORDS BUREAU
21 AUDUBON AVENUE
NEW YORK,NY 10032
See Social Sciences/Humanities: Education; Professional Organizations

ENGINEERING DEPARTMENT
STATE UNIVERSITY OF NEW YORK
BUFFALO, NY 14210
See Engineering: General; Educational
Institute

ENGINEERING EXAMINERS AND
BOILER INSPECTORS
2501 CITY HALL
BUFFALO, NY 14202
See Engineering: Pollution Abatement;
Government-State or Local

ENVIRONMENTAL ADVISORY
PANEL AT COLGATE
COLGATE UNIVERSITY
HAMILTON, NY 13346
See Chemistry: General; Educational Institute

ENVIRONMENTAL AFFAIRS
SECTION
1271 AVENUE OF AMERICAS
NEW YORK, NY 10020
See Engineering: Water Resources; Government-Federal

ENVIRONMENTAL CENTER OF
THE LOWER HUDSON VALLEY
MERCY COLLEGE
DOBBS FERRY, NY 10522
See Biology: Ecology; Educational Institute

ENVIRONMENTAL DEFENSE FUND,
INCORPORATED
POST OFFICE BOX 740
STONY BROOK, NY 11790
See Biology: Ecology; Professional Organizations

ENVIRONMENTAL DEFENSE FUND,
INCORPORATED
162 OLD TOWN
EAST SETAUKET, NY 11733
See Social Sciences/Humanities: Law/
Legislation; Professional Organizations

ENVIRONMENTAL EDUCATION
ASSOCIATION OF SUSQUEHANNA
616 PHEASANT LANE
ENDWELL, NY 13760
See Biology: Ecology; Educational Institute

ENVIRONMENTAL ENGINEERING
AND SCIENCE GRADUATE
PROGRAM
MANHATTAN COLLEGE
BRONX, NY 10711
See Engineering: Water Resources; Educational Institute

ENVIRONMENTAL ENGINEERING
AND SCIENCE, CIVIL
ENGINEERING DEPARTMENT
MANHATTAN COLLEGE
BRONX, NY 10471
See Engineering: General; Educational
Institute

ENVIRONMENTAL HEALTH
DEPARTMENT, HOOKER
CHEMICAL COMPANY
277 PARK AVENUE
NEW YORK, NY 10017
See Chemistry: General; Industrial/Commercial

ENVIRONMENTAL HEALTH
SERVICE, COUNTY HEALTH
DEPARTMENT
363 ALLEN STREET
HUDSON, NY 12534
See Engineering: Pollution Abatement;
Government-State or Local

ENVIRONMENTAL HEALTH
SERVICES DIVISION
845 CENTRAL AVENUE
ALBANY, NY 12208
See Engineering: Water Resources; Government-State or Local

ENVIRONMENTAL HEALTH
SERVICES, BROOME COUNTY
HEALTH DEPARTMENT
62068 WATER STREET
BINGHAMTON, NY 13901
See Engineering: Pollution Abatement;
Government-State or Local

ENVIRONMENTAL HEALTH
SERVICES, COUNTY HEALTH
DEPARTMENT
COUNTY OFFICE BUILDING
LOCKPORT, NY 14094
See Engineering: Pollution Abatement;
Government-State or Local

ENVIRONMENTAL HEALTH
SERVICES, COUNTY HEALTH
DEPARTMENT
311 BALDWIN STREET
ELMIRA, NY 14901
See Engineering: Pollution Abatement;
Government-State or Local

ENVIRONMENTAL HEALTH
SERVICES, HEALTH
DEPARTMENT
409 MADISON AVENUE
ALBANY, NY 12201
See Engineering: Pollution Abatement;
Government-State or Local

ENVIRONMENTAL LABORATORY
OF LAKE ONTARIO
STATE UNIVERSITY OF NEW YORK
AT OSWEGO
OSWEGO, NY 13126
See Biology: Ecology; Field Station/Laboratory

ENVIRONMENTAL MANPOWER
OFFICE
50 WOLF ROAD
ALBANY, NY 12201
See Engineering: Water Resources; Government-State or Local

ENVIRONMENTAL MEDICINE
INSTITUTE
NEW YORK UNIVERSITY MEDICAL
CENTER
NEW YORK, NY 10001
See Interdisciplinary: General; Educational Institute

ENVIRONMENTAL MEDICINE
INSTITUTE
NEW YORK UNIVERSITY MEDICAL
CENTER, LONG MEADOW
TUXEDO, NY 10987
See Engineering: General; Educational
Institute

ENVIRONMENTAL PROTECTION
AGENCY, REGION 2
26 FEDERAL PLAZA
NEW YORK, NY 10007
See Interdisciplinary: General; Unclassified

ENVIRONMENTAL PROTECTION
BUREAU, DEVELOPMENT
DEPARTMENT
87 NEPPERHAN AVENUE
YONKERS, NY 10701
See Social Sciences/Humanities: Housing
; Government-State or Local

ENVIRONMENTAL QUALITY
MANAGEMENT CENTER
CORNELL UNIVERSITY
ITHACA, NY 14850
See Interdisciplinary: General; Educational Institute

ENVIRONMENTAL RESEARCH
PROGRAM
NEW YORK UNIVERSITY
NEW YORK, NY 10019
See Biology: Ecology; Government-Federal

ENVIRONMENTAL RESEARCH, SCHOOL OF ENGINEERING AND SCIENCES
NEW YORK UNIVERSITY
NEW YORK, NY 10001
See Engineering: General; Educational Institute

ENVIRONMENTAL SANITATION, HEALTH DEPARTMENT
406 ELIZABETH STREET
UTICA, NY 13501
See Engineering: Pollution Abatement; Government-State or Local

ENVIRONMENTAL SCIENCE AND ENGINEERING
COLUMBIA UNIVERSITY
NEW YORK, NY 10022
See Engineering: General; Educational Institute

ENVIRONMENTAL SCIENCE AND FORESTRY COLLEGE
STATE UNIVERSITY OF NEW YORK AT SYRACUSE
SYRACUSE, NY 13210
See Interdisciplinary: General; Government-State or Local

ENVIRONMENTAL SCIENCE CENTER
COLLEGE OF NEW ROCHELLE
NEW ROCHELLE, NY 10801
See Biology: Ecology; Educational Institute

ENVIRONMENTAL SCIENCE PROGRAM
ADELPHI UNIVERSITY
GARDEN CITY, NY 11530
See Interdisciplinary: General; Educational Institute

ENVIRONMENTAL SCIENCE PROGRAM
LONG ISLAND UNIVERSITY
GREENVALE, NY 11548
See Chemistry: General; Educational Institute

ENVIRONMENTAL SCIENCE PROGRAM
RENSSELAER POLYTECHNICAL INSTITUTE
TROY, NY 12181
See Interdisciplinary: General; Educational Institute

ENVIRONMENTAL SCIENCE PROGRAM
STATE UNIVERSITY COLLEGE
CORTLAND, NY 13045
See Chemistry: General; Educational Institute

ENVIRONMENTAL SCIENCE PROGRAM
STATE UNIVERSITY COLLEGE

OSWEGO, NY 13126
See Chemistry: General; Educational Institute

ENVIRONMENTAL SCIENCE PROGRAM
STATE UNIVERSITY OF NEW YORK AT BINGHAMTON
BINGHAMTON, NY 13901
See Chemistry: General; Educational Institute

ENVIRONMENTAL SCIENCE PROGRAM
UNION COLLEGE AND UNIVERSITY
SCHENECTADY, NY 12308
See Interdisciplinary: General; Educational Institute

ENVIRONMENTAL SCIENCE PROGRAM
VASSAR COLLEGE
POUGHKEEPSIE, NY 12601
See Chemistry: General; Educational Institute

ENVIRONMENTAL SCIENCE PROGRAM
WEBB INSTITUTE OF NAVAL ARCHITECTURE
GLEN COVE, NY 11542
See Engineering: General; Educational Institute

ENVIRONMENTAL SCIENCE PROGRAM
WELLS COLLEGE
AURORA, NY 13026
See Chemistry: General; Educational Institute

ENVIRONMENTAL SCIENCES AND ENGINEERING PROGRAM
COLUMBIA UNIVERSITY
NEW YORK, NY 10023
See Engineering: General; Educational Institute

ENVIRONMENTAL SCIENCES GROUP, STATE UNIVERSITY COLLEGE
1300 ELMWOOD AVENUE
BUFFALO, NY 14222
See Chemistry: General; Educational Institute

ENVIRONMENTAL SCIENCES TRAINING COMMISSION
DEPARTMENT OF MEDICINE AT CORNELL
CORNELL, NY 10021
See Biology: Ecology; Government-Federal

ENVIRONMENTAL STUDIES CENTER, QUEENS COLLEGE
65-30 KISSENA BOULEVARD
FLUSHING, NY 11367
See Chemistry: General; Educational Institute

ENVIRONMENTAL STUDIES GROUP, ROCHESTER INSTITUTE OF TECHNOLOGY
1 LOMB DRIVE
ROCHESTER, NY 14623
See Chemistry: General; Educational Institute

ENVIRONMENTAL STUDIES PROGRAM
ALFRED UNIVERSITY
ALFRED, NY 14802
See Interdisciplinary: General; Educational Institute

ENVIRONMENTAL STUDIES PROGRAM
CORNELL UNIVERSITY
ITHACA, NY 14850
See Interdisciplinary: General; Educational Institute

ENVIRONMENTAL STUDIES PROGRAM
HOBART COLLEGE
GENEVA, NY 14456
See Chemistry: General; Educational Institute

ENVIRONMENTAL STUDIES PROGRAM
ROCKLAND COUNTY CENTER
SUFFERN, NY 10901
See Social Sciences/Humanities: General; Educational Institute

ENVIRONMENTAL STUDIES PROGRAM
SAINT LAWRENCE UNIVERSITY
CANTON, NY 13617
See Interdisciplinary: General; Unclassified

ENVIRONMENTAL STUDIES PROGRAM
STATE UNIVERSITY COLLEGE
BROCKPORT, NY 14420
See Biology: Ecology; Educational Institute

ENVIRONMENTAL STUDIES PROGRAM
STATE UNIVERSITY COLLEGE
BUFFALO, NY 14201
See Interdisciplinary: General; Educational Institute

ENVIRONMENTAL STUDIES PROGRAM
STATE UNIVERSITY COLLEGE
OSWEGO, NY 13126
See Interdisciplinary: General; Educational Institute

ENVIRONMENTAL STUDIES PROGRAM
STATE UNIVERSITY COLLEGE
PLATTSBURGH, NY 12901
See Interdisciplinary: General; Educational Institute

ENVIRONMENTAL STUDIES PROGRAM
STATE UNIVERSITY OF NEW YORK AT STONY BROOK
STONY BROOK, NY 11790
See Interdisciplinary: General; Educational Institute

ENVIRONMENTAL STUDIES PROGRAM
UNIVERSITY OF ROCHESTER
ROCHESTER, NY 14627
See Social Sciences/Humanities: General; Educational Institute

ENVIRONMENTAL STUDIES PROGRAM
WILLIAM SMITH COLLEGE
GENEVA, NY 14456
See Chemistry: General; Educational Institute

ENVIRONMENTAL STUDIES PROGRAM, CANISIUS COLLEGE
2001 MAIN STREET
BUFFALO, NY 14208
See Interdisciplinary: General; Educational Institute

ENVIRONMENTAL STUDIES PROGRAM, CITY COLLEGE
CONVENT AVENUE AT 138TH STREET
NEW YORK, NY 10031
See Interdisciplinary: General; Educational Institute

ENVIRONMENTAL STUDIES PROGRAM, CORNELL UNIVERSITY
SCHOOL OF AGRICULTURE
ITHACA, NY 14850
See Interdisciplinary: General; Educational Institute

ENVIRONMENTAL STUDIES PROGRAM, HERBERT H LEHMAN COLLEGE
BEDFORD PARK BOULEVARD WEST
NEW YORK, NY 10468
See Chemistry: General; Educational Institute

ENVIRONMENTAL STUDIES PROGRAM, HUNTER COLLEGE
695 PARK AVENUE
NEW YORK, NY 10021
See Interdisciplinary: General; Educational Institute

ENVIRONMENTAL STUDIES PROGRAM, WAGNER COLLEGE
631 HOWARD AVENUE
STATEN ISLAND, NY 10301
See Chemistry: General; Educational Institute

ENVIRONMENTAL STUDIES, NEW YORK UNIVERSITY
WASHINGTON SQUARE
NEW YORK, NY 10003
See Interdisciplinary: General; Educational Institute

ENVIRONMENTAL STUDIES, POLYTECHNICAL INSTITUTE OF BROOKLYN
333 JAY STREET
BROOKLYN, NY 11201
See Interdisciplinary: General; Educational Institute

ENVIRONMENTAL STUDIES, SAINT JOHN'S UNIVERSITY
GRAND CENTRAL AND UTOPIA PARKWAYS
JAMAICA, NY 11432
See Interdisciplinary: General; Educational Institute

ENVIRONMENTAL STUDIES, UNIVERSITY OF ROCHESTER
RIVER BOULEVARD
ROCHESTER, NY 14627
See Interdisciplinary: General; Educational Institute

ENVIRONMENTAL STUDY, STATE UNIVERSITY OF NEW YORK AT ALBANY
1400 WASHINGTON AVENUE
ALBANY, NY 12222
See Interdisciplinary: General; Educational Institute

EXPERIMENTAL PATHOLOGY AND TOXICOLOGY INSTITUTE
ALBANY MEDICAL COLLEGE, UNION
ALBANY, NY 12208
See Interdisciplinary: General; Educational Institute

EXPERIMENTAL RADIOLOGY, SCHOOL OF MEDICINE
UNIVERSITY OF ROCHESTER
ROCHESTER, NY 14600
See Biology: General; Educational Institute

FAMILY SERVICE ASSOCIATION OF AMERICA
44 EAST 23RD STREET
NEW YORK, NY 10010
See Social Sciences/Humanities: General; Foundation

FIRE PREVENTION BUREAU, FIRE DEPARTMENT
470 EAST LINCOLN AVENUE
MT VERNON, NY 10550
See Engineering: Pollution Abatement; Government-State or Local

FORDHAM UNIVERSITY
FORDHAM ROAD
BRONX, NY 10458
See Interdisciplinary: General; Educational Institute

FOREIGN SERVICE VOLUNTARY AGENCY
44 EAST 23RD STREET
NEW YORK,NY 10010
See Social Sciences/Humanities: Employment/Unemployment; Government-Federal

FRIENDS OF AFRICA IN AMERICA
330 SOUTH BROADWAY
TARRYTOWN, NY 10591
See Biology: Ecology; Educational Institute

FRIENDS OF THE EARTH
30 EAST 42ND STREET
NEW YORK, NY 10017
See Biology: Ecology; Government-Federal

GAME CONSERVATION SOCIETY
BOX 54
ARMONK, NY 10504
See Interdisciplinary: General; Professional Organizations

GARDEN CLUB OF AMERICA
598 MADISON AVENUE
NEW YORK, NY 10022
See Biology: Ecology; Professional Organizations

GIRL SCOUTS OF USA
830 THIRD AVENUE
NEW YORK, NY 10022
See Interdisciplinary: General; Foundation

HEALTH DEPARTMENT
148 MARITINE AVENUE
WHITE PLAINS, NY 10601
See Engineering: Pollution Abatement; Government-State or Local

HEALTH, EDUCATION AND WELFARE REGION 2 OFFICE
26 FEDERAL PLAZA
NEW YORK, NY 10007
See Interdisciplinary: General; Government-Federal

HOUSING AND ENVIRONMENTAL STUDIES CENTER
CORNELL UNIVERSITY
ITHACA, NY 14850
See Social Sciences/Humanities: General; Educational Institute

HUGH MOORE FUND
60 EAST 42ND STREET
NEW YORK, NY 10017
See Social Sciences/Humanities: Population Studies/Family Planning; Foundation

HUMAN RESOURCES CONSERVATION COMMITTEE
COLUMBIA UNIVERSITY
NEW YORK, NY 10027

See Interdisciplinary: General; Educational Institute

INCINERATOR INSTITUTE OF AMERICA
BX 1, ONE STONE PLACE
BRONXVILLE, NY 10708
See Engineering: Pollution Abatement; Industrial/Commercial

INDUSTRIAL LABOR RELATIONS LIBRARY
CORNELL UNIVERSITY
ITHACA, NY 14850
See Social Sciences/Humanities: Labor/Relations/Unions; Educational Institute

INDUSTRIAL MEDICINE INSTITUTE, NEW YORK UNIVERSITY
550 FIRST AVENUE
NEW YORK, NY 10016
See Engineering: Pollution Abatement; Educational Institute

INDUSTRIAL RELATIONS AND PUBLIC AFFAIRS OFFICE
150 EAST 42ND STREET
NEW YORK, NY 10017
See Social Sciences/Humanities: Education; Government-State or Local

INDUSTRIAL RELATIONS COUNCIL INFORMATION SERVICE
1270 AVENUE OF THE AMERICAS
NEW YORK, NY 10020
See Social Sciences/Humanities: Labor/Relations/Unions; Industrial/Commercial

INLAND WATER RESOURCES CENTER
STATE UNIVERSITY OF NEW YORK
BUFFALO, NY 14214
See Interdisciplinary: General; Educational Institute

INSTITUTE ENVIRONMENTAL MEDICINE
NEW YORK UNIVERSITY MEDICAL CENTER
NEW YORK, NY 10016
See Biology: Ecology; Educational Institute

INTERNATIONAL EDUCATION BUREAU
809 UNITED NATIONS PLAZA
NEW YORK, NY 10017
See Social Sciences/Humanities: Education; Research Institute

INTERSTATE SANITATION COMMISSION
10 COLUMBUS CIRCLE
NEW YORK, NY 10019
See Engineering: Pollution Abatement; Government-State or Local

IRON AND STEEL INSTITUTE
150 EAST 42D STREET
NEW YORK, NY 10017
See Engineering: Pollution Abatement; Industrial/Commercial

KEEP AMERICA BEAUTIFUL, INCORPORATED
99 PARK AVENUE
NEW YORK, NY 10016
See Biology: Ecology; Professional Organizations

LAKE ERIE ENVIRONMENTAL STUDIES
STATE UNIVERSITY COLLEGE
FREDONIA, NY 14063
See Biology: Ecology; Educational Institute

LAMONT GEOLOGICAL OBSERVATORY, COLUMBIA UNIVERSITY
TORREY CLIFF
PALISADES, NY 10964
See Geology: General; Educational Institute

LARGE DAMS COMMISSION, ENGINEERS JOINT COUNCIL
345 EAST 47TH STREET
NEW YORK, NY 10017
See Engineering: Water Resources; Government-Federal

LEGISLATIVE REFERENCE LIBRARY
EDUCATION BUILDING
ALBANY, NY 12224
See Social Sciences/Humanities: Law/Legislation; Government-State or Local

MAIMONIDES HOSPITAL OF BROOKLYN
4802 TENTH AVENUE
BROOKLYN, NY 11219
See Interdisciplinary: General; Research Institute

MANAGEMENT AND HISTORY OF ENVIRONMENT
MINER INSTITUTE
CHAZY, NY 12921
See Interdisciplinary: General; Educational Institute

MANAGEMENT INSTITUTE
125 EAST 38TH STREET
NEW YORK, NY 10016
See Social Sciences/Humanities: Industrial Development; Professional Organizations

MANHATTAN COLLEGE
RIVERDALE
BRONX, NY 10471
See Engineering: General; Educational Institute

MARGARET SANGER RESEARCH BUREAU, INCORPORATED
17 WEST 16TH STREET
NEW YORK, NY 10011
See Social Sciences/Humanities: Population Studies/Family Planning; Research Institute

MARINE SCIENCE DEPARTMENT
STATE UNIVERSITY OF NEW YORK
BINGHAMTON, NY 13904
See Geology: General; Educational Institute

MARINE SCIENCES RESEARCH CENTER
STATE UNIVERSITY OF NEW YORK
STONY BROOK, NY 11790
See Engineering: Water Resources; Educational Institute

MECHANICAL ENGINEERS (AMERICAN SOCIETY)
345 EAST 42ND STREET
NEW YORK, NY 10017
See Engineering: General; Professional Organizations

MEDICAL ACADEMY
2 EAST 103RD STREET
NEW YORK, NY 10029
See Social Sciences/Humanities: General; Professional Organizations

MEDICAL DEPARTMENT
BROOKHAVEN NATIONAL LABORATORY
UPTON, NY
See Biology: General; Research Institute

MEDICAL DEPARTMENT, SCHOOL OF MEDICINE
525 EAST 68TH STREET
NEW YORK, NY 10021
See Biology: Ecology; Educational Institute

METEOROLOGY
785 WEST END AVENUE, APT 6-C
NEW YORK, NY 10025
See Interdisciplinary: General; Industrial/Commercial

NATIONAL ASSOCIATION OF RETARDED CHILDREN, INCORPORATED
420 LEXINGTON AVENUE
NEW YORK, NY 10017
See Social Sciences/Humanities: Mental Health; Research Institute

NATIONAL CAMPERS AND HIKERS ASSOCIATION
7172 TRANSIT ROAD
BUFFALO, NY 14221
See Biology: Ecology; Foundation

NATIONAL COUNCIL FOR STREAM INPROVEMENT
103 PARK AVENUE
NEW YORK, NY 10016
See Engineering: Pollution Abatement; Industrial/Commercial

NATIONAL RECREATION ASSOCIATION
8 WEST EIGHTH STREET
NEW YORK, NY 10011
See Social Sciences/Humanities: Recreation and Leisure; Research Institute

NATURAL HISTORY MUSEUM OF AMERICA
CENTRAL PARK WEST AT 79TH STREET
NEW YORK, NY 10024
See Interdisciplinary: General; Professional Organizations

NATURE STUDY SOCIETY OF AMERICA
MILEWOOD ROAD
VERBANK, NY 12585
See Biology: Ecology; Professional Organizations

NEAR EAST FOUNDATION
54 EAST 64TH STREET
NEW YORK, NY 10021
See Social Sciences/Humanities: Housing ; Foundation

NEW YORK CITY AFFAIRS CENTER
NEW SCHOOL FOR SOCIAL RESEARCH
NEW YORK, NY 10001
See Social Sciences/Humanities: Regional Planning; Educational Institute

NUCLEAR RESEARCH CENTER
STATE UNIVERSITY OF NEW YORK-BUFFALO, 3435 MAIN STREET
BUFFALO, NY 14214
See Physics: General; Government-State or Local

OCCUPATIONAL SAFETY AND HEALTH DEPARTMENT
26 FEDERAL PLAZA
NEW YORK, NY 10007
See Chemistry: General; Government-Federal

OCEANOGRAPHY AND MARINE BIOLOGY INSTITUTE
POST OFFICE BOX 432
OYSTER BAY, NY 11711
See Biology: Biophysics; Research Institute

OPEN SPACE INSTITUTE
145 EAST 52ND STREET
NEW YORK, NY 10022
See Social Sciences/Humanities: Regional Planning; Professional Organizations

ORNITHOLOGY LABORATORY
CORNELL UNIVERSITY
ITHACA, NY 14850
See Biology: Ecology; Educational Institute

OYSTER INSTITUTE OF NORTH AMERICA
22 MAIN STREET
SAYVILLE, NY 11782
See Interdisciplinary: General; Industrial/Commercial

PATHOLOGY DEPARTMENT, MOUNT SINAI SCHOOL OF MEDICINE
100TH AND FIFTH AVENUE
NEW YORK, NY 10029
See Biology: General; Educational Institute

PETROLEUM INDUSTRY RESOURCES FOUNDATION
60 EAST 42ND STREET
NEW YORK, NY 10017
See Interdisciplinary: General; Foundation

PHYSICS INSTITUTE
335 EAST 45TH STREET
NEW YORK, NY 10017
See Physics: General; Educational Institute

PLANNED PARENTHOOD, WORLD POPULATION DIVISION
810 7TH AVENUE
NEW YORK, NY 10019
See Social Sciences/Humanities: Population Studies/Family Planning; Foundation

PLANNED PARENTHOOD, WORLD POPULATION RESEARCH DEPARTMENT
515 MADISON AVENUE
NEW YORK, NY 10022
See Social Sciences/Humanities: Population Studies/Family Planning; Research Institute

PLANNING SERVICES OFFICE
488 BROADWAY
ALBANY, NY 12207
See Social Sciences/Humanities: General; Government-State or Local

PLANT INDUSTRY DIVISION, DEPARTMENT OF AGRICULTURE AND MARKETS
STATE CAMPUS BUILDING 8
ALBANY, NY 12226
See Engineering: Agricultural Engineering; Government-State or Local

POLITICAL ECOLOGY DEPARTMENT
STATE UNIVERSITY OF NEW YORK
OLD WESTBURY, NY 11568
See Social Sciences/Humanities: Politics; Educational Institute

POLITICAL PSYCHOLOGY INSTITUTE, BROOKLYN COLLEGE
BEDFORD AVENUE AND AVENUE H
BROOKLYN, NY 11210
See Social Sciences/Humanities: Politics; Educational Institute

POPULATION COUNCIL
245 PARK AVENUE
NEW YORK, NY 10017
See Social Sciences/Humanities: Population Studies/Family Planning; Educational Institute

PRATT INSTITUTE
215 RYERSON STREET
BROOKLYN, NY 11205
See Engineering: General; Educational Institute

PROGRAMMED INSTRUCTION CENTER
TEACHERS COLLEGE, COLUMBIA UNIVERSITY
NEW YORK, NY 10027
See Social Sciences/Humanities: Education; Educational Institute

PUBLIC ADMINISTRATION INSTITUTE
55 WEST 44TH STREET
NEW YORK, NY 10036
See Social Sciences/Humanities: General; Research Institute

PUBLIC HEALTH AND ADMINISTRATIVE MEDICINE SCHOOL
COLUMBIA UNIVERSITY
NEW YORK, NY 10027
See Interdisciplinary: General; Educational Institute

PUBLIC WORKS BOARD
LITTLE FALLS, NY 13365
See Engineering: Pollution Abatement; Government-State or Local

PURE WATER DIVISION, STATE HEALTH DEPARTMENT
84 HOLLAND AVENUE
ALBANY, NY 12208
See Engineering: Pollution Abatement; Government-State or Local

RADIATION DIVISION, ENVIRONMENTAL PROTECTION AGENCY
26 FEDERAL PLAZA, ROOM 847
NEW YORK, NY 10007
See Chemistry: Physical Chemistry; Government-State or Local

REGIONAL PLANNING ASSOCIATION, INCORPORATED
235 EAST 45TH STREET
NEW YORK, NY 10017
See Social Sciences/Humanities: Regional Planning; Research Institute

RESEARCH CENTER OF LAKE GEORGE
LAKE GEORGE, NY 12854
See Engineering: Water Resources; Educational Institute

RESEARCH CENTER OF WESTERN NEW YORK
STATE UNIVERSITY OF NEW YORK
BUFFALO, NY 14210
See Chemistry: General; Educational Institute

RESEARCH DEPARTMENT, INTERNATIONAL LADIES GARMENT WORKERS UNION
1710 BROADWAY
NEW YORK,NY 10019
See Social Sciences/Humanities: Labor/ Relations/Unions; Research Institute

RESEARCH DIVISION
CLARKSON COLLEGE OF TECHNOLOGY
POTSDAM, NY 13676
See Interdisciplinary: General; Educational Institute

RESEARCH LABORATORY
CORNELL ORNAMENTALS
FARMINGDALE, NY 11735
See Biology: General; Educational Institute

RESOURCE MANAGEMENT AND LAND PLANNING
SYRACUSE UNIVERSITY
SYRACUSE, NY 13210
See Biology: Ecology; Educational Institute

RESOURCES EVALUATION DIVISION
110 LIVINGSTON STREET
BROOKLYN, NY 11201
See Social Sciences/Humanities: Education; Government-State or Local

RUFFED GROUSE SOCIETY OF AMERICA
81 INDIAN SPRING LANE
ROCHESTER, NY 14618
See Biology: General; Professional Organizations

SAINT HUBERT SOCIETY OF AMERICA
STUDIO 1, 5 TUDOR CITY PLACE
NEW YORK, NY 10017
See Interdisciplinary: General; Industrial/ Commercial

SCENIC AND HISTORIC PRESERVATION SOCIETY
15 PINE STREET
NEW YORK,NY 10005
See Social Sciences/Humanities: General; Professional Organizations

SCIENCE FOR YOUTH NATIONAL FOUNDATION
145 EAST 52ND STREET
NEW YORK, NY 10022
See Biology: Ecology; Foundation

SCIENTISTS INSTITUTION FOR PUBLIC INFORMATION
30 EAST 68TH STREET
NEW YORK, NY 10021
See Biology: Ecology; Professional Organizations

SEVERSKY ELECTRONATOM CORPORATION
30 ROCKEFELLER PLAZA
NEW YORK, NY 10020
See Engineering: Pollution Abatement; Industrial/Commercial

SHELLFISH INSTITUTE OF NORTH AMERICA
22 MAIN STREET
SAYVILLE, NY 11782
See Biology: Ecology; Foundation

SMOKE ABATEMENT AND AIR POLLUTION CONTROL
724 O'CONNOR BUILDING, RIDGE ROAD
LACKWANNA, NY 14218
See Engineering: Pollution Abatement; Government-State or Local

SMOKE ABATEMENT COMMISSION
200 EAST THIRD STREET
JAMESTOWN, NY 14701
See Engineering: Pollution Abatement; Government-State or Local

SMOKE AND AIR POLLUTION CONTROL BUREAU
217 ARSENAL STREET
WATERTOWN, NY 13601
See Engineering: Pollution Abatement; Government-State or Local

SOCIAL HEALTH ASSOCIATION
1790 BROADWAY
NEW YORK, NY 10024
See Social Sciences/Humanities: Urban Problems; Research Institute

SOIL CONSERVATION SERVICES
MIDTOWN PLAZA, ROOM 400, 700 EAST WATER STREET
SYRACUSE, NY 13210
See Biology: Ecology; Government-State or Local

ST LAWRENCE DEVELOPMENT COMPANY
SEAWAY CIRCLE
MASSENA, NY 13662
See Engineering: General; Industrial/ Commercial

SUBURBAN AFFAIRS CENTER
ROCKLAND COMMUNITY COLLEGE
SUFFERN, NY 10901
See Social Sciences/Humanities: Urban Problems; Educational Institute

TECHNICIAN TRAINING PROGRAM
BROOME TECHNICAL COLLEGE
BINGHAMTON, NY 13904
See Interdisciplinary: General; Educational Institute

TECHNICIAN TRAINING PROGRAM
HUDSON VALLEY COMMISSION COLLEGE
TROY, NY 12151
See Interdisciplinary: General; Educational Institute

TECHNICIAN TRAINING PROGRAM
MORRISVILLE AGRICULTURAL-TECHNOLOGY
MORRISVILLE, NY 13408
See Interdisciplinary: General; Educational Institute

TECHNICIAN TRAINING PROGRAM
SULLIVAN COUNTY COMMUNITY COLLEGE
SOUTH FALLSBURG, NY 12779
See Interdisciplinary: General; Educational Institute

TRAIL CONFERENCE
GPO BOX 2250
NEW YORK, NY 10001
See Social Sciences/Humanities: Recreation and Leisure; Professional Organizations

TRAINING AND RESEARCH INSTITUTE OF THE UNITED NATIONS
801 UNITED NATIONS PLAZA
NEW YORK, NY 10017
See Biology: Ecology; Research Institute

TWENTIETH CENTURY FUND
41 EAST 70TH STREET
NEW YORK, NY 10021
See Social Sciences/Humanities: General; Foundation

URBAN ENVIRONMENT INSTITUTE
COLUMBIA UNIVERSITY
NEW YORK, NY 10022
See Social Sciences/Humanities: Urban Problems; Educational Institute

URBAN ENVIRONMENTAL STUDIES
POLYTECHNICAL INSTITUTE OF BROOKLYN
BROOKLYN, NY 11201
See Social Sciences/Humanities: General; Educational Institute

URBAN ENVIRONMENTAL STUDIES
RENSSELAER POLYTECHNIC INSTITUTE
TROY, NY 12181
See Social Sciences/Humanities: General; Educational Institute

VOCATIONAL FOUNDATION INCORPORATED
353 PARK AVENUE SOUTH
NEW YORK, NY 10010

See Social Sciences/Humanities: Employment/Unemployment; Professional Organizations

WATER INFORMATION CENTER, INCORPORATED
44 SIRTSINK DRIVE
PORT WASHINGTON, NY 11050
See Engineering: Water Resources; Educational Institute

WATER RESOURCES AND MARINE SCIENCES
CORNELL UNIVERSITY
ITHACA, NY 14850
See Engineering: Water Resources; Educational Institute

WATER RESOURCES CENTER
COLLEGE OF FORESTRY
SYRACUSE, NY 13210
See Engineering: Water Resources; Government-State or Local

WATER RESOURCES COMMISSION OF NEW YORK STATE
STATE OFFICE BUILDING
ALBANY, NY 12226
See Engineering: Water Resources; Government-State or Local

WATER SUPPLY, GAS AND ELECTRICITY DEPARTMENT OF NEW YORK CITY
MUNICIPAL BUILDING
NEW YORK, NY 10007
See Engineering: Water Resources; Government-State or Local

WILDLIFE RESTORATION FOUNDATION
17 WEST 60TH STREET
NEW YORK, NY 10023
See Interdisciplinary: General; Professional Organizations

WILLIAM GREEN HUMAN RELATIONS LIBRARY
25 EAST 78TH STREET
NEW YORK,NY 10021
See Social Sciences/Humanities: Labor/Relations/Unions; Professional Organizations

WORLD MEDICAL ASSOCIATION
10 COLUMBUS CIRCLE
NEW YORK, NY 10019
See Interdisciplinary: General; Professional Organizations

YOUTH CONFERENCE ON NATURAL BEAUTY AND CONSERVATION, NATIONAL
C/O GIRL SCOUTS OF US, 830 THIRD AVENUE
NEW YORK, NY 10022
See Biology: Ecology; Professional Organizations

ZOOLOGICAL SOCIETY OF NEW YORK
THE ZOOLOGICAL PARK
BRONX, NY 10460
See Interdisciplinary: General; Professional Organizations

Ohio

AIR POLLUTION BOARD
2211 SOUTH EIGHTH STREET
IRONTON, OH 45638
See Engineering: Pollution Abatement; Government-State or Local

AIR POLLUTION CENTER, PORTSMOUTH-IRONTON REGION
CITY BUILDING, 740 SECOND STREET
PORTSMOUTH, OH 45662
See Engineering: Pollution Abatement; Government-State or Local

AIR POLLUTION CONTROL
CITY HALL, 2935 MAYFIELD ROAD
CLEVELAND HEIGHTS, OH 44118
See Engineering: Pollution Abatement; Government-State or Local

AIR POLLUTION CONTROL DIVISION, CITY HEALTH DEPARTMENT
CITY HALL
CANTON, OH 44702
See Engineering: Pollution Abatement; Government-State or Local

AIR POLLUTION CONTROL, COUNTY HEALTH DEPARTMENT
CITY BUILDING
SANDUSKY, OH 44870
See Engineering: Pollution Abatement; Government-State or Local

AIR POLLUTION CONTROL, PUBLIC HEALTH AND WELFARE DEPARTMENT
2735 BROADWAY AVENUE
CLEVELAND, OH 44115
See Engineering: Pollution Abatement; Government-State or Local

AIR POLLUTION CONTROL, PUBLIC SAFETY DEPARTMENT
181 SOUTH WASHINGTON BOULEVARD
COLUMBUS, OH 43215
See Engineering: Pollution Abatement; Government-State or Local

AIR POLLUTION CONTROL, PUBLIC SERVICE DEPARTMENT
329 10TH STREET

LORAIN, OH 44052
See Engineering: Pollution Abatement; Government-State or Local

AIR POLLUTION CONTROL, SERVICES AND BUILDINGS DEPARTMENT
MUNICIPAL BUILDING, 101 WEST THIRD STREET
DAYTON, OH 45402
See Engineering: Pollution Abatement; Government-State or Local

AIR POLLUTION CONTROL, SEWERS DEPARTMENT
2400 BEEKMAN STREET
CINCINNATI, OH 45214
See Engineering: Pollution Abatement; Government-State or Local

AIR POLLUTION DEPARTMENT
MARKET STREET
STEUBENVILLE, OH 43952
See Engineering: Pollution Abatement; Government-State or Local

AMERICAN SOCIETY OF SANITARY ENGINEERING
228 STANDARD BUILDING
CLEVELAND, OH 44113
See Engineering: Pollution Abatement; Professional Organizations

AQUATIC ECOLOGY DEPARTMENT, JOHN CARROLL UNIVERSITY
UNIVERSITY HEIGHTS
CLEVELAND, OH 44118
See Biology: Ecology; Educational Institute

ARMCO ENVIRONMENTAL ENGINEERING
POST OFFICE BOX 1970
MIDDLETOWN, OH 45042
See Engineering: General; Industrial/Commercial

ATMOSPHERIC STUDIES PROGRAM
CASE WESTERN RESERVE UNIVERSITY
CLEVELAND, OH 44106
See Engineering: Pollution Abatement; Educational Institute

AUDUBON SOCIETY OF OHIO
3530 EPWORTH AVENUE
CINCINNATI, OH 45211
See Interdisciplinary: General; Professional Organizations

B A ARNESON INSTITUTE OF PRACTICAL POLLUTION
OHIO WESLEYAN UNIVERSITY
DELEWARE, OH 43015
See Social Sciences/Humanities: Politics; Educational Institute

**BEHAVIOR RESOURCES,
ANTHROPOMETRIC
LABORATORY**
ANTIOCH COLLEGE
YELLOW SPRINGS, OH 45387
See Social Sciences/Humanities: Psychology/Behavioral Science; Government-Federal

BUILDING DEPARTMENT
EUCLID, OH 44123
See Engineering: Pollution Abatement;
Government-State or Local

**BUSINESS RESEARCH DIVISION,
SCHOOL OF COMMERCE, OHIO
STATE UNIVERSITY**
1775 SOUTH COLLEGE ROAD
COLUMBUS,OH 43210
See Social Sciences/Humanities: General;
Educational Institute

**CHEMICAL ABSTRACTS SERVICE,
AMERICAN CHEMICAL SOCIETY**
OHIO STATE UNIVERSITY-
OLENTANGY R ROAD
COLUMBUS, OH 43210
See Engineering: Water Resources; Foundation

**CHEMISTRY AND CHEMISTRY
ENGINEERING DEPARTMENT**
BATTELLE MEMORIAL INSTITUTE
COLUMBUS, OH 43201
See Engineering: Chemical Engineering;
Educational Institute

**CHEMISTRY AND PHYSICS
DIVISION**
NATIONAL AIR POLLUTION
CONTROL, PUBLIC HEALTH
SECTION
CINCINNATI, OH 45227
See Engineering: Pollution Abatement;
Government-Federal

CHEMISTRY DEPARTMENT
OHIO STATE UNIVERSITY, 88 WEST
18TH AVENUE
COLUMBUS, OH 43210
See Engineering: Pollution Abatement;
Educational Institute

CINCINNATI GENERAL HOSPITAL
UNIVERSITY OF CINCINNATI
MEDICAL CENTER
CINCINNATI, OH 45229
See Engineering: General; Field Station/
Laboratory

**COMMUNITY ENVIRONMENTAL
MANAGEMENT BUREAU**
5555 RIDGE AVENUE
CINCINNATI, OH 45213
See Interdisciplinary: General; Government-State or Local

**COMMUNITY SERVICE
INCORPORATED**
114 EAST WHITEMAN STREET
YELLOW SPRINGS, OH 45387
See Social Sciences/Humanities: Community Development/Studies; Research
Institute

**CONSERVATION CONGRESS OF
OHIO**
6284 AUDREY, SW
CANTON, OH 44706
See Biology: Ecology; Professional Organizations

DEVELOPMENT DEPARTMENT
65 SOUTH FRONT STREET
COLUMBUS, OH 43215
See Engineering: Pollution Abatement;
Government-State or Local

**ENGINEERING DEPARTMENT,
HEALTH DEPARTMENT**
POST OFFICE BOX 118
COLUMBUS, OH 43216
See Engineering: Pollution Abatement;
Government-State or Local

**ENVIRONMENTAL CONTROL
ADMINISTRATION**
222 EAST CENTRAL PARKWAY
CINCINNATI, OH 45202
See Interdisciplinary: General; Unclassified

**ENVIRONMENTAL CONTROL
ADMINISTRATION, BUREAU
SOLID WASTE MANAGEMENT**
5555 RIDGE AVENUE
CINCINNATI, OH 45213
See Engineering: Water Resources; Educational Institute

**ENVIRONMENTAL HEALTH
DEPARTMENT, COLLEGE OF
MEDICINE**
UNIVERSITY OF CINCINNATI
CINCINNATI, OH 45219
See Biology: Ecology; Educational Institute

**ENVIRONMENTAL HEALTH
DIVISION, COUNTY HEALTH
DEPARTMENT**
325 EAST CENTRAL PARKWAY
CINCINNATI, OH 45202
See Engineering: Pollution Abatement;
Government-State or Local

**ENVIRONMENTAL HEALTH
INSTITUTE**
UNIVERSITY OF CINCINNATI
CINCINNATI, OH 45289
See Engineering: Pollution Abatement;
Educational Institute

**ENVIRONMENTAL RESEARCH
CENTER**
CINCINNATI, OH 45201
See Engineering: Pollution Abatement;
Research Institute

**ENVIRONMENTAL SCIENCE
PROGRAM**
ANTIOCH COLLEGE
YELLOW SPRINGS, OH 45387
See Interdisciplinary: General; Educational Institute

**ENVIRONMENTAL SCIENCE
PROGRAM**
COLLEGE OF WOOSTER
WOOSTER, OH 44691
See Geology: General; Educational Institute

**ENVIRONMENTAL SCIENCE
PROGRAM**
MIAMI UNIVERSITY
OXFORD, OH 45056
See Interdisciplinary: General; Educational Institute

**ENVIRONMENTAL SCIENCE
PROGRAM**
OHIO STATE UNIVERSITY
COLUMBUS, OH 43210
See Interdisciplinary: General; Educational Institute

**ENVIRONMENTAL SCIENCE
PROGRAM**
OHIO WESLEYAN UNIVERSITY
DELAWARE, OH 43015
See Chemistry: General; Educational Institute

**ENVIRONMENTAL SCIENCE
PROGRAM**
UNIVERSITY OF TOLEDO
TOLEDO, OH 43606
See Interdisciplinary: General; Educational Institute

**ENVIRONMENTAL SCIENCE
PROGRAM**
WITTENBERG UNIVERSITY
SPRINGFIELD, OH 45501
See Interdisciplinary: General; Educational Institute

**ENVIRONMENTAL SCIENCES
PROGRAM, CASE WESTERN
RESERVE UNIVERSITY**
2040 ADELBERT ROAD
CLEVELAND, OH 44106
See Interdisciplinary: General; Educational Institute

ENVIRONMENTAL STUDIES
UNIVERSITY OF CINCINNATI
CINCINNATI, OH 45221
See Interdisciplinary: General; Educational Institute

**ENVIRONMENTAL STUDIES
CENTER, XAVIER UNIVERSITY**
DANA AVENUE AND VICTORIA

PARKWAY
CINCINNATI, OH 45207
See Chemistry: General; Educational Institute

ENVIRONMENTAL STUDIES PROGRAM
BOWLING GREEN STATE UNIVERSITY
BOWLING GREEN, OH 43402
See Interdisciplinary: General; Educational Institute

ENVIRONMENTAL STUDIES PROGRAM
KENT STATE UNIVERSITY
KENT, OH 44240
See Interdisciplinary: General; Educational Institute

ENVIRONMENTAL STUDIES PROGRAM
OBERLIN COLLEGE
OBERLIN, OH 44074
See Chemistry: General; Educational Institute

ENVIRONMENTAL STUDIES PROGRAM
OHIO UNIVERSITY
ATHENS, OH 45701
See Interdisciplinary: General; Educational Institute

ENVIRONMENTAL STUDIES PROGRAM
YOUNGSTOWN STATE UNIVERSITY
YOUNGSTOWN, OH 44503
See Interdisciplinary: General; Educational Institute

ENVIRONMENTAL STUDIES PROGRAM, UNIVERSITY OF AKRON
302 EAST BUCHTEL AVENUE
AKRON, OH 44304
See Interdisciplinary: General; Educational Institute

ENVIRONMENTAL STUDIES PROJECT, CLEVELAND STATE UNIVERSITY
EUCLID AVENUE AT 24TH STREET
CLEVELAND, OH 44115
See Interdisciplinary: General; Educational Institute

ENVIRONMENTAL STUDIES, BATTELLE MEMORIAL INSTITUTE
505 KING AVENUE
COLUMBUS, OHIO
See Interdisciplinary: General; Research Institute

ENVIRONMENTAL STUDIES, UNIVERSITY OF DAYTON
300 COLLEGE PARK AVENUE
DAYTON, OH 45409
See Interdisciplinary: General; Educational Institute

FELS RESEARCH INSTITUTE
LIVERMORE STREET
YELLOW SPRINGS, OH 45387
See Social Sciences/Humanities: Psychology/Behavioral Science; Research Institute

FRANZ T STONE LABORATORY
1735 NEIL AVENUE
COLUMBUS, OH 43210
See Biology: General; Field Station/Laboratory

GEOLOGICAL RESOURCES DIVISION, NATURAL RESOURCES DEPARTMENT
1207 GRANDVIEW AVENUE
COLUMBUS, OH 43212
See Engineering: Pollution Abatement; Government-State or Local

GRANTS PROGRAM OFFICE, OCCUPATIONAL SAFETY AND HEALTH
1014 BROADWAY
CINCINNATI, OH 45202
See Engineering: Pollution Abatement; Government-Federal

HEALTH DEPARTMENT
MUNICIPAL BUILDING, ROOM 353
HAMILTON, OH 45010
See Engineering: Pollution Abatement; Government-State or Local

HEALTH DISTRICT- LAKE COUNTY
121 LIBERTY STREET
PAINESVILLE, OH 44077
See Engineering: Pollution Abatement; Government-State or Local

INTERNATIONAL SHADE TREE CONFERENCE
1827 NEIL AVENUE
COLUMBUS, OH 43210
See Biology: General; Professional Organizations

INTERPRETIVE NATURALISTS ASSOCIATION
1251 EAST BROAD STREET
COLUMBUS, OH 43205
See Interdisciplinary: General; Professional Organizations

LAKE CARRIERS ASSOCIATION
305 ROCKEFELLER BUILDING
CLEVELAND, OH 44121
See Engineering: Pollution Abatement; Professional Organizations

LIFE SCIENCES RESOURCES CENTER, KENT STATE UNIVERSITY
AGASSIZ HOUSE
KENT, OHIO
See Biology: General; Educational Institute

LIFE SUPPORT DIVISION
6570 AEROSPACE MEDICAL RESOURCE LABORATORY
WRIGHT-PATTERSON AF BASE, OH 45433
See Engineering: Pollution Abatement; Government-Federal

MARINE SCIENCES DIVISION, 9TH COAST GUARD DISTRICT
1240 EAST 9TH STREET
CLEVELAND, OH 44199
See Engineering: Water Resources; Government-State or Local

MECHANICAL ENGINEERING DEPARTMENT, BATTELLE MEMORIAL INSTITUTE
505 KING AVENUE
COLUMBUS, OH 43201
See Engineering: Pollution Abatement; Research Institute

MEDICAL RESEARCH DEPARTMENT
SAINT LUKES HOSPITAL
CLEVELAND, OH 44104
See Interdisciplinary: General; Research Institute

METEOROLOGY DIVISION, NATIONAL AIR POLLUTION ADMINISTRATION
PUBLIC HEALTH SERVICE
CINCINNATI, OH 45227
See Geology: General; Government-State or Local

NATIONAL ENVIRONMENTAL RESEARCH CENTER
OFFICE OF PUBLIC AFFAIRS
CINCINNATI, OH 45268
See Interdisciplinary: General; Unclassified

NATURAL RESOURCES INSTITUTION
124 W 17 AVENUE
COLUMBUS, OH 43210
See Engineering: Water Resources; Educational Institute

NATURALISTS SOCIETY OF AMERICA
WOOSTER COLLEGE
WOOSTER, OH 44691
See Biology: General; Professional Organizations

NUCLEAR SCIENCES AND ENGINEERING PROGRAM
UNIVERSITY OF CINCINNATI, 121 CHEMISTRY BUILDING
CINCINNATI, OH 45221
See Chemistry: General; Educational Institute

OCCUPATIONAL HEALTH PROGRAM, ENVIRONMENTAL CONSERVATION ADMINISTRATION

222 EAST CENTRAL PARKWAY
CINCINNATI, OH 45202
See Biology: Ecology; Government-State
or Local

OHIO BASIN REGIONAL LIBRARY
4676 COLUMBIA PARKWAY
CINCINNATI, OH 45226
See Engineering: Water Resources; Government-Federal

**OHIO VALLEY IMPROVEMENT
ASSOCIATION INCORPORATED**
4017 CAREW TOWER
CINCINNATI, OH 45202
See Engineering: Water Resources; Government-Federal

**PARKS AND RECREATION
ASSOCIATION**
60 EAST BROAD STREET
COLUMBUS, OH 43215
See Social Sciences/Humanities: Recreation and Leisure; Professional Organizations

PHYSICAL CHEMISTRY DIVISION
505 KING AVENUE, BATTELLE
MEMORIAL INSTITUTE
COLUMBUS, OH 43201
See Chemistry: General; Research Institute

**PLANT INDUSTRY DIVISION,
DEPARTMENT OF AGRICULTURE**
REYNOLDSBURG, OH 43068
See Engineering: Agricultural Engineering; Government-State or Local

POLLUTION CONTROL AGENCY
26 MAIN STREET
TOLEDO, OH 43605
See Engineering: Pollution Abatement;
Government-State or Local

PSYCHOMETRIC SOCIETY
231 HILLCREST DR
CINCINNATI, OH 45215
See Social Sciences/Humanities: Psychology/Behavioral Science; Research Institute

PUBLIC HEALTH SERVICE
222 EAST CENTRAL PARKWAY
CINCINNATI, OH 45202
See Interdisciplinary: General; Government-State or Local

PUBLIC LIBRARY AT CLEVELAND
325 SUPERIOR AVENUE
CLEVELAND, OH 44101
See Interdisciplinary: General; Research
Institute

REPUBLIC STEEL CORPORATION
6801 BRECKSVILLE ROAD
INDEPENDENCE, OH 44131
See Engineering: General; Industrial/
Commercial

**RESOURCES DIVISION, OHIO
STATE UNIVERSITY**
1775 SOUTH COLLEGE ROAD
COLUMBUS, OH 43210
See Social Sciences/Humanities: Psychology/Behavioral Science; Educational
Institute

**SCRIPPS FOUNDATION FOR
POPULATION RESEARCH**
218 HARRISON HALL, MIAMI
UNIVERSITY
OXFORD, OH 45056
See Social Sciences/Humanities: Population Studies/Family Planning; Foundation

SOIL CONSERVATION SERVICE
311 OLD FEDERAL BUILDING, 3RD
AND STATE STREETS
COLUMBUS, OH 43215
See Biology: Ecology; Government-Federal

**SOLID WASTE MANAGEMENT
OFFICE, ENVIRONMENTAL
PROTECTION AGENCY**
P.O. BOX 597
CINCINNATI, OH 45201
See Engineering: Pollution Abatement;
Unclassified

SOLID WASTE RESEARCH DIVISION
NATIONAL ENVIRONMENTAL
RESEARCH CENTER
CINCINNATI, OH 45268
See Engineering: Pollution Abatement;
Government-Federal

**URBAN AND INDUSTRIAL HEALTH
NATIONAL CENTER**
550 MAIN STREET
CINCINNATI, OH 45202
See Biology: Ecology; Government-Federal

**WATER DIVISION, OHIO
DEPARTMENT OF NATURAL
RESOURCES**
815 OHIO STATE OFFICE BUILDING
COLUMBUS, OH 43215
See Engineering: Water Resources; Government-State or Local

WATER HYGIENE
222 EAST CENTRAL PARKWAY
CINCINNATI, OH 45202
See Engineering: Water Resources; Government-Federal

**WATER POLLUTION CONTROL
BOARD, HEALTH DEPARTMENT**
POST OFFICE BOX 118
COLUMBUS, OH 43125
See Engineering: Pollution Abatement;
Government-State or Local

**WATER QUALITY SURVEY OF
LORAINE COUNTY**
147 DUMMOND ROAD
AVON LAKE, OH 44012
See Engineering: Water Resources; Educational Institute

**WATER RESOURCES CENTER,
OHIO STATE UNIVERSITY**
1791 NEIL AVENUE
COLUMBUS, OH 43210
See Engineering: Water Resources; Government-State or Local

**WATER SANITATION OF OHIO
RIVER VALLEY**
414 WALNUT STREET
CINCINNATI, OH 45202
See Engineering: Water Resources; Government-State or Local

Oklahoma

**AIR POLLUTION CONTROL,
ENVIRONMENTAL HEALTH
SERVICES**
3400 NORTH EASTERN BOULEVARD
OKLAHOMA CITY, OK 73105
See Engineering: Pollution Abatement;
Government-State or Local

**AIR POLLUTION SECTION,
HEALTH DEPARTMENT**
921 NE 23RD
OKLAHOMA CITY, OK 73105
See Engineering: Pollution Abatement;
Government-State or Local

**AQUATIC BIOLOGICAL
LABORATORY**
OKLAHOMA STATE UNIVERSITY
STILLWATER, OK 74074
See Biology: General; Field Station/Laboratory

**AR-WHITE-RED BASINS
COMMISSION, FEDERAL
BUILDING**
P O BOX 1467
MUSKOGEE, OK 74401
See Engineering: Water Resources; Government-State or Local

**BIOCHEMISTRY DEPARTMENT,
OKLAHOMA CITY UNIVERSITY**
2501 NORTH BLACKWELDER
OKLAHOMA CITY, OK 73106
See Biology: Biochemistry; Educational
Institute

CHEMISTRY DEPARTMENT
OKLAHOMA CITY UNIVERSITY
OKLAHOMA CITY, OK 73106
See Chemistry: General; Educational Institute

**CIVIL AEROMEDICAL INSTITUTE,
FEDERAL AVIATION
ADMINISTRATION**
POST OFFICE BOX 25082
OKLAHOMA CITY, OK 73125
See Interdisciplinary: General; Unclassified

COUNTY HEALTH DEPARTMENT
2111 LAHOMA ROAD
ENID, OK 73701
See Engineering: Pollution Abatement;
Government-State or Local

ENTOMOLOGY DIVISION,
DEPARTMENT OF AGRICULTURE
122 STATE CAPITOL BUILDING
OKLAHOMA CITY, OK 73105
See Engineering: Agricultural Engineer-
ing; Government-State or Local

ENVIRONMENTAL HEALTH
DIVISION, COUNTY HEALTH
DEPARTMENT
4616 EAST 15TH STREET
TULSA, OK 74112
See Engineering: Pollution Abatement;
Government-State or Local

ENVIRONMENTAL HEALTH
SERVICES
3400 NORTH EASTERN AVENUE
OKLAHOMA CITY, OK 73105
See Engineering: General; Government-
State or Local

ENVIRONMENTAL INSTITUTE,
OKLAHOMA STATE UNIVERSITY
STILLWATER, OK 74074
See Interdisciplinary: General; Educa-
tional Institute

ENVIRONMENTAL PROTECTION
AGENCY
LABORATORY
ADA, OK 74820
See Engineering: Pollution Abatement;
Government-Federal

ENVIRONMENTAL RESEARCH
CENTER
UNIVERSITY OF TULSA
TULSA, OK 74104
See Biology: Ecology; Educational Insti-
tute

ENVIRONMENTAL SCIENCE
PROGRAM
OKLAHOMA STATE UNIVERSITY OF
AGRICULTURE
STILLWATER, OK 74074
See Engineering: Agricultural Engineer-
ing; Educational Institute

ENVIRONMENTAL STUDIES
PROGRAM
UNIVERSITY OF OKLAHOMA
NORMAN, OK 73069
See Interdisciplinary: General; Educa-
tional Institute

FACULTY EXCHANGE, BUREAU OF
GOVERNMENT RESEARCH
UNIVERSITY OF OKLAHOMA
NORMAN, OK 73069
See Social Sciences/Humanities: Law/
Legislation; Educational Institute

FISHERIES RESEARCH CENTER
UNIVERSITY OF OKLAHOMA
NOBLE, OK 73068
See Biology: General; Educational Insti-
tute

GEOLOGICAL SURVEY OF
OKLAHOMA
830 VAN VLEET OVAL, ROOM 163
NORMAN, OK 73069
See Geology: General; Government-State
or Local

INDIAN HEALTH SERVICE OF
OKLAHOMA CITY
388 OLD POST OFFICE AND
COURTHOUSE BUILDING
OKLAHOMA CITY, OK 73102
See Engineering: Water Resources; Gov-
ernment-Federal

LEGISLATIVE REFERENCE AND
RESEARCH DIVISION, STATE
LIBRARY
109 STATE CAPITOL
OKLAHOMA CITY,OK 73105
See Social Sciences/Humanities: Law/
Legislation; Government-State or Local

MAMMALOGISTS SOCIETY OF
AMERICA
OKLAHOMA STATE UNIVERSITY
STILLWATER, OK 74074
See Biology: General; Professional Organ-
izations

PETROLEUM GEOLOGISTS
(AMERICAN ASSOCIATION)
BOX 979
TULSA, OK 74101
See Engineering: General; Professional
Organizations

PETROLEUM RESEARCH CENTER
AT BARTLESVILLE
POST OFFICE BOX 1398
BARTLESVILLE, OK 74003
See Engineering: Chemical Engineering;
Government-Federal

SOIL CONSERVATION SERVICES
FARM ROAD AND BRUMLEY
STREET, AGRICULTURE
BUILDING
STILLWATER, OK 74074
See Biology: Ecology; Government-State
or Local

UNITED STATES DEPARTMENT OF
THE INTERIOR
POST OFFICE DRAWER 1619
TULSA, OK 74101
See Engineering: General; Government-
Federal

WATER RESOURCES BOARD OF
OKLAHOMA
2241 NW 40TH STREET
OKLAHOMA CITY, OK 73112
See Engineering: General; Government-
State or Local

WATER RESOURCES BUREAU
UNIVERSITY OF OKLAHOMA
NORMAN, OK 73069
See Engineering: Water Resources; Edu-
cational Institute

WATER RESOURCES RESEARCH
INSTITUTE
OKLAHOMA STATE UNIVERSITY
STILLWATER, OK 74074
See Engineering: General; Educational
Institute

WILDLIFE FEDERATION OF
OKLAHOMA
7404 NW 30TH STREET
BETHANY, OK 73008
See Biology: Ecology; Foundation

WORLD NEIGHBORS,
INCORPORATED
5116 NORTH PORTLAND AVENUE
OKLAHOMA CITY, OK 73112
See Social Sciences/Humanities: Population Studies/Family Planning; Research Institute

Oregon

AIR POLLUTION
1010 NORTHEAST COUCH STREET
PORTLAND, OR 97232
See Engineering: Pollution Abatement;
Field Station/Laboratory

AIR POLLUTIONAL REGIONAL
AUTHORITY OF PORTLAND
104 SW 5TH AVENUE
PORTLAND, OR 97204
See Biology: Ecology; Government-State
or Local

APPLIED SCIENCE DEPARTMENT
PO BOX 751, PORTLAND STATE
UNIVERSITY
PORTLAND, OR 97207
See Engineering: Pollution Abatement;
Educational Institute

BONNEVILLE POWER
ADMINISTRATION
P O BOX 3621
PORTLAND, OR 97208
See Engineering: Water Resources; Gov-
ernment-Federal

CHEMISTRY DEPARTMENT
UNIVERSITY OF OREGON
EUGENE, OR 97403
See Biology: Biochemistry; Educational
Institute

ENGINEERING SCHOOL
OREGON STATE UNIVERSITY
CORVALLIS, OR 97331
See Engineering: General; Educational
Institute

**ENVIRONMENTAL HEALTH
  PROGRAM**
OREGON TECHNICAL INSTITUTE
KLAMUTH FALLS, OR 97601
See Biology: Ecology; Educational Institute

**ENVIRONMENTAL HEALTH
  SCIENCE CENTER**
OREGON STATE UNIVERSITY
CORVALLIS, OR 97330
See Biology: Ecology; Educational Institute

**ENVIRONMENTAL QUALITY
  DEPARTMENT**
1234 SOUTHWEST MORRISON
  STREET
PORTLAND, OR 97205
See Engineering: Pollution Abatement;
Government-State or Local

**ENVIRONMENTAL RESEARCH
  CENTER, NATIONAL**
CORVALLIS, OR 97330
See Biology: Ecology; Research Institute

**ENVIRONMENTAL SCIENCE
  PROGRAM**
WILLIAMETTE UNIVERSITY
SALEM, OR 97301
See Chemistry: General; Educational Institute

**ENVIRONMENTAL STUDIES
  CENTER**
UNIVERSITY OF OREGON
EUGENE, OR 97403
See Interdisciplinary: General; Educational Institute

**ENVIRONMENTAL STUDIES
  PROGRAM**
OREGON STATE UNIVERSITY
CORVALLIS, OR 97331
See Interdisciplinary: General; Educational Institute

**ENVIRONMENTAL STUDIES
  PROGRAM, REED COLLEGE**
3203 SOUTH EAST WOODSTOCK
  BOULEVARD
PORTLAND, OR 97202
See Chemistry: General; Educational Institute

**ENVIRONMENTAL STUDIES
  PROGRAM, UNIVERSITY OF
  PORTLAND**
5000 NORTH WILLIAMETTE
  BOULEVARD
PORTLAND, OR 97203
See Chemistry: General; Educational Institute

**FOREST SERVICE REGION 6
  OFFICE**
319 SW PINE STREET, BOX 3623
PORTLAND, OR 97208
See Engineering: Agricultural Engineering; Government-Federal

**FORESTRY AND CONSERVATION
  ASSOCIATION**
1326 AMERICAN BANK BUILDING
PORTLAND, OR 97205
See Biology: Ecology; Professional Organizations

HEALTH DIVISION OF OREGON
1400 SW 5TH AVENUE, STATE
  OFFICE BUILDING
PORTLAND, OR 97201
See Engineering: Water Resources; Government-State or Local

**INDIAN HEALTH SERVICE,
  PORTLAND AREA**
ROOM 200, 921 SW WASHINGTON
  STREET
PORTLAND, OR 97205
See Engineering: Water Resources; Government-State or Local

**LABORATORY SERVICES,
  DEPARTMENT OF AGRICULTURE**
635 CAPITOL NORTH EAST
SALEM, OR 97301
See Engineering: Agricultural Engineering; Government-State or Local

**MARINE BIOLOGICAL INSTITUTE
  OF OREGON**
UNIVERSITY OF OREGON
CHARLESTON, OR 97420
See Biology: General; Educational Institute

MECHANICAL ENGINEERING
OREGON STATE UNIVERSITY
CORVALLIS, OREGON 97331
See Engineering: General; Educational Institute

OCEAN RESOURCES PROGRAM
OREGON STATE UNIVERSITY
CORVALLIS, OR 97330
See Interdisciplinary: General; Educational Institute

OCEANOGRAPHY DEPARTMENT
OREGON STATE UNIVERSITY
CORVALLIS, OR 97330
See Interdisciplinary: General; Educational Institute

**OCEANOGRAPHY RESEARCH
  PROGRAM, OREGON STATE
  UNIVERSITY**
OCEANOGRAPHY BUILDING
CORVALLIS, OR 97331
See Interdisciplinary: General; Educational Institute

**PACIFIC COOPERATIVE WATER
  POLLUTION LABORATORY**
104 BIOLOGICAL SCIENCES
  BUILDING, OREGON STATE
  UNIVERSITY
CORVALLIS, OR 97331
See Biology: General; Educational Institute

**PACIFIC NORTHWEST WATER
  LABORATORY**
PITTOCK BLOCK
PORTLAND, OR 97205
See Engineering: Water Resources; Government-Federal

**PESTICIDE REGULATION
  DIVISION, U S DEPARTMENT OF
  AGRICULTURE**
511 NORTH W BROADWAY
PORTLAND, OR 97207
See Engineering: Agricultural Engineering; Government-Federal

**PUBLIC WELFARE COMMISSION,
  OREGON**
PUBLIC SERVICE BUILDING
SALEM, OR 97310
See Social Sciences/Humanities:
Welfare(Child Public Social);
Government-State or Local

SOIL CONSERVATION SERVICES
1218 SW WASHINGTON STREET
PORTLAND, OR 97205
See Biology: Ecology; Government-State or Local

**WATER POLLUTION AND
  FISHERIES COOPERATIVE
  RESEARCH LABORATORY**
315 EXTENSION HALL, OREGON
  STATE UNIVERSITY
CORVALLIS, OR 97331
See Engineering: Pollution Abatement;
Field Station/Laboratory

**WATER RESOURCE RESEARCH
  INSTITUTE, OREGON
  UNIVERSITY**
114 COVELL HALL
CORVALLIS, OR 97331
See Physics: General; Educational Institute

WEATHER MEASURE NORTHWEST
P O BOX 1776
EUGENE, OR 97401
See Interdisciplinary: General; Field Station/Laboratory

**WILDLIFE FEDERATION OF
  OREGON**
811 SW 6TH AVENUE, ROOM 216
  EXECUTIVE BUILDING
PORTLAND, OR 97204
See Biology: Ecology; Foundation

Pennsylvania

**AIR ENVIRONMENTAL STUDIES
  CENTER**
PENNSYLVANIA STATE UNIVERSITY
UNIVERSITY PARK, PA 16802
See Biology: Ecology; Educational Institute

AIR MANAGEMENT SERVICES, PHILADELPHIA DEPARTMENT OF HEALTH
1701 ARCH STREET, 6TH FLOOR
PHILADELPHIA, PA 19103
See Engineering: Pollution Abatement; Government-State or Local

AIR POLLUTION BUREAU, PUBLIC SAFETY DEPARTMENT
MUNICIPAL BUILDING
ERIE, PA 16501
See Engineering: Pollution Abatement; Government-State or Local

AIR POLLUTION CONTROL ASSOCIATION
4400 FIFTH AVENUE
PITTSBURGH, PA 15213
See Engineering: Pollution Abatement; Professional Organizations

AIR POLLUTION CONTROL BOARD
601 W GERMANTOWN PIKE
PLYMOUTH MEETING, PA 19462
See Engineering: Pollution Abatement; Government-State or Local

AIR POLLUTION CONTROL BOARD OF GREATER YORK
32 WEST KING STREET
YORK, PA 17401
See Engineering: Pollution Abatement; Government-State or Local

AIR POLLUTION CONTROL DISTRICT
1516 MAIN STREET
NORTHAMPTON, PA 18067
See Engineering: Pollution Abatement; Government-State or Local

AIR POLLUTION CONTROL, ALLEGHENY COUNTY HEALTH DEPARTMENT
301 39TH STREET
PITTSBURGH, PA 15201
See Engineering: Pollution Abatement; Government-State or Local

AIR POLLUTION CONTROL, BOARD OF HEALTH, KIRBY HEALTH CENTER
71 NORTH FRANKLIN STREET
WILKES-BARRE, PA 18701
See Engineering: Pollution Abatement; Government-State or Local

AIR POLLUTION CONTROL, BUREAU OF HEALTH AND SANITATION
1510 EAST PAPER MILL ROAD
PHILADELPHIA, PA 19118
See Engineering: Pollution Abatement; Government-State or Local

AIR POLLUTION CONTROL, HEALTH BUREAU
MUNICIPAL BUILDING
WASHINGTON, PA 15301
See Engineering: Pollution Abatement; Government-State or Local

AIR POLLUTION CONTROL, HEALTH DEPARTMENT
POST OFFICE BOX 90
HARRISBURG, PA 17120
See Engineering: Pollution Abatement; Government-State or Local

AIR POLLUTION DIVISION, MINE SAFETY APPLIANCE COMPANY
201 NORTH BRADDOCK AVENUE
PITTSBURGH, PA 15208
See Engineering: Pollution Abatement; Industrial/Commercial

AIR QUALITY AND NOISE CONSERVATION, ENVIRONMENTAL RESOURCES DEPARTMENT
P O BOX 2351
HARRISBURG, PA 17105
See Engineering: Pollution Abatement; Government-State or Local

ALUMINUM CORPORATION OF AMERICA
1501 ALCOA BUILDING
PITTSBURGH, PA 15219
See Social Sciences/Humanities: Community Development/Studies; Foundation

AMERICAN INSTITUTE FOR RESEARCH
410 AMBERSON AVENUE
PITTSBURGH,PA 15232
See Social Sciences/Humanities: General; Professional Organizations

APPALACHIAN REGION-ANTHRACITE DEPOSITS, ENVIRONMENTAL AFFAIRS
19 NORTH MAIN STREET
WILKES-BARRE, PA 18701
See Engineering: Pollution Abatement; Government-Federal

ATOMIC ENERGY COMMISSION PITTSBURGH NAVAL REACTORS OFFICE
POST OFFICE BOX 109
WEST MIFFLIN, PA 15122
See Chemistry: Physical Chemistry; Government-State or Local

BIOLOGY DEPARTMENT
CEDAR CREST COLLEGE
ALLENTOWN, PA 18104
See Biology: General; Educational Institute

BIOSCIENCES INFORMATION SERVICE
2100 ARCH STREET
PHILADELPHIA, PA 19103
See Social Sciences/Humanities: Psychology/Behavioral Science; Research Institute

BITUMINOUS COAL RESEARCH, INCORPORATED
350 HOCHBERG ROAD
MONROEVILLE, PA 15146
See Engineering: Pollution Abatement; Research Institute

BOONE AND CROCKETT CLUB, CARNEGIE MELLON UNIVERSITY
4400 FORBES AVENUE
PITTSBURGH, PA 15213
See Interdisciplinary: General; Professional Organizations

CITY PLANNING COMMISSION, PHILADELPHIA
JUNIPER AND FILBERT STREETS
PHILADELPHIA, PA 19107
See Social Sciences/Humanities: Community Development/Studies; Government-State or Local

CIVIL ENGINEERING DEPARTMENT
950 BEH, UNIVERSITY OF PITTSBURGH
PITTSBURGH, PA 15213
See Engineering: Water Resources; Educational Institute

CONSERVANCY OF WESTERN PENNSYLVANIA
204 FIFTH AVENUE
PITTSBURGH, PA 15222
See Biology: Ecology; Professional Organizations

CONSERVATION EDUCATION CENTER
CLARION STATE COLLEGE
CLARION, PA 16214
See Engineering: Agricultural Engineering; Educational Institute

CYCLICAL STUDIES FOUNDATION
124 SOUTH HIGHLAND AVENUE
PITTSBURGH, PA 15206
See Interdisciplinary: General; Foundation

EARTH AND MINERAL SCIENCES COLLEGE
PENNSYLVANIA STATE UNIVERSITY, 503 DEIKE BUILDING
UNIVERSITY PARK, PA 16802
See Engineering: Pollution Abatement; Educational Institute

ENVIRONMENTAL PROTECTION AGENCY REGION 3 OFFICE
POST OFFICE BOX 12900
PHILADELPHIA, PA 19108
See Engineering: Pollution Abatement; Government-State or Local

ENVIRONMENTAL QUALITY PROGRAMS OFFICE
PENNSYLVANIA STATE UNIVERSITY
UNIVERSITY PARK, PA 16802
See Interdisciplinary: General; Educational Institute

ENVIRONMENTAL RADIATION, GRADUATE SCHOOL OF PUBLIC HEALTH
UNIVERSITY OF PITTSBURGH
PITTSBURGH, PA 15213
See Physics: General; Educational Institute

ENVIRONMENTAL SCIENCE CENTER
MERCYHURST COLLEGE
ERIE, PA 16501
See Biology: Ecology; Educational Institute

ENVIRONMENTAL SCIENCE PROGRAM
ALLEGHENY COLLEGE
MEADVILLE, PA 16335
See Interdisciplinary: General; Educational Institute

ENVIRONMENTAL SCIENCE PROGRAM
BRYN MAWR COLLEGE
BRYN MAWR, PA 19010
See Chemistry: General; Educational Institute

ENVIRONMENTAL SCIENCE PROGRAM
HAVERFORD COLLEGE
HAVERFORD, PA 19041
See Chemistry: General; Educational Institute

ENVIRONMENTAL SCIENCE PROGRAM
LEHIGH UNIVERSITY
BETHLEHEM, PA 18015
See Interdisciplinary: General; Educational Institute

ENVIRONMENTAL SCIENCE PROGRAM
THIEL COLLEGE
GREENVILLE, PA 16125
See Chemistry: General; Educational Institute

ENVIRONMENTAL SCIENCE PROGRAM
UNIVERSITY OF PENNSYLVANIA
PHILADELPHIA, PA 19104
See Interdisciplinary: General; Educational Institute

ENVIRONMENTAL SCIENCE PROGRAM
UNIVERSITY OF SCRANTON
SCRANTON, PA 18510
See Chemistry: General; Educational Institute

ENVIRONMENTAL SCIENCE PROGRAM
WESTMINSTER COLLEGE
NEW WILMINGTON, PA 16142
See Chemistry: General; Educational Institute

ENVIRONMENTAL SCIENCE PROGRAM, ROOM 407
KIRKBRIDE HALL-WIDENER COLUMBIA
CHESTER, PA 19013
See Engineering: General; Educational Institute

ENVIRONMENTAL SCIENCES GROUP, DREXEL UNIVERSITY
32ND STREET AND CHESTNUT STREET
PHILADELPHIA, PA 19104
See Interdisciplinary: General; Educational Institute

ENVIRONMENTAL SCIENCES GROUP, ST JOSEPH'S COLLEGE
54TH AND CITY LINE AVENUE
PHILADELPHIA, PA 19131
See Chemistry: General; Educational Institute

ENVIRONMENTAL SCIENCES LABORATORY, GENERAL ELECTRIC COMPANY
POST OFFICE BOX 8555
PHILADELPHIA, PA 19101
See Interdisciplinary: General; Industrial/Commercial

ENVIRONMENTAL SCIENCES PROGRAM AT WILKES COLLEGE
ENVIRONMENTAL SCIENCES RESEARCH INSTITUTION
WILKES BARRE, PA 18703
See Biology: Ecology; Research Institute

ENVIRONMENTAL SCIENCES PROJECT, DUQUESNE UNIVERSITY
600 FORBES AVENUE
PITTSBURGH, PA 15219
See Interdisciplinary: General; Educational Institute

ENVIRONMENTAL SERVICES, HEALTH BUREAU
CITY HALL
ALLENTOWN, PA 18101
See Engineering: Pollution Abatement; Government-State or Local

ENVIRONMENTAL STUDIES
143 SOUTH THIRD STREET
PHILADEPHIA, PA 19106
See Biology: Ecology; Government-State or Local

ENVIRONMENTAL STUDIES INSTITUTE, CARNEGIE-MELLON UNIVERSITY
500 FORBES AVENUE
PITTSBURGH, PA 15213
See Interdisciplinary: General; Educational Institute

ENVIRONMENTAL STUDIES PROGRAM
BROAD STREET AND MONTGOMERY AVENUE
PHILADELPHIA, PA 19122
See Interdisciplinary: General; Educational Institute

ENVIRONMENTAL STUDIES PROGRAM
BUCKNELL UNIVERSITY
LEWISBURG, PA 17837
See Interdisciplinary: General; Educational Institute

ENVIRONMENTAL STUDIES PROGRAM
SWARTHMORE COLLEGE
SWARTHMORE, PA 19081
See Interdisciplinary: General; Educational Institute

ENVIRONMENTAL STUDIES PROGRAM
VILLANOVA UNIVERSITY
VILLANOVA, PA 19085
See Interdisciplinary: General; Educational Institute

ENVIRONMENTAL STUDIES PROGRAM, LA SALLE COLLEGE
OLNEY AVENUE AT 20TH STREET
PHILADELPHIA, PA 19141
See Chemistry: General; Educational Institute

ENVIRONMENTAL STUDIES, UNIVERSITY OF PITTSBURGH
5TH AND BIGELOW STREETS
PITTSBURGH, PA 15213
See Interdisciplinary: General; Educational Institute

FELS RESEARCH INSTITUTE, SCHOOL OF MEDICINE
TEMPLE UNIVERSITY
PHILADELPHIA, PA 19140
See Biology: Ecology; Educational Institute

GAME BREEDERS OF NORTH AMERICA, SHOOTING PREVENTION ASSOCIATION
EAST MOUNTAIN ROAD, ROAD 2
HEGINS, PA 18947
See Interdisciplinary: General; Professional Organizations

GREAT LAKES RESEARCH INSTITUTE
1120 G DANIEL BALDWIN BUILDING
ERIE, PA 16501
See Interdisciplinary: General; Research Institute

HEALTH AND ENVIRONMENTAL SANITATION, PUBLIC SAFETY DEPARTMENT
CITY HALL, 423 WALNUT STREET
HARRISBURG, PA 17101
See Engineering: Pollution Abatement; Government-State or Local

HEALTH BUREAU
EIGHTH AND WASHINGTON
STREETS
READING, PA 19601
See Engineering: Pollution Abatement;
Government-State or Local

HEALTH LAW CENTER
130 DE SOTO STREET
PITTSBURGH, PA 12513
See Engineering: Water Resources; Educational Institute

**HEALTH LAW CENTER,
UNIVERSITY OF PITTSBURGH**
130 DE SOTO STREET
PITTSBURGH,PA 15213
See Social Sciences/Humanities: Law/
Legislation; Educational Institute

**HEALTH, EDUCATION, AND
WELFARE REGION 3**
POST OFFICE BOX 12900
PHILADELPHIA, PA 19108
See Interdisciplinary: General; Unclassified

**INDUSTRIAL AND PUBLIC
RELATIONS DEPARTMENT**
BETHLEHEM STEEL CORPORATION
BETHLEHEM, PA 18016
See Engineering: General; Industrial/
Commercial

**INDUSTRIAL HEALTH
FOUNDATION**
5231 CENTER AVENUE
PITTSBURGH, PA 15232
See Interdisciplinary: General; Research
Institute

**INSTRUMENT SOCIETY OF
AMERICA**
400 STANWIX STREET
PITTSBURGH, PA 15222
See Engineering: Pollution Abatement;
Professional Organizations

**INTERCOLLEGIATE OUTING CLUB
ASSOCIATION**
310 NORTH 37TH STREET
PHILADELPHIA, PA 19104
See Biology: Ecology; Professional Organizations

**INTERSTATE RELATIONS,
GOVERNOR'S OFFICE**
STATE CAPITOL
HARRISBURG, PA 17120
See Engineering: Pollution Abatement;
Government-State or Local

**JONES AND LAUGHLIN STEEL
CORPORATION**
3 GATEWAY CENTER
PITTSBURGH, PA 15230
See Engineering: General; Industrial/
Commercial

**LAND AND WATER RESOURCES
INSTITUTE, PENNSYLVANIA
STATE UNIVERSITY**

102 RESEARCH BUILDING 3
UNIVERSITY PARK, PA 16802
See Engineering: Water Resources; Educational Institute

LIMNOLOGY DEPARTMENT
19TH STREET AND PARKWAY
PHILADELPHIA, PA 19100
See Biology: General; Foundation

**MARINE AND ENVIRONMENTAL
STUDIES CENTER**
LEHIGH UNIVERSITY
BETHLEHEM, PA 18015
See Interdisciplinary: General; Research
Institute

**MARINE SCIENCES CONSORTIUM
OF PENNSYLVANIA**
MILLERSVILLE, PA 17551
See Biology: General; Educational Institute

**MINING AND SAFETY RESEARCH
CENTER, BUREAU OF MINES**
4800 FORBES AVENUE
PITTSBURGH, PA 15213
See Engineering: Pollution Abatement;
Government-Federal

**OCCUPATIONAL HEALTH
DEPARTMENT**
GRADUATE SCHOOL OF PUBLIC
HEALTH, UNIVERSITY OF
PITTSBURGH
PITTSBURGH, PA 15213
See Engineering: Pollution Abatement;
Educational Institute

**OCCUPATIONAL SAFETY AND
HEALTH, HEALTH, EDUCATION
AND WELFARE**
POST OFFICE BOX 12900
PHILADELPHIA, PA 19108
See Engineering: Pollution Abatement;
Government-State or Local

**PENNSYLVANIA FEDERATION OF
SPORTSMEN'S CLUBS**
925 SOUTH JEFFERSON STREET
JEANNETTE, PA 15664
See Biology: Ecology; Foundation

**PHARMACY AND SCIENCE,
PACIFIC COLLEGE**
43RD AND KINGSESSING AVENUE
PHILADELPHIA, PA 19104
See Chemistry: General; Educational Institute

**POLITICAL SOCIAL SCIENCES
ACADEMY**
3937 CHESTNUT STREET
PHILADELPHIA, PA. 19104
See Social Sciences/Humanities: General;
Research Institute

**POPULATION DIVISION, PUBLIC
HEALTH SCHOOL**
UNIVERSITY OF PITTSBURGH
PITTSBURGH, PA 15213

See Social Sciences/Humanities: Population Studies/Family Planning; Educational Institute

POPULATION STUDIES CENTER
UNIVERSITY OF PENNSYLVANIA,
3718 LOCUST STREET
PHILADELPHIA, PA 19104
See Social Sciences/Humanities: Population Studies/Family Planning; Educational Institute

**PUBLIC HEALTH AND SAFETY
BUREAU**
400 SOUTH EIGHTH STREET
LEBANON, PA 17042
See Engineering: Pollution Abatement;
Government-State or Local

**PUBLIC HEALTH LIBRARY
GRADUATE SCHOOL,
UNIVERSITY OF PITTSBURGH**
130 DE SOTO STREET
PITTSBURGH, PA 15213
See Biology: General; Educational Institute

**PUBLIC SAFETY DIVISION,
HEALTH BUREAU**
FIFTH AND WELSH STREETS
CHESTER, PA 19013
See Engineering: Pollution Abatement;
Government-State or Local

**RADIATION DIVISION,
ENVIRONMENTAL PROTECTION
AGENCY**
POST OFFICE BOX 12900
PHILADELPHIA, PA 19108
See Chemistry: Physical Chemistry; Government-State or Local

**RADIATION HEALTH, UNIVERSITY
OF PITTSBURGH**
508 SCAIFE HALL
PITTSBURGH, PA 15213
See Interdisciplinary: General; Educational Institute

RADIATION PROTECTION
3 GATEWAY CENTER, BOX 2278
PITTSBURGH, PA 15230
See Engineering: General; Government-State or Local

**RESEARCH INSTITUTE OF GREAT
LAKES**
1120 G DANIEL BALDWIN
BUILDING
ERIE, PA 16501
See Engineering: Water Resources; Educational Institute

RESEARCH LABORATORY
BENJAMIN FRANKLIN PARKWAY
PHILADELPHIA, PA 19103
See Interdisciplinary: General; Research
Institute

RESEARCH WATER BIOLOGY
GANNON COLLEGE
ERIE, PA 16501

See Biology: General; Educational Institute

SCIENCES RESEARCH INSTITUTE
PHILADELPHIA, PA 19100
See Engineering: Pollution Abatement; Research Institute

SCIENTIFIC RESOURCES CORPORATION
MONTGOMERYVILLE, PA 18936
See Biology: Ecology; Industrial/Commercial

SOCIAL RESPONSES IN SCIENCES SOCIETY
37 HERMAN STREET
PHILADELPHIA,PA 19144
See Social Sciences/Humanities: General; Professional Organizations

SOIL AND WATER CONSERVATION COMMISSION
2301 NORTH CAMERON STREET
HARRISBURG, PA 17120
See Engineering: Water Resources; Government-State or Local

SOIL CONSERVATION SERVICES
BOX 985, FEDERAL SQUARE STATION
HARRISBURG, PA 17108
See Biology: Ecology; Government-State or Local

SUN OIL COMPANY
POST OFFICE BOX 426
MARCUS HOOK, PA 19061
See Engineering: Pollution Abatement; Industrial/Commercial

TOPOGRAPHY BUREAU, GEOLOGICAL SURVEY
PENNSYLVANIA DEPARTMENT OF ENVIRONMENTAL RESOURCES
HARRISBURG, PA 17120
See Geology: General; Government-State or Local

UNITED STATES STEEL CORPORATION
525 WILLIAM PENN PLACE
PITTSBURGH, PA 15230
See Engineering: General; Industrial/Commercial

URBAN AND ENVIRONMENTAL STUDIES
DREXEL UNIVERSITY
PHILADELPHIA, PA 19104
See Engineering: Pollution Abatement; Educational Institute

WASTE WATER RENOVATION AND CONSERVATION PROJECT
PENNSYLVANIA STATE UNIVERSITY
UNIVERSITY PARK, PA 16802
See Engineering: Pollution Abatement; Research Institute

WATER DEPARTMENT OF PHILADELPHIA
1160 MUNICIPAL SERVICES BUILDING, JOHN KENNEDY AND 15TH STREETS
PHILADELPHIA, PA 19107
See Engineering: General; Government-State or Local

WATER QUALITY MANAGEMENT BUREAU
POST OFFICE BOX 2351, H AND W BUILDING
HARRISBURG, PA 17120
See Engineering: Water Resources; Government-State or Local

WATER RESOURCES ASSOCIATION OF DELAWARE RIVER BASIN
21 SOUTH 12TH STREET
PHILADELPHIA, PA 19107
See Engineering: Water Resources; Professional Organizations

WOMEN'S NATIONAL FARM AND GARDEN ASSOCIATION
BOX 204
VALENICIA, PA 10659
See Engineering: Agricultural Engineering; Professional Organizations

Rhode Island

AIR POLLUTION AND MECHANICAL EQUIPMENT INSTITUTE
112 UNION STREET
PROVIDENCE, RI 02903
See Engineering: General; Government-State or Local

AIR POLLUTION CONTROL, HEALTH DEPARTMENT
204 HEALTH BUILDING
PROVIDENCE, RI 02908
See Engineering: Pollution Abatement; Government-State or Local

AUDUBON SOCIETY OF RHODE ISLAND
40 BOWEN STREET
PROVIDENCE, RI 02903
See Interdisciplinary: General; Educational Institute

BLACKSTONE RIVER WATERSHED ASSOCIATION
133 KENYON AVENUE
PAWTUCKET, RI 02801
See Engineering: Water Resources; Foundation

BROWN UNIVERSITY
PROVIDENCE, RI 02912
See Interdisciplinary: General; Educational Institute

CHEMISTRY DEPARTMENT
BROWN UNIVERSITY
PROVIDENCE, RI 02912
See Chemistry: General; Educational Institute

CONSERVATION COMMISSION OF RHODE ISLAND
VETERANS MEMORIAL BUILDING, RM 302
PROVIDENCE, RI 02903
See Biology: Ecology; Government-State or Local

CONSERVATION COMMISSIONS OF RHODE ISLAND
20 FIRGLADE AVENUE
EAST PROVIDENCE, RI 02915
See Biology: Ecology; Government-State or Local

ECOLOGY ACTION FOR RHODE ISLAND
286 THAYER STREET
PROVIDENCE, RI 02906
See Biology: Ecology; Educational Institute

ECOLOGY ACTION FOR SOUTHERN RHODE ISLAND
PO BOX 9
KINGSTON, RI 02881
See Biology: Ecology; Government-State or Local

ENTOMOLOGY DIVISION, DEPARTMENT OF AGRICULTURE AND CONSERVATION
83 PARK STREET
PROVIDENCE, RI 02903
See Engineering: Agricultural Engineering; Government-State or Local

ENVIRONMENTAL BIOLOGY INSTITUTE
UNIVERSITY OF RHODE ISLAND
KINGSTON, RI 02836
See Biology: General; Educational Institute

ENVIRONMENTAL COUNCIL OF RHODE ISLAND
40 BOWEN STREET
PROVIDENCE, RI 02903
See Biology: Ecology; Government-State or Local

ENVIRONMENTAL HEALTH, DEPARTMENT OF HEALTH
DAVIS STREET
PROVIDENCE, RI 02908
See Engineering: Water Resources; Government-State or Local

ENVIRONMENTAL PROTECTION AGENCY LABORATORY
NARRAGANSETT, RI 02882
See Biology: Ecology; Field Station/Laboratory

**ENVIRONMENTAL SCIENCE
PROGRAM**
PROVIDENCE COLLEGE
PROVIDENCE, RI 02918
See Chemistry: General; Educational Institute

**ENVIRONMENTAL STUDIES
PROGRAM**
RHODE ISLAND UNIVERSITY
KINGSTON, RI 02881
See Interdisciplinary: General; Educational Institute

LIFE SCIENCES INSTITUTE
BROWN UNIVERSITY
PROVIDENCE, RI 02912
See Social Sciences/Humanities: General; Educational Institute

**MARINE WATER QUALITY
LABORATORY**
P O BOX 277, LIBERTY LANE AND FAIRGROUNDS ROAD
WEST KINGSTON, RI 02892
See Engineering: Water Resources; Government-Federal

**MARINE WATER QUALITY
LABORATORY, NATIONAL**
POST OFFICE BOX 277
WEST KINGSTON, RI 02892
See Biology: Ecology; Government-Federal

METEOROLOGY DEPARTMENT
UNIVERSITY OF RHODE ISLAND
KINGSTON, RI 02881
See Interdisciplinary: General; Educational Institute

OUTDOOR WRITER'S ASSOCIATION
244 RICHMOND DR
WARWICK, RI 02888
See Interdisciplinary: General; Professional Organizations

**SHELLFISH SANITATION
NORTHEAST RESEARCH CENTER**
NARRAGANSETT, RI 02882
See Engineering: Agricultural Engineering; Government-Federal

**SOIL AND WATER CONSERVATION
ASSOCIATION OF RHODE ISLAND**
TOURTELLOT HILL ROAD
CHEPACHET, RI 02814
See Biology: Ecology; Government-State or Local

SOIL CONSERVATION SERVICE
UNITED STATES POST OFFICE
EAST GREENWICH, RI 02818
See Biology: Ecology; Government-State or Local

**WATER POLLUTION CONTROL
DIVISION, STATE HEALTH
DEPARTMENT**
335 STATE OFFICE BUILDING
PROVIDENCE, RI 02903
See Engineering: Pollution Abatement; Government-State or Local

**WATER RESOURCES CENTER OF
RHODE ISLAND**
UNIVERSITY OF RHODE ISLAND
KINGSTON, RI 02881
See Engineering: Water Resources; Educational Institute

**WATER SUPPLY RESEARCH
LABORATORY, ENVIRONMENTAL
PROTECTION AGENCY**
SOUTH FERRY ROAD
NARRAGANSETT, RI 02882
See Engineering: Pollution Abatement; Government-Federal

**WILDLIFE FEDERATION OF
RHODE ISLAND**
40 BOWEN STREET
PROVIDENCE, RI 02903
See Biology: Ecology; Foundation

ZERO POPULATION GROWTH
POST OFFICE BOX 89
KINGSTON, RI 02881
See Social Sciences/Humanities: Population Studies/Family Planning; Foundation

South Carolina

**AIR POLLUTION CONTROL
SECTION, COUNTY HEALTH
DEPARTMENT**
334 CALHOUN STREET
CHARLESTON, SC 29401
See Engineering: Pollution Abatement; Government-State or Local

**AIR POLLUTION TECHNOLOGY
ADVANCE BOARD**
145 WEST BROAD STREET
SPARTANBURG, SC 29301
See Engineering: General; Government-State or Local

**ATOMIC ENERGY COMMISSION,
SAVANNAH RIVER OPERATIONS**
POST OFFICE BOX A
AIKEN, SC 29801
See Geology: General; Government-Federal

**CROP PESTICIDE STATE
COMMISSION**
CLEMSON, SC 29631
See Engineering: Agricultural Engineering; Government-State or Local

ENGINEERING COLLEGE
CLEMSON UNIVERSITY
CLEMSON, SC 29631
See Engineering: General; Educational Institute

**ENVIRONMENTAL PROTECTION
AGENCY LABORATORY**
BEARS BLUFF, SC 29910
See Biology: Ecology; Field Station/Laboratory

**ENVIRONMENTAL RESOURCES
INSTITUTE**
DEPARTMENT OF CHEMICAL ENGINEERING, UNIVERSITY OF SOUTH CAROLINA
COLUMBIA, SC 29208
See Engineering: Water Resources; Educational Institute

**ENVIRONMENTAL SCIENCE
PROGRAM**
CLEMSON UNIVERSITY
CLEMSON, SC 29631
See Interdisciplinary: General; Educational Institute

**ENVIRONMENTAL SCIENCE
PROGRAM**
THE CITADEL
CHARLESTON, SC 29401
See Interdisciplinary: General; Educational Institute

**ENVIRONMENTAL STUDIES
PROGRAM**
FURMAN UNIVERSITY
GREENVILLE, SC 29613
See Chemistry: General; Educational Institute

**ENVIRONMENTAL STUDIES
PROGRAM**
UNIVERSITY OF SOUTH CAROLINA
COLUMBIA, SC 29208
See Interdisciplinary: General; Educational Institute

**ENVIRONMENTAL SYSTEMS
ENGINEERING**
CLEMSON UNIVERSITY
CLEMSON, SC 29631
See Engineering: Water Resources; Educational Institute

**INSPECTION SERVICES OFFICE, U
S DEPARTMENT OF
AGRICULTURE**
3202 DEVINE STREET, OFFICE H
COLUMBIA, SC 29205
See Engineering: Agricultural Engineering; Government-Federal

**MARINE BIOLOGICAL
LABORATORY, FORT JOHNSON**
COLLEGE OF CHARLESTON, RT 1
CHARLESTON, SC 29401
See Biology: General; Field Station/Laboratory

POLLUTION CONTROL AUTHORITY
2600 BULL STREET, J MARION SIMS BUILDING
COLUMBIA, SC 29201
See Engineering: Pollution Abatement; Government-State or Local

PUBLIC WORKS DEPARTMENT
1735 MAIN STREET
COLUMBIA, SC 29201
See Engineering: General; Government-State or Local

**SOIL CONSERVATION SERVICES,
FEDERAL BUILDING**
901 SUMTER STREET
COLUMBIA, SC 29201
See Biology: Ecology; Government-State
or Local

**STATE DEVELOPMENT BOARD OF
SOUTH CAROLINA**
WADE HAMPTON BOULEVARD,
BOX 927
COLUMBIA, SC 29202
See Engineering: Water Resources; Government-State or Local

**WATER AND POLLUTION
CONTROL ASSOCIATION**
STATE BOARD OF HEALTH
COLUMBIA, SC 29201
See Engineering: Pollution Abatement;
Government-State or Local

**WATER POLLUTION CONTROL
AUTHORITY**
J MARION SIMS BUILDING
COLUMBIA, SC 29201
See Engineering: Pollution Abatement;
Government-State or Local

**WILDLIFE FEDERATION OF
SOUTH CAROLINA**
LONE STAR ROAD
ELLORE, SC 29047
See Biology: Ecology; Foundation

South Dakota

**ATMOSPHERIC SCIENCES
INSTITUTE**
SOUTH DAKOTA SCHOOL OF
MINES AND TECHNOLOGY
RAPID CITY, SD 57701
See Engineering: Pollution Abatement;
Educational Institute

**ENVIRONMENTAL SCIENCE
PROGRAM**
SOUTH DAKOTA SCHOOL OF
MINES & TECHNOLOGY
RAPID CITY, SD 57701
See Interdisciplinary: General; Educational Institute

ENVIRONMENTAL STUDIES
SOUTH DAKOTA STATE
UNIVERSITY
BROOKINGS, SD 57006
See Interdisciplinary: General; Educational Institute

**ENVIRONMENTAL STUDIES
PROGRAM**
AUGUSTANA COLLEGE
SIOUX FALLS, SD 57102

See Chemistry: General; Educational Institute

**ENVIRONMENTAL STUDIES
PROGRAM**
UNIVERSITY OF SOUTH DAKOTA
VERMILLION, SD 57069
See Interdisciplinary: General; Educational Institute

**GAME, FISHERIES AND PARKS
DEPARTMENT OF SOUTH
DAKOTA**
PIERRE, SD 57501
See Engineering: Water Resources; Government-State or Local

**GEOLOGICAL SURVEY OF SOUTH
DAKOTA**
SCIENCES CENTER, UNIVERSITY
OF SOUTH DAKOTA
VERMILLION, SD 57069
See Geology: General; Educational Institute

GOVERNMENT RESEARCH BUREAU
UNIVERSITY OF SOUTH DAKOTA
VERMILLION, SD 57069
See Social Sciences/Humanities: Politics;
Educational Institute

HEALTH DEPARTMENT
PIERRE, SD 57501
See Engineering: Pollution Abatement;
Government-State or Local

**INDIAN HEALTH CENTER,
ABERDEEN AREA**
405 CITIZENS BUILDING
ABERDEEN, SD 57401
See Engineering: Water Resources; Government-State or Local

**LEGISLATIVE RESOURCES
COUNCIL, SOUTH DAKOTA**
STATE CAPITOL
PIERRE, SD 57501
See Social Sciences/Humanities: Law/
Legislation; Government-State or Local

**MINES AND TECHNOLOGY
SCHOOL OF SOUTH DAKOTA**
INSTITUTION OF ATMOSPHERIC
SCIENCES
RAPID CITY, SD 57701
See Geology: General; Educational Institute

**NATIONAL WILDLIFE
FEDERATION**
REGION 9
SIOUX FALLS, SD 57101
See Biology: Ecology; Foundation

**OCCUPATIONAL SAFETY AND
HEALTH DIVISION**
STATE HEALTH OFFICE

PIERRE, SD 57501
See Interdisciplinary: General; Government-State or Local

**PLANT INDUSTRY DIVISION,
DEPARTMENT OF AGRICULTURE**
PIERRE, SD 57501
See Engineering: Agricultural Engineering; Government-State or Local

**RADIOLOGICAL HEALTH
DIVISION, STATE HEALTH
OFFICE**
STATE DEPARTMENT OF HEALTH
PIERRE, SD 57501
See Interdisciplinary: General; Government-State or Local

RAPTOR RESEARCH FOUNDATION
UNIVERSITY OF SOUTH DAKOTA
VERMILLION, SD 57609
See Biology: General; Foundation

**SANITARY ENGINEERING AND
ENVIRONMENTAL PROTECTION**
DEPARTMENT OF HEALTH
PIERRE, SD 57501
See Engineering: Pollution Abatement;
Government-State or Local

**SOIL AND WATER CONSERVATION
COMMISSION OF SOUTH
DAKOTA**
STATE CAPITOL
PIERRE, SD 57501
See Engineering: Water Resources; Government-State or Local

SOIL CONSERVATION SERVICES
239 WISCONSIN AVENUE, SW PO
BOX 1357
HURON, SD 57350
See Biology: Ecology; Government-State
or Local

STATE CHEMICAL LABORATORY
VERMILLION, SD 57069
See Chemistry: General; Government-State or Local

**WATER RESOURCES COMMISSION
OF SOUTH DAKOTA**
STATE OFFICE BUILDING 1
PIERRE, SD 57501
See Engineering: Water Resources; Government-State or Local

**WILDLIFE FEDERATION OF
SOUTH DAKOTA**
1217 SOUTH LAKE AVENUE
SIOUX FALLS, SD 57105
See Biology: Ecology; Foundation

Tennessee

**AIR POLLUTION CONTROL
BUREAU**
CITY HALL, 11TH STREET

CHATTANOOGA, TN 37402
See Engineering: Pollution Abatement;
Government-State or Local

**AIR POLLUTION CONTROL,
ENVIRONMENTAL HEALTH
BUREAU**
814 JEFFERSON AVENUE
MEMPHIS, TN 38105
See Engineering: Pollution Abatement;
Government-State or Local

**AIR POLLUTION CONTROL,
PUBLIC HEALTH DEPARTMENT**
727 CORDELL HULL BUILDING
NASHVILLE, TN 37219
See Engineering: Pollution Abatement;
Government-State or Local

**ATMOSPHERIC AND WATER
POLLUTION, BIOLOGY
DEPARTMENT**
CARSON NEWMAN COLLEGE
JEFFERSON CITY, TN 37760
See Engineering: Pollution Abatement;
Educational Institute

**ATOMIC ENERGY COMMISSION,
OAK RIDGE OPERATIONS**
POST OFFICE BOX E
OAK RIDGE, TN 37830
See Geology: General; Government-Federal

BIOLOGY DEPARTMENT
MID-APPALACHIAN COLLEGE
COUNCIL
KNOXVILLE, TN 37921
See Biology: General; Educational Institute

**BUILDING AND AIR POLLUTION
CONTROL DEPARTMENT**
CITY HALL, 225 WEST CENTER
STREET
KINGSPORT, TN 37660
See Engineering: Pollution Abatement;
Government-State or Local

**CONSERVANCY COUNCIL OF
MIDDLE TENNESSEE**
NASHVILLE CHILDRENS MUSEUM
NASHVILLE, TN 37210
See Engineering: General; Professional
Organizations

**CONSERVATION DEPARTMENT,
DIVISION OF GEOLOGY**
G-5 STATE OFFICE BUILDING
NASHVILLE, TN 37219
See Geology: General; Government-State
or Local

**CONSERVATION LEAGUE OF
TENNESSEE**
1507 COLLEGE HEIGHTS DRIVE
JOHNSON CITY, TN 37601
See Biology: Ecology; Foundation

EASTERN DECIDUOUS FOREST
OAK RIDGE NATIONAL
LABORATORY
OAK RIDGE, TN 37830
See Biology: Ecology; Research Institute

**ECOLOGICAL SCIENCES
INFORMATION CENTER, OAK
RIDGE LABORATORY**
BUILDING 3017
OAK RIDGE, TN 37830
See Biology: Ecology; Government-Federal

**ENGINEERING DESIGN OFFICE,
TENNESSEE VALLEY AUTHORITY**
607 UNION BUILDING
KNOXVILLE, TN 37902
See Engineering: Water Resources; Government-Federal

ENGINEERING SCHOOL
BOX 1826, STATION B, 24TH
AVENUE, SOUTH
NASHVILLE, TN 37203
See Engineering: Water Resources; Educational Institute

**ENVIRONMENTAL AND WATER
RESOURCES ENGINEERING
DEPARTMENT**
VANDERBILT UNIVERSITY
NASHVILLE, TN 37201
See Interdisciplinary: General; Educational Institute

**ENVIRONMENTAL MUTAGEN
INFORMATION CENTER,
BIOLOGICAL DIVISION**
POST OFFICE BOX Y
OAK RIDGE, TN 37830
See Biology: Biochemistry; Government-Federal

**ENVIRONMENTAL SCIENCE
PROGRAM**
FISK UNIVERSITY
NASHVILLE, TN 37203
See Chemistry: General; Educational Institute

**ENVIRONMENTAL SCIENCE
PROGRAM**
TENNESSEE TECHNOLOGY
UNIVERSITY
COOKEVILLE, TN 38501
See Interdisciplinary: General; Educational Institute

ENVIRONMENTAL STUDIES
UNIVERSITY OF TENNESSEE
KNOXVILLE, TN 37901
See Biology: General; Educational Institute

**ENVIRONMENTAL STUDIES
PROGRAM**
EAST TENNESSEE STATE

UNIVERSITY
JOHNSON CITY, TN 37601
See Chemistry: General; Educational Institute

**ENVIRONMENTAL STUDIES
PROGRAM**
MEMPHIS STATE UNIVERSITY
MEMPHIS, TN 38111
See Chemistry: General; Educational Institute

**ENVIRONMENTAL STUDIES
PROGRAM**
UNIVERSITY OF THE SOUTH
SEWANEE, TN 37375
See Chemistry: General; Educational Institute

**ENVIRONMENTAL STUDIES
PROGRAM, UNIVERSITY OF
TENNESSEE**
CUMBERLAND AVENUE
KNOXVILLE, TN 37916
See Interdisciplinary: General; Educational Institute

**ENVIRONMENTAL STUDIES,
VANDERBILT UNIVERSITY**
21ST AVENUE AND WEST END
NASHVILLE, TN 37203
See Interdisciplinary: General; Educational Institute

**FOOD AND DRUG DIVISION,
DEPARTMENT OF AGRICULTURE**
BOX 9039, MELROSE STATION
NASHVILLE, TN 37204
See Engineering: Agricultural Engineering; Government-State or Local

**FORESTRY ASSOCIATION OF
TENNESSEE**
SEWANEE, TN 37372
See Biology: Ecology; Professional Organizations

**FORESTRY DEVELOPMENT
DIVISION**
TENNESSEE VALLEY AUTHORITY
NORRIS, TN 37828
See Engineering: Water Resources; Government-Federal

**GEOLOGY DIVISION, TENNESSEE
DEPARTMENT OF
CONSERVATION**
G-5 STATE OFFICE BUILDING
NASHVILLE, TN 37219
See Engineering: Water Resources; Government-State or Local

GOVERNOR'S OFFICE
STATE OFFICE BUILDING
NASHVILLE, TN 37219
See Engineering: Pollution Abatement;
Government-State or Local

HEALTH AND PHYSICS DIVISION
OAK RIDGE NATIONAL
LABORATORY
OAK RIDGE, TN 37831
See Biology: General; Government-Federal

**HEALTH AND SAFETY DIVISION,
TENNESSEE VALLEY AUTHORITY**
715 EDNEY BUILDING, 11TH AND
MARKET STREETS
CHATTANOOGA, TN 37401
See Engineering: Water Resources; Government-Federal

HEALTH DEPARTMENT
311 23RD AVENUE NORTH
NASHVILLE, TN 37203
See Engineering: Pollution Abatement;
Government-State or Local

HOME FEDERAL BUILDING
MARKET STREET
KNOXVILLE, TN 37902
See Engineering: Water Resources; Government-Federal

**NUCLEAR SAFETY INFORMATION
CENTER**
PO BOX Y, OAK RIDGE NATIONAL
LABORATORY
OAK RIDGE, TN 37831
See Engineering: General; Government-Federal

**OAK RIDGE ASSOCIATED
UNIVERSITIES**
POST OFFICE BOX 117
OAK RIDGE, TN 37830
See Chemistry: Physical Chemistry; Government-Federal

**OBSTETRICS AND GYNECOLOGY
DEPARTMENT, SCHOOL OF
MEDICINE**
VANDERBILT UNIVERSITY
NASHVILLE, TN 37203
See Biology: General; Educational Institute

**PESTICIDE REGULATION
DIVISION DEPARTMENT OF
AGRICULTURE**
SUITE 104, TILLMAN STREET
MEMPHIS, TN 38111
See Engineering: Agricultural Engineering; Government-Federal

PUBLIC HEALTH DEPARTMENT
SIXTH AVENUE NORTH, CORDELL
HULL BUILDING
NASHVILLE, TN 37219
See Social Sciences/Humanities: General;
Educational Institute

PUBLIC WELFARE DEPARTMENT
STATE OFFICE BUILDING
NASHVILLE, TN 37219

See Social Sciences/Humanities:
Welfare(Child Public Social);
Government-State or Local

**RADIATION PROTECTION
(INTERNATIONAL)**
OAK RIDGE NATIONAL
LABORATORY
OAK RIDGE, TN 37830
See Physics: General; Research Institute

**SCENIC RIVERS ASSOCIATION OF
TENNESSEE**
BOX 3104
NASHVILLE, TN 37219
See Biology: Ecology; Professional Organizations

SOIL CONSERVATION SERVICE
561 UNITED STATES COURT HOUSE
NASHVILLE, TN 37203
See Interdisciplinary: General; Unclassified

**STREAM POLLUTION CONTROL,
PUBLIC HEALTH DEPARTMENT**
620 CORDELL HULL BUILDING
NASHVILLE, TN 37219
See Engineering: Pollution Abatement;
Government-State or Local

**WATER CONTROL PLANNING
DIVISION**
HOME FEDERAL BUILDING,
MARKET STREET
KNOXVILLE, TN 37902
See Engineering: Water Resources; Government-State or Local

WATER RESOURCES CENTER
1000 WHITE AVENUE
KNOXVILLE, TN 37916
See Engineering: Water Resources; Educational Institute

**WATER RESOURCES DIVISION,
DEPARTMENT OF
CONSERVATION**
2611 WEST END AVENUE
NASHVILLE, TN 37203
See Engineering: Water Resources; Government-State or Local

**WILDERNESS PLANNING OF
TENNESSEE CITIZENS**
130 TABOR ROAD
OAK RIDGE, TN 37830
See Biology: Ecology; Professional Organizations

Texas

AGRICULTURE DEPARTMENT
CAPITOL STATION
AUSTIN, TX 78710

See Engineering: Agricultural Engineering; Government-State or Local

**AIR AND WATER POLLUTION
CONTROL, HARRIS COUNTY
HEALTH DEPARTMENT**
BOX 6031
PASADENA, TX 77502
See Interdisciplinary: General; Government-State or Local

AIR CONTROL BOARD
1100 WEST 49TH STREET
AUSTIN, TX 78756
See Engineering: Pollution Abatement;
Government-State or Local

**AIR POLLUTION CONTROL
DEPARTMENT**
CITY HALL
TEMPLE, TX 76501
See Engineering: Pollution Abatement;
Government-State or Local

**AIR POLLUTION CONTROL
PROGRAM, ENVIRONMENTAL
HEALTH DIVISION**
1936 AMELIA COURT
DALLAS, TX 75235
See Engineering: Pollution Abatement;
Government-State or Local

**AIR POLLUTION CONTROL, CITY-
COUNTY HEALTH UNIT**
1700 THIRD STREET
WITCHITA FALLS, TX 76301
See Engineering: Pollution Abatement;
Government-State or Local

**AIR POLLUTION CONTROL,
COUNTY HEALTH DEPARTMENT**
POST OFFICE BOX 2039
TYLER, TX 75701
See Engineering: Pollution Abatement;
Government-State or Local

**AIR POLLUTION CONTROL,
HEALTH DEPARTMENT**
1115 NORTH MACGREGOR STREET
HOUSTON, TX 77025
See Engineering: Pollution Abatement;
Government-State or Local

**AIR POLLUTION DIVISION,
COUNTY HEALTH DEPARTMENT**
TEXAS TECHNOLOGY UNIVERSITY
LUBBOCK, TX 79409
See Interdisciplinary: General; Educational Institute

ANTHROPOLOGY DEPARTMENT
UNIVERSITY OF TEXAS
AUSTIN, TX 78712
See Social Sciences/Humanities: General;
Educational Institute

ATMOSPHERIC STUDIES CENTER
UNIVERSITY OF HOUSTON
HOUSTON, TX 77000
See Engineering: Pollution Abatement;
Educational Institute

**BALCONES RESEARCH CENTER,
UNIVERSITY OF TEXAS**
ROUTE 4 BOX 189
AUSTIN, TX 78700
See Engineering: General; Educational
Institute

BIOLOGY DEPARTMENT
NORTH TEXAS STATE UNIVERSITY
DENTON, TX 76203
See Biology: General; Educational Institute

BIOLOGY DEPARTMENT
RICE UNIVERSITY
HOUSTON, TX 77001
See Biology: General; Educational Institute

**CHEMICAL ENGINEERING
DEPARTMENT**
UNIVERSITY OF TEXAS
AUSTIN, TX 78712
See Engineering: Pollution Abatement;
Educational Institute

**CITY-COUNTY HEALTH
DEPARTMENT**
1202 JARVIS STREET, BOX 998
LUBBOCK, TX 79408
See Engineering: Pollution Abatement;
Government-State or Local

**CONSERVATION
COMMUNICATIONS
ASSOCIATION**
POST OFFICE BOX 310
LUFKIN, TX 75901
See Interdisciplinary: General; Industrial/
Commercial

**CONSERVATION COUNCIL OF
TEXAS**
730 EAST FRIAR TUCK LANE
HOUSTON, TX 77024
See Biology: Ecology; Professional Organizations

**CONSERVATION DISTRICTS
FOUNDATIONS, DAVIS
CONSERVATION LIBRARY**
PO BOX 776, 408 MAIN STREET
LEAGUE CITY, TX 77573
See Interdisciplinary: General; Foundation

COOLING TOWER INSTITUTE
3003 YALE STREET
HOUSTON, TX 77018
See Engineering: Water Resources; Professional Organizations

**CORROSION END ASSOCIATION
(NATIONAL)**
980 M & M BUILDING
HOUSTON, TEX 77002
See Chemistry: General; Government-Federal

DOWELL SCHLUMBERGER
1300 FIRST CITY EAST BUILDING
HOUSTON, TX 77002
See Social Sciences/Humanities: Industrial Development; Industrial/Commercial

**ECOLOGY BUREAU AND GEOLOGY
BUREAU**
18TH AND RED RIVER STREET,
BOX X UNIVERSITY STATION
AUSTIN, TX 78712
See Engineering: Water Resources; Educational Institute

**EDUCATION RESEARCH AND
SERVICES BUREAU**
CULLEN BOULEVARD, UNIVERSITY
OF HOUSTON
HOUSTON,TX 77002
See Social Sciences/Humanities: Education; Educational Institute

ENGINEERING COLLEGE
UNIVERSITY OF TEXAS
AUSTIN, TX 78712
See Engineering: General; Educational
Institute

**ENGINEERING DIVISION, PUBLIC
HEALTH DEPARTMENT**
1800 UNIVERSITY DRIVE
FORT WORTH, TX 76107
See Engineering: Pollution Abatement;
Government-State or Local

**ENVIRONMENTAL EDUCATION
OFFICE**
1114 COMMERCE STREET
DALLAS, TX 75202
See Social Sciences/Humanities: Education; Government-State or Local

**ENVIRONMENTAL HEALTH
DEPARTMENT, UNIVERSITY OF
TEXAS**
POST OFFICE BOX 20186
HOUSTON, TX 90007
See Biology: General; Educational Institute

**ENVIRONMENTAL HEALTH
ENGINEERING LABORATORY**
ENGINEERING LABORATORY
BUILDING 305
AUSTIN, TX 78712
See Engineering: Water Resources; Educational Institute

**ENVIRONMENTAL HEALTH,
METROPOLITAN HEALTH
DEPARTMENT**

131 WEST NUEVA STREET
SAN ANTONIO, TX 78285
See Engineering: Pollution Abatement;
Government-State or Local

**ENVIRONMENTAL PROTECTION
AGENCY REGION 6 OFFICE**
1114 COMMERCE STREET
DALLAS, TX 75202
See Engineering: Pollution Abatement;
Government-State or Local

**ENVIRONMENTAL SCIENCE AND
ENGINEERING PROGRAM**
RICE UNIVERSITY
HOUSTON, TX 77001
See Engineering: Pollution Abatement;
Educational Institute

**ENVIRONMENTAL SCIENCE
PROGRAM**
BAYLOR UNIVERSITY
WACO, TX 76703
See Chemistry: General; Educational Institute

**ENVIRONMENTAL SCIENCE
PROGRAM**
NORTH TEXAS STATE UNIVERSITY
DENTON, TX 76203
See Chemistry: General; Educational Institute

**ENVIRONMENTAL SCIENCE
PROGRAM**
SAM HOUSTON STATE COLLEGE
HUNTSVILLE, TX 77340
See Interdisciplinary: General; Educational Institute

**ENVIRONMENTAL SCIENCE
PROGRAM**
TEXAS AGRICULTURAL AND
MECHANICAL UNIVERSITY
COLLEGE STATION, TX 77843
See Interdisciplinary: General; Educational Institute

**ENVIRONMENTAL SCIENCE
PROGRAM**
TEXAS TECHNOLOGY COLLEGE
LUBBOCK, TX 79406
See Interdisciplinary: General; Educational Institute

**ENVIRONMENTAL SCIENCE
PROGRAM**
TRINITY UNIVERSITY
SAN ANTONIO, TX 78212
See Chemistry: General; Educational Institute

**ENVIRONMENTAL SCIENCE
PROGRAM**
UNIVERSITY OF TEXAS AT
ARLINGTON
ARLINGTON, TX 76010

See Interdisciplinary: General; Educational Institute

ENVIRONMENTAL SCIENCES AND ENGINEERING LABORATORY
DEPARTMENT OF CHEMICAL ENGINEERING, RICE UNIVERSITY
HOUSTON, TX 77001
See Engineering: Water Resources; Educational Institute

ENVIRONMENTAL SCIENCES AND ENGINEERING PROGRAM
UNIVERSITY OF HOUSTON-3801 CULLEN
HOUSTON, TX 77004
See Engineering: Pollution Abatement; Government-State or Local

ENVIRONMENTAL STUDIES GROUP
TEXAS CHRISTIAN UNIVERSITY
FORT WORTH, TX 76129
See Biology: Ecology; Educational Institute

ENVIRONMENTAL STUDIES INSTITUTE
BAYLOR UNIVERSITY
WACO, TX 76703
See Interdisciplinary: General; Educational Institute

ENVIRONMENTAL STUDIES PROGRAM
LAMAR STATE COLLEGE OF TECNOLOGY
BEAUMONT, TX 77704
See Interdisciplinary: General; Educational Institute

ENVIRONMENTAL STUDIES PROGRAM
SOUTHERN METHODIST UNIVERSITY
DALLAS, TX 75222
See Interdisciplinary: General; Educational Institute

ENVIRONMENTAL STUDIES PROGRAM
TEXAS ARTS AND INDUSTRIES UNIVERSITY
KINGSVILLE, TX 78363
See Engineering: General; Educational Institute

ENVIRONMENTAL STUDIES PROGRAM
TEXAS WOMANS UNIVERSITY
DENTON, TX 76204
See Biology: Ecology; Educational Institute

ENVIRONMENTAL STUDIES PROGRAM
UNIVERSITY OF TEXAS AT AUSTIN
AUSTIN, TX 78712

See Interdisciplinary: General; Educational Institute

ENVIRONMENTAL STUDIES PROGRAM
UNIVERSITY OF TEXAS AT EL PASO
EL PASO, TX 79999
See Interdisciplinary: General; Educational Institute

ENVIRONMENTAL STUDIES, RICE UNIVERSITY
POST OFFICE BOX 1982
HOUSTON, TX 77001
See Interdisciplinary: General; Educational Institute

ENVIRONMENTAL STUDIES, UNIVERSITY OF HOUSTON
3801 CULLEN ROAD
HOUSTON, TX 77004
See Interdisciplinary: General; Educational Institute

FEED AND FERTILIZER CONTROL SERVICE
COLLEGE STATION, TX 77843
See Engineering: Agricultural Engineering; Government-State or Local

GOVERNMENT RESEARCH BUREAU, LYNDON B JOHNSON SCHOOL OF PUBLIC AFFAIRS
UNIVERSITY OF TEXAS
AUSTIN, TX 78712
See Social Sciences/Humanities: General; Educational Institute

HEALTH DEPARTMENT
IRVING AND COLLEGE STREETS, BOX 1751
SAN ANGELO, TX 76901
See Engineering: Pollution Abatement; Government-State or Local

HEALTH DEPARTMENT
1149 PEARL STREET, 601 COURTHOUSE
BEAUMONT, TX 77701
See Engineering: Pollution Abatement; Government-State or Local

HEALTH DEPARTMENT
1207 OAK STREET
LA MARQUE, TX 77568
See Engineering: Pollution Abatement; Government-State or Local

HEALTH DEPARTMENT OF NUECES COUNTY
1811 NORTH SHORELINE DRIVE
CORPUS CHRISTI, TX 78403
See Engineering: Pollution Abatement; Government-State or Local

HEALTH, EDUCATION AND WELFARE REGION 6 OFFICE
1114 COMMERCE STREET

DALLAS, TX 75202
See Interdisciplinary: General; Government-Federal

HOGG FOUNDATION FOR MENTAL HEALTH
UNIVERSITY OF TEXAS
AUSTIN, TX 78712
See Social Sciences/Humanities: Mental Health; Educational Institute

HYDROLOGY OFFICE, NATIONAL WEATHER SERVICES, SOUTHERN OFFICE
ROOM 10E09, 819 TAYLOR STREET
FORT WORTH, TX 76102
See Engineering: Water Resources; Government-State or Local

INTERNATIONAL BOUNDARIES AND WATER COMMISSION, US AND MEXICO
POST OFFICE BOX 1859
EL PASO, TX 79950
See Engineering: General; Government-Federal

MARINE SCIENCES AND MARITIME RESOURCES, TEXAS A AND M UNIVERSITY
BUILDING 311 FT CROCKETT
GALVESTON, TX 77550
See Interdisciplinary: General; Educational Institute

MARINE SCIENCES INSTITUTE
UNIVERSITY OF TEXAS
PORT ARANSAS, TX 78373
See Biology: Ecology; Educational Institute

NATIONAL WILDLIFE FEDERATION
REGION 8
PORT ARTHUR, TX 77640
See Biology: Ecology; Foundation

OBSTETRICS AND GYNECOLOGY DEPARTMENT, SCHOOL OF MEDICINE
UNIVERSITY OF TEXAS
SAN ANTONIO, TX 78229
See Biology: General; Educational Institute

OCCUPATIONAL HEALTH AND RADIATION CONTROL, ENVIRONMENTAL HEALTH
1100 WEST 49TH STREET
AUSTIN, TX 78756
See Engineering: Pollution Abatement; Government-State or Local

OCCUPATIONAL SAFETY AND HEALTH, HEALTH, EDUCATION AND WELFARE
1114 COMMERCE STREET
DALLAS, TX 75202

See Engineering: Pollution Abatement;
Government-State or Local

**ODESSA-ECTOR COUNTY HEALTH
DEPARTMENT**
200 WEST THIRD STREET
ODESSA, TX 79761
See Engineering: Pollution Abatement;
Government-State or Local

**PESTICIDE REGULATION
DIVISION, U S DEPARTMENT OF
AGRICULTURE**
POST OFFICE BOX 6050
FORT WORTH, TX 76115
See Engineering: Agricultural Engineering; Government-Federal

**PUBLIC HEALTH SCHOOL,
UNIVERSITY OF TEXAS**
POST OFFICE BOX 20186
HOUSTON, TX 77025
See Biology: Ecology; Educational Institute

**RADIATION DIVISION,
ENVIRONMENTAL PROTECTION
AGENCY**
1114 COMMERCE STREET
DALLAS, TX 75202
See Chemistry: Physical Chemistry; Government-State or Local

RESEARCH CENTER, GRADUATE
UNIVERSITY OF TEXAS
DALLAS, TX 75205
See Interdisciplinary: General; Educational Institute

**RESEARCH IN WATER CENTER,
UNIVERSITY OF TEXAS AT
AUSTIN**
BALCONES RESEARCH CENTER-RT
4-189
AUSTIN, TX 78757
See Engineering: Water Resources; Educational Institute

**SOCIAL PSYCHOLOGY
DEPARTMENT, PUBLIC HEALTH
SCHOOL**
UNIVERSITY OF TEXAS
HOUSTON, TX 77025
See Social Sciences/Humanities: Psychology/Behavioral Science; Educational Institute

**SOIL AND WATER CONSERVATION
BUILDING**
1014 FIRST NATIONAL BANK
BUILDING
TEMPLE, TX 76501
See Engineering: Water Resources; Government-State or Local

**SOIL AND WATER CONSERVATION
FOUNDATION, DAVIS LIBRARY**
P O BOX 776, 408 MAIN STREET

LEAGUE CITY, TX 77573
See Engineering: Water Resources; Foundation

SOIL CONSERVATION SERVICES
16-20 MAIN STREET, PO BOX 648
TEMPLE, TX 76501
See Biology: Ecology; Government-State or Local

**SOUTH WESTERN RESEARCH
INSTITUTE**
LIBRARY 8500 CULEBRA, P O
DRAWER 28510
SAN ANTONIO, TX 78284
See Interdisciplinary: General; Research Institute

**SOUTHWEST CENTER FOR
ADVANCED STUDY**
BOX 8478
DALLAS, TX 75205
See Geology: Geophysics; Research Institute

SPORTSMEN'S CLUBS OF TEXAS
311 VAUGHN BUILDING
AUSTIN, TX 78701
See Biology: Ecology; Foundation

URBAN STUDIES INSTITUTE
SOUTHERN METHODIST
UNIVERSITY
DALLAS, TX 75201
See Social Sciences/Humanities: Urban Problems; Educational Institute

**WATER DEVELOPMENT BOARD OF
TEXAS**
POST OFFICE BOX 13087, CAPITAL
STATION
AUSTIN, TX 78711
See Engineering: Water Resources; Government-State or Local

WATER QUALITY BOARD OF TEXAS
1108 LAVACA STREET
AUSTIN, TX 78701
See Engineering: Water Resources; Government-State or Local

WATER RESOURCES CENTER
COLLEGE OF CIVIL
ENGINEERING, TEXAS
TECHNICAL COLLEGE
LUBBOCK, TX 79409
See Engineering: Water Resources; Educational Institute

WATER RESOURCES INSTITUTE
TEXAS A AND M UNIVERSITY
COLLEGE STATION, TX 77843
See Engineering: Water Resources; Educational Institute

WELDER WILDLIFE FOUNDATION
BOX 1400
SINTON, TX 78387
See Biology: Ecology; Foundation

**WILDLIFE PROTECTION COUNCIL
OF TEXAS**
3132 LOVERS LANE
DALLAS, TX 75225
See Biology: Ecology; Professional Organizations

ZOOLOGY DEPARTMENT
UNIVERSITY OF TEXAS
AUSTIN, TX 78712
See Interdisciplinary: General; Educational Institute

Utah

AGRICULTURE DEPARTMENT
ROOM 412, STATE CAPITOL
BUILDING
SALT LAKE CITY, UT 84114
See Engineering: Agricultural Engineering; Government-State or Local

BIOLOGY DEPARTMENT
UNIVERSITY OF UTAH
SALT LAKE CITY, UT 84112
See Engineering: Pollution Abatement;
Educational Institute

ECOLOGY CENTER
UTAH STATE UNIVERSITY
LOGAN, UT 84321
See Biology: Ecology; Educational Institute

**ECONOMIC RESOURCES
INSTITUTE**
UTAH STATE UNIVERSITY
LOGAN, UT 84321
See Biology: General; Research Institute

**EMPLOYMENT SECURITY
DEPARTMENT**
P O BOX 2100
SALT LAKE CITY, UT 84110
See Social Sciences/Humanities: Employment/Unemployment; Government-State or Local

ENGINEERING IN UTAH
442 CAPITOL BUILDING
SALT LAKE CITY, UT 84101
See Engineering: Water Resources; Government-State or Local

**ENVIRONMENTAL AND
BIOLOGICAL RESEARCH
INSTITUTE**
UTAH UNIVERSITY
SALT LAKE CITY, UT 84101
See Biology: General; Educational Institute

**ENVIRONMENTAL HEALTH
DIVISION, CITY HEALTH
DEPARTMENT**
610 SOUTH SECOND STREET, EAST
SALT LAKE CITY, UT 84111

See Engineering: Pollution Abatement; Government-State or Local

ENVIRONMENTAL HEALTH DIVISION, COUNTY HEALTH DEPARTMENT
2570 GRANT AVENUE
OGDEN, UT 84401
See Engineering: Pollution Abatement; Government-State or Local

ENVIRONMENTAL HEALTH SECTION, STATE HEALTH DEPARTMENT
44 MEDICAL DRIVE
SALT LAKE CITY, UT 84113
See Engineering: Pollution Abatement; Government-State or Local

ENVIRONMENTAL SCIENCE PROGRAM
BRIGHAM YOUNG UNIVERSITY
PROVO, UT 84601
See Interdisciplinary: General; Educational Institute

ENVIRONMENTAL SCIENCE PROGRAM
UNIVERSITY OF UTAH
SALT LAKE CITY, UT 84112
See Interdisciplinary: General; Educational Institute

ENVIRONMENTAL STUDIES PROGRAM
UNIVERSITY OF UTAH GRADUATE SCHOOL
SALT LAKE CITY, UT 84112
See Interdisciplinary: General; Educational Institute

ENVIRONMENTAL STUDIES PROGRAM
UTAH STATE UNIVERSITY
LOGAN, UT 84321
See Interdisciplinary: General; Educational Institute

GEOLOGICAL AND MINERALOGICAL SERVICE OF UTAH
UNIVERSITY OF UTAH
SALT LAKE CITY, UT 84112
See Engineering: Water Resources; Government-State or Local

MINES BUREAU OF UNITED STATES
1600 EAST FIRST SOUTH STREET
SALT LAKE CITY, UT 84112
See Engineering: General; Government-Federal

NATIONAL WEATHER SERVICE, WESTERN REGION
11188 FEDERAL BUILDING, 125 SOUTH STATE STREET
SALT LAKE CITY, UT 84111
See Engineering: Water Resources; Government-Federal

NATURE STUDY SOCIETY
1523 36TH STREET
OGDEN, UT 84403
See Social Sciences/Humanities: Education; Professional Organizations

NATURE STUDY SOCIETY OF AMERICA
1144 EAST 3RD STREET
SALT LAKE CITY, UT 84101
See Biology: Ecology; Field Station/Laboratory

PLANT SCIENCE DEPARTMENT
UTAH STATE UNIVERSITY
LOGAN, UT 84321
See Biology: General; Educational Institute

POLLUTION RESEARCH CENTER
UTAH STATE UNIVERSITY
LOGAN, UT 84321
See Biology: Ecology; Educational Institute

SOIL CONSERVATION SERVICES
FEDERAL BUILDING, 125 SOUTH STATE STREET, ROOM 4012
SALT LAKE CITY, UT 84111
See Biology: Ecology; Government-State or Local

UPPER COLORADO RIVER COMMISSION
355 SOUTH FOURTH E STREET
SALT LAKE CITY, UT 84111
See Engineering: Water Resources; Government-Federal

WILDLIFE AND OUTDOOR RECREATION FEDERATION OF UTAH
1102 WALKER BANK BUILDING
SALT LAKE CITY, UT 84111
See Biology: Ecology; Foundation

Virginia

AGRICULTURE DEPARTMENT
8822 FIRCREST PLACE
ALEXANDRIA, VA 22308
See Engineering: Agricultural Engineering; Government-Federal

AIR POLLUTION CONTROL
BOX 6084, PRINCESS ANN STATION
VIRGINIA BEACH, VA 23450
See Engineering: Pollution Abatement; Government-State or Local

AIR POLLUTION CONTROL BOARD
9TH STREET, STATE OFFICE BUILDING
RICHMOND, VA 23201
See Engineering: Pollution Abatement; Government-State or Local

AIR POLLUTION CONTROL BUREAU
CITY HALL
HOPEWELL, VA 23860
See Engineering: Pollution Abatement; Government-State or Local

AIR POLLUTION CONTROL DEPARTMENT
209 CHURCH AVENUE, SW
ROANOKE, VA 24011
See Engineering: Pollution Abatement; Government-State or Local

AIR POLLUTION CONTROL, COVINGTON-ALLEGHENY COUNTY
COVINGTON, VA 24426
See Engineering: Pollution Abatement; Government-State or Local

AIR POLLUTION, PUBLIC SAFETY DEPARTMENT
501 NORTH NINTH STREET
RICHMOND, VA 23219
See Engineering: Pollution Abatement; Government-State or Local

ALEXANDRIA HEALTH DEPARTMENT
517 ST ASAPH STREET
ALEXANDRIA, VA 22314
See Engineering: Pollution Abatement; Government-State or Local

BUILDING INSPECTION BUREAU
HAMPTON, VA 23369
See Engineering: Pollution Abatement; Government-State or Local

CLEARING HOUSE FOR FEDERAL SCIENCES-TECHNOLOGY INFORMATION
5285 PORT ROYAL ROAD
SPRINGFIELD, VA 22151
See Interdisciplinary: General; Unclassified

CONSERVATION AND RURAL DEVELOPMENT
1417 MONTAGUE DRIVE
VIENNA, VA 22180
See Biology: Ecology; Government-Federal

CONSERVATION AND RURAL DEVELOPMENT
3833 ROBERTS LANE NORTH
ARLINGTON, VA 22207
See Biology: Ecology; Government-Federal

CONSERVATION COUNCIL OF NORTHERN VIRGINIA
POST OFFICE BOX 304
ANNANDALE, VA 22003
See Biology: Ecology; Professional Organizations

DEFENSE DEPARTMENT
6304 STONEHAM LANE
MCLEAN, VA 22101
See Interdisciplinary: General; Unclassified

DEFENSE DOCUMENTATION CENTER, DEFENSE SUPPLY AGENCY
DEPARTMENT DEFENSE, CAMERON STATION
ALEXANDRIA, VA 22314
See Interdisciplinary: General; Unclassified

ECOLOGY AND ENVIRONMENTAL CONSERVATION OFFICE
6822 SORRELL DRIVE
MCLEAN, VA 22101
See Biology: Ecology; Government-Federal

ECOLOGY STUDIES PROGRAM
1616 HUNTER MILL ROAD
VIENNA, VA 22180
See Biology: Ecology; Government-Federal

ENVIRONMENTAL EDUCATION, NATIONAL PARK SERVICES SOUTHEAST OFFICE
POST OFFICE BOX 10008
RICHMOND, VA 23240
See Biology: Ecology; Government-State or Local

ENVIRONMENTAL HEALTH BUREAU
401 COLLEY AVENUE
NORFOLK, VA 23507
See Engineering: Pollution Abatement; Government-State or Local

ENVIRONMENTAL HEALTH DIVISION, COUNTY HEALTH DEPARTMENT
4080 CHAIN BRIDGE ROAD
FAIRFAX, VA 22030
See Engineering: Pollution Abatement; Government-State or Local

ENVIRONMENTAL RESOURCES DEVELOPMENT LABORATORY
UNITED STATES DEPARTMENT OF ARMY
FORT BELVOIR, VA 22060
See Engineering: General; Government-Federal

ENVIRONMENTAL SCIENCE PROGRAM
UNIVERSITY OF RICHMOND
RICHMOND, VA 23173
See Interdisciplinary: General; Educational Institute

ENVIRONMENTAL SCIENCE PROGRAM
UNIVERSITY OF VIRGINIA
CHARLOTTESVILLE, VA 22903
See Interdisciplinary: General; Educational Institute

ENVIRONMENTAL STUDIES
HOLLINS COLLEGE
HOLLINS COLLEGE, VA 24020
See Biology: General; Educational Institute

ENVIRONMENTAL STUDIES CENTER
VIRGINIA POLYTECHNIC INSTITUTE/STATE UNIVERSITY
BLACKSBURG, VA 24061
See Interdisciplinary: General; Research Institute

ENVIRONMENTAL STUDIES PROGRAM
COLLEGE OF WILLIAM AND MARY
WILLIAMSBURG, VA 23185
See Chemistry: General; Educational Institute

ENVIRONMENTAL STUDIES PROGRAM
OLD DOMINION UNIVERSITY
NORFOLK, VA 23508
See Engineering: General; Educational Institute

FEDERAL WATER POLLUTION CONTROL ADMINISTRATION
1921 JEFFERSON DAVIS HIGHWAY
ARLINGTON, VA 22212
See Interdisciplinary: General; Unclassified

FORESTRY AND SOIL CONSERVATION DIVISION
5708 18TH ROAD NORTH
ARLINGTON, VA 22205
See Biology: Ecology; Government-Federal

FORESTRY ASSOCIATION EXECUTIVES NATIONAL COUNCIL
301 EAST FRANKLIN STREET
RICHMOND, VA 23219
See Interdisciplinary: General; Professional Organizations

GOVERNOR'S OFFICE
STATE CAPITOL
RICHMOND, VA 23219
See Engineering: Pollution Abatement; Government-State or Local

HEALTH, EDUCATION, AND WELFARE DEPARTMENT
1100 CREST LANE
MCLEAN, VA 22010
See Interdisciplinary: General; Unclassified

HUMAN RESOURCES RESEARCH ORGANIZATION
300 NORTH WASHINGTON STREET
ALEXANDRIA, VA 22314
See Social Sciences/Humanities: Employment/Unemployment; Research Institute

INSPECTION DIVISION, PUBLIC WORKS DEPARTMENT
427 PATTON STREET, BOX 1159
DANVILLE, VA 24541
See Engineering: Pollution Abatement; Government-State or Local

ISAAC WALTON LEAGUE OF AMERICA
1800 NORTH KENT STREET, SUITE 806
ARLINGTON, VA 22209
See Biology: Ecology; Foundation

MARINE ENVIRONMENTAL PROTECTION DIVISION
11567 LINKS DRIVE
RESTON, VA 22070
See Engineering: Pollution Abatement; Government-Federal

MARINE SCIENCES INSTITUTE OF VIRGINIA
WACHAPREAGUE, VA 23480
See Biology: General; Research Institute

MARINE SCIENCES INSTITUTE OF VIRGINIA
SCHOOL OF MARINE SCIENCES, WILLIAM AND MARY COLLEGE
GLOUCESTER POINT, VA 23062
See Biology: Ecology; Government-State or Local

MINERAL RESOURCES DIVISION, VIRGINIA DEPARTMENT OF CONSERVATION
POST OFFICE BOX 3667
UNIVERSITY STATION
CHARLOTTESVILLE, VA 22903
See Geology: General; Government-State or Local

NATIONAL AIR POLLUTION CONTROL
801 NORTH RANDOLPH STREET
ARLINGTON, VA 22203
See Engineering: Pollution Abatement; Government-Federal

NATIONAL WATER COMMISSION
800 NORTH QUINCY STREET
ARLINGTON, VA 22203
See Interdisciplinary: General; Unclassified

ORNITHOLOGY SOCIETY OF VIRGINIA
6207 NEWMAN ROAD
FAIRFAX, VA 22030
See Interdisciplinary: General; Professional Organizations

OUTDOOR RECREATION BUREAU
111 PRINCESS STREET
ALEXANDRIA, VA 22314
See Social Sciences/Humanities: Recreation and Leisure; Government-Federal

PESTICIDE REGULATION DIVISION
POST OFFICE BOX 8348
RICHMOND, VA 23226
See Engineering: Agricultural Engineering; Government-Federal

**PESTICIDE REGULATION,
DEPARTMENT OF AGRICULTURE**
203 NORTH GOVERNOR STREET,
ROOM 304
RICHMOND, VA 23219
See Engineering: Agricultural Engineering; Government-State or Local

**POPULATION AND ECONOMIC
RESOURCES**
UNIVERSITY OF VIRGINIA
CHARLOTTESVILLE, VA 22903
See Social Sciences/Humanities: Population Studies/Family Planning; Research Institute

PUBLIC WORKS DEPARTMENT
CITY HALL, 118 MAIN STREET
NEWPORT NEWS, VA 23601
See Engineering: Pollution Abatement;
Government-State or Local

**RADIATION BIOLOGY DIVISION,
DEPARTMENT OF RADIATION**
MEDICAL COLLEGE OF VIRGINIA
RICHMOND, VA 23219
See Biology: General; Government-State
or Local

RESEARCH MANAGEMENT
4633 DENPAT CENTER
ANNANDALE, VA 22003
See Biology: Ecology; Government-Federal

**RURAL DEVELOPMENT AND
CONSERVATION, DEPARTMENT
OF AGRICULTURE**
3833 ROBERTS LANE NORTH
ARLINGTON, VA 22207
See Engineering: General; Government-Federal

**SANITARY ENGINEERING BUREAU,
DIVISION OF ENGINEERING,
HEALTH DEPARTMENT**
1314 EAST GRACE STREET
RICHMOND, VA 32319
See Engineering: Water Resources; Government-State or Local

**SCIENCE-TECHNOLOGY
INFORMATION,
CLEARINGHOUSE**
NATIONAL BUREAU OF
STANDARDS
SPRINGFIELD, VA 22151
See Engineering: General; Government-Federal

**SOIL AND WATER CONSERVATION
COMMISSION OF VIRGINIA**
10 SOUTH 10TH STREET
RICHMOND, VA 23216
See Engineering: Water Resources; Government-State or Local

SOIL CONSERVATION SERVICE
7504 VENICE COURT
FALLS CHURCH, VA 22043
See Engineering: Agricultural Engineering; Government-State or Local

SOIL CONSERVATION SERVICES
FEDERAL BUILDING, 400 NORTH
EIGHTH STREET, ROOM 7408
RICHMOND, VA 23240
See Biology: Ecology; Government-State
or Local

**SOIL CONSERVATION SERVICES,
ENGINEERING DIVISION**
6312 24TH STREET, N
ARLINGTON, VA 22207
See Engineering: General; Government-Federal

**SOIL CONSERVATION SERVICES,
RIVER BASIN DIVISION**
5233 POMMEROY DRIVE
FAIRFAX, VA 22030
See Engineering: Water Resources; Government-Federal

**SOIL CONSERVATION SERVICES,
WATERSHED PLANNING
DIVISION**
1318 JULIANA PLACE
ALEXANDRIA, VA 22304
See Engineering: Water Resources; Government-Federal

**SOIL SURVEY OPERATIONS
DIVISION**
1624 WOODMAN DRIVE
MCLEAN, VA 22101
See Engineering: Agricultural Engineering; Government-Federal

**SPORT FISHERIES AND WILDLIFE
BUREAU**
8207 DUSINANE CENTER
MCLEAN, VA 22101
See Interdisciplinary: General; Unclassified

**STANDARDS AND COMPLIANCE
OFFICE**
PUBLIC HEALTH SERVICE
ARLINGTON, VA 22203
See Engineering: Pollution Abatement;
Government-Federal

UNITED STATES NAVY
3406 FIDDLERS GREEN
FALLS CHURCH, VA 22044
See Interdisciplinary: General; Government-State or Local

UNITED WAY OF AMERICA
801 NORTH FAIRFAX STREET
ALEXANDRIA, VA 22314
See Social Sciences/Humanities: General;
Foundation

WATER CONTROL BOARD
4010 WEST BROAD STREET
RICHMOND, VA 23230

See Engineering: Pollution Abatement;
Government-State or Local

WATER DEPARTMENT
SIXTH AND TAYLOR STREETS
LYNCHBURG, VA 24501
See Engineering: Pollution Abatement;
Government-State or Local

WATER RESOURCES COUNCIL
10212 VALE ROAD
VIENNA, VA 22180
See Engineering: Water Resources; Government-Federal

**WATERSHED ADMINISTRATION,
SOIL CONSERVATION SERVICE**
218 NORTH COLUMBUS STREET
ARLINGTON, VA 22203
See Engineering: Water Resources; Government-Federal

**WATERSHED PLANNING, SOIL
CONSERVATION SERVICES**
9005 STRATFORD LANE
ALEXANDRIA, VA 22308
See Engineering: Water Resources; Government-Federal

**WILDLIFE FEDERATION OF
VIRGINIA**
5608 WAYCROSS DRIVE
ALEXANDRIA, VA 22310
See Biology: Ecology; Foundation

Vermont

**ANTI-POLLUTION LEAGUE OF
CONNECTICUT VALLEY**
134 MAIN STREET
BRATTLEBORO, VT 05301
See Engineering: Pollution Abatement;
Government-State or Local

**AQUATIC INCORPORATED
CONSULTANTS**
1025 AIRPORT DRIVE
SOUTH BURLINGTON, VT 05401
See Biology: Ecology; Professional Organizations

**AUDUBON SOCIETY OF GREEN
MOUNTAIN**
POST OFFICE BOX 33
BURLINGTON, VT 05401
See Biology: Ecology; Foundation

**CONSERVATION ASSOCIATION OF
VERMONT**
CHESTER DEPOT, VT 05144
See Biology: Ecology; Government-State
or Local

**CONSERVATION SOCIETY OF
SOUTHERN VERMONT**
BOX 256
TOWNSHEND, VT 05353
See Biology: Ecology; Government-State
or Local

ECOLOGY ACTION
BOX ONE
WOODSTOCK, VT 05091
See Biology: Ecology; Government-State
or Local

**ENVIRONMENTAL ACTION
COMMITTEE**
BOX 99, BILLINGS CENTER
BURLINGTON, VT 05401
See Biology: Ecology; Government-State
or Local

**ENVIRONMENTAL AWARENESS
COMMITTEE**
GREEN MOUNTAIN COLLEGE
POULTNEY, VT 05741
See Biology: Ecology; Government-State
or Local

**ENVIRONMENTAL CENTER OF
VERMONT**
WOODSTOCK, VT 05091
See Interdisciplinary: General; Educational Institute

ENVIRONMENTAL CLUB
SOUTH BURLINGTON HIGH
SCHOOL
SOUTH BURLINGTON, VT 05401
See Biology: Ecology; Government-State
or Local

**ENVIRONMENTAL PROGRAMS
COMMISSION**
UNIVERSITY OF VERMONT
BURLINGTON, VT 05401
See Biology: Ecology; Educational Institute

ENVIRONMENTAL QUALITY
11 PIERSON DRIVE
SHELBURNE, VT 05482
See Biology: Ecology; Government-State
or Local

**ENVIRONMENTAL STUDIES
PROGRAM**
MIDDLEBURY COLLEGE
MIDDLEBURY, VT 05753
See Biology: Ecology; Educational Institute

**GEOLOGICAL SURVEY OF
VERMONT**
UNIVERSITY OF VERMONT
BURLINGTON, VT 05401
See Geology: General; Educational Institute

**INDUSTRIAL HYGIENE DIVISION,
VERMONT HEALTH
DEPARTMENT**
32 SPAULDING BUILDING, BOX 607
BARRE, VT 05641
See Engineering: Pollution Abatement;
Government-State or Local

**MERCK FOREST FOUNDATION,
INCORPORATED**

POST OFFICE BOX 485
MANCHESTER, VT 05254
See Biology: Ecology; Professional Organizations

**NATURAL RESOURCE COUNCIL OF
VERMONT**
26 STATE STREET
MONTPELIER, VT 05602
See Biology: Ecology; Educational Institute

**NATURAL RESOURCES
CONSERVATION ASSOCIATION
OF VERMONT**
CHESTER DEPOT, VT 05144
See Biology: Ecology; Professional Organizations

NATURE CONSERVANCY
JERICHO, VT 05465
See Biology: Ecology; Foundation

**OPTIMUM POPULATION,
INCORPORATED**
CHARLOTTE, VT 05445
See Social Sciences/Humanities: Population Studies/Family Planning; Foundation

**PLANT PESTICIDE CONTROL
DIVISION, DEPARTMENT OF
AGRICULTURE**
STATE OFFICE BUILDING, 116
STREET
MONTPELIER, VT 05602
See Engineering: Agricultural Engineering; Government-State or Local

RESOURCE CENTER OF VERMONT
UNIVERSITY OF VERMONT
BURLINGTON, VT 05410
See Interdisciplinary: General; Educational Institute

**SOIL CONSERVATION COUNCIL OF
VERMONT**
UNIVERSITY OF VERMONT
BURLINGTON, VT 05401
See Interdisciplinary: General; Educational Institute

SOIL CONSERVATION SERVICES
96 COLLEGE STREET
BURLINGTON, VT 05401
See Biology: Ecology; Government-Federal

SPORTSMENS CLUBS FEDERATION
RFO-WESTBORO
WESTBORO, VT 05494
See Social Sciences/Humanities: Recreation and Leisure; Professional Organizations

**STUDENTS CONCERNED FOR THE
ENVIRONMENT**

MIDDLEBURY UNION HIGH
SCHOOL
MIDDLEBURY, VT 05753
See Biology: Ecology; Educational Institute

**WATER RESOURCES DEPARTMENT
OF VERMONT**
STATE OFFICE BUILDING
MONTPELIER, VT 05602
See Engineering: Water Resources; Government-State or Local

ZERO POPULATION GROWTH
BOX 0913
MIDDLEBURY, VT 05753
See Social Sciences/Humanities: Population Studies/Family Planning; Foundation

ZERO POPULATION GROWTH
303 PEARL STREET
BURLINGTON, VT 05401
See Social Sciences/Humanities: Population Studies/Family Planning; Foundation

Washington

**AIR POLLUTION CONTROL
AUTHORITY**
1200 FRANKLIN STREET
VANCOUVER, WA 98660
See Engineering: Pollution Abatement;
Government-State or Local

**AIR POLLUTION CONTROL
AUTHORITY**
207 PIONEER BUILDING
MT VERNON, WA 98273
See Engineering: Pollution Abatement;
Government-State or Local

**AIR POLLUTION CONTROL
BRANCH, ENVIRONMENTAL
PROTECTION AGENCY**
1200 6TH AVENUE
SEATTLE, WA 98101
See Engineering: Pollution Abatement;
Government-Federal

**AIR POLLUTION CONTROL, CITY
HEALTH DEPARTMENT**
817 NORTH JEFFERSON
SPOKANE, WA 99201
See Engineering: Pollution Abatement;
Government-State or Local

**AIR POLLUTION CONTROL,
HEALTH DEPARTMENT**
1510 SMITH TOWER
SEATTLE, WA 98104
See Engineering: Pollution Abatement;
Government-State or Local

AIR RESOURCE PROGRAM
CIVIL ENGINEERING
   DEPARTMENT, 301 MORE HALL
SEATTLE, WA 98105
See Engineering: Pollution Abatement;
Educational Institute

**APPLIED PHYSICS LABORATORY,
   UNIVERSITY OF WASHINGTON**
1013 NE 40TH STREET
SEATTLE, WA 98105
See Physics: General; Educational Institute

**ATOMIC ENERGY COMMISSION,
   RICHLAND OPERATIONS**
POST OFFICE BOX 550
RICHLAND, WA 99352
See Geology: General; Government-Federal

BIOLOGICAL LABORATORY
2725 MONTLAKE BOULEVARD,
   EAST
SEATTLE, WA 98102
See Biology: Ecology; Government-Federal

**BIOLOGICAL STATION, WALLA
   WALLA COLLEGE**
RT 3 BOX 555 ROSARIO BEACH
ANACORTES, WA 98221
See Biology: General; Educational Institute

**BIOLOGICAL STRUCTURE
   DEPARTMENT, SCHOOL OF
   MEDICINE**
UNIVERSITY OF WASHINGTON
SEATTLE, WA 98105
See Biology: General; Educational Institute

**BIRD BANDING ASSOCIATION
   (WESTERN)**
3041 ELDRIDGE
BELLINGHAM, WA 98225
See Interdisciplinary: General; Professional Organizations

**BOTANICAL GARDENS, AMERICAN
   ASSOCIATION**
UNIVERSITY OF WASHINGTON
   ARBORETUM
SEATTLE, WA 98105
See Biology: General; Professional Organizations

CHEMISTRY DEPARTMENT
WASHINGTON STATE UNIVERSITY
PULLMAN, WA 99163
See Chemistry: General; Educational Institute

**CONSERVATION COUNCIL OF
   NORTH CASCADES**
POST OFFICE BOX 156, UNIVERSITY
   STATION
SEATTLE, WA 98501

See Biology: Ecology; Professional Organizations

ECOLOGY DEPARTMENT
WASHINGTON STATE
OLYMPIA, WA 98504
See Biology: Ecology; Government-State or Local

**ENGINEERING DEPARTMENT OF
   SEATTLE**
910 MUNICIPAL BUILDING
SEATTLE, WA 98104
See Engineering: Water Resources; Government-State or Local

**ENVIRONMENTAL AND
   RADIOLOGICAL SCIENCES**
BATTELLE NORTHWEST POST
   OFFICE 999
RICHLAND, WA 99352
See Engineering: General; Educational Institute

**ENVIRONMENTAL CONSERVATION
   DIVISION, NORTHWEST
   FISHERIES CENTER**
2725 MONTLAKE BOULEVARD EAST
SEATTLE, WA 98112
See Chemistry: General; Government-Federal

**ENVIRONMENTAL EDUCATION,
   NATIONAL PARK SERVICES
   NORTHWEST OFFICE**
4TH AND PIKE BUILDING
SEATTLE, WA 98101
See Biology: Ecology; Government-State or Local

**ENVIRONMENTAL HEALTH
   DEPARTMENT, UNIVERSITY OF
   WASHINGTON**
F356 HEALTH SCIENCES
   BUILDING, ROAD-94
SEATTLE, WA 98195
See Interdisciplinary: General; Educational Institute

**ENVIRONMENTAL PROTECTION
   AGENCY LABORATORY**
GIG HARBOR, WA 98335
See Biology: Ecology; Field Station/Laboratory

**ENVIRONMENTAL PROTECTION
   AGENCY REGION 10**
1200 SIXTH AVENUE
SEATTLE, WA 98101
See Interdisciplinary: General; Unclassified

**ENVIRONMENTAL PROTECTION
   AGENCY, REGION LABORATORY**
15345 NE 36TH STREET
REDMOND, WA 98052
See Chemistry: General; Government-Federal

**ENVIRONMENTAL RESEARCH
   CENTER**

WASHINGTON STATE UNIVERSITY
PULLMAN, WA 99163
See Interdisciplinary: General; Educational Institute

**ENVIRONMENTAL SCIENCE
   PROGRAM**
SEATTLE UNIVERSITY
SEATTLE, WA 98122
See Interdisciplinary: General; Educational Institute

**ENVIRONMENTAL SCIENCE
   PROGRAM**
UNIVERSITY OF WASHINGTON
SEATTLE, WA 98105
See Interdisciplinary: General; Educational Institute

**ENVIRONMENTAL SERVICES,
   CROWN ZELLERBACH**
904 NORTHWEST DRAKE STREET
CAMAS, WA 98607
See Engineering: Pollution Abatement;
Industrial/Commercial

**ENVIRONMENTAL STUDIES
   COLLEGE**
HUXLEY COLLEGE
BELLINGHAM, WA 98225
See Interdisciplinary: General; Educational Institute

**ENVIRONMENTAL STUDIES
   PROGRAM**
EVERGREEN STATE COLLEGE
OLYMPIA, WA 98501
See Interdisciplinary: General; Educational Institute

**ENVIRONMENTAL STUDIES
   PROGRAM**
PACIFIC LUTHERAN UNIVERSITY
TACOMA, WA 98447
See Chemistry: General; Educational Institute

**ENVIRONMENTAL STUDIES
   PROGRAM**
UNIVERSITY OF PUGET SOUND
TACOMA, WA 98416
See Interdisciplinary: General; Educational Institute

**ENVIRONMENTAL STUDIES
   PROGRAM**
WASHINGTON STATE UNIVERSITY
PULLMAN, WA 99163
See Interdisciplinary: General; Educational Institute

**ENVIRONMENTAL STUDIES,
   HUXLEY COLLEGE**
WESTERN WASHINGTON STATE
   COLLEGE
BELLINGTON, WA 98225
See Interdisciplinary: General; Educational Institute

EXPLORATORY FISHING AND GEAR RESOURCES BASE
2725 MONTLAKE BOULEVARD, EAST
SEATTLE, WA 98102
See Engineering: Water Resources; Government-Federal

FISHERIES CENTER, LABORATORY OF RADIATION BIOLOGY
UNIVERSITY OF WASHINGTON
SEATTLE, WA 98105
See Biology: General; Educational Institute

FISHERIES DISEASE LABORATORY
SAND POINT NAVAL AIR STATION
SEATTLE, WA 98115
See Biology: General; Government-Federal

FISHERIES NUTRITION LABORATORY
STAR ROUTE
COOK, WA 98615
See Biology: General; Government-Federal

FLOOD CONTROL DIVISION, DEPARTMENT OF ECOLOGY
335 GENERAL ADMINISTRATION BUILDING
OLYMPIA, WA 98501
See Engineering: Water Resources; Government-State or Local

FOOD SCIENCE LABORATORY
2725 MONTLAKE BOULEVARD, EAST
SEATTLE, WA 98102
See Biology: Biochemistry; Government-Federal

GENETICS DEPARTMENT, SCHOOL OF MEDICINE
UNIVERSITY OF WASHINGTON
SEATTLE, WA 98105
See Biology: General; Educational Institute

GOOD OUTDOOR MANNERS ASSOCIATION
POST OFFICE BOX 7095
SEATTLE, WA 98133
See Social Sciences/Humanities: Recreation and Leisure; Educational Institute

GRAIN AND CHEMICAL DIVISION, U S DEPARTMENT OF AGRICULTURE
BOX 128
OLYMPIA, WA 98501
See Engineering: Agricultural Engineering; Government-State or Local

HEALTH DEPARTMENT OF WASHINGTON

PUBLIC HEALTH BUILDING
OLYMPIA, WA 98501
See Engineering: Water Resources; Government-State or Local

HEALTH, EDUCATION AND WELFARE REGION 10 OFFICE
1321 SECOND AVENUE
SEATTLE, WA 98101
See Interdisciplinary: General; Government-Federal

INDUSTRIAL HYGIENE SECTION, STATE OF WASHINGTON
DEPARTMENT OF LABOR AND INDUSTRY
OLYMPIA, WA 98501
See Biology: Biochemistry; Industrial/Commercial

INDUSTRIAL RESEARCH DIVISION
WASHINGTON STATE UNIVERSITY
PULLMAN, WA 94662
See Engineering: Pollution Abatement; Educational Institute

LABOR AND INDUSTRY DEPARTMENT
GENERAL ADMINISTRATION BUILDING
OLYMPIA, WA 98502
See Social Sciences/Humanities: Labor/Relations/Unions; Government-State or Local

LABORATORIES OF FRIDAY HARBOR
UNIVERSITY OF WASHINGTON
FRIDAY HARBOR, WA 98250
See Biology: General; Educational Institute

MARINE FISHERIES SERVICE, NORTHWEST FISHERIES CENTER
2725 MONTLAKE BOULEVARD, EAST
SEATTLE, WA 98112
See Biology: General; Government-Federal

MARINE MAMMAL DIVISION
NAVAL SUPPORT ACTIVITY 192
SEATTLE, WA 98115
See Biology: Ecology; Government-Federal

MARINE SCIENCES DIVISION, 13TH COAST GUARD DISTRICT
618 2ND AVENUE
SEATTLE, WA 98104
See Engineering: Water Resources; Government-State or Local

MEDICAL SCHOOL
UNIVERSITY OF WASHINGTON
SEATTLE, WA 98105
See Engineering: Pollution Abatement; Educational Institute

MOUNTAINEERS
719 DIKE STREET

SEATTLE, WA 98101
See Biology: Ecology; Foundation

NORTH-WEST WATER SUPPLY RESEARCH LABORATORY
6702 TYEE DRIVE
GIG HARBOR, WA 98335
See Interdisciplinary: General; Unclassified

NUCLEAR ENGINEERING DEPARTMENT, UNIVERSITY OF WASHINGTON
303 BENSON HALL
SEATTLE, WA 98105
See Engineering: General; Educational Institute

OCCUPATIONAL SAFETY AND HEALTH, HEALTH, EDUCATION AND WELFARE
1321 SECOND AVENUE
SEATTLE, WA 98101
See Engineering: Pollution Abatement; Government-State or Local

OCEANOGRAPHY DEPARTMENT
UNIVERSITY OF WASHINGTON
SEATTLE, WA 98105
See Interdisciplinary: General; Educational Institute

PACIFIC FISHERIES PRODUCTS TECHNOLOGY CENTER
2725 MONTLAKE BOULEVARD EAST
SEATTLE, WA 98112
See Chemistry: General; Government-Federal

PACIFIC NORTHWEST LABORATORY
P O BOX 999
RICHLAND, WA 99352
See Interdisciplinary: General; Field Station/Laboratory

POPULATION RESEARCH AND CENSUS BUILDING
UNIVERSITY OF WASHINGTON
SEATTLE, WA 98105
See Social Sciences/Humanities: Population Studies/Family Planning; Educational Institute

PULP AND PAPER ASSOCIATION
2633 EASTLAKE AVENUE EAST
SEATTLE, WA 98102
See Engineering: Pollution Abatement; Industrial/Commercial

RADIATION DIVISION, ENVIRONMENTAL PROTECTION AGENCY
1200 6TH AVENUE
SEATTLE, WA 98101
See Chemistry: Physical Chemistry; Government-State or Local

RADIATION ECOLOGY LABORATORY, FISHERIES CENTER

UNIVERSITY OF WASHINGTON
SEATTLE, WA 98195
See Biology: Ecology; Educational Institute

SHELLFISH SANITATION NORTHWEST LABORATORY
ROUTE 4, BOX 4519
GIG HARBOR, WA 98335
See Engineering: Agricultural Engineering; Government-Federal

SOIL CONSERVATION SERVICES
W 920 RIVERSIDE AVENUE
SPOKANE, WA 99201
See Biology: Ecology; Government-Federal

SPORTSMENS COUNCIL OF WASHINGTON
BOX 569
VANCOUVER, WA 98660
See Biology: Ecology; Foundation

STUDENT CONSERVATION ASSOCIATION
OLYMPIC VIEW DRIVE, ROUTE 1, BOX 573A
VASHON, WA 98070
See Biology: Ecology; Professional Organizations

TECHNOLOGICAL LABORATORY
2725 MONTLAKE BOULEVARD, EAST
SEATTLE, WA 98102
See Engineering: Water Resources; Government-Federal

WATER POLLUTION CONTROL COMMISSION
BOX 829
OLYMPIA, WA 98501
See Engineering: Pollution Abatement; Government-State or Local

WATER RESOURCES CENTER OF WASHINGTON
WASHINGTON STATE UNIVERSITY
PULLMAN, WA 99163
See Biology: General; Research Institute

ZOOLOGY AND BIOLOGY, HISTORY OF SCIENCES, ADMINISTRATION
EVERGREEN STATE COLLEGE
OLYMPIA, WA 98501
See Biology: General; Educational Institute

Wisconsin

AGRICULTURE COLLEGE
UNIVERSITY OF WISCONSIN
MADISON, WI 53706
See Engineering: Agricultural Engineering; Educational Institute

AGRONOMY SOCIETY OF AMERICA
677 SOUTH SEGOE ROAD
MADISON, WI 53711
See Engineering: Agricultural Engineering; Professional Organizations

AIR POLLUTION AND HEATING INSPECTION DEPARTMENT
CITY HALL
GREEN BAY, WI 54301
See Engineering: Pollution Abatement; Government-State or Local

AIR POLLUTION CONTROL DEPARTMENT
9722 WEST WATERTOW PLANK
WAUWATOSA, WI 53226
See Engineering: Pollution Abatement; Government-State or Local

AIR POLLUTION CONTROL, HEALTH DEPARTMENT
CITY HALL
OSKOSH, WI 54901
See Engineering: Pollution Abatement; Government-State or Local

AUDUBON NORTH CENTRAL COUNCIL
536 LAPLANT STREET
GREEN BAY, WI 54302
See Biology: Ecology; Foundation

BIOCHEMISTRY DEPARTMENT, AGRICULTURE AND LIFE SCIENCES COLLEGE
UNIVERSITY OF WISCONSIN
MADISON, WI 53706
See Biology: Biochemistry; Educational Institute

BIOLOGY DEPARTMENT
DOMINICAN COLLEGE
RACINE, WI 53402
See Biology: General; Educational Institute

BIRD BANDING ASSOCIATION (INLAND)
BOX 152
BAILEYS HARBOR, WI 54202
See Interdisciplinary: General; Professional Organizations

CASPER-NATRONA COUNTY HEALTH DEPARTMENT
265 SOUTH WASHINGTON
CASPER, WY 82601
See Engineering: Pollution Abatement; Government-State or Local

CONSERVATION EDUCATION ASSOCIATION
BOX 450
MADISON, WI 53701
See Social Sciences/Humanities: Education; Foundation

DEPARTMENT OF RADIOLOGY
UNIVERSITY OF WISCONSIN
MADISON, WI 53706

See Interdisciplinary: General; Educational Institute

EMPLOYERS MUTUAL OF WAUSAU
407 GRANT STREET
WAUSAU, WI 54402
See Social Sciences/Humanities: General; Government-State or Local

ENVIRONMENTAL HEALTH DIVISION, CITY HEALTH DEPARTMENT
6TH STREET, CITY HALL
LA CROSSE, WI 54601
See Biology: Ecology; Government-State or Local

ENVIRONMENTAL SCIENCE PROGRAM
LAWRENCE UNIVERSITY
APPLETON, WI 54911
See Chemistry: General; Educational Institute

ENVIRONMENTAL SCIENCE PROGRAM
UNIVERSITY OF WISCONSIN
MADISON, WI 53706
See Interdisciplinary: General; Educational Institute

ENVIRONMENTAL SCIENCE PROGRAM
WISCONSIN STATE UNIVERSITY - STEVENS POINT
STEVENS POINT, WI 54481
See Chemistry: General; Educational Institute

ENVIRONMENTAL SCIENCES COLLEGE
UNIVERSITY OF WISCONSIN
GREEN BAY, WI 54301
See Biology: General; Educational Institute

ENVIRONMENTAL STUDIES INSTITUTE, UNIVERSITY OF WISCONSIN
1225 W DAYTON STREET
MADISON, WI 53706
See Interdisciplinary: General; Educational Institute

ENVIRONMENTAL STUDIES PROGRAM
BELOIT COLLEGE
BELOIT, WI 53511
See Chemistry: General; Educational Institute

ENVIRONMENTAL STUDIES PROGRAM
UNIVERSITY OF WISCONSIN
SUPERIOR, WI 54880
See Interdisciplinary: General; Educational Institute

**ENVIRONMENTAL STUDIES
PROGRAM**
WISCONSIN STATE UNIVERSITY-
EAU CLAIRE
EAU CLAIRE, WI 54701
See Chemistry: General; Educational Institute

**ENVIRONMENTAL STUDIES
PROGRAM, UNIVERSITY OF
WISCONSIN**
3203 NORTH DOWNER AVENUE
MILWAUKEE, WI 53211
See Social Sciences/Humanities: General;
Educational Institute

**ENVIRONMENTAL STUDIES,
MARQUETTE UNIVERSITY**
1131 WEST WISCONSIN AVENUE
MILWAUKEE, WI 53233
See Interdisciplinary: General; Educational Institute

**FOOD SCIENCES DEPARTMENT,
UNIVERSITY OF WISCONSIN**
BABCOCK HALL
MADISON, WI 53706
See Social Sciences/Humanities: Community Development/Studies; Educational Institute

**FOREST SERVICE REGION 9
OFFICE**
633 WEST WISCONSIN AVENUE
MILWAUKE, WI 53203
See Engineering: Agricultural Engineering; Government-Federal

**GEOLOGICAL AND NATURAL
HISTORY SURVEY**
SCIENCE HALL, UNIVERSITY OF
WISCONSIN
MADISON, WI 53706
See Physics: General; Government-State or Local

**GOVERNMENT AFFAIRS
INSTITUTE, UNIVERSITY OF
WISCONSIN EXTENSION**
610 LANGDON STREET
MADISON, WI 53706
See Social Sciences/Humanities: Urban Problems; Educational Institute

GREAT LAKES STUDIES CENTER
UNIVERSITY OF WISCONSIN-
MILWAUKEE
MILWAUKEE, WI 53201
See Biology: Ecology; Educational Institute

HEALTH DEPARTMENT
CITY HALL, 225 NORTH ONEIDA
APPLETON, WI 54911
See Engineering: Pollution Abatement; Government-State or Local

HEALTH DEPARTMENT
CITY OFFICE BUILDING
BELOIT, WI 53511

See Engineering: Pollution Abatement; Government-State or Local

HEALTH DEPARTMENT
SAFETY BUILDING
EAU CLAIRE, WI 54701
See Engineering: Pollution Abatement; Government-State or Local

HEALTH DEPARTMENT
18 NORTH JACKSON STREET
JANESVILLE, WI 53545
See Engineering: Pollution Abatement; Government-State or Local

HEALTH DEPARTMENT
407 GRANT STREET
WAUSAU, WI 54401
See Engineering: Pollution Abatement; Government-State or Local

**HEALTH DEPARTMENT
LABORATORY**
CITY HALL, 1323 BROADWAY
SUPERIOR, WI 54880
See Engineering: Pollution Abatement; Government-State or Local

**HYDRAULICS AND SANITATION
LABORATORY**
UNIVERSITY OF WISCONSIN
MADISON, WI 53706
See Interdisciplinary: General; Educational Institute

**LAND MANAGEMENT
CURRICULUM**
UNIVERSITY OF WISCONSIN
RIVER FALLS, WI 54022
See Social Sciences/Humanities: Recreation and Leisure; Educational Institute

**LEGISLATIVE REFERENCE
BUREAU**
STATE CAPITOL
MADISON,WI 53702
See Social Sciences/Humanities: Law/Legislation; Government-State or Local

LIMNOLOGY LABORATORY
UNIVERSITY OF WISCONSIN
MADISON, WI 53706
See Interdisciplinary: General; Field Station/Laboratory

MAN IN HIS ENVIRONMENT
DOMINICAN COLLEGE
RACINE, WI 53401
See Interdisciplinary: General; Educational Institute

**NATURAL RESOURCES
ASSOCIATION OF WISCONSIN**
RT 1, BOX 390
STEVENS POINT, WI 54481
See Interdisciplinary: General; Professional Organizations

**NATURAL RESOURCES
DEPARTMENT OF WISCONSIN**
POST OFFICE BOX 450
MADISON, WI 53701
See Engineering: Water Resources; Government-State or Local

NATURAL RESOURCES SCHOOL
COLLEGE OF AGRICULTURE AND
LIFE SCIENCES
MADISON, WI 53700
See Biology: Ecology; Educational Institute

**ORNITHOLOGICAL SOCIETY OF
WISCONSIN**
288 EAST SOMO AVENUE
TOMAHAWK, WI 54487
See Interdisciplinary: General; Professional Organizations

**OUTDOOR WRITERS ASSOCIATION
OF AMERICA, INCORPORATED**
4141 WEST BRADLEY ROAD
MILWAUKEE, WI 53209
See Social Sciences/Humanities: General;
Professional Organizations

PAPER CHEMISTRY INSTITUTE
1043 EAST SOUTH RIVER STREET
APPLETON, WI 54911
See Engineering: Pollution Abatement;
Educational Institute

**PESTICIDE CONTROL,
DEPARTMENT OF AGRICULTURE**
HILL FARM BUILDING, ROOM 202-B
MADISON, WI 53702
See Engineering: Agricultural Engineering; Government-State or Local

PUBLIC HEALTH DEPARTMENT
817 FRANKLIN STREET
MANITOWOC, WI 54220
See Engineering: Pollution Abatement; Government-State or Local

**PULP MANUFACTURERS
RESEARCH LEAGUE**
P O BOX 436, 1043 EAST SOUTH
RIVER STREET
APPLETON, WI 54911
See Engineering: Water Resources; Educational Institute

**REGIONAL PLANNING
COMMISSION OF SE WISCONSIN**
916 NORTH EAST AVENUE
WAUKESHA, WI 53187
See Engineering: Water Resources; Government-State or Local

**RESOURCES BUREAU, WISCONSIN
DEPARTMENT OF NATURAL
RESOURCES**
BOX 450
MADISON, WI 53701
See Engineering: Water Resources; Government-State or Local

RESOURCES CONSERVATION COUNCIL OF WISCONSIN
BOX 707
MELLEN, WI 54546
See Biology: Ecology; Professional Organizations

RESOURCES DEVELOPMENT DIVISION, DEPARTMENT OF NATURAL RESOURCES
1 WEST WILSON STREET
MADISON, WI 53702
See Engineering: Water Resources; Government-State or Local

SCIENTIFIC LAND MANAGEMENT CURRICULUM
WISCONSIN STATE UNIVERSITY
RIVER FALLS, WI 54022
See Interdisciplinary: General; Educational Institute

SEAMAN NUCLEAR CORPORATION
3846 WEST WISCONSIN AVENUE
MILWAUKEE, WI 53208
See Chemistry: General; Industrial/Commercial

SMOKE INSPECTION DIVISION, BUILDING INSPECTION DEPARTMENT
210 MONONA AVENUE
MADISON, WI 53709
See Engineering: Pollution Abatement; Government-State or Local

SMOKE INSPECTIONS, PUBLIC HEALTH DEPARTMENT
41 WEST SECOND STREET
FOND DU LAC, WI 54935
See Engineering: Pollution Abatement; Government-State or Local

SOIL CONSERVATION SERVICES
4601 HAMMERSLEY ROAD, PO BOX 4248
MADISON, WI 53711
See Biology: Ecology; Government-State or Local

SOIL SCIENCES SOCIETY OF AMERICA
677 SOUTH SEGOE ROAD
MADISON, WI 53711
See Engineering: Water Resources; Foundation

SOIL-WATER CONSERVATION, 204 SOILS BUILDING
UNIVERSITY OF WISCONSIN
MADISON, WI 53706
See Biology: Ecology; Government-State or Local

TYMPANUCHUS CUPIDO PINNATUS SOCIETY
611 EAST WISCONSIN AVENUE, P O BOX 1156

MILWAUKEE, WI 53201
See Interdisciplinary: General; Professional Organizations

UNIVERSITY OF WISCONSIN
BIOTRON, BIRGE HALL
MADISON, WI 53706
See Biology: General; Educational Institute

WATER CHEMISTRY PROGRAM
UNIVERSITY OF WISCONSIN
MADISON, WI 53706
See Interdisciplinary: General; Educational Institute

WATER RESOURCES CENTER HYDRAULICS-SANITATION LABORATORY
UNIVERSITY OF WISCONSIN
MADISON, WI 53706
See Engineering: Water Resources; Educational Institute

ZOOLOGY DEPARTMENT
UNIVERSITY OF WISCONSIN
MADISON, WI 53706
See Interdisciplinary: General; Educational Institute

West Virginia

AIR POLLUTION CONTROL
CITY HALL, 1500 CHAPLINE STREET
WHEELING, WV 26003
See Engineering: Pollution Abatement; Government-State or Local

AIR POLLUTION CONTROL COMMISSION
4108 MACCORKLE AVENUE, SOUTH EAST
CHARLESTON, WV 25304
See Engineering: Pollution Abatement; Government-State or Local

APPALACHIAN STUDIES AND DEVELOPMENT
295 COLISEUM
MORGANTOWN, WV 26506
See Engineering: Pollution Abatement; Government-State or Local

BROOKS BIRD CLUB, INCORPORATED
707 WARWOOD AVENUE
WHEELING, WV 26003
See Interdisciplinary: General; Professional Organizations

CIVIL ENGINEERING DEPARTMENT

EVANSDALE CAMPUS
MORGANTOWN, WV 26506
See Engineering: Pollution Abatement; Industrial/Commercial

CONSUMER PROTECTION, DEPARTMENT OF AGRICULTURE
CAPITOL BUILDING, ROOM EAST-109
CHARLESTON, WV 25305
See Engineering: Agricultural Engineering; Government-State or Local

COOPERATIVE EXTENSION SERVICE
295 COLISEUM
MORGANTOWN, WV 26506
See Engineering: Pollution Abatement; Government-State or Local

ENGINEERING COLLEGE
WEST VIRGINIA UNIVERSITY
MORGANTOWN, WV 26506
See Engineering: Pollution Abatement; Educational Institute

ENVIRONMENTAL HEALTH CENTER
WEST VIRGINIA UNIVERSITY
MORGANTOWN, WV 26505
See Biology: Ecology; Educational Institute

ENVIRONMENTAL STUDIES PROGRAM
MARSHALL UNIVERSITY
HUNTINGTON, WV 25701
See Chemistry: General; Educational Institute

GEOLOGIC AND ECONOMIC SURVEY OF WEST VIRGINIA
WEST VIRGINIA UNIVERSITY
MORGANTOWN, WV 26505
See Engineering: Water Resources; Government-State or Local

INDUSTRIAL RELATIONS BOARD, WEST VIRGINIA UNIVERSITY
344 ARMSTRONG
MORGANTOWN, WV 26506
See Social Sciences/Humanities: Labor/Relations/Unions; Educational Institute

NATURAL RESOURCES DEPARTMENT OF WEST VIRGINIA
1709 WASHINGTON STREET EAST
CHARLESTON, WV 25311
See Interdisciplinary: General; Foundation

RECREATION AND PARK ASSOCIATION
OGLEBAY PARK

WHEELING, WV 26003
See Social Sciences/Humanities: Recreation and Leisure; Government-Federal

RESEARCH OFFICE, LABOR DEPARTMENT
1800 WASHINGTON STREET, EAST
CHARLESTON,WV 25305
See Social Sciences/Humanities: Labor/Relations/Unions;   Government-State or Local

SANITARY ENGINEERING DIVISION, WEST VIRGINIA HEALTH DEPARTMENT
1800 WASHINGTON STREET, EAST
CHARLESTON, WV 25311
See Engineering: Water Resources; Government-State or Local

SOIL CONSERVATION SERVICES
209 PRAIRIE AVENUE, PO BOX 865
MORGANTOWN, WV 26505
See Biology: Ecology; Government-State or Local

WATER RESOURCES DIVISION, DEPARTMENT OF NATURAL RESOURCES
1201 GREENBRIER STREET
CHARLESTON, WV 25311
See Engineering: Water Resources; Government-State or Local

WATER RESOURCES INSTITUTE
WEST VIRGINIA UNIVERSITY
MORGANTOWN, WV 26505
See Engineering: Water Resources; Educational Institute

WILD ANIMAL PROPAGATION TRUST
OGLEBAY PARK
WHEELING, WV 26003
See Interdisciplinary: General; Professional Organizations

WILDLIFE FEDERATION OF WEST VIRGINIA
BOX 38
DURBIN, WV 26264
See Biology: Ecology; Foundation

ZOOLOGICAL PARKS AND AQUARIUMS ASSOCIATION OF AMERICA
OGLEBAY PARK
WHEELING, WV 26003
See Biology: General; Professional Organizations

Wyoming

ECONOMIC PLANNING AND DEVELOPMENT DEPARTMENT
210 W 23RD STREET
CHEYENNE, WY 82001
See Social Sciences/Humanities: Regional Planning; Government-State or Local

ENGINEERING DEPARTMENT OF WYOMING
STATE CAPITOL BUILDING
CHEYENNE, WY 82001
See Engineering: Water Resources; Government-State or Local

ENVIRONMENTAL RESEARCH INSTITUTE
BOX 156
MOOSE, WY 83012
See Biology: Ecology; Research Institute

ENVIRONMENTAL SANITATION DIVISION
STATE OFFICE BUILDING
CHEYENNE, WY 82001
See Engineering: Pollution Abatement; Government-State or Local

INDUSTRIAL HYGIENE, PUBLIC HEALTH DEPARTMENT
STATE OFFICE BUILDING
CHEYENNE, WY 82001
See Engineering: Pollution Abatement; Government-State or Local

LABORATORIES DIVISION, UNIVERSITY OF WYOMING
P O BOX 3228, CHEMISTRY-ZOOLOGY BUILDING, ROOM 405
LARAMIE, WY 82071
See Engineering: Water Resources; Government-State or Local

LARAMIE ENERGY RESEARCH
POST OFFICE BOX 3395
UNIVERSITY STATION
LARAMIE, WY 82070
See Engineering: Chemical Engineering; Government-Federal

NATURAL RESOURCES RESEARCH INSTITUTE, COLLEGE OF ENGINEERING, UNIVERSITY OF WYOMING
BOX 3038, UNIVERSITY STATION
LARAMIE, WY 82070
See Engineering: General; Field Station/Laboratory

PLANT INDUSTRY DIVISION, WYOMING DEPARTMENT OF AGRICULTURE
308 CAPITOL BUILDING
CHEYENNE, WY 82001
See Engineering: Agricultural Engineering; Government-State or Local

SOIL CONSERVATION SERVICE
FEDERAL OFFICE BUILDING, POST OFFICE BOX 2440
CASPER, WY 82601
See Interdisciplinary: General; Unclassified

SOIL, WATER AND WEATHER DIVISION, WYOMING DEPARTMENT OF AGRICULTURE
313 CAPITOL BUILDING

CHEYENNE, WY 82001
See Engineering: General; Government-State or Local

WATER RESOURCES RESEARCH INSTITUTE, UNIVERSITY OF WYOMING
BOX 3038, UNIVERSITY STATION
LARAMIE, WY 82070
See Engineering: Water Resources; Unclassified

WILDLIFE FEDERATION OF WYOMING
BOX 1406
CASPER, WY 82601
See Biology: Ecology; Foundation

WYOMING NATURAL
210 WEST 23RD STREET
CHEYENNE, WY 82001
See Engineering: Water Resources; Government-State or Local

Puerto Rico

ECONOMIC AND SOCIAL ANALYSIS BUREAU, PUERTO RICO PLANNING
STOP 22
SANTURCE, PR 00909
See Social Sciences/Humanities: General; Government-State or Local

EDUCATIONAL RESEARCH DIVISION
UNIVERSITY OF PUERTO RICO
RIO PIEDRAS, PR 00931
See Social Sciences/Humanities: Education; Government-State or Local

ENVIRONMENTAL STUDIES PROGRAM
UNIVERSITY OF PUERTO RICO
RIO PIEDRAS, PR 00931
See Interdisciplinary: General; Educational Institute

HEALTH DEPARTMENT
POST OFFICE BOX 9232
SAN JUAN, PR 00908
See Engineering: Agricultural Engineering; Government-State or Local

MARINE BIOLOGY INSTITUTE
UNIVERSITY OF PUERTO RICO
MAYAGUEZ, PUERTO RICO
See Biology: General; Educational Institute

PLANNING SOCIETY, INTER-AMERICA
1505 PONCE DE LEON AVENIDA
SANTURCE, PR 00903
See Social Sciences/Humanities: Regional Planning; Research Institute

SOCIAL SCIENCE RESEARCH CENTER
UNIVERSITY OF PUERTO RICO
RIO PIEDRAS, PUERTO RICO 00931
See Social Sciences/Humanities: General;
Educational Institute

SOIL CONSERVATION SERVICES, CARIBBEAN AREA
GPO BOX 4868
SAN JUAN, PR 00936
See Interdisciplinary: General; Unclassified

SUPERIOR EDUCATION COUNCIL
UNIVERSITY OF PUERTO RICO
RIO PIEDRAS, PR 00931
See Social Sciences/Humanities: Education; Government-State or Local

TROPICAL FORESTRY INSTITUTE
POST OFFICE BOX AQ
RIO PIEDRAS, PR 00923
See Engineering: Agricultural Engineering; Government-Federal

TROPICAL METEOROLOGY INSTITUTE
UNIVERSITY OF PUERTO RICO
RIO PIEDRAS, PR 00931
See Interdisciplinary: General; Educational Institute

WATER RESOURCES AUTHORITY OF PUERTO RICO
POST OFFICE BOX 4267
SAN JUAN, PUERTO RICO 00905
See Engineering: Water Resources; Government-Federal

Virgin Islands

CARIBBEAN CONSERVATION ASSOCIATION
COLLEGE OF THE VIRGIN ISLANDS
ST THOMAS, VI 00801
See Social Sciences/Humanities: Regional Planning; Research Institute

CONSERVATION SOCIETY OF VIRGIN ISLANDS
BOX 750
ST THOMAS, VI 00801
See Biology: Ecology; Professional Organizations

ENVIRONMENTAL SANITATION BUREAU
CHARLOTTE AMALIE BOX 1442
ST THOMAS, VI 00801
See Engineering: Water Resources; Government-State or Local

ISLAND RESOURCES FOUNDATION, INCORPORATED
POST OFFICE BOX 4187
ST THOMAS, VI 00801
See Interdisciplinary: General; Foundation

URUGUAY

DEFENSE MINISTRY
25 DEL MAYO 279
MONTEVIDEO, URUGUAY
See Biology: General; Government-Federal

FISHERIES RESOURCE INSTITUTE, UNIVERSITY OF URUGUAY
ALBERTO LASPLACES 1550
MONTEVIDEO, URUGUAY
See Biology: General; Educational Institute

NATURAL HISTORY MUSEUM, MINISTRY OF CULTURE
BUENOS AIRES 652
MONTEVIDEO, URUGUAY
See Biology: General; Government-Federal

OCEANOGRAPHIC AND FISHERIES SERVICE
JULIO HERRERA Y OBES 1467
MONTEVIDEO, URUGUAY
See Biology: General; Government-Federal

SCIENCE AND TECHNOLOGY DEPARTMENT
JUAN LINDOLFO CUESTAS 1401
MONTEVIDEO, URUGUAY
See Biology: General; Government-Federal

SCIENCES AND HUMANITIES FACULTY
CERRITO 73,
MONTEVIDEO, URUGUAY
See Biology: General; Educational Institute

VENEZUELA

ANTHROPOLOGY-SOCIOLOGY DIVISION
LA SALLE FOUNDATION
CARACAS, VENEZUELA
See Social Sciences/Humanities: General; Foundation

FISHERIES INVESTIGATION CENTER
CUMANA
ESTADO SUCRE, VENEZUELA
See Interdisciplinary: General; Unclassified

FOOD TECHNOLOGY DEPARTMENT, UNIVERSITY OF CENTRAL VENEZUELA
ORIENTE 10098
CARACAS, VENEZUELA
See Interdisciplinary: General; Educational Institute

LIVESTOCK AND AGRICULTURE MINISTRY
TORRES NORTE
CARACAS, VENEZUELA
See Biology: General; Government-Federal

MARGARITE MARINE BIOLOGICAL STATION
ESTADO NUEVA ESPARTA, VENEZUELA
See Biology: General; Industrial/Commercial

MARINA DIVISION
LA SALLE FOUNDATION
CARACAS, VENEZUELA
See Biology: Ecology; Foundation

OCEANOGRAPHIC INSTITUTE
UNIVERSITY OF ORIENTE, CUMANA
ESTADO SUCRE, VENEZUELA
See Interdisciplinary: General; Educational Institute

SCIENCE INVESTIGATIONS INSTITUTE OF VENEZUELA
APARTADO 1827
CARACAS, VENEZUELA
See Interdisciplinary: General; Government-State or Local

TROPICAL ZOOLOGY INSTITUTE
UNIVERSITY OF CENTRAL VENEZUELA
APARTADO SAB, VENEZUELA
See Biology: General; Educational Institute

VEN DEVELOPMENT CORPORATION
EDIFICO N, CENTRO SI BOL
CARACUS, VENEZUELA
See Biology: General; Industrial/Commercial

WALES

CHEMISTRY DEPARTMENT
GLAMORGAN COLLEGE OF TECHNOLOGY
TREFOREST, GLAMORGAN, WALES
See Chemistry: General; Educational Institute

CHEMISTRY DEPARTMENT
UNIVERSITY COLLEGE OF WALES
ABERYSTWYTH, WALES
See Chemistry: General; Educational Institute

MARINE SCIENCE LABS, NERC UNITED
MENAI BRIDGE
ANGLESEY, WALES
See Interdisciplinary: General; Field Station/Laboratory

MARINE SCIENCES LABORATORY, UNIVERSITY COLLEGE OF NORTH WALES
MENAI BRIDGE, WALES
See Biology: General; Educational Institute

PLANT PATHOLOGY DEPARTMENT
WELSH PLANT BREEDING STATION
PLAS GOGERDDAU,
CARDIGANSHIRE, WALES
See Biology: Biochemistry; Field Station/Laboratory

WATER AND CLEAN AIR RESEARCH CENTER
STRIP MILLS DIVISION OF BRITISH STEEL
PORT TALBOT, GLAMORGANSHIRE, WALES
See Engineering: Pollution Abatement; Industrial/Commercial

WEST GERMANY

AGRICULTURAL SCIENCES, GERMAN ACADEMY
MUGGELSEEDAMM 310
DDR 1162 BERLIN, WEST GERMANY
See Biology: General; Educational Institute

APPLIED BOTANY STATE INSTITUTION, HAMBURG UNIVERSITY
ERIKASTR 130
HAMBURG 20, WEST GERMANY
See Biology: Ecology; Educational Institute

APPLIED GEOPHYSICS INSTITUTE
THERESIEN STRASSE, UNIVERSITY OF MUNICH
MUNICH 2, WEST GERMANY
See Physics: General; Field Station/Laboratory

BOTANISCH STAATSSAMMIUNG
MENZINGER STRASSE 67
8000 MUNICH 19, WEST GERMANY
See Biology: General; Research Institute

CHEMISTRY INSTITUTION MARBURG
L BAHNHOFSTRASSE 7
355 MARBURG, WEST GERMANY
See Chemistry: Physical Chemistry; Educational Institute

FISHERIES RESEARCH, FEDERAL INSTITUTE
PALMAILLE 9
HAMBURG-ALTONA, WEST GERMANY
See Biology: General; Government-Federal

FOREST BOTANY INSTITUTE
BERTOLDSTRASSE 17
78 FREIBURG 1 BR, WEST GERMANY
See Biology: General; Educational Institute

FORESTRY INSTITUTION, UNIVERSITY OF FREIBURG
FREIBURG/BR
SONNHALDE 77, WEST GERMANY
See Biology: General; Educational Institute

FORSCHUNGSSTELLE LIMNOLOGIE
ACADEMY OF SCIENCE
JENA-L, WEST GERMANY
See Engineering: General; Educational Institute

GEOLOGISCH-PALAONTOLOGISCHES INSTITUTION
DER TECHNOLOGY HOCHSCHULE DARMST
61 DARMSTADT, WEST GERMANY
See Geology: General; Educational Institute

GEOLOGY DEPARTMENT, UNIVERSITY OF MUNICH
RICHARD WAGNER STRASSE 10-11
MUNICH 2, WEST GERMANY
See Geology: Paleontology; Educational Institute

GEOLOGY INSTITUTE
UNIVERSITY OF WURZBURG
WURZBURG, WEST GERMANY
See Geology: General; Educational Institute

GEOLOGY INSTITUTE, UNIVERSITY OF BONN
NUSSALLEE 8
53 BONN, WEST GERMANY
See Geology: General; Educational Institute

GEOLOGY-PALEONTOLOGY INSTITUTE, UNIVERSITY MAINZ
MAINZ-GONSENHEIM
AN DER PRALL 1, WEST GERMANY
See Geology: General; Educational Institute

GEOPHYSICS INSTITUTE
GIVENBECKERS WEG 61
44 MUNSTER/WESTF, WEST GERMANY
See Geology: General; Educational Institute

HYDROBIOLOGY AND FISCHEREIWISS INSTITUTE
2 HAMBURG-ALTONA 1
OLBERSWEG 24, WEST GERMANY
See Biology: General; Educational Institute

HYDROGRAPHIC INSTITUTE
BERNHARD NOCHT-STRASSE 78

HAMBURG 4, WEST GERMANY
See Physics: General; Government-State or Local

INSTITUTION OF BRENNSTOFFCHEM
RHEIN-WESTF TH AACHEN
BONN, WEST GERMANY
See Chemistry: General; Educational Institute

LIMNOLOGY FLUSSTATION, SCHLITZ
STEINWEG 21, 6407 SCHLITZ
HESSEN, WEST GERMANY
See Biology: Ecology; Educational Institute

LIMNOLOGY, MAX-PLANCK-INSTITUTION
D-232 PLON (HOLSTEIN)
POSTFACH 165, WEST GERMANY
See Biology: General; Research Institute

MARINE RESEARCH INSTITUTE
HANDELSHAFEN 12
BREMERHAVEN, WEST GERMANY
See Biology: General; Research Institute

MARINE SCIENCE INSTITUTE, UNIVERSITY OF KIEL
NIEMANNSWEG 11
23 KIEL, WEST GERMANY
See Biology: General; Educational Institute

MAX-PLANCK INSTITUTION OF BIOLOGY
CORRENSSTRASSE 41
TUBINGEN, WEST GERMANY
See Biology: General; Educational Institute

MECRESKUNDE INSTITUTE, UNIVERSITY OF HAMBURG
HEIMHUDER STR 71
2 HAMBURG 13, WEST GERMANY
See Geology: General; Educational Institute

MECRESKUNDE, UNIVERSITY OF KIEL
HOHENBERGSTR 2
KIEL, WEST GERMANY
See Geology: General; Educational Institute

MINERAL INSTITUTION, UNIVERSITY OF SAARLANDES
66 SAARBRUCKEN 15
BONN, WEST GERMANY
See Geology: Geochemistry; Educational Institute

MINERAL INSTITUTION, UNIVERSITY WURZBURG
PLEICHERTORSTR 34
WURZBURG, WEST GERMANY
See Geology: General; Educational Institute

**MINERAL-PETROLEUM INSTITUTE,
    UNIVERSITY OF COLOGNE**
ZULPICHER STRASSE 47
COLOGNE, WEST GERMANY
See Geology: Geochemistry; Educational
Institute

**ORGANIC CHEMISTRY INSTITUTE,
    TECHNICAL UNIVERSITY**
BERLIN, WEST GERMANY
See Chemistry: General; Educational In-
stitute

**ORGANIC CHEMISTRY INSTITUTE,
    UNIVERSITY OF GIESSEN**
LUDUIGSTR 21
63 GIESSEN, WEST GERMANY
See Chemistry: General; Educational Institute

**PALEONTOLOGY DEPARTMENT,
    UNIVERSITY OF BONN**
NUSSALLEE 8
53 BONN, WEST GERMANY
See Geology: Paleontology; Educational
Institute

**PHYSICS-CHEMISTRY INSTITUTE,
    TECHNISCHE HOCHSCULE**
51 AACHEN, POSTFACH D TH
BONN, WEST GERMANY
See Chemistry: Physical Chemistry; Educational Institute

**PLANT GEOGRAPHY
    INTERNATIONAL SOCIETY**
3261 TODENMANN UBER RINTEN
BONN, WEST GERMANY
See Biology: Ecology; Research Institute

RESEARCH DEPARTMENT
BEMERODERSTRASSE 61
HANNOVER-KIRCHRONE, WEST
GERMANY
See Biology: General; Research Institute

**SYSTEMATIC GEOBOT
    INSTITUTION, GOTTINGEN
    UNIVERSITY**
UNTERE KARSPULE 2
GOTTINGEN, WEST GERMANY
See Biology: Ecology; Educational Insti-
tute

**WATER POLLUTION RESEARCH
    ASSOCIATION, HYDROBIOLOGIE
    INSTITUTE**
PALMOILLE 55
2 HAMBURG-50, WEST GERMANY
See Engineering: Pollution Abatement;
Research Institute

**ZOOLOGIC INSTITUTION, JUSTUS
    LIEBIG UNIVERSITY**
LUDWIGSTRASSE 23
GIESSEN, WEST GERMANY
See Biology: General; Educational Insti-
tute

**ZOOLOGY DEPARTMENT,
    UNIVERSITY OF GOTTINGEN**
GOTTINGEN, WILHELMSPLATZL
BONN, WEST GERMANY
See Biology: Ecology; Educational Insti-
tute

ZOOLOGY INSTITUTE
61 DARMSTADT
BONN, WEST GERMANY
See Biology: General; Educational Institute

**ZOOLOGY INSTITUTE, UNIVERSITY
    OF ERLANGEN-NURNBERG**
UNIVERSITATSSTRASSE 19
852 ERLANGEN, WEST GERMANY
See Biology: Ecology; Educational Institute

YUGOSLAVIA

BIOLOGICAL INSTITUTE
DUBROVNIK, YUGOSLAVIA
See Biology: General; Research Institute

BIOLOGY INSTITUTE
TESLOVA 19
LJUBLJANA, YUGOSLAVIA
See Biology: General; Educational Insti-
tute

GEOLOGY DEPARTMENT
CARLI CAPLINA 31
BELGRADE, YUGOSLAVIA
See Geology: General; Educational Insti-
tute

MARINE BIOLOGY INSTITUTE
ROVINJ, YUGOSLAVIA
See Biology: General; Research Institute

**OCEANOGRAPHY AND FISHERIES
    INSTITUTE**
114 RT MARJONA
SPLIT, YUGOSLAVIA
See Biology: General; Research Institute

ZANZIBAR

**MARINE FISHERIES RESOURCES
    LABORATORY ORGANIZATION
    OF EAST AFRICA**
POST OFFICE BOX 668
ZANZIBAR
See Biology: General; Field Station/Lab-
oratory